BRIEF CONTENTS

NINTH EDITION

Prebles' ARTFORMS

An Introduction to the Visual Arts

PATRICK FRANK

California State University, Monterey Bay

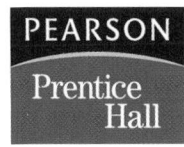

PEARSON

Prentice Hall

Upper Saddle River, NJ 07458

Library of Congress Cataloging-in-Publication Data

Frank, Patrick
   Prebles' artforms : an introduction to the visual arts / Patrick Frank. — 9th ed.
      p. cm.
   Includes bibliographical references and index.
   ISBN 0-13-514132-X (alk. paper)
   1. Composition (Art) 2. Visual perception. 3. Art--History.
   I. Preble, Duane. Artforms. II. Title. III. Title: Artforms.
      N7430.P69 2008
      701'.8--dc22

2007050151

Editor in Chief: Sarah Touborg
Senior Acquisitions Editor: Amber Mackey
Editorial Assistant: Carla Worner
Assistant Editor: Alexandra Huggins
Director of Marketing: Brandy Dawson
Executive Marketing Manager: Marissa Feliberty
Multimedia Specialist: Alison Lorber
Senior Managing Editor: Mary Rottino
Project Manager: Barbara Marttine Cappuccio
Production Assistant: Marlene Gassler
Senior Operations Specialist: Brian Mackey
AV Project Manager: Gail Cocker-Bogusz
Senior Art Director: Pat Smythe
Interior Design: Judy Allan
Cover Design: Ray Cruz / Pat Smythe
Cover Image: Xul Solar. Dragon. 1927, © Pan Klub
   Foundation—Xul Solar Museum, Buenos Aires.

Pearson Imaging Center
Site Supervisor: Joe Conti
Project Coordinator: Corrin Skidds
Scanner Operators: Corrin Skidds / Robert Uibelhoer /
   Ron Walko
Director, Image Resource Center: Melinda Patelli
Manager, Rights and Permissions: Zina Arabia
Manager, Visual Research: Beth Brenzel
Manager, Cover Visual Research and Permissions:
   Karen Sanatar
Image Permission Coordinator: Debbie Latronica
Photo Researchers: Francelle Carapetyan / Clare Maxwell
Composition/Full-Service Project Management:
   Natalie Hansen / Sandra Reinhard, Black Dot Group
Printer/Binder: Courier Kendallville
Cover Printer: Phoenix Color, Corp.

Pearson Education LTD.
Pearson Education Australia PTY, Limited
Pearson Education Singapore, Pte. Ltd
Pearson Education North Asia Ltd

Pearson Education, Canada, Ltd
Pearson Educación de Mexico, S.A. de C.V.
Pearson Education—Japan
Pearson Education Malaysia, Pte. Ltd

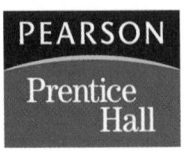

10 9 8 7 6 5 4 3 2
ISBN 10: 0-13-514132-X
ISBN 13: 978-0-13-514132-8
a la Carte version ISBN 10: 0-20-569750-X

ABOUT THE COVER

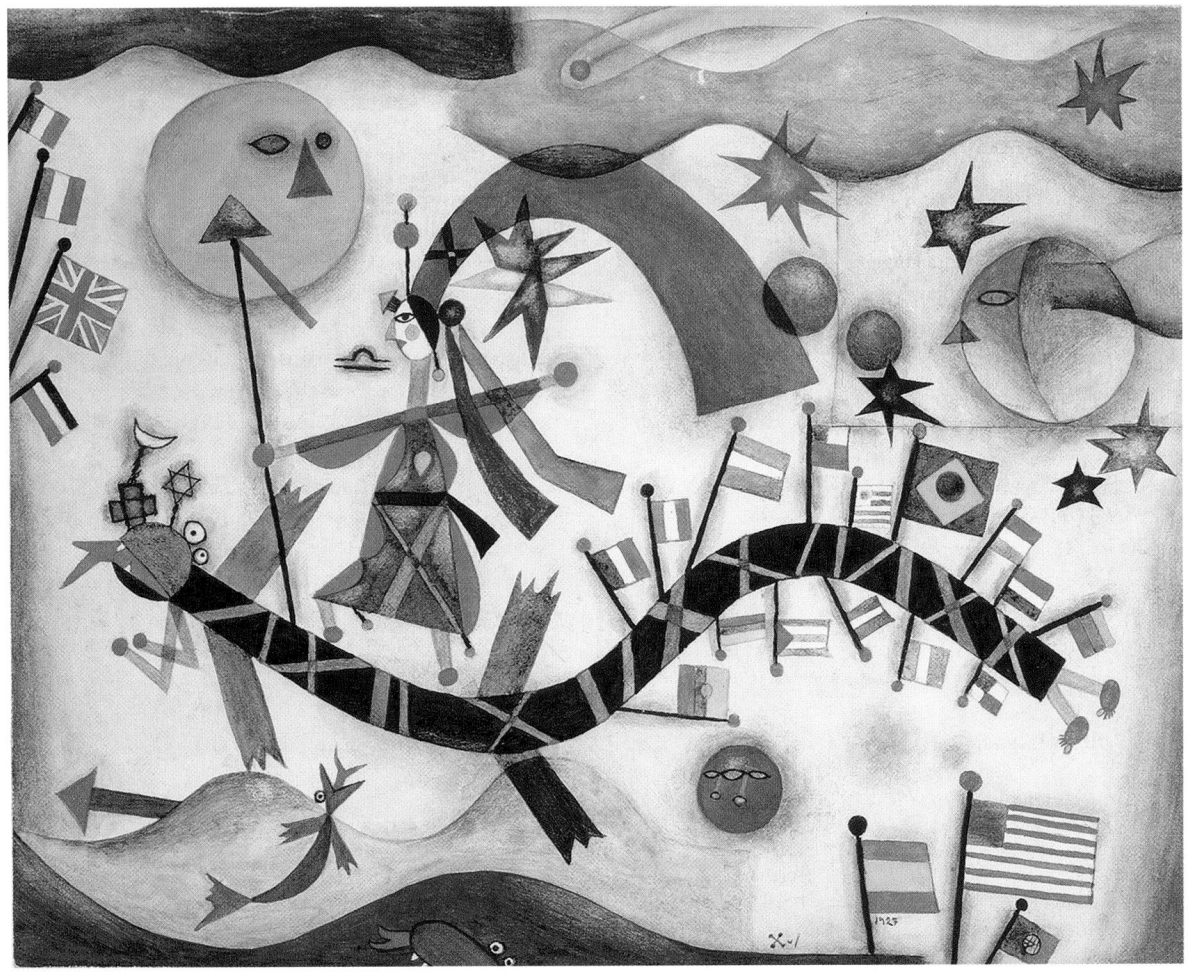

Xul Solar. DRAGON. 1927.
Watercolor on paper. 10″ x 12⅝″.
Fundación Pan Klub, Museo Xul Solar, Buenos Aires.

What can you say about an artist who named himself after the sun? The pseudonym he invented was Xul Solar, the first name a backward spelling of *lux* (Latin for light). He lived a quiet life in an apartment in Buenos Aires, where for forty years he painted visions of worlds that none but he had seen. One of the best of these is his 1927 watercolor DRAGON, in which a sorcerer rides a giant dragon across a sun- and moon-spangled sky. The dragon's body is adorned with the flags of many nations; its head sports symbols of three major religions: Judaism, Islam, and Christianity. The painting expresses the artist's vision of global understanding between all religions and nationalities. Because art can indeed serve as a vehicle for comprehension between peoples and cultures, DRAGON makes a fitting cover for this book, which holds the same hope.

TO ALL WHO COME TO KNOW THE ARTIST WITHIN

CONTENTS

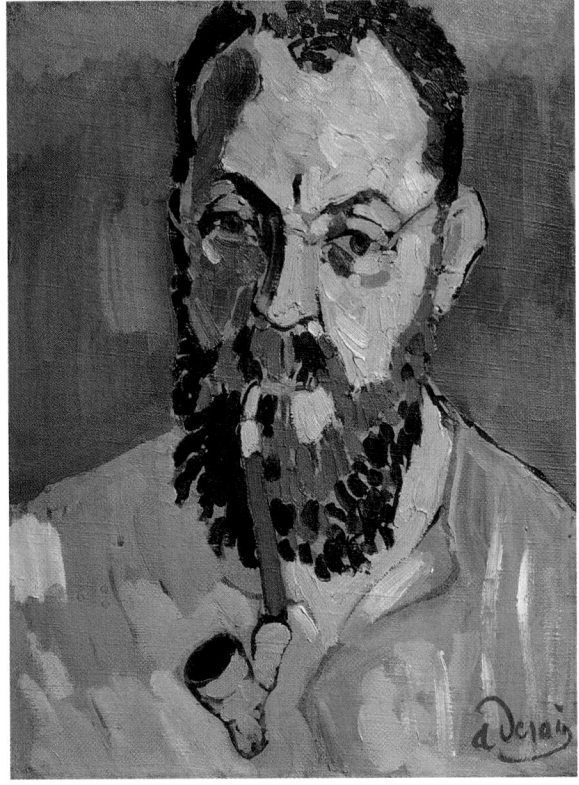

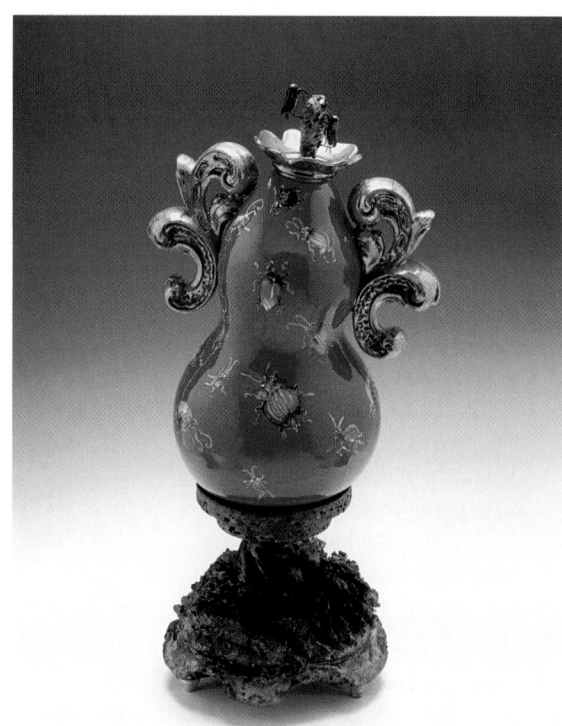

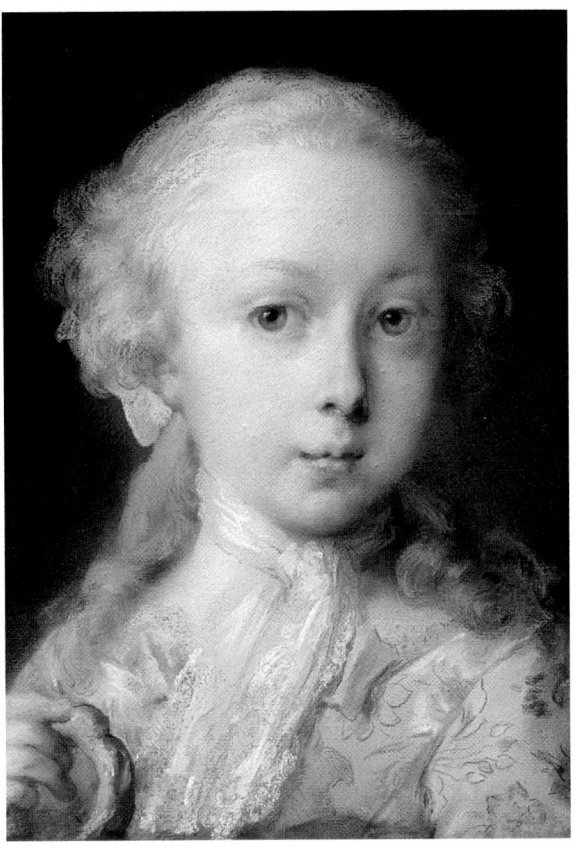

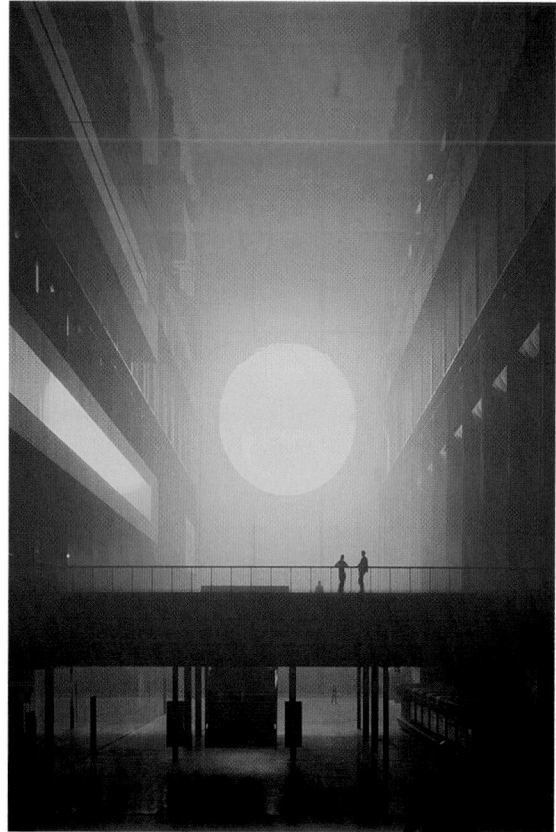

ABOUT THE AUTHOR

Patrick Frank has taught in several higher education environments, from rural community colleges to private research universities. His recent scholarly work has focused on Latin American graphic arts. He is author of *Posada's Broadsheets: Mexican Popular Imagery 1890–1910* and *Los Artistas del Pueblo: Prints and Workers' Culture in Buenos Aires* (University of New Mexico Press). He has curated five exhibitions of Latin American prints. He has also edited a volume of artists' writings, *Readings in Latin American Modern Art* (Yale University Press). He served as collaborating author in the revision of the modern section of Marilyn Stokstad's *Art History* (third edition). He earned M.A. and Ph.D. degrees at George Washington University in Washington, D.C., and is currently an adjunct faculty member in the Department of Visual and Public Art at California State University, Monterey Bay. His involvement with ARTFORMS began when he first taught from it in 1991.

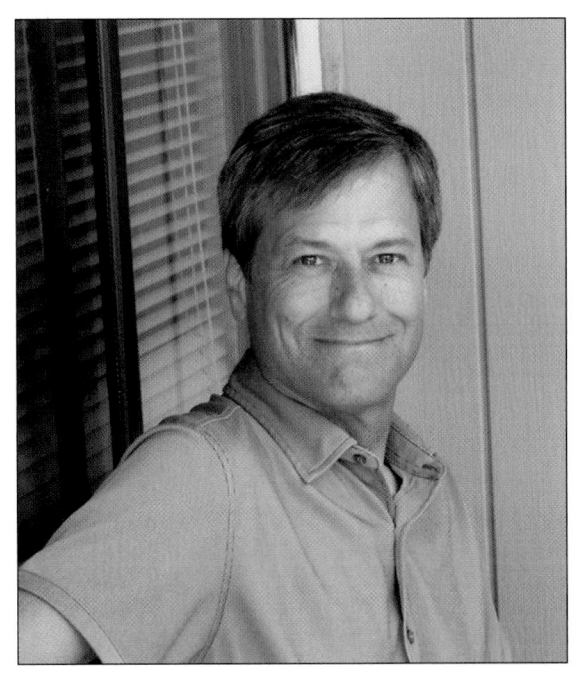

PATRICK FRANK

ACKNOWLEDGMENTS

I greatly appreciate the help and encouragement of the many people who have been directly involved in this ninth edition. A few people deserve special mention for their major contributions.

Senior Acquisitions Editor Amber Mackey was a constant source of creative ideas on how to present our new material. Project Manager Barbara Cappuccio kept us all on track. Researching and acquiring pictures gets more complicated with each edition as ARTFORMS reaches further across the globe, and photo researchers Francelle Carapetyan and Clare Maxwell were in every way equal to the at-times strange demands that I placed upon them. Editorial project manager Natalie Hansen of Black Dot Group shepherded this book from manuscript to printed page with an inspiring mix of patience, diligence, and friendliness. I received valuable assistance on specialized content areas from Charles James, Philip James, Shyla McGill, and Monica Blackmun Visonà. Many artists opened their studios and homes to me as I was researching this book; I greatly appreciate their generosity just as I hope that I have communicated the vigor and inspiration of their creativity. All of these persons made special contributions to this book, and their efforts and dedication mark its every page.

I am also grateful to original authors Duane and Sarah Preble. As this book continues to evolve to meet changing times, it will always remain faithful to the original vision that they had.

I express my appreciation to the following reviewers, who offered many helpful suggestions during the revision of the text:

Stephen Strickland, *Faulkner State Community College*
Kefly X. Reed, *Bishop State Community College*
Christine Dupont-Patz, *Metropolitan State College of Denver*
Patricia Sterritt, *College of the Albemarle*
Charlotte Lowry Collins, *Kennesaw State University*
Marleen Hoover, *San Antonio College*
Amy E. Johnson, *Otterbein College*
Robert McColl, *Saint Mary's University*
Lynn Metcalf, *Saint Cloud State University*
Amanda L. Rogers, *Middle Tennessee State University*
Michael Sevick, *University of Michigan- Flint*
Patricia Drew, *California State University-Fullerton*
Helen Barnes, *Butler Community College*

Leo Tolstoy wrote that art can be a "means of union" for people, "joining them together in the same feelings." I hope that this book facilitates such unions, because if we study and enjoy the cultural productions of the world's peoples, we will build strong bridges of human understanding.

PATRICK FRANK

PREFACE

From the first edition in 1972, ARTFORMS has been as visually exciting as the individual works of art that are reproduced in it. ARTFORMS grew out of a desire to introduce art through an engaging visual experience. It is written and designed to help readers build an informed foundation for individual understanding and enjoyment of art. By introducing art theory, practice, and history in a single volume, this book aims to draw students into a new or expanded awareness of the visual arts. The goal is to engage readers in the process of realizing their innate creativity.

The title of this book has a dual meaning. Besides the expected discussion of the various forms of art, the title also reflects the fact that art does indeed help to form us as people. As we create forms, we are in turn formed by what we have created. Several years ago, the title was changed to PREBLES' ARTFORMS, acknowledging the pioneering contribution of the original authors, Duane and Sarah Preble, to the study of art. Their vision and spirit have touched hundreds of thousands of students who have studied ARTFORMS.

Beyond fostering appreciation of major works of art, this book's primary concern is to open students' eyes and minds to the richness of the visual arts as unique forms of human communication and to convey the idea that the arts enrich life best when we experience, understand, and enjoy them as integral parts of the process of living.

ORGANIZATION

- *Part One: Art Is . . .* (Chapters 1 and 2) introduces the nature of art, aesthetics, and creativity, and discusses the purposes of art and visual communication. Strongly believing that we are all artists at heart, I include an essay on children and their *Early Encounters with the Artist Within,* and a section on the works of untrained artists.

- *Part Two: The Language of Visual Experience* (Chapters 3–5) presents the language of vision, visual elements, and principles of design. Experience with the language of visual form introduced in those chapters provides a foundation for developing critical thinking and for considering evaluation and art criticism, discussed in Chapter 5.

- The visual and verbal vocabulary covered in *Part Two* prepares the reader to sample the broad range of art disciplines, media, and processes presented in *Part Three: The Media of Art* (Chapters 6–13). In this part we consider the classical media used in drawing, painting, sculpture, and architecture and the latest developments in photography, video, film, digital imaging, and industrial design.

- *Part Four: Art as Cultural Heritage* (Chapters 14–19) and *Part Five: The Modern World* (Chapters 20–24) introduce historic world styles and related cultural values. Three chapters cover artistic traditions outside the Western world. That each new technique in the history of art relies heavily on its predecessors becomes obvious in these chapters.

- *Part Six: The Postmodern World* and its Chapter 25 discuss art of the present generation and the multifaceted and changing roles of artists today. It includes a section on the Global Present, emphasizing the international aspects of the contemporary art world.

In addition to a revised *Glossary, Pronunciation Guide,* and *Selected Readings,* the back matter of PREBLES' ARTFORMS includes a brief listing of Web sites related to art: Images, artists, museums, art organizations, magazines, and other sources. The three-page Timeline is illustrated and includes additional information on both Western and non-Western art.

Special Features

Throughout the book, three types of essays enrich the presentation. *Biography* essays profile important artists from across time. *Art in the World* essays address how art affects our society once it leaves the artist's studio and how we may encounter these issues in our everyday lives. *Artists at Work* essays highlight interviews with six contemporary artists, showing that artists' creativity is a rational process of making choices in order to arrive at a statement that expresses their vision.

NEW TO THE NINTH EDITION

In keeping with the philosophy of the text, the Ninth Edition of PREBLES' ARTFORMS **is a careful blending of the strengths of its earlier editions—** clear organizational structure, straightforward writing, and high quality images—with significant new content.

- *Contemporary Art.* I continue to expand our coverage of the most recent creativity as I keep this book at the top of its field in coverage of contemporary art. In this edition are 55 new images by living artists, 40% of them women and 25% of them global. There are new biographical essays on Andy Warhol, architect Thom Mayne, and art blogger Tyler Green. I also rewrote the final section on The Global Present in Chapter 25, and rewrote and reorganized the section on Digital Art in Chapter 9.

- *Art Repatriation and Looting.* These issues continue to roil the museum world, and will likely do so in the future. I wrote a new essay on the Italian government's recently asserted claims, which appears in Chapter 15, and I updated the staggering cost of art looting in Iraq with new information for the essay in Chapter 18.

- *Latin American Modern Art.* In response to growing demand and increased museum exposure, there is a new section in Chapter 22 that covers the beginnings of modern art in Latin America. This naturally complements the many works by Latino artists throughout the first half of the book.

- *Motion Graphics.* The digital revolution continues to influence visual creativity. I visited the studios of several motion graphics creators who work in this new and dynamic branch of design, and the result is a new section on them in Chapter 10.

- *Street Art.* Some of today's most challenging creations are not done legally, but rather take the form of graffiti or street art. I interviewed several of these artists while preparing a new section for Chapter 25. Other artists who partake of the Street Art aesthetic are considered in other chapters on art media.

- *Graphic Novels.* Formerly known as comics, graphic novels have recently taken on striking new levels of depth and a much wider range of subjects. In recognition of this fact, I wrote a new section on this art form near the end of Chapter 6, which briefly summarizes the history of that exciting medium.

I have always welcomed feedback and input from readers, students, and teachers. Here is a direct way to communicate with me: **Please send any thoughts, concerns, questions, and comments to this e-mail address: patrickfrank@artformstext.com.**

PATRICK FRANK
Monterey, California

The Prentice Hall Digital Art Library DVD

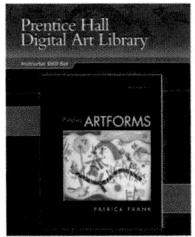

Instructors who adopt PREBLES' ARTFORMS are eligible to receive this unparalled resource. The Prentice Hall Digital Art Library contains every image in the book in the highest resolution and pixilation possible for optimal projection and one-click download.

INSTANT DOWNLOAD

This powerful resource offers every image in jpeg format and in customizable PowerPoint slides with an instant download function.

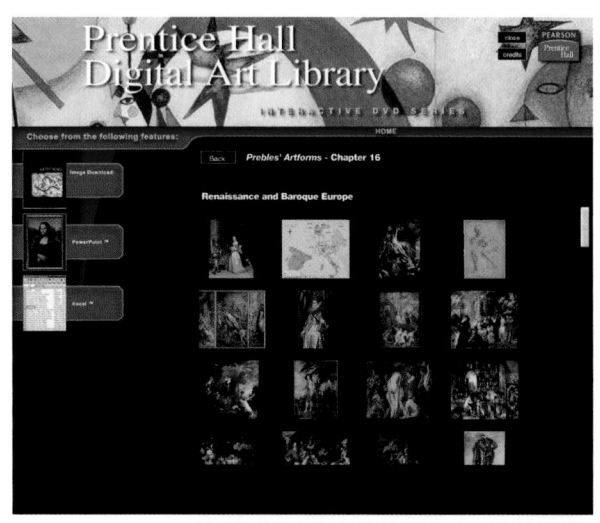

SAVE DETAIL

Save Detail functionality allows you to zoom in and save any detail of an image to your hard drive, which you can then import into PowerPoint.

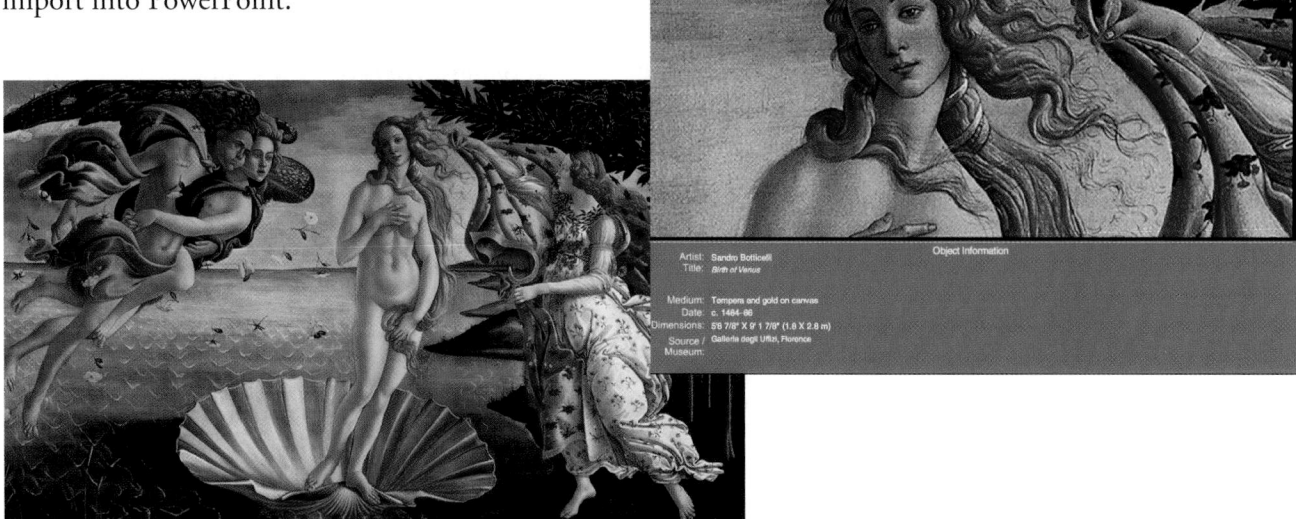

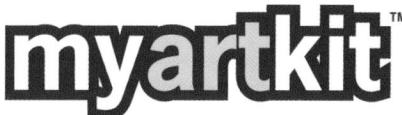

MyArtKit is a state-of-the-art interactive and instructive solution for use in art appreciation courses. It is designed to be used as a supplement to a traditional lecture course, or to completely administer an online course. MyArtKit provides a robust suite of teaching and learning resources including chapter quizzes with feedback, e-Flashcards of every image in the book, video clips, and many more dynamic activities. MyArtKit offers you and your students a unique, interactive experience that helps bring art to life.

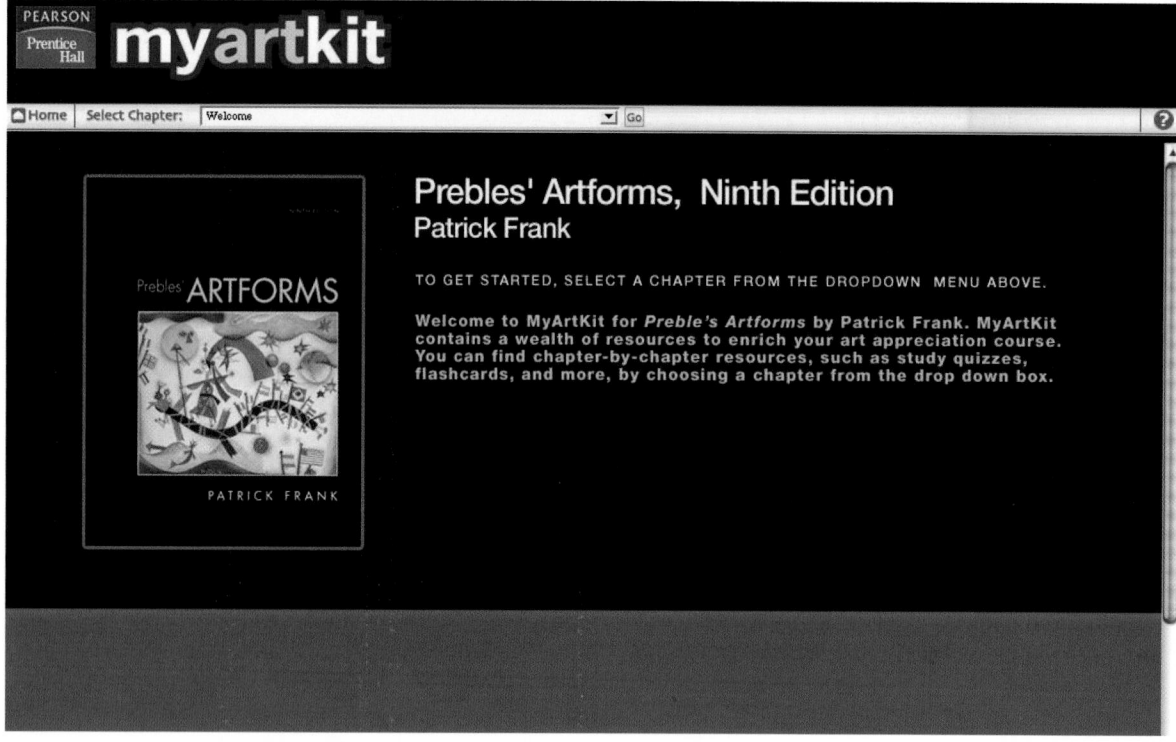

E-FLASHCARDS

Interactive e-Flashcards offer all the benefits of traditional flashcards in a student-friendly and printable online format. Each e-Flashcard is accompanied by a critical thinking question to help students further analyze the individual works of art.

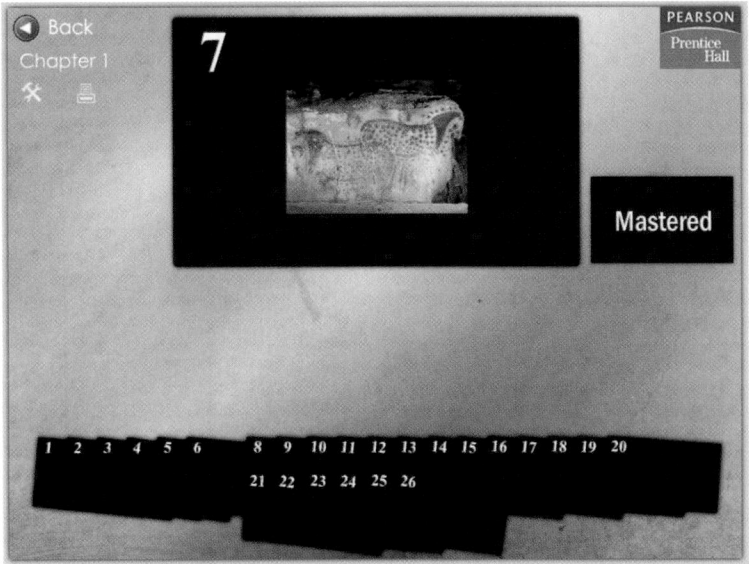

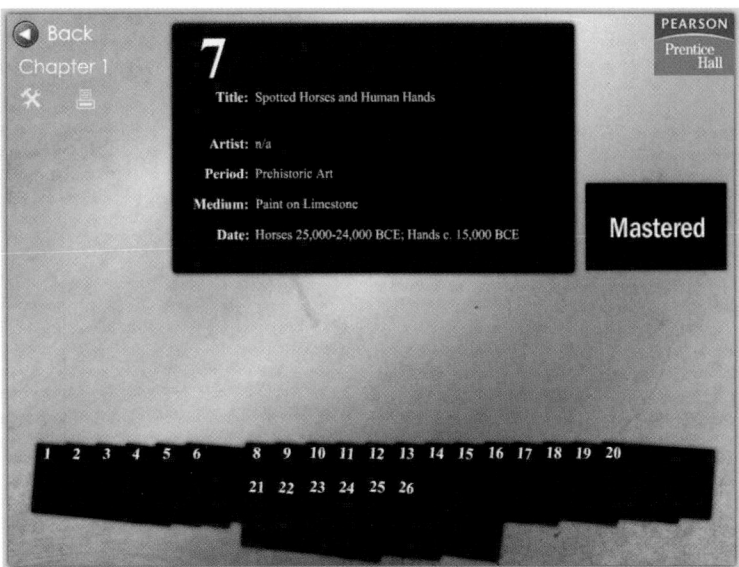

GUIDED TOUR

Interactive Guided Tours give
students an in-depth look at
selected images from the text.
Zoom in for a close-up look at
particular details of the object
and their meanings. Guided
Tours help students develop
the skills to closely "read" an
image.

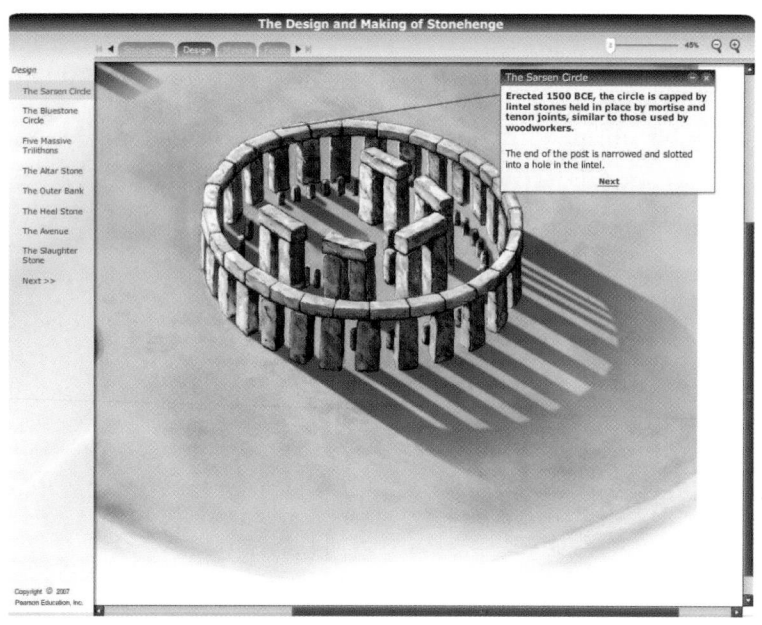

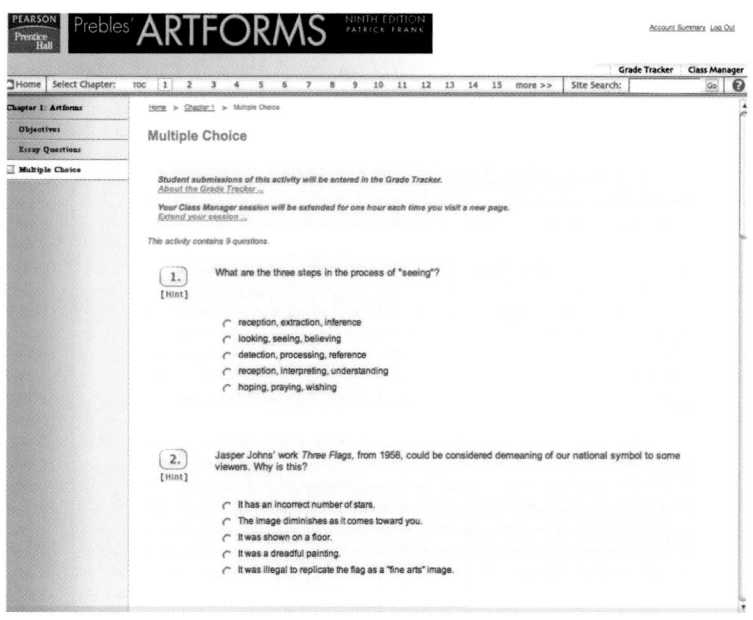

QUIZZES

Self-study quizzes with
targeted feedback for each
chapter allow students to
review their knowledge of the
material and concepts.
Explanatory feedback directs
students to the relevant section
of the textbook.

Faculty and Student Resources *to accompany the text*

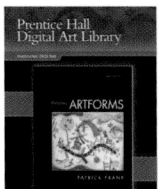 **The Prentice Hall Digital Art Library DVD.** Instructors who adopt PREBLES' ARTFORMS are eligible to receive this unparalled resource, which contains every image in the book in the highest resolution and pixilation possible for optimal projection and one-click download. This powerful resource offers every image in jpeg format and in customizable PowerPoint slides with an instant download function. Save Detail functionality allows you to zoom in and save any detail of an image to your hard drive, which you can then import into PowerPoint. ISBN: 0-13-603371-7.

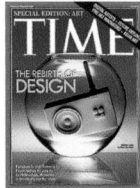 **MyArtKit** is a state-of-the-art interactive and instructive solution for use in art appreciation courses. MyArtKit gives you and your students access to a wealth of resources all geared to meet the individual teaching and learning needs of your classroom. For more information, please visit www.myartkit.com.

■ **TIME Magazine Special Edition: Art.** From environmental design to exhibition reviews to performance art, this issue offers the same accessible writing style and bold coverage/photography for which TIME is known. This is the perfect complement for discussion groups, in-class debates, or research assignments. Available at a nominal cost when packaged with PREBLES' ARTFORMS. ISBN: 0-13-191848-6.

■ **ArtNotes.** This notebook lecture companion for students features thumbnail reproductions of the works in the text, with captions and page references for each. Space is provided next to each object for note taking in class. Available at a nominal cost when packaged with PREBLES' ARTFORMS. ISBN: 0-13-603369-5.

■ **Companion Web site at www.prenhall.com/preble.** This site features unique study and support tools for every chapter of PREBLES' ARTFORMS: Objectives, Internet projects, image links, and more. Multiple-choice and short-answer quizzes provide instant scoring and feedback to help students' self-study, or students can e-mail essay responses and graded quizzes directly to their instructors.

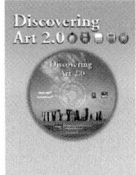 **Discovering Art 2.0 CD-ROM**—contained in every new copy of PREBLES' ARTFORMS. This interactive CD-ROM offers students a highly visual exploration of art. Students will see and hear video demonstrations of studio processes, view images in a virtual image gallery, and learn how—and where—to visit a museum. Plus, interactive exercises help students to review and reinforce the material under study.

■ *Understanding the Art Museum* **by Barbara Beall-Fofana.** This handbook gives students essential museum-going guidance to help them make the most of their experience seeing art outside of the classroom. Case studies are incorporated into the text, and a list of major museums in the United States and key cities across the world is included. ISBN: 0-13-195070-3.

■ **Instructor's Manual with Test Bank.** Designed for both the novice and seasoned professor, this invaluable guide includes the following for each chapter: An overview, objectives, outline, key terms, lecture and discussion ideas, assignments and hands-on projects, further resources, and a test bank. The test bank contains multiple-choice, true/false, short-answer, and essay questions. Contact your local Prentice Hall representative for more information. ISBN: 0-13-604415-8.

■ **TestGen.** This commercial-quality computerized test management program for Windows™ or Macintosh® allows instructors to select test bank items to design their own examinations. Contact your local Prentice Hall sales representative for more information. ISBN: 0-13-604416-6.

For details about these resources, or to order a value package for PREBLES' ARTFORMS, contact your local Pearson sales representative (use our rep locator at www.prenhall.com), or e-mail us: art_service@prenhall.com.

PART ONE

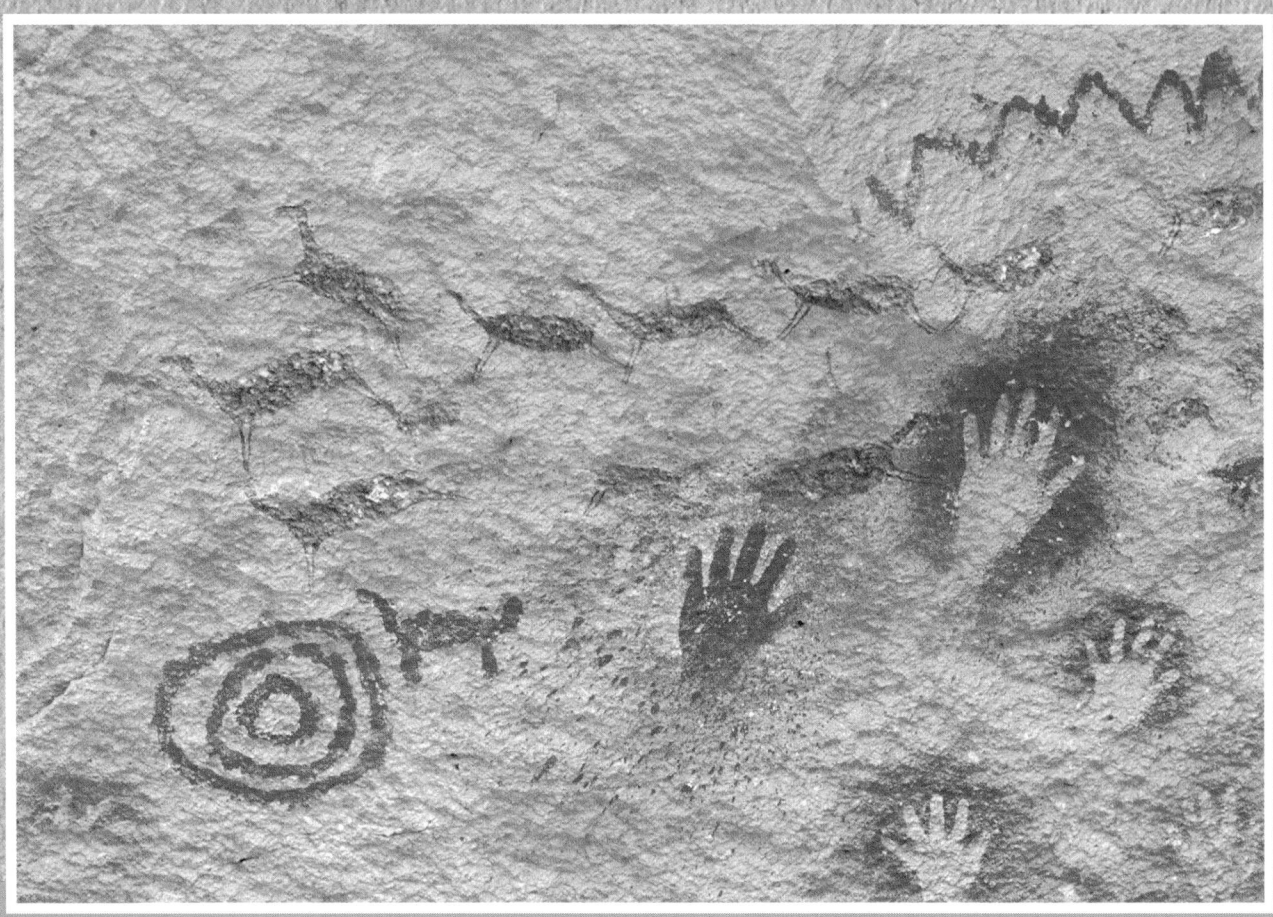

DEER AND HANDS.
Las Manos Cave, Argentina. c. 15,000 B.C.E.

ART IS...

CONSIDER...

Have you ever tried to explain something to someone—then used a pencil to show exactly what you meant?

Are any paintings, posters, or photographs displayed where you live or work? If so, how do you feel about them? Do they enhance your life?

Do you think artists are born with special gifts, or do you think they acquire skills through practice and effort?

Most of us were active artists as children, and then we stopped making art. Do you still draw or paint or take photographs? If not, why not?

Do you think that most societies use art in the same way? Is art a concept, a process, or is it objects? Can societies with no word for art still have art?

THE NATURE OF ART

When Barnett Newman's painting CATHEDRA went back on view at the Stedelijk Museum in Amsterdam in 2002, few viewers realized that it had been attacked with a carpet knife five years previously. The attacker grievously damaged the work, leaving an ugly array of parallel horizontal gashes along most of its 18-foot width. Specialists took more than four years to restore it, traveling the world to see similar paintings, consulting the artist's archives and associates, laboriously mixing trial shades of paint, and even building replicas of CATHEDRA to slash and restore themselves.

We might immediately think that the attacker was insane, but this is not true. Rather, his own actions showed his sanity: After the crime he had stayed in the museum, calmly awaiting arrest, passing out leaflets to explain his action. He was not against all art, he said, only "abstract art and realism." He was tried and sentenced to a fine and a two-year prison term.

So what drove him to do this? Slashing a painting is a rash, extreme, and even a criminal act, but if he was not insane, then perhaps he was like us. He acted on his feelings in a way that landed him in jail, but the fact is that art can arouse many deep feelings in almost everyone. Works of art have stirred all of us at one time or another, awakening memories, thoughts, passions, drives, pleasures, and pains. The goal of this book is to help deepen that encounter.

Not all of us regularly create works of art, but all of us are creative in some way. We create a home life. We create relationships. We create events, goals, projects, and accomplishments. Even a common act such as arranging furniture in a room or pictures on the wall is creative and allows us self-expression. Visual art is one type of human creativity, and art viewers, when contemplating a work, create their own responses to it. When we respond to a work of art, we activate our own creativity; the artist's work evokes the artist within us.

At its best, an encounter with art is not a one-way street. That is, humans form art works, and then the art forms us. Hence the title of this book: *Artforms*. Art forms us by telling us things, embellishing our lives, elevating our spirits, showing us who we are, waking us up to injustice, or just flooring us with beauty.

It may not be apparent at first, but Newman painted CATHEDRA with a spiritual intent. He wanted to evoke the mightiness and transcendence of God, without referring to any specific religion. The title comes from the Greek word for throne, *kathedra*, from which we get the word *cathedral*. Newman said that the work depicts "the throne of God. His blue robe fills the holy space." Just as we might approach the seat of God with awe and wonder, Newman hoped to inspire such feelings in us as we contemplate this 18-foot painting with its intensely blue space.

1   Barnett Newman.
CATHEDRA. 1951.
Oil on canvas, 96″ × 213″.
Stedelijk Museum, Amsterdam. © 2009 Artists Rights Society (ARS), NY.

Understanding the artist's intent can help us appreciate CATHEDRA, but art does not need to be "understood" to be enjoyed. Like life itself, it can simply be experienced. Yet the more we understand about what art can offer, the richer our experience will be.

WHAT IS ART?

Within this book a *work of art* is the visual expression of an idea or experience formed with skill through the use of a medium. A *medium* is a particular material, along with its accompanying technique. (The plural is *media*.) Artists select media to suit the ideas and feelings they wish to present. When a medium is used in such a way that the object or performance contributes to our understanding or enjoyment of life, we experience the final product as art.

Media in use for many centuries include clay, fiber, stone, wood, and paint. By the mid-twentieth century, modern technology had added new media, including video and computers, to the nineteenth-century contributions of photography and motion pictures. Art made with a combination of different materials is referred to as *mixed media*.

When people speak of *the arts*, they are usually referring to music, dance, theater, literature, and the visual arts. Each art form is perceived in different ways by our senses, yet each grows from a common need to give expressive substance to feelings, ideas, insights, and experiences. In this book, the focus is the visual arts, including drawing, painting, sculpture, film, architecture, and design.

Much of our communication is verbal, yet any single medium of expression has its limitations. Some ideas and feelings can be communicated only

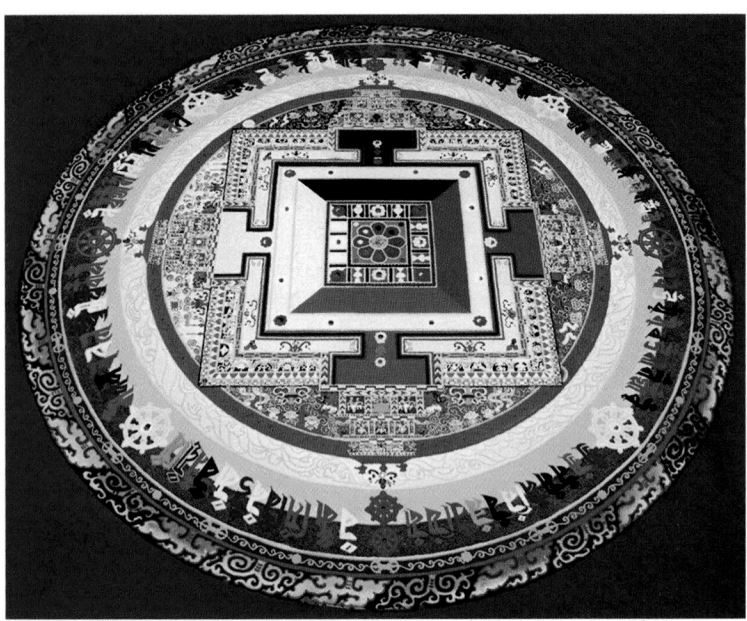

2   WHEEL OF TIME.
Tibetan sand mandala. 1997.
Photograph: José R. Lopez, *New York Times* Pictures.

through visual forms, while other insights can be expressed best through music. American painter Georgia O'Keeffe said: "I found that I could say things with colors and shapes that I couldn't say in any other way—things I had no words for."[1] The arts communicate meanings that go far beyond ordinary verbal exchange, and artists use the entire range of thought, feeling, and observation as the subjects of their art.

THE NEED TO BE CREATIVE

All societies produce objects that communicate beyond words and meet physical, spiritual, or aesthetic needs. Some objects—from simple tools to vast temple complexes—have been designed to meet many of these needs simultaneously.

In the context of Tibetan Buddhism, art making is a meditative collaborative process requiring concentration and focused attention. In 1997, three Tibetan monks from the American Nagyal Monastery spent three weeks at the Asia Society in New York City making a traditional *mandala* (a sacred circle). Working eighteen-hour days for three weeks, they produced the WHEEL OF TIME by

carefully pouring colored sand. The monks followed ancient traditional practices as they created their contemporary symbol. After celebrating and sharing the work, they destroyed it to symbolize the impermanence of life.

Visual creativity can take almost any form. A film director places actors and cameras on a stage in order to emphasize a certain aspect of the script. A Hopi potter takes clay from the ground near her home and shapes it into a water jar. A graphic designer seated at a computer screen arranges a composition of typefaces, images, and colors in order to help get his message across. A carver in Japan fashions wood into a Buddha that will aid in meditation at a monastery. Most of us have at some time selected and arranged posters or pictures on our walls. All of these actions involve artistic creativity, the use of visual imagery to communicate beyond what mere words can say.

Because our high-tech, multicultural society has few shared traditions, we have few traditional art forms. Most of us tend to think of "art" as something produced only by "artists"—uniquely gifted people. Because art is often separated from community life in contemporary society, many people believe they have no artistic talent. This belief makes them hesitate to create their own art or even to explore the art of others. Today, works we call art are often displayed in galleries and museums—far removed from the everyday life experiences of the people who created them or view them.

This situation is unfortunate; people living in highly technological societies need art as much as the members of traditional societies need art. Science and the arts serve humanity in complementary ways. Both involve creative thinking and problem solving. Science seeks answers to questions about the outer, physical world; these answers form the basis of our technology. The arts foster the development of our inner world—the intuitive, emotional, spiritual, and creative aspects of being human. Reality is explained through the sciences and revealed through the arts. People need both science and art if they are to balance function with meaning.

History provides the best evidence of our need for the arts. When a dictator or conquering group seeks domination over a people, and perhaps has already won a military victory, the next step is to find ways to destroy the culture—to eliminate the language, traditions, and the arts of the oppressed. Artists of all kinds are among the first to be controlled or silenced. Hitler's and Saddam Hussein's control of the arts, and the suppression of the languages and ritual arts of Native Americans, immediately come to mind.

As groups and individuals, we can survive incredible physical hardships more easily than the loss of our personal creativity and cultural foundations. Our languages, our arts, our traditions, and beliefs are at the core of who we are.

PURPOSES AND FUNCTIONS OF ART

Art can inform, embellish, inspire, arouse, awaken, and delight us. Art can challenge us to think and see in new ways, and help each of us to develop a personal sense of beauty and truth. It can also deceive, humiliate, and anger us. A given work of art may serve several functions all at once.

When we look at art we cannot always know exactly what its creators had in mind. To understand their purposes and functions, let us examine some works as examples.

Art for Communicating Information

Because art makes a statement that can be understood by a broad spectrum of people, it has often been used to impart information and ideas. During the Middle Ages in Europe, stained-glass windows and stone sculpture of the cathedrals taught Bible stories to an illiterate population.

At Chartres Cathedral, near Paris, a stained-glass window called THE TREE OF JESSE depicts the genealogy of Jesus Christ, beginning with the Jewish

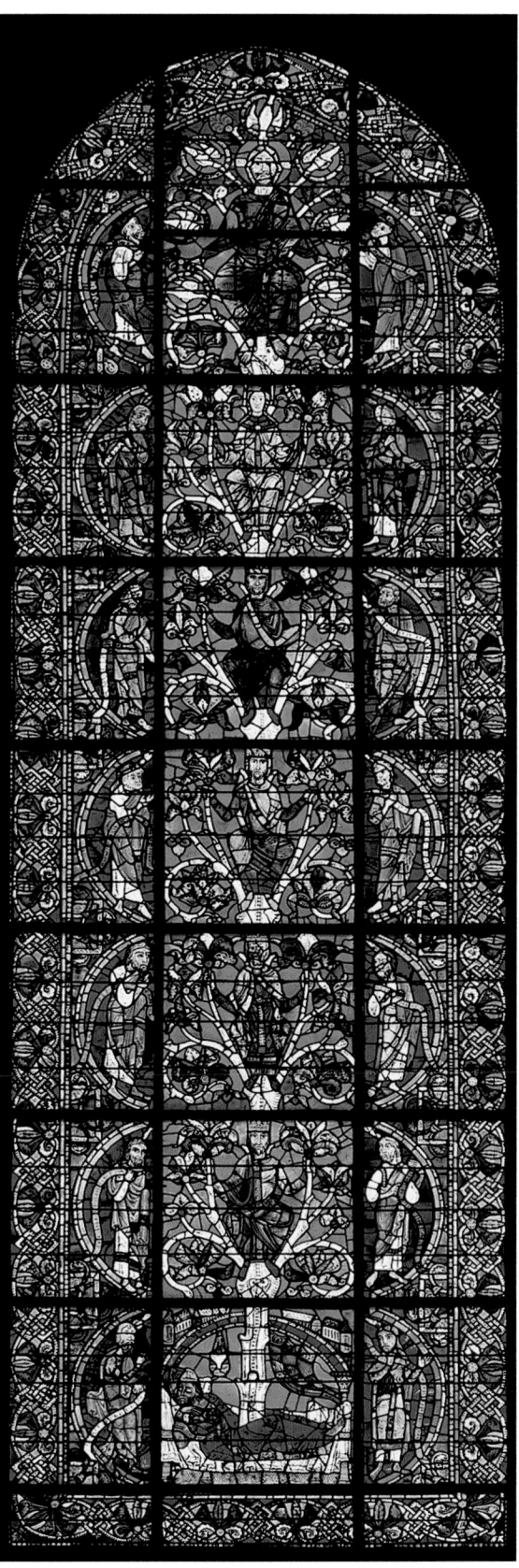

3   THE TREE OF JESSE.
    West facade, Chartres Cathedral. c. 1150–1170.
    Stained glass.
    Photograph: Laura Lushington, Sonia Halliday Photographs.

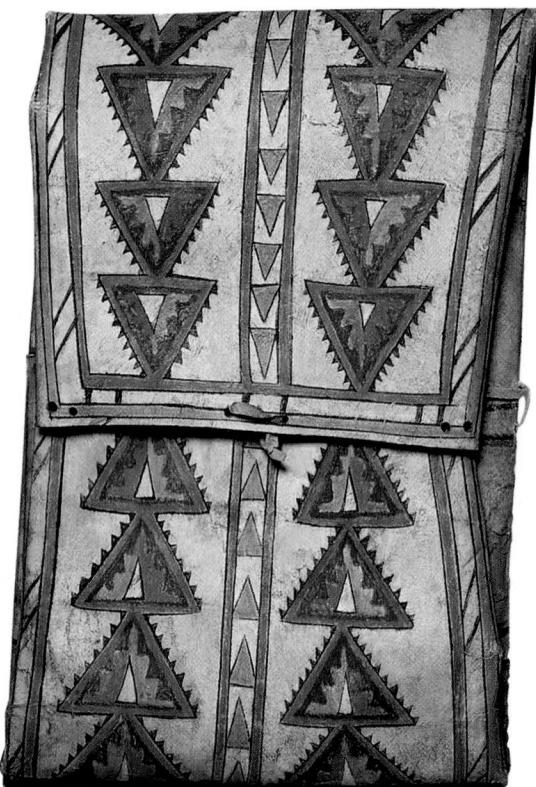

4   BLACKFEET PARFLECHE. 1885.
Rawhide, pigment. 21″ × 14″.
University of Pennsylvania Museum, Philadelphia. (Neg. #T4-826)

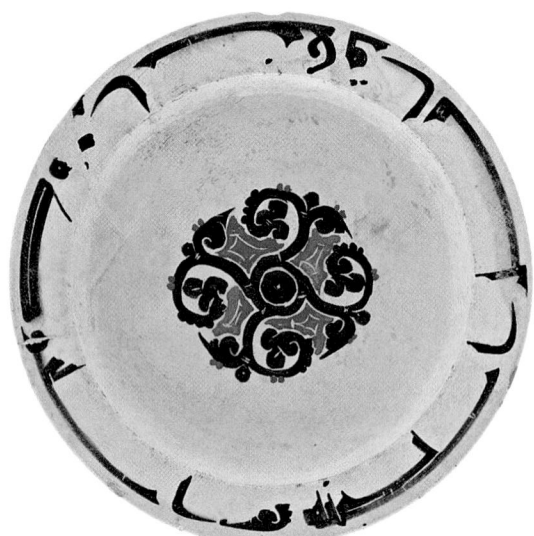

5   DISH.
10th Century. East Iran.
Lead-glazed earthenware with colored slips. Diameter 8¼″.
Courtesy Freer Gallery of Art, Smithsonian Institution,
Washington, D.C. (F1965.27)

patriarch Jesse (at the bottom below the tree). The vertical sequence presenting the four kings culminates in depictions of Mary the mother of Jesus, and at the top, Christ himself. Many later artists—especially portrait painters—following in the European tradition, have had as their primary goal the mere recording of information for posterity.

Art continues to inform nonliterate as well as literate people around the world. Photography, film, and television have proven to be particularly useful for recording and communicating. Through artistic presentation, information often becomes more accessible and memorable than it would be through words alone.

Art for Day-to-Day Living

Objects of all kinds, from ancient, carefully crafted flint knives to sleek sports cars, have been conceived to delight the eye as well as to serve more obviously useful functions. Well-designed utilitarian objects and spaces—from chairs to communities—bring pleasure and efficiency into our daily lives. For example, the BLACKFEET PARFLECHE is a rawhide envelope that was useful for carrying personal goods in that nomadic Native American society. However, it is also decorated with colorful symbolic forms that refer to the tribe's communal life and to the forces of nature. Women made these parfleches by stretching out pieces of rawhide in the sun to dry, then applying paints pigmented with earthen powders.

Many societies value the artistic embellishment of everyday things. This DISH from ancient Persia is simply decorated in a few colors. The circular patterns in the central motif echo the shape of the plate itself. Dancing around its border is a line of stylized Arabic writing from Muslim scripture, which underlines the plate's function in hospitality: "Generosity is one of the qualities of the people of Paradise."

In a general sense, the visual arts include all human creations in which visual form has been a major consideration during their design and production. Nearly all the objects and spaces we use in our private and public lives were designed by artists and designers. The best of our buildings, towns, and cities have been designed with the quality of their visual form—as well as their other functions—in mind. Each of us is involved with art and design whenever we make decisions about how to style our hair, what clothes to wear, or how to furnish and arrange our living spaces. As we make such choices, we are engaged in universal art-related processes—making visual statements about who we are and the kind of world we like to see around us.

Art for Worship and Ritual

In many societies, the arts have a spiritual component. Spiritual and/or magical purposes apparently motivated the making of the world's earliest carvings and cave paintings. Long before the developments of farming and writing, the arts helped sustain bands of hunter-gatherers. What motivated prehistoric peoples to carve, draw, and paint? Survival needs? The desire to record events? The need to magically control the animals they hunted for food? Or simply the urge to create?

Among the best-known ritual structures built by stone-age human beings is the complex of huge boulders at STONEHENGE, England. It was constructed at a time when religion and science were one unified quest for understanding. Four series of giant stones, surrounding an altar stone, stand within a circular trench 300 feet in diameter. Most archaeologists agree that STONEHENGE was built in several phases, around 2000 B.C.E., to serve some sort of religious or scientific function. Because many of the stones in the structure align with celestial phenomena such as solar and lunar movements, many art historians think that this structure served a spiritual function, showing humans their place in the cosmic cycle. Most likely it was also a backdrop for various rituals.

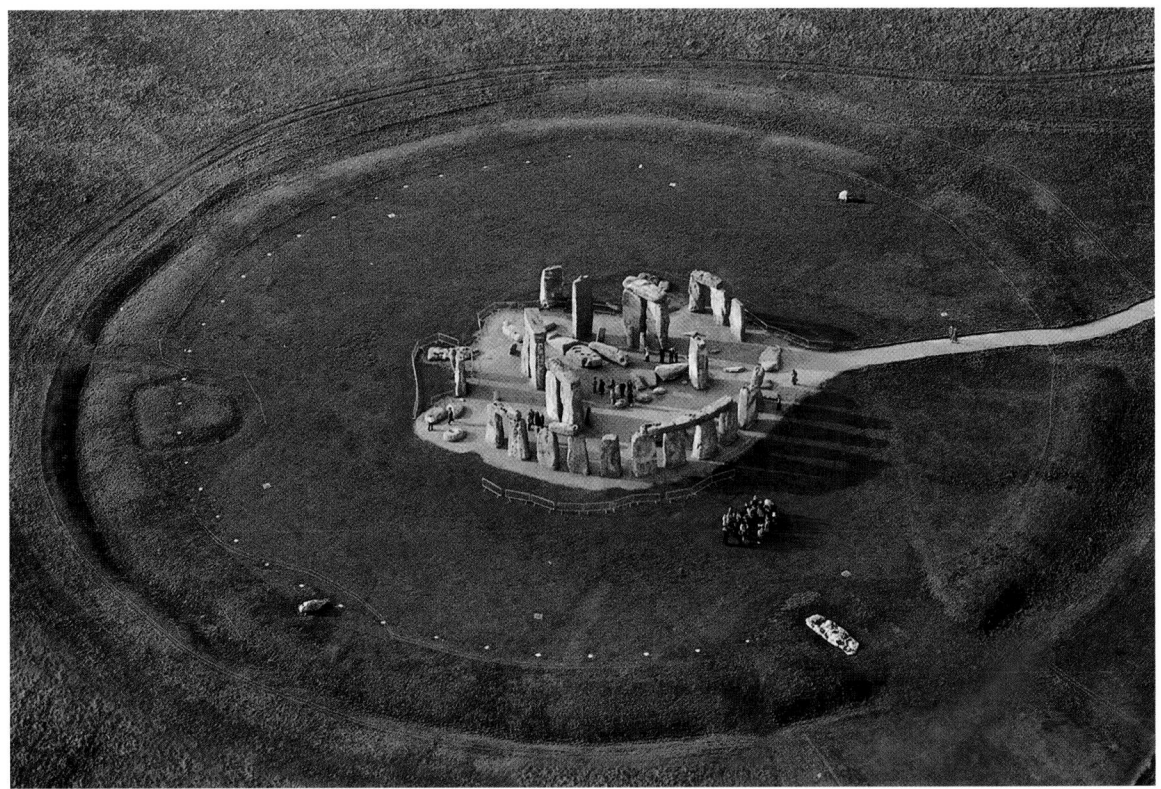

6   STONEHENGE. c. 2000 B.C.E.
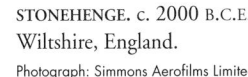   Wiltshire, England.
Photograph: Simmons Aerofilms Limited.

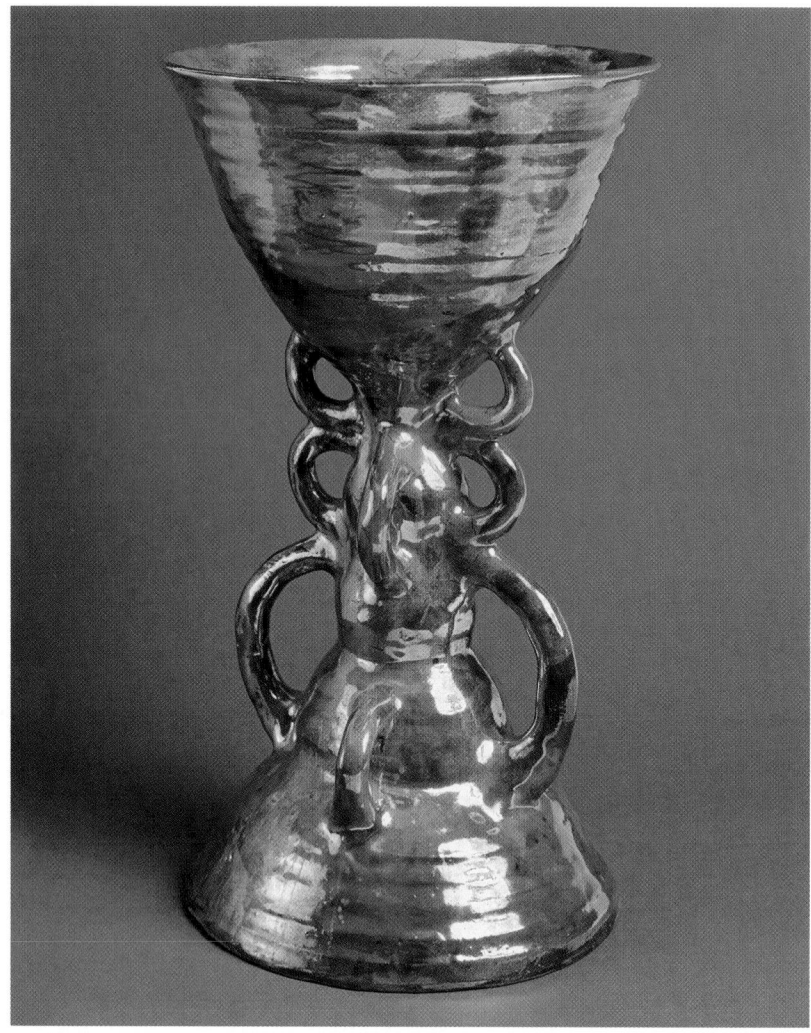

7   Beatrice Wood.
CHALICE. 1986.
Pottery. 7⅝″ × ⅞″.
The Newark Museum/Art Resource, NY.

Many objects created for ritual use look precious, befitting their use in divine ceremonies. The CHALICE by American potter Beatrice Wood seems to radiate warm light. Muslim potters centuries ago developed the technique for producing this glowing, metallic surface; here the artist applied it to a shape that she formed with earthenware. The profile of the piece shows its origins in the natural forms of the earth, as it lacks straight lines and square edges. Its resemblance to a human form may echo the Christian belief that Christ is present in the ritual. The CHALICE has many handles that seem to invite eager grasping. These handles are symmetrical, positioned so that the most natural approach to it is to stand before it and hold it up, which is in fact what priests do in the Roman Catholic Mass. The CHALICE could hold consecrated wine for Christian ritual, but its earthy, rounded shape and glowing body make it a compelling decorative piece as well.

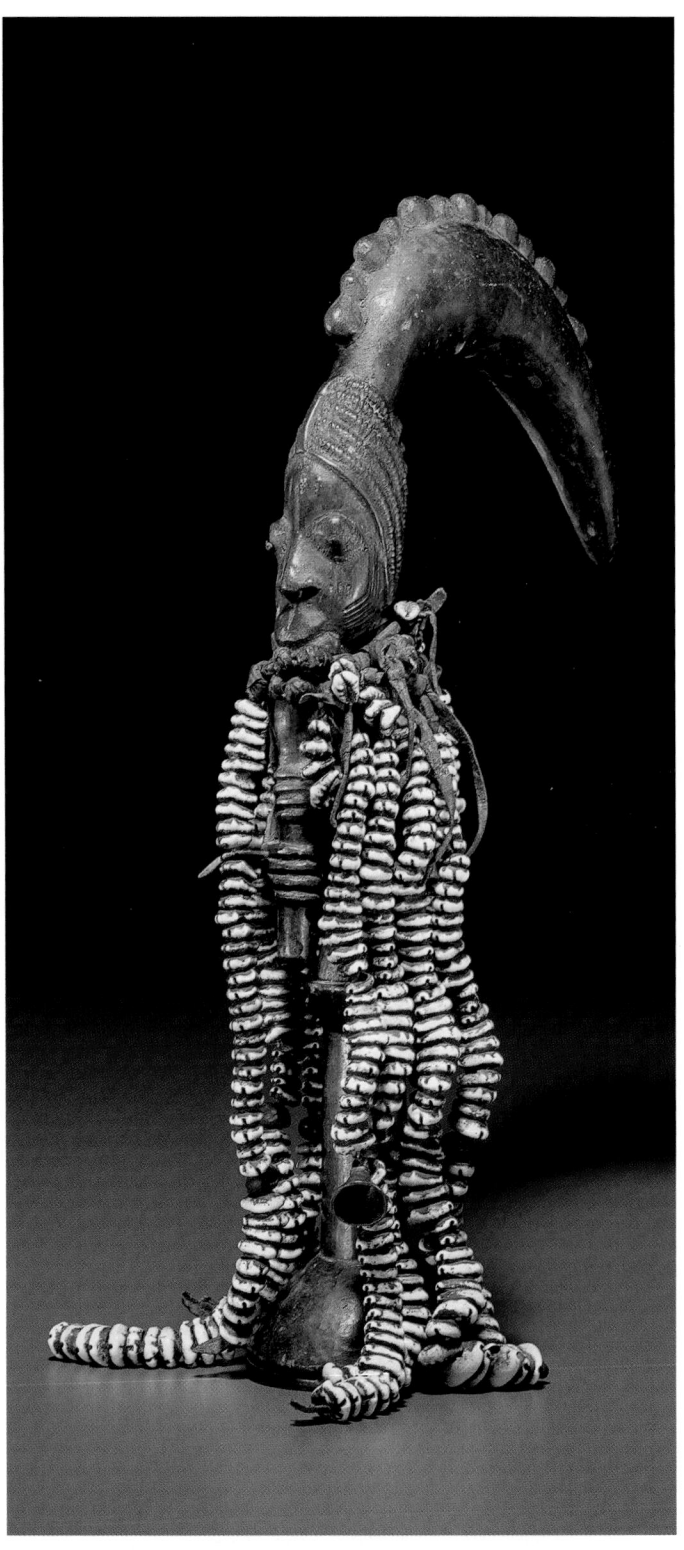

A great deal of African art has a spiritual emphasis, as worshippers use objects in rituals to attract the attention of the gods. The DANCE WAND IN HONOR OF ESHU is draped with strands of the shells that were used as currency, alluding to Eshu's lordship of the marketplace. A worshipper uses the statue by hanging it over a shoulder and literally dancing with it to the appropriate chants and songs. The bulbs protruding from Eshu's bladelike hairdo signify the medicines that Eshu uses.

Art continues to fulfill personal, spiritual needs for many people, and all of the world's major religions have used art to inspire and instruct the faithful.

Art for Personal Expression

Certain artists reveal themselves and their heritage so clearly that we feel we know them. Seventeenth-century Dutch artist Rembrandt van Rijn expressed his attitude toward life through well over one thousand paintings, drawings, and prints.

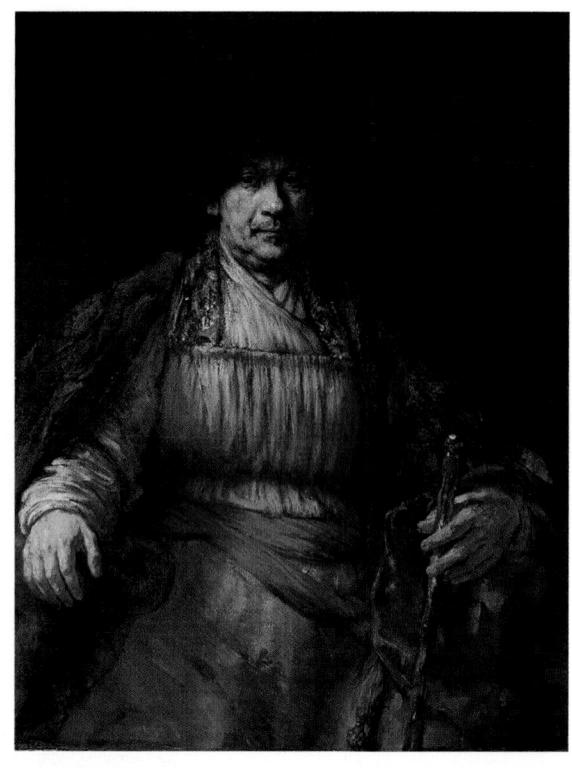

From the age of twenty until his death at sixty-three, Rembrandt drew and painted dozens of self-portraits. He was fascinated by the expressive possibilities of the human body and found himself to be the most readily available model. Like a good actor, he used his own face as a resource for studying life.

In most of his self-portraits, Rembrandt viewed himself straightforwardly and with the same curiosity that he brought to his other human subjects. Rembrandt's SELF-PORTRAIT of 1658 is brought to life by the eyes, which suggest a person of penetrating insight. By examining himself objectively, he went beyond himself; he created a statement about how it feels to be alive, to be human.

Korean-American artist Yong Soon Min projects an altogether contemporary sense of the self in her mixed-media piece DWELLING. Born in a small village in Korea just before the end of the Korean War, she and her mother joined her father in California when she was seven. Thus while she was raised mainly in the United States, it is not her native land; yet on trips back to Korea she feels distant from her country of origin as well.

DWELLING expresses this alienation and absence. The artist inserted personal mementoes into a traditional Korean-style dress and hung it over a pile of books, maps, and photographs. Inside the dress, barely visible, is a script from a Korean poet, which gives voice to the loss of identity. The

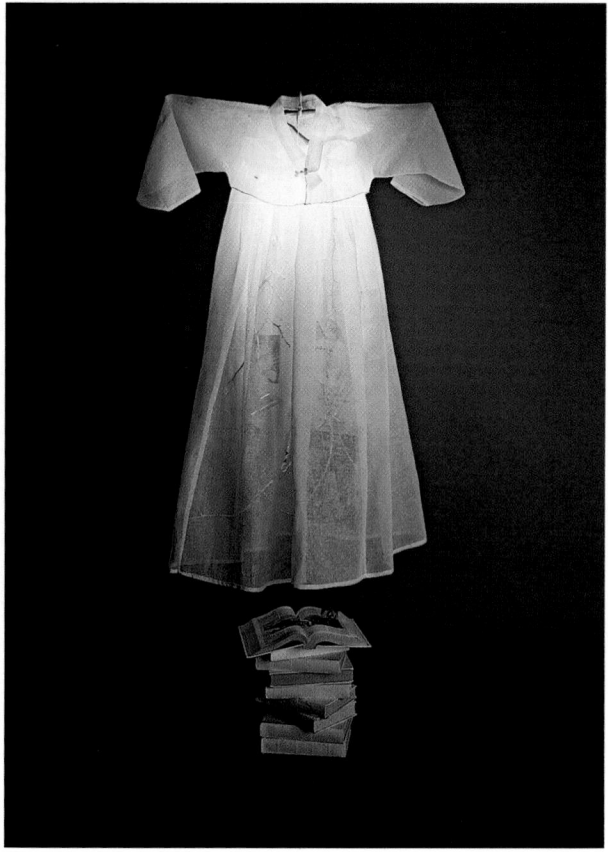

9 Rembrandt van Rijn.
SELF-PORTRAIT. 1658.
Oil on canvas. 52⅝″ × 40⅞″.
© The Frick Collection, New York.

10 Yong Soon Min.
DWELLING. 1994.
Mixed media. 72″ × 42″ × 28″.
Photo by Erik Landsberg. Courtesy of the artist.

hauntingly empty dress seems to await a Korean occupant who will never put it back on. This sense of divided nationality is increasingly common among Americans, many of whom were born elsewhere.

Twentieth-century American artist Romare Bearden was fascinated by the pageant of daily life he witnessed in the rural South and in Harlem, New York. Bearden created memorable images of humanity by observing, distilling, then reconstructing the life he saw around him. In PREVALENCE OF RITUAL: TIDINGS an angel seems to console or embrace an introspective young woman. Borrowed picture fragments with a few muted colors make up an otherwise gray world. There is a mood of melancholy and longing. Does the train suggest departure from this world or escape to the lure of a better life in the North?

In ROCKET TO THE MOON, collage fragments build a scene of quiet despair and stoic perseverance. A barely visible rocket heads for the moon, while urban life remains punctuated by a red stoplight. The artist makes an ironic visual statement: Bearden placed America's accomplishments in space next to our inner cities' stalled social and economic progress.

Rembrandt and Bearden were concerned with the effectiveness of their communication to others, but equally important was their own inner need for expression. Within the broad range of the visual arts, there is a considerable difference in the amount and type of personal expression. Not all art is meant to express the personality of the maker; the designs of a coin or a telephone offer much less information about the personal concerns of the artist than do the designs of a painting or a piece of sculpture.

Yet an element of self-expression exists in all art, even when the art is produced cooperatively by many individuals, as in filmmaking and architecture. In each case, the intended purpose for the art affects the nature and degree of the personal expression.

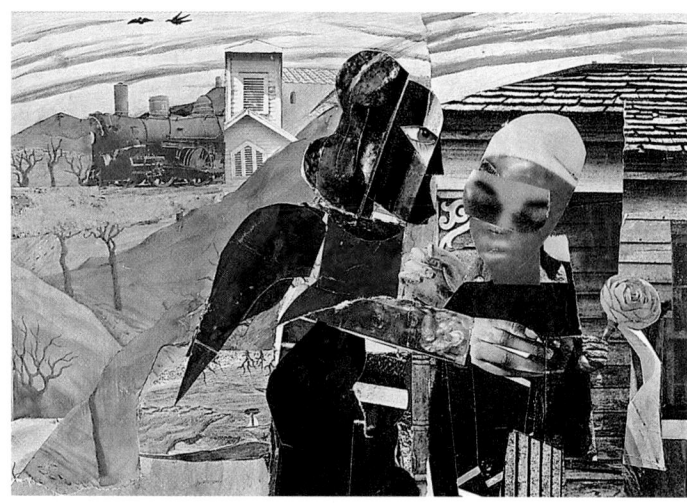

11 Romare Bearden.
PREVALENCE OF RITUAL: TIDINGS. 1967.
Photomontage. 36″ × 48″.
© Romare Bearden Foundation/Licensed by VAGA, New York, NY.

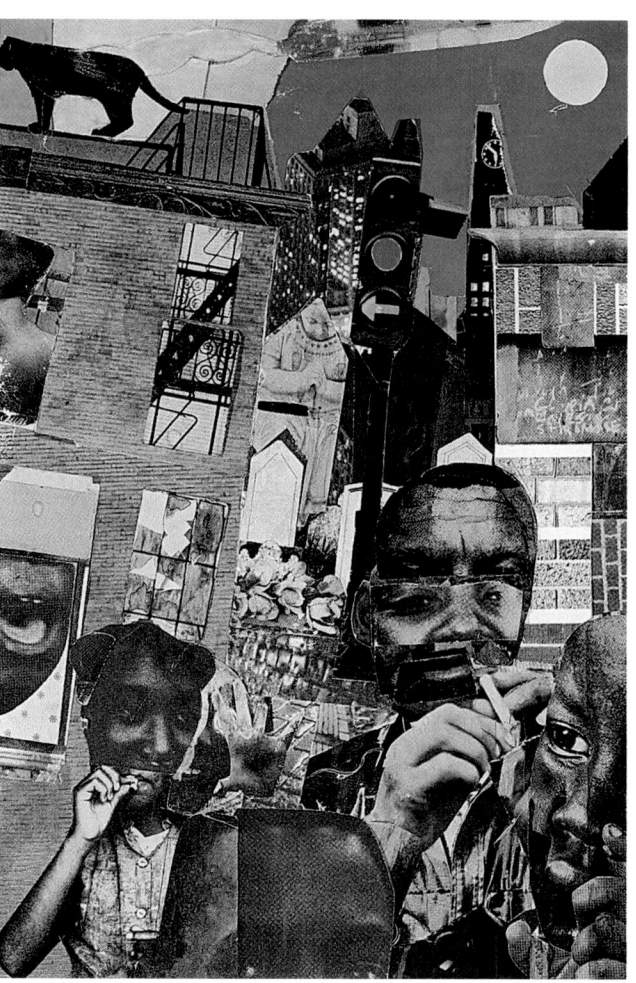

12 Romare Bearden.
ROCKET TO THE MOON. 1971.
Collage on board. 13″ × 9¼″.
© Romare Bearden Foundation/Licensed by VAGA, New York, NY.

ROMARE
Bearden
1911–1988

ROMARE BEARDEN paid tribute to the richness of his African-American experience through his art. He sought:

to paint the life of my people as I know it ... because much of that life is gone and it had beauty.[2]

The child of educated, middle-class parents, Bearden spent his early childhood in rural North Carolina, then moved north with his family to Harlem, in New York City. He had a brief stint as a professional baseball player for the Boston club of the now-defunct Negro Leagues. He attended New York University, where he earned a degree in education and drew cartoons for the *NYU Medley*. He went on to draw humorous and political cartoons for magazines and a newspaper. During the Depression he attended the Art Students League in New York, where he was encouraged to say more in his drawings than he said in his cartoons. He held his first exhibition in a private studio in 1940—about the same time that he became a social worker in New York, a job he held on and off until 1966.

After serving in the army during World War II, Bearden used his G.I. Bill education grant to study at the Sorbonne in Paris. There he came to know a number of intellectuals and writers of African descent, including poet Leopold Senghor and novelist James Baldwin. Bearden was inspired to make the philosophical perspective of his ethnic heritage a cornerstone of his art. He said of his experience at the Sorbonne, "The biggest thing I learned was reaching into your consciousness of black experience and relating it to universals."[3]

Bearden was critical of programs that supported African-American artists by encouraging them to work in European academic traditions rather than those of their own lives. He believed that, just as African Americans had created their own musical forms such as jazz and blues, they should invent their own visual art. He urged fellow African-American artists to create art out of their own life experiences, as had jazz greats Ellington, Basie, Waller, and Hines, who were among Bearden's friends. Bearden himself was a musician and songwriter who said he painted in the tradition of the blues.

He combined his stylistic search with institutional activism. In 1963, he founded the Spiral Group, an informal group of African-American artists who met in his studio. A year later, he became art director of the Harlem Cultural Council, a group devoted to recognizing and promoting the arts of Harlem residents.

His study of art history led Bearden to admire Cubist and Surrealist paintings and African sculpture, as well as work by earlier European masters. These works of art were among the many important influences on his creative development. Also important was the rapid-cut style of contemporary documentary filmmakers. Bearden worked in a variety of styles prior to the 1960s, when he arrived at the combined collage and painting style for which he is best known.

Although he learned from direct association with the previous generation of international artists, Bearden's focus remained the

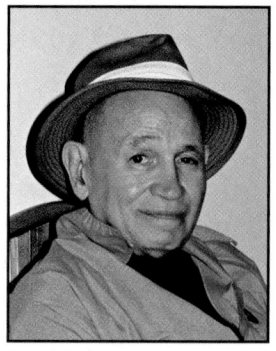

13   Romare Bearden.
Photograph: Bernard Brown and Associates.

African-American experience. He kept a list of key events from his life on the wall of his studio. Often, Bearden drew upon memories of his childhood in rural North Carolina. The idea of homecoming fascinated him. He said, "You can come back to where you started from with added experience and you hope more understanding. You leave and then return to the homeland of your imagination."[4]

Despite his emphasis on his own experiences, Bearden cannot simply be labeled an African-American artist because his work has meaning both for and far beyond that community. He said, "What I try to do with art is amplify." If he had just painted a North Carolina farm woman, "it would have meaning to her and people there. But art amplifies itself to something universal."[5]

Art for Social Causes

Artists in many societies have sought to criticize or influence values and public opinion through their work. Often the criticism is clear and direct, as with Francisco Goya's expression of outrage at the Napoleonic Wars in his country. THE DISASTERS OF WAR vividly documents atrocities committed by Napoleon's troops as they invaded Spain in 1808. In a similar vein is the work of Cuban-American artist Félix González-Torres. In 1990, he printed large sheets with photographs and information on all of the victims of gunfire in the United States in a randomly selected week. UNTITLED (DEATH BY GUN) was reproduced in what the artist called "endless copies," which were then placed in a stack on the floor of the art gallery, free for the taking by viewers. González-Torres said of these pieces, "I need the public to complete the work. I ask the public to help me, to take responsibility, to become a part of my work, to join in."[6]

Sometimes the artist's social comment is less obvious, but still sincere. The Chinese painter Bada Shanren of the seventeenth century, deeply dissatisfied with the foreign rulers of his country, frequently painted melons as a political statement. Melons are a symbol in China of new birth and new beginnings. The seeds inside the melons

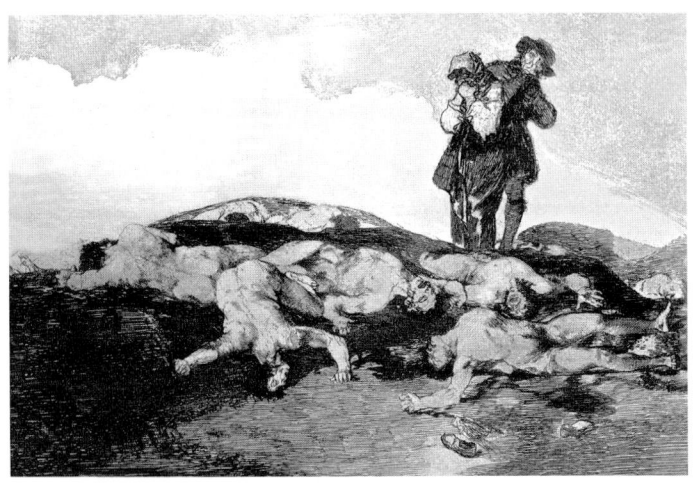

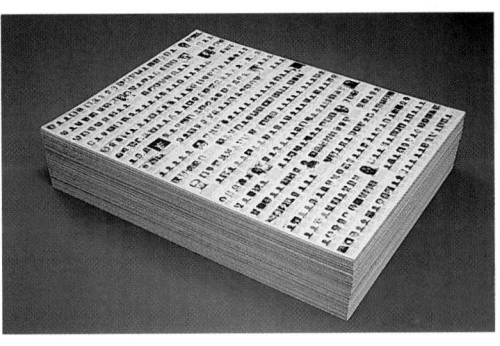

14   Francisco Goya.
THE DISASTERS OF WAR, NO. 18:
BURY THEM AND SAY NOTHING. 1818.
Etching and aquatint.
5⅞″ × 8⅜″.
S.P. Avery Collection, Miriam and Ira D.
Wallach Division of Art, Prints and Photographs.
The New York Public Library,
Astor, Lenox, and Tilden Foundations. Art Resource.

15   Félix González-Torres.
UNTITLED (DEATH BY GUN). 1990.
Offset print on paper. 44½″ × 32½″.
a. Installation view.
b. Single sheet.
The Museum of Modern Art, NY/Licensed by Scala-Art
Resource, NY. Purchased in part with funds from Arthur
Fleisher, Jr. and Linda Barth Goldstein.
Photograph: © 2002 The Museum of Modern Art, NY.

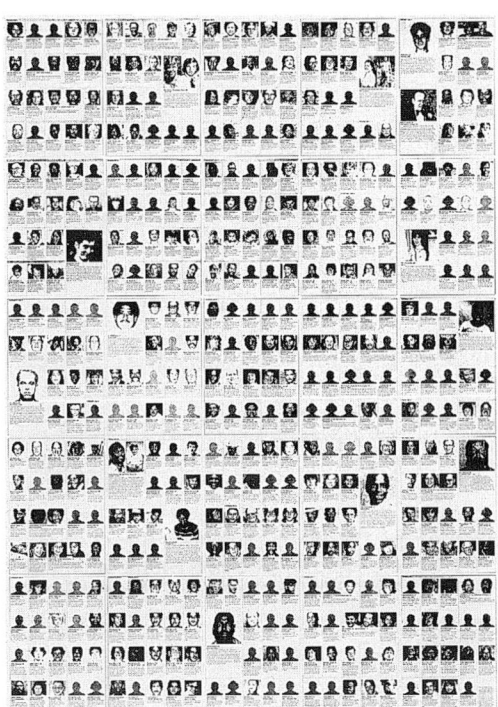

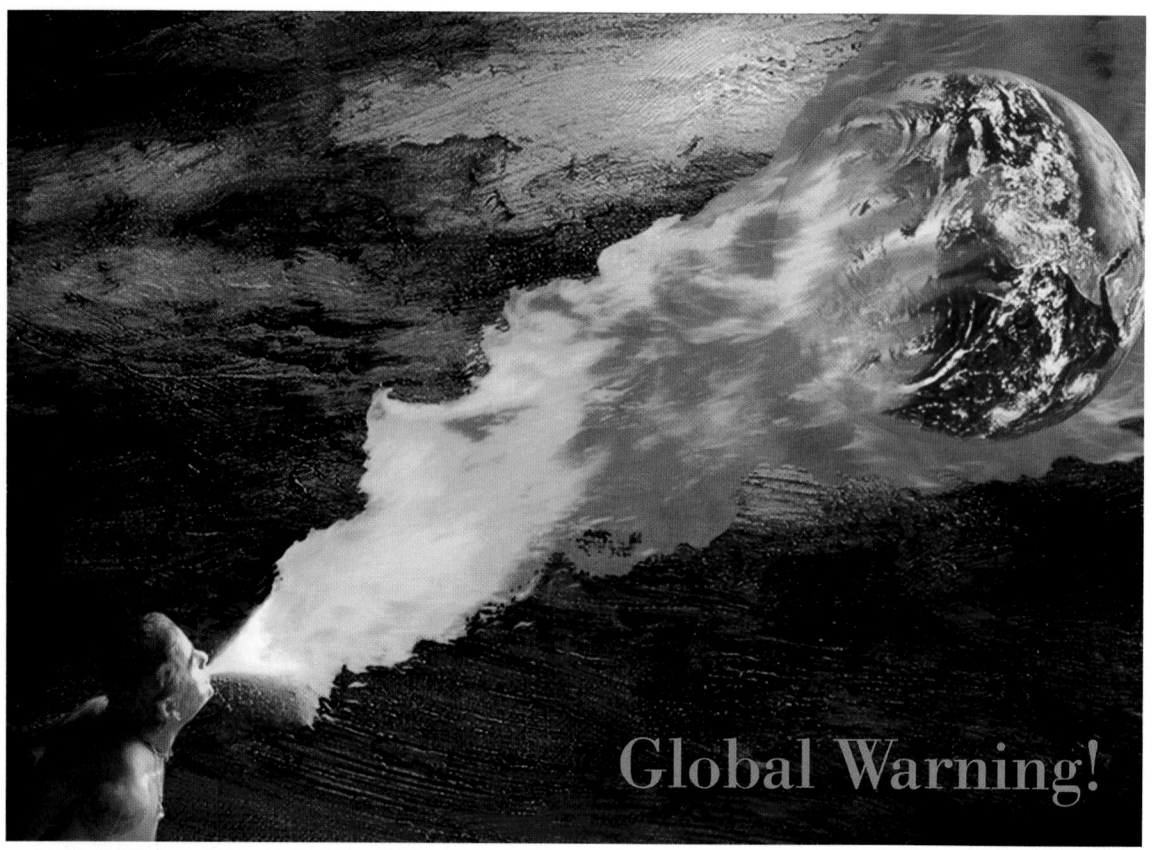

Global Warning!

16   Chaz Maviyane-Davies.
      GLOBAL WARNING. 1997.
      Poster for 3rd United Nations Convention on Climate
      Change, Kyoto.
      Courtesy of the artist.

symbolized the previous Chinese royal line to which the artist was still faithful. While not an outright protest, most educated persons understood the painter's intent.

Architecture, painting, and sculpture—and more recently film and television—have been used to project and glorify images of deities, political leaders, and now corporations. In seventeenth-century France, King Louis XIV built an enormous palace and formal garden at Versailles. His purpose was to symbolize the strength of his monarchy—to impress and intimidate the nobility with the Sun King's power (see Chapter 16).

Advertising designers often use the persuasive powers of art to present a version of the truth. We see their messages every day on television and in the media. Not all persuasive art is commercial, however. Art can be an effective instrument for educating, directing popular values, molding public opinion, and gaining and holding political power.

Global warming causes a great deal of concern today, but some artists have been calling attention to the problem for years. In 1997, Zimbabwean graphic designer Chaz Maviyane-Davies made the poster GLOBAL WARNING for a United Nations conference in Kyoto, Japan. Here we see the earth literally roasting under the impact of the hot breath of the man at the lower left. The poster leaves no doubt about the global nature of the problem, and also the idea that humans are causing it.

Maviyane-Davies was one of the few socially committed designers in his native Zimbabwe, and his commitment to art for social improvement brought him both controversy and wide renown.

When presidential elections were scheduled in Zimbabwe in 2002, the regime of Robert Mugabe took several steps to discourage voting, especially by persons who opposed the status quo. They failed to provide enough polling places in less friendly regions, forcing voters to travel long distances; they also harassed persons who attempted to register to vote. In the face of this threat, Maviyane-Davies began creating posters that denounced the situation, printing them on paper and distributing them free over the Internet. He established a "Portal of Truth" Web site and offered a new poster there each day in the month leading up to the elections. His artistic activism forced him into exile later that year.

The art of our culture reflects who we are and what our relationships are to our surroundings and to one another. Art can be pleasing and beautiful, but it can also shout us awake and inspire us to action. Today, when life demands cross-cultural understanding, open-mindedness, and creative problem solving, art can elevate our consciousness and thus deepen our humanity.

Art for Visual Delight

Many of us probably think of visual delight as the first function of art. Indeed, art can provide pleasure, enjoyment, amusement, diversion, and embellishment in our world. Art that is visually attractive and well crafted can "lift us above the stream of life," as a noted aesthetician once put it.[7] Absorbed in contemplating such works, we forget where we are for a moment.

Islamic art is particularly abundandant with lavish decorations of this sort. For example, the

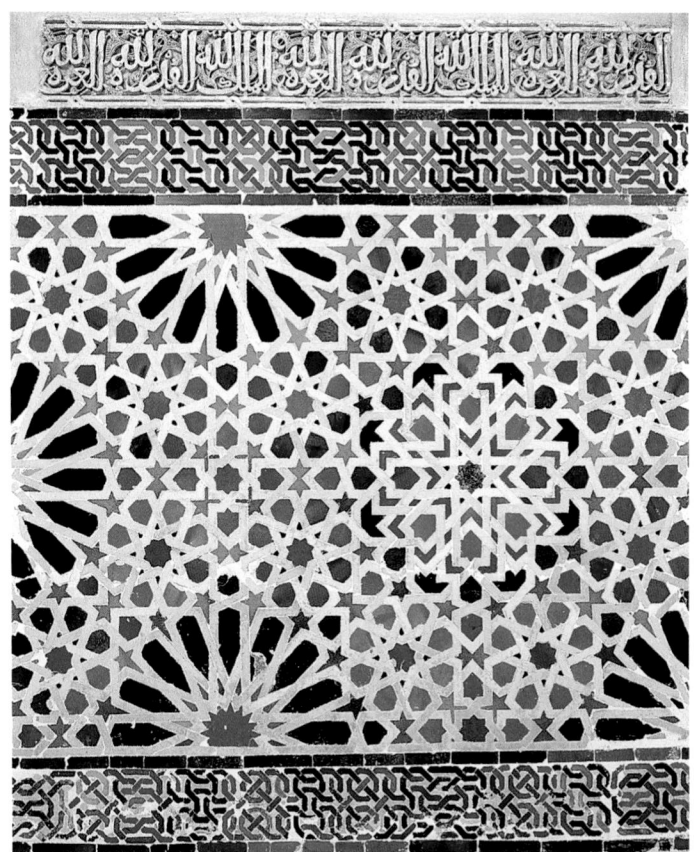

17 DECORATIVE PANEL FROM THE ALHAMBRA.
Granada, Spain. Nasrid Period, 14th Century.
Glazed mosaic tile. 60″ × 50⅝″.
Museo de la Alhambra. Photograph: Sheldan Collins.

fourteenth-century DECORATIVE PANEL FROM THE ALHAMBRA is made of colored mosaic tile laid in dazzling patterns. Our eyes follow pathways that enclose geometric figures of many different shapes, sizes, and colors. These small polygons are elements in a larger rhythm of black starbursts between rows of geometric interlace. The piece shown here is only a small fragment of the lower portion of a wall enclosing a room in the Alhambra, a palace that reached its full glory under the Nasrid rulers of Granada in the fourteenth century.

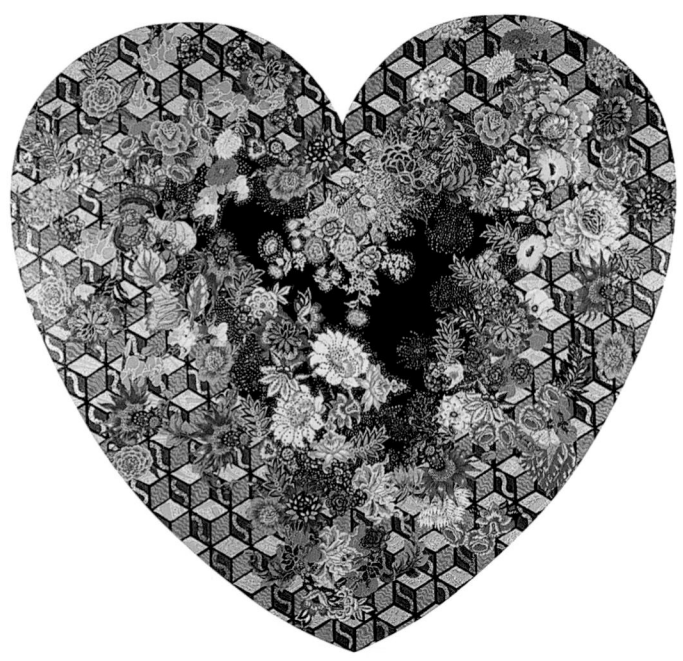

18   Miriam Schapiro.
      HEARTLAND. 1985.
      Acrylic, fabric, and glitter on canvas. 85″ × 94″.
      Collection of Orlando Museum of Art, Orlando, Florida.
      Gift of the Women for Special Acquisitions and the Council of 101, 87.1.

Some contemporary artists have achieved decorative effects with very different materials. Miriam Schapiro's HEARTLAND depends partly on sheer size for its impact, since it measures nearly seven by eight feet. Here, a rich texture of mixed media calls to mind traditional art forms of quilting and flower arranging, which were once considered the province of women. The piece actually combines paint, fabric, and glitter in a collage format whose feminine elements led Schapiro to coin the term "femmages" to describe them. The lush colors, bold patterns, and symbolic meanings of the shape of the work combine to create a garden of visual delight.

Like beauty, truth, and life itself, art is larger than any single definition. One widely used dictionary defines art in this way:

art, n. 1. the expression or application of creative skill and imagination, especially through a visual medium such as painting or sculpture.[8]

As we have seen from the works illustrated in just this chapter, it is difficult to arrive at a definition that includes all the possible forms of art. Hence, we will spend the rest of the book exploring them.

AWARENESS, CREATIVITY, AND COMMUNICATION

There are as many ways to create as there are creative people. The creative process often begins when one is inspired by an idea or faced with a problem.

VISUAL THINKING

Much of our thinking is visual thinking. To visualize is to use imagination and visual memory to preview events or plans before they occur. Most of the things we make begin with a mental picture. This is true for a meal, a vacation, a painting, or a building. All artists use visualization. Some plan their works by mentally picturing them as completed images; others visualize each step as they go along, letting one idea lead to another.

Our experiences influence both inner visualization and outer seeing. For example, ten people painting the same subject—even working from the same vantage point—will make ten different images based on their experiences, values, and interests. An English botanist, a Peruvian developer, and a Japanese photographer each see the same landscape differently.

We may also have a variety of responses to a given subject over time. When we look at a picture of a house, for example, we see an enclosed volume. On an intellectual level we may assume it contains rooms, while our emotions may lead us to make associations with "home." In creative visual thinking, we see objects before us and know their names, but

we also may associate them with feelings, and see them as shapes and colors, with relations to other remembered things. Thus, we draw from many levels of meaning, and integrate the complementary modes of rational and intuitive intelligence.

PERCEPTION AND AWARENESS

Of all our planet's resources, the most precious is human awareness.

DON FABUN[1]

Perception and awareness are closely related. To *perceive* is to become aware through the senses, particularly through sight or hearing. To be aware means to be conscious, to know something, and to understand through that awareness.

In the visual arts, we gain awareness through the sense of sight and through the development of visual thinking. Surprising as it may seem, much of our sensory awareness is learned. The eyes are blind to what the mind cannot see. The following story provides an unusually dramatic example.

Joey, a New York City boy with blind parents, was born with cerebral palsy. Because of his disabilities, as well as those of his parents, Joey was largely confined to his family's apartment. As he grew older, he learned to get around the apartment in a walker. His mother believed him to be of normal intelligence, yet clinical tests showed him to be blind and mentally retarded. At age five Joey was admitted to a school for children with a variety of disabilities, and for the first time he had daily contact with people who could see. Although he bumped into things in his walker and felt for almost everything, as a blind person does, it soon became apparent that Joey was not really blind. *He simply had never learned to use his eyes.* The combined disabilities of Joey and his parents had prevented him from developing normal visual awareness. After working with specialists and playing with sighted children for a year, his visual responses were normal. Those who worked with him concluded that Joey was a bright and alert child.

To varying degrees, we are all guided—or limited, as Joey was—in the growth of our awareness by parents, teachers, the mass media, and others who influence us.

Even common words and concepts can sometimes limit our sensory impressions. When we look at an object only in terms of a label or a stereotype, we miss the thing itself; we tend to see a vague something called "tree" or "chair" rather than *this* tree, this *particular* chair, or this *unique* object or person. As artist Robert Irwin pointed out, "seeing is forgetting the name of the thing one sees."[2]

As we become more conscious of our own sensory experiences, we open up new levels of awareness. Ordinary things become extraordinary when seen without prejudgment. Is Edward Weston's photograph of a pepper meaningful to us because we like peppers so much? Probably not. To help us see anew, Weston created a memorable image on a flat surface with the help of a common pepper. A time exposure of over two hours gave PEPPER #30 a quality of glowing light—a living presence that resembles an embrace. Through his sensitivity to form, Weston revealed how this pepper appeared to him. Notes from his *Daybook* communicate his enthusiasm about this photograph:

August 8, 1930

I could wait no longer to print them—my new peppers, so I put aside several orders, and yesterday afternoon had an exciting time with seven new negatives.

First I printed my favorite, the one made last Saturday, August 2, just as the light was failing—quickly

made, but with a week's previous effort back of my immediate, unhesitating decision. A week?—Yes, on this certain pepper,—but twenty-eight years of effort, starting with a youth on a farm in Michigan, armed with a No. 2 Bull's Eye [Kodak] 3½ × 3½, have gone into the making of this pepper, which I consider a peak of achievement.

It is a classic, completely satisfying—a pepper— but more than a pepper: abstract, in that it is completely outside subject matter … this new pepper takes one beyond the world we know in the conscious mind.[3]

Weston's photograph of a seemingly common object is a good example of the creative process at work. The artist was uniquely aware of something in his surroundings. He applied a great deal of creative effort in achieving the image he wanted. The photograph that resulted not only represents the object, but communicates a deep sense of wonder about the natural world and its processes. Thus, the work combines awareness, creativity, and communication.

LOOKING AND SEEING

Degrees of visual awareness can be distinguished by the verbs "look" and "see." Looking implies taking in what is before us in a purely mechanical way; seeing is a more active extension of looking. If we care only about function, we simply need to look quickly at a doorknob in order to grasp and turn it. But when we get excited about the shape and finish of a doorknob, or the bright clear quality of a winter day, we go beyond simple functional looking to a higher level of perception called "seeing."

The twentieth-century French artist Henri Matisse wrote about the effort it takes to move beyond stereotypes and to see fully:

To see is itself a creative operation, requiring an effort. Everything that we see in our daily life is more or less distorted by acquired habits, and this is perhaps more

19 Edward Weston.
   PEPPER #30. 1930.
   Photograph.
   Collection Center for Creative
   Photography, The University of Arizona.
   ©1981, Arizona Board of Regents.

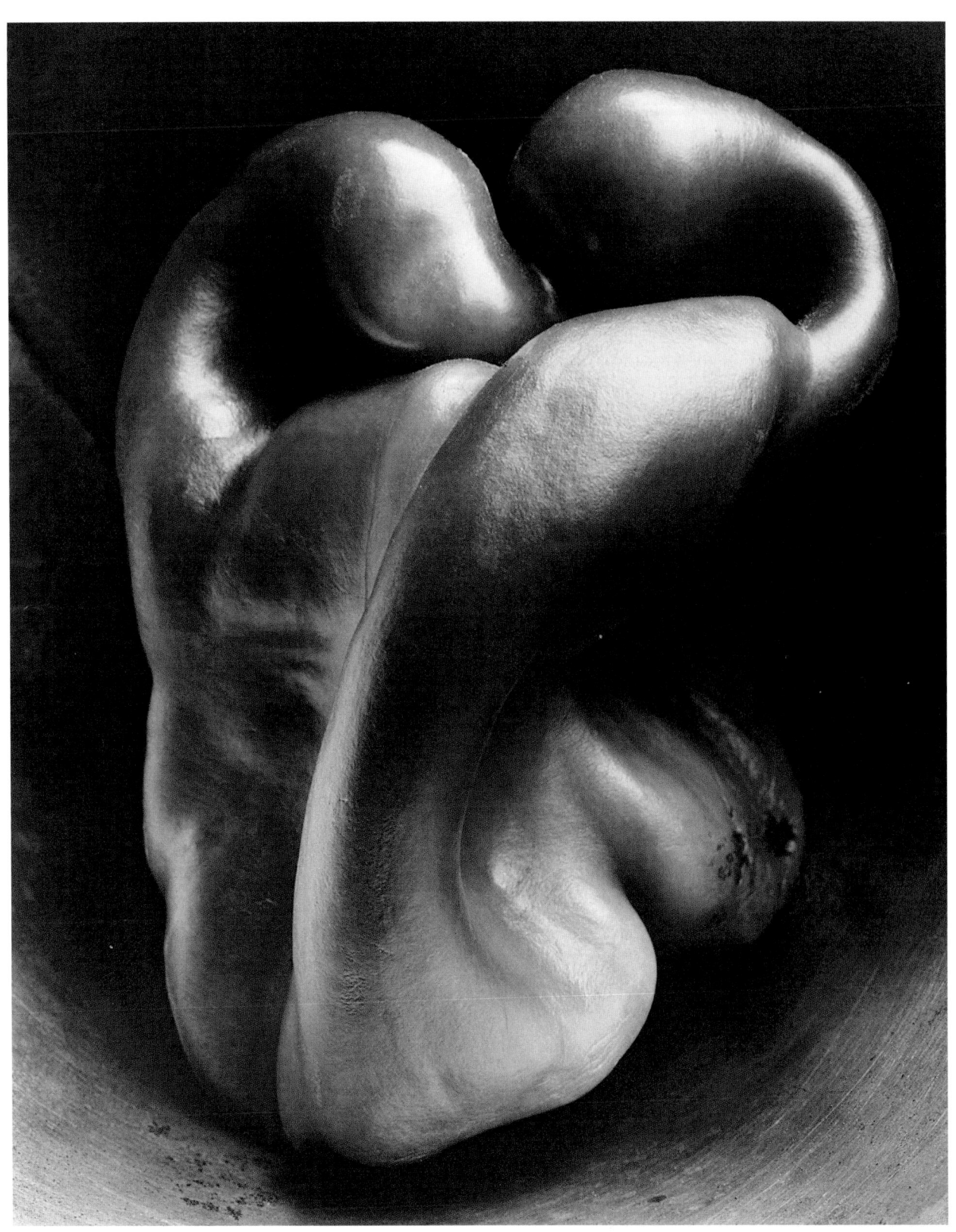

CHAPTER 2   AWARENESS, CREATIVITY, AND COMMUNICATION   **19**

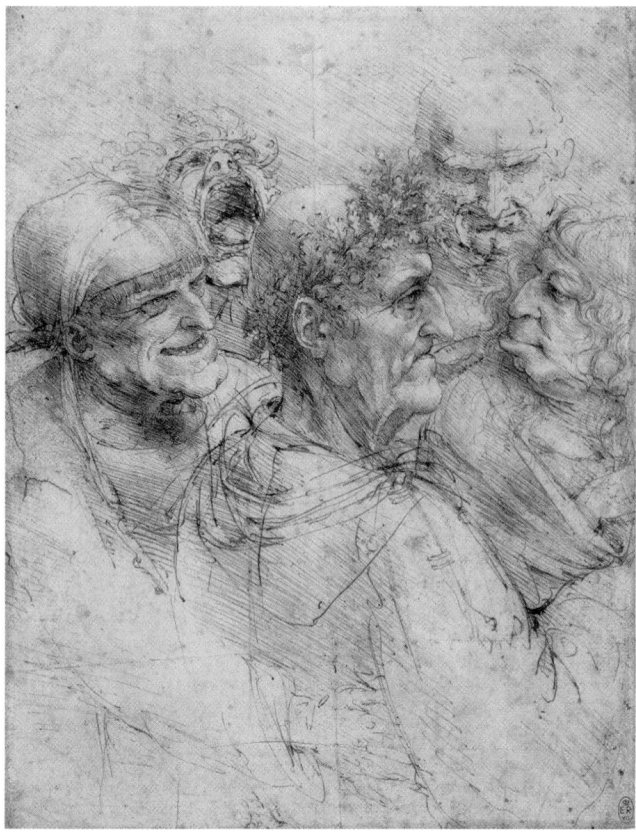

20   Leonardo da Vinci (1452–1519).
A MAN TRICKED BY GYPSIES. c. 1493.
Pen and brown ink. 10¼″ × 8½″.
The Royal Collection © 2004, Her Majesty Queen Elizabeth II.
Photo by EZM. RL12495.

evident in an age like ours when cinema, posters, and magazines present us every day with a flood of ready-made images which are to the eye what prejudices are to the mind. The effort needed to see things without distortion takes something very like courage.[4]

AESTHETICS, ART, AND BEAUTY

Aesthetics refers to an awareness of beauty or to that quality in a work of art or other manmade or natural form which evokes a sense of elevated awareness in the viewer. Some people equate the word "aesthetic" with taste. Many artists and art critics oppose this view, maintaining that art has nothing to do with taste; they think that so-called good taste can actually limit an honest response. "Good taste" almost always refers to an already established way of seeing.

Innovative artists, seeking new ways of seeing, often challenge the established conventions of taste.

Most cultures that have a definition of "beautiful" define it as something pleasing to the eye that is well-proportioned, harmonious, and often approximating an ideal of some sort. In the Western tradition works from Classical Greece or the Renaissance are most frequently described as beautiful. However, what is pleasing to the eye (and hence the sense of beauty) varies considerably across cultures.

Today we often use the word "beautiful" to refer to things that are simply pretty. "Pretty" means pleasant or attractive to the eye, whereas "beautiful" means having qualities of a high order, qualities that delight the eye, engage the intellectual or moral sense, or do all these things simultaneously. In the words of architect Louis Kahn, "Beautiful doesn't necessarily mean good-looking."[5]

Let us consider possibilities beyond the conventional or established standards of beauty and ugliness. If art's only function were to please the senses, ugliness would have no place in art. But since we don't expect all works of drama or literature to be pretty or pleasant, why should we have different expectations of the visual arts? Leonardo da Vinci, Vincent van Gogh, and Jean-Michel Basquiat—artists from different times and places—explored dimensions of "ugliness" in relation to their own concerns and personal modes of expression.

Street life fascinated Italian Renaissance artist Leonardo da Vinci. He was particularly interested in studying people of striking appearance, people either very beautiful or very ugly. Leonardo found ugliness to be as worthy of attention as beauty. In fact, he considered ugliness a variation of beauty, and this feeling can be seen in his A MAN TRICKED BY GYPSIES. In his *Treatise on Painting*, he advised others always to carry a pocket notebook in which to make quick drawings of what they observed. He also drew from memory, as described by sixteenth-century artist and biographer Giorgio Vasari:

Leonardo used to follow people whose extraordinary appearance took his fancy, sometimes throughout a

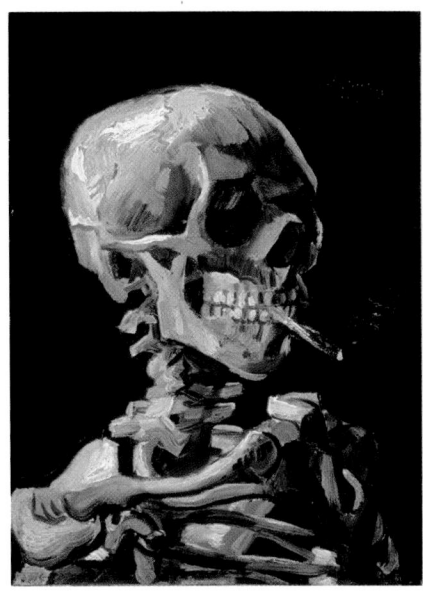

21 Vincent van Gogh.
SKULL WITH A BURNING CIGARETTE. 1885–1886.
Antwerp. Oil on canvas. 32″ × 24½″.
Van Gogh Museum (Vincent Van Gogh Foundation), Amsterdam.

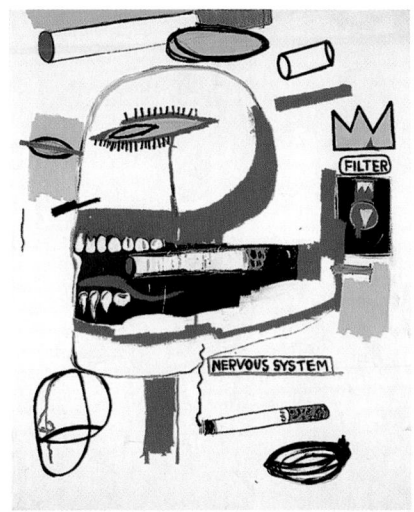

22 Jean-Michel Basquiat.
TOBACCO. 1984.
Acrylic and oil crayon on canvas. 86″ × 68″.
Courtesy Galerie Bruno Bischofberger, Zurich.
© 2002 Artists Rights Society (ARS), NY/ADAGP, Paris.

whole day, until be could draw them as well by memory as though they stood before him.[6]

Vincent van Gogh's SKULL WITH A BURNING CIGARETTE presents another aspect of what we humans consider ugly: reminders of death, the skeleton. The skeleton seems eerily lit as it basks in an earthy brown glow before an overwhelmingly dark background.

In contrast to the careful brushwork of van Gogh is the intentionally blunt, bad-boy, street-painting style of Jean-Michel Basquiat. Basquiat's direct approach, as seen in TOBACCO, evolved from his early experience as a teenage graffiti artist.

ART AND EXPERIENCE

Art encourages us to experience our lives more vividly by urging us to reexamine our thoughts and renew our feelings. The essence of art is the spark of insight and the thrill of discovery—first experienced by the maker, then built into the work of art, and finally experienced by the viewer. A noted philosopher once described the process:

To evoke in oneself a feeling one has experienced, and having evoked it . . . , then by means of movement,
line, color, sounds or forms expressed in words, so transmit that same feeling—this is the activity of art.[7]

As we live our lives, experiences flow past in a stream of what may seem like disconnected events and impressions. Art helps us to grasp the significance of the moment and the interrelationships of events—and thereby to experience life fully.

While animals seem keenly aware of their world through their senses, human beings have lost some of the ability to experience life intensely in the present moment. Caught up in thoughts and emotions, and often separated from direct experiences with nature, we risk adopting dulled, programmed responses to our environments.

The best art cuts through our tendency to prejudge our experience. Great art sharpens our perceptions by re-creating human experience in fresh forms, bringing a new sense of the significance and connectedness of life.

EARLY ENCOUNTERS WITH THE ARTIST WITHIN

I'd like to study the drawings of kids. That's where the truth is, without a doubt.
ANDRÉ DERAIN[8]

THE ARTS COME from inborn human needs to create and to communicate. They come from the desire to explore, confirm, and share special observations and insights—a fact readily apparent in nine-year-old Kojyu's SEARCHING FOR BUGS IN THE PARK. The arts are one of the most constructive ways to say "I did it. I made it. This is what I see and feel. I count. My art is me." Unfortunately, the great value of this discover-and-share, art-making process is only rarely affirmed in today's busy homes and schools.

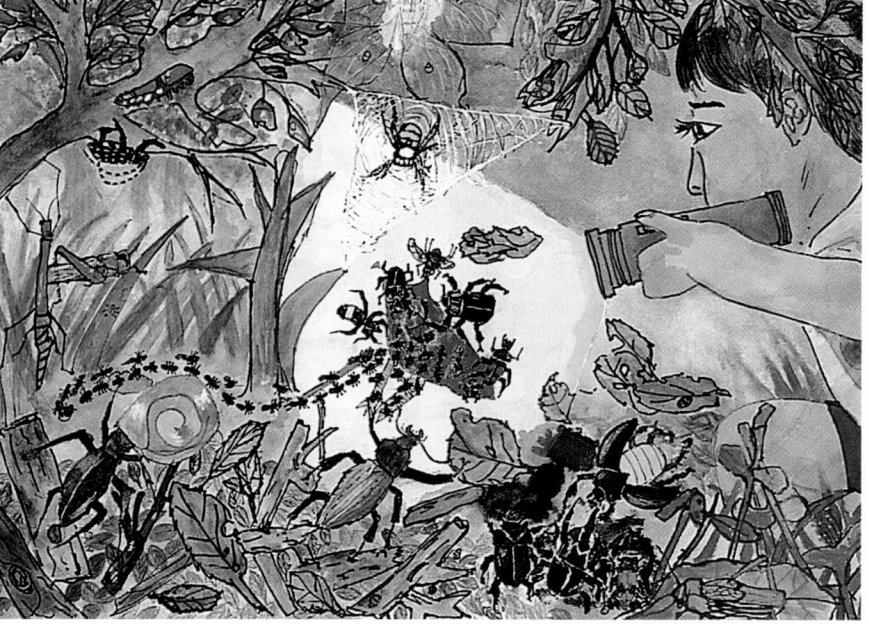

23   Kojyu, age 9.
SEARCHING FOR BUGS IN THE PARK.

We include art by children as the best way—other than actual hands-on art-making processes—to help you reexamine your relationship to your own creative powers and perhaps even to guide you as you prepare to become a parent, a teacher, or a caregiver for children.

Children use a universal visual language. All over the world, drawings by children ages two to six show similar stages of mental growth, from exploring with mark-making to inventing shapes to symbolizing things seen and imagined. Until they are about six years old, children usually depict the world in symbolic rather than realistic ways. Their images are more mental constructions than records of visual observations.

During the second year of life, children enjoy making marks, leaving traces of their movements. Sensitive exploration is visible in FIRST LINES, by a one-and-a-half-year-old child. After marking and scribbling, making circles and other shapes fascinates young children. The HOUSE shape is by a two-year-old. HAND WITH LINE AND SPOTS is by a three-year-old, as is the smiling portrait of GRANDMA in which self-assured lines symbolize a happy face, shoulders, arms, body, belly button, and legs.

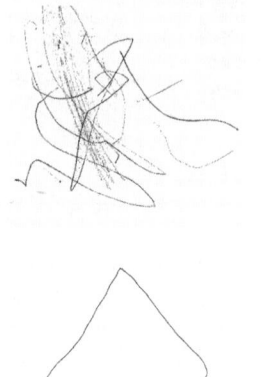

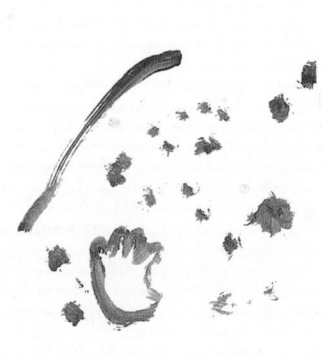

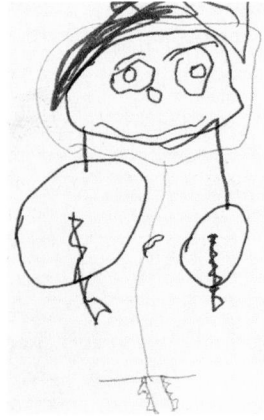

24   Anonymous Child, age 18 months. FIRST LINES.
25   Alana, age 2. HOUSE.
26   Jeff, age 3. HAND WITH LINE AND SPOTS.
27   Alana, age 3. GRANDMA.
Photographs: Duane Preble.

EARLY ENCOUNTERS WITH THE ARTIST WITHIN

28   Jason, almost 4.
MOTHER OCTOPUS
WITH BABIES.

29   Yuki, age 8.
I CAN RIDE, I CAN
RIDE MY UNICYCLE.
Photographs: Duane Preble.

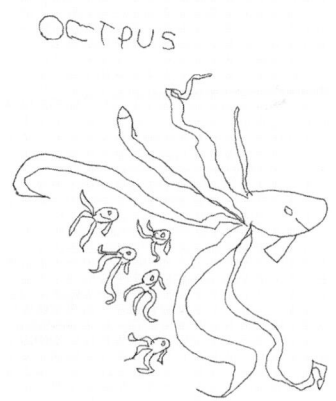

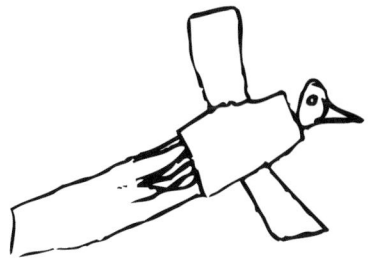

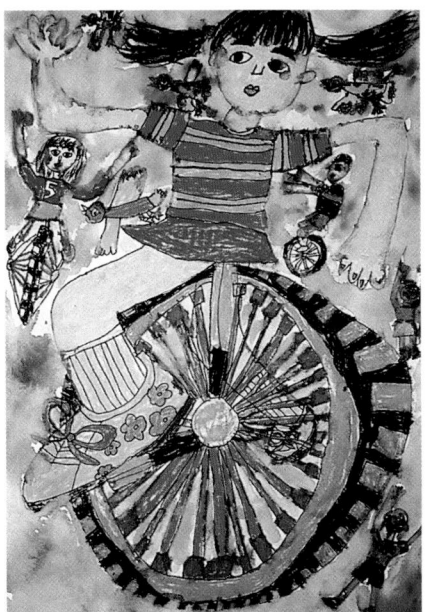

30   Anonymous Child. BIRDS.
a. This picture shows one child's drawing of a bird before exposure to coloring books.

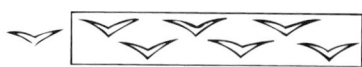

b. Then the child colored a workbook illustration.

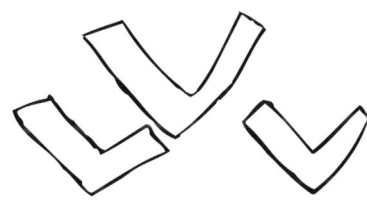

c. After coloring the workbook birds, the child lost creative sensitivity and self-reliance.
(a, b, and c) *Creative Mental Growth* by Victor Lowenfeld, © 1975, p. 23. Reproduced by permission of Pearson Education, Inc., Upper Saddle River, NJ.

Being the son of a saltwater fish collector, and watching an octopus, gave almost four-year-old Jason the idea for his drawing of a smiling MOTHER OCTOPUS WITH BABIES. The excitement of joyful play with friends on unicycles inspired eight-year-old Yuki's I CAN RIDE, I CAN RIDE MY UNICYCLE. Notice how she emphasized her own image by greatly exaggerating her size relative to others and how she included important information, such as her right leg seen through the spokes of the wheel.

Young children often demonstrate an intuitive sense of composition. Unfortunately, we lose much of this intuitive sense of balanced design as we begin to look at the world from a conceptual, self-conscious point of view. Most children who have been given coloring books, workbooks, and pre-drawn printed single sheets become overly dependent on such impersonal, stereotyped props. In this way, children often lose the urge to invent unique images based on their own experiences. A child's two drawings of BIRDS show this process: The child first interprets the bird in a personal, fresh way, but later adopts the trite forms of a conventional workbook. Without ongoing opportunities for personal expression, children lose self-confidence in their original creative impulses.

Children begin life as eager learners. If they are loved and cared for, they soon express enthusiasm for perceiving and exploring the world around them. Research shows that parents' ability to show interest in and empathy for their child's discoveries and feelings is crucial to the child's brain development. Before the age of one, and well before they talk, babies point tiny fingers at wonderful things they see. Bodies move in rhythm to music. Ask a group of four-year-olds "Can you dance?" "Can you sing?" "Can you draw?" and they all say, "Yes! Yes!" Ask twelve-year-olds the same questions, and they will too often say "No, we can't." Such an unnecessary loss has ominous implications for the spiritual, economic, social, and political health of society.

Most abilities observed in creative people are also characteristic of children during interactions with the world around them. What becomes of this extraordinary capacity? According to John Holt, author of *How Children Fail,*

We destroy this capacity above all by making them afraid—afraid of not doing what other people want, of not pleasing, or of making mistakes, of failing, of being wrong. Thus we make them afraid to gamble, afraid to experiment, afraid to try the difficult and unknown.[9]

CREATIVITY

The source of all art, science, and technology—in fact, all of civilization—is human imagination, or creative thinking. As scientist Albert Einstein declared, "Imagination is more important than knowledge."[10]

What do we mean by this ability we call creativity? Psychologist Erich Fromm wrote:

In talking about creativity, let us first consider its two possible meanings: creativity in the sense of creating something new, something which can be seen or heard by others, such as a painting, a sculpture, a symphony, a poem, a novel, etc., or creativity as an attitude, which is the condition of any creation in the former sense but which can exist even though nothing new is created in the world of things. . . .

What is creativity? The best general answer I can give is that creativity is the ability to see (or to be aware) and to respond.[11]

Creativity is as fundamental to experiencing and appreciating a work of art as it is to making one. Insightful seeing is itself a creative act; it requires open receptivity—putting aside habitual modes of thought.

Studies of creativity have described traits of people who have maintained or rediscovered the creative attitude. These include the abilities to:

- wonder and be curious
- be open to new experience
- see the familiar from an unfamiliar point of view
- take advantage of accidental events
- make one thing out of another by shifting its function
- generalize from particulars in order to see broad applications
- synthesize, integrate, find order in disorder
- be in touch with one's unconscious, yet be intensely conscious

- be able to analyze and evaluate
- know oneself, have the courage to be oneself in the face of opposition
- be willing to take risks
- be persistent: to work for long periods—perhaps years—in pursuit of a goal

As Fromm said, creativity is an *attitude*. We all have the potential to be creative, yet most of us have not been encouraged to develop our creativity.

Though certain aspects of creativity seem very similar worldwide, each culture has specific ways of thinking about the subject. In Chinese painting, for example, the artist is not expected merely to copy the appearance of the subject of the work, but rather to *understand* it deeply and communicate that understanding. In that tradition, paintings of bamboo are fairly common; but an artist who masters the subject is one who can go beyond mere appearances and harmonize his or her spirit with that of the plant. The eleventh-century poet and painter Su Xi once described the creative process as an intuitive grasping of the subject, not a laborious copying of its every detail: "Painters of today draw joint after joint and pile up leaf on leaf. How can that become a bamboo? When you are going to paint a bamboo, you must first realize the thing completely in your mind."[12] He once praised the artist Yu Ko by saying that Yu was transformed into the bamboos that he painted.

Native American pottery painters of the Southwest offer another perspective on creativity. These artists decorate their earthenware vessels with symbolic forms that are meant to recall the natural surroundings. Each tribal group generally uses a basic set of commonly understood symbols, which the artists, who traditionally are women, may vary and combine at will. When an anthropologist interviewed several of these potters in the 1920s, most said that they first dreamed of the designs that they would paint on their pots. Each said that she fully conceived the design in her mind before painting it.

Wherever it happens, artistic creativity is an asset to society. Creativity developed through art experiences enhances problem solving and communication in other areas of life. For all of us, opportunities for creative expression develop our abilities to integrate experiences of the outside world with those of our inner selves.

UNTRAINED AND FOLK ARTISTS

The urge to create is universal; it has little to do with art training. We satisfy our artistic sensibilities every day in a variety of ways. Those with little or no formal art education who make objects commonly recognized as art are usually described as either *untrained* artists or *folk artists.*

Art by untrained artists, also called *naive* or *outsider artists,* is made by people who are largely unaware of art history or the art trends of their time. Unlike folk art, which is made by people working within a tradition, art by untrained artists is personal expression created apart from any conventional practice or style.

Many untrained artists seem to develop their art spontaneously, without regard to art of the past or present. Anna Zemankova was a Czech housewife with no art training who at age fifty-two suddenly began making drawings. She would awaken each morning at about four o'clock and draw with pastel until seven. Seated at a special easel that her son designed, she seemed to work transfixed by some inner vision. All of her works are UNTITLED (M), but they seem to depict plant life. The imagery that she created resembles in some ways the local decorative arts of her region, such as embroideries or ceramic glazes, but the combination is completely her own. In later years she began embroidering on the drawings. She said that in her art she grew plants that did not grow elsewhere, and indeed they resemble no known species.

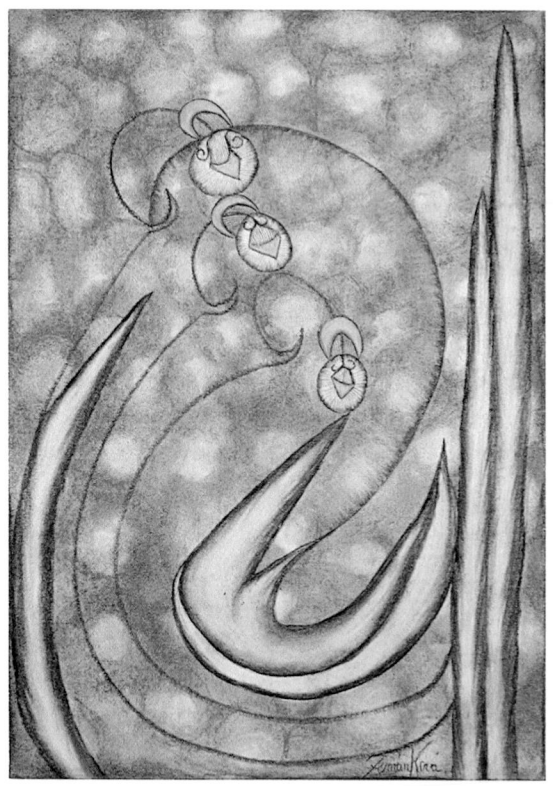

31   Anna Zemankova.
UNTITLED (M). c. 1970s.
Pastel on paper. 24¼″ × 17¾″.
Courtesy of the artist and Cavin-Morris Gallery, NY.

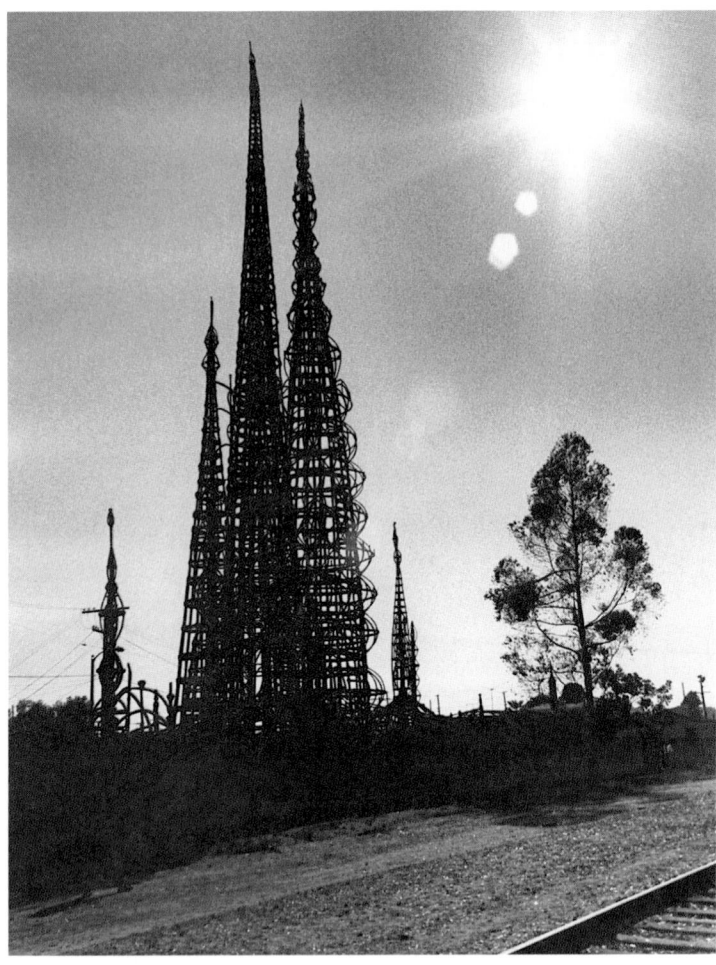

32 Sabatino "Simon" Rodia.
a. NUESTRO PUEBLO.
Watts, California, 1921–1954. Mixed media. Height 100′.
Photographs: Duane Preble.

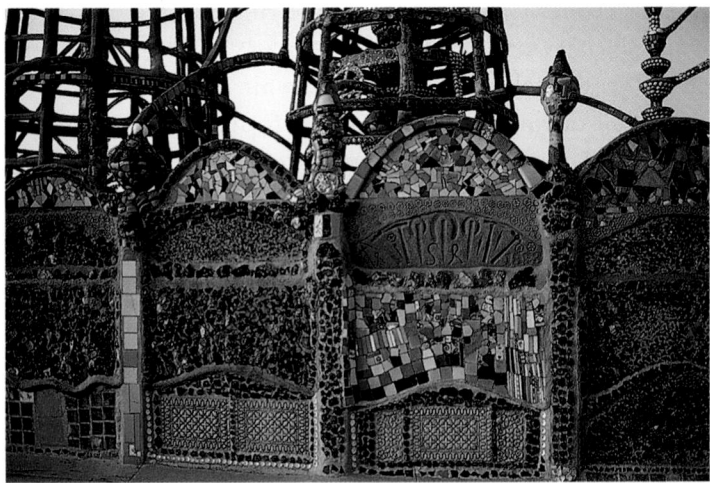

b. Detail of NUESTRO PUEBLO.
Enclosing wall with construction-tool impressions.

The sculptural spires in Watts, California, known commonly as "Watts Towers," were titled NUESTRO PUEBLO (OUR PEOPLE) by Sabatino Rodia, the Italian tile setter who built them. Rodia exemplifies the artist who visualizes new possibilities for ordinary materials. He worked on his cathedral-like towers for thirty-three years, making the fantastic structures from cast-off materials such as metal pipes and bed frames held together with steel reinforcing rods, mesh, and mortar. Incredibly, he built the towers without power tools, rivets, welds, or bolts.

As the towers rose in his tiny triangular backyard, he methodically covered their surfaces with bits and pieces of broken dishes, tile, melted bottle glass, shells, and other colorful "junk" from the vacant lots of his neighborhood. Rodia's towers and the ideas they represent are testimony to the artist's creativity and incredible perseverance.

Another striking work by an untrained artist in this century is the THRONE OF THE THIRD HEAVEN OF THE NATIONS' MILLENNIUM GENERAL ASSEMBLY, which James Hampton built in his garage over a fourteen-year span. The artist brought home pieces of furniture and other found objects, which he laboriously covered with gold and silver foil and arranged symmetrically. Hampton, a Baptist minister and night janitor at government buildings in Washington, D.C., believed that Jesus was coming again soon. His reading of the last book of the New Testament, Revelation, convinced him that when Jesus returned, he would need a throne to sit on. Between about 1950 and 1964, he actually built one. No one knew of this project until Hampton died, and relatives going through his possessions found this amazing work. It now occupies an entire gallery in the Smithsonian Institution.

Folk art applies to art by artists who are part of established traditions of style, theme, and craftsmanship. Most folk artists are untrained in traditional Western art skills, and create from an inner desire to communicate more than from professional commitment. Folk art can take many forms, including

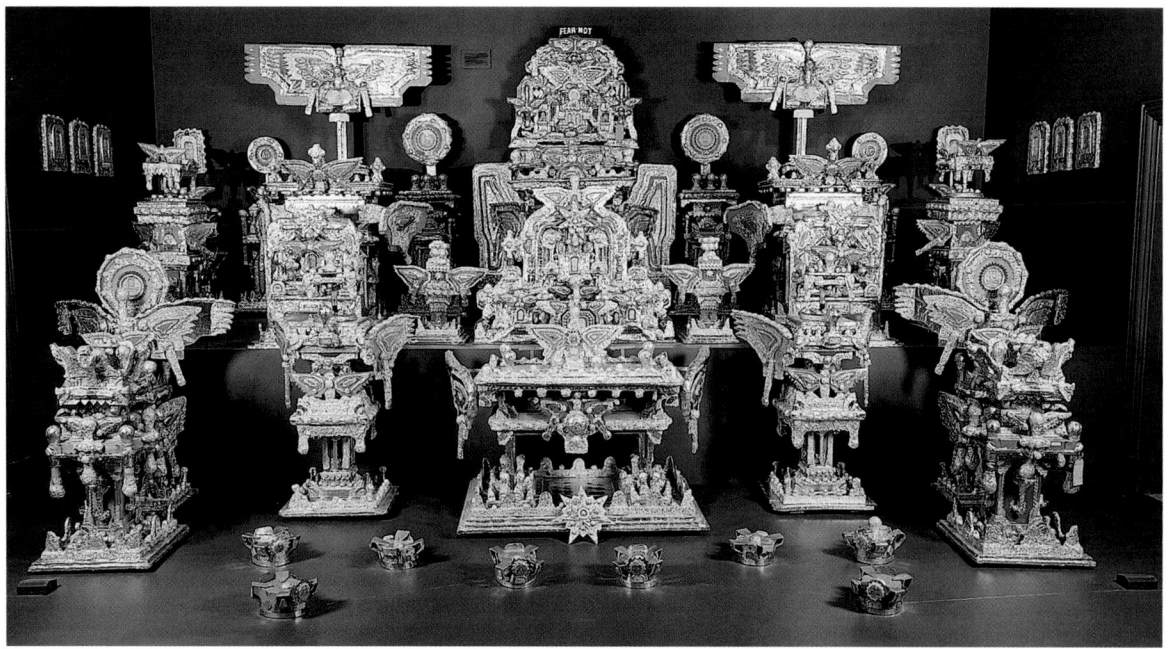

33   James Hampton.
      THRONE OF THE THIRD HEAVEN OF THE NATIONS' MILLENNIUM GENERAL ASSEMBLY. c. 1950–1964.
      Gold and silver aluminum foil, colored Kraft paper, plastic sheets over wood, paperboard, and glass.
      180 pieces. 10'6" × 27' × 14'6".
      © National Museum of American Art, Smithsonian, Washington, D.C./Art Resource, NY.

quilts, hand-stitched samplers, decorated weather vanes, or customized cars. Even convicts in the Southwest have a tradition of making ink drawings on prison-issued handkerchiefs. In earlier times, particularly in rural areas, communication and influences from beyond one's immediate community were limited, and thus many folk art traditions remained relatively unchanged for long periods.

When the Southwest was a Spanish colony, a folk tradition of religious imagery evolved in the Roman Catholic churches. Small panels and statues were made for private devotion in homes. Since the saints, or *santos*, were the most common subjects, the artists who painted or sculpted them were known as *santeros*. One of the most interesting of these traditional artists never signed any of his works. Since most are wood carvings from the Arroyo Hondo region of northern New Mexico, we know him only as the Arroyo Hondo Carver, and scholars attribute works to him only on the basis of style. His OUR LADY OF THE IMMACULATE CONCEPTION (on the following page) shows his typical method of carving, with its elongated figures and distant, other-worldly facial expressions. Compared with related folk arts of the same region, this piece also displays the carver's brighter color scheme. OUR LADY OF THE IMMACULATE CONCEPTION is usually represented without a Christ Child, but some folk artists ignore the usual rules of representation, as the carver has done here. The work probably came from a private family chapel that priests visited only occasionally.

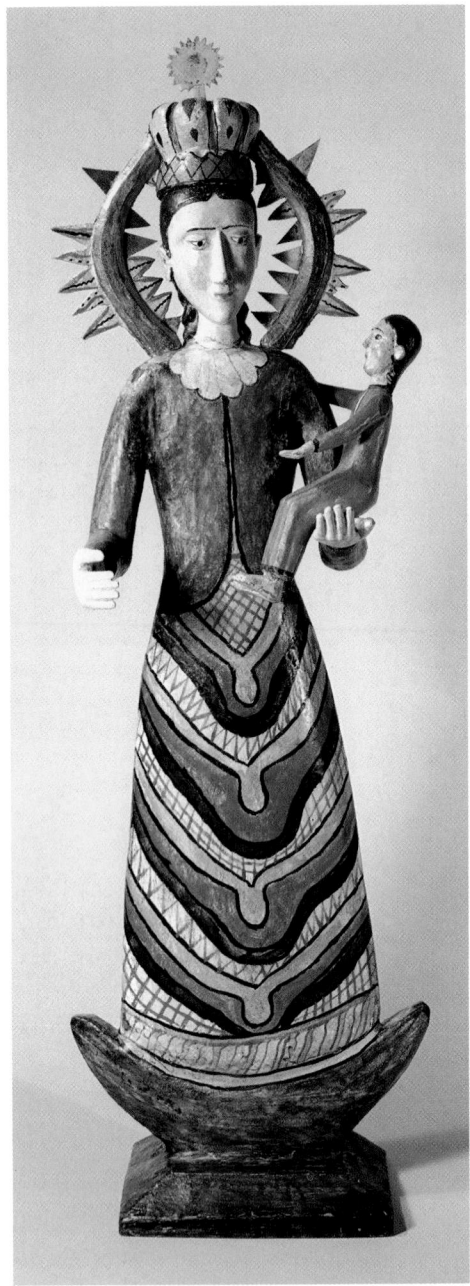

34 Arroyo Hondo Carver.
OUR LADY OF THE IMMACULATE CONCEPTION.
1830–1850.
Carved and painted wood, 29" high.
Taylor Museum, Colorado Springs Fine Arts Center,
Museum Purchase. TM3858.

TRAINED ARTISTS

In the past, the world's trained artists generally learned by working as apprentices to accomplished masters. (With a few notable exceptions, women were excluded from such apprenticeships.) Through practical experience, they gained necessary skills and developed knowledge of their society's art traditions. Today most art training takes place in art schools, or in college or university art departments. Learning in such settings develops sophisticated knowledge of alternative points of view, both contemporary and historical.

In contrast to untrained artists, who demonstrate unmannered originality, trained artists often show a self-conscious awareness of their relationship to art history. This can be either an asset or a burden. Knowledge of art history provides a wealth of material to draw from but can lead to an egocentric struggle to be profound and original.

Whether outsider, folk, or trained, artists must be independent thinkers and must have the courage to go beyond group mentality. In this way artists offer not what others have seen, but fresh insights that extend the experiences of those who see their art.

VISUAL COMMUNICATION

The language of vision determines, perhaps even more subtly and thoroughly than verbal language, the structure of our consciousness.

S. I. HAYAKAWA[13]

The most direct avenue to the mind is by way of the eyes. As philosopher and educator S. I. Hayakawa pointed out, our visual experience of the world is so profoundly influential that it constitutes a nonverbal language all its own. This is the language that art uses to communicate.

In art, the visual experience is essential. The words we use to describe that experience are simply a means of discussing our perceptions. Words can help us analyze and better understand the infinite ways in which artists communicate visually.

But, since words and visual images are two different "languages," talking about visual arts with words is always an act of translation one step removed from actually experiencing art. In fact, our eyes have their own connections to our minds and emotions. By cultivating these connections, we are able to take full advantage of what art has to offer.

In the context of art, how the artist interprets a subject is often more important than the actual subject being used. Subjects don't make art, artists do. How the image is composed, the materials and techniques employed, what is emphasized, and what is left out: all this becomes the basis for an in-depth experience of a work of art.

ART AND APPEARANCES

Art involves interpretation rather than replication. A real horse, a painting of a horse, and a sculpture of a horse each has its own reality—and each of these realities is substantially different from the others.

Artists may depict much of what they see in the physical world, they may alter appearances, or they may invent forms not seen in either the natural or human-made world. Regardless of their approaches, most artists invite viewers to see beyond mere appearances. The terms *representational*, *abstract*, and *nonrepresentational* (or *nonobjective*) are used to describe a work's relationship to the physical world.

Representational Art

Representational art (sometimes called *objective* or *figurative art*) depicts the appearance of things. It represents—presents again—objects we recognize from the everyday world. Objects that representational art depicts are called *subjects*.

Representational art includes a wide range of styles, from the fool-the-eye realism of William Harnett to personally expressive images such as those by Rembrandt (see page 10), to distortions such as those in Romare Bearden's art (page 11).

The most "real" looking paintings are in a style called *trompe l'oeil* (pronounced "tromp loy")—French for "fool the eye." Paintings in this illusionistic style impress us because they look so "real." In

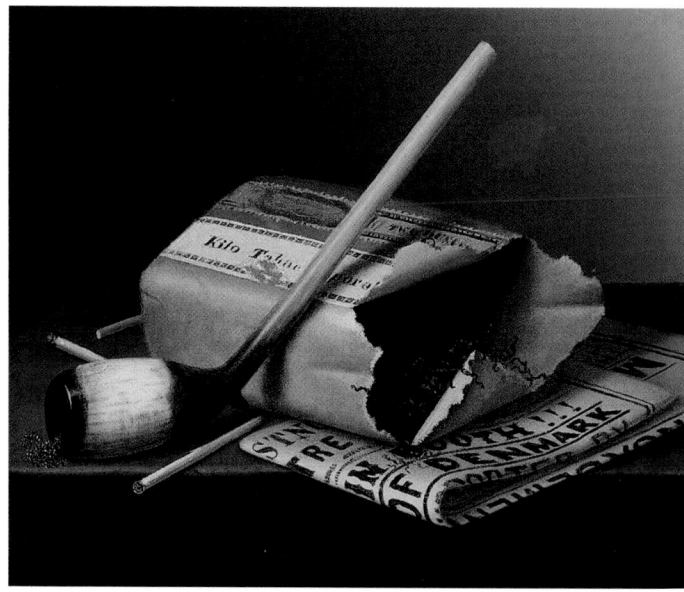

35 William Harnett.
A SMOKE BACKSTAGE. 1877.
Oil on canvas. 7″ × 8½″.
Honolulu Academy of Arts, Gift of John Wyatt Gregg Allerton, 1964. (3211.1).

Harnett's painting A SMOKE BACKSTAGE, the assembled objects are close to life-size, which contributes to the illusion. We almost believe that we could touch the pipe and match.

Belgian painter René Magritte shows a different relationship between art and reality in the work on the following page. The subject of the painting appears to be a pipe, but written in French on the painting are the words, "*Ceci n'est pas une pipe.*" ("This is not a pipe.") The viewer wonders, "If this is not a pipe, what is it?" The answer, of course, is that it is a painting! Magritte's title, THE TREASON OF IMAGES, suggests what the artist had in mind.

Matisse told of an incident that illustrated a similar view on the difference between art and nature. A woman visiting his studio pointed to one of his paintings and said, "But surely, the arm of this woman is much too long." Matisse replied, "Madame, you are mistaken. This is not a woman, this is a picture."[14]

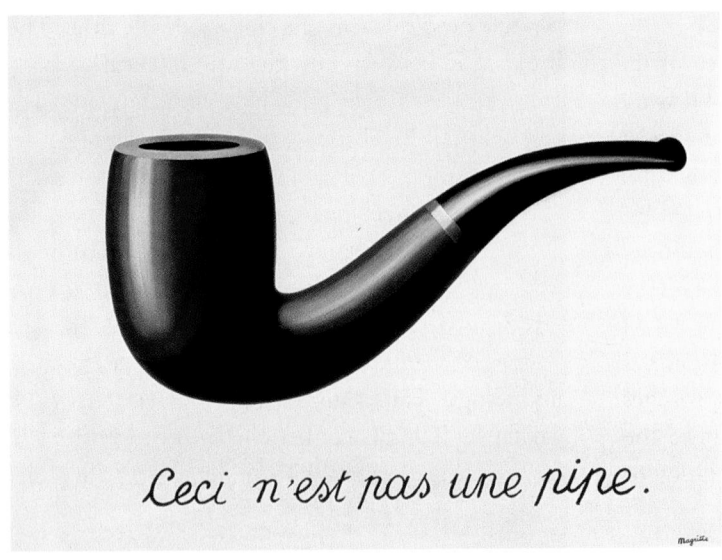

36   René Magritte. (1898–1967)
LA TRAHISON DES IMAGES
(CECI N'EST PAS UNE PIPE). 1929.
Oil on canvas. 23½″ × 32″.
Los Angeles County Museum of Art, Los Angeles, CA.
Art Resource, NY. Banque d'Images, ADAGP. © 2009
Artists Rights Society (ARS), NY.

California artist Ray Beldner further complicated the relationship between art and reality by creating a reproduction of Magritte's painting out of sewn dollar bills, and calling it THIS IS DEFINITELY NOT A PIPE. Modern artists are so famous these days, and their works sell for such high prices, that they may as well be "made of money." Beldner's point is that even representational art has a complex relationship to reality; artists do not merely paint what they see. Rather, they select, arrange, and compose reality to fit their personal vision. The process can take them several steps away from the fact of a pipe on a tabletop.

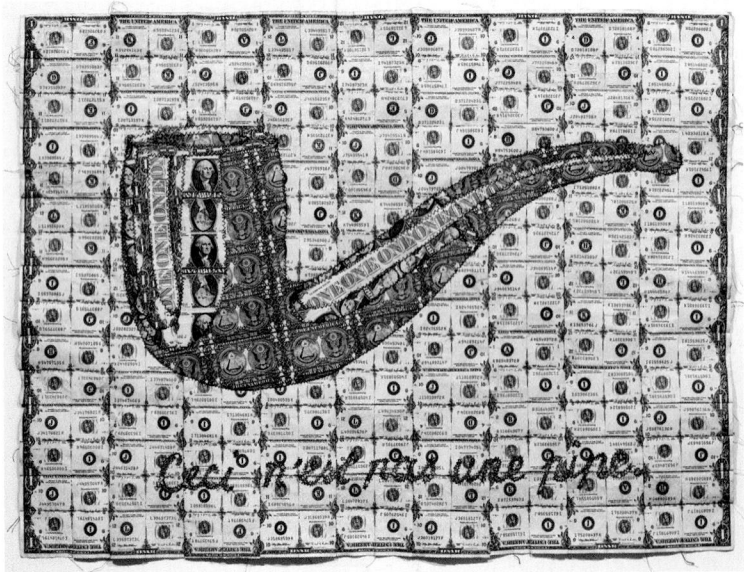

37   Ray Beldner.
THIS IS DEFINITELY NOT A PIPE. 2000.
Sewn currency. 24″ × 33″.
Courtesy of the artist and Catharine Clark Gallery,
San Francisco, CA.

Abstract Art

"To abstract" means to extract the essence of an object or idea. In art, the word *abstract* can mean either (1) works of art that have no reference at all to natural objects, or (2) works that depict natural objects in simplified, distorted, or exaggerated ways. In this book, we use abstract in the second sense.

In abstract art the artist changes the object's natural appearance in order to emphasize or reveal certain qualities. Just as there are many approaches to representational art, there are many approaches to abstraction. We may be able to recognize the subject matter of an abstract work quite easily, or we may need the help of a clue (such as a title). The interaction between how the subject actually looks and how an artist presents it is part of the pleasure and challenge of abstract art. In a basic sense, all art is abstraction because it is not possible for an artist to reproduce exactly what is seen.

Abstraction in one form or another is common in the art of many cultures. Native peoples of the Northwest coast decorate many objects with forms abstracted from the animals that populate their mythology. For example, the CHILKAT BLANKET woven by Tlingit women contains in its center a face of such a composite figure. Below the face,

38   CHILKAT BLANKET.
Tlingit. Before 1928.
Mountain goat wool and shredded cedar bark. 4′7″ × 5′4″.
Courtesy Department of Library Services,
American Museum of Natural History, New York.
Photograph: Steve Myers. Neg./Transparency no. 3804.

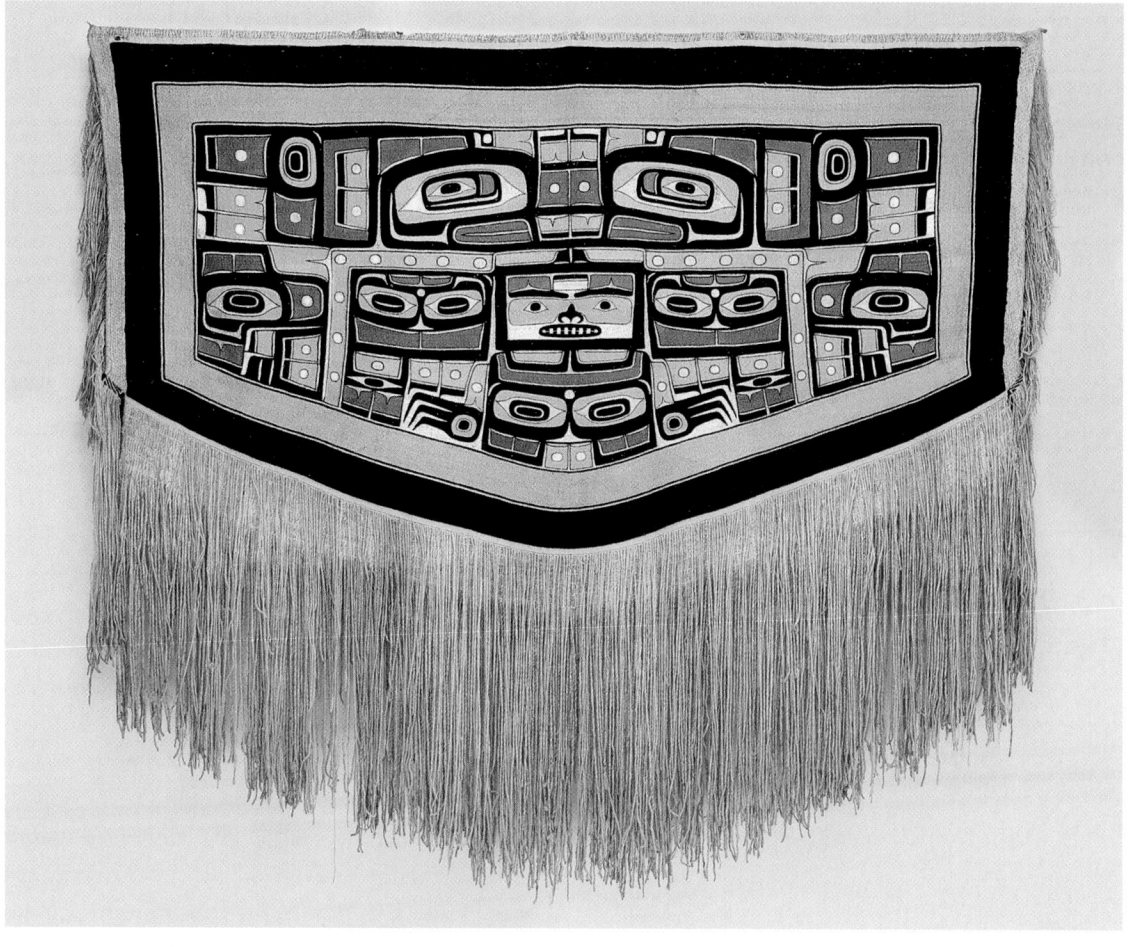

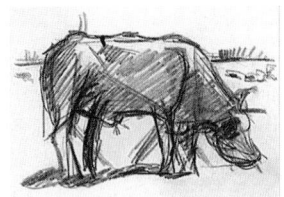

39 Theo van Doesburg (C.E.M. Kupper).
ABSTRACTION OF A COW.

Studies for composition
(THE COW). c. 1916.
Pencil on paper. Each 4⅝″ × 6¼″.
The Museum of Modern Art, NY/Licensed by Scala-Art
Resource, NY. Purchase.
Photograph © 2002 The Museum of Modern Art, NY.
© 2002 Artists Rights Society (ARS), NY/Beeldrecht,
Amsterdam.

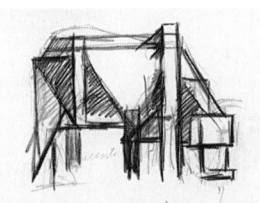

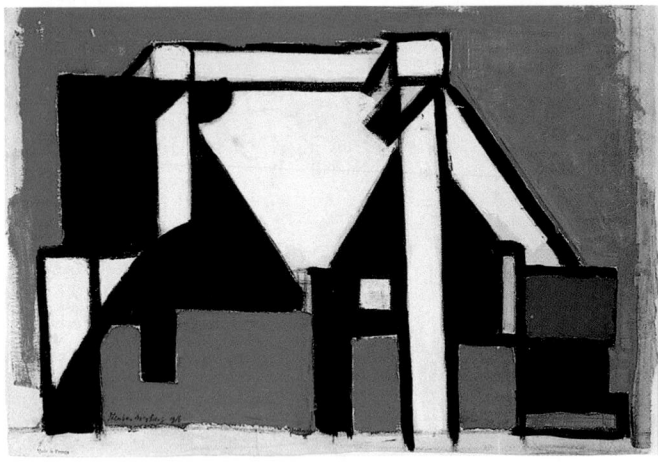

Theo van Doesburg (C.E.M. Kupper).
COMPOSITION (THE COW). c. 1917 (dated 1916).
Tempera, oil and charcoal on paper. 15⅝″ × 22¾″.
The Museum of Modern Art, NY/Licensed by Scala-Art Resource, NY. Purchase.
Photograph © 2002 The Museum of Modern Art, NY.
© 2002 the Artists Rights Society (ARS), NY/Beeldrecht, Amsterdam.

Theo van Doesburg (C.E.M. Kupper).
COMPOSITION (THE COW). c. 1917.
Oil on canvas. 14¾″ × 25″.
The Museum of Modern Art, NY/Licensed by Scala-Art Resource, NY.
Purchase. Photograph © 2002 The Museum of Modern Art, NY.
© 2002 Artists Rights Society (ARS), NY/Beeldrecht, Amsterdam.

along the bottom edge, claw feet point outward. Elsewhere in the design, shapes that symbolize eyes, fins, and wings of other animals fill the surface in a symmetrical arrangement. This blanket, once the prized possession of a high tribal official, was woven in a regional style. The weaver employed abstraction in the decorative use of meaningful symbols connecting seen and unseen spheres.

We see stages of abstraction in Theo van Doesburg's series of drawings and paintings, ABSTRACTION OF A COW. The artist apparently wanted to see how far he could abstract the cow through simplification and still have his image symbolize the essence of the animal. Van Doesburg used the subject as a point of departure for a composition made up of colored rectangles. If we viewed only the final painting, and none of the earlier ones, we would see it as a nonrepresentational painting.

Nonrepresentational Art

A great deal of the world's art was not meant to be representational at all. Amish quilts, many Navajo textiles, and most Islamic wood carvings consist primarily of flat patterns that give pleasure through mere variety of line, shape, and color. *Nonrepresentational* art (sometimes called *nonobjective* or *nonfigurative* art) presents visual forms with no specific references to anything outside themselves. Just as we can respond to the pure sound forms of music, so we can respond to the pure visual forms of nonrepresentational art.

While nonrepresentational art may at first seem more difficult to grasp than representational or abstract art, it can offer fresh ways of seeing. Absence of subject matter actually clarifies the way all visual form affects us. Once we learn how to "read" the language of vision, we can respond to art and the world with greater understanding and enjoyment.

Two widely different types of nonrepresentational art are pictured on the next page. In FOOTSCRAY, the work of the American painter-sculptor Nancy Graves, oil paint on canvas combines with brightly colored aluminum elements

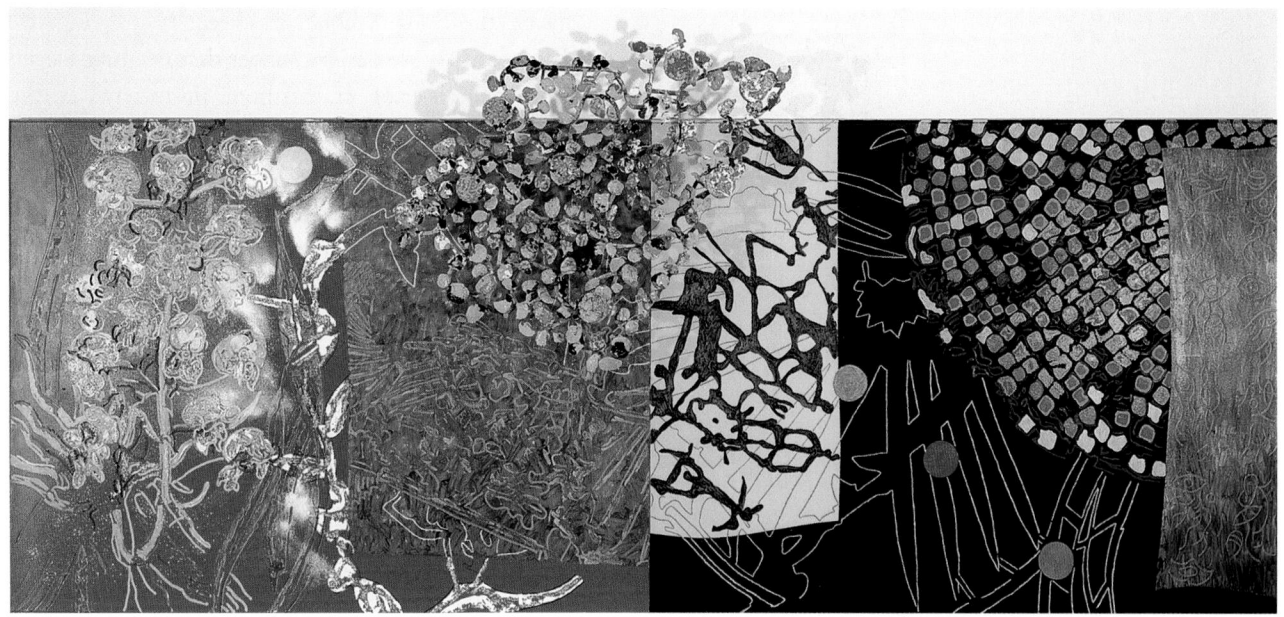

40   Nancy Graves.
        FOOTSCRAY, from the AUSTRALIAN SERIES. 1985.
        Oil, acrylic, and glitter on canvas with painted aluminum sculpture.
        6′4½″ × 14′5″ × 12½″ (diptych).
        © Nancy Graves Foundation/Licensed by VAGA, New York, NY.

that hover above the surface of the work. The forms in the piece suggest organic, exuberant motion.

In New Zealand, Maori women working in pairs weave strips of dyed flax into geometric patterns called TUKUTUKU PANELS. These patterns are traditional in Maori societies and they have names such as "sand flounder," "human ribs," and "albatross tears." The panels are woven in specific sizes to fit between the wooden uprights of meeting houses where religious ceremonies are held. A given meeting house may contain *tukutuku* panels of many different designs, giving the room a rich and varied visual texture.

Whereas the makers of the TUKUTUKU PANELS used naturally dyed flax to create elegantly rhythmic, yet strictly geometric, traditional designs, Graves employed manmade materials, bright synthetic colors, and a dynamic, irregular composition to create FOOTSCRAY. These contrasting works show that even in nonrepresentational art, an extremely wide variety of forms, compositions, moods, and messages is possible.

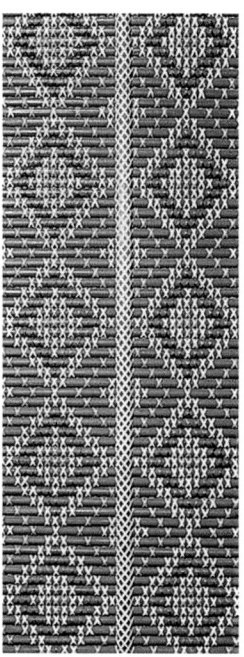 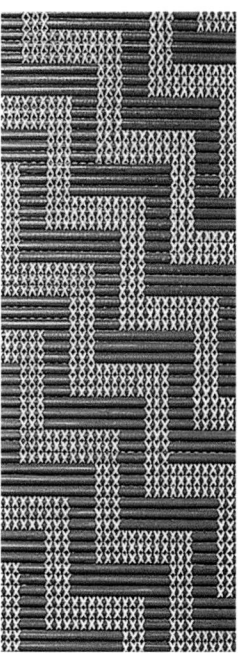

41   TUKUTUKU PANELS.
        Maori Peoples, New Zealand. 1930s.
        Dyed plaited flax strips over wood laths.
        Dimensions variable.
        The Museum of New Zealand, Te Papa Tongarewa, Wellington, New Zealand.
        F236, F238.

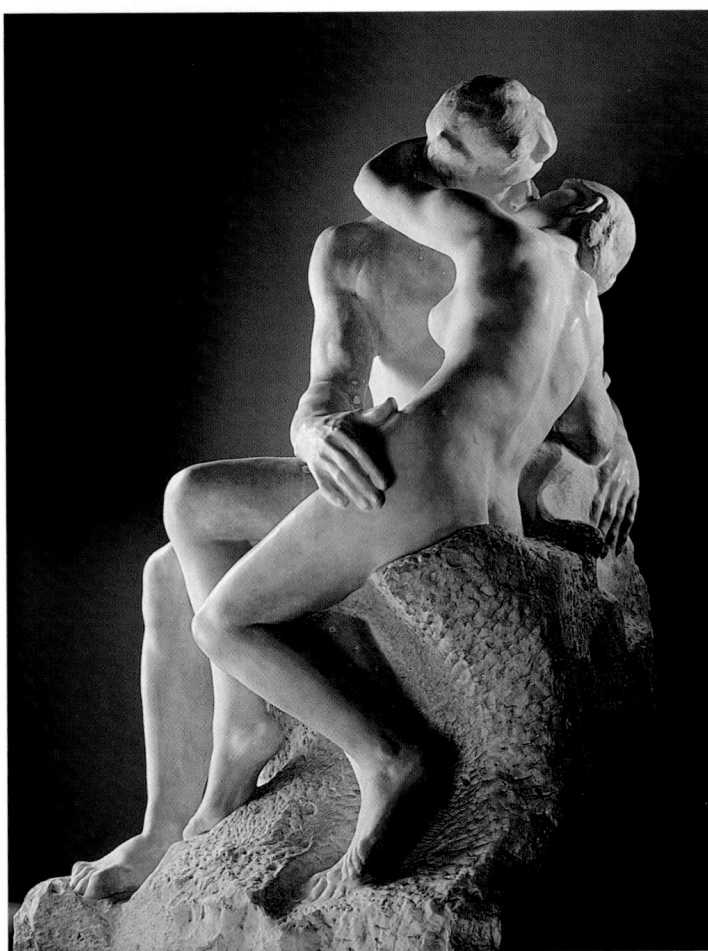

FORM AND CONTENT

Form is what we see; content is the meaning we get from what we see. In this book, *form* refers to the total effect of the combined visual qualities within a work, including such components as materials, color, shape, line, and design. *Content* refers to the message or meaning of the work of art—what the artist expresses or communicates to the viewer. Content determines form, but form expresses content; thus the two are inseparable. As form changes, content changes, and vice versa.

For example, the sign that represents the human heart is a symbol of love. If someone were to give you a huge, beautifully made red velvet valentine, so large it had to be pulled on a cart, you would probably be overwhelmed by the gesture. The content would be Love! But if you were to receive a faint photocopied outline of a heart on a cheap piece of paper, you might read the content as: *love*—sort of—a very impersonal kind. And if you were to receive a shriveled, greenish brown, slightly moldy image of a heart, you might read the content as *Ugh*!

One way to understand how art communicates experience is to compare works that have the same subject but differ greatly in form and content. THE KISS by Auguste Rodin and THE KISS by Constantin Brancusi show how two sculptors interpret an embrace. In Rodin's work, the life-size human figures represent Western ideals of the masculine and feminine: Rodin captured the sensual delight of that highly charged moment when lovers embrace. Our emotions are engaged as we overlook the hardness of the marble from which he carved it. The natural softness of flesh is heightened by the rough texture of the unfinished marble supporting the figures.

In contrast to Rodin's sensuous approach, Brancusi used the solid quality of a block of stone to express lasting love. Through minimal cutting of the block, Brancusi symbolized—rather than illustrated—the concept of two becoming one. He chose geometric abstraction rather than representational naturalism to express love. Rodin's work expresses the *feelings* of love while Brancusi's expresses the *idea* of love.

42   Auguste Rodin.
THE KISS. 1886.
Marble. Height 5′11¼″
Musée Rodin, Paris, France.
Photograph: Bruno Jarret.
© 2002 Artists Rights Society (ARS)
NY/ADAGP, Paris.

43   Constantin Brancusi.
THE KISS. c. 1916.
Limestone.
23″ × 13″ × 10″.
Philadelphia Museum of Art: The Louise and Walter Arensberg Collection.
Photograph: Graydon Wood, 1994.
1950-135-4.
© 2002 Artists Rights Society (ARS),
NY/ADAGP, Paris.

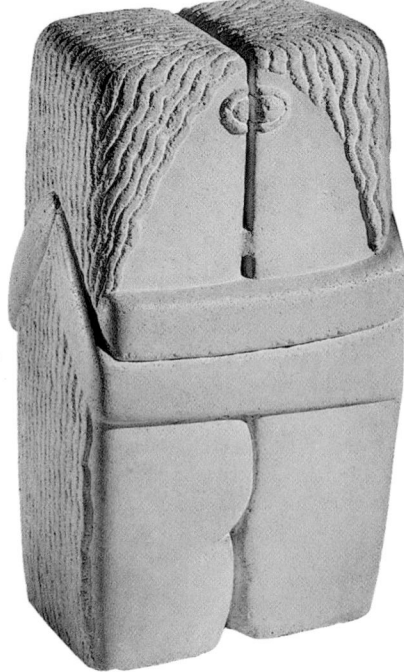

SEEING AND RESPONDING TO FORM

Obviously, artists expend effort to produce a work of art; less obvious is the fact that responding to a work of art also requires effort. The artist is the source or sender; the work is the medium carrying the message. We viewers must receive and experience the work to make the communication complete. In this way, we become active participants in the creative process.

Whether we realize it or not, learning to respond to form is part of learning to live in the world. We guide our actions by "reading" the forms of people, things, and events that make up our environment. Even as infants, we have an amazing ability to remember visual forms such as faces, and all through life we interpret events based on our previous experiences with these forms. Every form can evoke some kind of response from each of us.

Subject matter can interfere with our perception of form. One way to learn to see form without subject is to look at pictures upside down. Inverting recognizable images frees the mind from the process of identifying and naming things. Familiar objects become unfamiliar.

When confronted with something unfamiliar, we often see it freshly only because we have no idea what we are looking at. For example, Edward Burtynsky's photograph is likely to puzzle us for a moment, as we see lines and shapes in an environment almost totally white. We see only forms, few of them recognizable. Before we read the title and realize that the photograph represents a marble quarry, we have a moment of pure seeing that many artists also cultivate.

Another exercise in learning to see form is to search for images that resemble objects radically different from each other. Elliott Erwitt captured one such similarity in his 1968 photograph FLORIDA. The faucet on its bent pipe is a visual metaphor for the bird with its curved neck and thin legs.

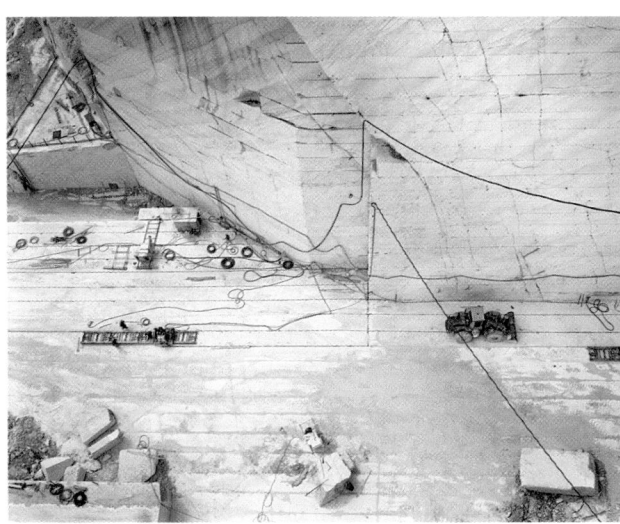

44 Edward Burtynsky.
CARRARA MARBLE QUARRIES NO. 24. 1993.
Photograph.
Charles Cowles Gallery, New York/Robert Koch Gallery,
San Francisco/Nicholas Metivier Gallery, Toronto, Canada.

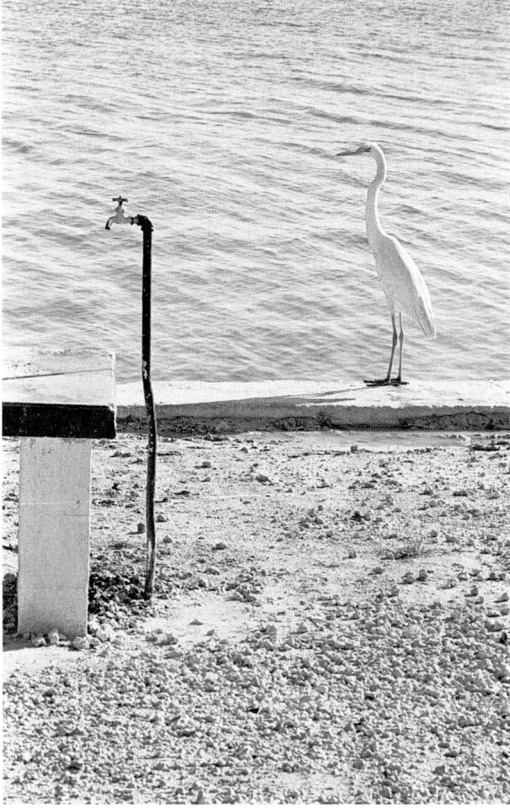

45 Elliott Erwitt.
FLORIDA. 1968.
Photograph.
Photograph: Elliott Erwitt, Magnum Photos Inc.

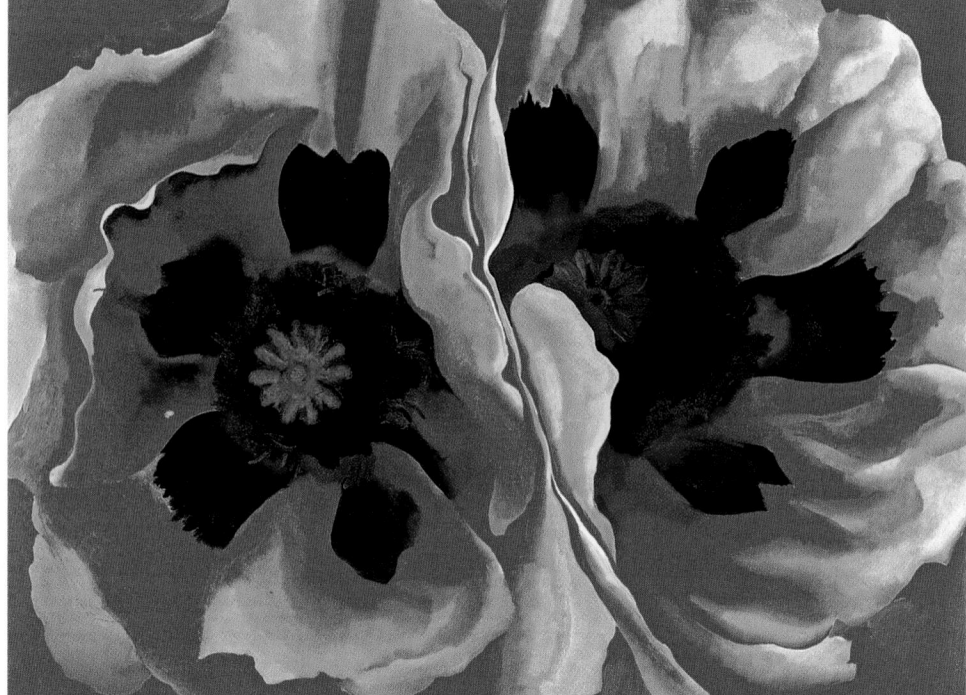

46 Georgia O'Keeffe.
ORIENTAL POPPIES. 1927.
Oil on canvas. 30" × 40⅛".
Collection Frederick R. Weisman
Art Museum, University of Minnesota,
Minneapolis, Museum Purchase.
© 2002 The Georgia O'Keeffe
Foundation/Artists Rights Society (ARS), NY.

47 Georgia O'Keeffe.
JACK-IN-THE-PULPIT NO. V. 1930.
Oil on canvas. 48" × 30".
Framed: 49⁷⁄₁₆" × 31⁷⁄₁₆" × 11¹¹⁄₁₆".
Alfred Stieglitz Collection, Bequest of Georgia
O'Keeffe. Photograph by Malcolm Varon
© 2001 Board of Trustees, National
Gallery of Art, Washington, D.C.
1987.58.4/PA.; © 2002 The Georgia O'Keeffe
Foundation/Artists Rights Society (ARS), NY.

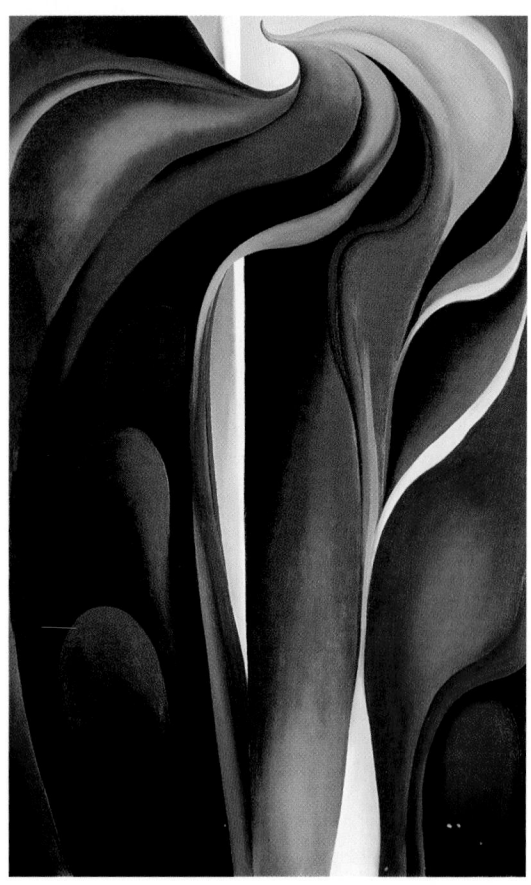

Georgia O'Keeffe responded to nature's forms in her own way. In paintings such as **ORIENTAL POPPIES** and **JACK-IN-THE-PULPIT NO. V,** she shared her awareness. She said of these paintings:

Everyone has many associations with a flower—the idea of flowers. Still—in a way—nobody sees a flower—really—it is so small—we haven't the time—and to see takes time, like to have a friend takes time. If I could paint the flower exactly as I see it no one would see what I see because I would paint it small like the flower is small.

So I said to myself—I'll paint what I see—what the flower is to me but I'll paint it big and they will be surprised into taking time to look at it.[15]

Those who have seen O'Keeffe's paintings of flowers and the American Southwest often go on to see actual flowers and desert landscapes in new ways.

ICONOGRAPHY

As we have noted, form conveys content even when no nameable subject matter is represented. But when subject matter is present, meaning is often based on traditional interpretations.

GEORGIA
O'Keeffe
A Personal Vision

1887–1986

DURING HER LONG, productive life, Georgia O'Keeffe became nearly as well known as her distinctive paintings. She represented, to many people, the popular concept of the isolated, eccentric "artist." She lived a spare, often solitary life, and approached both her life and her art in her own unique way.

O'Keeffe was born in Sun Prairie, Wisconsin, and spent her childhood on her family's farm. While in high school, she had a memorable experience that gave her a new perspective on the art-making process. As she passed the door to the art room, O'Keeffe stopped to watch as a teacher held up a jack-in-the-pulpit plant so that the students could appreciate its unusual shapes and subtle colors. Although O'Keeffe had enjoyed flowers in the marshes and meadows of Wisconsin, she had done all of her drawing and painting from plaster casts or had copied them from photographs or reproductions. This was the first time she realized that one could draw and paint from real life. Twenty-five years later she produced a powerful series of paintings based on flowers.

O'Keeffe studied at the Art Institute of Chicago, the Art Students League in New York, and Columbia University Teachers College. From Arthur Wesley Dow of Columbia she learned to appreciate Japanese design, to fill space in a beautiful way, and to balance light and dark. As a student she was also influenced by the first wave of European abstract paintings to reach the United States from Europe.

From 1912 to 1918, she spent four winters teaching school in the Texas Panhandle. The Southwest landscape left a strong impression on her and influenced her later decision to move to New Mexico—where the desert became her favorite subject.

O'Keeffe's first mature works, produced in 1915, consisted of abstract charcoal drawings suggesting natural forms and vivid watercolor landscapes. A friend of O'Keeffe's showed those drawings to influential photographer and gallery owner Alfred Stieglitz, who exhibited them in his avant-garde Gallery 291 in New York. Thus began one of the best-known artistic and romantic liaisons of the twentieth century. O'Keeffe and Stieglitz were married in 1924, and O'Keeffe's work was exhibited annually in various galleries owned by Stieglitz until his death in 1946. They were strong supporters of one another's work.

Although associated with American modern artists, O'Keeffe developed her own style, which is both

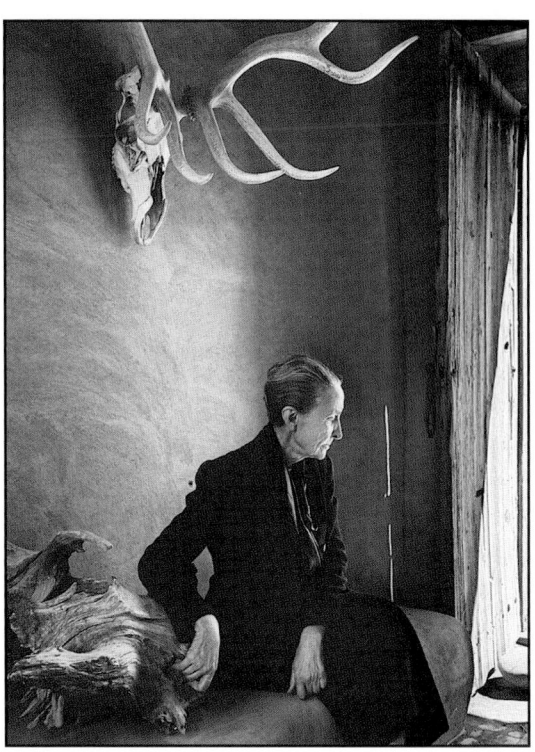

48   Yousuf Karsh.
GEORGIA O'KEEFFE. 1956.
Photograph.
Photograph: Yousuf Karsh,
Woodfin Camp & Associates, Inc.

sensuous and austere. Her paintings of the 1920s include the series of greatly enlarged flowers, landscapes, and geometrically structured views of New York City. In her mature style, O'Keeffe rejected realism in favor of simplified flat patterns and color harmonies inspired by Japanese art.

From 1929 to 1949 O'Keeffe spent summers in Taos, New Mexico, surrounded by the desert she loved. After Stieglitz died she settled permanently on an isolated ranch near the village of Abiquiu, where she remained until her death in 1986 at age ninety-eight. In people's minds she lives on as a model of creative individuality and strength.

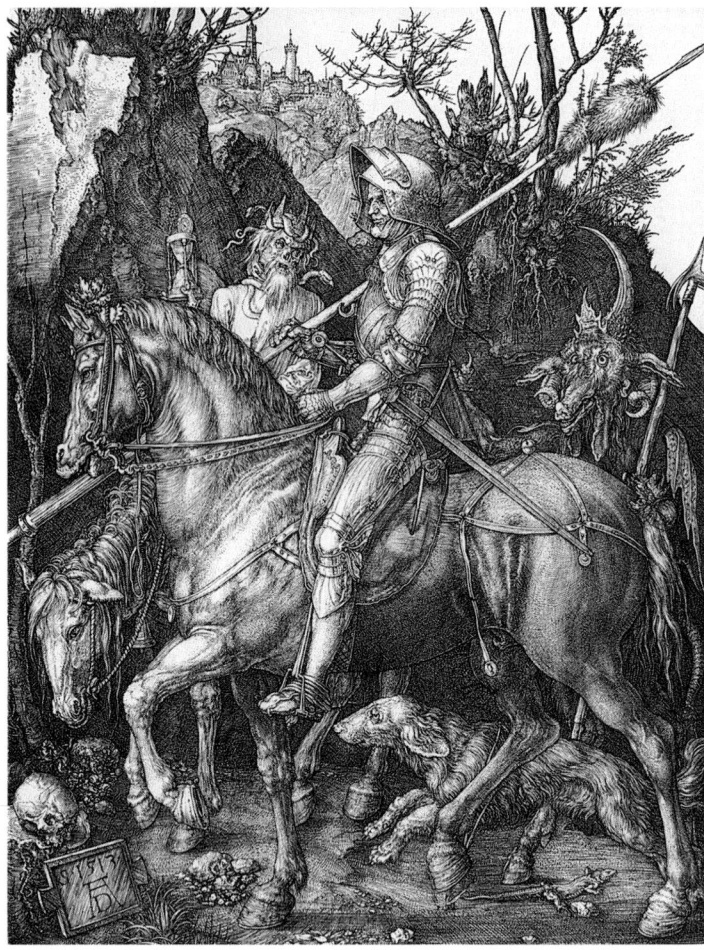

49   Albrecht Dürer.
THE KNIGHT, DEATH AND THE DEVIL. 1513.
Engraving. 9⅝″ × 7½″.
The Brooklyn Museum of Art, New York.
Gift of Mrs. Horace O. Havemeyer. 54.35.6.

Iconography is the symbolic meaning of signs, subjects, and images. Not all works of art contain iconography. In those that do, it is often the symbolism (rather than the obvious subject matter) that carries the deepest levels of meaning. The identification and specific significance of subjects, motifs, forms, colors, and positions are the central concern of iconographic interpretation.

Examples of iconography from different times and places reveal a wealth of cultural meanings. Today, the term iconography is usually associated with a religious or cultural area of study, such as Egyptian or Christian iconography.

The primary subject in Albrecht Dürer's THE KNIGHT, DEATH AND THE DEVIL is a man in armor on

horseback; behind him are a corpselike figure and a horned monster. The meanings of this imagery would have been well understood by viewers in Dürer's time because they were familiar with Christian iconography: the knight in armor symbolizes the dutiful Christian who follows the right path undistracted by Death and the Devil.

The knight must ride through the darkness of the "valley of the shadow of death" to reach the City of God, seen in the background. An hourglass in the hand of Death symbolizes human mortality or the brevity of life. Serpents in Death's hair are ancient symbols of death and also Christian symbols of the Devil. The dog, a symbol of faithfulness in both religion and marriage, symbolizes the faith the knight must have if he is to reach his goal. A lizard, representing evil, scurries in the opposite direction. Dürer organized all these separate references in a way that leaves no doubt that the Christian knight will reach his goal. The idealized form and dominant central position of the knight and his powerful horse convey a sense of assurance.

An excellent example of Hindu iconography called DESCENT OF THE GANGES was carved in a huge granite outcropping in the town of Māmallapuram, in southern India. Included in the large composition are more than a hundred human figures, deities, flying pairs of angels without wings, life-size elephants, and a variety of other animals, all converging at the Ganges River in an elaborate depiction of intertwining Hindu legends. As in Dürer's engraving, the composition is filled with symbolic subject matter.

The central gorge in the carving symbolizes the descent of the sacred Ganges from heaven to earth, making the land fertile. The cobra-like figures in the gorge are the King and Queen of the Nagas, serpent deities that portray the great river. While these figures occupy the center of the relief, other legends are illustrated around them.

In front of the largest elephant is a comical depiction of a cat and mice. According to an old folktale, a cat pretending to be an ascetic stood beside the Ganges with upraised paws and gazed at the sun. The cat convinced the mice that it was holy and thus worthy of worship. As the mice closed their eyes in reverence, the cat snatched them for dinner.

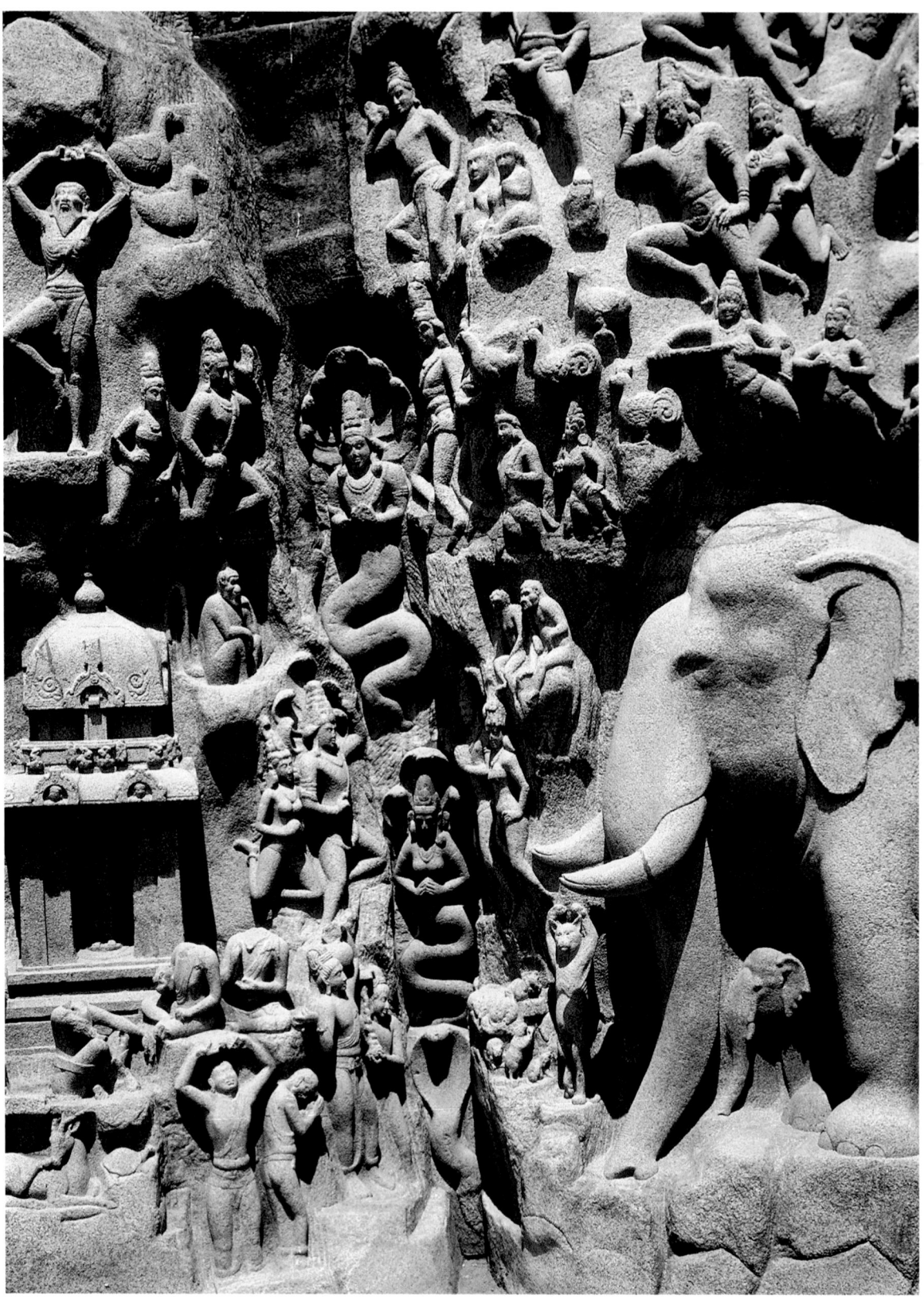

50 Detail of DESCENT OF THE GANGES.
Māmallapuram, India. 7th Century. Granite. Height approximately 30′.
Photograph: Duane Preble.

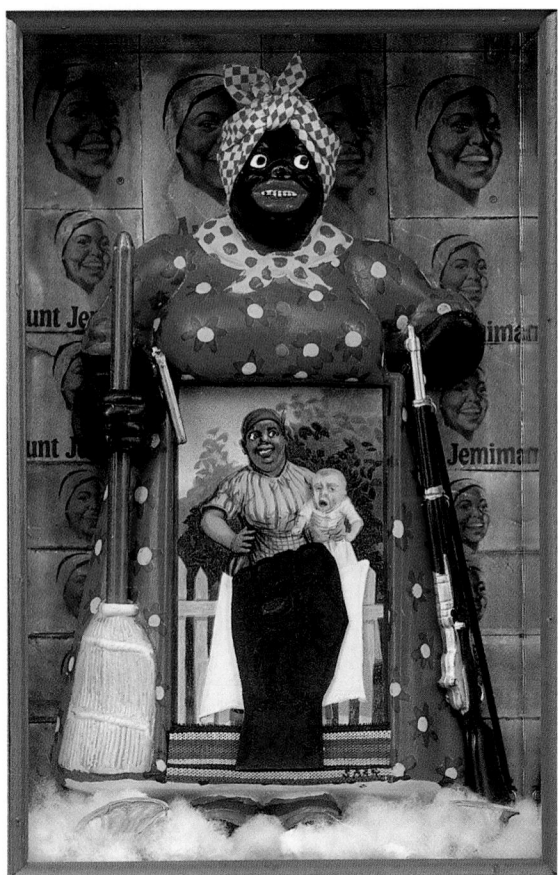

51 Betye Saar.
THE LIBERATION OF AUNT JEMIMA. 1972.
Mixed media. 11¾″ × 8″ × 2¾″.
University of California, Berkeley Art Museum. Purchased with the aid of funds
from the National Endowment for the Arts.
Photographed for the museum by Benjamin Blackwell.

The whole sculpture relates to the annual miracle of the return of the life-giving waters of the river. Appropriately, the many figures appear to be emerging from the stone as if from flowing water.

In modern America, the most pervasive art forms are mass media advertising images, and they too have their iconography. Some artists have used such commercial images to comment on their times. Betye Saar's THE LIBERATION OF AUNT JEMIMA is based on a stereotypical image of a black nanny from a box of cooking mix. The work confronts viewers with a startling group of faces and figures as the artist altered the imagery to allow Jemima to arm herself. Even now, decades after its creation, the figure of Aunt Jemima can dredge up painful feelings associated with racial stereotyping.

Contrasts between a broom and a rifle add to the message. The whole construction is punctuated with an icon of very different purpose: the defiant, upraised clenched fist, a salute and primary symbol of the Black Power movement. By making this hand large, and by placing it in the lower central position, in front of the woman holding the baby, Saar made her meaning abundantly clear: no more of this demeaning nonsense!

ARTISTS AT WORK

Carlos Frésquez

CONTEMPORARY Mexican-American artist Carlos Frésquez offers a wide range of iconographic symbols in his oil painting YELLOW WALL. "I am always searching for imagery," he said. The work is laden with images that are "very important to my culture." The diverse images in this work refer to pre-conquest Mexico, European modern art, television cartoons, and thrift shops. The faces in silhouette refer to the mixed heritage of Mexican Americans. When the boldness of some of these juxtapositions caused him to be labeled audacious, Frésquez replied, "Thank you." More of the conversation is available on the Web site that accompanies this book.

Carlos Frésquez. 52
MI CASA ES SU CASA: YELLOW WALL (WEST). 1997.
Mixed media with objects on panel. 11′ × 8′.
Courtesy of the artist.

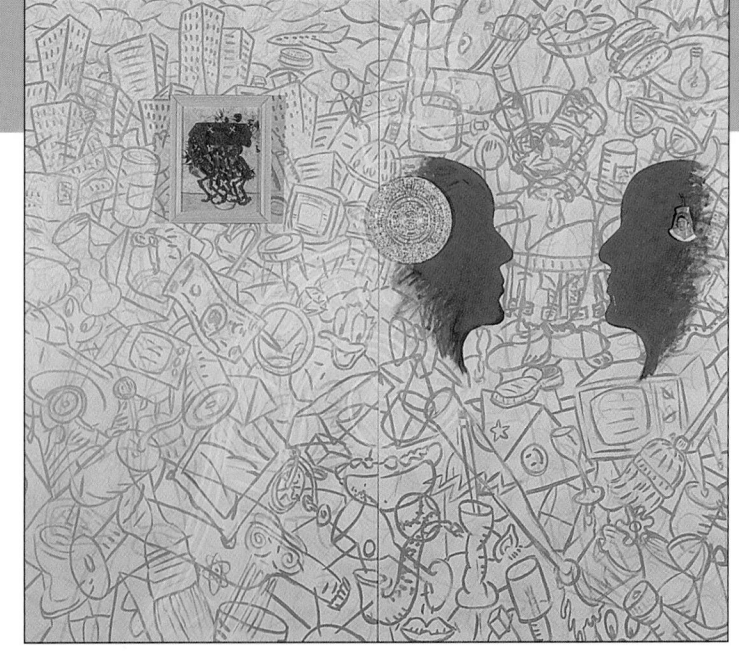

PART TWO

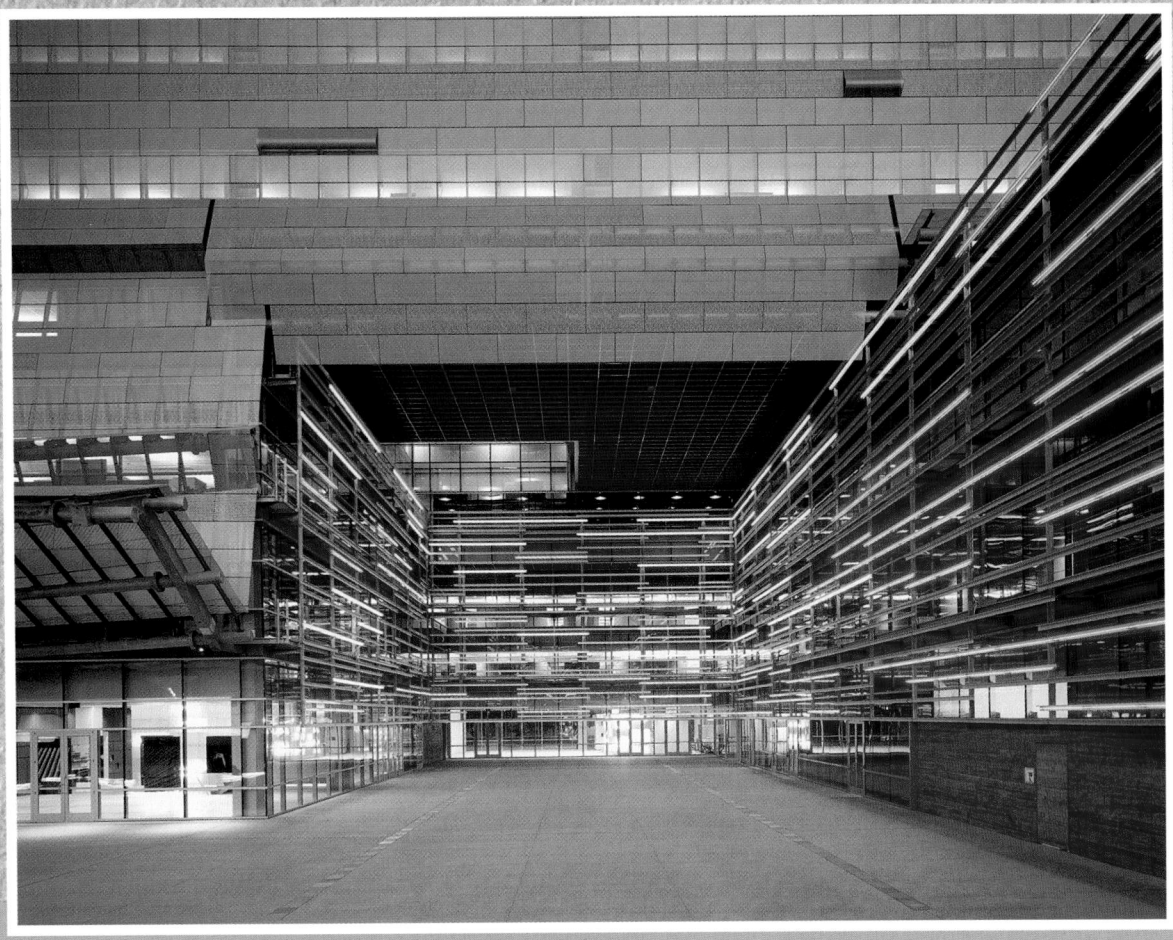

Keith Sonnier.
MOTORDOM. 2004.
Light Installation at Caltrans District 7
Headquarters, Los Angeles.

THE LANGUAGE OF VISUAL EXPERIENCE

CONSIDER...

Have you ever arranged a group of pictures on the wall of your home? How did you know when the arrangement looked "right"?

Have you ever been in a room where the space felt oppressive? What caused that feeling, and how would you change the space in order to alter the mood?

Why is handwriting sometimes accepted as legal evidence in court? What does that tell you about individual drawing styles?

How do cartoonists show the passage of time? How do they show movement? What other visual media can express time or movements?

Does color affect your emotions? What color would you choose to express sadness? Joy? Boredom? Anger? Do you avoid using certain colors in your clothing or in your art?

VISUAL ELEMENTS

Remember that a picture—before being a war horse, a nude woman, or some anecdote—is essentially a plane surface covered with colors assembled in a certain order.

MAURICE DENIS[1]

Painter Maurice Denis might have gone on to say that the *plane,* the two-dimensional picture surface, can also be covered with lines, shapes, textures, and other aspects of visual form (visual elements). Sculpture consists of these same elements organized and presented in three-dimensional space. Because of their overlapping qualities, it is impossible to draw rigid boundaries between the elements of visual form.

For example, a glance at Swiss artist Paul Klee's LANDSCAPE WITH YELLOW BIRDS reveals his playful interpretation of the subject. Fluid, curving *lines* define abstract *shapes.* Klee simplified and flattened the solid *masses* of natural plant and bird forms so that they read as flat shapes against a dark background *space.* Such abstraction emphasizes the fantastic, dreamlike quality of the subject. The whimsical positioning of the upside-down bird suggests a moment in *time* without *motion. Light* illuminates and enhances the yellow *color* of the birds and the unusual colors of the leaves. Surface *textures* provide further interest in each area of the painting.

This chapter introduces the visual elements identified in LANDSCAPE WITH YELLOW BIRDS: line, shape, mass, space, time, motion, light, color, and texture. Not all these elements are important, or even present, in every work of art; many works emphasize only a few elements. To understand their expressive possibilities, it is useful for us to examine—one at a time—some of the expressive qualities of each of the aspects of visual form.

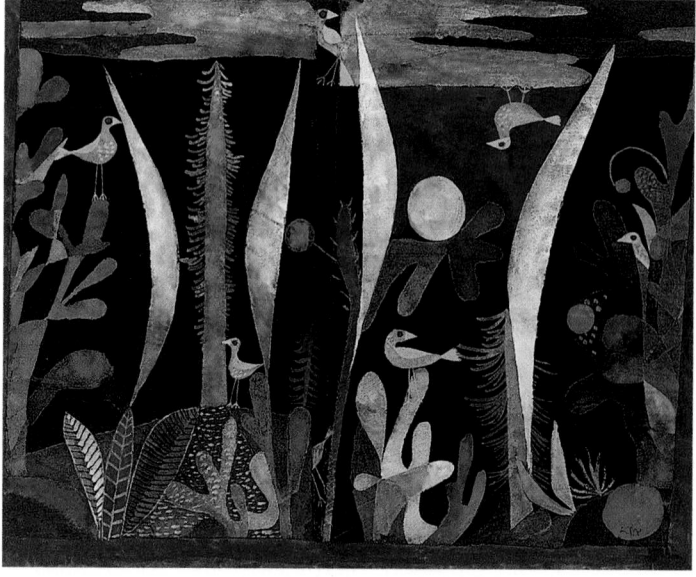

53   Paul Klee.
     LANDSCAPE WITH YELLOW BIRDS. 1923.
     Watercolor, newspaper, black base. *14″ × 17⅜″.*
     Photograph: Hans Hinz/Artothek.© 2005 Artists Rights Society
     (ARS), NY/VG Bild-Kunst, Bonn.

LINE

We write, draw, plan, and play with lines. Our individualities and feelings are expressed as we write our one-of-a-kind signatures or make other unmechanical lines. Line is our basic means for recording and symbolizing ideas, observations, and feelings; it is a primary means of visual communication. (An interactive exercise about line can be found on the *Discovering Art* CD.)

A line is an extension of a point. Our habit of making all kinds of lines obscures the fact that pure geometric line—line with only one dimension, length—is a mental concept. Such geometric lines, with no height or depth, do not exist in the three-dimensional physical world. Lines are actually linear forms in which length dominates over width. Wherever we see an edge, we can perceive the edge as a line—the place where one object or plane appears to end and another object or space begins. In a sense, we often "draw" with our eyes, converting edges to lines.

In art and in nature, we can consider *lines* as paths of action—records of the energy left by moving points. Many intersecting and contrasting linear paths form the composition in Ansel Adams' photograph RAILS AND JET TRAILS.

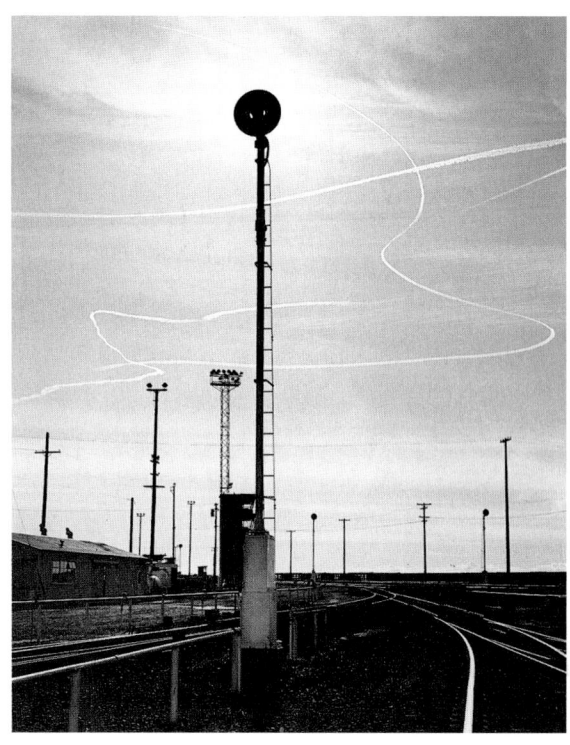

54 Ansel Adams.
RAILS AND JET TRAILS, ROSEVILLE, CALIFORNIA. 1953.
Photograph.

Characteristics of Line

Lines can be active or static, aggressive or passive, sensual or mechanical. Lines can indicate directions, define boundaries of shapes and spaces, imply volumes or solid masses, and suggest motion or emotion. Lines can also be grouped to depict light and shadow and to form patterns and textures. Note the line qualities in these LINE VARIATIONS.

55 LINE VARIATIONS.

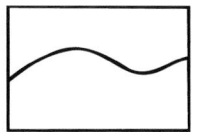

a. Actual line

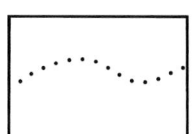

b. implied line

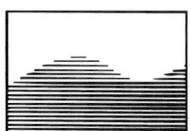

c. Actual straight lines and implied curved line

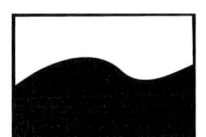

d. Line created by an edge

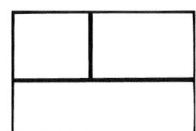

e. Vertical line (attitude of alert attention); horizontal line (attitude of rest).

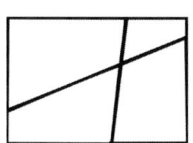

f. Diagonal lines (slow action, fast action).

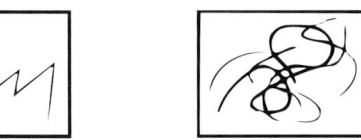

g. Sharp, jagged line.

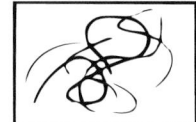

h. Dance of curving lines.

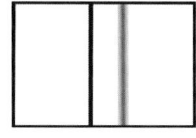

i. Hard line, soft line.

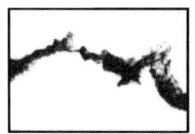

j. Ragged, irregular line.

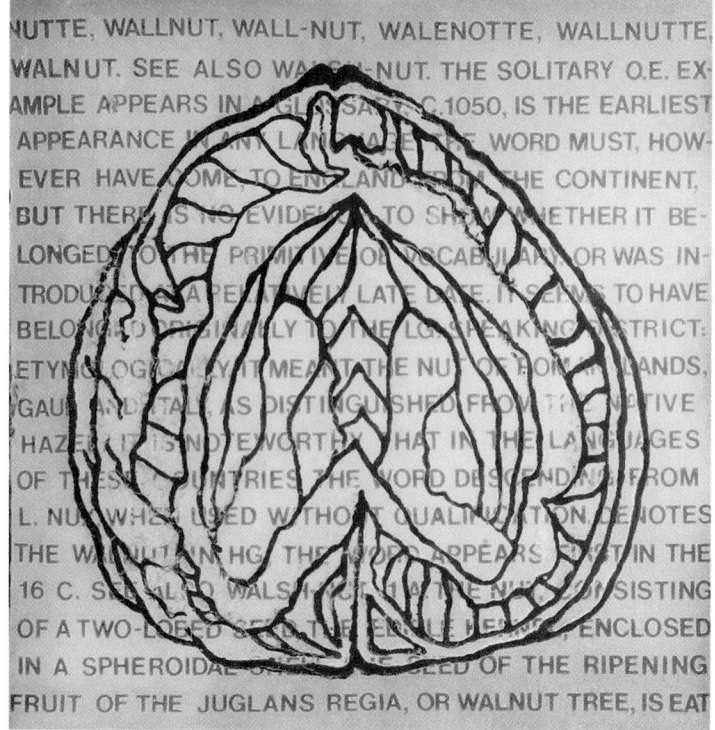

56 Abby Leigh. WALLENOTE. 2002.
   Linen on abaca on cotton, 30¾″ × 30¾″.
   Paper made at Dieu Donne Papermill.
   © Abby Leigh. Courtesy of the Betty Cuningham Gallery, NY.

Consider the range of uses artists found for lines in the works pictured on these two pages. In Abby Leigh's WALLENOTE, contour lines describe the edges of shapes inside a walnut. Most of us think first of line in this way, as outlining. Indeed, this is line's most basic function in art, and we probably started drawing in this way as children. Cartoonists work in a similar fashion. But artists have put lines to many other uses.

Bridget Riley created a powerful energy field of parallel, wavy lines in her painting CURRENT. We cannot focus steadily on one spot in this work, and as our eyes move, the work seems to vibrate even though nothing in it moves. Jackson Pollock made his DRAWING by pouring and dripping ink from a stick without touching the paper. The swirling lines tracked his expressive hand motions, varying the thickness with the speed of his wrist. The TWO ACROBATS by Alexander Calder are drawn in space using wire that the artist flexed into shape with pli-

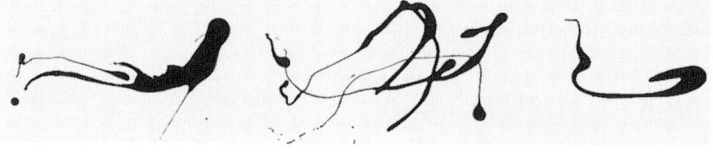

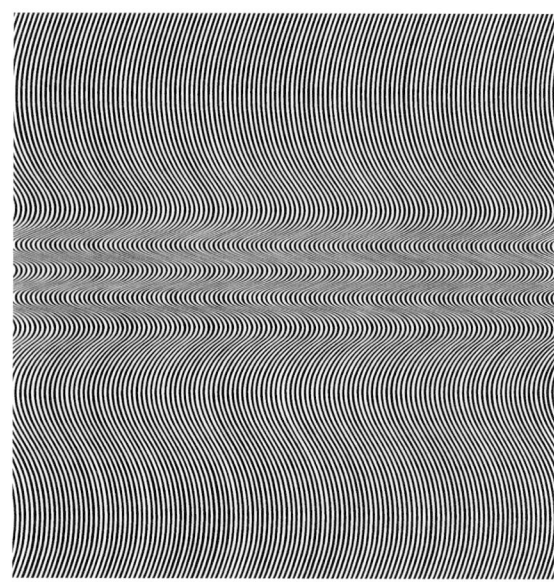

57 Bridget Riley.
   CURRENT. 1964.
   Synthetic polymer paint on composition board.
   58⅜″ × 58⅞″.
   © 2006 Bridget Riley. The Museum of Modern Art/Licensed by Scala-Art Resource, NY. Philip Johnson Fund. Photograph © 2001 The Museum of Modern Art, NY.

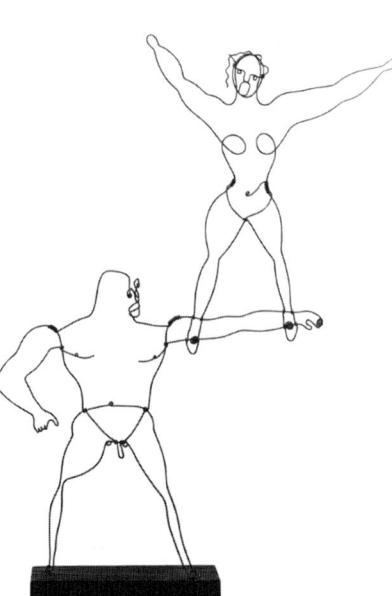

58 Jackson Pollock.
   DRAWING. 1950.
   Duco on paper.
   11⅛″ × 60″.
   Staatsgalerie, Stuttgart/Graphische Sammlung. © 2002 The Pollock-Krasner Foundation/Artists Rights Society (ARS), NY.

59 Alexander Calder.
   TWO ACROBATS. 1928.
   Brass wire.
   Height with base 34″.
   Honolulu Academy of Arts, Gift of Mrs. T.A. Cooke, Mrs. W.F. Dillingham, and Mrs. P.E. Spalding, 1937. #4595. © 2002 Estate of Alexander Calder/Artists Rights Society (ARS), NY.

ers; his whimsical lines captured their exuberant maneuvers. Many Japanese prints take as subject matter popular entertainers such as dancers and actors. The two prints pictured here use black contour lines in contrasting ways: WOMAN DANCER is curvy and sensuous, suggesting rhythmic motion, whereas Torii Kiyotada's ACTOR uses angular lines to express violent and swift action.

Many types of prints are made up almost entirely of lines, with little shading or color. Kiki Smith etched lines in a metal plate to create GINZER, a depiction of her cat. She painstakingly drew one line for each of GINZER'S hairs, it seems. The eyes and foot pads are slightly shaded, but all else was done with line. She successfully captured the cat's flexible limbs and back as GINZER reclined, but she also showed a hint of the cat's wild side in the mouth and alert eyes.

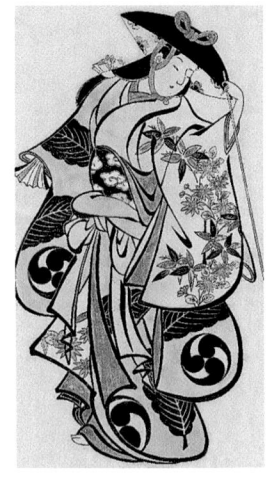

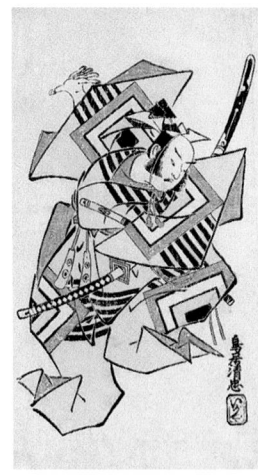

60 Attributed to Torii Kiyonobu I.
WOMAN DANCER WITH FAN AND WAND.
c. 1708.
Woodblock print.
$21^3/_40 \times 11^1/_20$.
The Metropolitan Museum of Art, New York. Harris Brisbane Dick Fund and Rogers Fund, 1949 (JP3098). Photograph: © 1979 The Metropolitan Museum of Art.

61 Torii Kiyotada.
AN ACTOR OF THE ICHIKAWA CLAN IN A DANCE MOVEMENT OF VIOLENT MOTION.
c. 1715.
Hand-colored woodcut. $11^1/_40 \times 60$.
The Metropolitan Museum of Art, New York. Harris Brisbane Dick Fund and Rogers Fund, 1949 (JP3075). Photograph: © 1979 The Metropolitan Museum of Art.

62 Kiki Smith.
GINZER. 2000.
Etching, aquatint, and drypoint on mold-made paper.
180×240.
Published by Harlan & Weaver, NY.

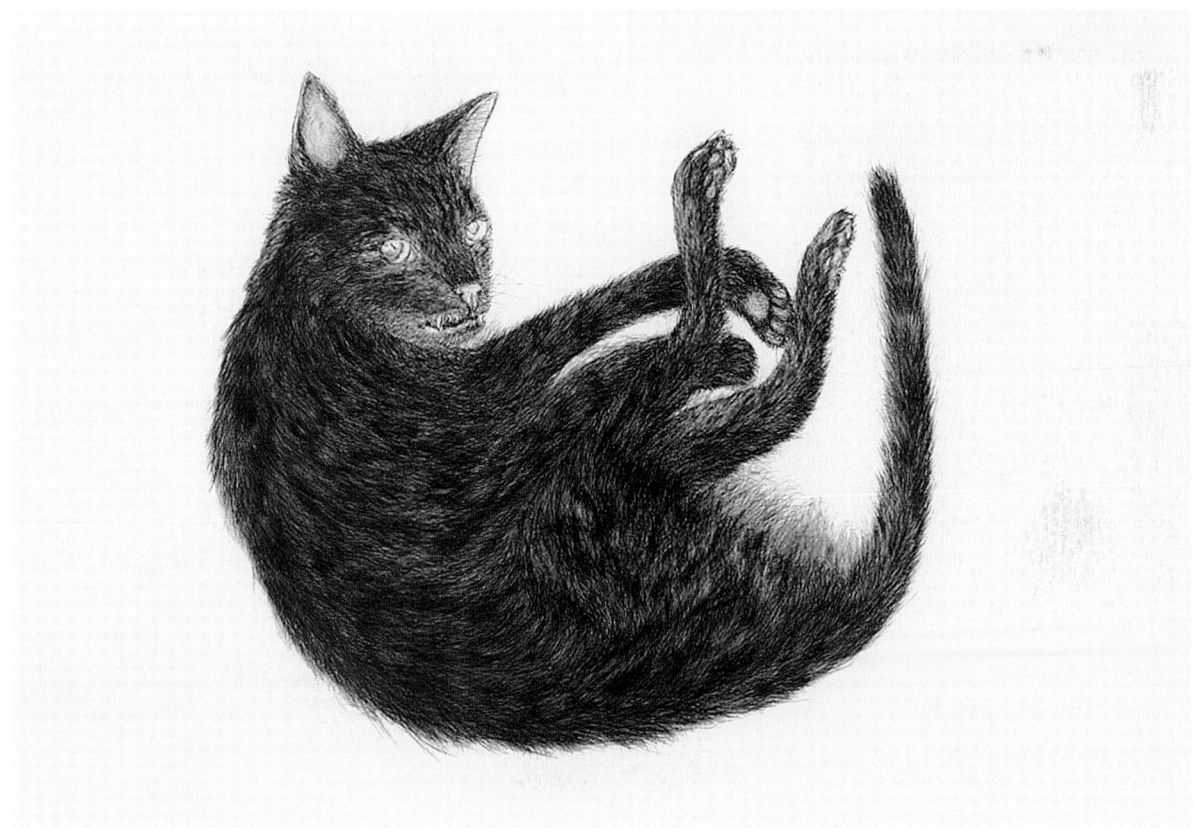

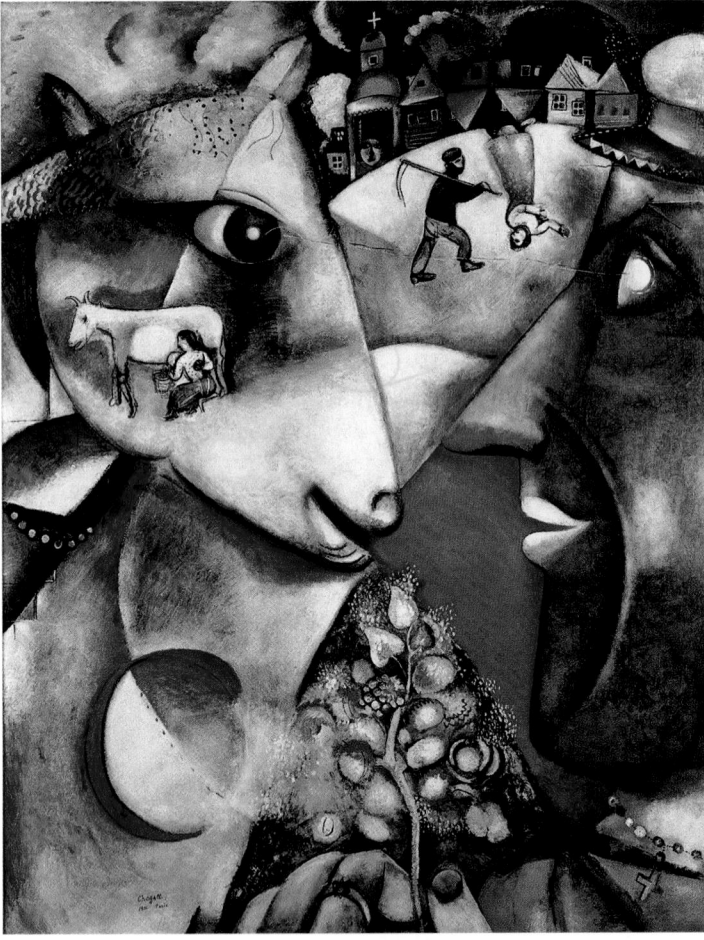

63   Marc Chagall.
I AND THE VILLAGE. 1911.
Oil on canvas. 75⁵/₈″ × 59⁵/₈″.
The Museum of Modern Art, NY/Licensed by Scala-Art Resource, NY. Mrs. Simon
Guggenheim Fund. Photograph © 2002 The Museum of Modern Art, New York.
© 2002 Artists Rights Society (ARS), NY/ADAGP, Paris.

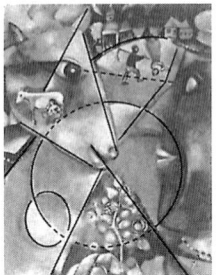

63b   Marc Chagall.
I AND THE VILLAGE. 1911.
Oil on canvas. 75⁵/₈″ × 59⁵/₈″.
The Museum of Modern Art, NY/Licensed by Scala-Art Resource, NY. Mrs. Simon
Guggenheim Fund. Photograph © 2002 The Museum of Modern Art, New York.
© 2002 Artists Rights Society (ARS), NY/ADAGP, Paris.

Implied Line

Implied lines suggest visual connections. Implied lines that form geometric shapes can serve as an underlying organizational structure. In I AND THE VILLAGE, Marc Chagall used implied lines to create a circle that brings together scenes of Russian Jewish village life. Notice that he also drew in the implied sightline between man and animal.

SHAPE

The words *shape*, *mass*, and *form* are sometimes used interchangeably. Here *shape* is used to refer to the expanse within the outline of a two-dimensional area or within the outer boundaries of a three-dimensional object. When we see a three-dimensional object in natural light, we see that it has mass, or volume. If the same object is silhouetted against a sunset, we may see it only as a flat shape. Enclosing lines or changing color sets a shape or mass apart from its surroundings so that we recognize it.

We can group the infinite variety of shapes into two general categories: geometric and organic. *Geometric shapes*—such as circles, triangles, and squares—tend to be precise and regular. *Organic shapes* are irregular, often curving or rounded, and seem relaxed and more informal than geometric shapes. The most common shapes in the human-made world are geometric. Although some geometric shapes exist in nature—in such forms as crystals, honeycombs, and snowflakes—most shapes in nature are organic. A related term with a similar meaning is *biomorphic*, which also suggests shapes based on natural forms.

In I AND THE VILLAGE, Chagall used a geometric structure of circles and triangles to organize the organic shapes of people, animals, and plants. He softened the severity of geometric shapes to achieve a natural flow between the various parts of the painting. Conversely, he abstracted natural subjects toward geometric simplicity in order to strengthen visual impact and symbolic content. (An interactive exercise showing how shapes function in other artworks is on the *Discovering Art* CD.)

When a shape appears on a *picture plane* (the flat picture surface), it simultaneously creates a second shape out of the background area. The subject or dominant shapes are referred to as *figures* or *positive shapes*; background areas are *ground* or *negative shapes*. The figure-ground relationship is a fundamental aspect of perception; it allows us to sort out and interpret what we see. Because we are conditioned to see only objects, and not the spaces between and around them, it takes a shift in awareness to see the negative shapes in A SHAPE OF SPACE. An artist, however, must consider both positive and negative shapes simultaneously, and treat them as equally important to the total effectiveness of an image.

Interactions between figure shapes and ground shapes are heightened in some images. NIGHT LIFE can be seen as white shapes against black or as black shapes against white, or the figure-ground relationship can shift back and forth. In both this and M.C. Escher's woodcut SKY AND WATER, the shifting of figure and ground contributes to a similar content: the interrelatedness of all things.

In the upper half of Escher's print, we see dark geese on a white ground. As our eyes move down the page, the light upper background becomes fish against a black background. In the middle, however, fish and geese interlock so perfectly that we are not sure what is figure and what is ground. As our awareness shifts, fish shapes and bird shapes trade places, a phenomenon called *figure-ground reversal*.

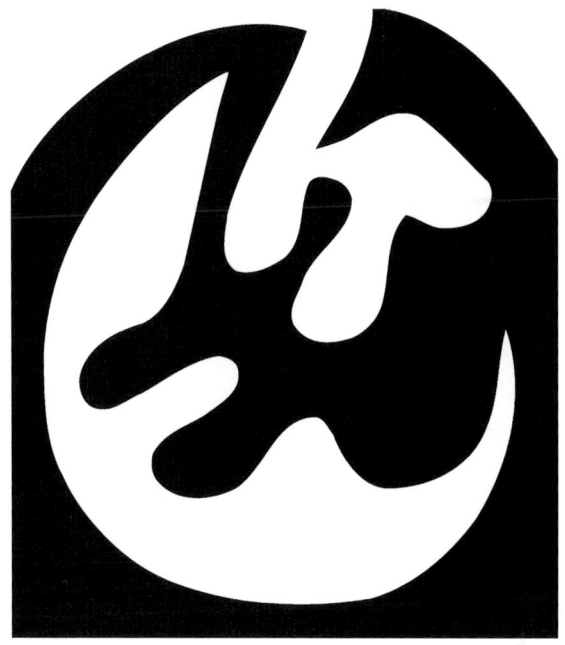

65   Duane Preble.
NIGHT LIFE.
Figure-ground reversal.

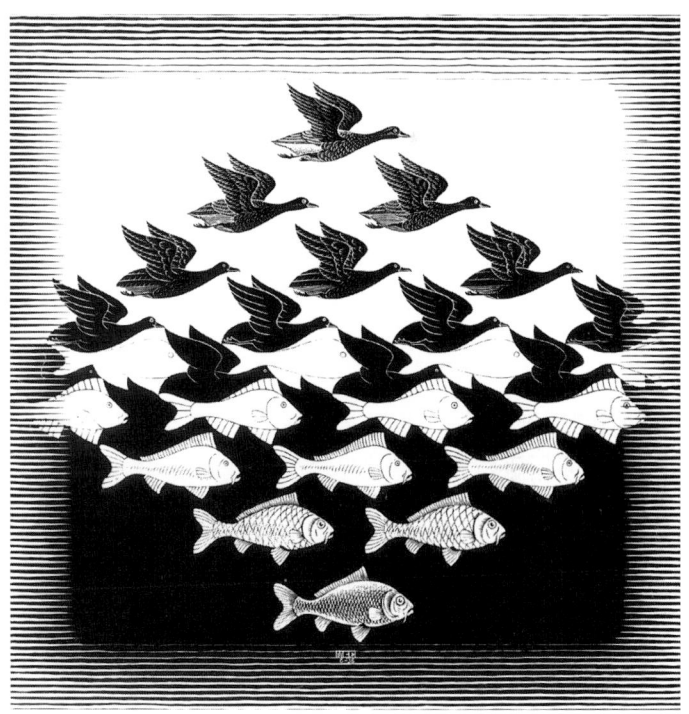

66   M. C. Escher.
SKY AND WATER I. 1938.
Woodcut. $17\frac{1}{8}'' \times 17\frac{1}{4}''$.

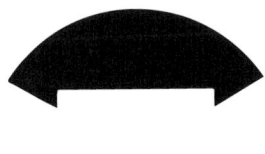

64   A SHAPE OF SPACE.
Implied shape.

MASS

Whereas a two-dimensional area is called a shape, a three-dimensional area is called a *mass*—the physical bulk of a solid body of material. When mass encloses space, the space is called *volume*. The word *form* is sometimes used instead of mass to refer to physical bulk.

Mass in Three Dimensions

Mass is often a major element in sculpture and architecture. Immense or bulky mass was an important characteristic of ancient Egyptian architecture and sculpture. Egyptians sought this quality and perfected it because it expressed their desire to make art for eternity.

QENNEFER, STEWARD OF THE PALACE, was carved from hard black granite and retains the cubic, block-like appearance of the quarried stone. None of the limbs projects outward into the surrounding space.

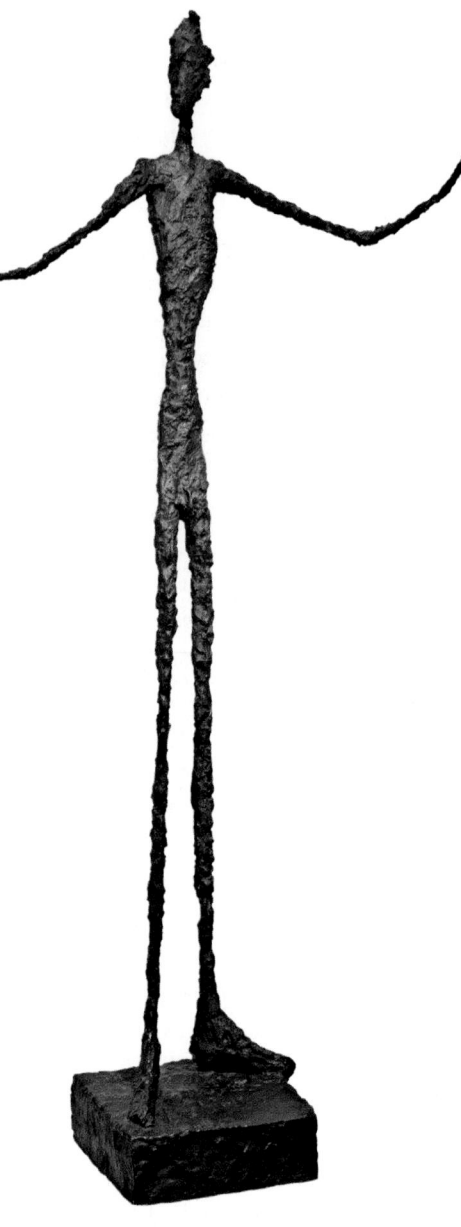

68   Alberto Giacometti.
MAN POINTING. 1947.
Bronze. $70^{1}/_{2}'' \times 40^{3}/_{4}'' \times 16^{3}/_{8}''$.
The Museum of Modern Art, NY/Licensed by Scala-Art Resource, NY. Gift of Mrs. John D. Rockefeller III. (678.1954) The Museum of Modern Art, NY. © 2009 Artists Rights Society (ARS), NY/ADAGP, Paris. Digital image The Museum of Modern Art/Licensed by Scala/Art Resource, NY.

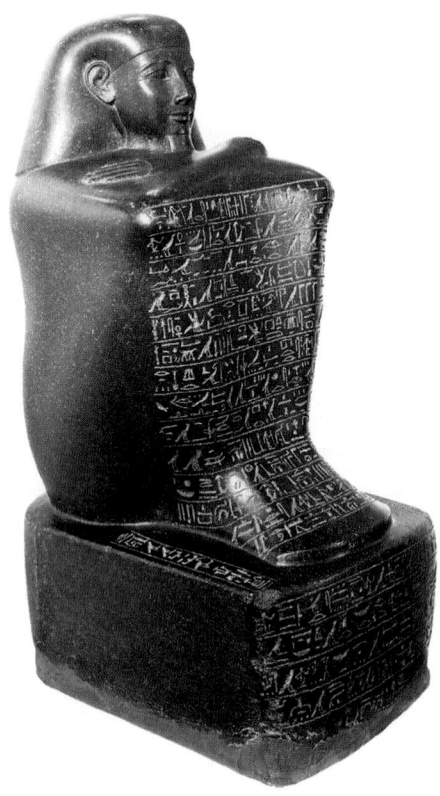

67   QENNEFER, STEWARD OF THE PALACE. c. 1450 B.C.E.
Black granite. Height 2'9".
The British Museum, Department of Egyptian Antiquities. © The British Museum.

The figure sits with knees drawn up and arms folded, the neck obscured by a ceremonial headdress. The body is abstracted and implied with minimal suggestion. This piece is a good example of *closed form*—form that does not openly interact with the space around it. Here, compact mass symbolizes permanence. Egyptian portrait sculpture acted as a symbolic container for the soul of an important person to ensure eternal afterlife.

In contrast to the compact mass of the Egyptian portrait, modern sculptor Alberto Giacometti's MAN POINTING conveys a sense of fleeting presence rather than permanence. The tall, thin figure appears eroded by time and barely existing. Because Giacometti used little solid material to construct the figure, we are more aware of a linear form in space than of mass. The figure reaches out; its *open form* interacts with the surrounding space, which seems to overwhelm it, suggesting the fragile, impermanent nature of human existence.

Giacometti's art reveals an obsession with mortality that began when he was twenty, following the death of an older companion. Later, expressing the fleeting essence of human life became a major concern visible in his work. For Giacometti, both life and the making of art were continuous evolutions. He never felt that he succeeded in capturing the changing nature of what he saw, and therefore he considered all of his works unfinished.

Mass in Two Dimensions

With two-dimensional media, such as painting and drawing, mass must be implied. In BREAD, Elizabeth Catlett drew lines that seem to wrap around and define a girl in space, implying a solid mass. The work gives the appearance of mass because the lines both follow the curvature of the head and build up dark areas to suggest mass revealed by light. Her use of lines convinces us that we are seeing a fully rounded person. (Interactive exercises showing how artists imply mass in two dimensions are found on the *Discovering Art* CD.)

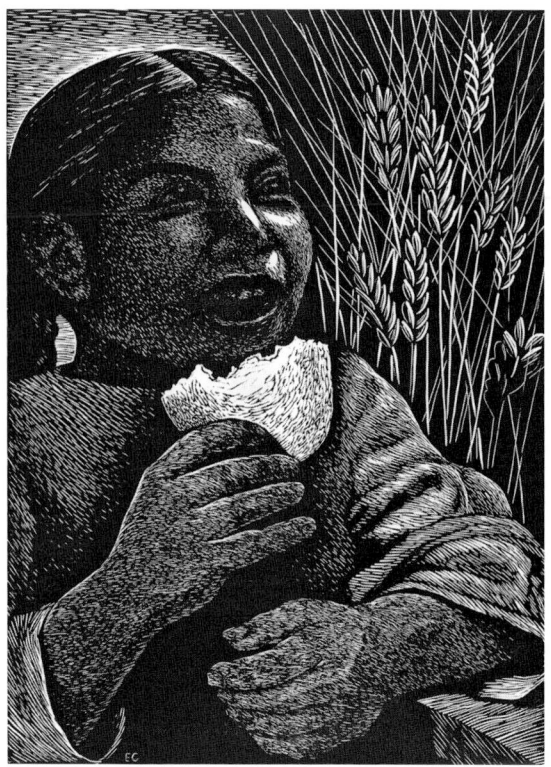

69   Elizabeth Catlett.
BREAD. 1962.
Linocut on paper.
Courtesy of the Library of Congress. © Elizabeth Catlett/
Licensed by VAGA, New York, NY.

SPACE

Space is the indefinable, general receptacle of all things—the seemingly empty space around us. It is continuous, infinite, and ever present. The visual arts are sometimes referred to as *spatial* arts because most of these art forms are organized in space. In contrast, music is a *temporal* art because musical elements are organized primarily in time. In film, video, and dance, form is organized in both time and space.

Space in Three Dimensions

Of all the visual elements, space is the most difficult to convey in words and pictures. To experience three-dimensional space, we must be in it. We

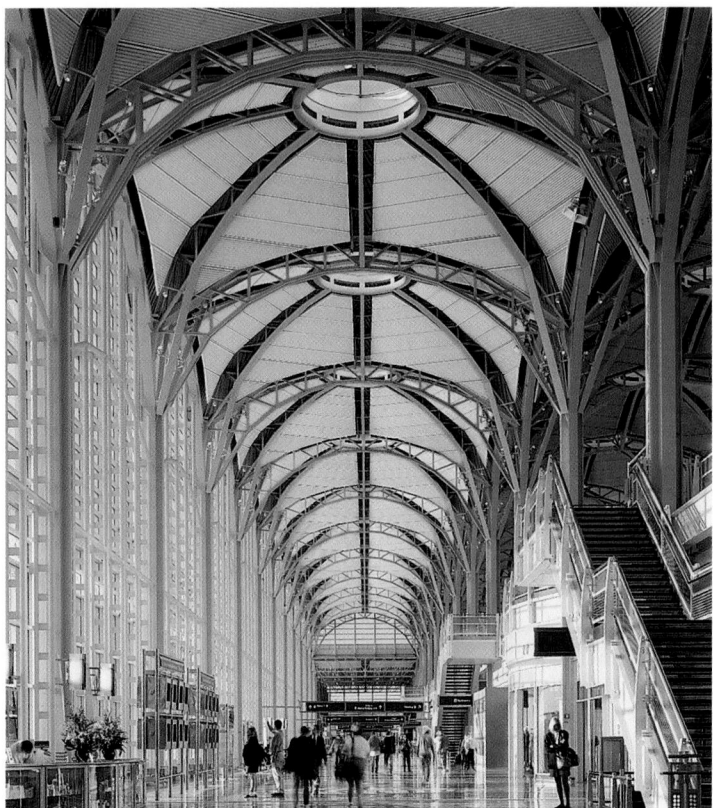

70   a. Cesar Pelli and Associates.
NORTH TERMINAL, RONALD REAGAN WASHINGTON
NATIONAL AIRPORT. 1997.
Photographer: Jeff Goldberg/Esto Photographics, Inc.

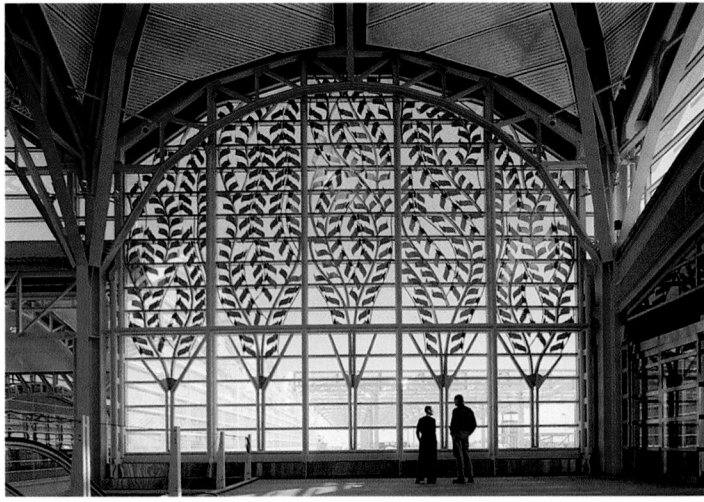

b. CLOSE-UP OF INTERIOR.
Photographer: Jeff Goldberg/Esto Photographics, Inc.

experience space beginning with our own positions in relation to other people, objects, surfaces, and voids at various distances from ourselves. Each of us has a sense of personal space—the area surrounding our bodies—that we like to protect, and the extent of this invisible boundary varies from person to person and from culture to culture.

Architects are especially concerned with the qualities of space. Imagine how you would feel in a small room with a very low ceiling. What if you raised the ceiling to fifteen feet? What if you added skylights? What if you replaced the walls with glass? In each case you would have changed the character of the space and, by doing so, would have radically changed your experience.

Whereas we experience the outside of a building as mass in space, we experience the inside as volume and as a sequence of enclosed spaces. Cesar Pelli's design for the NORTH TERMINAL at Ronald Reagan Washington National Airport takes the passenger's experience of space into account. There are many large windows that offer views of the runways and also of the Potomac River and the nearby Washington Monument. The interior is divided into many small domed modules: "The module has an important psychological value in that each one is like a very large living room in size," the architect said.[2] "It's a space that we experience in our daily life. . . . The domes make spaces designed on the scale of people, not on the scale of big machines."

Space in Two Dimensions

With three-dimensional objects and spaces, such as sculpture and architecture, we must move around to get the full experience. With two-dimensional works, such as drawing and painting, we see the space of the surface all at once. In drawings, prints, photographs, and paintings, the actual space of each picture's surface *(picture plane)* is defined by its edges—usually the two dimensions of height and width. Yet within these boundaries, a great variety of possible pictorial spaces can be implied, creating depth in the picture plane.

Paintings from ancient Egypt show little or no depth. Early Egyptian painters made their images clear by portraying objects from their most easily identifiable angles and by avoiding the visual confusion caused by overlap and the appearance of diminishing size. POND IN A GARDEN demonstrates this technique. The pond is shown from above while the trees, fish, and birds are all pictured from the side.

Implied Depth

Almost any mark on a picture plane begins to give the illusion of a third dimension: depth. Clues to seeing spatial depth are learned in early childhood. A few of the major ways of indicating space on a picture plane are shown in the diagrams of CLUES TO SPATIAL DEPTH.

When shapes overlap, we immediately assume from experience that one is in front of the other (diagram a). Overlapping is the most basic way to achieve the effect of depth on a flat surface. The effect of overlap is strengthened by *diminishing size*, which gives a sense of increasing distance between each of the shapes (diagram b). Our perception of distance depends on the observation that distant objects appear smaller than near objects. A third method of achieving the illusion of depth is *vertical placement:* objects placed low on the picture plane (diagram c on the preceding page) appear to be closer to the viewer than objects placed high on the plane. This is the way we see most things in actual space. Creating illusions of depth on a flat surface usually involves one or more such devices (diagram d).

When we look at a picture, we may be conscious of both its actual flat surface and the illusion of depth that the picture contains. Artists can emphasize either the reality or the illusion—or strike a balance between these extremes. For centuries, Asian painters have paid careful attention to the relationship between the reality of the flat picture plane as

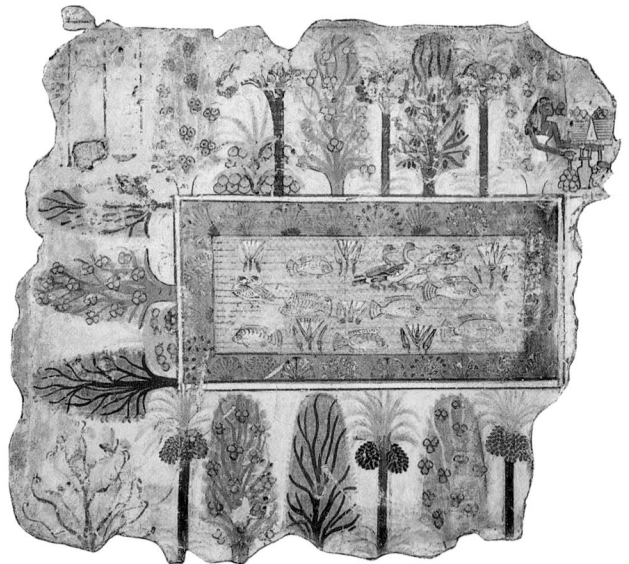

71   POND IN A GARDEN.
Wall painting from the tomb of Nebamun.
Egypt. c. 1400 B.C.E.
Paint on dry plaster.
Photograph: © The British Museum, London.

72   CLUES TO SPATIAL DEPTH.

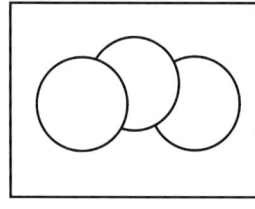

a. Overlap.

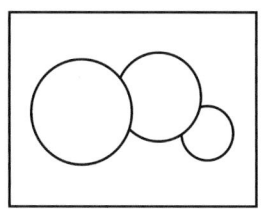

b. Overlap and diminishing size.

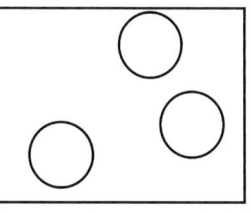

c. Vertical placement.

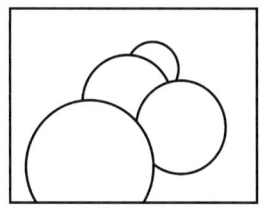

d. Overlap, vertical placement, and diminishing size.

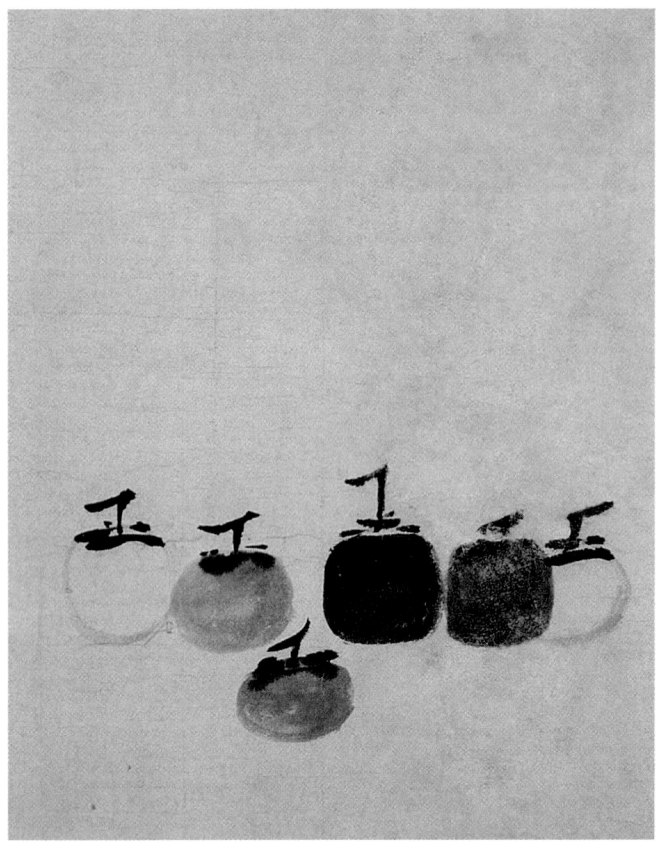

73 Mu Qi.
SIX PERSIMMONS. c. 1269.
Pen and ink on paper, width 14¼".
Daitoku-ji Monastery, Kyoto, Japan. The Bridgeman Art Library International Ltd.

well as the illusion of depth they wish to imply. Mu Qi's ink painting SIX PERSIMMONS has only a subtle suggestion of depth in the overlap of two of the persimmons. By placing the smallest persimmon lowest on the picture plane, Mu Qi further minimized the illusion of depth; because we interpret the lower part of the picture as being closer to us, we might expect the persimmon there to be larger.

The persimmons appear against a pale background that works as both flat surface and infinite space. The shapes of the fruit punctuate the open space of the ground. Imagine what would happen to this painting if some of the space at the top were cut off. Space is far more than just leftovers; it is an integral part of the total visual design.

Linear Perspective. In general usage, the word *perspective* refers to point of view. In the visual arts, *perspective* refers to any means of representing three-dimensional objects in space on a two-dimensional surface. In this sense it is correct to speak of the perspective of Persian miniatures, Japanese prints, Chinese Song Dynasty paintings, or Egyptian murals—although none of these styles is similar to the linear perspective system, which was developed during the Italian Renaissance. Different traditions, rather than mere skill, give us various ways of depicting depth.

In the West, we have become accustomed to *linear perspective* (also called simply *perspective*) to depict the way objects in space appear to the eye. This system was developed by Italian architects and painters in the fifteenth century, at the beginning of the Renaissance.

Linear perspective is based on the way we see. We have already noted that objects appear smaller when seen at a distance than when viewed close up. Because the spaces between objects also appear smaller when seen at a distance, parallel lines appear to converge as they recede into the distance, as shown in the first of the LINEAR PERSPECTIVE diagrams. Intellectually, we know that the edge lines of the road must be parallel, yet they seem to converge, meeting at last at what is called a *vanishing point* on the horizon—the place where land and sky appear to meet. On a picture surface, the horizon (or *horizon line*) also represents your eye level as you look at a scene.

Eye level is an imaginary plane, the height of the artist's eyes, parallel with the ground plane and extending to the horizon, where the eye level and ground plane appear to converge. In a finished picture, the artist's eye level becomes the eye level of anyone looking at the picture. Although the horizon is frequently blocked from view, it is necessary for an artist to establish a combined eye-level/horizon line to construct images using linear perspective.

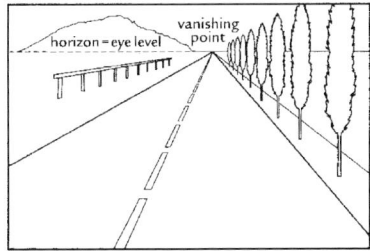

a. One-point linear perspective

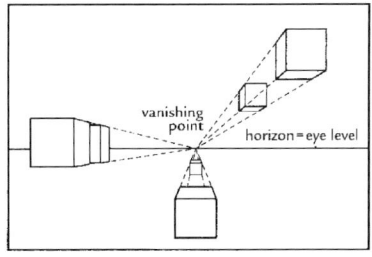

b. One-point linear perspective. Cubes above eye level, at eye level, and below eye level.

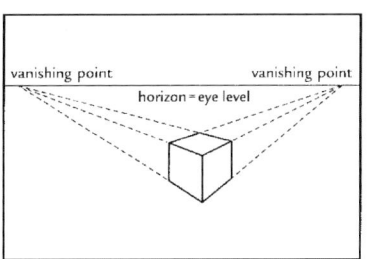

c. Two-point linear perspective.

With the LINEAR PERSPECTIVE system, an entire picture can be constructed from a single, fixed position called a *vantage point*, or *viewpoint*. Diagram a. shows one-point (one vanishing point) perspective, in which the parallel sides of the road appear to converge and trees in a row appear smaller as their distances from the vantage point increase.

Diagram b. shows cubes drawn in one-point linear perspective. The cubes at the left are at eye level; we can see neither their top nor their bottom surfaces. We might imagine them as buildings.

The cubes in the center are below eye level: We can look down on their tops. These cubes are drawn from a high vantage point, a viewing position above the subject. The horizon line is above these cubes and their perspective lines go up to it. We may imagine these as boxes on the floor.

The cubes at the right are above our eye level; we can look up at their bottom sides. These cubes are drawn from a low vantage point. The horizon line is below these cubes and their perspective lines go down to it. Imagine that these boxes are sitting on a glass shelf high above our heads.

In *one-point perspective*, all the major receding "lines" of the subject are actually parallel, yet visually they appear to converge at a single vanishing point on the horizon line. In *two-point perspective*, two sets of parallel lines appear to converge at two points on the horizon line, as in diagram c.

When a cube or any other rectilinear object is positioned so that a corner, instead of a side, is closest to us, we need two vanishing points to draw it. The parallel lines of the right side converge to the right; the parallel lines of the left side converge to the left. There can be as many vanishing points as there are sets and directions of parallel lines.

Horizontal parallel lines moving away from the viewer above eye level appear to go down to the horizon line; those below eye level appear to go up to the horizon line. (Linear perspective and spatial depth are explored on the *Discovering Art* CD.)

In THE SCHOOL OF ATHENS (on the following page), Raphael invented a grand architectural setting in the Renaissance style to provide an appropriate space for his depiction of the Greek philosophers Plato and Aristotle and other important thinkers. The size of each figure is drawn to scale according to its distance from the viewer; thus the entire group seems natural. Lines superimposed over the painting reveal the basic one-point perspective system used by Raphael. However, the cube in the foreground is not parallel to the picture plane or to the painted architecture and is in two-point perspective.

Raphael used perspective for emphasis. We infer that Plato and Aristotle are the most important figures in this painting because of their placement at the center of receding archways in the zone of greatest implied depth.

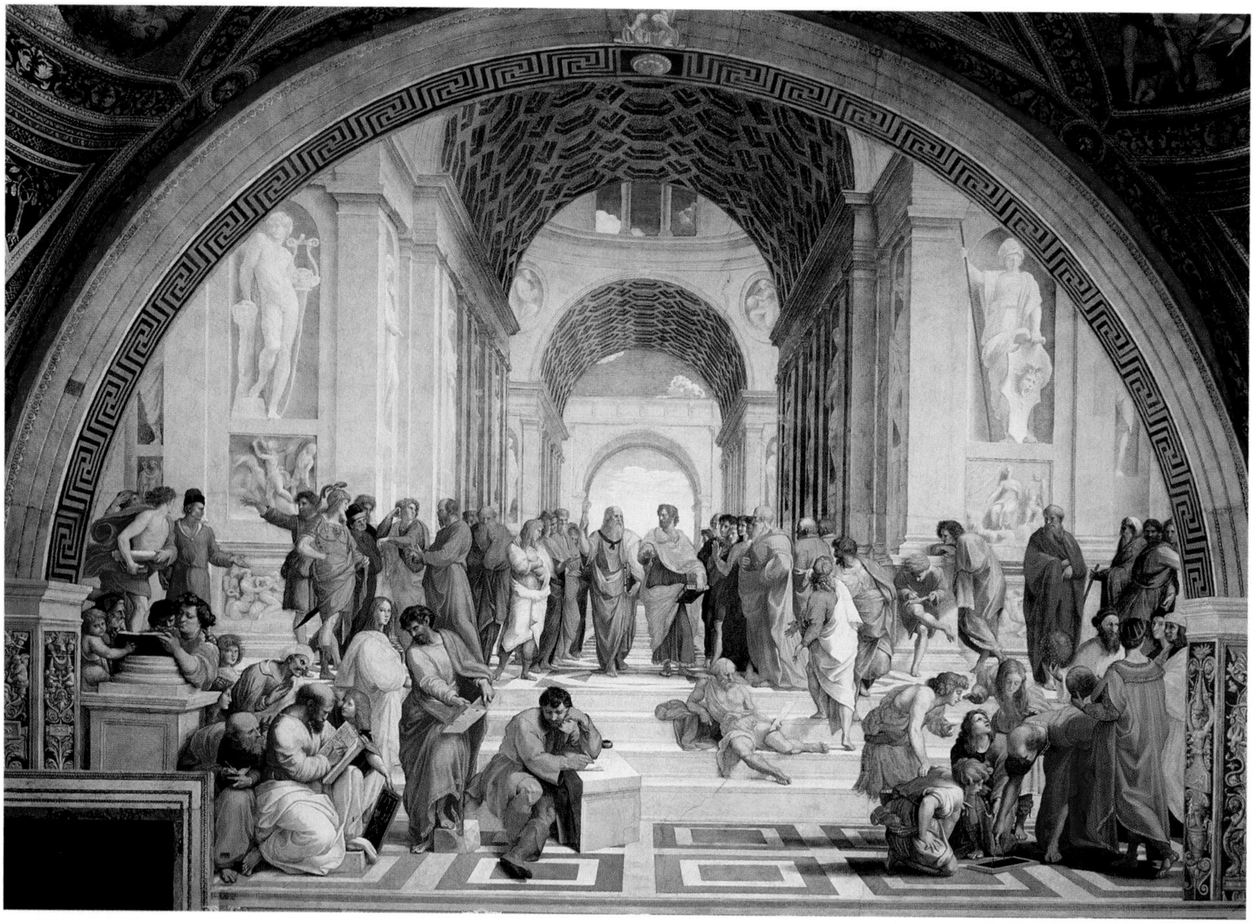

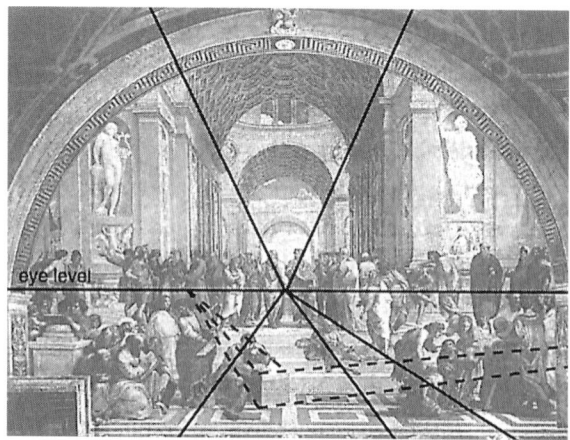

75 Raphael.

THE SCHOOL OF ATHENS. 1508. Fresco. Approximately 18′ × 26′.
Stanza della Segnatura, Vatican Palace, Vatican State. © Erich Lessing/Art Resource, NY.

eye level

Perspective lines showing eye level, main vanishing point, and left
vanishing point for the stone block in the foreground.

75b Raphael.

THE SCHOOL OF ATHENS. 1508.
Stanza della Segnatura, Vatican Palace, Vatican State.
© Erich Lessing/Art Resource, NY.

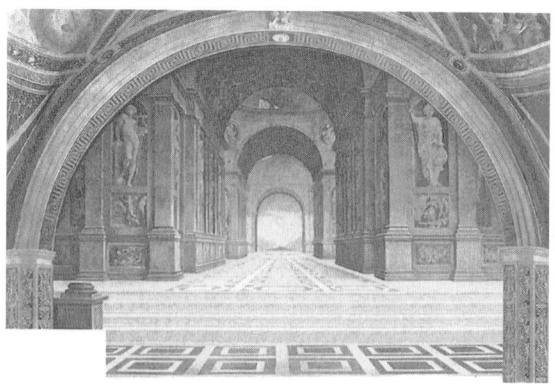

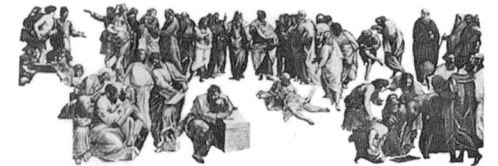

76 Study of Raphael's **THE SCHOOL OF ATHENS.**

If the figures are removed, as shown in the study of Raphael's THE SCHOOL OF ATHENS, our attention is pulled right through the painted setting into implied infinite space. Conversely, without their architectural background defined by perspective, Plato and Aristotle lose importance.

Atmospheric Perspective. *Atmospheric* or *aerial perspective* is a nonlinear means for giving an illusion of depth. The illusion of depth is created by changing color, value, and detail. In visual experience of the real world, as the distance increases between the viewer and faraway objects such as mountains, the increased quantity of air, moisture, and dust causes the distant objects to appear increasingly bluer and less distinct. Color intensity is diminished, and contrast between light and dark is reduced.

Asher Brown Durand used atmospheric perspective in his painting KINDRED SPIRITS to provide a sense of the vast distances in the North American wilderness. The illusion of infinite space is balanced by dramatically illuminated foreground details, by the figures of the men, and by Durand's lively portrayal of trees, rocks, and waterfalls. We identify with the figures of painter Thomas Cole and poet William Cullen Bryant as they enjoy the spectacular landscape. As in THE SCHOOL OF ATHENS, the implied deep space appears as an extension of the space we occupy.

Traditional Chinese landscape painters have another way of creating atmospheric perspective. In Shen Zhou's painting POET ON A MOUNTAIN TOP, (on the following page) near and distant mountains are suggested by washes of ink and color on white paper. The light gray of the farthest mountain implies space and atmosphere. Traditional Chinese landscape paintings present poetic symbols of landforms rather than realistic representations. Whereas KINDRED SPIRITS draws the viewer's eye into and through the suggested deep space, POET ON A MOUNTAIN TOP leads the eye across (rather than into) space.

A third system for suggesting depth is isometric perspective, which is employed by engineers and

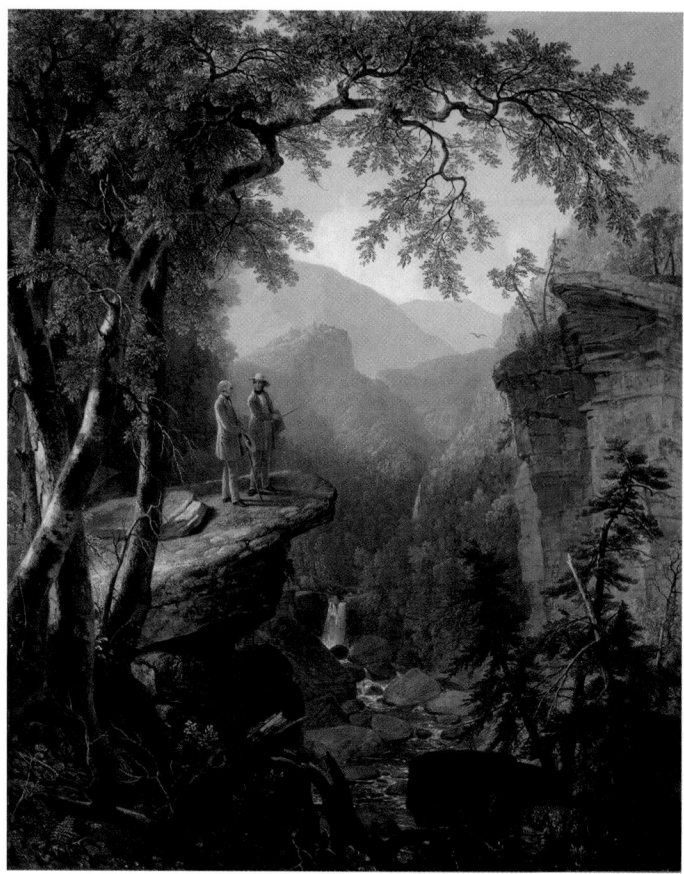

77   Asher Brown Durand.
KINDRED SPIRITS. 1849.
Oil on canvas. *44″ × 36″.*
Courtesy of the Crystal Bridges Museum of
American Art, Bentonville, AR.

is often used by traditional Asian artists. In isometric perspective, parallel lines remain parallel; they do not converge as they recede. Instead, rectangular planes that turn away from the viewer are drawn as parallelograms. The illustration ISOMETRIC PERSPECTIVE (on the following page) shows a cube drawn in isometric perspective. Industrial designers and architects also find isometric perspective useful because it enables them to maintain accurate measurements in working drawings. The detail from the Chinese hanging scroll EIGHTEEN SCHOLARS (on the following page) shows furniture and another hanging scroll in isometric perspective.

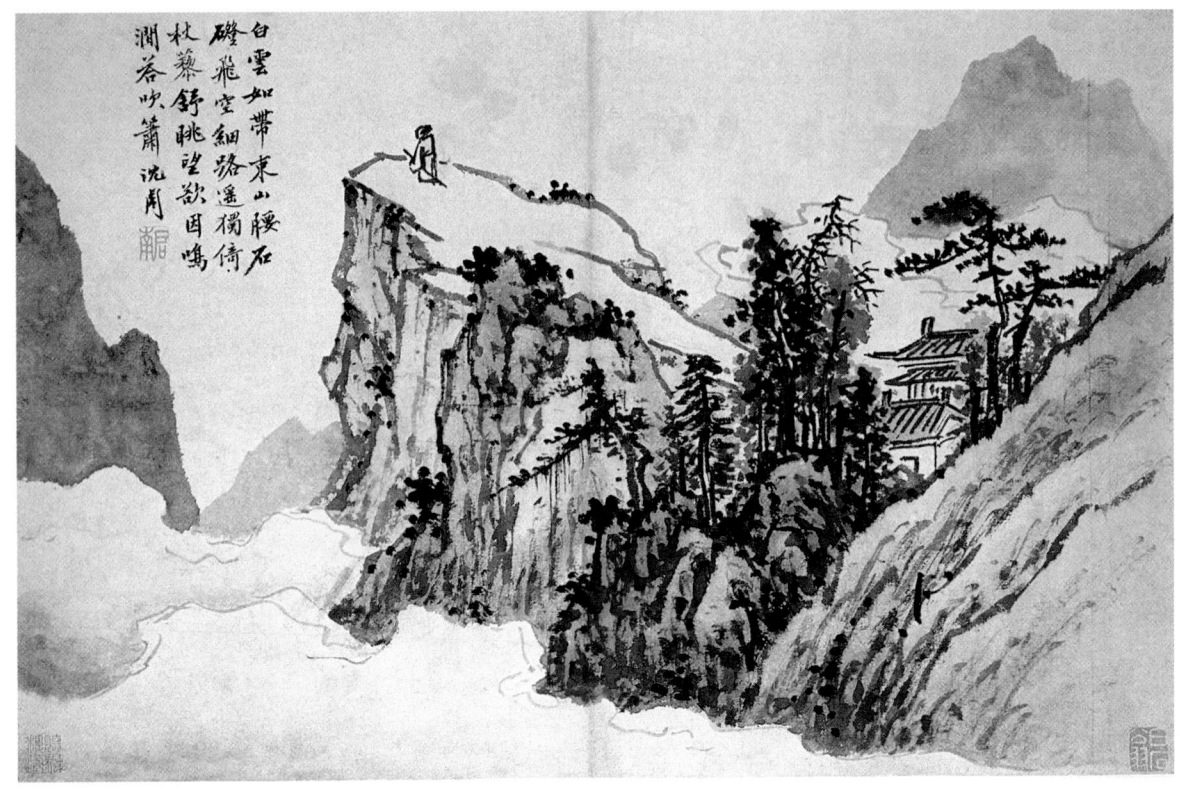

白雲如帶東山腰
磴飛空細路遙倚
杖藜舒眺望欲因鳴
澗落吹簫　沈周

78　Shen Zhou.
POET ON A MOUNTAIN TOP.
Series: **LANDSCAPE ALBUM: FIVE LEAVES**
Ming dynasty (1368–1644).
Album leaf mounted as a handscroll. Ink and watercolor on paper.
15¼″ × 23¾″ overall.
The Nelson-Atkins Museum of Art, Kansas City, Missouri. Purchase: Nelson Trust. 46–5½.

79　**ISOMETRIC PERSPECTIVE.**

80　Anonymous.
EIGHTEEN SCHOLARS.
Detail. Song dynasty (960–1279).
Hanging scroll. Ink and color on silk.
67⅞″ × 40¼″.
National Palace Museum, Taipei, Taiwan.

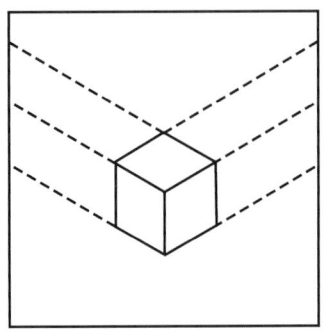

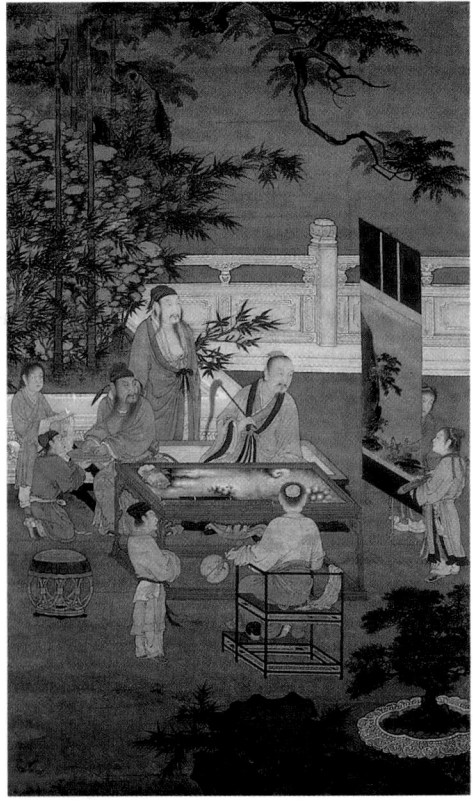

TIME AND MOTION

Time is the nonspatial continuum, the fourth dimension, in which events occur in succession. Because we live in an environment combining space and time, our experience of time often depends on our movement in space and vice versa. Although time itself is invisible, it can be made perceptible in art. Time and motion become major elements in visual media such as film, video, and kinetic (moving) sculpture.

Many traditional non-Western cultures teach that time is cyclic. The Aztecs of ancient Mexico, for example, held that the earth was subject to periodic destruction and recreation, and their calendar stone embodies this idea. At the center of the AZTEC CALENDAR STONE is a face of the sun god representing the present world, surrounded by four rectangular compartments that each represent one previous incarnation of the world. The whole stone is round, symbolizing the circular nature of time.

The Judeo-Christian tradition of Western culture teaches that time is linear—continually moving forward. The early Renaissance painter Sassetta implied the passage of linear time in his painted narration of THE MEETING OF SAINT ANTHONY AND SAINT PAUL. The painting depicts key moments during Saint Anthony's progression through time and space, including the start of his journey in the city, which is barely visible behind the trees. He first comes into view as he approaches the wilderness; we next see him encountering the centaur; finally, he emerges into the clearing in the foreground, where he meets Saint Paul. The road on which he travels implies continuous forward movement in time.

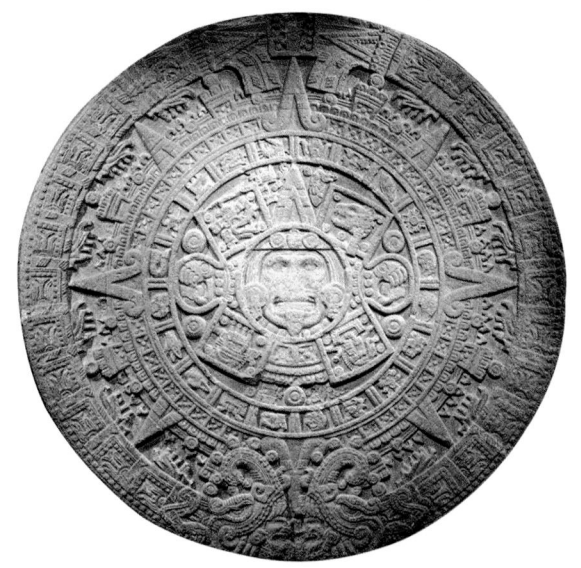

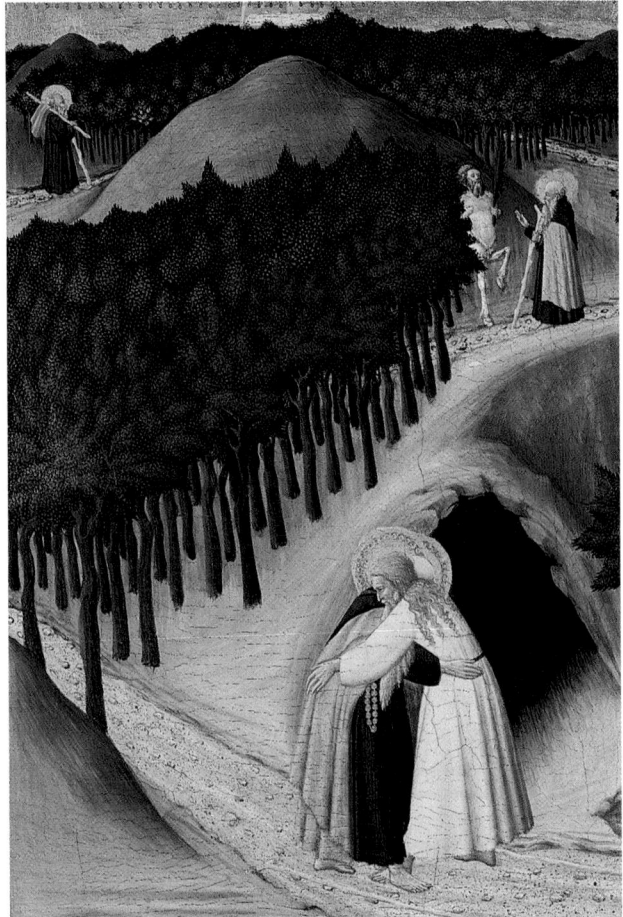

81   AZTEC CALENDAR STONE. 1479.
National Museum of Anthropology, Mexico City.
© Robert Frerck/Woodfin Camp and Associates/National Museum of Anthropology.

82   Sassetta and Workshop of Sassetta.
THE MEETING OF SAINT ANTHONY AND SAINT PAUL. c. 1440.
Tempera on panel, 18³/₄″ × 13⁵/₈″.
Samuel H. Kress Collection. Photograph: © 2001 Board of Trustees, The National Gallery of Art, Washington, D.C. 1939.1.239.(404)/PA.

Kristin Jones and Andrew Ginzel

CONTEMPORARY artists have found new ways to include time in their works. Kristin Jones and Andrew Ginzel suggest the passage of time in a clever way in their work called MNEMONICS, which was created for Stuyvesant High School in New York City. They embedded objects from remote times and places in more than 400 glass bricks distributed around the school in no apparent order. These include fragments from New York's past, sand from remote deserts, or pieces of ancient monuments such as the Great Wall of China. Each graduating class contributes its own brick as well, so that the building itself mirrors the passage of time.

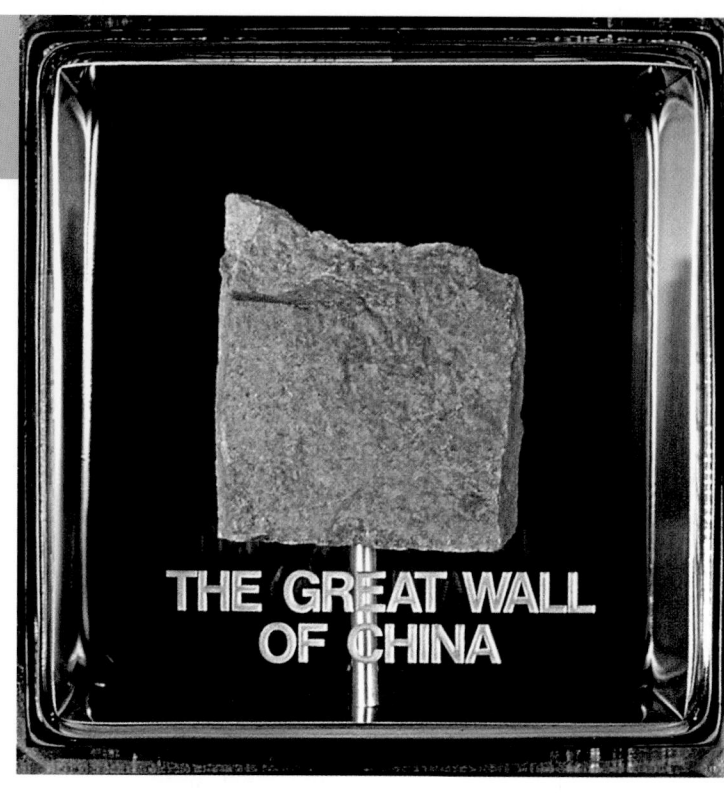

Kristin Jones and Andrew Ginzel. 83
MNEMONICS. 1992.
The New Stuyvesant High School, NYC.
Photograph courtesy of the artists.

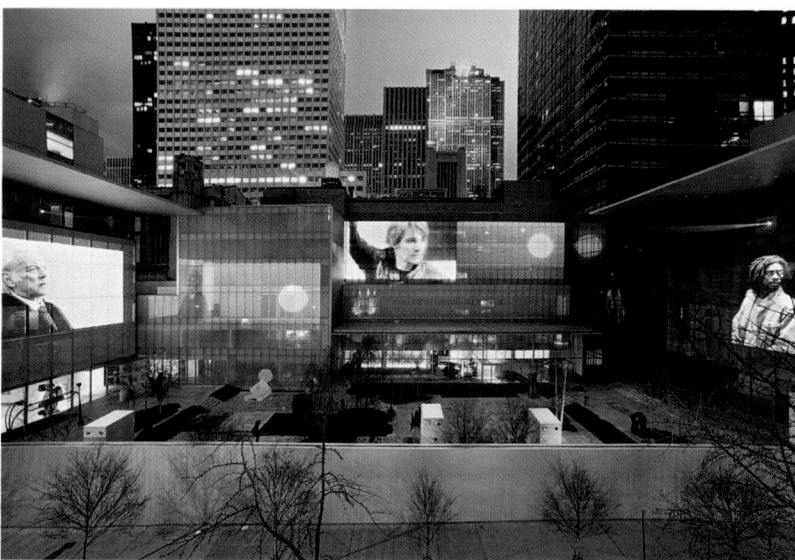

84 Doug Aitken.
SLEEPWALKERS. 2007.
Installation view.
The Museum of Modern Art, New York.
January 16 through February 12, 2007.
IN1991.25 The Museum of Modern Art,
New York, NY, U.S.A. Courtesy 303 Gallery,
New York.

Manipulated Time

Doug Aitken's 2007 video work SLEEPWALKERS manipulated time by presenting five parallel narratives of actors awakening at sunset and going about urban rounds in the city at night. The five actors played various roles, from bike messenger to corporate executive. Their stories were edited down to 13 minutes each, and projected in random sequence onto eight exterior walls of the Museum of Modern Art in New York. The piece interacted with viewers' urban errands as well, since the work was on view from 5 to 10 P.M. each night for a month. The artist said of the work, "I wanted to create something that transformed architecture into a moving, flowing space." As viewers moved about the city block that the museum occupies, they saw five workers in parallel narratives also moving about the city.

The word *movies* underscores the central feature of the filmmaker's art: the appearance of motion. In films, still pictures are shown at the rate of twenty-four images per second, creating the illusion of actual motion. Past, present, and future time can be implied and intermixed, and events that occur too quickly or too slowly to be perceived can be made visible by slowing them down or speeding them up.

Implied Motion

To give lifelike feeling, artists often search for ways to create a sense of movement. Sometimes movement itself is the subject or a central quality of the subject. An appealing depiction of movement, DANCING KRISHNA portrays the Indian Hindu god as a playful child who just stole his mother's butter supply and now dances with glee. The cast bronze medium provides the necessary strength to hold the dynamic pose as the energy-radiating figure stands on one foot, counterbalancing arms, legs, and torso.

A sense of motion can be created by actual or implied changes in position. In 1884, American painter and pioneer photographer Thomas Eakins used a single camera and a movable photographic plate to capture sequential images that show the movements of a MAN POLE VAULTING. Eakins also designed a camera with revolving discs to produce stop-action stills, anticipating the principle of the motion picture camera.

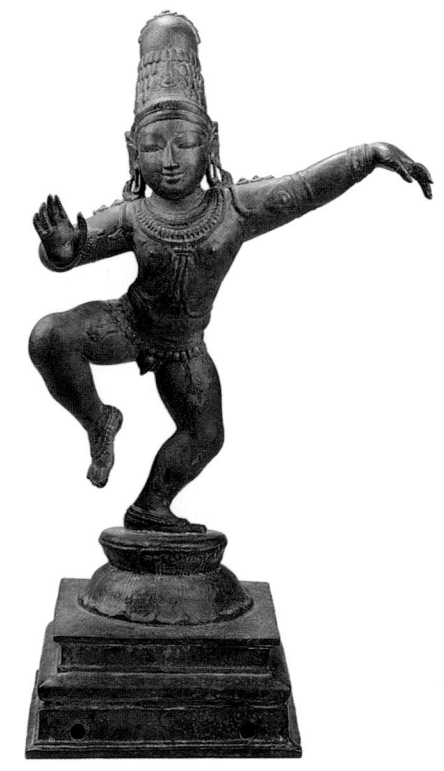

85   DANCING KRISHNA.
Tanjor, Tamil Nadu. South India. Chola dynasty.
c. 1300. Bronze, 23⅝".
Honolulu Academy of Arts. Partial gift of Mr. & Mrs. Christian H. Aall;
Partial purchase, The Jhamandas Watumull Family Fund, 1997. 8640.1.
Photograph: Shuzo Uemoto.

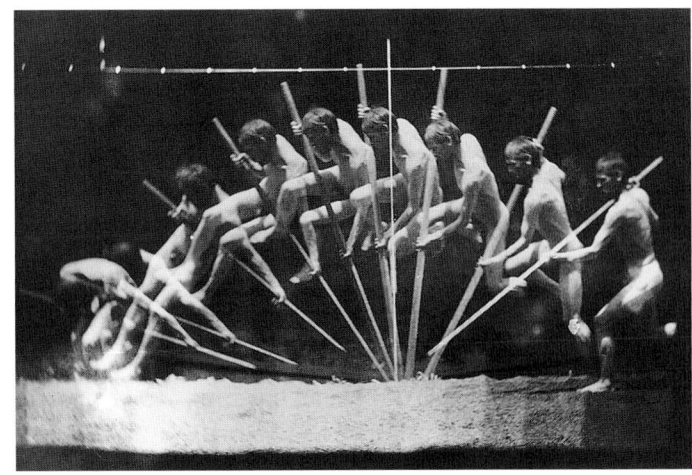

86   Thomas Eakins.
MAN POLE VAULTING. 1884.
Multiple-exposure photograph of George Reynolds. 3¼" × 4¾".
The Metropolitan Museum of Art, New York. Gift of Charles Bregler, 1941. 41.142.11.

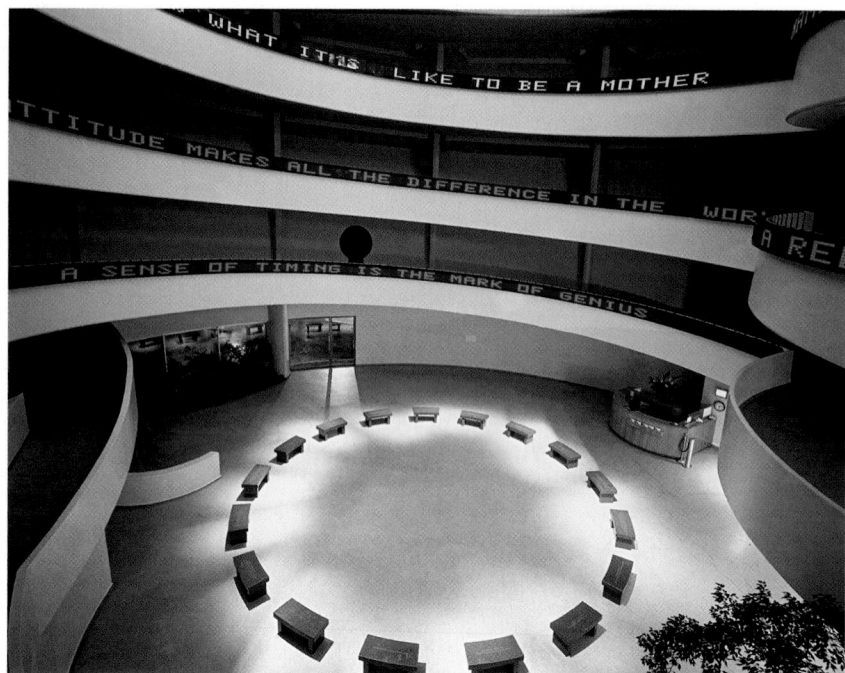

87   Jenny Holzer.
UNTITLED
(Selections from Truisms,
Inflammatory Essays, The Living
Series, The Survival Series, Under a
Rock, Laments, and Child Text), 1989.
Extended helical tricolor L.E.D. elec-
tronic display signboard. Site-specific
dimensions: 16½″ × 16′ × 6″.
Solomon R. Guggenheim Museum, New York. Partial
gift of the artist, 1989, 89.3626. Photograph by David
Heald © The Solomon R. Guggenheim Foundation,
New York. © 2005 Jenny Holzer/Arists Rights Society
(ARS), New York.

88   Alexander Calder.
BIG RED. 1959.
Painted sheet metal and steel wire.
74″ × 114″.
Collection of Whitney Museum of American Art,
New York. Purchase, with funds from the Friends
of the Whitney Museum of American Art, and
exchange 61.46. Photograph © 2001: Whitney
Museum of American Art. © 2005 Estate of
Alexander Calder/Artists Rights Society (ARS), NY.

Contemporary artist Jenny Holzer made a
clever use of implied motion in an UNTITLED work,
in which she installed light boards on the inner
edge of the spiral ramp in the Guggenheim
Museum in New York. These boards are commonly
used for advertising, but she populated this
extended helix with sayings of her own invention.
The sayings seem to process down the ramp in a
continuous flow, but in reality the lights go on and
off only at carefully programmed intervals. In this
welter of constantly shifting slogans, she hoped to
show how the mass media bombard us with input.

Actual Motion

Before the advent of electric motors, artists created
moving sculpture by harnessing the forces of wind
and water. Fountains, kites, banners, and flags have
been popular since ancient times.

Alexander Calder's mobiles, such as BIG RED,
rely on air movement to perform their subtle
dances. Calder, a leading inventor of kinetic sculpture, was one of the first twentieth-century artists
who made movement a major feature of their art.

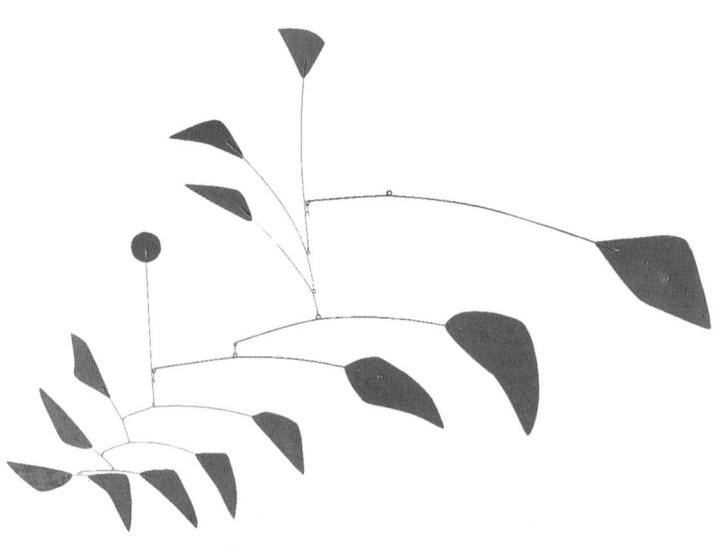

LIGHT

Our eyes are light-sensing instruments. Everything we see is made visible by the radiant energy we call light. Sunlight, or natural light, although perceived as white, actually contains all the colors of light that make up the visible part of the electromagnetic spectrum. Light can be directed, reflected, refracted, diffracted, or diffused. The various types of artificial light include incandescent, fluorescent, neon, and laser. The source, color, intensity, and direction of light greatly affect the way things appear; as light changes, surfaces illuminated by it also appear to change.

Seeing Light

A simple shift in the direction of light dramatically changes the way we perceive the sculpture of **ABRAHAM LINCOLN** by Daniel Chester French. When the monumental figure was first installed in the Lincoln Memorial in Washington, D.C., the sculptor was disturbed by the lighting: The character of the Lincoln figure was radically altered by sunlight reflected from the floor of the entrance to the building. Light alone had changed the content of French's portrait from wise leader to frightened novice. The problem was corrected by placing spotlights in the ceiling above the statue. Because the spotlights are stronger than the natural light reflected from the white marble floor, they illuminate the figure with the kind of overhead light we are accustomed to seeing.

Light coming from a source directly in front of or behind objects seems to flatten three-dimensional form and emphasize shape. Light from above or from the side, and slightly in front, most clearly reveals the form of objects in space.

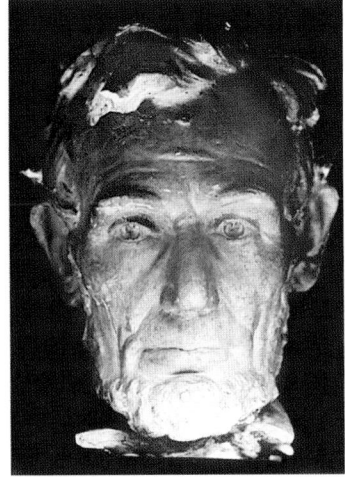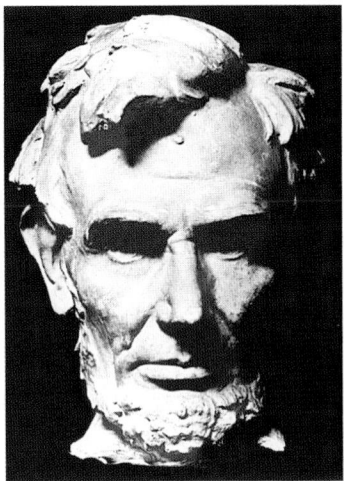

89   Daniel Chester French.
      ABRAHAM LINCOLN. Detail, seated statue, Lincoln Memorial.
      a. As originally lit by daylight.
      b. With the addition of artificial light.
      Historical professional composite photograph (1922) of full-size plaster model of head (1917–1918). 50½" tall. Chesterwood, A National Trust Historic Site, Stockbridge, MA. Photographer: De Witt Ward.

In the terminology of art, *value* (sometimes called *tone*) refers to the relative lightness and darkness of surfaces. Value ranges from white through various grays to black. Value can be considered a property of color or an element independent of color. Subtle relationships between light and dark areas determine how things look. To suggest the way light reveals form, artists use changes in value. A gradual shift from lighter to darker tones can give the illusion of a curving surface, while an abrupt value change usually indicates an abrupt change in surface direction.

Implied Light

The diagram **DARK/LIGHT RELATIONSHIPS** shows that we perceive relationships rather than isolated forms: the gray bar has the same gray value over

90   DARK/LIGHT RELATIONSHIPS.
      Value scale compared to uniform middle gray.

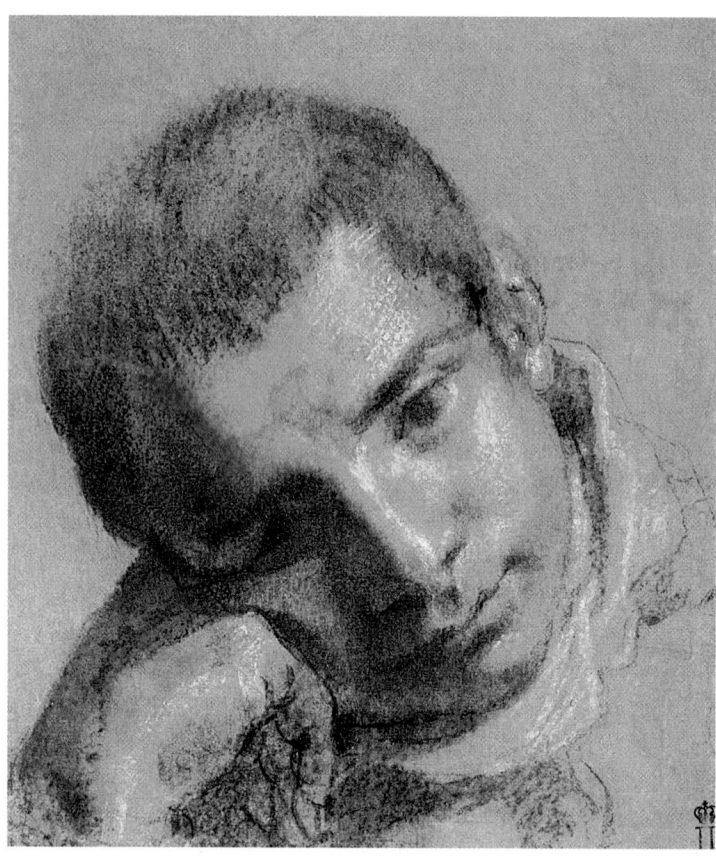

91 Annibale Carracci.
HEAD OF A YOUTH.
Charcoal and white chalk on green/gray paper.
10¾″ × 9½″.
Hermitage, St. Petersburg, Russia. The Bridgeman Art Library International Ltd.

stand in contrast both to the white highlights and to the color of the paper; the darkest area, at the left, forms a silhouette against the background.

The choice of colored paper is in some ways advantageous because we tend to perceive white areas as flooded with light. Middle-value paper tends to heighten the contrasts of light and dark within the subject itself.

The preoccupation with mass or solid form as revealed by light is a Western tradition that began in the Renaissance. Most of the world's pictoral art before the twentieth century did not show shadows. When the Japanese first saw Western portraits, they wanted to know why one side of the face was dirty!

Color, direction, quantity, and intensity of light strongly affect our moods, mental abilities, and general well-being. California architect Vincent Palmer has experimented with the color and intensity of interior light, and he has found that he can modify the behavior of his guests by changing the color of the light around them. Light quality affects people's emotions and physical comfort, thereby changing the volume and intensity of their conversations and even the lengths of their visits.

Light as a Medium

Some contemporary artists use artificial light as their medium. Keith Sonnier placed an array of neon tubes in the outdoor lobby of a new government building in Los Angeles and called it MOTORDOM, to express the reality of car culture that Southern Californians live with. The tubes slowly flicker in a pattern that repeats every five minutes, as if taillights are passing along the sides of the walls and around the lobby. The agency that commissioned the building operates the state's roads and bridges, making MOTORDOM particularly appropriate for that space.

Light used in combination with visual media and sound has become of increasing interest to contemporary artists. Lighting has also become important in performances of all kinds, including rock concerts and videos.

its entire length, yet it appears to change from one end to the other as the value of the background changes.

Using charcoal and white chalk on middle-value paper, Annibale Carracci used chiaroscuro (shading from light to dark) to create the illusion of roundness in his drawing HEAD OF A YOUTH. The face on its brighter side is close to the shade of the paper. At times the distinction between subject and background is difficult to see, as in the clothing. On the areas where light strikes the subject most directly, the artist used white chalk, as on the forehead and nose, making these areas brighter than the background. Areas around the mouth and chin are delicately shaded, showing that the artist is sensitive to the subtlest curves of the face. The shadowy areas

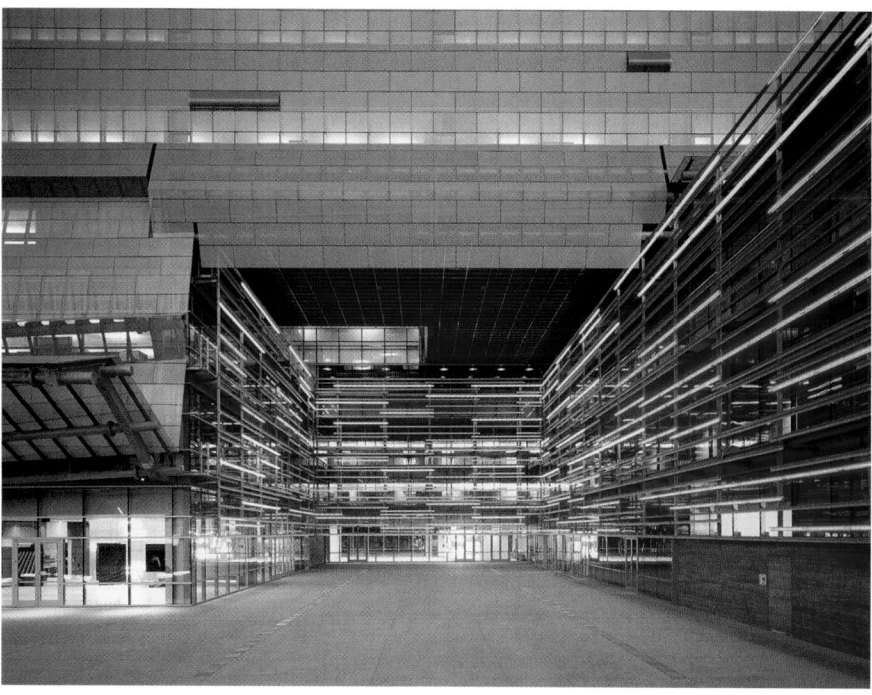

92 Keith Sonnier.
MOTORDOM. 2004.
Light Installation at Caltrans District
7 Headquarters, Los Angeles.
Architect: Thom Mayne and Morphosis.
Photo: Roland Halbe.

COLOR

Color, a component of light, affects us directly by modifying our thoughts, moods, actions, and even our health. Psychologists, as well as designers of schools, offices, hospitals, and prisons, have acknowledged that colors can affect work habits and mental conditions. People surrounded by expanses of solid orange or red for long periods often experience nervousness and increased blood pressure. In contrast, some blues have a calming effect, causing blood pressure, pulse, and activity rates to drop to below normal levels.

Dressing according to our color preferences is one way we express ourselves. Leading designers of everything from clothing and cars to housewares and interiors recognize the importance of individual color preferences, and they spend considerable time and expense determining the colors of their products.

Most cultures use color symbolically, according to established customs. Leonardo da Vinci was influenced by earlier European traditions when he wrote, "We shall set down for white the representative of light, without which no color can be seen; yellow for earth; green for water; blue for air; red for fire; and black for total darkness."[3] In traditional painting in North India, flat areas of color are used to suggest certain moods, such as red for anger and blue for sexual passion. The artist may paint the sky or the ground with a bright shade that relates not to the appearance of the area, but to the feeling appropriate to the work. In spoken Austrian German, yellow describes a state of envy or jealousy, while blue means intoxicated.

In China and Japan, traditional painters have often limited themselves to black ink on white. Before the mid-nineteenth century, color was used in limited, traditional ways in Western art. In the 1860s and 1870s, influenced by the new science of color, the French Impressionist painters revolutionized the way color was seen and used.

The Physics of Color

What we call "color" is the effect on our eyes of light waves of differing wavelengths or frequencies. When combined, these light waves make white light—the visible part of the electromagnetic spectrum. Individual colors are components of white light.

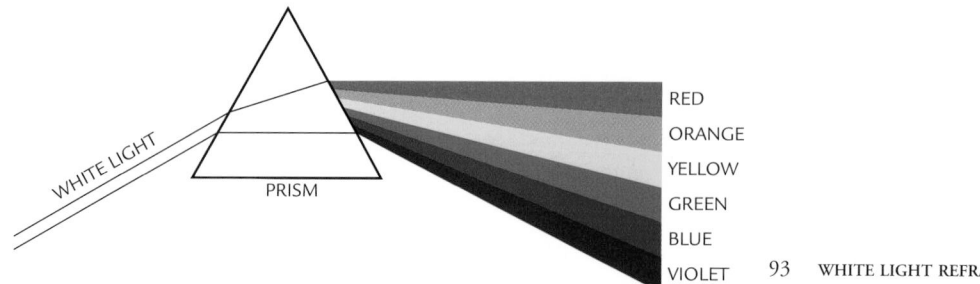

RED
ORANGE
YELLOW
GREEN
BLUE
VIOLET   93   WHITE LIGHT REFRACTED BY A PRISM.

WHITE LIGHT

PRISM

The phenomenon of color is a paradox: color exists only in light, but light itself seems colorless to the human eye. Objects that appear to have color are merely reflecting the colors that are present in the light that illuminates them. In 1666, British scientist Sir Isaac Newton discovered that white light is composed of all the colors of the spectrum. He found that when the white light of the sun passes through a glass prism, it is separated into the bands of color that make up the *visible spectrum*, as shown in the diagram WHITE LIGHT REFRACTED BY A PRISM.

Because each color has a different wavelength, each travels through the glass of the prism at a different speed. Red, which has the longest wavelength, travels more rapidly through the glass than blue, which has a shorter wavelength. A rainbow results when sunlight is refracted and dispersed by the spherical forms of raindrops, producing a combined effect like that of the glass prism. In both cases, the sequence of spectral colors is: red, orange, yellow, green, blue, and violet.

Pigments and Light

Our common experience with color is provided by light reflected from pigmented surfaces. Therefore, the emphasis in the following discussion is on pigment color rather than on color coming from light alone.

When light illuminates an object, some of the light is absorbed by the surface of the object and some is reflected. The color that appears to our eyes as that of the object (called *local color* or *object color*) is determined by the wavelengths of light being reflected. Thus, a red surface illuminated by white light (full-spectrum light) appears red, because it reflects mostly red light and absorbs the rest of the spectrum. A green surface absorbs most of the spectrum except green, which it reflects; and so on with all the hues.

When all the wavelengths of light are absorbed by a surface, the object appears black; when all the wavelengths are reflected, the surface appears white. Black and white are not true colors: white, black, and their combination, gray, are *achromatic* (without the property of hue) and are often referred to as *neutrals*.

Each of the millions of colors human beings can distinguish is identifiable in terms of just three variables: hue, value, and intensity.

- *Hue* refers to a particular wavelength of spectral color to which we give a name. Colors of the spectrum—such as yellow and green—are called hues.
- *Value* refers to relative lightness or darkness from white through grays to black. Pure hues vary in value. On the color chart shown in THE THREE DIMENSIONS OF COLOR, hues in their purest state are at their usual values. Pure yellow is the lightest of hues; violet is the darkest. Red and green are middle-value hues.

Black and white pigments can be important ingredients in changing color values. Black added to a hue produces a *shade* of that hue. For example, when black is added to orange, the result is a brown; when black is mixed with red, the result is maroon. White added to a hue produces a *tint*. Lavender is a tint of violet; pink is a tint of red.

- *Intensity*, also called *saturation*, refers to the purity of a hue or color. A pure hue is the most intense form of a given color; it is the hue at its highest saturation, in its brightest form. With pigment, if white, black, gray, or another hue is added to a pure hue, its intensity diminishes and the color is thereby dulled.

When the pigments of different hues are mixed together, the mixture appears duller and darker because pigments absorb more and more light as their absorptive qualities combine. For this reason, pigment mixtures are called *subtractive color mixtures*. Mixing red, blue, and yellow will produce a dark gray, almost black, depending on the proportions and the type of pigment used.

Most people are familiar with the three PIGMENT PRIMARIES: red, yellow, and blue. Printers use *magenta* (a bluish red), *yellow*, and *cyan* (a greenish blue) because magenta and cyan provide the specific purplish red and greenish blue that work best for four-color printing.

A lesser-known triad is the three LIGHT PRIMARIES: red-orange, green, and blue-violet—actual electric light colors that produce white light when combined. Such mixtures are called *additive color mixtures*. Combinations of the light primaries produce lighter colors: red and green light, when mixed, produce yellow light. Color television employs additive color mixture.

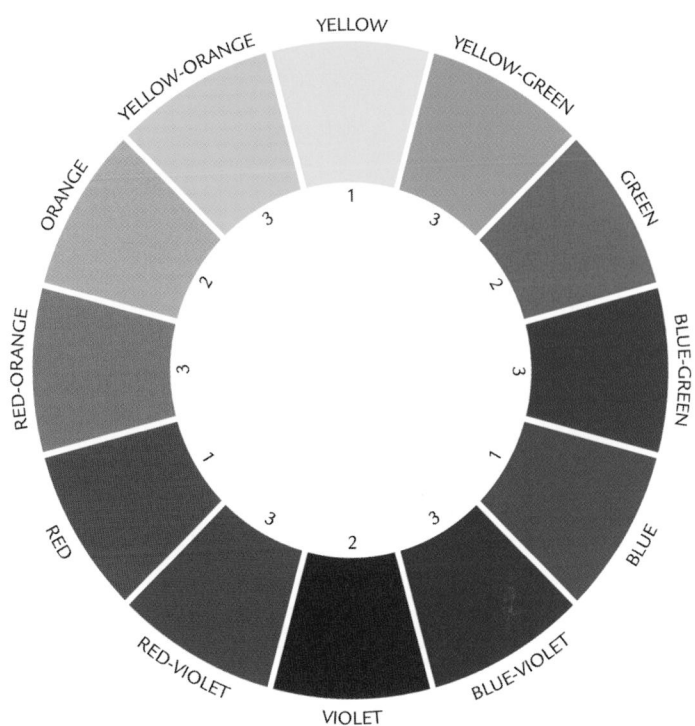

a. HUE—the color wheel.

b. VALUE—from light to dark. Value scale from white to black.

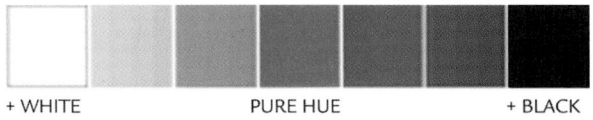

+ WHITE   PURE HUE   + BLACK

Value variation in red.

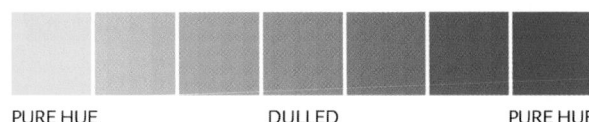

PURE HUE   DULLED   PURE HUE

c. INTENSITY—from bright to dull.

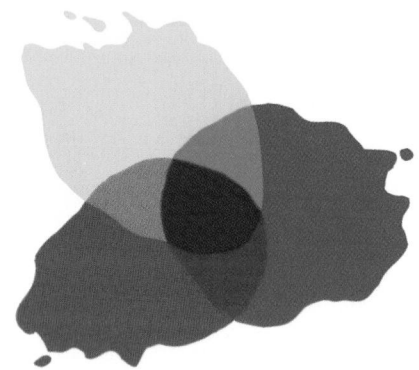

95   PIGMENT PRIMARIES: SUBTRACTIVE COLOR MIXTURE.

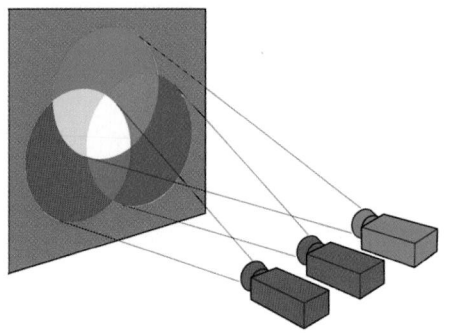

96   LIGHT PRIMARIES: ADDITIVE COLOR MIXTURE.

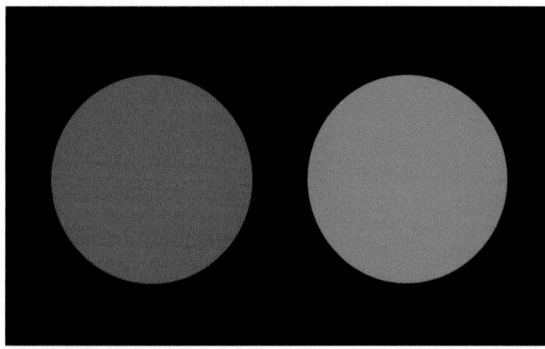

97   WARM/COOL COLORS.

Color Wheel

The color wheel is a twentieth-century version of a concept first developed in the seventeenth century by Sir Isaac Newton. After Newton discovered the spectrum, he found that both ends could be combined into the hue red-violet, making the color wheel concept possible. Numerous color systems have followed since that time, each with its own basic hues. The color wheel shown here is based on twelve pure hues and can be divided into the following groups:

- *Primay hues* (see 1 on the color wheel): red, yellow, and blue. These pigment hues cannot be produced by an intermixing of other hues. They are also referred to as primary colors.
- *Secondary hues* (see 2 on the color wheel): orange, green, and violet. The mixture of two primaries produces a secondary hue. Secondaries are placed on the color wheel between the two primaries of which they are composed.
- *Intermediate hues* (see 3 on the color wheel): red-orange, yellow-orange, yellow-green, blue-green, blue-violet, and red-violet. Each intermediate is located between the primary and the secondary of which it is composed.

The blue-green side of the wheel seems *cool* in psychological temperature, and the red-orange side is *warm*. Yellow-green and red-violet are the poles dividing the color wheel into warm and cool hues. The difference between warm and cool colors may come chiefly from association. Relative warm and cool differences can be seen in any combination of hues. Color affects our feelings about size and distance as well as temperature. Cool colors appear to contract and recede; warm colors appear to expand and advance, as in the WARM/COOL COLORS diagram.

Color sensations more vibrant than those achieved with actual pigment mixture can be obtained when dots of pure color are placed together so that they blend in the eye and mind, to create the appearance of other hues. This is called *optical color mixture*. For example, we see rich greens when many tiny dots or strokes of yellow-green and blue-green are placed close together. (View the interactive exercise Elements of Color and Light on the *ed* *Discovering Art* CD.)

Painter Georges Seurat worked with these effects in the 1880s as a result of his studies of Impressionist paintings and recent scientific discoveries of light and color. He wanted his paintings to capture the brilliance and purity of natural light. Seurat called his method divisionism; it is now usually called *pointillism*. The result is similar to modern four-color printing, in which tiny dots of ink in the printer's three primary colors—magenta (a bluish red), yellow, and cyan (a greenish blue)—are printed together in various amounts with black ink on white paper to achieve the effect of full color. Seurat, however, used no black. Compare the detail of Seurat's **A SUNDAY ON LA GRANDE JATTE** with the color separations and the enlarged detail of the reproduction of Botticelli's **BIRTH OF VENUS** (on the following page). The eye perceives subtle blends as it optically mixes tiny dots of intense color both in Seurat's painting and in four-color printing.

Color Schemes

Color groupings that provide distinct color harmonies are called *color schemes*.

Monochromatic color schemes are based on variations in the value and intensity of a single hue. In a monochromatic scheme, a pure hue is used alone with black and/or white, or mixed with black and/or white. Artists may choose a monochromatic color scheme because they feel that a certain color represents a mood. Pablo Picasso, for

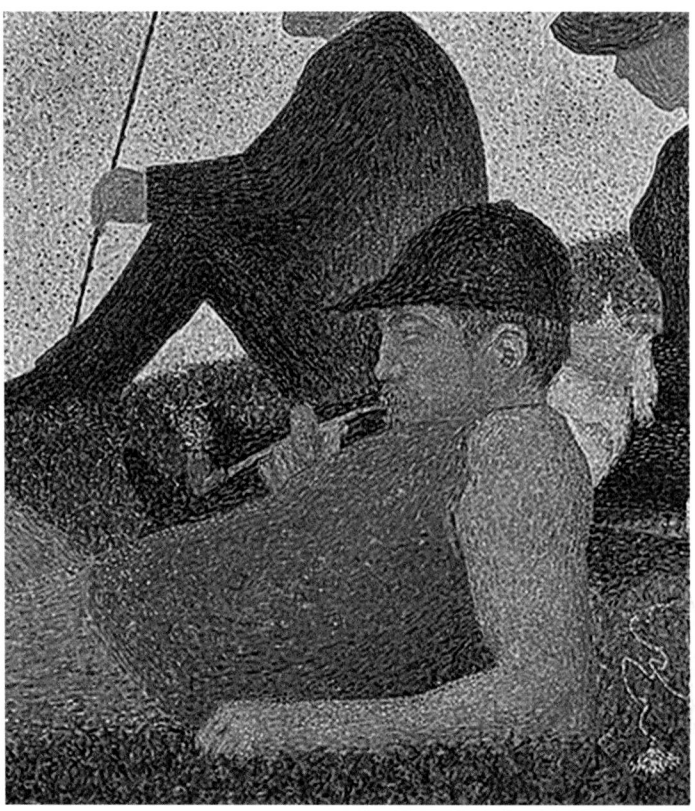

98 Georges Seurat.
Detail of A SUNDAY ON LA GRANDE JATTE. 1884–86.
Oil on canvas, 81¼″ × 121¼″.
Helen Birch Bartlett Memorial Collection. 1926.224.
© The Art Institute of Chicago. All Rights Reserved.

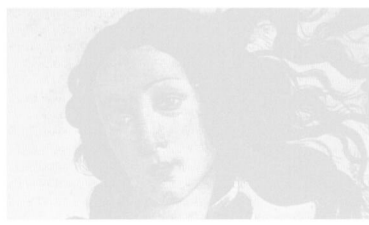

a. Yellow.

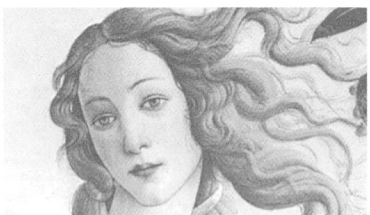

b. Magenta.

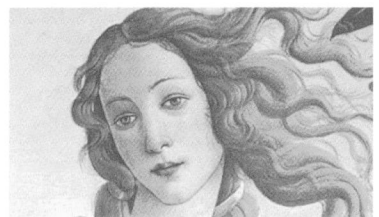

c. Yellow and magenta.

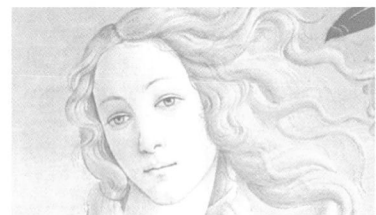

d. Cyan.

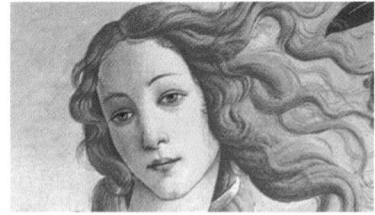

e. Yellow, magenta, and cyan.

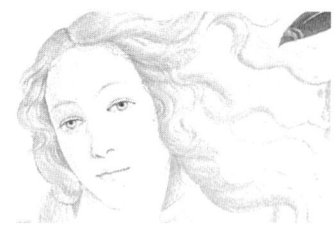

f. Black.

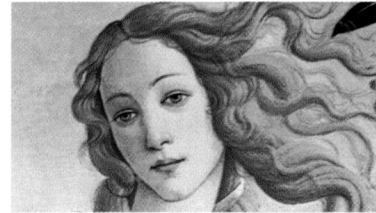

g. Yellow, magenta, cyan, and black.

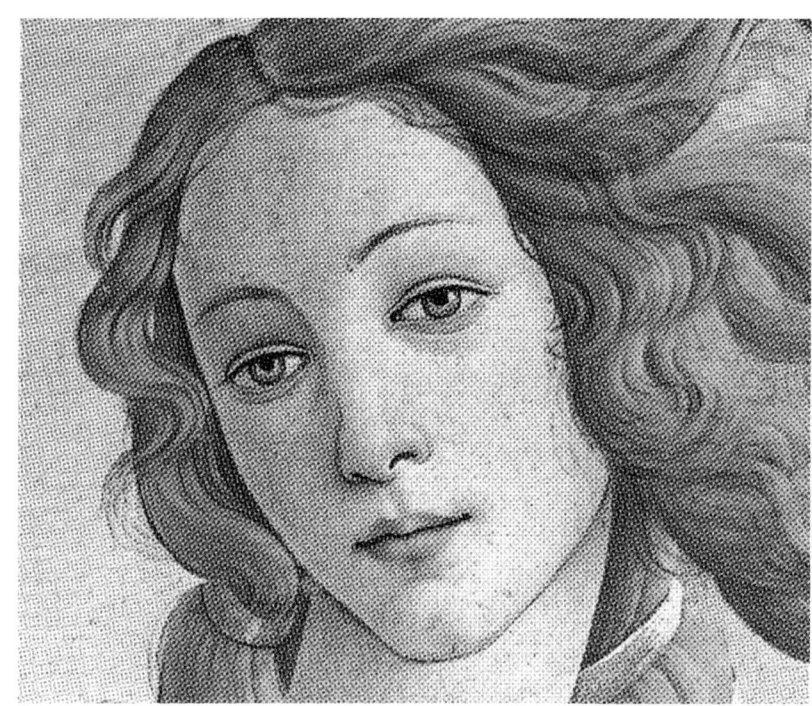

99 **COLOR PRINTING.**

h. Color printing detail of Sandro Botticelli's BIRTH OF VENUS, 1486. Detail. Tempera on canvas, 69″ × 52¾″. Uffizi, Florence, Italy.
Erich Lessing/Art Resource, NY.

example, made many blue paintings in the early years of the twentieth century, at a time in his life when he was poor. Other artists adopt the monochromatic color scheme as a kind of personal discipline, in order to experiment with the various shades and gradations of a relatively narrow band of the spectrum. James McNeill Whistler did just that in the 1870s when he embarked on a series of works called NOCTURNES. The series began when he noticed that after sunset the world becomes in effect more monochromatic as the brightest hues disappear. The challenge, which he met in NOCTURNE: BLUE AND GOLD—OLD BATTERSEA BRIDGE, is to create a visually rich surface with limited tonal means. The gold flecks are the only counterfoil to the monochromatic blue-green scheme.

Analogous color schemes are based on colors adjacent to one another on the color wheel, each containing the same pure hue, such as a color scheme of yellow-green, green, and blue-green. Tints and shades of each analogous hue may be used to add variations to such color schemes.

Jennifer Bartlett's three-dimensional installation VOLVO COMMISSION uses the analogous colors yellow-orange, yellow, and yellow-green, which are adjacent to one another in the spectrum and on the color wheel. The analogous color scheme supports the mood of quiet relaxation appropriate to the pleasant rural subject.

Complementary color schemes emphasize two hues directly opposite each other on the color wheel, such as red and green. When actually mixed together as pigments in almost equal amounts,

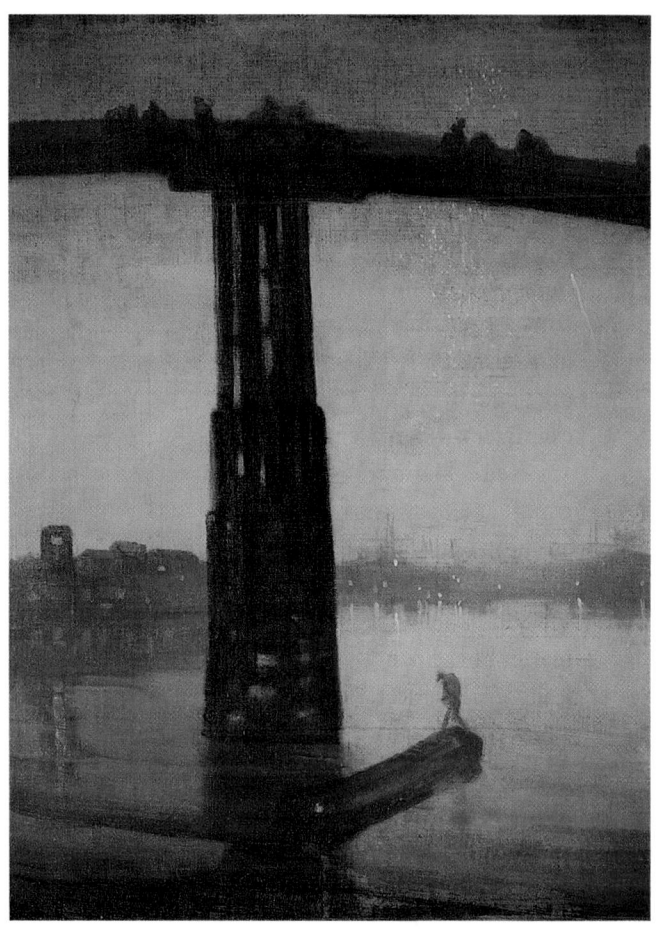

100 James McNeill Whistler.
NOCTURNE: BLUE AND GOLD—OLD BATTERSEA BRIDGE.
1872–1875.
Tate Gallery, London, Great Britain. © Erich Lessing/Art Resource, NY.

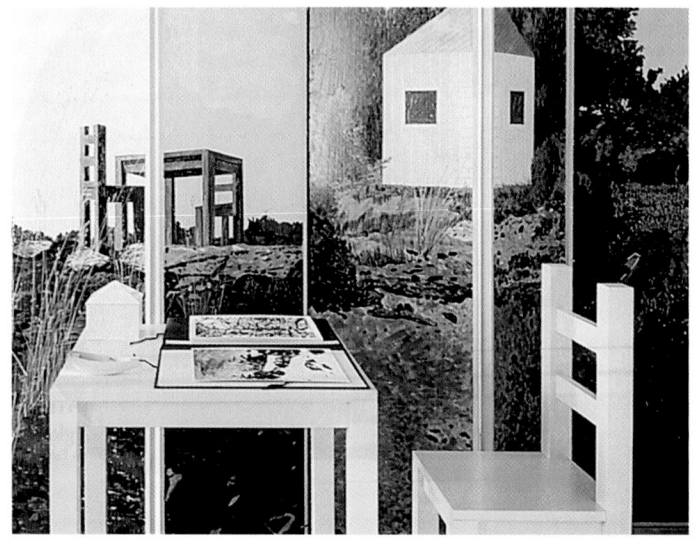

101 Jennifer Bartlett.
VOLVO COMMISSION. 1984.
Relaxation room, detail: table, painted wood, 29″ × 35″ × 35″; chair, painted wood, 35″ × 18″ × 18″; portfolio of twenty-four drawings, pen, brush, and ink on paper, 20″ × 16″; house cigarette box, painted wood, 5″ × 5″; boat ashtray, silver, 5″ × 2″; screen, enamel on six wood panels, 6′ × 10′3″.
Volvo Corporate Headquarters, Sweden. Courtesy of the artist.

PRINCIPLES OF DESIGN

Organized perception is what art is all about.

ROY LICHTENSTEIN[1]

We are continually affecting and being affected by design—our own designs and the designs of others. Whenever we select clothing, place items on a plate, arrange furniture, or hang pictures, we are designing. The process of selecting and ordering the objects and events in our daily lives is related to the design process in art. Like all of us, artists and designers organize visual elements to create meaningful and interesting form. In two-dimensional arts, such as painting and photography, this organization is usually called *composition*, but a broader term that applies to the entire range of visual arts is *design*. The word *design* indicates both the process of organizing visual elements and the product of that process.

Design addresses our basic need for meaningful order. Some designs are so well integrated that they have qualities beyond a mere sum of their parts. Such designs are said to be beautiful, interesting, absorbing, or surprising. Our desire to unify our experience of form is at the root of our appreciation for design.

There are no absolute rules for good design. However, there are principles and general guidelines for effective visual communication. We study them for the same reason artists do: to develop our innate design sense, to give ourselves a vocabulary for talking to one another about what we see, and to become more sensitive to the expressive and relational possibilities of form. In this chapter we look at seven key principles of design:

> unity and variety
> balance
> emphasis and subordination
> directional forces
> contrast
> repetition and rhythm
> scale and proportion

Together, these terms provide an understanding not only of how artists work, but also of how design affects us. The process at its best is a lively give-and-take between the intention and intuition of the designer and the character of the materials he or she uses.

UNITY AND VARIETY

Unity and variety are complementary concerns. *Unity* is the appearance or condition of oneness. In design, unity describes the feeling that all the elements in a work belong together and make up a coherent and harmonious whole. When a work of art has unity, we feel that any change would diminish its quality.

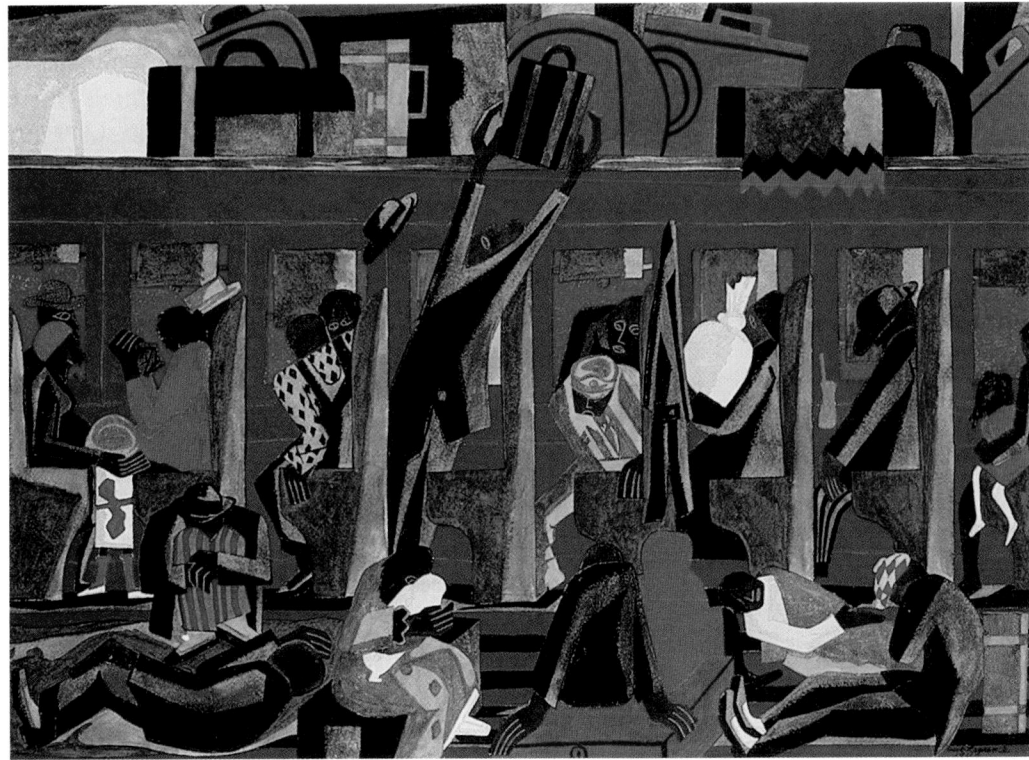

107 Jacob Lawrence.
GOING HOME. 1946.
Gouache.
21½″ × 29½″.
Private collection, courtesy of DC
Moore Gallery, NY. © 2006
Gwendolyn Knight Lawrence/
Artists Rights Society
(ARS), NY.
Photographer: Joe Painter.

Variety, on the other hand, provides diversity. Variety acts to counter unity. The sameness of too much unity is boring, and the diversity of uncontrolled variety is chaotic, but a balance between unity and variety creates life.

Artists select certain aspects of visual form to clarify and intensify the expressive character of their subjects or themes. In his painting GOING HOME, Jacob Lawrence balanced unity and variety. He established visual themes with the lines, shapes, and colors of the train seats, figures, and luggage, and then he repeated and varied those themes. Notice the varied repetition in the green chair seats and window shades. As a unifying element, the same red is used in a variety of shapes. The many figures and objects in the complex composition form a unified design through the artist's skillful use of abstraction, theme, and variation.

Lawrence was known for the lively harmony of his distinctive compositions. Although he worked

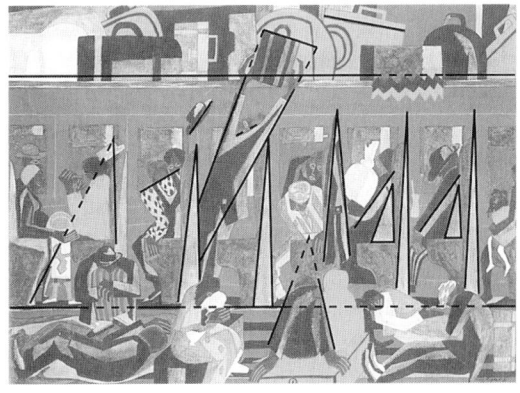

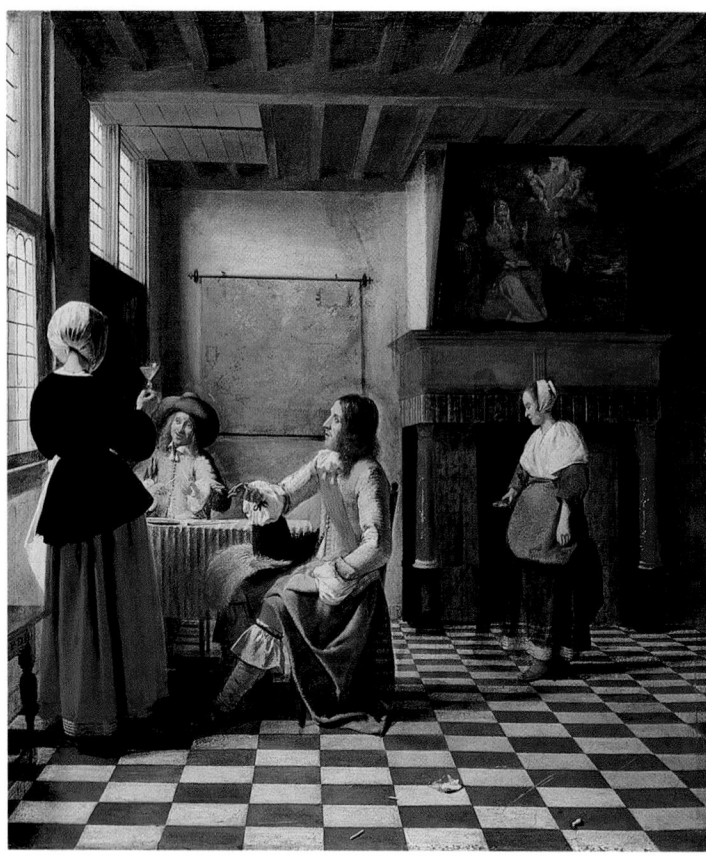

108 Pieter de Hooch.
INTERIOR OF A DUTCH HOUSE. 1658.
Oil on canvas. 29″ × 35″.
© National Gallery, London.

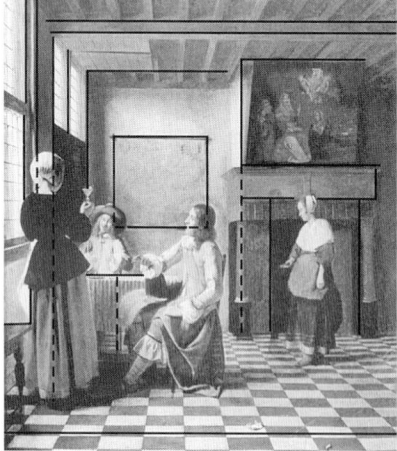

in a manner that may seem unsophisticated, he was always resolving his designs through adjustments of unity and diversity. Lawrence studied other artists' work, and he was influenced by painters who were design problem-solvers. He said, "I like to study the design to see how the artist solves his problems and brings his subjects to the public."[2]

The flat quality of GOING HOME contrasts with the illusion of depth in Pieter de Hooch's INTERIOR OF A DUTCH HOUSE. Each artist depicted daily life in a style relevant to his times. In both, the painter's depiction of space provides the unity in the composition. De Hooch "borrowed" the unity that architectural interior imposes in order to unify pictorial space and provide a cohesive setting for the interaction of figures.

Pattern refers to a repetitive ordering of design elements. In de Hooch's painting, the patterns of floor tiles and windows play off against the larger rectangles of map, painting, fireplace, and ceiling. These rectangular shapes provide a unifying structure. The nearly square picture plane itself forms the largest rectangle. He then created a whole family of related rectangles, as indicated in the accompanying diagram. In addition, the shapes and colors in the figures around the table relate to the shapes and colors of the figures in the painting above the fireplace—another use of theme and variation.

Alberto Giacometti's sculpture CHARIOT combines diverse elements—a standing female figure and two wheels. Unity is achieved through the thin lines and rough texture in the figure, wheels, and axle, as well as through the use of bronze for the entire piece. The unity of handling leads us to see the sculpture as a single mysterious entity. Our interest is held by the varied components and by the precariousness of the figure poised atop a two-legged table on two wheels. And these bring us to the principle called balance.

BALANCE

For sculptors such as Giacometti, balance is both a visual issue and a structural necessity. The interplay between the opposing forces of unity and variety is a common condition of life. The dynamic process of seeking balance is equally basic in art.

Balance is the achievement of equilibrium, in which acting influences are held in check by opposing forces. We strive for balance in life and in art, and we may lack peace of mind in its absence. In art, our instinct for physical balance finds its parallel in a desire for visual balance. A painting can depict an act of violence or imbalance—a frenzied battle or a fall from a tightrope; however, if the painting is unbalanced, it will lack the expressive power necessary to convince us that the battle was terrible, the fall disastrous. Instead, it will merely convince us that it is not a very good painting. (An interactive exercise on balance can be found on the *Discovering Art* CD.)

The two general types of balance are symmetrical (formal) and asymmetrical (informal).

Symmetrical Balance

Symmetrical balance is the near or exact matching of left and right sides of a three-dimensional form or a two-dimensional composition.

Architects often employ symmetrical balance to give unity and formal grandeur to a building's facade or front side. For example, in 1792 James Hoban won a competition for his DESIGN FOR THE PRESIDENT'S HOUSE, a drawing of a symmetrical, Georgian-style mansion. Today, two centuries and several additions later, we know it as the WHITE HOUSE.

Symmetrical design is useful in architecture because it is easier to comprehend than asymmetry. Symmetry imposes a balanced unity, making large complex buildings comprehensible in a glance. Symmetry connotes permanence and poise. We generally want our symbolically important buildings to seem motionless and stable. All the qualities that make symmetry desirable in architecture make it generally less desirable in sculpture and two-dimensional art. Too much symmetry can be boring. Although artists admire symmetry for its formal qualities, they rarely

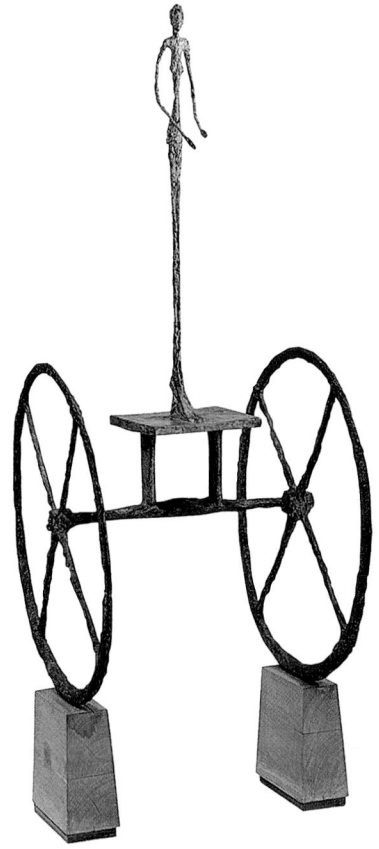

109 Alberro Giacometti.
CHARIOT. 1950.
Bronze. 57″ × 26″ × 26⅛″.
The Museum of Modern Art, NY/Licensed by Scala-Art Resource, NY.
Purchase. Photograph © 2002
The Museum of Modern Art, NY.
© 2002 Artists Rights Society (ARS), NY/ADAGP, Paris.

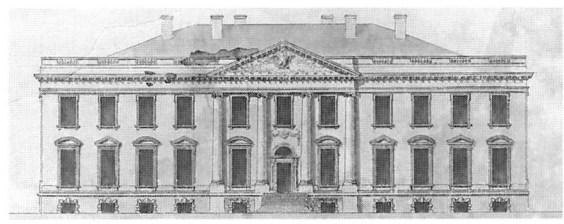

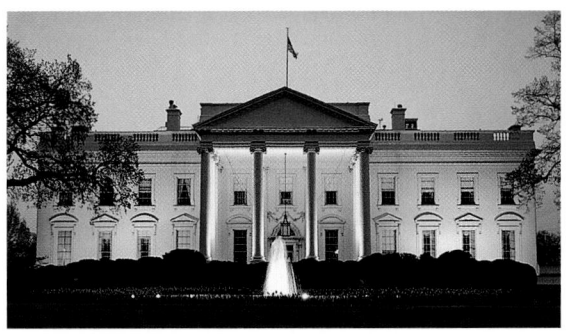

110 James Hoban.
A DESIGN FOR THE PRESIDENT'S HOUSE. 1792.
a. Elevation.
Maryland Historical Society, Baltimore.
b. WHITE HOUSE.
Front view. 1997.
Photograph: Antonio M. Rosario. Getty Images – The Image Bank.

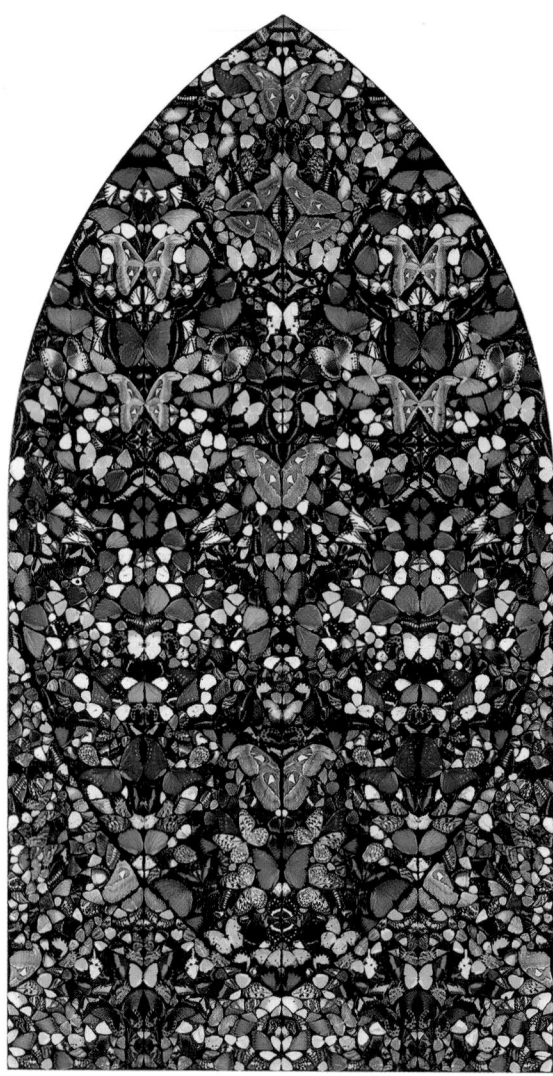

111 Damien Hirst.
POSTERITY—THE HOLY PLACE. 2006.
Butterflies and household gloss on canvas, 89⅝″ × 48″.
© Damien Hirst. Courtesy of Gagosian Gallery, Beverly Hills.
Photograph: Parcence Cuming Associates, Inc.

use it rigidly. Artists usually do not want their work to seem static.

Few works of art are perfectly symmetrical, but POSTERITY—THE HOLY PLACE by Damien Hirst is one. The artist formed it entirely out of butterflies, and it is symmetrical at every level: each butterfly, each unit of the composition, and the work as a whole. It resembles a stained-glass window, but is even more symmetrical than the one pictured on page 5. The stability of symmetry is a useful tool for religious art, which suggests the divine. But the sheer luminosity of POSTERITY—THE HOLY PLACE exceeds even that of a stained-glass window, because butterfly wings do not depend on direct sunlight to show brilliance. (The artist bought the butterflies from a dealer who raises them.) Because the work is made up of so many small parts, the levels of symmetry help to structure the composition. We can prove this by merely imagining a work of similarly large size without a symmetrical arrangement.

Asymmetrical Balance

With *asymmetrical balance*, the left and right sides are not the same. Instead, various elements are balanced—according to their size and meaning—around a felt or implied center of gravity. For example, in THE EVENING GLOW OF THE ANDO, the composition as a whole seems balanced, but only because dramatic imbalances are held in check. The strong diagonal of the wall and floor is accented by the heads of the two subjects, one of whom is reading a poem. This diagonal provides the principal focus of the composition. The curves of the water in the upper left have no counterpart except for the curves of the figures at the center. The lightness of the water and the tree branches is balanced by the solidly anchored candle lamp that the other figure is adjusting. The horizontal lines of the alcove and floor mats give a rhythm to the composition, which the principal diagonal often interrupts. The artist has engaged and balanced complex energies in a knowing and tasteful way typical of the best Japanese prints. Asymmetrical balance is difficult to achieve, but it is flexible, subtle, and dynamic.

What exactly are the visual weights of colors and forms, and how does an artist go about balancing them? As with design itself, there are no rules, only principles. Here are a few about visual balance:

- A large form is heavier, more attractive, or more attention-getting than a small form. Thus, two or more small forms can balance one large form.
- A form gathers visual weight as it nears the edge of a picture. In this way, a small form near an edge can balance a larger form near the center.
- A complex form is heavier than a simple form. Thus, a small complex form can balance a large simple form.

The introduction of color complicates these principles. Here are three color principles that overturn the three principles of form just given:

- Warm colors are heavier than cool colors. A single small yellow form can therefore balance a large dark blue form.
- Related to the point above, warm colors tend to advance toward the viewer, while cool colors tend to recede. This means that when considering two similar forms of opposing temperature, the warmer will be visually heavier because it seems closer to the viewer.
- Intense colors are heavier than weak or pale colors (tints and shades). Hence, a single small bright blue form near the center can balance a large pale blue form near an edge.
- The intensity, and therefore the weight, of any color increases as the background color approaches its complementary hue. Thus, on a green background, a small simple red form can balance a large complex blue form.

Although guidelines such as these are interesting to study and can be valuable to an artist if she or he gets "stuck," they are really "laboratory" examples. The truth is that most artists rely on a highly developed sensitivity to what "looks right" to arrive at a dynamic balance. Simply put, a picture is balanced when it feels balanced.

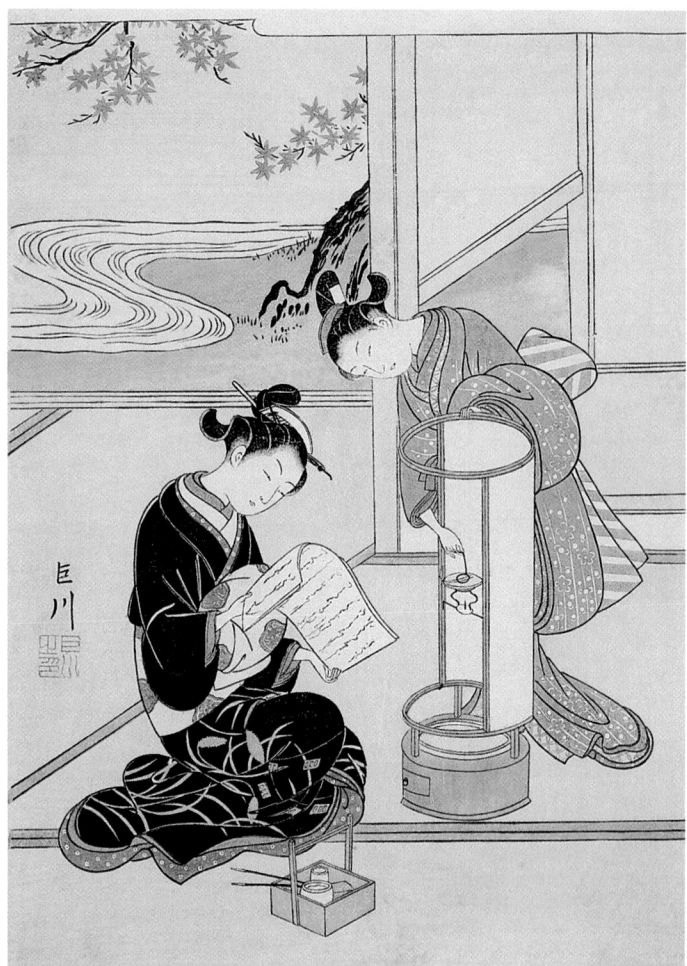

112 Suzuki Haranobu.
THE EVENING GLOW OF THE ANDO.
From the series EIGHT PARLOR VIEWS.
Edo period. 1766.
Color woodblock print. 11¼″ × 8½″.
The Art Institute of Chicago. Clarence Buckingham Collection, 1928.900.
Photograph: © 1997, The Art Institute of Chicago. All rights reserved.

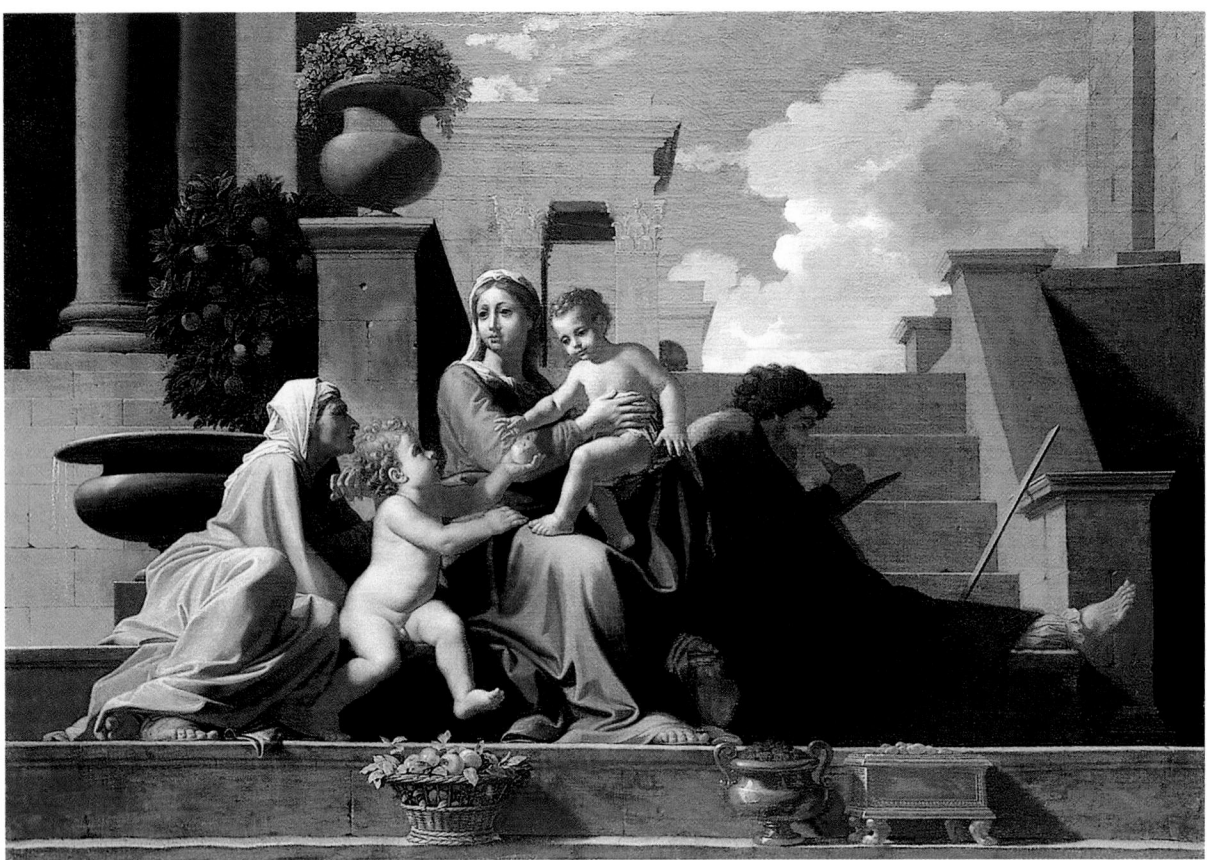

113 Nicolas Poussin.
THE HOLY FAMILY ON THE STEPS. 1648.
Oil on canvas. 28½″ × 44″.
© The Cleveland Museum of Art, 2001, Leonard C. Hanna, Jr., Fund, 1981.18.

A classic example of balance in Western art is Nicolas Poussin's HOLY FAMILY ON THE STEPS. Poussin combined both asymmetrical and symmetrical elements in this complex composition. He grouped the figures in a stable, symmetrical pyramidal shape. The most important figure, the infant Jesus, is at the center of the picture, the strongest position. In case we don't see that right away, Poussin guided our attention by making the traditional red and blue of Mary's robes both light and bright, and by placing Jesus' head within a halolike architectural space.

But then Poussin offset the potential inertness of this symmetry with an ingenious asymmetrical color balance. He placed Joseph, the figure at the right, in deep shadow, undermining the clarity of the stable pyramid. He created a major center of interest at the far left of the picture by giving St.

Elizabeth a bright yellow robe. The interest created by the blue sky and clouds at the upper right counterbalances the figures of St. Elizabeth and the infant John the Baptist. But the final master stroke that brings complete balance is Joseph's foot, which Poussin bathed in light. The brightness of this small, isolated shape with the diagonal staff above it is enough to catch our eye and balance the color weights of the left half of the painting.

While the overall composition of HOLY FAMILY ON THE STEPS is balanced asymmetrically, the painting's center of gravity is still the central vertical axis. In JOCKEYS BEFORE THE RACE, on the other hand, Edgar Degas located the center of gravity on the right. To reinforce it, he drew it in as a pole. At first glance, all our attention is drawn to our extreme right, to the nearest and largest horse. But the solitary circle of the sun in the upper left exerts a strong fascination. The red cap, the pale pink jacket of the distant jockey, the subtle warm/cool color intersection at the horizon, and the decreasing sizes of the horses all help to move our eyes over to the left portion of the picture, where a barely discernible but very important vertical line directs our attention upward.

In JOCKEYS BEFORE THE RACE, a trail of visual cues moves our attention from right to left. If we are sensitive to them, we will perform the act of balancing the painting. If we are not, the painting will seem forever unbalanced. Degas, who was known for his adventurous compositions, relied on the fact that seeing is an active, creative process and not a passive one.

Notice that both Poussin and Degas used strong diagonals in their designs. In the Poussin, Elizabeth's robe at the lower left begins an implied diagonal line that continues up through the cloud at the upper right. In the Degas, the large horse in the lower right, our first center of attention, is counter-balanced by the sun in the upper left. Diagonal opposition is common in asymmetrical compositions, and looking for it can often help you find the key to the balance.

A good way to explore a picture's balance is to imagine it painted differently. Block out Joseph's light-bathed foot in the Poussin, then see how the lack of balance affects the picture. Cover the jockey's red cap in the Degas and you'll see a spark of life go out of the painting.

Asymmetrical balance in architecture is difficult to show in photographs. In Frank Lloyd Wright's FALLINGWATER (page 226), we can sense that the asymmetrically placed horizontal forms are firmly held, visually, by the implied gravity of the vertical tower. But what we cannot see is how the play of forms would shift constantly if we were to walk around the house, how the forms maintain a balance that we could see from every angle.

Besides the visual balance we seek in all art, works of sculpture and architecture need structural balance or they will not stand up. Feelings about visual balance are intimately connected to our experience with actual physical balance. It appears that Beverly Pepper designed her large sculpture

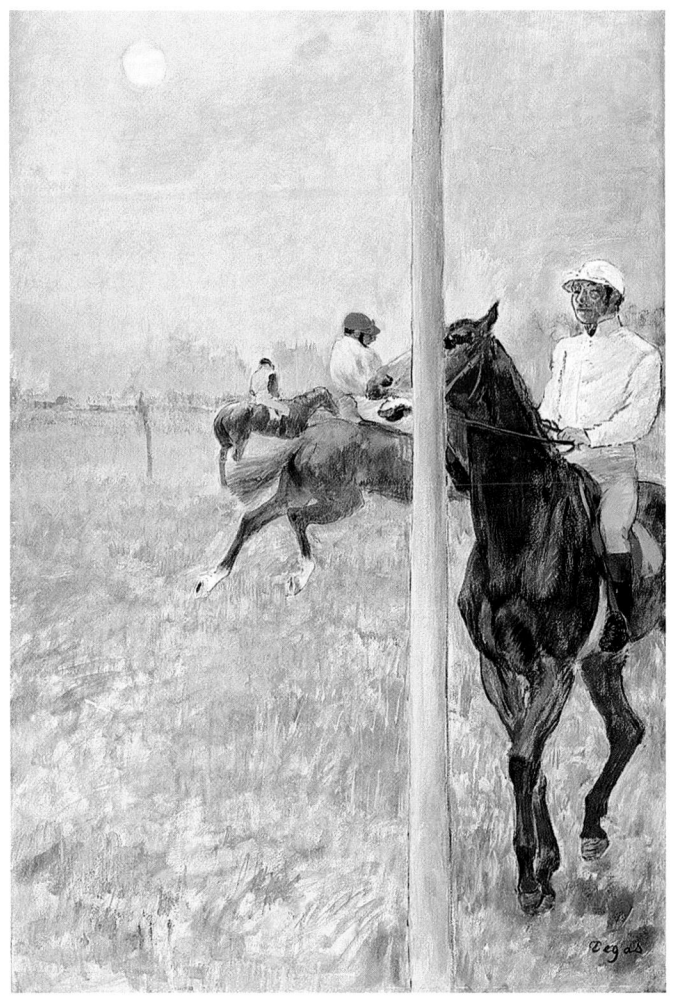

114 Edgar Degas.
JOCKEYS BEFORE THE RACE. c. 1878–1879.
Oil essence, gouache, and pastel. 42½″ × 29″.
The Barber Institute of Fine Arts, The University of Birmingham. Bridgeman Art Library.

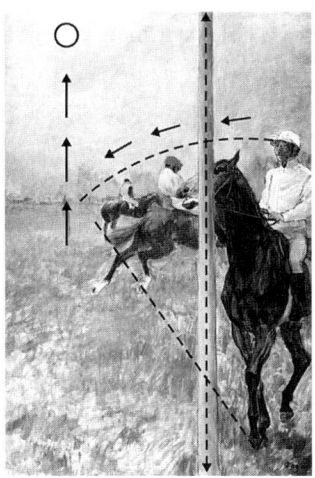

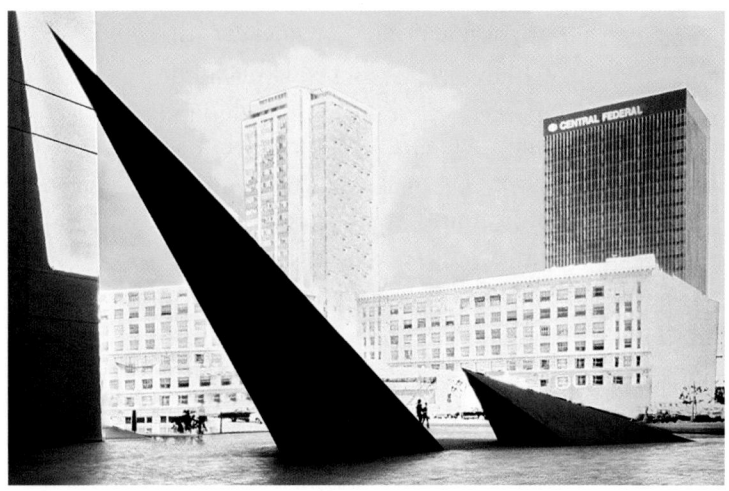

115 Beverly Pepper.
    EXCALIBUR. 1975–1976.
    San Diego Federal Courthouse.
    Steel painted black. 35′ × 45′ × 45′.
    Photograph: Courtesy of the artist.
    Beverly Pepper Studio.

EXCALIBUR to look somewhat unbalanced as a way of giving an intriguing tension to her soaring diagonal structures. We know the triangular forms are securely attached to the ground, yet they look precarious. If we view the work from this and other angles, the smaller piece seems to provide an anchor—a visual pull that acts as a counterweight to the larger form.

EMPHASIS AND SUBORDINATION

Emphasis is used to draw our attention to an area or areas. If that area is a specific spot or figure, it is called a *focal point*. Position, contrast, color intensity, and size can all be used to create emphasis.

Through *subordination*, an artist creates neutral areas of lesser interest that keep us from being distracted from the areas of emphasis. We have seen them at work in the two paintings we have just examined.

In HOLY FAMILY ON THE STEPS, Poussin placed the most important figure in the center, the strongest location in any visual field. In JOCKEYS BEFORE THE RACE, Degas took a different approach, using size, shape, placement, and color to create areas of emphasis *away* from the center. The sun is a separate focal point created through contrast (it is lighter than the surrounding sky area and the only circle in the painting) and through placement (it is the only shape in that part of the painting). Sky and grass areas, however, are muted in color with almost no detail so that they would be subordinate to, and thus support, the areas of emphasis.

DIRECTIONAL FORCES

Like emphasis and subordination, directional forces influence the attention we pay to parts of an artwork. Directional forces are "paths" for the eye to follow provided by actual or implied lines. Implied directional lines may be suggested by a form's axis, by the imagined connection between similar or adjacent forms, or by the implied continuation of actual lines. Studying directional lines and forces often reveals a work of art's underlying energy and basic visual structure.

Looking at JOCKEYS BEFORE THE RACE, we find that our attention is pulled to a series of focal points: the horse and jockey at the extreme right, the vertical pole, the red cap, the pink jacket, and the blue-green at the horizon. The dominant directional forces in JOCKEYS are diagonal. The focal points mentioned above create an implied directional line. The face of the first jockey is included in this line.

The implied diagonal line created by the bodies of the three receding horses acts as a related directional force. As our eyes follow the recession, encouraged by the attraction of the focal points, we perform the act of balancing the composition by correcting our original attraction to the extreme right.

Just as our physical and visual feelings for balance correspond, so do our physical and visual feelings about directional lines and forces. The direction of lines produces sensations similar to standing still (|), being at rest (—), or being in motion (/). Therefore, a combination of vertical and horizontal lines provides stability. For example, columns and walls and horizontal steps provide a stable visual foundation for HOLY FAMILY ON THE STEPS. The vertical pole and horizon provide stability in JOCKEYS by Edgar Degas.

Francisco Goya's print BULLFIGHT provides a fascinating example of effective design based on a dramatic use of directional forces. To emphasize the drama of man and bull, Goya isolated them in the foreground as large, dark shapes against a light background. He created suspense by crowding the spectators into the upper left corner.

Goya evoked a sense of motion by placing the bullfighter exactly on the diagonal axis that runs from lower left to upper right (diagram a). He reinforced the feeling by placing the bull's hind legs along the same line.

Goya further emphasized two main features of the drama by placing the man's hands at the intersection of the image's most important horizontal and vertical lines. He also directed powerful diagonals from the bull's head and front legs to the pole's balancing point on the ground (a). The resulting sense of motion to the right is so powerful that everything in the rest of the etching is needed to balance it.

By placing the light source to the left, Goya extended the bull's shadow to the right, to create a relatively stable horizontal line. The man looks down at the shadow, creating a directional force that causes us also to look. When we do, we realize that the implied lines reveal the underlying structure to be a stable triangle (diagram b). Formally, the triangle serves as a balancing force; psychologically, its missing side serves to heighten the tension of the situation.

The dynamism of the man's diagonal axis is so strong that the composition needed additional balancing elements; thus Goya used light to create two

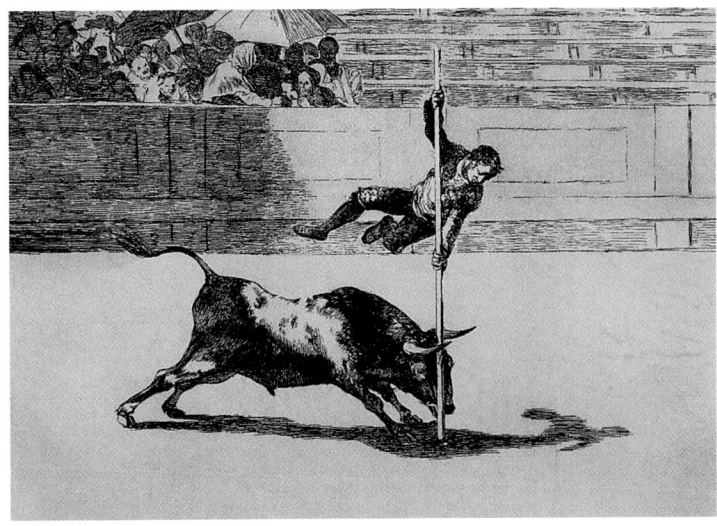

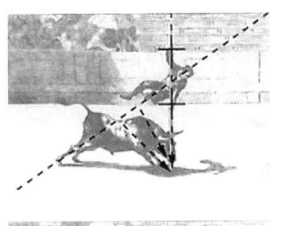
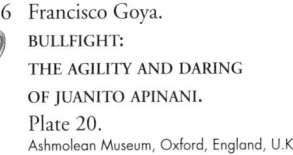
a.

116 Francisco Goya.
BULLFIGHT:
THE AGILITY AND DARING
OF JUANITO APINANI.
Plate 20.
Ashmolean Museum, Oxford, England, U.K.

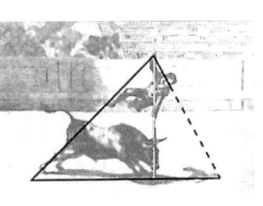
b.

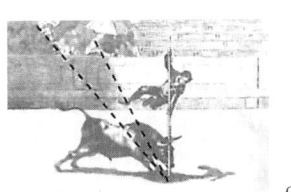
c.

more diagonals in the opposite direction (diagram c). The area of shadow in the background completes the balance by adding visual weight and stability to the left.

It has taken many words and several diagrams to describe the visual dynamics that make the design of Goya's etching so effective. However, our eyes take it in instantly. Good design is efficient; it communicates its power immediately.

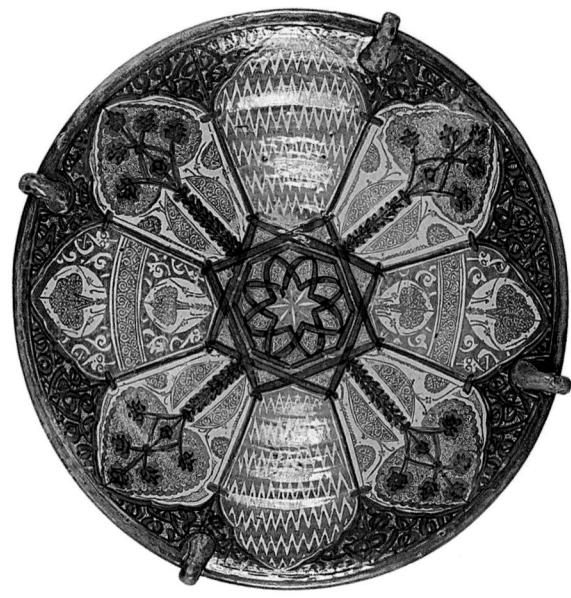

117   LUSTER-PAINTED BOWL.
Hispano-Moresque, Manises. Spain. c. 1400.
Tin-glazed earthenware painted in cobalt blue and luster.
Height 5½", diameter 17⅗".
Courtesy of the Hispanic Society of America, NY.

CONTRAST

Contrast is the juxtaposition of strongly dissimilar elements. Dramatic effects can be produced when dark is set against light, large against small, bright colors against dull. Without contrast, visual experience would be monotonous.

Contrast can be seen in the thick and thin areas of a single brush stroke. It can also be seen in the juxtaposition of regular geometric and irregular organic shapes, or in hard (sharp) and soft (blurred) edges. Contrast can provide visual interest, emphasize a point, and express content.

In the LUSTER-PAINTED BOWL, for example, the gold luster contrasts strongly with the blue accents. There is also a great deal of contrast among the eight petal-shaped segments that radiate from the central starburst. These segments are divided and decorated quite differently, creating a richly varied surface. Four of the petals have a blue tree shape, which evokes the idea of paradise described in the Quran, the Muslim holy book. They provide the major rhythm of the composition, while the other four petals alternate

between a simple zigzag and a doubled tree separated by a band. After a moment's look, we realize that the vivid and rich contrasts of this piece are subjected to a rigorous balancing scheme based on the repetition of radiating shapes. This discovery soon gives way to admiration for the designer's ability to harmonize such disparate elements.

REPETITION AND RHYTHM

The repetition of visual elements gives a composition unity, continuity, flow, and emphasis. As we saw earlier, de Hooch's INTERIOR OF A DUTCH HOUSE (page 76) is organized around the repetition of rectangular shapes.

In Raphael's MADONNA OF THE CHAIR, curved shapes echo the circular format of the painting. The curve of the edge of the painting is repeated in the curve of Mary's head, shoulder, and arm, and in the interlocking curve of the infant Jesus. The repeated curves provide flow and continuity, while the vertical axis of the chair post stabilizes the curving directional forces that dominate the composition.

In the visual arts, *rhythm* is created through the regular recurrence of elements with related variations. Rhythm refers to any kind of movement or structure of dominant and subordinate elements in sequence. We generally associate rhythm with temporal arts such as music, dance, and poetry. Visual artists also use rhythm, as an organizational and expressive device.

Japanese artist Ogata Korin used repetition and rhythm to charming effect in CRANES, one of a pair of folding screens. The landscape is a flat yet opulent background of gold leaf, interrupted only by a suggestion of a curving stream. The birds are severely simplified, their bodies and legs forming a pattern that is repeated with variations. The heads and beaks of the cranes create a strong directional force to our left, leading the eye to an ironically empty rectangle. The heads are held high, and their location near the top of the composition enhances this loftiness, making the birds seem pretentious. Their procession in marching steps in a seemingly straight line supports this note of humor.

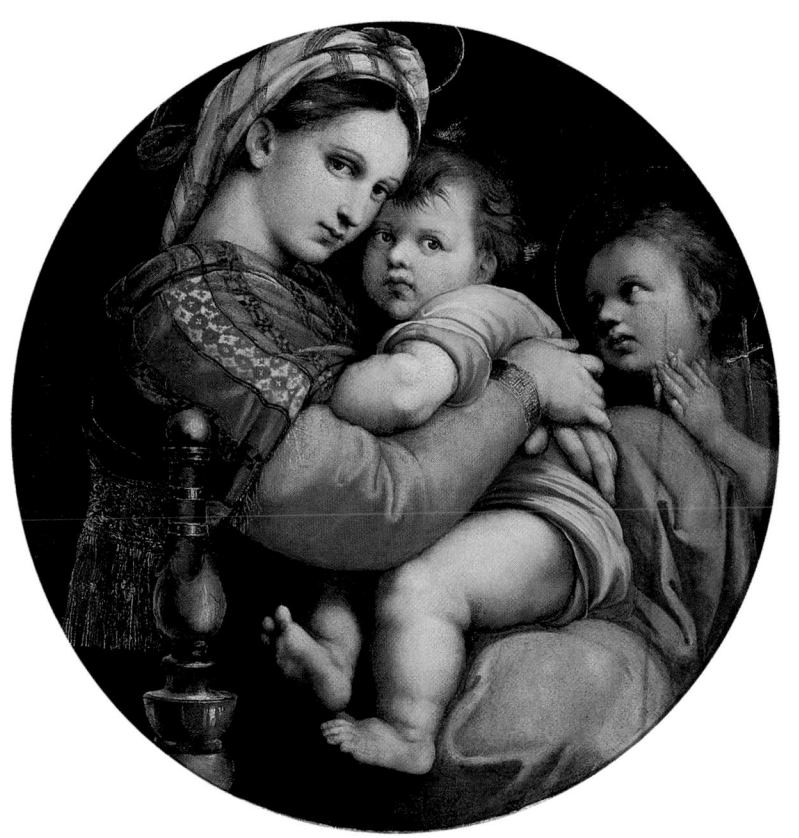

118 Raphael.
MADONNA OF THE CHAIR. c. 1514.
Oil on wood. Diameter 2′4″.
Pitti Gallery, Florence, Italy.
Photograph: Scala/Art Resource, NY.

119 Ogata Korin.
CRANES. c. 1700. Edo period.
Ink, color, and gold on paper. 65⅜″ × 146⅛″.
Freer Gallery of Art, Washington, D.C. Purchase, F1956.20.

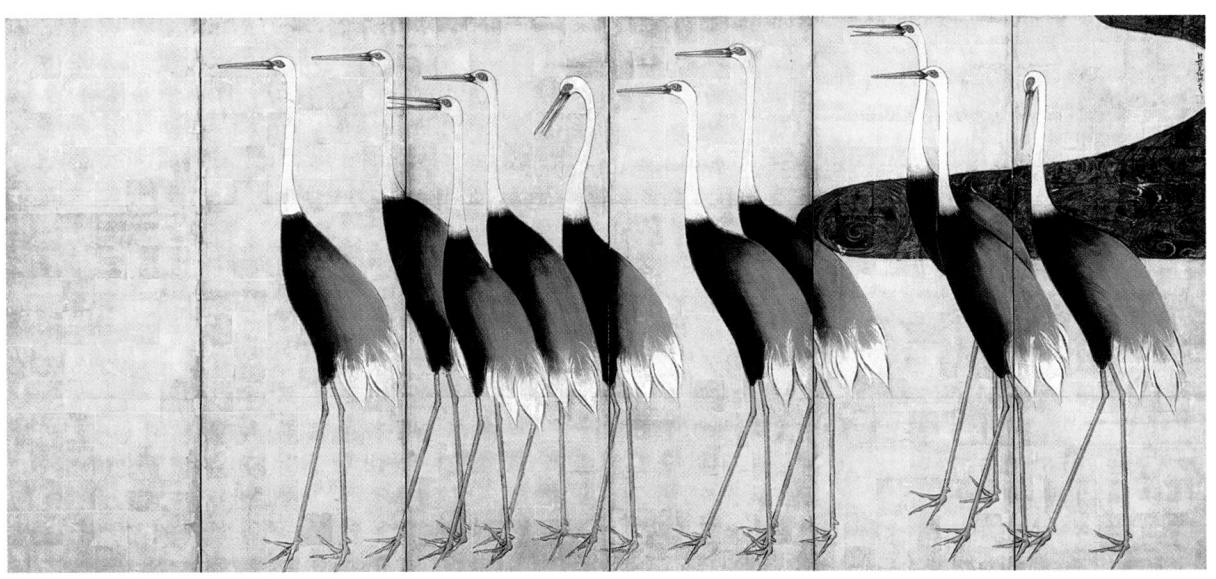

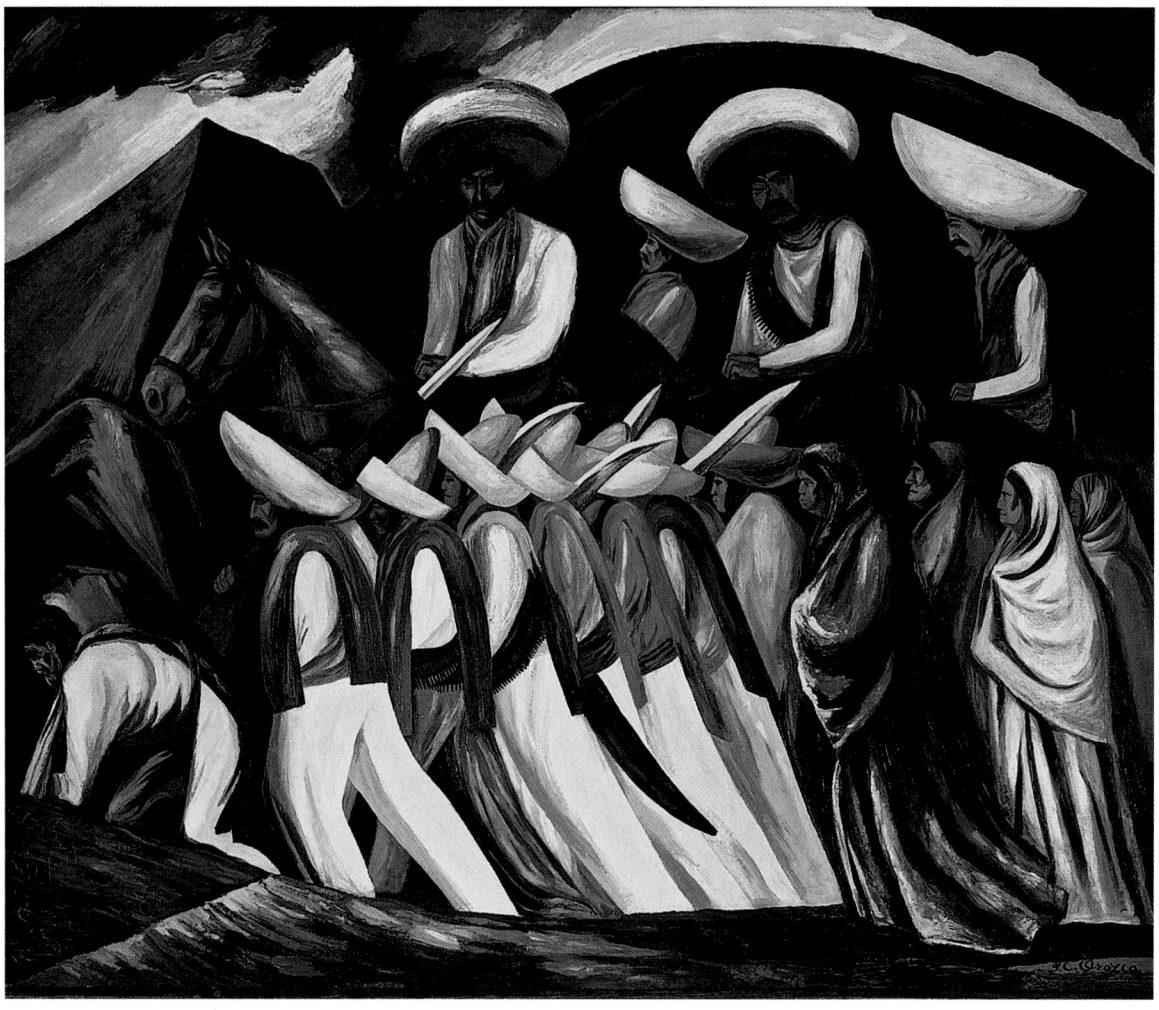

120 José Clemente Orozco.
ZAPATISTAS. 1931.
Oil on canvas. 45″ × 55″.
The Museum of Modern Art, New York. Anonymous gift.
Photograph © 2002 The Museum of Modern Art, New York. © Clemente V. Orozco.
Reproduction authorized by the Instituto Nacional de Bellas Artes.

A strong rhythm dominates José Clemente Orozco's ZAPATISTAS. The line of similar, diagonally placed figures grouped in a rhythmic sequence expresses the determination of oppressed people in revolt. The rhythmic diagonals of their hat brims, bayonets, and swords all contribute to a feeling of action. In fact, diagonal lines dominate the entire composition.

SCALE AND PROPORTION

Scale is the size relation of one thing to another. *Proportion* is the size relationship of parts to a whole.

Scale is one of the first decisions an artist makes when planning a work of art. How big will it be? We experience scale in relation to our own size, and this experience constitutes an important part of our response to works of art.

We see many relationships in terms of scale. You have probably noticed that when a short person stands next to a tall person, the short one seems shorter and the tall one taller. Their relationship exaggerates the relative difference in their heights. In the diagram SCALE RELATION-SHIPS, the inner circles at the center in both

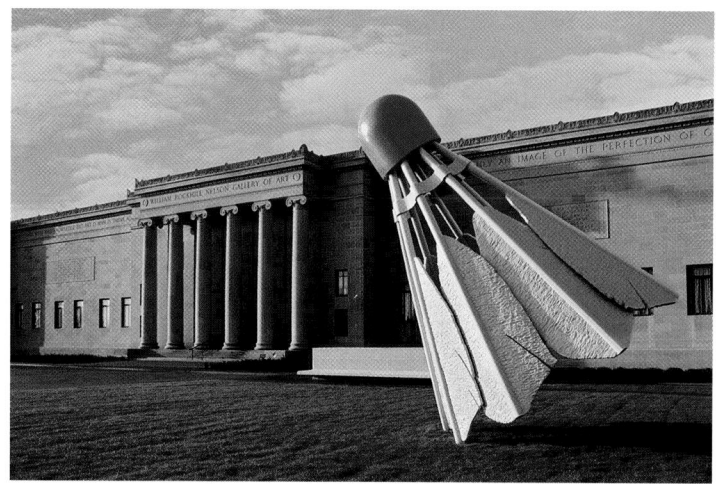

121 Claes Oldenburg and Coosje van Bruggen.
SHUTTLECOCKS. 1994. One of four.
Aluminum, fiberglass-reinforced plastic,
and paint. 215¾" × 209" × 191¾".
The Nelson-Atkins Museum of Art, Kansas City, MO.
Purchase: acquired through the generosity of the Sosland Family.
© Claes Oldenburg and Coosje van Bruggen, F94-1/1.
Photograph: Jamison Miller.

groups are the same size, but they appear to be quite different.

Claes Oldenburg and Coosje van Bruggen's SHUTTLECOCKS is a contemporary example of distortion of scale. The artists arrayed four huge metal shuttlecocks on the lawns outside the north and south façades of the Nelson-Atkins Museum of Art in Kansas City, Missouri. Each is an outlandish seventeen feet high and weighs over 5,000 pounds. Because badminton is played on grass, it appears that the shuttlecocks fell during a game among giants who used the museum as a net. SHUTTLECOCKS thus uses distortion of scale to poke gentle fun at the museum, mocking its rather prim look with a playfully irreverent attitude.

When the size of any work is modified for reproduction in a book, its character changes. The sizes of almost all the art objects in this book have been changed to fit the photographic reproductions of them on the pages. One of the few exceptions is Rembrandt's SELF-PORTRAIT IN A CAP. This tiny etching, which the artist did when he was twenty-four years old, is reproduced here the actual size of the original print. It captures a fleeting expression of intense surprise. At this scale, it reads as an intimate notation of human emotion. On the other hand, many large-sized works have been reduced in this book to tiny fractions of their actual

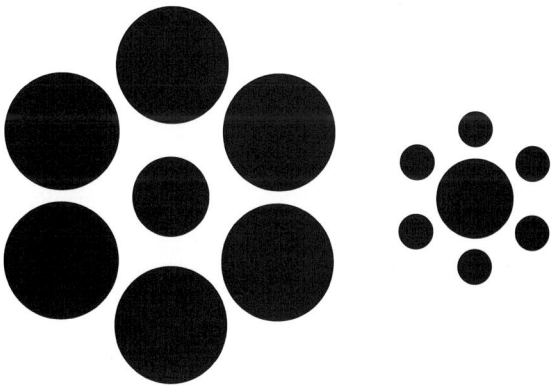

122 SCALE RELATIONSHIPS.

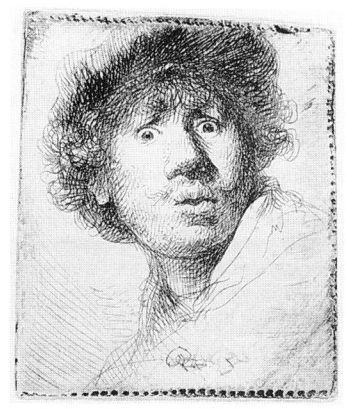

123 Rembrandt van Rijn.
SELF-PORTRAIT IN A CAP, OPEN
MOUTHED AND STARING. 1630.
Etching. 2" × 1⅞".
Copyright The British Museum.

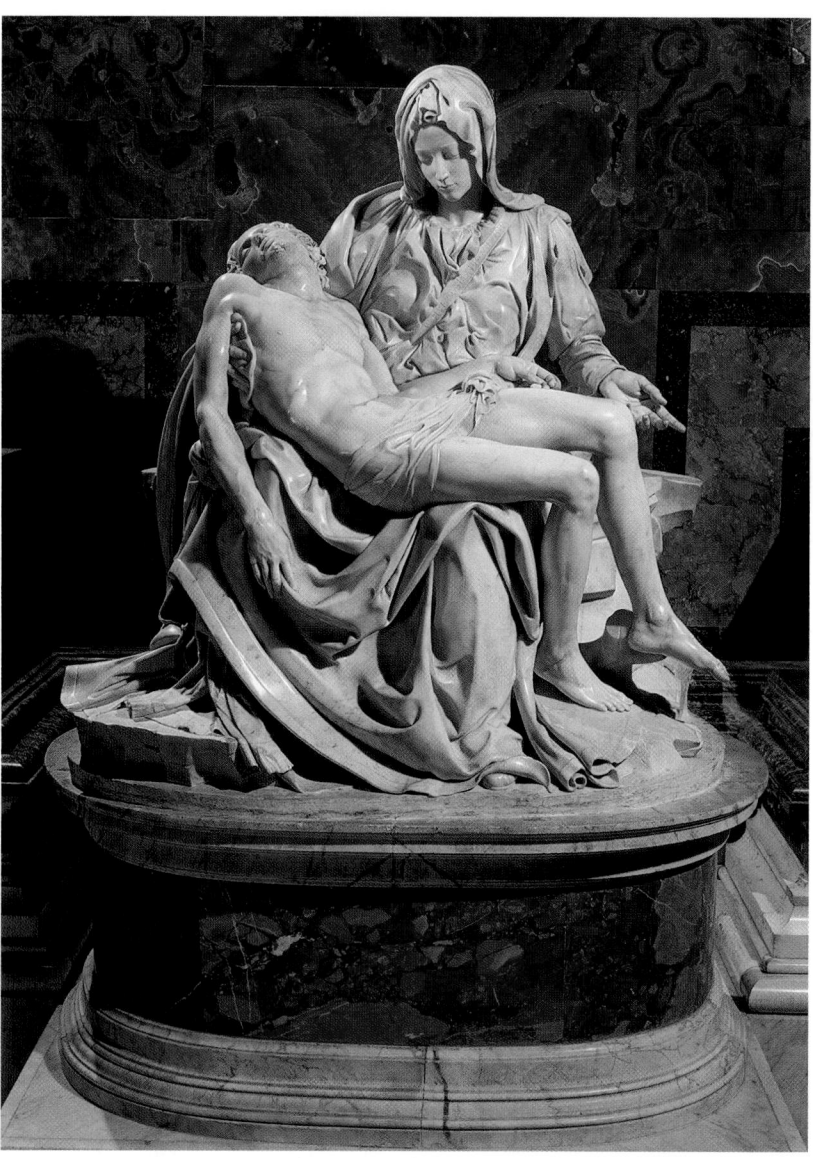

124 Michelangelo Buonarroti.
PIETÀ, 1501.
Marble. Height 6'8½".
St. Peter's Basilica, Vatican State.
© Canali Photobank.

sizes, thereby altering their impact. Because works of art are distorted in a variety of ways when they are reproduced, it is important to experience original art whenever possible.

The term *format* refers to the size and shape—and thus to the scale and proportion—of a two-dimensional picture plane, such as a piece of paper, a canvas, a book page, or a video screen. For example, the format of this book is a vertical 8½ by 11-inch rectangle, the same format used for com-

puter paper and most notebooks. Three common formats favored by traditional painters in China and Japan have been the long horizontal hand-scroll, the tall, vertical hanging scroll, and the fan. The circular or "tondo" format was used during the Renaissance by Raphael (see page 85) and others. Some recent artists have used huge formats.

The format an artist chooses affects the total composition (design) of a particular work. Matisse made this clear in his *Notes of a Painter*:

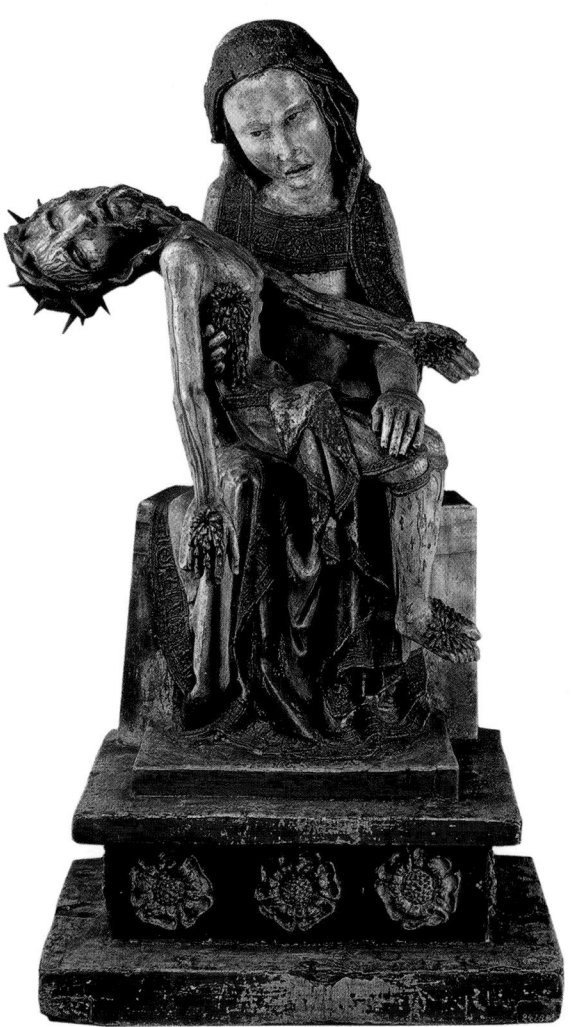

125 ROETTGEN PIETÀ. 1300–1325.
Painted wood, height 34½".
Rhenisches Landesmuseum, Bonn.

Composition, the aim of which should be expression, is modified according to the surface to be covered. If I take a sheet of paper of a given size, my drawing will have a necessary relationship to its format. I would not repeat this drawing on another sheet of different proportions, for example, rectangular instead of square.[3]

Size relationships within a work of art often express symbolic meaning. The use of unnatural proportions to show the relative importance of figures is called *hierarchical scale*. In Egyptian art, the relative importance of figures in a composition often dictates their size, so that rulers appear much larger than servants or captives.

Change in proportion can make a major difference in how we experience a given subject. This becomes apparent when we compare two *pietàs* (*pietà*, Italian for "pity," refers to a depiction of Mary holding and mourning over the body of Jesus).

Creating a composition with an infant on its mother's lap is much easier than showing a fully grown man in such a position. In his most famous PIETÀ, the young Michelangelo solved the problem by dramatically altering the human proportions of Mary's figure. Michelangelo made the heads of the two figures the same size but greatly enlarged Mary's body in relation to that of Christ, disguising her immensity with folds of drapery. Her seated figure spreads out to support the almost horizontal curve of Christ's limp body. Imagine how the figure of Mary would appear if she were standing. Michelangelo made Mary's body into that of a giant; if she were a living human being rather than a work of art, she would stand at least eight feet tall!

Because the proportions of the figure of Christ are anatomically correct and there are abundant naturalistic details, we overlook the proportions of Mary's figure; yet the distortion is essential to the way we experience the content of the work.

Compare Michelangelo's work with the ROETTGEN PIETÀ, created about two centuries earlier. Unlike the Renaissance work, the German sculptor carved both figures of similar height. Making Christ bony and emaciated helped to alleviate the problem of how Mary can support a person of similar size; Christ's gaunt body also expresses the truth of his suffering in a way that Michelangelo avoided. The sculptor of ROETTGEN PIETÀ also carved both heads larger, out of proportion to the sizes of their bodies. This distortion also helps to heighten the expressiveness of the work.

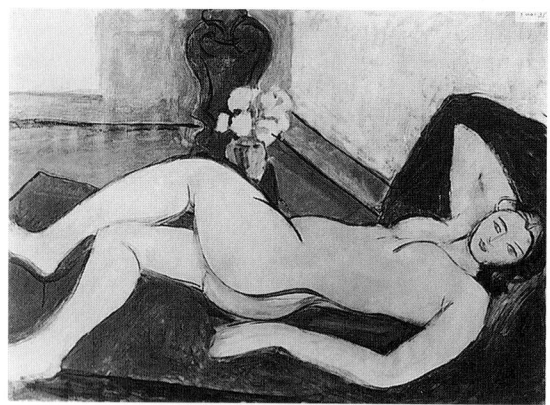

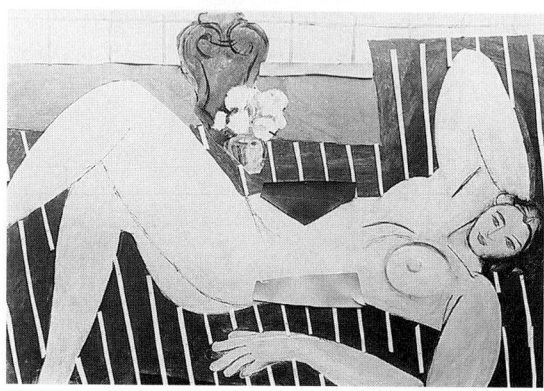

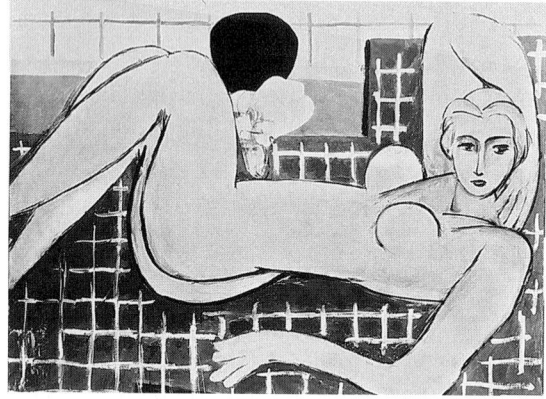

126 Henri Matisse.
Photographs of three states of LARGE RECLINING NUDE.
a. State I, May 3, 1935.
b. State IX, May 29, 1935.
c. State XIII, September 4, 1935.
The Baltimore Museum of Art. The Cone Collection.
© 2002 Succession H. Matisse, Paris/Artists Rights Society (ARS), NY.

DESIGN SUMMARY

A finished work affects us because its design seems inevitable. However, design is not inevitable at all. Faced with a blank piece of paper, an empty canvas, a lump of clay, or a block of marble, an artist begins a process involving many decisions, false starts, and changes in order to arrive at an integrated whole. This chapter has presented some of the principles of design that guide the art-making process.

By photographing the progress of his painting LARGE RECLINING NUDE, Henri Matisse left us a rare record of the process of designing. He took twenty-four photographs over a period of four months; three of them are reproduced here.

The first version (State I) is by far the most naturalistic: the proportions of the model's body on the couch and the three-dimensional space of the room seem ordinary. This stage of the work shows the traditional rules of picture construction, but this is only the start of a fascinating journey.

By State IX, Matisse had introduced a number of bold changes. Because the model's head and crooked right arm did not give the proper weight to that side of the composition, he greatly enlarged the arm. He added more curves to the torso, and he put the legs together to provide a balancing element on the left side. The space of the room now has a new look because he removed the diagonal; this change flattened the composition, highlighting its two-dimensional design. The model's left arm is now closer to a ninety-degree angle, which makes it seem to support more weight; this is a stronger effect than that of the rubbery arm in the first photo. The boldest change regards the couch. Now it is far larger, with vertical white stripes in a rhythmic pattern. Because the stripes are parallel, they do not function as perspective lines; rather, the couch appears to be tipped toward us. Matisse kept the potted flowers and the chair, but he simplified the chair and placed the flowers on the couch.

By the time the artist took our third photograph (State XIII), he had introduced even more changes, to compensate for some of the bold effects he had introduced earlier. The model's head is larger and placed upright, so that it fits better into the

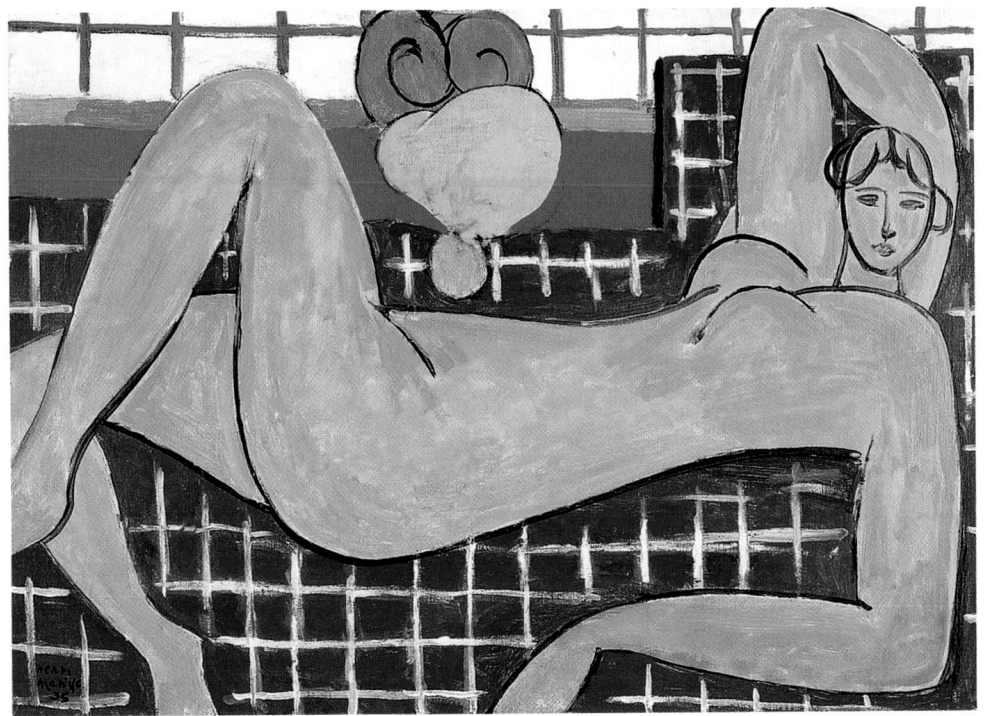

127 Henri Matisse (French, 1869–1954).
LARGE RECLINING NUDE.
1935.
Oil on canvas. 26″ × 36½″.
The Baltimore Museum of Art: The Cone Collection, formed by Dr. Claribel Cone and Miss Etta Cone of Baltimore, Maryland. BMA 1950.258.
© 2002 Succession H. Matisse, Paris/Artists Rights Society (ARS), NY.

shape of the raised arm. He simplified the curves of the torso and created a new position for the left arm, a compromise between its position in the first photo and the second one. The legs are now almost a unit, their bulky mass balancing the verticals and diagonals on the right. He added horizontal lines to the couch, making a pattern of squares that parallel the framing edges of the painting. This net-like motif is repeated in the larger squares on the back wall of the room. The composition is already interesting, but Matisse did not stop here.

The final version shows further refinements and a few discoveries. Because the model's left arm probably still seemed weak, Matisse finally fixed it in the corner of the work at a strong angle aligned with the picture frame. The head is smaller, because the new position of the arms provides enough visual weight on that side of the work. He intensified the pattern on the back wall, so that it now serves as a variation of the motif on the couch. He

gave new functions to the shapes and lines of the chair back and flowers by emphasizing their curves. They now echo the shapes of the body and balance the rigidity of the squares in the couch and wall. The position of the legs is the biggest change. By moving one of them down, he created a "pinwheel" effect that the arms carry through, adding a new circular element to the design of the whole. Finally, he repositioned the model's entire body at a slight angle from the horizontal.

Matisse's keen sense of design and restless experimentation produced a work in which powerful forces in the composition are balanced with seemingly simple means. He wrote that the expressiveness of a work does not rest merely on facial expressions or gestures of figures:

The entire arrangement of my picture is expressive: the place occupied by the figures, the empty spaces around them, the proportions, everything has its share.[4]

WHEN FRENCH artist Henri Matisse was eighteen years old, his father sent him to Paris to study law. A year later he passed his examinations and took a dull job as a clerk in a lawyer's office. Then an attack of appendicitis changed the direction of his life. During the long convalescence at his parents' home, his mother tried to amuse him with a gift of a box of paints, brushes, and a do-it-yourself book on painting. The result was extraordinary.

By the age of twenty-one, Matisse knew he wanted to be a painter. He returned to Paris and became a full-time art student. In the methodical manner of a lawyer, he began his artistic career by becoming thoroughly proficient in the traditional techniques of French art. Throughout his life he worked at adding to both his knowledge and his skills, while being careful to preserve his original freshness of vision.

For Matisse, a painting was a combination of lines, shapes, and colors before it was a depiction of nameable objects. His personal style was based on intuition; yet he acknowledged the importance of his years of study. He carefully assimilated influences from the arts of the Near East and Africa and from other painters.

Matisse's primary interest was to express his passion for life through the free use of visual form, with the human figure his main subject.

What interests me most is neither still life nor landscape but the human figure. It is through it that I best succeed in expressing the nearly religious feeling that I have towards life.[5]

His search for expressive means caused him to question or abandon many of the "rules" of art as it was then understood. For example, he often used colors that did not correspond to what the eye sees, but rather to what he felt inside. He also simplified and flattened his compositions, because he felt that adding too much detail took away feeling. For these and other innovations in painting style, he was once called a "wild beast"—*fauve* in French. The name stuck, and Fauvism took its place among the most important modern art movements.

Matisse sought to hide his own artistic struggles so that his work would appear effortless and light. He was concerned, however, that young people would think he had created his paintings casually—even carelessly—and would mistakenly conclude that years of disciplined work and study were unnecessary.

The dominant qualities in Matisse's art are lyric color and vitality. Behind the

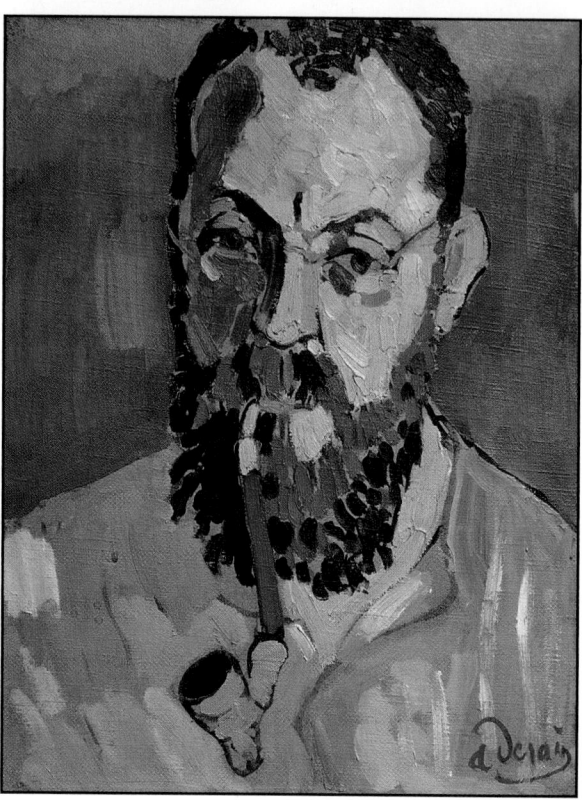

128   André Derain.
HENRI MATISSE. 1905.
Oil on canvas. 18″ × 13¾″.
Tate Gallery, London. Art Resource, NY.
© Artists Rights Society (ARS), NY.

playful appearance lie radiant big-heartedness, grace, and wisdom. Although he lived through both world wars and was aware of acute suffering, Matisse chose to express joy and tranquility in his art.

What I dream of is an art of balance, of purity and serenity, devoid of troubling or depressing subject matter, an art which might be for every mental worker . . . businessman or writer, like an appeasing influence, like a mental soother, something like a good armchair in which to rest from physical fatigue.[6]

EVALUATING ART

Before exploring further the many ways of making art, it is important to consider how to evaluate it. What makes a work of art worthwhile? Is it visually interesting? Is it moving? Is it skillfully done? Which criteria are even relevant to judging art? Who is qualified to make such judgments? As we consider answers to these questions, we will find that there are many ways of judging the quality of art. Further, we will see that our assessments of quality are usually connected to other values that we also hold about the function of art in society; hence our preferences generally embody these other deeply held beliefs.

EVALUATION

Have you ever heard someone say, "I don't know anything about art, but I know what I like"? Each of us expresses likes or dislikes many times a day. When we select one thing over another, or appreciate the specialness of something, we are evaluating.

The creative experience is also a process of selecting and evaluating. For the artist, the creative process involves selecting and evaluating each component before deciding to include it in the final form. After the work is complete, the viewer's enjoyment comes from recognizing the quality that has been achieved. How do viewers evaluate art to determine whether it has quality?

Quality is relative. How a work of art is evaluated varies from person to person, from culture to culture, and from age to age. In Mexico before the Spanish Conquest, the Aztecs judged art to be good if it continued the style of the Toltecs, an ancient neighboring people that the Aztecs admired. In traditional Chinese art criticism, painters were urged to go beyond mere representation of the outward appearance of their subject matter. Good art was a matter of successfully understanding and communicating the inner spirit or "life breath" of the subject. If an artist failed to attain this goal, the work was judged merely "skillful."

In the European tradition, few famous artists or styles have had unchanging reputations. For example, the Impressionist painters of the late nineteenth century were ridiculed by critics, museum curators, and the public. Their style differed too radically from those of their predecessors for easy acceptance in their own time. Today, Impressionist paintings have an honored place in museums and are eagerly sought by the public. Likewise, many artists who were celebrated in their times are forgotten today.

Value judgments about art necessarily involve subjectivity. It is not possible to measure artistic quality objectively in the same way that we measure the wingspan of an airplane or the capacity of a computer. In this regard it is useful for us to compare

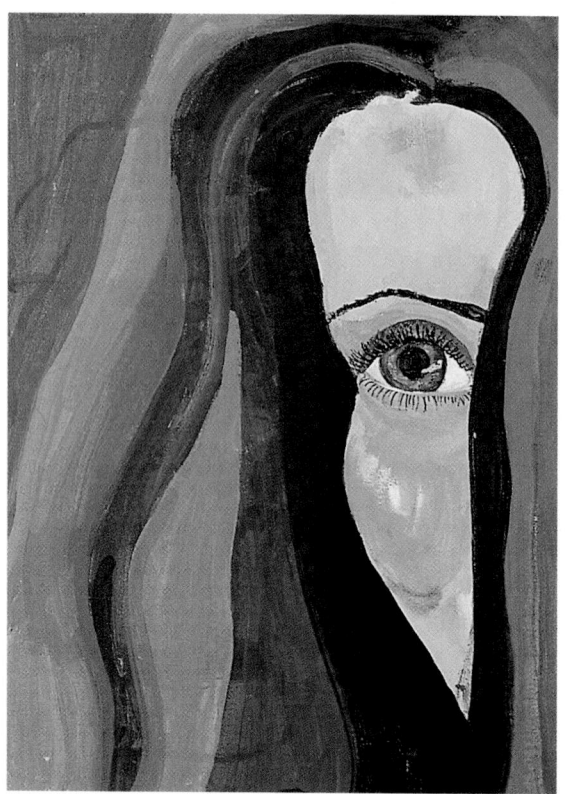

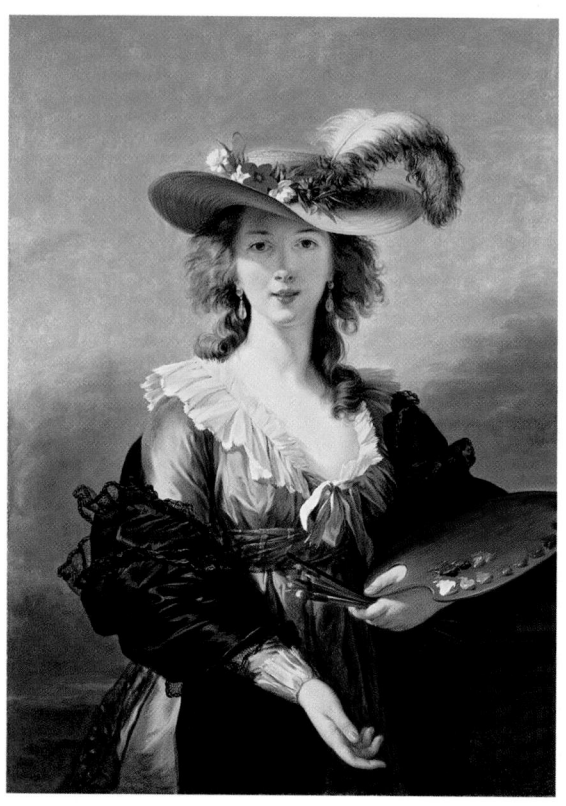

129   Dawn Marie Jigagian.
SHY GLANCE. 1976.
Acrylic on canvas. 18″ × 24″.
Museum of Bad Art, Dedham, MA.

130   Elizabeth Vigee-Lebrun.
SELF-PORTRAIT IN A STRAW HAT. 1782.
Oil on canvas, 38½″ × 27½″.
© National Gallery, London, NG1653.

SHY GLANCE, a work generally regarded as "bad," with SELF-PORTRAIT IN A STRAW HAT by Elizabeth Vigee-Lebrun. The painter of SHY GLANCE lacks skill in color shading (the cheek is blotchy), anatomy (the eyebrow is too narrow and the forehead bulges), composition (it is difficult to tell positive from negative space), and brushwork (the hair and eyelashes!). The feeling it communicates is almost embarrassingly sweet. In contrast, the SELF-PORTRAIT shows great assuredness in the use of paint to show anatomy. The light seems to fall naturally over the subject's face and shoulder. The eyes and face show a relaxed, confident glance. The two artists are poles apart in level of traditional skill.

Yet, today's viewers might find SHY GLANCE at least as interesting as the other work. The SELF-PORTRAIT, for all its skill, looks conventional, even ordinary. In contrast, SHY GLANCE has an obvious sincerity and enthusiasm that may be infectious.

The painter of SHY GLANCE showed great boldness in even bringing forth this work after such modest training. Hence, the level of traditional skill that an artist shows may be relevant to a judgment of quality, but rarely gives the final answer.

When we look at a work of art and find that we are pleased (or displeased), it is useful to ask why. What we find in a work of art depends on what we are looking for. Would we like art to dazzle our senses? Show great skill? Move our feelings? Inform us about the world around in which we live? Bare the artist's soul? These are personal value orientations that will lead us to make judgments about the works of art that we encounter. Expressing our taste in art thus involves our personality and our values more than other kinds of judgments. The type of art that we prefer reveals far more about us than does our favorite flavor of ice cream.

Evaluations of art also vary widely across cultures. We may feel baffled by works of art whose cultural roots are foreign to us. For example, Michelangelo's PIETÀ (see page 88) is recognized as a masterpiece in the West, but it may look strange to a person from a traditional Islamic culture, where representation of the human form in art is considered blasphemous. Likewise, the hastily brushed landscape painting by Shen Zhou (see page 56) may mystify Western viewers who are unfamiliar with the Zen Buddhist philosophies that helped to give it birth.

Whether you are approaching art for your own enjoyment or for a class assignment, it is most rewarding to begin with an open, receptive mind—to go beyond prejudgments. Give yourself time to get acquainted and to respond.

In addition to making drawings or composition studies of significant works, one of the best ways to become acquainted with a work of art is to write about it. Writing about visual form is a process of interpretation that will heighten your personal experience not only of the particular work you are writing about, but also of your future encounters with art and art making. Writing even a paragraph or brief essay causes you to take time to engage in seeing and responding to a work of art, to become conscious of the reasons for your initial gut-level reaction. Senses, emotions, and memories come together with knowledge as you think about how to communicate through words what you see and feel.

Start by considering what you see. Describe its physical qualities. What is it made of? How big is it? Go into detail about what you see. As you are writing, describe the work as if you were helping a blind person "see" it. What colors and shapes are used? What subjects (if any) are represented?

What you have just done is the beginning of formal analysis—a discussion of the way visual elements and design principles affect viewers' thoughts and feelings. Terms introduced in Chapters 2 through 4 will be helpful; use them to describe the use of elements such as line, shape, color, and space. How was the work designed? Is it balanced? What is emphasized? Rhythm? Proportion? Contrast? Does it have unity as well as variety?

Follow the analysis of form with a subjective interpretation of the meaning or symbolism of the work. How does the work make you feel? How or why does it evoke these feelings? Think again about your first description. At this point, go beyond "I like it" or "I don't like it." Get informed about the cultural background of the object and the artist, keeping in mind that the functions of art vary widely across the globe. If it came from a culture remote from your own, assess how it expresses the values of that culture.

Finally, try to determine what the work says about the artist who made it. Can you tell what the artist was trying to say? If so, how clearly was it said? Was saying it worth the effort? Is it a valuable statement from your point of view?

The process just described is a simplified version of the one used by an art critic.

ART CRITICISM

The term *art criticism* refers to making discriminating judgments, both favorable and unfavorable. The three steps outlined above correspond to the three dominant types of art criticism:

Formal theories, which focus attention on the composition of the work and how it may have been influenced by earlier works.
Sociocultural theories, which consider art as a product and of a culture and value system.
Expressive theories, which pay attention to the artist's attempt to express a personality or worldview.

These theories emphasize the work, the culture, and the artist respectively. Let us consider each in turn, as they might be used to analyze three paintings from various cultures that are pictured in this chapter.

Formal Theories

Critics who use formal theories look carefully at how a work is made: how the parts of the composition function to create a visual experience that may interest us or not. They generally believe that the most important influence on a work is other works that the artist has seen or studied. Because the formal organization of the work is the most important factor in evaluating it, the theories are called *formal*.

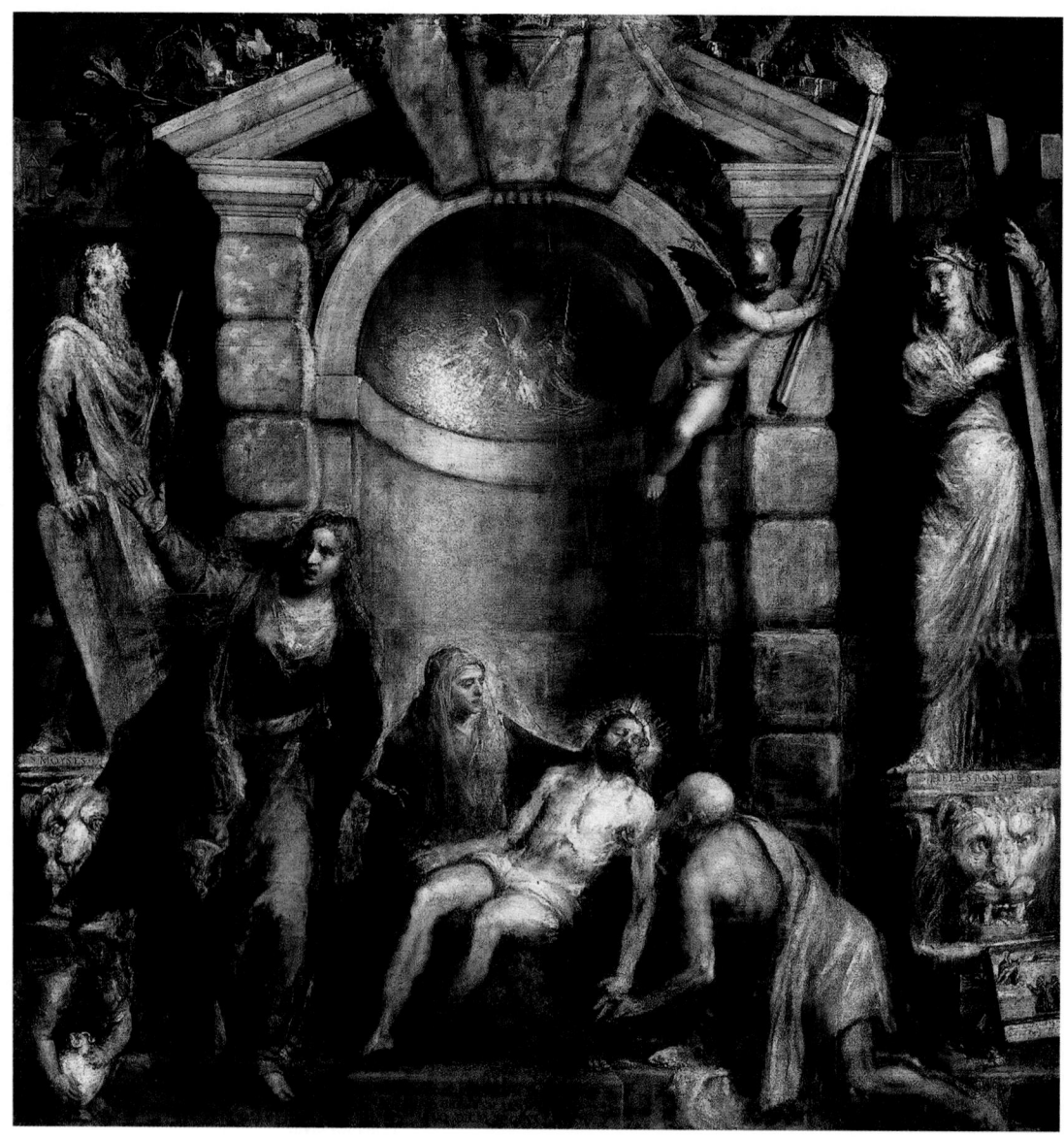

131 Titian.
PIETÀ. 1576.
Oil on canvas, 149″ × 136″.
Gallerie dell Accademia, Venice. Cat, no. 400.
Photograph: Scala-Art Resource, NY.

Formalist critics value innovation in style above all. They value such stylistic novelty because they believe that art can be an important source of refreshment, unconnected to our complicated and strife-tornworld.

For example, Titian's PIETÀ is very innovative in its brushwork. His immediate predecessors in Italian art were the Renaissance masters Raphael, Michelangelo, and Leonardo, among others. Titian understood the painting methods that they used, but he went beyond them by making his brushwork much bolder and looser, adding a new element of expressiveness to painting that influenced artists for generations to come. The work also uses an innovative composition: the center is an empty niche surrounded by a diagonal row of heads that is balanced by the two figures at the upper right.

From a formal perspective, the artists who created UMAR SLAYS A DRAGON successfully solved a

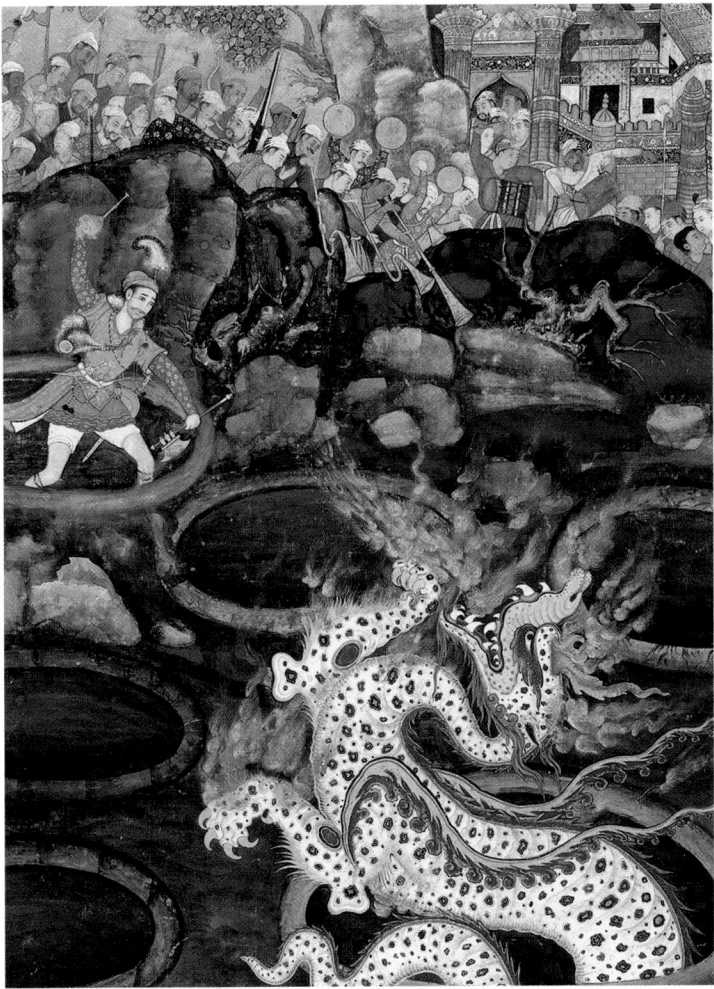

132 Attributed to Dasavanta and Tara.
UMAR SLAYS A DRAGON. 1567–72.
Gouache and color on paper, 24½″ × 20″.
MAK—Austrian Museum of Applied Arts/Contemporary Art, Vienna.

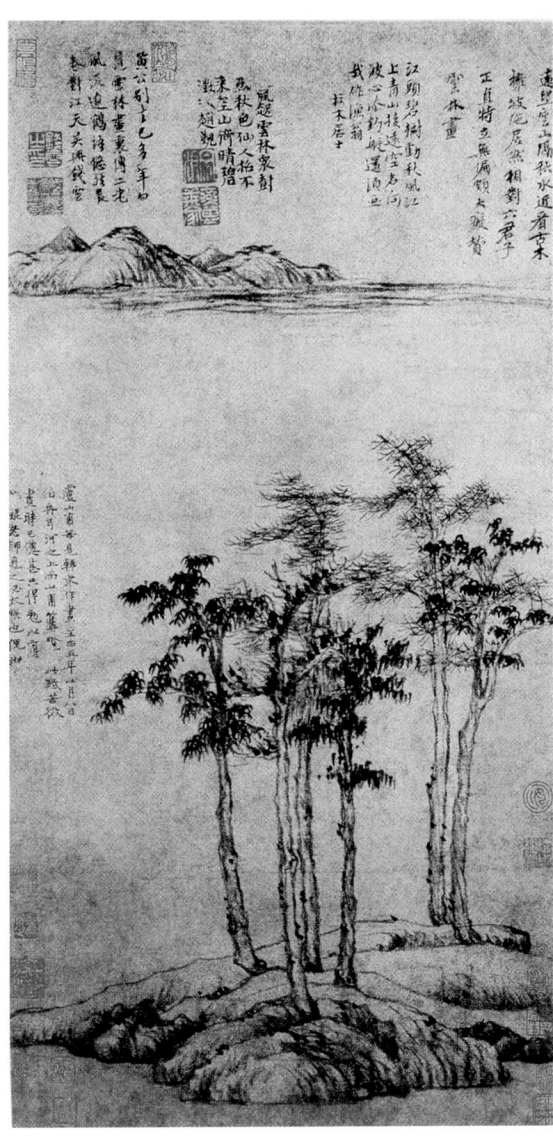

133 Ni Zan.
SIX GENTLEMEN (SIX TREES). 1345.
Hanging scroll, ink on paper, 24¼″ × 13″.
Shanghai Museum of Art, Shanghai, China/China Stock.

challenging problem: how to depict a monster in its lair dying a fiery death. They invented a dark, hellish region marked by circular pits, the better to show off the dragon within. The hero stands knee-deep in one of these pits, hurling firebombs that engulf the monster in flames. As is typical in Islamic painting, this work is a book illustration, but the artists improved on the work of their forebears by enlarging the format, further underlining the vivid action.

Ni Zan's SIX GENTLEMEN seems very calm by comparison, but it too is innovative in its form. Ni Zan worked in a very dry, austere style that was on the cutting edge of its times. The SIX GENTLEMEN of the title are the six trees of different species that he placed at the lower center. This arrangement, with the empty expanse of water at the center below the distant hills, proved very influential on later artists who wanted to communicate feelings of loneliness or stubborn endurance.

Sociocultural Theories

Critics who use these theories tend to look first at the environmental influences on a work of art: the economic system, the cultural values, and even the politics of the time; hence they are termed *sociocultural theories.* They are likely to favor works that either cogently embody important cultural values or memorably express resistance to them. Doing this type of criticism usually requires investigation of the culture that surrounds a work.

Titian's PIETÀ is an altarpiece, destined for public viewing in a chapel of the Church of the Frari in Venice; such works generally took up important Christian themes, and this one is no exception. However, he painted it during an epidemic of the plague, and its theme of mortality and grief takes on added meaning. The vacant niche may symbolize death, and Titian's eloquent depiction of the dead Christ must have given comfort to the many Venetians who lost relatives in the epidemic.

UMAR SLAYS A DRAGON illustrates a story from *The Adventures of Hamza,* an important literary work of ancient Persia. This particular work was created for the Mughal ruler Akbar, who enjoyed hearing stories recited as servants held the paintings up for viewing. This painting is a fairly typical hero narrative of the sort that Akbar favored, rendered in a vivid and engrossing way. Because Akbar was illiterate, he seems to have encouraged painters in his court to make works in larger format than preceding rulers had.

Ni Zan worked during the Yuan dynasty, when China was under foreign domination, and this fact influenced art in several ways. Most of the best artists refused to work for the foreign rulers, and hence were cut off from their usual sources of employment. This left artists freer to experiment, making the Yuan dynasty an important period of innovation in painting. Most educated persons of that period would

have seen symbolic meaning in the SIX GENTLEMEN (SIX TREES) standing by the water; they stand for endurance in the face of oppression.

Expressive Theories

All art works are made by people. The skill level, personal intent, mental state, gender, or mindset of the creator must play a role in the creative process. Artist-centered theories are thus termed *expressive* or *empathic theories.* Critics who favor this approach tend to look for powerful personal meanings, deep psychological insight, or profound human concern. These types of critical theories have been strongly influenced by psychoanalysis and by gender studies.

Titian painted the PIETÀ in the last year of his life; hence its somber reflection on death expresses the artist's own mortality. Indeed, the figure at the lower right in the red shawl is Titian himself. Many critics believe that his looser brushwork represents an "old age style" in which the artist cast off the restraint of his younger days.

Mughal artists never signed their works, and we do not know exactly who painted UMAR SLAYS A DRAGON. Not every culture values personal style to the extent that Western culture does, and hence this work is attributed to two artists on the basis of an educated guess by an expert. Although it is a memorable work, it yields little information about its makers.

In contrast, we know many details about Ni Zan's life; one fact that seems to have greatly influenced his painting is his abhorrence of dirt of any kind. He was so fastidiously clean that he regularly washed the trees on his property, according to legend. Most likely this personal proclivity influenced his dry and spare painting style, in which humans rarely appear.

Although we can describe, analyze, interpret, and appraise art, there is no single correct way to evaluate art. All three of these approaches have enjoyed favor at one time or another; at present, sociocultural theories seem to predominate. But the process of evaluation is rewarding from any viewpoint because it draws the viewer into the creative process.

TYLER
Green

CAN CORPORATE SPONSORSHIP ruin an art exhibition? Can a museum get too cozy with its sponsors from the business world? Have these problems surfaced recently?

Green works in today's fast-paced 24-hour news world where his blog, *Modern Art Notes*, is read by thousands daily. We might call him an art critic for the twenty-first century. He reviews shows on his blog, but he also presents art-world news such as who is being hired and fired, who has made major donations to whom, and which galleries are moving or expanding. His most important contribution has been to constantly police the ever-closer relationships between museums and large corporate sponsors, warning when he sees business money hovering too closely over what museums do.

For example, in 2006–2009, an exhibition on the most famous ruler of Egypt, King Tut, traveled to museums in five major cities. Most viewers probably thought that the museum staffs collaborated on the works to be borrowed, and planned the show to explore certain themes that would educate the public about ancient Egypt by showing beautiful artworks. But those viewers were wrong. The exhibition was put together by Anschutz Entertainment Group (AEG), a Denver-based company that also owns sports arenas, movie the-aters, and four professional soccer teams. The company joined with the National Geographic Society to borrow 130 objects from the Egyptian government, and then offered the show to museums as a profit-making venture. Museum staffs had no say in which works were borrowed or how they were exhibited, and AEG took charge of all advertising (one New York billboard called the Egyptian ruler "The King of Bling").

Green denounced this arrangement on his blog: "Museum ethics have become a joke, and some recent museum practices take hallowed halls big steps closer to installations at the Mall of America." The basic problem was that the museums that hosted the show basically rented out space to an entertainment company instead of curating the exhibition themselves. And the admission price was steep: $30 for adults, $15 for children. Green said that AEG is of course free to plan exhibitions, but art museums should not turn space over to them, because an art museum is not an entertainment company.

He also took aim at the Museum of Modern Art in New York (MOMA) when it showed work from the collection of UBS Financial Services. Corporate sponsorship of exhibitions is not new; it happens all the time. But companies that donate to museums usually do not determine the contents of the shows they

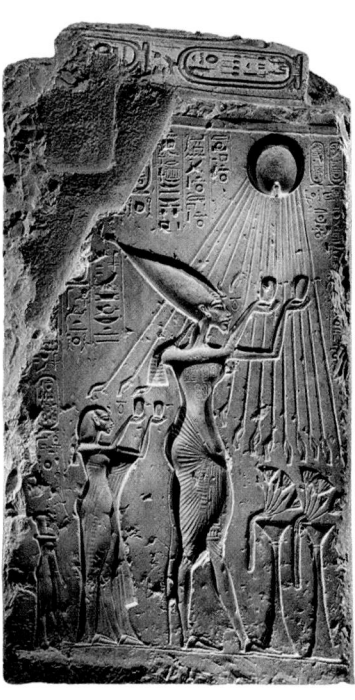

134   ATEN, AKHENHATEN, AND FAMILY. Balustrade.
From 2007 exhibition "Tutankhamun and the Golden Age of the Pharaohs."
Photograph: Kenneth Garrett.

sponsor. In the UBS case, instead of staging a show of contemporary art selected by its curators, MOMA let this company determine the show's content and thus helped to promote the UBS image. This makes MOMA, "the art world's corporate headquarters," said Green. (He also protested when the museum increased its admission charge after an expansion, calling it M$20MA.)

So what's the basic difference between traditional art criticism and blogging? Most art critics work for newspapers or magazines, where editors supervise what they cover and how much they write. In con-trast, a blog is a solo operation where the blogger alone determines all content. (Software makes this easy to do.) Green came to blogging from art journalism; he regularly contributes to *Fortune* magazine, *The New York Observer*, and *Bloomberg News*. He started *Modern Art Notes* in 2001, and it seems to be the most widely read art blog today.

Why blog? Says Green: "Many bloggers, myself included, have consciously rejected the 'traditional' art criticism model because it's confining and appropriate only for dino-media." Welcome to the twenty-first century.

ART *in the world*

VISITING IT

ART MUSEUMS CAN be mind-expanding or sleep-inducing, depending on how you approach them. It is a mistake to enter a museum with the belief that you should like everything you see—or even that you should see everything that is there. Without selective viewing, the visitor to a large museum is likely to come down with a severe case of museum exhaustion.

The English word museum comes from the Greek *mouseion,* "place of the muses." "Muse" indicates the spirit or power believed to be capable of inspiring and watching over poets, musicians, and other artists—or any source of inspiration. A museum is for musing, a place devoted to collecting, caring for, studying, and displaying objects of lasting value and interest.

Unfortunately, museum visitors are often overwhelmed by the many rooms full of art and background information. Some may feel that they should have an extensive knowledge of art history before they even enter a museum. Even the entrance to a museum can be a bit intimidating ("Step this way. Serious art. No smiling.") or it can be inviting and welcoming ("Come on in. Relax. Make yourself comfortable.").

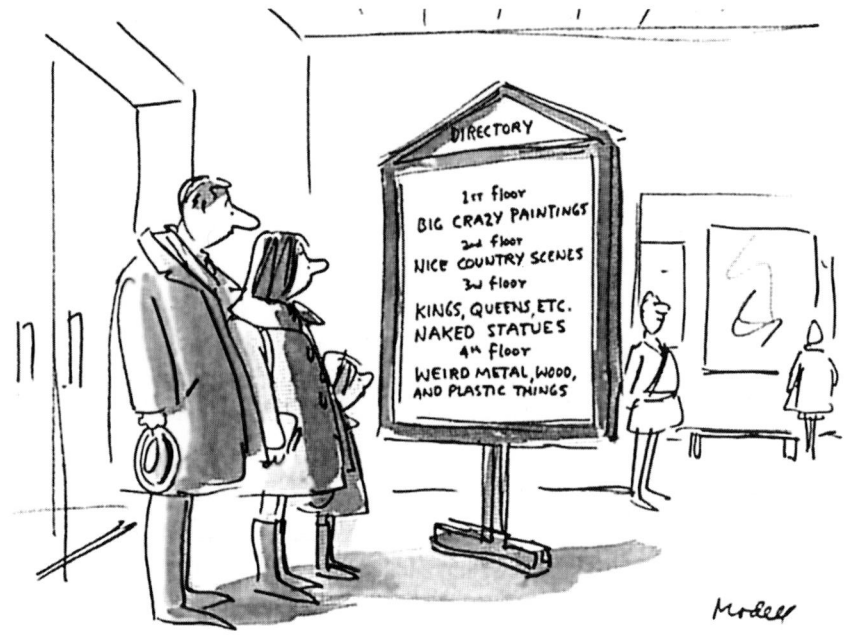

135   Frank Modell.
© The New Yorker Collection, 1983.

There is a way to enjoy an art museum without experiencing overload. If you were to go to a new restaurant and try to sample everything on the menu, you would probably get sick. In both restaurants and museums, selection is the key to a positive experience.

It makes sense to approach an art museum the way a seasoned traveler approaches a city for a first visit: Find out what there is to see. In the museum, inquire about the schedule of special shows, then see those exhibitions and outstanding works that interest you. Museums are in the process of rethinking their buildings and collections to meet the needs of changing populations and changing values. It is not unusual to find video exhibits, performances of all kinds, and film showings as part of regular museum programming.

If you are visiting without a specific exhibition in mind, follow your interests and instincts. Browsing can be highly rewarding. Zero in on what you feel are the highlights, savoring favorite works and unexpected discoveries.

The *Discovering Art CD* includes several hints and interactive exercises to help maximize the benefit from a museum visit, as well as links to several museum Web sites.

Don't stay too long in a museum. Take breaks. Perhaps there is a garden or cafe in which you can pause for a rest. The quality of your experience is not measured by the amount of time you spend in the galleries or how many works you see. The most rewarding experiences can come from finding something that "speaks" to you, then sitting and enjoying it in leisurely contemplation.

PART THREE

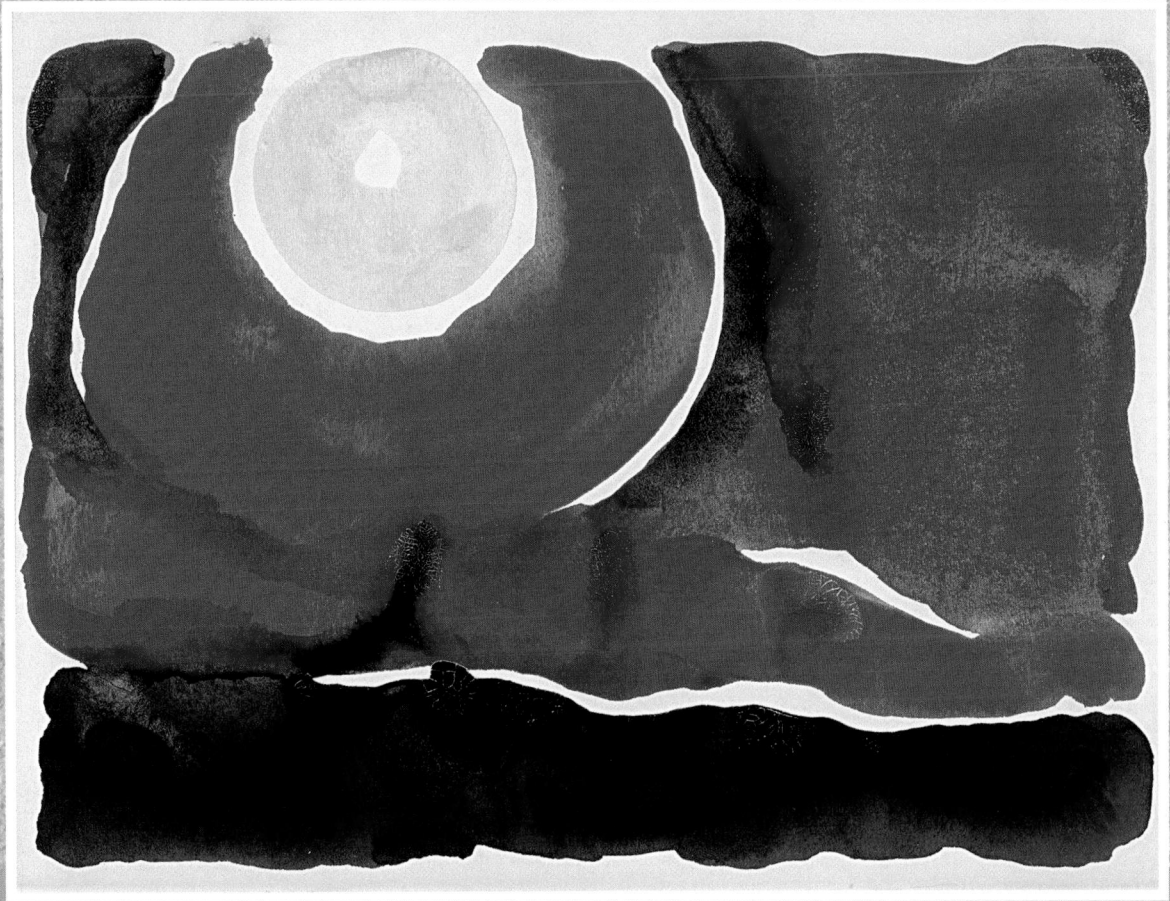

Georgia O'Keeffe.
EVENING STAR VI. 1917.
Watercolor on cream paper. 8⅞″ × 12″.

THE MEDIA OF ART

CONSIDER...

Have you ever said, I can't draw? Does not being able to draw mean you can't write your name or draw a map? What do people really mean when they say they can't draw?

In what ways does a sculpture of a human being differ from a painting of one?

Can exposure to television, with its immediacy and vivid action, dull one's response to paintings?

Does the camera ever lie?

Are new communications media such as the Internet, cell phones, and cable television bringing the world closer together? Are they building understanding between people of different cultures?

DRAWING

6

When my daughter was about seven years old, she asked me one day what I did at work. I told her that I worked at the college—that my job was to teach people to draw. She stared back at me, incredulous, and said, "You mean they forget?"

HOWARD IKEMOTO[1]

The desire to draw is as natural as the desire to talk. As children, we draw long before we learn to read and write. In fact, making letter forms is a kind of drawing—especially when we first learn to "write." Some of us continue to enjoy drawing; others return to drawing as adults. Those who no longer draw probably came to believe they did not draw well enough to suit themselves or others. Yet drawing is a learned process. It is a way of seeing and communicating, a way of paying attention.

In the most basic sense, to draw means to pull, push, or drag a marking tool across a surface to leave a line or mark. Most people working in the visual arts use drawing as a major tool for visual thinking—for recording and developing ideas.

Drawing is an immediate and accessible way to communicate through imagery. Through drawing we can share ideas, feelings, experiences, and imaginings. Sometimes a drawing does several of these things simultaneously.

When French sculptor Auguste Rodin saw a troupe of Cambodian folk dancers in 1906, he was so transfixed by their graceful movements that he

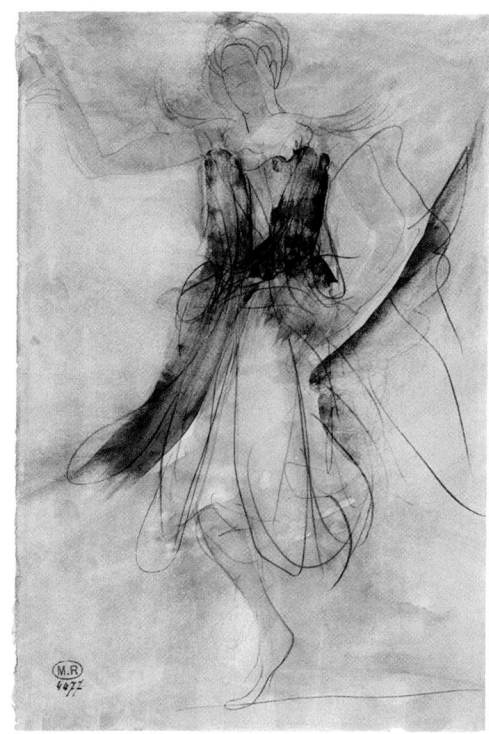

136 Auguste Rodin.
CAMBODIAN DANCER. 1906.
Graphite, watercolor, gouache, and crayon
on cream vellum paper. 11¾″ × 7⅞″.
Rodin Museum, Paris.

went to their rehearsals and made dozens of drawings. His **CAMBODIAN DANCER** is one of these, heightened with washes of watercolor and crayon. The drawing seems almost as spontaneous and fluid as the dancer's movements that inspired it.

Many people find it valuable to keep a sketchbook handy to serve as a visual diary, a place to develop and maintain drawing skills and to note whatever catches the eye or imagination. From sketchbook drawings, some ideas may develop and reach maturity as finished drawings or complete works in other media. Leonardo da Vinci kept many of his exploratory drawings and writings in notebooks. He drew this study of THREE SEATED FIGURES next to idea sketches for some mechanical devices.

Guillermo del Toro, director of *Hellboy, 3993*, and other films, keeps a SKETCHBOOK for jotting notes and ideas. The pages here show his musings about the desire for fame, meeting other directors, and sketches of some strange beings that found their way into his 2006 feature *Pan's Labyrinth*. (This film is discussed on page 160.)

A great deal of drawing is receptive; that is, we use it to attempt to capture the physical appearance of something before us. Many people use drawing in this way, as they take up a pencil or pen or chalk to render the fall of light on a jar, the leaves of a tree, arrangement of a landscape, the roundness of a body, or their own reflection in a mirror. This type of drawing can be a professional necessity for an artist, or recreation for the rest of us.

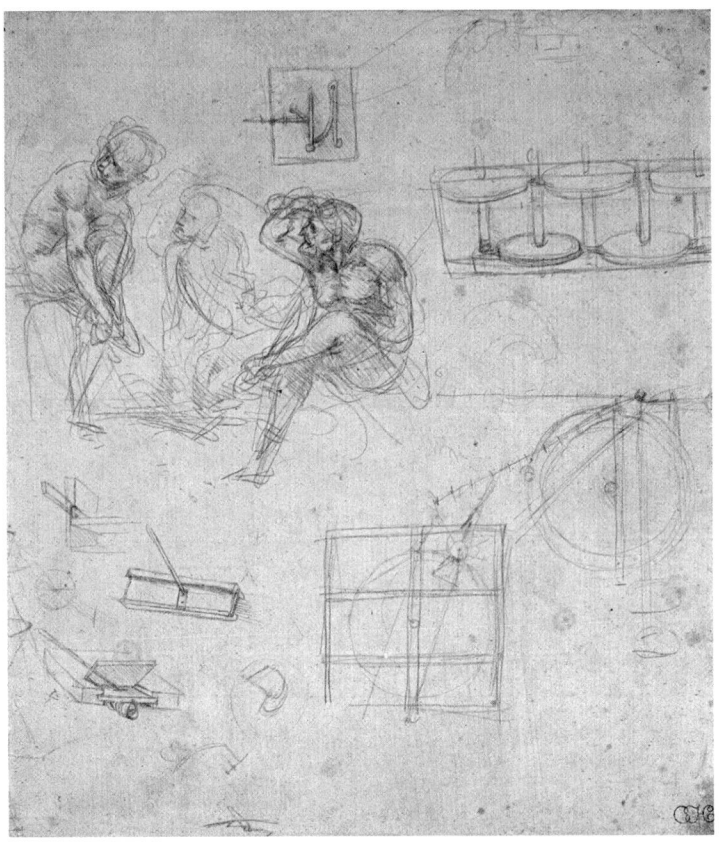

137 Leonardo da Vinci.
THREE SEATED FIGURES AND STUDIES OF MACHINERY. c. 1490.
Silver-point on very pale pink, prepared surface.
Ashmolean Museum, Oxford, England, U.K.

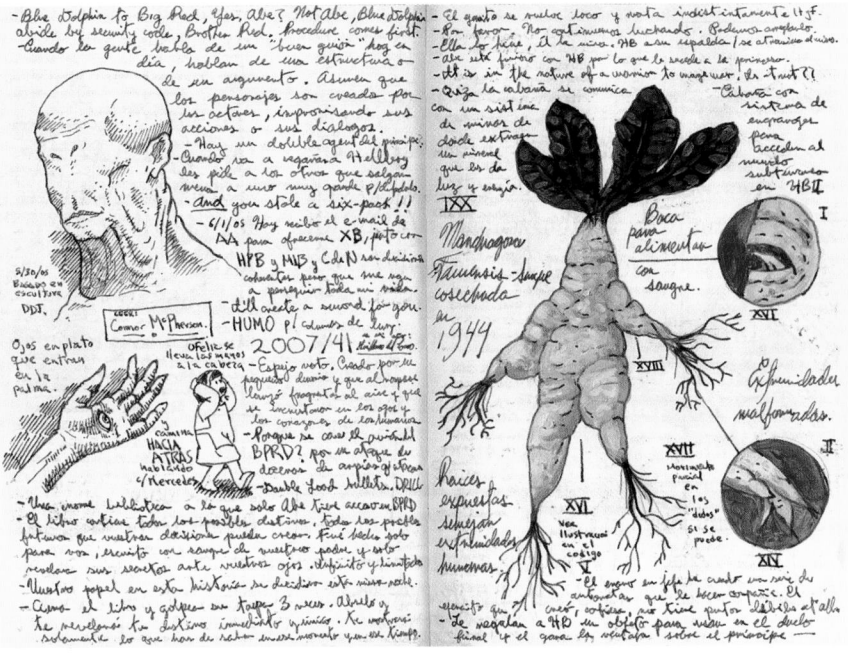

138 Guillermo del Toro.
Pages from SKETCHBOOK.
2006.
Photograph: Geoff Spear/courtesy of New Line Productions, Inc.

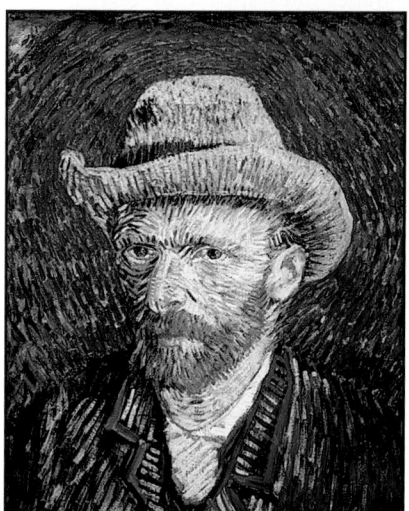

142 Vincent van Gogh.

ed SELF PORTRAIT WITH GRAY HAT. 1887.
Oil on canvas. 17¼″ × 14¾″.
Vincent van Gogh Foundation/Van Gogh Museum,
Amsterdam.

TODAY THE ART of Vincent van Gogh is internationally known and admired. It is hard to believe that van Gogh worked as an artist for only ten years and that during his lifetime his art was known only to a few. In fact, he sold only one painting.

Van Gogh was born in the Netherlands. His father was a minister, his grandfather a famous preacher; three uncles, and later his brother, were art dealers—a background that paved the way for Vincent's lifelong concern with both art and religion.

From age sixteen, he worked for a firm of art dealers, first in The Hague and later in London and Paris. During this period he began what was to become his famous correspondence with his brother Theo. It is primarily through these extraordinary letters (published in the book *Dear Theo*) that we have come to know van Gogh's short, intense, yet highly creative life.

After six years working for art dealers, he returned to the Netherlands to study theology. In 1878, at age twenty-five, he became a lay preacher among impoverished miners in Belgium. Although not successful at preaching, van Gogh was effective at nursing victims of mining disasters and disease. When his compassion spurred him to give most of his own clothes and other possessions to the poor, the missionary society that had hired him dismissed him for his literal interpretation of Christ's teachings.

Van Gogh remained in Belgium, living in acute poverty and spiritual turmoil until he decided to apply himself to becoming an artist. He made his commitment to art not because he possessed any obvious talent, but because he saw art as the means through which he could communicate with others. Although determined to be a painter, van Gogh believed that he had to master drawing before he allowed himself to use color. Miners and farm laborers were his first models. As he worked on developing his skill, Vincent—the name he used to sign his finished works—was supported by his brother Theo, who regularly sent money and provided encouragement through his letters.

Van Gogh studied briefly at the art academy in Antwerp, Belgium, but he was largely self-taught. In 1886 he joined his brother in Paris, where he met the leading French Impressionist and Post-Impressionist painters. Under their influence van Gogh's paintings, which had been limited to the somber tones of traditional Dutch painting, became much lighter and brighter in color (see his SELF PORTRAIT WITH GRAY HAT).

In 1888 he moved to southern France, where—in less than two years—he produced most of the paintings for which he is known. There, armed with the Impressionists' bright, free color, and inspired by the intense semitropical light, van Gogh took color even further. He developed a revolutionary approach to color based on the way colors and color combinations symbolize ideas and emotional content. His new understanding of expressive color led him to write that "the painter of the future will be a colorist such as has never existed."[4]

Van Gogh's use of pure colors and his bold strokes of thick paint created images of emotional intensity that had a great impact on artists—especially Expressionist painters—of the twentieth century. Before van Gogh, most Western painters used color to describe the appearance of their subjects. After van Gogh, painters began to realize that color could make visible feelings and states of mind.

From his teenage years, van Gogh's intense personality caused him to be rejected by the women with whom he fell in love, and later it drove away potential friends, such as Paul Gauguin. Such rejection contributed to several emotional breakdowns. Spells of fervent painting were interrupted by periods of illness and depression. Increasing illness led him voluntarily to enter a mental hospital for several months. After leaving the hospital he returned to Paris, then settled in a nearby town under the watchful eye of a doctor known to be a friend of artists. There, in a frenzy of creative productivity, he completed about seventy paintings in sixty-five days—the last two months of his fife. Van Gogh's loneliness and despair drove him to suicide at age thirty-seven.

An emphasis on the tragic aspects of van Gogh's now legendary life has produced a popular view of the man that tends to obscure his great contribution to art. In spite of his difficulties, van Gogh produced almost two thousand works of art within a mere ten years. Although most of his contemporaries could not see the value of his art, his paintings and drawings are displayed today in major museums worldwide, and exhibitions of his works attract record crowds.

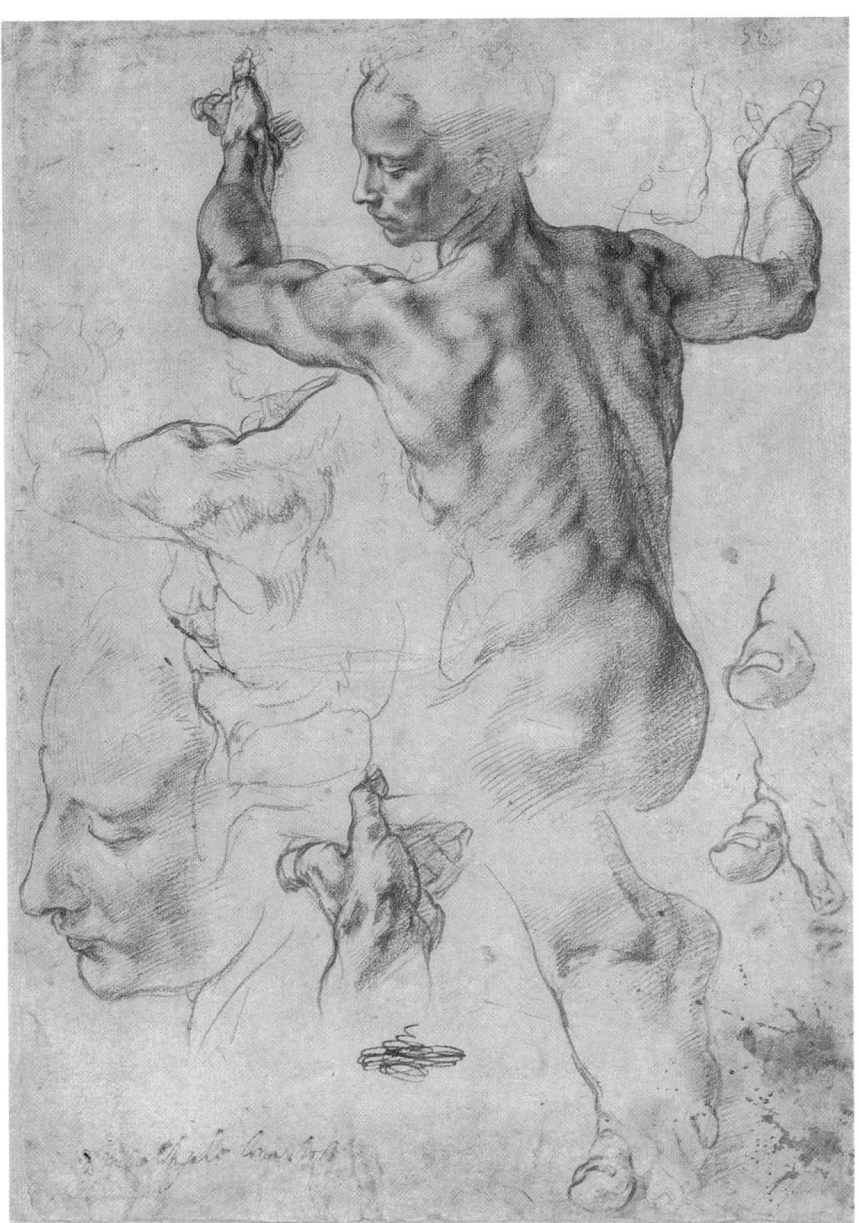

143 Michelangelo Buonarotti.
Studies for the LIBYAN SIBYL on the
Sistine Chapel ceiling. c. 1510.
Red chalk on paper. 11⅜″ × 8⅞₁₆″.
The Metropolitan Museum of Art, New York.
Purchase, Joseph Pulitzer Bequest, 1924 (24.197.2).
Photograph: © 1995 The Metropolitan Museum of Art.

PURPOSES OF DRAWING

A drawing can function in three ways:

- as a notation, sketch, or record of something seen, remembered, or imagined
- as a study or preparation for another, usually larger and more complex work such as a sculpture, a building, a film, a painting—or another drawing
- as an end in itself, a complete work of art

Michelangelo made detailed studies of the LIBYAN SIBYL for his finished painting of the figure on the ceiling of the Sistine Chapel.

This magnificent drawing of a mythical female figure was drawn from a male model. The studies are a record of search and discovery as Michelangelo carefully drew what he observed. His knowledge of anatomy helped him to define each muscle. The flow between the head, shoulders, and arms of the figure is based on Michelangelo's feeling for visual

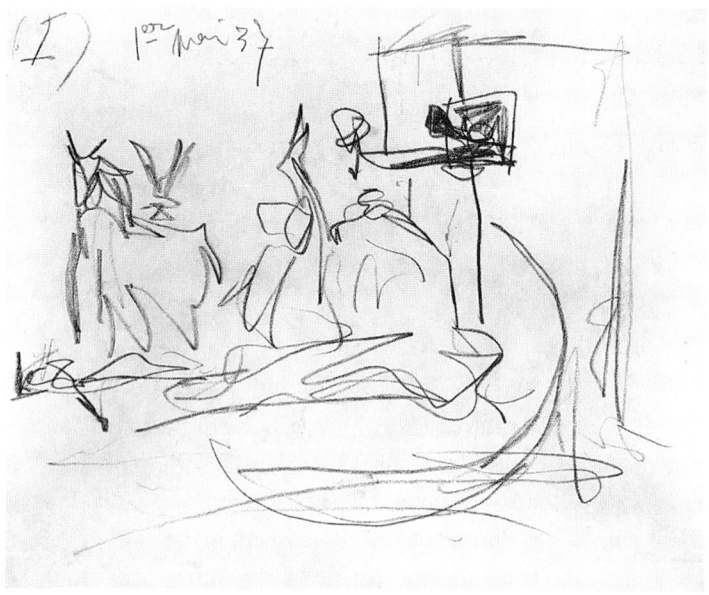

144 Pablo Picasso.
FIRST COMPOSITION STUDY FOR GUERNICA. May 1, 1937.
Pencil on blue paper. 8¼″ × 10⅝″.
Museo Nacional Centro de Arte Reina Sofía.
© 2002 Estate of Pablo Picasso/Artists Rights Society (ARS), NY.

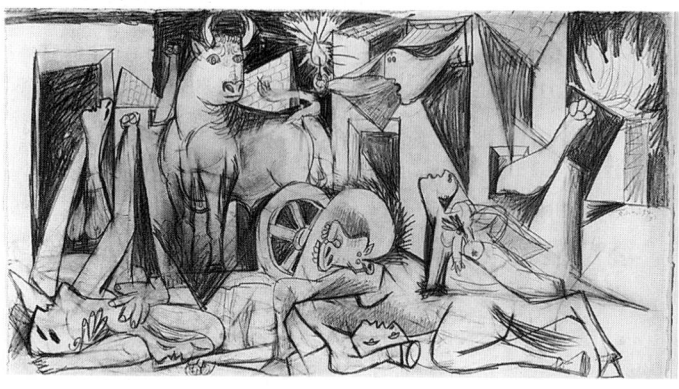

145 Pablo Picasso.
COMPOSITION STUDY FOR GUERNICA. May 9, 1937.
Pencil on white paper. 9½″ × 17⅞″.
Museo Nacional Centro de Arte Reina Sofía.
© 2002 Estate of Pablo Picasso/Artists Rights Society (ARS), NY.

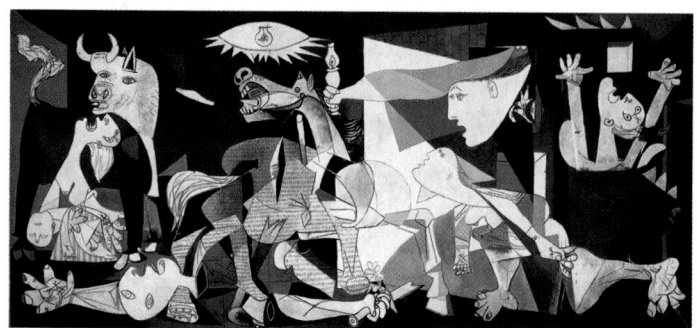

continuity as well as his attention to detail. The parts of the figure that he felt needed further study he drew repeatedly. To achieve the dark reds, Michelangelo evidently licked the point of the chalk.

A simple, tiny sketch, quickly done, can be the starting point for a far larger and more complex work. In such drawings an artist can work out problems of overall design or concentrate on small details. Picasso did many studies in preparation for a major painting, GUERNICA—a huge work measuring more than 11 feet high by 25 feet long (a larger reproduction appears on page 410). Forty-five of Picasso's studies are preserved; nearly all are dated.

The first drawing for GUERNICA shows what can be identified in later stages as a woman with a lamp, apparently an important symbol to Picasso. The woman leans out of a house in the upper right. On the left appears a bull with a bird on its back. Both the bull and the woman with the lamp are major elements in the final painting. The first drawing was probably completed in a few seconds, yet its quick gestural lines contain the essence of the large, complex painting.

Although artists do not generally consider their preliminary sketches as finished pieces, studies by leading artists are often treasured both for their intrinsic beauty and for what they reveal about the creative process. Picasso recognized the importance of documenting the creative process from initial idea to finished painting:

It would be very interesting to preserve photographically, not the stages, but the metamorphoses of a picture. Possibly one might then discover the path followed by the brain in materializing a dream. But there is one very odd thing to notice, that basically a picture doesn't change, that the first "vision" remains almost intact, in spite of appearances.[5]

146 Pablo Picasso.

GUERNICA. 1937.
Oil on canvas. 11′5½″ × 25′5¼″.
Museo Nacional Centro de Arte Reina Sofía, Madrid.
© John Bigelow Taylor/Art Resource NY.
© 2002 Estate of Pablo Picasso/Artists Rights Society (ARS), NY.

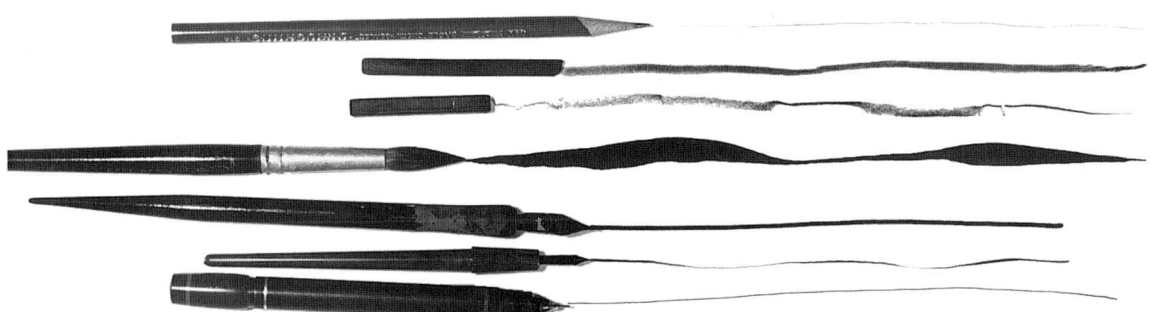

147 DRAWING TOOLS AND THEIR CHARACTERISTIC LINES.

Another type of preparatory drawing is the cartoon. The original meaning of cartoon, still used by art professionals, is a full-sized drawing made as a guide for a large work in another medium, particularly a fresco painting, mosaic, or tapestry.

In today's common usage, the word *cartoon* refers to a narrative drawing emphasizing humorous or satirical content. Cartoons and comics are among the most widely enjoyed drawings, and will be discussed later in this chapter.

Each drawing tool and each type of paper has its own characteristics. The interaction between these materials and the technique of the artist determines the nature of the resulting drawing. The illustration DRAWING TOOLS shows the different qualities of marks made by common drawing tools.

TYPES OF HATCHING shows how values can be built up with parallel lines, called *hatching,* or with *cross-hatching* of various types. Charles White used cross-hatched ink lines in PREACHER to build up the figure's mass and gesture in a forceful manner.

148 TYPES OF HATCHING.

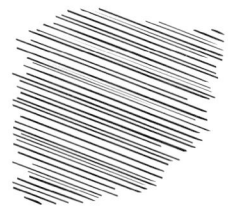 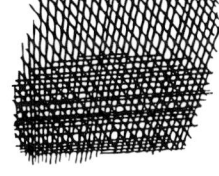 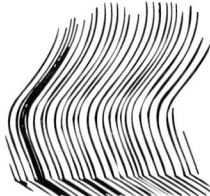

a. Hatching.   b. Cross-hatching.   c. Contour hatching.

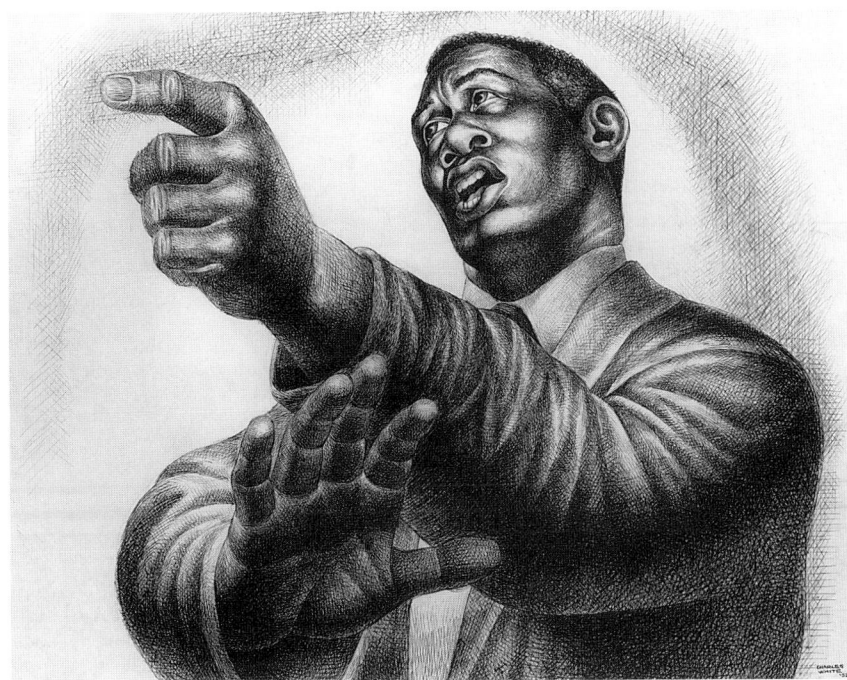

149   Charles White.
PREACHER. 1952.
Ink on cardboard.
21³⁄₈″ × 29³⁄₈″.
Collection of Whitney Museum of
American Art, New York.
Purchase. 52.25.
Photograph: Geoffrey Clements, NY.
© 2001: Whitney Museum of
American Art.

Through the use of *contour hatching*, White gave the figure a feeling of sculptural mass. The foreshortened right hand and forearm add to the drawing's dramatic impact.

DRY MEDIA

Dry drawing media include pencil, charcoal, conté crayon, and pastel. Drawing pencils include those made of graphite varying from soft (dark) to hard (light) and high-quality colored pencils in a wide range of colors.

Darkness and line quality are determined both by the degree of hardness of the pencil and by the texture of the surface to which it is applied. Paper with some *tooth* or surface grain receives pencil marks more readily than paper that is smooth. Pencil lines can vary in width or length, can be made by using the side of the pencil point in broad

strokes, and can be repeated as hatching. A considerable range of values can be produced by varying the pressure on a medium-soft drawing pencil.

A rich variety of values and inventive shapes made with light and dark grades of drawing pencils fills Judith Murray's drawing OBSIDIAN.

The sticks of charcoal used today are similar to those used by prehistoric peoples to draw on cave walls. With charcoal, dark passages can be drawn quickly. The various hard-to-soft grades now available provide a flexible medium for both beginning and advanced artists. Because not all charcoal particles bind to the surface of the paper, charcoal is easy to smudge, blur, or erase. This quality is both an advantage and a drawback: it enables quick changes, but finished works can easily smear. A completed charcoal drawing may be set or "fixed" with a thin varnish called *fixative*, which is sprayed over it to help bind the charcoal to the paper. Charcoal produces a wide range of light to dark values from soft grays to deep velvety blacks.

Georgia O'Keeffe took full advantage of charcoal in her drawing of a BANANA FLOWER. The potential for showing gradations of shade in charcoal provided her with the means to draw with powerful precision. Here she dramatized the structure of her subject as a monumental sculptural mass. Although O'Keeffe is best known for her colorful paintings of enlarged close-up views of flowers (see page 36), in this drawing she achieved a comparable impact with just black and white.

Conté crayon is a semi-hard chalk with enough oil in the binder to cause it to adhere to smooth paper. It can produce varied lines or broad strokes that are relatively resistant to smudging. Wax-based crayons, such as those given to children, are avoided by serious artists; they lack flexibility, and most fade over time. Because the strokes do not blend easily, it is difficult to obtain bright color mixtures with wax crayons.

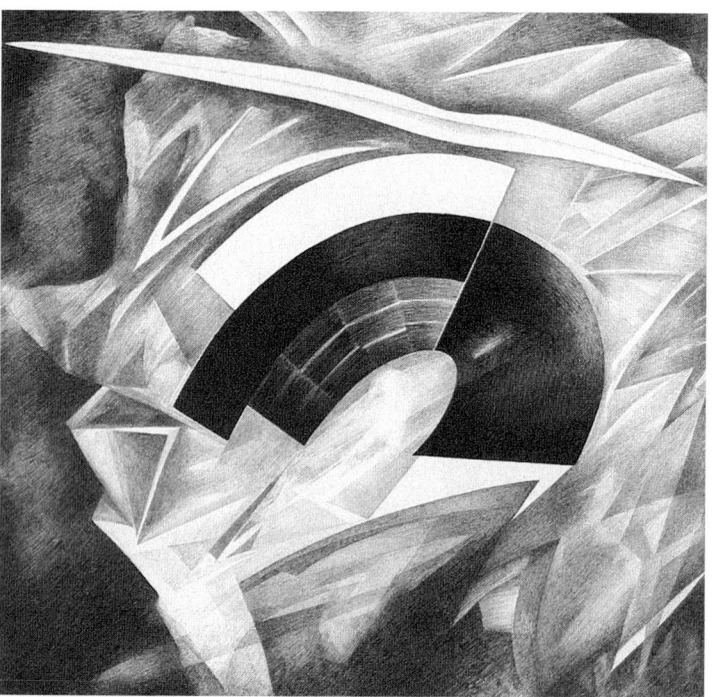

150 Judith Murray.
OBSIDIAN. 1988.
Pencil on arches paper. 17½″ × 19¼″.
Courtesy of the artist. Collection of Howard and Terry S. Walters, Summit, NJ.

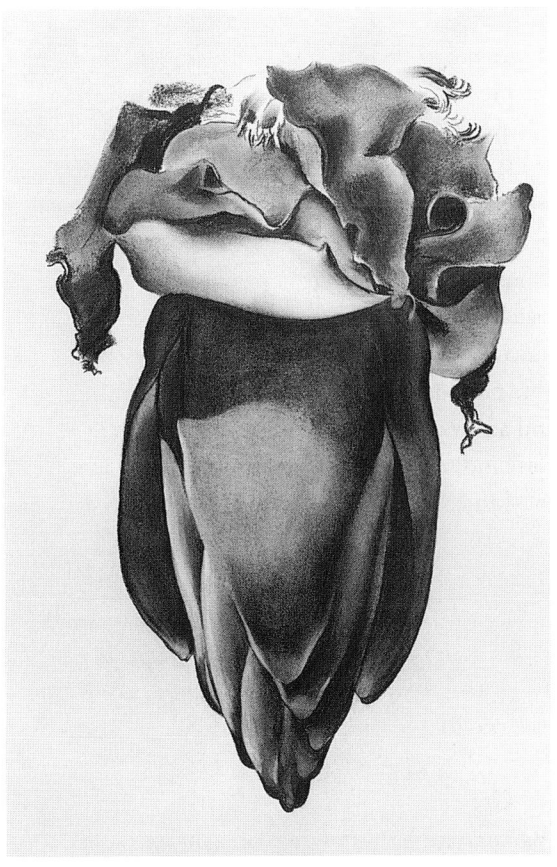

151 Georgia O'Keeffe.
BANANA FLOWER. 1933.
Charcoal and black chalk on paper. 21¾″ × 14¾″.
The Museum of Modern Art, NY/Licensed by Scala-Art Resource, NY. Given
anonymously (by exchange). Photograph © 2002 Museum of Modern Art, NY.
© 2002 The Georgia O'Keeffe Foundation/Artists Rights Society (ARS), NY.

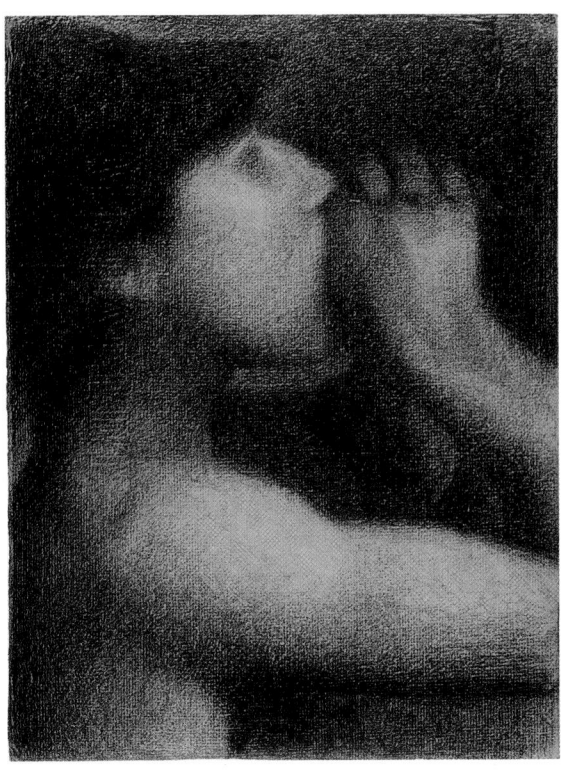

152 Georges Seurat.
L'ECHO, Study for UNE BAIGNADE, ASNIERES.
1882–1891.
Black conté crayon. 12¹⁵/₁₆″ × 9⁷/₁₆″.
Yale University Art Gallery, New Haven. Bequest of Edith Malvina K. Wetmore.
1966.80.11.

Georges Seurat used conté crayon to build up the illusion of three-dimensional form through value gradations (*chiaroscuro*) in his drawing L'ECHO. Seurat actually drew a multitude of lines; yet in the final drawing the individual lines are obscured by the total effect of finely textured light and dark areas. He selected conté crayon on rough paper as a means of concentrating on basic forms and on the interplay of light and shadow.

Natural chalks of red, white, and black have been used for drawing since ancient times. Pastes, produced since the seventeenth century, have characteristics similar to those of natural chalk. They have a freshness and purity of color because they are comprised mostly of pigment, with very little binding material. Because no drying is needed, there is no change in color, as occurs in some paints when they dry. Soft pastels do not allow for much detail—they force the user to work boldly. Blending of strokes with fingers or a paper stump made for the purpose produces a soft blur that lightly mixes the colors. Pastels yield the most exciting results when not over-worked.

Venetian portraitist Rosalba Carriera made dozens of works with pastels in the early eighteenth century. Her PORTRAIT OF A GIRL WITH A BUSSOLÀ shows her sensitivity to the medium. The hard, fine-grained pastels in common use at that time give the finished work a smooth surface that makes possible fine color shadings. Because of the artist's light, deft touch with short strokes of the pastel, the work resembles an oil painting in its appearance, an effect promoted by the very smooth paper. Carriera was in demand to make pastel portraits throughout Germany, France, and North Italy until poor eyesight forced her retirement in 1746.

French artist Edgar Degas shifted from oil painting to pastels in his later years, and occasionally he combined the two. He took advantage of the rich strokes of color and subtle blends possible with pastel. Although carefully constructed, his compositions look like casual, fleeting glimpses of everyday life. In LE PETIT DEJEUNER APRES LE BAIN, bold contours give a sense of movement to the whole design.

153 Rosalba Carriera.
PORTRAIT OF A GIRL WITH A BUSSOLÀ. 1725–1730.
Pastel on paper. 13⅜″ × 10½″.
Venice, Galleria dell'Accademia. Cat. 444.
Photograph: Cameraphoto/Art Resource, NY.

154 Edgar Degas.
LE PETIT DEJEUNER APRES LE BAIN
(JEUNE FEMME S'ESSUYANT). c. 1894.
Pastel on paper. 39¼″ × 23½″.
© 2002. Courtesy Christie's Images Limited, NY.

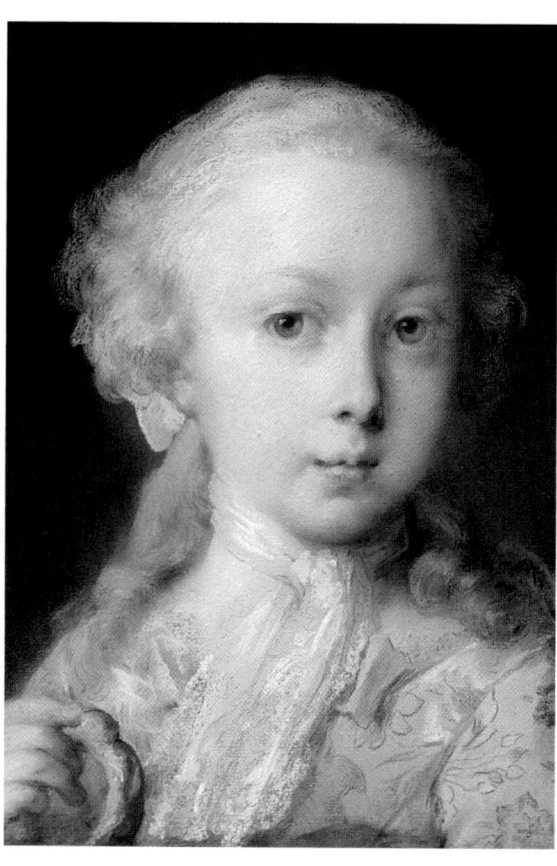

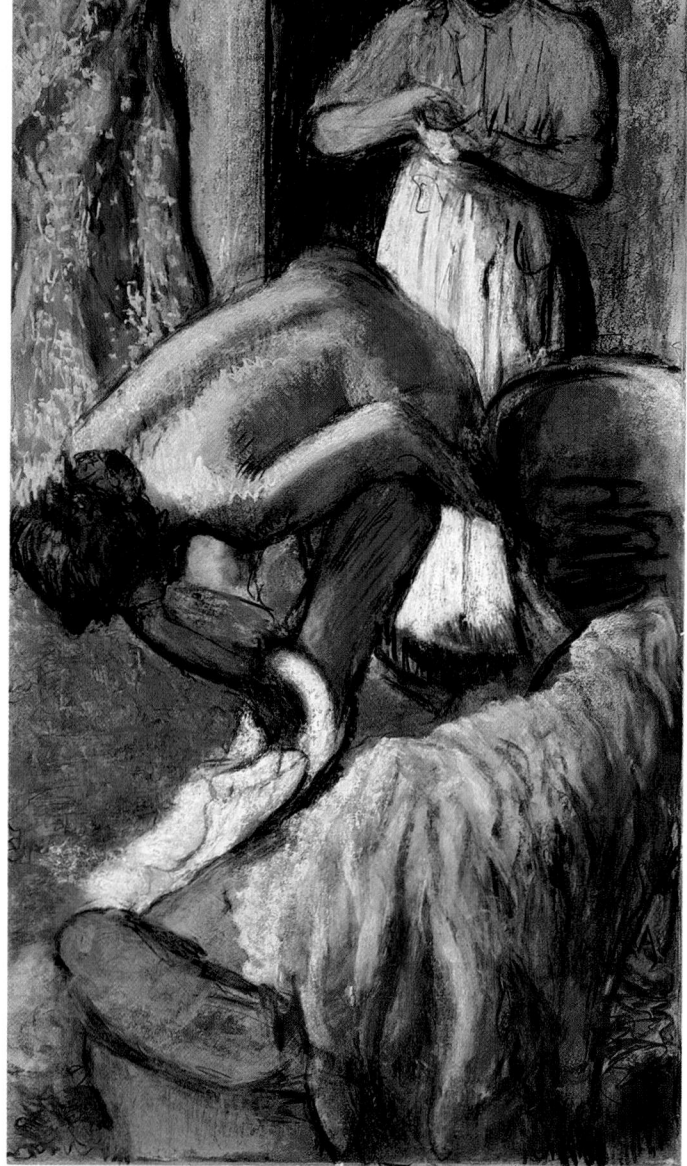

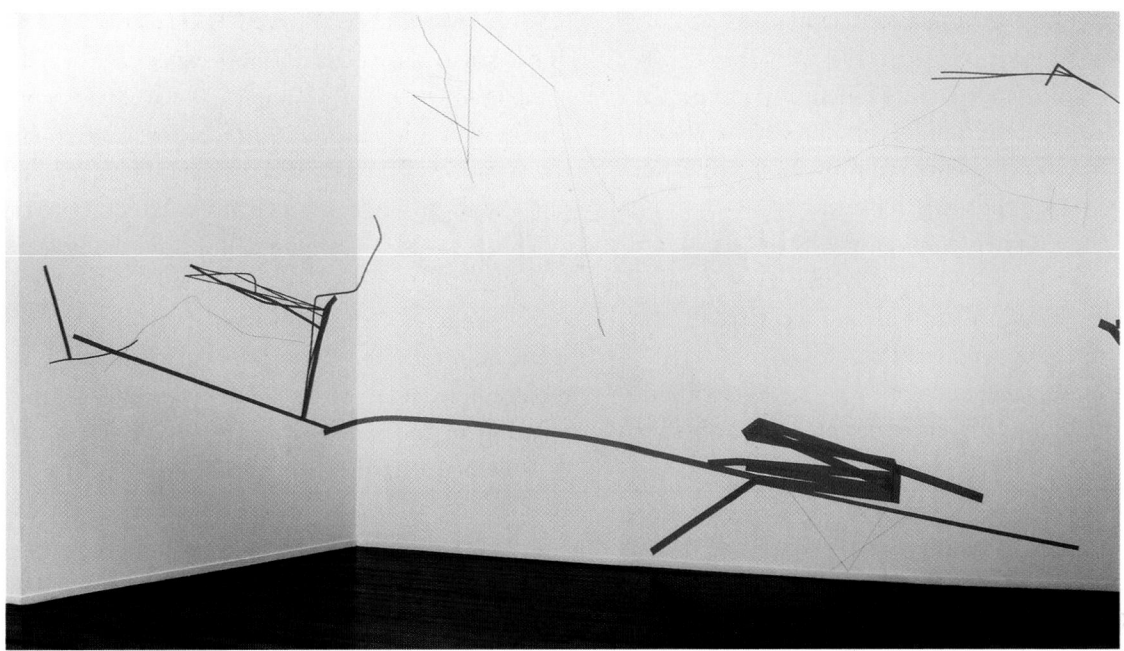

160 Christine Hiebert.
UNTITLED. 2004.
Installation at Margarete Roeder Gallery, New York.
Blue adhesive tape on wall; full drawing: running wall length 36′7″, wall height 11′6″.
Courtesy of the artist.

Christine Hiebert makes lines directly on walls with the blue tape that painters use to mask negative spaces. In works that she creates specifically for each exhibition, her lines affect our perception of the space. In her UNTITLED work from 2004, for example, she interrupted the clean horizontals and verticals of a gallery with diagonals of varying thickness. Her lines resemble drawn lines, but in fact she has "drawn" the tape across the walls. When the show is over, the tape comes off without leaving a trace.

Barry McGee takes drawing out of the realm of "fine art" and brings it to everyone's level. He made his 2006 UNTITLED work using pens bought at a drug store, "The same pens everyone has on the dashboard of their cars or in the office," he said. The four heads resemble doodles that we might make while talking on the phone or waiting in line. He used paper that he found in a dumpster, and a frame bought at a thrift store. He creates these works in bursts of 20 to 30 and then exhibits them in overlapping constellations, casually nailed to the

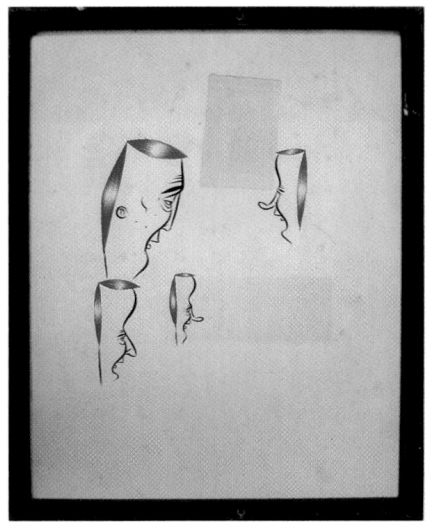

161 Barry McGee.
UNTITLED. 2006.
Ink on found paper in found frame. 10¾″ × 8¾″.
Gallery Paule Anglim, San Francisco.

wall. The work thus embodies an unpretentious "street art" style similar to the graffiti that he also makes. We will consider works by other street artists in Chapter 25.

PAINTING

For many people in the Western world, the word art means painting. The long, rich history of painting, the strong appeal of color, and the endless image-making possibilities explain painting's popularity.

Drawing and painting are related, overlapping processes. Paintings tend to be larger, more formal, more colorful, and usually take more time to complete than drawings—but there are many exceptions. There is no distinct separation between painting and drawing.

Painting is often drawing with paint. In Gerhard Richter's ABSTRACT PAINTING, the medium, paint, and the process of its application are a major part of the message. Richter's invented landscape suggests rugged forms in the foreground and an open, distant sky. Large brush strokes of thickly applied oil paint contrast with the smooth gradations of paint in the sky area.

The people who made the earliest cave paintings used natural pigments obtained from plants and nearby deposits of minerals and clays. Pigments used in cave paintings at Pont d'Arc, France—including blacks from charred woods and earth colors—have lasted more than 30,000 years.

By Rembrandt's time, the seventeenth century, painters or their assistants mixed finely ground pigments with oil by hand until the paint reached a desirable fineness and consistency. Today high-quality paints are conveniently packaged in tubes or jars, ready for immediate use.

Paints consist of three components: pigment, binder, and vehicle. The pigment provides color; the binder mixes with the pigment to hold the pigment particles together and to attach the pigment to the surface; and the vehicle spreads the pigment. With oil paints, linseed oil is the binder and turpentine (or its substitute) is the vehicle. With traditional tempera, egg yolk is the binder and water is the vehicle.

Powdered coloring agents called pigments have long been derived from plant, animal, and mineral sources. In the nineteenth and twentieth centuries, major advances in the chemical industry made it possible to produce synthetic pigments that extend the available range of colors. Since then, the durability of both natural and synthetic pigments has also improved. Most of the same pigments are used in manufacturing both the various paint media and the dry drawing media, such as colored pencils and pastels.

In the broad context of the visual arts, medium means both a material and its accompanying technique. In the context of painting, the word *medium* can also refer to the vehicle in which pigment is suspended in order to apply it.

Paints are usually applied to a flat support, such as stretched canvas for oils or paper for watercolors.

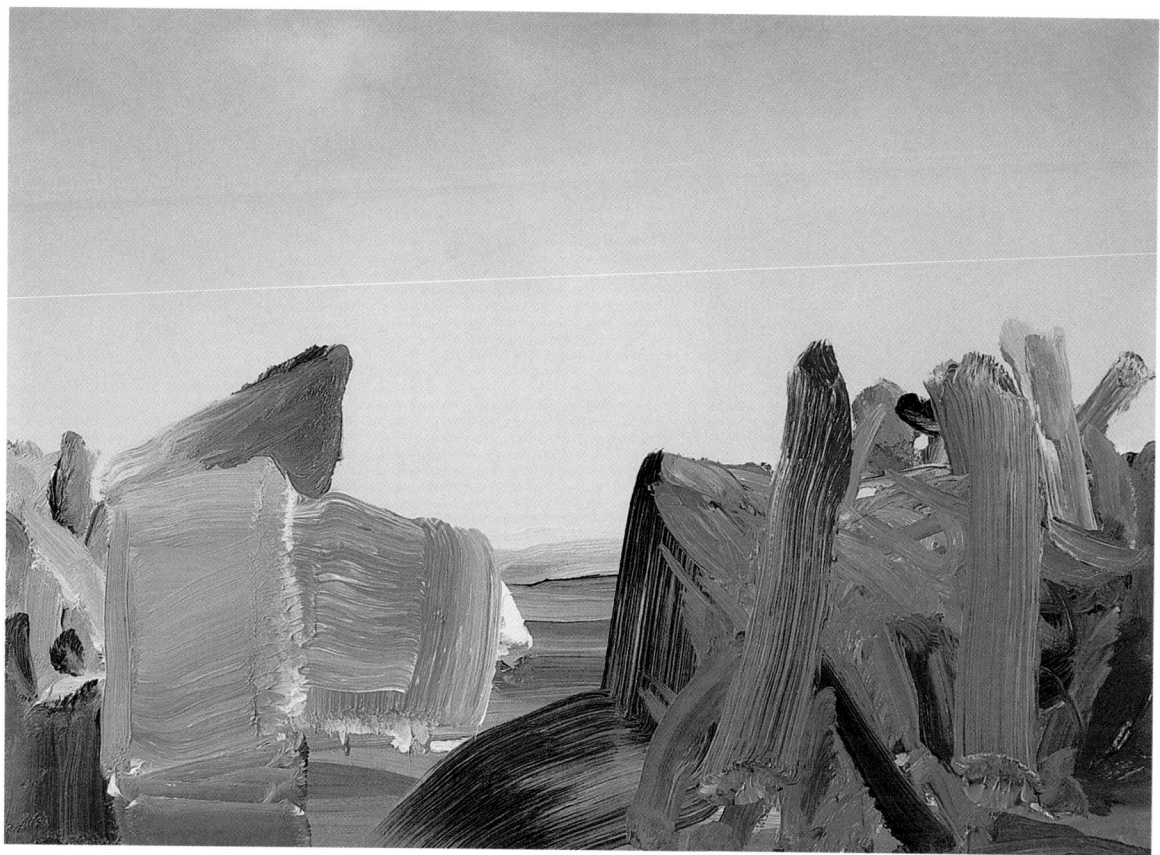

162 Gerhard Richter.
ABSTRACT PAINTING (551–4). 1984.
Oil on canvas. 17″ × 23⅝″.
Marian Goodman Gallery, NY.
© Gerhard Richter.

To achieve a ground (the prepared surface to which the paint is applied), the surface of the support (usually canvas) is prepared by sizing or priming, or both. Because supports are often too absorbent to permit controlled application of paint, a size, or sealer, is usually applied to lessen absorbency and fill in the pores of the material. For oil painting in particular, sizing is needed on canvas and paper to protect them from disintegrating from the drying action of linseed oil in oil paint. To complete the surface preparation for painting, an opaque primer, or ground, usually white, is often applied after or instead of sizing. Sizing and priming are unnecessary for watercolors; a paper surface provides both the support and the ground.

A student or beginning artist will want to experiment with the various types of paint available, learning firsthand the possibilities of each paint medium. Watercolor, tempera, oils, and synthetic or acrylic paints are among today's choices, but for the last five hundred years, oil paint has been the favorite medium of most Western painters. In recent years artists have begun to use synthetic (usually acrylic) paints for spraying, pouring, dripping, and other innovative methods of application. Each type of paint has unique advantages and disadvantages.

WATERCOLOR

Watercolor paintings are made by applying pigments suspended in a solution of water and gum arabic (a resin from the acacia tree) to white paper. Rag paper (made from cotton rag) is the preferred support because of its superior absorbency and

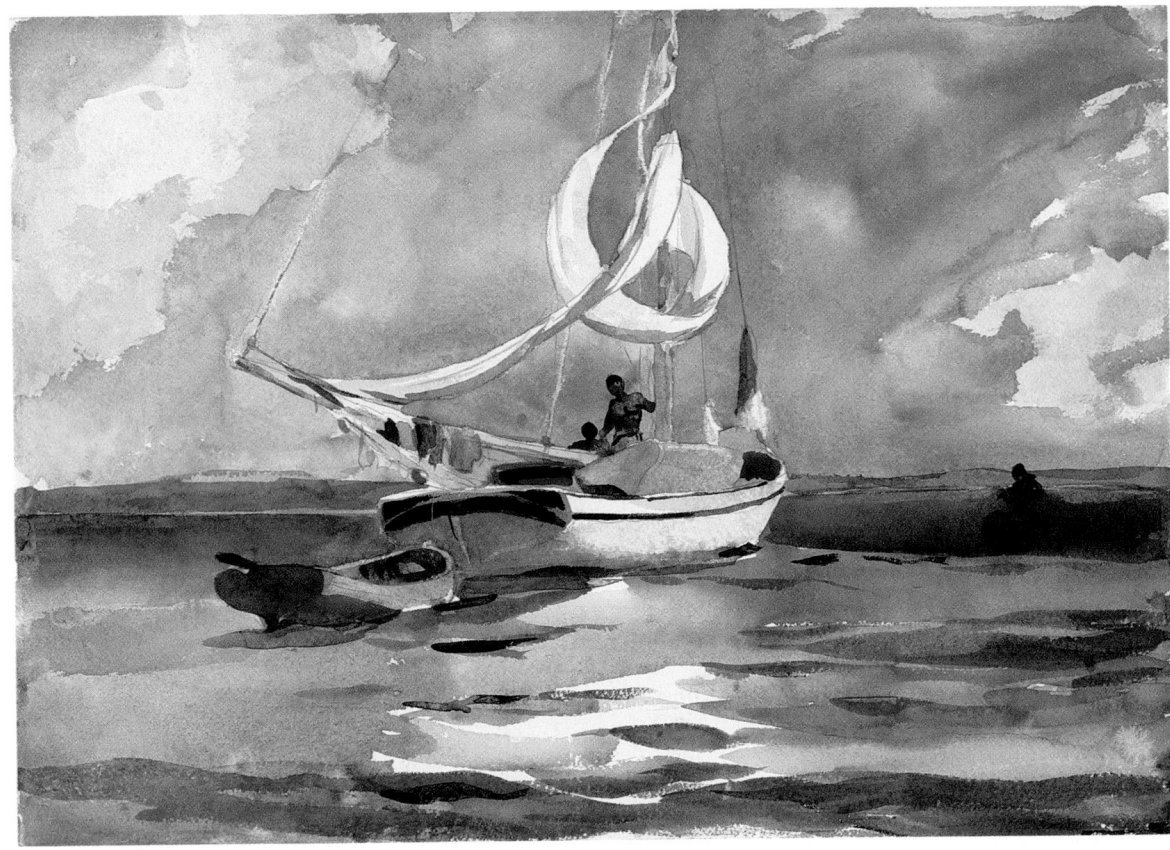

163　Winslow Homer.
SLOOP, NASSAU. 1899.
Watercolor and graphite on off-white wove paper. 14⅞″ × 21⁷⁄₁₆″.
The Metropolitan Museum of Art, NY. Lent by the Republic of Italy. L. 2006.10.
Image copyright: © The Metropolitan Museum of Art.

long-lasting qualities. Blocks of paint available in metal or plastic boxes are modern versions of the dried blocks of watercolor used for thousands of years. Professional artists use high-quality pigments sold in tubes.

Watercolor is basically a staining technique. The paint is applied in thin, translucent washes that allow light to pass through the layers of color and to reflect back from the white paper. Highlights are obtained by leaving areas of white paper unpainted. Opaque (nontranslucent) watercolor is sometimes added for detail. Watercolors are well suited to spontaneous as well as carefully planned applications. Despite the simple materials involved, watercolor is a demanding medium because it does not permit easy changes or corrections. If you overwork a watercolor, you lose its characteristic freshness.

Watercolor's fluid spontaneity makes it a favorite medium for painters who want to catch quick impressions outdoors. The translucent quality of watercolor washes particularly suits depictions of water, atmosphere, light, and weather.

American artist and illustrator Winslow Homer was one of the best watercolorists. In SLOOP, NASSAU, Homer used the bright whiteness of the bare paper to form the highlights of ocean waves, boat, and sails. From light pencil lines to finished painting, his whole process is visible. Homer captured the mood of weather—in this case, the particular qualities of light and color in the calm just before a storm. For Homer, a keen observer of nature, a quick impression made with watercolor was visually stronger than a painting filled with carefully rendered details.

Homer's spontaneous technique was well suited to watercolor; because it dries so quickly, watercolor does not allow for easy changes if the artist makes a mistake or decides to alter the composition.

Opaque watercolor (also called gouache) has been widely used for centuries. It was common in book illustration during the European Middle Ages, and also in traditional Persian art (see Chapter 18 for an example). Gouache is like watercolor except that the medium includes small amounts of chalk powder. It is popular in our times with designers and illustrators because of its ease of use and low cost. Jacob Lawrence used gouache to good advantage in his work GOING HOME (see page 74). Here we see the typical opaque appearance of the colors. The speed of application of gouache also helps to suggest the rapid movements of the figures in the work.

In traditional Chinese watercolor technique, the artist employs water-based black ink as well as color, and often uses the ink without color. The Chinese regard painting as descended from the art of calligraphy, which is also done with black ink. In Asia, black ink painting is a fully developed art form, accorded at least as much honor as painting with color.

We see excellent use of ink in LANDSCAPE by Qi Baishi. The artist used a variety of techniques. At the top of the mountain is a spot of dark black. The rest of this landmass is composed of brush strokes of varying density. Some strokes show a brush laden with dark ink; in others, the brush is relatively dry. At the base of the mountain, a layer of mist is suggested with lateral strokes of very light wash. The grasses below are also suggested with deftly varying strokes of ink. The artist included a little green color in both the grasses and the mountain, and he finished the work with two lines of calligraphy in different writing styles. Despite the obvious level of skill and care in the composition, the painting shows great freshness, as if it were painted in a single brief sitting. This work demonstrates mastery of a variety of brush strokes and control of ink in a wide range of tones, qualities admired in traditional Chinese painting.

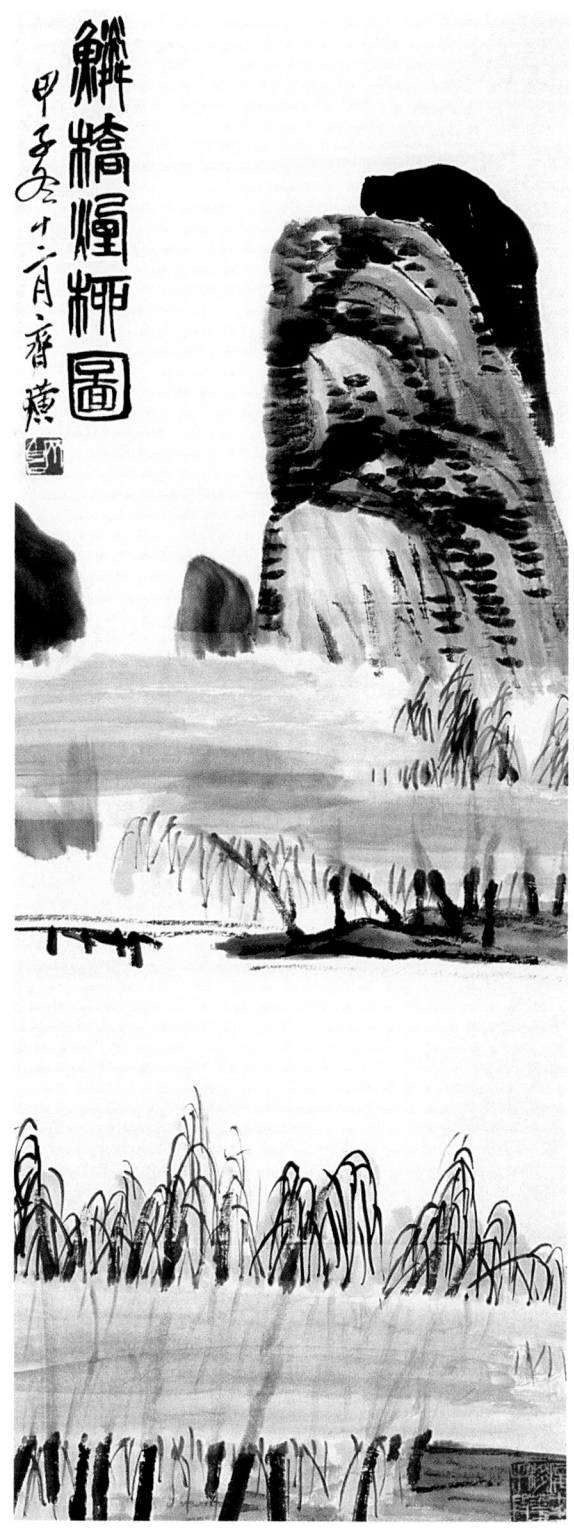

164   Qi Baishi.
LANDSCAPE. 1924.
Hanging scroll, ink and colors on paper. 40⅜" × 15⅜".
China National Art Gallery, Beijing. China Stock.

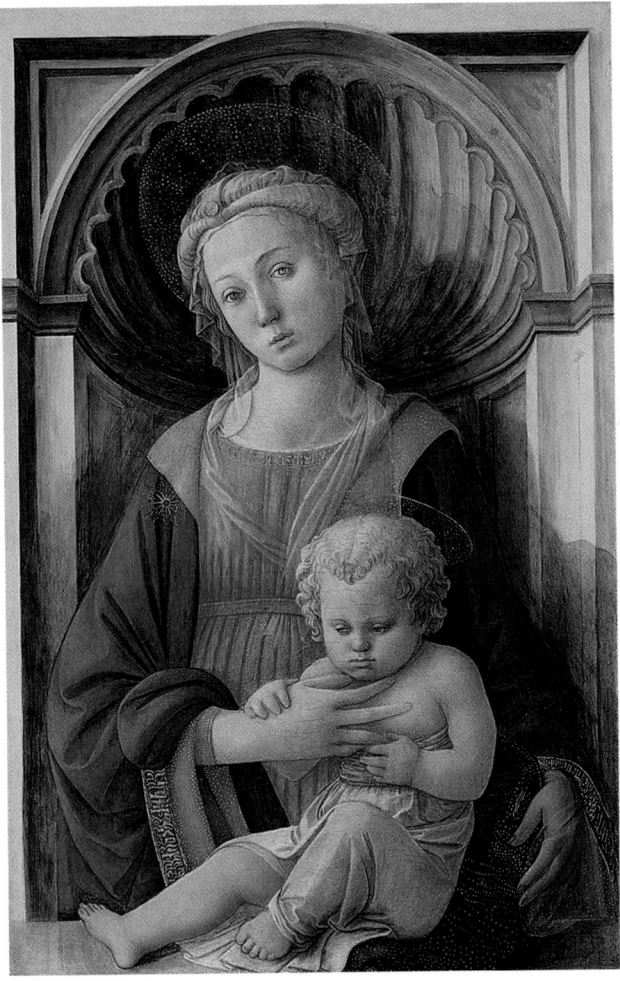

165 Fra Filippo Lippi.
MADONNA AND CHILD. c. 1440–1445.
Tempera on panel. 31⅜" × 20⅛".
National Gallery of Art, Washington, D.C. Samuel H. Kress Collection.
Photograph: © 2001 Board of Trustees, National Gallery of Art, Washington, D.C.
1939.1.290. (401)/PA.

TEMPERA

Tempera was used by the ancient Egyptians, Greeks, and Romans. Artists perfected it during the Middle Ages, when it was used for small paintings on wood panels. Since ancient times the principal tempera medium has been egg tempera, in which egg yolk, or occasionally egg white, is the binder. Today the word *tempera* is sometimes used for the water-based paints such as poster paints or paints with binders of glue or casein.

Egg tempera has a luminous, slightly matte (not shiny) surface when dry. Its clear, brilliant quality results from painting on a ground of very white gesso. Gesso, a preparation of chalk or plaster of Paris and glue, is applied to a support as a ground for tempera and oil paintings.

Egg tempera is good for achieving sharp lines and precise details, and it does not darken with age. However, its colors change during drying, and blending and reworking are difficult because tempera dries rapidly. Traditional tempera painting requires complete preliminary drawing and pale underpainting because of its translucency and the difficulty in making changes. Overpainting consists of applying layers of translucent paint in small, careful strokes. Because tempera lacks flexibility, movement of the support may cause the gesso and pigment to crack. A rigid support, such as a wood panel, is required.

In MADONNA AND CHILD, Fra Filippo Lippi methodically built up thin layers of color, creating a smooth, almost luminous surface. Tempera is well suited for depicting translucencies such as those he created in the halo and the sheer neck scarf. His naturalistic yet poetic portrayal brought a worldly dimension to religious subject matter.

OIL

In Western art, oil paint has been a favorite medium for five centuries. Pigments mixed with various vegetable oils, such as linseed, walnut, and poppyseed, were used in the Middle Ages for decorative purposes, but not until the fifteenth century did Flemish painters fully develop the use of paint made with linseed oil pressed from the seeds of the flax plant. In this early period, artists applied oil paint to wood panels covered with smooth layers of gesso, as in the older tradition of tempera painting. (The *Discovering Art* CD demonstrates how oil paint is made by mixing pigment, binder, and vehicle.)

The brothers Hubert and Jan van Eyck are credited with developing oil painting techniques and bringing them to their first perfection. They achieved glowing, jewel-like surfaces that remain amazingly fresh to the present day.

166 Jan van Eyck.
MADONNA AND CHILD WITH THE CHANCELLOR ROLIN. c. 1433–1434.
Oil and tempera on panel. 26″ × 24⅜″.
Musée du Louvre, Paris.
Photograph: © Erich Lessing. Art Resource, NY.

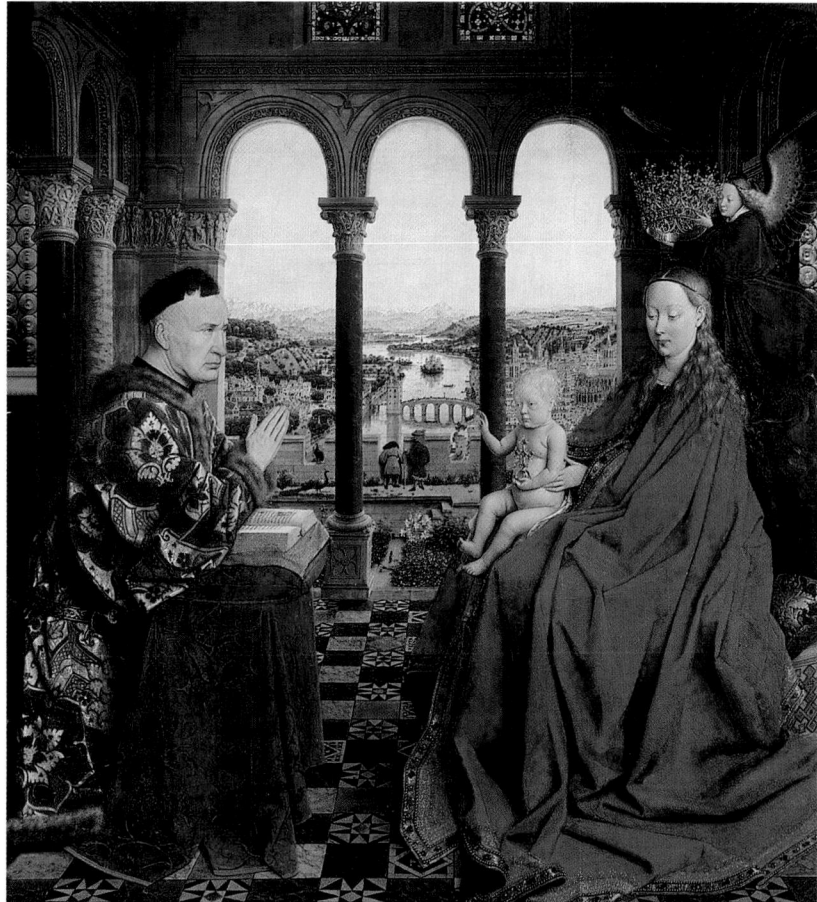

Jan van Eyck's MADONNA AND CHILD WITH THE CHANCELLOR ROLIN is an example of his early mastery of the oil technique. Jan painted it on a small gesso-covered wood panel. After beginning with a brush drawing in tempera, he proceeded with thin layers of oil paint, moving from light to dark and from opaque to translucent colors. The luminous quality of the surface is the result of successive oil glazes. A glaze is a very thin, transparent film of color applied over a previously painted surface. To produce glazes, oil colors selected for their transparency are diluted with glazing medium—usually a mixture of oil, thinner, and varnish. Glazes give depth to painted surfaces by allowing light to pass through and reflect from lower paint layers.

Here the sparkling jewels, the textiles, and the furs are each given their own refined textures. Within the context of the religious subject, the artist demonstrated his enthusiasm for the delights of the visible world. Veils of glazes in the sky area provide atmospheric perspective and thus contribute to the illusion of deep space in the enticing view beyond the open window. The evolution in the new oil painting technique made such realism possible.

Oil has many advantages over other traditional media. Compared to tempera, oil paint can provide both increased opacity—which yields better covering power—and, when thinned, greater transparency. Its slow drying time, first considered a

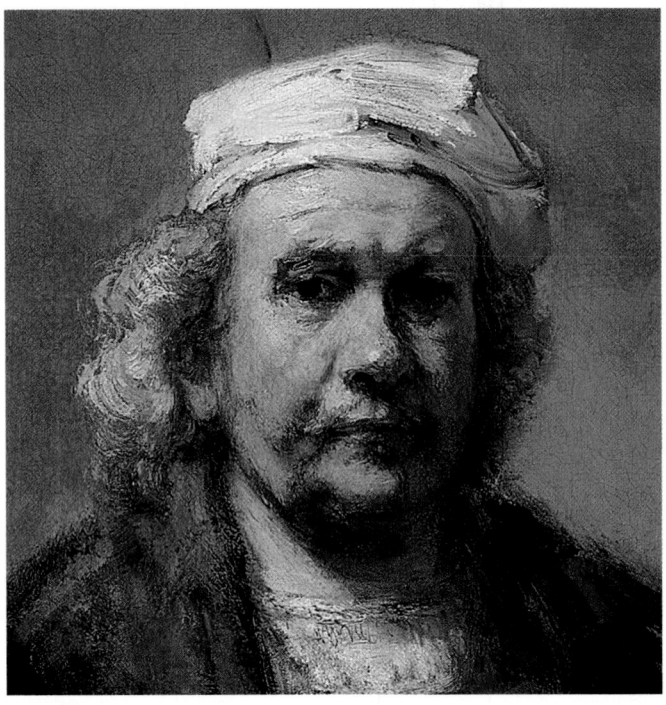

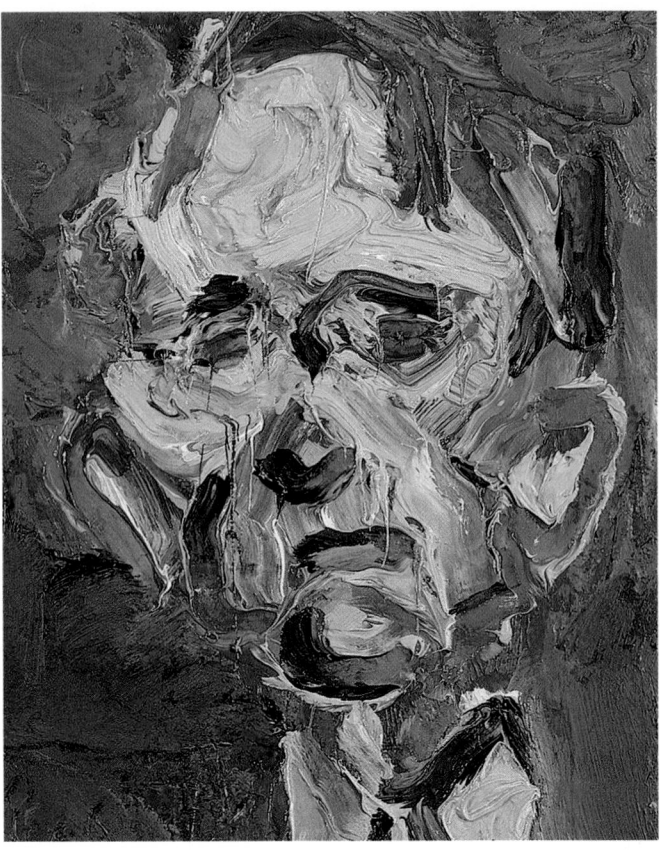

167 Rembrandt van Rijn.
Detail from SELF-PORTRAIT. 1663.
Oil on canvas. Full painting 45″ × 38″.
Kenwood House, London. English Heritage Photo Library.

168 Frank Auerbach.
HEAD OF MICHAEL PODRO. 1981.
Oil on board. 13″ × 11″.
Photograph: Marlborough Fine Art Ltd., London.

drawback, soon proved to be a distinct advantage, allowing artists to blend strokes of color and make changes during the painting process. Unlike pigment in tempera, gouache, and acrylics, pigment colors in oil change little when drying; however, oil medium (primarily linseed oil) has a tendency to darken and yellow slightly with age. Because of the flexibility of dried oil film, sixteenth-century Venetian painters who wished to paint large pictures could replace heavy wood panels with canvas stretched on wood frames. A painted canvas not only is light in weight, but also can be unstretched and rolled for transporting. Most oil painters today still prefer canvas supports.

Oil can be applied thickly or thinly, wet into wet or wet onto dry. When applied thickly, it is called impasto. When a work is painted wet into wet and completed at one sitting, the process is called the direct painting method.

Rembrandt used this method in his SELF-PORTRAIT. The detail here shows how the impasto of light and dark paint both defines a solid-looking head and presents the incredible richness of Rembrandt's brushwork.

In Rembrandt's SELF-PORTRAIT and in Frank Auerbach's HEAD OF MICHAEL PODRO, we see the artists' responsiveness to both the reality of their subjects and the physical nature of paint. Because the thick, paste-like quality of oil paint is celebrated rather than hidden, viewers participate in the process of conjuring up images when viewing Rembrandt's rough strokes and Auerbach's smears and globs of paint. Both paintings project strong images when seen at a distance and show rich tactile surfaces when viewed close up.

The wide range of approaches possible with oil paint becomes apparent when we compare Jan van Eyck's subtly glazed colors with the impasto surfaces of Rembrandt and Auerbach.

In one sense, the story of painting is about the visual magic that people around the world have been able to conjure up with various paint media.

Joan Mitchell used oil paint to spontaneously recreate emotional states in abstract visual form. BORDER is painted very loosely in a complex mix of rich, sensuous colors. The composition is subtly symmetrical (note the light vertical green stripe near the top center), and colors are applied with a combination of care and abandon. To arrive at the bright and lush yellows, blues, greens, and reds, the artist avoided overmixing her colors. The varying textures of the work show spontaneous, expressive execution. She made the yellow strokes with a dry brush; she allowed some of the blues to run; reds give accents at carefully selected points. We can actually follow the creation of this work, layer by layer and color by color, as we look at this embodiment of a warm—even exciting—mood.

Some contemporary artists use oil in ways that show the influence of digital arts and animation. Inka Essenhigh's 2003 work ESCAPE POD, for example, resembles a still from an animated science-fiction film. The work's title refers to the small craft that space travelers use in case of disaster, and some kind of accident seems to have happened here. The slick surfaces and subtle gradations of tone in this work make good use of the characteristics of oil paint.

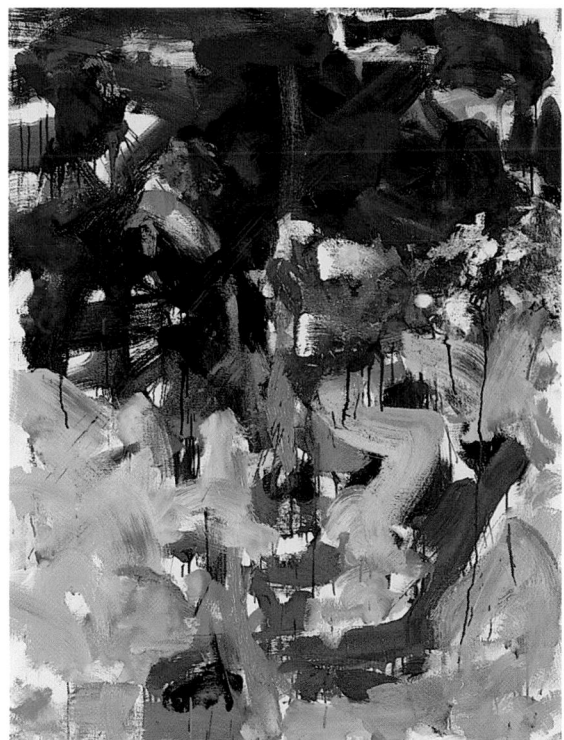

169 Joan Mitchell.
BORDER. 1989.
Oil on canvas. 45½″ × 35″.
© The Estate of Joan Mitchell. Courtesy Robert Miller Gallery.

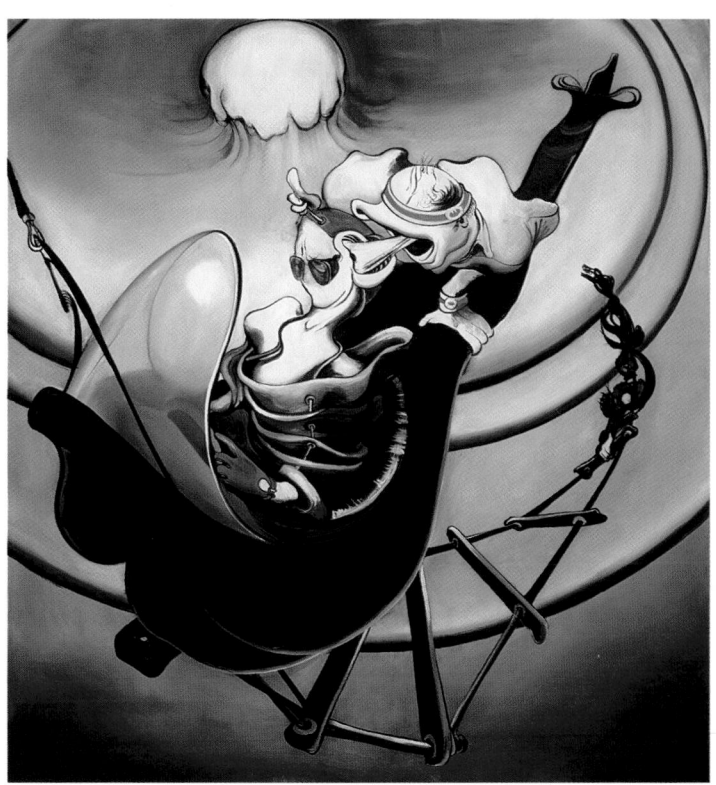

170 Inka Essenhigh.
ESCAPE POD. 2003.
Oil on canvas. 50″ × 50″.
Courtesy of 303 Gallery, NY.

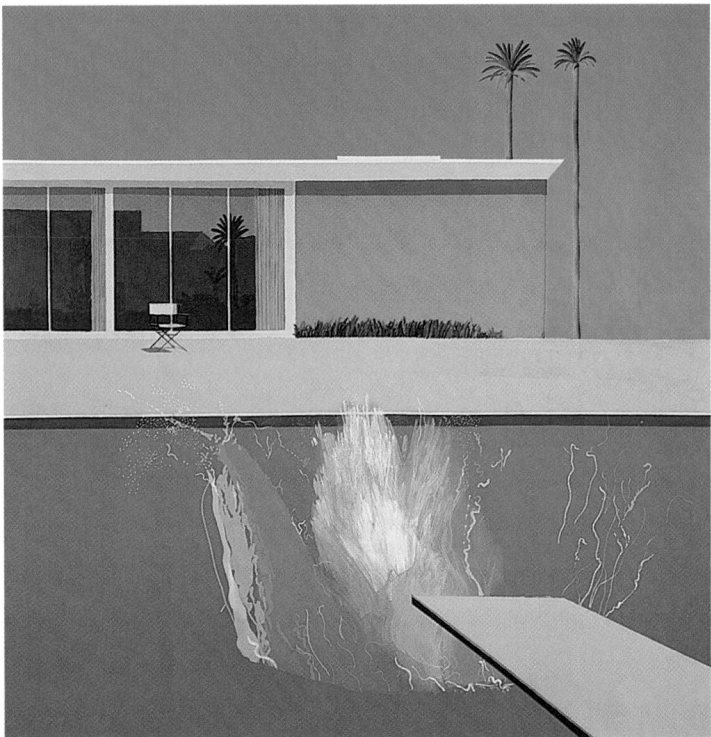

171 David Hockney.
A BIGGER SPLASH. 1967.
Acrylic on canvas. 96″ × 96″.
© The Tate Gallery, London. Art Resource, NY.

ACRYLIC

Foremost among the synthetic painting media currently in wide use are acrylics. Pigments are suspended in acrylic polymer medium, which provides a fast-drying, flexible film. These relatively permanent paints can be applied to a wider variety of surfaces than traditional painting media. Most acrylics are water-thinned yet water-resistant when dry. Because acrylic resin medium is highly transparent, colors can maintain a high degree of intensity. Unlike oils, acrylics rarely darken or yellow with age. Their rapid drying time restricts blending and limits reworking, but it greatly reduces the time involved in layering processes such as glazing.

Acrylics work well when paint is applied quickly with little blending—witness the splash in David Hockney's A BIGGER SPLASH—or when it is brushed on in flat areas as in the rest of the painting. The strong contrast between the dramatic freedom of the paint application of the splash and the thinly painted, geometric shapes of house, chair, pool rim, and diving board gives lively energy to the suburban scene.

In recent years many painters have used airbrushes to apply acrylics and other types of paint. An airbrush is a small-scale paint sprayer capable of projecting a fine, controlled mist of paint. It provides an even paint application without the personal touch of individual brush strokes, and it is therefore well suited to the subtle gradations of color values found in many paintings of the 1960s and 1970s, such as Audrey Flack's WHEEL OF FORTUNE. Graffiti artists, of course, also favor spray guns because of the quickness of execution.

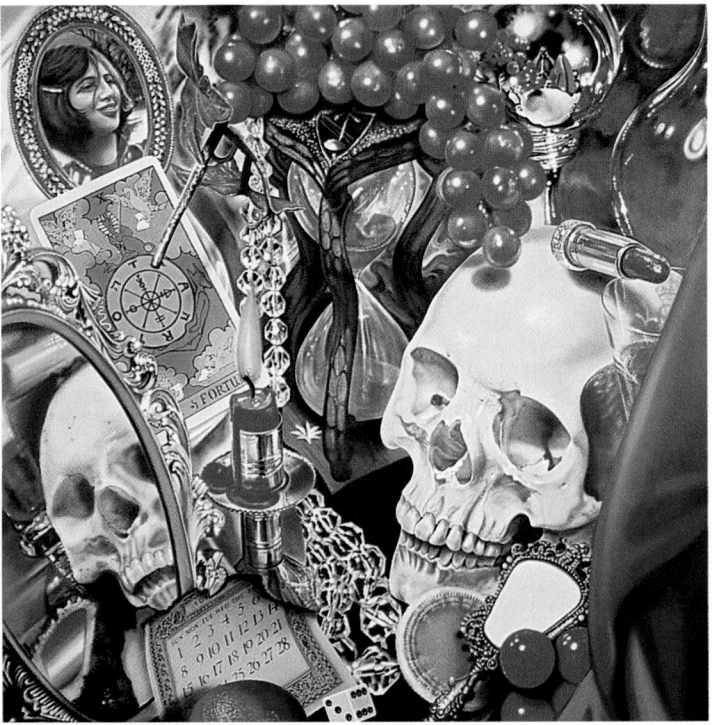

172 Audrey Flack.
WHEEL OF FORTUNE. 1977–1978.
Oil over acrylic on canvas. 96″ × 96″.
Courtesy of Louis K. Meisel Gallery, NY.

FRESCO

True fresco, or *buon fresco*, is an ancient wallpainting technique in which very finely ground pigments suspended in water are applied to a damp lime-plaster surface. Generally, a full-size drawing called a cartoon is completed first, then transferred to the freshly laid plaster wall before painting. Because the plaster dries quickly, only the portion of the wall that can be painted in one day is prepared; joints are usually arranged along the edges of major shapes in the composition.

The painter works quickly in a rapid staining process similar to watercolor. Lime, in contact with air, forms transparent calcium crystals that chemically bind the pigment to the moist lime-plaster wall. The lime in the plaster thus becomes the binder, creating a smooth, extremely durable surface. Once the surface has dried, the painting is part of the wall. Notice the texture of the plaster in the detail from Diego Rivera's DETROIT INDUSTRY.

Completion of the chemical reaction occurs slowly, deepening and enriching the colors as the fresco ages. Colors reach their greatest intensity fifty to one hundred years after a fresco is painted, yet the hues always have a muted quality.

The artist must have the design completely worked out before painting, because no changes can be made after the paint is applied to the fresh plaster. It may take twelve to fourteen straight hours of work just to complete two square yards of a fresco painting. Fresco technique does not permit the delicate manipulation of transitional tones; but the luminous color, fine surface, and permanent color make it an ideal medium for large murals. (A mural is any wall-sized painting; fresco is one possible medium for such a work.)

Fresco secco (dry fresco), another ancient wallpainting method, is done on finished, dried lime-plaster walls. With this technique, tempera paint is applied to a clean, dry surface or over an already

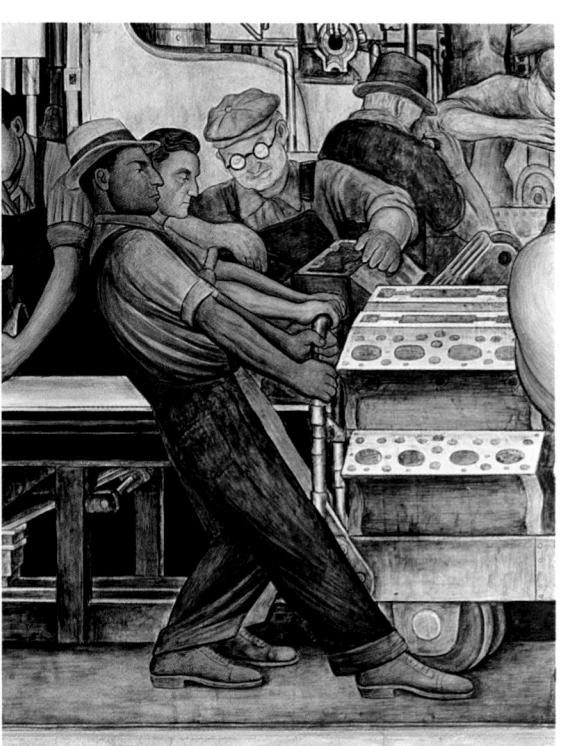

173 Diego Rivera.
Detail from DETROIT INDUSTRY. 1932–1933.
Fresco.
Detroit Institute of Arts, MI. Gift of Edsel B. Ford. Bridgeman Art Library.

dried true fresco to achieve greater color intensity than is possible with true fresco alone.

Fresco has been used in Asian and Western cultures for at least four thousand years. In Renaissance Italy it was the favored medium for painting on church walls. Probably the best known fresco paintings are those by Michelangelo on the Sistine Chapel ceiling in the Vatican in Rome. After the Renaissance and Baroque periods, fresco became less popular, eclipsed by the more flexible oil medium. How-ever, a revival of the fresco technique began in Mexico in the 1920s, encouraged by the new revolutionary government's support for public murals.

By leading the revival in fresco mural painting for public buildings, Diego Rivera broke away from the limited studio and gallery audience and made art a part of the life of the people. His style blends European and native art traditions with contemporary subject matter. He created DETROIT INDUSTRY in the lobby of the Detroit Institute of Arts.

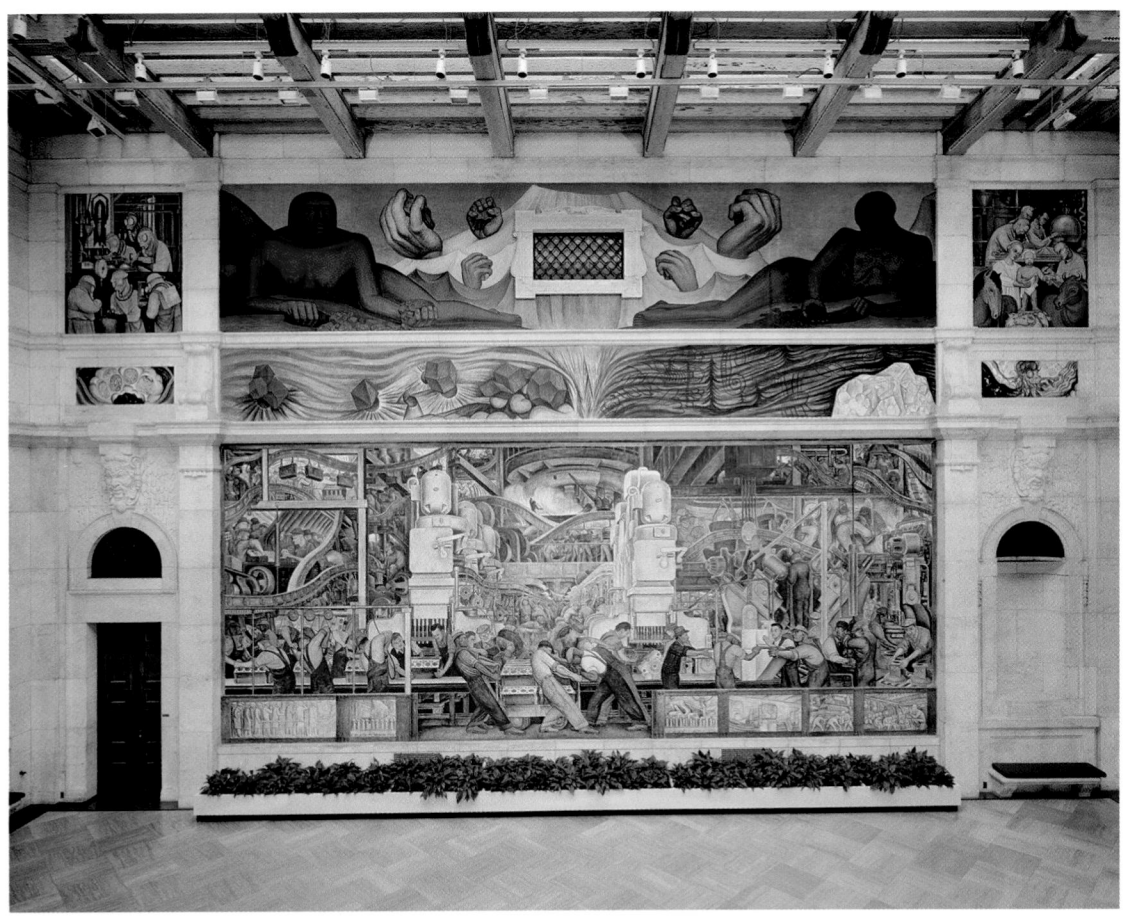

174   Diego Rivera.
DETROIT INDUSTRY. 1932–1933.
Fresco.
Detroit Institute of Arts, MI. Gift of Edsel B. Ford. Bridgeman Art Library.

THE GREAT WALL OF LOS ANGELES

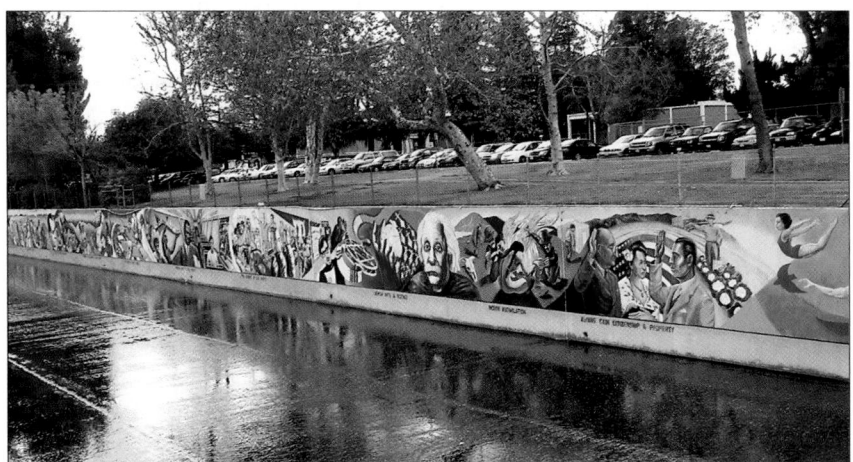

175   Judith F. Baca.
View of GREAT WALL OF LOS ANGELES. 1976–1983.
Tujunga Wash, Studio City, CA.
Photograph: Patrick Frank.

THE WORLD'S largest painting is fourteen feet high and stretches for a half mile along the side wall of a drainage ditch in the San Fernando Valley. Not able to take it in all at once, viewers must contemplate it from a bike path or through the windows of their passing cars. This colossal project is the brainchild of Judy Baca, who for twenty years has combined art with community activism.

She was inspired by the mural paintings of Mexican artists of the 1920s and 1930s, who decorated public buildings with scenes of their country's history and life. They showed through their work how art could become, rather than a luxurious private possession, a vehicle of community awareness and empowerment. Baca recalls recruiting over four hundred teenagers and young adults to help make

THE GREAT WALL OF LOS ANGELES over a period of several summers beginning in 1976.

Baca recalls how the idea was born:

When I first saw the wall, I envisioned a long narrative of another history of California: one which included ethnic peoples, women, and minorities who were so invisible in conventional textbook accounts. The discovery of California's multicultured peoples was a revelation to me.[1]

THE GREAT WALL presents a sweeping panorama of the history of California. Beginning with the Native American cultures of the area, it continues with the Roman Catholic missions and moves on to the Anglicization of the state when it became part of the United States with the Treaty of Guadalupe Hidalgo in

1848. The twentieth-century section includes the Dust Bowl migrants of the 1930s, the dawn of the movie and aviation industries, and the impact of World War II.

Many parts of the mural highlight histories that are often left untold. One panel tells graphically how the building of Dodger Stadium in 1962 dislodged a Mexican-American neighborhood. Another depicts the forced incarceration of Japanese Americans in "relocation" camps after the Pearl Harbor attack that started World War II in the Pacific. A third deals with the blacklisting of dozens of Hollywood writers for suspected Communist affiliations during the height of the Cold War. THE GREAT WALL's size parallels its expansive, inclusive vision of the history of California.

Getting it done was a monumental task. Baca paid all

of the workers, to help both the pocketbooks and the pride of the young people she recruited. Many of the Mural Makers were former gang members, juvenile delinquents, or ex-offenders on parole; painting the mural was their first job. She organized the workers into crews, taking care that each unit was multi-ethnic.

The mural's impact on the lives of those who painted it is well documented. Many disadvantaged youths got needed job skills. Social service referrals to counseling or drug treatment were readily available. For the first time, hundreds learned of their history and how it related to the state as a whole. One participant recalled, "After my first year on the mural, I left with a sense of who I was and what I could do that was unlike anything I'd ever felt before."[2]

PRINTMAKING

The term *printmaking* describes a variety of techniques developed to create multiple copies of a single image. So much in our society is printed—newspapers, books, posters, magazines, greeting cards, billboards—that it is hard to imagine a time in which all illustrations were produced by hand, one at a time. Before 1415, every book and manuscript in Europe was hand-lettered and hand-illustrated. In contrast, thousands of copies of *Artforms* are printed in a few hours by a mechanical printing method called *offset lithography*.

The technologies for both printing and papermaking came to Europe from China. By the ninth century, the Chinese were printing pictures; by the eleventh century, they had invented (but seldom used) movable type. Printmaking was developed in Europe during the fifteenth century—first to meet the demand for inexpensive religious icons and playing cards, then to illustrate books printed with the new European movable type. Since the fifteenth century, the art of printmaking has remained closely associated with the illustration of books.

As recently as the late nineteenth century, printmakers were still needed to copy drawings, paintings, and even early photographs by making plates to be used, along with movable type, for illustrating newspapers and books. However, as photomechanical methods of reproduction were developed in the late nineteenth century, handwork played a decreasing role in the printing process. Artists, however, have continued to use the old handcrafted printmaking processes to take advantage of their uniquely expressive properties. By designing and printing multiple originals, today's printmakers can sell their works for much less than one-of-a-kind paintings. Such works, conceived as *original prints*, are not to be confused with reproductions.

One of the best definitions of an original print comes from artist June Wayne: "It is a work of art, usually on paper, which has siblings . . . They all look alike, they were all made at the same time from the same matrix, the same creative impulse, and they are all originals. The fact that there are many of them is irrelevant."[1]

Nearly all original prints are numbered to indicate the total number of prints *pulled*, or printed, in the edition, and to give the number of each print in the sequence. The figure 6/50 on a print, for example, would indicate that the edition totaled fifty prints and that this was the sixth print pulled.

As part of the printmaking process, artists make prints called progressive proofs at various stages to see how the image on the block, plate, stone, or screen is developing. When a satisfactory stage is reached, the artist makes a few prints for his or her record and personal use. These are marked AP, meaning *artist's proof*.

Printmaking methods range from simple to complex. Traditionally, these methods are divided into four basic categories: relief, intaglio, planographic (lithography), and stencil (screenprinting). (The *Discovering Art* CD provides live examples of these methods.) Contemporary artists are using the old methods in new ways, sometimes combining them with digital techniques; we will consider some of these new directions at the end of this chapter.

RELIEF

In a *relief* process, the printmaker cuts away all parts of the printing surface not meant to carry the ink, leaving the design to be printed "in relief" at the level of the original surface (see the RELIEF diagram on page 133). The surface is then inked, and the ink is transferred to paper with pressure. Relief processes include *woodcut* (or *woodblock*), *wood engraving*, and *linoleum cut* (or *linocut*). Marks made by rubber stamps, fingerprints, and wet tires are examples of relief-printed marks in the everyday world.

The traditional woodcut process lends itself to designs with bold black-and-white contrast. The image-bearing block of wood, usually a soft wood, is a plank cut along the grain. Because the woodcut medium does not easily yield shades of color, artists who use it are generally drawn by the challenge of working in black and white only. Others use woodcut because they enjoy the feel of carving a fresh block of wood. Color can be printed with single or multiple blocks. As with most printmaking techniques, when more than one color is used, individually inked blocks—one for each color—are carefully *registered* (lined up) to ensure that colors will be exactly placed in the final print.

Block printing from woodcuts originated in China, where the desire to spread the Buddhist religion greatly influenced the type of prints produced. THE DIAMOND SUTRA is one of the world's oldest surviving documents. It opens with a woodblock print of the Buddha, surrounded by attendants and guardians, preaching to an old man seen in the lower left. (The swastika on the Buddha's chest is an ancient symbol of his enlightenment.) An inscription states that it was made in 868 for free distribution, an apparent act of religious goodwill. The hard wood of this early print makes possible the many fine lines in the design, which is similar in style to

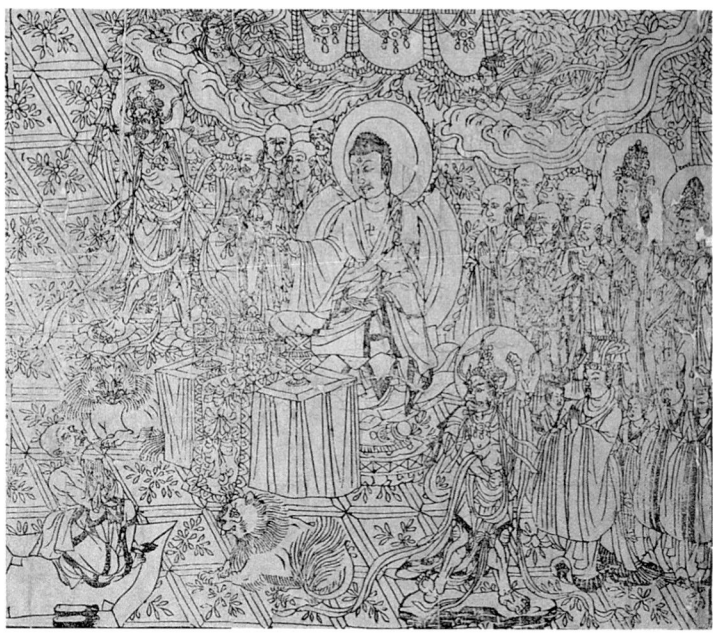

176 Section of THE DIAMOND SUTRA.
Chinese Buddhist text, 868.
Scroll, woodblock print on paper.
Length of entire scroll 18′.
By permission of The British Library. OR.8210f2.

stone carvings from the same time period. This scroll is in excellent condition despite its age, because it was hidden in a cave for many centuries.

Woodblock printing flourished in Japan in the seventeenth through the nineteenth centuries. Japanese woodblock prints were made through a complex process that used multiple blocks to achieve subtle and highly integrated color effects. Because they were much cheaper than paintings, these prints were the preferred art form for middle-class people who lived in the capital city of Edo (now known as Tokyo). Their subject matter included famous theater actors, nightlife, landscapes, and even erotic pictures. Japanese prints were among the first objects of Asian art to be appreciated by European artists, and many Impressionist and Post-Impressionist painters were strongly influenced by them.

Japanese artist Hokusai's color woodcut prints have become well known around the world. Hokusai worked in close collaboration with highly skilled carvers to realize the final prints. For each of his woodcuts, specialists transferred Hokusai's

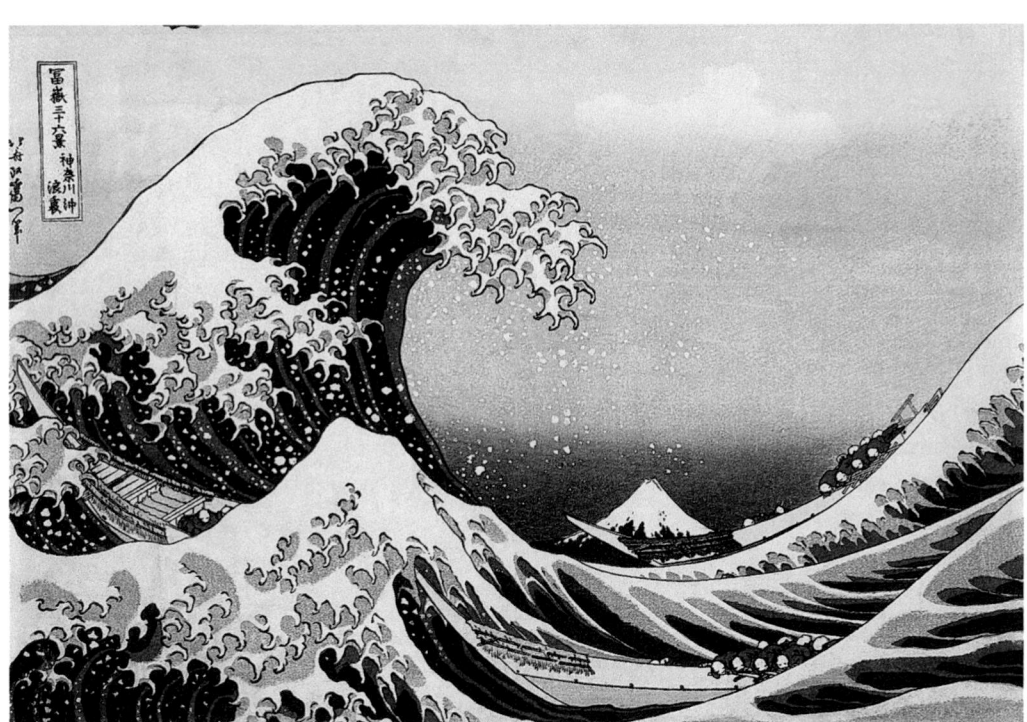

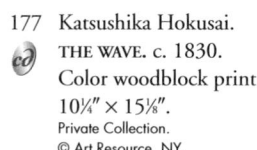

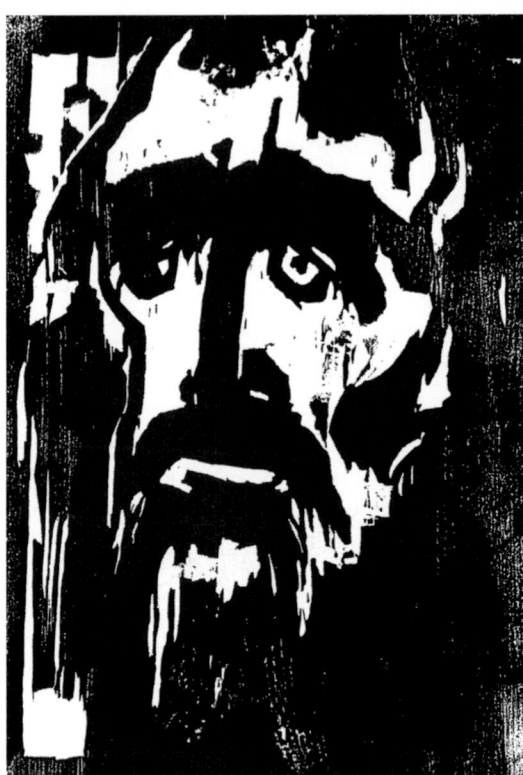

178 Emil Nolde.
PROPHET. 1912.
Woodcut.
Image 12½″ × 8¹³/₁₆″.

watercolor brush painting to as many as twenty blocks, cut the blocks, and then inked each one with a separate color. In Hokusai's print THE WAVE, a clawing mountain of water threatens tiny fishermen in their boats. The rhythmic curves of the churning sea even dwarf Mount Fuji, which nonetheless stands firm in the distance. This imaginative rendering captures the awesome power of the sea. This print is one of Hokusai's thirty-six views of Mount Fuji seen from various locations.

The detail in Hokusai's print is quite different from the roughness of the woodcut PROPHET by German artist Emil Nolde. Each cut in this block is expressive of an old man's face and reveals the character of the wood and the wood-cutting process. The simplified light-and-dark pattern of the features gives emotional intensity to the image. Nolde's direct approach is part of the long tradition of German printmaking that includes the prints of Albrecht Dürer.

The linoleum cut is a modern development in relief printing. The artist starts with the rubbery, synthetic surface of linoleum, and just as in woodcut, gouges out the areas not intended to take ink. The material is softer than wood, has no grain, and can be cut with equal ease in any direction.

An example of a linoleum cut (or linocut) is SHARECROPPER by Elizabeth Catlett, in which the even, white gouges betray the soft material. This work also typifies Catlett's lifelong devotion to creating dignified images of African Americans.

INTAGLIO

Intaglio printing is the opposite of relief: areas below the surface hold the ink (see the INTAGLIO diagram below). *Intaglio* comes from the Italian *intagliare*, "to cut into." The image to be printed is either cut or scratched into a metal surface by steel- or diamond-tip tools, or etched into the surface by acid. To make a print, the printmaker first daubs the plate with viscous printer's ink, then wipes the surface clean, leaving ink only in the etched or grooved portions. Damp paper is then placed on the inked plate, which then passes beneath the press roller. A print is made when the dampened paper picks up the ink in the grooves. The pressure of the roller creates a characteristic plate mark around the edges of the print. Intaglio printing was traditionally done from polished copper plates, but now zinc, steel,

aluminum, and even plastic are often used. Engraving and etching are the two principal intaglio processes.

Engraving

In *engravings*, lines are cut into the polished surface of the plate with a *burin*, or engraving tool. This exacting process takes strength and control. Lines are made by pushing the burin through the metal to carve a groove, removing a narrow strip of metal in the process. Engraving grew out of the inscription and decoration of jewelry. A clean line is desired; thus, any rough edges of the groove must be smoothed down with a scraper. Engraved lines cannot be as freely drawn as etched lines because of the pressure needed to cut the grooves. The precise, smooth curves and parallel lines typical of engravings are obvious in the engraved portraits that appear on the paper currency we use.

We can see the complex richness of engraved lines in Albrecht Dürer's engraving THE KNIGHT, DEATH AND THE DEVIL, reproduced close to its actual size (on the following page). Thousands of

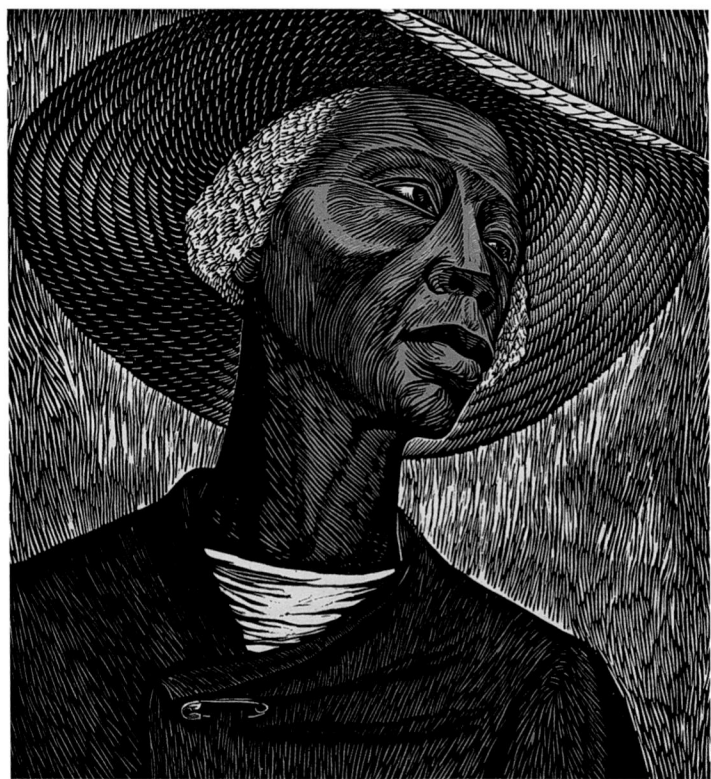

179 Elizabeth Catlett.
SHARECROPPER. 1970.
Color linocut on cream Japanese paper. 15⅓″ × 10¼″.
The Art Institute of Chicago. Restricted gift of Mr. and Mrs. Robert S. Hartman. 1992. 182.
Photograph: © 2002 The Art Institute of Chicago. All rights reserved.
© Elizabeth Catlett. Licensed by VAGA, NY.

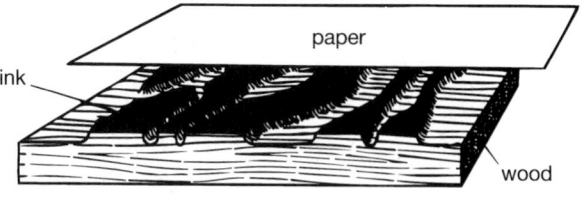

180 RELIEF.

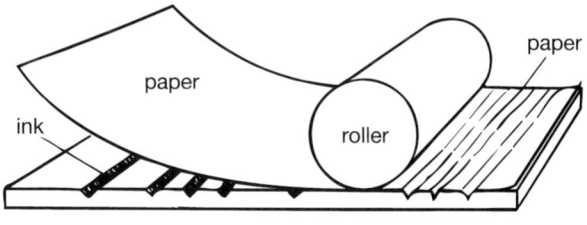

181 INTAGLIO.

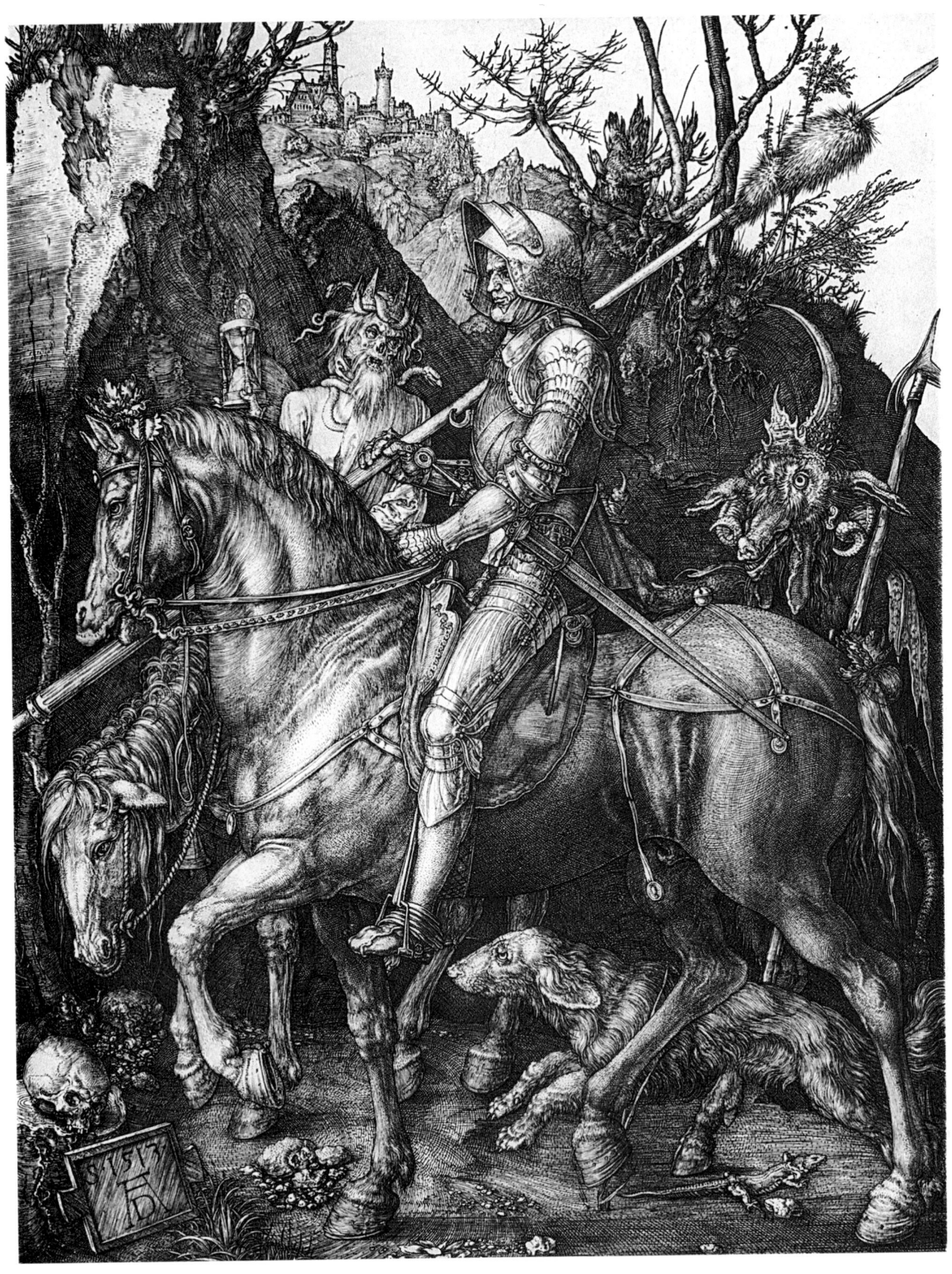

fine lines define the shapes, masses, spaces, values, and textures of the depicted objects. The precision of Dürer's lines seems appropriate to the subject—an image of the noble Christian knight moving with resolute commitment, unswayed by the forces of chaos, evil, and death that surround him (a discussion of the print's iconography appears on page 38).

Etching

The process of making an *etching* begins with the preparation of a metal plate with a *ground*—a protective coating of acid-resistant material that covers the copper or zinc. The printmaker then draws easily through the ground with a pointed tool, exposing the metal. Finally, the plate is immersed in acid. Acid "bites" into the plate where the drawing has exposed the metal, making a groove that varies in depth according to the strength of the acid and the length of time the plate is in the acid bath.

Because they are more easily produced, etched lines are generally more relaxed or irregular than engraved lines. We can see the difference in line quality between an engraving and an etching—the freedom versus the precision—by comparing the lines in Rembrandt's etching CHRIST PREACHING with the lines in Dürer's engraving THE KNIGHT, DEATH AND THE DEVIL.

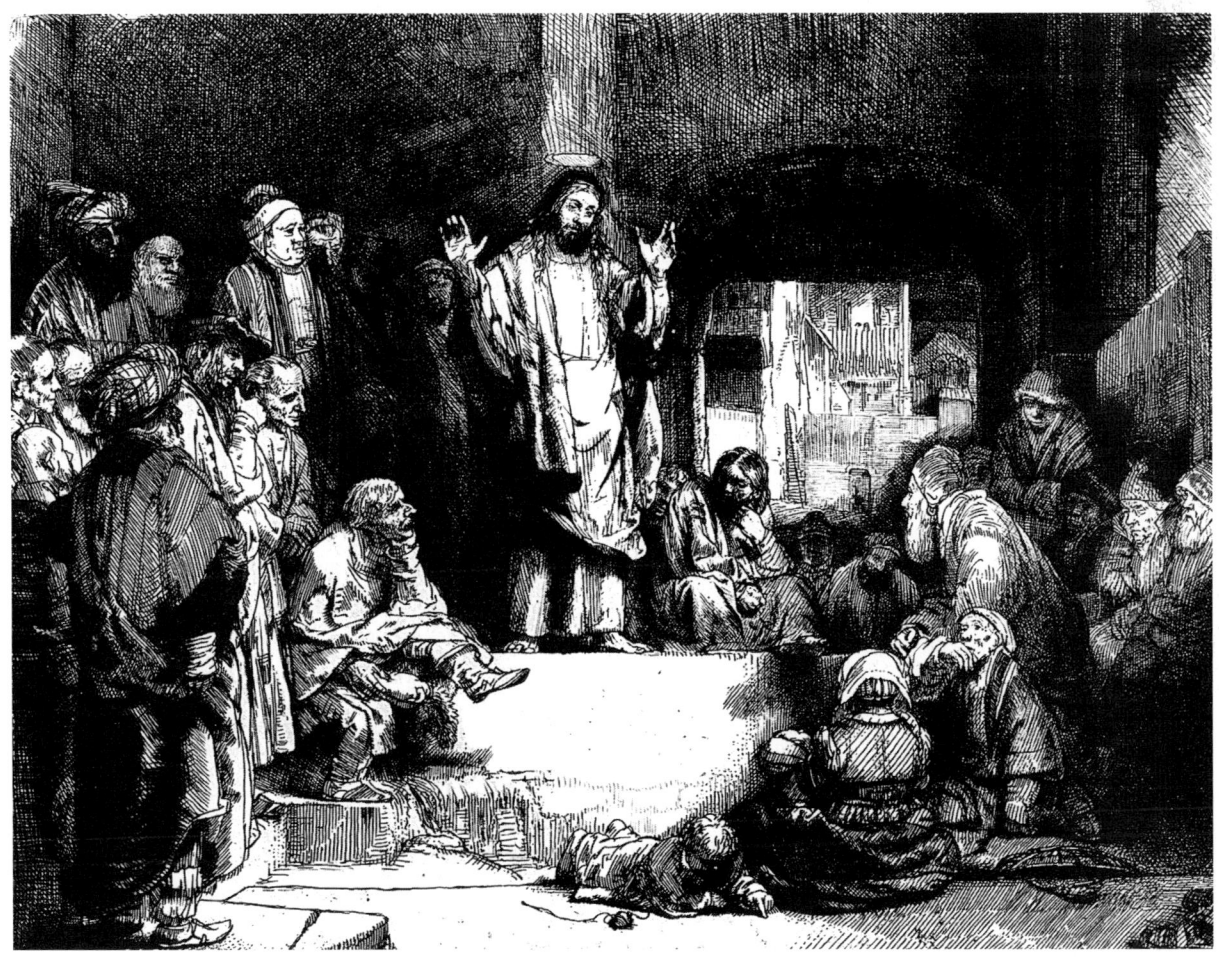

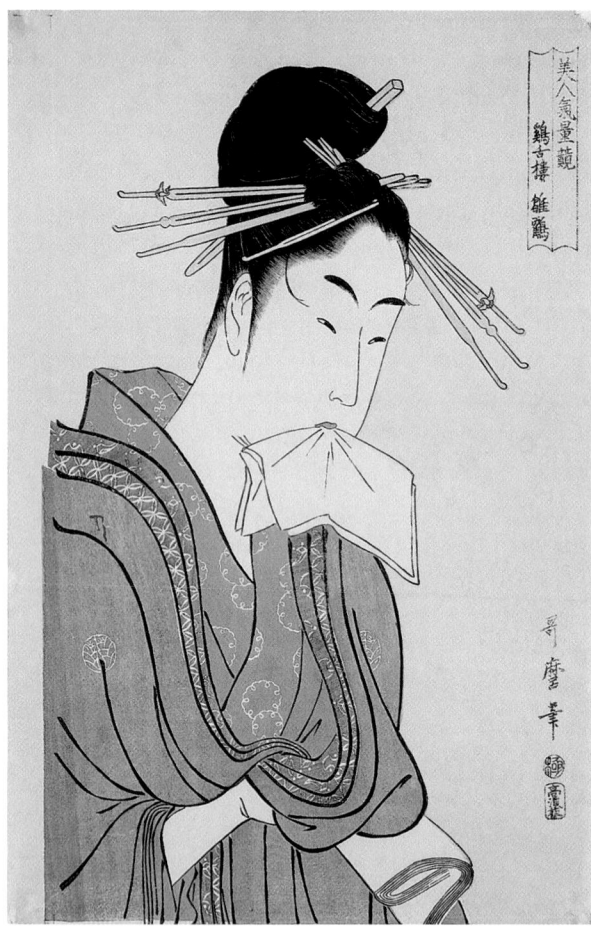

184 Kitagawa Utamaro.
A COMPETITIVE SHOWING OF BEAUTIES:
HINZAURU OF THE HEIZETSURO. c. 1796.
Woodblock print. 15⅓″ × 10⅛″.
Clarence Buckingham Collection, 1925.3047.
Photograph courtesy of the Art Institute of Chicago.

In CHRIST PREACHING, Rembrandt's personal understanding of Christ's compassion harmonizes with the decisive yet relaxed quality of the artist's etched lines. This etching shows Rembrandt's typical use of a wide range of values. Skillful use of light and shadow draws attention to the figure of Christ and gives clarity and interest to the whole image. In a composition in which each figure is similar in size, Rembrandt identifies Jesus as the key figure by setting him off with a light area below, a light vertical band above, and implied lines of attention leading to him from the faces of his listeners.

Aquatint is an etching process used to obtain shaded areas in black-and-white or color prints. Contemporary aquatints are prepared with acid-resistant spray paints. When the plate is placed in acid, the exposed areas between the paint particles are eaten away to produce a rough surface capable of holding ink. Values thus produced can vary from light to dark, depending on how long the plate is in the acid. Because aquatint is not suited to making thin lines, it is usually combined with a linear print process such as engraving, drypoint, or line etching. Francisco Goya used such a combination in his print from the series THE DISASTERS OF WAR on page 13. Goya achieved the lightly colored sky and some of the shading on the ground by using aquatint along with etched lines.

American artist Mary Cassatt's prints and paintings show the influence of the strong flat shapes and elegant lines of Japanese woodblock prints. She was especially drawn to the work of Kitagawa Utamaro, who frequently made prints depicting fashionable ladies. Cassatt owned many prints by Utamaro, including A COMPETITIVE SHOWING OF BEAUTIES: HINZAURU OF THE HEIZETSURO in which a woman holds a scarf in her lips while dressing. Cassatt borrowed the composition of this work for her own print THE LETTER . She made the colored areas with aquatint; for the fine lines she used drypoint, an acid-free method in which she simply scratched the metal plate with a diamond-tipped tool to leave a shallow groove for the ink.

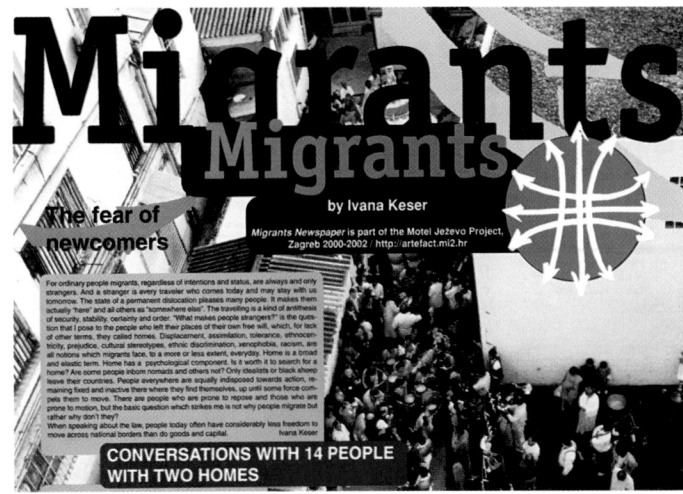

195   Ivana Keser.
      MIGRANTS NEWSPAPER. 2002.
      Detail of cover. Offset, eight pages. 16½″ × 11¾″.
      Courtesy of the artist.

gallery for viewers to take at no charge. She has made almost a dozen editions so far, taking up subjects as various as utopia, gardening, city life, community art, globalization, and **MIGRANTS.** Each issue presents a personal perspective on the matter at hand. She learned graphic design from working on a newspaper, and her publications amount to her own interventions in the flow of mass media that we all live with. Her art is disposable, but she does not mind if people throw her creations in the trash because, she says, "That's the future of all publications." She does not like the daily news that the media present, so she makes her own.

Because digital prints are in theory infinitely reproducible without loss of quality, some artists have devised novel means of controlling the size of an edition. The English duo Gilbert and George (who do not use their last names) in 2007 made a print available for free downloading on the Internet for thirty-six hours. The edition was limited not by the number of downloads or printouts but by the clock.

Argentine artist Alicia Candiani combines digital and traditional technologies in prints that question stereotypical representations of women. In LA HUMANIDAD (Humanity), she used traditional Japanese woodcut techniques to print a map of the world on paper whose texture and color resemble human skin. Just beneath this grid, she printed a digital image of her own wet body in a pose based on the physical disciplines of yoga. The background includes digitally altered versions of dressmaking patterns. Thus, the artist used ancient and contemporary techniques to map woman on the surface of the earth.

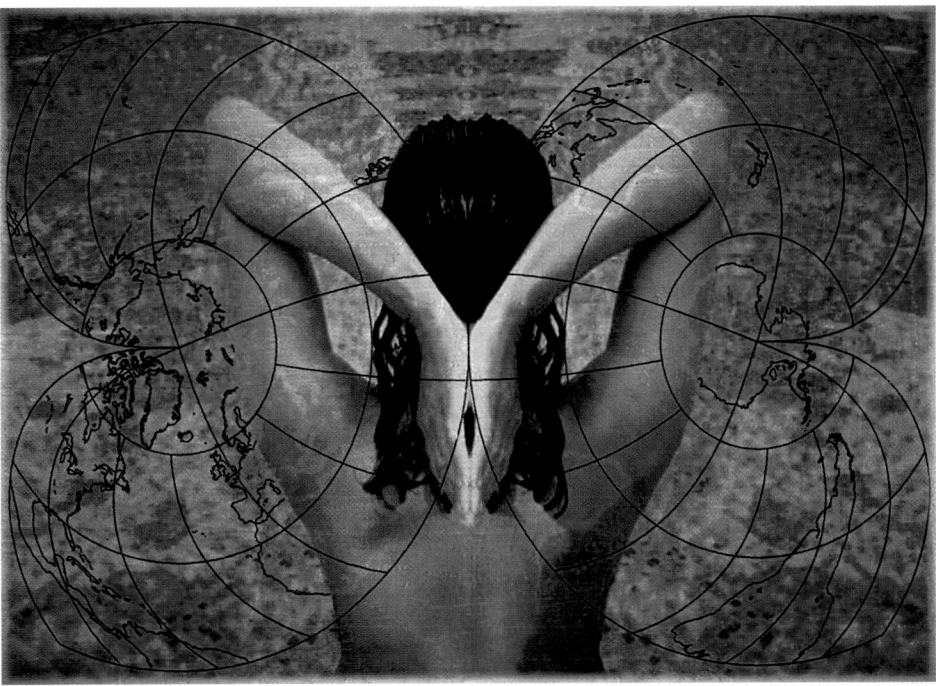

196   Alicia Candiani.
      LA HUMANIDAD. 2004.
      From Continents series:
      Humanity.
      Digital print on clear film and
      waterbased woodcut on Buthan
      paper. 27″ × 40″.
      Courtesy of the artist.

CAMERA ARTS
AND DIGITAL IMAGING

While captivated by photography, film, or video, we can easily forget that the camera arts are recent extensions of a long pictorial tradition. Each new technique in the history of art relies heavily on its predecessors.

Photography has been influenced by Western painting, and in turn it has influenced painting. Cinematography grew from still photography. Television is influenced by painting, photography, and cinematography. Digital arts are influenced by all of these. In turn, television and other photographic imagery influence the more traditional visual and performing arts. Apart from all these mutual influences, cameras and computers provide means through which both past and present art can be reproduced and enjoyed by people in all parts of the world.

PHOTOGRAPHY

Many nineteenth-century inventions changed the way we live; but of all of them, photography had the greatest impact on the way we see. As an art form, photography reveals the photographer's personal way of seeing and responding.

Photography literally means "light-writing," although a more accurate description would be "light-drawing." Like drawing, photography can be either an art form or a practical tool. Beyond its many uses in journalism, science, advertising, public relations, and other fields—as well as for recording family history—photography offers the artist a powerful means of expression.

Beyond selecting camera, lens, and subject, a skilled photographer makes many choices about light, angle, focus, distance, and composition. The best photographers have learned to visualize their photographs before releasing the shutter. American photographer Ansel Adams spoke of the need to give considerable time and effort to the making of a photograph for the result to be worthwhile.

I have often thought that if photography were difficult in the true sense of the term—meaning that the creation of a simple photograph would entail as much time and effort as the production of a good watercolor or etching—there would be a vast improvement in total output. The sheer ease with which we can produce a superficial image often leads to creative disaster. We must remember that a photograph can hold just as much as we put into it, and no one has ever approached the full possibilities of the medium.[1]

Edwin Land, who developed the Polaroid instant camera, also emphasized the process of making a photograph when he described how even automatic, "instant" cameras can help us learn to see:

At its best, photography can be an extra sense, or a reservoir for the senses. Even when you don't press the trigger, the exercise of focusing through a camera can make you better remember thereafter a person or a moment. When we had flowers in this office recently to use as test objects, it was a great experience to take pictures of them. I learned to know each rose. I now know more about roses and leaves, and that enriched my life. Photography can teach people to look, to feel, to remember in a way that they didn't know they could.[2]

The Evolution of Photography

The basic concept of the camera preceded actual photography by more than three hundred years. The desire of Renaissance artists to make accurate depictions of nature was the original impetus behind the eventual invention of photography.

The forerunner of the modern camera was the *camera obscura*, literally "dark room." The concept of photography grew out of the observation that reflected sunlight passing through a small hole in the wall of a darkened room projects onto the opposite wall an inverted image of whatever lies outside. In the fifteenth century, Leonardo da Vinci described the device as an aid to observation and picture making.

As a fixed room, or even as a portable room, the camera obscura was too large and cumbersome to be widely used. In the seventeenth century, when it was realized that the person tracing the image did not have to be inside, the CAMERA OBSCURA evolved into a portable dark box. During the course of this pre-camera evolution, a lens was placed in the small hole to improve image clarity. Later an angled mirror was added to right the inverted image, enabling anyone, skilled or unskilled, to trace the projected pictures with pen or pencil (see the table model CAMERA OBSCURA).

It was not until about 1826 that the first vague photographic image was made by Joseph Nicéphore Niépce. He recorded and fixed on a sheet of pewter an image made by exposing the sensitized metal

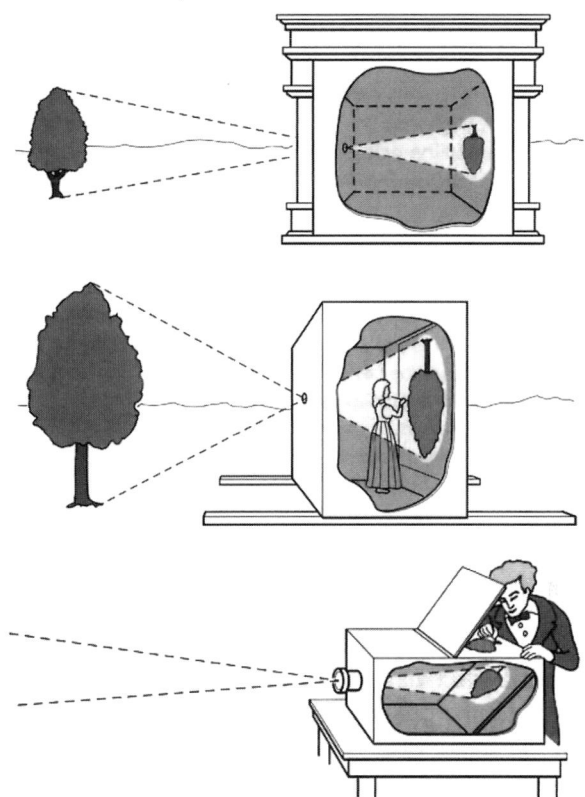

197 EVOLUTION OF THE CAMERA OBSCURA, PREDECESSOR OF THE MODERN CAMERA.
a. Sixteenth-century camera obscura.
b. Seventeenth-century portable camera obscura.
c. Seventeenth–nineteenth-century table model camera obscura.

plate to light for eight hours. During the next decade, the painter Louis Daguerre further perfected Niépce's process and produced some of the first satisfactory photographs, known as *daguerreotypes*.

At first, because the necessary exposure times were so long, photography could record only stationary objects. In Daguerre's photograph of LE BOULEVARD DU TEMPLE (on the following page), taken in Paris in 1839 (the year his process was made public), the streets appear deserted because moving figures made no lasting light impressions on the plate. However, one man, having his shoes shined, stayed still long enough to become part of

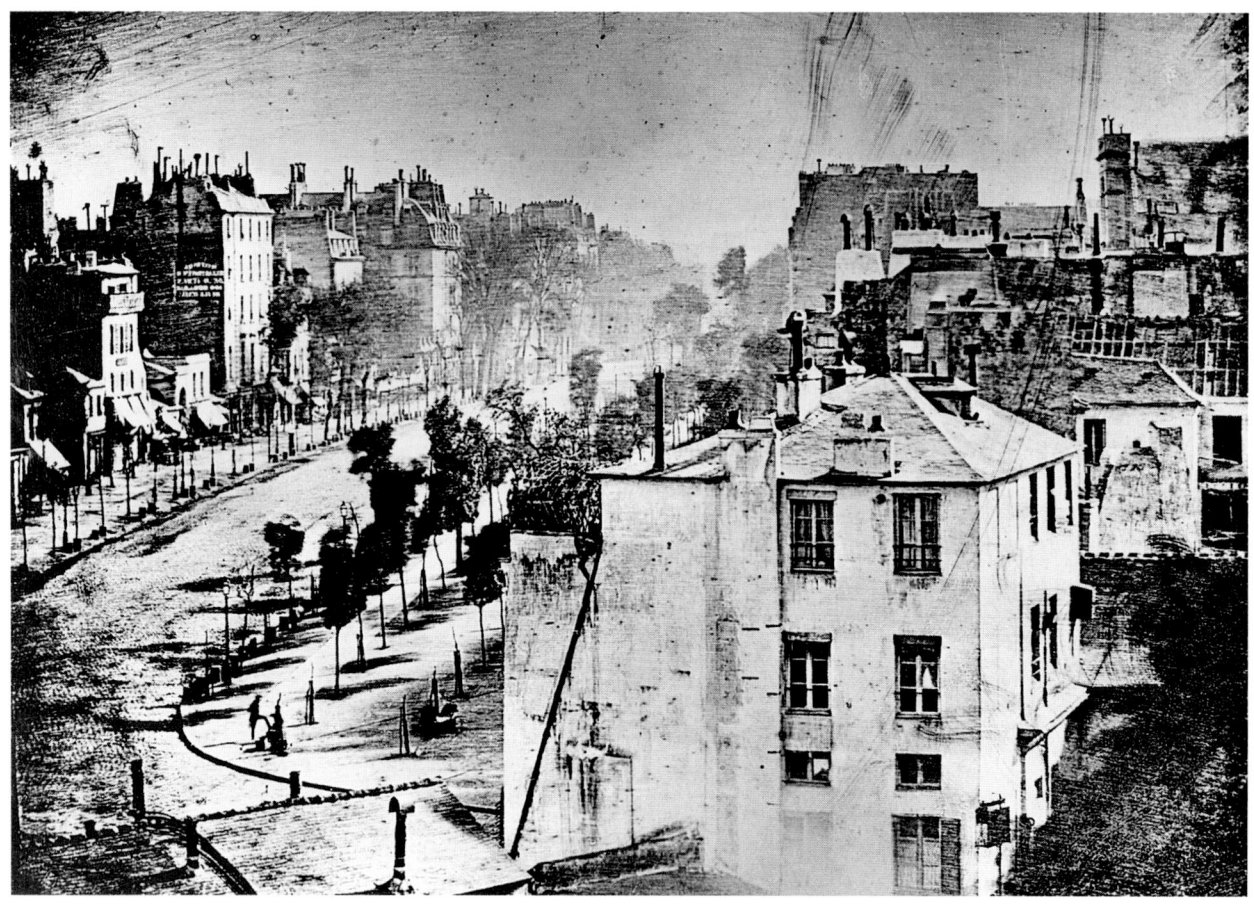

198   Louis Jacques Mandé Daguerre.
LE BOULEVARD DU TEMPLE. 1839.
Daguerreotype.
Bayerisches National Museum, Munich (R6312).

the image. He is visible on the corner in the lower left, the first person to appear in a photograph. It was a significant moment in history: At last images of people and things could be made without the hand of a trained artist. Although some painters at the time felt the new medium was unfair competition and spelled the end of their art, the invention of photography actually marked the beginning of a period when art would be more accessible to all through photographic reproductions; it also marked not the end but the beginning of new approaches to painting, complemented by the new art of photography.

Before the development of the camera, it was usually only royalty and the wealthy who could afford to have their portraits painted. By the mid-nineteenth century, people of average means were going in great numbers to photography studios to sit unblinking for several minutes in bright sunlight to have their portraits made with the camera.

From the beginning, portrait photography was heavily influenced by the traditions of portrait painting. The art of portrait photography was raised to the level of art by Julia Margaret Cameron. By 1864, she had become an avid photographer and had begun to create some expressive portraits. Cameron pioneered the use of close-ups and carefully controlled lighting to enhance the images of her subjects, who were often family members and famous friends. Her

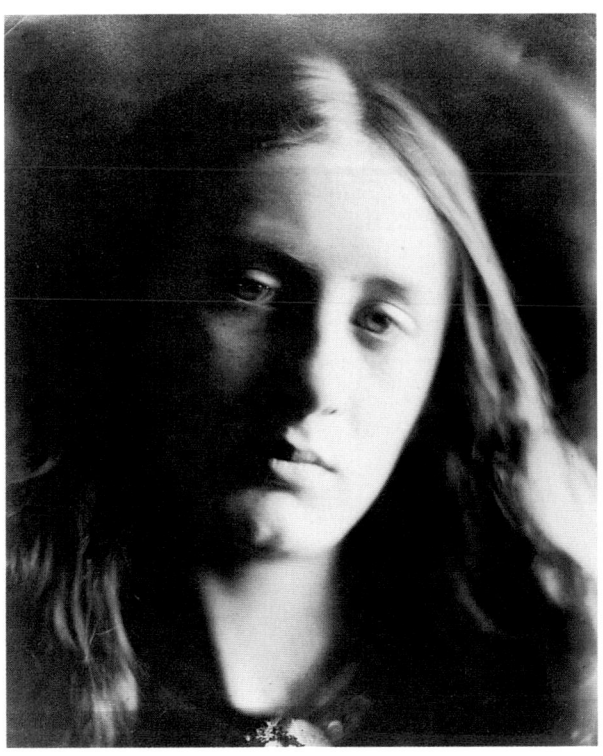

199 Julia Margaret Cameron.
JULIA JACKSON. 1866.
Albumen silver print from wet-collodion glass negative.
13¼″ × 11″.
Gernsheim Collection, Harry Ransom Humanities Research
Center, The University of Texas at Austin.

portrait of JULIA JACKSON is an excellent example. Cameron's use of raking light and a soft focus combine with Jackson's intense gaze and slight tilt of the head to suggest thoughtful energy.

Many nineteenth-century photographers looked for ways to duplicate what painters had already done—and thereby failed to find their medium's unique strengths. Painters, meanwhile—partially freed by photography from their ancient role as recorders of events, places, and people—looked for other avenues to explore. Yet some leading painters were greatly influenced by photography.

Photography as an Art Form

In the beginning, the public was reluctant to put photography on the same plane as other art forms because of its reliance on a mechanical device. Today, however, most people agree that the camera can be a vehicle for personal expression, symbolic communication, and eye-catching compositions. An early crusader in the art photography movement was

American Alfred Stieglitz, who opened a photography gallery in New York City in 1905. He also founded an influential magazine, *Camera Work*, which published photography along with essays about modern art and culture.

Stieglitz's own photography was almost always "straight"—that is, produced with no technical manipulation of the negative. In his 1903 photograph THE FLATIRON BUILDING (on the following page), Stieglitz arranged visual fields so that they echo each other. The basic shape of the foreground tree is answered in the stand of trees in the middle ground, but the fork of its branches also suggests the angle of the building (the "Flatiron" of the title). Like the foreground tree, this building seems to emerge from the ground, an impression supported by the row of seats in the snowy park. The recession of the ground from front to back of the picture is contradicted above the horizon, where the Flatiron and the black tree branches seem to touch. In his early photographs, Stieglitz showed the poetry he saw in urban reality.

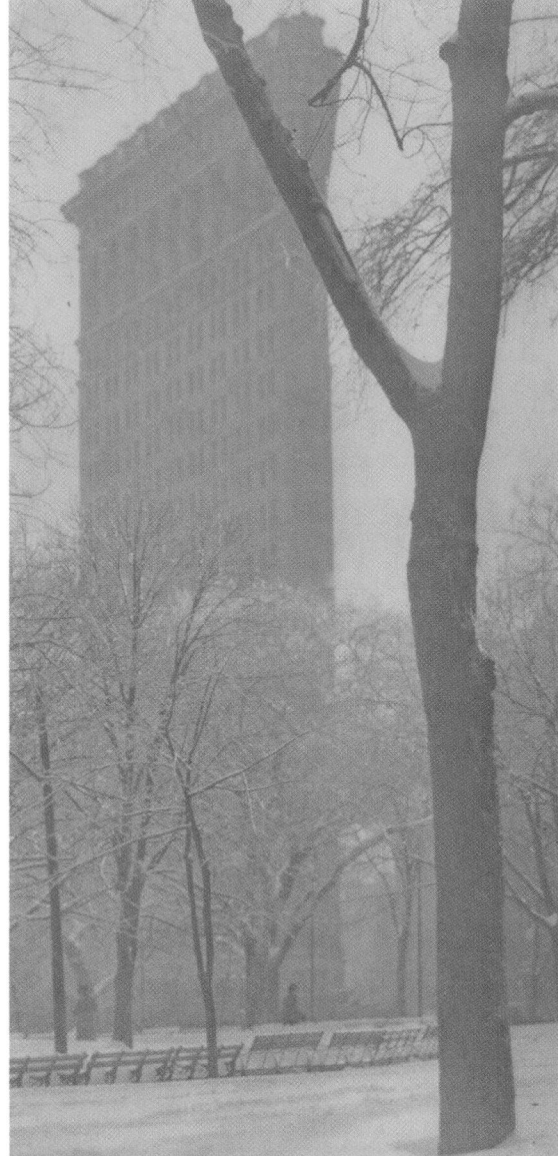

French photographer Henri Cartier-Bresson captured a subtle moment of urban drama in PLACE DE L'EUROPE BEHIND THE GARE ST. LAZARE, PARIS. Here he released the shutter at exactly the right moment to capture a man leaping over a puddle. The man's shape is echoed in both his own reflection and that of the dancer in the poster behind, just as semicircular ripples find a parallel in the round shapes close by in the water. For Cartier-Bresson, good photography is a matter of capturing the decisive moment:

To me, photography is the simultaneous recognition, in a fraction of a second, of the significance of an event as well as of a precise organization of forms which give that event its proper expression.[3]

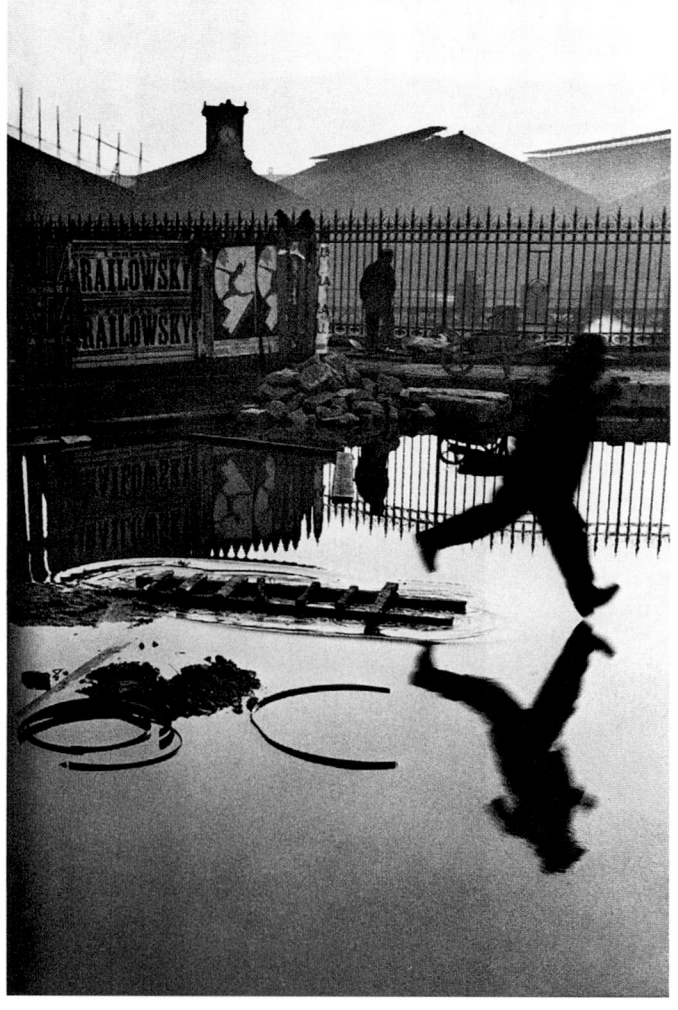

200 Alfred Stieglitz (1864–1946).
THE FLATIRON BUILDING. 1903.
Photograph from *Camera Work* (Vol. IV, 1903).
Plate I from Camera Work. NY, Number 4, October 1903.
Gravure on vellum 12⅞″ × 6⅝″.
Purchase (403.1976). Digital Image © The Museum of Modern Art/Licensed by
SCALA / Art Resource, NY © 2009 Artists Rights Society (ARS), NY.

201 Henri Cartier-Bresson.
PLACE DE L'EUROPE BEHIND THE GARE ST. LAZARE, PARIS. 1932.
Photograph.
© Henri Cartier-Bresson. Magnum Photos.

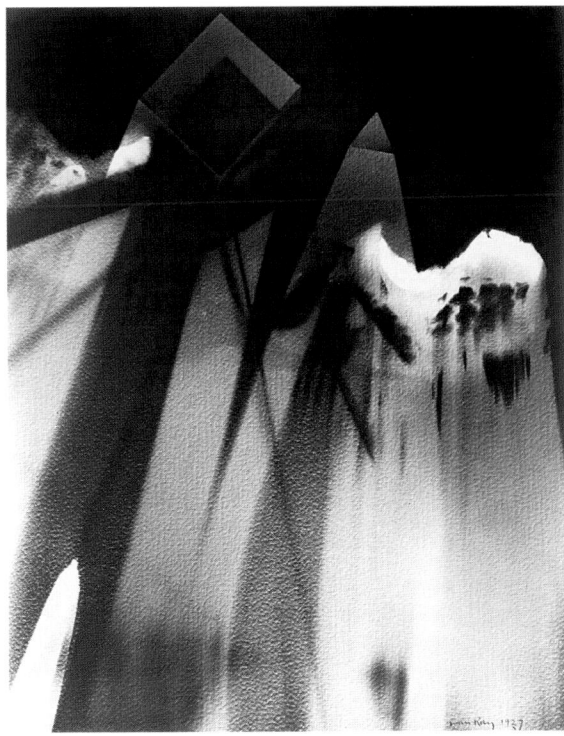

202 Man Ray.
RAYOGRAPH. 1927.
Gelatin silver print, 11½″ × 9⅛″.
Courtesy of George Eastman House, Rochester, NY.
© 2005 Man Ray Trust. Artists Rights Society (ARS), NY. ADAGP, Paris.

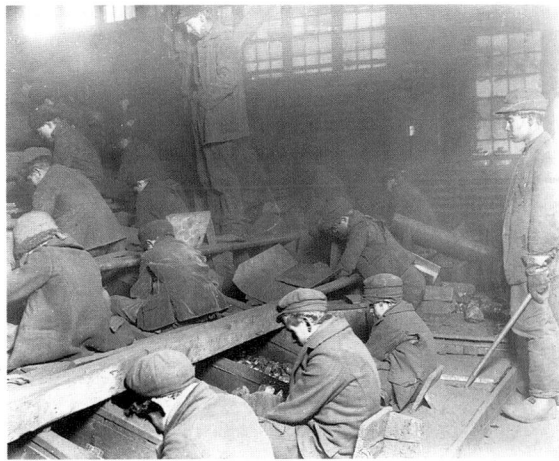

203 Lewis Hine.
COALBREAKERS, PENNSYLVANIA. 1910.
Gelatin silver print.
Courtesy George Eastman House, Rochester, NY.

Other photographers went beyond the camera itself to achieve more inventive effects. Man Ray made innovative photographs, which he called RAYOGRAPHS, by placing objects on light-sensitive paper and exposing them to sunlight. The rayographs are not really photographs, because they are not "pictures" of anything. Rather, they are visual inventions recorded on film. Sometimes, as in the work pictured here, it is not clear what the original subject was.

Photography and Social Change

Each generation produces its own memorable photographs. Such photographs move us not only because of the way their subjects are presented, but because we know the photographer was there. We join the photographer as witnesses. The significance of such images lies not simply in their ability to inform us, but in their power to stir our emotions.

Only a few decades after the invention of the medium, photographers began to bring public attention to suffering caused by war, poverty, hunger, and neglect. The new tool made visual statements believable in ways that no other media could. Of all the arts, photography is uniquely suited not only to documenting events and social problems, but to bringing about empathetic awareness that can lead to reform.

Early in this century, long before television, American sociologist Lewis Hine photographed working children. COALBREAKERS, PENNSYLVANIA is one of a series of photographs that show young children working long hours in coal yards, cotton mills, and food-processing factories. These photographs brought such abuses to the attention of the public and played a significant role in the creation of child labor laws.

During the 1930s, Margaret Bourke-White introduced the concept of the photographic essay—an approach that was soon adopted by other photographers. A *photo essay* is a collection of photographs on a single subject, arranged to tell a story or convey a mood in a way not possible with a single photograph. Photo essays are now an important part of international journalism. See also her photograph LOUISVILLE FLOOD VICTIMS on the *Discovering Art* CD.

FEW PHOTOGRAPHERS HAVE had a greater impact on the American public than Margaret Bourke-White. A pioneer in photojournalism, she made memorable images of most of the world's major events for nearly thirty years.

Her early family environment encouraged her to expand the boundaries of a woman's traditional role: "Learning to do things fearlessly was considered important by both my parents," she said.[4] She began to use a camera seriously when she took a group of landscape photographs in upstate New York that she sold to help pay her tuition at Cornell University. By 1927, she had her own studio in Cleveland, where she specialized in photographing industrial buildings such as steel mills.

Her life changed radically in the spring of 1929, when she got a call from Henry Luce, the publisher of *Time* magazine. He was founding a new magazine of American business, to be called *Fortune*, and he wanted to pioneer a new visual approach. Bourke-White recalled Luce's concept: "Pictures and words would be conscious partners . . . The camera would act as interpreter, recording what modern industrial civilization is, how it looks, how it meshes."

Thus began one of the most important partnerships in American journalism. She photographed American businesses from all angles, capturing everything "from the steam shovel to the board of directors." She climbed on buildings, stood in swamps, and suspended herself in midair, as we can see in MARGARET BOURKE-WHITE ATOP THE CHRYSLER BUILDING. Luce sent her to Russia to record the process of industrialization under Stalin's five-year plan.

When the Depression took hold in the United States, Bourke-White collaborated on a book documenting its effects. With writer Erskine Caldwell, she made *You Have Seen Their Faces,* a record of individual suffering and endurance in the face of the economic crisis. In 1936, when Henry Luce founded *Life,* Bourke-White became its lead photographer. Her photograph of the Fort Peck Dam in Montana was used as the cover for the first issue.

Her work with *Life* anchored the rest of her career. She recalled, "I loved the swift pace of *Life* assignments, the exhilaration of stepping over the threshold into a new land. Everything could be conquered. Nothing was too difficult. And if you had a stiff deadline to meet, all the better. You said yes to the challenge."[6] The Air

Force sent her as a war correspondent to most of the battlefronts of Europe in World War II, and she was among the photographers who recorded the liberation of the Buchenwald concentration camp in 1945.

Her pace hardly slackened when the war ended. Besides regular assignments within the U.S. borders, she witnessed and photographed for the rest of the world the decolonization of India, the Korean War, and struggles of South African gold miners. She was negotiating to be the first photographer sent to the moon when Parkinson's disease forced her retirement.

She said that she never recalled consciously choosing between marriage and a career, but as she grew older she realized that hers was "a life into which marriage doesn't fit very well. If I had had children, I would have charted a widely different life. . . . Perhaps I would have worked on children's books instead of going to wars. . . . One life is not better than the other; it is just a different life."[7] What settled the matter for her was probably this feeling: "There is nothing else like the exhilaration of a new story boiling up. To me this was food and drink."[8]

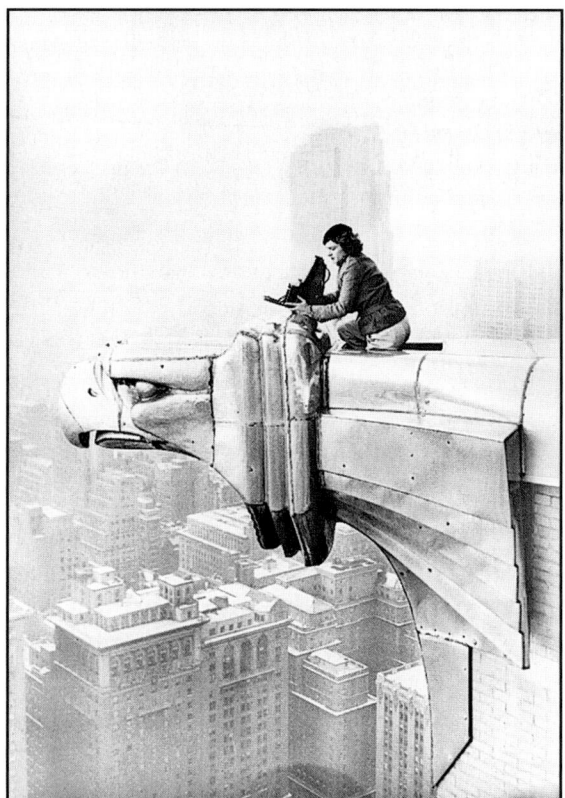

204 MARGARET BOURKE-WHITE ATOP THE CHRYSLER BUILDING. 1934.
LIFE Magazine © TimePix.
Photograph: Oscar Grauber.
Courtesy of Margaret Bourke-White Estate.

This was the very role I believed photography should play . . . I could see that this whole concept would give photography greater opportunities than it had ever had before.[5]

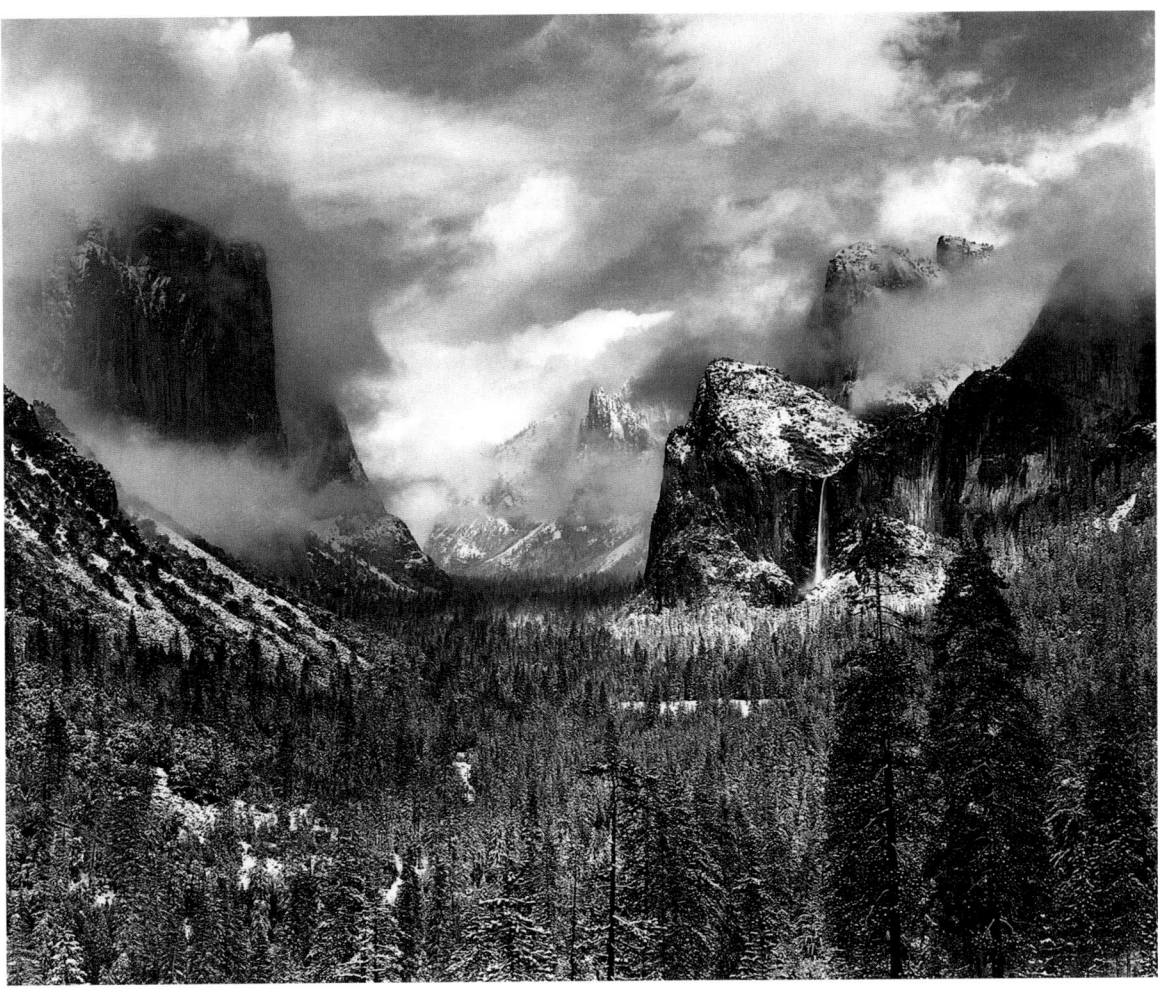

205 Ansel Adams.
CLEARING WINTER STORM, YOSEMITE NATIONAL PARK, CALIFORNIA. 1944.
Photograph.

In addition to focusing on social problems, photography has aided environmentalists. Ansel Adams used his photographs to increase public awareness of the need for conservation of the natural environment. The CLEARING WINTER STORM, YOSEMITE NATIONAL PARK reflects the symphonic grandeur of nature's design. It renders the cathedral-like Yosemite Valley as an orchestration in black and white where stark rock mingles with soft mist.

Adams viewed aspects of nature as symbols of spiritual life, capable of transcending the conflicts of society. In his majestic black-and-white photographs, nature becomes a timeless metaphor for spiritual harmony.

Color Photography

Photography began as a black-and-white (sometimes brown-and-white) process. For the first one hundred years, black and white was the only practical option for photographers. Through much of the twentieth century, technical problems with color persisted: film and printing papers were expensive, and, over time, color prints faded. Even when fairly accurate color became practical, many photographers felt that color lacked the abstract power of the black-and-white image.

The development of color photography began in 1907 with the invention of positive color transparencies. In 1932, the Eastman Kodak Company

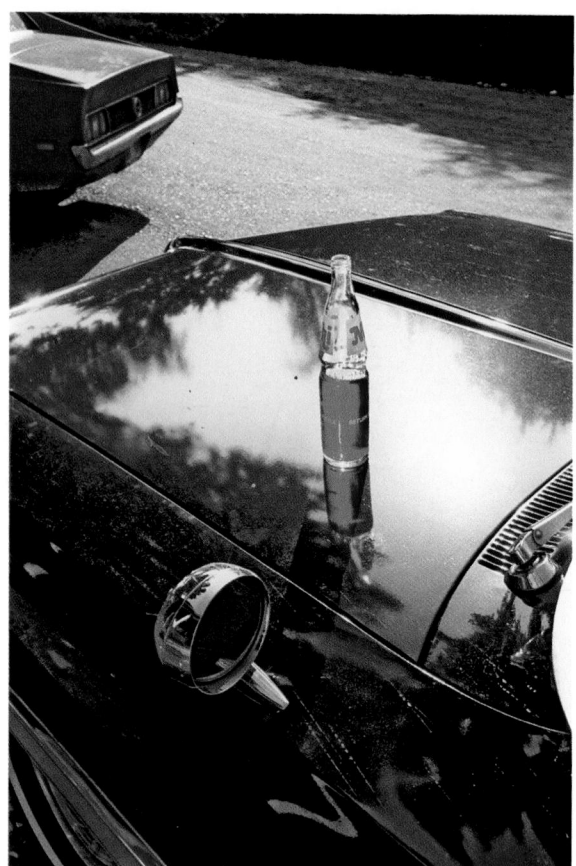

206　William Eggleston.
UNTITLED (NEHI BOTTLE ON CAR HOOD).
From *Los Alamos Portfolio*. 1974. Color photograph.
Eggleston Artistic Trust.

began making color film. Then, in 1936, the invention of Kodachrome substantially improved the versatility and accuracy of color film. Later progress improved the relative permanence of color prints.

Through the 1960s, most art photographers disdained color film, first because the negatives were unstable, later because color was associated with family snapshots and tourist photographs. But when William Eggleston exhibited his color work at the Museum of Modern Art in 1976, the world took notice and a new branch of art photography was born.

Eggleston's pictures from the *Los Alamos Portfolio* are elegant compositions of everyday things. In the UNTITLED photo (NEHI BOTTLE ON CAR HOOD) shown here, two cars block out an abstract composition of off-balance diagonals against a paved background darkened by wedges of shadow. The soda bottle seems perfectly positioned to both anchor the composition and capture the sunlight. Besides the skillful arrangement, the photo rivets our attention because it immediately evokes a world: a casual social setting in some American rural area on a warm afternoon. To prove the validity of Eggleston's commitment to color photography, all we have to do is imagine this work in black and white.

Pushing the Limits

Artists have explored a variety of techniques to go beyond photography's assumed limits. For example, Los Angeles artist Wallace Berman used an early version of the photocopy machine as a camera to make UNTITLED (B-3 MASTERLOCK) and other photo collages in the middle 1960s. He held a transistor radio in his hand and laid it on the glass bed of a Verifax machine. The resulting print gave him the base for embedding other images where the radio speaker was, so that instead of hearing different stations, we see different images. The addition of Hebrew letters to some frames adds a mysterious note.

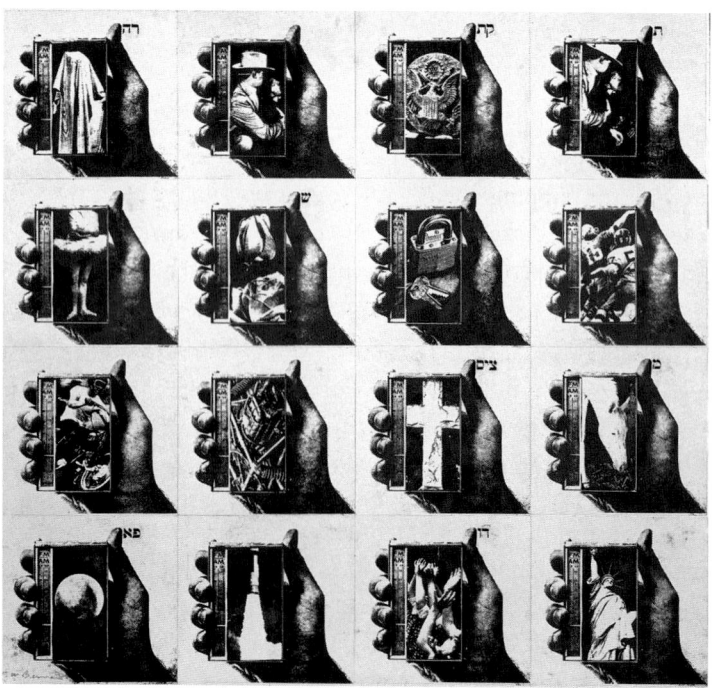

207　Wallace Berman.
UNTITLED (B-3 MASTERLOCK). 1965.
Verifax collage. 24″ × 25″.
Hirshhorn Museum and Sculpture Garden. Joseph H.
Hirshhorn Purchase Fund, 1990. (90–21).

Sonia Landy Sheridan pioneered the use of the imaging ability of computers as artists' tools. These tools support her research in the creative use of imaging technology, which she calls "generative systems." In FLOWERS, the translucent colors that fill the background were produced by shining fluorescent and tungsten lights into a color copy machine. Trained as a traditional artist, Sheridan began to shift in the late 1960s to creative uses of technological processes. Rather than wait for technology to catch up to her ideas, she worked with the 3M Company to develop tools to generate some of the images she envisioned.

The advent of digital photography, coupled with the expanding capabilities of photo-editing computer programs, is now radically altering the art of photography. Images that were once "handcrafted" in the darkroom can now be adjusted using a keyboard and mouse. Editing software allows many types of alterations, from resizing to color alterations to layering of images.

The invention of photography and the increasing availability of photographs and cameras have changed art more than any other invention to date, liberating it from its former narrative and documentary roles. Now, with computers, artists are empowered to explore personal thoughts and meanings even more freely.

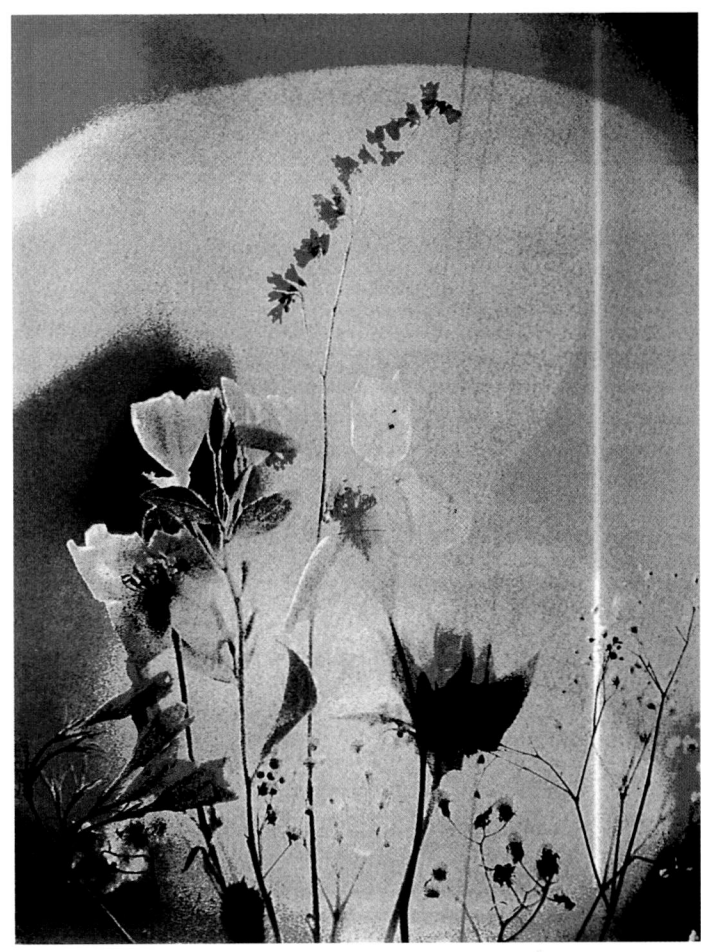

208 Sonia Landy Sheridan.
FLOWERS. 1976
3M color-in-color print. 8½″ × 11″.
Courtesy of the artist.

FILM: THE MOVING IMAGE

For thousands of years, artists have attempted to depict motion and how events occur over time. Prehistoric people portrayed animals in cave paintings and carvings in ways that suggested action. Assyrians, Egyptians, and Romans presented time progressions in low-relief sculpture; French artists of the Middle Ages painted frescoes in strips to show episodes from biblical stories; and Chinese and Japanese artists painted scrolls that told stories in visual segments as their paintings were unrolled a section at a time. But only with the development of movies in the late nineteenth century did motion and time find full, lifelike expression.

Before movies, it was discovered that looking at rapidly changing short sequences of still drawings gave the illusion of motion. By spinning drawings of various stages of a movement in a *magic lantern*, or flipping them in a *flip book*, viewers experienced a flickering appearance of movement. The magic lantern/flip book phenomena led the way to the invention of cinematography. When camera lenses and film evolved to the point where they could capture clear photographs of each stage of an object in motion, technology made motion pictures possible.

Leland Stanford (the founder of Stanford University) made a bet in 1870 that all four of a horse's hooves came off the ground when it ran. To settle the bet, Eadweard Muybridge lined up a series of still cameras close together along the side of a racetrack; each camera was fixed with a string to be tripped by

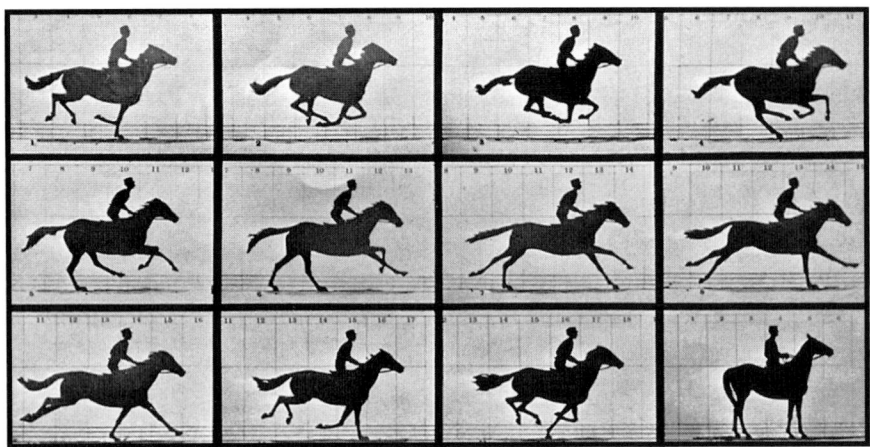

209 Eadweard Muybridge.
THE HORSE IN MOTION.
1878.
Photographs.
Courtesy of the Library of Congress.

the horse's front legs as it ran by. When the resulting pictures of THE HORSE IN MOTION were reviewed, it was evident that all four hooves left the ground. When Muybridge projected his still photographs in rapid succession, he discovered that the horse appeared to gallop. Others soon began experimenting with sequences of projected photographs, and cinematography was born, changing forever the way we see movement.

The illusion of motion is made possible by the *persistence of vision*, the brief retention of an image by the retina of our eyes after a stimulus is removed; and the process of *perception*, by which the mind attempts to make sense of incomplete information.

Film and Visual Expression

First and foremost, a movie is a visual experience. Film's rhythmic, time-based structure makes motion picture photography a very different sort of visual art from painting or even from still photography. Whereas a painter or photographer designs a single moment, a filmmaker must design sequences that work together in time as well as space.

Each piece of film photographed in a continuous running of the camera is called a *shot*. Film makes possible a dynamic relationship among three kinds of movement: the movement of objects within a shot; the movement of the camera toward and away from the action; and the movement created by the sequence of shots.

Much of the power of film comes from its ability to reconstruct time. Film is not inhibited by the constraints of clock time; it can convincingly present the past, the present, and the future, or it can mix all three in any manner. Film time can affect us more deeply than clock time, because film sequences can be constructed to approximate the way we feel about time. In addition to editing, filmmakers can manipulate time by slowing or accelerating motion. The filmmaker's control over time, sequence, light, camera angle, and distance can create a feeling of total, enveloping experience so believable that it becomes a new kind of reality.

Making a film is a collaborative effort, coordinated and given a coherent form by the director. Leading directors create their own styles and are known for certain kinds of content.

Technical Developments: Creating a New Language of Vision

The recognition of film as a significant art form came slowly. At first, film was nothing more than a novelty. In order to gain public acceptance, early filmmakers tried to make their movies look like filmed theatrical performances. Actors made entrances and exits in front of a fixed camera as though it too were a member of the audience at a stage play. Early films not only were limited to a fixed view, but also were silent because the technology for recording sound on film was not perfected until more than thirty years after the invention of motion picture photography. Total reliance on the visual image forced pioneer filmmakers to develop the visual language of film that continues to be basic to the art.

Between 1907 and 1916, American director D. W. Griffith helped bring the motion picture from its infancy as an amusement to full stature as a means of artistic expression. Griffith introduced the moving camera by releasing it from its fixed, stagebound position in order to better express narrative content. The camera was placed where it would best reveal the dramatic meaning of each scene. A scene thus came to be composed of several shots taken from different angles, thereby greatly increasing the viewer's feeling of involvement.

Assembling a scene from several shots involves *film editing*, a process in which the editor selects the best shots from raw footage, then reassembles them into meaningful sequences and finally into a total, unified progression.

Later, Griffith used parallel editing to compare events occurring at the same time in different places (person in danger and approach of would-be rescuer) or in different times, as in his film INTOLERANCE, in which he cut back and forth among four stories set in four periods of history.

One of film's most characteristic techniques was discovered when Griffith's camera operator accidentally let the shutter of his camera close slowly, causing the light to gradually darken. Griffith decided that this might be a good way to begin and end love scenes. *Fading in* or *fading out* remains a common transition between scenes.

Griffith was the first to use the close-up and the longshot while most movies were still stagebound. A *close-up* shows only the actor's face. Today the close-up is one of the most widely used shots;

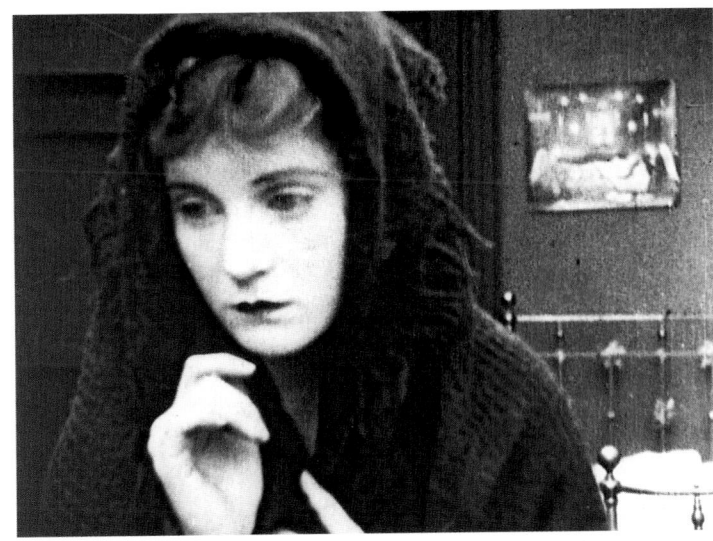

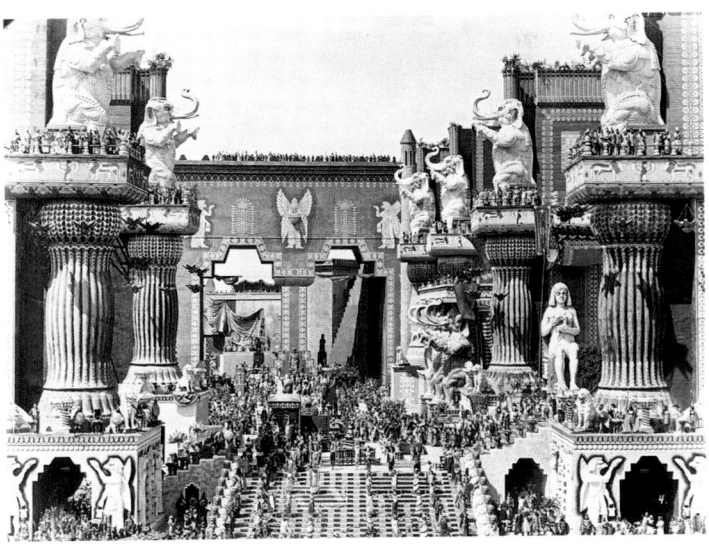

210 D. W. Griffith.
INTOLERANCE. 1916.
Film stills.
a. Close-up ("Little Dear One").
b. Longshot ("Belshazzar's Feast").
The Museum of Modern Art Film Stills Archive, New York.

but when Griffith first wanted to try a close shot, his cameraman balked at the idea of a head without a body! In a *longshot* the camera photographs from a distance to emphasize large groups of people or a panoramic setting.

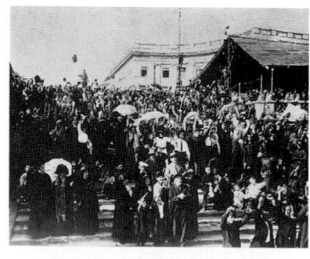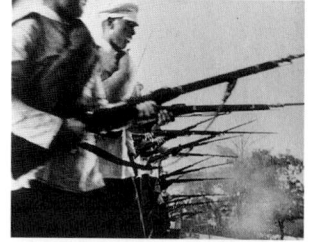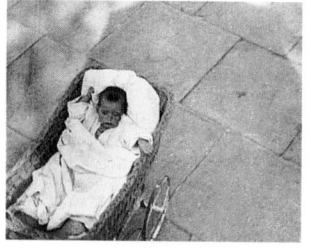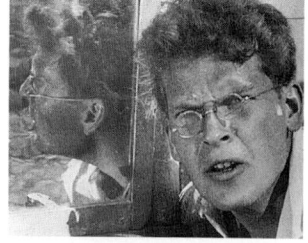
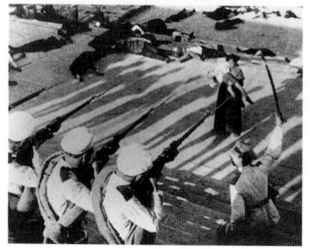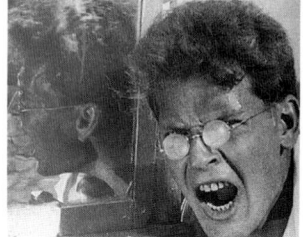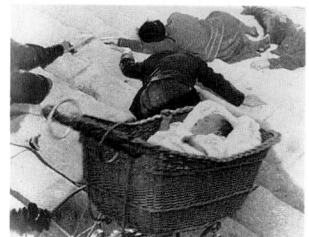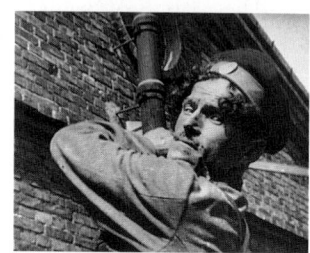

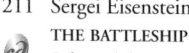 211 Sergei Eisenstein.
THE BATTLESHIP POTEMKIN. 1925.
Selected frames from Odessa Steps sequence.
Film stills.
The Museum of Modern Art Film Stills Archive, New York.

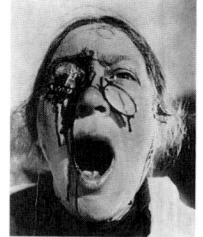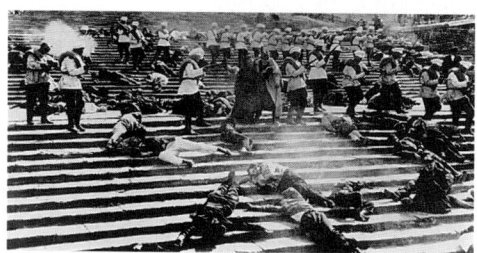

An International Language

When films were silent, movies could be produced in many countries for an international audience, without concern for language barriers. Following the Russian Revolution in 1917, Sergei Eisenstein emerged as a major film artist, honored as much in the West as in the Soviet Union. Eisenstein greatly admired Griffith's film techniques; after careful study, he developed them further, becoming one of the first filmmakers to produce epic films of high quality.

One of Eisenstein's major contributions was his skilled use of montage to heighten dramatic intensity. *Montage*, introduced by Griffith in 1916, is the editing technique of combining a number of very brief shots, representing distinct but related subject matter, in order to create new relationships, build strong emotion, or indicate the passage of time. With the use of montage, a great deal seems to happen simultaneously, in a short time.

In his film THE BATTLESHIP POTEMKIN, Eisenstein created one of the most powerful sequences in film history: the terrible climax of a failed revolt. The montage of brief shots, edited into a sequence of no more than a few minutes, effectively portrays the tragedy of the historic event. Rather than shoot the entire scene with a wide-angle lens from a spectator's perspective, Eisenstein intermixed many close-ups to give viewers the sensation of being caught as participants in the middle of the violence. The juxtaposition of close-ups and longshots gives audiences a powerful sense of the fear and tragedy that took place.

Charlie Chaplin came to prominence about 1915, when pressure from audiences and industry competition caused "stars" to be created and publicized. After starting his career as a member of a pantomime troupe, he became not only the leading comedian of his time, but also a director, producer, writer, and even composer. He built a team consisting of cameraman, leading lady, and comic actors, who worked with him for many years. A perfectionist, he reshot particular scenes dozens, even hundreds of times. Chaplin chose to stay with the silent tradition in CITY LIGHTS (except for music and sound effects), even though "talkies" were then being made by all other Hollywood filmmakers.

The arrival of sound in 1927 added a new dimension to film, but it did not change the medium's fundamental visual grammar. Color was introduced in the 1930s; the wide screen and three-dimensional images in the 1950s; 360-degree projection was first seen by the public in the 1960s. Most of these techniques, however, had been conceived of and researched by 1910.

After World War I, Hollywood became the film capital of the world. In the 1930s, most Hollywood films simply repeated plot formulas already proven successful at the box office. During that decade, the major studios all adhered voluntarily to the Motion Picture Production Code, which attempted to regulate the moral content of films. The Code forbade profanity in the script, as well as depictions of nudity, sexual activity, drug use, interracial romance, and ridicule of the clergy. It also prohibited the glamorization of crime, so that all gangsters had to be arrested or killed in the end. Studios submitted scripts to the Code authorities prior to shooting, and any film that lacked a Code seal of approval had no chance of wide distribution. At times, Code strictures were relaxed somewhat: Clark Gable's famous farewell to Vivien Leigh in *Gone With the Wind* ("Frankly, my dear, I don't give a damn.") remained in the film, but the producer paid a fine of $5,000 for it. The Code's authority declined in succeeding decades, but remained in effect until 1968, when the Motion Picture Association of America introduced the Ratings system that is still in force.

In 1941, at age twenty-five, Orson Welles made his film debut with CITIZEN KANE, an international landmark in filmmaking. Welles coauthored the script,

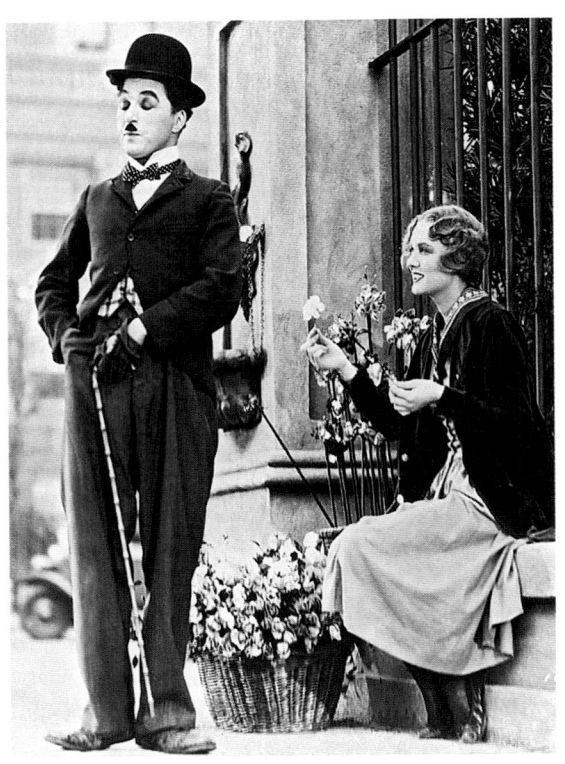

212 Charlie Chaplin.
CITY LIGHTS. 1931.
Film still.
The Museum of Modern Art Film Stills Archive, New York.

213 Orson Welles.
 CITIZEN KANE. 1941.
Film still.
The Museum of Modern Art Film Stills Archive, New York.

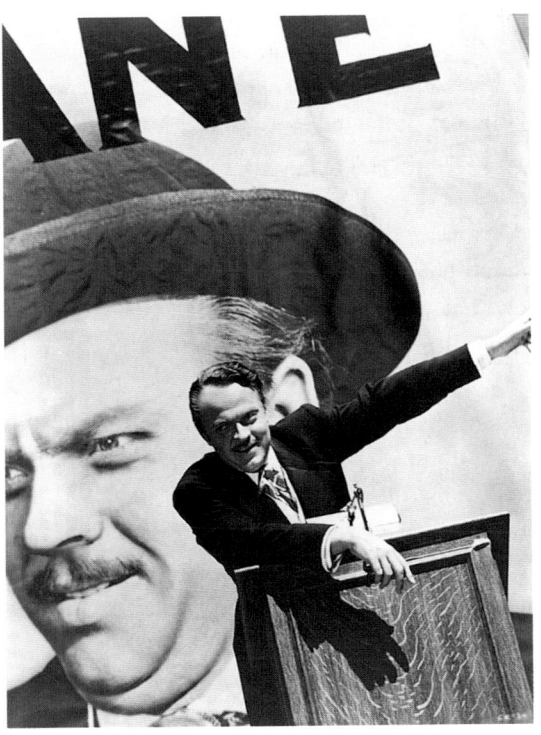

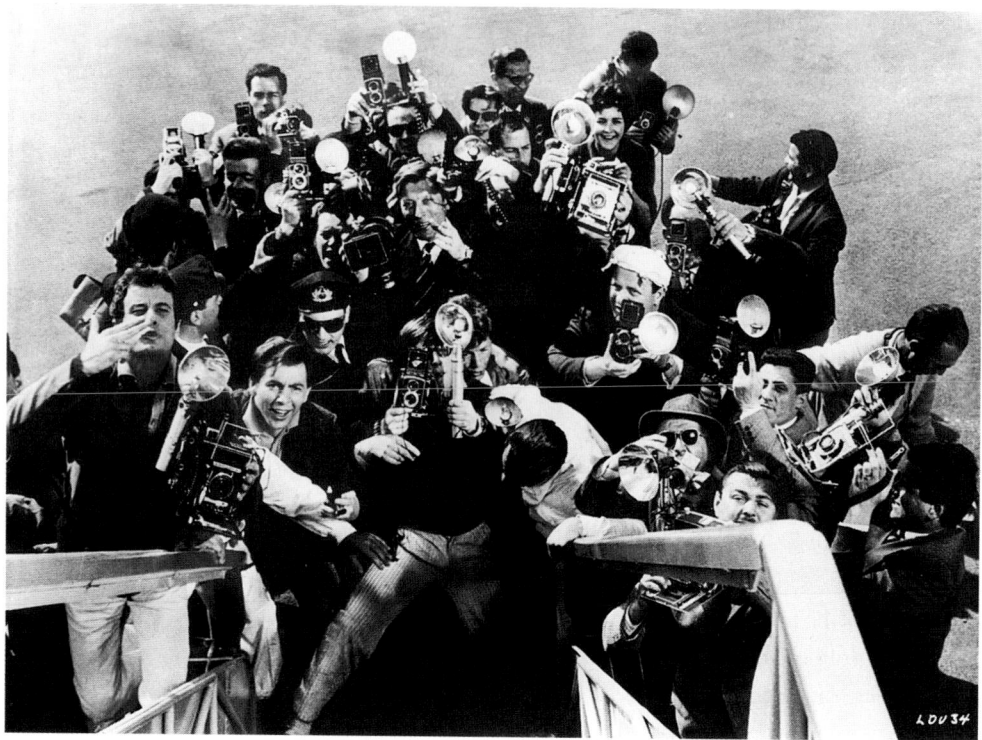

214   Federico Fellini.
LA DOLCE VITA. 1961.
Film still.
Everette Collection, Inc.

directed, and played the leading role in the thinly dis-
guised account of the life of newspaper tycoon William
Randolph Hearst. Because of its outstanding aesthetic
quality and meaningful social message, CITIZEN KANE
immediately set new standards for filmmaking. Welles
and his cinematographer, Gregg Toland, pioneered the
use of extreme camera angles. The low angle camera
presents Kane (Welles) as a towering presence; another
such angle is the tilt, which emphasizes Kane's crooked
politics.

Italian director Federico Fellini's 1961 film LA
DOLCE VITA (The Sweet Life) foreshadows many of
today's critiques of the mass media. Marcello Mas-
troianni played the lead character, a tabloid journalist also named Marcello who makes his career
reporting on sensations, scandals, and celebrities.

The protagonist follows the lifestyles of the
rich and famous, dutifully attending spectacles of
all kinds, from the exploits of American movie stars
to decadent parties to religious visions. He frolics

in a fountain at 4 A.M. with Anita Ekberg. He joins
the media circus as thousands throng to a small
town where two children say they saw the Virgin
Mary. One of these fellow travelers is a photographer friend named Paparazzo, and ever since this
film's release intrusive photographers throughout
the world have been called *paparazzi*.

Questioned about his tendency to exaggerate all
he reports on, Marcello replies defensively, "The
public demands exaggeration; but reasonably, when
permitted, I can report events without exaggeration." At a party where the discussion has turned to
art, Marcello announces that the art he prefers is "a
living art; a clear, honest style, without rhetoric and
without subterfuge." In fact, he devotes his life to
rhetoric and subterfuge, as he later tells a friend, "I
am just wasting my days, uselessly." In the end,
Marcello proves unable to resist the temptations of
the "Sweet Life," as he plunges headlong into the
world he reported on.

Animation and Special Effects

Beginning with the development of FANTASIA in the late 1930s, Disney animators have meticulously explored the possibilities of animation. With FANTASIA, released in 1940, Disney created a new form of film that integrated classical music, painting, dance, and drama with a mix of human and cartoon characters as the stars.

The group effort began with a story conference in which artists and musicians brainstormed ways to realize Walt Disney's initial concept. Ideas were portrayed on storyboards outlining the story from which the director choreographed the action. A *storyboard*, a series of drawings or paintings arranged in a sequence like a comic strip, was used to visualize the major shots in the film. Layout artists made the story come alive as the spatial relationships were worked out. Animators dramatized individual characters in each action sequence. Disney's goal was always to create characters who gave the illusion—at twenty-four frames per second—that they were not just moving, but thinking and feeling. Inkers traced the drawings onto cels (clear plastic sheets) for each frame and painters painted the reverse side. Each cel was then photographed, often using Disney's innovative multiplane camera for heightening the illusion of depth.

In recent years, some of the biggest box office successes have employed special effects made possible by a merging of old techniques and new technology. Teams of artists and technicians work with producer-directors such as George Lucas, creator of the STAR WARS trilogy, to provide working sketches, models, animation, and sets that are fantastic yet believable.

Industrial Light and Magic (ILM), the special-effects division of George Lucas's company, Lucasfilm Ltd., was the leading special-effects studio of the late 1970s and 1980s. The ILM team took ideas from script to storyboard to models to film. ILM spent at least a week on a sequence that lasts less than two seconds in the finished film. Only with computers can the complex alignment of all the elements of camera, light, model, and background be achieved.

Some of the best animated films in recent years have been made in Japan, where meaningful characters combine with epic story lines in visually

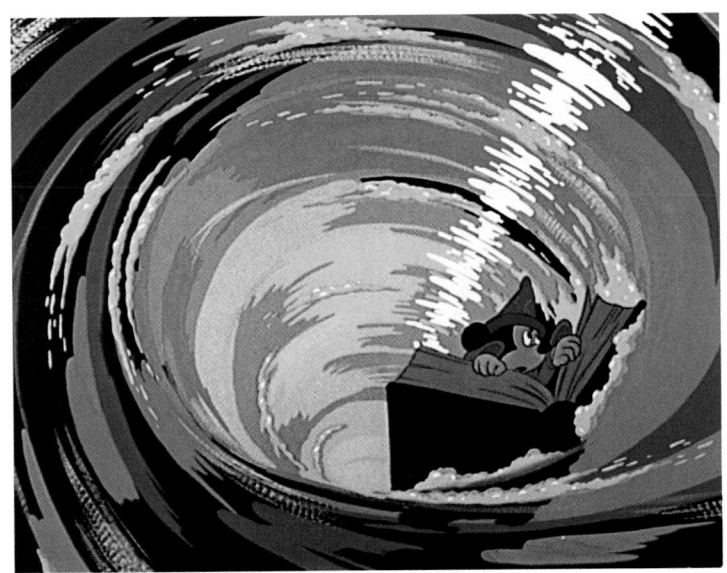

215 Walt Disney.
FANTASIA. 1940.
Film still. *The Sorcerer's Apprentice.*
Photograph: © The Walt Disney Studios. Photofest.

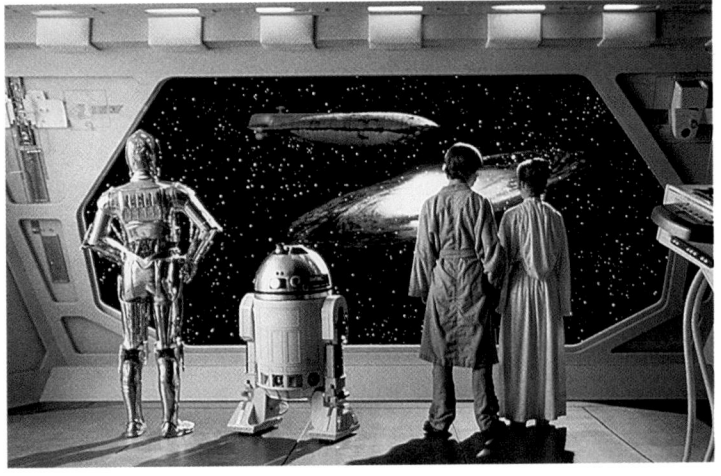

216 George Lucas.
STAR WARS. 1977.
Film still.
Lucasfilm Ltd.
Picture Desk, Inc. Kobal Collection.

stunning productions. One of the best of these was METROPOLIS, a frightening vision of a future society in which robots have evolved but people remain as greedy and unpredictable as ever. The film is notable for its exploration of human qualities in machines, as well as its impressive urban landscapes.

A new kind of film that shows today's more global society is the international co-production. Companies from several countries may collaborate on these films as they avoid some of the stereotypes of Hollywood. A recent example was PAN'S LABYRINTH, a joint Spanish-American production by Mexican director Guillermo del Toro. The film shows what happens when imagination and reality intersect in the life of an 11-year-old girl in fascist-dominated Spain. Her difficult life under a cruel stepfather leads her to take refuge in a fantasy world populated by tiny flying fairies and trees that move, led by a faun who represents a kingdom beyond this world. He recognizes her as royalty, but she must first prove her status by performing certain tasks that cross the line between her fantasies and "real" existence. The film's principal theme is how imagination can help us cope with adversity, and its many vivid sets and characters are testimony to the director's visual creativity (see pages from his

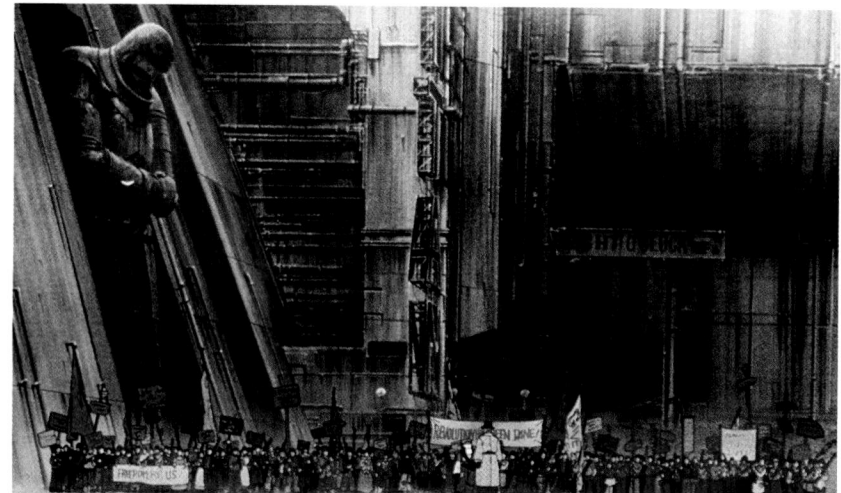

217 METROPOLIS. 2002.
Film still. Animated film
directed by Rintaro.
Sony Pictures Entertainment.
© 2001 Tezuka Productions. Metropolis Committee. All Rights Resercved.

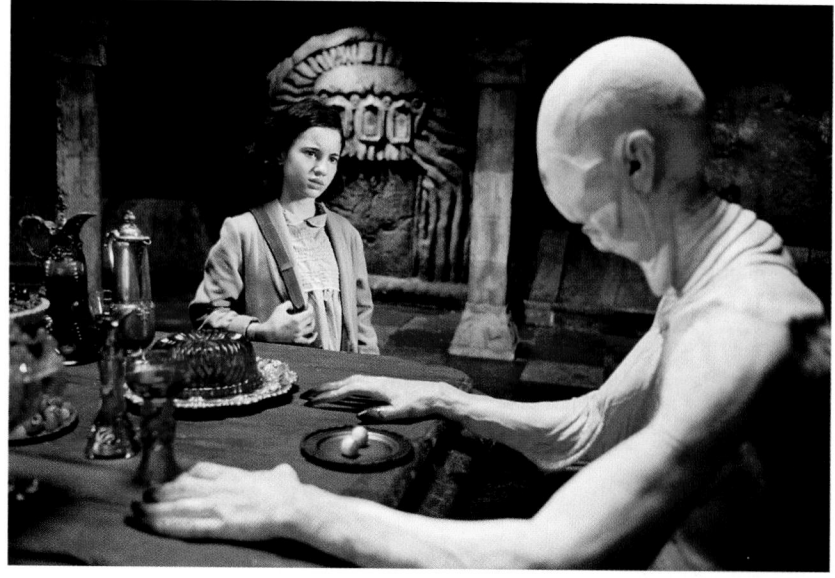

218 PAN'S LABYRINTH. 2006.
Film still. Film directed by
Guillermo del Toro.
Warner Brothers. Picturehouse.
© 2006 Picturehouse.

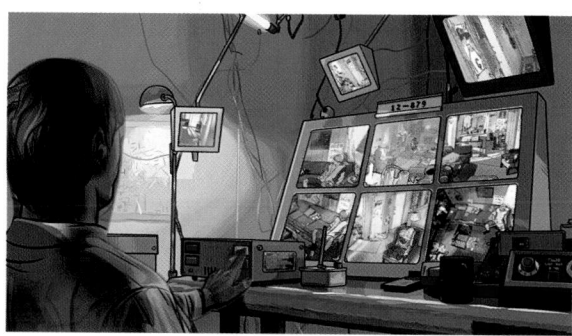

219 A SCANNER DARKLY. 2006.
Film still. Film directed by Richard Linklater.
Warner Independent Pictures.

SKETCHBOOK on page 103). PAN'S LABYRINTH has moments of both stunning beauty and aching horror. Del Toro refuses to tell us which is real and which imaginary, leaving the final decision to us.

Today, most major Hollywood film studios are owned by large international corporations, and they have discovered that they can draw audience interest around the world with movies that employ luxurious special effects with a fast story line. To aid international receipts, these "blockbusters" generally do not rely on character development or social comment for their success, and they are promoted together with merchandise such as clothing or toys derived from the film, to aid their appeal to younger audiences.

Closer to the cutting edge of cinema is the 2006 film A SCANNER DARKLY, based on a grim futuristic novel by science fiction writer Philip K. Dick. The story takes place "seven years from now," after the war on drugs has obviously been lost. The main character is both an addict and a drug enforcement officer, and his supervisor sends him on a mission to spy, in effect, on himself. To create the feeling of unreality that is the film's stock in trade, director Richard Linklater used rotoscoping, a technique for animating live-action digital video. The film's brightly colored frames dramatically reduce the star-quality of the main actors, but also heighten the film's allegorical meanings. The story

ends tragically, with a scrolling list of the novelist's friends whose lives were damaged by drugs.

TELEVISION AND VIDEO

Television, literally "vision from afar," is the electronic transmission of still or moving images and sound by means of cable or wireless broadcast. Television is primarily a distribution system for advertising, news, and entertainment. Video is the medium for television; it can also be an art form.

Video Art

The Sony corporation set the stage for the beginning of video art in 1965 when it introduced the first portable video recording camera, the Portapak. Although it was cumbersome, some artists were drawn to the new medium because of its unique characteristics: The instant feedback of video does away with development times necessary for film. Video works can be stored on inexpensive cassettes that can be erased and re-recorded. In addition, because a video signal can be sent to more than one monitor, it allows flexibility of presentation.

Early videos by artists were relatively simple, consisting mainly of recordings of the artists themselves performing, or of dramatic scenes staged with only a few actors or props. Because no editing was possible, and the black-and-white image was incompatible with the color resolution of television broadcasts of the time, the medium was most suited to private screenings for small groups. In 1972, the compatibility issue was resolved with the introduction of standardized ¾-inch tape; this allowed artists to work with television production equipment, and even to broadcast the results of their labors. The 1980s brought vast improvements in video technology in the form of lighter cameras, color, and computerized editing.

In the short history of video art, some artists have consistently tried to expand the limits of the medium's technical capacities. A leader in this movement was the Korean-born artist Nam June Paik. With the help of foundation grants, he worked in partnership with public television labs in Boston to develop the first video synthesizer. This

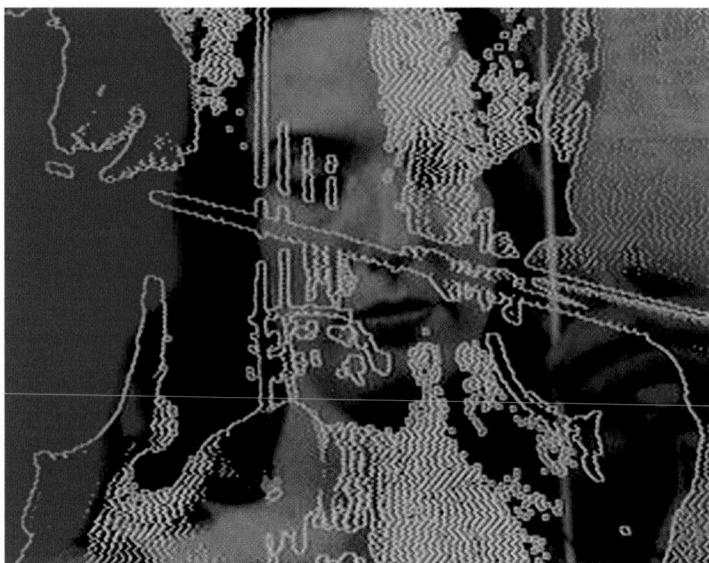

220 Nam June Paik and John Godfrey.
GLOBAL GROOVE. 1987.
Video.
Courtesy of Electronic Arts Intermix, New York.

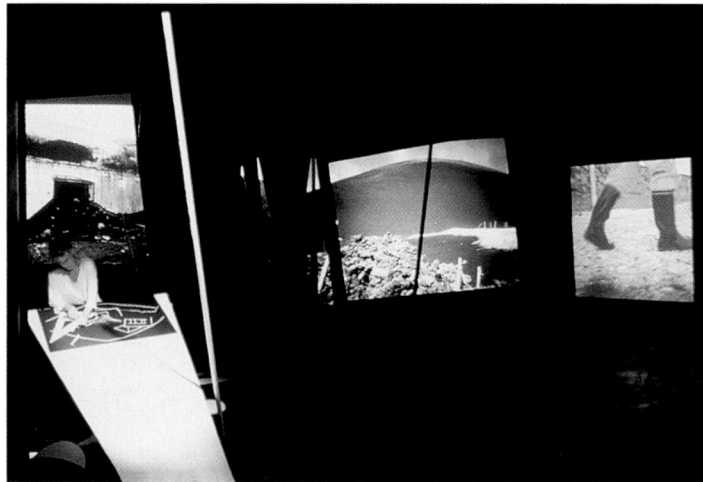

221 Joan Jonas.
VOLCANO SAGA. 1987.
Performance still.
Performing Garage, NY. Pat Hearn Gallery, NYC.

machine generated brilliant color patterns that could be programmed to develop from black-and-white input. Using it, he created GLOBAL GROOVE, a 1987 program that was broadcast over a public station in New York City.

Other video artists have used the medium to create and tell stories using themselves as actors. In her VOLCANO SAGA, Joan Jonas tells a story of a memorable trip to Iceland. Caught in a fierce windstorm, she was blown off the road and lost consciousness. Awakened by a local woman who offers help, the artist is magically transported back to ancient times in the company of Gundrun, a woman from Icelandic mythology who tells her dreams. The artist sympathizes with Gundrun's struggles in her ancient society, and returns to her New York home feeling kinship with women of the past. In the video, images move back and forth between past and present with the aid of overlays and an evocative musical score.

Today's video artists often use the medium as an element in three-dimensional installations. Dara Birnbaum's HOSTAGE uses five monitors arranged in an ascending arc together with target figures. The screens display borrowed images from a 1977 television news broadcast of a German hostage explaining his captors' demands. These are interrupted with cuts to American news reports of various other hostage-takings. The gallery environment is activated with sensors, so that viewers, by moving about, cause the cuts from one scene to another, and are thus held "hostage" themselves by being implicated in how the story unfolds on the screens.

DIGITAL ART FORMS

The artmaking capacity of computer-linked equipment ranges from producing finished art, such as color prints, film, and videos, to generating ideas for works that are ultimately made in another medium. Computers are also used to solve design problems by facilitating the visualization of alternative solutions. The computer's capacity to store images-in-progress enables the user to save unfinished images while exploring ways of solving problems in the original. Thus sculptors, photographers, filmmakers, designers, and architects can take advantage of the tools created by programmers of computer software.

The multipurpose characteristics of the computer have accelerated the breakdown of boundaries between media specializations. A traditional painter working with a computer can easily employ photo imaging or even add movement and sound to a work. A photographer can retouch, montage, change values, "paint over," or color black-and-white images. Digital technology facilitates the writing, design, and printing of books such as *Artforms*.

Early computer art looks dull by today's standards. The first exhibition of computer-generated digital imagery took place in a private art gallery in 1965; few claimed that it was art. Most of the earliest digital artists used computers to make drawings with a plotter, a small ink-bearing, wheeled device that moves over a piece of paper drawing a line in one color according to programmed instructions. With the help of technicians, Vera Molnar made some of the most visually interesting of these early efforts, such as her 1976 **PARCOURS: (MAQUETTE FOR AN ARCHITECTURAL ENVIRONMENT)**. The computer was programmed to make variations on a basic set of plotter movements, yielding a work that

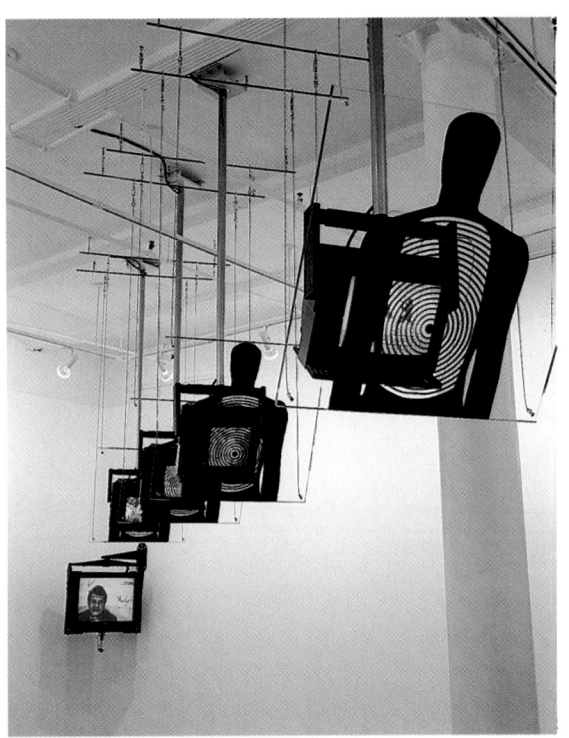

222   Dara Birnbaum.
HOSTAGE. 1994.
Six-channel video and interactive laser installation with Peerless ceiling and wall mounts, and designed ceiling mounts and plexiglass shields.
Dimensions site specific.
Photograph: Geoffrey Clements, Installation: Paula Cooper Gallery, NY.
Courtesy of Paula Cooper Gallery.

223   Vera Molnar.
**PARCOURS:
(MAQUETTE FOR AN
ARCHITECTURAL
ENVIRONMENT).**
1976. Computer
drawing.
© 2005 Artists Rights Society
(ARS), NY. ADAGP, Paris.
Courtesy of the artist.

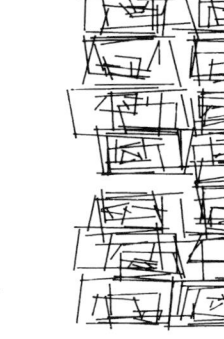
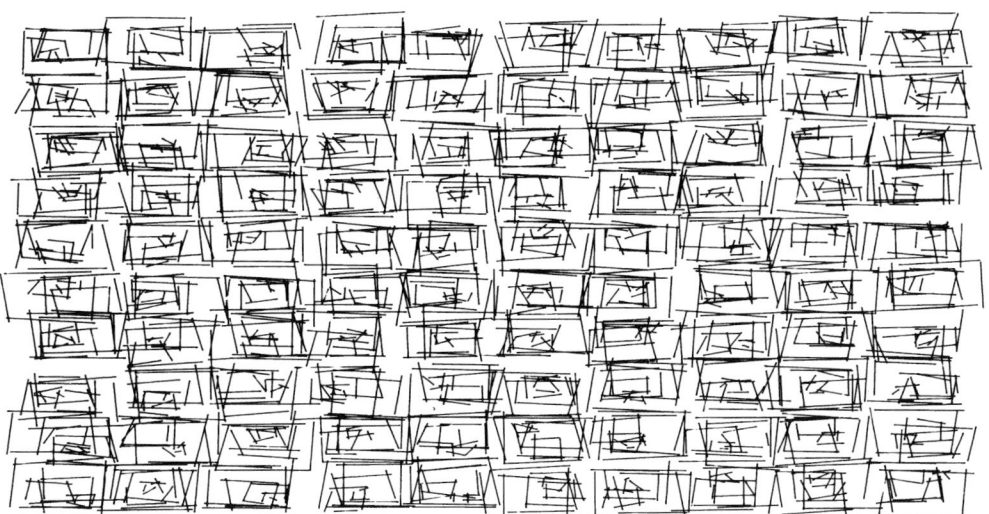

resembles a drawing quickly done by hand. In many of these early types of computer art, the plotter's motions were not entirely predictable, a fact that added to the attractiveness of the images. The expense and complexity of computer technology in those years, however, kept all but a few pioneer artists away from the medium.

The advent of faster computers, color printers, and interactive graphics radically changed the scenario in the middle 1980s; as the computer's capabilities grew, more artists began to take interest.

Camilla Benolirao Griggers used video editing in her work ALIENATIONS OF THE MOTHER TONGUE. She began with a fashion photograph and introduced incremental changes in the subject's face, bit by bit, until by the last frame we have a horrifying image of destruction. She combined all the stages of the frame's evolution into a five-minute video that evolves from something glamorous and desirable into a cry of pain.

This work shows how digital technology has undercut the traditional truth value of photography. If images are so easy to manipulate, then the camera can indeed be made to lie. Seeing is no longer believing, in the traditional sense of the term.

The digital artists considered so far use the computer to create art for the wall or the video screen; in that sense they are more traditional than the ones we consider next. This is because the digital revolution, besides generating new ways of making art, has also given rise to new ways of presenting it.

The newest digital medium is the World Wide Web, and many artists take advantage of its free universal distribution to create works expressly for viewing there. Some create works for posting to their own web pages; in addition there are several sites that specialize in exhibiting Web works and thus function like interactive galleries. A few museums have added collections of Web works to their sites as well. Like other branches of digital art, Web works have evolved rapidly since the first examples came out in the middle 1990s, in accordance with the increasing capabilities of Web browsers and plug-in programs. An early pioneer in Web works was James Johnson, whose ONE THOUSAND WORDS is discussed in the accompanying box.

Near the edge of the envelope in Web works is Annette Weintraub, whose 2001 piece THE MIRROR THAT CHANGES joins high-tech execution with social awareness. The title comes from a quote by Leonardo da Vinci: "Water is the mirror that changes with the color of its subject." On opening the work, we see nine vertical bars, each a portion of a photograph of water. A soundtrack of flowing liquid is a constant background. Clicking on one of the bars enlarges it and presents its related content, which may include video, sound, layered images, voice tracks, or scrolling text. The words that pass and the voices we hear may inform us about past wars fought over water, delight us with poetic quotes from literature

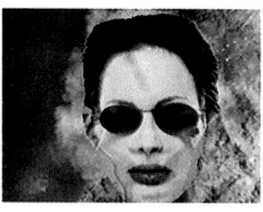
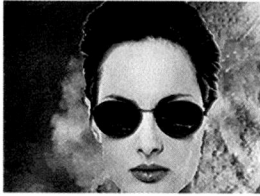
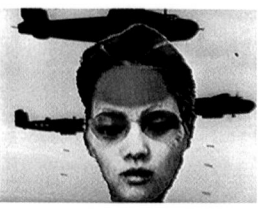
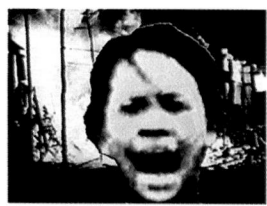

224   Camilla Benolirao Griggers.
ALIENATIONS OF THE MOTHER TONGUE. 1996.
Video with digital graphics and animation.
5 minutes.
Courtesy of the artist.

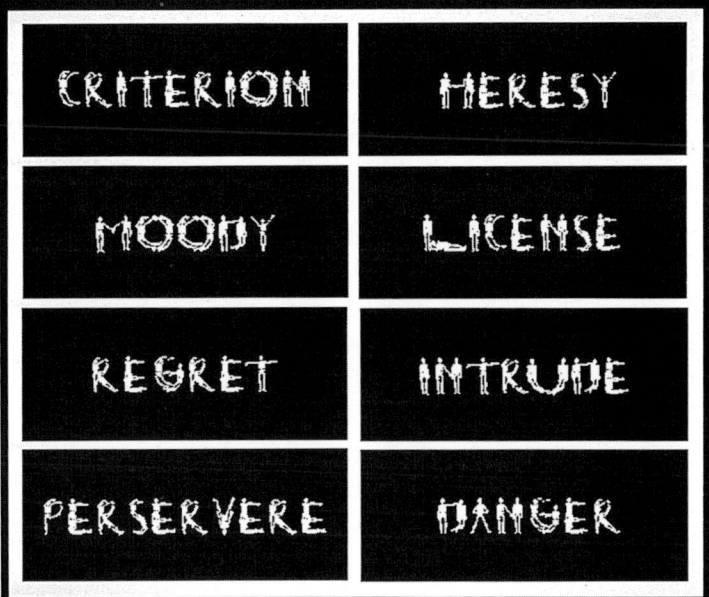

225 James Johnson.
Screenshot from ONE THOUSAND WORDS. 1998.
WWW work. 7½″ × 9″.
© James Johnson. http://spot.colorado.edu/~johnsoja/1KWords.html

James Johnson

James Johnson, who began his digital art career working with a plotter, makes Web works whose complexity is not apparent to the casual user. His interactive work ONE THOUSAND WORDS presents the viewer with an array. Clicking on any word will change it to another by selecting randomly from a large store. In this way, meanings and their combinations shift at random at a speed that the user determines. The work generates a welter of meanings, all presented in a unique type font that the artist himself invented.

One of the many ways in which Web works differ from other kinds is that copyright protection is severely weakened, because viewers can download and print in unlimited quantities any phase of a Web work. This does not worry Johnson, who says that art should be a gift. See the *Artforms* Web site for more of this interview.

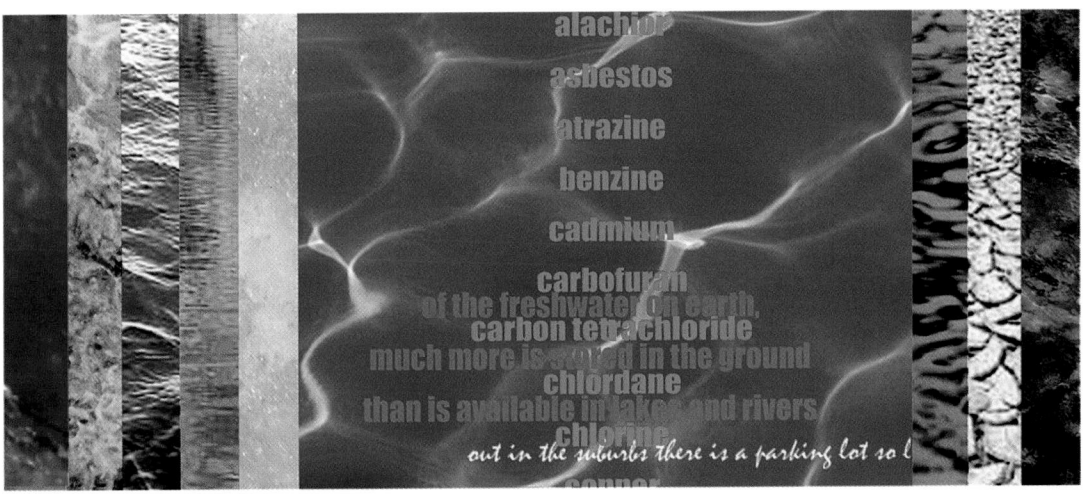

226 Annette Weintraub.
Screenshot from THE MIRROR THAT CHANGES. 2003.
Interactive WWW work.
http://www.virtualthemeworld.com/mirror/flashindex.html. Courtesy of the artist.

about water, or wake us up to current crises that involve water ("We will never have more water on earth than we have right now"). The work's wealth of information, presented in easily accessible layers with elegant presentation, make it a standout.

If Weintraub's piece raises awareness of our natural environment, Rui Filipe Antunes made a digital video work in 2006 that creates its own seemingly natural world. He describes XTNZ as a garden, made of slowly evolving shapes that resemble life forms, but they are in fact computer-drawn modules driven by software. They grow and interact, accompanied by both natural and manufactured sounds. The artist created these various "life forms," divided them into families, and turned them loose in a digital environment to see what would happen. The title is based on David Cronenberg's feature film *eXistenZ*, which deals with the question of real and virtual reality, and indeed the shapes of XTNZ could be real if not for the dreamy, fluorescent colors. The work is available for viewing at any time, because the artist created a YouTube channel for it.

As we all know, almost anything can be found on the Internet, and Natalie Bookchin took advantage of this abundance in creating the digital video LOCATION SECURED in 2006. She surfed the Internet to gather random examples of surveillance camera footage from about a dozen locations around the world, and then strung them together into a 12-minute film. For a soundtrack she used the recorded telephone conversations of President Lyndon Johnson from 1963 to 1965, alternating with telephone calls placed to Dr. Ruth Westheimer's radio program *Sexually Speaking* (yes, both were freely available for listening on the Internet). Sometimes the video footage is poor, as when rain distorts the camera lens, or vegetation blocks the view, or the equipment is of low quality. But as we look at a Japanese garden, for example, we hear President Johnson's staff discussing where to find him in the White House. Over footage of janitors sweeping a gymnasium somewhere, a woman complains because her boyfriend started asking out her twin sister. These odd juxtapositions are very common in today's cyber-driven world, but when the artist puts them together for display in an art gallery, the jarring effect is magnified. And because all of the material that she gathered deals with private realities, LOCATION SECURED highlights the issue of what is public and what is private, an urgent concern in a time when surveillance is increasing.

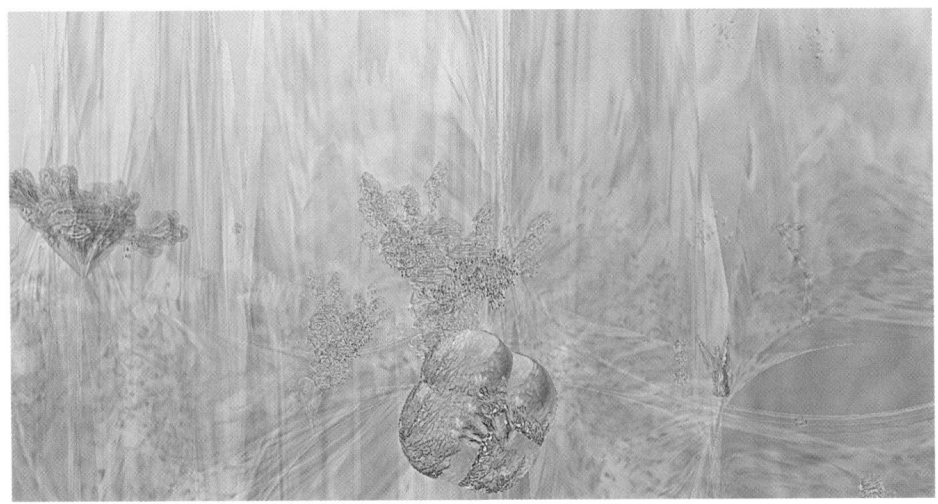

227 Rui Filipe Antunes.
Still from XTNZ. 2006
Digital video.
Courtesy of the artist.

Lynn Hershman Leeson directly confronted the issue of simulation when she created the video cyborg DiNA in 2004. "The title comes from the phrase 'digital DNA.'" DiNA appears on a video installation in which viewers walk up to a microphone and interact with the virtual woman on the screen before them. DiNA is running for the imaginary office of Telepresident, and in her slightly disembodied cybervoice she invites viewers to use the microphone to raise questions and concerns. DiNA's responses sound surprisingly intelligent for a machine, but she is linked to the Internet and searches in real time for text to use in response to viewer input. After interacting with DiNA for a few minutes, viewers learn that she takes moderately liberal positions on abortion and capital punishment, for example. Most viewers conclude either that DiNA could indeed run for office, or that she seems more thoughtful than most politicians. Her campaign slogan was "Artificial intelligence is better than no intelligence." In an age when telling the real from the pre-packaged is difficult, DiNA complicates the issue in a memorable way. The artist created a campaign Web site in time for the 2004 elections and stocked it with "live footage," just to ensure that DiNA's positions on the issues could be available to voters.

In short, digital art has evolved as quickly as computers themselves. Many artists today include digital technology in their works in one way or another. The need for a separate category "digital art" is subject to further debate. Whether it remains a medium with its own properties, or becomes integrated into others, is a decision best left for the future. For the present, the art world as a whole has been quick to adopt many aspects of digital technology, as the essay on the following page shows.

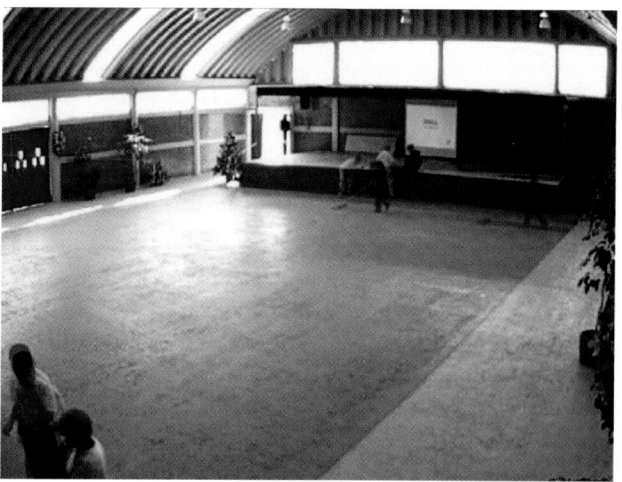

228 Natalie Bookchin.
Still from LOCATION SECURED. 2006.
Digital video. 12 minutes.
Courtesy of the artist.

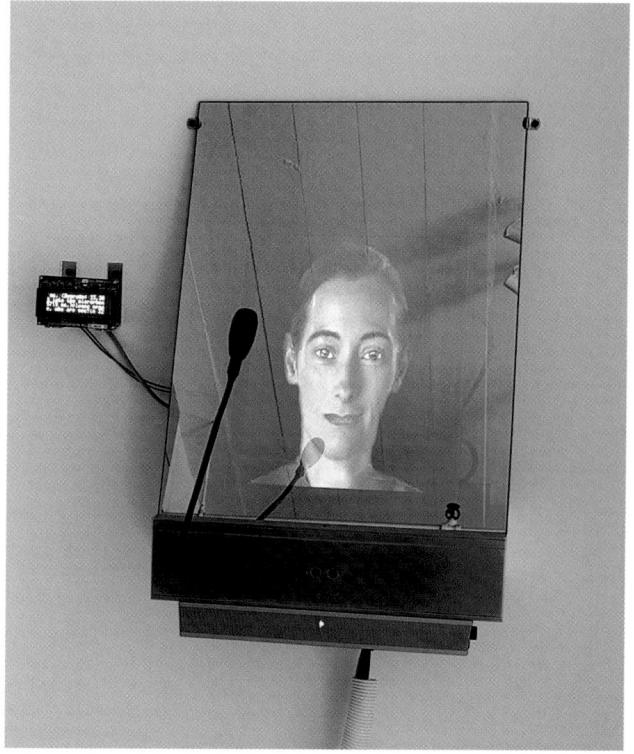

229 Lynn Hershman Leeson.
DiNA. 2004.
Artificially intelligent agent, network connection, custom software, video, and microphone. Dimensions variable.
Courtesy Bitforms Gallery, New York.

ART *in the world*

THE IMPACT of digital technology on the creation of artworks has been important, but the impact has been greater in other areas connected to art. Computers are now integral to the analysis, preservation, and sale of artworks. Indeed, the new technology has taken root in these areas sooner than it has in artists' studios.

There are several on-line art magazines, where Internet surfers can go to find out where art shows are held and read reviews of current exhibitions in many parts of the world. Critical issues surrounding art are discussed, and scholars present new findings. Because the quality of images visible on a computer screen is below that of a printed page, digital magazines are far from replacing hard copy; for now they function as a supplement to paper-based art criticism and analysis.

Museum Web sites become more sophisticated with each passing year. Most museums have them, and usually they contain information about current special exhibitions, as well as on-line viewing of artworks from their collections. Some museums create education modules on their sites so that the Internet public can learn in depth about the art on display. The most advanced museum Web sites have pioneered new methods of digital browsing of artworks, placing more and more of the collection on-line and allowing for close-up, high-resolution views of selected parts of works. In this way they have narrowed the quality gap between screen images and printed photographs.

Likewise, the new technology has had an important impact on conservation of artworks. From small pottery fragments dug up at an archaeological site, for example, computer programs can digitally reconstruct an entire piece. New three-dimensional laser scanners can track every square millimeter of sculptural works from several angles at once, making exact recordings of every surface possible. Painting conservators use computer-assisted mass spectrometers to analyze the chemical content of paint surfaces in order to aid in their cleaning and restoration.

On a more mundane level, there are several Web sites that track and post information on stolen artworks. Dealers and auction houses make frequent recourse to such sites, to check on the legal status of works that they may buy or sell.

Increasingly, the Internet is an important venue for the sale of artworks as well. Many galleries and dealers have Web sites that post works for sale, saving art collectors a great deal of browsing time. On-line auctions are another fast-growing trend. Only a small portion of these will last, partly because it is difficult to assess the quality, much less the authenticity, of a work posted on-line. In addition, deceptive practices such as price collusion and false bids are easy to bring about and difficult to trace. For these reasons, most of the high-value works will continue to sell at live auctions and in dealers' galleries. But there is little doubt that on-line auctions of artworks are here to stay because of the ease with which they bring in a wider public. On-line auctions are a highly visible phenomenon, widely reported in the media. But they represent only one facet of the continuing impact that computer technology is having on the art world.

There is one area that is still relatively untouched by digital technology: the study of artworks. Only a tiny fraction of documents relating to the history of art have been placed on-line. Thus, most art research still requires much more time in the library than at the computer screen. More important, no digital experience can quite take the place of standing before an actual work, or of meeting the person who created it face to face.

GRAPHIC DESIGN

Every manufactured object, printed image, and constructed space has been designed by someone. From clothing to airplanes, from homes to public buildings and community spaces, design is a necessity, not an afterthought.

DESIGN DISCIPLINES

Professional designers can enhance living by including aesthetics as well as utility in the design of the human-made world. Their designs shape and express our cultural values. Some designers see themselves as artists, while others think of themselves as creative problem solvers. The design concepts introduced in Chapter 4 provide a basis for understanding how designers enhance the visual, informational, and mechanical qualities of our material environment.

As consumers, we discover that some things are well designed and some are not. When the form and function of an object do not complement each other, the object is poorly designed. Good design solves problems; bad design creates problems.

Design disciplines include, but are not limited to, graphic design, industrial design, motion graphics, textile design, clothing design, interior design, architecture, and environmental design. In this chapter, the focus is on graphic design, motion graphics, and industrial design.

Of all art forms, we encounter graphic design most frequently in our daily life. We interact with graphic design on an almost constant basis; most designers have chosen it as their profession because they relish that close interaction with people in all situations. Our encounters with graphic design are usually casual and unintended; we do not seek out graphic design the way we might seek other art forms in a gallery or museum. This fact gives designers an unequalled opportunity to attract, inform, persuade, delight, bore, offend, or repel us.

Text dominates Russian designer Aleksandr Rodchenko's sketch for a 1923 sign. GIVE ME SUN AT NIGHT! exclaims the text in the upper left. "Where do we find this?" reads the inscription just below. "Buy it at GUM," is the answer, referring to

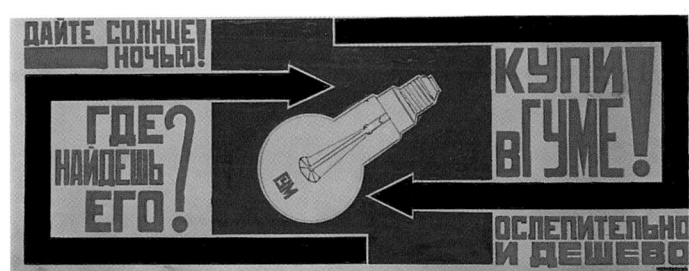

230 Aleksandr Rodchenko and Vladimir Maiakovskii.
GIVE ME SUN AT NIGHT.
Design for Poster. 1923.
Gouache, ink, pencil, gelatin silver print. 4⅜″ × 18″.
Merrill C. Berman Collection. Photograph by Jim Frank.
© Estate of Aleksandr Rodchenko. Licensed by VAGA, New York, NY.

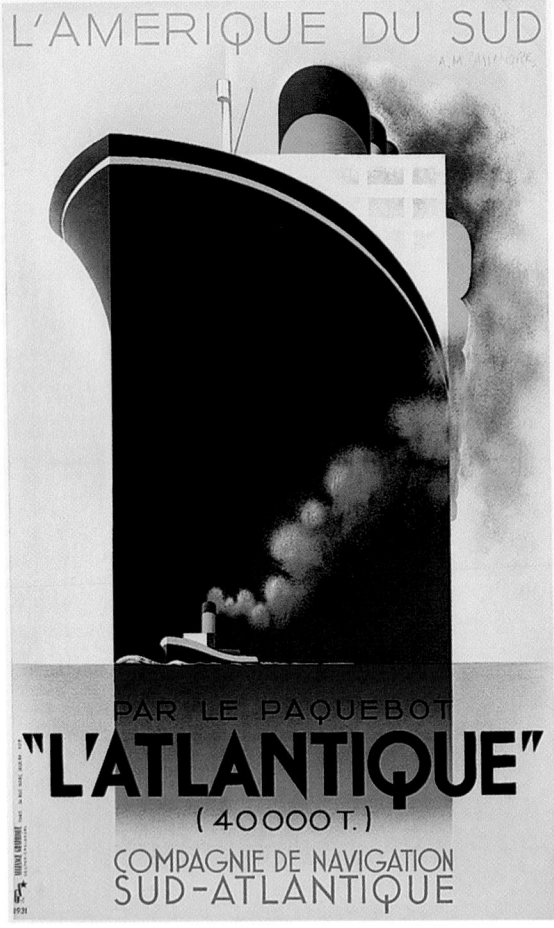

231 Cassandre (Adolpe Jean-Marie Noreau).
L'ATLANTIQUE. 1932.
Lithograph. 39½″ × 24½″.
Merrill C. Berman Collection. Photograph by Jim Frank.
© 2002 Artists Rights Society (ARS), NY.

Moscow's largest department store. In the lower right, a slogan hammers the point home: "Blinding and cheap." In the center, surrounded by arrows, is the lightbulb that will illuminate everyone at night. The designers had the task of convincing people to buy a product that was not widely used at the time, so the tone is emphatic.

Graphic design often has the goal of getting us to do something. The French designer Cassandre designed the poster L'ATLANTIQUE in 1932 to promote travel by ship. The text of the poster merely informs viewers that the ship weighs forty thousand tons, and frequently goes to South America under the auspices of the Sud-Atlantique Steamship Company. The designer lets the image do most of the persuading in this poster, and it dominates the composition. The angle of view is from below, as if we were bobbing on the ocean surface as the ship looms majestically above. The implication is that if we travel by ship, we participate in something larger than life.

GRAPHIC DESIGN

The term *graphic design* refers to the process of working with words and pictures to create solutions to problems of visual communication. Much of graphic design involves designing materials to be printed, including books, magazines, brochures, packages, posters, and imagery for electronic media. Such design ranges in scale and complexity from postage stamps and trademarks to billboards, film, video, and Web pages.

Graphic design is a creative process employing art and technology to communicate ideas. With control of symbols, type, color, and illustration, the graphic designer produces visual compositions meant to attract, inform, and persuade a given audience. A good graphic designer can memorably arrange image and text for the benefit of both.

Logos and Symbols

In our age, when image seems to be everything, companies spend large sums on graphic design to present the best "identity package." A *logo* is an identifying mark, or trademark, based primarily on letter forms. A *symbol* is an identifying mark based on pictorial (rather than typographic) sources. Corporations finely calibrate logos and symbols to present a distinctive and memorable appearance.

An organization's logo may even change over time, reflecting a different cultural climate, a different set of goals, or new management. When the National Aeronautics and Space Administration (NASA) was founded in the late 1950s, the first of the NASA LETTERHEAD used a celestial globe with the Earth, the Moon, and a stylized arrow symbolizing space flight (a). In 1973, with space travel more commonplace, the logo was changed to the stylized initials in red (b). The letters "A" symbolize rocket nose cones in this second NASA logo.

In the early 1990s, in the aftermath of federal budget cuts and in a demoralized environment caused by the explosion of the space shuttle Challenger, the logo was redesigned again. NASA decided to return to a version of its previous logo, which administrators thought better exemplified an optimistic and exploratory mood (c). This time they used the color blue to symbolize the heavens.

In today's media-saturated world, where excessive familiarity can be deadening, keeping a corporate identity package both contemporary and recognizable is a big challenge. One of the most original solutions to this problem is the SAKS FIFTH AVENUE LOGO by Michael Bierut of Pentagram. Most people have been familiar with the Saks brand for years; for most of its history it used logos based on elegant cursive script to decorate its shopping bags. Bierut cut the old logo into 64 equal squares and reassembled them randomly, making the new logo both recognizable and utterly new. Moreover, the logo can be continuously varied by shifting the squares or adjusting their scale. Thus, said Bierut, the new logo "creates consistency without sameness," a worthwhile motto for the present.

Typography

Letter forms are art forms. *Typography* is the art and technique of composing printed material from letter forms (*typefaces* or *fonts*). Designers, hired to meet clients' communication needs, frequently create designs that relate nonverbal images and printed words in complementary ways.

Just a few decades ago, when people committed words to paper, their efforts were handwritten or typewritten—and nearly all typewriters had the same typeface, the name of which was unknown to most users. Now anyone who uses a computer can select fonts and can create documents that look typeset, producing desktop publications such as newsletters and brochures. But computer pro-

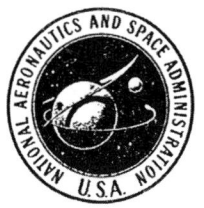

a. 1959. Logo designer James Modarelli.

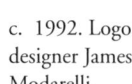

b. 1974. Designers Danne & Blackburn, NYC. 1973

c. 1992. Logo designer James Modarelli.

232 NASA LETTERHEAD.
Cooper-Hewitt, National Design Museum. Smithsonian Institution. Gift of NASA.

grams, like pencils, paintbrushes, and cameras, are simply tools: They can facilitate artistic aims if their operator has artistic sensibilities.

Since the Chinese invention of printing in the eleventh century, thousands of typefaces have been created—helped recently by digital technology. For the text of *Artforms*, Adobe Garamond was selected for its elegance and readability.

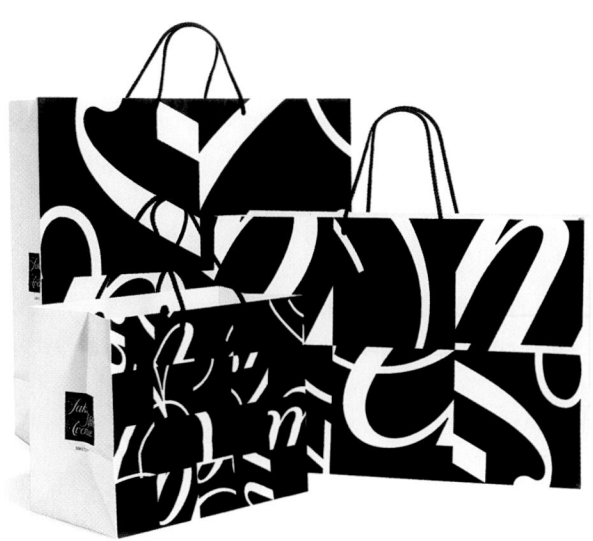

233 Michael Bierut.
SAKS FIFTH AVENUE LOGO. 2007.
Design Firm: Pentagram.
Courtesy of Saks Fifth Avenue.

Nobel
Armada
Garage Gothic

234 Tobias Frere-Jones.
THREE TYPEFACES: NOBEL™, ARMADA™, GARAGE GOTHIC™.
1992–1994.
The Font Bureau, Boston.

Many European-style typefaces are based on the capital letters carved in stone by early Romans. **Roman** letters are made with thick and thin strokes, ending in *serifs*—short lines with pointed ends, at an angle to the main strokes. In typesetting, the term "roman" is used to mean "not italic." Sans serif (without serifs) typefaces have a modern look due to their association with modernist designs. They are actually ancient in origin. **Black letter** typefaces are based on Northern medieval manuscripts and are rarely used today.

Today, many type designers are redesigning and updating old fonts, keeping in mind readability and contemporary preferences. Tobias Frere-Jones reworked the **NOBEL** font, updating a style invented in 1929 in Holland. He developed the font **ARMADA** to refer to the arches of nineteenth-century urban warehouses; his GARAGE GOTHIC is meant to recall the printing on parking garage tickets.

Heidi Cody took a more ironic stance with her 2000 work AMERICAN ALPHABET. She found all twenty-six letters in the initials of corporate logos. She said, "I try to get viewers to consciously acknowledge how indoctrinated, or 'branded' they are."[1]

Posters, Advertisements, and Other Graphics

A poster is a concise visual announcement that provides information through the integrated design of typographic and pictorial imagery. In a flash, an effective poster attracts attention and conveys its message. The creativity of a poster designer is directed toward a specific purpose, which may be to advertise or to persuade.

The concept of the modern poster is more than a hundred years old. In the nineteenth centry, most posters were lithographs, and many artists made extra income by designing them. Henri de Toulouse-Lautrec was the most important of these, as we saw on page 140. Early lithographic posters were all hand-drawn; designers added color to their work by printing the same sheet with multiple stones, one for each color. In the 1920s and 1930s, advances in printing methods made high-quality mass production possible, including the printing of photographs at large scale with text. Since the 1950s, radio, television, and print advertising have overshadowed posters. Although they now play a lesser role than they once did, well-designed posters can still fulfill needs for instant communication.

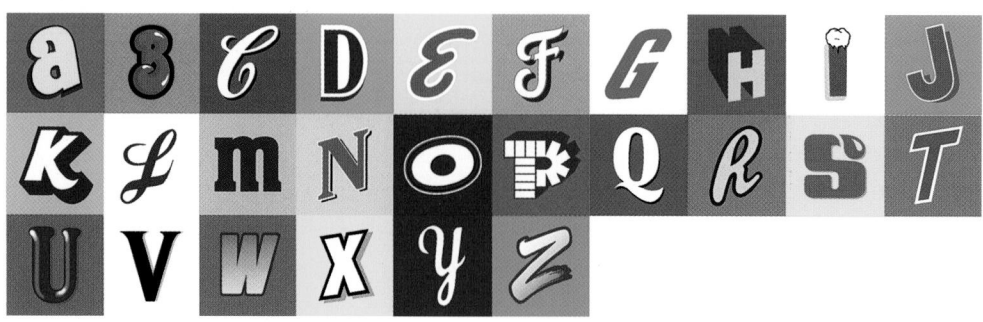

235 Heidi Cody.
AMERICAN ALPHABET. 2000.
Lightbox installation.
Roebling Hall Gallery, Brooklyn, NY.
© 2000 Heidi Cody.

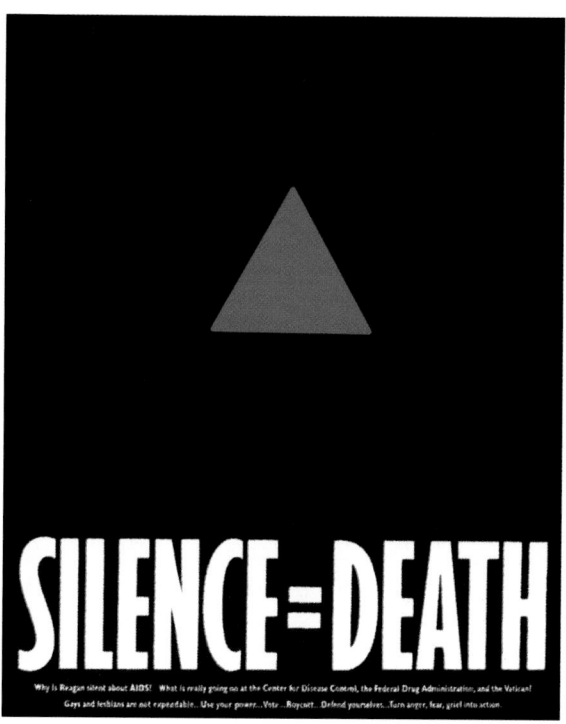

236 SILENCE=DEATH. 1986.
Poster. Offset lithograph.
Designed and published by the Silence=Death Project,
New York.
© Avram Finkelstein, Brian Howard, Oliver Johnston, Charles Kreloff, Christopher
Lione, Jorge Soccoras.

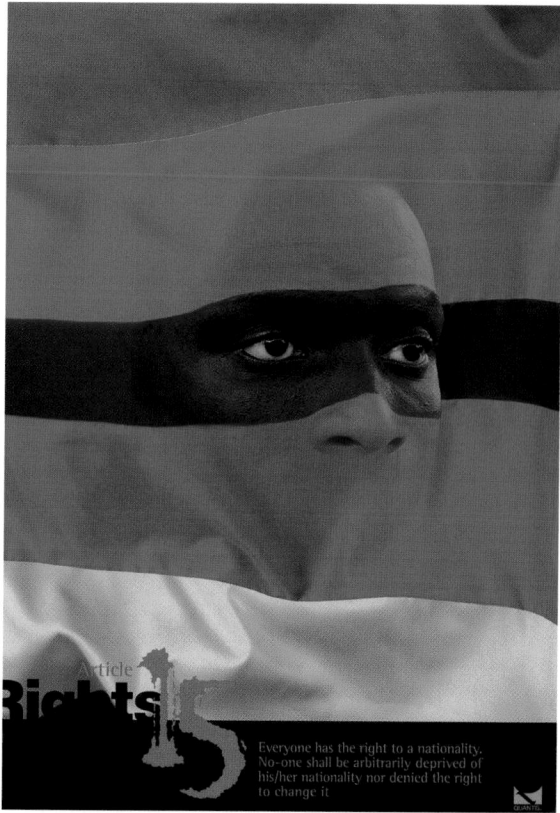

237 Chaz Maviyane-Davies.
ARTICLE 15: EVERYONE HAS THE RIGHT TO NATIONALITY
AND TO CHANGE IT. 1996.
Offset poster.
Courtesy of the artist.

For example, the AIDS crisis presented a new set of social issues in many American cities during the 1980s. The SILENCE=DEATH poster was produced as advocacy by a group of six gay men who founded the Silence=Death Project in 1986. The composition as a whole is meant to resemble a corporate logo. The purple triangle is an inverted version of the insignia homosexuals were forced to wear in Nazi concentration camps. The slogan suggests that the causes, treatment, and prevention of AIDS need to be discussed openly. It is not until the viewer comes close enough to read the inscription at the bottom of the poster that the epidemic is mentioned at all. This emblem became the logo of the movement known as ACT UP (AIDS Coalition to Unleash Power), and is still used on posters, T-shirts, bumper stickers, billboards, and handbills.

Many social causes find vivid expression in posters. The Black Panther Party, an African American activists organization, made many creative (and militant) posters in the 1960s and 1970s. At the same time, the Chicano movement commissioned many artists to make silkscreens promoting the causes of Mexican-Americans. An example of the latter is the poster by Ester Hernández on page 141.

Some posters remind us of our rights rather than urge us to change our behavior. Chaz Maviyane-Davies in 1996 based a set of posters on the United Nations Universal Declaration of Human Rights. His poster ARTICLE 15 includes text that guarantees the right to a nationality. He used the face of a black man who watches hopefully between the stripes of a flag, because a great many images of Africans that we see in the media are associated with disaster or famine. Maviyane-Davies has also made more urgent graphic appeals, as the essay on the next page shows. As long ago as 1977, he was warning us about the effects of global climate

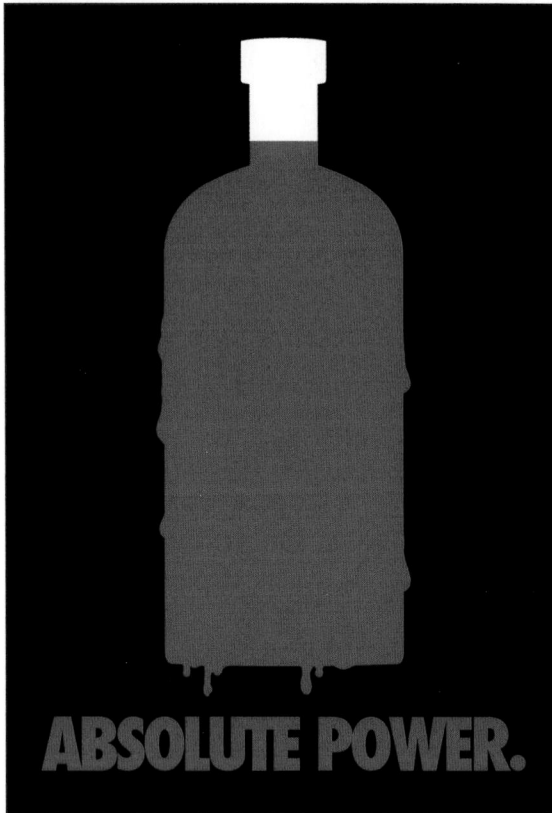

238   Chaz Maviyane-Davies.
ABSOLUTE POWER. 2002.
Offset poster.
Courtesy of the artist.

CHAZ MAVIYANE-DAVIES
grew up in Zimbabwe when it was still a British colony. His first jobs were low-paying drafting tasks for a telecommunications company. He recalled, "discrimination was the order of the day so very few opportunities existed for me to pursue anything outside of the life that a racist government had planned for me."[2] He went to London and earned an M.A. degree at the Central School of Art and Design. While he was away, Zimbabwe became independent under the leadership of the Patriotic Front party headed by Robert Mugabe. He established a graphic design firm called the Maviyane Project in the capital, Harare. Most of his clients were charities, public service agencies, and nongovernmental organizations.

As years passed, the Mugabe regime became more and more suspicious and repressive of alternative viewpoints. Maviyane-Davies tried to remain apart from the growing fray, but found it difficult. He recalled, "Designers can choose to be active or passive in what they do, regardless of their ideology—but if they think they are neutral they should be careful whose interests they really serve." By trying to remain neutral, he grew to believe that he was only giving support to the regime.

His work took a step toward militancy when the Mugabe government began restricting participation in the 2000 legislative elections. Suddenly opposition parties had trouble getting candidates on the ballot, and voters were prevented from registering in many areas. Maviyane-Davies created dozens of posters for free distribution encouraging people to keep democracy alive.

The Mugabe regime began using many of the same procedures during the 2002 presidential campaigns, even imprisoning the leading candidate for treason. Maviyane-Davies again swung into action, making posters for free distribution on paper and over the Internet. One of these is ABSOLUTE POWER, a simple design based on a popular drink advertisement in which the designer changed the original beverage into blood.

This graphic agitation must have been effective: The government forced Maviyane-Davies to leave the country in 2003. He now teaches graphic design and continues his public service work. One of his best-known projects was a set based on the United Nations Universal Declaration of Human Rights. He said the series "grew out of the indignation I have always felt in the way that Africans are constantly portrayed. For many, 'Africa' conjures up images of a continent torn apart by hatred and brutality, corpses and corruption. Ignore these images and the continent has no other identity. And yes, as an African I've experienced life on a continent where in many parts, fundamental human rights are obliterated with blood and sadness, as conflict and turmoil leave only despair and hopelessness in their wake." Hence the series gives prominence to black persons.

His advice for aspiring designers: "I'd just say believe in yourself, really believe in yourself; research, work as hard as you can at the process and not the ends, strive to realize your vision, listen with your eyes and ears and use your soul."

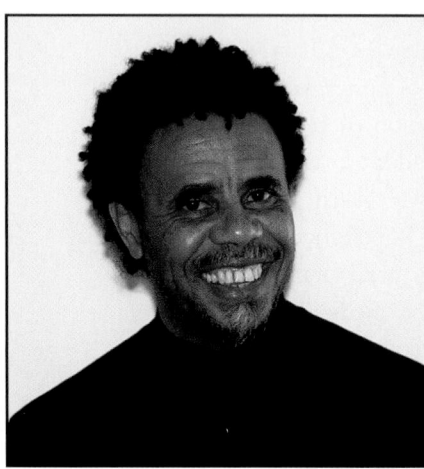

239   Chaz Maviyane-Davies.
Courtesy of Chaz Maviyane-Davies.

change. See his poster for a United Nations Convention, pictured on page 14.

Humor has great appeal. Maira Kalman's NEW YORKER COVER gently mocks the boisterous subcultures of Manhattan and environs with exotic-sounding names. Some of these are Botoxia, Hiphopabad, Trumpistan, and al-Zeimers. Published in December 2001, the design allowed New Yorkers to laugh at themselves again after the tragedy of September 11. English graphic designer Jonathan Barnbrook took a more sarcastic tone with his TOMAHAWK FONT, which is based on the script found on missiles that the military uses to strike suspected terrorist camps.

Subcultures often have their own unique design styles. For example, when the Globe Poster company promoted NORTH AMERICAN TOUR '94, it used a brightly colored and highly readable style that its designers had pioneered a generation before. Globe set the standard for promotional design on behalf of soul, gospel, and blues performers, and the "Globe Style" is still the norm in many areas of the United States for such functions, giving almost instant recognizability.

The subculture of punk music developed its own design style, which does not look designed at all. The Sex Pistols released their first single, GOD SAVE THE QUEEN (on the following page), to coincide with the Silver Jubilee celebrations of the twenty-fifth year of

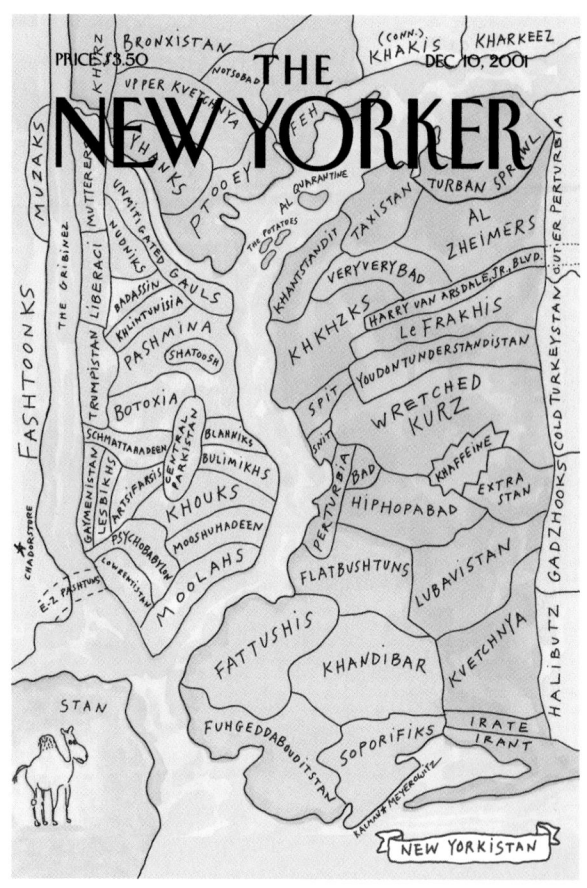

240 Maira Kalman and Rick Meyerowitz.
NEWYORKISTAN.
NEW YORKER COVER. December 10, 2001.
© 2001 Conde Nast Publications, Inc. Reprintted by permission. All rights reserved.

241 Jonathan Barnbrook.
TOMAHAWK FONT SAMPLE. 2003.
Courtesy of the artist.

242 NORTH AMERICAN TOUR '94. 1994.
Globe Poster Printing Corporation, Francis Cicero.
Silkscreen and offset lithography. 33¾" × 22¹⁄₁₆".
Cooper-Hewitt National Design Museum. Smithsonian Institution. Gift of Globe Poster Printing Corp., 1997–54–2.

>>TOMAHAWK
FOR ALL YOUR
GRAPHIC
PRE-EMP+IVE
S+RIKES

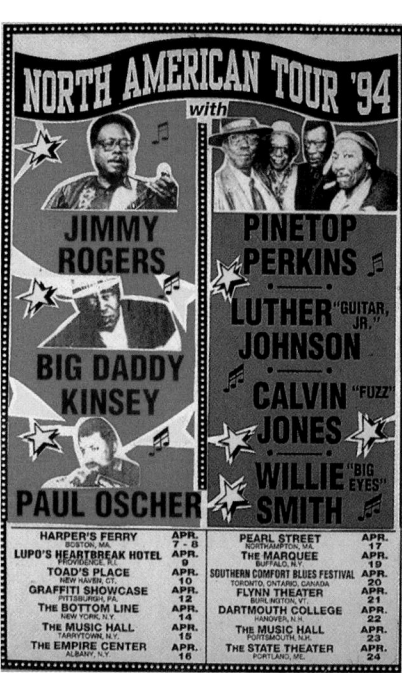

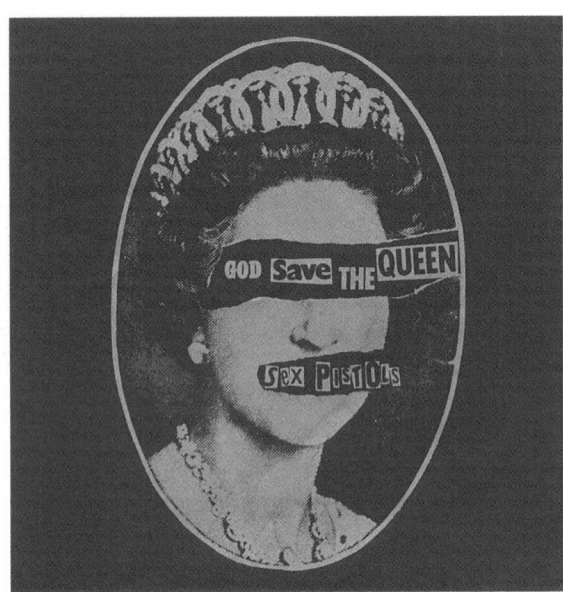

243 Jamie Reid.
GOD SAVE THE QUEEN. 1977.
Album cover.
Virgin Records. Arcova Publishing Ltd.

the reign of Queen Elizabeth. The song was so controversial that it was banned from the airways, yet it became the number one selling song. Twenty-five years later, the book *100 Best Record Covers of All Time* judged Jamie Reid's cover the best record cover ever produced.

Book cover designs function like corporate logos, uniting image and text to extend the message of a book and condense it into a single memorable page that shoppers will see in bookstores. Chip Kidd is a leader in this field, as evidenced by his work on the cover for DRY: A MEMOIR. This book tells the story of an advertising executive's fast-paced life fueled by excessive drinking, and his eventual recovery from alcoholism. Kidd's cover resembles a dry landscape where water once flowed around the title letters, just as liquor once flowed through the author's life. The designer counted his work a success when a bookstore customer once asked the sales clerk for a copy that had not suffered water damage.

MOTION GRAPHICS

The cutting edge of design right now is in the field of motion graphics, in which a designer uses visual effects, live action, and animation to create a two-dimensional project that moves. Designers combine these techniques in various ways for time-based sequences in Web sites, television commercials, and music videos.

Motion graphics as a discipline began in the 1950s with title sequences for Hollywood movies. Most title sequences were merely slow scrolls of names until the arrival of Saul Bass, and his collaboration with Alfred Hitchcock. Bass said in an interview that an opening title sequence for a film can "create a climate for the story that is to follow," because "the audience involvement with a film should really begin with the first frame."

Thus for the 1960 film PSYCHO, he split the name of the movie into three horizontal sections

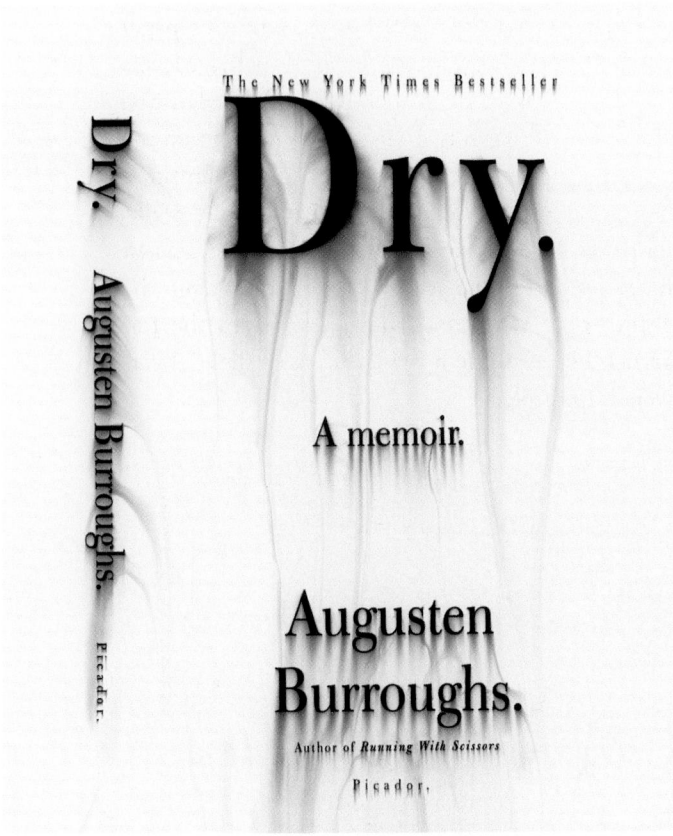

244 Chip Kidd.
Cover for DRY: A MEMOIR. 2003.
Book by Augusten Burroughs.
Publisher: Picador. Photo: Geoff Spear.

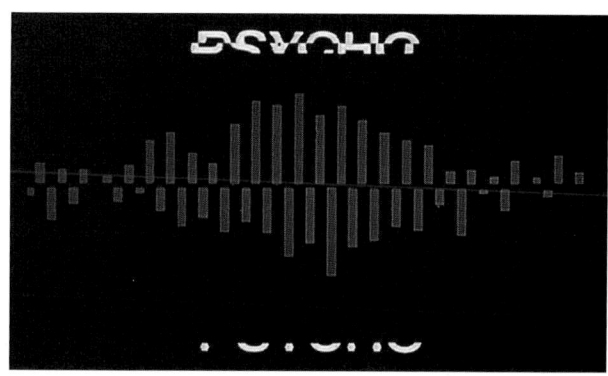

245 Saul Bass.
     Title sequence for PSYCHO. 1960.
     Film directed by Alfred Hitchcock.
     Paramount Pictures.

that grind against each other before flying apart, pushed by an array of moving vertical bars. The fast motion of the sequence captures the restless energy and surging passions of the film, just as the title's fragmentation parallels the psychic breakdown of the film's main character, a murderer. Bass created the PSYCHO title sequence by moving actual bars and letters on tracks and photographing them, an extremely tedious process.

The arrival of advanced digital editing in the 1990s ensured the takeoff of motion graphics. The new computer applications enable designers to create each frame of a sequence with all the freedom that photo editing allows. Thus motion graphics designers are increasingly directors of short but intense projects that combine input from many sources.

The most original use of the new technologies came with Kyle Cooper's work on the title sequence of SE7EN, which like PSYCHO, is a dramatic crime story. The title sequence has a plot of its own, as a man with bandaged fingers assembles and stitches together a booklet about murder and sexual deviance. Layered images, film clips, and spoiled type nervously twitch across the screen along with the hand-lettered credits, over a soundtrack by the Nine Inch Nails. Most important, this haunting close-up sequence has a function in the

script: It introduces the audience to the mind of the killer, who does not appear until 40 minutes into the film. Cooper said that his aptitude for vivid graphics came in part from his earlier study at Yale with Paul Rand, one of America's legendary designers.

Cooper's tense style was widely imitated in credits for other thriller and sci-fi films, but the motion graphics medium is capable of almost any mood. When Stardust Studios made a television commercial for HUGO BOSS (on the following page) in 2006, they staged actor Jonathan Rhys Meyers walking through an exuberantly animated urban environment that surges and sways like kelp on the seabed. Buildings spring up and turn on their sides, passersby morph into bouncing balls, sidewalks fold like Japanese screens, and a lamppost lies down to become the tone arm of a turntable before the entire scene swirls and rushes back into the fragrance bottle. Only a few years ago, these effects were impossible.

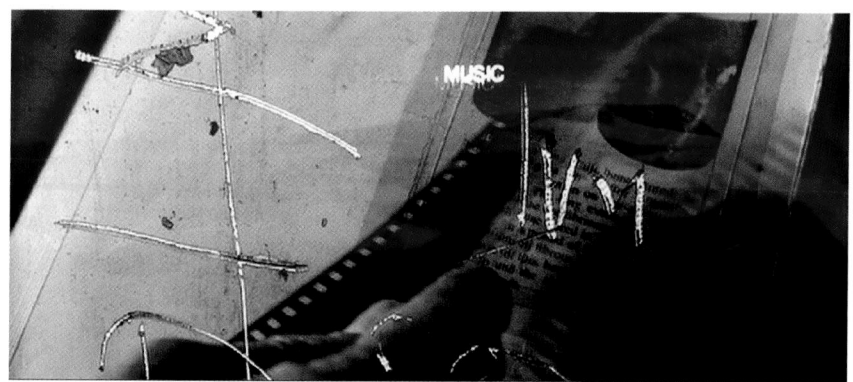

246 Kyle Cooper.
     Title sequence for SE7EN. 1995.
     Film directed by David Fincher.
     New Line Cinema-Time Warner.

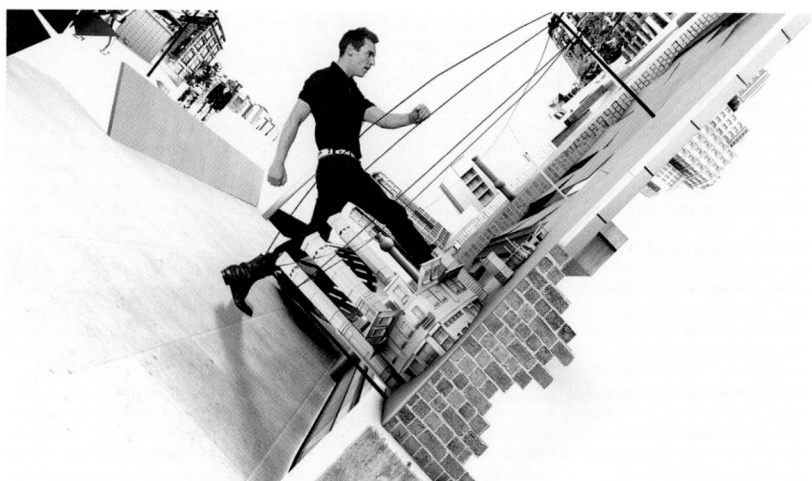

247 Stardust Studios.
HUGO BOSS COMMERCIAL. 2006.
Motion graphics television spot.
Jake Banks, creative director.

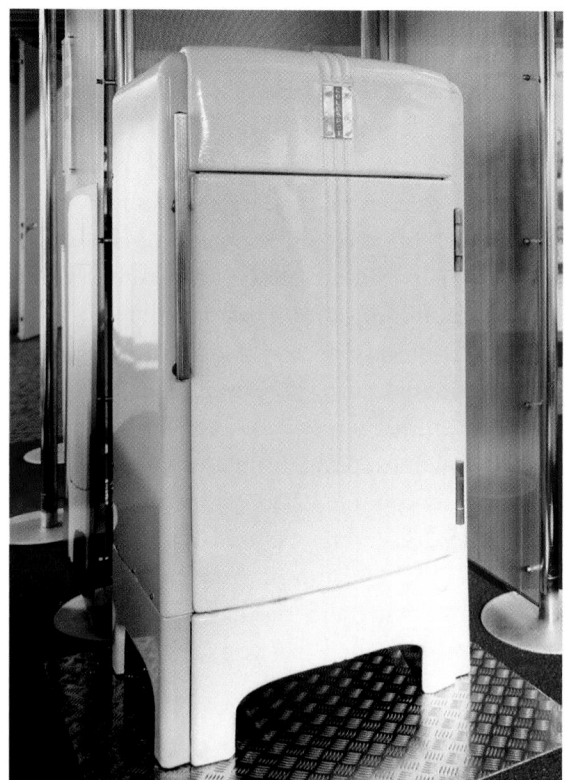

248 Raymond Loewy.
COLDSPOT SUPER SIX REFRIGERATOR. 1934.
Sears, Roebuck & Co.
Whirlpool Corporation. AKG-images, London.

INDUSTRIAL DESIGN

We all handle designed products every day, and industrial designers work to make these products more beautiful and useful. We close this chapter by examining four common objects that made history by integrating utility, technology, and cutting-edge design.

Probably the person most responsible for making industrial design into a profession was the French-born American Raymond Loewy. He established his first firm in 1919, and went to work designing window displays for Macy's department store. Probably the most important industrial designer of the twentieth century, his office was responsible for the Shell Oil Company logo, the exterior of the Greyhound bus, the Lucky Strike cigarette package, the Coke machine, and even the external markings on the presidential jet Air Force One. His sloped-roof design for the 1952 Studebaker car influenced a generation of autos toward a more sleek look.

Before 1934, most refrigerators were plain boxes on thin, high legs; Loewy's COLDPSOT SUPER SIX was revolutionary. He flexed the front into an attractive curve with tasteful corrugations; he also lowered the legs and integrated them into the front panel. He installed a new handle that could be activated with a touch, and used nonrusting aluminum shelves inside. He even replaced the motor so that the machine would hum rather than buzz. After these aesthetic and practical improvements, sales of refrigerators quadrupled. Loewy summarized his design philosophy in the acronym MAYA, which stands for Most Advanced Yet Acceptable; it has become a byword in the design community.

The Sony Corporation of Japan used transistor technology in home radios for several years, but sales did not take off until they released the TR-610 in 1957. The new transistor radio was a better fit for the hand, and consumers could select the color of its elegant exterior. It also had a wire loop that swung out to allow placement on a table, and a larger speaker. The model sold nearly a half million units during its two years of shelf life. The name Sony was itself invented near the time of the release of the TR-610, in order to facilitate global sales. The name is a combination of the Latin *sonus* ("sound") and the endearing nickname Sonny. This corporate brand name is not obviously tied to any nationality, and is far easier to pronounce than the company's previous name, Tokyo Tsushin Kogyo.

Sony introduced the FM band into its transistor radios the next year, thus beginning a long chain of innovations in personal audio that lasted for decades. In the 1970s, the company united miniature headphones with the new cassette technology and invented the Walkman. When compact disc recordings became feasible in the 1980s, Sony developed a portable player that soon became known as the "boom box." The advent of consumer

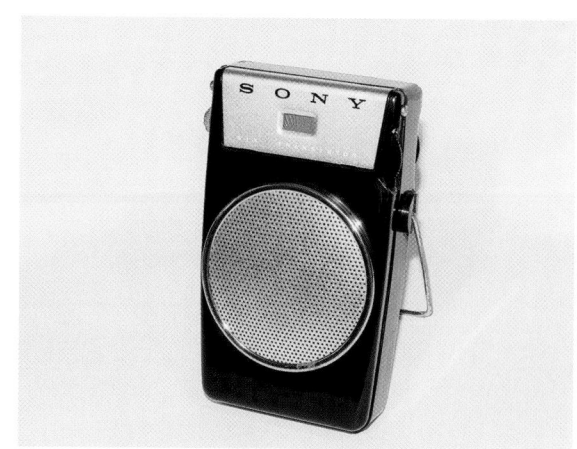

249   Sony Corporation.
   TR-610 TRANSISTOR RADIO. 1957.
   Enrico Tedeschi.

digital audio as the century turned led to a proliferation of personal mp3 players by Sony and other companies.

New technology and sleek design came together in the **APPLE MACINTOSH** computer in 1984. With its curvy, off-white exterior and new mouse-driven user interface, this model set off the Silicon Valley boom. Designed with an eye for "the rest of us" rather than button-down business types or techno-savvy geeks, the Macintosh was promoted as a vehicle of personal creativity. Its graphical user interface

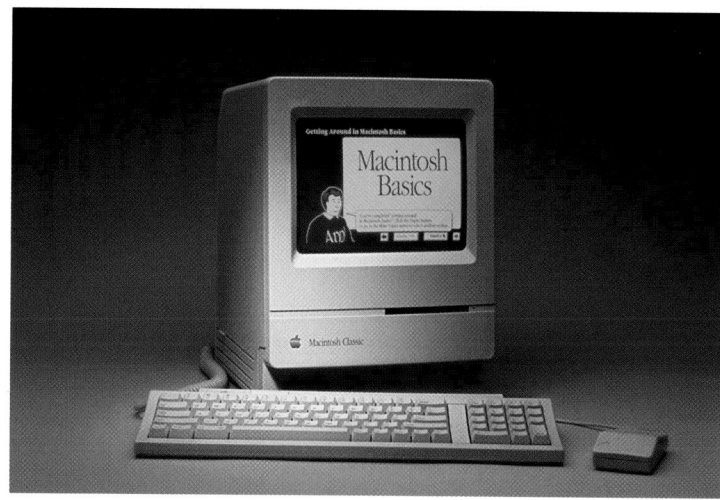

250   Frogdesign/Harmut Esslinger.
   APPLE MACINTOSH. 1984.
   Personal Computer.
   Apple Computer, Inc.
   Photograph: Will Mosgrove.

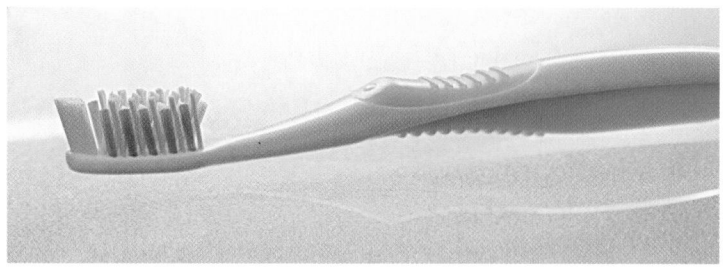

251 Lunar Design.
ORAL-B CROSS-ACTION TOOTHBRUSH. 1999.
Sandbox Studio. Gerard Furbershaw.

made most tasks much easier than the old command-line interface, and it had a small footprint on the personal desktop. It was also one of the first new products to be introduced to the public in a television advertisement during the Super Bowl football championship.

The MACINTOSH came out just as desktop computers were making great leaps in processing power. The machine's ease of use and faster speeds contributed to a radical decentralization of the design industry in the 1990s; one person at a workstation could now do the work of an entire team.

The ORAL-B CROSS-ACTION TOOTHBRUSH came directly out of the Silicon Valley environment. Consumer research determined that people generally hold toothbrushes in one of five ways. The Oral-B company commissioned Lunar Design to create a new brush to more comfortably accommodate all of them while delivering the bristles at a more effective angle than traditional rectangular brushes. The designers used ergonomics, three-dimensional computer modeling, and advanced resin materials to create the new brush in 1999. It became an industry leader and set a new aesthetically pleasing and effective norm for what had been a very common object.

From toothbrushes to office buildings, good design can make the difference between an effective product and a failure.

SCULPTURE

Sculpture exists in space, as we do. The total experience of a sculpture is the sum of its surfaces and profiles. Even when touching is not permitted, perceiving its tactile quality is an important part of the way we experience sculpture.

FREESTANDING AND RELIEF SCULPTURE

Sculpture meant to be seen from all sides is called *in-the-round* or *freestanding.* As we move around it, our experience of a sculpture is the sum of its surfaces and profiles. No one had to suggest moving around Calder's OBUS to the little girl in our photograph. A single photograph shows only one view of a sculpture under one kind of light; thus, unless we can see many photographs or, better yet, a video, or best of all, view the piece firsthand, we receive only a limited impression of the sculpture.

A sculpture that is not freestanding but projects from a background surface is in relief. In *low-relief* (or *bas-relief*) sculpture, the projection from the surrounding surface is slight. As a result, shadows are minimal. Coins, for example, are works of low-relief sculpture stamped from molds. A high point in the art of coin design was reached on the island of Sicily during the classical period of ancient Greece. The APOLLO coin, shown here slightly larger than actual size, has a strong presence in spite of being in low relief and very small.

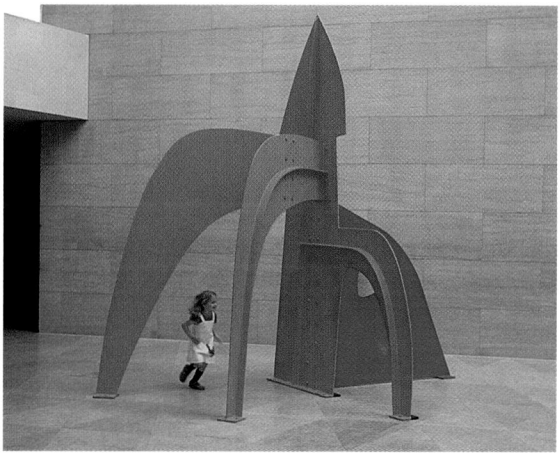

252 Alexander Calder.
OBUS. 1972.
Painted sheet metal. 142½″ × 152″ × 89⅝″.
Mr. & Mrs. Paul Mellon Collection. Photograph © 2001 Board of Trustees, National Gallery of Art, Washington, D.C. 1983.1.49.(A-1859)/SC. © 2002. Estate of Alexander Calder. Artists Rights Society (ARS), NY. Photograph: Duane Preble.

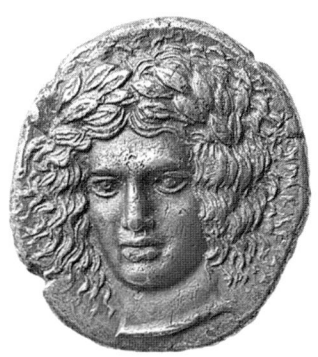

253 APOLLO. c. 415 B.C.E.
Greek silver coin.
Diameter 1⅛″.
Photograph: Hirmer Fotoarchiv, Munich Germany.

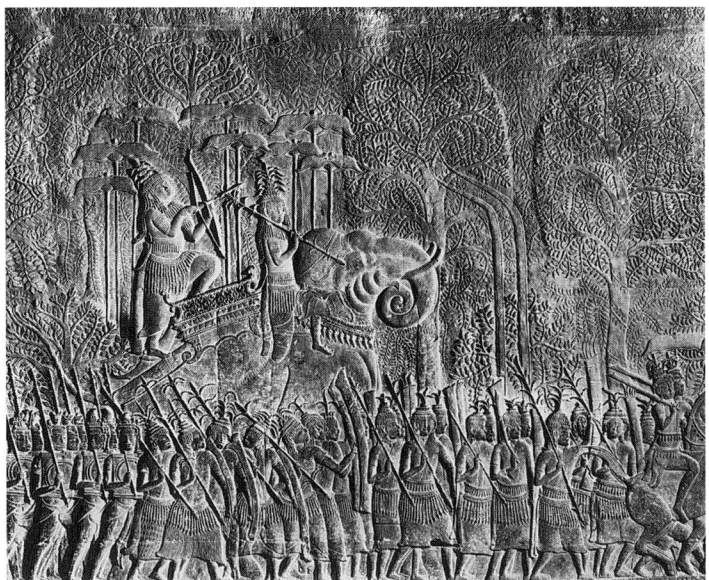

254 ARMY ON THE MARCH.
Angkor Wat, Cambodia, 1100–1150.
Sandstone.
Eliot Elisofon, LIFE Magizine © TimePix.

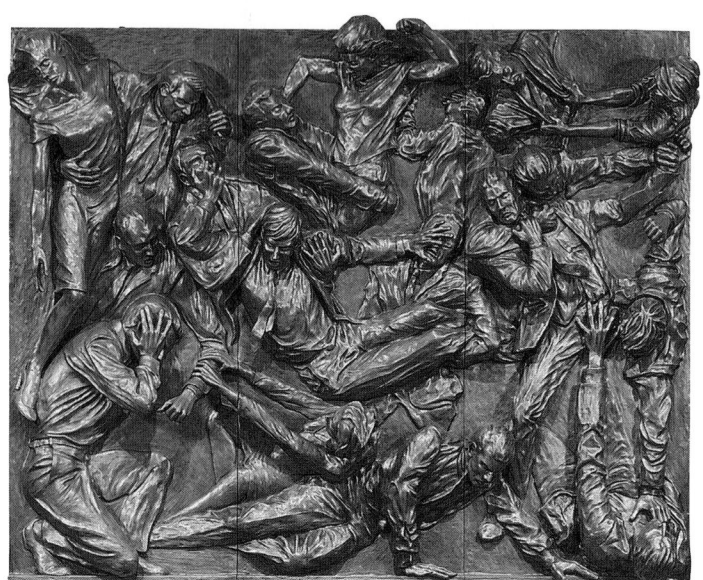

255 Robert Longo.
CORPORATE WARS: WALL OF INFLUENCE. 1982.
Middle portion.
Cast aluminum. 7′ × 9′.
Photograph: Courtesy of Metro Pictures.

Some of the world's best and most varied low-relief sculptures are found at the temple of Angkor Wat in Cambodia. This vast temple complex was the center of the Khmer empire in the twelfth cen-tury. It was here that Khmer kings sponsored an extensive program of sculpture and architecture. Within the chambers of the complex, carvings are in such delicate low relief that they seem more like paintings than sculpture. One scene depicting an ARMY ON THE MARCH is a king's army commanded by a prince. The rhythmic pattern of the spear-carrying soldiers contrasts with the curving pat-terns of the jungle foliage in the background. The soldiers and background provide a setting for the prince, who stands with bow and arrow poised in his carriage on the elephant's back. Intricate detail covers entire surfaces of the stone walls.

In *high-relief* sculpture, more than half of the natural circumference of the modeled form projects from the surrounding surface, and figures are often substantially undercut.

This is the case with Robert Longo's CORPORATE WARS: WALL OF INFLUENCE, where male and female figures convulse in painful conflict. Much of the composition is high-relief; in only a few areas are limbs and garments barely raised above the back-ground surface. Dynamic gestures and the diagonal placement of torsos and limbs make the sculpture very active. The emotional charge of the piece sug-gests that Longo is horrified by the intense compe-tition of corporate life.

METHODS AND MATERIALS

Traditionally, sculpture has been made by model-ing, casting, carving, constructing, and assembling, or a combination of these processes. (The tech-niques of modeling, casting, and carving can be seen on the *Discovering Art* CD.)

Modeling

Modeling is a *manipulative* and often *additive* process. Pliable material such as clay, wax, or plaster is built up, removed, and pushed into a final form.

Tool marks and fingerprint impressions are vis-ible on the surface as evidence of the modeling technique employed to make BALLPLAYER WITH THREE-PART YOKE AND BIRD HEADDRESS. Body vol-ume, natural gesture, and costume detail are clearly defined. The ancient Maya, who lived in what are

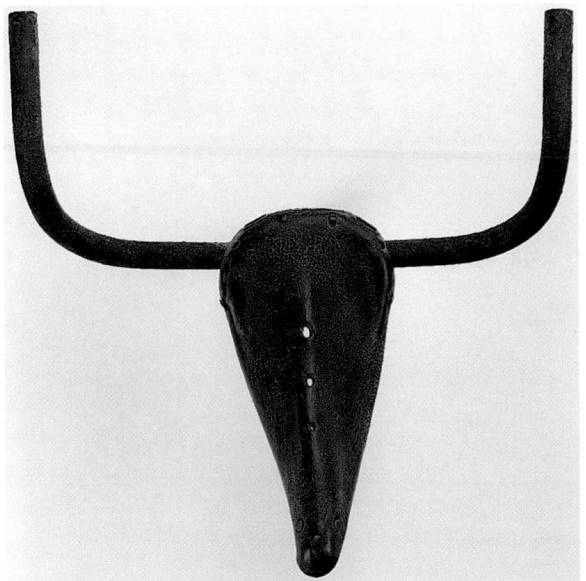

269 Pablo Picasso.
BULL'S HEAD. 1943.
Bronze. Seat and handles of a bicycle. Height 16⅛".
Photo by Bernice Hatala. Musée Picasso, Paris, France.
© Reunion des Musées Nationaux/Art Resource, NY.
© 2005 Estate of Pablo Picasso/Artists Rights Society (ARS), NY.

Picasso found a wealth of ready-made ingredients from salvaged fragments of daily life. For his assemblage BULL'S HEAD he cut the creative process to a single leap of awareness. Describing how it happened, Picasso said:

One day I found in a pile of jumble an old bicycle saddle next to some rusted handle bars... In a flash they were associated in my mind ... The idea of this BULL'S HEAD came without my thinking of it ... I had only to solder them together...[3]

Some assemblages gather meaning from the juxtaposition of real objects. Roberto Visani brought a tripod stand, a rifle, and a crutch together in his installation YOU SEE THE HUT YET YOU ASK "WHERE SHALL I GO FOR SHELTER." The phrase TRIBAL WAR inscribed across the top of the crutch indicates the recent events in Africa that partly inspired the work. Yet the assemblage was also influenced by music: The artist heard a concert

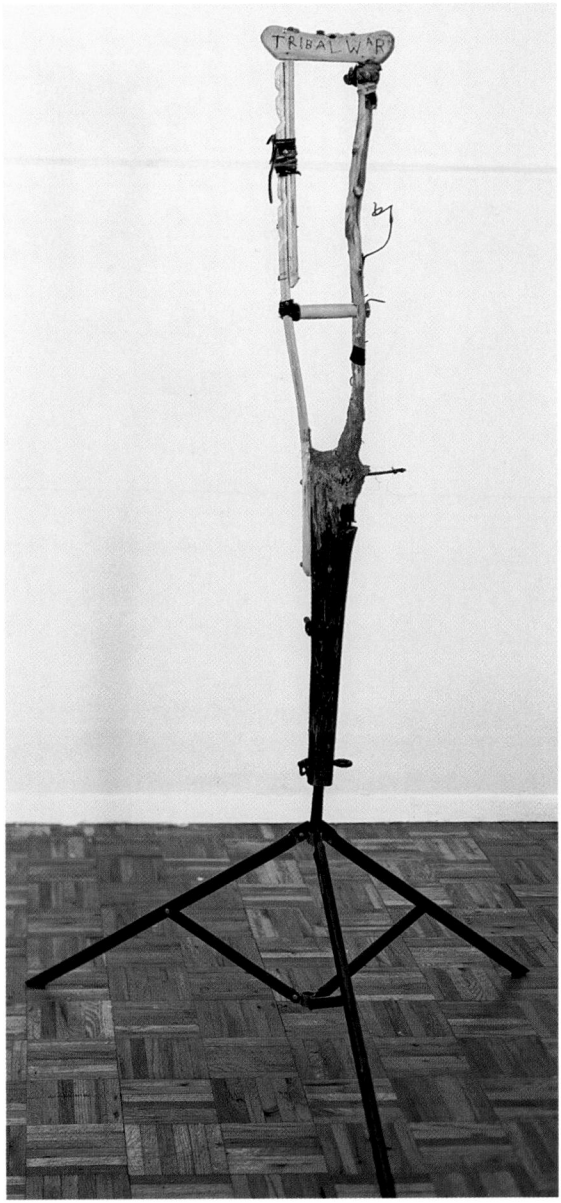

270 Roberto Visani.
TRIBAL WAR, from YOU SEE THE HUT YET YOU ASK "WHERE SHALL I GO FOR SHELTER." 2000–2003.
61" × 35" × 34".
Detail from mixed-media installation.
Courtesy of the artist.

by Afro beat artist and political activist Fela Kuti while traveling in Ghana, and was inspired by a line in one of Kuti's songs: "Tell the man with the gun that the people who teach our people fear, render the whole country defenseless."

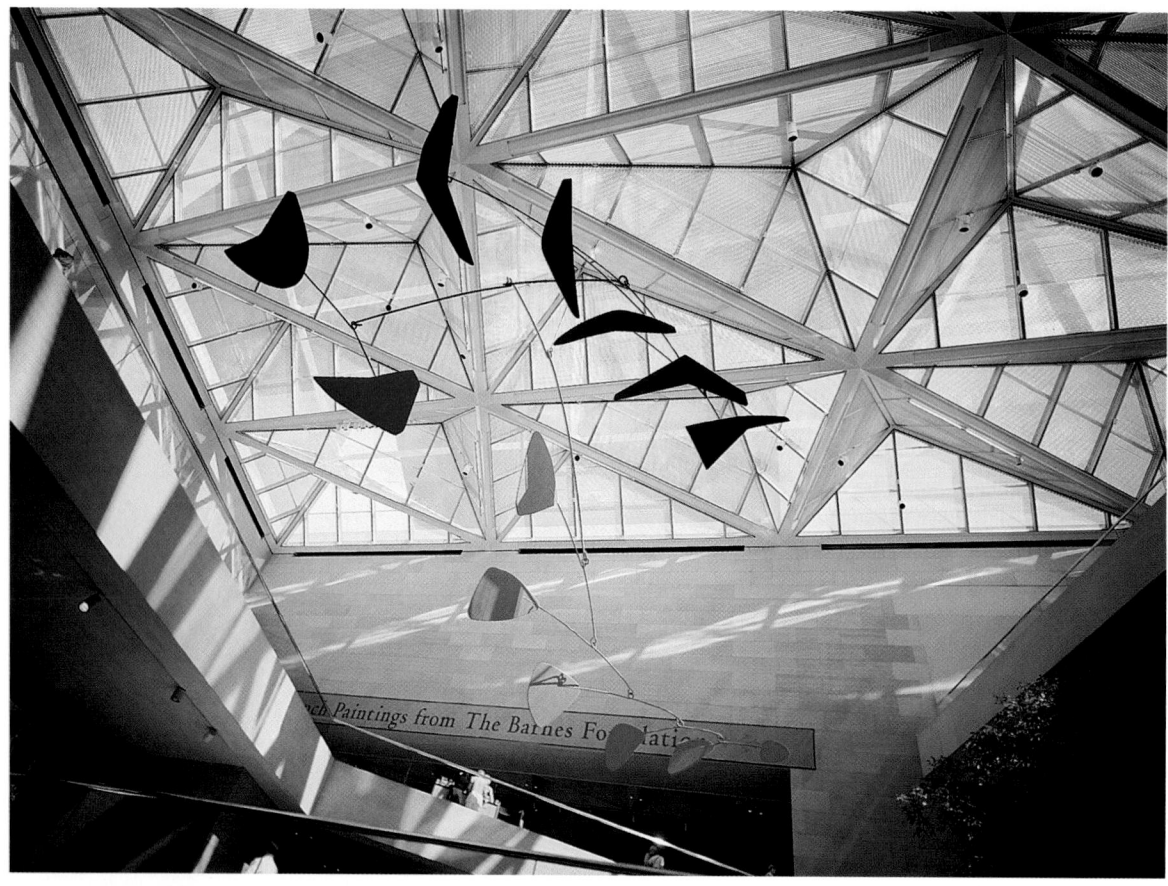

271 Alexander Calder.
UNTITLED. 1976.
Painted aluminum and tempered steel. 29'10½" × 76'.
Gift of the Collectors Committee. Photograph © 2001 Board of Trustees, National Gallery of Art, Washington, D.C.
1977.76.1.(A-1799)/SC. © 2002 Estate of Alexander Calder. Artists Rights Society (ARS), NY.

KINETIC SCULPTURE

Alexander Calder was among the first to explore the possibilities of *kinetic sculpture*, or sculpture that moves. Marcel Duchamp named Calder's kinetic sculptures *mobiles*—a word Duchamp had coined for his own work in 1914. Sculptors' traditional emphasis on mass is replaced in Calder's work by a focus on shape, space, and movement. By 1928, he was designing inventive wire and sheet-metal constructions (see page 44). Calder's huge UNTITLED mobile is the centerpiece of the contemporary wing of the National Gallery of Art in Washington, D.C.; indoor air currents impel its slow, graceful movement.

MIXED MEDIA

Today's artists frequently use a variety of media in a single work. Rather than being presented as a long list of materials, such combinations are often identified only as *mixed media*. The media may be two-dimensional, three-dimensional, or a mixture of the two. Often, the choice of media expresses some cultural or symbolic meaning.

Cai Guo Qiang retold an ancient Chinese war story in his large work BORROWING YOUR ENEMY'S ARROWS: A crafty general dared the enemy to shoot at his boats as he floated by; the enemy obliged with such enthusiasm that the arrows helped the general's laden boats float higher.

When Lara Schnitger drapes and stretches fabric over wooden armatures, she creates both a sculpture and a hollow interior space. The work of this Los Angeles-based artist straddles the boundary between sculpture and fashion design, just as the figures she creates hover nervously between human and some other living thing. In GRIM BOY, for example, she used various dark-colored fabrics together with beads and fur to suggest a mannequin from hell. This tense, lurking figure seems to exude the nervous energy of an adolescent combined with the quick eye of a bird. But it stands six feet tall, like a gangling teenager, and the work's title may remind us of a brooding, trenchcoat-clad youth. There is an additional feminist message to most of Schnitger's work as well, because she is doing a sort of "dressmaking," a traditional woman's art form. Rather than creating beautiful adornments, though, she fashions curious quasi-human beings.

For almost four decades, Korean-born Nam June Paik was the artist most identified with the fusion of art and technology. In Chapter 9, Paik was introduced as among the first to use video as an art medium. Here, we consider him as a major mixed-media artist.

From the beginning of his career, Paik refused to conform to the demands of only one creative medium. He began by studying musical composition before moving on to visual art. In the 1960s he achieved art-world notoriety for creating a cello made from television monitors. He composed several works for his "TV cello." For a 1978 installation, he recorded videotapes of green landscapes, and played them on monitors placed in a bed of live plants. A more recent installation included video monitors, sounds, projected imagery, and brightly colored laser beams.

In 1974 Paik envisioned a totally new kind of super highway made up of interactive technologies that would enable a new level of communication around the world. His 1997–1998 traveling installation exhibit, the *Electronic Super Highway*, filled with his recent assemblages, incorporates more than 650 working television monitors. He calls it "Cybertown." What could be more "mixed"

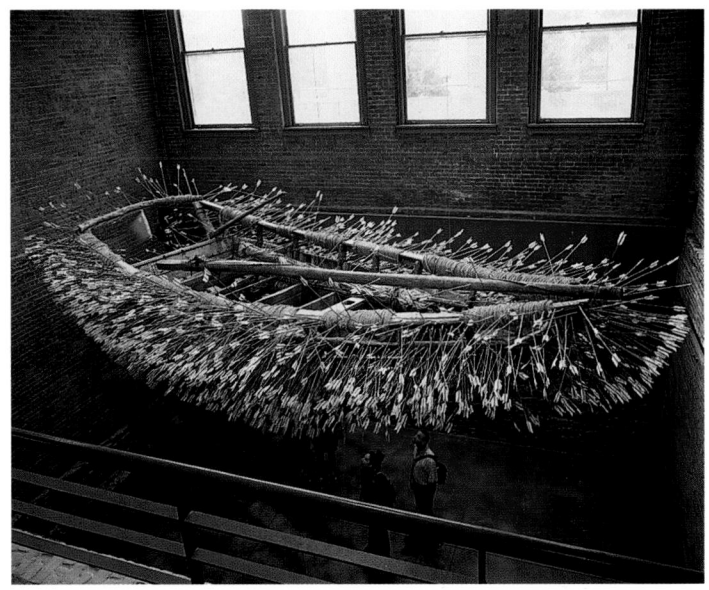

272 Cai Guo Qiang.
BORROWING YOUR ENEMY'S ARROWS. 1998.
Wooden boat, straw, bamboo, arrows, flags, and fan. Length 32½′.
Photo: Hiro Ihara. Courtesy of the artist.

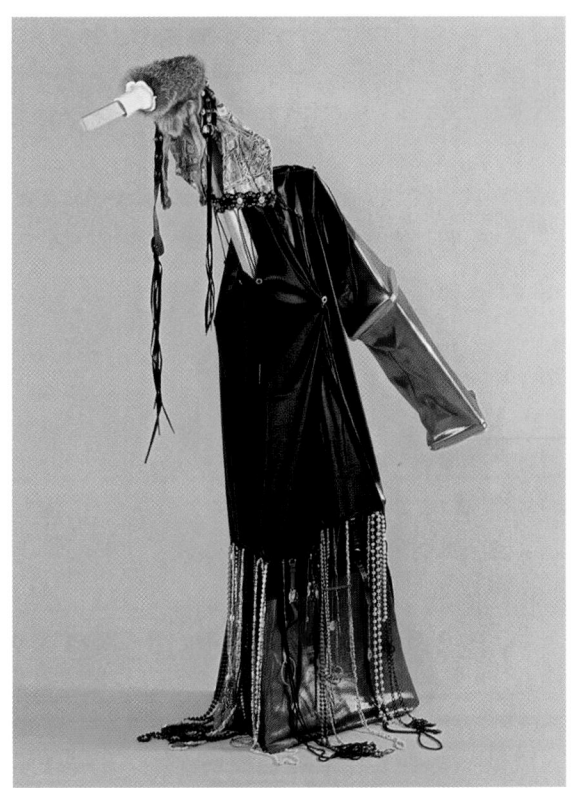

273 Lara Schnitger.
GRIM BOY. 2005.
Wood, fabric, and mixed media. 71″ × 59″ × 20″.
Anton Kern Gallery, NY.

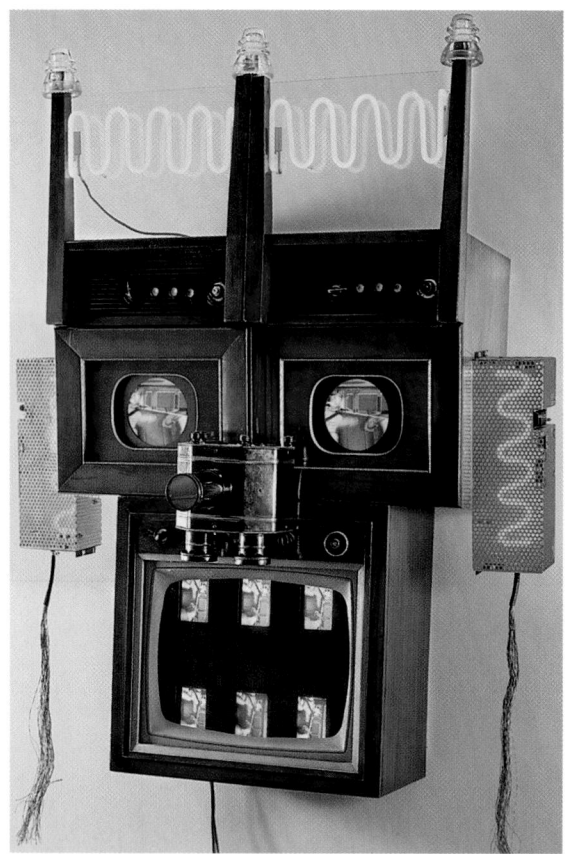

274 Nam June Paik.
INTERNET DWELLER: WOL.FIVE.YDPB. 1994.
Two Panasonic 10″ televisions, six KTV 5″ televisions, six
vintage television cabinets, projector, lantern, glass insulators,
neon, one laser disc player, one original Paik laser disc.
Courtesy Carl Solway Gallery, Cincinnati, Ohio.
Photographers: Chris Gomien and Tom Allison.

than the ingredients of Paik's humorous INTERNET
DWELLER: WOL.FIVE.YDPB listed in the caption of
the piece shown here?

INSTALLATIONS

Many artists now use the three-dimensional
medium of *installation* to tell a story visually. An
installation artist transforms a space by bringing into
it items of symbolic significance. This medium is
most similar to constructed sculpture, but the artist
constructs an entire environment within the gallery.

Many art critics regard Cady Noland as a pioneering American installation artist. In the middle
1980s, she began arranging rooms with symbolic
items that seemed to comment on contemporary
culture. Typical is a 1989 work called THIS PIECE
DOESN'T HAVE A TITLE YET. Here we see row upon

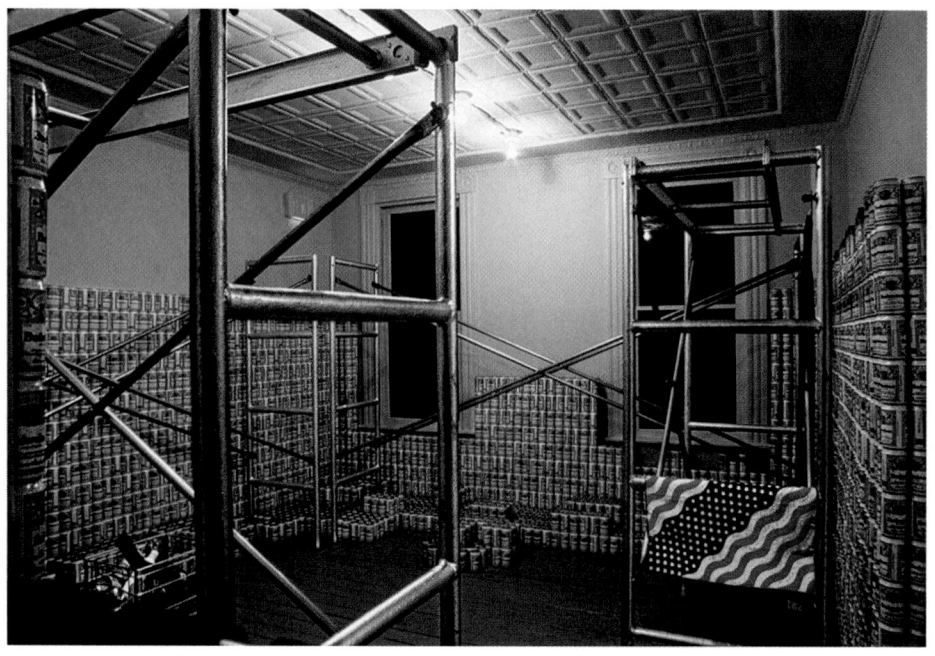

275 Cady Noland.
THIS PIECE
DOESN'T HAVE A
TITLE YET. 1989.
Installation,
dimensions
variable.
The Mattress Factory,
Pittsburgh.

row of beer cans, held in place by aluminum frames. Once we notice the American flag, we immediately see that the beer cans use the same colors. We might also reflect on how some beer commercials encourage us to associate their product with nationalism or with America. After all, "consumption" is an American thing to do. The aluminum scaffolding resembles the structure of bleachers commonly assembled for sports events. The artist left some tools lying about, to suggest that this is a special occasion that required larger audience seating. Beer, sports, and nationalism: three elements of American culture that Noland brought together in her installation. We might not notice this constellation much in everyday life, but seeing it in an art gallery raises our awareness of how often they go together.

When the Tate Modern took over an old power plant in London in 2000, the museum inherited a uniquely large space for indoor art: a huge atrium nearly 500 feet long that it now uses for large-scale temporary installations. One of the most striking of these installations so far has been THE WEATHER PROJECT by Danish artist Olafur Eliasson. He installed a huge semicircular sun of bright lamps and then covered the ceiling in mirrors, so that the yellow orb seems whole. The lights that illuminated it were single-frequency bulbs, which created an intense yellow glow throughout the hall. A few strategically placed fans blew mist from melting dry ice, creating clouds that lazily gathered and dispersed.

Museum officials estimated that THE WEATHER PROJECT drew two million visitors over its five-month run during the bleak London winter of 2003–2004. Viewers basked in the seeming warmth of a huge yellow sun that never set. They watched the passing indoor weather. They lay on the floor and looked at their reflections on the ceiling 115 feet above. The installation generally served as a space of communal meditation.

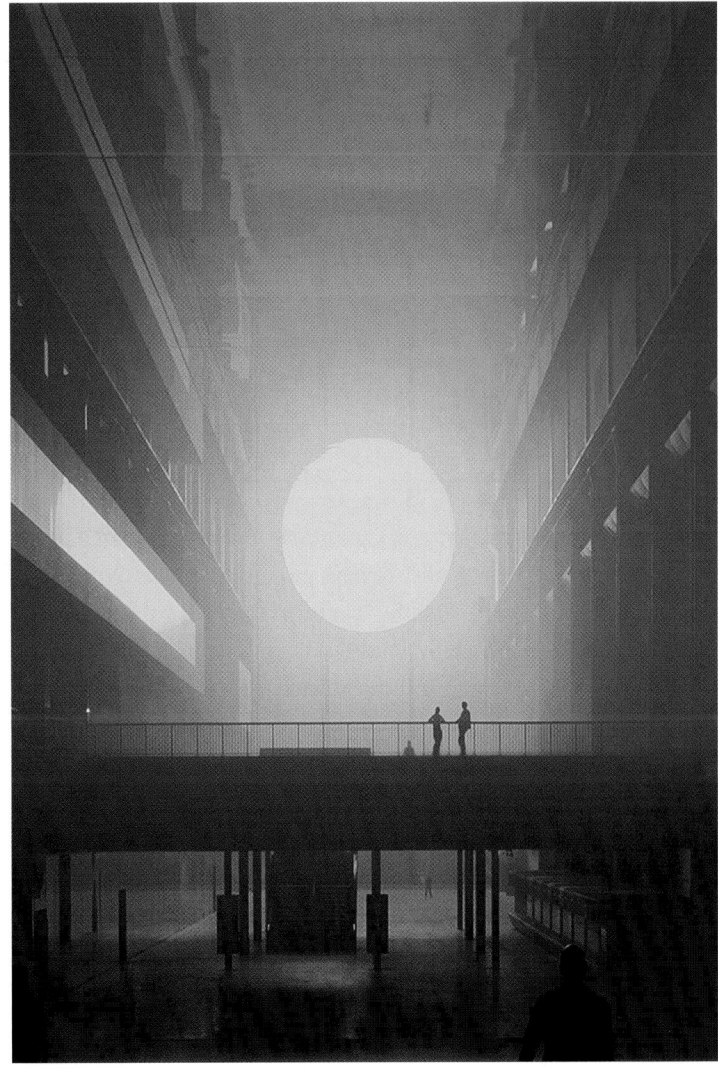

276 Olafur Eliasson.
THE WEATHER PROJECT. 2003–2004.
Installation in Turbine Hall, Tate Modern, London
(The Universal Series). Monofrequency lights, projection foil, haze machines, mirror foil, aluminium, and scaffolding. 26.7 m x 155.4 m. Photo: Jens Ziehe.
Courtesy the artist; neugerriemschneider. Berlin: and Tanya Bonakdar Gallery, New York © Olafur Eliasson 2003

CLAY, GLASS, METAL, WOOD, FIBER

Ever since the Renaissance, we in the West have tended to rank the "crafts" a little below the "arts." We have generally considered craft objects to be useful things, such as dishes, blankets, or jewelry, whereas art (painting and sculpture) is meant to be only looked at and thought about, in a gallery or on a wall in someone's home. Crafts are made with different media (clay, glass, wood, fiber) from those of art (paint, marble, bronze). Craft objects tend to be decorative, whereas art generally makes a personal statement.

Artists and craft workers have rebelled against this discrimination at various times. For example, in the 1870s William Morris in England urged artists to turn away from the "fine arts" and devote their skills to making everyday objects. Most works of art in the West are unique and very expensive things; only the wealthy can afford them, while the rest of us visit them in museums or look at copies in books. Morris thought that if artists devoted their skills and taste to the creation of things for common use, then everyone's life would be enriched. (His belief was influenced by the Socialist politics that he also practiced.) Hence the artists in his workshop made dishes, wallpaper, furniture, and fabrics, all by hand like craft workers of the Middle Ages. Unfortunately, the shop could never get its prices low enough to please either the founder or the public.

A similar idea led to the creation of the Bauhaus in Germany in 1919, though it had a more modern approach. The school was the union of an art academy and a craft workshop, and there too, students and teachers cultivated the "fine arts" side by side with the "applied arts" of furniture-making, graphic design, typography, and even architecture. The emphasis here was on modern mass-production rather than hand crafting, as the artists' designs were destined to be made in factories. The goal was similar to that of the Morris workshop: to bring craft and art together and let artists use their skills to enrich objects we use every day. But because Adolph Hitler disliked modern art, the school was subject to Nazi harassment in the early 1930s and forced to close.

The most recent push against this barrier began in the 1970s, when many artists began making unique objects for gallery exhibition out of craft media. Viewers at that time increasingly appreciated the high level of skill, taste, and labor that go into the best craft work such as quilts, dishes, and stained glass. Industry and mass production reduced the demand for handmade things for daily use. Craft and art thus began to draw together, and the barrier between them began to break down.

This change in attitude brought Western thought in line with that of other cultures around the world and throughout history, which have not separated art and craft. Most of the world's cultures have always regarded an excellent piece of pottery as highly as a painting, and a book illustration as equal in merit to a piece of sculpture; Western society is arriving at this view as well. In 2002, the

American Craft Museum changed its name to the Museum of Contemporary Arts and Design; the following year, the California College of Arts and Crafts became the California College of the Arts.

Some of the artists who adopted craft media in the 1970s had a feminist intent. Miriam Schapiro borrowed techniques from quilting for large works such as PERSONAL APPEARANCE #3. She selected and cut out pieces of fabric and glued them to the surface of the canvas, where they joined forces with acrylic paint in colorful, exuberant compositions. Traditional craft media such as textiles and ceramics have for centuries been a woman's province. Schapiro and many others feel that relegating craft to a lower status demeans the achievements of women throughout history. Regarding her effort to heal the breach, to elevate craft, and join it with art, Schapiro said, "I dovetail my feminism with decoration."[1]

In this chapter, we will consider several media formerly associated with crafts: clay, glass, metal, wood, and fiber. By looking at traditional and contemporary examples, we will see that separating "art" from "craft" is nearly impossible, and that it is better to simply think of them all as art forms.

CLAY

Bits of broken clay pots found in archaeological sites provide valuable clues to thousands of years of human civilization. Since humans began to live in settled communities, clay has been a valuable art material. Clay is extremely flexible in the artist's hands, yet it hardens into a permanent shape when exposed to heat, a process known as *firing*.

The art and science of making objects from clay is called *ceramics*. A person who works with clay is a *ceramist*; one who specializes in making dishes is a *potter*. A wide range of objects, including tableware, dishes, sculpture, bricks, and many kinds of tiles, is made of clay. Most of the basic ceramic materials were discovered, and processes developed, thousands of years ago.

Clays are generally categorized in one of three broad types. *Earthenware* is typically fired at a relatively low temperature (approximately 1,100°C to 1,150°C), and is porous after firing. It may vary from red to brown to tan. Earthenware is the most

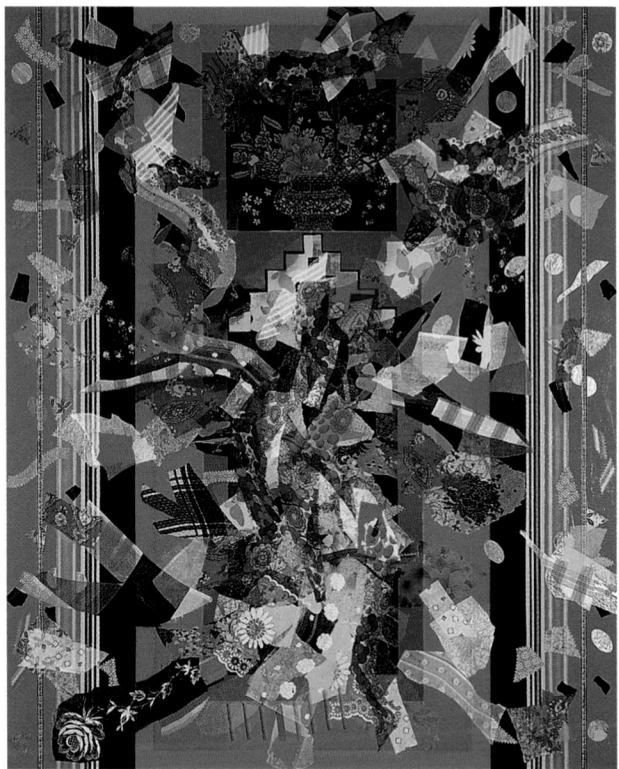

277   Miriam Schapiro.
PERSONAL APPEARANCE #3. 1973.
Acrylic and fabric on canvas. 60″ × 50″.
Collection Marilyn Stokstad, Lawrence, Kansas. Courtesy of Bernice Steinbaum Gallery, Miami, FL. Photo: Robert Hickerson.

common of the three types, and a great many of the world's pots have been made from it. *Stoneware* is fired at a higher temperature (1,200°C to 1,300°C) and is not porous. It is usually grayish or brown. Combining strength with easy workability, stoneware is the preferred medium of most of today's art potters. *Porcelain* is the rarest and most expensive of the three types. Made from deposits of decomposed granite, it becomes white and translucent after firing at a typically high temperature (1,350°C to 1,500°C). Also nonporous, it rings when struck. Porcelain was first developed in China, and even today in England and America the finest white dishes are called "China," no matter where they are made.

With any type of clay, the ceramic process is relatively simple. Ceramists create functional pots or purely sculptural forms from soft, damp clay using hand-building methods such as slab, coil, or modeling, or by *throwing*—that is, by shaping clay on a rapidly revolving wheel. Invented in Mesopotamia about six thousand years ago, the potter's wheel allows potters to produce circular forms with great speed and uniformity. In the hands of a skilled worker, the process looks effortless—almost magical—but it takes time and practice to perfect the technique.

After shaping, a piece is thoroughly dried. Next it is fired in a *kiln* (a kind of oven) where heat chemically transforms the clay into a hard, stone-like substance. (Some techniques for making and decorating ceramic pieces are demonstrated in the Modeling section of the *Discovering Art* CD.)

Two kinds of liquids are commonly used to decorate ceramics, though rarely on the same piece. A *slip* is a mixture of clay and water about the consistency of cream, sometimes colored with earthen powders. With this relatively simple technique, only a limited range of colors is possible, but many ancient cultures made a specialty of this type of pottery decoration.

A *glaze* is a specially formulated liquid paint for clay with a silica base. During firing, the glaze vitrifies (turns to a glass-like substance) and fuses with the clay body, creating a nonporous surface. Glazes can be colored or clear, translucent or opaque, glossy or dull, depending on their chemical composition. Fir-

ing changes the color of most glazes so radically that the liquid that the potter applies to the vessel comes out of the kiln an entirely different color.

Recent works by two of today's leading ceramists will help to show the possibilities of this medium; both are vessels with handles, but they show widely divergent styles. Betty Woodman's DIVIDED VASES (CHRISTMAS) have an exuberant, free-form look that preserves the expressiveness of spontaneous glaze application. The handles are actually flat perforated panels that still show traces of the working process. She used earthenware, a relatively coarse clay that is conducive to natural shapes like the bamboo segments that the vase bodies suggest. She threw each in three pieces on the wheel, and then joined them before adding the handles. The DIVIDED VASES have a fresh look, as if they just came out of the firing kiln.

Adrian Saxe's FUTURE KINGS OF THE WORLD seems precious by comparison. He used porcelain for the main body, working it into a gourd-like

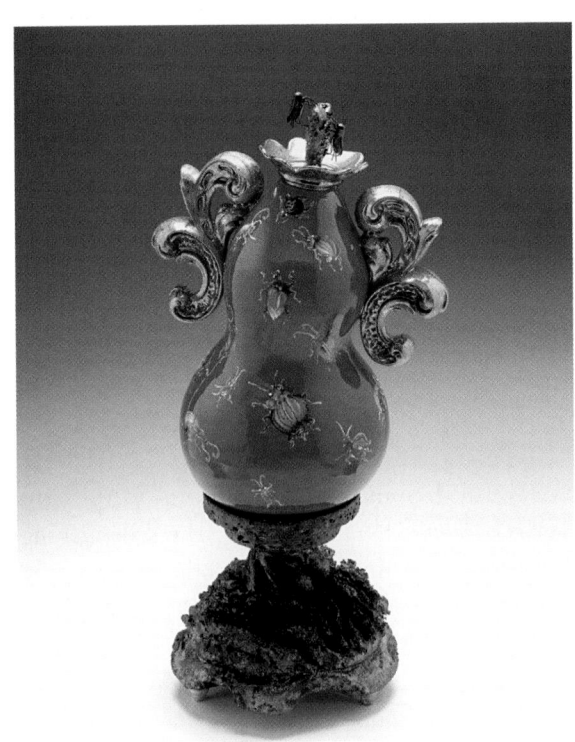

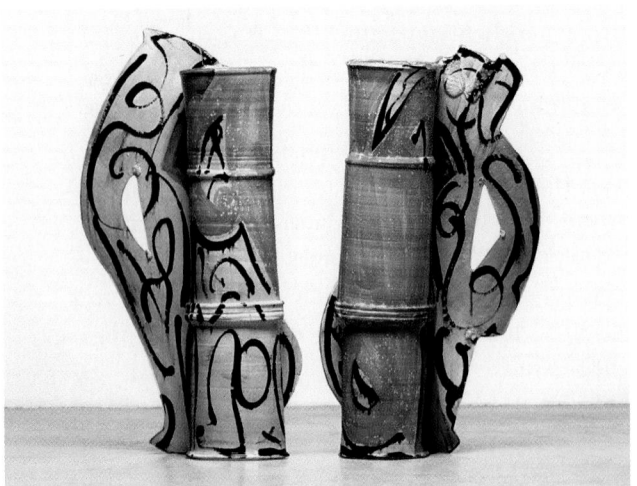

278   Betty Woodman.
divided vases (christmas): view b. 2004.
Glazed earthenware, epoxy resin, lacquer, and paint.
341/20 ¥ 390 ¥ 70.
Frank Lloyd Gallery, Santa Monica.
Courtesy of the artist and Max Protetch Gallery, NY.

279   Adrian Saxe.
RULERS OF THE FUTURE WORLD. 2004.
Porcelain, stoneware, overglaze enamel, lusters, mixed media. 26¼″ × 13¼″ × 10″.
Frank Lloyd Gallery, Santa Monica.

Nampeyo

NAMPEYO WAS BORN into the Snake Clan in the village of Hano, on land that the Hopis called First Mesa. Her name means "Snake That Does Not Bite." There were no paved roads leading to the village, and the nearest city—Winslow, Arizona—was three days' journey away. Her family responded to her early artistic interests by sending her to a neighboring village to learn pottery making from her grandmother, one of the few who still made pots.

Nampeyo began picking up broken shards of pottery from the nearby site of an ancient Hopi village called Sikyatki. This village had been abandoned before the Spanish Conquest. She was fascinated by the ancient designs and began to incorporate them into her own pots.

In 1895, the anthropologist Jesse Walter Fewkes arrived to dig and study the ruins of Sikyatki. Nampeyo's husband helped Fewkes with the digging and told what he knew about the Hopi peoples. Fewkes and his assistants unearthed hundreds of burials, finding many ancient Hopi pots in excellent condition. Among these were many seed jars, low pots with a narrow opening and abstract designs in brown or black over a rich yellow body.

Nampeyo studied and copied these pots, invigorated by the work of her ancestors, and she mastered the shape of the traditional seed jar. Once she learned the vocabulary of symbols, she found that she could freely adapt and combine them, rather than merely copy ancient models. She told an anthropologist, "When I first began to paint, I used to go to the ancient village and pick up pieces of pottery and copy the design. That is how I learned to paint. But now I just close my eyes and see designs and I paint them."[2] She discovered that there was a ready market for pottery with the ancient designs. In this effort she was a pioneer. The relatively rare ancient pottery had always found buyers among a few select collectors; however, when Nampeyo began making pots in that style, to her delight she found that she could easily sell her entire production. She used the new income to support her entire extended family, and allevi-

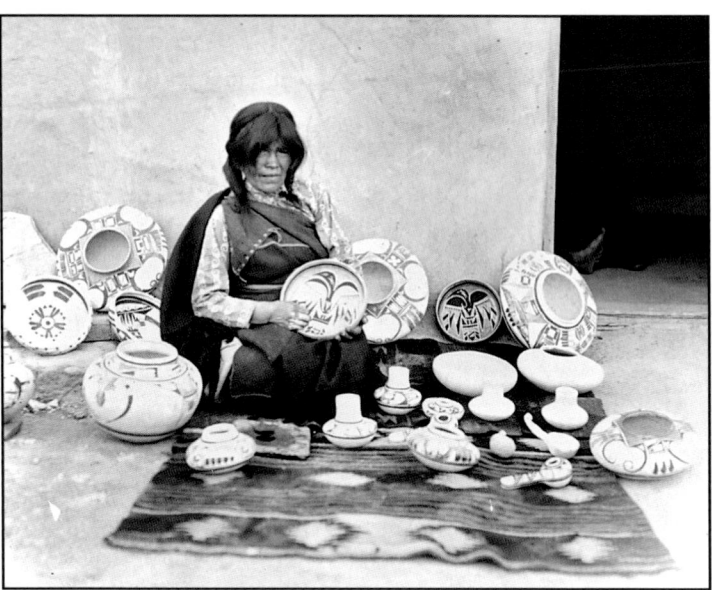

280　NAMPEYO DECORATING POTTERY. 1901.
Displaying pottery: ollas, dippers, bowls, vases.
Courtesy of the Southwest Museum, Los Angeles. Photograph: Adam Clark Vroman. N42363.

ate some of the poverty on First Mesa.

Her success became a pattern that other Indian artists would follow. In the Pueblo of San Ildefonso, María Martínez and her husband, in collaboration with anthropologist Edgar Hewitt, soon reintroduced ancient black pottery from that Pueblo. Lucy Lewis of Ácoma was similarly inspired by ancient designs. The revival of Pueblo and Hopi pottery contributed to the creation, in 1932, of the American Indian Arts and Crafts Board, the first government attempt to encourage Native creators to practice their traditional art forms.

Nampeyo continued to produce work until she began to lose her eyesight in the 1920s. Her husband painted some of her designs until his death in 1932. Today, her great-granddaughters continue the tradition.

shape before tipping it slightly off-axis. The overly elegant handles recall antique picture frames, while the rough vase quotes the style of traditional Chinese pottery. The work's title shows the artist's sarcastic mindset: The FUTURE KINGS OF THE WORLD are insects, two of which crawl up the cap.

Some present-day potters use ancient methods, firing their pots in open fires that reach only low and generally varied temperatures. A pioneer in the rediscovery of past techniques was the Hopi potter Nampeyo. Working in the 1890s in collaboration with anthropologists and archaeologists who were digging ancient ruins near her village, she learned the long-forgotten symbolic vocabulary of ancient wares, and in the process revitalized her own work and that of many other potters, as the accompanying essay shows.

In the mid-1950s, Peter Voulkos brought ceramic tradition together with modern art expression, and thus extended the horizons for both art and craft. He and a group of his students led the California sculpture movement that broke through preconceptions about the limits of clay as a medium for sculpture. With his rebellious spirit, Voulkos revitalized ceramic art and helped touch off new directions in other craft media. If most movements to unite art and craft involved artists moving toward craft, Voulkos reversed the process. He was trained as a potter, and had a studio that sold dishes in upscale stores until the middle 1950s. Then he began to explore abstract art, and he found ways to incorporate some of its techniques into his ceramic work. At first he took a fresh approach to plates: He flexed them out of shape and scratched their surface as if they were paintings, thereby rendering them useless in the traditional sense. His first exhibition of these works in 1959 caused a great deal of controversy, because most people did not think of stoneware as an art medium. Yet none could deny the boldness of his inventions. His monumental GALLAS ROCK brings the emotional energy of Abstract Expressionist painting (see Chapter 23) to three-dimensional form. He said that the basis of this work is "the core cylinder inside, with other cylinders going in different directions to take the weight of the slabs. . . . Outside and inside grew together." While working on it, he had to "relate everything at the same time and still keep the spontaneity."[3]

Both Peter Voulkos and Toshiko Takaezu were influenced by the earthiness and spontaneity of some traditional Japanese ceramics, as well as by expressionist painting, yet they have taken very different

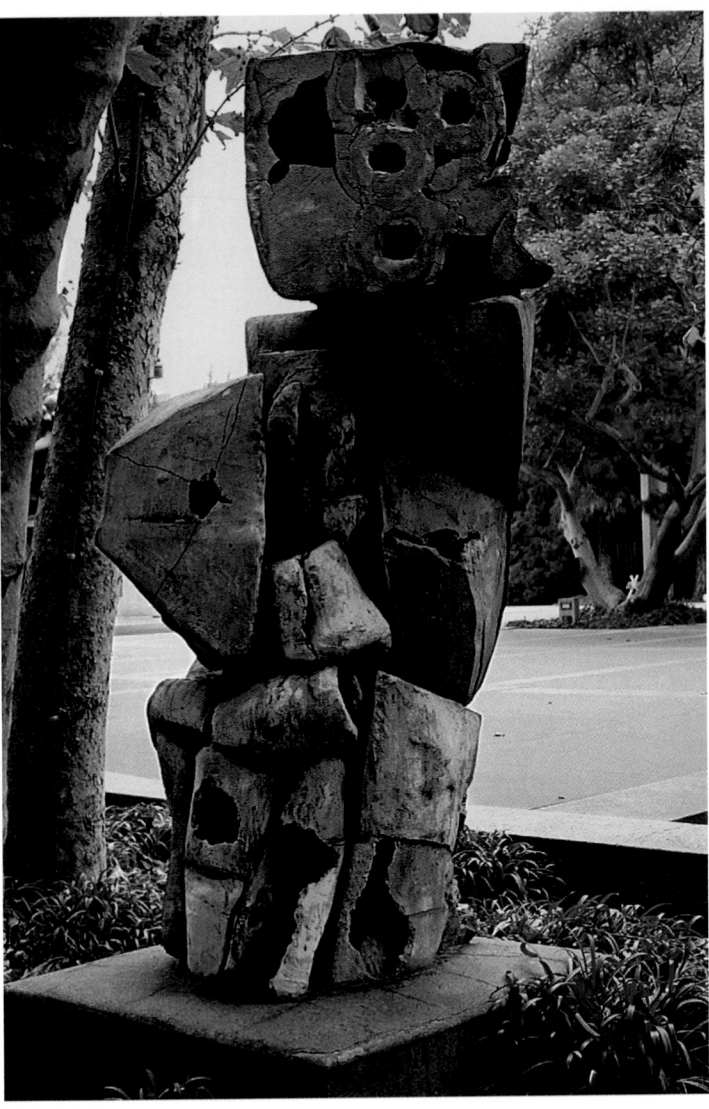

281 Peter Voulkos.
GALLAS ROCK. 1960.
Glazed ceramic. Height 6'.
University of California at Los Angeles.
Photograph: Duane Preble.

directions. Voulkos's pieces are rough and aggressively dynamic, whereas Takaezu's MAKAHA BLUE II offers subtle, restrained strength. By closing the top of container forms, she turns vessels into sculptures, thus providing surfaces for rich paintings of glaze and oxide. She reflected on her love of the clay medium:

When working with clay I take pleasure from the process as well as from the finished piece. Every once in a while I am in tune with the clay, and I hear music, and it's like poetry. Those are the moments that make pottery truly beautiful for me.[4]

Ceramic processes evolved very slowly until the twentieth century, when new formulations and even synthetic clays became available. Other changes have included more accurate methods of firing and improved techniques and equipment. The most significant change of all has come in the use of clay as a sculptural art form.

GLASS

Glass has been used for at least four thousand years as a material for practical containers of all shapes and sizes. During the Middle Ages, stained glass was used extensively in Gothic churches and cathedrals (see page 5). Elaborate, blown-glass pieces have been made in Venice since the Renaissance. Glass is also a fine medium for decorative inlays in a variety of objects—including jewelry.

Glass is an exotic and enticing art medium. One art critic wrote, "Among sculptural materials, nothing equals the sheer eloquence of glass. It can assume any form, take many textures, dance with color, bask in clear crystallinity, make lyrics of light."[5]

Chemically, glass is closely related to ceramic glaze. As a medium, however, it offers a wide range of unique possibilities. Hot or molten glass is a sensitive, amorphous material that is shaped by blowing, casting, or pressing into molds. As it cools, glass solidifies from its molten state without crystallizing. After it is blown or cast, glass may be cut, etched, fused, laminated, layered, leaded, painted, polished, sandblasted, or slumped (softened for a

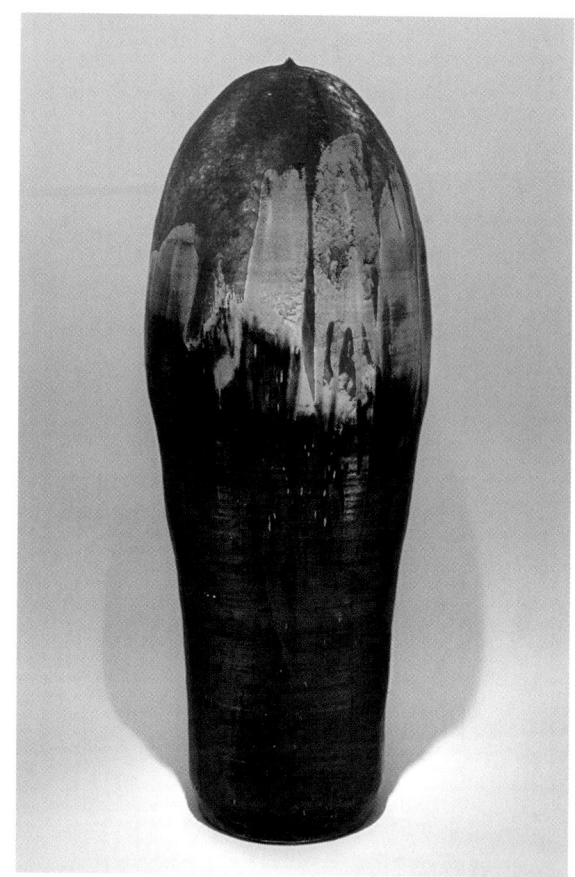

282 Toshiko Takaezu.
MAKAHA BLUE II. 2002.
Stoneware. 18½″ × 48″.
Courtesy of the artist and Charles Cowles Gallery, NY.

controlled sag). The fluid nature of glass produces qualities of mass flowing into line as well as translucent volumes of airy thinness.

Although it is said that the character of any material determines the character of the expression, this statement is particularly true of glass. Molten glass requires considerable speed and skill in handling. The glassblower combines the centering skills of a potter, the agility and stamina of an athlete, and the grace of a dancer to bring qualities of breath and movement into crystalline form.

The person most responsible for making glass into an art form was Harvey Littleton. Formerly a ceramic artist, he started a glassblowing studio on

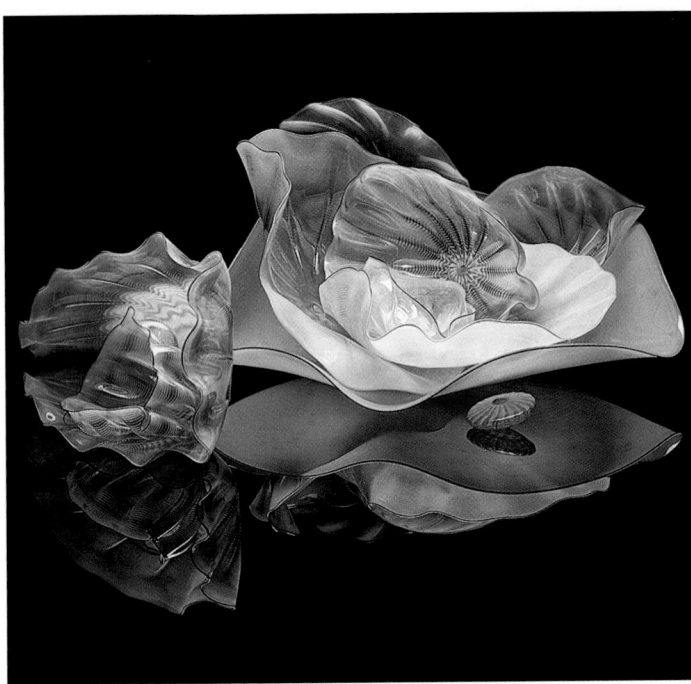

283 Dale Chihuly.
MAUVE SEAFORM SET WITH BLACK LIP WRAPS from the
"SEAFORMS" SERIES. 1985.
Blown glass.
Courtesy of Dale Chihuly. Photograph: Dick Busher.

the grounds of the Toledo Museum of Art in Ohio in 1962 and began experimenting with artistic glassmaking. With help from industrial technicians, he soon settled at the University of Wisconsin, where he began the first instructional studio. A generation of glassworkers studied with him, and they fanned out to start more than fifty other university glass studios within ten years.

The fluid and translucent qualities of glass are used to the fullest in Dale Chihuly's SEAFORM SERIES. Chihuly, a Littleton student, produces such pieces with a team of glass artists working under his direction. In this series, he arranged groups of pieces and carefully directed the lighting to suggest delicate undersea environments.

METAL

Metal's primary characteristics are strength and formability. The various types of metal most often used for crafts and sculpture can be hammered, cut, drawn out, welded, joined with rivets, or cast. Early metalsmiths created tools, vessels, armor, and weapons.

A high point of metalwork production was reached in the Islamic cultures of the Middle East in the thirteenth and fourteenth centuries, when techniques of shaping and inlaying were practiced with unparalleled sophistication. The D'ARENBERG BASIN, named after a French collector who owned it for many years, was made for the last ruler of the Ayyubid dynasty in Syria in the mid-thirteenth century. The body of the basin was first cast in brass; its extremely intricate design included lowered areas into which precisely cut pieces of silver were placed. Although most of the silver pieces are only a fraction of an inch in size, they enliven a carefully patterned design that occupies several finely proportioned horizontal bands. The lowest band is a decorative pattern based on repeated plant shapes. Above is a row of real and imaginary animals that decorates a relatively narrow band. The next band depicts a scene of princely pleasure, as well-attired people play polo. The uppermost contains more plant shapes between the uprights of highly stylized Arabic script that expresses good

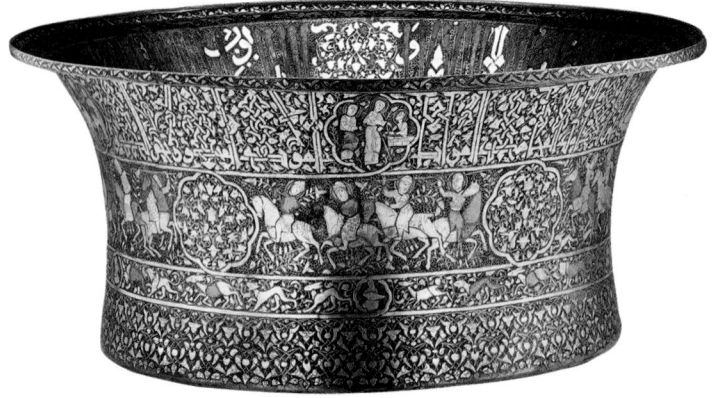

284 D'ARENBERG BASIN.
Syria. Mid-13th century.
Brass with silver inlay. 9" × 20".
Freer Gallery of Art, Smithsonian Institution, Washington, D.C. F1955.10.

wishes to the owner of the piece. A central panel in this upper row depicts a scene from the life of Christ, who is regarded as an important figure in the Muslim religion.

Cal Lane combines some of the intricate metalwork of Middle Eastern pieces with scenes ripped from today's headlines, in works such as FILIGREE CAR BOMBING. She worked for years as a welder, a woman in a traditionally male occupation. After cleaning up the shop at night, she sometimes laid delicate pieces of lace over half-finished jobs as a kind of visual joke for her male coworkers when they arrived the next morning. The juxtaposition ended up fertilizing her own art, as she began perforating shovels and scrap metal pieces with the intricate lace patterns. She felt an affinity for lacemaking, an art form traditionally practiced by women, so she began to "feminize" pieces of metal, creating lacy surfaces in sheets of metal with her oxyacetylene blowtorch.

To make FILIGREE CAR BOMBING, she used parts from a car that had been demolished in an accident. Making the lace patterns with the torch resembled both drawing and carving. She said that the process of making "becomes evidence of the handmade, as in a lace doily or a drawing, but in a hard, cold, heavy-duty, structural steel plate." Installed in the gallery, the lace patterns cast shadows on the floor below. The result is a kind of visual oxymoron, as a wrecked car becomes handmade, light, and airy.

WOOD

The living spirit of wood is given a second life in handmade objects. Growth characteristics of individual trees remain visible in the grain of wood long after trees are cut, giving wood a vitality not found in other materials. Its abundance, versatility, and warm tactile qualities have made wood a favored material for human use and for art pieces.

Virginia Dotson makes elegant works that straddle the boundary between useful things and objects just for contemplation. Her bowl CROSSWINDS includes two kinds of wood that have been inlaid, laminated, and turned on a lathe. While

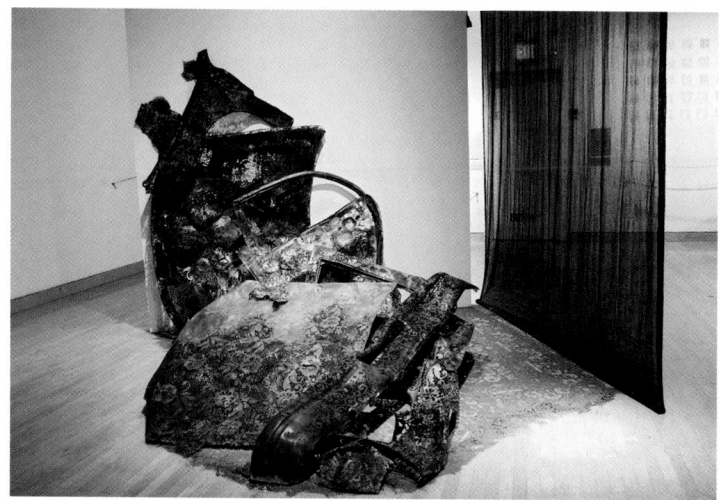

285 Cal Lane.
FILIGREE CAR BOMBING. 2007.
Found automobile parts, dirt. 6′6″ × 8′ × 9′.
Courtesy Foley Gallery, NY.

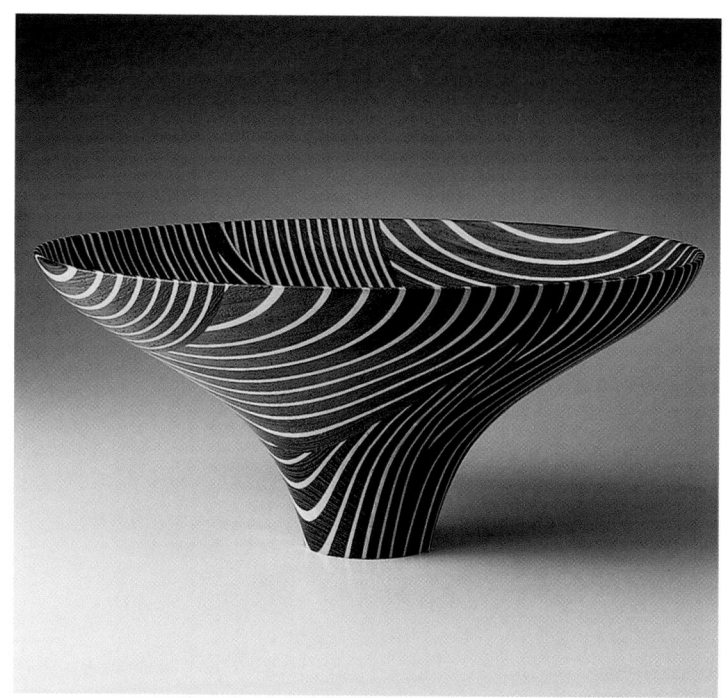

286 Virginia Dotson.
CROSSWINDS. 1989.
Wenge and maple, laminated and turned.
5¾″ × 13⅛″ × 13⅛″.
Ronald C. Wornick Collection.

devoted to wood as a medium, she favors interaction with other types of artists. She said, "I love to look at work in other media and talk about common concerns with weavers, quilters, metal, and glass artists. This type of interaction has provided many insights for the personal involvement I have with my work."[6]

Most furniture purchased today is produced by industrial mass-production methods. However, those with the skill to make their own—or enough money to buy custom pieces—can enjoy living with handcrafted furniture.

Sam Maloof makes unique pieces of furniture and also repeats some designs he finds particularly satisfying. His DOUBLE ROCKING CHAIR and other designs show his thorough understanding of wood and of the hand processes he uses to shape wood into furniture. Flowing curves result from his sensitive melding of form and function. Although he employs assistants who help him duplicate his best designs, he limits quantity. Because he enjoys knowing that each piece is cut, assembled, and finished according to his own high standards, Maloof has rejected offers from manufacturers who want to mass-produce his designs. He prefers to retain quality control and the special characteristics that are inevitably lost when even the best designs are factory-produced rather than handmade. Many pieces of furniture are pleasing to look at, and many are comfortable to use, but relatively few fulfill both functions so successfully.

FIBER

Fiber art includes such processes as weaving (both loom and nonloom techniques), stitching, basketmaking, surface design (dyed and printed textiles), wearable art, and handmade papermaking. These fiber processes use natural and synthetic fibers in both traditional and innovative ways. Artists working with fiber (as with artists working in any medium) draw on the heritage of traditional practices and also explore new avenues of expression.

All weaving is based on the interlacing of lengthwise fibers, *warp*, and cross fibers, *weft* (from which we get the word *weave*). Weavers create patterns by changing the numbers and placements of interwoven threads, and they can choose from a variety of looms and techniques. Simple hand looms can produce very sophisticated, complex weaves. A large tapestry loom, capable of weaving hundreds of colors into intricate forms, may require several days of preparation before work begins.

Some of the world's most spectacular carpets came from Islamic Persia during the period of the Safavid dynasty in the sixteenth century. Here, weavers employed by royal workshops knotted carefully dyed wool over a network of silk warps and wefts. THE ARDABIL CARPET, long recognized as one of the greatest Persian carpets, contains about three hundred such knots, over fine silk threads, per square inch. Thus, this carpet required approximately 25 million knots!

The design of the carpet is centered on a sunburst surrounded by sixteen oval shapes. Two mosque lamps of unequal size share space with an intricate pattern of flowers. At the corners of the main field, quarters of the central design are repeated. A small panel at the right gives the date and the name of an artist, who must have been the designer. Another inscription is a couplet by Hafiz,

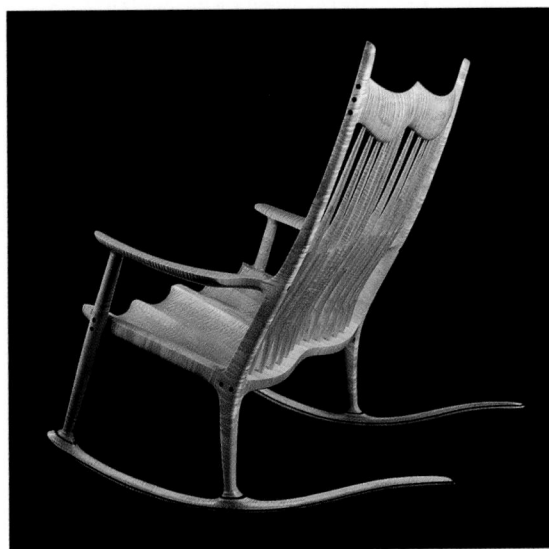

287 Sam Maloof.
DOUBLE ROCKING CHAIR. 1992.
Fiddleback maple and ebony.
42⅜" × 42" × 44½".
Courtesy of the artist.

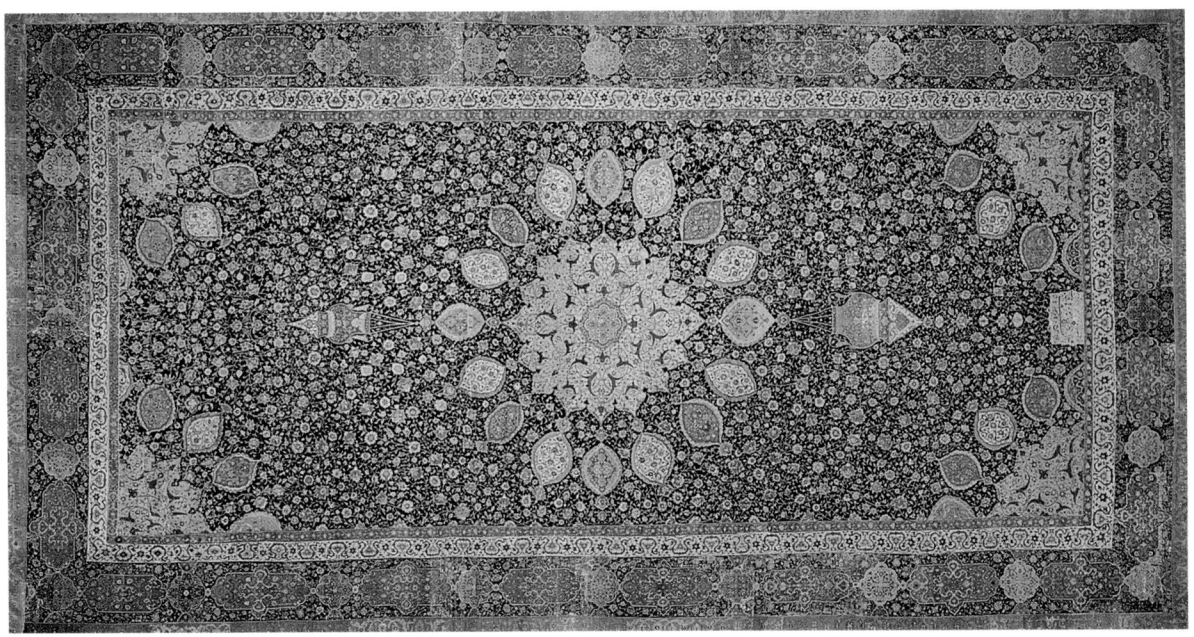

288   **THE ARDABIL CARPET.** Tabriz. 1540.
     Wool pile on silk warps and wefts. 34′ × 17′6″.
     V & A Picture Library.

the bestknown lyrical poet in Iran: "I have no refuge in this world other than thy threshold. My head has no resting-place other than this doorway."

Prolific, highly influential contemporary artist Diane Itter created a major body of work consisting of off-loom, small-scale knotted structures made of linen threads. PATTERN SCAPE is one of Itter's many pieces made with a technique she developed. Working from the center out, through patterned repetition, she constructed complex color-rich forms thread by thread. Of her work she said:

I have come to realize what it is about the textile arts that fascinates me. Among other things … it is the capacity to be both painter and sculptor at the same time. That is, the visual image is created by the integration of color and structure—one cannot exist without the other. In addition, the textile arts allow me a way of working which is both personal and intimate yet potentially monumental in concept and universal in nature. By limiting both my technique (knotting) and my materials (linen) I am able to concentrate all my energies on full exploration of the visual image.

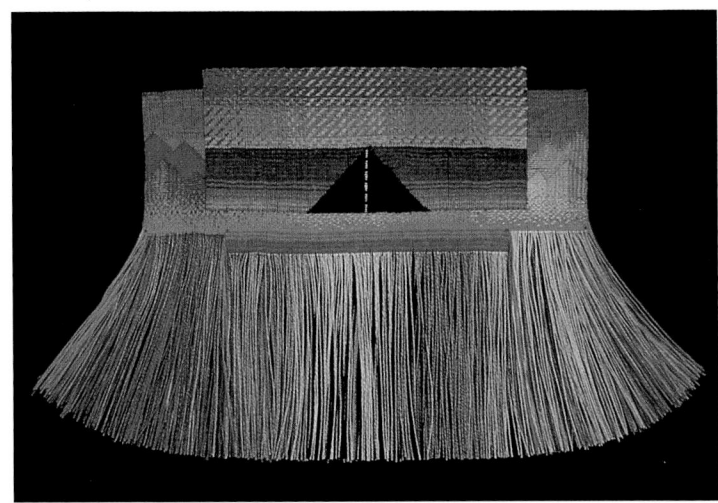

289   Diane Itter.
     PATTERN SCAPE. 1985.
     Linen, knotted. 10″ × 11″.
     Photo courtesy of the Museum of Arts & Design, NY, from the exhibition "Craft Today: Poetry of the Physical," 1986.

After many years of working, I am still fascinated by the infinite variety of images I can create within the set limits.[7]

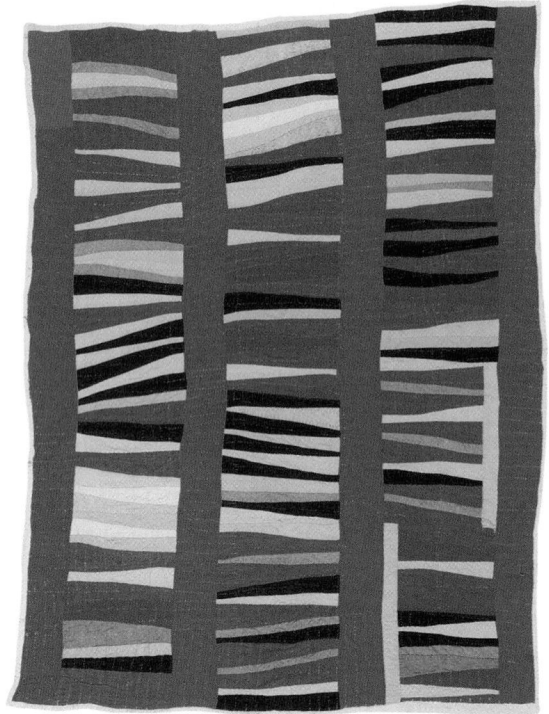

290 Jessie Pettway.
BARS AND STRING-PIECE COLUMNS. ca. 1950s.
Cotton, 95″ × 76″.
©2003 Tinwood Alliance collection, Atlanta (www.tinwoodmedia.com).
Photo: Steve Pitkin/Pitkin Studios.

In some African-American communities, women have carried on a traditional of quilt making for generations. One of the most active groups has been meeting in Gees Bend, Alabama for over a hundred years, where the quilters gather to share fabric, discuss neighborhood news, and encourage creativity. Jessie Pettway made BARS AND STRING-PIECE COLUMNS from leftover pieces of cloth. This quilt, like many produced at Gees Bend, resembles some kinds of African textiles (see Chapter 19). Many Gees Bend quilters create their work with only a minimum of advance planning, and this lends their work a look of spontaneity and exuberance. The coincidental resemblance to modern art also attracts the attention of collectors.

Quilt making is often a collaborative type of art, facilitating interaction between creators as they share ideas and fabric pieces. New York fiber artist Cat Mazza is using this example to turn her knitting into political activism. She is organizing fiber workers to create a new kind of petition in opposition to the sweatshop conditions that many workers around the world face. At her Web site, she invites fiber artists to create 4″ × 4″ textile squares by knitting or crocheting, and then send them to her as a handmade signature on the NIKE BLANKET PETITION that she is assembling. She also sponsors workshops to teach others the basics of fiber arts and encourage them to aid the effort. She photographs all the submitted squares and posts them to her Web site, along with the names and locations of the petitioners. At the end of the three-year project, she will attach all the squares together and present the result to the head of the Nike Corporation. The goal is to make a Nike logo 14 feet wide, surrounded by a huge multicolored border.

Polly Apfelbaum dyes fabrics to create installations that show the influence of both modern abstract art and feminism. She said that she wanted to do a contemporary version of the traditional crazy quilt, in which random fragments of leftover cloth are stitched together in dazzling patterns. In this way she claims descent from the women who

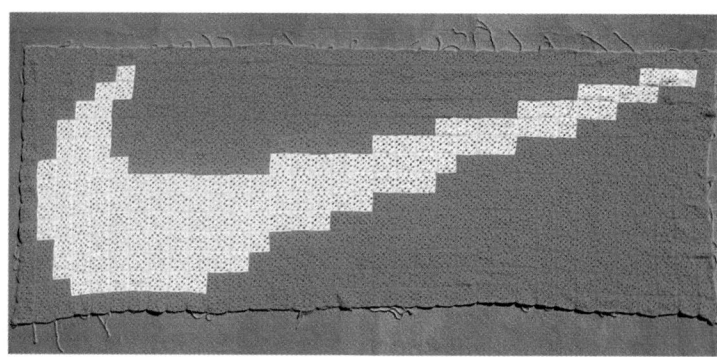

291 Cat Mazza.
NIKE BLANKET PETITION. 2007–2010.
Crocheted wool. 56″ × 11′8″.
Courtesy of the artist.

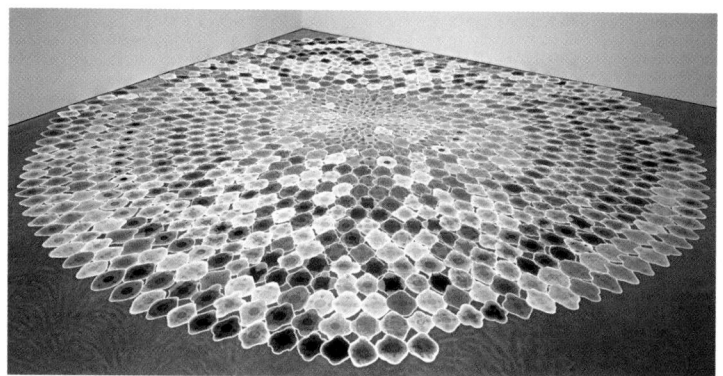

have traditionally woven and sewn most textiles. In BLOSSOM, she used bright colors to stain oval-shaped pieces of velvet. She attached them together to heighten the resemblance to quilts, and then installed them on the floor of a gallery. The resulting work resembles a quilt, a carpet, and a luxurious bed of flower petals. She applied fabric dye to each part with a squeeze bottle. For this piece, she prevented the dye from reaching the edge of each oval, leaving a white border that sets each color apart. Her dyeing process resembles painting, but the works she creates are closer to sculpture and textile art. She sometimes calls her works "fallen paintings," because placing the work on the floor allows viewers to interact with the work from more angles.

Faith Ringgold's paintings, quilts, and soft sculptures speak eloquently of her life and ideas. Happy memories of her childhood in Harlem in the 1930s provide much of her subject matter. MRS. JONES AND FAMILY represents Ringgold's own family. Commitments to women, the family, and cross-cultural consciousness are at the heart of Ringgold's work. With playful exuberance and insight, she draws on history, recent events, and her own experiences for her depictions and narratives of class, power, race, and gender. Her sophisticated use of naiveté gives her work the appeal of the best folk art, but her work has also dealt with more urgent themes such as unemployment and race discrimination. See the biographical essay on the next page.

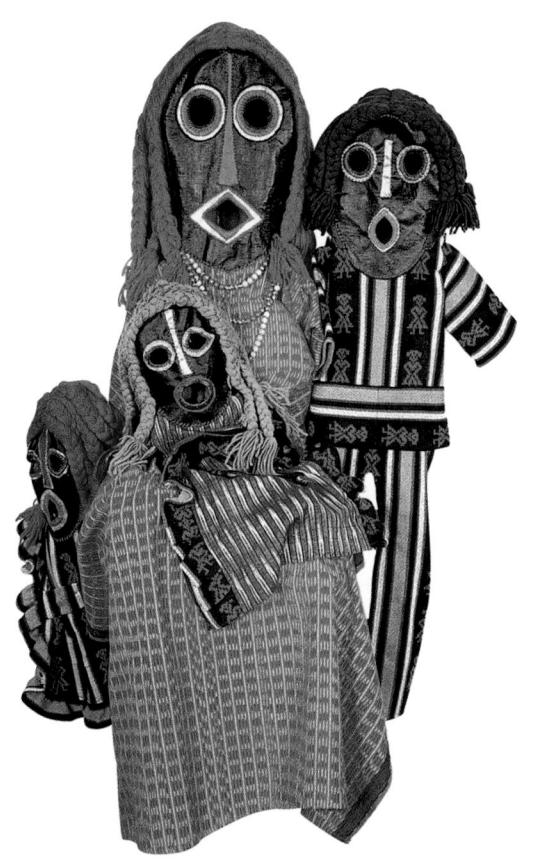

293　Faith Ringgold.
MRS. JONES AND FAMILY. 1973.
Soft sculpture, mixed media. 74″ × 69″.
Artist's collection. © 1973 Faith Ringgold.

Ringgold

Stitched into History

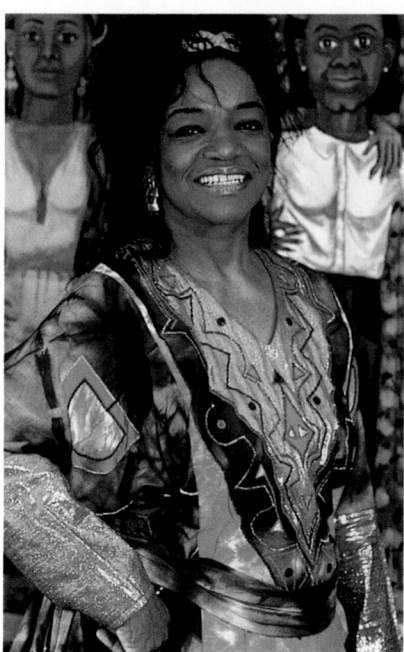

294 Faith Ringgold.
With detail of THE PURPLE QUILT. 1986.
© Faith Ringgold, Inc. Photographer: C'Love.

A PROLIFIC CREATOR of many art forms, from paintings to quilts to children's books, Faith Ringgold has taken the reality of racial discrimination and made from it uplifting stories about finding sustenance and overcoming adversity.

Born in Harlem to working-class parents, she was encouraged as a child to succeed by their example. Acknowledging the double disadvantage of being an African-American woman, her parents taught her that "you have to be twice as good to go half as far."[9] Her mother was a seamstress and fashion designer, her father a sanitation truck driver. After receiving bachelor's and master's degrees in art from City College of New York, she taught in New York City public schools from 1955 to 1972. She later recalled that the experience of teaching children encouraged her own creativity: "They showed me what it is to be free, to be able to express yourself directly."[10]

During the early years of her teaching career, she painted landscapes. But the civil rights movement of the 1960s encouraged her to address directly in her art the issues of inequality that seemed then to be present everywhere. She sought advice from the elder African-American artist Romare Bearden (see page 12), who included her work in a group show in Harlem in 1966. She also took part in several protest actions at New York museums, urging greater inclusion of African-American artists and more outreach to ethnic minority neighborhoods.

Leaving her teaching position in 1972, she began to devote full time to art. She also began a ten-year collaboration with her mother in the creation of works on cloth. Quilt making had been a family tradition as far back as her great-great-grandmother, who had made them as a slave in Florida. Now the mother-daughter team collaborated on a new type of textile art that included images and stories on the sewn fragments. In addition to continuing ancient African textile art traditions, these cloth works were also portable.

Her themes are highly varied. Some are personal and autobiographical, such as *Change: Faith Ringgold's Over 100 Pound Weight Loss Performance Story Quilt*. Others expose injustice, such as *The Slave Rape Series*, which dealt with the mistreatment of African women in the slave trade. Some are about important African-American cultural figures, such as *Sonny's Quilt*, which depicts the jazz saxophonist Sonny Rollins, performing as he soars over the Brooklyn Bridge.

Typical of the artist's "Story Quilts" is TAR BEACH, which tells the story of the fictional Cassie, an eight-year-old character who is based on Ringgold's own childhood memories. She would go up to the asphalt roof of her apartment building ("Tar Beach") with her family on hot nights, because there was no air-conditioning in the home. Cassie describes Tar Beach as a magical place, with a 360-degree view of tall buildings and the George Washington Bridge in the distance. She dreams that she can fly, that she can do anything she imagines, as she lies on a blanket with her little brother. She dreams that she can give her father the union card that he has been denied because of his race. She dreams that she can let her mother sleep late, and eat ice cream every day for dessert. She even dreams that she can buy the building her father works in, and that her mother won't cry when her father can't find work. The quilt depicts the two children on the blanket, and her parents playing cards with the neighbors next to a table set with snacks and drinks. TAR BEACH was later made into a children's book, one of four that Ringgold has written.

The combination of fantasy and hard reality in this work, with imagination the key to overcoming obstacles, is typical of Ringgold's work as well as her life. Near the end of her memoir, she said, "I don't want the story of my life to be about racism, though that has played a major role. I want my story to be about attainment, love of family, art, helping others, courage, values, dreams coming true."[11]

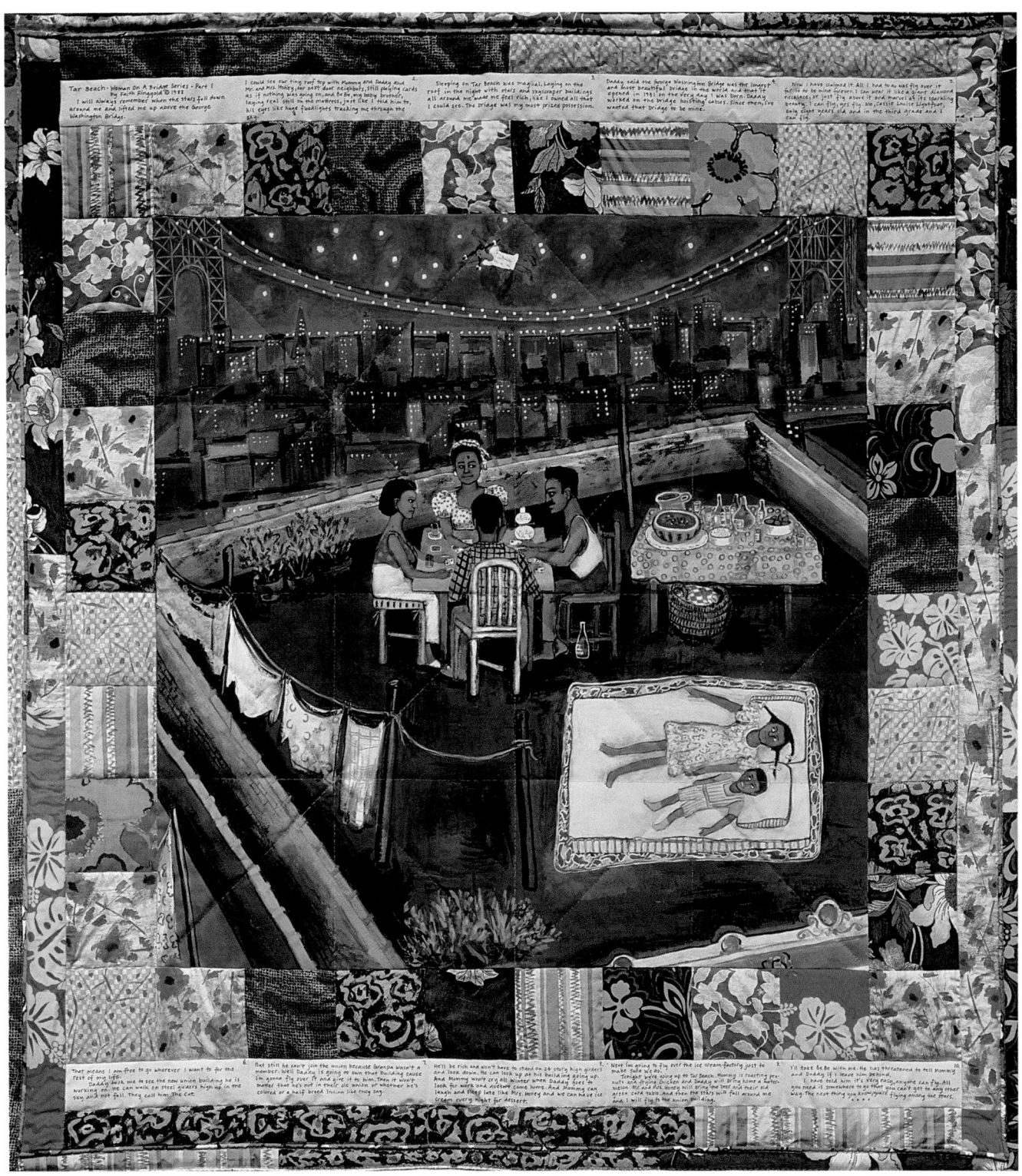

295 Faith Ringgold.
TAR BEACH. 1988.
Acrylic pieced and printed fabric. 74″ × 69″.
Collection: Solomon R. Guggenheim Museum, NY. © Faith Ringgold Inc.

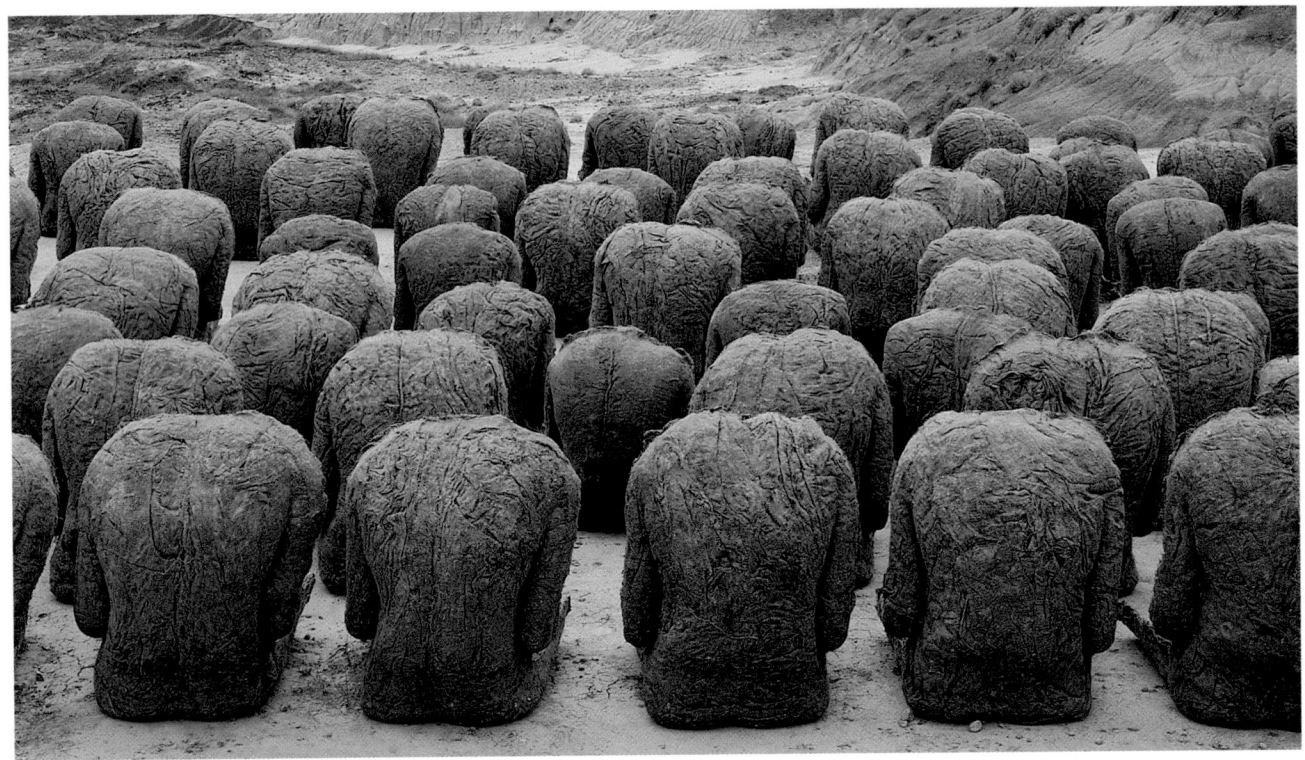

296 Magdalena Abakanowicz.
BACKS (IN LANDSCAPE). 1976–1982.
80 pieces, burlap and glue.
Photograph: © 1982 Dirk Bakker.
© Magdalena Abakanowicz.
Courtesy of Marlborough Gallery, NY.

Innovations in off-loom fiber work have taken the fiber arts into the realm of sculpture in a variety of ways. Magdalena Abakanowicz has been at the leading edge of nontraditional uses of fiber since the 1960s. Her powerful series called BACKS has an unforgettable quality—at once personal and universal. The earthy color and textures of the formed burlap suggest the capacity to endure dire hard-ships and to survive with strength. Her forms have what she feels all art must have: mysterious, bewitching power. The artist spoke of her motives:

I want the viewer to penetrate the inside of my forms. For I want him to have the most intimate contact with them, the same contact one can have with clothes, animal skins, or grass.[8]

ARCHITECTURE

Architecture has great potential for enhancing our lives. Every day we live, work, and move about in indoor and outdoor spaces that have been designed by individuals or teams. No matter how simple or complex, how rich or how poor our life situations, we can find comfort in making our surroundings beautiful. Margaret Courtney-Clarke's photograph of a woman painting an image of a chicken on the mud wall of her house embodies this idea. The title, BEAUTIFYING THE SPACE IN WHICH WE LIVE MAKES LIFE MORE BEARABLE, says it all.

In our modern and more specialized society, creative architects and environmental designers make their designs after considering the needs and concerns of clients and those who will live with their designs. The work of professionals is in turn maintained, enhanced, or modified by those who use the spaces.

ARCHITECTURE IS . . .

Architecture is a frequently overlooked and misunderstood art form because it is generally considered a necessity rather than an expressive statement. In fact, it is both. As the art form that often surrounds us in our daily lives, architecture has long made human survival both possible and enjoyable.

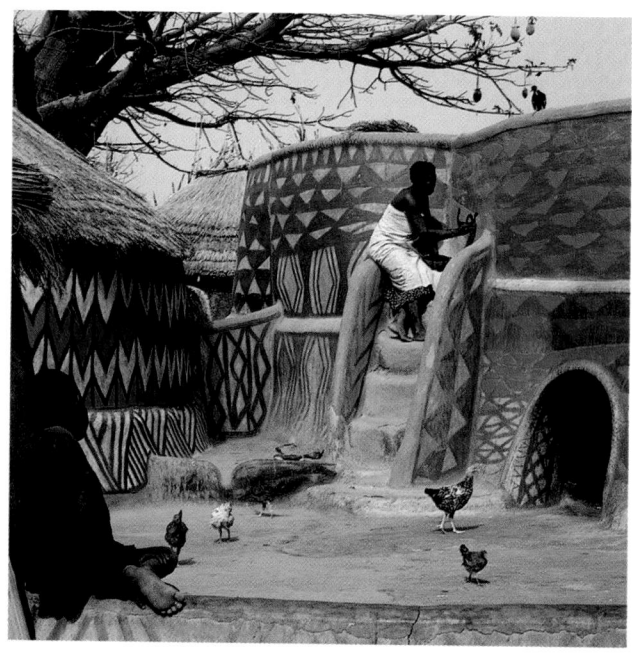

297　Margaret Courtney-Clarke.
BEAUTIFYING THE SPACE IN WHICH WE LIVE MAKES LIFE MORE BEARABLE.
From *African Canvas*, Namibia. 1990.
Photograph.
© Margaret Courtney-Clarke.

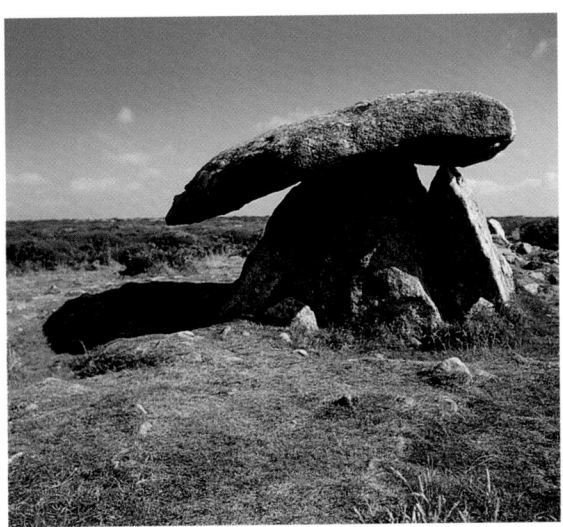

298 DOLMEN.
Crocuno, north of Carnac, France.
Photographer: James Lynch. Ancient Art and Architecture Collection, Ltd.

Architecture is the art and science of designing and constructing buildings for practical, aesthetic, and symbolic purposes. Because it grows out of basic human needs and aspirations, architecture records a society's values. For at least five thousand years, people around the world have built impressive structures that go beyond providing mere shelter.

Throughout most of recorded history, people built their own homes. The essential skills were passed on from generation to generation. Among the world's oldest surviving structures is the DOLMEN located in northwestern France. Its builders simply massed huge boulders to create an enclosed tomb.

Yet before industrialization and the growth of cities, the building crafts became specialized. In order to provide livable housing for the world's growing population, educated people need knowledge of architectural possibilities. One way to begin learning what it takes to design buildings is to get directly involved with creating and building one. When architect Frank Lloyd Wright started an architecture school in Arizona, for example, he required his students to make their own dwellings from simple materials.

We come to understand a building through a succession of experiences in time and space. We cannot see or experience a building all at once as we do a painting; to enjoy the pleasures architecture offers, often we must explore buildings inside and out.

Walk around your house or apartment. How do you respond to the entrance? The height of the ceilings? Wall and floor colors, textures, materials? Window sizes and placements? The stairs, if any? Have you ever noticed how your response changes as you move from a dark, low-ceilinged entranceway to a bright, high-ceilinged room?

An Art and a Science

No matter what sort of structure they are building, architects address and integrate three key issues: function (how a building is used); form (how it looks); and structure (how it stands up). As an art, architecture both creates interior spaces and wraps them in an expressive shape.

As a science, architecture is a physics problem: How does a structure hold up its own weight and the loads placed on it? Architecture must be designed to withstand the forces of compression, or pushing ($\rightarrow\leftarrow$); tension, or pulling ($\leftarrow\rightarrow$); bending, or curving ($\mathcal{L}\,\mathcal{J}$); and any combination of these physical forces.

Like the human body, contemporary architecture has three essential components. These are a supporting skeleton or frame; an outer skin; and operating equipment, similar to the body's vital organs and systems. The equipment includes plumbing; electrical wiring; appliances; and systems for cooling, heating, and circulating air as needed. In earlier centuries, structures of wood, earth, brick, or stone had no such equipment, and the skeleton and skin were often one.

Styles, Materials, and Methods

The evolution of architectural techniques and styles has been determined by the materials available and by the changing needs and values of society. In ancient times, when nomadic hunter-gatherers became farmers and village dwellers, housing evolved from caves, huts, and tents to more substantial structures. During the Middle Ages, the tallest buildings were stone churches; during our own age of commerce, the tallest buildings are office towers.

Because early building designers (as well as those in nonindustrialized countries today) made structures only out of the materials at hand, regional styles developed that blended with their sites and climates. Modern transportation and the spread of advanced technologies now make it possible to build almost anything anywhere. The consequence is a loss of a sense of place. Urban architecture in many parts of the world now looks very much alike.

Wood, Stone, and Brick. Since the beginning of history, most structures have been made of wood, stone, earth, or brick. Each of these natural materials has its own strengths and weaknesses. For example, wood, which is light, can be used for roof beams; whereas stone, which is heavy, can be used for load-bearing walls but is not effective as a beam. Much of the world's major architecture has been constructed of stone because of its permanence, availability, and beauty. In the past, entire cities were slowly built by cutting and placing stone upon stone.

Dry Masonry. Probably the simplest building technique is to pile stones atop one another. The process has been used to make such rudimentary structures as markers, piles, and cairns throughout the world. When such massing is done with a consistent pattern, the result is called masonry. In dry masonry, where no mortar is used, the weight of the stones themselves holds the structure up. If the stones are cut or shaped before use, they are *dressed*.

The GREAT ZIMBABWE ("Great Stone House") in East Africa is an elliptical structure that gave its name to the country in which it is located. Built sometime in the twelfth century, it was abandoned about three hundred years later. GREAT ZIMBABWE is nearly round, with several conical structures inside whose original function is still unknown. Its walls, made of dressed local stone, are approximately thirty feet high. For added stability, the walls were built up to fifteen feet thick at the base, tapering slightly toward the top. Roofing was probably grass or thatch held together with sticks. The structure is the largest of a group of ancient stone dwellings that formed a trading city that may have held as many as twenty thousand people at its height. Though the outer walls of GREAT ZIMBABWE have openings in selected locations for entry and exit, there are no windows; because these tend to weaken masonry walls, only structures that are considerably smaller can use them without external support.

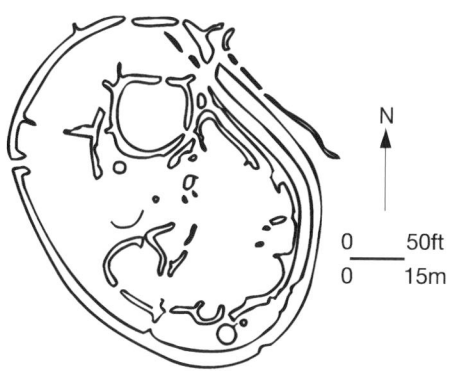

299 GREAT ZIMBABWE.
Zimbabwe. Before 1450.
Height of wall 30′.

a. Plan.
b. Interior.
Casement Creative Services, Inc., ARPS/The Casement Collection.

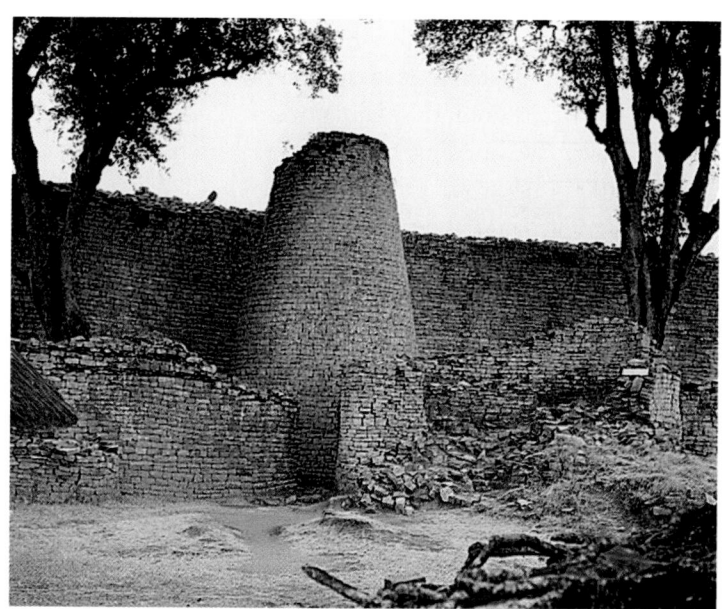

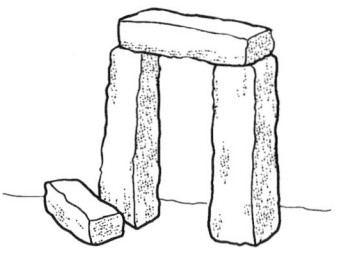

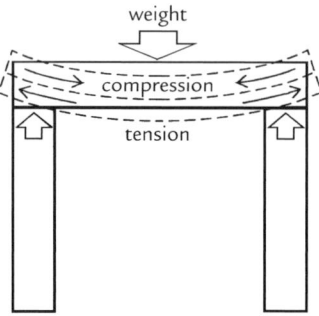

weight

compression

tension

300 POST-AND-BEAM CONSTRUCTION.

GREAT ZIMBABWE is the largest ancient stone structure in Africa south of the great pyramids of Egypt, which are also built of dry masonry. Other notable examples of such buildings are Machu Picchu in Peru and the ancient pueblos of the American Southwest, such as Mesa Verde.

Post and Beam. Prior to the twentieth century, two dominant structural types were in common use: post-and-beam (also called post-and-lintel) and arch systems, including vaulting. Most of the world's architecture, including modern steel structures, has been built with POST-AND-BEAM CONSTRUCTION. Vertical posts or columns support horizontal beams and carry the weight of the entire structure to the ground.

The form of post-and-beam buildings is determined by the strengths and weaknesses of the materials used. Stone beam lengths must be short and columns (posts) relatively thick to compensate for stone's brittleness. Wood beams may be longer, and posts thinner, because wood is lighter and more flexible. The strength-to-weight ratio of modern steel makes it possible to build with far longer beams and thus to create much larger interior spaces.

Bundled reeds provided the model for the monumental post-and-beam Egyptian temples at Luxor. A row of columns spanned or connected by beams is called a *colonnade*, as seen in the COLONNADE AND COURT OF AMENHOTEP III. Most ancient Egyptian temples were symmetrical, with aisles for processions that connected adjacent pavilions. Their arrangement was also generally hierarchical, with the more remote precincts accessible only to the higher-ranking priests.

Following the lead of the Egyptians, the Greeks further refined stone post-and-beam construction. For more than two thousand years, the magnificence of the Parthenon and other classical Greek architecture (see Chapter 15) has influenced the designers of a great many later buildings.

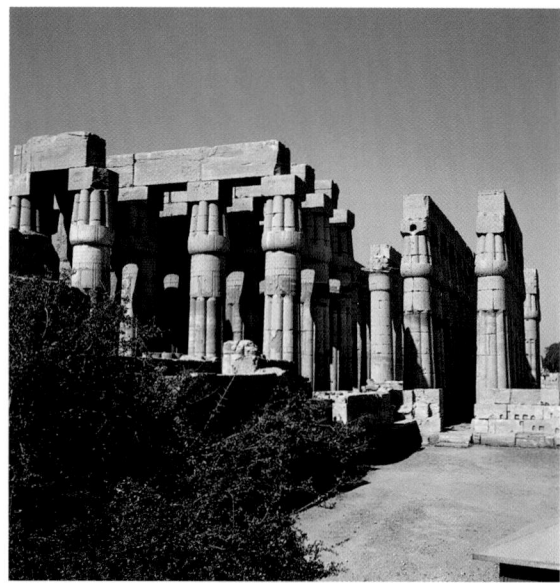

301 COLONNADE AND COURT OF AMENHOTEP III.
Temple of Amun-Mut-Khonsu. View of the great court with double row of papyrus-clustered columns.
18th dynasty. Luxor, Thebes, Egypt. c. 1390 B.C.E.
Alistar Duncan © Dorling Kindersley.

Round Arch, Vault, and Dome. (View these basic elements of architecture using the interactive exercises on the *Discovering Art* CD.) Both Egyptian and Greek builders had to place their columns relatively close together because stone is weak under the load-bearing stresses inherent in a beam. The invention of the semicircular ROUND ARCH allowed builders to transcend this limitation and create new architectural forms. When extended in depth, the ROUND ARCH creates a tunnel-like structure called a BARREL VAULT. Roman builders perfected the round arch and developed the GROIN VAULT, formed by the intersection of two barrel vaults.

A *vault* is a curving ceiling or roof structure, traditionally made of bricks or blocks of stone tightly fitted to form a unified shell. In recent times, vaults have been constructed of materials such as cast reinforced concrete.

Early civilizations of western Asia and the Mediterranean area built arches and vaults of brick, chiefly for underground drains and tomb chambers. But it was the Romans who first used the arch extensively in above-ground structures. They learned the technique of stone arch and vault construction from the Etruscans, who occupied central Italy between 750 and 200 B.C.E.

A round stone arch can span a longer distance and support a heavier load than a stone beam because the arch transfers the load more efficiently. The Roman arch is a semicircle made from wedge-shaped stones fitted together with joints at right angles to the curve. During construction, temporary wooden supports carry the weight of the stones. The final stone that is set in place at the top is called the *keystone*. When the keystone is placed, a continuous arch with load-bearing capacity is created and the wood support is removed. A series of such arches supported by columns forms an ARCADE.

Roman builders created cities, roads, and aqueducts throughout their vast empire in most of Europe, the Near East, and North Africa. The aqueduct called PONT DU GARD, near Nimes, France, is one of the finest remaining examples of the functional beauty of Roman engineering. The combined height of the three levels of arches is 161 feet. Dry

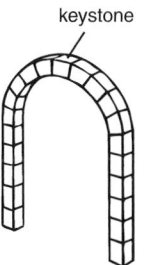

keystone

302 ROUND ARCH.

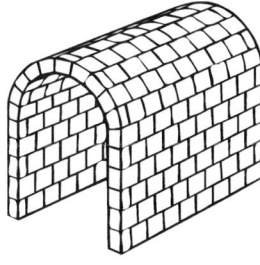

303 BARREL VAULT.

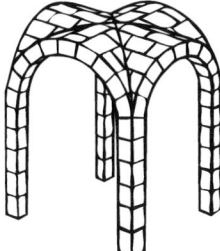

304 GROIN VAULT.

305 ARCADE.

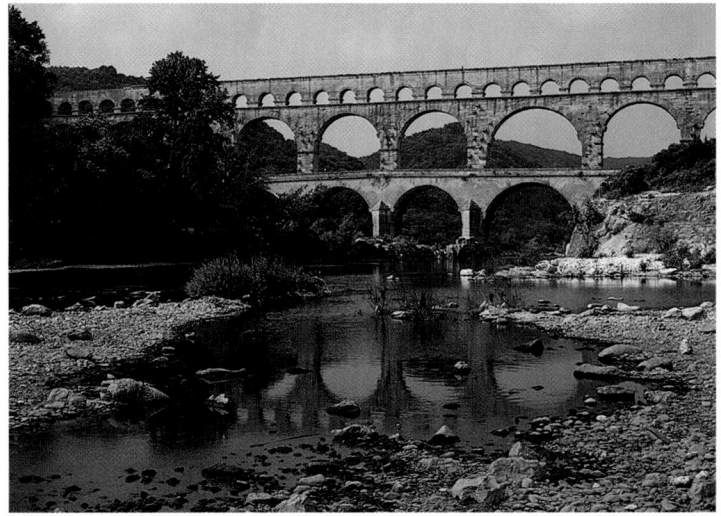

306 **PONT DU GARD.**
Nimes, France. 15 C.E.
Limestone. Height 161', length 902'.
Photograph: Duane Preble.

masonry blocks, weighing up to two tons each, make up the large arches of the two lower tiers. Water was once carried in a conduit at the top, with the first level serving as a bridge for traffic. That the aqueduct is still standing after two thousand years attests to the excellence of its design and construction.

Roman architects borrowed Greek column design and combined it with the arch, enabling them to greatly increase the variety and size of their architectural spaces. The Romans also introduced concrete as a material for architecture. Cheap, stonelike, versatile, and strong, concrete allowed the Romans to cut costs, speed construction, and build on a grand scale.

An arch rotated 180 degrees on its vertical axis creates a DOME. Domes may be hemispherical, semihemispherical, or pointed. In general usage the word *dome* refers to a hemispherical vault built up from a circular or polygonal base. The weight of a dome pushes downward and outward all around its circumference. Therefore, the simplest support is a cylinder with walls thick enough to resist the downward and outward thrust.

One of the most magnificent domes in the world was designed for the Byzantine cathedral of HAGIA SOPHIA (Holy Wisdom) in Istanbul, Turkey. It was built in the sixth century as the central sanctuary of the Eastern Orthodox Christian Church. After the Islamic conquest of 1453, *minarets* (towers) were added and it was used as a mosque. It is now a museum. The dome of HAGIA SOPHIA rests on curving triangular sections called *pendentives* over a square base.

HAGIA SOPHIA'S distinctive dome appears to float on a halo of light—an effect produced by the

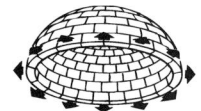

307 DOME.
   a. Dome (arch rotated 180°).

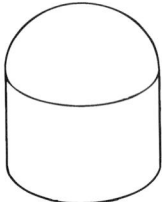

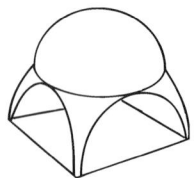

b. Dome on a cylinder.   c. Dome on pendentives.

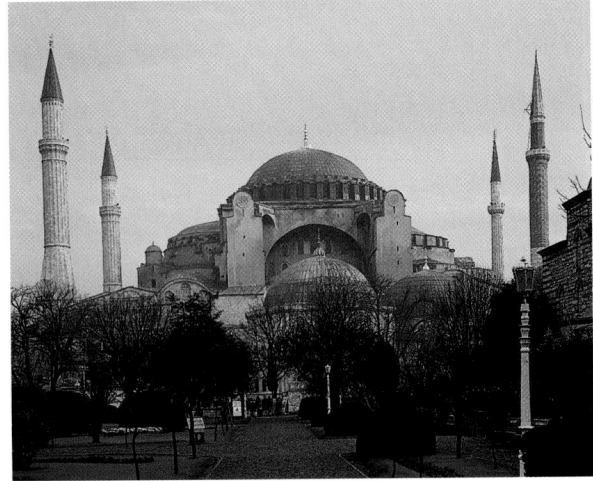

308 HAGIA SOPHIA. 532–535.
   Istanbul, Turkey.
   a. Exterior.

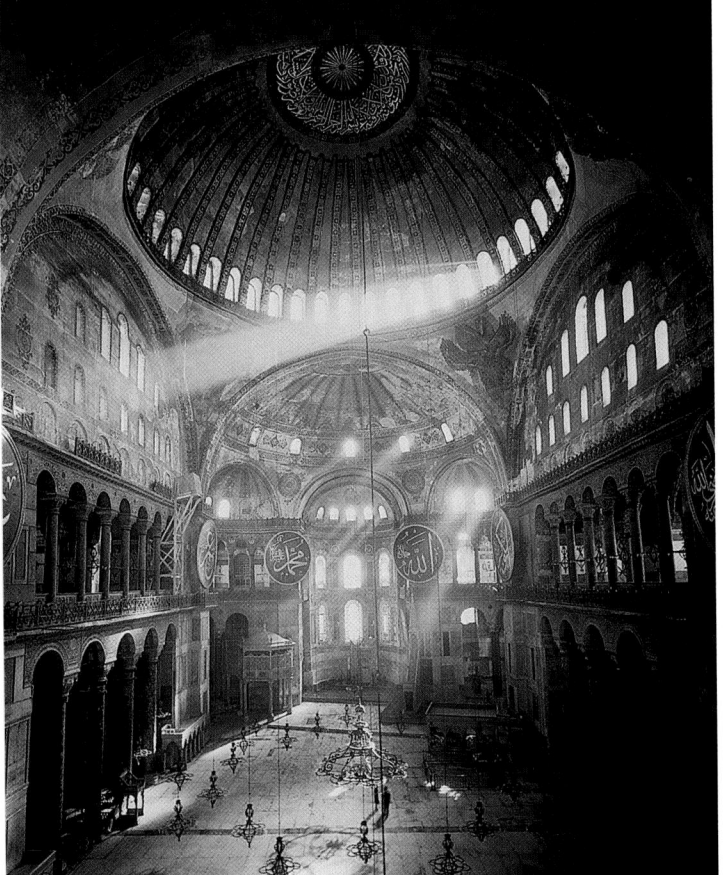

b. Interior.
Photographs: Erich Lessing/Art Resource, NY.

row of windows encircling its base. The huge dome is supported on what appears to be a larger dome with its top and sides removed. *Pendentives* carry the enormous weight from the circular base of the upper dome downward to a square formed by supporting walls.

Pointed Arch and Vault. After the round arch, the pointed GOTHIC ARCH was the next great structural advance in the Western world. This new shape seems a small change, but its effect on the building of cathedrals was spectacular. Vaults based on the pointed arch made it possible to build wider naves. It was not merely the geometry of the pointed arch, but also the exterior buttresses and the trusses supporting the roof that allowed builders to go higher and to make thinner walls with larger window areas as we see in NOTRE DAME DE CHARTRES.

Although a pointed arch is steeper and therefore sends its weight more directly downward, a substantial sideways thrust must still be countered. Gothic builders accomplished this by constructing elaborate supports called *buttresses* at right angles to the outer walls. In the most developed Gothic cathedrals, the outward force of the arched vault is carried to large buttresses by stone half-arches called FLYING BUTTRESSES.

By placing part of the structural skeleton on the outside, Gothic builders were able to make their cathedrals higher and lighter in appearance. Because the added external support of the buttresses relieved the cathedral walls of much of their structural function, large parts of the wall could be replaced by enormous stained-glass windows, allowing more light (a symbol of God's grace and love) to enter the sanctuary. From the floor of the sanctuary to the highest part of the interior above the main altar, the windows increase in size. Stones carved and assembled to form thin ribs and pillars make up the elongated columns along the nave walls, which emphasize verticality and give the cathedral its apparent upward thrust. (We discuss the stylistic features of Gothic architecture in more detail in Chapter 16.)

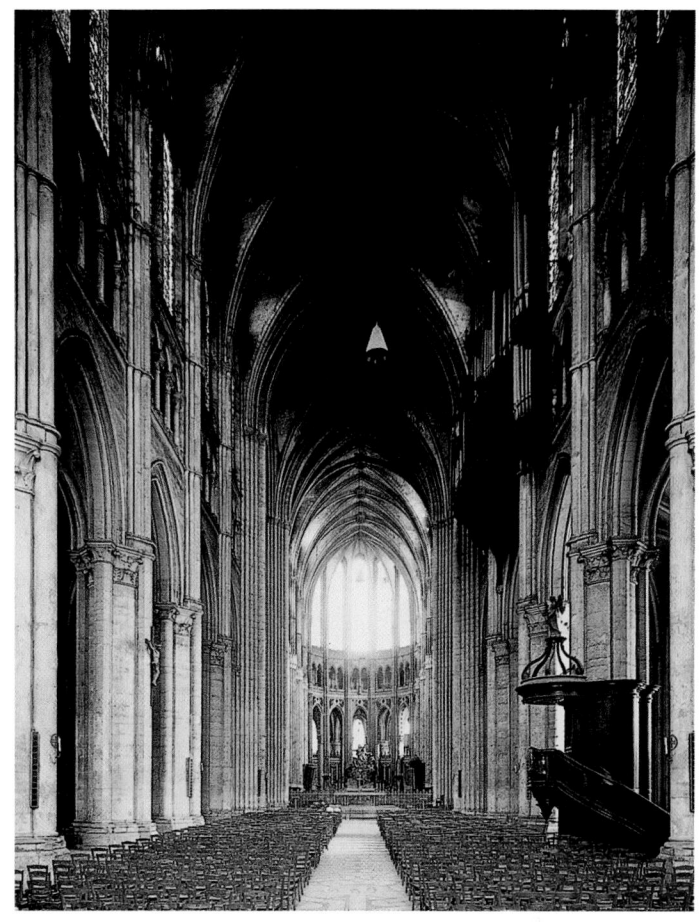

309 NOTRE DAME DE CHARTRES.
Chartres, France. 1145–1513.
Interior, nave. Height 122′, width 53′, length 130′.
Scala/Art Resource, NY.

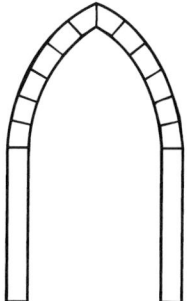

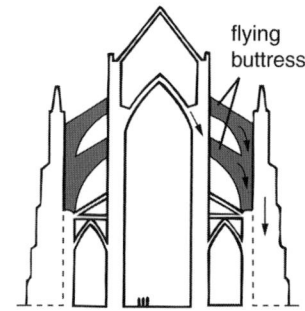

flying buttress

310 GOTHIC ARCH.   311 FLYING BUTTRESSES.

After the Gothic pointed arch and vault, no basic structural technique was added to the Western architectural vocabulary until the nineteenth century. Instead, architects designed a variety of structures—at times highly innovative—by combining elements from different periods. Forms and ornamentation from the Greek and Roman periods were revived again and again and given new life in different contexts.

In the nineteenth century, eclectic and revival architecture consisted primarily of elements applied to exteriors, whereas interior spaces were designed in more contemporary ways, often taking advantage of new technical resources. By the mid-nineteenth century, the world was being transformed by science and industry. Major changes in

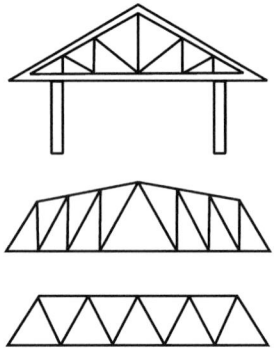

312 TRUSSES.

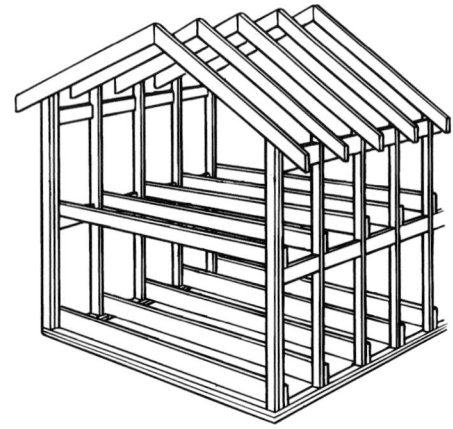

313 BALLOON FRAME.

materials and techniques have continued at an accelerating pace until the present. New inventions of the industrial age led to a revolution in architecture. First cast iron, then steel, then steel-reinforced concrete, electricity, and the invention of the high-speed elevator gave architects a set of materials and technologies that changed the design of buildings.

Truss and Balloon Frame Construction. It is possible to build strong structures with relatively thin wooden boards. One method is to use TRUSSES, such as those used for structural support in Gothic cathedral roofs. A *truss* is a triangular framework used to span, reinforce, or support. Another method is balloon framing, in which heavy timbers are replaced with thin studs held together only with nails. In the nineteenth century, the availability of cheap wood in the United States led to the BALLOON FRAME innovation in wood construction for houses and other small structures. Old-timers, who were unwilling to use the new method, called it balloon framing because they thought it was as fragile as a balloon. The method—widely used since its 1833 introduction—helped to make possible the rapid settlement of America's Western frontier.

Cast Iron. Cast iron became technically useful during the Industrial Revolution, and it led to new types of structures in which heavy, load-bearing walls were no longer needed. Iron has much greater strength than most stone and can span much larger distances. The engineering of structures with iron was a prelude to the development of steel toward the end of the nineteenth century and steel-reinforced concrete in the twentieth.

After the iron industry was established, cast and wrought iron became important building materials. Stronger and more fire-resistant than wood, iron led to lighter exterior walls and more flexible uses of interior space. Factories, bridges, and railway stations were among the new types of buildings for which cast iron was used.

The CRYSTAL PALACE, designed by Joseph Paxton, was a spectacular demonstration of what cast

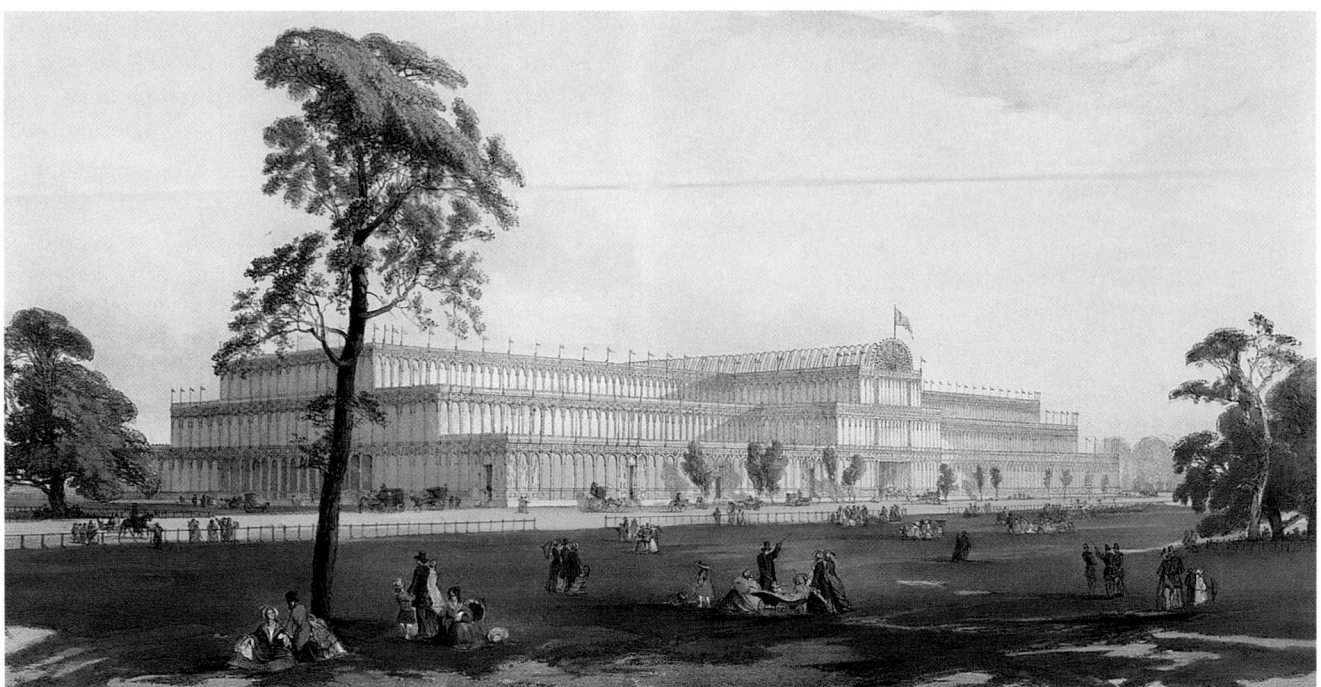

314   Joseph Paxton.
CRYSTAL PALACE.
London. 1850–1851. Cast iron and glass.
Victoria and Albert Museum, London. Crown Copyright.
Photograph: Stock Montage, Inc. © The Newberry Library.

iron could do. It was built for the Great Exhibition of the Works of Industry of All Nations, the first international exposition, held in London in 1851. The building was designed to show off the latest mechanical inventions. It was built (from prepared materials) in six months and enclosed twenty-one acres of park land! This was the first time new industrial methods and materials were eloquently presented in architecture. In its day, the CRYSTAL PALACE was recognized as a highly original expression of the spirit of the new age.

In this building there was no borrowing of earlier styles. Paxton used relatively lightweight, factorymade *modules* (standard-size structural units) of cast iron and glass. By freeing himself from past styles and masonry construction, Paxton created a whole new architectural vocabulary. The light, decorative quality of the glass and cast-iron units was created not by applied ornamentation, but by the structure itself. Paxton, inspired by leaf structures,

said, "Nature gave me the idea." The modular units provided enough flexibility for the entire structure to be assembled on the site, right over existing trees, and later disassembled and moved across town.

Paxton's design was a new application of the concept "form follows function," expressed earlier by Renaissance architect Leon Battista Alberti and later made famous by American architect Louis Sullivan.

In Paris, the 984-foot *Eiffel Tower* (see the *Discovering Art* CD for a picture), designed and built by civil and aeronautic engineer Gustave Eiffel in 1889, epitomizes the inventive spirit of the new cast-iron structures of the mid- to late-nineteenth century. At the time of its design and construction, the tower was highly controversial because of its disruption of the low skyline of Paris. (All cities were low-rise then.) When it was built, it was the world's tallest freestanding structure. Even now, as the city's most visible symbol, it dominates the Paris skyline.

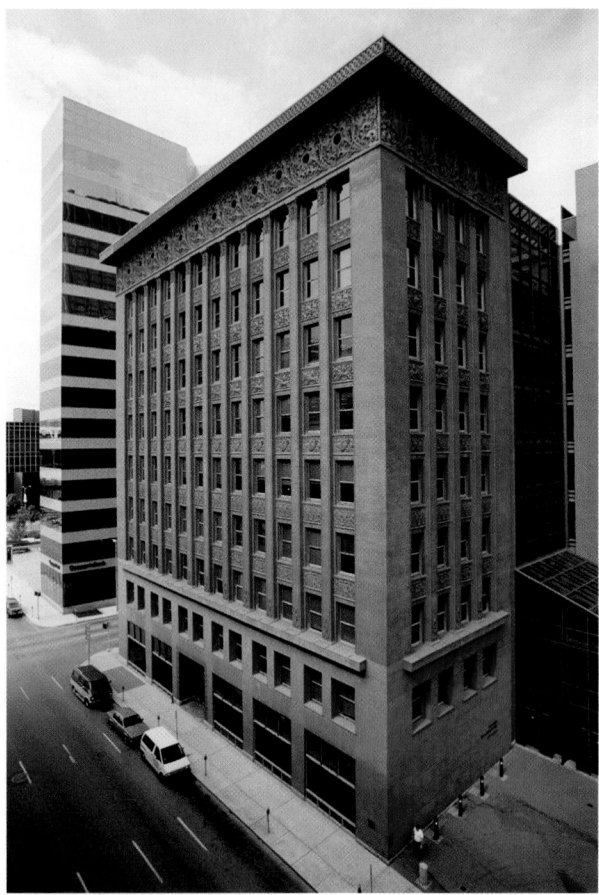

315 Louis Sullivan.
WAINWRIGHT BUILDING.
St. Louis, Missouri. 1890–1891.
Photograph: Hedrich Blessing, LTD.

Steel and Reinforced Concrete. The next breakthrough in construction methods for large structures came between 1890 and 1910 with the development of high-strength structural steel, used by itself and as the reinforcing material in reinforced concrete. The extensive use of cast-iron skeletons in the mid-nineteenth century had prepared the way for multistory steel-frame construction in the late 1880s.

Steel frames and elevators, together with rising urban land values impelled a fresh approach to structure and form. The movement began to take shape in commercial architecture, symbolized by early skyscrapers, and found one of its first opportunities in Chicago, where the big fire of 1871 had cleared the way for a building boom.

Leading the Chicago school was Louis Sullivan, regarded as the first great modern architect. Sullivan, like Paxton, rejected references to past buildings and sought to meet the needs of his time by using new methods and materials. Sullivan had a major influence on the early development of what became America's and the twentieth century's most original contribution to architecture: the "skyscraper."

Among the first of these skyscrapers was Sullivan's WAINWRIGHT BUILDING in St. Louis, Missouri, which was made possible by the invention of the elevator and by the development of steel for the structural skeleton. The building boldly breaks with nineteenth-century tradition. Its exterior design reflects the internal steel frame and emphasizes the height of the structure by underplaying horizontal elements in favor of tall vertical shafts. Sullivan demonstrated his sensitivity and adherence to the harmony of traditional architecture by dividing the building's facade into three distinct zones, reminiscent of the base, shaft, and capital of Greek columns. These areas also reveal the various functions of the building, with shops at the base, offices in the central section, and utility rooms at the top. The heavily ornamented band at the top (cornice) stops the vertical thrust of the piers located between the office windows.

The interdependence of form and function is found throughout nature. Sullivan's observation that "form ever follows function" eventually helped architects to break with their reliance on past styles and to rethink architecture from the inside out.[1]

In this spirit a new architecture arose in Europe between 1910 and 1930. Younger architects rejected decorative ornamentation and eclecticism, as well as traditional stone and wood construction, and they broke away from the earlier idea of a building as a mass. The resulting International Style expressed the function of each building, its underlying structure, and a logical (often asymmetrical) plan.

With a simple drawing of the DOMINO CONSTRUCTION SYSTEM, Le Corbusier—French architect, painter, and city planner—demonstrated the basic components of steel-column and reinforced-concrete-slab construction. This concept was used

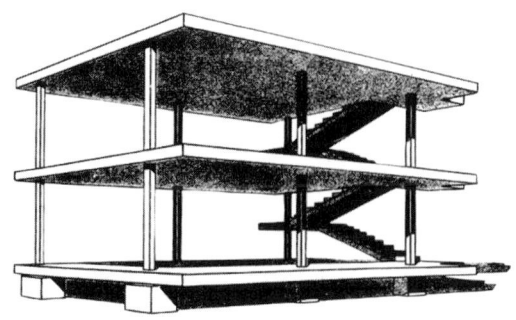

316 Le Corbusier.
DOMINO CONSTRUCTION SYSTEM. 1914–1915.

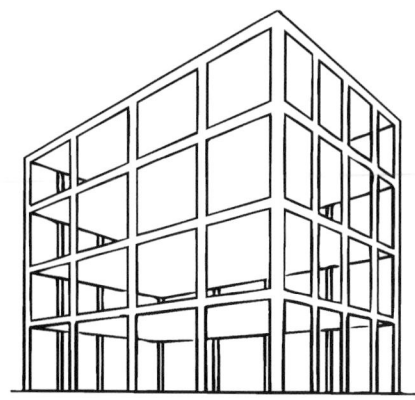

317 STEEL-FRAME CONSTRUCTION.

extensively later in the century as architects adopted the look, and sometimes the principles, of the International Style. Le Corbusier's idea of supporting floors and roof on interior load-bearing columns instead of load-bearing walls made it possible to vary the placement of interior walls and the nature of exterior coverings. His sense of style was inspired by the efficiency of machines and an awareness of the importance of natural light.

Walter Gropius carried out the principles of the International Style in his new building for the BAUHAUS when the school moved to Dessau, Germany. The workshop wing, built between 1925 and 1926, follows the basic concept illustrated in Le Corbusier's drawing. Because the reinforced-concrete floors and roof were supported by steel columns set back from the outer edge of the building, exterior walls did not have to carry any weight: they could be *curtain walls* made of glass. Even interior walls were non-load-bearing and could be placed anywhere they were needed.

In the United States, the development of the high-rise building reached a climax in New York. On the city's small, heavily populated Manhattan Island, tall buildings provided a way to supply ever more residential and commercial space. By 1915, New York was suffering from poor air circulation and reduction of sunlight because so many skyscrapers were built straight up from the sidewalk. By the 1920s, a new *set-back* law required architects to terrace their structures back from the street to allow sunlight to enter what were becoming dark canyons.

Le Corbusier's idea for alleviating urban crowding by using tall, narrow buildings surrounded by open space, and Sullivan's concept for high-rise buildings that express the grid of their supporting STEEL-FRAME CONSTRUCTION came together in the

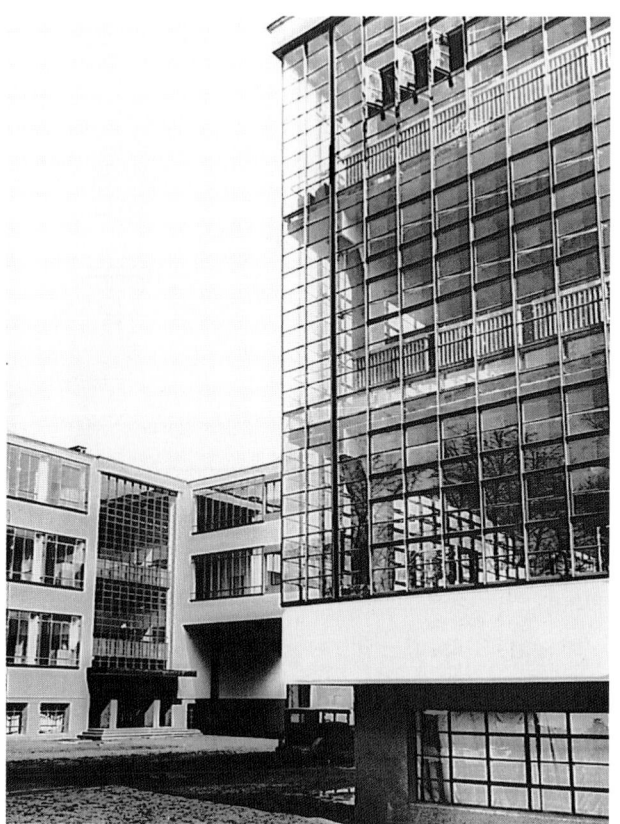

318 Walter Gropius.
BAUHAUS.
Dessau, Germany. 1925–1926.
Bauhaus-Archiv Berlin. Photograph: Lucia Moholy
© VG Bild Kunst, Berlin, Germany 2001; © 2005 Artists Rights Society (ARS), NY.

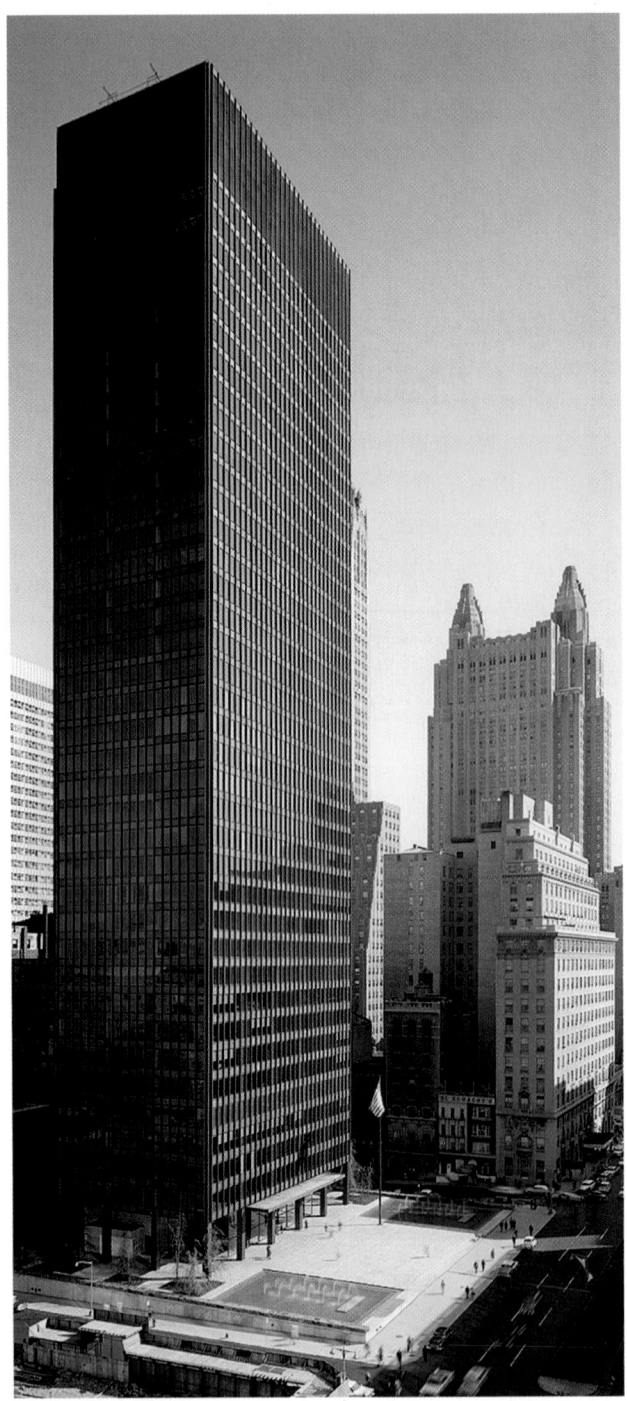

SEAGRAM BUILDING, designed by Ludwig Mies van der Rohe and Philip Johnson. Non-load-bearing glass walls had been a major feature of Mies's plans for skyscrapers conceived as early as 1919, but it was not until the 1950s that he had the chance to build such structures. In the SEAGRAM BUILDING, interior floor space gained by the height of the building allowed the architects to leave a large, open public area at the base. The vertical lines emphasize the height and provide a strong pattern that is capped by a top section designed to give a sense of completion. The austere design embodies Mies's famous statement "Less is more."

Mies van der Rohe was a leading proponent of the International Style, which had an enormous, if sometimes negative, influence on world architecture. It often replaced unique, place-defining regional styles. By mid-century, modern architecture had become synonymous with the International Style. The uniformity of glass-covered rectilinear grid structures was considered the appropriate formal dressing for the bland anonymity of the modern corporation.

Recent Innovations.   By the second half of the twentieth century, improved construction techniques and materials, new theories regarding structural physics, and computer analyses of the strengths and weaknesses in complex structures led to the further development of fresh architectural forms such as the SHELL STRUCTURE and the SUSPENSION STRUCTURE.

Eero Saarinen's 1962 TWA TERMINAL was for many years the epitome of the excitement of flight. A boldly shaped SHELL STRUCTURE at JFK International Airport, the terminal's soaring wings symbolized the glamour and speed of air travel. Increasing

319   Ludwig Mies van der Rohe and Philip Johnson.
SEAGRAM BUILDING.
New York. 1956–1958.
Photograph: Ezra Stoller © Esto.

320   Eero Saarinen.
SHELL STRUCTURE (TWA TERMINAL).
Kennedy Airport, New York. 1956–1962.

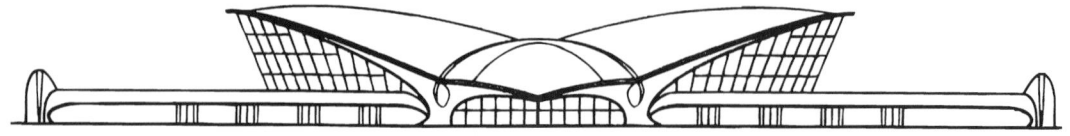

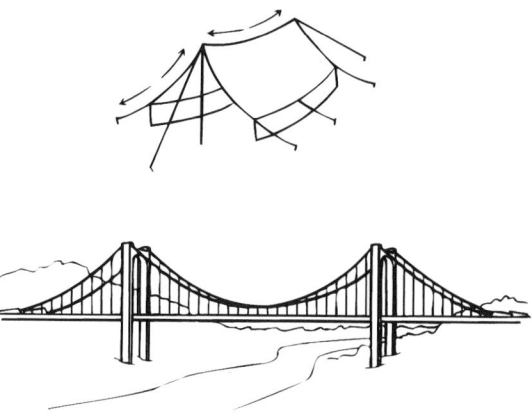

321 SUSPENSION STRUCTURE.

security needs and the bankruptcy of the airline forced its closure in 2001. A budget carrier has recently taken it over, and soon the TWA TERMINAL will serve as a gateway to a larger structure more accommodating to contemporary air travel. Although the original structure will not have the same function as before, it will remain intact. See Suggested Web Sites at the back of this book for a link to a 360-degree panorama of the building's unique interior.

The most dramatic use of the suspension technology in a major public building was in the JEPPESEN TERMINAL BUILDING at Denver International Airport. Its roof is a giant tent composed of fifteen acres of woven fiberglass, making it the largest suspension building on Earth. This white roofing material lets in large amounts of natural light without conducting heat, and it is coated with Teflon for water resistance and easy cleaning. Its exterior design was inspired by the snow-capped Rocky Mountains, which are visible from inside.

Architecture's first technical innovation of the twenty-first century is carbon fiber, and it may have an important impact on how we build in the future. Scientists found that heating carbon atoms in an oxygen-free environment fuses them together into some of the lightest and strongest materials known to humans. Certain aircraft parts, racing car bodies, and bicycle frames already use carbon fiber. Shaping this fiber carefully and coating it with polyester or nylon yields a new material that can be literally woven to create a building.

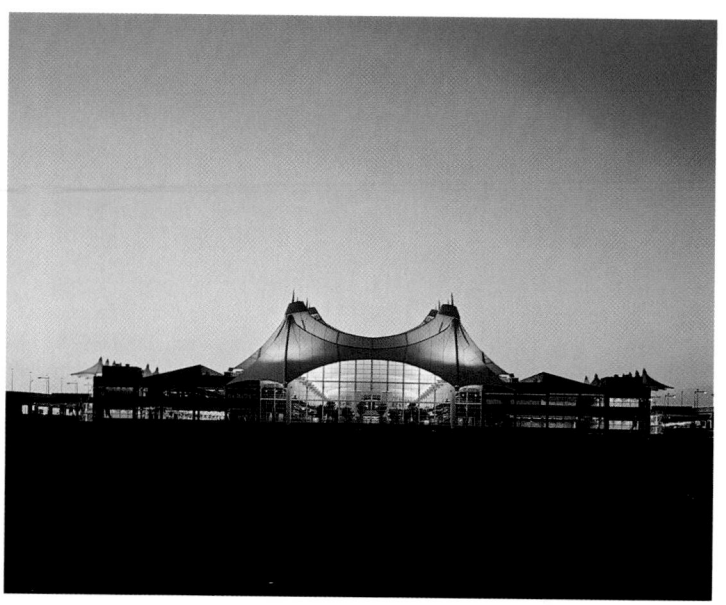

322 JEPPESEN TERMINAL BUILDING.
Denver International Airport.
1994. Fentress-Bradburn Architects.
Timothy Hursley Photography/Fentress Bradburn Architects Ltd.

The architectural firm of Testa and Weiser has explored the possibilities of carbon fiber, writing computer programs that make possible a completely new approach to structure. For example, their CARBON TOWER is a plan for a 40-story skyscraper supported by one-inch-thick filaments woven into a helix-shaped web. The tower will have no columns

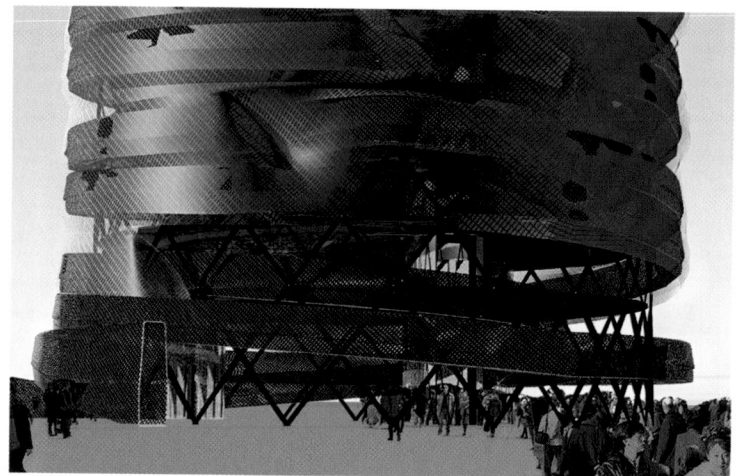

323 Testa and Weiser.
CARBON TOWER. 2005.
Model of proposed 40-story skyscraper.

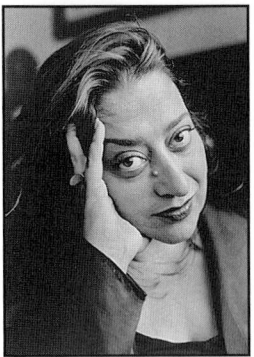

324 Zaha Hadid.
Photograph: Michael Wilson,
1998. Courtesy The
Contemporary Arts Center,
Cincinnati, Ohio.

ONE OF THE most creative and controversial architects now at work is Zaha Hadid. Indeed, many of her buildings have remained in the planning stages because they are too radical to be built. But her realized projects are adventurous designs that radically alter the viewer's experience of space.

Born in Baghdad, as a young girl she worked weaving carpets. She has said that their intricate and dazzling designs later influenced her design ideas. She studied architecture at London's Architectural Association, where she was constantly challenged to reinvent modern architecture. This private academy was an incubator of new ideas where the teachers often threw practicality to the winds. Hadid's graduation project was to redesign a busy bridge over the Thames River so that people could live on it. The fact that few would want to live on a heavily trafficked bridge bothered neither her nor her teachers, who pronounced it excellent.

Most people's experience of built space comes from rectangular, orderly, self-contained, often symmetrical rooms. Her plans often give such a break from these kinds of spaces that she was soon termed a Deconstructive architect. That is, she makes buildings in such a way that they look flexed, twisted, crushed, or shattered: constructed and not constructed at the same time. She uses digital animation programs to help her visualize and develop her ideas.

We see her skills to good advantage at the CONTEMPORARY ARTS CENTER in Cincinnati. The center shows only temporary exhibitions with no permanent collection, so the trustees wanted the building to reflect the unpredictable nature of contemporary art. The building has a translucent skin on the outside, so that passersby on the street will see some of the art displayed within. The entry lobby is planned to be an inviting space, with galleries visible above as if suspended from the ceiling. A ramp with switchbacks gives access to the exhibition spaces while providing periodic glimpses of the lobby and the city outside. Each of these galleries is radically different in shape and structure, so that viewers cannot predict what sort of space lies ahead. Thus, viewers proceed along a ramp toward yet-unseen works whose very unpredictability can be exciting, interesting, and stimulating.

Hadid is concerned about modern urban life, which is getting more closed-in and crowded in many parts of the world. Referring to Tokyo, she said, "In such a dense city, light and air are valuable commodities. We must release these spaces from their constricted sites and breathe light and air into the urban condition."[2] She sees her loose and open spaces helping to contribute to the liberation of people from surroundings that are at times oppressive.

Hadid's practice has ranged widely. She has made an archaeological museum in Vienna, a music video pavilion in Holland, a sports complex in Abu Dhabi, the Irish Prime Minister's residence, and a ski jump in Austria. For these and other projects she was awarded the Pritzker Prize in 2004.

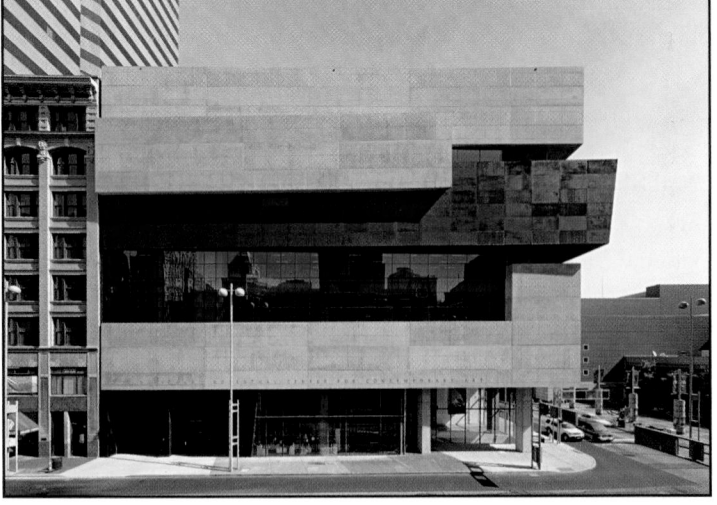

325 Zaha Hadid.
CONTEMPORARY ARTS CENTER. Cincinnati, Ohio. 2003.
The Lois and Richard Rosenthal Center for Contemporary Art.
Photograph: Roland Halbe. Courtesy The Contemporary Arts Center, Cincinnati, Ohio.
© 2003 office of Zaha Hadid.

and no central core, and its exterior walls can be paper-thin and translucent. The expense of the CARBON TOWER makes its realization today very difficult, but the future potential is enormous.

In recent years architect Frank O. Gehry has designed several major show places for the performing and visual arts. The GUGGENHEIM MUSEUM BILBAO (GMB), completed at the harbor's edge in Bilbao, Spain, in the fall of 1997, is a spectacular example of Gehry's concept of architecture as functional sculpture. The design—he calls it a "metallic flower"—is a dramatic limestone and titanium-clad cluster of soaring, all-but-dancing volumes climaxing in a gigantic, glass-enclosed atrium. Museum director Thomas Krens envisioned a museum that would celebrate the ever-evolving, at times large-scale inventions of leading contemporary artists while also featuring the art of the architecture—a great world-class museum for world-class art.

With its interplay of organic forms and spaces, the museum is the major element in an urban-renewal plan aimed at cleaning up and revitalizing the deteriorated port area in which it is built. In its sculptural break from traditional rectangular structures, the Bilbao museum relates to the ground-breaking main Guggenheim Museum in New York, designed in the 1950s by Frank Lloyd Wright. The GMB presents today's art objects in a space that offers an awesome experience in itself.

Like cathedrals or civic buildings of the past, art museums today are showplaces for the most recent ideas in architecture. Both GMB and the CONTEMPORARY ARTS CENTER in Cincinnati are innovative inside and out.

Designing with Nature

Major influences on American domestic architecture came from Japan through Frank Lloyd Wright. Wright was among the first to use open planning in houses. In a break with the tradition of closed, box-like houses, Wright eliminated walls between rooms, enlarged windows, and discovered that one of the best ways to open a closed-in room was to

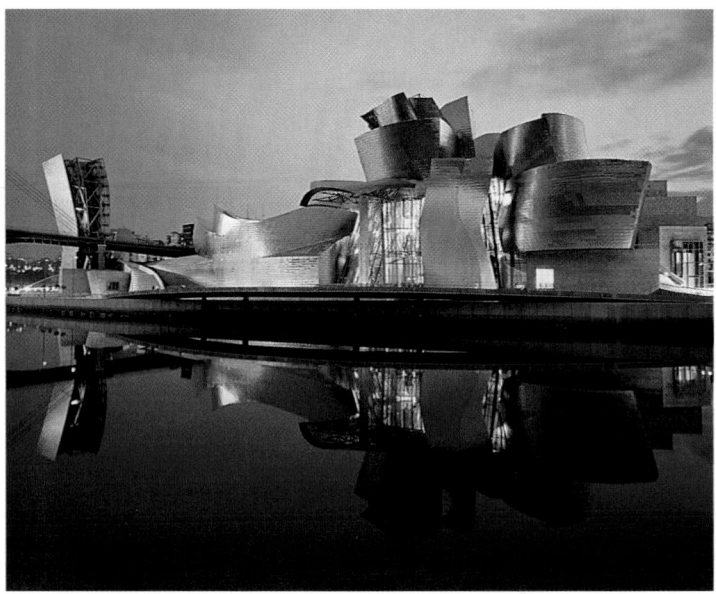

326 Frank O. Gehry.
GUGGENHEIM MUSEUM BILBAO.
Bilbao, Spain. 1997.
© FMGB Guggenheim Bilbao Museo, 2002.
Photographer: Erika Ede. All rights reserved.

place windows in corners. With these devices, he created flowing spaces that opened to the outdoors, welcomed natural light, and related houses to their sites and climates. Sliding glass doors were influenced by the sliding paper-covered *shoji* doors in traditional Japanese architecture.

Wright also made extensive use of the cantilever. When a beam or slab is extended a substantial distance beyond a supporting column or wall, the overhanging portion is called a *cantilever*. Before the use of steel and reinforced concrete, cantilevers were not used to a significant degree because the available materials could not extend far enough to make the concept viable.

One of the boldest and most elegant uses of the principle occurs in Wright's KAUFMANN RESIDENCE (on the following page) (also known as FALLINGWATER) at Bear Run, Pennsylvania. Horizontal masses cantilevered from supporting piers echo the rock ledges on the site and seem almost to

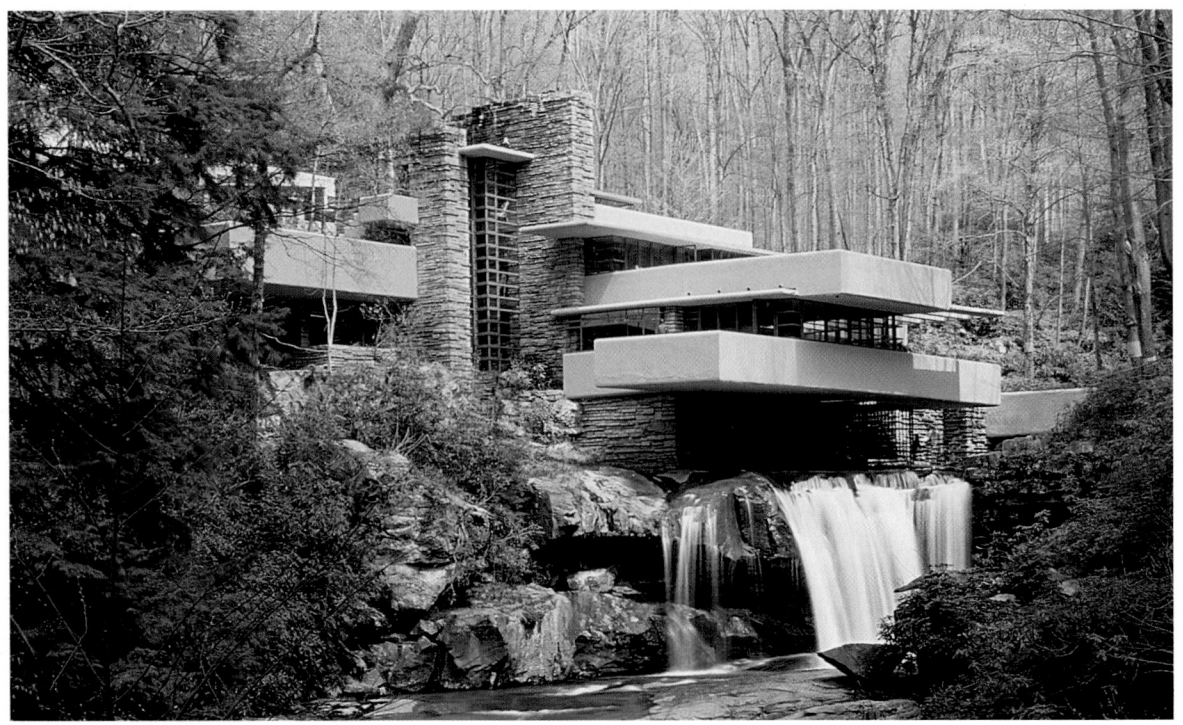

327   Frank Lloyd Wright.
FALLINGWATER (EDGAR KAUFMANN RESIDENCE).
Bear Run, Pennsylvania. 1936.
Esta Photographics, Inc.

float above the waterfall. Vertical accents were influenced by surrounding tall, straight trees. The intrusion of a building on such a beautiful location seems justified by the harmony Wright achieved between the natural site and his equally inspiring architecture.

GREEN BUILDING

Modern glass-box style buildngs like the SEAGRAM BUILDING (on page 222) are tremendously inefficient. They require a great deal of both cooling in summer and heating in winter. Moreover, because the heated or cooled interior air is so expensive, ventilation is usually minimized, which can cause indoor pollution to rise to uncomfortable levels. More and more architects in recent years are thinking of ways to reduce the impact of building on the environment and to make the interiors more healthful. At Harare, Zimbabwe, an office complex meets this goal with a design that respects local culture. THE EASTGATE COMPLEX (on page 228) is the first building in the world based on the heating and cooling principles of Africa's temperature-efficient termite mounds. Architect Mick Pearce designed an office block that would have a comfortable year-round indoor climate with no air-conditioning and almost no heating in a place where outside temperatures range from 35°F at night to 104°F during the day. Amazingly, the building uses less than ten percent of the energy consumed by conventional buildings of its size and density. Instead of an energy-gobbling glass skin, Pearce took what he calls a Gothic approach, inspired in part by the headdresses of the local Shona tribe and by the earthy textures of termite mounds.

In the United States, the Green Building Council gives annual awards for leadership in environmentally sensitive design. Architects can submit

FRANK
Lloyd Wright   *Radical Innovator*
1867–1959

FRANK LLOYD WRIGHT, the most influential twentieth-century American architect, was born in Wisconsin, the son of a Baptist minister.

At age eighteen, Wright took a job with a local builder while studying civil engineering part-time at the University of Wisconsin. In 1887, he went to Chicago, where he worked as an apprentice in the newly formed architectural firm of Adler & Sullivan. When Louis Sullivan was designing the WAIN-WRIGHT BUILDING (page 220), Wright was his chief draftsman. Eager to do his own work, Wright began designing houses on his own at night. Sullivan took offense at this practice, and Wright left the firm. Wright, however, was strongly influenced by Sullivan and continued throughout his life to refer to him as *Lieber Meister* (beloved master).

By 1893, Wright had opened his own office in the rapidly growing community of Oak Park, Illinois, where he designed a series of houses with low horizontal lines that echoed the flat prairie landscape. This distinctive approach became known as his Prairie Style.

That same year, at the Columbian Exposition in Chicago, Wright saw a Japanese tea house. The encounter led to a deep interest in Japanese architecture and long stays in

Japan. He found the asymmetrical balance, large extended eaves, and flexible open plan (with sliding doors and walls) of traditional Japanese houses more sensitive to nature and to human life than the often static symmetry of traditional American homes.

Wright brought his own poetic sense of nature into harmony with the new materials and the engineering technology of the machine age. In terms of both structure and aesthetics, Wright was a radical innovator. He used poured reinforced concrete and steel cantilevers in houses at a time when such construction was usually confined to commercial structures. His KAUFMANN RESIDENCE is dramatically cantilevered over a waterfall, and two of his major buildings were designed with flowing interior spaces and spiral ramps. Among his many notable buildings was the structurally innovative Imperial Hotel in Tokyo, built between 1916 and 1922. His use of the cantilever in this hotel was criticized as a violation of sound construction—until the devastating quake of 1923, when it remained one of the few undamaged buildings in the city.

In his later years, Wright continued his large practice and devoted considerable time to writing and to teaching apprentices in his workshop-homes. Throughout his career Wright was

guided by his awareness that buildings have a profound, life-shaping influence on the people who inhabit them.

Among Wright's many unrealized projects was a plan for a mile-high skyscraper. His last major work was the controversial Solomon R. Guggenheim Museum, built in the late 1950s. Its immense spiraling ramp enables viewers to see exhibitions in a clearly defined continuous path, but the sloping, eye-filling space tends to overpower the presentation of other works of art.

Wright's guiding philosophy is most apparent in his houses, where his concern for simplicity and his sensitivity to the character of space and materials express what he defined as an organic ideal for architecture. According to Wright, the word *organic* goes beyond its strictly biological meaning to refer to the integration of all aspects of a form, the part to the whole and the whole to the part. Thus, in architecture, one should deter-

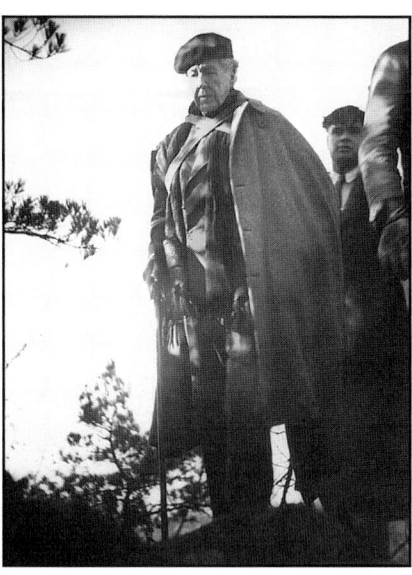

328   FRANK LLOYD WRIGHT. 1936.
Photograph: Edmund Teske. Courtesy The Frank Lloyd Wright Archives, Scottsdale, AZ.

mine the form of a building by designing in terms of the unique qualities of the site, proceeding from the ground up, and honoring the character of the natural conditions as well as the materials and purposes of the structure. Wright spoke of organic architecture as having a meaning beyond any preconceived style:

Exalting the simple laws of common sense—or of super-sense if you prefer—determining form by way of the nature of materials, the nature of purpose so well understood that a bank will not look like a Greek Temple, a university will not look like a cathedral, nor a fire-engine house resemble a French château. . . . Form follows function? Yes, but more important now [with organic architecture] form and function are one.[3]

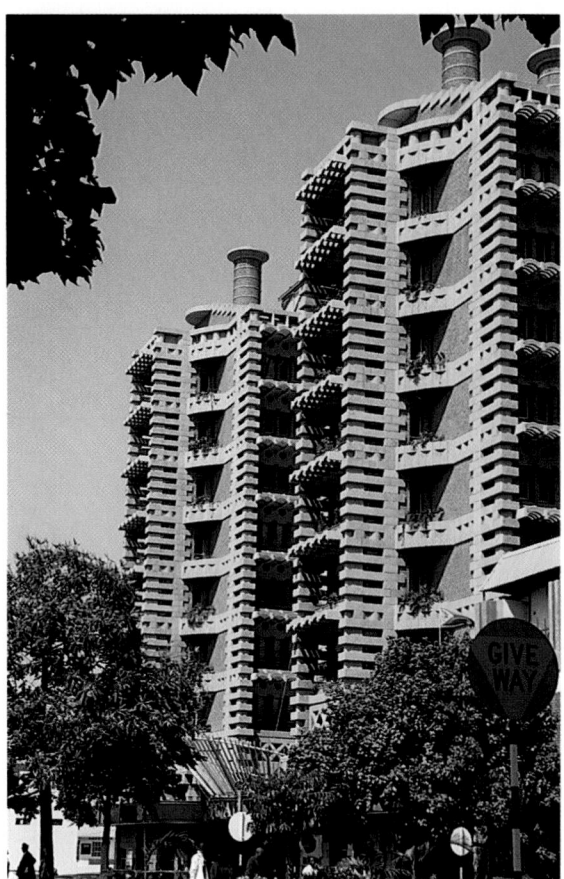

a. Exterior.

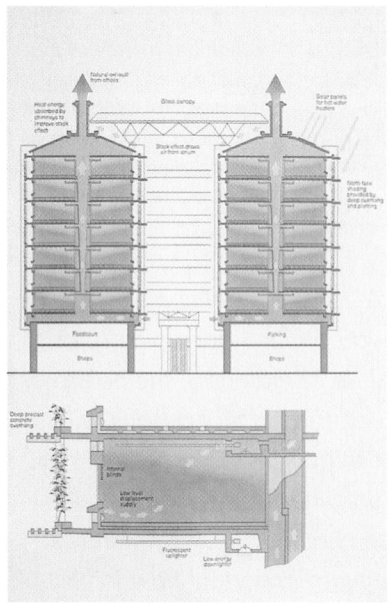

b. Energy use.
Courtesy Pearce McComish Partnership Architects, Harare.

329 Mick Pearce.
THE EASTGATE COMPLEX.
Harare, Zimbabwe. 1996.
Wide Angle (PVT) Ltd.

their plans to the Council for rating, and the Council assigns points for such factors as harmony with prevailing wid or sunshine patterns, indoor energy efficiency, use of recycled water, and reduction of transportation costs for materials. The Council then makes annual awards for Leadership in Energy and Environmental Design, presenting Silver, gold, and Platinum certificates each year to projects that reach designated point levels.

The highest award they have yet given went in 2005 to the ALBERICI CORPORATE HEADQUARTERS outside St. Louis. This corporate campus is an encyclopedia of green design ideas: A majority of the building material was purchased locally, saving air pollution and transportation costs. Thirty percent of this material came from recycled sources. All rainwater is captured and re-used. (Outdoor native plants require no irrigation in any case.) A wind turbine on-site generates a fifth of the building's energy needs. The parking area is not made of asphalt, to minimize the "heat island" effect. All windows are oriented to maximize daylight, and ninety percent of the 200 employees have an outside view. Soy-based paint and sustainably harvested woods were used throughout. As a result, the ALBERICI CORPORATE HEADQUARTERS uses less than half of the energy of a typical office building of its size, and the company spun off a consulting firm to help others duplicate its achievement.

In the quest to build green, some architectural firms embrace more radical solutions. For example, when a Southern California artist wanted a new

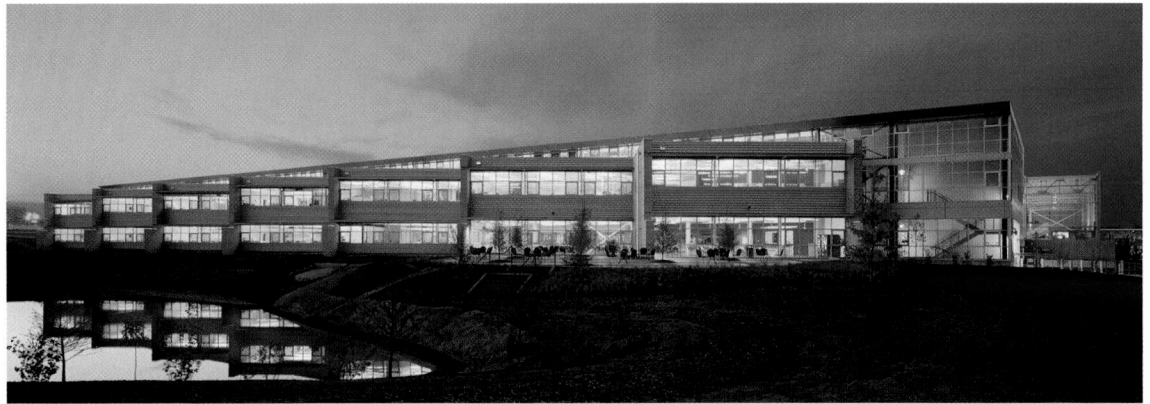

330   Mackey Mitchell Architects.
      ALBERICI CORPORATE HEADQUARTERS. 2005.
      Overland, MO.

home with curving roof lines, architect David Hertz bought a retired 747 passenger aircraft, cut it into pieces and used most of its exterior in the 747 WING HOUSE. The upper fuselage will serve as roofing for the guest house and the studio, just as the wings will cover the main dwelling. The upturned nose cone will serve as a meditation room, with the cockpit windows facing straight up to the sky. What color to paint it is a problem, because the Federal Aviation Administration demanded that it not be mistaken for a crashed plane lying in pieces on the ground. Still, building with this recycled material is cheaper than starting fresh. And the plane made the ultimate "soft landing."

Each year more buildings are built green, but not all appear innovative from the outside. This is because some green designers prefer to redesign existing buildings rather than build new ones.

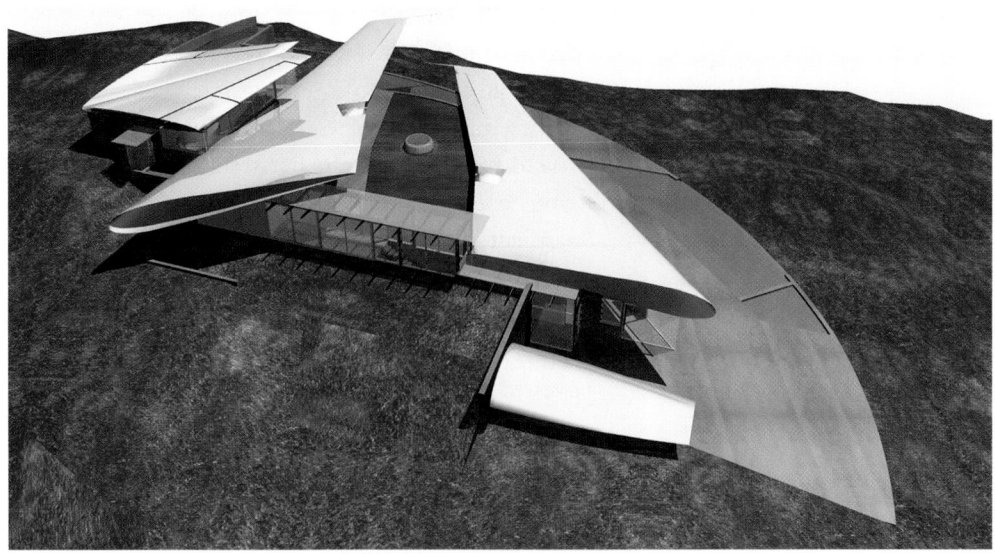

331   David Hertz and Syndesis.
      747 WING HOUSE. 2008. Digital Model.
      Malibu, CA.

By imagination and reason, we turn experience into foresight. We become the creators of our future, and cease to be slaves of our past.

WILL DURANT[4]

The evolutionary jump that lies ahead is . . . a tall one, for it means no more or less than changing ourselves by changing our surroundings, and learning to do this by choice and not by chance.

HUMPHRY OSMOND[5]

MOMENT-TO-MOMENT, day-to-day, we influence our surroundings and, in turn, are influenced by them. The original title of this book was *Man Creates Art Creates Man*, referring to the fact that "art" is not just pictures on the wall, or special performances, but the whole world of creative awareness and actions available to all. What human beings have invented and are inventing has an enormous impact on who we are and how we live. The process of caring for the spaces we live in is essential. Our sense of ourselves and our attitudes about life determine the way we live. Art is one name for how we manifest our being in the world—from the clothing we

choose to wear to the spaces we select and shape for living.

What qualities in our surroundings make life both sustainable and worthwhile? What is behind the making of sense-pleasing, soul-satisfying places? How can neighbors work together to create and sustain rewarding communities? How can we work with nature to sustain and create viable and beautiful living environments for all? Such questions are behind the art of environmental design.

The more aware we are of what is possible, the more we can make a positive difference in our own lives and in the lives of others. Art cannot be forced or dictated; sources of aesthetic pleasure vary from person to person. Yet, when enough members of a community are aware of aesthetic values and realize that they affect results, whether they are consciously involved in the decision making or not, the rewarding art of placemaking can begin.

Environmental issues are best addressed from the perspectives of many disciplines, including the sciences and the arts.

Some issues should be obvious: One doesn't build for a desert what would be best in a rain forest; one makes optimal use of natural light in indoor spaces to save energy costs. The visual arts heighten awareness (design/aesthetic sensitivity) and help develop visual thinking, making it possible to visualize options. The principles of effective visual design— such as harmony, proportion, balance, unity, and variety, introduced in Chapter 4—apply as much to environmental design as to any of the other visual arts.

Many of us spend much of our time "capsulized." In a given work day, we might go from a home capsule to a car capsule to an elevator capsule to an office capsule, with only a distant through-windows contact with the larger environment. In this context, we are capsulized both physically and mentally; one state contributes to the other. How can we influence environmental decision making if we are not really in touch with our physical surroundings? The capsule is a metaphor for a mental box—a mind-set that limits understanding of what is possible.

Feng shui, the ancient Chinese art of placement, teaches that everything has a life force *(qi)*. If the environment is not harmonious, people will become ill, unhappy, and unproductive. Mystical meaning, practicality, and aesthetic sensibility are combined in this art that may deal with ecology, architecture, and the arrangement of furniture. In practice, Feng shui functions as both an art and a science.

When our senses are insulted by visual pollution and chaos, life is "diseased." While good design is not a cure-all, indoor and outdoor living spaces that are life supporting, rather than degrading, will reward our senses and greatly enhance our well-being. The goal is to see, to be aware of the art of living, and to enjoy the results of our own creative contributions.

PART FOUR

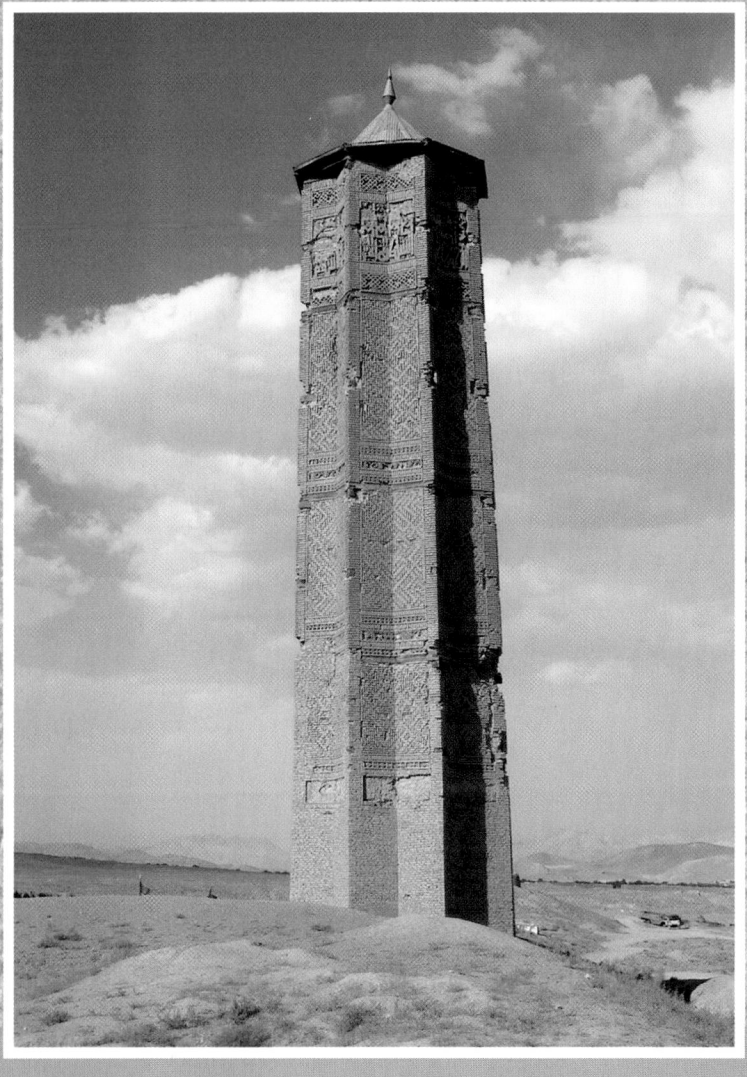

GHAZNI MINARET, Afghanistan.
Early twelfth century. Height 65′.

ART AS CULTURAL HERITAGE

CONSIDER...

Picasso once said, "If a work of art cannot live always in the present it must not be considered at all." What do you think he meant?

Glance through Chapters 17 to 19 without reading the text. How much can you learn about each civilization by looking at its art and architecture? For example, compare the Indian temple with the Japanese palace.

What differences are apparent in each culture's view of beauty?

When you think of historic culture, what comes to your mind: dates, images, or political events?

Notice the change in the subject matter as you glance through Chapter 20. How would you characterize the artistic interests of the eighteenth and nineteenth centuries, when compared with those of the Renaissance in Chapter 16?

FROM THE EARLIEST ART
TO THE BRONZE AGE

Art history makes history visible and accessible. It is a record of how the people of the past—our ancestors—lived, felt, and acted in widely separated parts of the world at different periods of time.

Art history differs from other kinds of history because works of art from the past are with us in the present. One-to-one communication occurs even when artist and viewer are separated by thousands or even tens of thousands of years. This communicative power of art makes it possible for us to glimpse some of the experiences of those whose lives preceded ours, to better understand societies other than our own, and to see beyond our own cultural boundaries. Although interesting, old science is no longer of practical use; but old art can be as life-enriching as new art.

Our knowledge of art history is constantly growing. Excavations and restorations continue to bring ancient works to light. In rare cases such as the excavations of Pompeii in Italy, an entire city is being revealed.

Modern techniques of photo reproduction, printing, and electronic transmission have helped to make the art of the whole world available to us. Through reproductions, we can now see more fine works of ancient Egyptian and Chinese art, for example, than the people of those cultures were themselves able to see.

As numbers of years can be confusing when we study art history, let's consider numbers in terms of generations. Since the beginning of human life on Earth, the average time interval between the birth of parents and the birth of their offspring has varied from about eighteen to thirty-three years. When we figure that roughly twenty-five years is the average generation, we can come closer to the people of the past by realizing that most of us have three generations within our own families, and many have four. The United States became a country only ten generations ago; the Italian Renaissance occurred just twenty-five generations ago; Jesus Christ lived eighty generations ago; the Buddha (Siddhartha Gautama) lived about one hundred generations ago. In fact, the end of the prehistoric period occurred less than three hundred generations ago.

There is no "better" or "best" when we compare the art of different societies, or even the art of different times within the same society. Rather, differences in art reflect differences in points of view. Pablo Picasso put the subject of art history in perspective in this way:

To me there is no past or future in art. If a work of art cannot live always in the present it must not be considered at all. The art of the Greeks, the Egyptians, the great painters who lived in other times, is not an art of the past; perhaps it is more alive today than it ever was. Art does not evolve by itself, the ideas of people evolve and with them their mode of expression.[1]

THE PALEOLITHIC PERIOD

Roughly two million years ago, in east central Africa, early hominids made crude stone-cutting tools. The making of these tools enabled our predecessors to extend their skills and thereby gain a measure of control over their surroundings. From such beginnings, human beings developed the abilities to reason and to visualize: to remember the past, to relate it to the present, and to imagine possible futures. As we became form-creating creatures, our ability to conceive mental images—and the development of hands capable of making those images—set us apart from other animals. Imagination is our special advantage.

About one million years ago in Africa, and more recently in Asia and Europe, people made more refined tools by chipping flakes from opposite sides of stones to create sharp cutting edges. It took another 250,000 years or so for human beings to develop choppers and hand axes that were symmetrical and refined in shape. An awareness of the relationship of form to function, and of form as enjoyable in itself, was the first step in the history of art.

Sprinkled powders and beads accompany many widely dispersed gravesites from about 100,000 years ago. These finds suggest to archaeologists that humans at that time practiced ritual burial, though the meaning of these decorative additions is unknown.

Recent discoveries have enlivened the debate about when art began. In 2002, archaeologists digging in the Blombos Cave in South Africa unearthed what may qualify as the earliest art that we know of. In a soil layer 77,000 years old, they found some pieces of ENGRAVED OCHRE bearing marks that appear to be symbols. The marks form an abstract pattern of parallel diagonal lines between horizontal bars. Any practical use for the markings is highly unlikely; rather, they seem symbolic or at least decorative, making these ochres the oldest decorated objects yet found. In 2004, researchers in the same cave found a similarly ancient set of beads pierced for stringing. Many archaeologists concluded that this African site contains the first known instances of artistic creativity.

More sophisticated examples of Paleolithic art were discovered during the last hundred years at many locations around the world. Current scientific dating places the earliest of these findings at about 40,000 years ago, toward the end of the last Ice Age. As the southern edge of the European ice sheet slowly retreated northward, hunter-gatherers

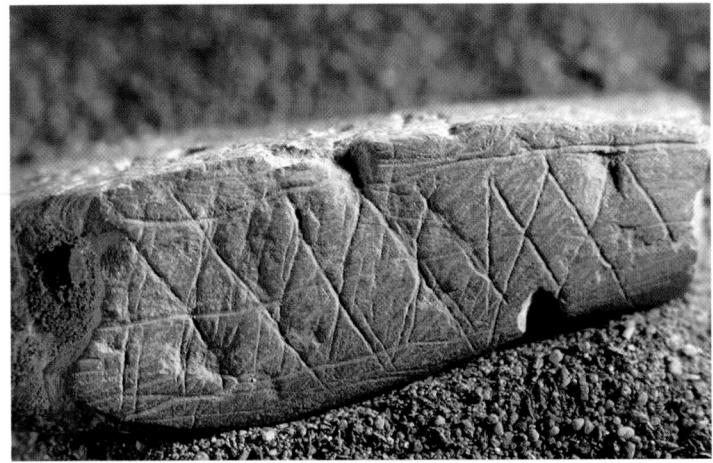

332 ENGRAVED OCHRE. From Blombos Cave, South Africa. c. 75,000 B.C.E. Length 4″.

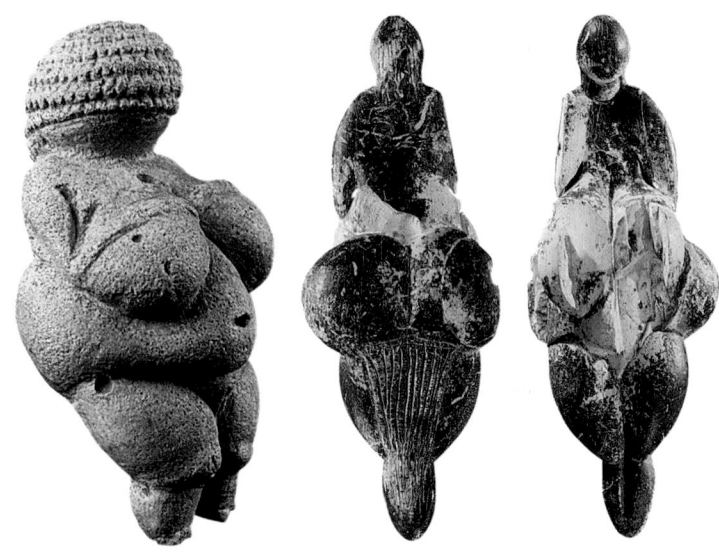

333 WOMAN OF WILLENDORF. c. 25,000–20,000 B.C.E. Limestone. Height 4½″.
Naturhistorisches Museum, Vienna. Photograph: Erich Lessing. Art Resource, NY.

334 WOMAN OF LESPUGUE.
Mammoth ivory. Height 7¹³⁄₁₆″.
a. back view
b. front view
Musee de l'Homme, Paris, France. © Scala. Art Resource, NY.

followed the animals that they hunted for food. They carved and painted images of these animals on cave walls deep in the earth.

Hand-size carvings of female figures have been found in the areas now called Eastern and Western Europe. Shown here are two of the best known: the WOMAN OF WILLENDORF and WOMAN OF LESPUGUE.

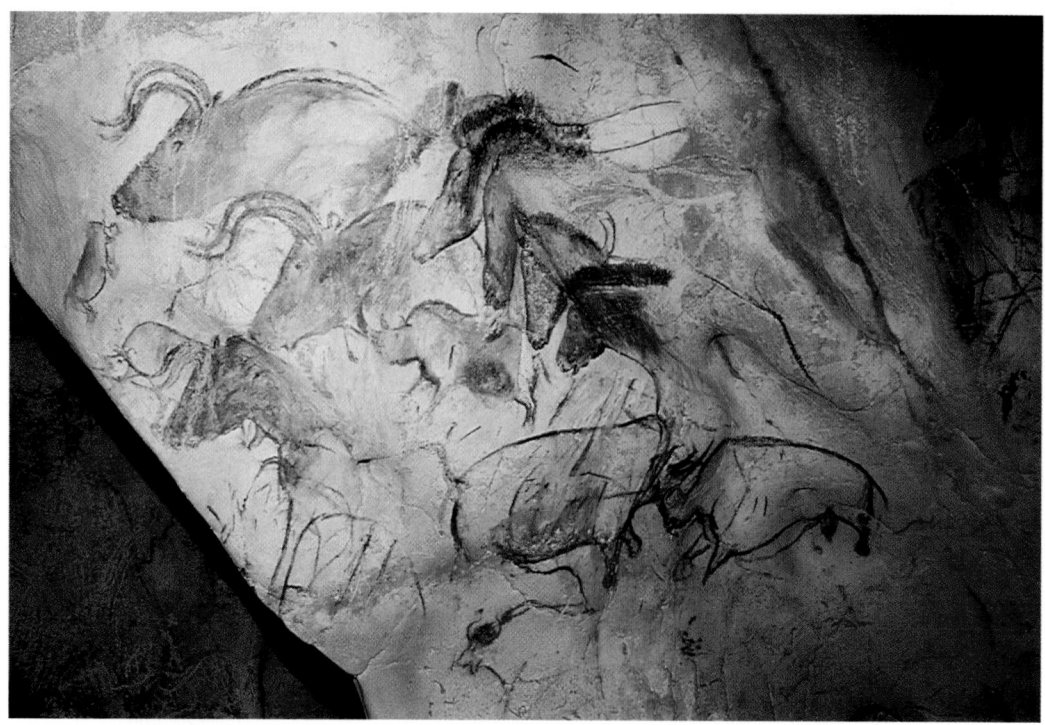

335 WALL PAINTING OF ANIMALS. Chauvet Cave, Pont d'Arc, France. c. 28,000 B.C.E.
Photograph: Jean Clottes/Carbis/Sygma.

In each of these figures, the exaggerated emphasis on hips and breasts implies a specific purpose that we can only guess. We might assume that prehistoric people gave primary credit to women for the most evident creative act: the birth of a new person. These figures may be the earliest known works of religious art, depicting the Paleolithic image of the Creator—the Great Mother Goddess. We refer to the Paleolithic period as the Stone Age, but that is mainly because only stone artifacts have survived. Some details on these figures suggest that their makers also practiced the arts of twining and braiding. For example, recent researchers believe that the WOMAN OF LESPUGUE wears a skirt made from braided cords, and the WOMAN OF WILLENDORF may sport a cap.

Human figures rarely appear in Paleolithic paintings; those that do tend to be more simplified and abstract than the images of animals. Animals portrayed in sculpture and paintings of this period have an expressive naturalism. The oldest known paintings were found in 1994 in the Chauvet Cave in south central France. The WALL PAINTING OF ANIMALS is among dozens of 30,000-year-old images painted with charcoal and earthen pigments on the cave walls. The unknown artists depicted in a lifelike fashion horses, rhinoceroses, tigers, and other large animals, many of them now extinct. Explorers found nearby a bear's skull placed in the middle of a flat stone slab in what may have been an altar.

The Lascaux Cave in southern France contains examples of the magnificent art of the late Paleolithic period. On walls of the inner chambers, large and small animals were portrayed in as many as thirteen different styles, from small and delicate to very large and bold. The largest bull at Lascaux (pictured on the *Discovering Art* CD) is eighteen feet in length. Successive images were painted over earlier ones. Each of the vigorous, naturalistic styles

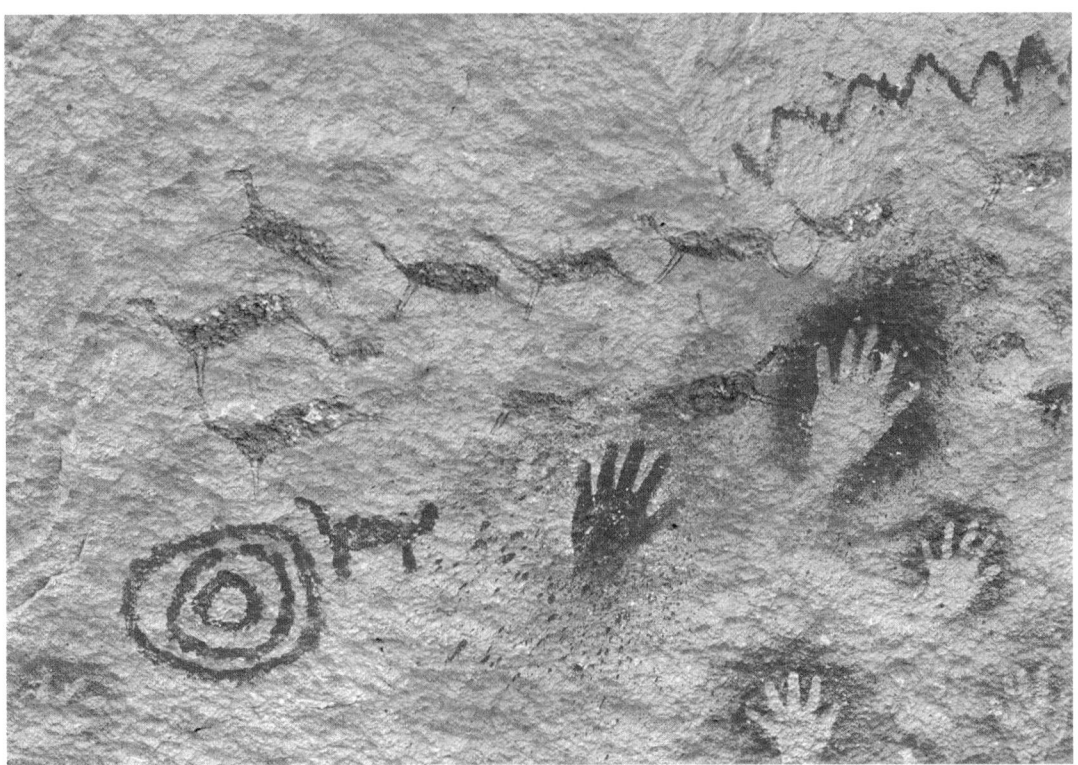

336 DEER AND HANDS. Las Manos Cave, Argentina. c. 15,000 B.C.E.
Bruce Coleman Inc. Photograph: Des and Jen Barlett.

was made in a different time period. Depictions are obviously based on careful observation gained through considerable contact with the animals that roamed the land at that time. The paintings were made by the light of oil-bearing stone lamps. At Lascaux, and at many other Paleolithic sites, geometric signs or symbols often appear along with the animal and occasional human figures.

Scholars long believed that the purpose of naturalistic Paleolithic art was to bring the spirits of animals into rituals related to the hunt. Many authors accept this theory. However, careful study of footprints and other archaeological remains has recently led some experts to theorize that Lascaux and similar sites were used as sanctuaries where youth were initiated in ceremonies based on symbolic and metaphysical associations with the portrayed animals.

Paleolithic Age people, in what is now southern Argentina, made paintings of their hands, probably by blowing earth colors as they placed their hands against the cave wall. DEER AND HANDS is similar to hand impressions and paintings of animals found on many continents.

Much of the world's Paleolithic art is found in caves, but large parts of this heritage are above ground, etched in stones in many locations around the world. These rock art carvings, also known as *petroglyphs*, are made by scratching or pecking the surface of exposed stone. One of the largest petroglyph complexes is in the Dampier Archipelago off the northwest coast of Australia. There we see the MURUJUGA PETROGLYPHS (on the following page), thousands of carvings that depict humans, animals. and mythic beings. Like the cave paintings, the purpose of the petroglyphs is a matter of conjecture.

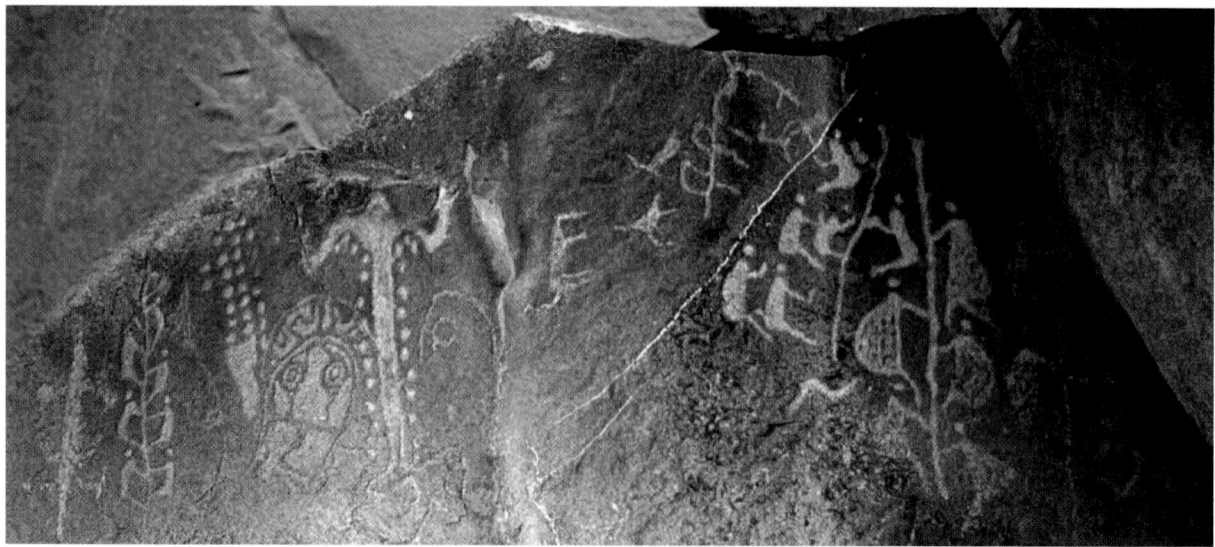

337 MURUJUGA PETROGLYPHS.
Up to 10,000 years old.
Dampier Archipelago, Western Australia.

Their age is also difficult to determine, because they are in exposed locations apart from soil sediments. A great deal of the world's rock art is also endangered for this reason; the MURUJUGA PETROGLYPHS, for example, have been eroded by acid rain, and economic development in the area threatens their outright destruction.

THE NEOLITHIC PERIOD

The transition from Old Stone Age, or Paleolithic, to New Stone Age, or Neolithic, cultures marked a major turning point in human history. Although there are comparable sites around the world, the New Stone Age seems to have occurred first in the Middle East, between 9000 and 6000 B.C.E., when people made the gradual transition from the precarious existence of nomadic hunters and food gatherers to the relatively stable life of village farmers and herders. The agricultural revolution—this major shift from nomadic groups to small agricultural communities—stabilized human life and produced early architecture and other technological developments. Out of neccessity, people learned

new techniques for working with seasonal rhythms. Because food and seeds had to be stored, it is not surprising that clay storage pots are among the most significant artifacts of the period.

Neolithic art reflects the great shift in living patterns. The vigorous, naturalistic art of Paleolithic hunters was largely replaced by the geometrically abstract art of Neolithic farmers. From about 10,000 to 3000 B.C.E., emphasis was placed on abstract designs used to enhance articles of daily use. The motifs, or dominant themes, used on clay pots were often derived from plant and animal forms.

The painted EARTHENWARE BEAKER is from Susa, the first developed city on the Iranian plateau. Solid bands define areas of compact decoration. The upper zone consists of a row of highly abstract long-necked birds, below which appears to be a band of dogs running in the opposite direction. The dominant image is an ibex or goat abstracted into triangular and circular shapes. The significant difference between the naturalism of Paleolithic animal art and the abstraction of Neolithic art becomes clear when we compare this goat with the naturalistic bulls of Chauvet or Lascaux.

Some of the finest Neolithic pottery was made in China. The well-preserved BURIAL URN (on the following page) from Kansu Province is decorated with a bold interlocking design, which may have been abstracted from spirals observed in nature. The design in the center of the spirals is probably derived from the bottoms of cowrie shells.

THE BEGINNINGS OF CIVILIZATION

Artifacts indicate that early civilizations emerged independently, at different times, in many parts of the world. We use the term *civilization* to distinguish cultures, or composites of cultures, that have fairly complex social orders and relatively high degrees of technical development. Key elements are food production through agriculture and animal husbandry, occupational specialization, writing, and production of bronze by smelting lead and tin. All of these developments were made possible by the move to cooperative living in urban as well as agricultural communities.

Among the earliest major civilizations were those in four fertile river valleys: the Tigris and Euphrates Rivers in Iraq, the Nile River in Egypt, the Indus River in west Pakistan and India, and the Yellow River in northern China.

The ancient civilizations of Mesopotamia and Egypt were almost parallel in time, arising in the fourth millennium B.C.E. and lasting some three thousand years. Yet they were quite different from each other. Urban civilization developed earlier in Mesopotamia than it did in Egypt. The Nile Valley of Egypt was protected by formidable deserts, making it possible for the Egyptians to enjoy thousands of years of relatively unbroken self-rule. The Tigris–Euphrates Valley of Mesopotamia, however, was vulnerable to repeated invasion; the area was ruled by a succession of different peoples. Each civilization therefore developed its own distinctive art forms.

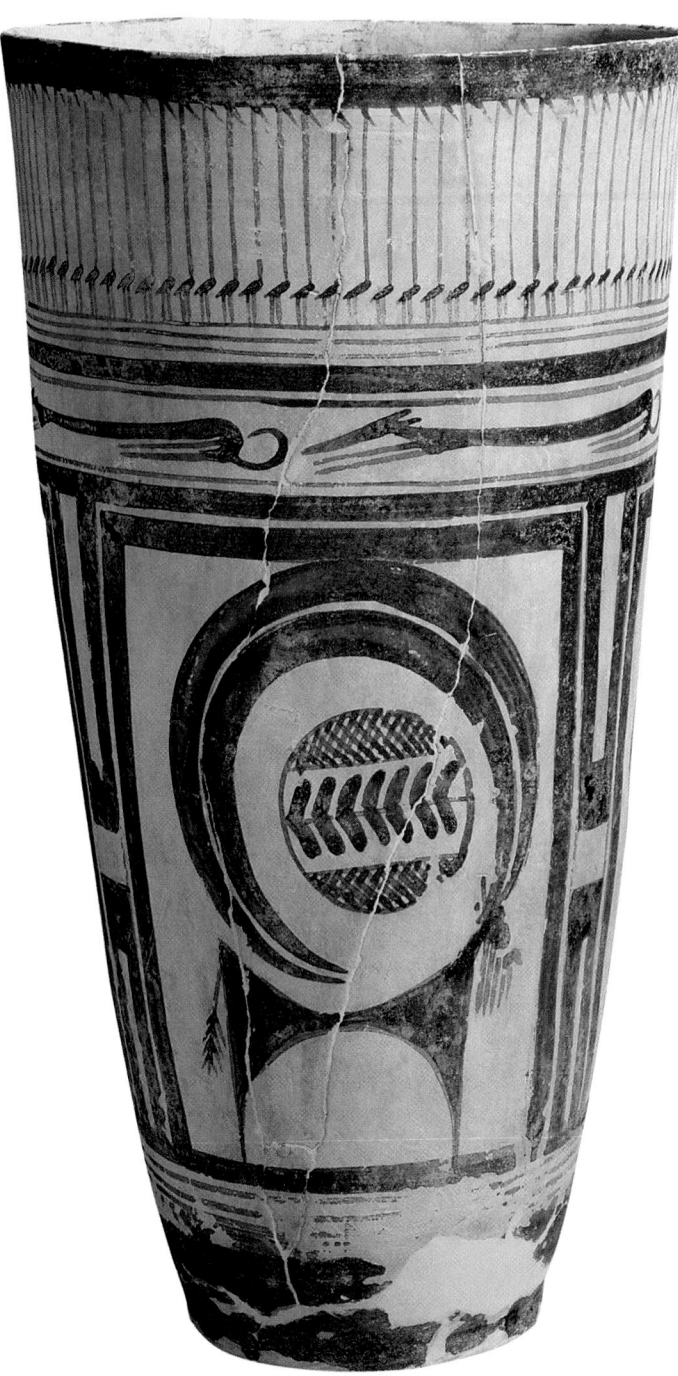

338   EARTHENWARE BEAKER. Susa, Iran. c. 4000 B.C.E.
Painted terra cotta. Height 11¼".
Musée du Louvre, Paris.
© Reunion de Musée Nationaux. Art Resource, NY.

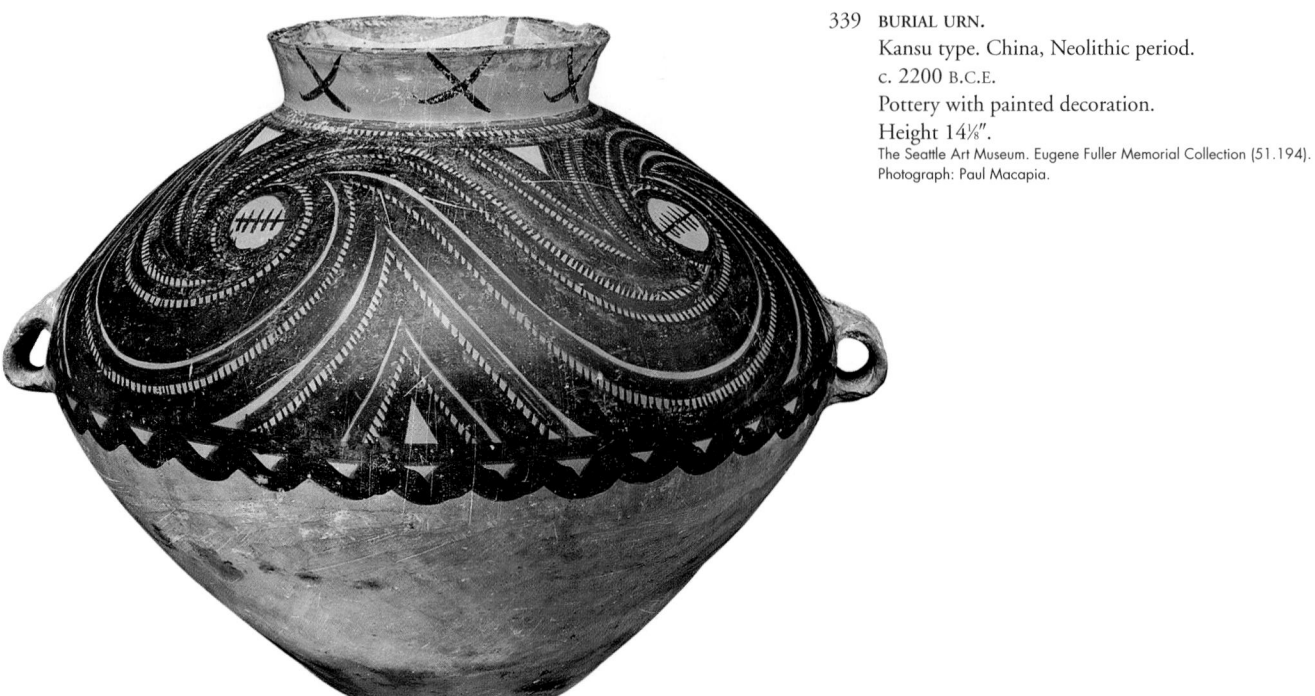

339 **BURIAL URN.**
Kansu type. China, Neolithic period.
c. 2200 B.C.E.
Pottery with painted decoration.
Height 14⅛″.
The Seattle Art Museum. Eugene Fuller Memorial Collection (51.194).
Photograph: Paul Macapia.

MESOPOTAMIA

The Greeks named the broad plain between the Tigris and Euphrates Rivers Mesopotamia, "the land between the rivers." Today, this plain is part of Iraq. The first Mesopotamian civilization arose in the southernmost part of the plain in an area called Sumer. The Sumerian people developed the world's first writing, the wheel, and the plow.

In the city-states of Sumer, religion and government were one; authority rested with priests who claimed divine sanction as they elected their rulers. The Sumerians worshiped a hierarchy of nature gods in temples set on huge platforms called *ziggurats*, which stood at the center of each city-state. Ruins of many early Mesopotamian cities are still dominated by eroding ziggurats, such as the

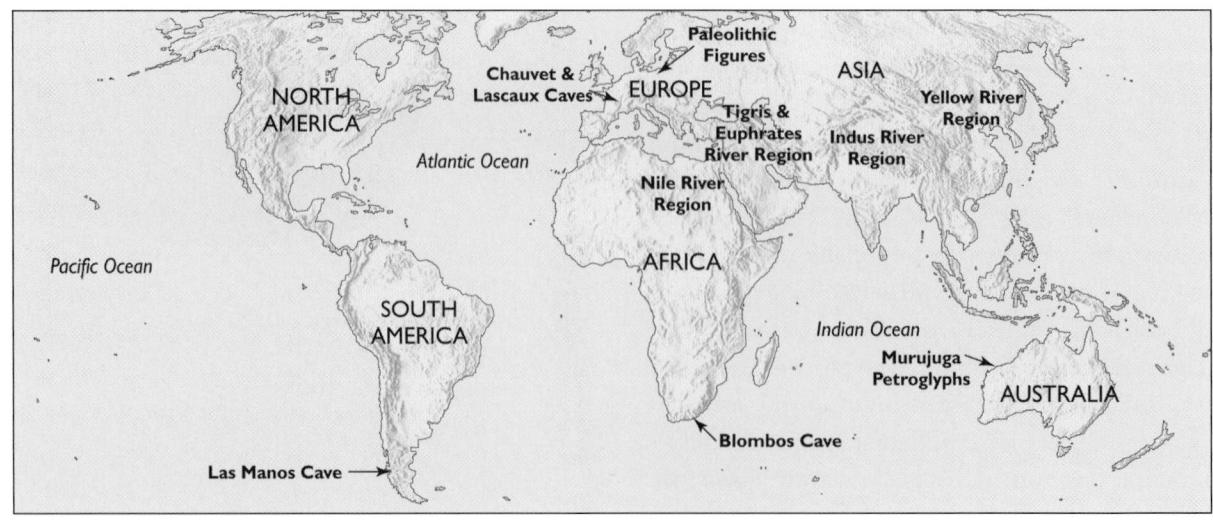

340 EARLIEST CENTERS OF CIVILIZATION, 3500–1500 B.C.E.

ZIGGURAT OF UR-NAMMU. The biblical Tower of Babel was probably a ziggurat.

Ziggurats symbolized the concept of the "sacred mountain" that links heaven and earth. They were filled with sun-baked bricks and faced with fired bricks often glazed in different colors. Two or more successively smaller platforms stood on the solid base, with a shrine on the uppermost platform. On these heights, close to heaven, the city's deities might dwell, and there the ruling priests and priestesses had their sanctuaries. A lack of stone led to the use of brick and wood for building, and consequently very little Mesopotamian architecture remains.

We can imagine the splendor of Sumerian court life by studying the reconstruction of the elegant royal LYRE found in the king's tomb in the ancient city of Ur. The narrative panel on the front and the bull's head are original. The bearded bull's head is a symbol of royalty often seen in Mesopotamian art. In contrast, the bulls and other imaginary animals inlaid on the harp's soundbox are depicted in a simplified narrative style. They take on human roles, as do the animals in the later Greek fables of Aesop.

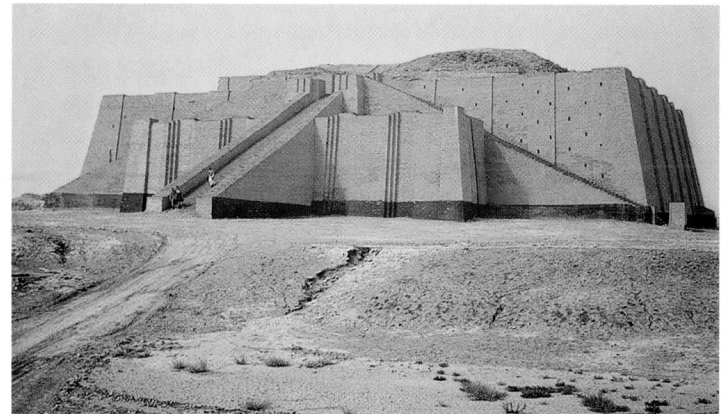

341 ZIGGURAT OF UR-NAMMU.
Iraq. c. 2100 B.C.E.
Photograph: Superstock.

342 LYRE.
From "The King's Grave" tomb RT 789. Ur. c. 2650–2550 B.C.E.
Reconstructed. Wood with gold, lapis lazuli, shell, and silver.
a. Front plaque.
b. Soundbox.
University of Pennsylvania Museum of Archaeology and Anthropology. Philadelphia. B 17694T4-29C. #T4–109C3.

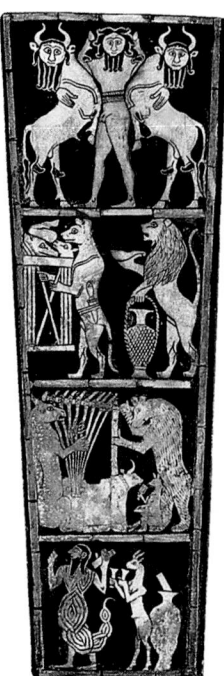

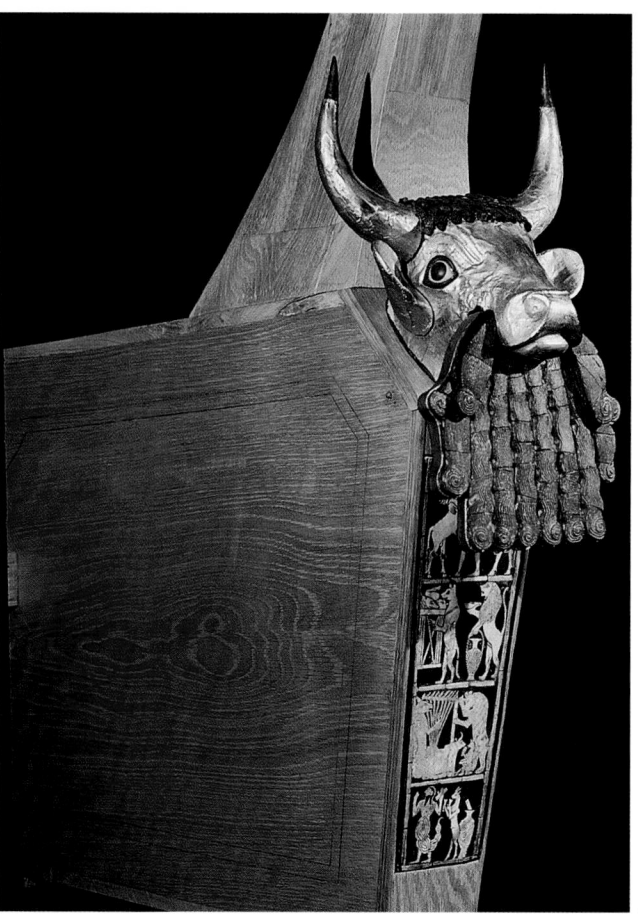

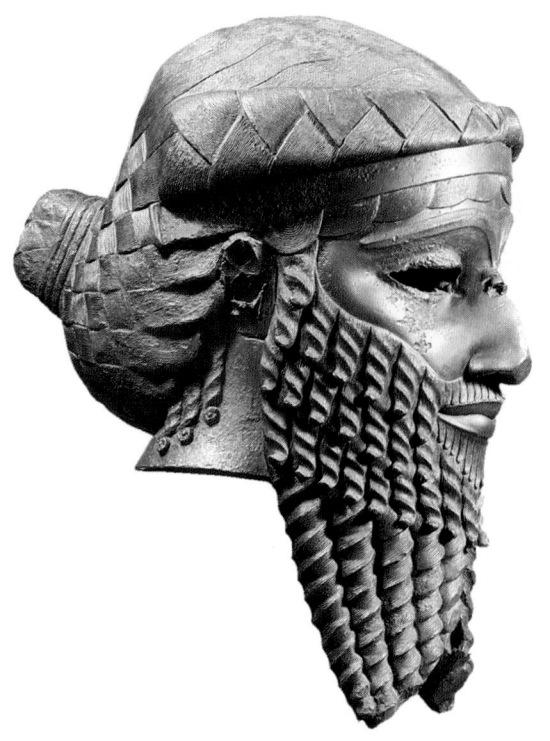

343 HEAD OF AN AKKADIAN RULER.
Nineveh. c. 2300–2200 B.C.E.
Bronze. Height 12″.
Photograph: Himer Fotoarchiv, Munich, Germany.

The upper panel, which shows a man embracing two bearded bulls, is a type of heraldic design developed by the Sumerians that was to influence the art of many later cultures. Both the upper panel and the panel at the bottom—a goat attending a scorpion-man—are believed to be scenes from the great classic of Sumerian literature, the *Epic of Gilgamesh*.

The region of Mesopotamia north of Sumer was called Akkadia. By about 2300 B.C.E., the scattered city-states of Sumer had come under the authority of a single Akkadian king. The magnificent HEAD OF AN AKKADIAN RULER portrays such an absolute monarch. Clearly, this highly sophisticated work evolved from a long tradition. The elaborate hairstyle and rhythmic patterning show the influence of Sumerian stylization. The handsome face expresses calm inner strength. Such superb blending of formal design with carefully observed naturalism

is a characteristic of both later Mesopotamian and Egyptian art.

Mesopotamia was an area of continual local rivalries, foreign invasions, and the rise and fall of military powers, yet this disorder did not prevent the development and continuity of cultural traditions.

EGYPT

Deserts on both sides of the Nile diminished outside influences and enabled Egypt to develop distinctive styles of architecture, painting, and sculpture that remained relatively unchanged for 2500 years—longer than the time from the birth of Christ to today. In our age of rapid cultural and technological change, it is difficult to imagine such artistic stability.

Among the most impressive and memorable works of Egyptian civilization are THE GREAT PYRAMIDS, gigantic mountain-like structures built as burial vaults for pharaohs—rulers who were considered god-kings. Legions of workers cut huge stone blocks, moved them to the site, and stacked them, without mortar, to form the pyramidal structure. The interiors are mostly solid, with narrow passageways leading to small burial chambers.

Egyptian religious belief focused intently on life after death. Preservation of the body and care for the dead were considered essential for extending life beyond the grave. Upon death, bodies of royalty and nobility were embalmed; together with accompanying artifacts, tools, and furniture, they were then buried in pyramids or in hidden underground tombs. Architects put great effort into preventing access to these funerary structures. As a result, most of what we know about ancient Egypt comes from such tombs.

Names of many Egyptian architects are known in association with their buildings. A striking and well-preserved example is the FUNERARY TEMPLE OF QUEEN HATSHEPSUT, designed by Senmut, the queen's chancellor and architect. Complementing the majestic cliffs of the site, the ramps and colonnades provide an elegant setting for ritual pageantry.

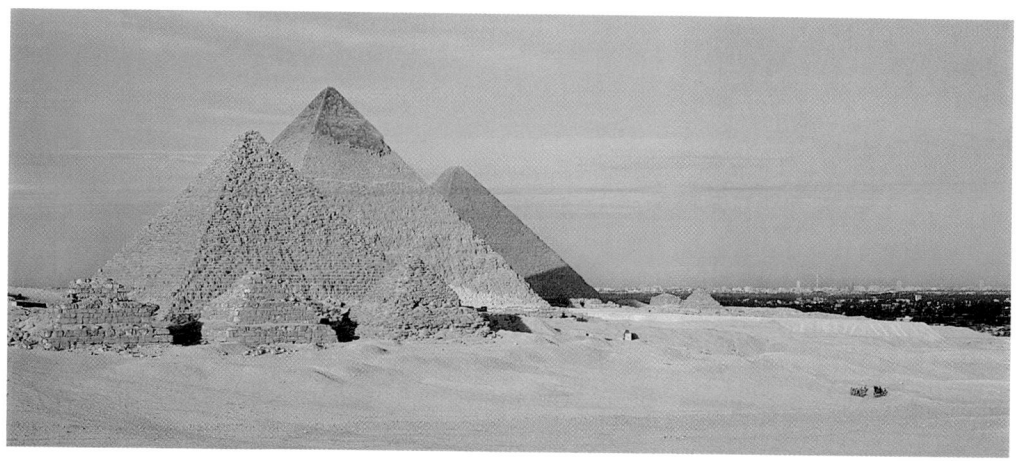

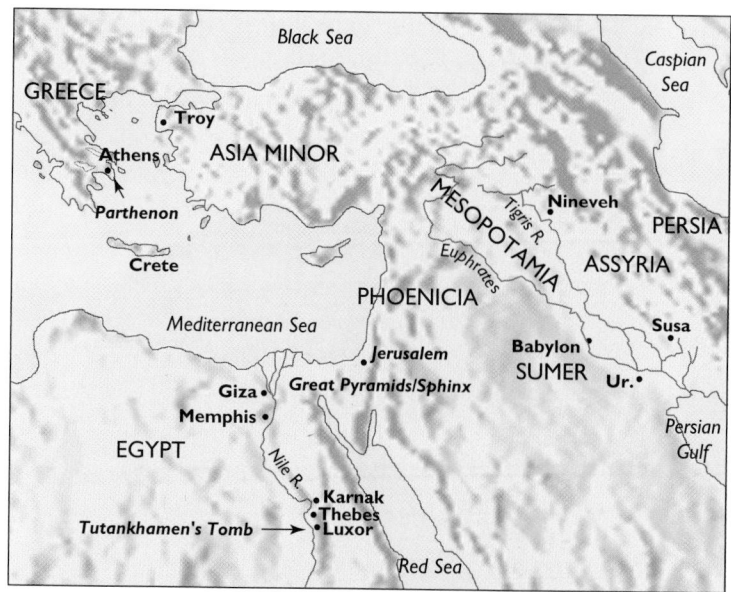

344   **THE GREAT PYRAMIDS.** Giza, Egypt.
Pyramid of Mycerinus, c. 2500 B.C.E.;
Pyramid of Chefren, 2650 B.C.E.;
Pyramid of Cheops, c. 2570 B.C.E.
© SEF. Art Resource, NY.

345   **THE ANCIENT MIDDLE EAST.**

346   **FUNERARY TEMPLE OF QUEEN**
HATSHEPSUT.
Deir el-Bahari. c. 1490–1460 B.C.E.
Tom Till Photography. © Tom Till.

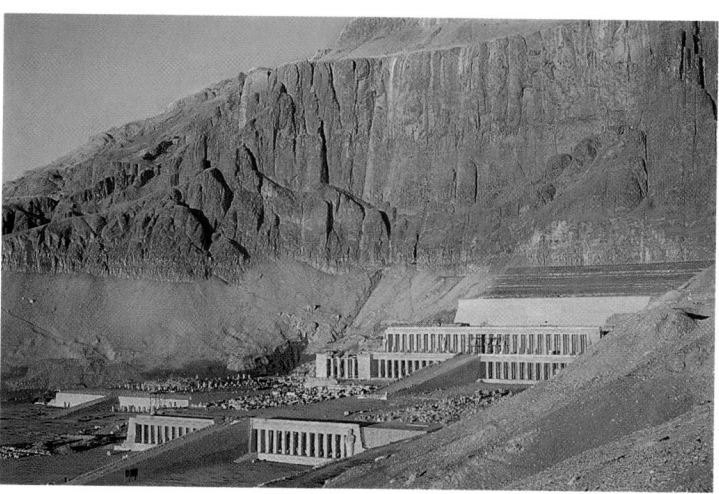

Egyptian sculpture is characterized by compact, solidly structured figures that embody qualities of strength and geometric clarity found in Egyptian architecture. The final form of a piece of sculpture was determined by an underlying geometric plan that was first sketched on the surface of the stone block. The sculptor of KING MYCERINUS AND QUEEN KHAMERERNEBTY paid considerable attention to human anatomy yet stayed within the traditionally prescribed geometric scheme. The strength, clarity, and lasting stability expressed by the figures result from this union of naturalism and abstraction. With formal austerity, the couple stands in the frontal pose (straight forward, not turning) that had been established for royal portraits. Even so, the figures express warmth and vitality; the queen touches Mycerinus in a sympathetic, loving way. Typical of sculpture of this era are the formal pose with left foot forward, the false ceremonial beard, and figures that remain attached to the block of stone from which they were carved.

Tutankhamen ("King Tut"), who died at age eighteen, is the best-known Egyptian ruler because his was the only Egyptian royal tomb discovered in modern times with most of its contents intact. The volume and value of the objects in the small tomb make it clear why grave robbers have been active in Egypt since the days of the first pharaohs. Tutankhamen's inlaid gold MASK FROM MUMMY CASE is but one of hundreds of extraordinary artifacts from the tomb. Its formal blend of naturalism and abstract idealism is distinctly Egyptian.

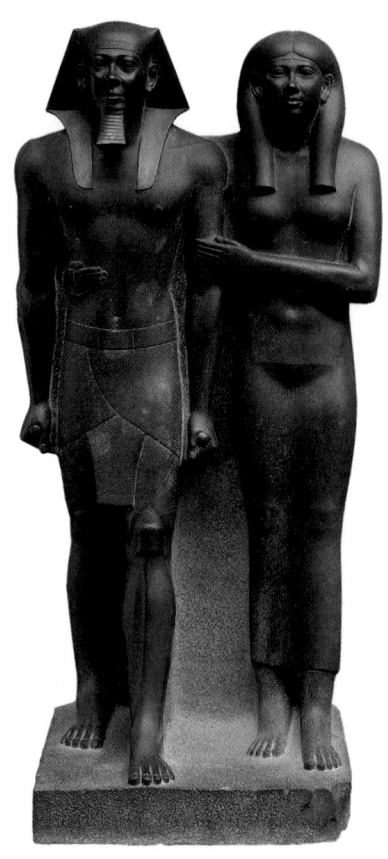

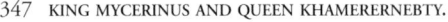

347 KING MYCERINUS AND QUEEN KHAMERERNEBTY.
Giza, Egypt. Dynasty 4, 2532–2510 B.C.E.
Schist. 56″ × 22½″ × 21¾″.

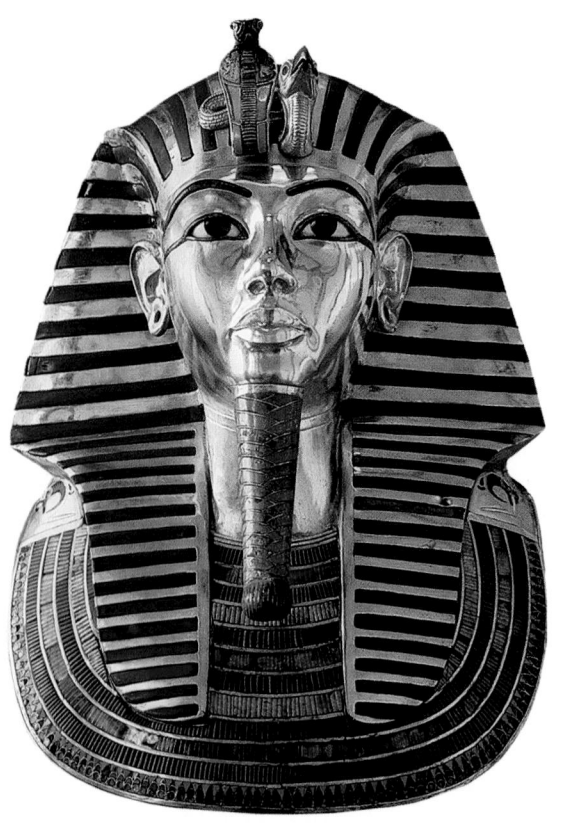

348 MASK FROM MUMMY CASE.
Tomb of Tutankhamen. c. 1340 B.C.E.
Gold inlaid with enamel and semiprecious stones.
Height 21¼″.
Egyptian Museum, Cairo.
Photograph: Superstock, Inc.

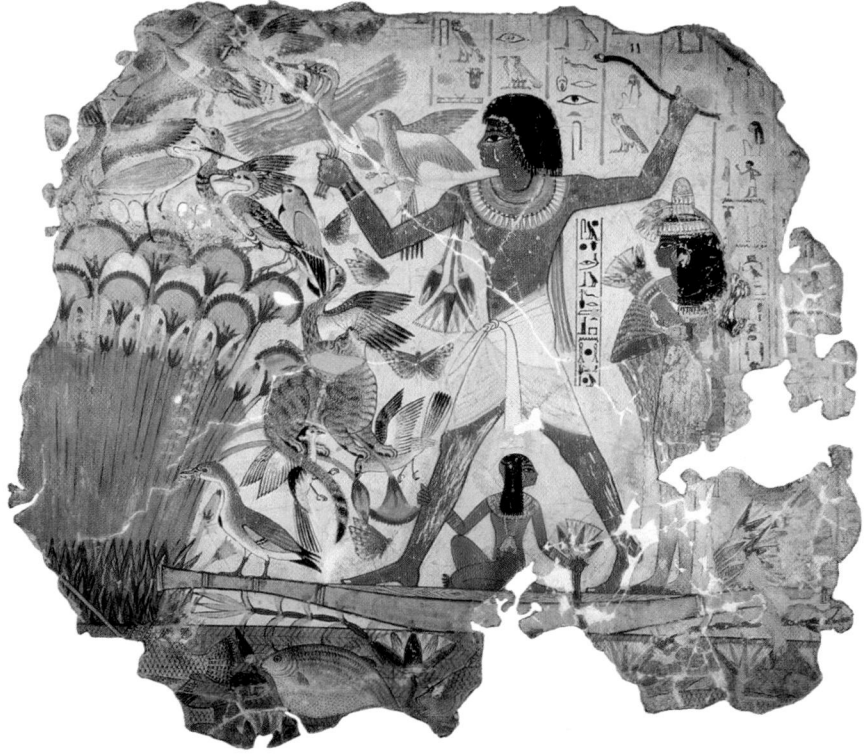

349   WALL PAINTING FROM THE TOMB OF NEBAMUN.
       Thebes, Egypt. c. 1450 B.C.E.
       Paint on dry plaster.
       © British Museum, London.

Egyptian artists in all media generally depicted the human figure either in a completely frontal position or in profile. Egyptian artists portrayed each object and each part of the human body from what they identified as its most characteristic angle, thus avoiding the ambiguity caused by random or chance angles of view (see also page 51).

In the WALL PAINTING FROM THE TOMB OF NEBAMUN, the painter of the hunting scene presents a wealth of specific information without making the painting confusing. Flat shapes portray basic elements of each subject in the clearest, most identifiable way. The head, hips, legs, and feet of the nobleman who dominates this painting are shown from the side, while his eye and shoulders are shown from the front. Sizes of human figures are determined by social rank, a system known as *hierarchic scale*; the nobleman is the largest figure, his wife is smaller, his daughter smaller still.

The family stands on a boat made of papyrus reeds; plants grow on the left at the shore. The entire painting is teeming with life, and the artist has even taken great care to show life below the water's surface. Attention to accurate detail lets us identify species of insects, birds, and fish. The hieroglyphics—the picture writing of ancient Egyptian priesthood—can be seen behind the figures.

Egyptian art greatly influenced that of early Greece, and the Greeks later developed one of the most important styles in Western art. To this period we now turn.

THE CLASSICAL AND MEDIEVAL WEST

The Classical cultures of Greece and Rome dominated Western civilization from the fifth century B.C.E. until the decline of Rome in the fifth century C.E. The later periods of Roman rule of Europe also saw the rise of Christianity, a faith that brought a wealth of new subjects to Western art. The period between the fall of Rome and the beginning of the Renaissance is referred to as the Middle Ages or Medieval Period, a term that does little justice to the creativity of that era. Meanwhile, Eastern Europe was dominated by the Byzantine Empire, headquartered in Constantinople (today's Istanbul). Byzantine Christianity is today known as the Orthodox Church. Hence, Christianity of one form or another was a major force in the art of both Eastern and Western Europe for a thousand years.

GREECE

The Greeks distinguished themselves from other peoples of Europe and Asia by their attitude toward being human. They came to regard humankind as the highest creation of nature—the closest thing to perfection in physical form, coupled with the power to reason. Greek deities had human weaknesses, and Greek mortals had godlike strengths.

With this attitude came a new concept of the importance of the individual. The Greek focus on human potential and achievement led to the development of democracy and to the perfection of naturalistic images of the human figure in art. The philosopher Plato taught that behind the imperfections of transitory reality was the permanent, ideal form. Thus, to create the ideal individual (the supreme work of nature) became the goal of Greek artists.

Greek civilization passed through three broad stages: the Archaic period, the Classical period, and the Hellenistic period. In the art of the Archaic period (from the late seventh to the early fifth centuries B.C.E.), the Greeks assimilated influences from Egypt and the Near East. Greek writers of the time tell us that Greek painters were often better known than Greek sculptors. Yet what we now see of Greek painting appears only on pottery because very few wall paintings survive. The elegant EUPHRONIOS KRATER shows the level of achievement of Greek potters and painters. It is in the Archaic "red-figure" style and depicts a scene from Homer's *Odyssey*: the dead Trojan warrior Sarpedon, wounds gushing blood, being carried off to eternity by the gods of Sleep and Death. The painter Euphronios signed the work; the word KRATER refers to the vessel's shape, traditionally used for mixing ceremonial beverages. This work was in the collection of the Metropolitan Museum for many years, but when the Italian government gathered information to prove that it was illegally exported, the Metropolitan was forced to return it. (For more on this story, see the essay on page 250.)

The Greeks honored individual achievement by creating numerous life-size nude male and clothed female figures. The Archaic-style KOUROS has a rigid frontal position that is an adaptation from Egyptian sculpture. (*Kouros* is Greek for male

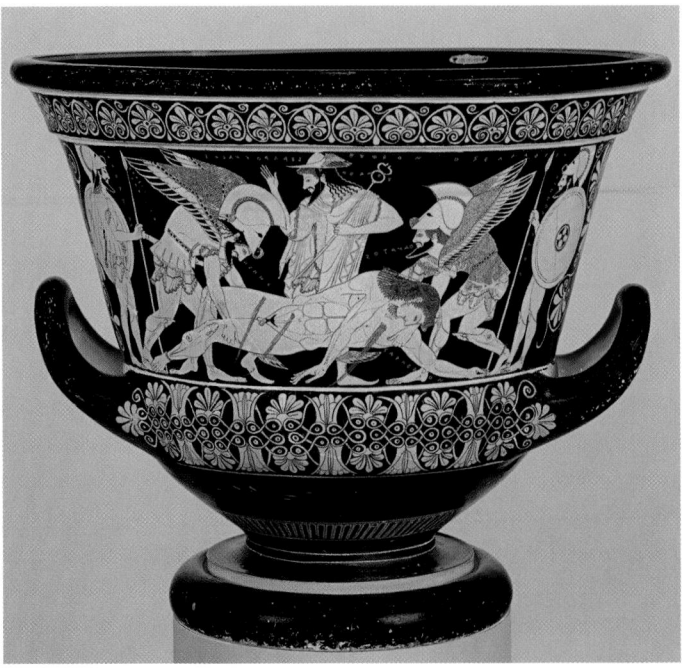

350 EUPHRONIOS KRATER. c. 515 B.C.E.
Terracotta. Height 18″, diameter 21¾″.
Metropolitan Museum of Art. Lent by the Republic of Italy.
Photograph: © The Metropolitan Museum of Art.

351 KOUROS. Statue of a youth. c. 610–600 B.C.E.
Marble. Height 76″.
The Metropolitan Museum of Art, New York. Fletcher Fund, 1932.
32.11.1. Photograph: © The Metropolitan Museum of Art.

youth; *kore* is the word for female youth.) The Egyptian figure of MYCERINUS (page 242) and the KOUROS both stand with arms held straight at the sides, fingers drawn up, and left leg forward with the weight evenly distributed on both feet.

In spite of the similarity of stance, however, the character of Greek sculpture is already quite different from that of Egyptian. The KOUROS is freestanding, and it honors an individual who was not a supernatural ruler.

Within one hundred years after the making of the KOUROS figure, Greek civilization entered its Classical phase (480–323 B.C.E.). Greek aesthetic principles from this period provide the basis for the concept of classicism. *Classical* art emphasizes rational simplicity, order, and restrained emotion. The rigid poses of Egyptian and early Greek figures gave way to a greater interest in anatomy and more relaxed poses. Sculpture became increasingly naturalistic as well as idealized and began to show the body as alive and capable of movement.

The statue known as the SPEAR BEARER is an excellent example of Greek Classicism. The sculptor Polykleitos wrote a treatise on the perfect proportions

352 Polykleitos.
SPEAR BEARER (DORYPHOROS).
Roman copy after Greek original
bronze of 450–440 B.C.E.
Marble, height 6′6″.
Museo Acheologico Nazionale, Naples.
Scala/Art Resource, NY.

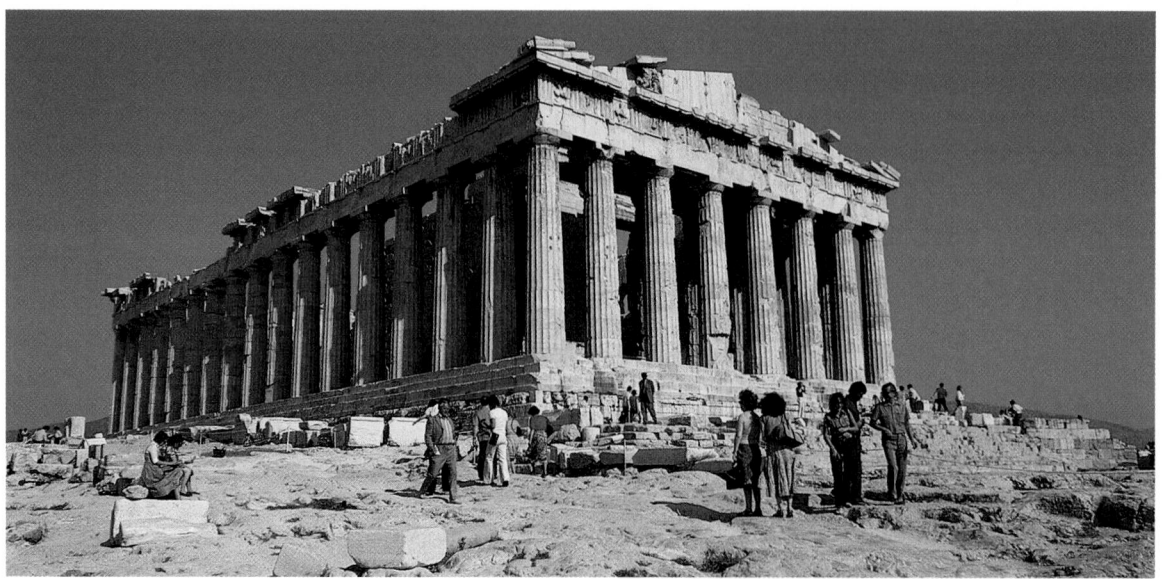

353 Ictinus and Callicrates.
PARTHENON. Acropolis, Athens. 448–432 B.C.E.
a. View from the northwest.

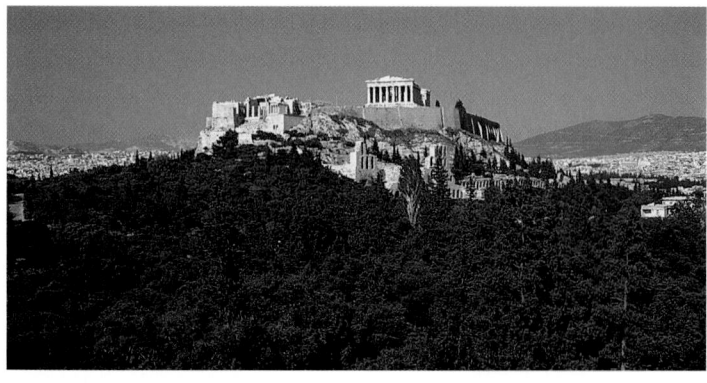

b. View from the southwest.
Photographs: Duane Preble.

of the human form and created this statue as an example. Neither the book nor the original statue survives, but both are known from documents and later copies. Polykleitos envisioned the human body as a harmonious set of divinely inspired ratios. By studying numerous models, he arrived at what he thought were the ideal proportions of the human body. Hence, the SPEAR BEARER combines actual observations with mathematical calculation.

The statue depicts an athlete who once held a spear on his left shoulder. Typical of Classical art, the figure is in the prime of life, and blemish-free. It is not a portrait of an individual but rather a vision of the ideal. He bears most of his weight on one leg in a pose known as *contrapposto*, meaning counterpoised. The Greeks and then the Romans used this pose to give a lifelike quality to figures at rest. Centuries later, their sculpture would inspire Renaissance artists to use the same technique.

The city-state of Athens was the artistic and philosophical center of Classical Greek civilization. Above the city, on a large rock outcropping called the Acropolis, the Athenians constructed one of the world's most admired structures, the PARTHENON. Today, even in its ruined state, the PARTHENON continues to express the ideals of the people who created it.

The largest of several sacred buildings on the Acropolis, the PARTHENON was designed and built as a gift to Athena Parthenos, goddess of wisdom, arts, industries, and prudent warfare, and protector of the Athenian navy.

When Ictinus and Callicrates designed the PARTHENON, they were following Egyptian tradition in temple design based on the post-and-beam system of construction (see page 214). In the

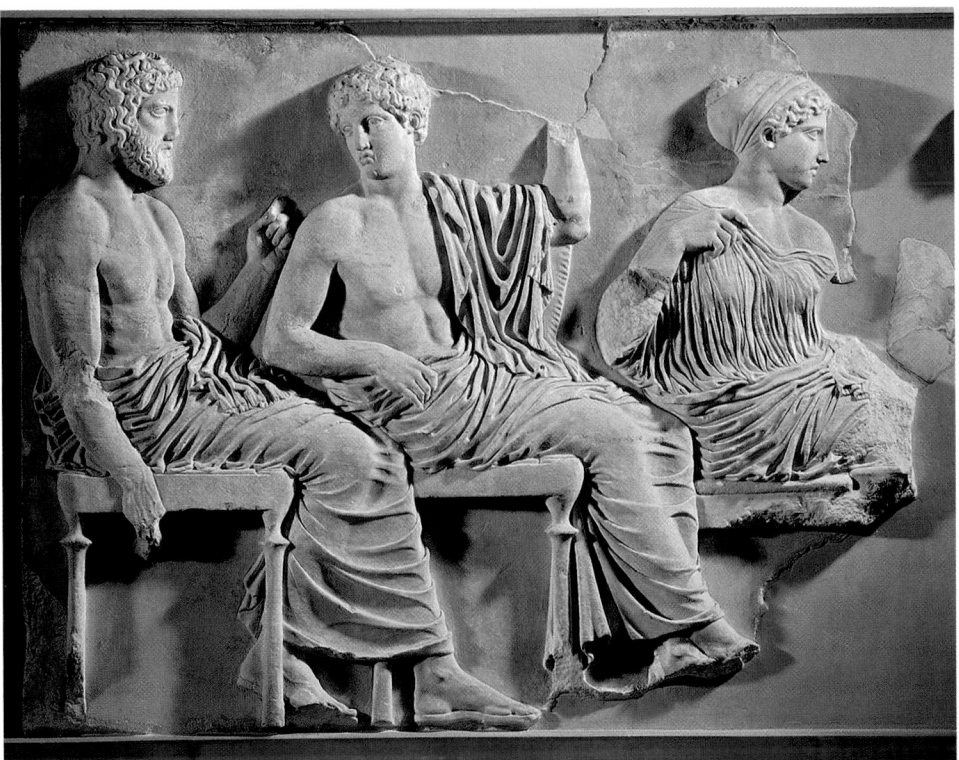

PARTHENON, the Greek temple concept reached its highest form of development. The structure was located so that it could be seen against the sky, the mountains, or the sea from vantage points around the city, and it was the focal point for processions and large outdoor religious ceremonies. Rites were performed on altars placed in front of the eastern entrance. The interior space was designed to house a forty-foot statue of Athena. The axis of the building was carefully calculated so that on Athena's birthday the rising sun coming through the huge east doorway would fully illuminate the towering (now lost) gold-covered statue.

In its original form, the PARTHENON exhibited the refined clarity, harmony, and vigor that are the basis of the Greek tradition. The proportions of the PARTHENON are based on harmonious ratios. The ratio of the height to the widths of the east and west ends is approximately 4 to 9. The ratio of the width to the length of the building is also 4 to 9. The diameter of the columns relates to the space between the columns at a ratio of 4 to 9, and so on.

None of the major lines of the building is perfectly straight. Many experts believe that the subtle deviations were designed to correct optical illusions. The columns have an almost imperceptible bulge (called *entasis*) above the center, which causes them to appear straighter than if they were in fact straight-sided, and this gives the entire structure a tangible grace. Even the steps and tops of doorways rise slightly in perfect curves. Corner columns, seen against the light, are somewhat larger in diameter to counteract the diminishing effect of strong light in the background. The axis lines of the columns lean in a little at the top. If extended into space, these lines would converge 5,856 feet above the building. These unexpected variations are not consciously seen, but they are felt, and they help make the building visually appealing.

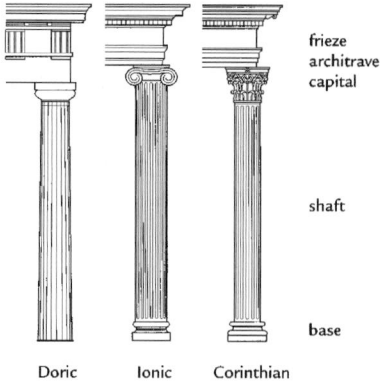

frieze
architrave
capital

shaft

base

Doric   Ionic   Corinthian

354 ARCHITECTURAL ORDERS.

355 VENUS DE MEDICI. 3rd century B.C.E.
Marble. Height 5'.
Uffizi Gallery, Florence. Photograph: Scala/Art Resource, NY.

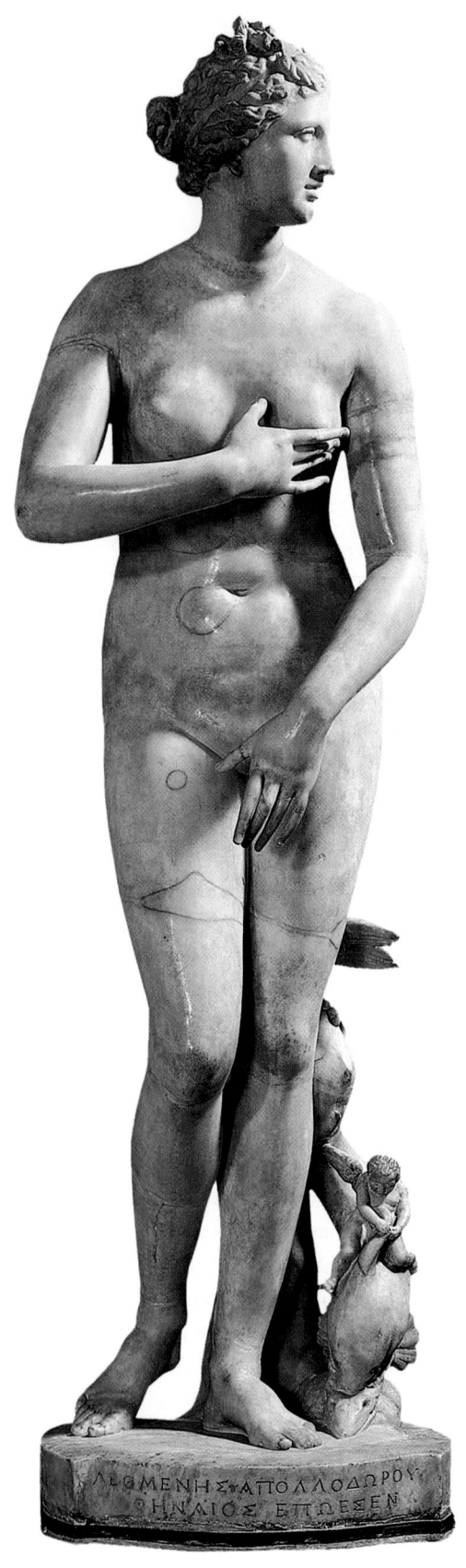

The Greeks developed three ARCHITECTURAL ORDERS: Doric, Ionic, and Corinthian. Each order comprises a set of architectural elements and proportions. The most telling details for identification of the orders are the three types of *capitals* used at the tops of columns. Doric, which came first, is simple, geometric, and sturdy; Ionic is taller and more dynamic than Doric; Corinthian is complex and organic. (See the *Discovering Art* CD for an interactive exercise and a video demonstration of Classical Architecture.)

Although today we see Greek temples as white stone structures, some of the upper portions of exterior surfaces were once brightly painted. Parts of sculpture were also painted.

Some of the finest Greek sculpture was made for the upper areas of the PARTHENON. Running along the exterior wall of the inner temple was a 524-foot-long relief sculpture of a procession in honor of Athena. As with the other figures on the FRIEZE (on the preceding page), the gods Poseidon, Apollo, and Artemis are depicted in ideal human form—noble and perfect.

VENUS DE MEDICI is a third-century B.C.E. Roman copy of a fourth-century B.C.E. Greek original. (Aphrodite, the Greek goddess of love and beauty, was known to the Romans as Venus.) This copy was inspired by an Aphrodite by Praxitiles, one of the most famous sculptors of the Classical period. Because it was made to symbolize a goddess rather than to portray a real woman, the figure is more ideal than natural. Its refined profile is one of the most obvious features of the Greek idealization of human figures. But we can sense the emerging Hellenistic sensibility in the figure's sensuality—a mortal element foreign to Classical ideals. A similarly beautiful male figure is the VICTORIOUS YOUTH, a subject of the essay on the following page.

After the decline of the Greek city-states at the end of the fourth century B.C.E., the art of the Mediterranean changed. Though it continued to be strongly influenced by earlier Greek art, and was often executed by Greek artists, it was often produced for non-Greek patrons. Thus, Mediterranean art during this era is called *Hellenistic*, meaning Greek-like. The transition from Classical to Hellenistic coincided with the decline of Athens as a city-state after it fought a useless war with the neighboring city of Sparta, and with the rise of an absolute monarchy in Macedonia that soon took over the entire peninsula. Most historians date the period from approximately the death of Alexander the Great (323 B.C.E.) to the Roman conquest of Egypt (30 B.C.E.). Artists turned from the idealized restraint of the Classical period to the subjective and imperfect aspects of life and humanity.

In the Hellenistic period, Greek art became more dynamic and less idealized. Everyday activities, historical subjects, myths, and portraiture became more common subjects for art. Late, or Hellenistic, Greek art contrasts with Classical Greek art in that it is more expressive and frequently shows exaggerated movement.

THE LAOCOÖN GROUP is a Roman copy of a Hellenistic work. In Greek mythology, Laocoön was the Trojan priest who warned against bringing the wooden horse into Troy during the Trojan War. Later, he and his sons were attacked by serpents, an act the Trojans interpreted as a sign of the gods' disapproval of Laocoön's prophecy. Laocoön is shown in hierarchic proportion to his sons.

The rationalism, clarity, and restraint of Classical sculpture have given way to writhing movement, tortured facial expressions, and strained muscles expressing emotional and physical anguish. When this sculpture was unearthed in Italy in 1506, it had an immediate influence on the young Michelangelo.

ROME

The Hellenistic era saw the rise of Rome, a formidable new force in the Mediterranean. By the second century B.C.E., Rome had become the major power in the Western world. At its height, the Roman Empire would include western Europe, North Africa, and the Near East as well as the shores of the Mediterranean. The governance of a

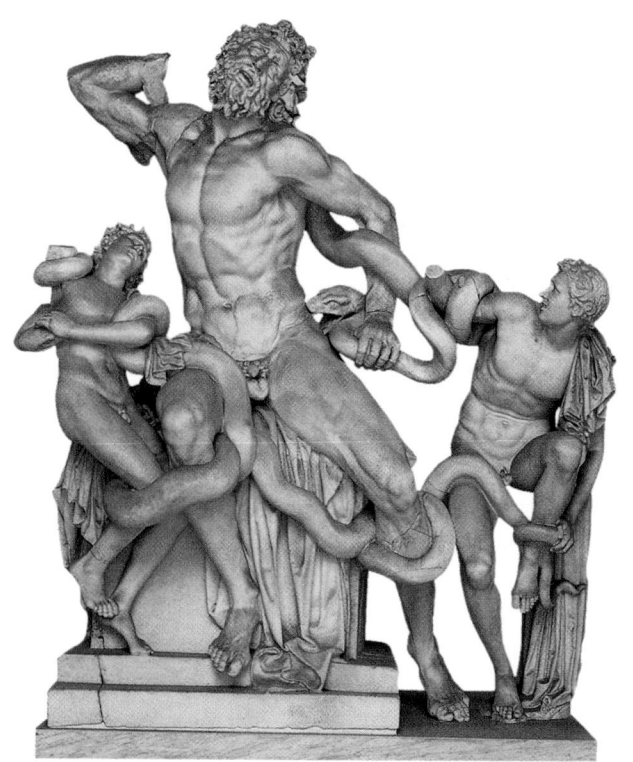

356 THE LAOCOÖN GROUP.
Roman copy of a 1st- or 2nd-century B.C.E.
Greek original, perhaps after Agesander, Athenodorus, and Polydorus of Rhodes. c. 1st century C.E.
Marble. Height 95¼".
Vatican Museum, Vatican State, Rome.
Photograph: Giraudon/Art Resource, NY.

ART *in the world*

BY ANY STANDARD, the VICTORIOUS YOUTH is an important piece of Classical Greek art. Depicting a hero of the ancient Olympic games, it is one of the few life-size Greek bronzes ever recovered intact. But it is also the subject of an international criminal trial that highlights some of the most wrenching issues in the museum world today. It is now on display in a U.S. museum, but Italy claims it was looted.

Fishermen found the statue in 1964 when it tore their nets off Italy's eastern coast. They sold it to two brothers, local cement makers, for about the equivalent of $36,000. Any antiquities found in Italy become property of the state, and the brothers did not want to lose their investment, so they entrusted it to the local priest, who hid it under a staircase. When the authorities heard of its existence and came to investigate, it was gone. They prosecuted the brothers and imprisoned them for four months, but the brothers never said to whom they sold the VICTORIOUS YOUTH.

In 1971, a German antiquities dealer announced that he had bought the work in Brazil. He restored it and claimed that it was created by Lysippos, personal sculptor to Alexander the Great. Six years later, the Getty Museum in California bought the work for just under $4 million, a

record price at the time. (Meanwhile, back at the fishing village, 8,000 citizens signed a petition demanding its return to them.)

The Italian government began efforts to recover the piece in 1989. Most recently, VICTORIOUS YOUTH headed a list of 47 objects that Italy says that the Getty Museum is holding illegally. They presented this list to the Getty in 2005 along with a criminal indictment against the Getty curator of antiquities, accusing her of purchasing illegally excavated and looted works. In summer 2007, the museum returned 40 of the listed works but kept VICTORIOUS YOUTH. Citing the work's origin in international waters and its lack of a clear ownership trail proving fraud, the Getty director refused to send it away.

But Italy is recently winning case after case when it alleges illegal export. The Boston Museum of Fine Arts returned 13 illegally acquired pieces in September 2006. The Metropolitan Museum entered negotiations regarding one of its most prized possessions, the EUPHRONIOS KRATER, in the same year (this work is pictured on page 245). The museum had bought the work in 1972, under conditions that the director at the time knew were suspicious, from an art dealer who was later indicted for illegal trafficking. Under the Metropolitan's agree-

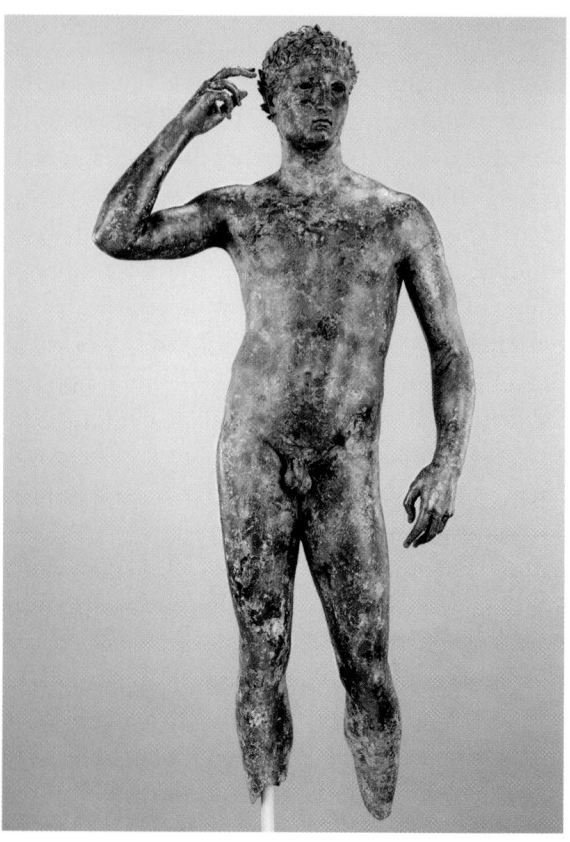

357 VICTORIOUS YOUTH. 300–100 B.C.E.
Bronze. Height 59⅝".
The J. Paul Getty Museum, Villa Collection,
Malibu, California.

ment, the KRATER remained in New York as a loan from the Italian government (as it is listed in our caption) until 2008, when it returned to Italy.

Italy's newfound assertiveness comes from solid evidence: A 1995 raid on a dealer's warehouse yielded thousands of photographs of illegally excavated ancient pieces, provided an extensive paper trail of loot, and earned the dealer a prison sentence. The Italian prosecutor entrusted with these matters, Maur-

izio Fiorilli, presents the evidence to museums, and they generally cooperate in returning illegally acquired works.

Not always willingly, though. Metropolitan Museum director Philippe de Montebello told an interviewer, "Italian museum storerooms are engorged with works of art. It's not as if they needed them. This is a political statement."[1] But prosecutor Fiorilli is equally blunt: "You can't do culture based on fraud and theft."[1]

multitude of unique peoples and cultures was a prime example of the Roman genius for order and practical politics. Roman culture has affected our lives in many areas: our systems of law and government, our calendar, festivals, religions, and languages.

The Romans were a practical, materialistic people, and their art reflects these characteristics. They made few changes in the general style of Greek art, which they admired, collected, and copied. But not all Roman art was imitative. Roman portraiture of the Republican period, such as the HEAD OF AN OLD MAN, achieved a high degree of individuality rarely found in Greek sculpture. The representationally accurate style probably grew out of the Roman custom of making wax death masks of ancestors for the family shrine or altar. Later, these images were recreated in marble to make them more durable. Roman sculptors observed and carefully recorded those physical details and imperfections that give character to each person's face.

The Romans' greatest artistic achievements were in civil engineering, town planning, and architecture. They created utilitarian and religious structures of impressive beauty and grandeur that had major influence on later Western architecture. As we saw in Chapter 13, the outstanding feature of Roman architecture was the semicircular arch, which the Romans utilized and refined in the construction of arcades, barrel vaults, and domes (see the diagrams on pages 215–216).

By developing the structural use of concrete combined with semicircular arch and vault construction, the Romans were able to enclose large indoor spaces. Although a type of concrete was commonly used in Roman construction, the quality of cement (the chemically active ingredient in concrete) declined during the Middle Ages, and concrete was not widely used again until it was redeveloped in the nineteenth century.

In the PANTHEON (on the following page), a major temple dedicated to all the gods, Roman builders created a domed interior space of immense scale. The building is essentially a cylinder, capped by a hemispherical dome, with a single entrance framed by a Greek porch, or *portico*. Because THE INTERIOR

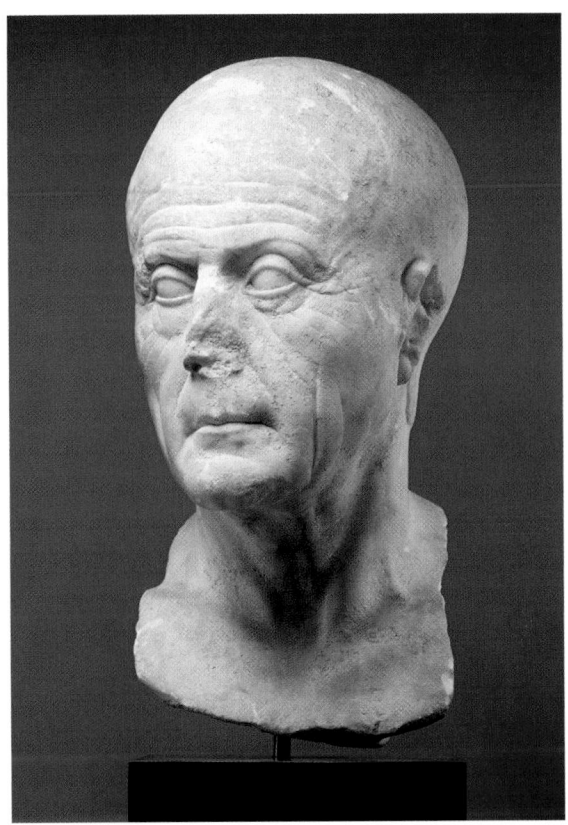

358 HEAD OF AN OLD MAN.
Marble. 25 B.C.E.–10 C.E.
Height 13¾".
The J. Paul Getty Museum, Villa Collection, Malibu, California.

OF THE PANTHEON is dimly lit and difficult to photograph, we see it in a famous 1734 painting.

Whereas Greek temples such as the PARTHENON were designed both as inner sanctuaries for priests and as focal points for outdoor religious ceremonies, the PANTHEON was built as a magnificent, awe-inspiring interior space that complemented its once opulent exterior. To meet their preference for spacious interiors, the Romans developed many other great domed and vaulted buildings.

The PANTHEON'S circular walls, which support the huge dome, are stone and concrete masonry, twenty feet thick and faced with brick. The dome diminishes in thickness toward the crown, and it is patterned on the interior surface with recessed squares called *coffers*, which both lighten and strengthen the structure. Originally covered with gold, the coffered ceiling symbolizes the dome of

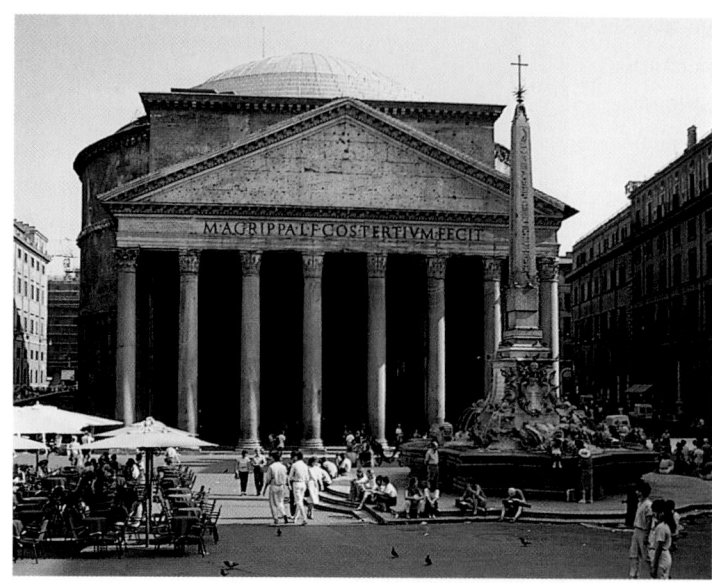

359 PANTHEON. Rome. 118–125 C.E.
a. View of the entrance.
Photograph: Duane Preble.

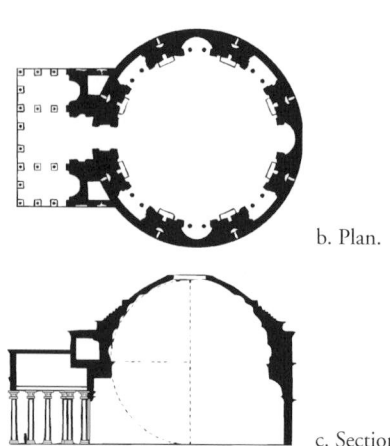

b. Plan.

c. Section.

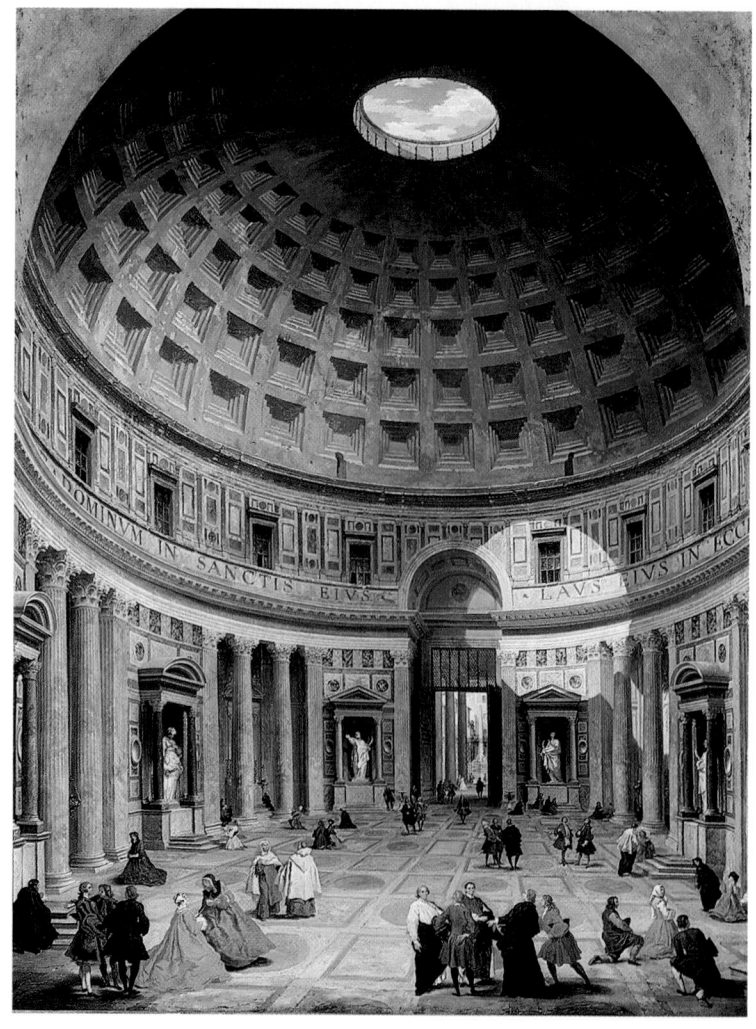

360 Giovanni Paolo Panini.
THE INTERIOR OF THE PANTHEON,
ROME. c. 1734.
Oil on canvas. 50½″ × 39″.
Samuel H. Kress Collection.
Photograph: Richard Carafelli.
© 2001 Board of Trustees, National Gallery of Art,
Washington, D.C.1939.1.24.(135)/PA.

heaven. It was designed so that the distance from the summit to the floor is equal to the 143-foot diameter—making it a virtual globe of space. At the dome's crown, an opening called an *oculus*, or eye, thirty feet in diameter, provides daylight and ventilation to the interior. Neither verbal description nor views of the exterior and interior can evoke the awe many visitors experience on entering the PANTHEON.

Wall paintings are among the most interesting art produced during the period of the Roman Empire. The majority known to us come from Pompeii, Herculaneum, or other towns buried—and thus preserved—by the eruption of Mt. Vesuvius in 79 C.E. In the first century, Roman artists continued the late Greek tradition of portraying depth in paintings of landscapes and urban views. The ROMAN PAINTING from a villa near Naples presents a complex urban scene painted with an unsystematic form of perspective. As is typical of Roman painting, the receding lines are not systematically related to one another to create a sense of common space, nor is there controlled use of the effect of diminishing size relative to distance. Perhaps the artist intended viewers simply to enjoy the pleasing interwoven shapes, patterns, colors, and varied scale rather than to "enter" the illusory space. After the collapse of the Roman Empire, even such suggestions of space were no longer applied, and the knowledge was forgotten until it was rediscovered and developed as a scientific system during the Renaissance, more than one thousand years later.

EARLY CHRISTIAN AND BYZANTINE ART

The Romans first regarded Christianity as a strange cult and suppressed it through law. This forced the followers of Christ to worship and hide their art in underground burial chambers called *catacombs*. The earliest Christian art was a simplified interpretation of Greco-Roman figure painting, with a new emphasis on storytelling through images of Christ and other biblical figures as well as through symbols. In contrast to major changes in the size relationships between figures (*hierarchical scale*) in later

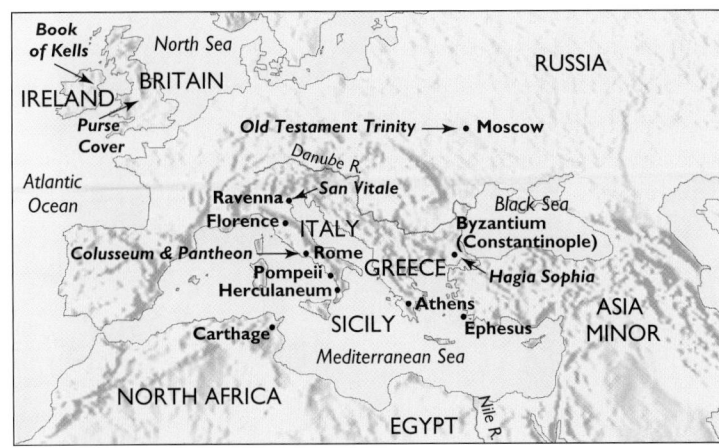

361 EUROPE FROM 117 TO 1400.

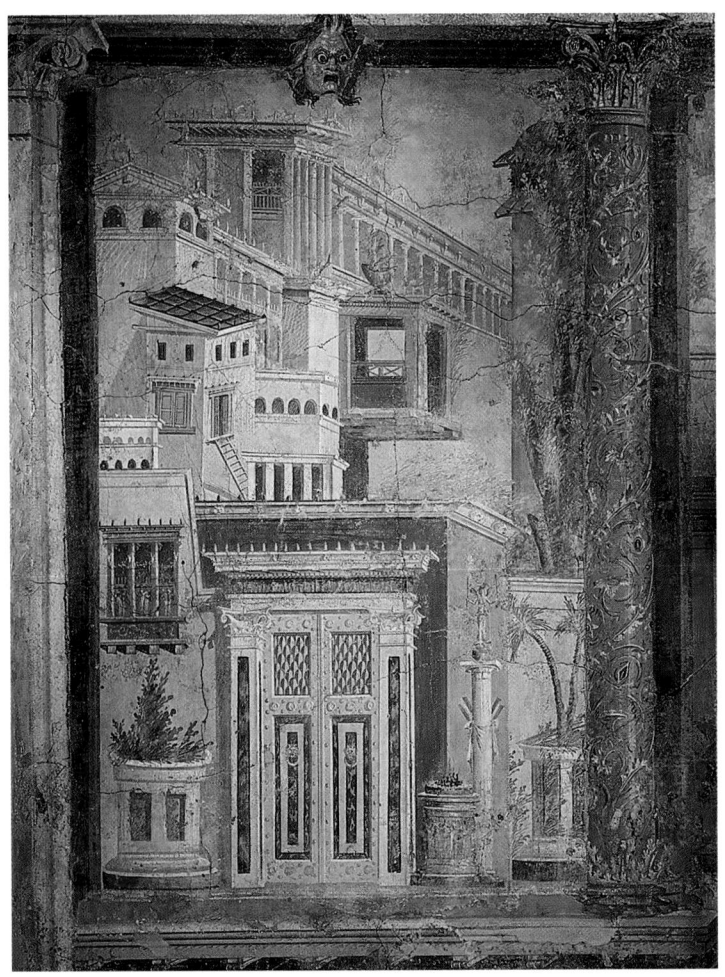

362 ROMAN PAINTING.
Detail of west wall in a villa at Boscoreale. 1st century B.C.E.
Fresco on lime plaster. Height 8′.
The Metropolitan Museum of Art, New York. Rogers Fund, 1903. 03.14.13.
Photograph: © 1986 The Metropolitan Museum of Art.

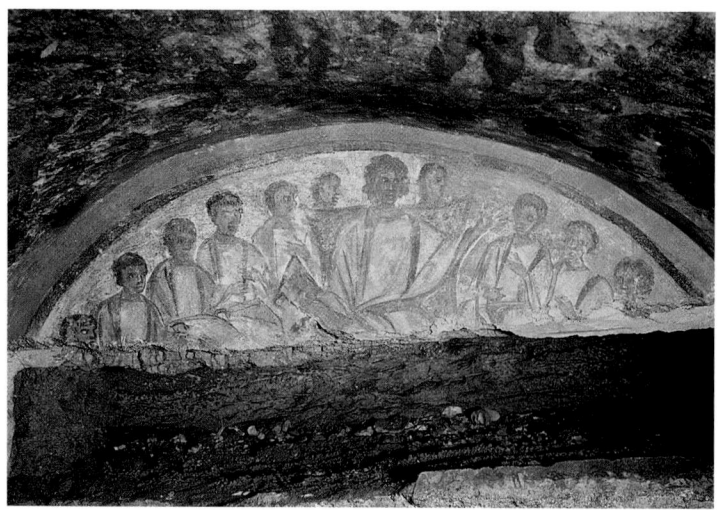

363 CHRIST TEACHING HIS DISCIPLES.
Catacomb of Domitilla, Rome. Mid-4th century C.E.
Photograph: Scala/Art Resource, NY.

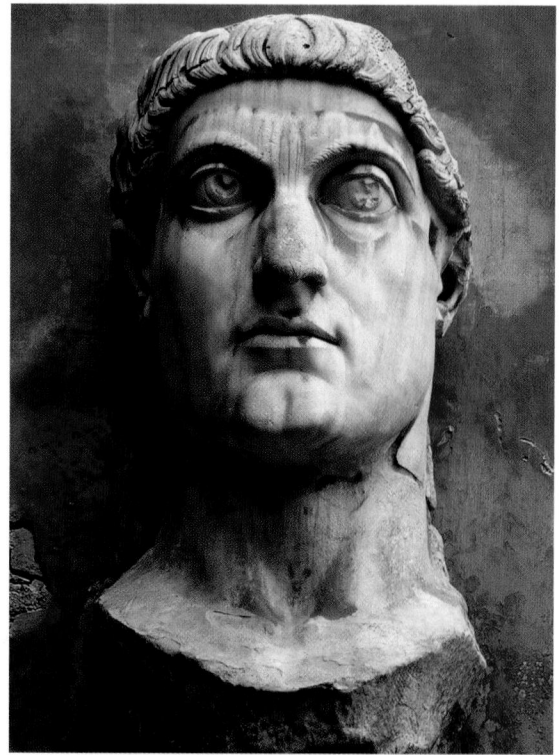

364 HEAD OF CONSTANTINE.
c. 312 C.E.
Marble. Height 8'.
Museo dei Conservatori, Rome.
Photograph: Duane Preble.

Byzantine art, CHRIST TEACHING HIS DISCIPLES shows Christ only slightly larger than the faithful who surround him.

By the time Emperor Constantine acknowledged Christianity in 312, Roman attitudes had changed considerably. The grandeur of Rome was rapidly declining. As confidence in the material world fell, people turned inward to more spiritual values. The new orientation was reflected in art such as the colossal marble HEAD OF CONSTANTINE, once part of an immense figure. The superhuman head is an image of imperial majesty, yet the large eyes and stiff features express an inner spiritual life. The late Roman style of the facial features, particularly the eyes, is very different from the naturalism of earlier Roman portraits.

In 330, Constantine moved the capital of the Roman Empire east from Rome to the city of Byzantium, which he renamed Constantinople (present-day Istanbul). Although he could not have known it, the move would effectively split the empire in two. In 395, the Roman Empire was officially divided, with one emperor in Rome and another in Constantinople—the center of what became known as Byzantium or the Byzantine empire. Over the course of the next century, the entire empire was repeatedly attacked by nomadic Germanic tribes. They placed one of their own on the Imperial throne in 476, a convenient marker for the end of the Roman Empire.

Byzantium successfully repelled its invaders; Rome was not so fortunate. Under relentless attack from the Germanic tribes, and weakened from within by military rebellions and civil wars, the political unity of the Western Roman Empire decayed, ushering in the era in Europe known as the Middle Ages.

The eastern portion of the empire, however, did not collapse. Indeed, the Byzantine Empire survived well into the fifteenth century. Founded as a Christian continuation of the Roman Empire, Byzantium developed a rich and distinctive artistic style that continues today in the mosaics, paintings, and architecture of the Orthodox church of Eastern Europe.

Not only did Constantine grant Christianity official recognition, he also sponsored an extensive building program. Thus, in the late Roman and early Byzantine empires, we find the first flowering of Christian art and architecture. For example, Christians adapted the Roman *basilica*, or assembly hall, for use in public worship. For the Romans, a basilica was a long hall flanked by columns with a semicircular *apse* at each end where government bodies and law courts met. One of the earliest Christian churches was OLD ST. PETER'S BASILICA in Rome. Its long central aisle, now called the *nave*, ends in an apse, as in a Roman building. Here, Christians placed an altar.

Round or polygonal buildings crowned with domes had been used in earlier buildings such as Roman baths, and later in the PANTHEON. Beginning in the fourth century, such buildings were built for Christian services and took on Christian meaning. Domed, central-plan churches have dominated the architecture of Eastern Orthodox Christianity ever since.

In contrast to the external grandeur of Greek and Roman temples, early Christian churches were built with an inward focus. Their plain exteriors gave no hint of the light and beauty that lay inside.

The rapid construction of many large churches created a need for large paintings or other decorations to fill their walls. Mosaic technique was perfected and widely used in Early Christian churches. Whereas other cultures knew the art of attaching pieces of colored glass and marble (tesserae) to walls and floors, early Christians used smaller tesserae, with a greater proportion of glass, in a wider range of colors. Thus they achieved a new level of brilliance and opulence.

We see the transition from Early Christian to Byzantine styles in the churches of Ravenna, an old Roman city about 80 miles south of Venice. Hoping to avoid the Germanic invasions, the Roman emperor moved his capital there in 404. When the Western empire fell in 476, Ravenna remained an important adminstrative center. However, emperor Justinian sent an army from his capital in Constantinople and reconquered it in 540, turning it into a showplace of Byzantine culture on the Italian peninsula.

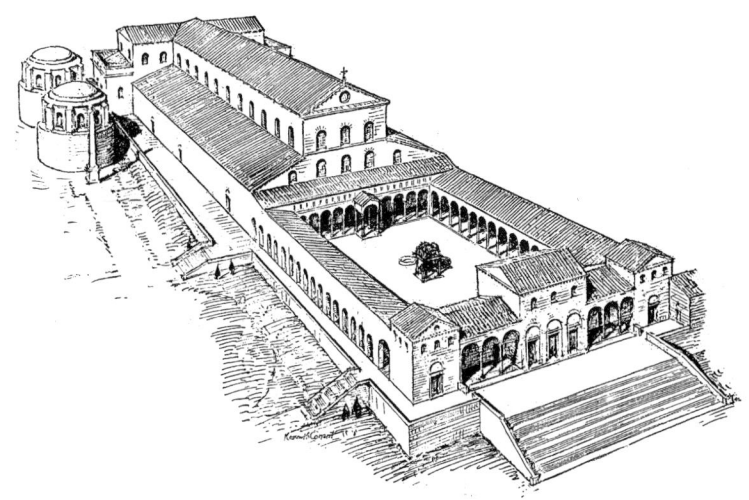

365 OLD ST. PETER'S BASILICA. Rome. c. 320–335.
   a. Reconstruction drawing.
   Restoration study by Kenneth J. Conant.
   Courtesy of the Francis Loeb Library, Graduate School of Design, Harvard University.

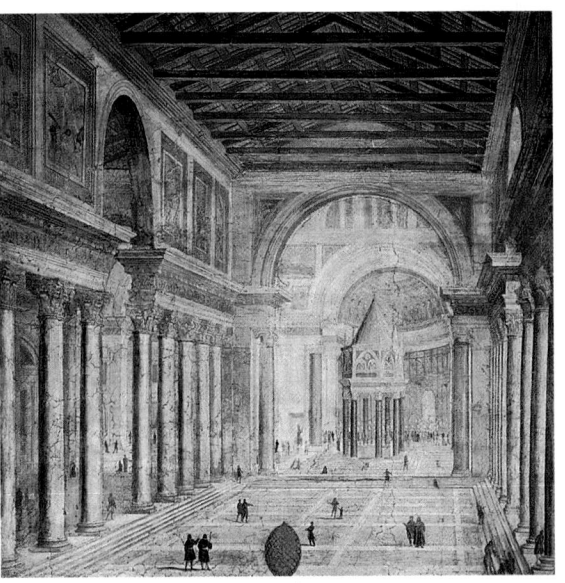

b. Interior view of basilica of Old Saint Peter's.
Fresco. S. Martino ai Monti, Rome, Italy.
Photograph: Scala/Art Resource, NY.

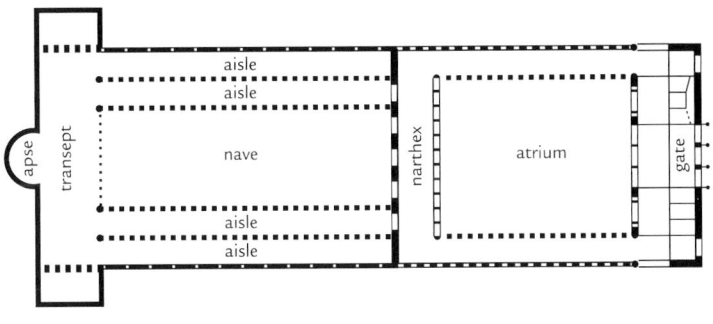

c. Plan.

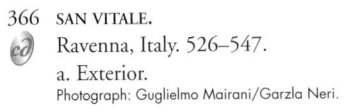

366 **SAN VITALE.**
Ravenna, Italy. 526–547.
a. Exterior.
Photograph: Guglielmo Mairani/Garzla Neri.

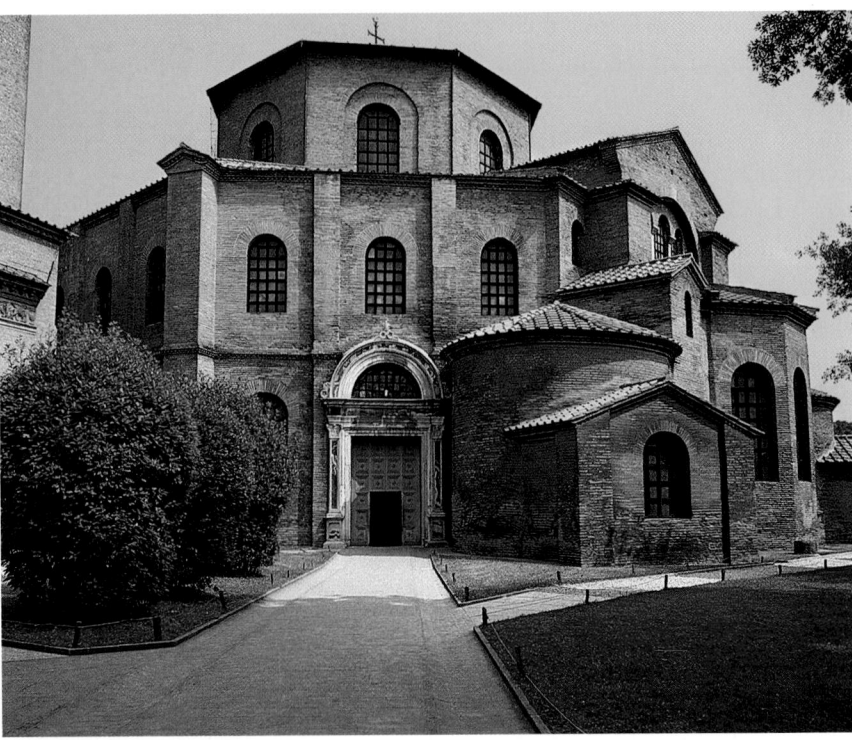

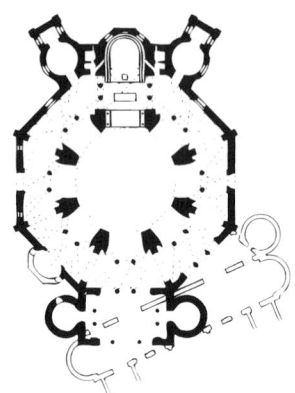
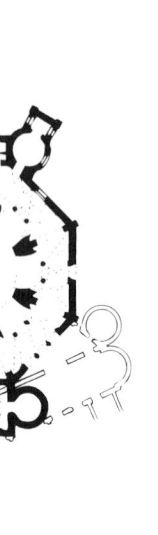

b. Plan.

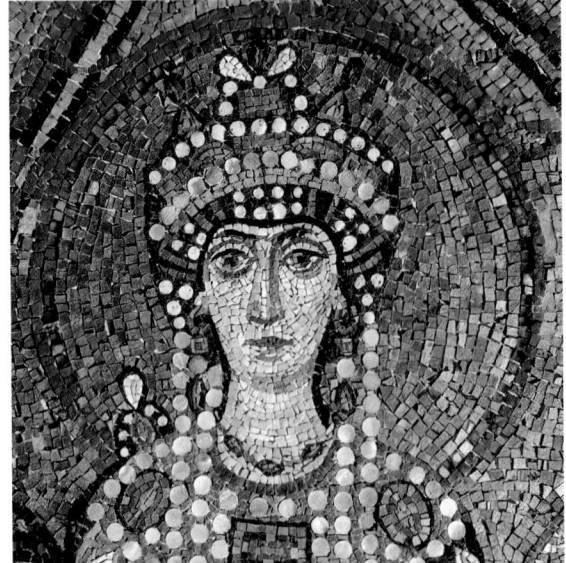

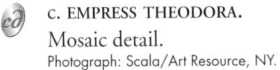
c. **EMPRESS THEODORA.**
Mosaic detail.
Photograph: Scala/Art Resource, NY.

The most important sixth-century Byzantine church is SAN VITALE in Ravenna. The glittering mosaic compositions that cover most of the interior surfaces depict the figures of Emperor Justinian and EMPRESS THEODORA in addition to religious figures and events. In a blending of religious and political authority, Justinian and Theodora are shown with halos, analogous to Christ and Mary, yet both are royally attired and bejeweled.

The elongated, abstracted figures provide symbolic rather than naturalistic depictions of the Christian and royal figures. Emphasis on the eyes is a Byzantine refinement of the stylized focus seen in the HEAD OF CONSTANTINE (page 254). Figures are depicted with heavy outline and stylized shading. The only suggestion of space has been made by overlap. Background and figures retain a flat, decorative richness typical of Byzantine art.

The arts of the Early Christian period were affected by an ongoing controversy between those who sought to follow the biblical prohibition against the making of images and those who wanted pictures to help tell the sacred stories. The

Byzantine style developed as a way of inspiring the illiterate while keeping the biblical commandment that forbids the making of graven images. The Byzantine theory was that highly stylized (abstract) and decorative images could never be confused with a real person (as a naturalistic work might be). As a result, the naturalism and sense of depth found in Roman painting gradually gave way to Byzantine stylization.

The apse mosaic in the interior of SAN VITALE shows Christ dressed in royal purple and seated on an orb that symbolizes the universe. He is beardless, in the fashion of Classical gods. With his right hand, he passes a crown to San Vitale, who stands in a depiction of the biblical paradise along with other saints and angels. The appearance of all of these figures owes something to Roman art, but in keeping with Byzantine style, they stand motionless and stare straight ahead. In their heavenly majesty, they seem to soar above human concerns. At the highest point in the aisle, where the groin vaults come together, we see a lamb, which symbolizes Christ and his self-sacrifice.

Between the sixth century and the twelfth, the Byzantine empire was wracked by the Iconoclastic Controversy, a debate over religious images that at times turned violent. In 726, Byzantine Emperor Leo III ordered the destruction of all images of Christ, Mary, the saints, and the angels. He and his party believed that such images encouraged idolatry, or worship of the image rather than the divine being. They were soon termed Iconoclasts, or image-breakers, and they punished persons who owned images by flogging or blinding them. (The Iconoclasts did not resist all decoration: they permitted jewelled crosses and pictures of leafy paradises, for example.) Those who favored images (the Iconophiles) argued that just as Christ was both god and human, an image of Christ combines the spiritual and the physical.

Although the Emperor's decree was not uniformly enforced, the controversy lasted for more

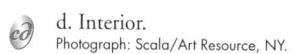

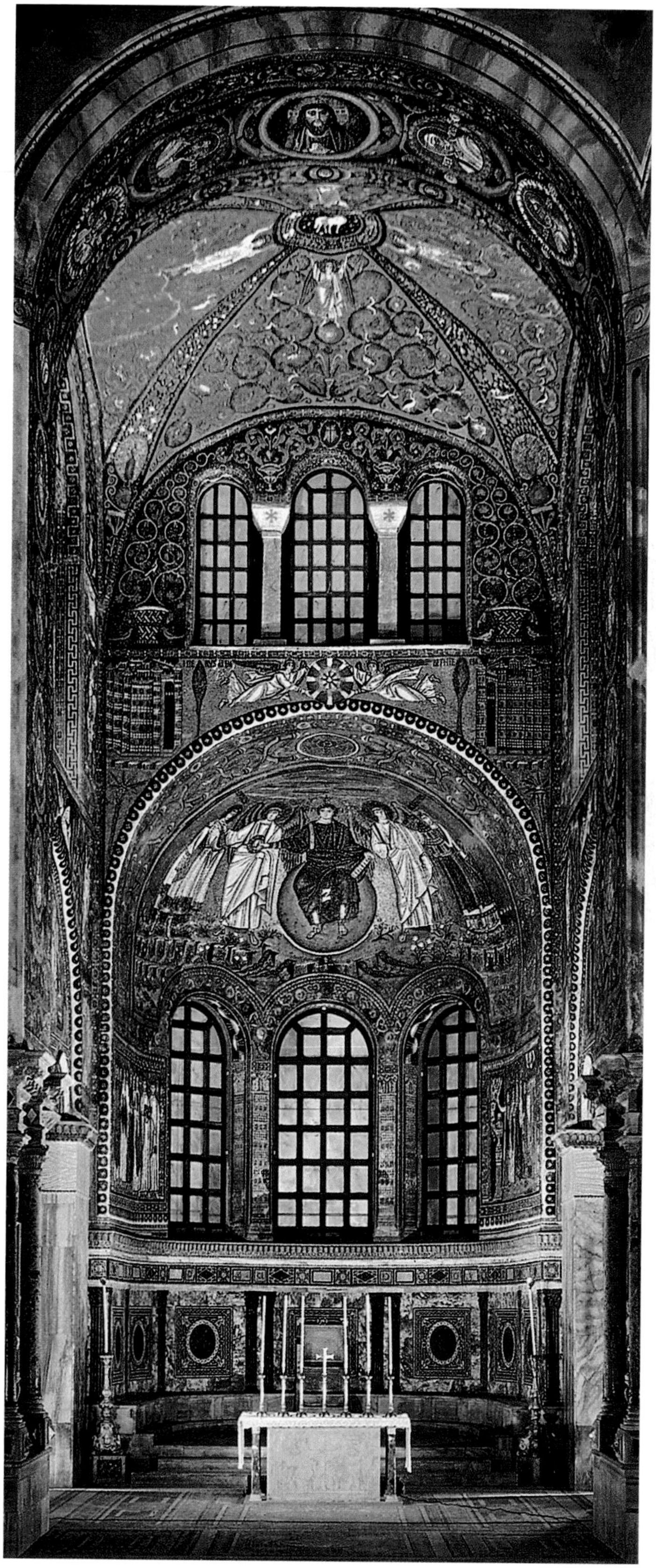

d. Interior.
Photograph: Scala/Art Resource, NY.

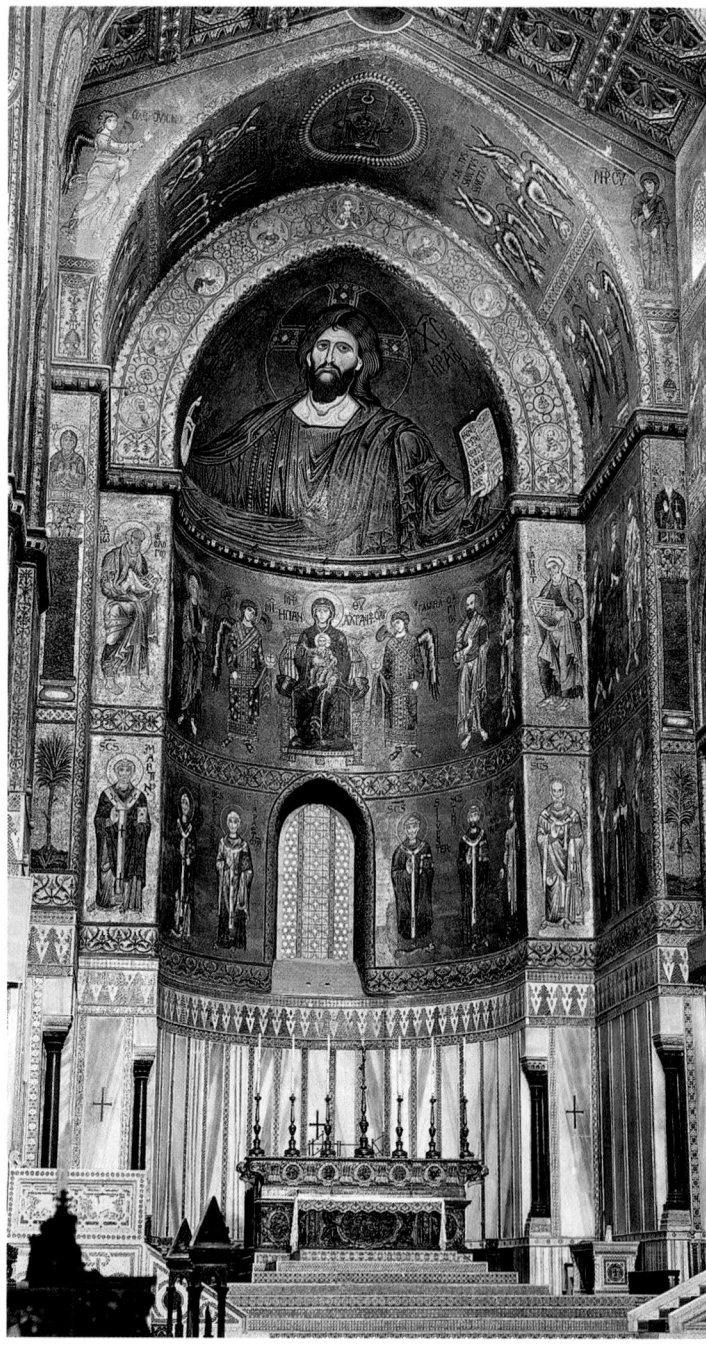

367 CHRIST AS PANTOCRATOR WITH MARY AND SAINTS.
Apse mosaic. Cathedral of Monreale, Sicily.
Late 12th century.
Photograph: Scala/Art Resource, NY.

than a hundred years, and it contributed to the split between the Roman Catholic and Eastern Orthodox churches. There was a political struggle as well: The Iconoclasts favored the Emperor's power over that of local monasteries, which were wealthy with sumptuous images. The dispute finally came to an end in 843, when Empress Theodora officially overturned Leo's decree.

As the controversy subsided, the inside of the dome of Hagia Sophia was adorned with a new kind of image, Christ as ruler of the universe—Christ as Pantocrator. This mosaic (now destroyed) became the inspiration for similar portrayals in smaller Byzantine churches such as the Cathedral of Monreale, Sicily, where the mosaic of CHRIST AS PANTOCRATOR WITH MARY AND SAINTS shows typical Byzantine style employing hierarchic scale to express the greater magnitude of Christ relative to Mary, the saints, and angels portrayed in rows below him.

By the tenth and eleventh centuries, Byzantine artists had created a distinct style that expressed Eastern Orthodox Christianity and also met the needs of a lavish court. The style had its roots in the Early Christian art of the late Roman Empire, as we have seen. But it also absorbed Eastern influences, particularly the flat patterns and nonrepresentational designs of Islam. Eastern influence continued with the hierarchical sizing and placement of subject matter in Byzantine church decoration.

The Byzantine style is still followed by painters and others working within the tradition of the Eastern Orthodox church. Clergy closely supervise the iconography and permit little room for individual interpretation. Artists of the Eastern Orthodox faith seek to portray the symbolic or mystical aspects of religious figures rather than their physical qualities. The figures are painted in conformity to a precise formula. Small paintings, referred to as *icons* (from the Greek *eikon*, meaning image), are holy images that inspire devotion but are not worshiped in themselves. The making of portable icon paintings grew out of mosaic and fresco traditions.

Even within the relatively tight stylistic confines of the Orthodox style, occasionally an artist is

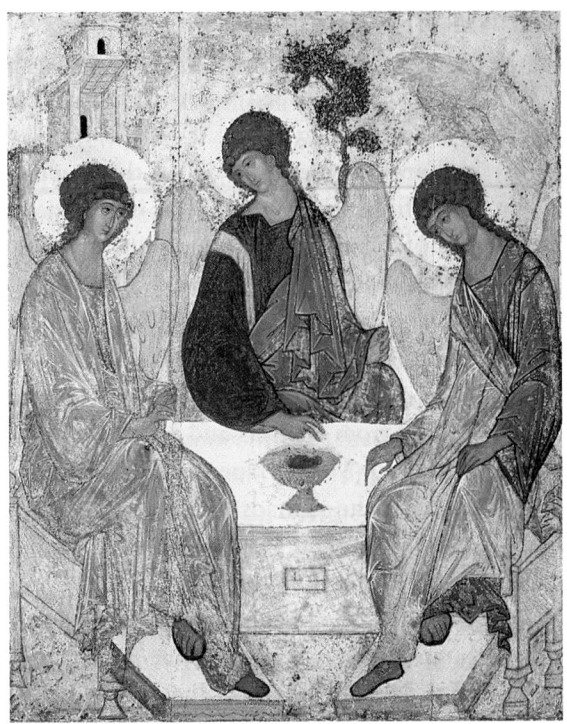

368 Andrei Rublev.
OLD TESTAMENT TRINITY. c. 1410–1420.
Tempera on panel. 55½″ × 44½″.
Tretyakov Gallery, Moscow.
Photograph: Scala/Art Resource, NY.

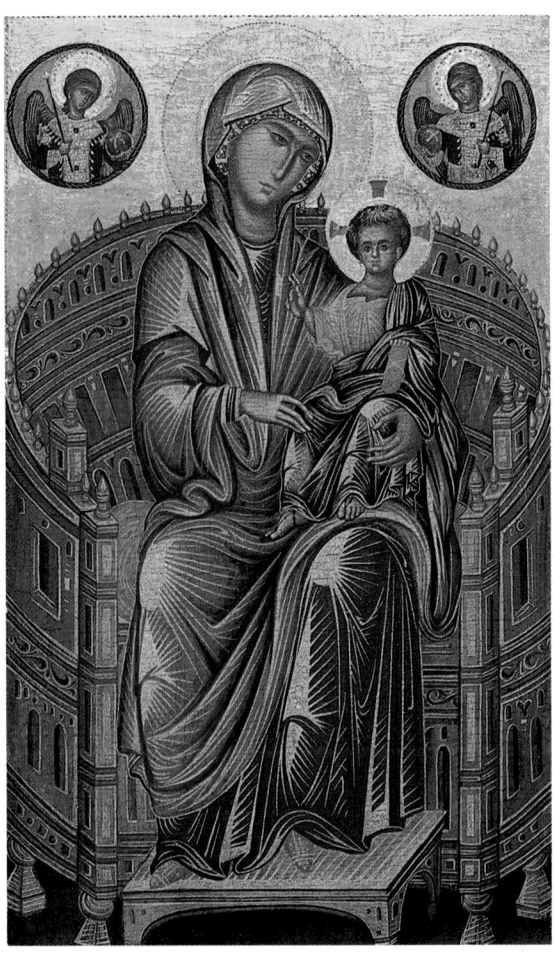

369 Byzantine School.
MADONNA AND CHILD ON A CURVED THRONE.
Byzantine, 13th century.
Tempera on panel.
32⅛″ × 19⅜″; framed 35¾″ × 22¹⁵⁄₁₆″ × 3″.
Photograph © 2001 Board of Trustees, National Gallery of Art, Washington, D.C.
Andrew W. Mellon Collection. 1937.1.1.(1)/PA.

able to make icons that not only have the required easy readability but also communicate powerful feeling. Such an artist was Andrei Rublev, one of the most highly regarded painters in Russian history. His OLD TESTAMENT TRINITY depicts a story in which Jewish patriarch Abraham entertained three strangers who later turned out to be angels: Christians have seen this story as foreshadowing their doctrine of the trinity. Rublev gave the scene a sweetness and tenderness through subtle facial expressions and elongation of bodies. The bright colors add intensity to the work, even in its present poor state.

The design of the icon painting MADONNA AND CHILD ON A CURVED THRONE is based on circular shapes and linear patterns. Mary's head repeats the circular shape of her halo; circles of similar size enclose angels, echoing the larger circle of the throne. The lines and shapes used in the draped robes that cover the figures give scarcely a hint of the bodies beneath. Divine light is symbolized by the gold background that surrounds the throne in which the Virgin Mary sits. The large architectural throne symbolizes Mary's position as Queen of the City of Heaven. Christ appears as a wise little man, supported on the lap of a heavenly, supernatural mother.

In order that they be worthy of dedication to God, icons are usually made of precious materials. Gold leaf was used here for the background and costly lapis lazuli for the Virgin's robe.

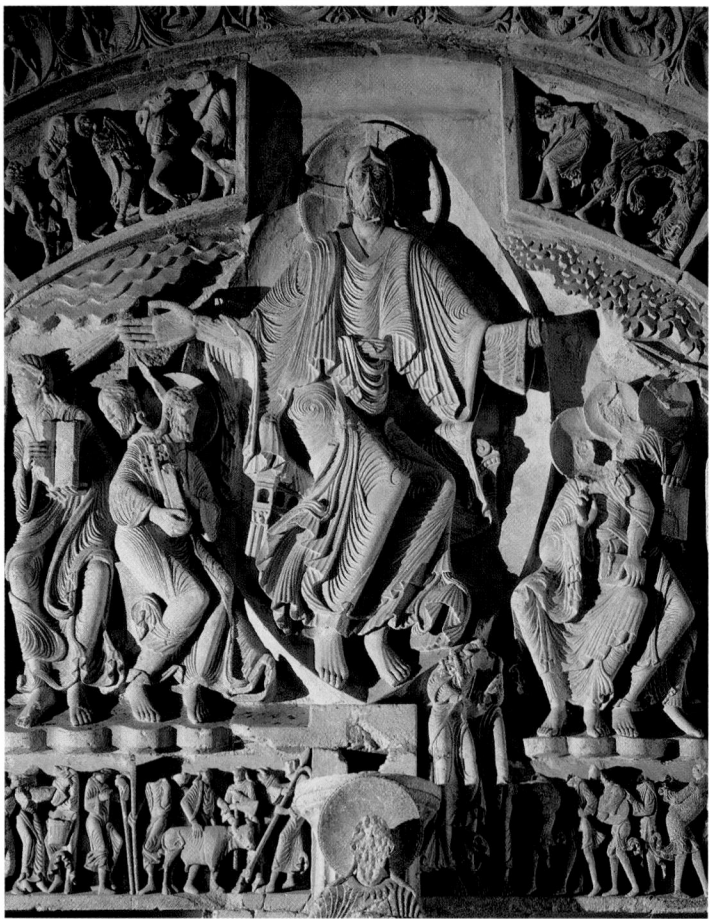

373 Detail of CHRIST OF THE PENTECOST.
Saint Madeleine Cathedral, Vézelay, France. 1125–1150.
Stone. Height of the tympanum 35½″.
Photograph: Dagli Orti. Picture Desk, Inc./Kobal Collection.

Romanesque churches feature imaginative stone carvings that are an integral part of the architecture. Subjects and models came from miniature paintings in illuminated texts, but sculptors gradually added a degree of naturalism not found in earlier medieval work. In addition to stylized and at times naive figures from biblical stories, relief carvings include strange beasts and decorative plant forms. The largest and most elaborate figures were placed over the central doorways of churches. Such figures were the first large sculpture since Roman times.

Deviation from standard human proportions enabled sculptors to give appropriately symbolic form to figures such as CHRIST OF THE PENTECOST. The mystical energy and compassion of Christ are expressed in this relief carving above the doorway of Saint Madeleine Cathedral at Vézelay, France. As worshippers enter the sanctuary, the image above them depicts Christ at the time he asked the Apostles and all Christians to take his message to the world. The image of Christ is larger in scale than the other figures, showing his relative importance. The sculptor achieved a monumental quality by making the head smaller than normal and by elongating the entire figure. Swirling folds of drapery are indicated with precise curves and spirals that show the continuing influence of the linear energy of the animal style and the CHI-RHO MONOGRAM. In abstract terms, the spiraling motion suggests Christ's cosmic power. (See the *Discovering Art* CD for a video demonstration of medieval architecture of the Romanesque and succeeding Gothic periods.)

Gothic

We see the restless energy of Europeans in the frequent changes in attitude that resulted in the changing styles of Western art. The Romanesque style had lasted barely a hundred years when the Gothic style began to replace it in about 1145. The shift is seen most clearly in architecture, as the Romanesque round arch was superseded by the pointed Gothic arch, developed in the mid-twelfth century (discussed on page 217).

Gothic cathedrals were expressions of a new age of faith that grew out of medieval Christian theology and mysticism. The light-filled, upward-reaching structures symbolize the triumph of the spirit over the bonds of earthly life, evoking a sense of joyous spiritual elation. Inside, the faithful must have felt they had actually arrived at the visionary Heavenly City.

Gothic cathedrals such as NOTRE DAME DE CHARTRES (Our Lady of Chartres) were the center of community life. In many cases, they were the

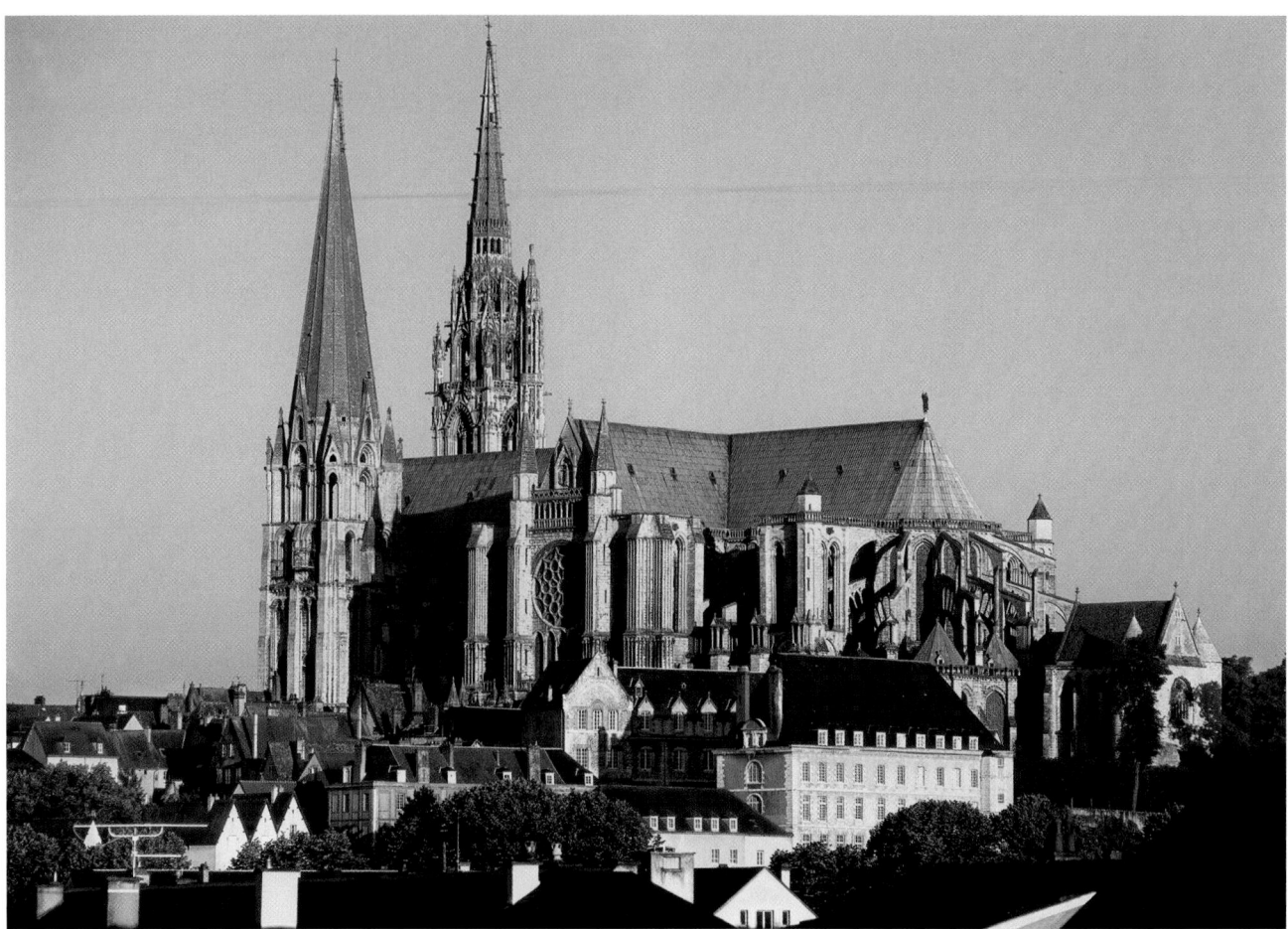

374 NOTRE DAME DE CHARTRES.
Chartres, France. 1145–1513.
Cathedral length 427'; facade height 157'; south tower height 344'; north tower height 377'.
a. View from the southeast.
© John Elk, III.

only indoor space that could hold all the townspeople at once; thus, they were used for meetings, concerts, and religious plays. But most of all, they were places of worship. Above the town of Chartres, the cathedral rises, its spires visible for miles around.

The entire community cooperated in the building of NOTRE DAME DE CHARTRES, although those who began its construction never saw its final form. The cathedral continued to grow and change in major ways for more than three hundred years. Although the basic plan is symmetrical and logically organized, the architecture of CHARTRES has a rich, enigmatic complexity that is quite different from the easily grasped totality of the classical PARTHENON.

Chartres was partially destroyed by fire in 1194 and then rebuilt in the High Gothic style. One of the first cathedrals based on the full Gothic system, it helped set the standard for Gothic architecture in Europe. In its WEST FRONT, Chartres reveals the transition between the early and late phases of Gothic architecture. The massive lower walls and

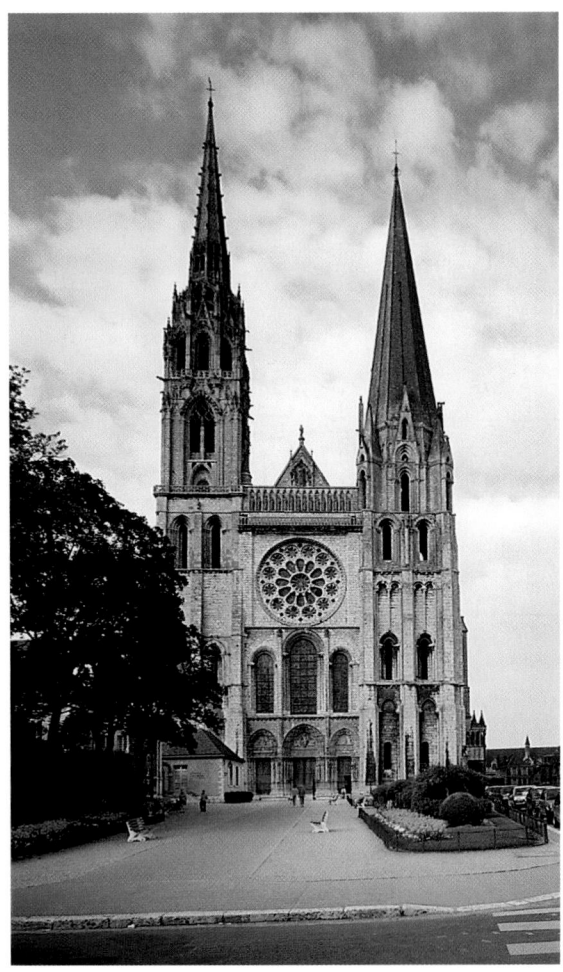

b. WEST FRONT.
Photograph: Duane Preble.

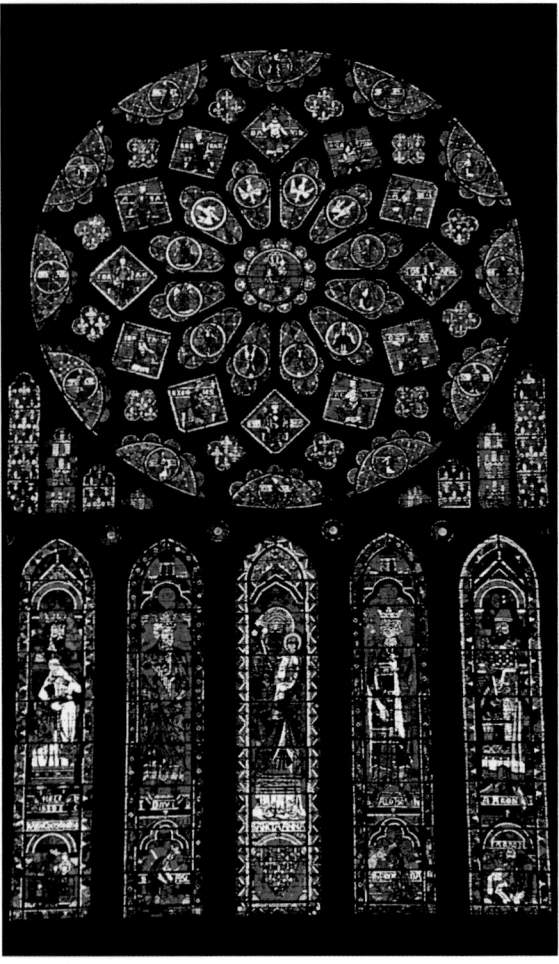

c. "ROSE DE FRANCE" WINDOW. c. 1233.
Photograph: Duane Preble.

round arch portals were built in the mid-twelfth century. The north tower (on the left) was rebuilt with the intricate flamelike or *flamboyant* curves of the late Gothic style early in the sixteenth century, after the original tower collapsed in 1506.

Magnificent stained-glass windows of this period are so well integrated with the architecture that one is inconceivable without the other. The scriptures are told in imagery that transforms the sanctuary with showers of color, changing hour by hour. At Chartres, the brilliant north rose window, known as the ROSE DE FRANCE, is dedicated to the Virgin Mary, who sits in majesty, surrounded by doves, angels, and royal figures of the celestial hierarchy. See also the interior photo on page 217.

The statues of the OLD TESTAMENT PROPHET, KINGS, AND QUEEN to the right of the central doorway at the west entrance of CHARTRES are among the most impressive remaining examples of early Gothic sculpture. The kings and queen suggest Christ's royal heritage and also honor French monarchs of the time. The prophet on the left depicts Christ's mission as an apostle of God. In contrast to active, emotional Romanesque sculpture, the figures are passive and serene. Their elongated forms allow them to blend readily with the vertical emphasis of the architecture.

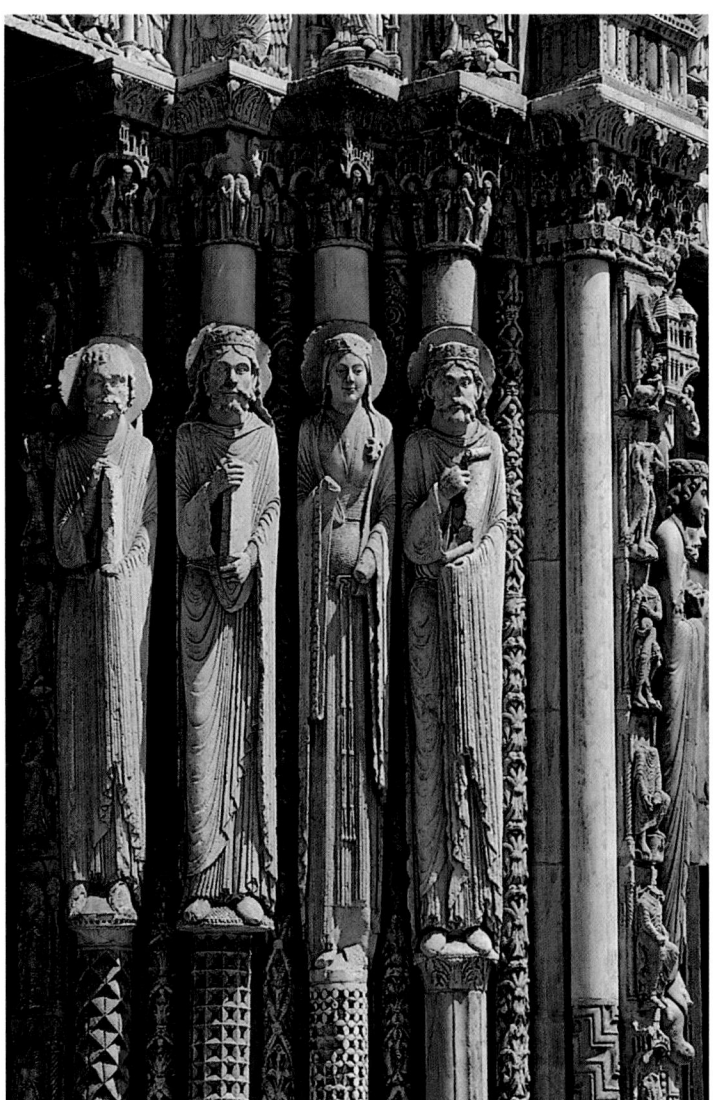

 d. OLD TESTAMENT PROPHET, KINGS, AND QUEEN.
c. 1145–1170.
Doorjamb statues from West (or Royal) Portal.
Photograph: Duane Preble.

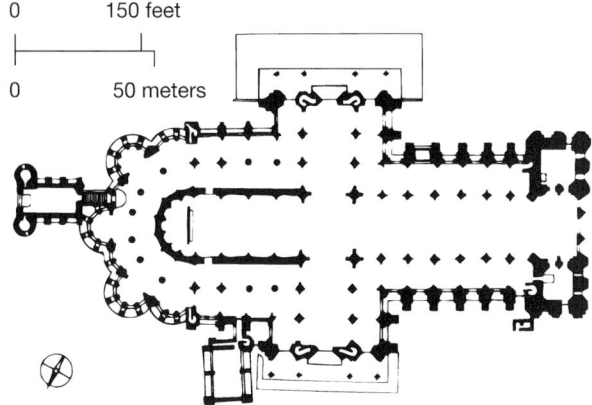

e. Plan based on Latin cross.

Although they are part of the total scheme, the figures stand out from the columns behind them. Their draped bodies, and especially their heads, reveal a developing interest in portraying human features. Such interest eventually led again to full portraiture and freestanding figures.

The cathedral relates to an idea expressed by Abbot Suger, the man credited with starting the Gothic era. At the Abbey church of St. Denis, where Suger began the Gothic style, he had an inscription placed on the entrance door stating his idea of the church's spiritual purpose:

Whoever you may be, if you are minded to praise this door,
Wonder not at the gold, nor at the cost, but at the work.
The work shines in its nobility; by shining nobly,
May it illumine the spirit, so that, through its trusty lights,
The spirit may reach the true Light in which Christ is the Door.
The golden door proclaims the nature of the Inward:
Through sensible things, the heavy spirit is raised to the truth;
From the depths, it rises to the light.[2]

RENAISSANCE AND BAROQUE EUROPE

A shift in attitude occurred in Europe as the religious fervor of the Middle Ages was increasingly challenged by logical thought and the new philosophical, literary, and artistic movement called *humanism*. Leading humanist scholars did not discard theological concerns, yet they supported the secular dimensions of life, pursued intellectual and scientific inquiry, and rediscovered the classical literature and art of Greece and Rome. The focus gradually shifted from God and the hereafter to humankind and the here and now.

THE RENAISSANCE

For many Europeans, the Renaissance was a period of achievement and worldwide exploration—a time of discovery and rediscovery of the world and of the seemingly limitless potential of individual human beings. The period began to take shape in the fourteenth century, reached its clear beginning in the early fifteenth century, and came to an end in the early seventeenth century. However, Renaissance thinking continues to influence our lives today, not only in Western countries but in all parts of the world where individualism, modern science, and technology influence the way people live. In art, new and more scientific approaches were brought to the quest for representational accuracy. The resulting naturalism dominated Western art for more than four hundred years.

The intellectuals of the time were the first in European history to give their own era an identifying name. They named their period the *Renaissance*—literally, Rebirth—an apt description for the period of revived interest in the art and ideas of classical Greece and Rome. Fifteenth-century Italians believed they were responsible for the rebirth of "the glory of ancient Greece," which they considered the high point of Western civilization. In fact, classical Greek books about philosophy, astronomy, mathematics, and medicine did not disappear completely, although medieval Christians neglected them. Muslim scholars in Spain, Egypt, and Iraq maintained respect for the Greeks and translated their works into Arabic for their libraries. Muslim and European scholars of the thirteenth and fourteenth centuries then recovered these works and made them available in Latin. In essence, the Renaissance was a period of new and renewed understanding that transformed the medieval European world, and laid the foundation for modern society.

In art, we can trace the beginnings of this new attitude to the fourteenth century. Whereas Gothic and Byzantine painters continued to employ relatively flat symbolic styles, Gothic sculptors were moving from stylized abstraction toward greater naturalism and individuality in their figures.

The humanist enthusiasm for classical antiquity and a growing secularism led to revolutionary thinking in many areas. The first writer to reveal evidence of Renaissance thinking was the Italian poet Dante Alighieri, who lived during the thirteenth and fourteenth centuries and belonged primarily to the

Middle Ages. The last major writer of the Renaissance was William Shakespeare, who lived three centuries later.

New values combined with technological advances brought forth a new style of art. Painting and sculpture were liberated from their medieval roles as supplements to architecture. Artists, who had been viewed as anonymous workers in the Middle Ages, came to be seen as individuals of creative genius.

The art of the Renaissance evolved in different ways in northern and southern Europe because the people of the two regions had different backgrounds, attitudes, and experiences. The Gothic style reached its high point in the north while Byzantine and Greco-Roman influences remained strong in the south. Italian Renaissance art grew from classical Mediterranean traditions that were human-centered and often emphasized monumentality and the ideal. In contrast, the art of the northern Renaissance evolved out of pre-Christian, nature-centered religions that became God-centered through conversion to Christianity.

The earliest precursor of the Renaissance was Italian painter and architect Giotto di Bondone, known as Giotto. He departed from the abstract, Byzantine style by portraying the feelings and physical nature of human beings. His innovative depictions of light, space, and mass gave a new sense of realism to painting. In LAMENTATION, Giotto depicted physical as well as spiritual reality. His figures are shown as individuals within a shallow, stagelike space, and their expressions portray personal feelings of grief not often seen in medieval art.

In retrospect, Giotto is considered not only a precursor of the Renaissance, but also the reinventor of naturalistic painting, which had not been seen in Europe since the decline of Rome a thousand years earlier. This "realism" is still an important current in Western painting.

The ancient Greeks had been concerned with idealized physical form; Roman artists had emphasized physical accuracy; and artists of the Middle Ages had focused on spiritual concerns rather than physical existence. In the Renaissance, as attention shifted from heaven to earth, artists portrayed

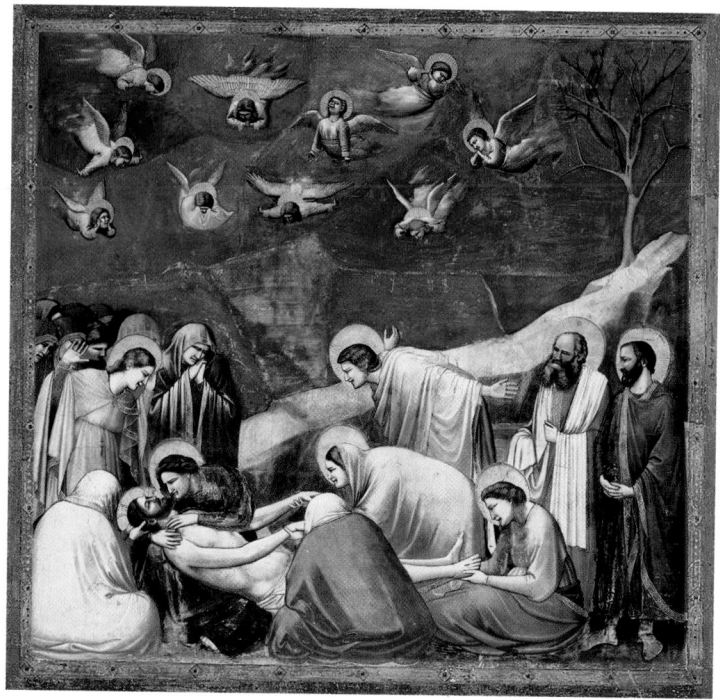

375   Giotto di Bondone. LAMENTATION.
Scrovegni Chapel, Padua, Italy. c. 1305.
Fresco. 72″ × 78″.
Photograph: Alinori/Art Resource, NY.

Christian subjects in human terms. Italian leaders expressed a desire to equal or surpass the glory of ancient Greece and Rome and to imbue their achievements with the light of Christian understanding.

Italy was the principal homeland of the Renaissance. In time the movement spread northward, but it did not flourish everywhere in Europe; it came late to Spain and Portugal, and it barely touched Scandinavia.

The Renaissance in Italy

Artistic and intellectual developments in the Italian city-states were aided by a flourishing economy set against a divided and chaotic political background. The wealth of Italian merchants enabled them to compete with one another, and with church officials and nobility, for the recognition and power that came with art patronage.

Italian architects, sculptors, and painters sought to integrate Christian spiritual traditions with the rational ordering of physical life in earthly space. Artists began an intense study of anatomy and light,

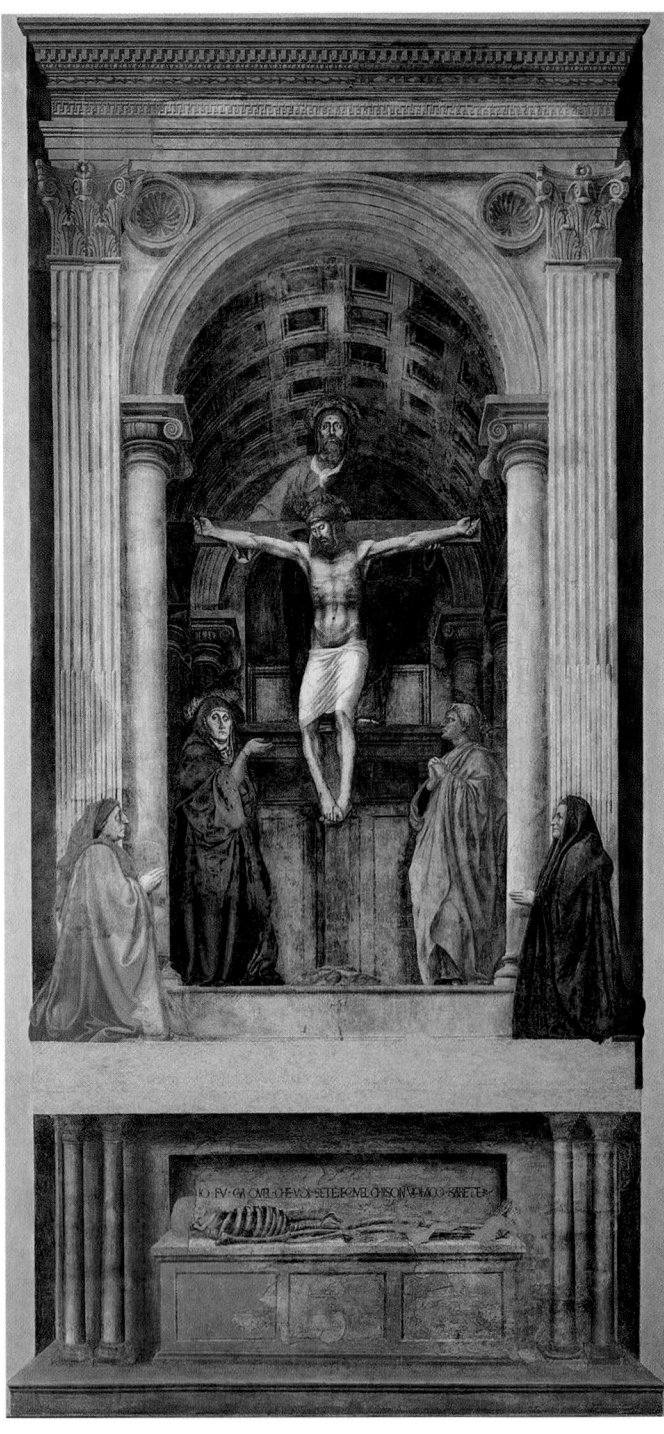

376 Masaccio.
THE HOLY TRINITY.
Santa Maria Novella, Florence. 1425.
Fresco. 21′10½″ × 10′5″.
Photograph: Scala/Art Resource, NY.

and they applied geometry to the logical construction of implied space through the use of linear perspective (see page 272). In turn, the careful observation of nature initiated by Renaissance artists aided the growth of science.

About one hundred years after Giotto, Masaccio became the first major painter of the Italian Renaissance. In his fresco THE HOLY TRINITY, the composition is centered on an open chapel in which we see the Trinity; God the father, Christ the son, and between their heads a white dove symbolizing the Holy Spirit. Within the niche, Mary the mother of Jesus stands, gesturing to Christ; opposite her is St. John. Kneeling outside are the donors who paid for the painting, a husband and wife who headed a powerful banking family of that time. He is wearing the red robe that marks him as a member of the Florence city council. Below, a skeleton is lying on a sarcophagus beneath the inscription, "I was what you are, and what I am you shall become." If we view the painting from top to bottom, we move from spiritual reality to temporal reality.

THE HOLY TRINITY was the first painting based on the systematic use of linear perspective. Although perspective was known to the Romans in a limited way, it did not become a consistent science until architect Filippo Brunelleschi rediscovered and developed it in Florence early in the fifteenth century. Masaccio used perspective to construct an illusion of figures in three-dimensional space. The single vanishing point is below the base of the cross, about five feet above ground, at the viewer's eye level. Masaccio's perspective is so precise that we can see the interior of the illusionary chapel as a believable extension of the space we occupy. The setting also reveals Masaccio's knowledge of the new Renaissance architecture developed by Brunelleschi, which he based on Roman prototypes.

The figures in THE HOLY TRINITY have a physical presence that shows what Masaccio learned from the work of Giotto. In Giotto's work, however, body and drapery still appear as one; Masaccio's figures are clothed nudes, with garments draped like real fabric.

During the Italian Renaissance, the nude became a major subject for art, as it had been in Greece and Rome. Unclothed subjects are rare in medieval art and appear awkward, their bodies graceless. In contrast, sculpted and painted figures by Italian Renaissance artists appear as strong and natural as the Greek and Roman nudes that inspired them.

The great range and vitality of work by sculptor Donatello had a lasting influence on later Renaissance sculpture and on European sculpture and painting for four centuries. Donatello brought the Greek ideal of what it means to be human into the Christian context. As a young adult he made two trips to Rome, where he studied medieval (Byzantine, Romanesque, and Gothic) as well as classical Greek and Roman art.

Donatello shows himself as an ambitious artist even in his early work. His bronze figure of DAVID was the first life-size, freestanding nude statue since Roman times. In it Donatello went beyond the classical ideal by including the dimension of personal expressiveness.

Although he was greatly attracted to the classical ideal in art, Donatello's sculpture was less idealized and more naturalistic than that of ancient Greece. He chose to portray the biblical shepherd, David—slayer of the giant Goliath and later king of the Jews—as an adolescent youth rather than as a robust young man. The sculptor celebrated the sensuality of the boy's body by clothing him only in hat and boots. It is not so much the face, but every shift in the figure's weight and angle that is expressive. The youth's position is derived from classical contrapposto. The few nudes that appeared in medieval art showed little sensual appeal and often portrayed shame and lust. Under the influence of humanist scholars who sought to surpass the Greeks and Romans in the nobility of form, the nude became a symbol of human worth and divine perfection, a representation of the "immortal soul."

During the Renaissance, artists received growing support from the new class of wealthy merchants and bankers, such as the Medici family, who, with great political skill and a certain ruthlessness, dominated the life of Florence and Tuscany. It is likely that Donatello created his bronze

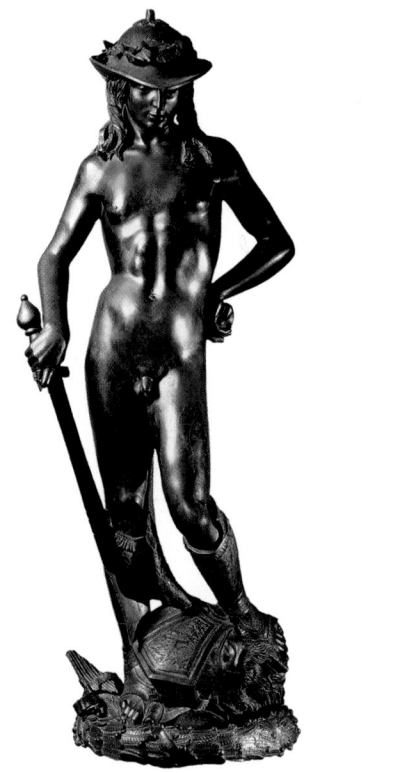
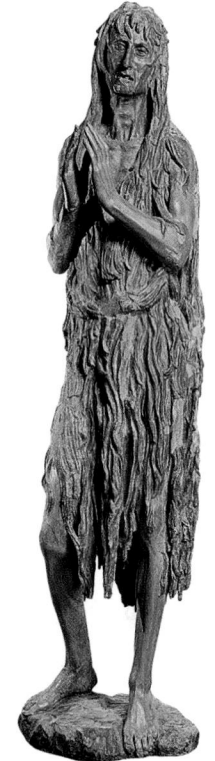

377 Donatello.
DAVID. c. 1425–1430.
Bronze. Height 62¼".
Museo Nazionale del Bargello, Florence. Photograph: Scala/Art Resource, NY.

378 Donatello.
MARY MAGDALEN. c. 1455.
Wood, partially gilded. Height 74".
Museo dell'Opera del Duomo, Florence. Photograph: Scala/Art Resource, NY.

DAVID as a private commission for Cosimo de Medici, for the courtyard of the Medici palace.

A major influence on Donatello and other Renaissance artists was the renewal of Neoplatonist philosophy, embraced by the Medici family and their circle of philosophers, artists, historians, and humanists. These intellectuals believed that all sources of inspiration or revelation, whether from the Bible or classical mythology, are a means of ascending from earthly existence to mystical union with "the One." In this context, Donatello's DAVID was intended to be a symbol of divine beauty.

Donatello's work displayed a wide range of expression, from lyric joy to tragedy to extremes of religious passion. In contrast to the youthful and somewhat brash DAVID, Donatello's MARY MAGDALEN

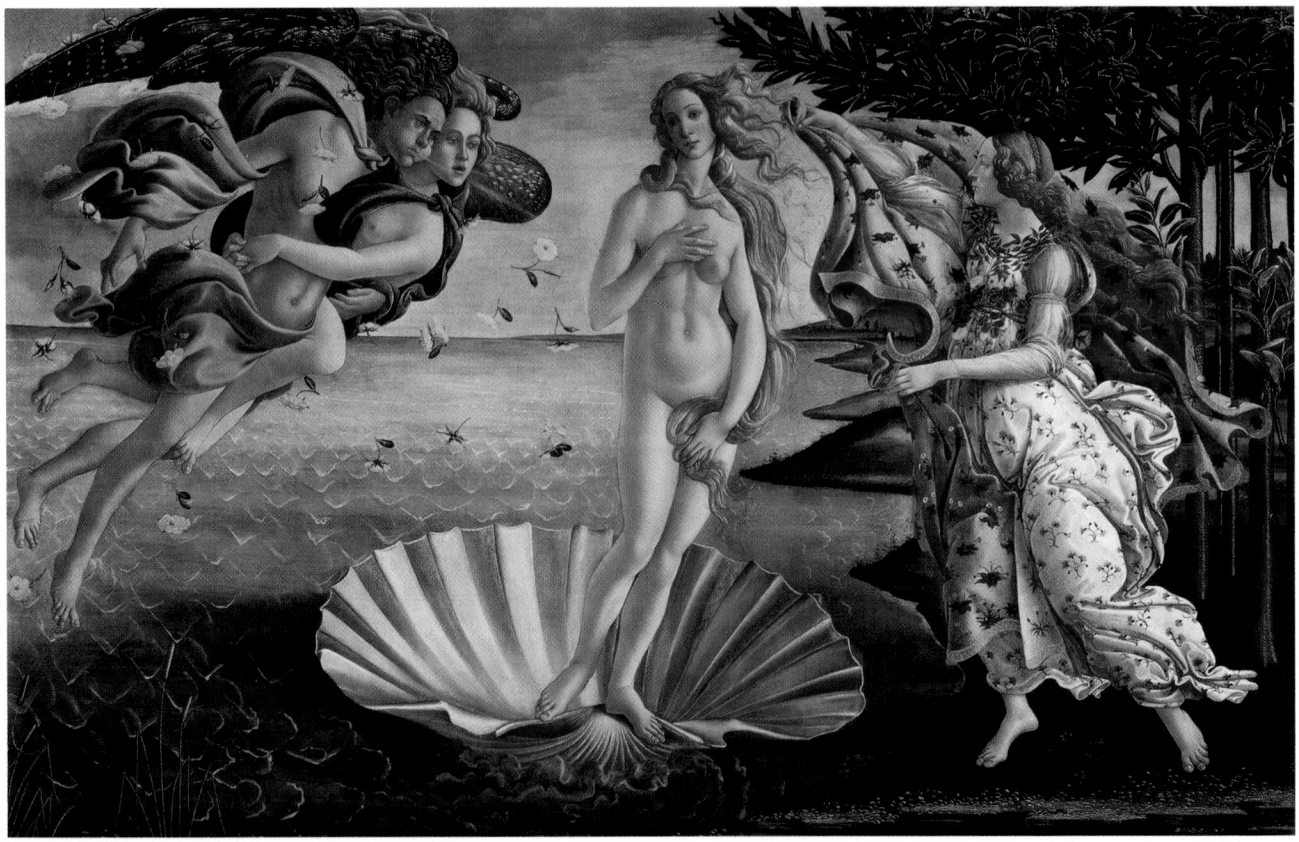

379   Sandro Botticelli.
BIRTH OF VENUS. c. 1480.
Tempera on canvas. 5′8⅞″ × 9′1⅞″.
Uffizi Gallery, Florence.
Photograph: Scala/Art Resource, NY.

is haggard and withdrawn—a forcefully expressive figure of old age and repentance. For this late work, Donatello chose painted wood, the favorite medium of northern Gothic sculptors.

Another Medici commission is Sandro Botticelli's BIRTH OF VENUS, one of the first paintings of an almost life-size nude since antiquity. The large painting, completed about 1480, depicts the Roman goddess of love just after she was born from the sea. She is being blown to shore by a couple symbolizing the wind. As she arrives, Venus is greeted by a young woman who represents Spring. The lyric grace of Botticelli's lines shows Byzantine influence. The background is decorative and flat, giving almost no illusion of deep space. The figures appear to be in relief, not fully three-dimensional.

The posture and gestures of modesty were probably inspired by a third-century B.C.E. Greco-Roman sculpture of Venus that Botticelli must have seen in the Medici family collection (see page 248). In her posture of introspection and repose, Botticelli's Venus combines the classical Greek idealized human figure with a Renaissance concern for thought and feeling.

To place a nude "pagan" goddess at the center of a large painting, in a position previously reserved for the Virgin Mary, was revolutionary. Botticelli's focus on classical mythology was—like Donatello's—based on Neoplatonist philosophy, a central preoccupation of the business-oriented, secular art patrons who commissioned most Renaissance art.

The High Renaissance

Between about 1490 and 1530—the period known as the High Renaissance—Italian art reached a peak of accomplishment in the cities of Florence, Rome, and Venice. The three artists who epitomized the period were Leonardo, Michelangelo, and Raphael. They developed a style of art that was calm, balanced, and idealized, reconciling Christian theology with Greek philosophy and the science of the day.

Leonardo da Vinci was motivated by strong curiosity and an optimistic belief in the human ability to understand the fascinating phenomena of the physical world. He believed that art and science are two means to the same end: knowledge.

Leonardo showed his investigative and creative mind in his journals, where he documented his research in notes and drawings (see also pages 20 and 103). His notebooks are filled with studies of anatomy and ideas for mechanical devices, explorations that put him in the forefront of the scientific development of his time. His study of THE INFANT IN THE WOMB has a few errors, yet much of the drawing is so accurate that it could serve as an example in one of today's medical textbooks.

Leonardo was one of the first to give a clear description of the *camera obscura* (see page 145), an optical device that captures light images in much the same way as the human eye. The concept of photography began with the Renaissance desire to create an equivalent to our visual perception of reality.

So frequently has Leonardo's world-famous portrait of MONA LISA been reproduced that it has become a cliché and the source of innumerable spoofs. Despite this overexposure, it still merits careful attention. It was one of Leonardo's favorite paintings. We can still be intrigued by the mysterious mood evoked by the faint smile and the strange, other-worldly landscape. The ambiguity is heightened by the hazy light quality that gives a sense of atmosphere around the figure. This soft blurring of the edges—in Leonardo's words, "without lines or borders in the manner of smoke"—achieved through subtle value gradations, is called *sfumato* and was invented by Leonardo.[1] MONA

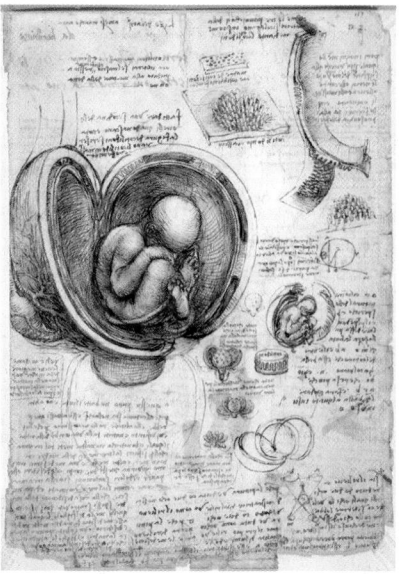

380 Leonardo da Vinci.
THE INFANT IN THE WOMB. c. 1510.
Pen and ink. 11⅞″ × 8⅜″.
The Royal Collection
© 2004 Her Majesty Queen Elizabeth II.
Photograph: EZM. RL19102r.

381 Leonardo da Vinci.
MONA LISA.
c. 1503–1506.
Oil on wood.
30¼″ × 21″.
Musée du Louvre, Paris.
Photograph: Scala/Art Resource, NY.

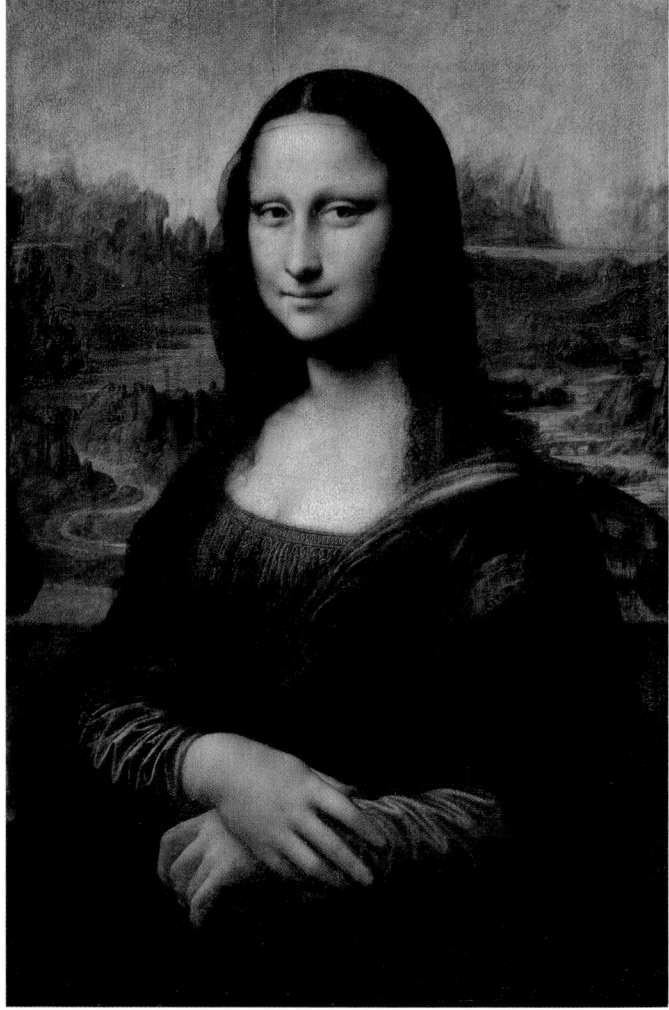

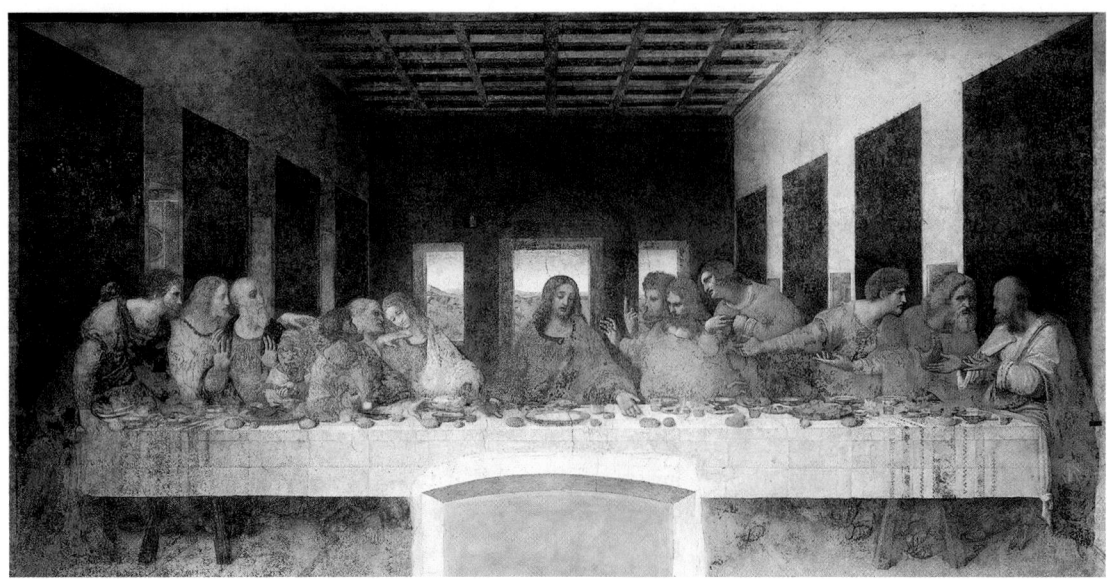

382 Leonardo da Vinci. THE LAST SUPPER.
Santa Maria delle Grazie, Milan. c. 1495–1498. Experimental paint on plaster. 14'5" × 28'¼".
Photograph: Scala/Art Resource, NY.

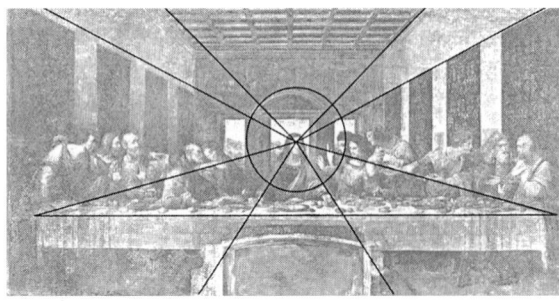

a. Perspective lines as both organizing structure and symbol of content.

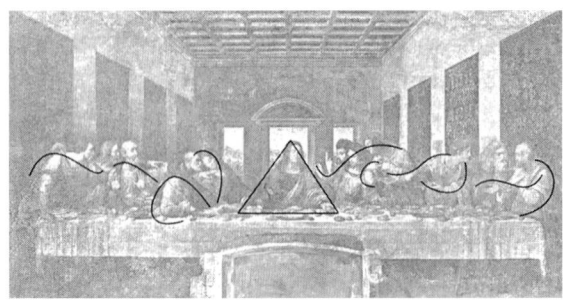

b. Christ's figure as stable triangle, contrasting with active turmoil of the disciples.

LISA'S rich, luminous surface was achieved through the application of glazes (thin, translucent layers of paint). Moreover, this work is a portrait, a type of art almost unknown in the medieval period.

The impact of Renaissance humanism becomes apparent when we compare THE LAST SUPPER by Leonardo with the Byzantine mosaic CHRIST AS PANTOCRATOR on page 258. In the Byzantine painting, Christ is portrayed as a lofty being of infinite power. In Leonardo's painting, Jesus sits across the table from us—an accessible person who reveals his divinity in an earthly setting.

The naturalist style of the work contains a hidden geometry, which structures the design and strengthens the painting's symbolic content. The interior is based on a one-point linear perspective system, with a single vanishing point in the middle of the composition, behind the head of Christ. Leonardo placed Christ in the center, at the point of greatest implied depth, associating him with infinity. Over Christ's head an architectural pediment suggests a halo, further setting him off from the irregular shapes and movements of the surprised disciples on either side. In contrast to the anguished figures surrounding him, Christ is shown with his arms outstretched in a gesture of acceptance, his image a stable triangle.

LEONARDO
da Vinci

The Artist as Scientist

1452–1519

LEONARDO DA VINCI— painter, sculptor, architect, town planner, writer, musician, scientist, engineer, and inventor—is the prototypical "Renaissance man," an extremely versatile individual with a record of high achievement in many fields.

Leonardo was the son of a young notary, Piero da Vinci, and a peasant girl of whom nothing is known. He grew up an only child in his father's household. In his mid-teens, he was apprenticed to Andrea del Verrochio, a leading artist in nearby Florence. Botticelli was one of his fellow apprentices.

Leonardo was a magnetic person, and people sought his company, yet he remained essentially solitary. He formed few friendships over the course of his life, and he never married.

At age thirty he began seventeen years in the service of the Duke of Milan, primarily as a military engineer and secondarily as a court painter, sculptor, and architect. He also entertained the court as a musician and satirist and designed scenery and costumes for pageants. During this period he painted several important works, including THE LAST SUPPER.

It was also in Milan that he started to keep notebooks. Along with his few paintings, Leonardo's notebooks are his great legacy. They contain a lifetime of observations, inventions, and plans, all drawn in meticulous detail and annotated in secretive mirror writing. In his research drawings, he anticipated the development of such twentieth-century technology as the airplane, the parachute, and the armored tank. His range of subjects was enormous: Mathematics, anatomy, architecture, astronomy, optics, botany, geology, cartography, aeronautics, mechanics, civil engineering, urban planning, hydraulics, and weaponry all captured Leonardo's interest and benefited from his research.

Milan fell to French invaders in 1499 and Leonardo fled to Venice, where he was again employed as a military engineer. From there he went to Florence and worked on a portrait of an obscure merchant's third wife, the MONA LISA. The French called him back to

Milan in 1506. He stayed until they were driven out six years later; then, hoping the Pope would have use for him, he journeyed to Rome.

Now in his sixties, Leonardo was increasingly haunted by a sense of futility. No building or invention of his had ever been built, no sculpture cast. Patrons had used his endless skills in frivolous or ignoble ways. Bored with what he could already do exquisitely well, he had left many paintings unfinished and ruined others with technical experiments. "Tell me if anything at all was done," he wrote over and over in his last notebooks. "Tell me if anything at all . . ."[2]

Yet what little he had finished was so spectacular that his fame was well established. In 1516, the new King of France, Francis I, offered Leonardo a house, a stipend, and the title of First Painter and Engineer and Architect to the King. The title was a formality; Francis expected nothing in return but the honor of Leonardo's presence and the pleasure of his conversation. He died in Cloux, near Amboise, France, in 1519.

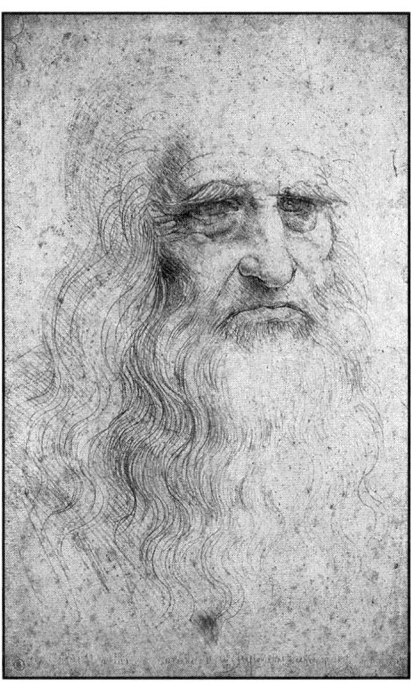

383 Leonardo da Vinci.
SELF-PORTRAIT. c. 1512.
Chalk on paper.
13" × 8¼".
Biblioteca Reale, Turin, Italy.
Photograph: Scala/Art Resource, NY.

Buonarroti

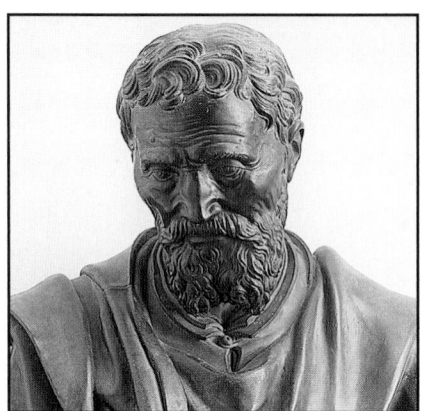

384 Damele da Volterra.
MICHELANGELO BUONARROTI. 1565.
Detail of bronze bust.
Height of entire work 32".
Accademia, Florence.
Photograph: Alinari/Art Resource, NY.

MICHELANGELO BUONARROTI was so greatly admired by his contemporaries that the poet Aristo referred to him as "Michael, more than human, Angel divine." Two biographies of Michelangelo were published in his lifetime. His noble, if difficult character and his mistrust of human nature—including his own—make his life one of the most interesting known to us from the sixteenth century.

Michelangelo's father was a member of the minor nobility of Florence, who lived off the remains of the family fortune. Michelangelo's mother was unable to nurse him, so the infant was sent to stay with a wet nurse. The nurse's husband was a quarry worker in an area where stonecutting was a way of life. Michelangelo returned to his parents only for visits because his mother continued to suffer poor health. She died when Michelangelo was six years old. For four more years he continued to live as the son of the stonecutter and his wife, visiting his father only occasionally. He could neither read nor write, but he learned to use hammer and chisel.

When he was ten his father remarried, and Michelangelo returned home and was enrolled in school for the first time. In three years he learned to read and write in Italian but absorbed little else. Michelangelo drew whenever he could and neglected his other studies. He decided to leave school to become an artist, starting as an apprentice to the painter Ghirlandaio. His father and uncles looked down on artists and thought it a disgrace to have one in the house. Michelangelo's father never realized the importance of the arts, even when Michelangelo gained fame and fortune.

After a year, Michelangelo transferred to the school in the Medici gardens, where he was inspired by the beauty of the Medici collection of contemporary Italian, ancient Greek, and Roman art. He studied there for several years, in the company of the leading artists and scholars of the time. During the turmoil following the death of his patron, Lorenzo de Medici, Michelangelo left Florence for Rome. In Rome he completed the first of his major sculptures, including the PIETÀ, at the age of twenty-four (see page 88). His handling of the difficult subject and the beautiful finish of the work established his reputation and led to important commissions, including DAVID, when he returned to Florence. For the rest of his life, he went back and forth between Florence and Rome.

Although he considered himself primarily a sculptor, Michelangelo's painting on THE SISTINE CHAPEL ceiling is one of the Western world's most acclaimed works of art. The project was made enormous by Michelangelo himself; although the original plan called for twelve figures, Michelangelo included over three hundred.

No other artist has left such worthy accomplishments in four major art forms: sculpture, painting, architecture, and poetry. If he had not been an architect, sculptor, and painter, Michelangelo might have been known to us as a writer. Perhaps the most revealing writings are his poems, which express his innermost feelings about his mind and soul as well as his art.

In his later years, in addition to architectural commissions—including the rebuilding of St. Peter's in Rome—Michelangelo worked as a city planner, completed some of his most important sculpture, and wrote many of his finest sonnets.

Michelangelo was very different from Leonardo, who was twenty-three years older. Michelangelo saw human beings as unique, almost godlike, whereas Leonardo saw them as one part of nature, which he viewed as a scientist as well as an artist. Michelangelo believed that in an artist's hands, "life" could be created through inspiration from God. For Michelangelo, sculpture and the process of its creation reflected people's struggle with their imperfect selves—souls in turmoil, bound in their bodies.

Michelangelo's life spanned nearly a century. From the time he was apprenticed at age thirteen until six days before his death at eighty-nine, he worked continuously. His last words were, "I regret that I have not done enough for the salvation of my soul and that I am dying just as I am beginning to learn the alphabet of my profession."[3]

In 1501, when he was twenty-six years old, Michelangelo obtained a commission from the city of Florence to carve a figure of David from an eighteen-foot block of marble that had been badly cut and then abandoned by another sculptor. The biblical hero David was an important symbol of freedom from tyranny for Florence, which had just become a republic. Other Renaissance artists such as Donatello had already given the city images of the young David, but it was Michelangelo's figure that gave the most powerful expression to the idea of David as hero, the defender of a just cause.

Michelangelo took DAVID'S stance, with the weight of the body on one foot, from Greek sculpture. But the positions of the hands and tense frown indicate anxiety and readiness for conflict. Through changes in proportion and the depiction of inner feeling, Michelangelo humanized, then made monumental, the classical Greek athlete.

Michelangelo worked for three years on this sculpture. When it was finished and placed in the town square, most citizens of Florence were filled with admiration for the work. With this achievement, Michelangelo became known as the greatest sculptor since the Greeks.

Equally praised as a painter, Michelangelo had just begun work on what he thought would be his main sculptural commission, the tomb of Pope Julius II, when the Pope ordered him to accept a commission to paint THE SISTINE CHAPEL (on the following page) in the Vatican. Michelangelo began work on the ceiling in 1508 and finished it four years later. The surface is divided into three zones. In the highest are nine panels of scenes from Genesis, including THE CREATION OF ADAM (on the following page). The next level contains prophets and sibyls (female prophets). The lowest level consists of groups of figures, some of which have been identified as Christ's biblical ancestors. *The Last Judgment*, painted later, fills the end wall above the altar.

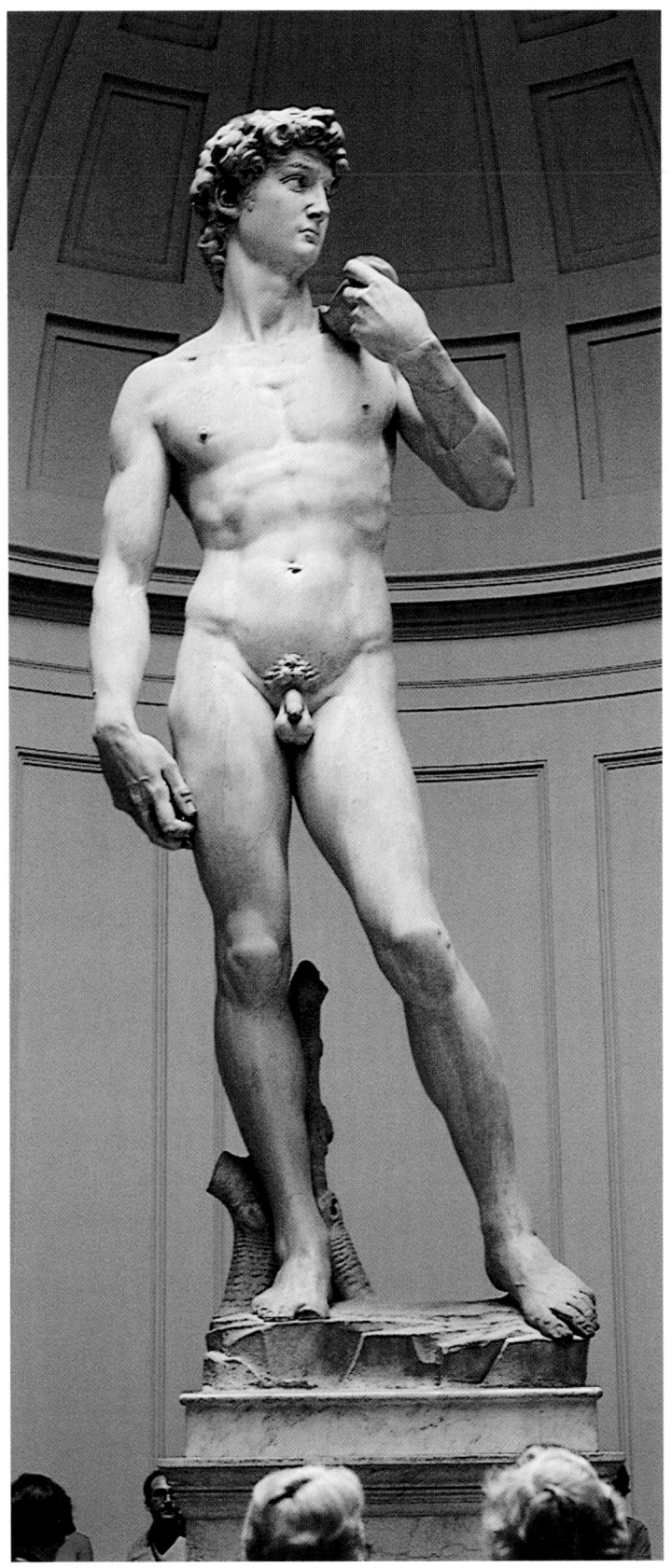

385   Michelangelo Buonarroti.
DAVID. 1501–1504.
Marble. Height of figure 14′3″.
Accademia, Florence.
Photograph: Duane Preble.

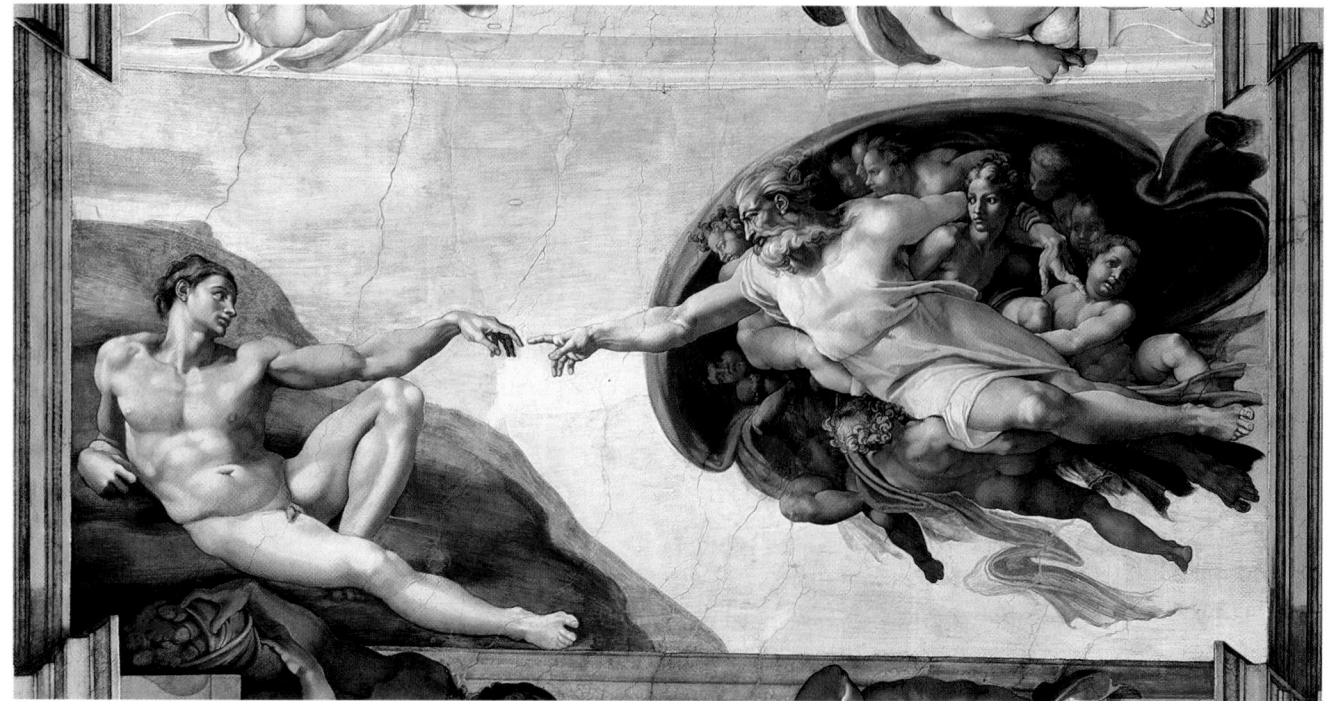

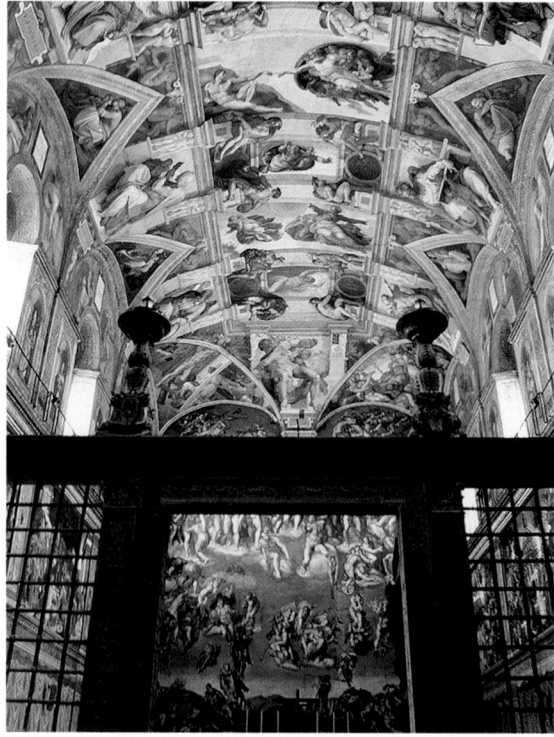

386 Michelangelo Buonarroti.
Frescoes on the ceiling and walls of THE SISTINE CHAPEL.
Vatican, Rome. 1508–1512.

a. THE CREATION OF ADAM, Fresco in the Sistine Chapel.
Vatican Museums, Rome, Italy.

b. THE SISTINE CHAPEL
Vatican Museums, Rome, Italy. © Reuters NewMedia Inc./Corbis.

The most-admired composition on the ceiling is the majestic portrayal of THE CREATION OF ADAM, in which God reaches out to give life to the first man. Eve, not yet mortal, stares at Adam from behind God's left arm.

The work powerfully expresses the Renaissance humanist concept of God: an idealized, rational man who actively tends every aspect of creation and has a special interest in humans. Michelangelo invented this powerful image, which does not exist in the Bible, to tell the story of the relationship between God and people from a Renaissance point of view.

Raphael Sanzio's warmth and gentleness were in sharp contrast to Leonardo's solitary, intellectual nature and Michelangelo's formidable moodiness. Of these three major creators of the High Renaissance, Raphael was the youngest and, in his life and art, the most expressive of the clarity and balance that marked the art of the period. His paintings present his awareness of the divine in human beings, the insight that was the driving enthusiasm of Italian Renaissance.

Raphael innovated in most types of painting that he attempted. For example, in MADONNA OF THE CHAIR (page 85) he arranged the figures so that their arms and heads echo the circular frame, while the vertical chair stabilizes the work. This composition is crowded yet perfectly legible; it is also adventurous in its use of bright contrasting colors.

In THE SCHOOL OF ATHENS (page 54) we see one of the clearest summations of Renaissance beliefs. He organized the complex composition into symmetrical sub-groups, all revolving around the central figures of Plato and Aristotle under the arch. Perspective lines help to frame our focus on them. Most of the figure poses in this work are based in Classical antiquity. More important, THE SCHOOL OF ATHENS elevates human reason by presenting a philosophical discussion among learned people as an ideal. The Pope commissioned this work for the wall of a meeting room, so that persons discussing church business could be inspired by an ideal meeting of great people from the past.

For Pope Leo X (a Medici descendant), Raphael made a series of cartoons for tapestries that would decorate the walls of the Sistine Chapel, below Michelangelo's ceiling. The tapestries have faded, but the cartoons retain most of the original vivid colors. Leo wished to glorify the early church by commissioning illustrations of important events in the Acts of the Apostles, and Raphael responded by creating memorable and dramatic works. PAUL PREACHING AT ATHENS is a diverse yet well-organized composition, as Paul preaches to the philosophically inclined Athenians. Among the audience is the Pope, just to the left of Paul. The message of this work, that reason can transmit religious truth, perfectly expresses Renaissance beliefs.

The Renaissance in Northern Europe

As the Early Renaissance was unfolding in Italy, a parallel new interest in realism arose in northern Europe, where artists were even more concerned than the Italians with depicting life in the real world. Jan van Eyck was a leading painter in Flanders, the region of present-day Belgium and adjacent parts of France and The Netherlands. He was one of the first to use linseed oil as a paint medium (see also pages 122–123). The fine consistency and

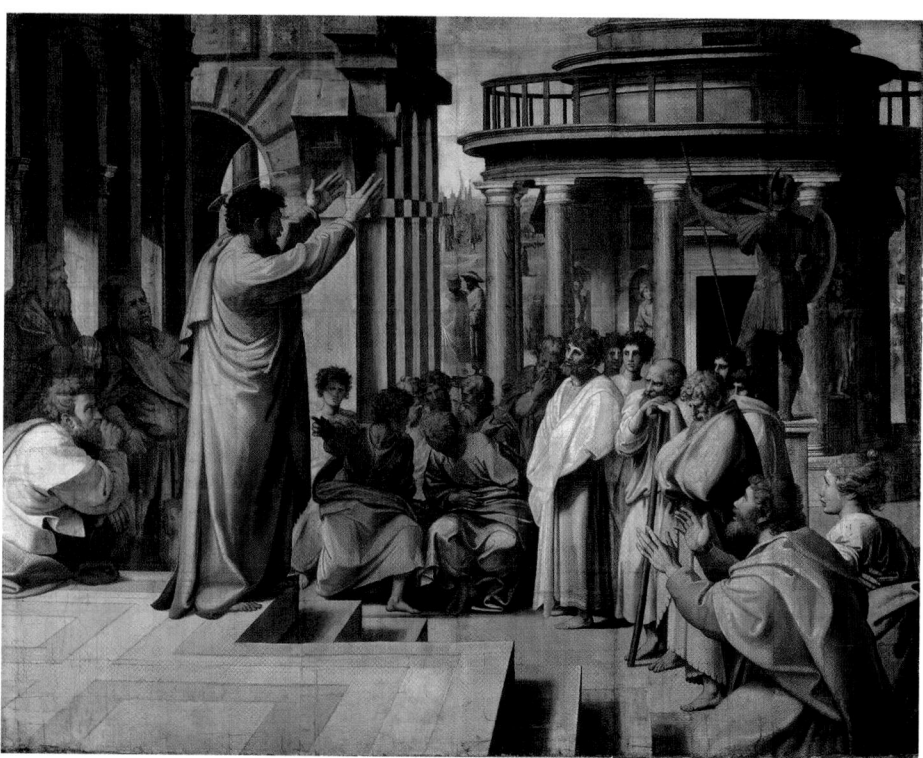

387 Raphael.
PAUL PREACHING AT ATHENS.
1515–1516.
Watercolor on paper mounted on canvas. 11′5½″ × 14′6¾″.
Victoria and Albert Museum, London.
Art Resource, NY.

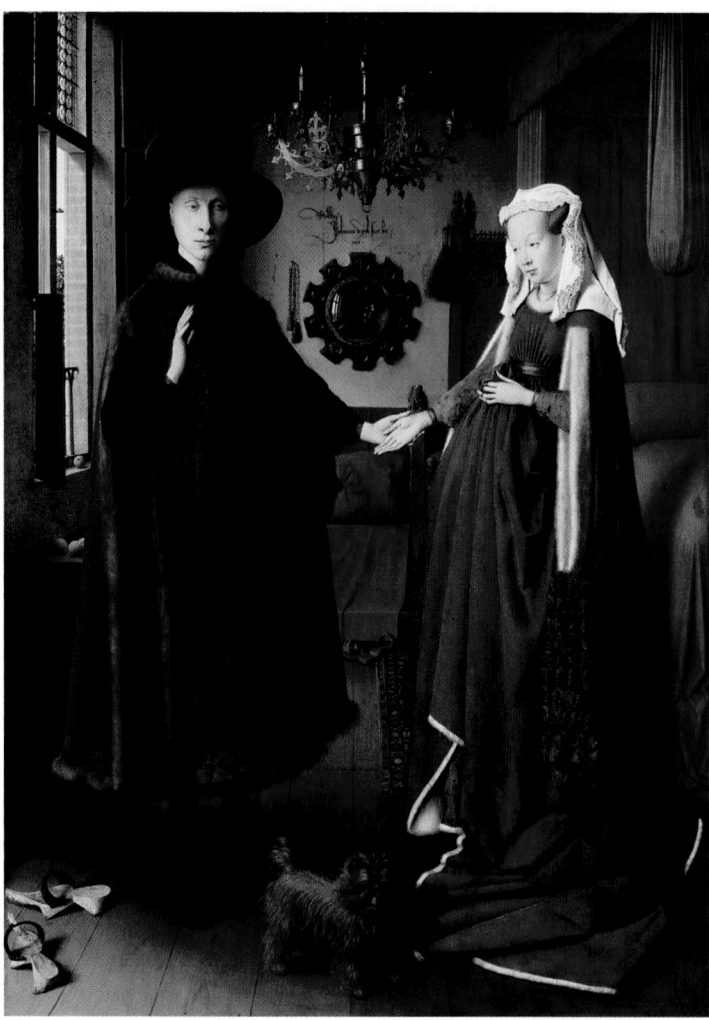

388 Jan van Eyck.
THE ARNOLFINI PORTRAIT. 1434.
Oil on oak panel. 33½″ × 23½″.
National Gallery, London, U.K.
Photograph: Bridgeman Art Library International Ltd.

tures, and the physical likenesses of particular people. Human figures and their interior settings took on a new, believable presence.

In spite of van Eyck's realistic detail, THE ARNOLFINI PORTRAIT has a Gothic quality in its traditional symbolism, formality, and vertical emphasis of the figures. The work likely commemorates a wedding, although other theories have been offered. At the time the portrait was commissioned, the Church did not always require the presence of clergy for a valid marriage contract, and thus it was easy to deny that a marriage had taken place. Van Eyck's painting is thought to be a testament to the oath of marriage between the two of them. As witness to the event, Jan van Eyck placed his signature and the date, 1434, directly above the mirror—and he himself appears to be reflected in the mirror (see detail on page 73).

Today the painting's Christian iconography, well understood in the fifteenth century, needs explanation. Many of the ordinary objects portrayed with great care have sacred significance. The single lighted candle in the chandelier symbolizes the presence of Christ; the amber beads and the sunlight shining through them are symbols of purity; the dog indicates marital fidelity. The bride's holding up her skirt suggestively in front of her stomach may indicate her willingness to bear children. Green, a symbol of fertility, was often worn at weddings.

In the early sixteenth century in Germany, Northern Renaissance master Albrecht Dürer further developed the practice of presenting instructive symbolism through detailed realism. His engraving THE KNIGHT, DEATH AND THE DEVIL (page 134) combines Christian symbols with familiar subjects in the Flemish tradition of van Eyck.

Pieter Bruegel developed a new artistic vision of the North European landscape. As a young man he traveled extensively in France and Italy. Under the influence of Italian Renaissance painting, Bruegel developed a broader sense of composition and spatial depth. The focus of Bruegel's paintings was the lives and surroundings of common people, and toward the end of his life he did a series of

flexibility of the new oil medium made possible a brilliance and transparency of color that were previously unattainable. His oil paintings remain in almost perfect condition, attesting to his skill and knowledge of materials. Italian artists admired and imitated the innovations of van Eyck and other Flemish and Dutch artists.

On the same type of small wooden panels previously used for tempera painting, van Eyck painted in minute detail, achieving an illusion of depth, directional light, mass, rich implied tex-

Vermeer gave equal attention to the details and the way each detail relates to the whole composition. Notice, for example, the immense care given to the rendering of the subtle surface qualities of the wall with its nail holes and stains.

During the Baroque period, French artists adopted Italian Renaissance ideas but made them their own; by the end of the seventeenth century, France had begun to take the lead in European art.

We can glimpse another view of seventeenth-century European life in the royal architecture and garden design of the French royal palace of VERSAILLES, built for King Louis XIV. The main palace and its gardens exemplify French Baroque architecture and landscape architecture. Throughout the palace and gardens, cool classical restraint and symmetry balance the romance of Baroque opulence and grand scale.

VERSAILLES expressed the king's desire to surpass all others in the splendor of his palace. It is an example of royal extravagance, originally set in fifteen thousand acres of manicured gardens, twelve miles south of Paris. The vast formal gardens, with their miles of clipped hedges, proclaimed the king's desire to rule even over nature. This palace, which was also a governmental center, played an important role in the program of absolute monarchy that Louis XIV personified. Never more than here is the Baroque style allied with aristocracy.

Early in eighteenth-century France, the heavy, theatrical qualities of Italian Baroque art gradually gave way to the decorative *Rococo* style, a light, playful version of the Baroque. The curved shapes of shells were copied for elegantly paneled interiors and furniture, and they influenced the billowing shapes found in paintings. The arts moved out of the marble halls of palaces such as VERSAILLES and into fashionable town houses (called hotels) such as the HÔTEL DE SOUBISE.

The enthusiastic sensuality of the Rococo style was particularly suited to the extravagant and often frivolous life of the French court and aristocracy. Some of the movement, light, and gesture of the Baroque remained, but now the effect was one of lighthearted abandon rather than dramatic action or quiet repose. Rococo paintings provided romantic

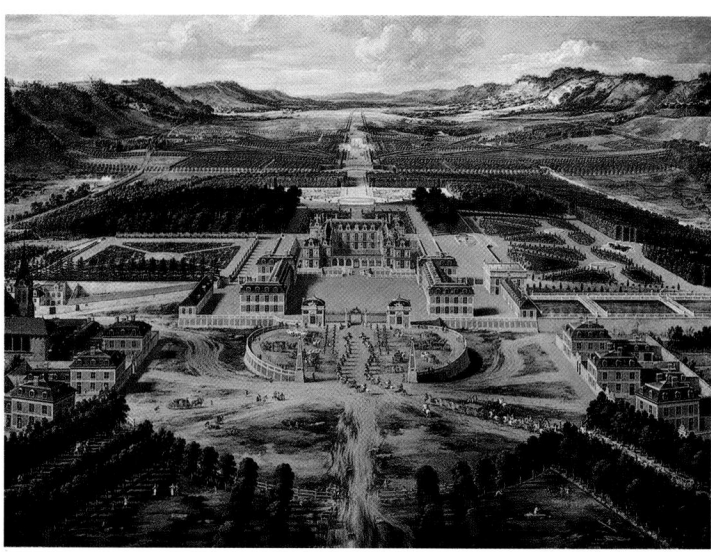

401   Pierre Patel.
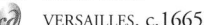   VERSAILLES. c.1665.
Chateau de Versailles et de Trianon, Versailles, France. Photograph: Giraudon/Art Resource, NY.

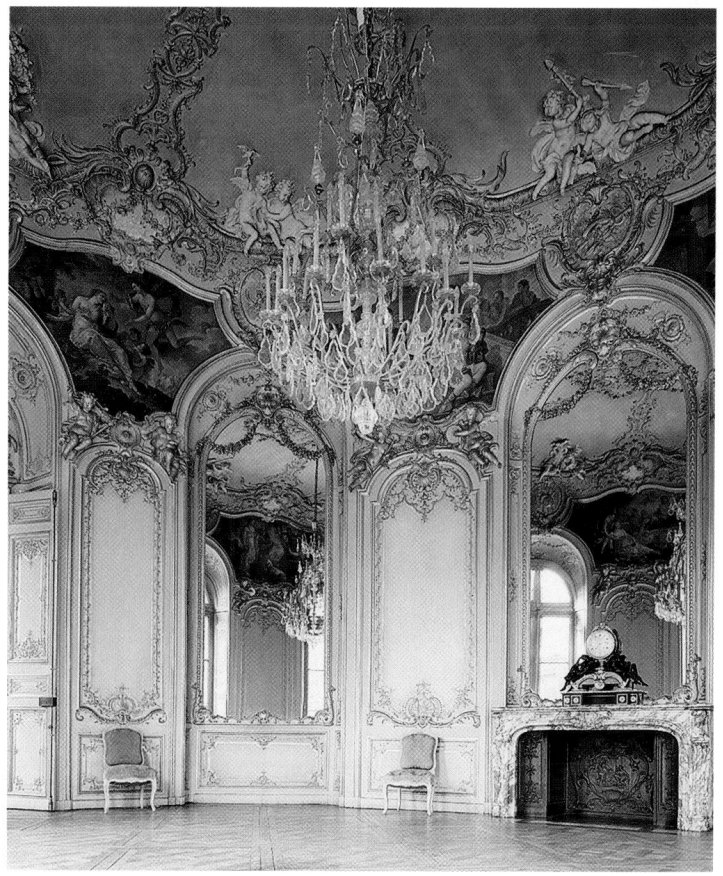

402   Germain Boffrand.
SALON DE LA PRINCESSE, HÔTEL DE SOUBISE.
Paris. Begun 1732.
Photograph: Hirmer Fotoarchiv, Munich, Germany.

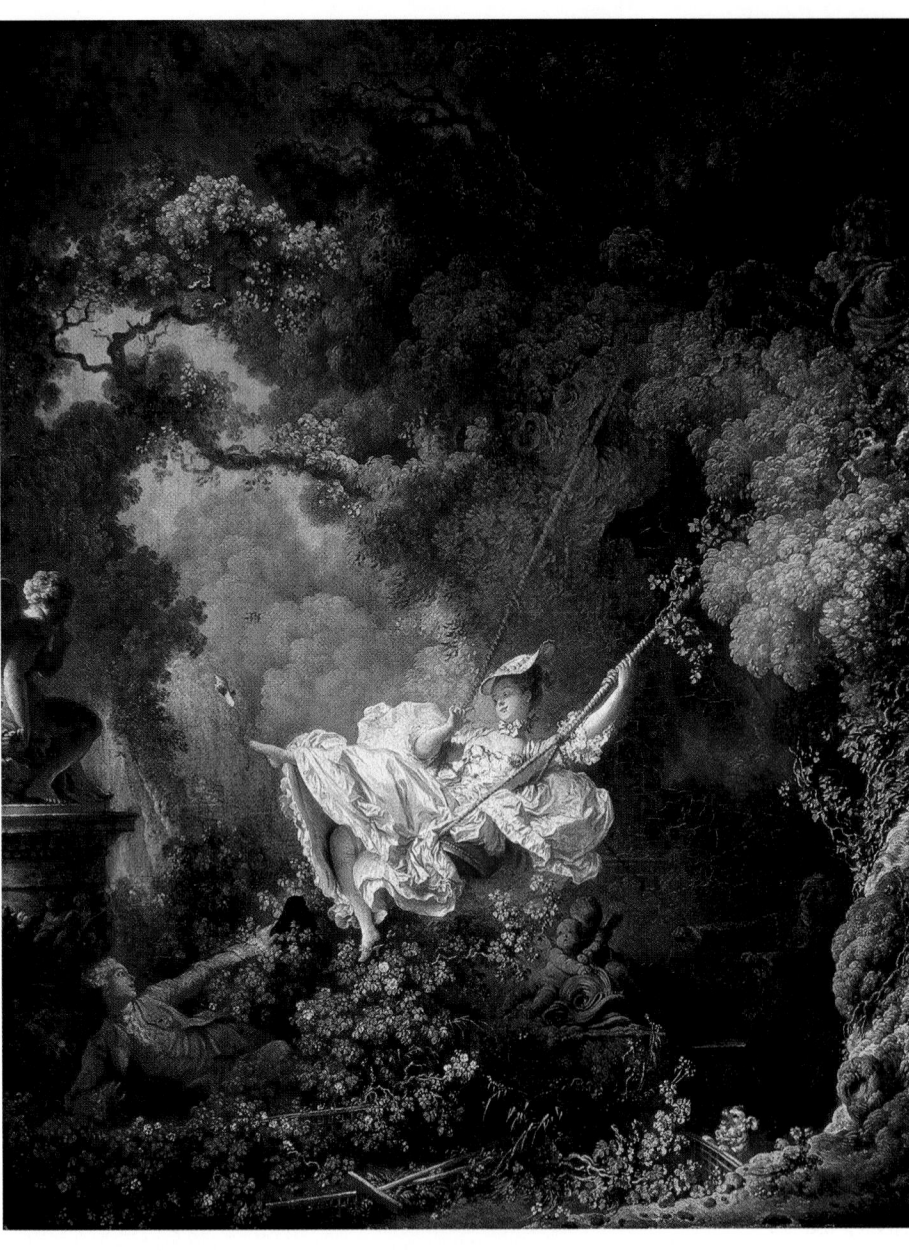

403 Jean Honoré Fragonard.
THE SWING. 1767.
Oil on canvas. 31⅞" × 25¼".
The Wallace Collection, London.

visions of life free from hardships, in which courtship, music, and festive picnics filled the days.

The aristocratic life of ease and dalliance is nowhere better depicted than in Jean-Honoré Fragonard's painting THE SWING. A well-dressed and idle young woman, attended by a dimly visible bishop, swings in a garden. At the lower left, a youth hides in the bushes and admires her. The story line of the work is provided by her flying shoe, which has come off and will soon land in the young man's lap. Fragonard learned the lessons of the Baroque well, as we can see in the off-balance composition arranged along the diagonal, and the contrasts of light and dark visible in the lush garden. But Baroque drama gives way here to the sensual abandon and light-as-air subject matter of the Rococo at its best.

Or worst. The next generation of French artists and intellectuals would rebel against the social irresponsibility portrayed in this type of art, which they saw as merely fluffy. The Enlightenment was already breaking out across western Europe, and its new ideas of social equality and scientific inquiry would soon shake European art and culture to its core.

ENGENDERING IT

THE CONDITIONS for producing great art—or for excelling in any discipline—include family support, educational opportunity, community support, and patronage, as well as aptitude. Many artists now considered "great" benefited from most of these advantages. Yet the situation has been and still is discouraging, even hostile at times, for anyone who is not born white, moderately affluent, and male. Obstacles begin with the attitudes of parents, teachers, and others in power. What is amazing is that so many women have achieved so much in the face of gender-based discrimination.

During the Renaissance in Italy, it became socially and politically acceptable for aristocrats to educate daughters a well as sons in the social arts. Although the idea was simply to produce women who could write poetry, dance, sing, paint, and excel in the art of conversation so that they would make good companions for aristocratic men, some women became highly accomplished artists. However, most were denied access to the training necessary for professional careers.

Sofonisba Anguissola was the first female artist of the Renaissance to achieve recognition throughout Europe. Anguissola studied with a portrait painter, and her well-publicized success led other male artists to accept female students. While still in her twenties, she became court painter to King Philip II of Spain. Her SELF-PORTRAIT of 1556 evokes a mysterious mood.

European women artists were more numerous and better known during the Baroque period. Among the most remarkable was Artemisia Gentileschi, daughter of well-known artist Orazio Gentileschi. Although some of today's art historians consider Artemisia a better painter than her father, until recently her work received limited recognition because she was a woman.

Her painting JUDITH AND THE MAIDSERVANT WITH THE HEAD OF HOLOFERNES tells the Bible story of the heroic Judith who beheaded an enemy general. The intensity of the moment is communicated clearly in this Baroque work. The drama is intensified by bold use of theatrical light, sweeping curves, dramatic gestures, and warm colors.

Because women were not allowed to study from the nude in art academies, most of the women who achieved distinction in the visual arts depended on the help of fathers or close male friends who were artists. A list of such women includes Rosa Bonheur (see chapter 21) and Marietta Robusti, both daughters of artists; Berthe Morisot, an Impressionist who was closely associated with Edouard Manet; and Mary Cassatt (see page 136), who was a close friend of Edgar Degas.

The art world made great strides toward gender equality in the twentieth century, but the goal has not yet been achieved.

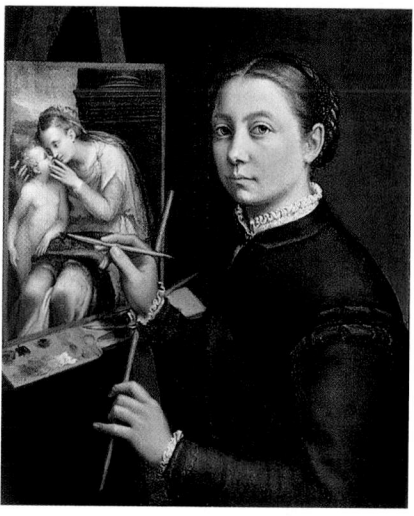

404   Sofonisba Anguissola.
SELF-PORTRAIT. 1556.
Oil on canvas. 25″ × 22⅜″.
Museum Zamek, Lancut Poland. © The Bridgeman Art Library International Ltd.

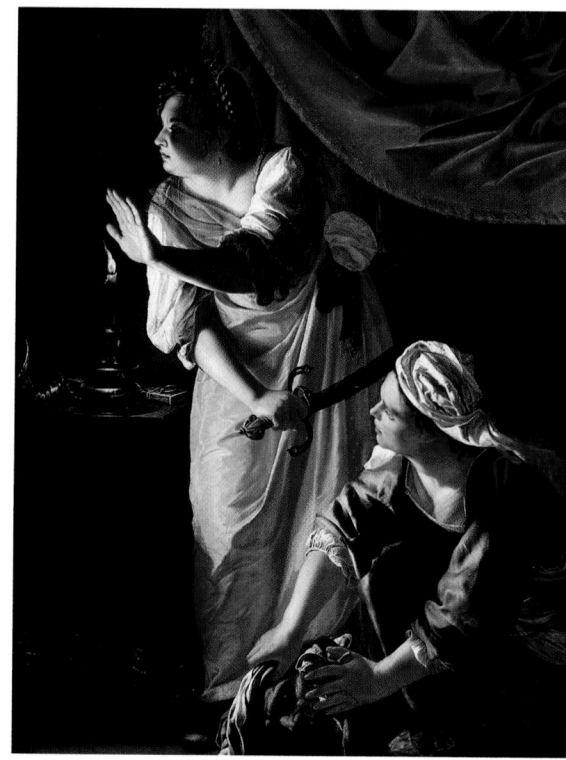

405   Artemisia Gentileschi.
JUDITH AND THE MAIDSERVANT WITH THE HEAD OF HOLOFERNES. c. 1625.
Oil on canvas. 6′½″ × 4′7¾″.
Gift of Mrs. Leslie H. Green. Photograph © 1984 The Detroit Institute of Arts.

ART *in the world*

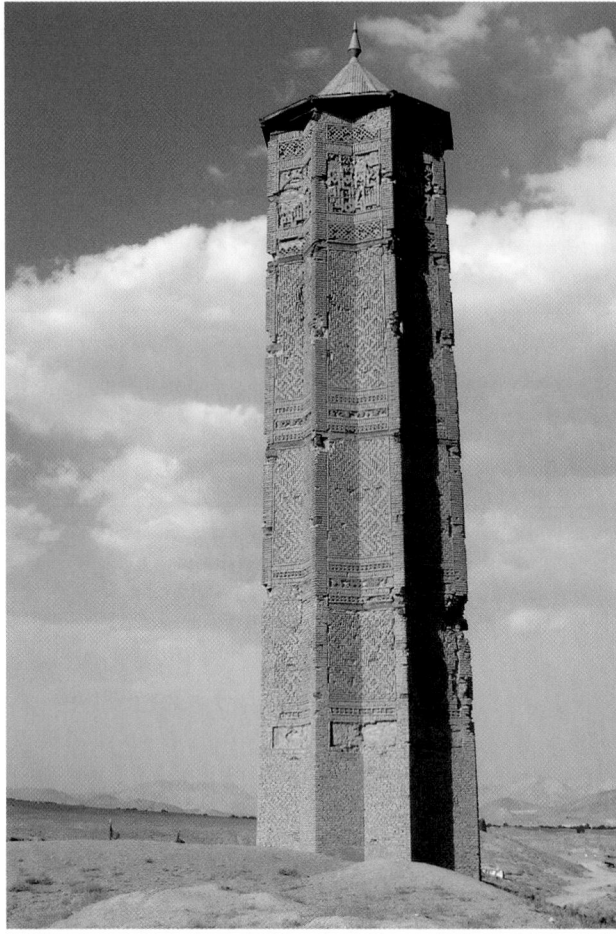

406 GHAZNI MINARET, Afghanistan.
Early twelfth century. Height 65'.
Photo courtesy World Monuments Fund, by Najim M. Azadzoi.
Architect/Planner, Azod Architects, Newton, MA.

MUCH OF THE ART of the past that we enjoy today would have perished but for art restorers who cared for it. Because art preserves tangible evidence of cultural history, preserving it is essential. But because art is subject to all the vicissitudes of nature and humanity, preserving it can also be very difficult.

A major work that has suffered grievously from both nature and humans is the beloved PARTHENON, a masterwork of world architecture (see page 246). After it served the Greeks as a temple of Athena, conquering Romans turned it into a brothel. Christians later used it as a church. The Turks of the Ottoman Empire refurbished it as a mosque for Muslim worship. When the Venetians attacked in 1687, the Turks converted it into an ammunition dump. In that year it was hit by Italian artillery and exploded.

In 1803, the British ambassador to the Ottoman court removed most of the marble sculpture from the building and took it to London, where it now remains. On the way, one of his ships ran aground and had to be salvaged. Overzealous cleaners in the British Museum in the 1930s scrubbed the surface of the sculptures with wire brushes, hopelessly damaging them. Meanwhile, what remains of the original building languishes under the impact of Athenian air pollution.

Every kind of art material presents its own particular set of challenges to restorers. Most restorers of painting and sculpture today are trained in chemistry. They carefully analyze the surface and layers of works in their charge, often using a computer-aided process called *mass spectrography*. This chemical diagnosis informs them of the work's level of stability and suggests restorative methods.

Restorers' decisions about how to treat a work can be hotly debated. Restorers of the MONA LISA, for example, decided in the late 1990s not to remove the last layer of varnish from its surface, for fear of damaging Leonardo's paint underneath. This decision was hailed as respectful in some quarters and derided as too timid in others. In contrast, restorers of Leonardo's LAST SUPPER recently added watercolor to the surface of the work, filling in gaps; this more assertive treatment was equally controversial for the opposite reasons.

However, for every high-profile work that is stabilized in a wealthy county, hundreds of others slowly decay in poorer areas where resources are not as plentiful. These threatened works include important buildings in addition to paintings and sculpture.

The World Monuments Fund (WMF) watches out for these, and publishes a list of the world's *One Hundred Most Endangered Sites* every two years. Sites pictured in this book that have appeared on the list include the ancient city of Teotihuacan in Mexico; Machu Picchu in Peru; the Amenhotep Temple in Luxor, Egypt; the Roman city of Pompeii; Hagia Sophia in Istanbul; the Angkor Wat temple complex in Cambodia; and Borobudur in Indonesia. The Taj Mahal in India has been on the list twice.

The GHAZNI MINARETS in Afghanistan were on the 2004 WMF list. Erected in the twelfth century, these towers rise some 65 feet above the surrounding desert, their star-shaped shafts coated in priceless terracotta decorations. The surface deterioration is serious in itself, yet the structures are located in an embattled country. Consevation of this and other monuments will require international cooperation.

TRADITIONAL ARTS OF ASIA

The human presence in Asia dates back to the Paleolithic period. In Asia there occurred a similar development of ancient cultures, from hunting and gathering to agricultural village societies, to Bronze Age kingdoms, and so on. (For examples of ancient Asian art, see Chapter 14.) Culturally as well as geographically, India is at the core of the continent. Many ideas that later permeated Asian societies originated in India and radiated outward. However, because each region of Asia also had its own local culture, outright borrowing was rare. Rather, we can trace the passage of ideas and art styles across the continent as they were adapted and modified in various locations.

INDIA

In the 1930s, excavations at the sites of the ancient city of Harappā revealed the remains of a well-organized society with advanced city planning and a high level of artistic production. Harappā served as a focal point for a civilization that extended for a thousand miles along the fertile Indus Valley between three thousand and five thousand years ago. (Most of this valley, where Indian culture began, became part of Pakistan after Indian independence in 1947.)

Ancient Indus Valley sculpture already shows the particularly sensual naturalism that characterizes much of later Indian art. This quality enlivens the small, masterfully carved MALE TORSO from Harappā. Comparing this figure with the classical Greek SPEAR BEARER on page 245 is highly instructive. Whereas the MALE TORSO seems fleshy, the sculptor of SPEAR BEARER focused on the underlying bone structure of the body.

Relatively few works of art survive from the period between 1800 B.C.E., when the Indus Valley civilization declined, and 300 B.C.E., when the first Buddhist art appeared. Nevertheless, the years in that interval were important ones for the development of Indian thought and culture.

Starting around 1500 B.C.E., the Indian subcontinent was infiltrated and gradually taken over by nomadic Aryan tribes from the northwest. The

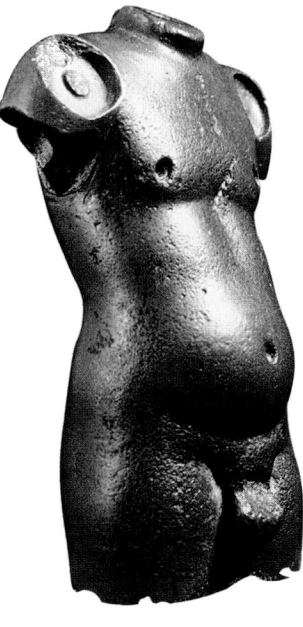

407 MALE TORSO.
Harappā, Indus Valley.
c. 2400–2000 B.C.E.
Limestone.
Height 3½".
Photograph: Prithwish Neogy.
Courtesy of Duane Preble.

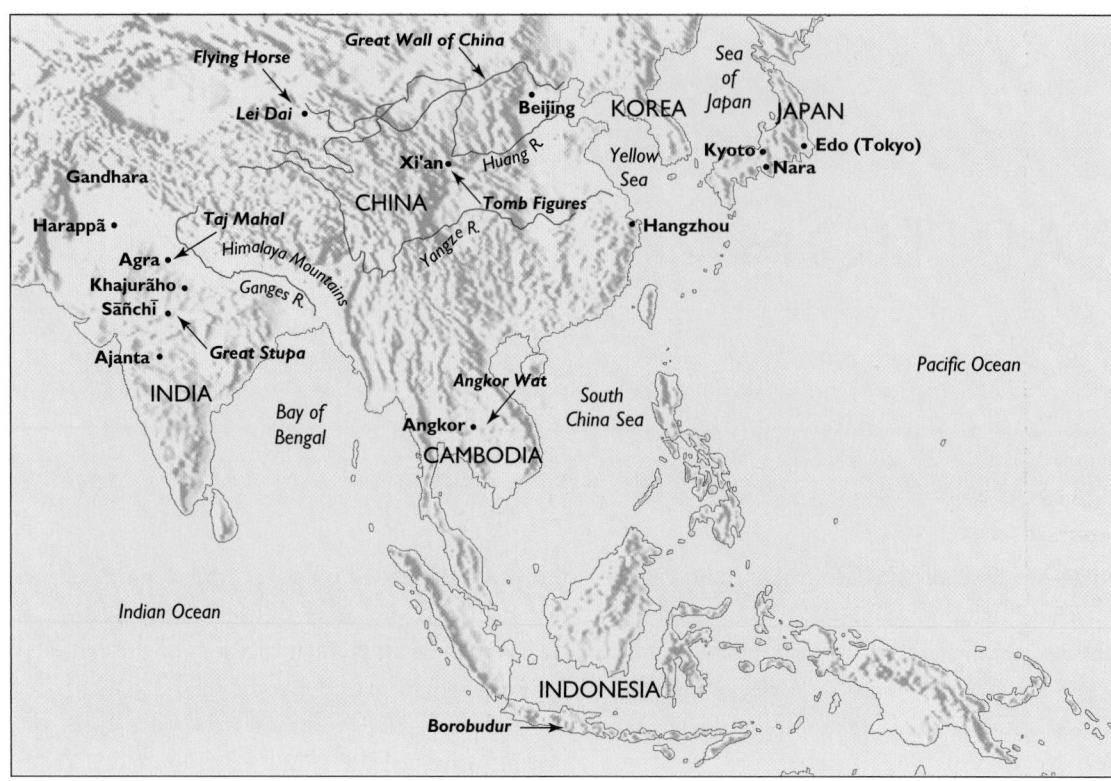

408 HISTORICAL MAP OF ASIA.

Aryans' beliefs, gods, and social structure formed the foundation of the subsequent development of Indian civilization. Key Aryan beliefs that influenced later Indian thought include the idea that the universe evolves in repeated cycles of creation and destruction; that individuals are reincarnated after death; and that there is one supreme form of wisdom. These beliefs were spelled out in the main forms of Aryan literature, the Vedas (hymns) and Upanishads (philosophical works)—texts still regarded as sacred by many Indians.

The Aryans, being nomads, left behind very little of what we might call art. What came into being as Indian art is a synthesis of indigenous Indian art forms and the religious ideas of the nomadic Aryans.

Many Indian religions developed from the core beliefs of the Aryans. Their literature, for example, was accepted as scripture by Hindus. In the sixth century B.C.E., two influential spiritual leaders preached variations on Hindu beliefs. They were Siddhartha Gautama (563–483 B.C.E.), founder of

Buddhism, and Mahavira (599–527 B.C.E.), founder of Jainism. Although most Indians today are Hindus, Buddhism dominated the formative years of the development of Indian art, and it became a major cultural factor elsewhere in Asia.

Buddhist Art

The Buddhist religion began when Siddhartha Gautama achieved enlightenment. Seeking an answer to the question of human suffering, he arrived at what Buddhists call the Four Noble Truths: (1) Existence is full of suffering. (2) The cause of suffering is desire. (3) To eliminate suffering, one must eliminate desire. (4) To eliminate desire, one must follow the Eightfold Path of right views, right aspirations, right speech, right conduct, right livelihood, right effort, right mindfulness, and right contemplation. He also taught that if one achieves enlightenment, the endless cycle of death and rebirth will be broken, and the believer will experience a final rebirth in a pure spiritual realm. Siddhartha began to attract followers in the late sixth century B.C.E.; they called him the "Enlightened One" or the Buddha.

Early Buddhism did not include the production of images. Eventually, however, religious practice needed visual icons as support for contemplation, and images began to appear. The many styles of Buddhist art and architecture vary according to the cultures that produced them. As Buddhism spread from India to Southeast Asia and across central Asia to China, Korea, and Japan, it influenced (and was influenced by) native religious and aesthetic traditions.

An excellent example of early Indian Buddhist art is the domelike structure called the *stupa*, which evolved from earlier burial mounds. At the GREAT STUPA at Sanchi, four gates are oriented to the four cardinal directions. The devout walk around the stupa in a ritual path, symbolically taking the Path of Life around the World Mountain. Such stupas were erected at sacred locations, and relics (items belonging to a holy person) were usually buried in their core.

The four gateways to the GREAT STUPA include layers of sculpture in relief. These tell the story of the Buddha's life, but without depicting him directly. The characteristic sensuousness that we observed in the MALE TORSO from Harappā still enlivens these early monuments.

We can trace the EVOLUTION OF BUDDHIST ARCHITECTURE from its origin in India to its later

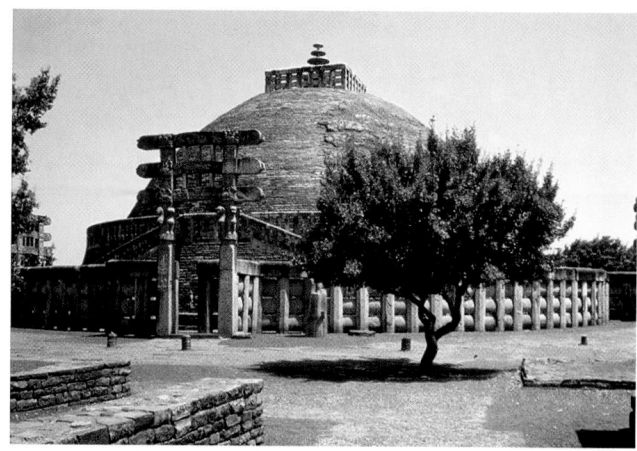

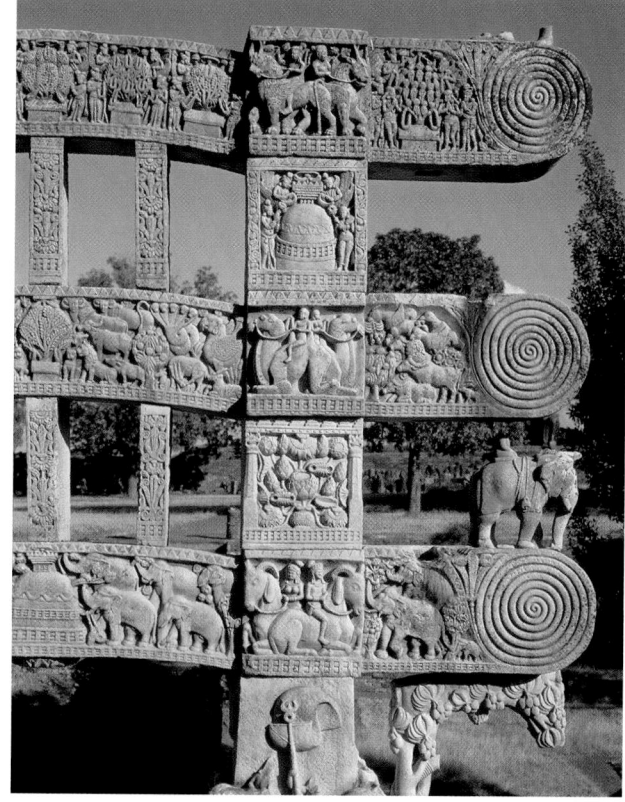

409 a. GREAT STUPA.
Sanchi, India. 10 B.C.E.–15 C.E.
Photograph: Prithwish Neogy.
Courtesy of Duane Preble.

b. Eastern gate of THE GREAT STUPA.
Photograph: Borromeo. Art Resource, NY.

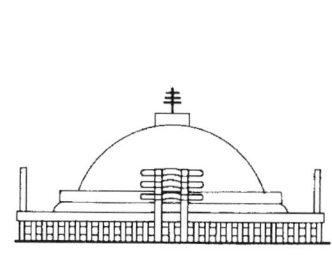
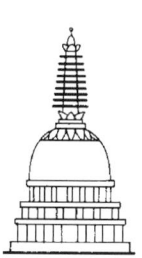
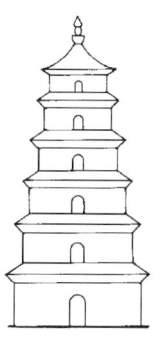
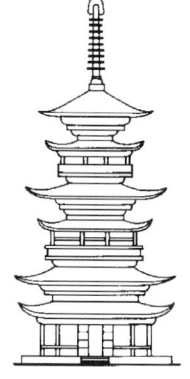

410 EVOLUTION OF BUDDHIST ARCHITECTURE.
a. Early Indian stupa. 3rd century to early 1st century B.C.E.
b. Later Indian stupa. 2nd century C.E.
c. Chinese pagoda. 5th to 7th centuries C.E.
d. Japanese pagoda. 7th century C.E.

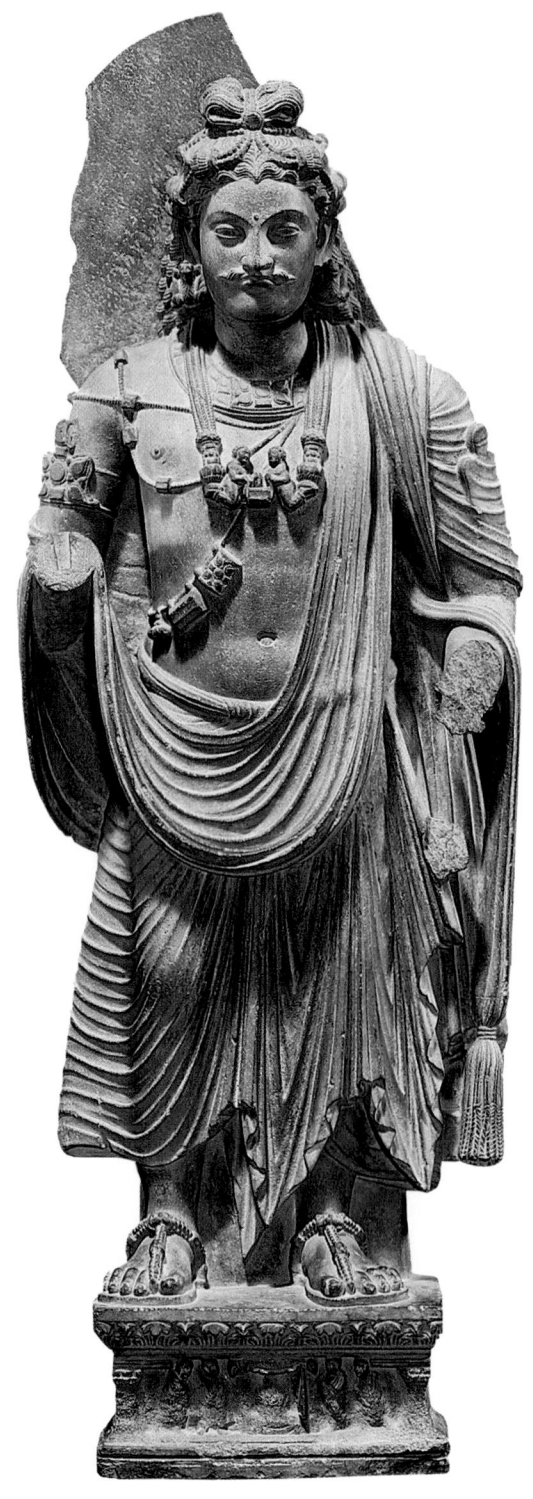

manifestations in other parts of Asia. Buddhist pagodas developed from a merging of the Indian stupa and the traditional Chinese watchtower. The resulting broad-eaved tower structure was in turn adopted and changed by the Japanese.

Indian art was influenced by Western art when Alexander the Great conquered large parts of what is now Pakistan and Afghanistan in the fourth century B.C.E. This region, called Gandhara, continued its contacts with the Roman Empire during its peak years. Buddhist sculptors in the region developed a distinctive style of working that owes about equal amounts to East and West; the STANDING BODHISATTVA is an excellent example. Here the sculptor shows a knowledge of the realism of Roman portraiture, as well as the classical Greek method of showing a subject's body beneath the folds of the drapery in the legs. The subject, however, is Buddhist. A *bodhisattva* is a person who is on the point of achieving enlightenment, but delays it in order to remain on earth and teach others. Bodhisattva are usually depicted wearing rich garments and jewels.

The Indian Gupta dynasty (c. 320–540) is notable for major developments in politics, law, mathematics, and the arts. In the visual arts, the Gupta style combines native Indian ways of seeing with the naturalism of the Gandhara. Although slightly damaged, the carved stone STANDING BUDDHA is a fine example of Gupta sculpture. In its cool, idealized perfection, the refined Gupta style marks a period of high achievement in Indian art. The simplified mass of the figure seems to push out from within as though the body were inflated with breath. The rounded form is enhanced by curves repeated rhythmically down the figure. The drapery seems wet as it clings to and accentuates the softness of the body.

We can see similar elegance and linear refinement in the noble figure known as the "BEAUTIFUL BODHISATTVA" PADMAPANI, part of a series of elaborate paintings in the Ajanta Caves in Central India. The fine linear definition of the figure accents full, rounded shapes, exemplifying the relaxed opulence of the Gupta style. This was the principal style exported when Buddhism began to spread to China and Southeast Asia.

411 STANDING BODHISATTVA.
N.W. Pakistan, Gandhara region. Late 2nd century C.E. Kushana period. Gray schist. Height 43⅛".
Courtesy of Boston Museum of Fine Arts, Boston. Helen and Alice Colburn Fund. 37.99. Reproduced with permission.
© Museum of Fine Arts, Boston. All rights reserved.

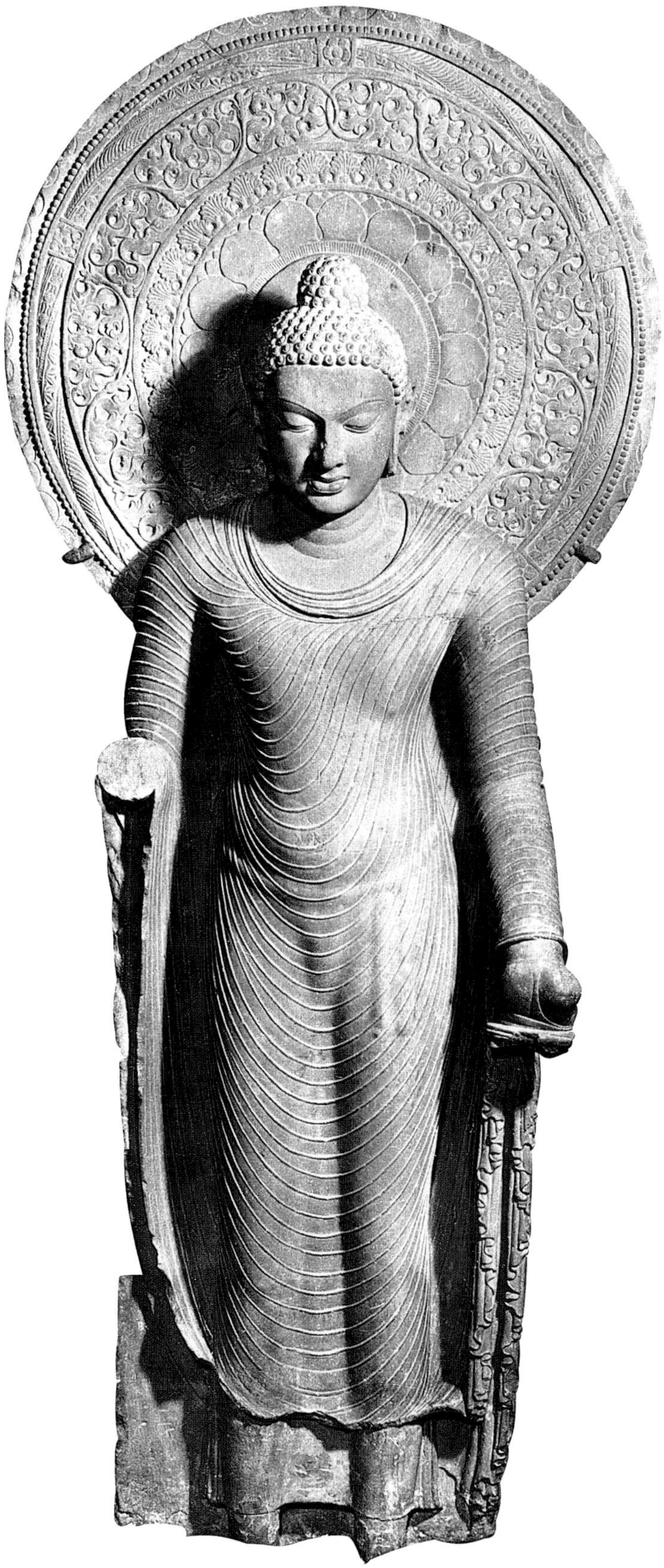

412 STANDING BUDDHA. 5th century.
Red sandstone. Height 5'3".
Indian Museum, Calcutta.

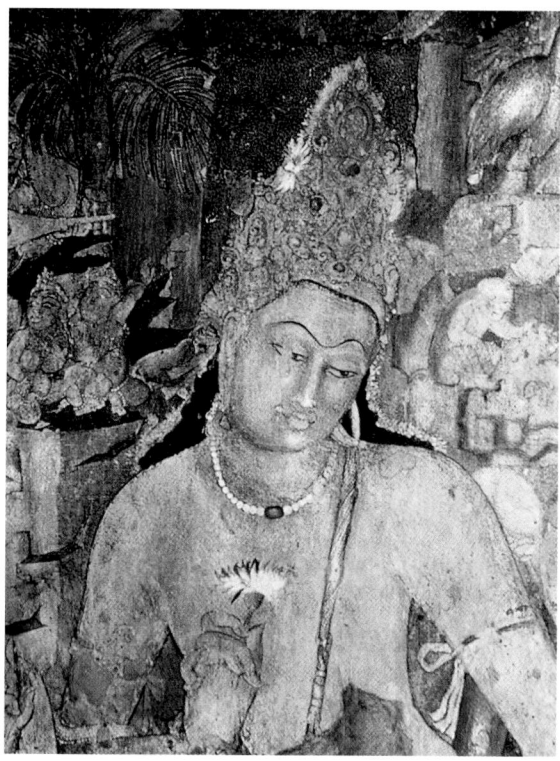

413 "BEAUTIFUL BODHISATTVA" PADMAPANI.
Detail of a fresco from Cave 1. Ajanta, India. c. 600–650.
Duane Preble.

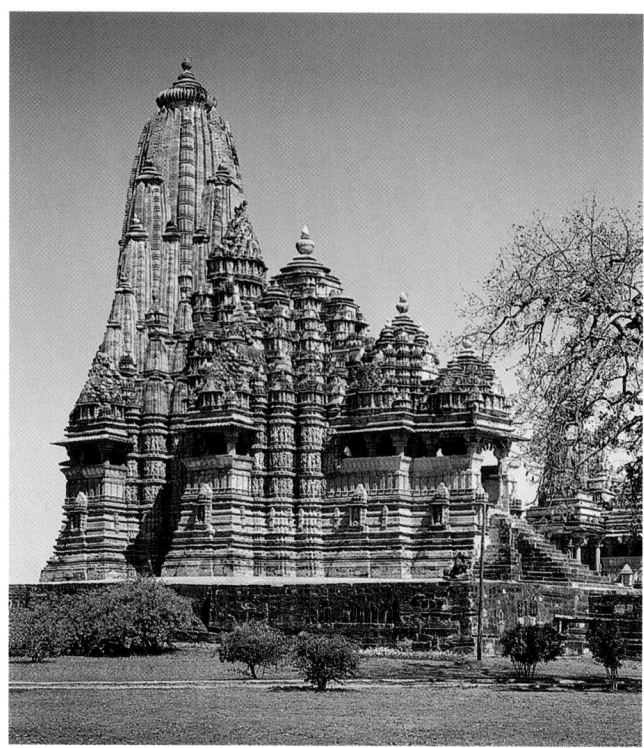

414 KANDARYA MAHADEVA TEMPLE.
Khajurāho, India. 10th–11th centuries.
a. Exterior
Photograph: Borromeo. Art Resource, NY.

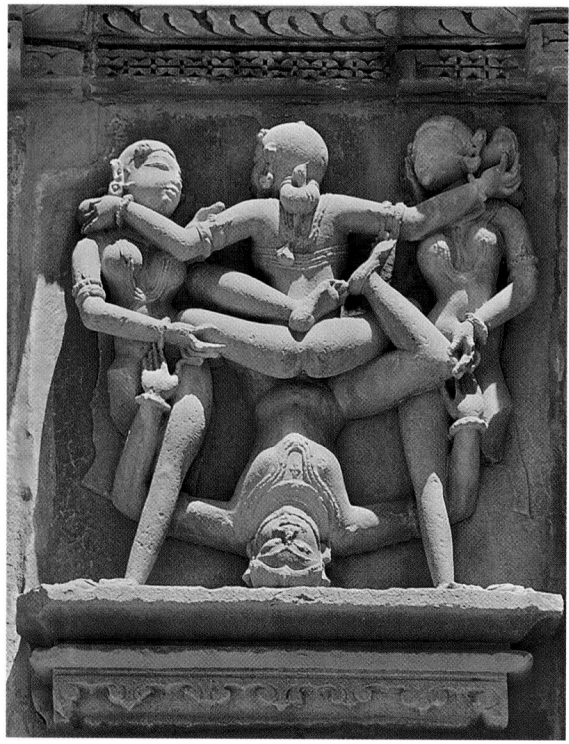

b. Scene from KANDARYA MAHADEVA TEMPLE.
Chandella dynasty, 1025–50 C.E. Khajuraho,
Madhya Pradesh, India.
Photograph: Borromeo. Art Resource, NY.

Hindu Art

Hinduism recognizes three principal gods: Brahma, the creator of all things; Vishnu, the sustainer; and Shiva, the destroyer. These three gods intervene in human affairs at appropriate moments either to guarantee the continuing evolution of the cosmos, or to restore the proper balance of good and evil forces in the world. Most Hindu devotional practices are done individually (rather than in a group as is common in Christian worship), and Shiva is the god most often venerated in architecture and sculpture.

The Hindu temple is a major architectural form of India, and one of the world's most distinctive. It typically includes two parts: a porch, for the preparation and purification of the worshiper, and the Womb Chamber, called in Sanskrit the *garba griha*, the sacred room where an image of the god is kept.

The KANDARYA MAHADEVA TEMPLE at Khajurāho in north central India is one of the most spectacular and best preserved. A stairway leads to not

one, but several porches, which allow access to the *garba griha*. The sacred chamber is marked on the outside by a tall tower that has replicas of itself on its sides. The rounded projecting forms, symbolizing both male and female sexuality, seem to celebrate the procreative energy existing in nature and within ourselves.

Shown here is one of hundreds of erotic scenes from the abundant sculpture on the outside of KANDARYA MAHADEVA TEMPLE. To the Hindu worshiper, union with God is filled with a joy analogous to the sensual pleasure of erotic love. The natural beauty and fullness of the human figures emphasize maleness and femaleness. Fullness seems to come from within the rounded forms, as we saw in the more ancient MALE TORSO from Harappā. The intertwining figures symbolize divine love in human form—an allegory of ultimate spiritual unity.

The complex corps of Hindu gods and goddesses depicted in Indian art represents all aspects of

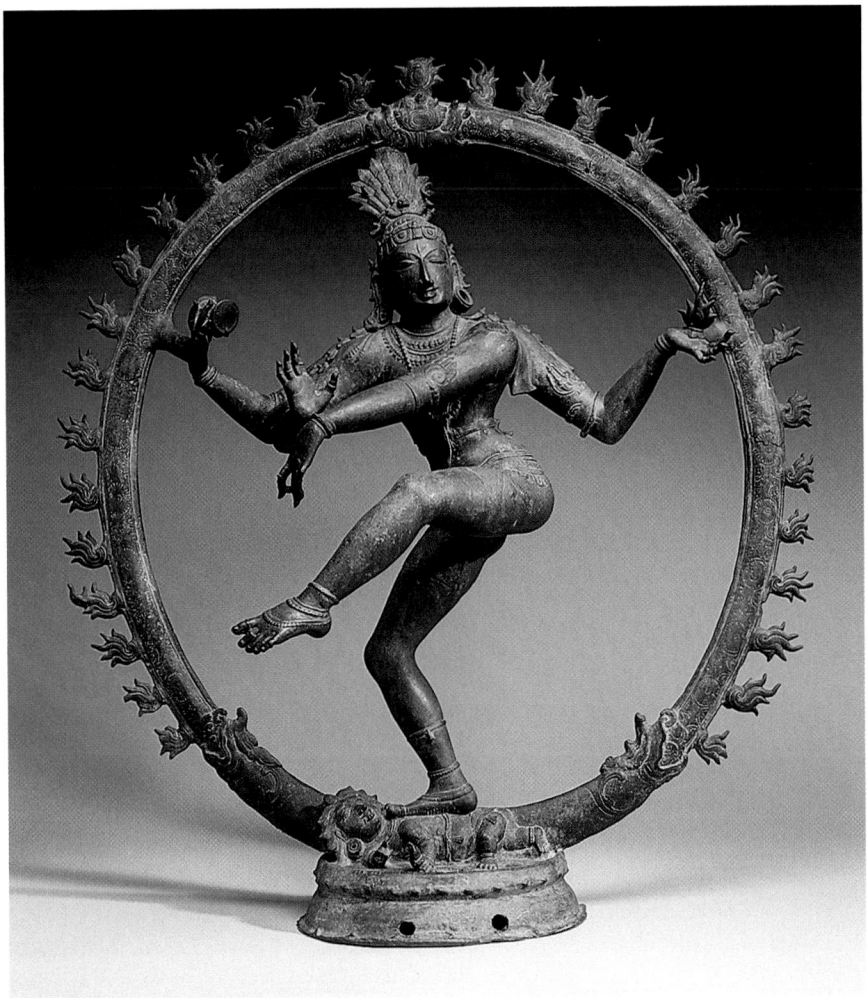

415 NĀTARĀJA, SHIVA AS KING OF DANCE.
South India, Chola Period, 11th century.
Bronze. 43⅛″ × 40″.
© 2001 The Cleveland Museum of Art.
Purchase from the J.H. Wade Fund. 1930.331.

human aspiration and experience. In later Hindu belief, Shiva encompasses in cyclic time the creation, preservation, dissolution, and re-creation of the universe. To show these roles, Shiva takes various forms in Hindu sculpture. In an eleventh-century image from South India, NĀTARĀJA, SHIVA AS KING OF DANCE, performs the cosmic dance within the orb of the sun. He tramples on the monster of ignorance as he holds sacred symbols in his hands. The encircling flame is the purifying fire of destruction and creation. He taps on a small drum to mark the cosmic rhythm of death and rebirth. As he moves, the universe is reflected as light from his limbs. The sculpture implies movement so thoroughly that motion seems contained in every aspect of the piece. Each part is alive with the rhythms of an ancient ritual dance. Multiple arms increase the sense of movement, while his face is composed and impassive, indicating that there is nothing to fear.

Most of India was conquered by Islamic Mughal rulers in the early sixteenth century. The Mughal style of painting (to be discussed in the following chapter) influenced Indian art after the Mughal domain receded again in the seventeenth and eighteenth centuries. Several local Indian art styles arose in the foothills of the Himalaya as artists again took

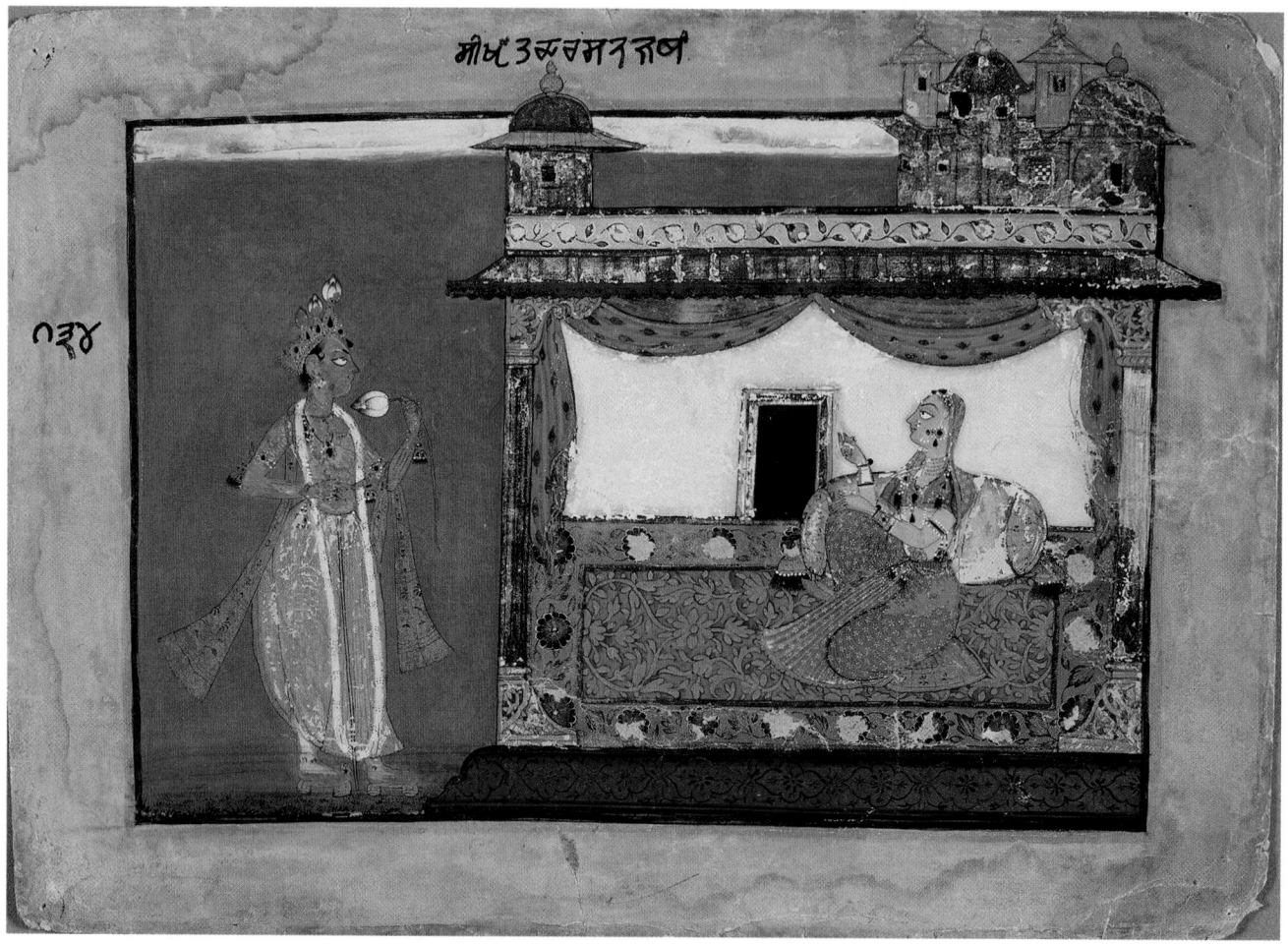

मीष उच्चप्सत्रष

प्रिथ

416 THE APPROACH OF KRISHNA. c. 1660–1670.
Color, silver, and beetle wings on paper. 6⅞″ × 10¼″.
© The Cleveland Museum of Art. Edward L. Whittemore Fund. 1965.249.

up traditional Hindu subjects; we see the Basholi style to good advantage in THE APPROACH OF KRISHNA. A woman waits breathlessly for her lover, the blue-skinned god Krishna. Like many other Indian works, this painting uses erotic desire as a symbol for the spiritual longing for union with the divine. The inscription reads, "Friend, give up your waywardness of mind." The bright red and blue colors symbolize the emotional states of expectancy and desire for the crowned and bejeweled Krishna, who brings a fragrant flower.

We will consider modern Indian art in Chapters 24 and 25.

SOUTHEAST ASIA

The Bronze Age in Southeast Asia began when that metal was first imported into the region about 800 B.C.E. Soon thereafter, the major cultural division of the region appeared: The eastern coast, encompassing most of what is now Vietnam, fell under Chinese influence; most of the remainder willingly adopted and transformed cultural influences from India.

Buddhism and Hinduism both spread southward and eastward from India with traders and merchants. Early Southeast Asian art is primarily Buddhist; later monuments combine motifs, gods, and figures from both religions. Each region of

417 BOROBUDUR. c. 800.
   Java, Indonesia, Asia
   a. Aerial view.
   Photograph: Robert Harding Word Imagery.

   b. CORRIDOR at Borobudur.
   First Gallery.
   Photograph: Werner Forman Archive, Ltd.

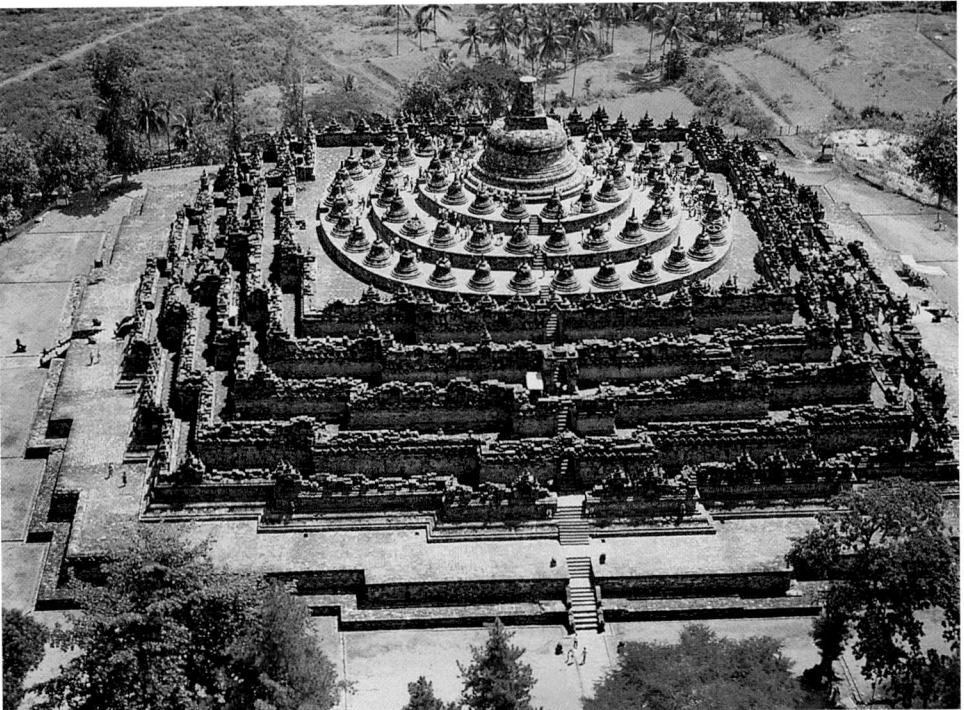

Southeast Asia developed its own interpretation of the major Indian styles.

By any standard, BOROBUDUR must rank among the major works of world art. Built about 800 C.E. on the island of Java (now part of Indonesia), it is an extremely elaborate version of an Indian stupa, or sacred mountain. Rising from a relatively flat plain, it stands above the local surroundings, measuring 105 feet high and 408 feet on a side. It is oriented to the four cardinal directions, with stairways at the four midpoints.

Pilgrims who come for spiritual refreshment may enter at any opening, and then walk around and climb the various terraces in a clockwise direction. More than ten miles of relief sculpture adorn the various CORRIDORS, telling stories that duplicate the journey to enlightenment. On the lower levels, the reliefs deal with the struggle of existence and the cycle of death and rebirth. Then come reliefs depicting the life of the Buddha. As pilgrims walk in these corridors, the high walls prevent them from seeing out, and the curves in the path limit the view ahead. Upper terrace reliefs depict the ideal world of paradise. However, there is still more to come.

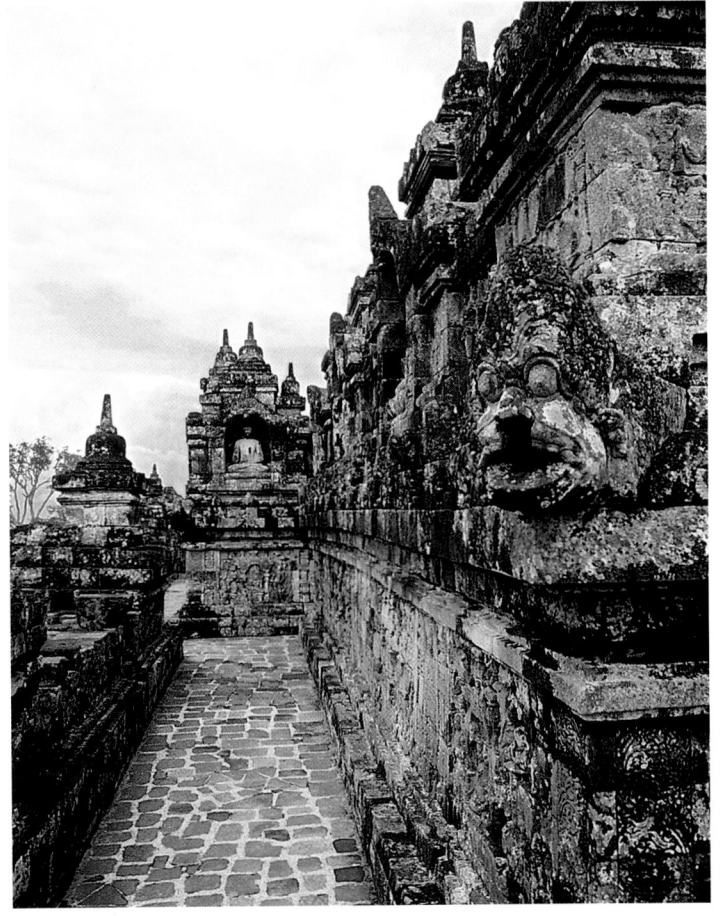

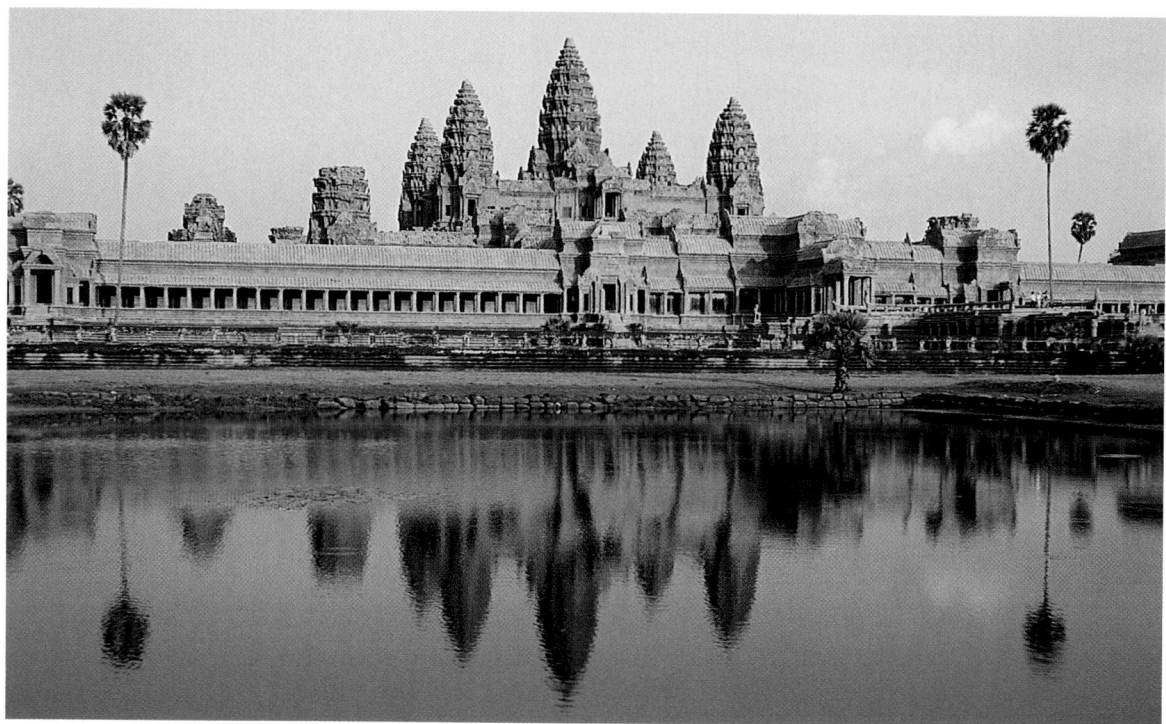

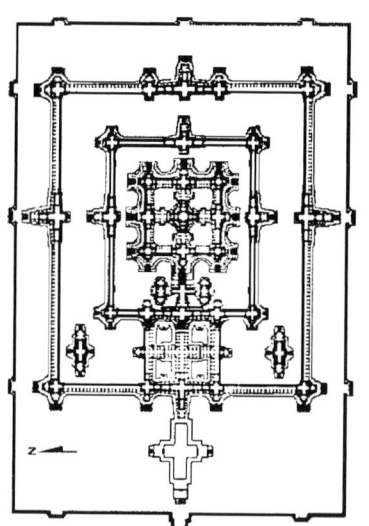

418 ANGKOR WAT.
c. 1120–1150.
a. West entrance.
Photograph: John Elk, Ill.
Bruce Coleman Inc.

b. Plan.

The final four circular levels permit the pilgrim to look out over the landscape and take in the broad view, suggesting enlightenment. Each of the seventy-two small hollow stupas contains a statue of a seated Buddha that is only dimly visible from the outside. At the very top is a sealed stupa whose contents the pilgrim can just guess at. Thus, BOROBUDUR presents the Buddhist conception of the pathway through the cycles of birth and death, which culminates in enlightenment.

The sacred mountain of BOROBUDUR was a principal influence on the Cambodian temple of ANGKOR WAT, which was erected in the twelfth century near the capital of the Khmer empire. This was the most prosperous period in Cambodia's history, as the rulers mastered the science of irrigation and were able to make the jungles produce abundant crops. The people at that time seemed to accord their rulers near-divine status because the many stone carvings of Buddhas, Bodhisattvas, and Hindu gods appear also to be portraits of real people. The two religions were apparently considered compatible.

The temple, which faces due west, was originally surrounded by moats, as if to remind everyone that management of water was the source of wealth. The many corridors have corbelled roofs, and inside they are decorated with low relief sculpture depicting primarily Hindu myths about the god Vishnu. (See one of the best of these, ARMY ON THE MARCH, on page 182.) The ruler of Cambodia thought of himself

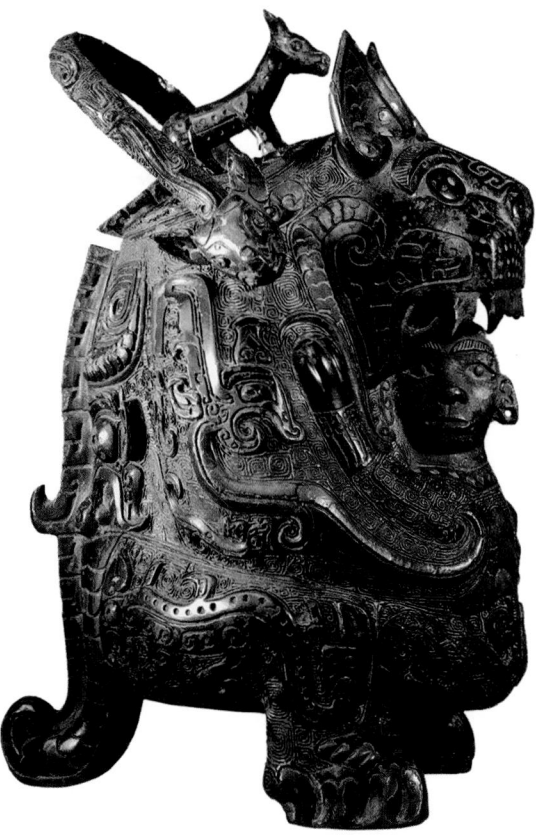

419 RITUAL VESSEL (LA TIGRESSE).
China. Shang dynasty. c. 1100–1000 B.C.E.
Cast bronze. Height 14″.
© Phototheque des Musées de la Ville de Paris.
Marie de Paris.
Photograph: L. De Graces.

as a descendant of Vishnu, guarding the fertility of his domain. This emphasis on fertility in the design of ANGKOR WAT extends to the tops of the towers, which resemble sprouting buds.

CHINA

Chinese civilization up to the modern period was characterized by the interaction of three traditions: Confucianism, Daoism, and Buddhism. The first two are Chinese creations, while Buddhism came from India. All three have interacted with and influenced each other, imparting richness and variety to Chinese culture. Before these traditions developed, however, distinctive Chinese arts were already flourishing.

Some of the world's finest cast-bronze objects were produced in China during the Shang dynasty (sixteenth to eleventh centuries B.C.E.). In the RITUAL VESSEL, there is an overall compactness. As on other Shang containers, surfaces are covered with an intricate composite of animal forms: sometimes fragments of animals are combined, sometimes complete animals are depicted. In this piece, a deer acts as a handle for the lid; just behind the deer, an elephant's trunk comes out of a tiger's mouth, providing a third support. The man seems about to be devoured—his head is shown within the ferocious jaw of the tiger spirit—yet at the same time his hands are relaxed as he reaches to the animal for protection. An intriguing aspect of this vessel is the gentle expression on the man's face in relation to the aggressive though protective power of the animal.

Most bronze vessels were used in rituals in honor of ancestors. The Chinese believed that one's ancestors live eternally in the spiritual realm, and from there they can influence worldly affairs for better or worse. These beliefs evolved into Confucianism, a moral and ethical system developed by Confucius (Kong Fuzi, 551–479 B.C.E.). Confucius was no mystic; asked once about honoring the spirits, he replied, "You do not even honor man; how can you honor the spirits!" Cautious innovation and respect for tradition characterize much Chinese art because of his influence.

In the hope of improving their afterlife, many persons were buried with most of their possessions. No one, however, was more vain in collecting objects for their burial than the emperor Qin Shihuangdi, who at the time of his death in 210 B.C.E. had unified China in something like its present form. (His dynastic name, Qin—pronounced chin—is the root of the word *China*.) So intent was he on guarding his afterlife that he ordered a massive army of life-size clay soldiers made for his protection. The TERRA COTTA WARRIORS (on the following page) number about six thousand in all, among them cavalrymen, archers, and foot soldiers. These lifelike figures in their huge tomb were discovered in 1974, in an extraordinary archaeological find.

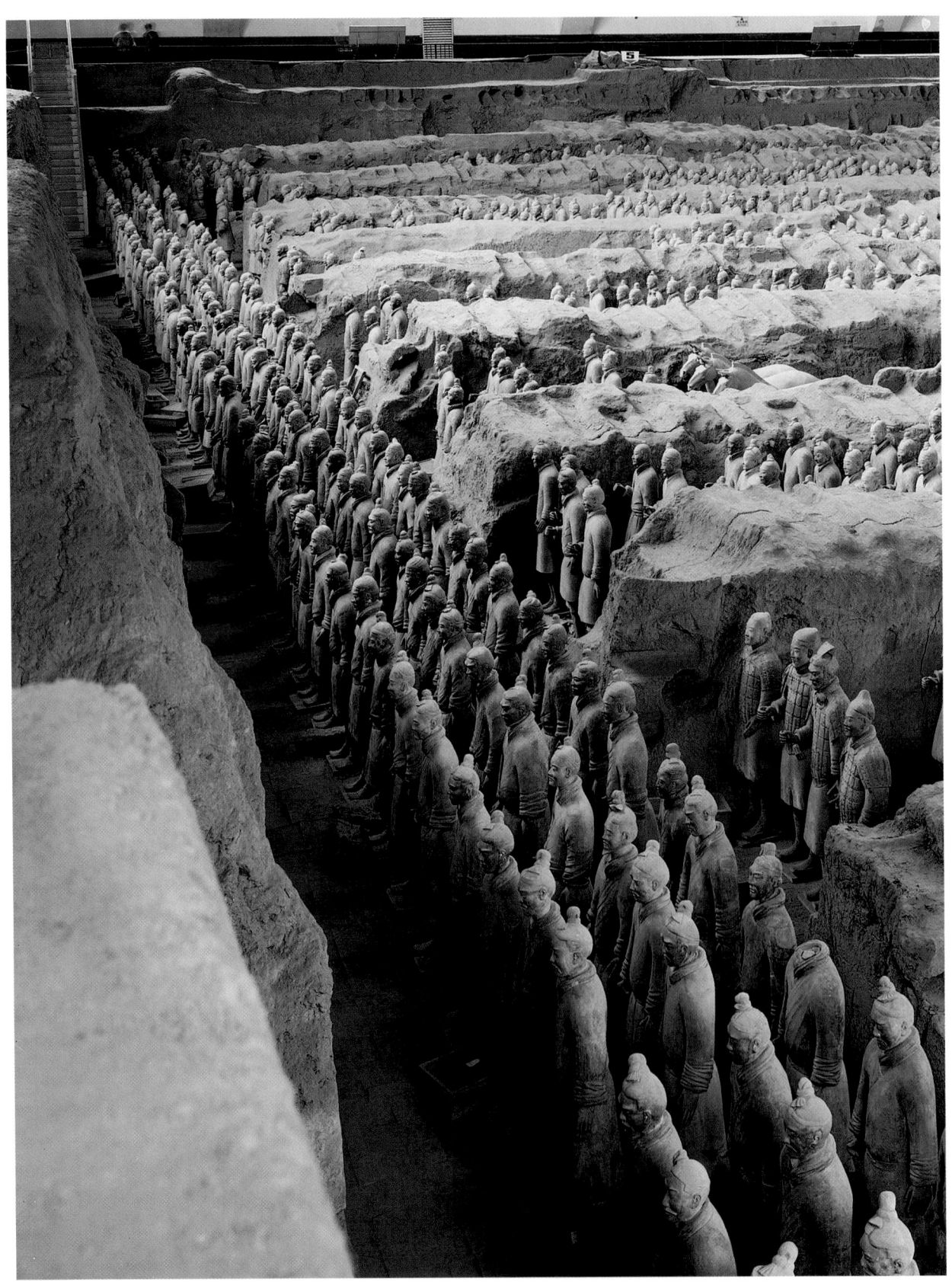

420 TERRA COTTA WARRIORS.
Pit No. 1, Museum of the First Emperor of Qin.
Shaanxi Province, China. Qin dynasty. c. 210 B.C.E.
Photograph: Hamilton Photography and Film Company.

The tombs from the Han dynasty (206 B.C.E.–221 C.E.) have yielded most of the surviving artwork from that period in China, and from these remains we can learn a great deal about what interested and motivated at least the upper classes.

A recently excavated work from this period is the magnificent second-century FLYING HORSE found in Gansu Province. The sculptor gave a feeling of weightlessness to the horse by delicately balancing it on one hoof atop an abstract representation of a flying swallow. The curvaceous form and powerful energy of this elegant horse is vividly captured in a way that is typically Chinese.

Horses were prized possessions of royalty and aristocracy. Throughout Chinese history, they frequently appear in art as strong, noble animals. The horse is one of the twelve signs of the traditional Chinese zodiac, and persons born in the Year of the Horse are said to possess strength, speed, and endurance.

Here the artist has understood the basic energy or life force of the animal, and rendered it faithfully. The quest to understand and depict this inner force, or *qi* in Chinese, animates a great deal of art production through the centuries in China.

The concept of *qi* derives from Daoist beliefs about the harmony of the universe. Daoists believe that the best life is one of harmony with the force

421 FLYING HORSE.
Eastern Han dynasty. 2nd century.
Bronze. 13½″ × 17¾″.
Wu–Wai, Kansu.
National Museum, Beijing, China.
Photograph: Erich Lessing. Art Resource, NY.

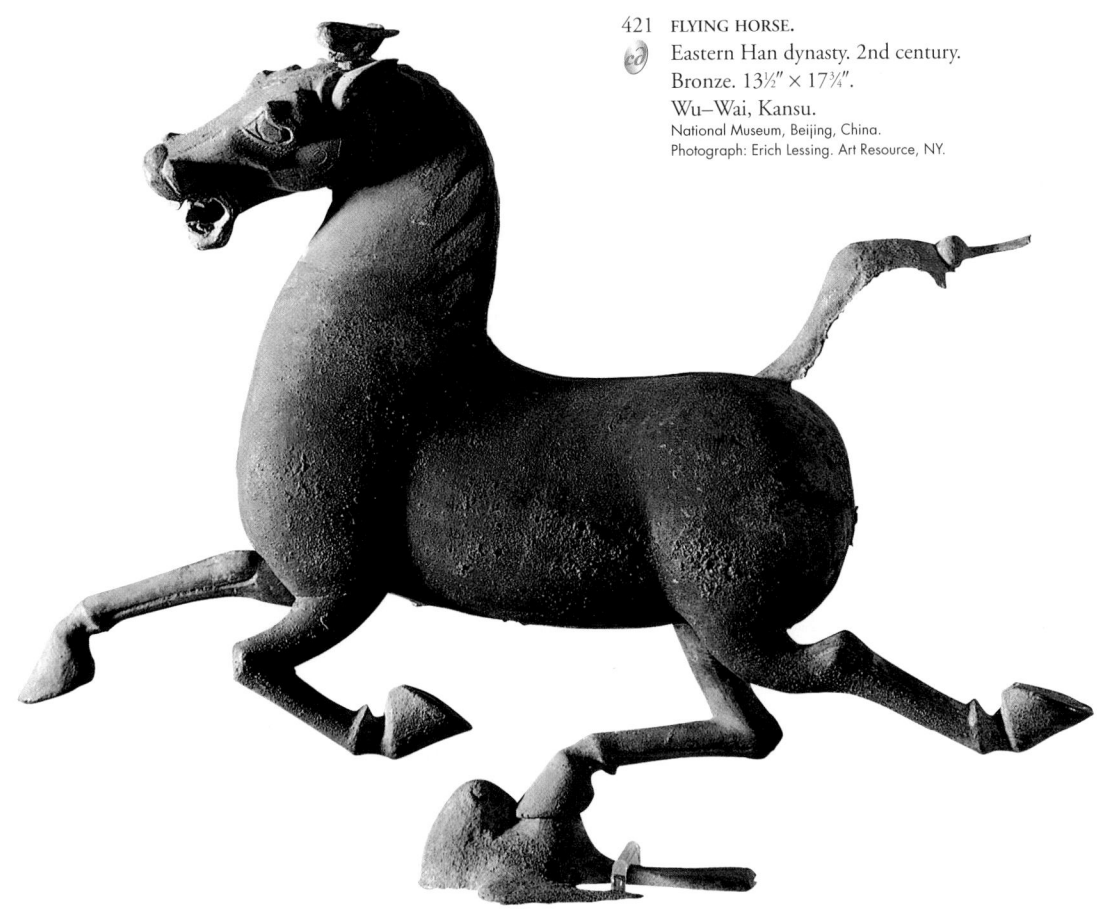

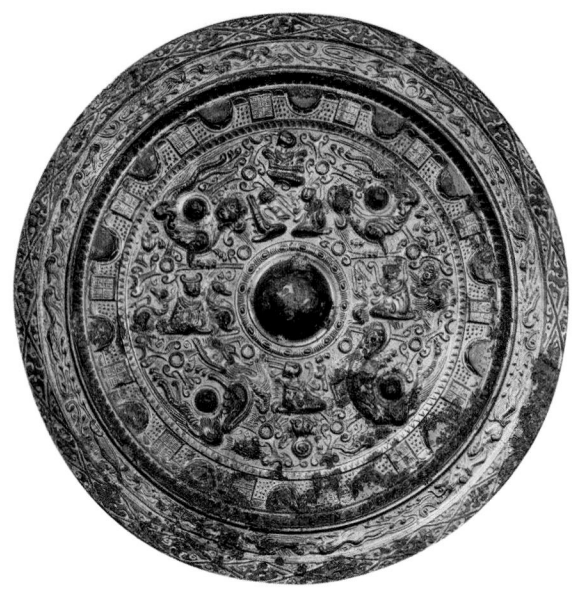

422 MIRROR WITH XIWANGMU.
Early Six Dynasties Period (317–581).
Bronze. Diameter 7¼".
© Cleveland Museum of Art.
The Severance and Greta Millikin Purchase Fund, 1983.213.

that animates all created beings. According to traditional Daoism, achieving this harmony will make one immortal; the MIRROR WITH XIWANGMU honors such a person. Also known as the Queen Mother of the West, she achieved the Dao and dispensed immortality from her home on faraway Jade Mountain. The mirror (which is shiny on the other side) depicts Xiwangmu seated at the left of the mirror's central bulb. Opposite her is the Lord Duke of the East; according to Daoist mythology, the two meet each year on the seventh day of the seventh month. Just outside their circle, an inscription wishes good fortune to the mirror's owner. In the outer bands are other heavenly beings and circles of clouds, which symbolize the endless cycle of time.

In painting, we see clearly the Chinese reverence for nature. Traditionally, Chinese painters sought to manifest the spirit residing in every form. According to Daoism, a secret force called the Dao (or "the way" in English) animates all creation. A painter was taught to meditate before wielding a brush in order to achieve a balance between the impression received through the eyes and the perception of the heart and mind. After prolonged contemplation of nature, the artist painted from memory, working with ink and light color on silk or paper. Through painting, individuals nourished spiritual harmony within themselves and revealed divine energy to others. Daoism focuses on the relative nature of all things: There can be no death without life, no good without evil, no East without West. Behind the duality and illusion of the so-called real world is the unifying Dao. It is in this way that the universe functions, as one can see in the effortless flow of interacting forces of nature.

The Northern Song dynasty (960–1126) was a particularly important period for painting in China. During the eleventh century, a group of artist-intellectuals developed a new spirit in artistic expression. Many of these painters, who were poets, political leaders, and accomplished calligraphers, held that the artist's true character and emotions could be expressed through the abstract forms of calligraphic characters—and even through individual brush strokes. They were critical of those who painted for commercial rather than aesthetic reasons.

Long valued in China, calligraphy is traditionally considered an art equal to painting. Since ancient times, Chinese leaders of all kinds have been expected to express the strength of their character through elegant writing. By introducing calligraphic brush techniques for expressive purposes, painters sought to elevate painting to the levels that calligraphy and poetry had already attained. Huai-su, in AUTOBIOGRAPHY, and later masters drew inspiration from fourth-century Daoist poet, statesman, and master calligrapher Wang Xizhi. His style of writing, an improvement on earlier styles, has served as an inspirational model for generations of calligraphers to the present day. The stature of Wang Xizhi in China is comparable to that of Shakespeare and Rembrandt in the West and indicates the Chinese people's long-standing admiration for great calligraphy. Unfortunately, only a few original examples of his writing survive.

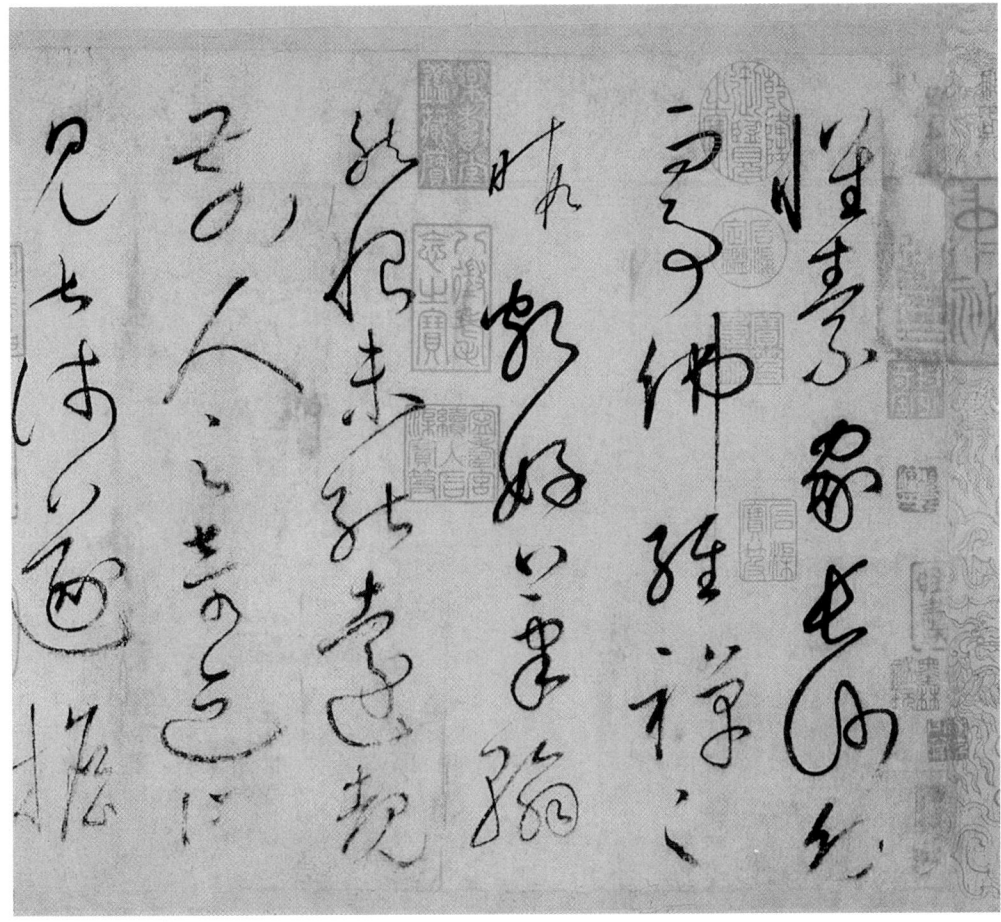

423 Huai-su.
Detail of AUTOBIOGRAPHY.
Tang dynasty, 7th–10th centuries.
Ink on paper.
National Palace Museum, Taipei, Taiwan, Republic of China.

The flowering of calligraphy as an art form was due partly to the popularity of the new, looser style of writing that freed scholars from the angular formality of the characters that were used in official script. The fluid script enabled artists and poets to express themselves in a personal and spontaneous manner. With the spontaneous, gestural design of each brush stroke, the artist conveys the emotional as well as the intellectual content of the word or character being written. Poetry lies in the execution of the stroke as well as the phrase. In China, painting and writing are closely related, and Chinese artists often include poems within their paintings. The same brushes and ink are used for both, and in both each brush stroke is important in the total design. Artists "paint" their poems as much as they "write" their paintings.

Contemporaries of the court painter Fan Kuan regarded him as the greatest landscape painter of the Song dynasty. In his large hanging scroll

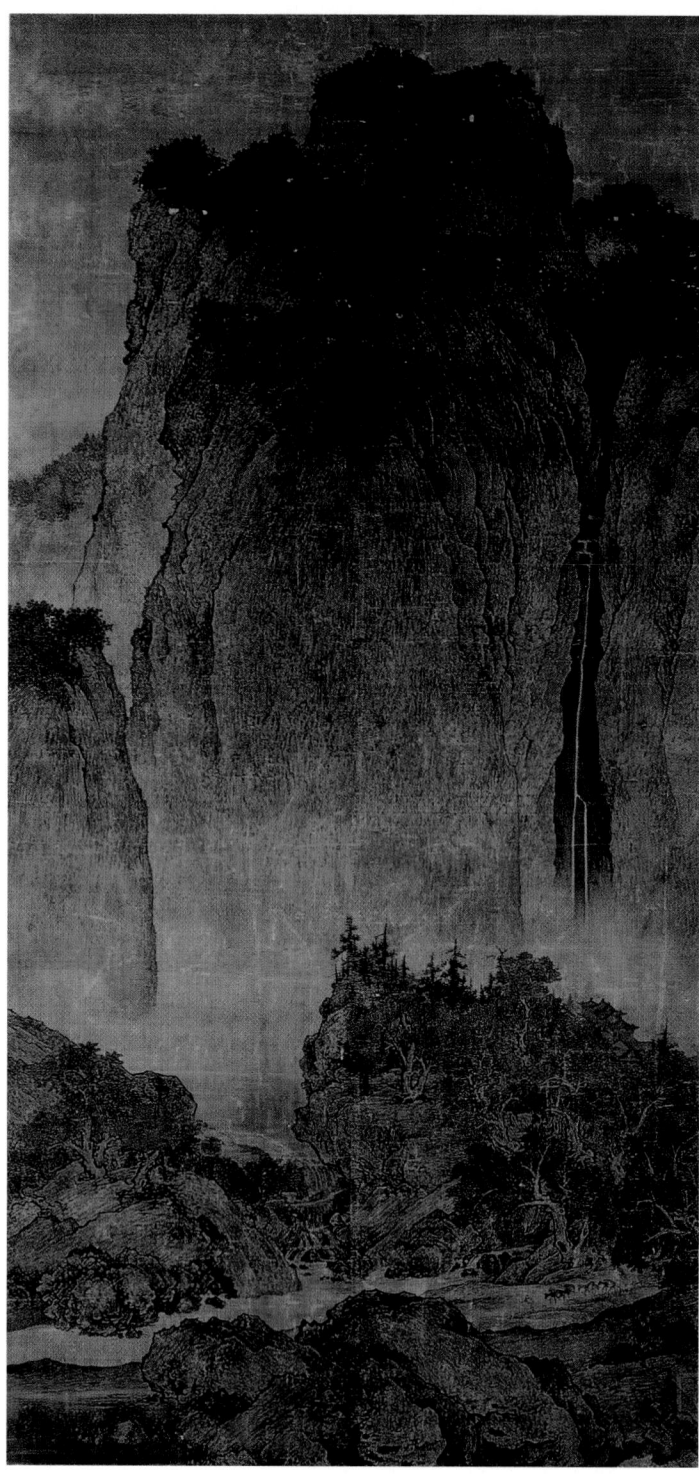

424 Fan Kuan.
TRAVELERS AMONG MOUNTAINS AND STREAMS.
Song dynasty. Early 11th century.
Hanging scroll, ink on silk. Height 81¼".
National Palace Museum, Taipei, Taiwan, Republic of China.

TRAVELERS AMONG MOUNTAINS AND STREAMS, intricate brushwork captures the spirit of trees and rocks. Artists used many kinds of brush strokes, each identified by descriptive names such as "raveled rope," "raindrops," "ax cuts," "nailhead," and "wrinkles on a devil's face." Here "raindrop" and other types of brush strokes suggest the textures of the vertical face of the cliff. Men and donkeys, shown in minute scale, travel a horizontal path dwarfed by high cliffs rising sharply behind them. To highlight the stylized waterfall as the major accent in the design, Fan Kuan painted the crevice behind the waterfall in a dark wash and left the off-white silk unpainted to suggest the falling water. The vertical emphasis of the composition is offset by the almost horizontal shape of the light area behind the rocks in the lower foreground. The massive centrality of the composition is typical of the efforts of Northern Song artists to capture the more powerful aspects of nature.

When a vertical line intersects a horizontal line, the opposing forces generate a strong center of interest. Fan Kuan took advantage of this phenomenon by extending the implied vertical line of the falls to direct the viewer's attention to the travelers. Figures give human significance to the painting and, by their small scale, indicate the vastness of nature. Fan Kuan achieved his monumental landscape in part by grouping the fine details into a balanced design of light and dark areas.

The painting embodies ideas of Daoism and Confucianism, China's two major philosophical and spiritual traditions, in which nature is both emptiness and substance, interacting passive and active forces (yin and yang) that regulate the universe. One achieves harmony on Earth through a balance of these forces—female and male, void and solid, dark and light.

In both central and southern China, steep, mist-shrouded peaks have inspired Chinese painters for centuries. In the seventeenth century, Li Li-Weng wrote, "First we see the hills in the painting, then we see the painting in the hills." His words remind us that, although art depends on our perception of nature, art also helps us to see nature with fresh eyes.

A Mongol invasion from the north dislocated China's Song dynasty rulers in 1125. (These were the same Mongols who under Genghis Khan and his relatives eventually occupied an empire stretching from Korea to Eastern Poland and Baghdad to Siberia.) The Song court and art academy moved south to Hangzhou, where a new painting style arose.

If the earlier Northern Song style was monumental and philosophical, the Southern Song was intimate and personal, emphasizing poetic views of relatively smaller landscapes. One of the leaders in the new style was Ma Yuan, a fifth-generation descendant of academy teachers who was a favorite of the emperor. Ma's painting WATCHING THE DEER BY A PINE SHADED STREAM captures a contemplative moment in which a scholar or official enjoys a respite on a wooded path. Ma's way of depicting pine branches gives the work an ethereal calm. The brushwork is as meticulous as in the preceding Northern Song, but the composition is relatively adventurous as it fades away into mist at the upper left. This composition is so off-balance that the artist's contemporaries referred to him as "one-corner Ma" because of his tendency to leave large areas of his works unpainted. Such boldness responds to Daoist beliefs, however, because without the voids we would not appreciate the fullness.

Most of the important painters of the Song dynasty were associated with official art academies or government service. During the following Yuan dynasty (1279–368), the final conquest of China by Mongols radically altered this scenario. The most creative artists refused to paint or teach for the foreign government; rather, they lived outside official sponsorship. Devoting themselves to a life of art and poetry, they created a new style called *literati painting*.

The Yuan dynasty literati painters made many innovations in brushwork and subject matter. They used the brush in new ways and saw old subjects with fresh eyes. An example is Ni Zan's SIX GENTLEMEN, pictured on page 97. Ni's style was even more personal and idiosyncratic than that of Southern Song dynasty painters.

The literati also pioneered the painting of bamboo. They did this because they saw symbolic meanings in its resistance to wind and storms. Just

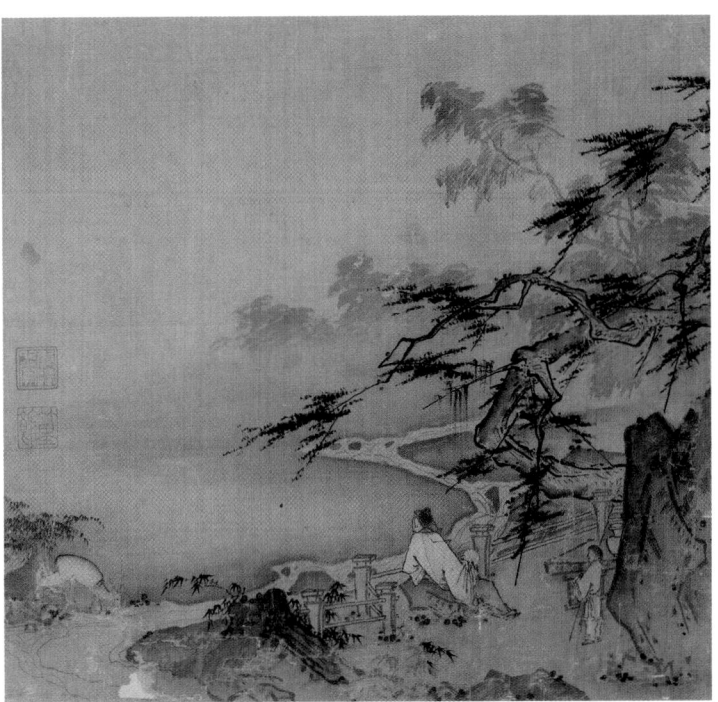

425 Ma Yuan.
WATCHING THE DEER BY A PINE SHADED STREAM. c. 1200.
Album leaf, ink on silk. 9½" × 10".
© Cleveland Museum of Art. Gift of Mrs. A. Dean Perry, 1997.88.

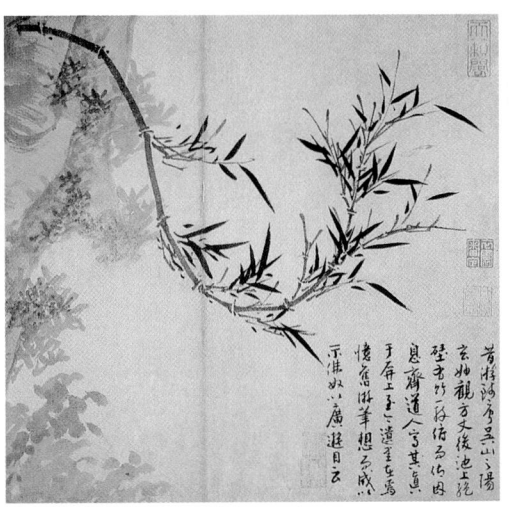

426 Wu Chen.
ALBUM LEAF from manual of ink bamboo. 1350.
Ink on paper. 16⅞" × 20½".
National Palace Museum, Taipei, Taiwan, Republic of China.

as bamboo bends without breaking, so must the creative artist in foreign-controlled China. A leading bamboo painter was Wu Chen, whose ALBUM LEAF is regarded as a masterpiece of the type.

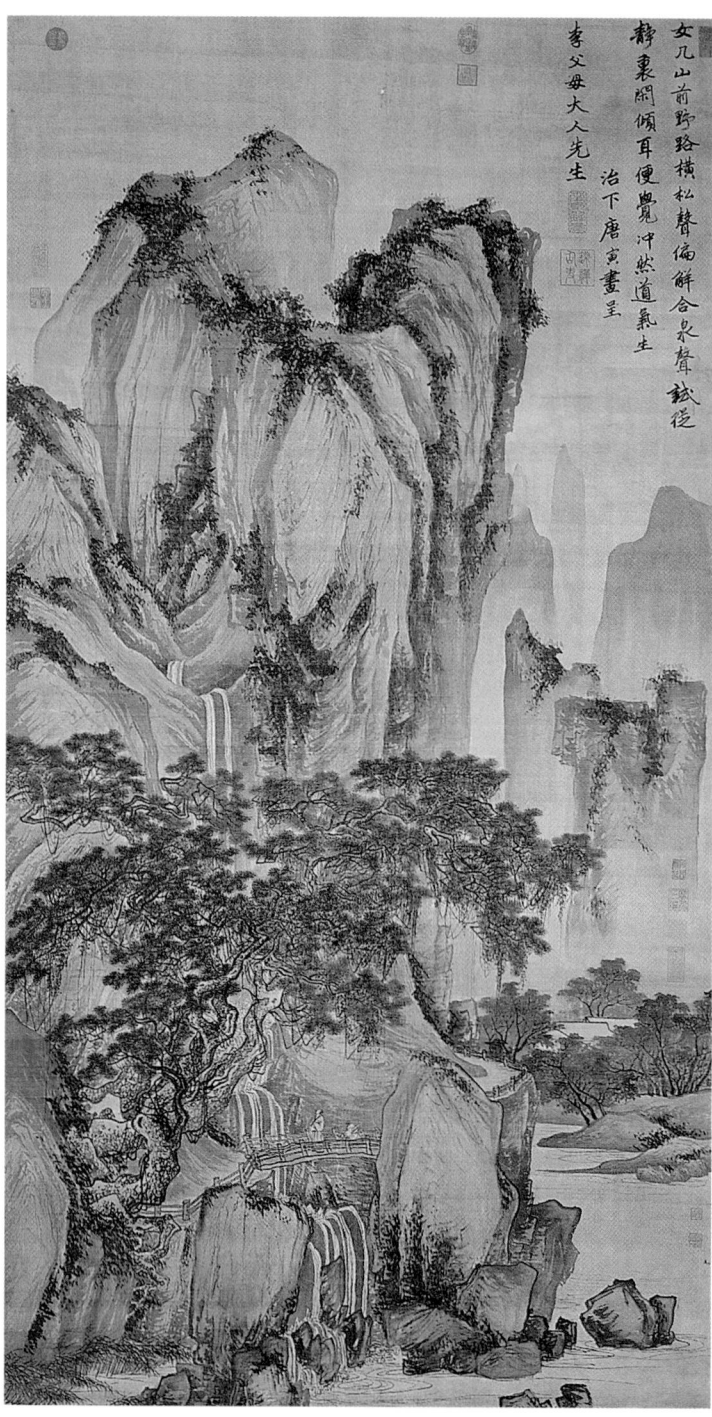

女几山前野路横松聲偏
静裏閒倾耳便覺冲然道氣
女几山前野路横松聲偏解翳泉聲
静裏閒倾耳便覺冲然道氣生

李父母大人先生
治下唐寅畫呈

In order to help assimilate their rich tradition, Chinese painters often copy (with personal variations) the works of earlier artists. Even fully mature painters will often produce a work in the style of an older master they particularly admire. This tendency reveals one of the basic precepts of Confucianism: respect for the past. The idea that a painter must fully comprehend tradition before expressing individuality was a hallmark of the artists who worked for the Imperial court in the sixteenth and seventeenth centuries, and they produced many works in which this homage is clear.

One of the most successful of these academic painters was Tang Yin, who worked in the early sixteenth century during the Ming dynasty (1368–1744). His painting WHISPERING PINES ON A MOUNTAIN PATH owes a great deal to Fan Kuan's work TRAVELERS AMONG MOUNTAINS AND STREAMS. The manner of painting the rocks and the overall composition clearly show that Tang was studying the work of Fan Kuan. In addition, Tang's inscribed poem shows his study of Daoism. The last three lines read:

The whispering pines dissolve in the rush of the
*   waterfall.*
I listen with quiet absorption
And feel the spirit of Dao rising within me.[1]

The Chinese have traditionally held ceramic arts in high regard, and the history of pottery in China is primarily the story of Imperial sponsorship and nearly continuous technical advances. During the Song dynasty, Chinese potters learned to use earth-toned glazes that slowly ran down the surface of stoneware bowls, creating interesting accidental designs. Other vessels were allowed to crack after firing, as the glaze cooled more quickly than the body; collectors especially prized vases with a balanced pattern of cracks. Later in the same dynastic period, Chinese potters developed the creamy and rich blue-green glaze whose color is so indescribable that Westerners named it

427   Tang Yin.
WHISPERING PINES ON A MOUNTAIN PATH.
Ming dynasty. c. 1516.
Hanging scroll. 76″ × 40″.
National Palace Museum, Taipei, Taiwan, Republic of China.

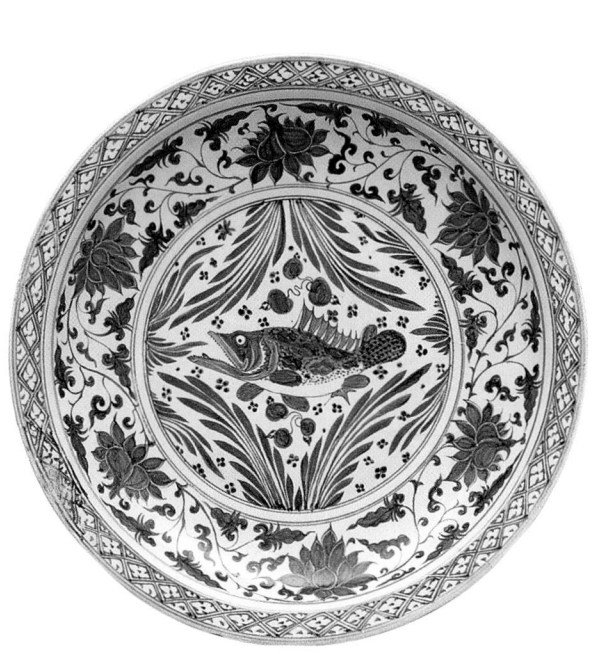

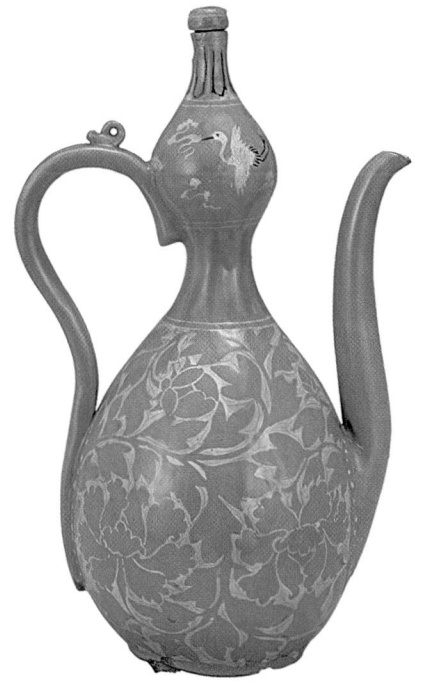

428 PORCELAIN PLATE.
Mid-14th century. Yuan dynasty.
Painted in underglaze blue. Diameter 18″.
Metropolitan Museum of Art. Purchase, Mrs. Richard E. Linburn Gift.
Photograph: © 1989 Metropolitan Museum of Art. 1987.10.

429 WINE PITCHER.
Koryo dynasty. Mid-12th century.
Stoneware with celadon glaze and inlaid white and black slip.
Height 13½″.
National Museum of Korea, Seoul. National Treasure No. 116.

Celadon after the hero's garments in a famous French play.

Probably the best-known type of Chinese ceramic is porcelain, made from a rare type of clay that when fired becomes pure white. Early porcelains, such as the PORCELAIN PLATE pictured here, were decorated with blue because that was the only color that could withstand the high temperatures necessary to fire porcelain correctly. The Chinese were the first to develop this type of pottery. Porcelain emerges translucent from the oven, and it rings when struck; this led the Chinese to conclude that their best dishes contained music. After it was first imported into the Western world, European workshops tried for generations to duplicate its translucency and deep blue colors. In the Ming dynasty,

potters discovered how to glaze porcelain in almost any color through multiple firings.

Throughout Asia, potters in different provinces and countries produced their own variations on Chinese ceramic styles. The WINE PITCHER shown here is an exquisite example of a Korean adaptation of the Chinese blue-green celadon, with the addition of a new style of decoration. The potter etched out the background behind the flower decorations in the lower part of the vessel, and also etched the shapes of the flying cranes above. The potter then filled these lowered areas with white and black *slip* (liquid clay) before firing the vessel for the final time. This slip-inlay technique is a Korean invention, and here the smooth surface complements the graceful curves of the double-gourd shape and

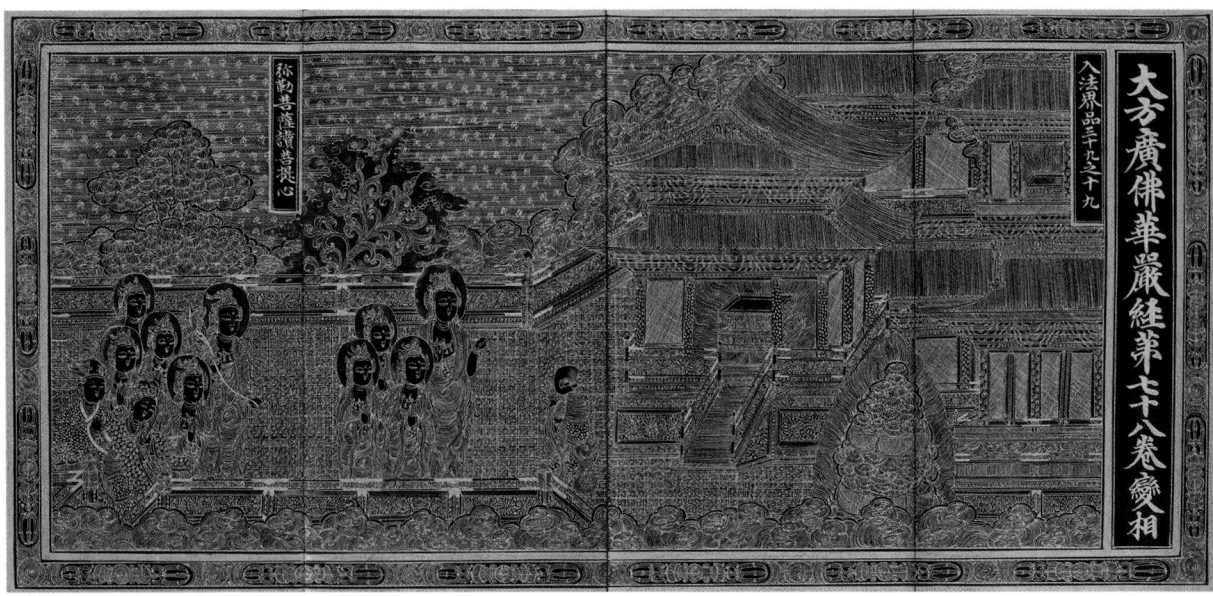

430   AVATAMASKA SUTRA, Vol. 12, 13th–14th century.
      Korea, Goryeo period.
      Gold and silver text on indigo blue paper. 12⅜″ × 4⅝″
      The Cleveland Museum of Art.
      The Severance and Greta Millikin Purchase Fund, 1994.25.

elegant handle of the pitcher. The shapes and decorations of this piece work so well together that the Korean government designated the WINE PITCHER a national treasure.

Korea developed some of its own art forms despite the influential presence of nearby China and Japan. We see one of these in the AVATAMASKA SUTRA, a book page produced in the mid-fourteenth century. A sutra is a book of Buddhist teachings, and this one includes the important teaching that all beings have the Buddha nature. The Korean artists who illustrated it used fine strands of gold and silver to depict a gallery of immortals and divine beings.

Chinese painting after the Yuan dynasty evolved down two parallel paths. Within the academies, artists copied old masters and innovated cautiously; outside them, the literati took a bolder and freer approach. One of the boldest of the latter was Bada Shanren, a descendant of Ming dynasty royalty who lived in the early part of the succeeding Qing dynasty (1644–1912). The Qing, like the Yuan,

were foreign. Because the Qing persecuted descendants of the Ming, Bada lived the life of a recluse, taking refuge in a monastery and later faking madness. Witnesses reported that he would wander the streets in rags, shouting. On the door of the abandoned building where he lived, he scrawled the word "dumb" (mute), and when visitors came he would laugh and drink with them, but would not talk. This behavior lasted about five years. In 1684, he gave up his faked insanity and lived in his provincial capital, trading paintings for food. His works, such as CICADA ON A BANANA LEAF, combine free execution with subtle political comments. The cicada is a symbol of rebirth in Chinese mythology, and in Bada's painting it signifies a hope for the resurrection of the failed Ming.

Bada's art remained almost unknown until the declining years of the Qing. Then, as artists began to radically question their tradition, Bada's wildness was an important precursor to more modern experiments in Chinese painting, as we shall see in Chapter 24.

JAPAN

Throughout its history, Japanese culture has been marked by alternating periods of nationalism, in which typically Japanese forms have prospered, and periods of eager borrowing of foreign influences.

The indigenous religion of Japan is an ancient form of nature and ancestor worship called Shinto. In this religion, forests, fields, waterfalls, and huge stones are considered holy places where gods dwell. The Shinto shrines at Ise occupy a sacred site within a forest. With only a few lapses, the present MAIN SHRINE at Ise has been completely and exactly rebuilt every twenty years since the late seventh century. Builders take wood for the shrine from the forest with gratitude and ceremonial care. As a tree is cut into boards, the boards are numbered so that the wood that was joined in the tree is reunited in the shrine. No nails are used; the wood is fitted and pegged. In keeping with the Shinto concept of purity, surfaces are left unpainted and the roof is natural thatch. The shrines at Ise combine simplicity with subtlety. Refined craftsmanship, sculptural proportions, and spatial harmonies express the ancient religious and aesthetic values of Shinto.

The first major wave of cultural borrowing took place in the seventh century, when Japanese emperor Shotoku sent emissaries to China to study that civilization. They returned very impressed with many aspects of Chinese culture. For example, the emperor enthusiastically adopted Buddhism, making it the official religion. (Many Shinto gods became sacred beings in Japanese Buddhism.) Japanese Buddhist sculpture from this period was heavily influenced by Chinese sculpture, which the Japanese reinterpreted with subtle changes. Shotoku also encouraged the Japanese aristocracy to learn Chinese and use Chinese script. Confucian teachings about social order and respect for tradition were also adopted, along with many aspects of Chinese art and architecture. In fact, because much of Chinese ancient architecture has not survived, the best place to study it is in Japan on the Yamato plain near Kyoto, where Shotoku set up his capital and the emperors lived for centuries after.

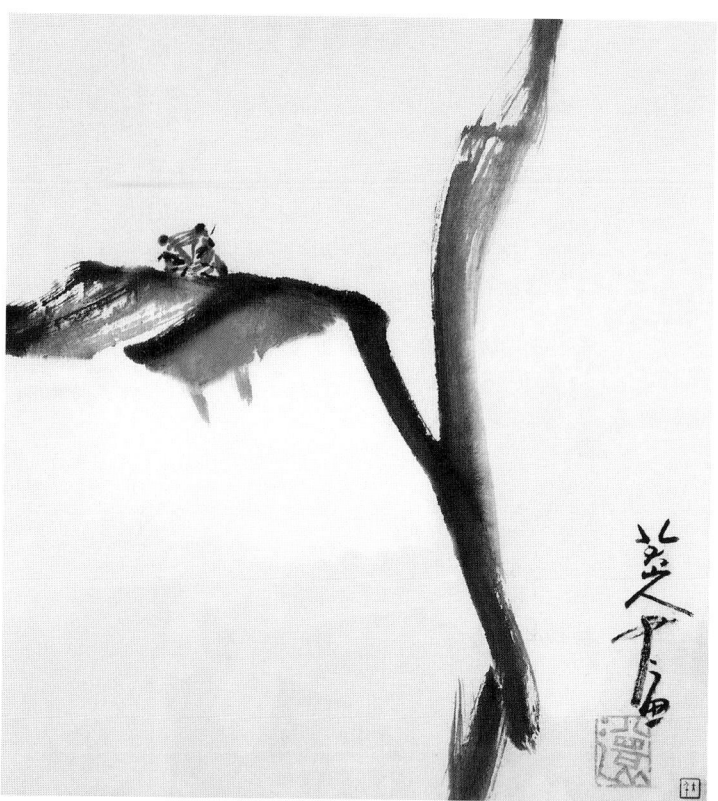

431 Bada Shanren.
CICADA ON A BANANA LEAF.
Qing dynasty. 1688–1689.
Leaf "f" from an album *Flowers and Birds*. Ink on paper.
Freer Gallery of Art, Smithsonian Institution, Washington, D.C. F1955.21e.

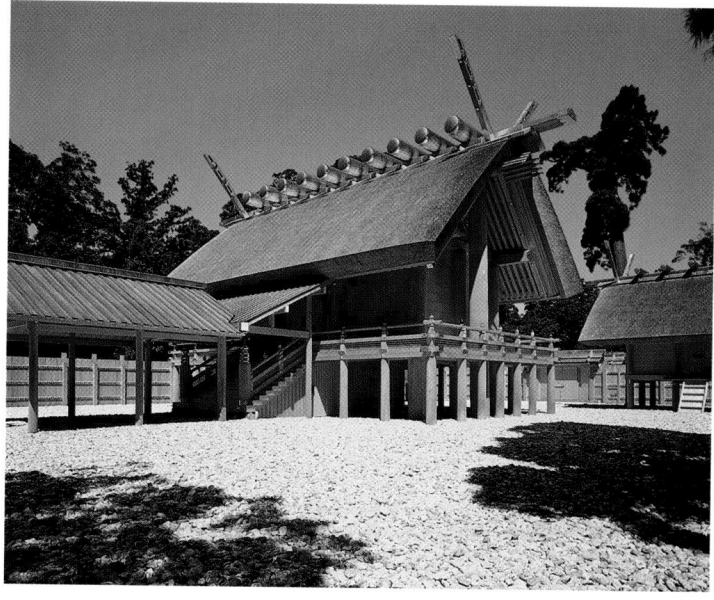

432 MAIN SHRINE. Ise, Japan. c. 685. Rebuilt every twenty years.
Photograph: Kyoto News International, Inc.

The temple complex of HORYUJI exemplifies the Buddhist monastery as it existed in both China and Japan. In the center of the courtyard, we can see the many-storied pagoda, which has a symbolic function relating to its descent from Chinese watchtowers and Indian stupas (see page 293). Next to it is the KONDO, or Golden hall, a meditation hall where Buddha statues are kept. In the center of one wall is a gate house; opposite it along the back wall is a larger lecture hall, where monks hear religious teaching. The oldest parts of HORYUJI date from the late seventh century, and are among the world's oldest surviving wooden buildings.

To hold up a two-story structure with a heavy tile roof, Japanese architects (influenced by Chinese predecessors) developed an elaborate bracketing system for the KONDO at Horyuji. The empty second story is merely an accent to show the importance of the building, but it also demonstrates the skill of the architect.

Japan has the oldest surviving royal family of any society. This longevity has been made possible by frequent military interventions in which the generals ruled on behalf of the emperors, as in the Kamakura

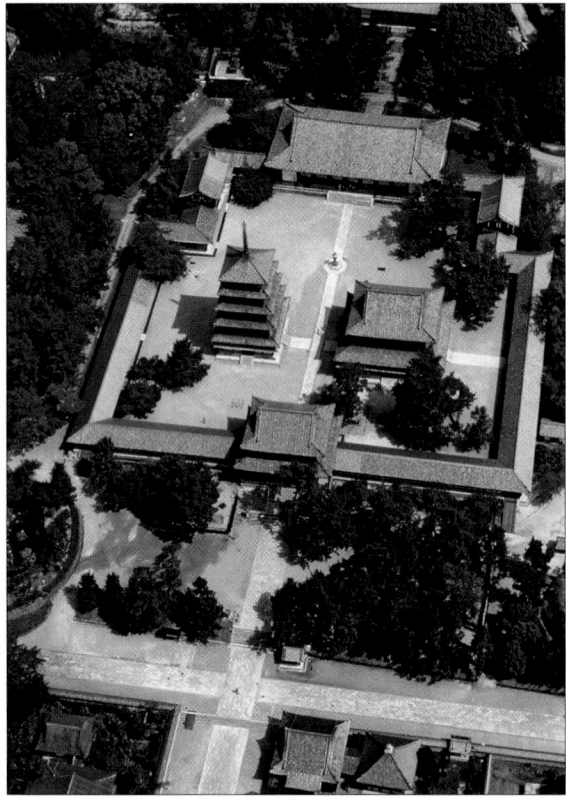

433 **HORYUJI TEMPLE.** Nara, Japan. c. 690.

a. Pagoda and a section of the lecture hall (Kondo).
Photograph: Kaz uyoshi Miyoshi. Pacific Press Service.
Galileo Picture Services, LLC.

b. **KONDO,** Structural diagram.
From *The Art and Architecture of Japan,* Robert Treat Paine and Alexander Coburn Soper, Penguin, London, 1981.
By permission of Yale University Press, Pelican History of Art.

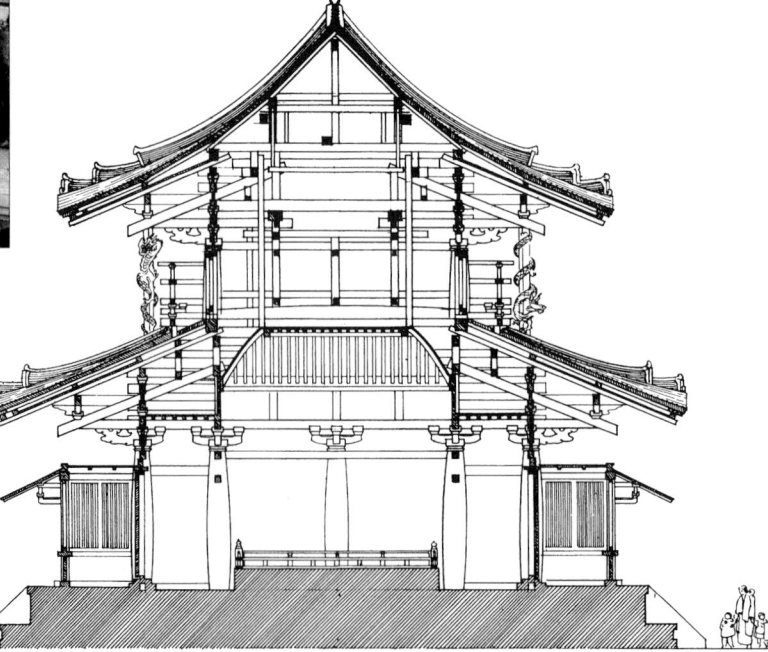

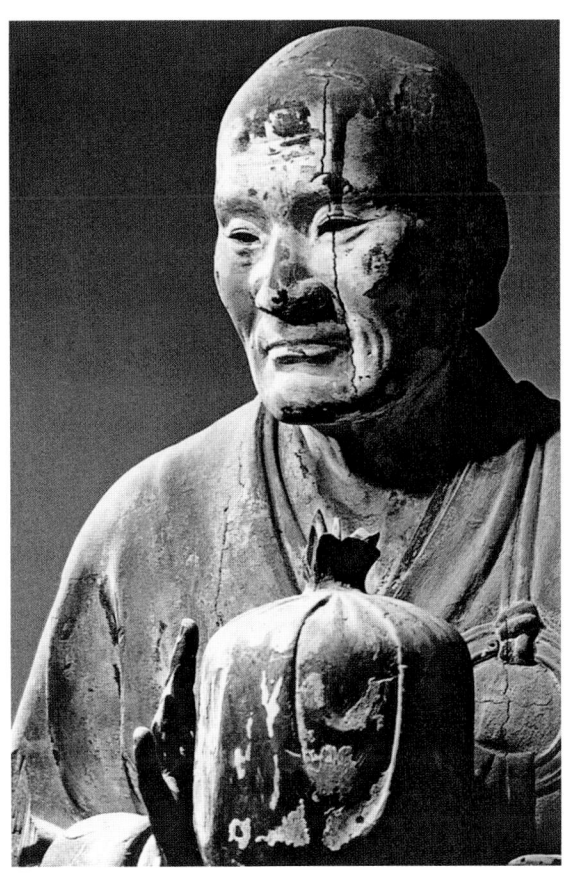

434 Unkei. Detail of MUCHAKU. c. 1208.
Wood. Height 75″.
Kofuku-ji Temple, Nara, Japan.

435 BURNING OF THE SANJO PALACE. From the HEIJI
MONOGATARI EMAKI (illustrated Scrolls of the Events of the
Heiji Era), Japan. Second half of the 13th century.
Kamakura period.
Handscroll, ink and colors on paper. 16¼″ × 275″.
Fenollosa-Weld Collection. Courtesy of Museum of Fine Arts, Boston.
© 2006 Museum of Fine Arts, Boston. Reproduced with permission.
All rights reserved.

period (1185–1333). The dominant taste of the leaders at that time favored a vigorous realism in art, and this is reflected in the wood portrait statue of the detail of MUCHAKU. Unkei, one of the greatest sculptors of Japan, created this life-size work depicting a legendary Buddhist priest from India holding a cloth-covered round box. The vividness of the facial expression and the delicacy of the hand gesture belie the wooden material from which he carved it.

Japanese painters of this period found the handscroll particularly effective for long narrative compositions that depict the passage of time. BURNING OF THE SANJO PALACE is from the HEIJI MONOGATARI

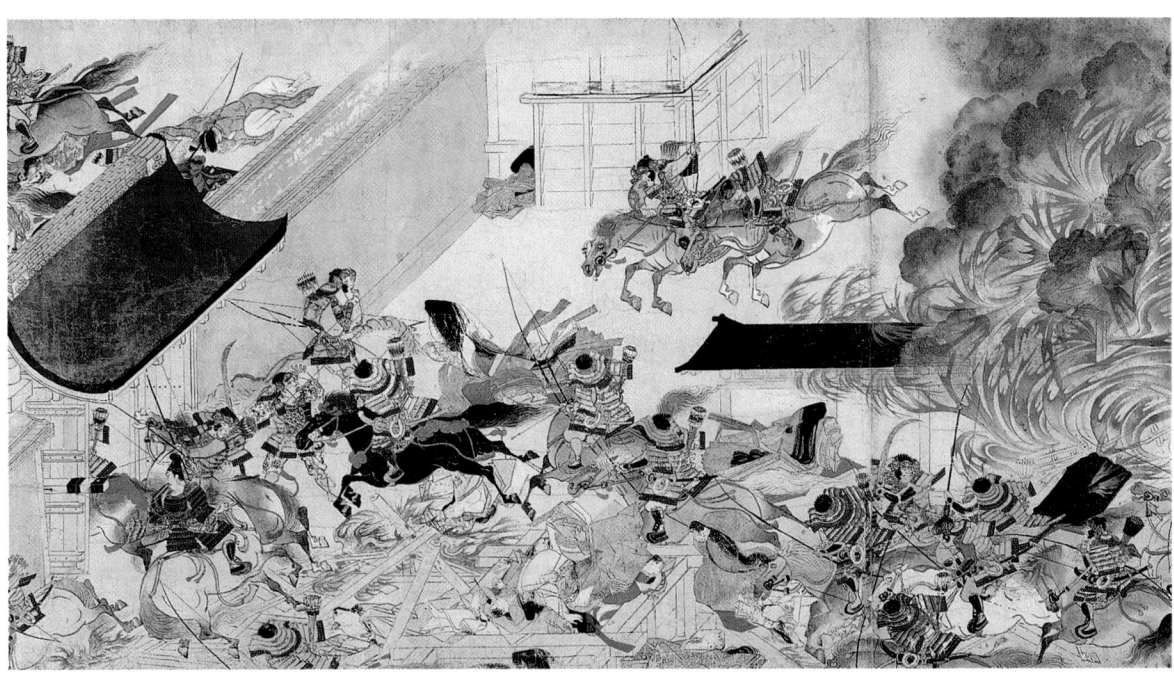

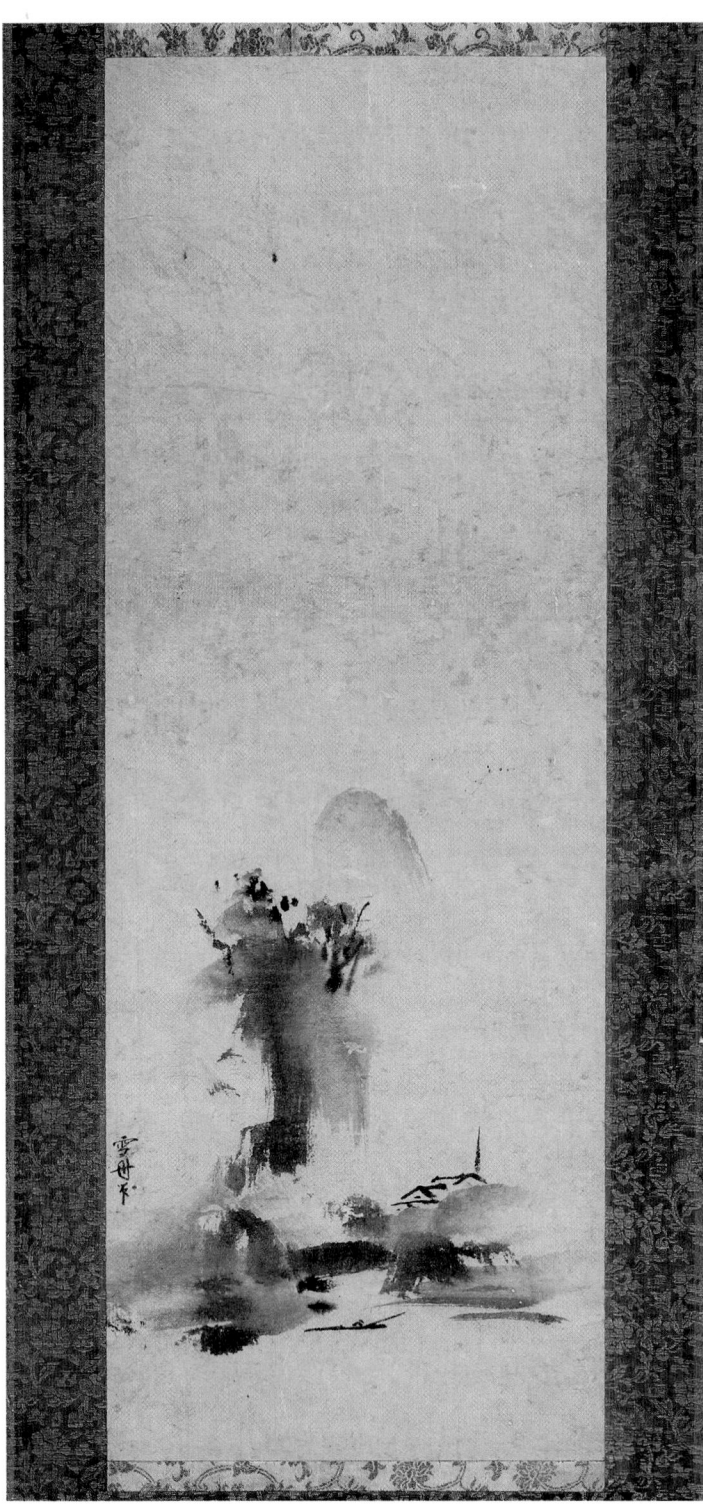

436 Sesshū Toyo.
HABOKU LANDSCAPE. 1400s–early 1500s.
Hanging scroll, ink on paper.
28¼″ × 10½″.
© The Cleveland Museum of Art. The Norweb Collection, 1955.43.

EMAKI, a scroll that describes the Heiji insurrection of 1160. As the scroll is unrolled from right to left, the viewer follows a succession of events expertly designed to tell the story. Through effective visual transitions, the horror and excitement of the action are connected. The story builds from simple to complex events, reaching a dramatic climax in the scene of the burning palace, a highly effective depiction of fire. The color of the flames emphasizes the excitement of the historic struggle. Parallel diagonal lines and shapes, used to indicate the palace walls, add to the sense of motion and provide a clear geometric structure in the otherwise frantic activity of this portion of the scroll. Today, such dramatic events are presented through film or television.

Zen Buddhism, which came to Japan from China in the thirteenth century, provided a philosophical basis within which aesthetic activities were given meaning beyond their physical form. Zen teaches that enlightenment can be attained through meditation and contemplation. The influence of Zen on Japanese aesthetics can be seen in spontaneous and intuitive approaches to poetry, calligraphy, painting, gardens, and flower arrangements.

Zen Buddhist priest Sesshū is considered the foremost Japanese master of ink painting. In 1467, he traveled to China, where he studied the works of Southern Song masters and saw the countryside that inspired them. Chinese Chan (Zen) paintings, such as Mu Qi's SIX PERSIMMONS (page 52) were greatly admired by the Japanese, and many were brought to monasteries in Japan.

Sesshū adapted the Chinese style and set the standard in ink painting for later Japanese artists. He painted in two styles. The first was formal and complex, while the second was a simplified, somewhat explosive style, later called *haboku*, meaning "flung ink." HABOKU LANDSCAPE is abstract in its simplification of forms and freedom of brushwork. Sesshū suggested mountains and trees with single, soft brush strokes. The sharp lines in the center foreground indicating a fisherman, and the vertical line above the rooftops representing the staff of a wine shop, are in contrast to the thin washes and darker accents of the suggested landscape.

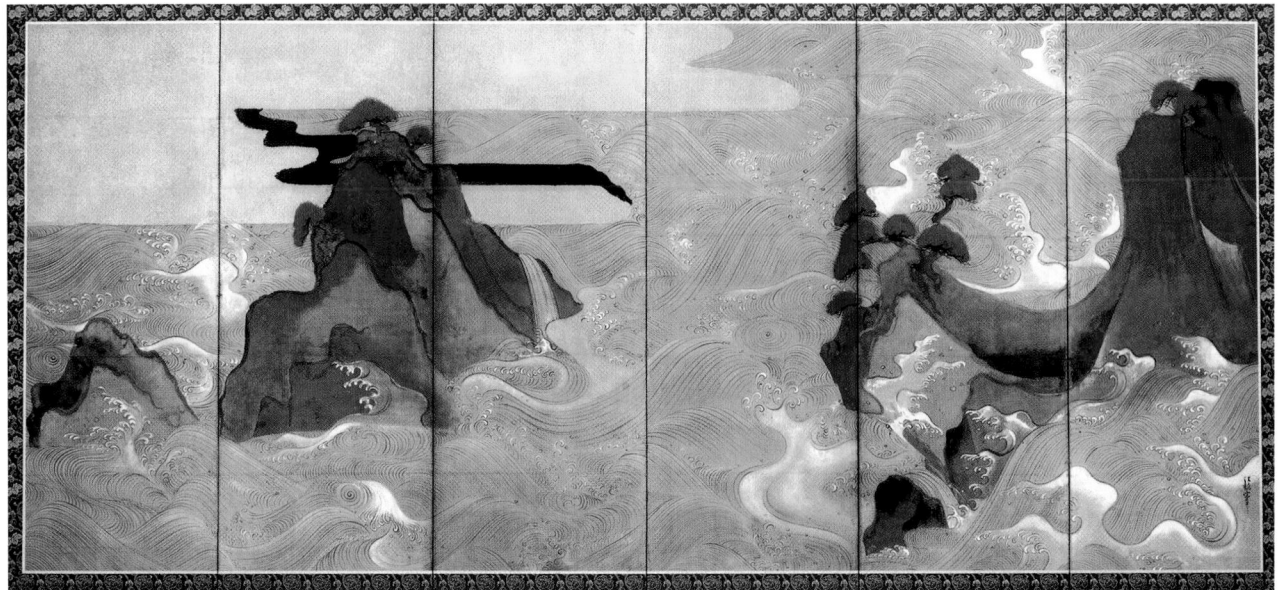

437 Tawaraya Sōtatsu.
WAVES AT MATSUSHIMA. 17th century. Edo period.
Folding screen, ink, color, gold, and silver on paper. Image, 59¹³⁄₁₆″ × 145⅝″.
Courtesy of the Freer Gallery of Art, Smithsonian Institution, Washington, D.C. Gift of Charles Lang Freer, (F1906.231).

In traditional Japan, folding screens provided privacy by separating areas within rooms. Artists have used the unique spatial properties of the screen format in highly original ways. In contrast to the European easel paintings that function like a window in the wall, a painted screen within the living space of a home becomes a major element in the interior.

Tawaraya Sōtatsu's large screen WAVES AT MATSUSHIMA consists of a pair of six-panel folding screens. The screens are designed so that together or separately they form complete compositions. The subject is a pair of islands where there were very old Shinto shrines.

In keeping with well-established Japanese artistic practices, Sōtatsu created a composition charged with the churning action of waves, yet as solid and permanent in its design as the rocky crags around which the waters leap and churn. He translated his sensitive awareness of natural phenomena into a decorative, abstract design. Spatial ambiguity in the sky and water areas suggests an interaction that the viewer should feel, rather than read as a literal transcription of nature. In addition to rhythmic patterns that fill much of the surface, boldly simplified shapes and lines are contrasted with highly refined details and eye-catching surprises. A flat, horizontal gold shape in the upper left, accentuated with a black line, signifies a cloud and reaffirms the picture plane. The strongly asymmetrical design, emphasis on repeated patterns, and relatively flat spatial quality are all often used in Japanese painting from the sixteenth to the nineteenth centuries.

By the mid-seventeenth century, the art of woodcut printing had developed to meet the demand for pictures by the newly prosperous middle class. Japanese artists took the Chinese woodcut technique and turned it into a popular art form. For the next two hundred years, hundreds of thousands of these prints were produced. The prints are called *ukiyo-e*, meaning "pictures of the floating world," because they depict scenes of daily life, such as landscapes, popular entertainments, and portraits of theater actors.

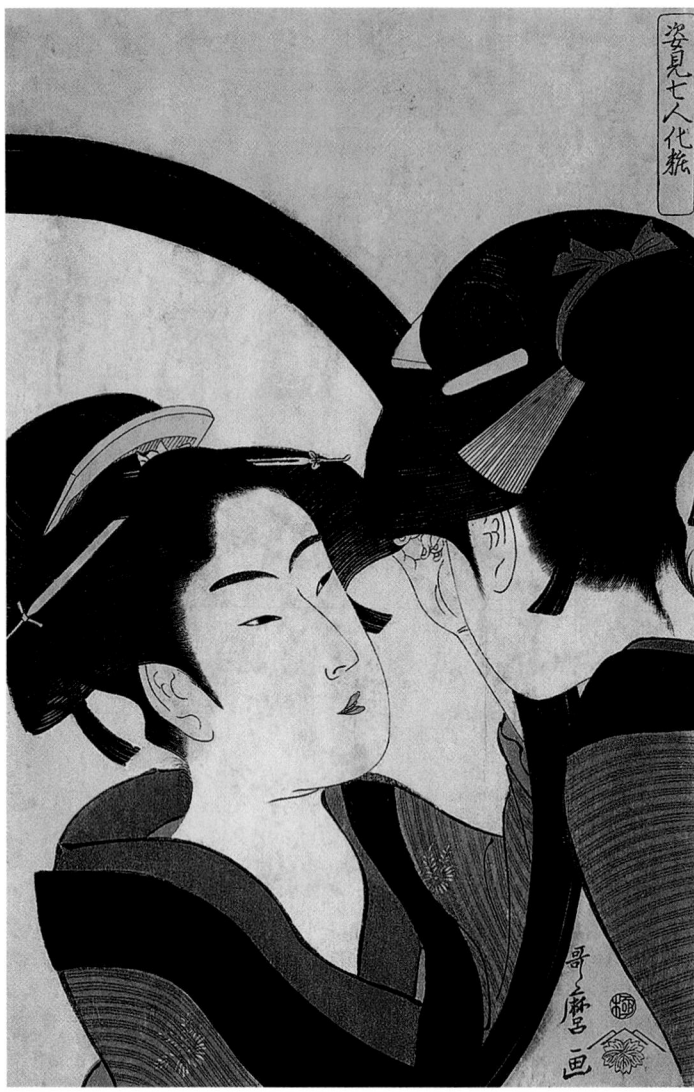

438 Kitagawa Utamaro.
REFLECTED BEAUTY, SEVEN BEAUTIES APPLYING MAKE-UP:
OKITA. c. 1790.
Woodblock print. 14¼" × 9½".
Honolulu Academy of Arts. Gift of James A. Michener, 1969. 15,490.

Kitagawa Utamaro's woodcut REFLECTED BEAUTY transforms the then ordinary subject into a memorable image consisting of bold, curving outlines and clear, unmodeled shapes. As with many Japanese paintings and prints, flat shapes are emphasized by the absence of shading. The center of interest is the reflected face of the woman, set off by the strong curve representing the mirror's edge. In contrast to Western composition with centered balance and subjects well within the frame, here the figure is thrust in from the right, and cut off abruptly by the edge of the picture plane, rather than being presented completely within the frame. This type of radically cropped composition was one of the elements of Japanese art that influenced European artists in the nineteenth century.

Japanese architects show a similar interest in asymmetry, casualness, and surprise. KATSURA DETACHED PALACE, a seventeenth-century Japanese imperial villa, was built in Kyoto beside the Katsura River, whose waters were diverted into the garden to form ponds. All elements—land, water, rocks, and plants—were integrated in a garden design that blends human-made and natural elements. Because many of the palace walls are sliding screens, they provide flexible interconnections between interior and exterior spaces.

In contrast to a European royal palace, KATSURA seems humble. The complex was planned with no grand entrance either to the grounds or to the buildings. Instead, one approaches the palace along garden paths, watching unexpected views open up. Earth contours, stones, and waterways are combined to symbolize—on a small scale—mountains, rivers, fields, inlets, and beaches. The tea house, which borrows from modest country dwellings, is constructed of common, natural materials. It provides the appropriate setting for the tea ceremony, which embodies the attitudes of simplicity, naturalness, and humility that permeate the entire palace grounds.

Domestic architecture has long been an important part of Japanese art. Modest houses, as well as palaces and Buddhist temples, have traditionally employed many of the structural and aesthetic

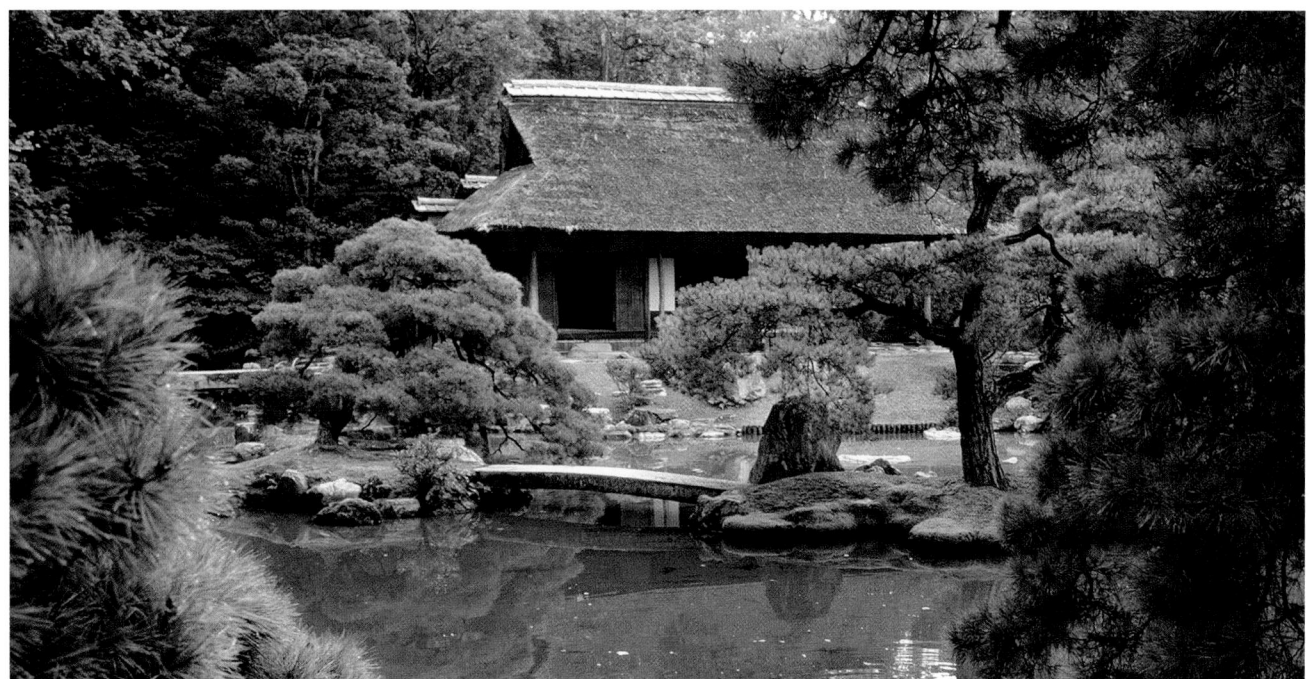

439 **KATSURA DETACHED PALACE.** Kyoto, Japan. 17th century.

a. Gardens and tea house.
Photograph: Ric Ergenbright. Henry Westheim Photography.

b. Imperial villa and gardens.
Photograph: Robert Holmes. Corbis.

c. Interior of tea house.
Photograph: Ric Ergenbright. Henry Westheim Photography.

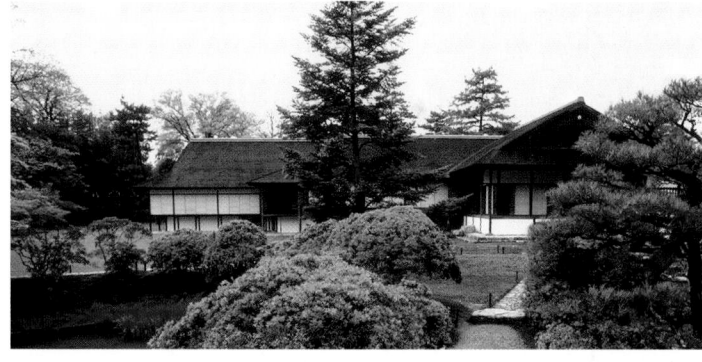

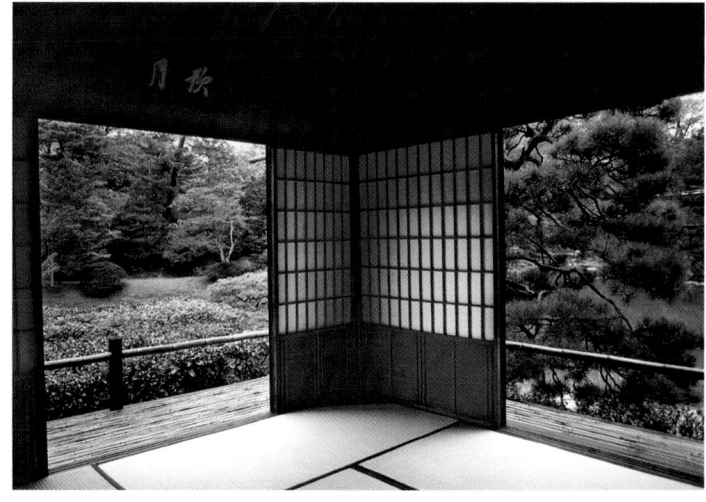

principles of Shinto shrines. In the past, Japanese homes were related to the land and were often set in or built around a garden. Today, small gardens provide intimacy with natural beauty, even in crowded city environments.

Traditional Japanese houses, such as those at KATSURA, are built of wood using post-and-beam construction. The result is essentially a roof on posts, allowing walls to be sliding screens rather than supports. The Japanese use of unpainted wood and the concept of spatial flow between indoors and outdoors have been major influences on modern architects in the West.

In the nineteenth century, European commerce and missionary work began to have a decisive impact across Asia. Various parts of Asia reacted differently to this new influence. India submitted, not

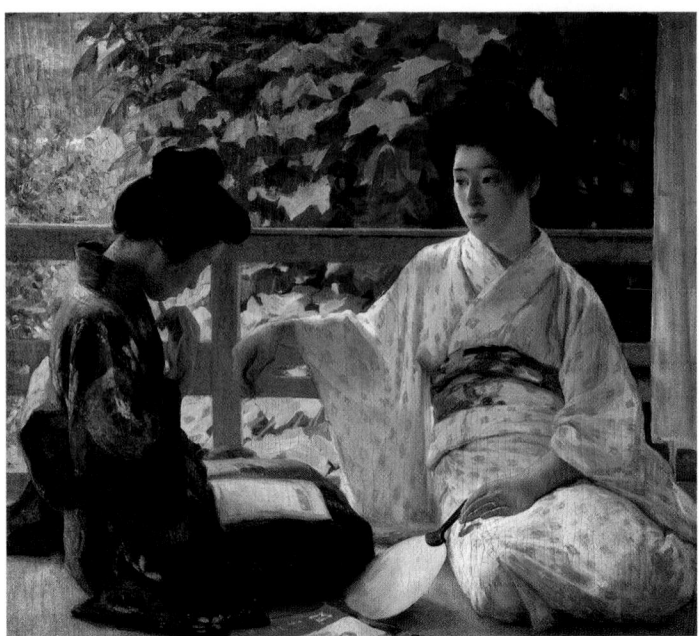

440 Mitsutani Kunishiro.
UPSTAIRS. 1910.
Oil on canvas. 105 × 120 cm.
Tokyo National Museum, Japan.
Image: TNM Image Archives.

always willingly, to colonial status under England. The Chinese tried to severely limit foreign influence on their culture, leading to conflicts that lasted into the twentieth century. The Japanese, in contrast, welcomed foreigners while avoiding colonization. A revolt in 1868 restored the Emperor to power, and he began a vigorous program of cultural importation from the West, which seems to continue even today.

The new policy of openness had an immediate impact on the arts. The government gave stipends for Japanese artists to study in Europe, and invited Western artists and scholars to teach in Japanese universities. We see the results of this hybridization in paintings such as UPSTAIRS by Mitsutani Kunishiro. He studied in Paris near the turn of the twentieth century, and the work reflects his knowledge of painting in natural light gleaned from looking at Impressionist and Post-Impressionist paintings. At the same time, the subject matter is Japanese.

Cultural trading between East and West continues into the present. We will consider some modern Asian artists in Chapters 24 and 25.

THE ISLAMIC WORLD

Islam is one of the three major world religions built on the teachings of the religious seers of the Middle East. Although based on the revelations to the prophet Mohammed, Islam shares some fundamental beliefs and religious history with its predecessors Judaism and Christianity. An adherent of Islam is called a Muslim—Arabic for "one who submits to God."

The Islamic calendar begins in 622 C.E. with the Hegira, Mohammed's emigration to what is now the city of Medina on the Arabian peninsula. The new religion spread quickly into much of what was once the Eastern Roman and Byzantine empires, then fanned out to include North Africa, Spain, and parts of Europe. Within one hundred years of the Prophet's death, Christian armies were repelling Muslim troops from Tours in central France. Islam is now the principal religion in the Middle East, North Africa, and some parts of Asia.

The Muslims facilitated their rule by allowing the peoples of conquered lands to retain their own religions and cultures, as the Romans had done. This strategy enabled the Muslims, who had little art of their own in their early history, to adapt earlier artistic traditions. At its height, from the ninth through the fourteenth centuries, Islamic culture synthesized the artistic and literary traditions and scientific knowledge of the entire ancient world.

Unlike the medieval Christians, who rejected pre-Christian civilization and scholarship, Muslims adapted and built on the achievements of their predecessors. Muslim scholars translated the legacy of Greek, Syrian, and Hindu knowledge into Arabic, and Arabic became the language of scholarship from the eighth through the eleventh centuries for Muslims as well as many Christians and Jews. As medieval Europe languished from intolerance, isolationism, and feudalism, Islamic civilization flourished, producing outstanding achievements in the arts, sciences, administration, and commerce that were not attained in Europe until the height of the Renaissance, in the late fifteenth century.

Traditional Muslims frown upon the representation of human figures in art that will be used in a religious context. Many Muslims believe that if an artist were to try to recreate the living forms of humans, he or she would be competing with Allah (God) who created everything. Mohammed also prohibited any pictures of himself while he was alive, claiming that he was not in any way exceptional—he was only a messenger. Thus, figural arts are rare in Islamic religious art, where more attention was given to geometry and to writing.

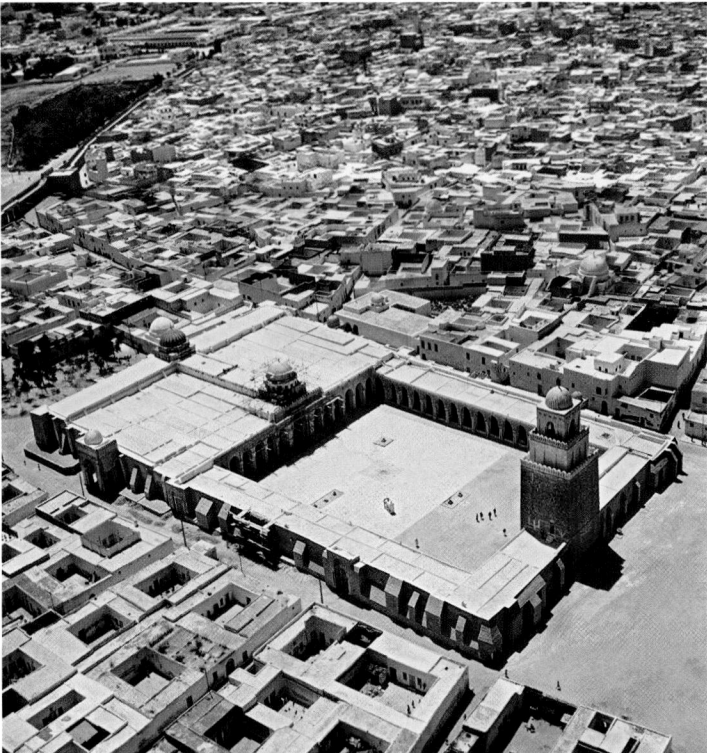

441 GREAT MOSQUE.
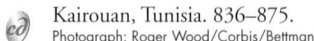
Kairouan, Tunisia. 836–875.
Photograph: Roger Wood/Corbis/Bettmann.

ARAB LANDS

When Islam first began to spread, local rulers took responsibility for building houses of worship in their territories. Early rulers often adapted abandoned buildings, converting them into *mosques*. (The word is based on the Arabic *masjid*, which means "place of prostration.") The typical mosque must be big enough to accommodate all male worshipers for Friday prayers, during which they hear a sermon and bow down in the direction of Mecca, Islam's most holy city. The basic plan of a mosque is based on the design of the Prophet's house, which had an open courtyard bordered by porches held up with columns. Often, mosques include one or more *minarets* (towers), which mark the building's location and are used by chanters who ascend and call the faithful to prayer.

An early mosque that still stands in something resembling its original condition is the GREAT MOSQUE in Kairouan, Tunisia. The open courtyard is surrounded by porches, with a minaret over the main entrance in the center of one short side. The deeper covered area opposite the minaret shelters the *mihrab*, the niche in the end wall that points the way to Mecca.

The ceramic arts are highly valued in Islam, and Arab potters in Iraq made a major advance when they perfected the luster technique, probably in the ninth century. This glaze effect, which imparts a metallic sheen to the surface of a vessel, is one of the most difficult to control in ceramics, and was equated in those days with alchemy, the effort to convert simple materials into gold. Most luster pottery was for the exclusive use of nobles and rulers. The PITCHER shown here has a very thin body, indicating that it was probably intended only for decorative purposes. The Arabic script on the piece expresses praise and good wishes to the owner.

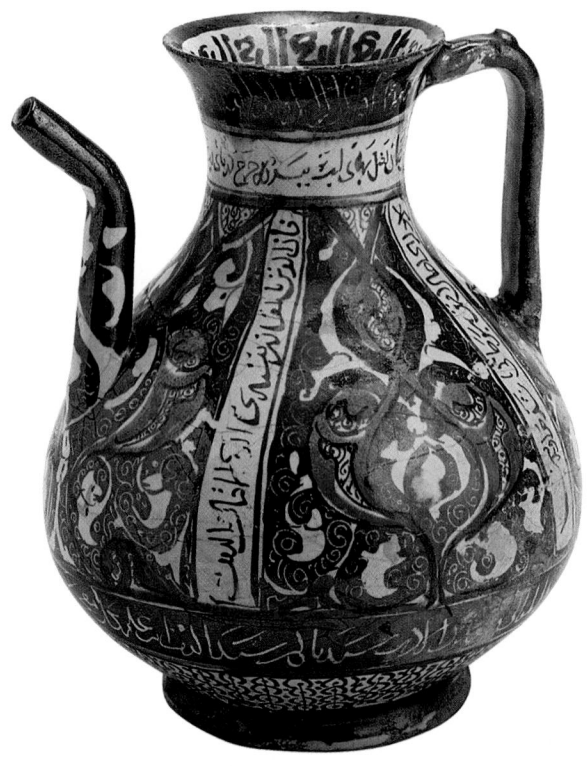

442 PITCHER (SPOUTED EWER).
Kashan. Early 13th century.
Luster over tin glaze.
Height 6⅔".
Reproduced by permission of the Syndics of the
Fitzwilliam Museum, Cambridge, from the Ades Loan Collection.

SPAIN

Muslims first conquered Spain for Islam in the eighth century, but soon the region (together with bordering North Africa) became a distinct Muslim culture with important scientists, poets, philosophers, architects, and artists (see, for example, the Spanish LUSTER-PAINTED BOWL on page 84). Some of Europe's best libraries were in the Spanish Muslim cities of Córdoba and Granada, and respect for books and learning was higher here than in most other areas of the continent.

Calligraphy is a highly honored Islamic art because it is used to enhance the beauty of the word of God. The most respected practice for a calligrapher is the art of writing the words of the Koran, the sacred text of Islam, which Muslims believe was revealed in Arabic by God to Mohammed. In the Islamic world, the written TEXT OF THE KORAN is the divine word in visible form. According to Islamic tradition, God's first creation was the *qalam*, the slantcut reed pen.

The decorative qualities of Arabic scripts combine well with both geometric and floral design motifs. We saw them combined in the PITCHER, but they work together with unforgettable effect in the COURT OF THE LIONS, which contains elaborate stucco arches resting on 124 white marble columns. Many of the walls seem to consist entirely of translucent webs of intricate decoration in marble, alabaster, glazed tile, and cast plaster. Light coming through the small openings in the decoration gives many of the rooms and courtyards a luminous splendor. Just above the columns is a horizontal band of calligraphy that says, "There is no victor save God." (For another example of Spanish Muslim decoration, see the DECORATIVE PANEL FROM THE ALHAMBRA on page 15.)

The COURT OF THE LIONS is part of the much larger Alhambra, the royal palace and fort of the Muslim rulers in Granada. Occupying a commanding hill, the Alhambra was a self-contained city, with meeting rooms, royal residences, gardens, and housing for workers of various kinds. This was one of the last strongholds of Muslim rule in Spain, and when the last ruler abandoned it in 1492, the Spanish rulers kept it intact.

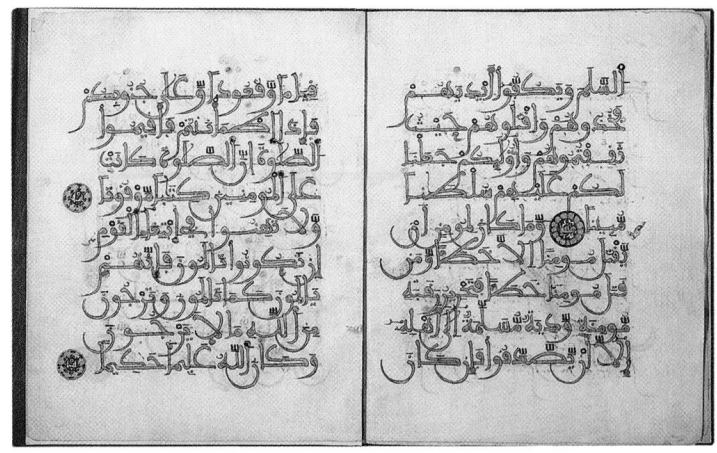

443   TEXT OF THE KORAN.
North Africa or Spain. 11th century. Colors on parchment.
MS no. 1544. Reproduced by kind permission of the Trustees of the Chester Beatty Library, Dublin.

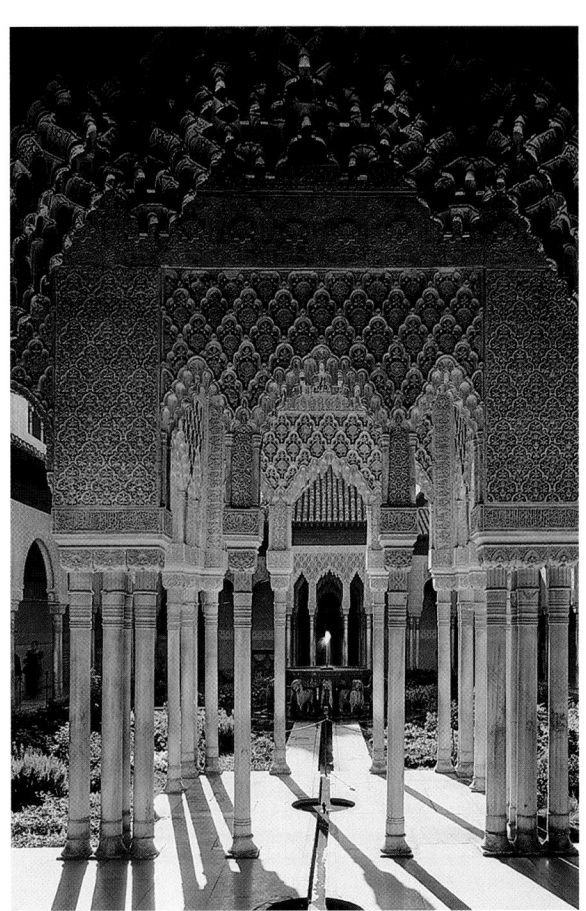

444   COURT OF THE LIONS, ALHAMBRA.
Granada, Spain. 1309–1354.
Photograph: SuperStock, Inc.

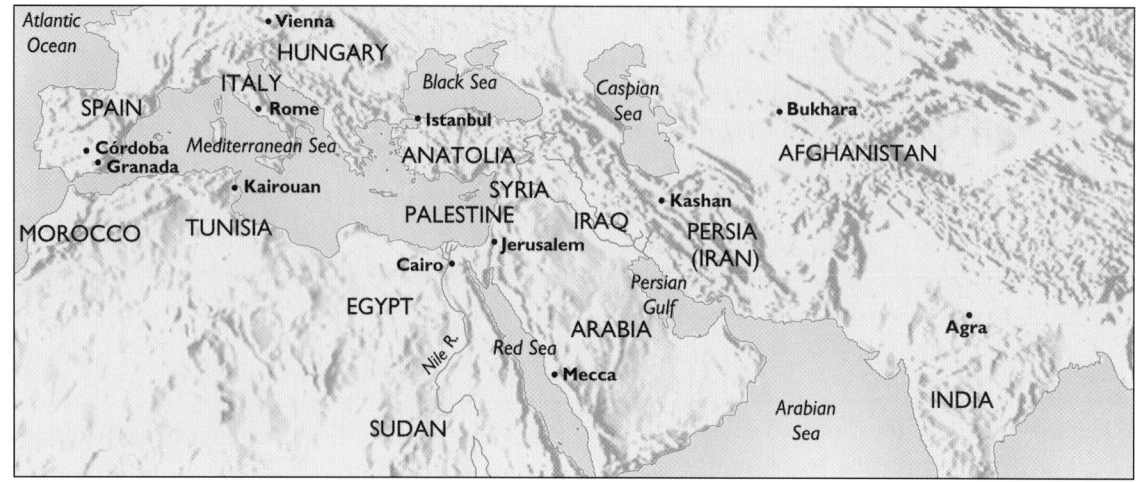

445 THE ISLAMIC WORLD.

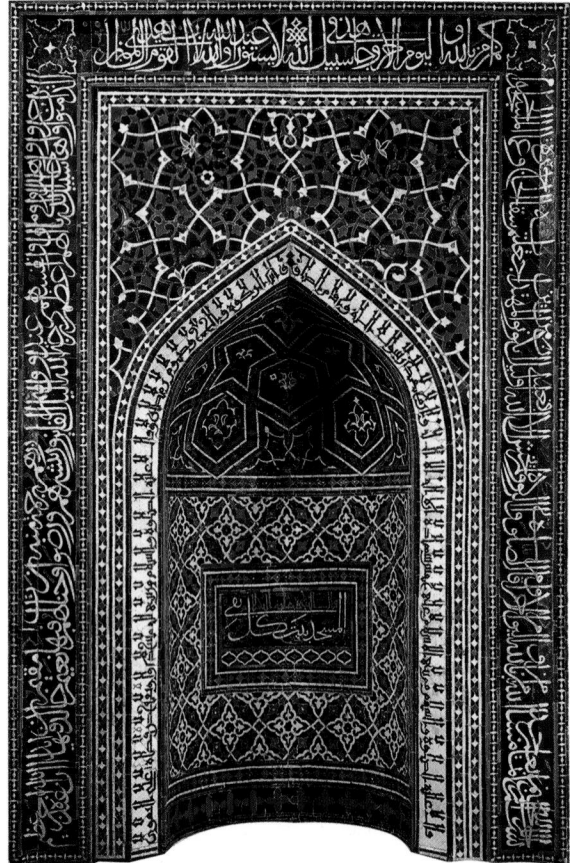

446 MIHRAB. Persia (Iran). c. 1354.
Glazed ceramic, cut and assembled in mosaic.
11'3" × 7'6".
The Metropolitan Museum of Art.
Harris Brisbane Dick Fund, 1939. 39.20.
Photograph: © The Metropolitan Museum of Art.

PERSIA

Probably the best-known item of Persian art in the West is the carpet (see page 205 for the ARDABIL CARPET, one of the most impressive). Carpets were not only prized possessions; they were important to the history of Islamic arts as a means of spreading design ideas. Relatively portable, a carpet is a repository of motifs and compositions. Many decorative schemes on buildings or pottery were influenced by carpet design from distant regions.

Decorating architecture with tiles is an important offshoot of the ceramic arts, and this technique reached a peak of achievement in Persia. The MIHRAB shown here was taken from a mosque, where it pointed the way to Mecca for worshipers. The disavowal of images in the religious context means that the art cannot tell a story with human figures, as is common in the West. Instead, Islamic art uses extremely intricate designs that satisfy the sensuous urge for beauty while also engaging the mind's desire for order and pattern. Muslims often used writing, as seen here on the outer band, which contains well-known verses from the Koran about the value of building mosques. In this way, a work such as this one can be absorbing to look at, spiritually uplifting, and aesthetically pleasing.

The MIHRAB has been separated from its original site, but it provides an example of the richness of

Persian decorative arts. Such techniques were often applied to entire buildings, as we see at the MIR-I-ARAB MADRASA in Uzbekistan. A *madrasa* is a Muslim theological school where the history of Islam and the interpretation of the Koran are taught. This one was named for its founder, a member of the philosophical Muslim sect known as Sufism.

The well-proportioned array of openings in two stories provides a counterpoint to the *iwan*, the large covered porch at the center. Behind are two domes, one marking the lecture hall and the other the founder's tomb. Most surfaces are dazzling with tiles in floral, geometric, and epigraphic patterns, showing how color is often integral to Islamic architecture.

Persian painters rank among the world's great illustrators, as they made pictures to accompany handwritten copies of their major literary works. These illustrated books were prized possessions of the aristocracy. One of the finest illustrations is SULTAN SANJAR AND THE OLD WOMAN, from the *Khamseh*, or "Five Poems," by Nizami (on the following page). The story is an allegory on vanity: The sultan was out riding with his courtiers one day when an old woman approached him, complaining that she had been robbed by one of his soldiers. Sanjar dismissed her, saying that her troubles were nothing compared to his with his military campaigns. The woman then confronted him, saying, "What good is conquering foreign armies when you can't make your own behave?"

The work is a careful composition with luxurious details in the fabrics, vegetation, and clouds. Subtle gestures help to tell the story, which takes place in the center. The method of rendering rocks in Persian painting owes a great deal to Chinese art, which the Persians knew (compare with TRAVELERS AMONG MOUNTAINS AND STREAMS on page 306), but the Persian artist made some of these resemble faces. These paintings were most often produced in workshops, so that we do not generally know the artists' names; but in this case it seems fairly certain that the work is by Sultan-Muhammad, one of the two or three most highly regarded painters of Safavid Persia.

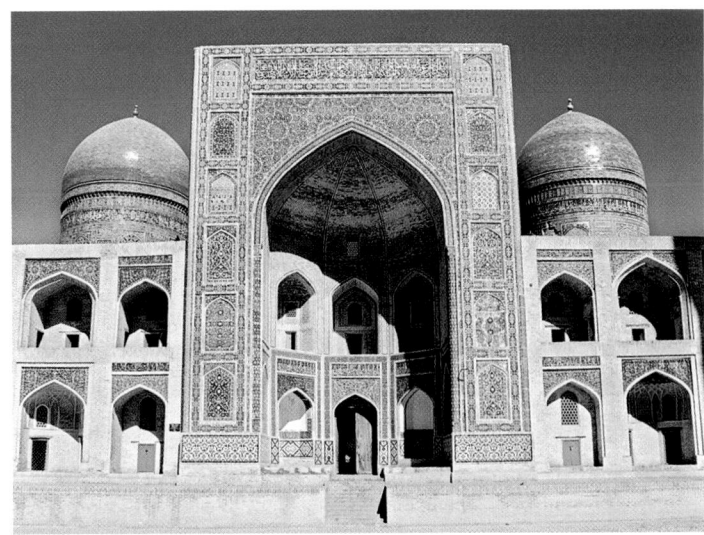

447 MIR-I-ARAB MADRASA.
Bukhara, Uzbekistan. 1535–1536. Facade.
Photograph: David Flack.

INDIA: THE MUGHAL EMPIRE

Heirs to both Persian and Mongol traditions, the Mughal rulers of the Indian subcontinent governed a wide mix of cultures in the sixteenth and seventeenth centuries. Their subjects were Hindu, Jain, Zoroastrian, and even a few Christians. Only a minority (the upper classes) were Muslim. This meant that in the Mughal Empire, Islam evolved further from its Arab roots than anywhere up to that time.

Governing such a diverse people led the Mughal rulers to a level of tolerance unknown elsewhere in the world. Akbar, for example, who ruled from 1556 to 1605, ordered his ministers to learn about the various religions practiced in his realm, and he hired tutors to teach them. He also established a new religion that combined elements of all, and made himself the head of it, the better to resolve disputes. When Jesuit missionaries from Baroque Rome visited him, he entertained them lavishly, and bought Western religious prints from them for his art collection. He encouraged figural representation in art, saying that trying to copy God's handiwork by making pictures would lead artists to a deeper respect for divine creativity.

Under the influence of the empire's cultural mix, and the tolerant curiosity of most of its rulers,

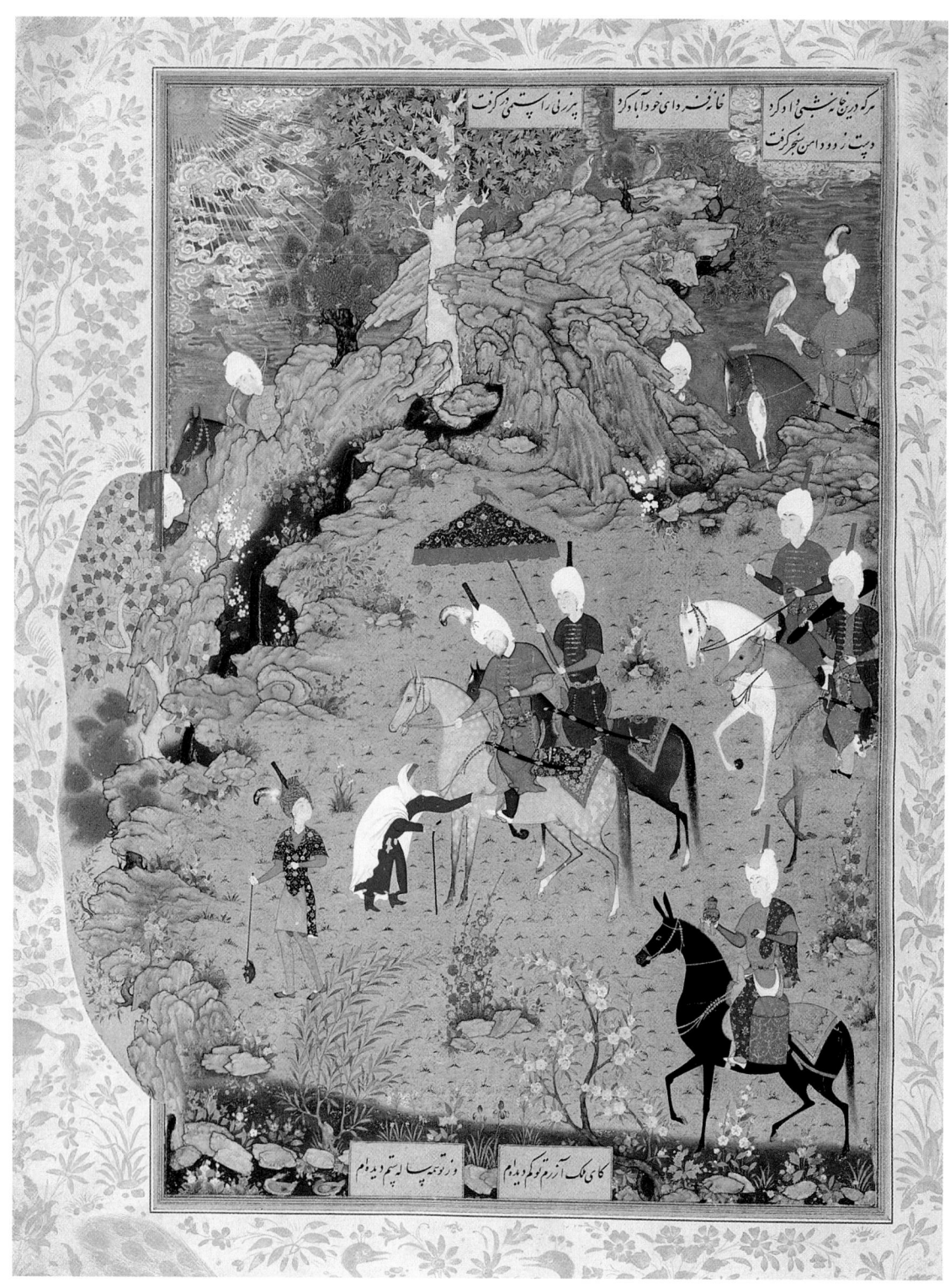

448 Attributed to Sultan-Muhammad.
SULTAN SANJAR AND THE OLD WOMAN, from the KHAMSEH (FIVE POEMS) of Nizami, folio 181. 1539–1543.
Gouache on paper. 14½″ × 10″.
By permission of The British Library.

a Mughal painting style evolved that combined elements of European naturalism with Persian love of color and attention to detail. When a Portuguese trader brought to the court a turkey (which came not from Europe but the New World), the ruler Jahanghir ordered his favorite artist to make a picture of it. The result is TURKEY-COCK, one of the most vivid depictions of wildlife ever realized. The surrounding text tells the details of the gift. The boldness of its impact is equaled by the fineness of its details.

The last Mughal ruler to hold the realm together was Shah Jahan, who also created the most memorable piece of Mughal art, the TAJ MAHAL. Erected on the banks of a river between a guest house and a small mosque, the TAJ MAHAL (which means "Crown of the Palace") is a tomb for the ruler's favorite wife, who had died in childbirth. It sits at one end of a four-part paradise garden that recalls the description of Paradise in the Koran. The surface of the white marble exterior seems to change colors by catching sunlight at various angles. The proportions of the bulb-shaped dome make the building look light, as if it barely touches the ground. The walls seem paper-thin, with arch openings in a graceful rhythm. The paradise motif of the garden is continued in the long inscription over the central doorway arch, which contains the most important chapter from the Koran describing the afterlife. The TAJ MAHAL'S combination of otherworldliness, beauty, and devotion draws visitors from across the world.

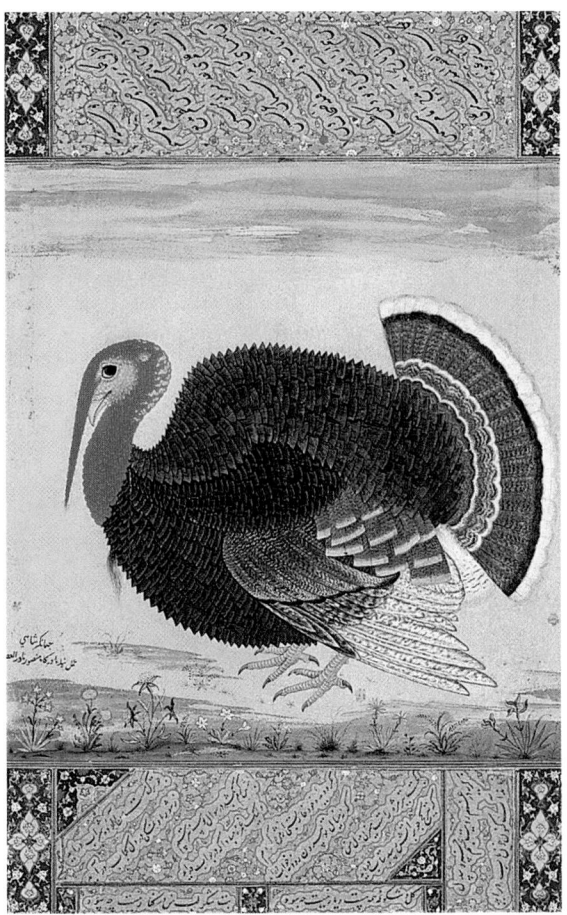

449 Mansur.
TURKEY-COCK. c. 1612.
Gouache on paper, painted image. 5¼″ × 5″.
Victoria and Albert Museum, London.
Courtesy of the Trustees of the Victoria and Albert Museum, IM 135–1921.
Victoria and Albert Picture Library.

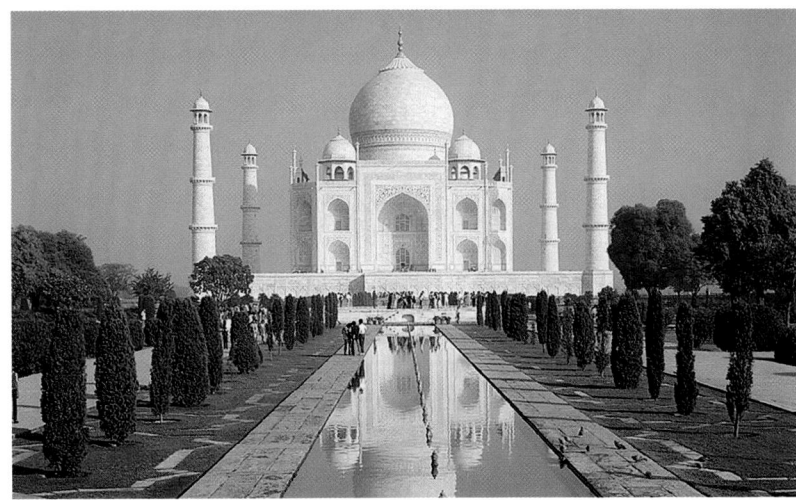

450 TAJ MAHAL.
Agra, India. 1632–1648.
Library, Getty Research Institute, Los Angeles.
Photograph: Wim Swaan Collection (96.P.21).

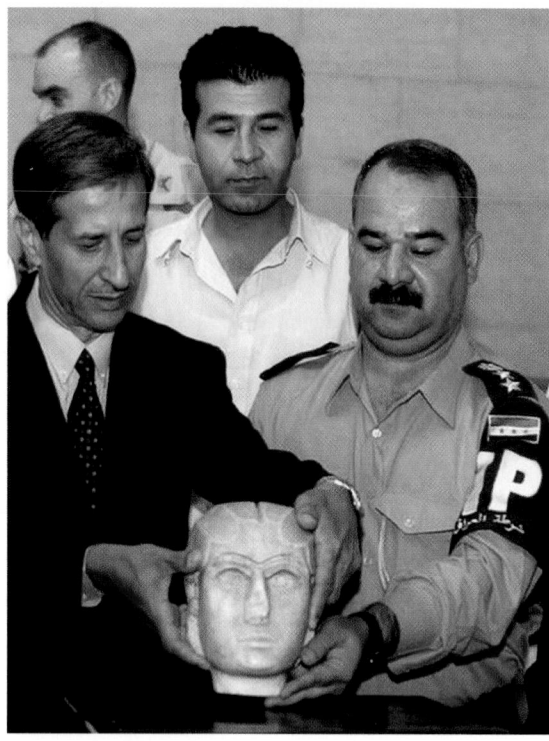

451 HEAD FROM WARKA. 3500–3000 B.C.E.
Marble. Height: 8".
Displayed by Iraqi authorities after its recovery.
Photograph: John Simmons.

IN JUNE 2004, Iraqi police staged a sting operation. Posing as art dealers, a squad of undercover agents met a group of looters about 55 miles south of Baghdad. Before they were arrested, the looters sold the agents several hundred illegally excavated objects from the ancient city of Babylon. Among them were statues, bowls, jewelry, and writing tablets. The price: $100 a crate. Their value to cultural history: immeasurable.

This case was a rare success in the effort to stop a massive problem. The looting of Iraq's cultural heritage began as a trickle after the first Persian Gulf war in 1991. The terms that ended that war stopped Saddam Hussein's army from its usual policing of the hundreds of Bronze Age villages that dot the country's river valleys. The looting continued throughout the 1990s. Once spirited across the border, the artifacts entered the international art trade.

The river valley region in central and southern Iraq is often termed the cradle of civilization. This is where agriculture was discovered, where people first lived in villages, and where writing was invented. Valuable archaeological sites are numerous.

Looters grew considerably bolder during and after the most recent war in 2003. After invading U.S. troops left the Iraqi National Museum unguarded, robbers entered and grabbed thousands of pieces in a three-day spree. About 4,000 items were later recovered, but the losses still amount to about 8,000 pieces, including ancient pottery, jewelry, musical instruments, religious objects, and statues of clay, wood, and precious metals.[1] Among the most grievous losses was the 5,000-year-old HEAD FROM WARKA, a marble face of a woman, perhaps a goddess, with sensitively carved features. It was later found in an orchard.

In the provinces, the looting of buried ancient cities continues apace. "In the big sites there is organized looting where people are bussed by the antiquities dealers," said Dr. Elizabeth Stone of Stony Brook University. "Police who tried to sort out the looters at Umma [city] were outgunned. The looters came with their own guards. The illegal antiquities trade is no different from the illegal drugs trade. There are major cities being totally destroyed."[2]

The U.S. Defense Department has increased its efforts to train soldiers in recognizing and protecting historic resources. In mid-2007, the Army distributed 4,000 special sets of playing cards to troops. Each card has information about historic Iraqi sites and tips on helping to care for them. The face of the Queen of Clubs, for example, shows a soldier talking to an Iraqi citizen above this text: "Ancient sites matter to the local community. Showing respect wins hearts and minds."

One ancient city that is well-protected is Ur with its ziggurat (see page 239). This important site is enclosed within a U.S. military base.

Several international treaties govern the care of art in wartime. The Geneva Conventions, which set forth rules for treatment of prisoners of war, also prohibit acts of hostility against monuments or works of art. The 1954 Hague Convention for the Protection of Cultural Property in the Event of Armed Conflict imposes obligations on warring parties and occupying armies to preserve art and artifacts from damage. These treaties have rarely been followed.

AFRICA, OCEANIA, AND THE AMERICAS

Most of us in the West tend to think of art as something to go and see in a museum. This is where most art is kept, after all. A museum is a special place set aside for us to contemplate the creativity of past and present generations. Or perhaps art is something that decorates our homes. Most of us arrange paintings or sculptures (or reproductions of them) as embellishments of our personal spaces.

In this chapter we will consider traditional arts from Africa, Oceania, and the Americas, regions where art is not created solely for visual pleasure or embellishment. These cultures did not set aside places for the care and enjoyment of art. Rather, the cultures we consider here found uses for art in religious ritual, civic life, and community functions.

Some Western art has also fulfilled these functions, but we mostly keep artworks in special places outside of our daily lives. The cultures we will consider here have a different view.

AFRICA

The arts of the African continent are extremely varied, and the diversity of style reflects the variety of cultures on the continent. North of the Sahara, the art forms of Africa generally fall under the influence of Egyptian, Roman, or (most recently) Islamic traditions. These cultures were covered in previous chapters; here we will focus on sub-Saharan Africa.

Humanity originated in Africa. We have already seen one of the world's oldest known decorated objects, the ENGRAVED OCHRE on page 233. We have also seen the GREAT ZIMBABWE, the large stone structure pictured on page 213. But because most ancient African art was made from perishable materials, little remains from before the thirteenth century.

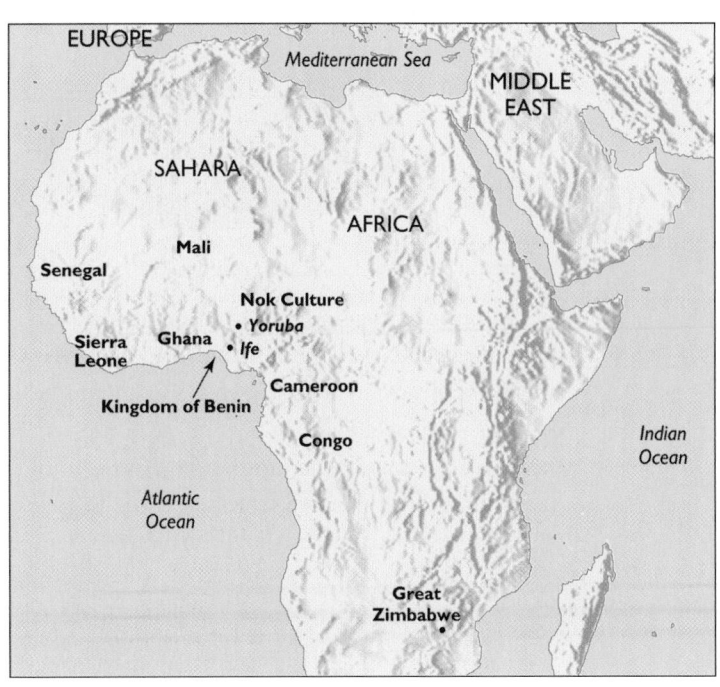

452 AFRICA.

453 HEAD.
   Nok culture, Nigeria.
   500 B.C.E.–200 C.E.
   Terra cotta. Height 14½".
   National Museum, Lagos, Nigeria.
   Photograph: Werner Forman Archive.

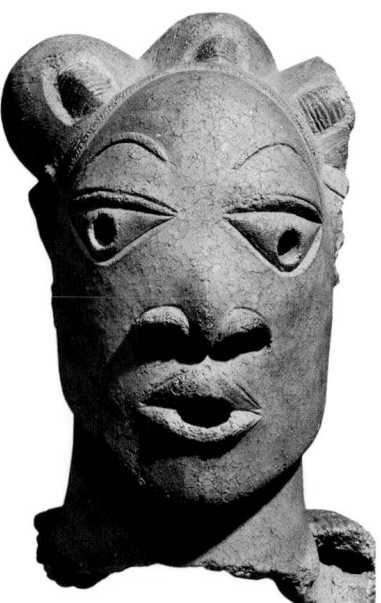

454 MALE PORTRAIT HEAD.
   Ife, Nigeria.
   13th century.
   Bronze. Height 11⁷⁄₁₆".
   Photograph: Frank Willet.

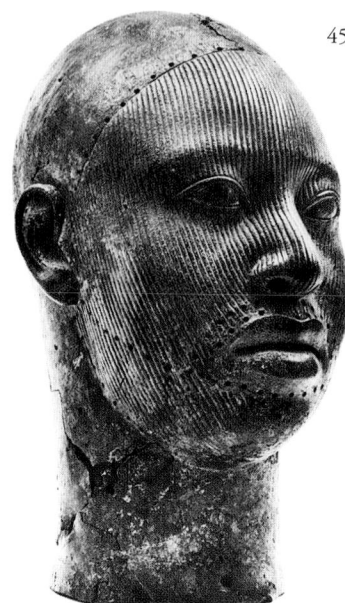

455 BENIN HEAD. Nigeria.
   16th century.
   Bronze. 8⅝" × 9¼".
   The Metropolitan Museum of Art,
   New York. The Michael C. Rockefeller
   Memorial Collection. Bequest of Nelson
   A. Rockefeller, 1979. 1979.206.86.
   Photograph by Schecter Lee. © 1986 The
   Metropolitan Museum of Art.

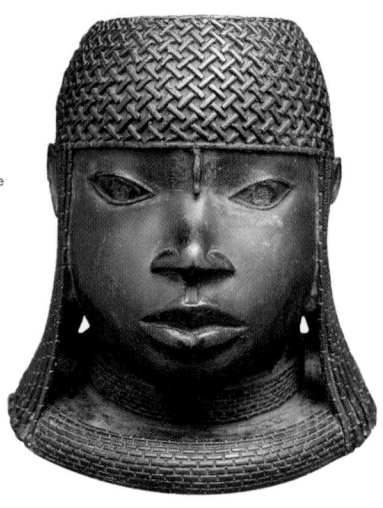

Tin miners digging in central Nigeria accidentally unearthed the oldest surviving examples of sub-Saharan art, such as the HEAD from the Nok culture. Archaeological evidence indicates that these works, of which hundreds have been found, date from the time of the Greeks and the Romans. Modeled in *terra cotta* (unglazed earthenware), they are nearly life-size. The heads, which are broken at the neck, were probably once attached to torsos. Their finely carved hair ornaments and facial features show that there had been sophisticated wood carving in that region. The vivid facial expression of the HEAD makes it seem like a portrait of an individual, but at the same time there is a degree of abstraction in the treatment of the eyes and nose. Little else has survived from the Nok culture. Although we know little about it, it seems to have heavily influenced other cultures of West Africa.

Concurrent with the Gothic era in twelfth-century Europe, a naturalistic style of court portraiture was being produced for the royal court of Ife, a sacred Yoruba city in southwestern Nigeria. The MALE PORTRAIT HEAD demonstrates the Ife skill in lost-wax bronze casting. Such thin-walled, hollow metal casting probably represents the culmination of generations of cultural influences. Scarification lines emphasize facial contours; rows of small holes probably held a beaded veil.

Ife probably influenced the sculptural arts of neighboring Benin. The BENIN HEAD exemplifies another court style, developed in Benin, that was somewhat abstract in comparison to the naturalism of Ife portrait sculpture.

Bronze casting in Benin was an art form devoted exclusively to glorifying the king (or *oba*). The technology was a closely guarded secret, which only licensed royal artisans could practice. Most of the Benin heads are portraits of royalty or other distinguished ancestors. The heads were generally placed in altars that successive generations tended.

When sixteenth-century Europeans first arrived in the kingdom of Benin, they were impressed by cast bronze sculptures, palaces, and a city that compared favorably to their own capital cities. The ivory PENDANT MASK from Benin was carved in the sixteenth century, and modern versions are still worn on the oba's chest, or at his waist during ceremonies. This PENDANT MASK portrays a Queen Mother who stares out with a serene expression. She wears a crown that depicts alternating human heads and salamanders. The human heads are meant to represent Portuguese traders and sailors who regularly visited Benin and, at times, helped the king in diplomatic disputes with neighboring peoples. A close examination of the figures reveals round caps and long mustaches. The salamanders symbolize immortality, because they seem to rise up alive from the mud each year. The two vertical marks in the Queen Mother's brow are shallow slots that held consecrated ointments during ceremonies.

The Bamana people of Mali are renowned for their carved wooden antelope figure headdresses, which young men attach to basketry caps and wear on top of their heads during agricultural ceremonies. When a new field is cleared, the most diligent male workers are selected to perform a dance of leaps in imitation of the mythical *tyi wara*, who taught human beings how to cultivate crops. The dance always includes both male and female TYI WARA DANCERS: the female is identified by a baby on her back, the male by a stylized mane. Abstracted antelope bodies become energized, almost linear forms. Rhythmic curves are accented by a few straight lines in designs that emphasize an interplay of solid mass and penetrating space.

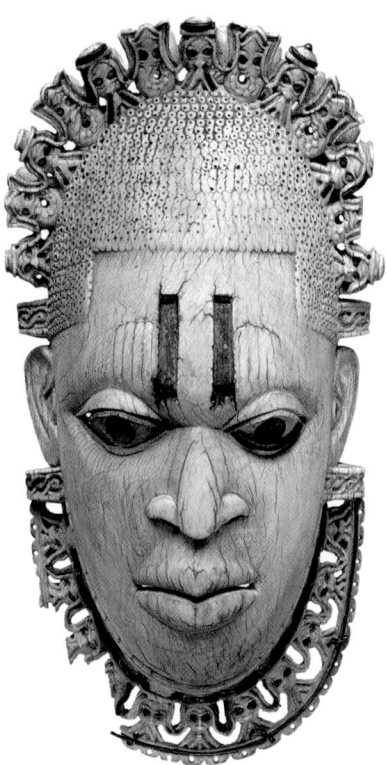

456 PENDANT MASK.
Nigeria. Early 16th century. Ivory, iron, copper. Height 9⅜″.
The Metropolitan Museum of Art. The Michael C. Rockefeller Memorial Collection. Gift of Nelson A. Rockefeller, 1972 (1978.412.323). Photograph by Schecter Lee. © 1986 The Metropolitan Museum of Art.

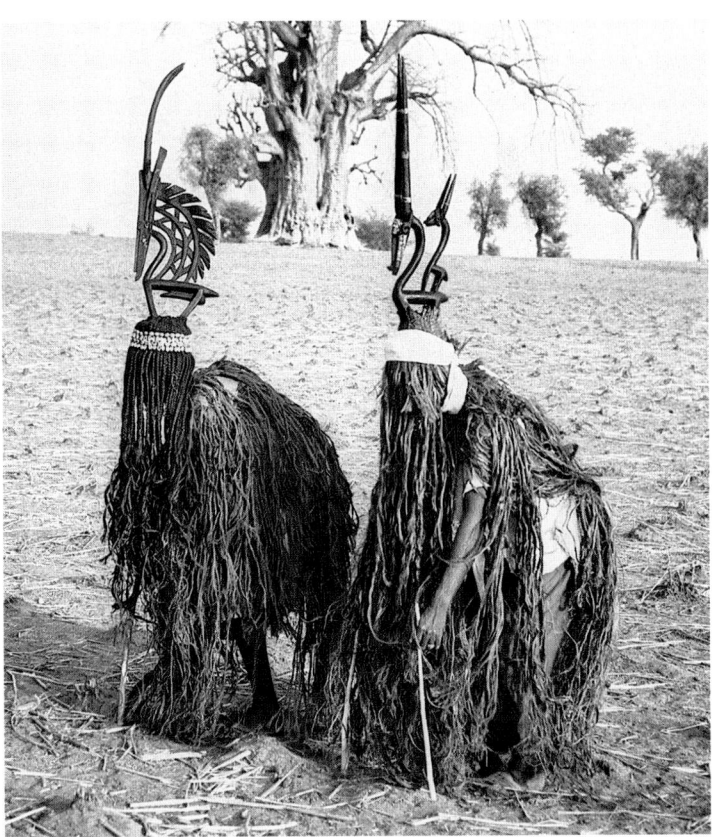

457 TYI WARA DANCERS.
Mali.
Photograph: Dr. Pascal James Imperato.

458 LARGE DANCE HEADDRESS.
Bamenda area, Cameroon, Africa.
19th century.
Wood. Height 26½".
Museum Rietberg, Zurich.
Edward von der Heydt Collection.
Photograph: Wettsin and Kauf.

459 Olembe Alaye.
HOUSE POST.
Yoruba, Nigeria. Mid-20th century.
Wood and paint. Height 83".
UCLA, Fowler Museum of Cultural History.

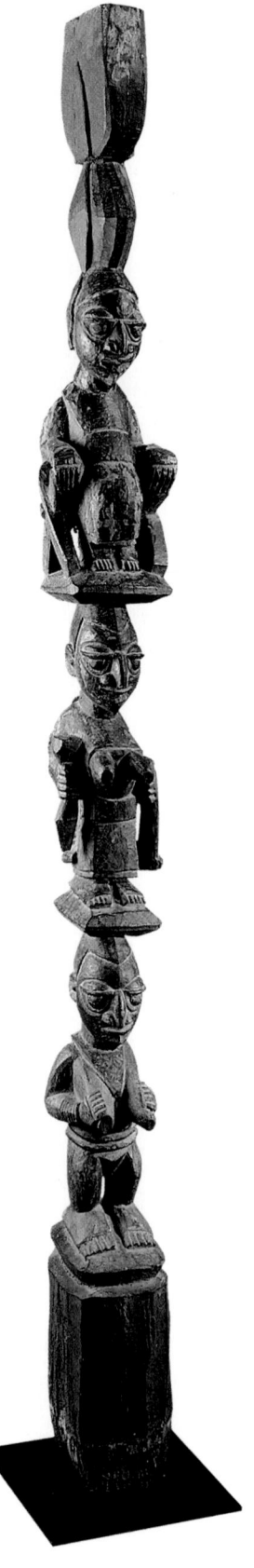

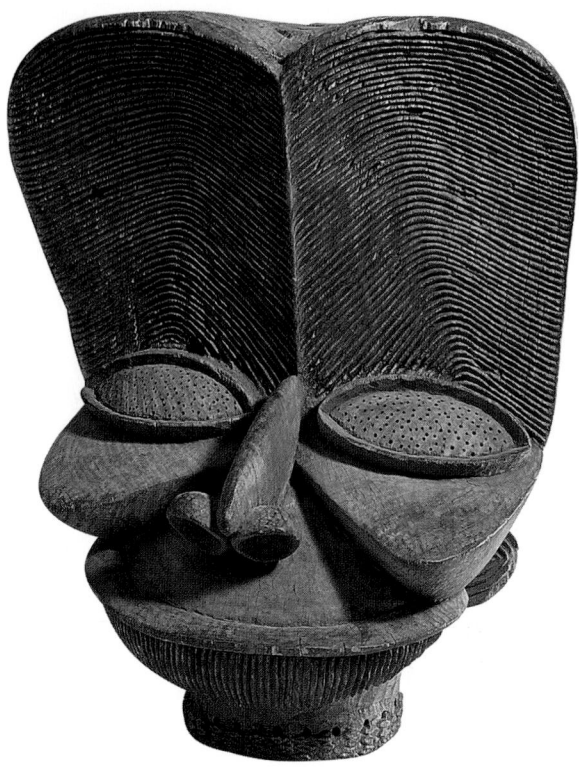

The bold, uninhibited style of art of the grass-lands region of Cameroon looks far removed from the aristocratic styles of Ife and Benin, even though it also was developed for royal courts. The separate areas of the LARGE DANCE HEADDRESS are clearly defined by different patterns and textures. This heavy sculpture, worn by court officials, does not copy the human head but reinterprets it.

The Yoruba peoples of Nigeria have a tradition of figural woodcarving that makes use of diminutive proportions and almond-shaped parts. The HOUSE POST by Olembe Alaye is not only a literal support for a roof; it is also a meditation on the idea of support. Stacked in this composition are (from the top) an elder of the tribe seated in a folding chair, a woman holding a baby on her back, and a second woman holding her breasts in a traditional gesture of welcoming and respect. All three of these people are important to the maintenance of the society, as they represent wisdom, nurturing, and hospitality. All three personify characteristics that support the community.

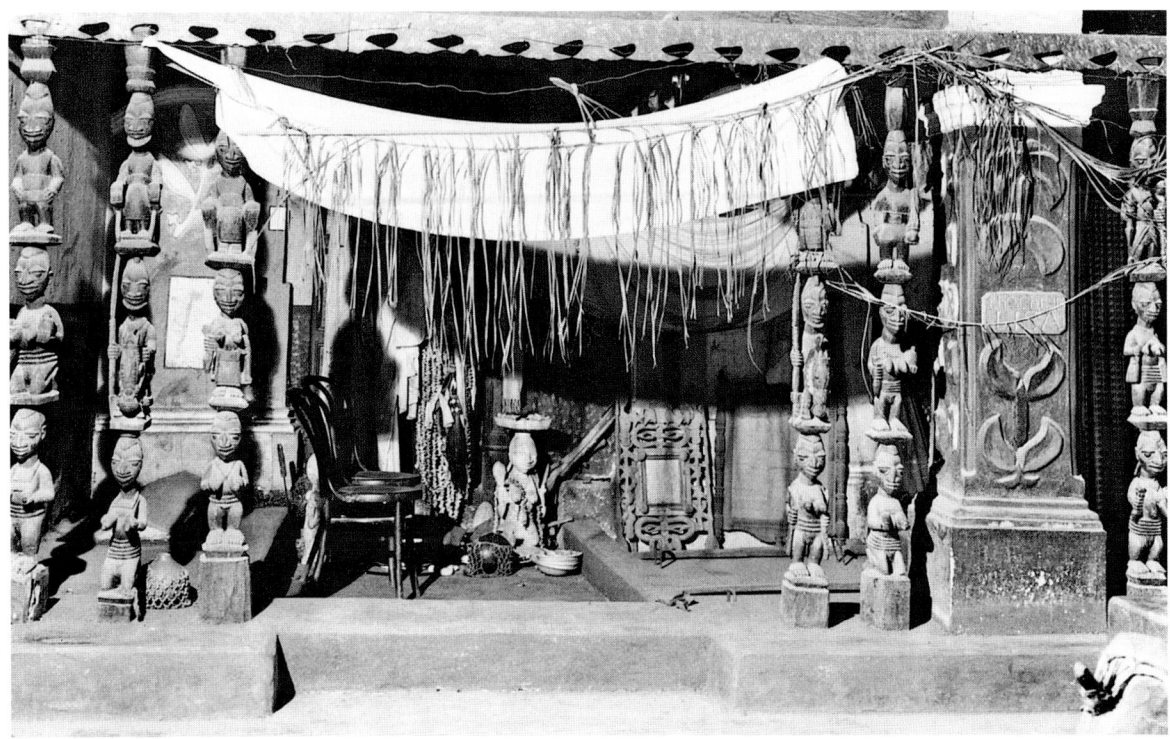

The HOUSE POST takes on added meaning when we see it on location in a 1959 photograph of the TOMB OF FORMER CHIEF LISA. The chief was the "pillar of the community"; placing these posts at the front of his tomb added significance and honor to his memory. He is buried among other emblems of support that, all together, comprise tribal life.

Not all African art has been made for royal or honorific uses. As with the antelope figures discussed earlier, much art is intended to influence future events for the better. An example is the POWER FIGURE from Congo. Someone who feels a need for spiritual power to solve a problem, answer a question, settle a dispute, or promote a favorable outcome might make use of one of these figures. First, the person buys a plain wooden statue. In itself, it has no power. Then a diviner or spirit counselor helps the purchaser add things to it. They may paint part of it, hang articles of clothing on it, attach charms to it, or drive nails into it. With each addition, the figure gains power, because each addition symbolizes an offered prayer, and each has a

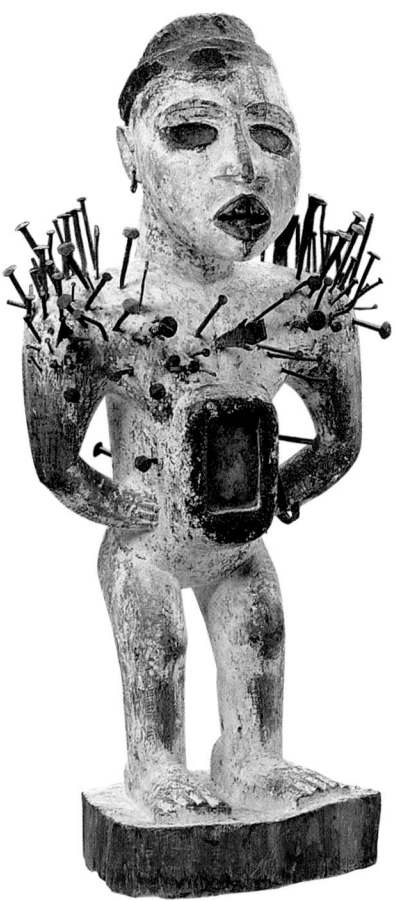

460 TOMB OF FORMER CHIEF LISA.
Ondo, Nigeria. The HOUSE
POST is third from left.
Photograph: W. Fagg, 1959.
William B. Fagg Archive, UCLA Fowler
Museum of Cultural History.

461 POWER FIGURE (NKONDE).
Kongo people. Democratic
Republic of Congo,
19th–20th century.
Wood, glass, iron nail, pigment,
metal, mirror, sacred material.
24″ × 12″ × 8″.
Gift of William E. and Bertha L. Teel,
1991.1064. Museum of Fine Arts, Boston.
Photograph: © 2004 Museum of Fine Arts.
Boston.

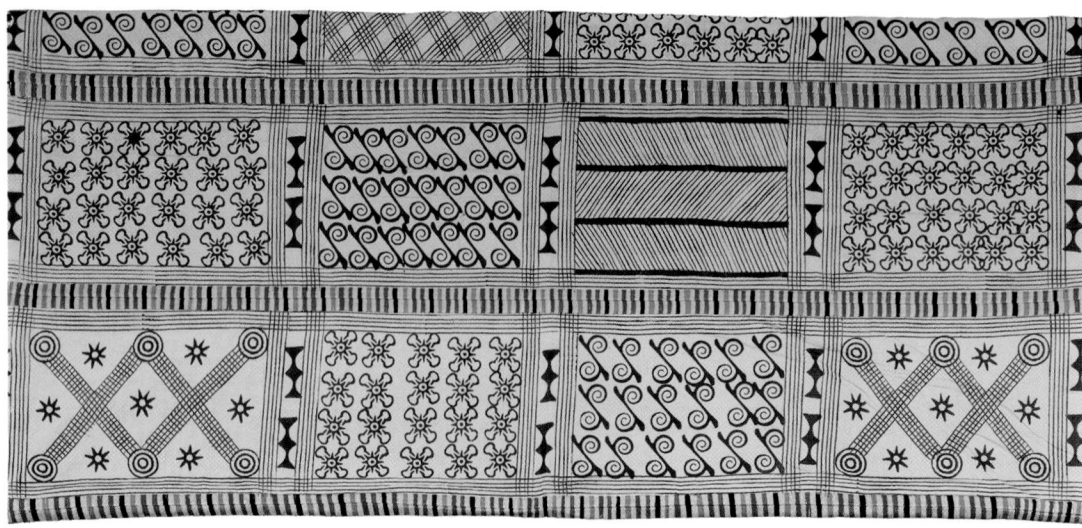

462 ADINKRA CLOTH (detail).
Ashante, Ghana.
© Fowler Museum of Cultural History, UCLA. Photograph: Don Cole.

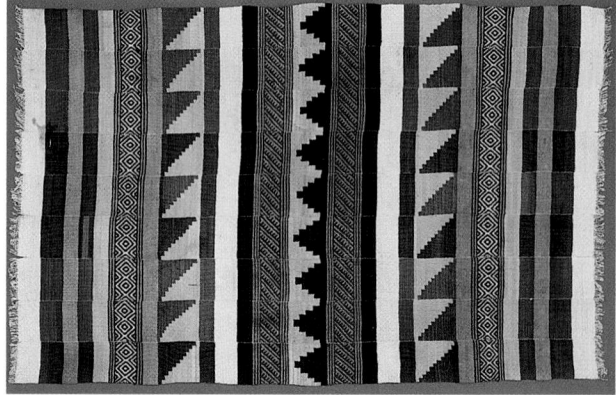

463 TEXTILE (KPOKPO). Mende peoples, Sierra Leone and Liberia.
Cotton, indigo dye, kola nut dye. 81½″ × 49½″.
National Museum of African Art and Museum of Natural History.
Purchased with funds provided by the Smithsonian Collections Acquisition Program,
1983–85, EJ10408. Photograph: Franko Khoury.

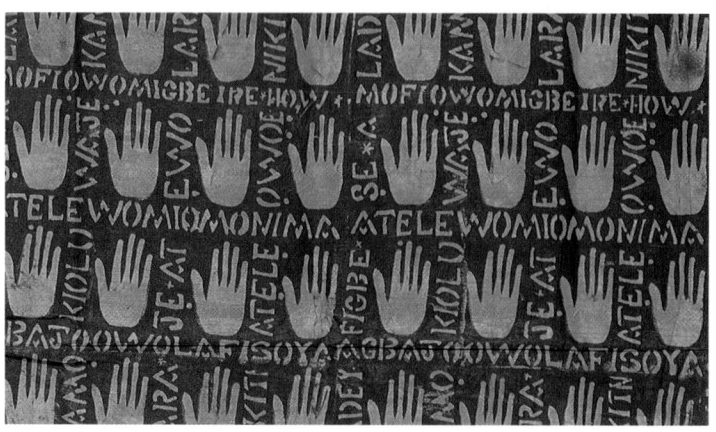

symbolic meaning. A POWER FIGURE such as the one pictured may have so much force that it must be shielded from public view and handled with extreme care. However, after a time the power in the figure is spent, and it becomes practically worthless.

The textile arts are highly developed in Africa, and many cloth styles have specific uses. The stamped ADINKRA CLOTH from the Ashante region of Ghana, for example, was worn in mourning. Artists made stamps from carved gourds and dipped them in dye boiled from tree bark.

In many African textile traditions, long, narrow strips of cloth are woven and then sewn together to make a piece of fabric large enough for a garment or blanket. For the TEXTILE from Sierra Leone, women wove strips with varied design motifs together so that the rhythmic patterns of the lengthwise pieces would line up to form crosswise stripes. Natural dye colors, rhythmic motifs, and subtle patterns were combined in elegant harmonies.

Making ADIRE CLOTH such as the piece pictured here requires a stencil made from a sheet of tin.

464 ADIRE CLOTH, detail of "Women's Wrapper with Human Hands and Proverbs." Yoruba, Lagos, Nigeria. 1984.
Dark and light blue cotton cloth, paste-resist and stencils, natural indigo dye. Sewn in three pieces, with two borders added. 62″ × 76″.
Collection of Flora Edouwaye Stewart Kaplan, New York.
Photograph: Sheldan Collins.

Women lay the stencils over the cloth, and press flour-and-water paste into the openings. When the stencil is lifted off, the patches of paste remain on the cloth and resist the action of the deep blue indigo dye. The rest of the fabric takes on the typical deep blue color after repeated soakings, leaving the words and designs a lighter shade. The ADIRE CLOTH contains repeated handprints, together with traditional Nigerian proverbs and sayings about the hand, such as "My hand is my closest friend."

African art was a principal influence on Western modern art; we will consider this in Chapter 21. Modern art has also flowered in Africa; this will be a subject of Chapters 24 and 25.

OCEANIA AND AUSTRALIA

Oceania is the collective name for the thousands of Pacific islands that comprise Melanesia, Micronesia, and Polynesia (including New Zealand). These islands were settled by migrants from Southeast Asia over a very long period, lasting from about 26,000 B.C.E., when New Guinea and Irian Jaya were populated, until about 800 C.E., when migrants reached New Zealand. Although it is difficult to generalize about Oceanic art, because the cultures, physical environments, and raw materials vary greatly over an enormous area, a few traditional beliefs seem to have been held in common across the Pacific, and these have influenced the creation of art.

First is the belief that the world as we know it was created by the union of the Earth Mother and the Sky Father. Their contact created life forms on the planet's surface. The Oceanic traditions view ancestors as intermediaries between people and the gods. Because ancestors who now live in the spirit world can intercede and influence future events, Oceanic artists have created many objects to honor or placate them. Another widely shared concept is *mana*, or spiritual power. *Mana* may reside in persons, places, or things. Many art forms of Oceania were intended to possess this power, which can keep adversity at bay, promote community well-being, and enhance personal power and wisdom.

Oceanic peoples developed very little pottery because of a shortage of clay, and they were not

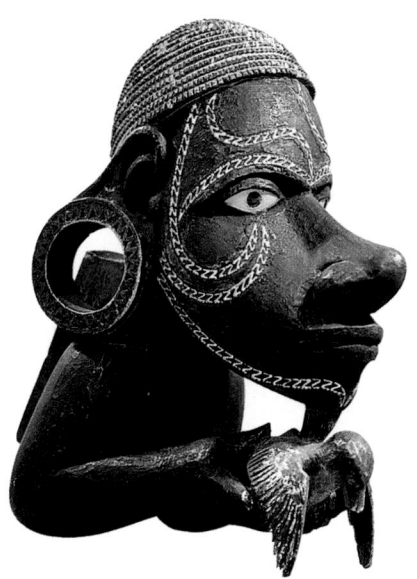

465 PROTECTIVE PROW FIGURE FROM A WAR CANOE.
New Georgia Island, Solomon Islands. 19th century.
Wood with mother-of-pearl. Height 6½".
Museum fur Volkerkunde, Basle, Switzerland. Werner Forman/Art Resource, NY.

acquainted with metal until traders introduced it in the eighteenth century. For tools, they used stone, bone, or shell; for houses, canoes, mats, and cloth, they used wood, bark, and small plants. Feathers, bone, and shells were employed not only for utensils and sculpture, but for personal adornment.

In the Solomon Islands and New Ireland (part of Melanesia), woodcarvings and masks are designed to serve ritual purposes. In the art of many Melanesian societies, birds appear with human figures to act as guides or messengers between the physical world of the living and the spiritual world of deceased ancestors. The bird held by the PROTECTIVE PROW FIGURE FROM A WAR CANOE from the Solomon Islands guides voyagers by acting as a protective spirit that watches out for shoals and reefs. Although the carving is only the size of a hand, it looks much larger because of the boldness of its form. The exaggerated nose and jaw help give the head its forward thrust. Against the blackened wood, inlaid mother-of-pearl provides strongly contrasting white eyes and rhythmically curving linear ZZZ bands.

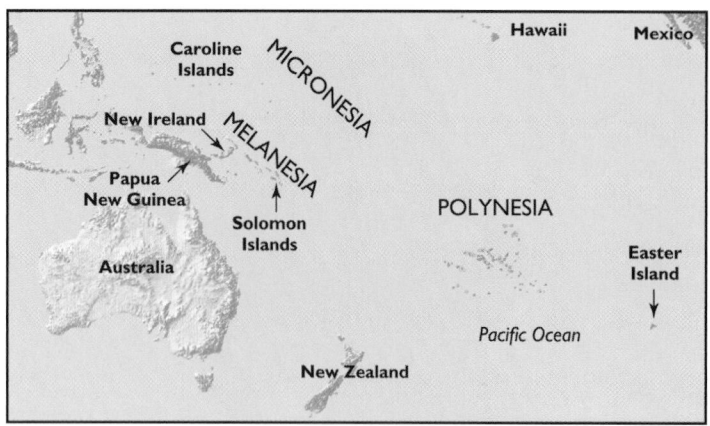

466 OCEANIA AND AUSTRALIA.

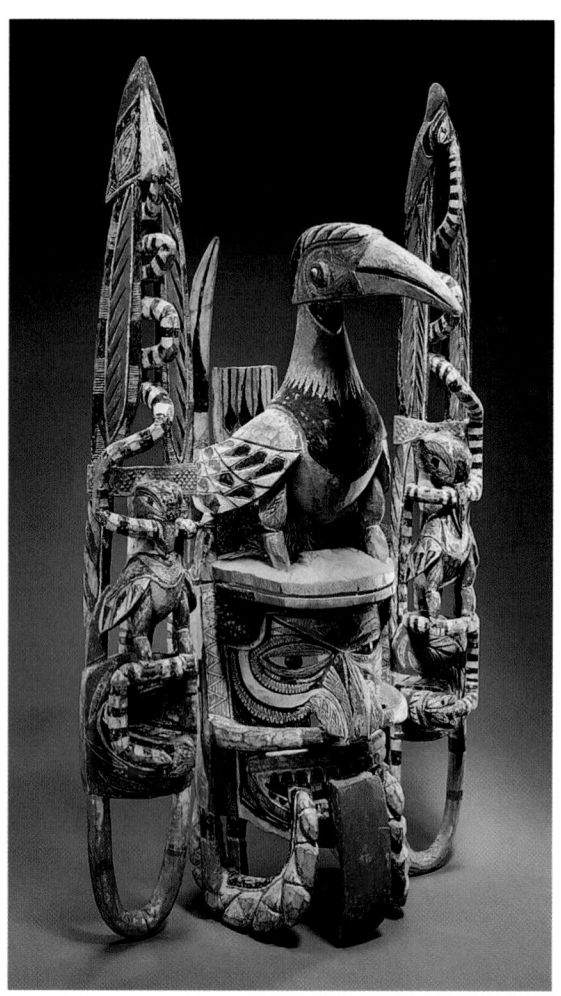

467 MASK. New Ireland. c. 1920.
Painted wood, vegetable fiber, shell. 37½″ × 21⅓″.
Photograph by Don Cole. © UCLA Fowler Museum of Cultural History.

In New Ireland, masks are made for funerary rites that commemorate tribal ancestors, both real and mythical. In this MASK, the elaborately carved, openwork panels are painted in strong patterns that accentuate—and at times oppose—the dynamic forms of the carving. Snail-shell eyes give the mask an intense expression. As in the Solomon Islands CANOE PROW FIGURE, a bird plays a prominent role. In the wings of this mask, chickens hold snakes in their mouths, a reference to the opposition of sky and earth. Anthropologists believe that this mask was used to remove bad influences from a ceremonial house. Once it had fulfilled its function, it was regarded as "used up," and was discarded.

Carvings made in Micronesia and in much of Polynesia are streamlined and highly finished. The Kapingamarangi COCONUT GRATER shows a fine

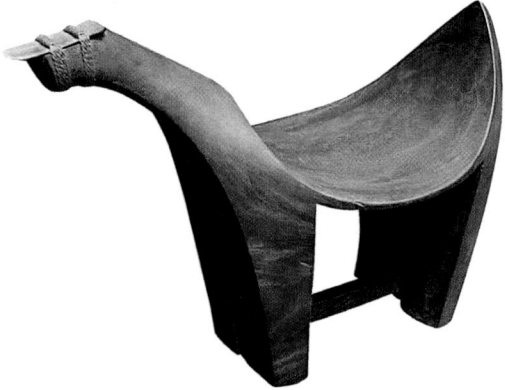

468 COCONUT GRATER.
Kapingamarangi, Caroline Islands. 1954.
Wood, shell blade attached with sennet.
Height 19½″.
Courtesy of Keahonui Rosehill Newhouse.

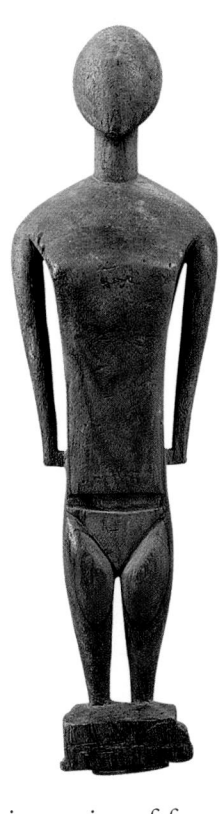

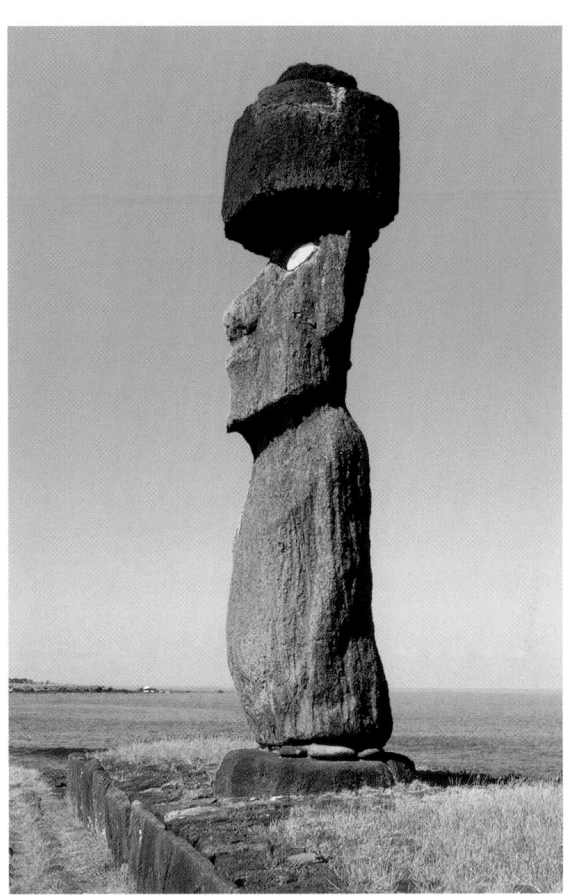

469 STANDING FEMALE FIGURE.
Nukuoro Atoll, Central
Carolines. 19th century.
Wood. Height 15⅞".
Honolulu Academy of Arts, by Exchange,
1943 (4752).

470 MOAI.
Easter Island.
Photolibrary.com.
Photograph: Nick Green.

471 AUMAKUA.
Wooden image from Forbes
Cave, Hawaii.
Koa wood. Height 29".
Photograph: Seth Joel, Bishop Museum.

integration of form and function. One sits on the "saddle" of the animal-like form and grates coconuts using the serrated blade at its head. The STANDING FEMALE FIGURE from Nukuoro Atoll has a similar distinctive spare quality. Although Kapingamarangi and Nukuoro are in the southern part of Micronesia, their culture is Polynesian.

Polynesia covers a large, triangular section of the Pacific, from New Zealand to Hawaii to Easter Island. Widely separated Polynesian islands and island groups developed greatly varied arts that include both delicate and boldly patterned bark cloth, featherwork, shellwork, woodcarvings, and huge rock carvings.

The original inhabitants of Easter Island left more than 600 carved MOAI before European explorers first visited the island in the 1770s. These stone figures, which are up to seventy feet tall, are statues of torsos and heads, set on flat stone platforms. The meaning of these figures is unknown, but they are thought to represent ancestors who have taken on spiritual power. Many Polynesian cultures accord similar homage to ancestors, but none on the scale we see here.

An outstanding example of semi-abstract Hawaiian sculpture is the forceful AUMAKUA

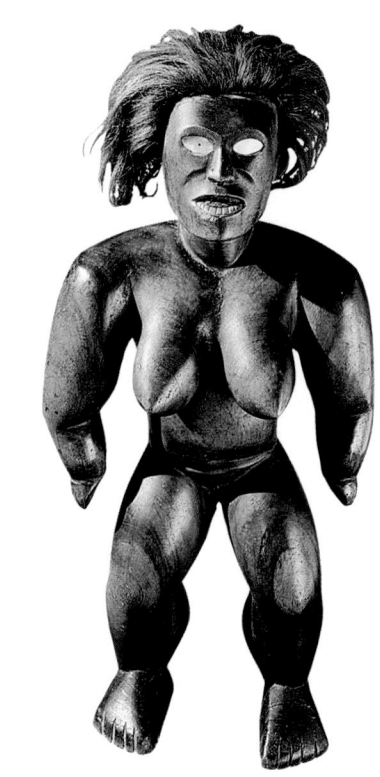

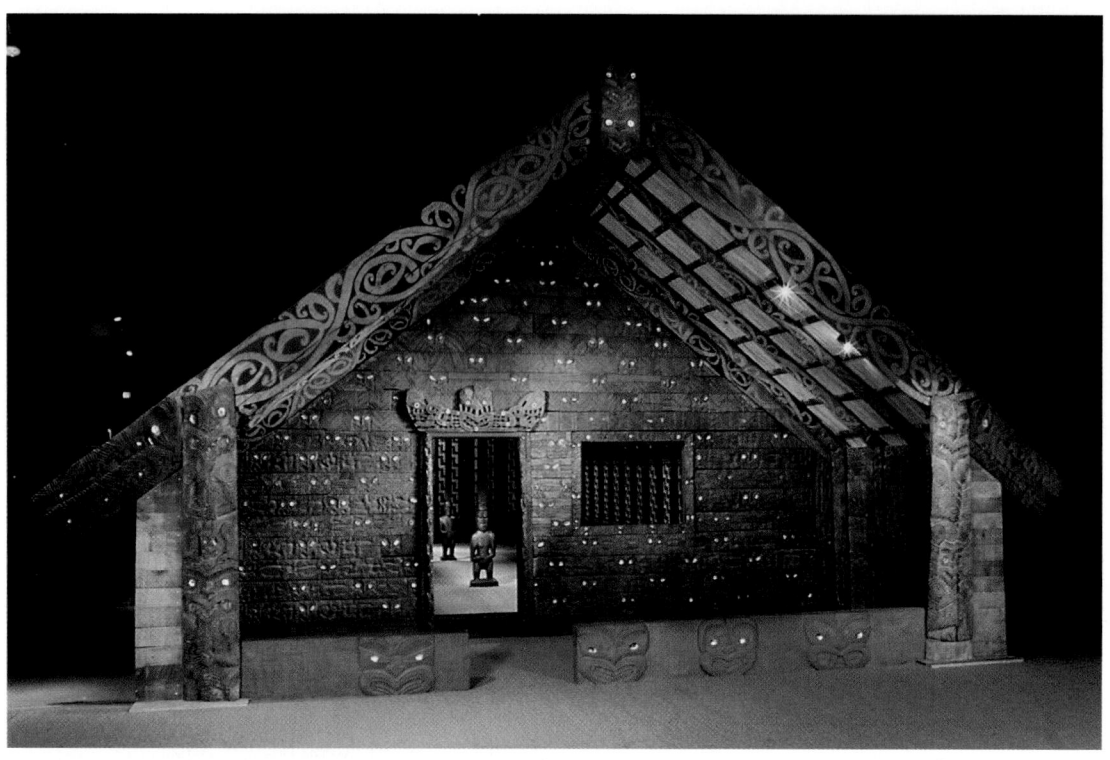

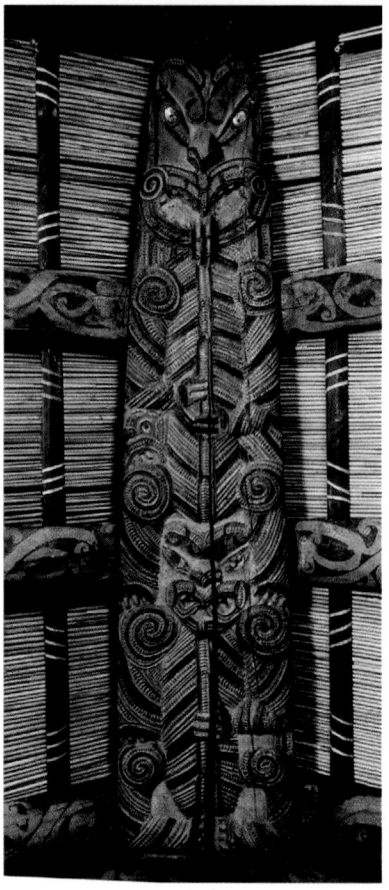

472 MAORI MEETING HOUSE.
Called "Ruatepupuke."
New Zealand. 1881.
Length 56'.
Height 13'10".
© 1993, The Field Museum, Chicago.
Neg. # A112508.3c.
Photograph: Diane Alexander White,
Linda Dorman.

a. Front view.
b. Ridge pole.

(ancestral deity) found in the lava-tube burial cave of a chief or high priest. By eliminating extraneous details and carefully articulating the parts of the body, the sculptor increased the impact of the female figure's bold stance. Its power is enhanced by the attached reddish human hair, shell eyes, and open mouth with bone teeth. The arms-out, knees-bent, feet-apart position gives the figure a strong presence. Full upper arms taper to small forearms and even smaller hands. There is consistent use of full, rounded, almost inflated mass. The well-polished dark wood and inset material show a high degree of craftsmanship.

Many art forms come together in the MAORI MEETING HOUSE, which is a typical structure of traditional New Zealand. Such houses are used for extended family gatherings and rituals in honor of ancestors. The house pictured is named Ruatepupuke in honor of the ancient ancestor of a clan that lives in the eastern corner of the north island.

Not only is the house named for the ancestor, it is meant to symbolize his presence. His face is at the top of the gable; the ridge represents his back; the rafters are his ribs; the front gable boards, which

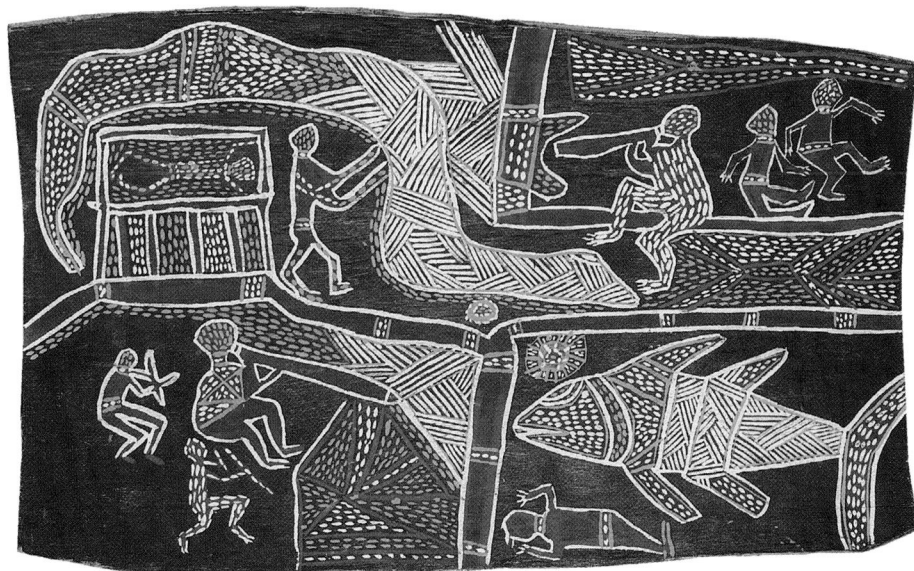

473 Bunia.
FUNERARY RITES AND SPIRIT'S
PATHWAY AFTER DEATH.
Australian bark painting.
Groote Eylantdt, Arnhem Land.
Northern Australia.
Axel Poignant Archive.

symbolize his arms, are painted in patterns that
suggest growing ferns; the front posts symbolize his
legs. The faces of numerous other ancestors are
carved in relief across the front of the house;
most noticeable are the eyes of each, which are
made from inlaid abalone shell. Through the doorway can be seen two center posts that hold up
the ridge pole; these also represent ancestors. The
inner walls alternate relief carvings with abstract
patterns in matted flax called Tukutuku panels (see
page 33).

The ridge pole above the porch is a relief carving
of the Earth Mother and the Sky Father, who are the
ancestors of all life forms. The degree of abstraction
in these figures is typical of Maori carving, with
swirling bands and spirals used in body decoration
and derived from plant forms. This single board was
carved in 1881; it cracked after drying unevenly. The
slightly ferocious aspect of these figures indicates
that they inhabit the spirit world, and this carving
attempts to communicate some of their *mana*.

The human presence in Australia dates back
forty thousand years. (See the MURUJUGA PETRO-
GLYPHS on page 236.) For tens of thousands of years
before the invention of writing, Native Australians
maintained an intimate bond with nature, as
demonstrated by their art. While most other human
groups gradually changed from wandering food for-
agers to settled farmers, manufacturers, and merchants, Native Australians continued to live as semi-
nomadic hunter-gatherers without clothing or
permanent shelters and with only a few simple but
highly effective tools.

The recognition of their dependence on nature
is evident in nearly all art done by Native Australians
and other tribal peoples. Native Australians see the
bond between themselves and nature as a close relationship established by creative beings in the mythical or Eternal Dreamtime. The many disciplines and
practices related to spiritual life vary from tribe to
tribe, but Dreamtime spirits are prominent in nearly
all Native Australian groups.

In the bark painting entitled FUNERARY RITES
AND SPIRIT'S PATHWAY AFTER DEATH, animal and
human symbols tell a story, with time segments
shown in four sections. In the upper left section, a
dying man lies on a funeral platform; in the lower
left, a *didjeridu* player and two dancers perform for
him until he dies. In the upper right, the spirit of the
dying man and his two wives also dance until he
dies. After his death, the man's spirit leaves the platform and begins the journey to the spirit world;
along the way he crosses over the great snake. In the
lower right, he uses a stone to kill a large fish for food

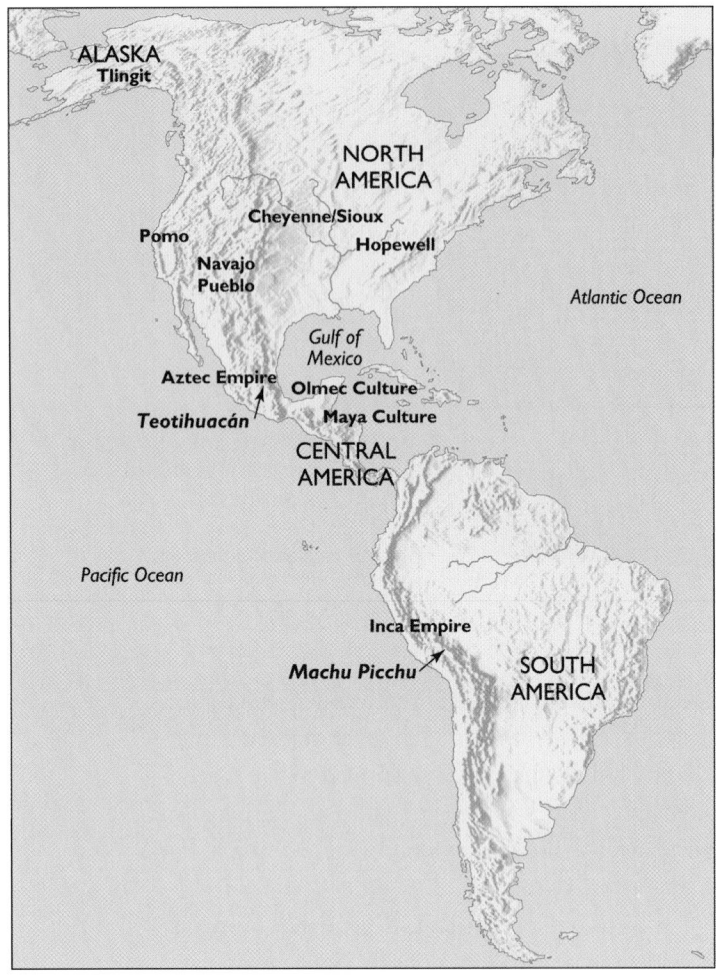

474 AMERICAS.

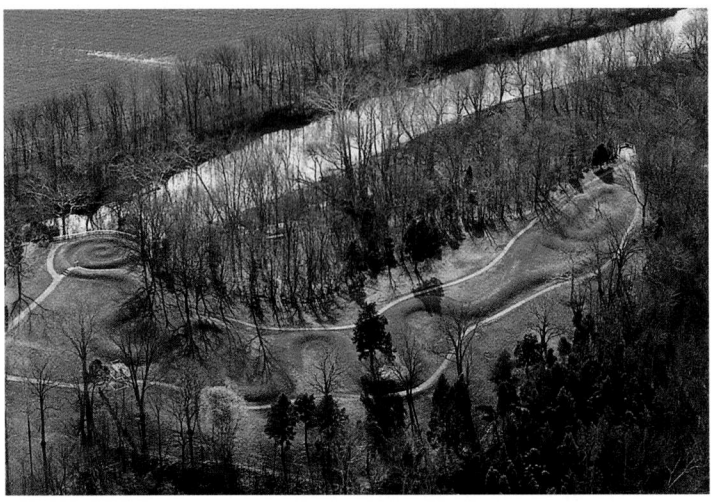

475 GREAT SERPENT MOUND.
Ohio. Adena culture. 100 B.C.E.–500 C.E.
Uncoiled length 1,254′.
Photograph: Mark C. Burnett/Photo Researchers, Inc.

for the journey. Native Australian artists began using paint and canvas in the 1970s, but their imagery has remained relatively constant for hundreds of years.

NATIVE NORTH AMERICA

Native peoples lived in North America for thousands of years before Europeans arrived on the continent. The oldest human-made artifacts—stone hearths and simple tools—may be twenty thousand to thirty thousand years old. (See DEER AND HANDS on page 235.) Some carved bone tools and spear points are about ten thousand years old. However, surviving objects that most people would consider art are much more recent.

The Hopewell culture flourished from the second century B.C.E. to the sixth century C.E. Large Hopewell burial mounds, most of which were built in what is now Ohio, contained rich offerings placed in elaborate log tombs. The largest of these Hopewell structures is the GREAT SERPENT MOUND, now a park near the town of Peebles. The mound-builders first outlined the writhing design with rows of stones, then piled dirt between them. The serpent has a spiral tail, and its curving body ends with open jaws holding a large oval object. When it was first studied in the mid-nineteenth century, the snake's body was 4 feet 10 inches tall and 27 feet wide. If it were extended, it would be over 1,200 feet long. This mysterious structure is one of hundreds of such earth works that early peoples built in the Midwest.

Hopewell artists included wood and stone carvers, potters, coppersmiths, and specialists who worked in shell and mica. The HAND-SHAPED CUTOUT, found in a burial mound, has a striking, abstract quality; elongated fingers and a glowing surface strengthen its mysterious presence. Cut from a glistening, translucent sheet of mica, it seems to celebrate the coordination of eye and hand, mind and spirit, that is the source of all art.

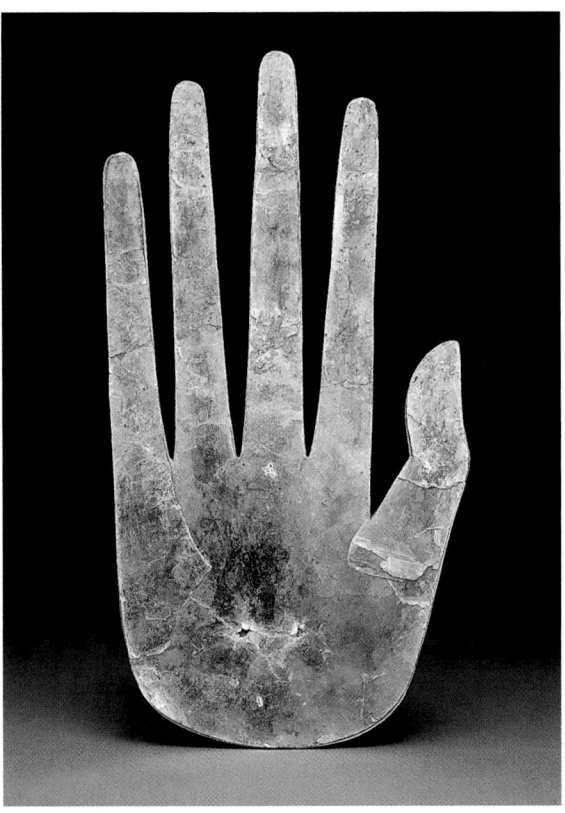

476 HAND-SHAPED CUTOUT.
Hopewell Mound, Ohio. c. 150.
Mica. 11⅛″ × 6″.
Ohio Historical Society, Columbus.
Photograph: © 1985 The Detroit Institute of Arts.

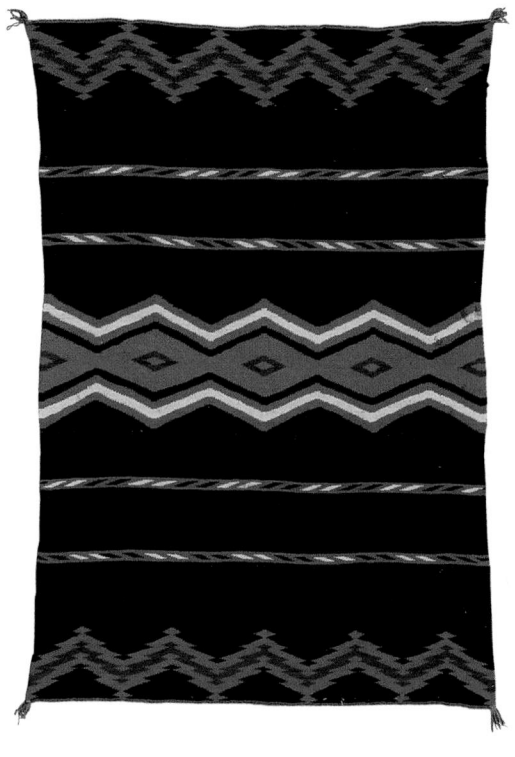

477 BLANKET, BANDED BACKGROUND.
Navajo. 1870–1875.
Length 75″.
Natural History Museum of Los Angeles County.
William Randolph Hearst Collection.

Native Americans today produce an astonishing variety of artworks, depending on their cultural tradition and the materials available in their region. In most cases, native art forms that are now practiced vigorously went through a period of disuse in the late nineteenth century when Indian reservations were first set up. Today many Native American artists are making traditional works, and many more are working in contemporary and even "cutting edge" styles. This section focuses on the traditional arts; contemporary work is a subject of Chapter 25.

The Navajo of Arizona have been resourceful weavers for more than two centuries. The oldest surviving blankets are relatively simple designs, but interactions with other Native American groups, with white settlers, and with the international art market have transformed their art. While many men weave blankets today, the art form was traditionally a woman's province.

The nineteenth-century BLANKET, BANDED BACKGROUND, shown here is made from hand-carded wool dyed with organic pigments. The chevron shapes indicate the influence of Mexican serapes, weavings that the Navajo saw during the period in the 1860s when they were uprooted by the U.S. Army and held in captivity in New Mexico. The advent of the art market led the Navajo to assimilate a great many new influences.

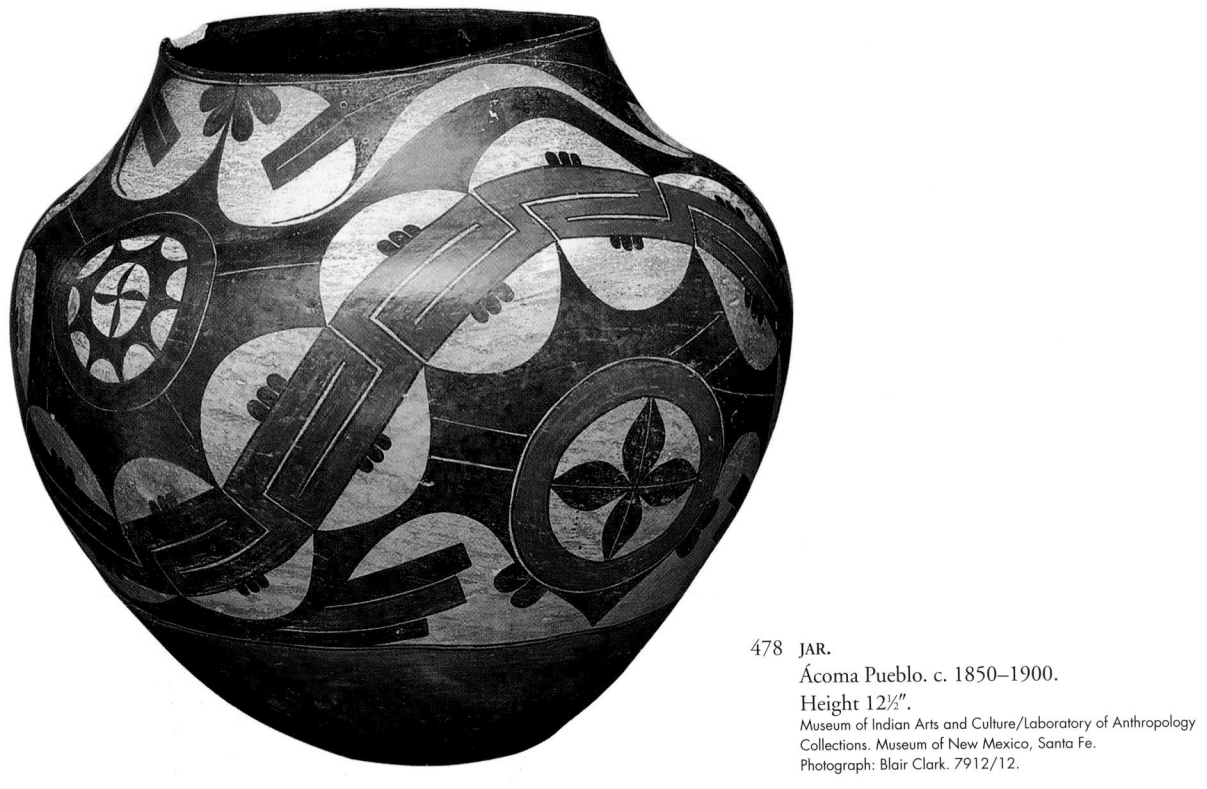

478 JAR.
Ácoma Pueblo. c. 1850–1900.
Height 12½″.
Museum of Indian Arts and Culture/Laboratory of Anthropology
Collections. Museum of New Mexico, Santa Fe.
Photograph: Blair Clark. 7912/12.

The Pueblo peoples of the Southwest are best known for pottery, which is traditionally done by women. Each Pueblo has its own style; the JAR that we see here is from Ácoma. These pots are made from local earthen clays and shaped without a wheel. The artists fire them in open fires and decorate them with pigments from earthen powders. The abstract symbols in Pueblo pots generally do not have a fixed meaning, but refer to the forces of nature or to community life. Pueblo pottery traditions are quite active now, but it was not always so. Near the beginning of the twentieth century, there was little being made until Nampeyo and others revived the ancient techniques (see essay on page 199).

Most Pueblo peoples recognize the spirits of invisible life forces. These spirits, known in Zuni Pueblo and neighboring Hopi areas as *kachinas*, are impersonated by masked and costumed male members of the tribes, who visit the villages in a variety of forms, including birds, animals, clowns, and demons. During ceremonies they dance, present kachina figures to delighted children, provide humor, and occasionally give public scoldings. The carved and painted kachinas, such as the HOPI KACHINA shown on the following page, are made by Hopi and Zuni fathers and uncles as a means of teaching children their sacred traditions.

Native Americans of the Pacific Coast region produce fine baskets. In northern California, Pomo artists made baskets of such incredible tightness that they can hold water. They vary greatly in size, shape, and decoration, from large containers up to four feet in diameter to tiny gift baskets less than a quarter of an inch across. Pomos wove strong geometric designs into many of their baskets and used ornaments such as feathers and shells to embellish others.

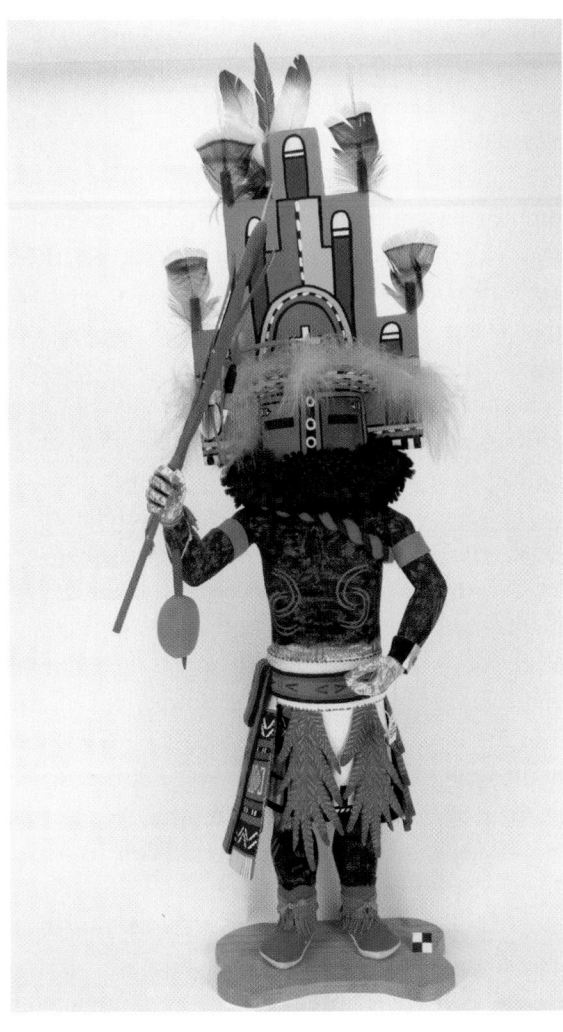

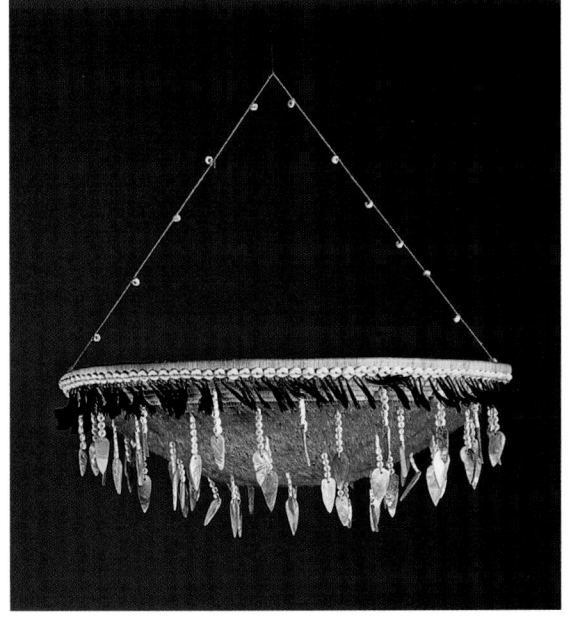

479 Marshall Lomakema.
HOPI KACHINA, HUMIS KATSINA FIGURE. 1971.
Shungopovi, Arizona. Height: 34″.
Painted wood.
Courtesy of National Museum of the American
Indian/Smithsonian Institution. 24/7577.
Photograph: Carmelo Guadagno.

Women were responsible for the highest artistic achievements in Pomo culture: the brightly colored FEATHER BASKETS. As with Pueblo pottery, the art of basketmaking was traditionally passed down in families from mother to daughter and aunt to niece. The instruction was frequently accompanied by training in other tribal traditions. Treasured pieces were made as gifts designed solely to delight the eye.

Plains Indians practiced the traditional art of painting on buffalo hides. Women generally made abstract paintings on useful objects, such as the BLACKFEET PARFLECHE on page 6. Men traditionally made representational paintings of their deeds in

480 POMO FEATHER BASKET.
California. 1937.
Feathers, beads, and shells. 13½″ × 3¼″.
Courtesy of the Southwest Museum, Los Angeles.
811.6.1683/CT294.
Photograph: Larry Reynolds.

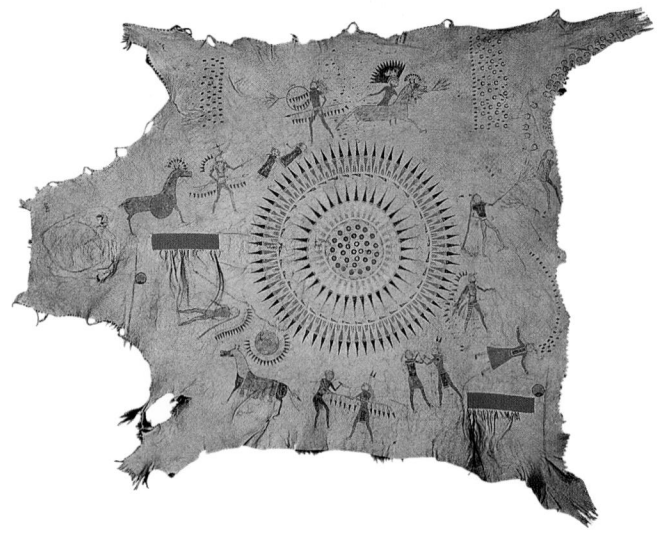

481 Mato Tope (Four Bears).
ROBE WITH MATO TOPE'S EXPLOITS. c. 1835.
Buffalo hide, red wool cloth, sinew, dyed porcupine quills,
horsehair and human hair; brown, yellow, and black pigment.
63″ × 83¾″.
Ethnographic Collection of the Bern Historical Museum. Photograph: S. Rebsamen.

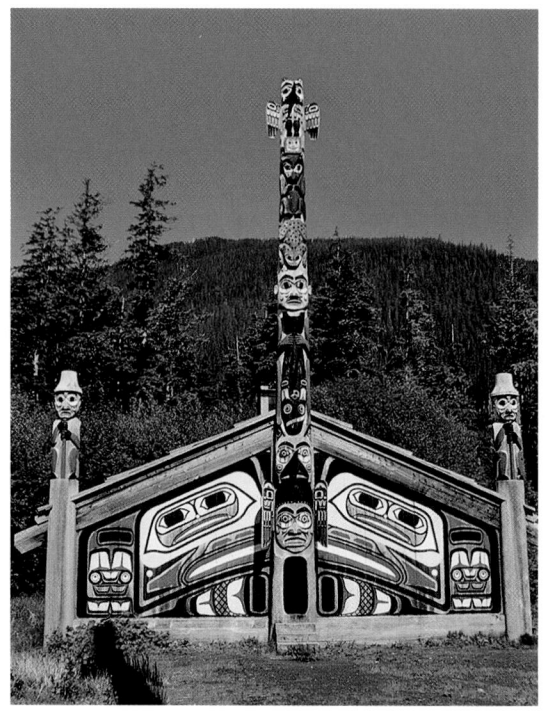

482 **TLINGIT COMMUNITY HOUSE.**
Ketchikan, Alaska.
Photograph: Steve McCutcheon.

battle, as we see in the ROBE WITH MATO TOPE'S EXPLOITS. Mato Tope stretched this hide in the sun to dry and then painted it with organic pigments in a water-based solution. Exploit paintings are typically full of action, with the moving figures seen in profile views with no horizon line. The best examples date from before European contact, but these are very rare. Our example was collected by a fur trader and sent back to Switzerland. Later hides depict battles with U.S. Army troops. With the disappearance of the buffalo and the creation of reservations, artists began to use watercolor and pencil on ledger books supplied by trading posts. One of the best-known of these warrior-artists was Howling Wolf, who is the subject of the accompanying essay.

Northwest Coast tribes developed highly imaginative arts to depict their mythology. Elegant abstractions of animal subjects typify the painting and sculpture of the Tlingit and other tribes that inhabit the coastline from Seattle to Alaska. On house walls, boxes, blankets, and even dishes, major features of a symbolic animal form are laid out in two-dimensional abstract patterns. With its wide, gently sloping roof, elaborately painted facade, and totem poles, the TLINGIT COMMUNITY HOUSE is characteristic of the art and architecture of the region. A *totem* is an object such as an animal or plant that serves as an emblem of a family or clan; it often symbolizes original, prehuman ancestors. The word itself, from a Native American language of the Upper Midwest, means "he is related to me."

The flat surfaces of the TLINGIT COMMUNITY HOUSE show abstract shapes of beavers, bears, whales, and ravens. The totem pole at the center consists of such stacked symbols, which help a family clan to remember its history back to mythological times, much like a family crest.

HOWLING
Wolf
1849–1927

Warrior, Captive, and Artist

PLAINS NATIVE AMERICAN artist Howling Wolf's drawings reflect not only the artist's unique personal journey, but also larger currents of Native and white relations during a troubled time.

Born into the Southern Cheyenne tribe, Howling Wolf excelled from an early age at the arts of warfare. The young Howling Wolf counted his first act of bravery in 1867, when he was wounded while trying to capture the lead horse of a supply train sent to reinforce white settlers in Kansas. He soon rose in the ranks of the tribe to become a leader alongside his father.

With the arrival of large numbers of white people, however, the nature of Plains warfare evolved toward greater physical danger and the use of firearms. In this style of fighting, the U.S. Army was far more efficient than the Plains warriors, and Native peoples saw their lands steadily reduced.

In 1875, Howling Wolf was captured and subjected to an experiment that both changed his life and influenced the future course of U.S. government treatment of Native Americans. Both Howling Wolf and his father were among seventy-two captives that the Army regarded as particularly dangerous. In September 1875 they were sent to Fort Marion on the coast of Florida, under the command of Captain Richard

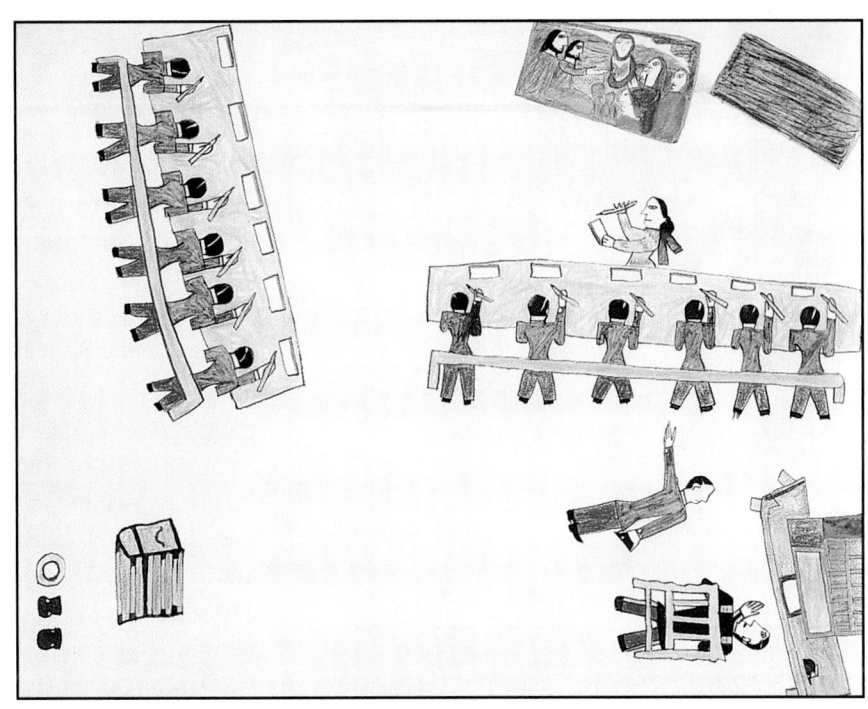

483 Howling Wolf. CLASSROOM AT FORT MARION. 1876.
Colored pencil on paper. 8½" × 11".
Courtesy of the New York State Library, Manuscript and Special Collections Section, Albany.

Pratt, whose goal was to "civilize" them. The warriors would take Christian names, cut their hair, wear uniforms, and attend classes with teachers who would instill the skills of white society.

The experiment lasted three years, during which time Howling Wolf learned to read and write. He also made drawings that clearly show his inner struggle between his traditional values and the new ones he was being asked to adopt. In CLASSROOM AT FORT MARION, twelve former warriors are seated obediently at their desks as a teacher attempts to show them how to use a pen. Above the

teacher's head is a chalkboard, and a larger rectangle shows a religious painting of the sort that commonly hung in classrooms of that time. In this picture within the picture, Howling Wolf experimented with Western perspective.

The rest of the work hovers guardedly between the flatness of traditional Plains painting and the demands of rendering three-dimensional blocks of space in the desks, the warriors, and the chest at the lower left. A confrontation seems to take place in the lower right corner, as a warrior remonstrates with an officer at his desk. In the

uneasiness of the spacing, the rigidity of the poses, and the ambiguous multiple viewpoints in this work we can clearly see Howling Wolf's wary suspension between two cultures.

Howling Wolf was released from Fort Marion after three years. Resigned to giving up the struggle with white settlers, he returned to the Cheyenne reservation in Oklahoma, where he functioned more as a tribal leader than as an artist. Few works from his later life survive.

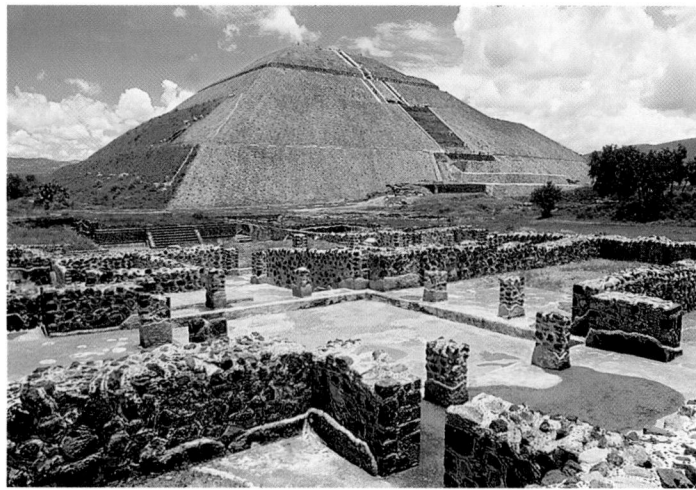

484 PYRAMID OF THE SUN.
cd Teotihuacan. 1st–7th century C.E.
700' wide, 200' high.
Photograph: John S. Flannery/Bruce Coleman Inc.

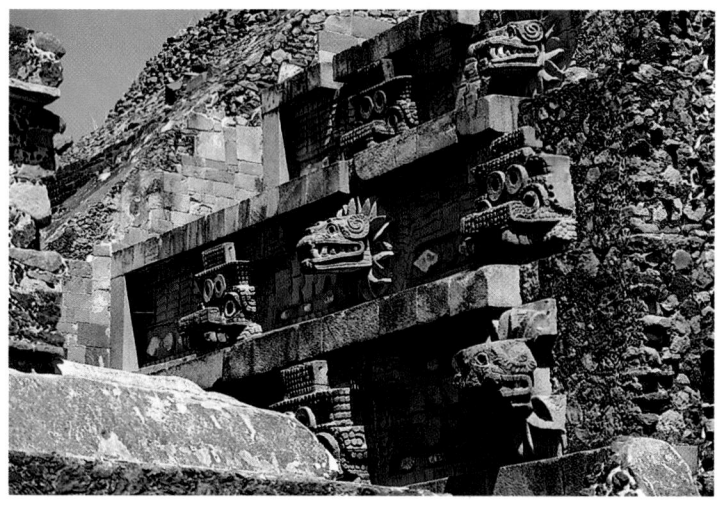

485 Detail of TEMPLE OF THE FEATHERED SERPENT.
cd Teotihuacan. 150–200 C.E.
Photograph: © Dr. E. R. Degginger/Color-Pic, Inc.

PRE-COLUMBIAN CENTRAL AND SOUTH AMERICA

A variety of agricultural civilizations flourished in Mexico from about the time of Christ until the Spanish conquest of the 1520s. These cultures influenced one another through trade and conquest, and as a result they share many cultural forms, among them pyramids, calendars, and some important gods and myths. The earliest was the Olmec, who inhabited the Gulf Coast near what is now Veracruz (see the Olmec MASSIVE STONE HEAD on page 187). Probably more influential were the people who built the city of Teotihuacan, located in the central valley about forty miles north of where Mexico City is today.

The PYRAMID OF THE SUN in Teotihuacan is among the largest in the world, covering slightly more ground than the largest of the Great Pyramids of Giza in Egypt. It rises only about half as high, and imitates the shape of the surrounding mountains. Many ancient Mexican cultures believed that humanity first emerged from a hole in the ground, and this pyramid may mark the spot: it sits over a deep cave. The pyramid is aligned to face the sunset on August 12, the date corresponding to the beginning of time in the Maya calendar. As we can see in the photograph, THE PYRAMID OF THE SUN was at the center of a large city, which archaeologists calculate was the world's sixth largest at its peak in 600 C.E.

At one end of the central avenue of Teotihuacan lies the TEMPLE OF THE FEATHERED SERPENT, which has sculptural decorations that influenced several other cultures. Alternating on the layers of the temple are relief heads of the Storm God, with its goggle eyes and scaly face, and the Feathered Serpent, its fanged head emerging from a plumed wreath. Teotihuacan itself was abandoned after burning in a mysterious fire in about the year 750 C.E. However, both of these gods were widely adopted by later cultures in ancient Mexico.

The Maya, whose descendants still live in what are now parts of Mexico, Guatemala, and Honduras, developed a written language, an elaborate calendar, advanced mathematics, and large temple complexes of stone.

The hundreds of stone temples at Tikal suggest that Maya priests had great power. TEMPLE I, built during the classical Maya period, 300–900 C.E., rises over a great plaza in a Guatemalan rain forest. The two-hundred-foot-high pyramid has a temple at the top consisting of three rooms. Another Maya temple pyramid contained a burial chamber deep inside, similar to those found in Egyptian pyramids. Walls and roofs of Maya stone temples were richly carved and painted.

An excellent example of Maya sculpture from one such temple is LINTEL 24 from Yaxchilan, a site on the border between Mexico and Guatemala. This stone relief is best understood with the help of the written symbols along its edges, which have been recently decoded. Standing is the king, Lord Shield Jaguar, holding a flaming torch. The sculptor seems to have rendered effortlessly the casual fall of the feathers in his headdress. His wife Lady Xoc kneels before him performing a ritual. She draws blood from her pierced tongue, which she will blot with the pieces of paper in the basket in front of her. She wears richly patterned clothing that hints at highly developed textile arts of that time (none of which, unfortunately, survive). Her elaborate headdress is crowned with the goggle-eyed storm god, who looks almost directly upward from the back of Lady Xoc's head. Especially noteworthy are the sculptor's evocation of the fleshiness of the figures, their subtle interaction, and the rich textures of their clothing. The writing on the work describes the action and even gives its date, 28 October 709.

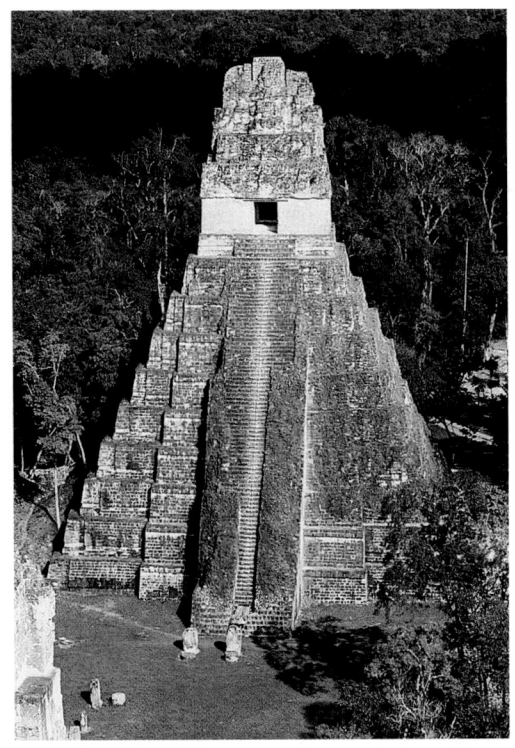

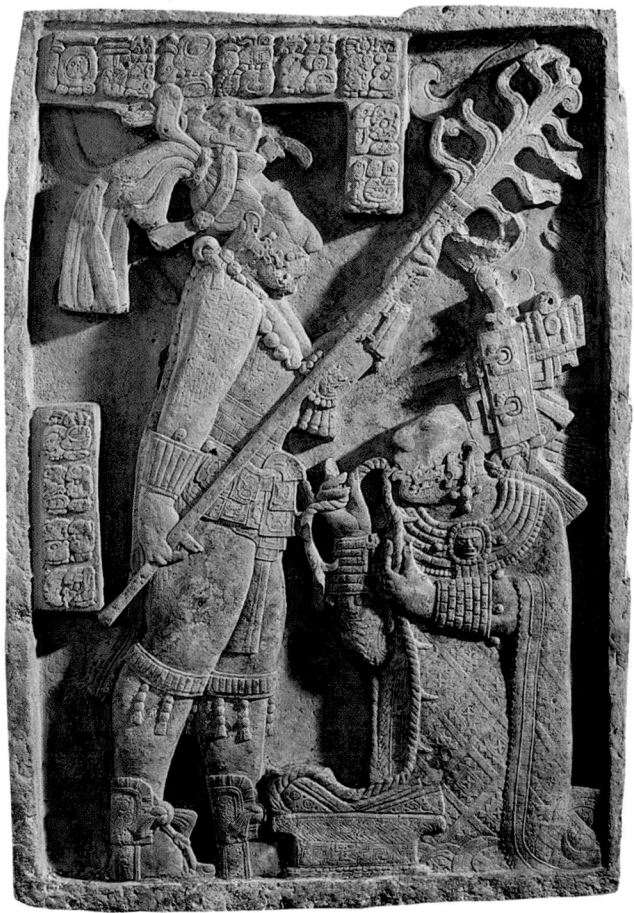

486 TEMPLE I. Maya.
Tikal, Guatemala. c. 300–900 C.E.
Photograph: Hans Namuth/Photo Researchers, Inc.

487 LINTEL 24.
Yaxchilan, Maya. 709 C.E.
Limestone. Height: 43″.
© Copyright British Museum.

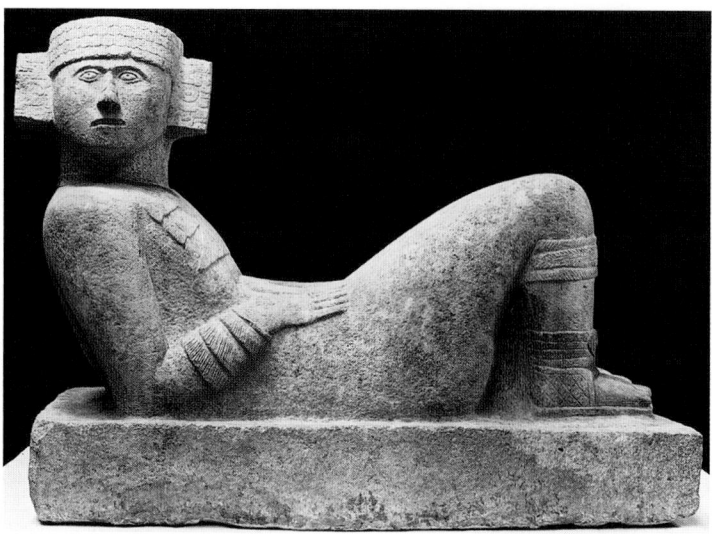

488 CHACMOOL. 10th–12th century. Toltec.
Stone. Length 42".
Photograph: © Giraudon/Art Resource, NY.

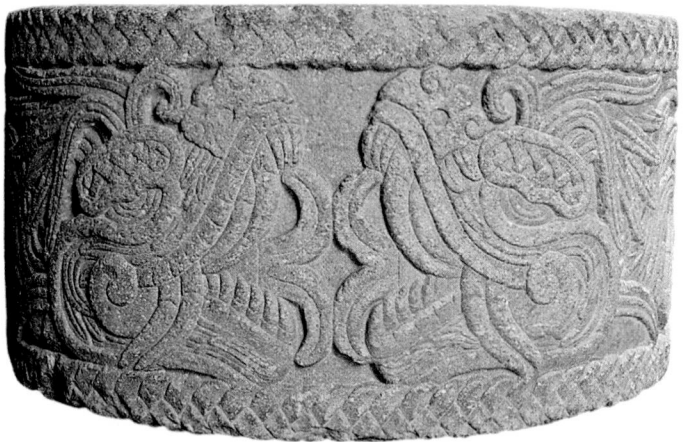

489 VESSEL OF THE FEATHERED SERPENT QUETZALCOATL.
Aztec. 1450–1521. Stone.
Height 19".
Museo Nacional de Antropologia, Mexico City.

The Toltec civilization that developed in central Mexico between the ninth and thirteenth centuries forms a bridge between the decline of the Maya and the rise of the Aztecs. During a time of conflict and change, the Toltecs initiated a major new era in the highlands of central Mexico, distinguished by architectural innovations and massive carved figures. A Toltec form that also occurs in Aztec and Maya art is the recumbent figure from Chichen Itza known by the Mayan name CHACMOOL. The bowl at the figure's waist held sacrificial offerings. Reclining figures such as this one were a strong influence on the modern sculpture of Henry Moore, whose RECUMBENT FIGURE is pictured in Chapter 22.

The Aztecs were the most powerful kingdom in Mexico at the time of the Spanish Conquest; their art is in many respects a summation of preceding styles. The Aztecs (who called themselves the Mexica) settled in the early fourteenth century in the area where Mexico City now stands. Their principal temple was a dual pyramid in honor of the storm god and a war god, where they made human sacrifices of the prisoners they had taken in warfare with neighboring peoples. The Aztecs believed that such sacrifices were necessary in order to honor and recreate the self-sacrifice that the feathered serpent had performed in ancient times in order to ensure the continuation of the world. They believed that this original sacrifice had occurred at Teotihuacan, which they knew as an uninhabited ruin.

The feathered serpent is frequently depicted in Aztec sculpture, but rarely with more horrific effect than in the VESSEL OF THE FEATHERED SERPENT QUETZALCOATL, a vessel for sacrificial offerings. Two snakes face each other, their fangs and split tongues forming a symmetrical design. The rather menacing aspect of this piece is typical of much Aztec stone sculpture, which reflects the militaristic and regimented nature of Aztec society. When the

which three brothers pledge to take the sword offered by their father to defend Rome. With such paintings, David gave revolutionary leaders an inspiring image of themselves rooted in history. "Take courage," was the painting's message, "your cause is a noble one and has been fought before."

David's Neoclassicism, seen in the rational, geometric structure of his composition, provides strong contrast to the lyrical softness of Rococo designs. The painting has the quality of classical (Greco-Roman) relief sculpture, with strong side light emphasizing the figures in the foreground. Even the folds in the garments are more like carved marble than soft cloth. The background arcade gives strength to the design and provides a historically appropriate setting for the Roman figures. The two center columns separate the three major parts of the subject. Vertical and horizontal lines parallel the edges of the picture plane, forming a stable composition that resembles a stage set.

The women at the right of the OATH OF THE HORATII seem overcome by emotion, unable to participate in the serious decisions required of men who would defend their homeland. This painting reflects what was commonly believed at that time: that women were unfit for public life. Their exclusion from most professions was also true of the art world, where women were banned from academy classes in which unclothed models were used. If a woman did succeed as an artist, it was because she either could afford private study or came from an artistic family.

In the works of the Neoclassicist Angelica Kauffmann, who overcame such obstacles, we see a different vision of woman's abilities. Born in Switzerland and trained by her father, Kauffmann spent six years in Italy before settling in London in 1768. She was elected a full member of the British Royal Academy two years later, the last woman to be so honored until the 1920s. Her work CORNELIA, POINTING TO HER CHILDREN AS HER TREASURES was painted a year after David's OATH OF THE HORATII. Cornelia is at the center of the work, talking to a friend seated at the right. The friend shows a string

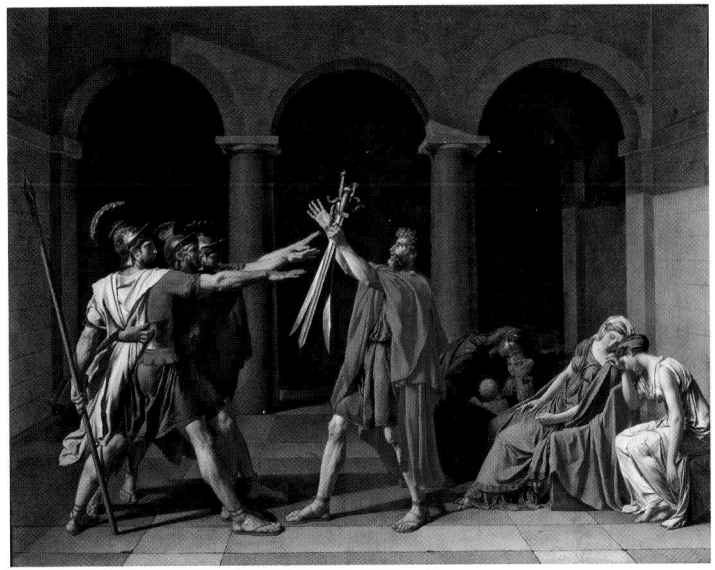

493   Jacques-Louis David.
OATH OF THE HORATII. 1784.
Oil on canvas. 10'10" × 14'.
Musée du Louvre, Paris.
Photograph: Scala. Art Resource, NY.

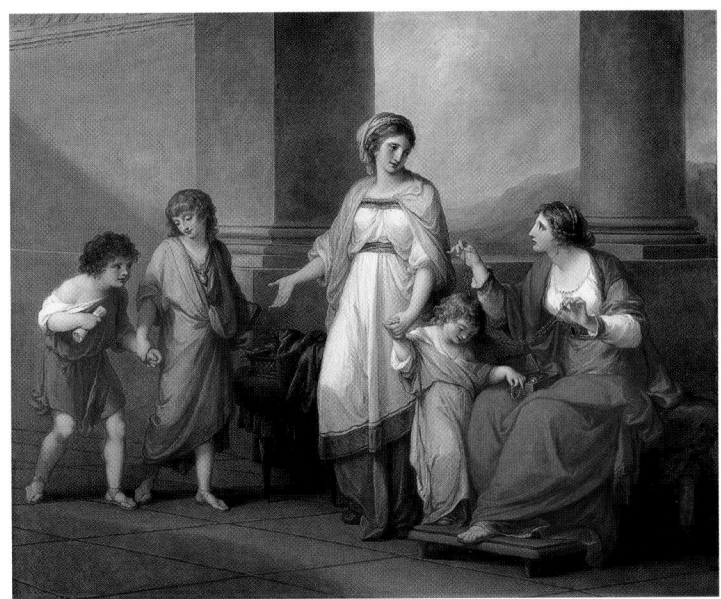

494   Angelica Kauffmann.
CORNELIA, POINTING TO HER CHILDREN AS HER TREASURES. c. 1785.
Oil on canvas. 40" × 50".
Virginia Museum of Fine Arts, Richmond. The Adolf D. and Wilkins C. Williams Fund.
Photograph: Ann Hutchison. © Virginia Museum of Fine Arts. 75.22/50669.2.

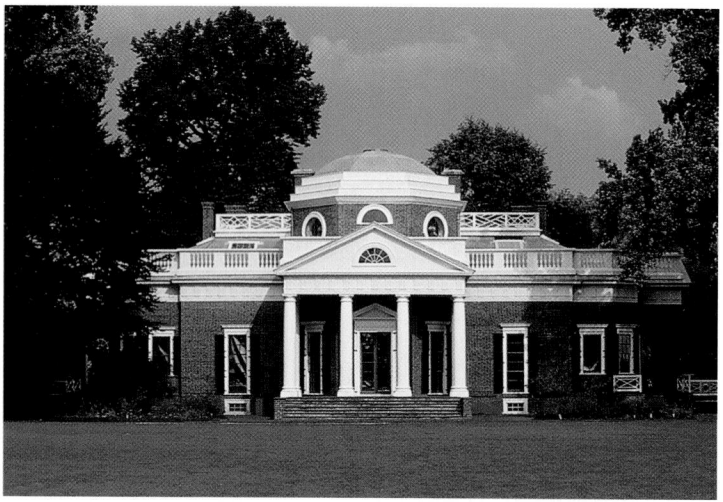

495 Thomas Jefferson.

MONTICELLO. Charlottesville, Virginia. 1793–1806.
Courtesy of the Thomas Jefferson Memorial Foundation, Inc.

of jewels as if boasting about them, to which Cornelia replies that her children are her jewels. Indeed, to a student of Roman history, this was true: Cornelia's children adopted her well-known democratic beliefs and went on to become important figures in the development of the Roman political system.

The new classical (that is, Neoclassical) spirit also infected architecture. American architecture achieved international stature for the first time with the work of statesman-architect Thomas Jefferson. His original design for his home, MONTICELLO, was derived from Palladio's Renaissance reinterpretation of Roman country-style houses (see page 280). Then, during his years in Europe as Minister to France (1784–1789), Jefferson carefully studied French, Italian, and Roman architecture. Thus, when he rebuilt his home between 1793 and 1806, he had the second story removed from the center of the building and replaced by a dome on an octagonal drum. He added a large Greco-Roman portico (a porchlike roof supported by columns), making the entire design reminiscent of the PANTHEON (see page 252) by way of contemporary French Neoclassical architecture. In comparison with the first MONTICELLO, the second version has a monumental quality that reflects Jefferson's increasingly classical conception of architecture.

Both MONTICELLO and Jefferson's designs for the University of Virginia show the Roman phase of Neoclassical American architecture, often called the Federal Style. Jefferson aimed for an architecture capable of expressing the values of the new American republic. In its fusion of classical Greek, Roman, Renaissance (Palladian), and eighteenth-century forms, his architecture shows an originality that sets it apart. Jefferson's Neoclassical style is reflected in much of American architecture before the Civil War. Neoclassical architecture can be found in practically every city in the United States, and it continues to dominate Washington, D.C.

ROMANTICISM

The Enlightenment celebrated the power of reason; however, an opposite reaction, Romanticism, soon followed. This new wave of emotional expression motivated the most creative artists in Europe from about 1825 to 1850. The word Romanticism comes from *romances*, popular medieval tales of adventure written in romance languages.

Whereas Neoclassicism refers to a specific style, *Romanticism* refers to an attitude that inspired a number of styles. Romantic artists, musicians, and writers held the views that imagination and emotion are more valuable than reason, that nature is less corrupt than civilization, and that human beings are essentially good. Romantics championed the struggle for human liberty and celebrated nature, rural life, common people, and exotic subjects in art and literature. They wanted to assert the validity of subjective experience and to escape Neoclassicism's fixation on classical forms.

Spanish artist Francisco Goya was a Romantic painter and printmaker. A contemporary of David, he was aware of the French Revolution and he personally experienced some of the worst aspects of the ensuing Napoleonic era, when French armies invaded Spain and much of the rest of Europe. Goya at first welcomed Napoleon's invading army because his sympathies were with the French Revolution and he had lost confidence in the king of Spain. But he soon discovered that the occupying army was destroying rather than defending the

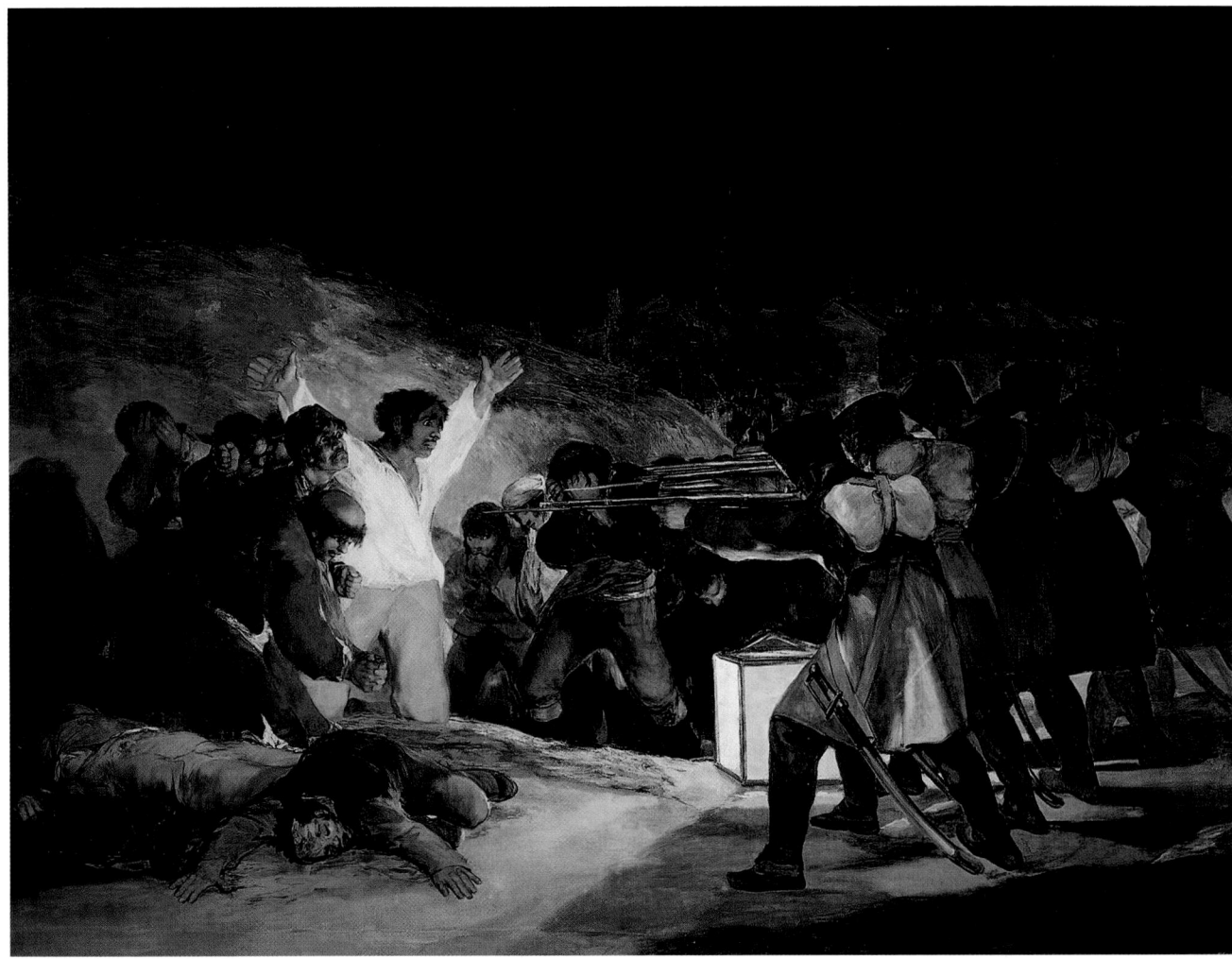

496 Francisco de Goya.
THE THIRD OF MAY 1808. 1814.
Oil on canvas. 8'9" × 13'4".
Museo del Prado, Madrid.
Photograph: Arixiu Mas, Barcelona. Derechos reservados.
© Museo Nacional Del Prado, Madrid.

ideals he associated with the Revolution. Napoleon's troops occupied Madrid in 1808; on May 2, a riot broke out against the French in the central square. Officers fired from a nearby hill, and the cavalry was ordered to cut down the crowds. The following night, firing squads were set up to shoot anyone who appeared in the streets. Later, Goya vividly and bitterly depicted these brutalities in his powerful indictment of organized murder, THE THIRD OF MAY 1808, painted in February 1814.

The painting is enormous, yet so well conceived in every detail that it delivers its message instantly. A structured pattern of light and dark areas organizes the scene, giving it impact and underscoring its meaning. Goya focuses attention on the soldiers by means of value shifts that define a wedge shape formed by the hill and the brightly lighted area on the ground. Mechanical uniformity marks the faceless firing squad, in contrast to the ragged group that is the target. From the soldiers' dark shapes, we are led by the light and the lines of the rifles to the man in white. The focal point is this man, raising his arms in a gesture of defiance. THE THIRD OF MAY 1808 is not a mere reconstruction of

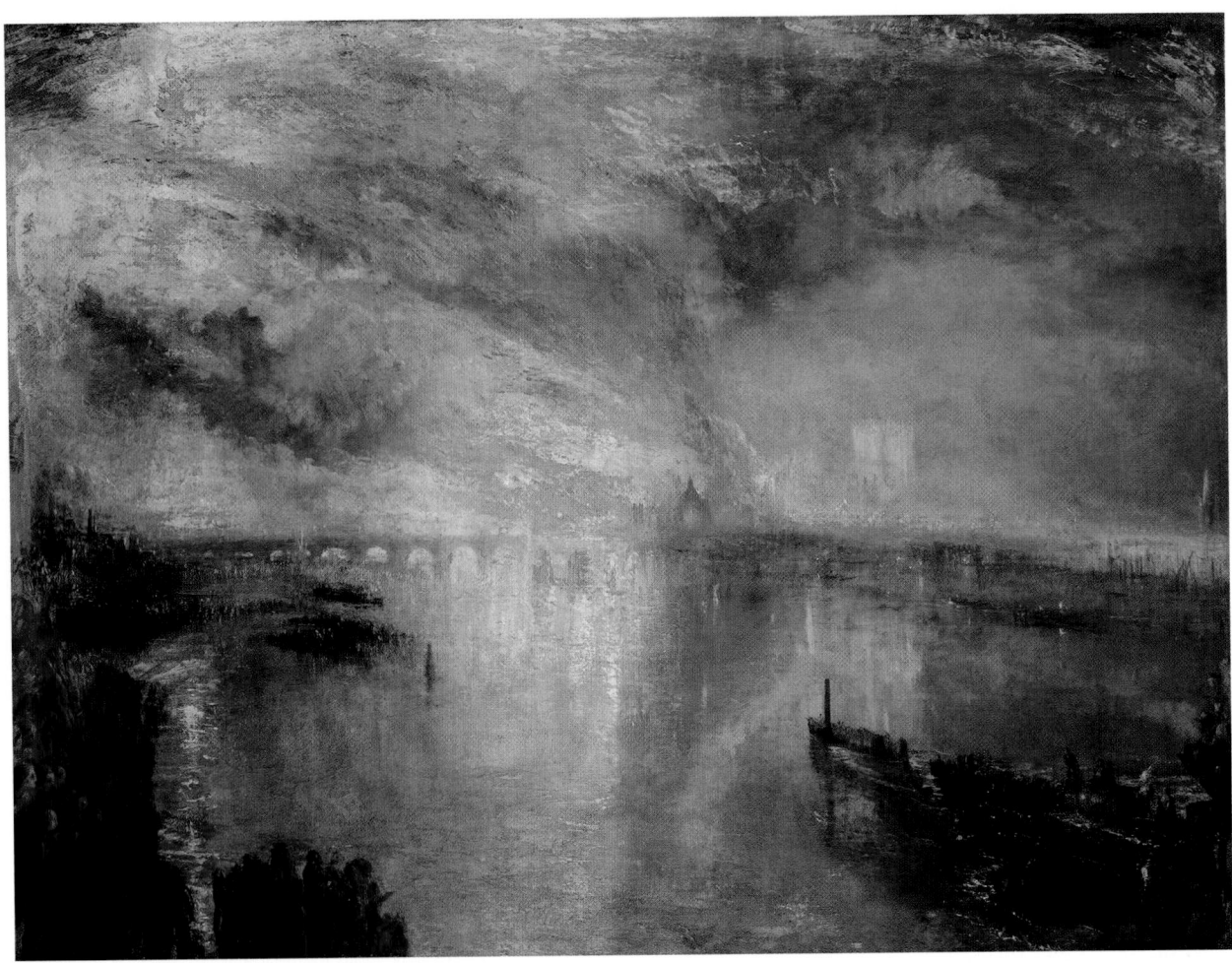

497　J. M. W. Turner.
THE BURNING OF THE HOUSES OF LORDS AND COMMONS. 1834.
Oil on canvas. 36½″ × 48½″.
© Cleveland Museum of Art, Bequest of John L. Severance. 1942.647.

history; it is a universal protest against the brutality of tyrannical governments.

Goya's THE THIRD OF MAY 1808 deals with events that took place only seven years before the artist took up the brush; a preoccupation with current events (rather than a mythological past) is one characteristic of the Romantic movement. When the British houses of Parliament burned in a disastrous fire one night in 1834, the artist J. M. W. Turner witnessed the event and made several sketches that soon became paintings. His work THE BURNING OF THE HOUSES OF LORDS AND COMMONS typifies the Romantic movement in several ways.

The brushwork is loose and expressive, as if he created the painting in a storm of passion. The colors are bright and vivid. Although the work depicts an event that happened only a few months before, the artist introduced distortions and exaggerations. According to contemporary reports, the flames did not leap up into the night as the artist shows them. Moreover, the Thames River has a curve that would partially block the view; Turner "straightened" the river to afford a wide horizon.[1] Turner made these departures from factual accuracy in order to convey the feeling of the event, as an English national symbol burned. This emphasis on feeling over fact is Romantic. Turner's loose painting style influenced

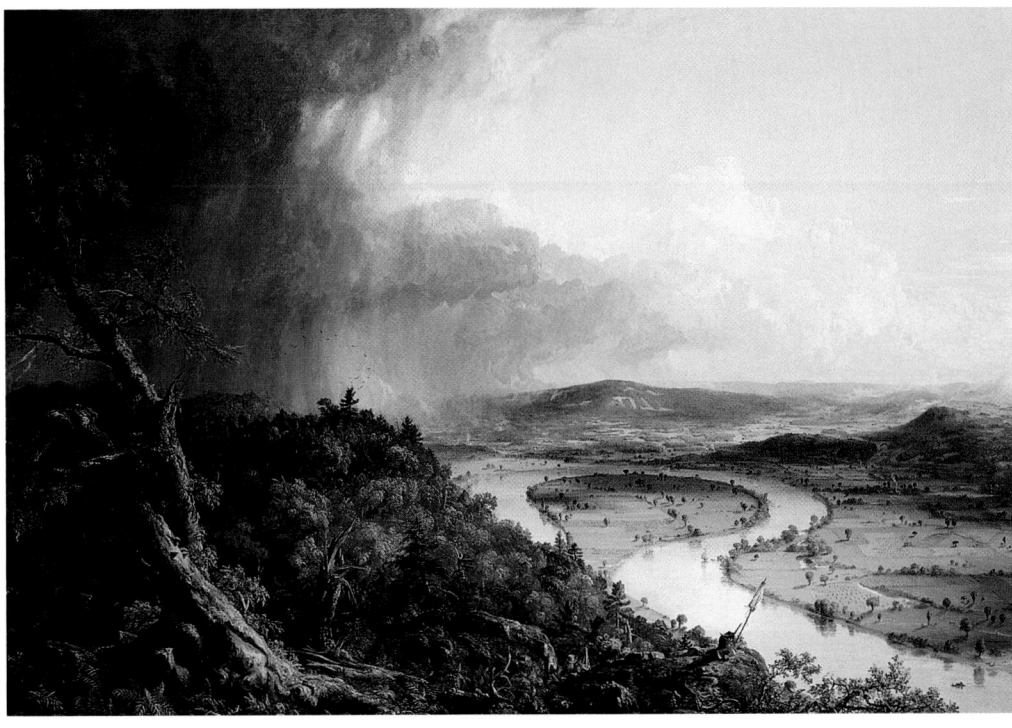

498 Thomas Cole.
THE OXBOW. 1836.
Oil on canvas.
51½″ × 76″.
The Metropolitan Museum of Art,
New York. Gift of Mrs. Russell Sage,
1908. 08.228.
Photograph: © 1995 The
Metropolitan Museum of Art.

499 Robert S. Duncanson.
BLUE HOLE, LITTLE MIAMI
RIVER. 1851.
Oil on canvas.
29¼″ × 42¼″.
Cincinnati Art Museum. Gift of
Norbert Heermann and Arthur
Helwig. 1926.18.

the later Impressionist movement, but there are important differences between them, as we shall see.

Many Romantic artists also painted the landscape, finding there a reflection of their own emotional states. Romantic landscape painting flourished especially in the United States, where Thomas Cole founded the Hudson River School in the 1830s. Like Turner, Cole began with on-site oil and pencil sketches, then made his large paintings in his studio. The broad, panoramic view, carefully rendered details, and light-filled atmosphere of paintings such as THE OXBOW became the inspiration for American landscape painting for several generations; see also Asher Durand's KINDRED SPIRITS on page 55.

In nineteenth-century America it was difficult to obtain the education necessary to become a professional artist; for an African-American it was almost impossible. Nevertheless, with the help of antislavery sponsors, a few succeeded.

Robert S. Duncanson was one of the first African-American artists to earn an international reputation. As the son of a Scots-Canadian father and an African-American mother, he may have had

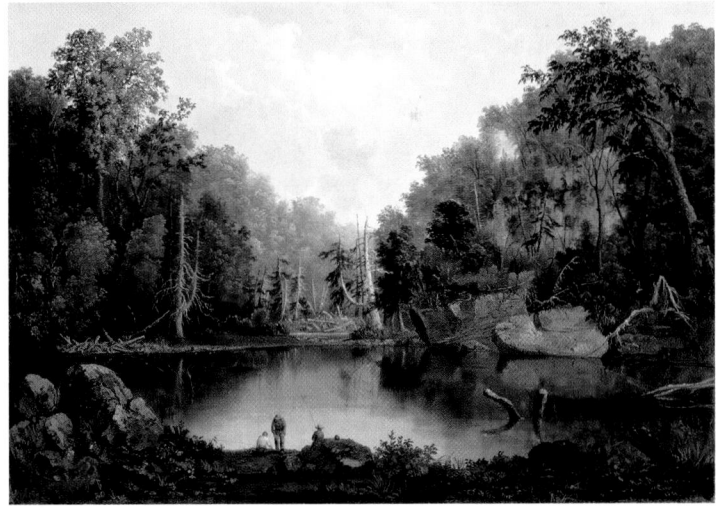

an easier time gaining recognition as an artist than those who did not straddle the color line. Prior to settling in Cincinnati, he studied in Italy, France, and England, and he was heavily influenced by European Romanticism. With BLUE HOLE, LITTLE MIAMI RIVER, Duncanson reached artistic maturity. He modified the precise realism of the Hudson River School with an original, poetic softening. He

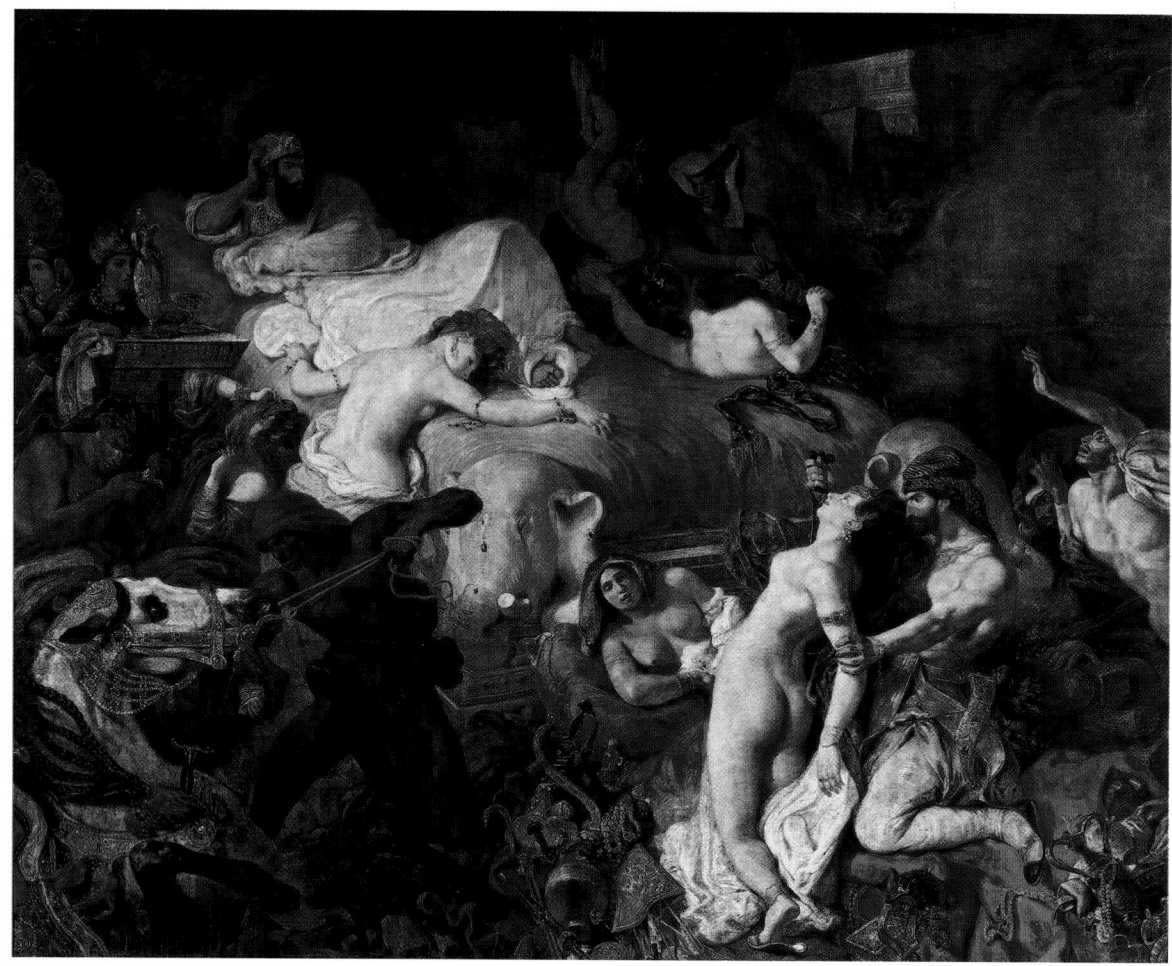

500 Eugène Delacroix.
THE DEATH OF SARDANAPALUS. 1827.
Oil on canvas. 12′1½″ × 16′2⅞″.
Musée du Louvre, Paris.
© Photograph: Kavaler/Art Resource, NY.

orchestrated light, color, and detail to create an intimate and engaging reverie of a person in nature.

In France, the leading Romantic painter was Eugène Delacroix. Delacroix's painting THE DEATH OF SARDANAPALUS exhibits the many qualities that distinguish Romanticism from the Neoclassicism of David and his followers. The story is based on an imaginative piece of literature by Lord Byron: Sardanapalus is an Assyrian king in a hopeless military situation. Rather than surrender, he takes poison and orders all of his favorite possessions brought before him and destroyed in an orgy of violence. Delacroix composed this writhing work along a diagonal, and lit it using strong chiaroscuro in a way that recalls

certain Baroque paintings (see page 284). His brushwork is loose and open, or *painterly*, not at all like the cool precision of Neoclassicism. Delacroix used all of these devices in order to enhance the viewer's emotional response to a horrifying, if imagined, event. The Romantic painters in general stressed strong viewer involvement, use of color in painterly strokes, and dramatic movement, in contrast to the detached rationality and clear idealism of the Neoclassicists.

PHOTOGRAPHY

Landscape and portrait painters initially saw photography as a threat to their livelihood. In fact, the camera freed painters from the roles of narrator and

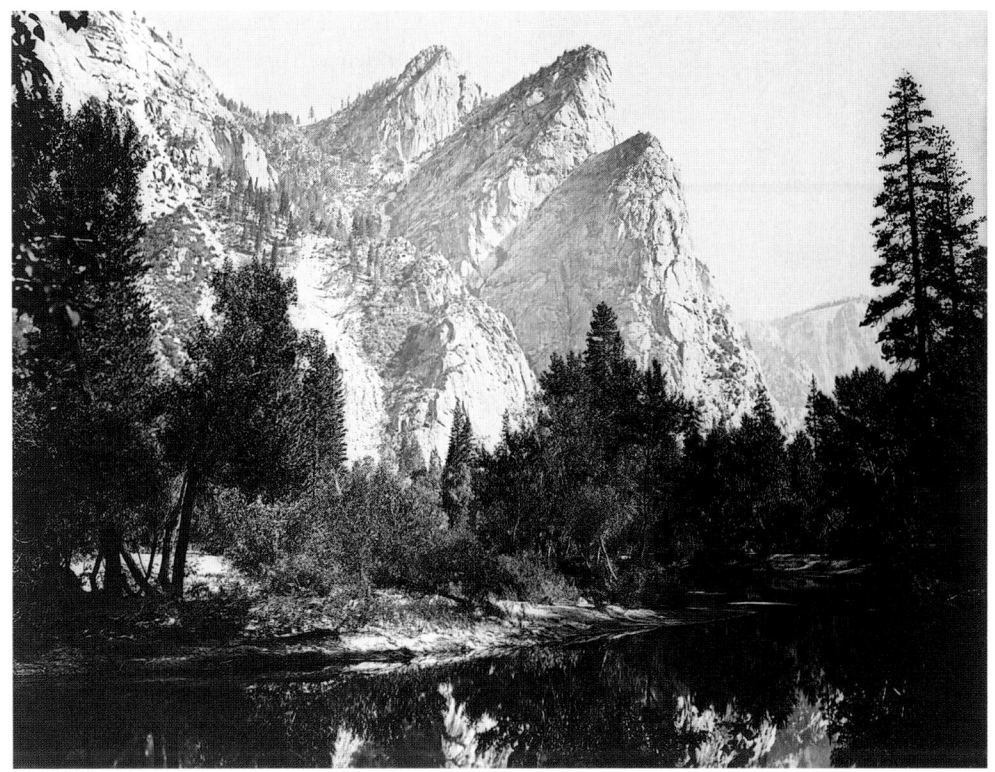

501 Carleton E. Watkins.
THE THREE BROTHERS. 1861.
Photograph.
Courtesy of the Library of Congress.

illustrator, allowing them to explore dimensions of visual experience that were largely out of reach in Western art since the Renaissance. At the same time, photography offered new opportunities to infuse images of objective reality with personal visions.

In its first two generations, the new medium was put to many uses. The perfection of glass-plate negatives in the 1850s made possible reproductions of photographs, though the technology was still quite cumbersome to use. Photographers had to smear glass plates with just the right amount of toxic chemicals, expose the plate for the correct number of seconds, and develop the negative almost immediately.

Carleton Watkins in 1861 journeyed into the Sierra Nevada to photograph THE THREE BROTHERS in Yosemite valley. This image is part of a portfolio of landscape photographs that he made for sale, signing each one as if it were a painting. These photographs were widely circulated, and they influ-

enced the U.S. Congress to set aside Yosemite as a national park.

Delacroix was one of the first to recognize the difference between camera vision and human vision. He believed that photography was potentially of great benefit to art and artists. In an essay for students, Delacroix wrote:

A daguerreotype is a mirror of the object; certain details almost always overlooked in drawing from nature take on in it characteristic importance, and thus introduce the artist to complete knowledge of construction as light and shade are found in their true character.[2]

Félix Tournachon, called Nadar, was—like many other photographers—an artist who came to prefer photography to drawing and printmaking. He gained fame as a balloonist, and from a hot air balloon he made the first aerial photographs. He

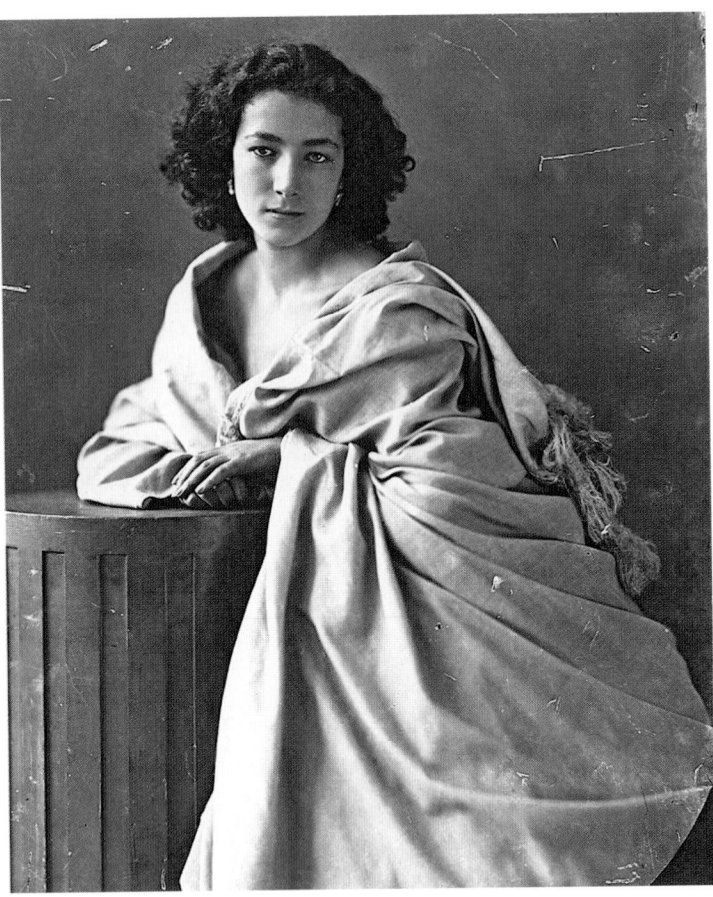

502 Nadar (Félix Tournachon).
SARAH BERNHARDT. 1855.
Photograph printed from a collodion negative.
International Museum of Photography of George Eastman House, Rochester, NY.

even took the first underground photographs in the sewers and catacombs of Paris, using artificial lighting techniques and long exposures.

Nadar recognized that photography was merely a mechanical process and that the photographer had to be intelligent and creative in order to make significant works of art with a camera. The most notable artists, writers, and intellectuals of Paris went to him to have their portraits made. His photograph of French actress SARAH BERNHARDT is an evolutionary link between the Romantic painted portraits of nineteenth-century women and the glamour photography of today. Another pioneer portrait photographer was Julia Cameron, who began photographing at age forty-eight and created an impassioned body of work (see page 147).

As both a tool and a way of seeing, photography influenced the next major stylistic development: Realism.

Both Neoclassicism and Romanticism had their beginnings in rebellion. But by mid-century each had become institutionalized, functioning as a conservative force in French artistic life. At the state-sponsored École des Beaux Arts, or School of Fine Arts, students were taught by members of the Academy of Fine Arts (an organization of government-approved artists) that "great painting" demanded "classical" technique and "elevated" subject matter found in history, mythology, literature, or exotic locations.

Delacroix accused Academy members of teaching beauty as though it were algebra. Today, we still use the term *academic art* for generally unimaginative works that follow stale formulas laid down by an academy or school, especially the French Academy of the nineteenth century.

French Academy members played a major role in selecting artists for a huge annual exhibition known as the Salon. Participating in the Salon was virtually the only way an artist might become known to the public. The history of the rest of the nineteenth century is largely one of rebellion against such institutions and authority figures. Vast changes in art and the artist's role in society were about to topple the dominance of the French Academy.

REALISM

Realism describes a style of art and literature that depicts ordinary existence without idealism, exoticism, or nostalgia. We have seen it before the nineteenth century, notably in Roman sculpture and Flemish and Dutch painting. By mid-century, a growing number of artists were dissatisfied with both the Neoclassicists' and the Romantics' attachment to mythical, exotic, extraordinary, and historical subjects. They believed that art should deal with human experience and observation. They knew that people in the nineteenth century were living a new kind of life, and wanted art to show it.

In the 1850s, French painter Gustave Courbet revived Realism with new vigor by employing a

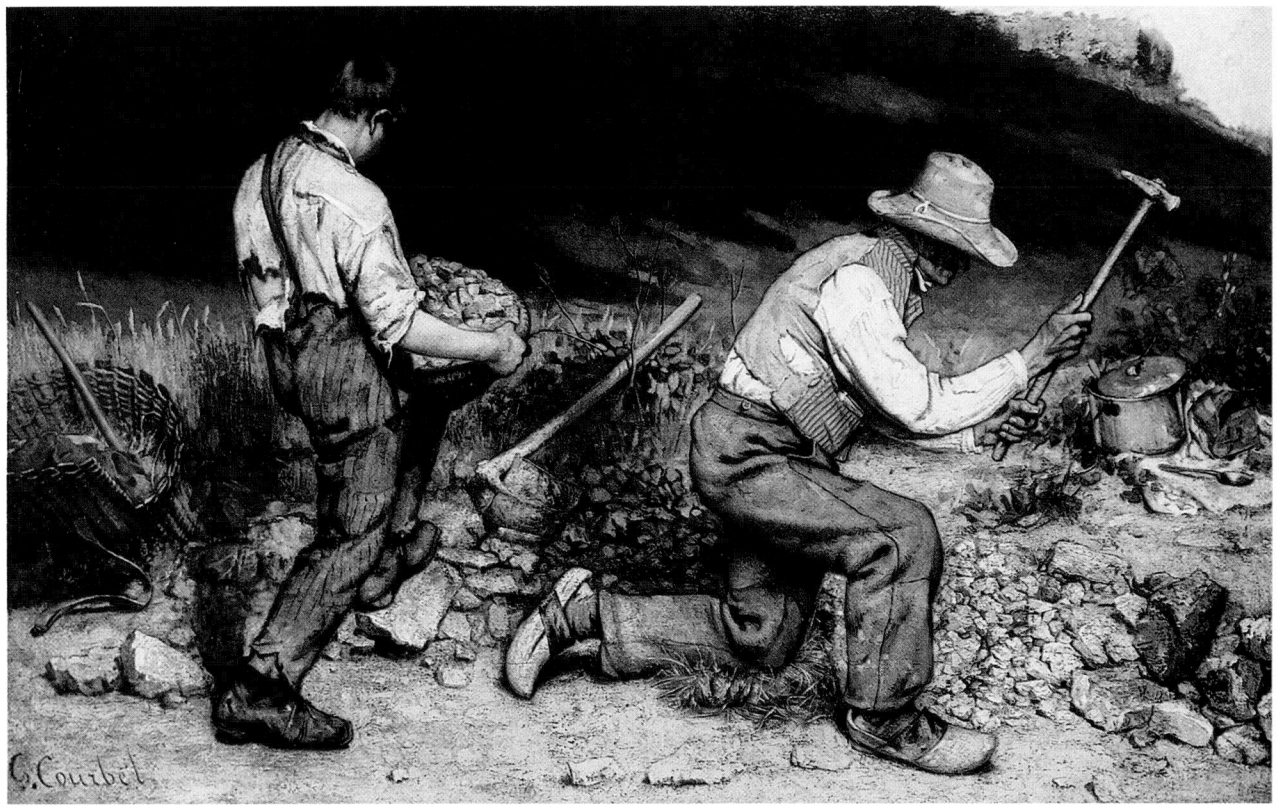

503 Gustave Courbet.
THE STONE BREAKERS. 1849.
(destroyed in 1945).
Oil on canvas. 5'5" × 7'10".
The Bridgeman Art Library International Ltd.

direct, painterly technique for the portrayal of the dignity of ordinary things and common life. In doing so, he laid the foundation for a rediscovery of the extraordinary visual qualities of everyday experience.

THE STONE BREAKERS shows Courbet's rejection of Romantic and Neoclassical formulas. His subject is neither historical nor allegorical, religious nor heroic. The men breaking stones are ordinary road workers, presented almost life-size. Courbet did not idealize the work of breaking stones or dramatize the struggle for existence; he simply said, Look at this.

Courbet's detractors were sure that he was causing artistic and moral decline by painting what they considered unpleasant and trivial subjects on a grand scale. They accused him of raising "a cult of ugliness" against cherished concepts of Beauty and the Ideal. Realism was perceived as nothing less than the enemy of art, and many believed that pho-

tography was the source and the sponsor of this disaster. When THE STONE BREAKERS was exhibited in Paris in the Salon of 1850, it was attacked as unartistic, crude, and socialistic. The latter charge actually had some validity. Courbet was in fact a lifelong radical who espoused anarchist philosophies. He believed that most governments were oppressive institutions that only served the wealthy, and that average people could better meet their needs by banding together in voluntary associations for such functions as public works, banking, and policing. Beginning in 1855, Courbet practiced what he preached and set up his own exhibits—the beginning of the continuing practice of independent shows organized by artists themselves.

Courbet was one of the first to finish his paintings outdoors, working directly from nature. Previously, most landscape painting had been done in

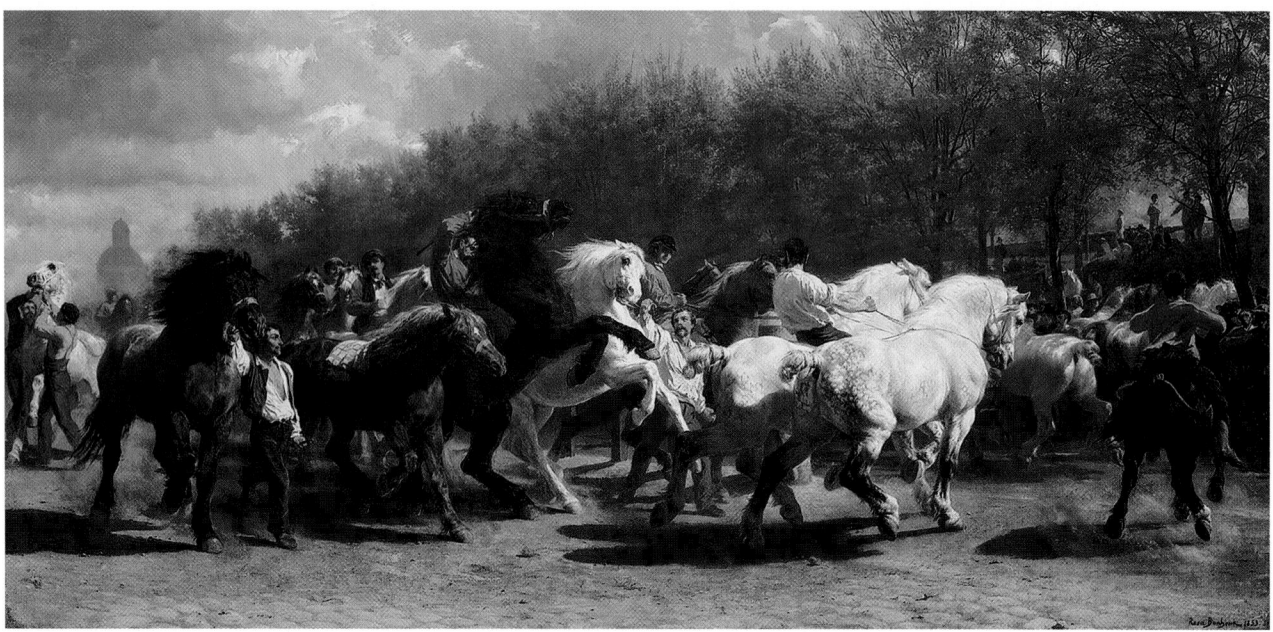

504 Rosa Bonheur.
THE HORSE FAIR. 1853–1855.
Oil on canvas. 8′ × 16′7½″.
The Metropolitan Musuem of Art, NY. Gift of Cornelius Vanderbilt, 1887.
Photograph: © 1997 The Metropolitan Museum of Art, NY.

the artist's studio from memory, sketches, and reference materials such as rocks and plants brought in from outside. When portable tubes of oil paint became available in 1841, oil painting outdoors became practical. By working directly from subjects outdoors, painters were able to capture first impressions. This shift in practice opened up whole new ways of seeing and painting.

Of his own work, Courbet said,

To know in order to create, that was my idea. To be able to represent the customs, the ideas, the appearance of my own era . . . to create living art; that is my aim.[3]

Realism of a more popular sort was practiced by Rosa Bonheur, who specialized in painting rural scenes with animals. In THE HORSE FAIR, she captured the surging energy of a group of horses offered for sale, some of them untamed. Many scholars believe that the figure on horseback in the blue-green coat near the center of the picture is a portrait of the artist wearing men's clothing. If so, it was one of several unconventional personal charac-

teristics that she adopted in order to help her career (see accompanying essay).

The Realist paintings of American artist Thomas Eakins are remarkable for their humanity and insight into the everyday world. A comparison of the paintings of Eakins and those of his teacher, Jean Léon Gérôme, shows the contrast between Realism and officially sanctioned academic art. The attitude Eakins presented is one of great respect for the beauty of the ordinary human being. Gérôme may have been equally interested in ordinary beauty, yet he created a painting based on classical and academic ideals. Eakins's insistence on painting people the way they actually look led him to escape the bondage of stylization imposed by the rules of the academy; it also led to shock and rejection by the public and much of the art world.

In the academic painting PYGMALION AND GALATEA (on page 362), Gérôme placed the woman, Galatea, on a pedestal, both literally and figuratively. The Greek myth of Pygmalion tells of a sculptor who carved a statue of a woman so

ROSA Bonheur
Flouting Social Conventions
1822–1899

THE LIST OF AWARDS that Rosa Bonheur earned in her lifetime was impressive by any standard: First Medal at the Paris Salon; Grand Cross of the French Legion of Honor; Commander of the Order of Isabella the Catholic; Member of the Order of King Leopold of Belgium. She was the first woman ever to receive most of these honors. She was also a friend to Queen Victoria of England and the French Emperor Napoleon III. Yet Rosa Bonheur also led an unusual personal life that showed the difficulties that a woman of her day had to face if she wanted a career.

Her most important early influence was her father, Raymond, a drawing teacher. He was a Saint-Simonian Socialist—that is, he believed all wealth should be shared because everybody was equal; girls were as worthy as boys and should be raised the same way. These beliefs are somewhat radical even today, but he took them even further. He believed that a new savior would come to the human race, as Christ had done in ancient times, and that this new Messiah would be a woman. Hence he took special pains to educate his daughters, an unusual step for that period.

Rosa Bonheur decided as a teenager to become an artist, and benefited from her father's teaching; in fact, she soon surpassed him. Because the Academy forbade women from studying the nude model, she decided to specialize in painting country scenes with animals. There was a ready market for such works, partly because France was industrializing and people from the country were moving to the city in great numbers. People wanted to remember country life, and Bonheur became their painter. A few Parisian artists had already specialized in this subject, but she soon surpassed them too.

The main problem inherent in her career choice was that she would have to do things that women just did not do: spend a lot of time on farms and ranches, become an expert rider, and sketch animal anatomy in slaughterhouses. All of these she did, apparently with pleasure.

She found that she could do her work with more ease and comfort if she cut her hair short and wore trousers. Cutting the hair was not a problem, but for a woman to wear trousers in public was illegal. Well, not exactly: She had to get a permit from the local police and renew it every six months. The stack of papers was found among her possessions after she died.

She was not the first woman to adopt a male appearance as a career move. The novelist Amandine Dupin, eighteen years older than Bonheur, had scandalized Paris by wearing men's clothing and using the pen name George Sand; Bonheur admired her.

How else might a woman advance her career in a male-dominated society? Bonheur always insisted that her only goals were convenience and career advancement: "If, however, you see me dressed as I am, it is not in the least in order to make me into an original, but simply in order to facilitate my work. Consider that, at a certain period in my life, I spent whole days at the slaughterhouse."[4]

She never married, regarding it as a hindrance. Rather, she lived most of her life with her friend Natalie Micas in a home filled with pets. The two of them were active in the Society for the Prevention of Cruelty to Animals. Her favorite males, she said, were the bulls that she painted.

Meanwhile, her work kept selling and gaining honors. She bought a country estate next to the Emperor's family home. When Empress Eugenie arrived at her door to present her with the Legion of Honor, the artist kept Her

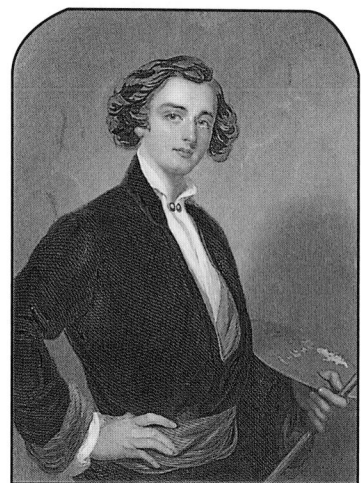

505 W. H. Mote.
ROSA BONHEUR. 1856.
Engraving after R. Buckner.
Picture Collection, The New York Public Library, Astor, Lenox and Tilden Foundations. Art Resource, NY.

Majesty waiting while she threw a robe on over her pants.

To the end of her life, Bonheur lived the dichotomy of the successful and honored career woman forced into an unconventional personal life. Accused of seeming unfeminine, she defended herself in a way that rings as a call for women's equality:

Why wouldn't I be proud of being a woman? My father, that enthusiastic apostle of humanity, repeated to me many times that woman's mission was to uplift the human race, that she was the Messiah of future centuries. I owe to his doctrines the great and proud ambition that I conceived for the sex to which I take glory in belonging, and whose independence I will uphold until my last day. Moreover, I am persuaded that the future belongs to us.[5]

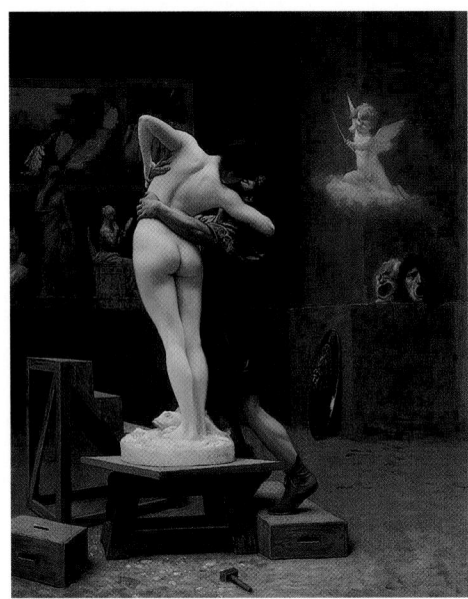

beautiful that he fell in love with his sculpture. Pygmalion prayed to Aphrodite, goddess of love, who responded by making the figure come to life. The sentimental approach (note the cupid), smooth finish, and mild eroticism are typical of academic art. In his painting WILLIAM RUSH CARVING HIS ALLEGORICAL FIGURE, Eakins presented a Realist view of the sculptor's trade: A model poses as the artist chisels away at the left; nineteenth-century decorum demanded that a chaperone be

506 Jean Léon Gérôme.
PYGMALION AND GALATEA. c. 1860.
Oil on canvas. 35″ × 27″.
The Metropolitan Museum of Art, New York. Gift of Louis C. Raegner, 1927.
Photograph: © 1989 The Metropolitan Museum of Art, 27. 200.

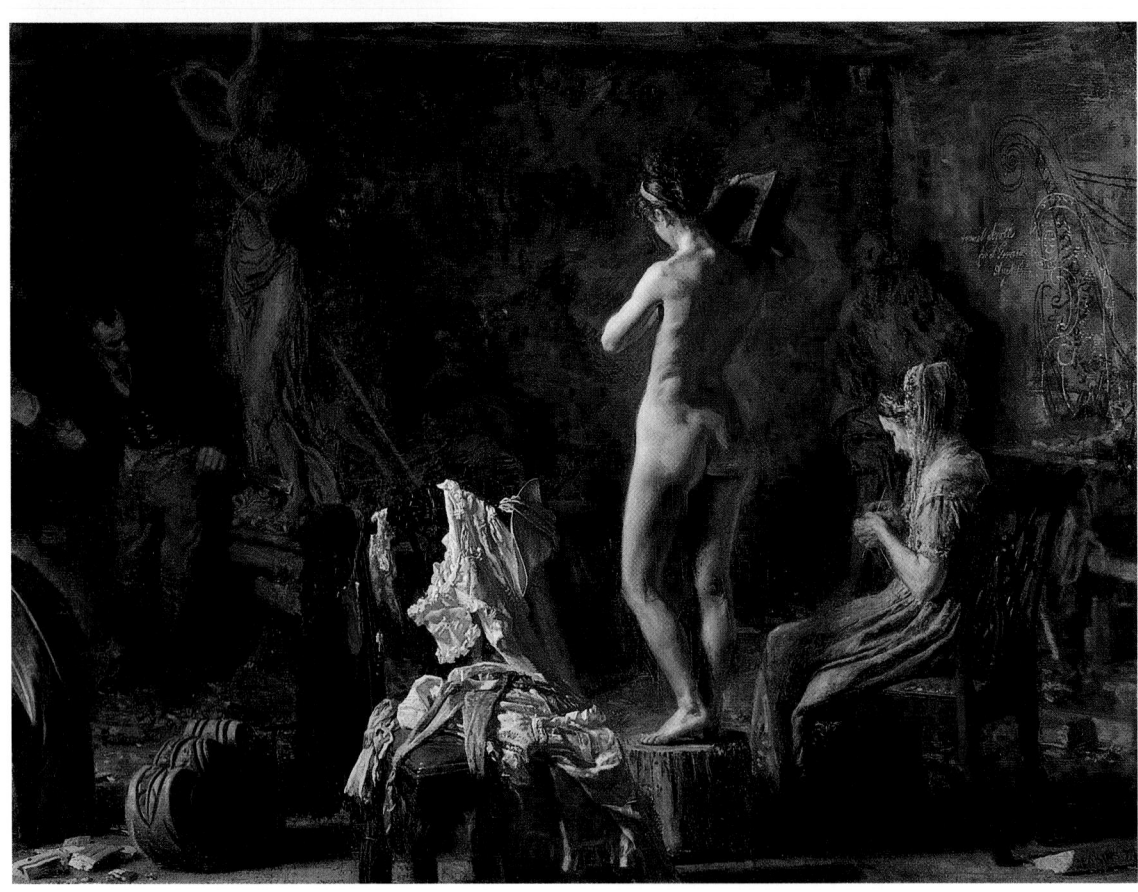

507 Thomas Eakins.
WILLIAM RUSH CARVING HIS ALLEGORICAL FIGURE OF THE SCHUYLKILL RIVER. 1876–1877.
Oil on canvas on Masonite. 20⅛″ × 26⅛″.
Philadelphia Museum of Art. Gift of Mrs. Thomas Eakins and Miss Mary A. Williams, 1929–184–27.
Photograph: Graydon Wood, 2000.

present. Eakins selected this subject because William Rush was the first American artist to use nude models, bringing controversy on himself in the 1820s.

We can see Eakins's influence in the work of his student and friend Henry Ossawa Tanner, who was the best known African-American painter before the twentieth century. At the age of thirteen, Tanner watched a landscape painter at work and decided to become a painter. While studying with Eakins at the Academy of Fine Arts in Philadelphia, Tanner changed his subject matter from landscapes to scenes of daily life. In 1891, after an exhibition of his work was largely ignored, Tanner moved to France, where he remained for most of the rest of his life. He found less racial prejudice in Paris than in the United States. His paper "The American Negro in Art," presented at the 1893 World's Congress on Africa in Chicago, voiced the need for dignified portrayals of blacks, and he offered his painting THE BANJO LESSON as a model.

The lively realism of THE BANJO LESSON reveals Tanner's considerable insight into the feelings of his subjects, yet he avoids the sentimentality that was common in many late nineteenth-century American paintings. This painting shows the influence of Eakins in its detail and the influence of the Impressionists in Tanner's use of light and color.

The most important predecessor of Impressionism in French art is without a doubt Edouard Manet, who was the most controversial artist in Paris in the 1860s. He studied with an academic master, but soon broke away from traditional teaching in an effort to update the art of the Old Masters (Veronese, Velázquez, and Rembrandt, for example) by infusing painting with a dose of realism inherited from Gustave Courbet. In addition, Manet often flattened out the figures in his paintings under the influence of the Japanese prints that he knew and admired. His loose, open brushwork and sometimes commonplace subjects were an inspiration to younger painters who led the Impressionist movement. Manet's painting

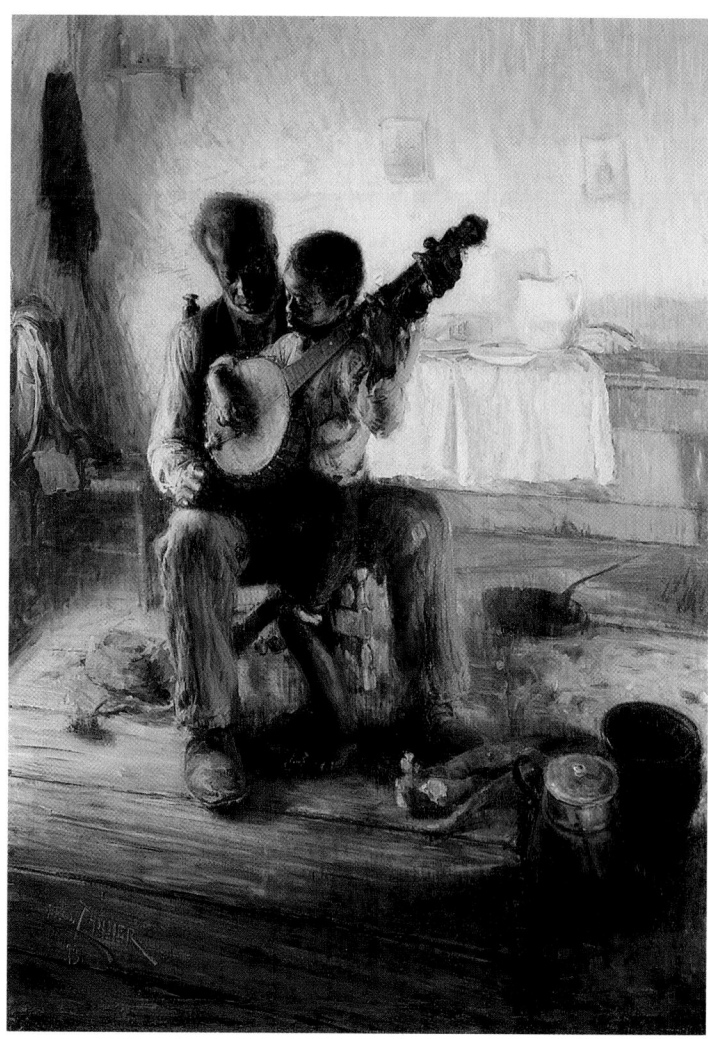

508   Henry Ossawa Tanner.
THE BANJO LESSON. 1893.
Oil on canvas. 49″ × 35½″.
Hampton University Museum, Hampton, Virginia.

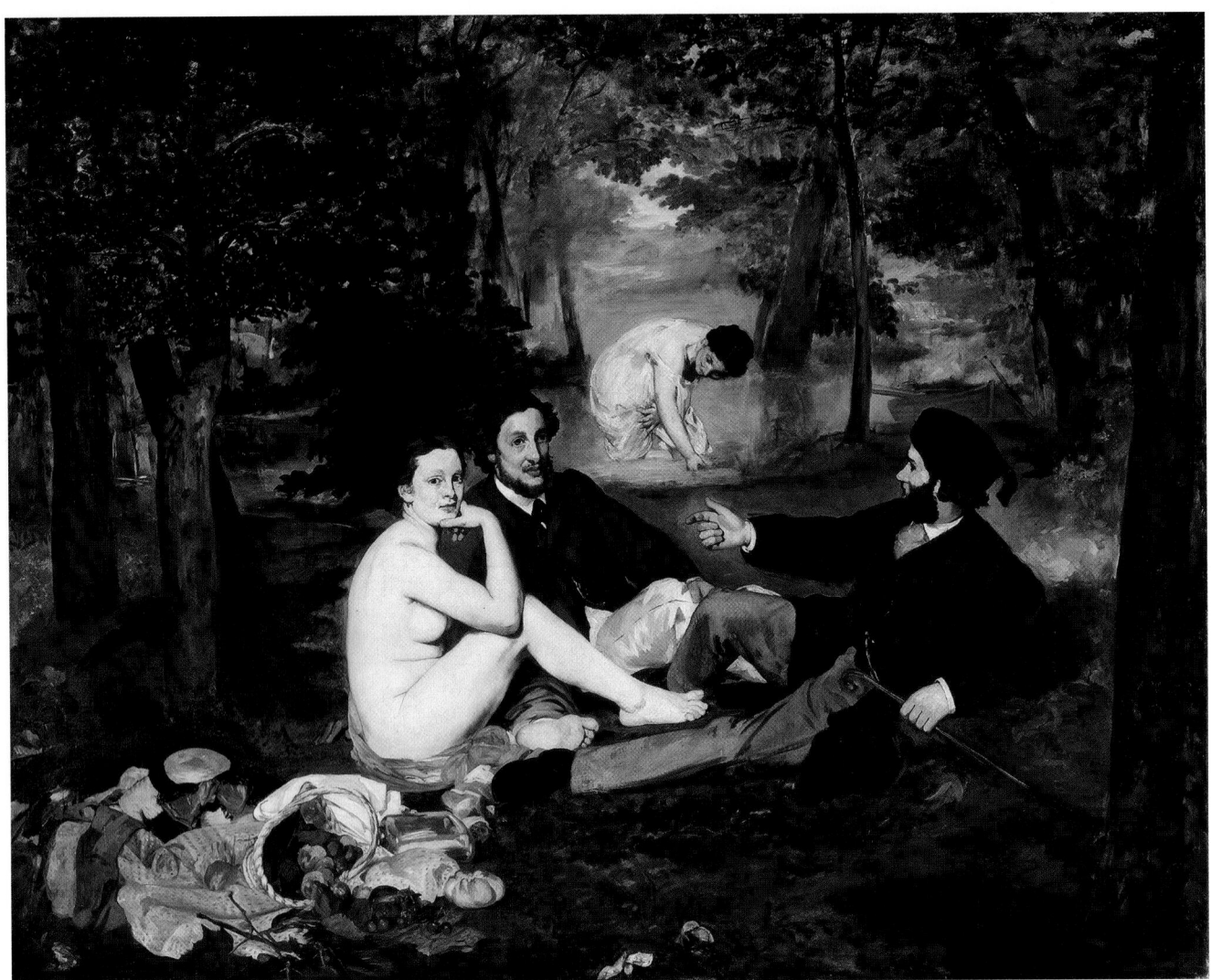

509 Edouard Manet.
LUNCHEON ON THE GRASS (LE DÉJEUNER SUR L'HERBE). 1863.
Oil on canvas. 84″ × 106″.
Musée d' Orsay, Paris. © Reunion des Musées Nationaux. Art Resource, NY. © 2008 Artist Rights Society (ARS), NY.
Photograph: Herve Lewandowski.

LUNCHEON ON THE GRASS scandalized French critics and the public—because of the way it was painted as well as the subject matter. Manet painted the female figure without shading, employed flat patches of color throughout the painting, and left bare canvas in some places. He concentrated on the interplay among the elements of form that make up the composition: light shapes against dark, cool colors accented by warm colors, directional forces, and active balance. Manet's concern with visual issues over content or storytelling was revolutionary.

Renaissance illusion of depth is greatly diminished here. Manet's emphasis on the interaction of dark and light shapes and his de-emphasis of both chiaroscuro and perspective cause us to look at the surface of the painting rather than simply through it as an illusionary window onto nature.

The juxtaposition of a female nude with males dressed in clothing of the time shocked viewers, but such a combination was not new. Nude and clothed figures in landscape derives from a tradition going back to Renaissance and even Roman compositions

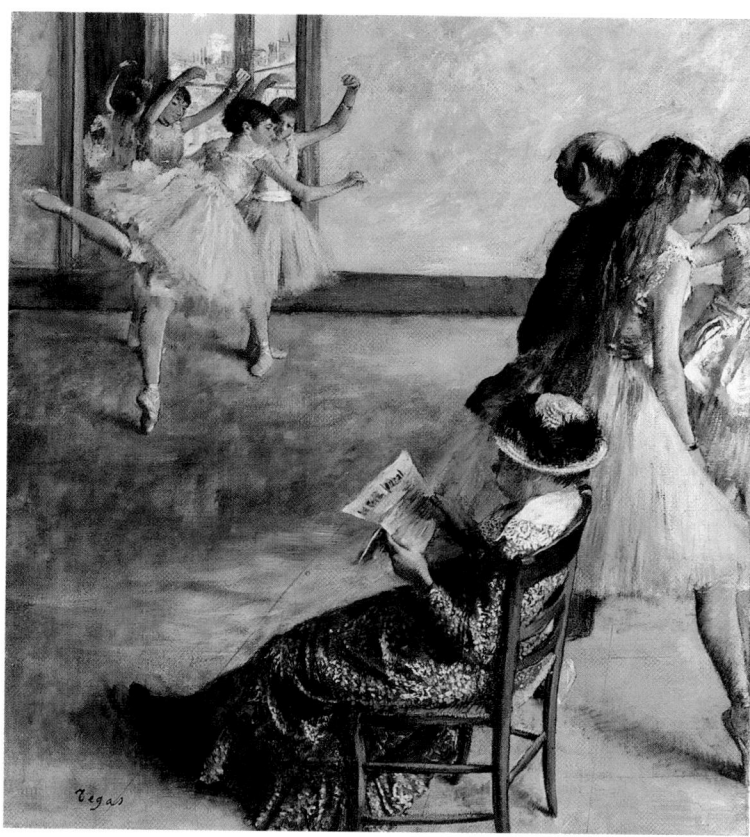

514 Edgar Degas.
THE BALLET CLASS. c. 1879–1880.
Oil on canvas. 32⅜″ × 30¼″.
Philadelphia Museum of Art.
Purchased with the W. P. Wilstach Fund.
W1937-2-1.

technology, and a taste for fashion—and the Impressionists chronicled their lives.

Edgar Degas exhibited with the Impressionists, although his approach differed from theirs. He shared with the Impressionists a directness of expression and an interest in portraying contemporary life, but he combined the immediacy of Impressionism with a highly inventive approach to design. Degas, along with the Impressionists, was influenced by the new ways of seeing and composing that he saw in Japanese prints and unposed street-scene photography.

Conventional European compositions placed subjects within a central zone. Degas, however, used surprising, lifelike compositions and effects that often cut figures at the edge. The tipped-up ground planes and bold asymmetry found in Japanese prints inspired Degas to create paintings filled with intriguing visual tensions, such as those in THE BALLET CLASS, in which two diagonal groups of figures appear on opposite sides of an empty center.

Degas depicted ballet classes in ways that showed their unglamorous character. Often, as here, he was able to turn his great ability to the task of defining human character and mood in a given situation. The painting builds from the quiet, disinterested woman in the foreground, up to the right, then across to the cluster of dancing girls, following the implied sightline of the ballet master. The stability of the group on the right contrasts with the smaller, irregular shape of the girls before the mirror. Degas managed to balance spatial tensions between near and far and to create interesting contrasts between stable and unstable, large and small. He emphasized the line in the floor, which he brought together with the top of the woman's newspaper to guide the viewer's eye. The angle of the seated woman's foot brings us around to begin again.

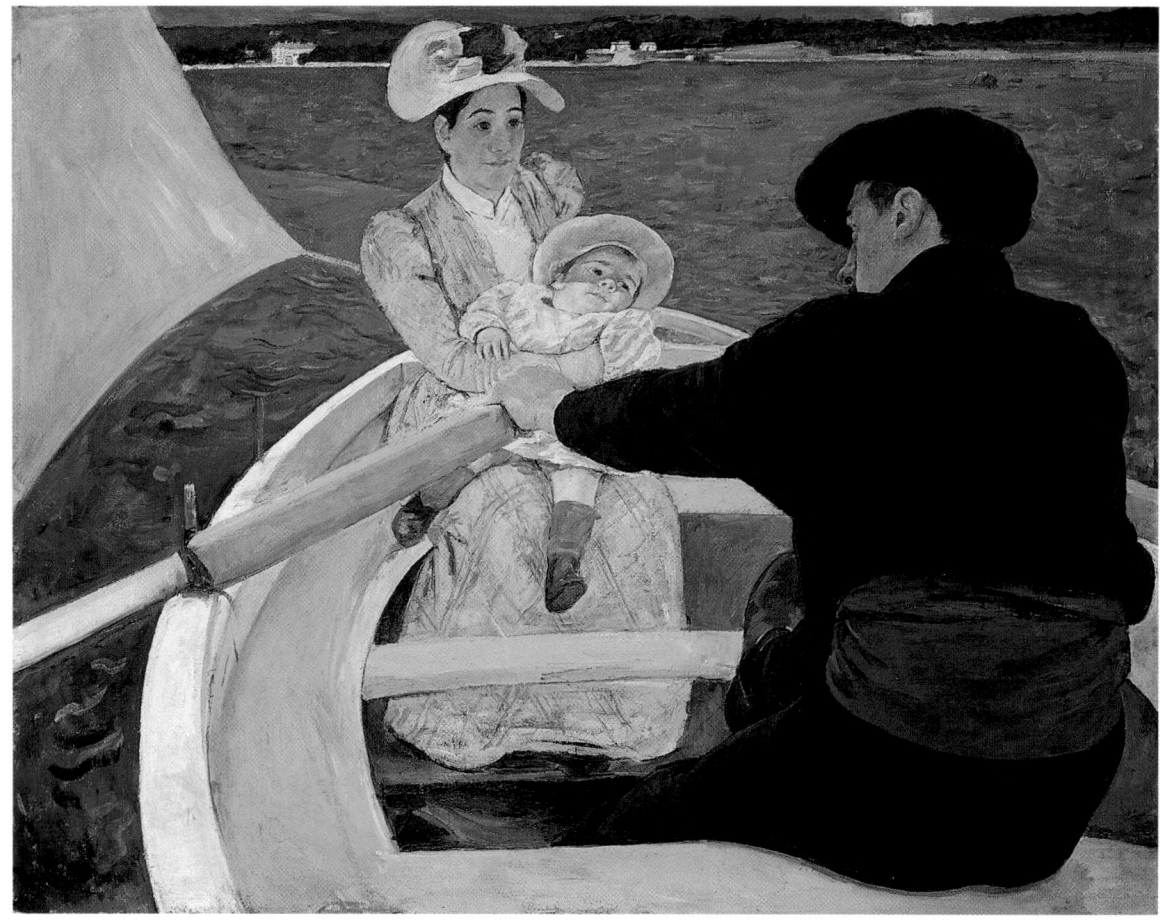

515 Mary Cassatt.
 THE BOATING PARTY. 1893–1894.
Oil on canvas. 35⁷⁄₁₆″ × 46⅛″.

Chester Dale Collection.
Photograph: © 2001 Board of Trustees, National Gallery of Art,
Washington, D.C. 1963.10.94.(1758)PA.

American painter Mary Cassatt went to Paris in the late 1860s to further her artistic development. She was strongly influenced by the work of Manet and Degas. Following an invitation by Degas, she joined and exhibited with the Impressionists. Later, she was among the many European and American artists who were influenced by Japanese prints and casual compositions of late nineteenth-century do-it-yourself photography. A resemblance to Japanese prints is readily apparent in the simplicity and bold design of THE BOATING PARTY. Cassatt refined her subject in sweeping curves and almost flat shapes.

There is, in addition, subtle feminist content in this work. The difference in clothing styles between the woman and the man shows that she has hired him to take her and the child out for a boat ride. This was an unusually assertive thing for a woman to do for herself in those days, and the glances between all three persons in the painting show some of the social tension that would have accompanied this event. The work is typical of Cassatt in its focus on the world of women and their concerns.

Painters such as Manet, Monet, Renoir, Degas, and Cassatt rejected the artificial poses and limited color prescribed by the Academy. Because they rebelled against accepted styles, they made few sales in their early years. Many who were considered outsiders, set apart from the conventional art of their time, we now consider masters of nineteenth-century art and precursors of twentieth-century art.

The Impressionist group disbanded after its exhibition in 1886, but its influence was immeasurable—in spite of the fact that Impressionist paintings were looked upon with indifference, even hostility, by most of the public and the critics until the 1920s. From the perspective of our time, Impressionism was the most important artistic movement of the nineteenth century.

French artist Auguste Rodin was at least as important to sculpture as his contemporaries, the Impressionist and Post-Impressionist painters, were to painting. Rodin became the first sculptor since Bernini (see page 283) to return sculpture to the status of a major art form, renewed with emotional and spiritual depth.

In 1875, after training as a sculptor's helper, Rodin traveled to Italy where he was impressed by the work of the Renaissance masters Donatello and Michelangelo. Rodin was the first to use Michelangelo's unfinished pieces (see page 187) as an inspiration for making rough finish an expressive quality. In contrast to Michelangelo, however, Rodin was primarily a modeler rather than a carver.

In 1880, he was commissioned to make a bronze door, *The Gates of Hell*, for a proposed museum of decorative arts. The large project was unfinished at Rodin's death, but many of the figures that are part of the door, including THE THINKER, modeled in clay and cast in bronze, and THE KISS, carved in marble (page 34), were enlarged as independent pieces. Of THE THINKER, Rodin wrote that his first inspiration had been Dante, but he rejected the idea of a thin, ascetic figure.

Guided by my first inspiration I conceived another thinker, a naked man, seated upon a rock, his feet drawn under him, he dreams. The fertile thought slowly elaborates itself within his brain. He is no longer dreamer, he is creator.[7]

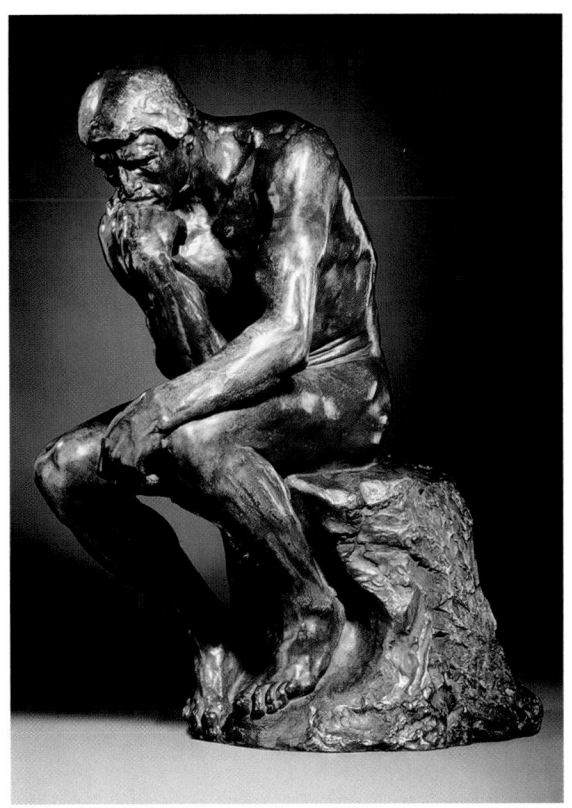

516 Auguste Rodin.
THE THINKER (LE PENSEUR). c. 1910.
Bronze. Life-size.
Christie's Images. SuperStock.

In the place of Christ in judgment, often seen over the doorways of medieval churches, Rodin projected the universal artist/poet as creator, judge, and witness, brooding over the human condition. Rodin combined a superb knowledge of anatomy with modeling skill to create the fluid, tactile quality of hand-shaped clay. He restored sculpture as a vehicle for personal expression after it had lapsed into mere decoration and heroic monuments.

THE POST-IMPRESSIONIST PERIOD

Post-Impressionism refers to trends in painting starting in about 1885 that followed Impressionism. The Post-Impressionist painters did not share a single style; rather, they built on or reacted to Impressionism in highly individual ways. Some felt that Impressionism had sacrificed solidity of form and composition for the sake of momentary impressions.

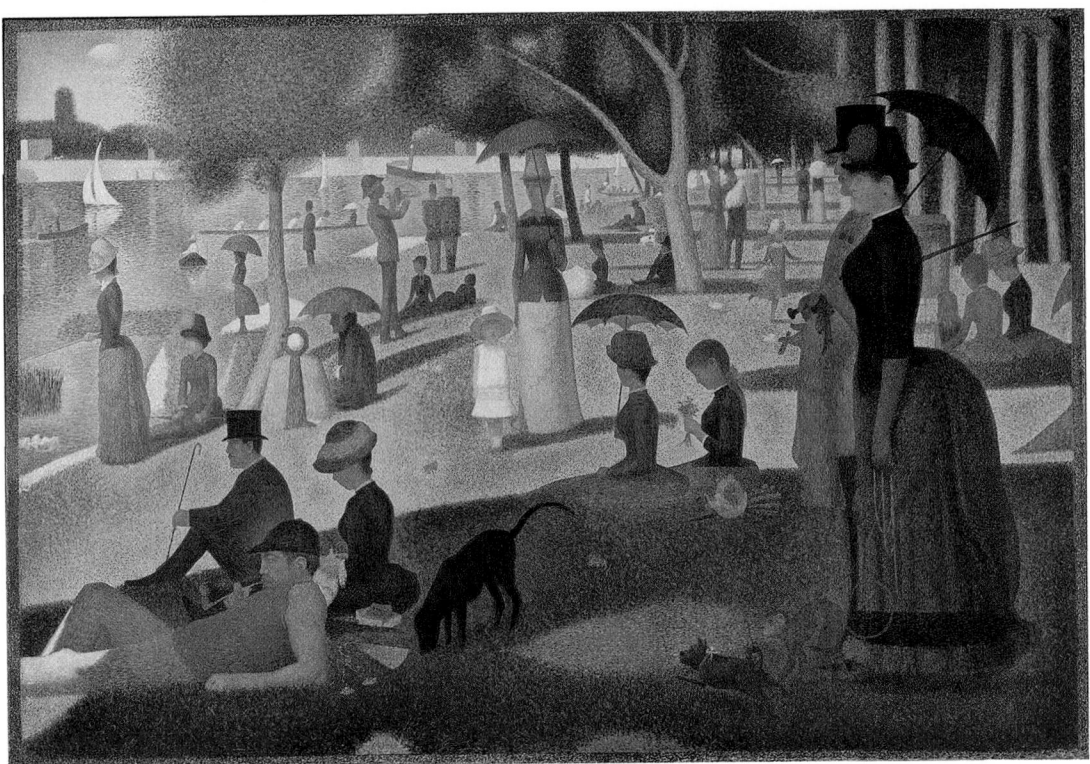

517 Georges Seurat.
A SUNDAY ON LA GRANDE JATTE. 1884–1886.
Oil on canvas. 81″ × 120⅜″.
Helen Birch Bartlett Memorial Collection. 1926.224.

Others felt that Impressionism's emphasis on the direct observation of nature and everyday life did not leave enough room for personal expression or spiritual content. Among those whose works best exemplify Post-Impressionist attitudes were Dutch artist Vincent van Gogh and French artists Paul Gauguin, Georges Seurat, and Paul Cézanne.

Gauguin and van Gogh brought to their work expressive, emotional intensity and a desire to make their thoughts and feelings visible. They often used strong color contrasts, shapes with clear contours, bold brushwork, and, in van Gogh's case, vigorous paint textures. Their art greatly influenced twentieth-century expressionist styles.

Seurat and Cézanne were interested in developing formal structure in their paintings. Each in his own way organized visual form to achieve structured clarity of design. Their paintings influenced twentieth-century formalist styles.

Cézanne and Seurat based their work on the observation of nature, and both used visibly separate strokes of color to build rich surfaces. Seurat's large painting A SUNDAY ON LA GRANDE JATTE has the subject matter, light, and color qualities of Impressionism, but this is not a painting of a fleeting moment. It is a carefully constructed composition of lasting impact. Seurat set out to systematize the optical color mixing of Impressionism and to create a more solid, formal organization with simplified shapes. He called his method *divisionism*, but it is more popularly known as *pointillism*. With it, Seurat tried to develop and apply a "scientific" technique. He arrived at his method by studying the principles of color optics that were being formulated at the time. Through the application of tiny dots of color, Seurat achieved a vibrant surface based on optical mixture (see page 67 for a detail).

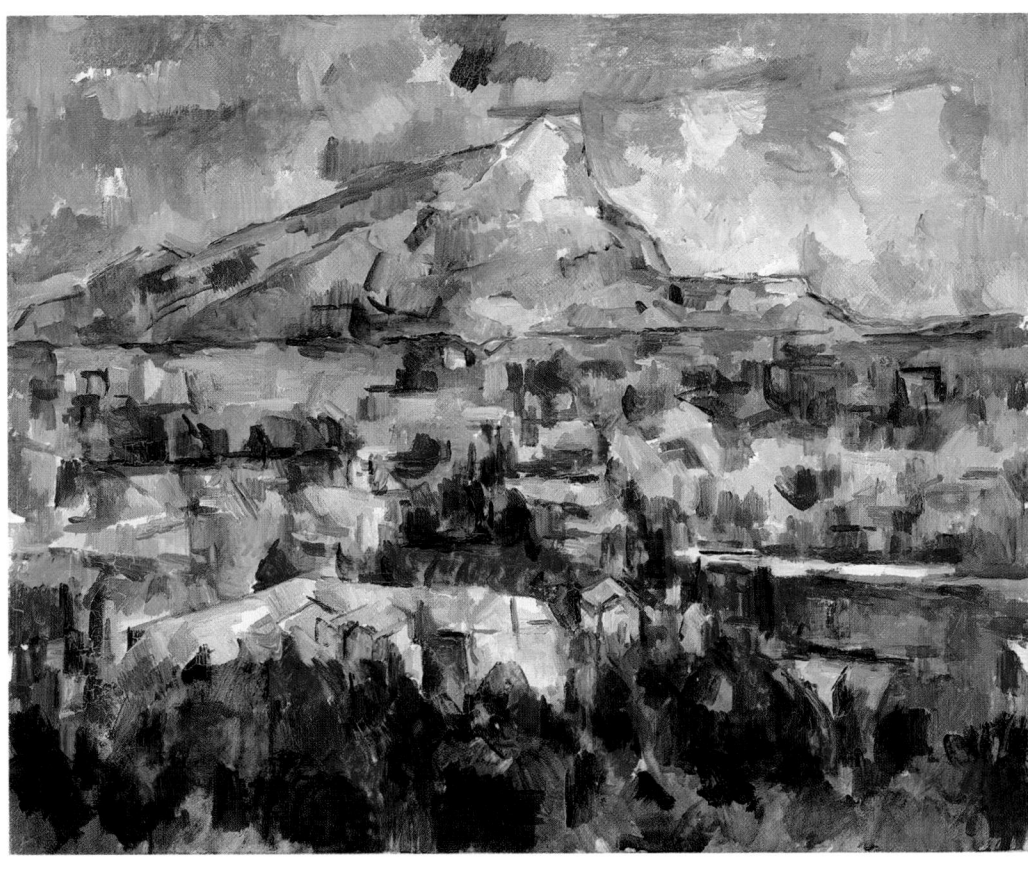

518 Paul Cézanne.
MONT SAINTE-VICTOIRE.
1902–1904.
Oil on canvas.
27½″ × 35¼″.
Philadelphia Museum of Art.
The George W. Elkins Collection.
E1936-1-1.

Seurat preceded A SUNDAY ON LA GRANDE JATTE with more than fifty drawn and painted preliminary studies in which he explored the horizontal and vertical relationships, the character of each shape, and the patterns of light, shade, and color. The final painting shows the total control that Seurat sought through the application of his method. The frozen formality of the figures seems surprising, considering the casual nature of the subject matter; yet it is precisely this calm, formal grandeur that gives the painting its strength and enduring appeal.

Like Seurat, Cézanne sought to achieve strength in the formal structure of his paintings. "My aim," he said, "was to make Impressionism into something solid and enduring like the art of the museums."[8]

Cézanne saw the planar surfaces of his subjects in terms of color modulation. Instead of using light and shadow in a conventional way, he relied on carefully developed relationships between adjoining strokes of color to show solidity of form and receding space. He questioned, then abandoned, linear and atmospheric perspective and went beyond the appearance of nature, to reconstruct it according to his own interpretation.

Landscape was one of Cézanne's main interests. In MONT SAINTE-VICTOIRE, we can see how he flattened space yet gave an impression of air and depth with some atmospheric perspective and the use of warm advancing and cool receding colors. The dark edge lines around the distant mountain help counter the illusion of depth. There is an important interplay between the illusion of depth and the fact of strokes of color on a flat surface. Cézanne simplified the houses and trees into patches of color that suggest almost geometric planes and masses. His open (not blended) brush strokes and his concept of a geometric substructure in nature and art offered a new range of possibilities to later artists. Of the many painters working in France around the turn of the century, Cézanne had the most lasting effect on the course of painting in the twentieth century. His art both built on, and departed from, Impressionism.

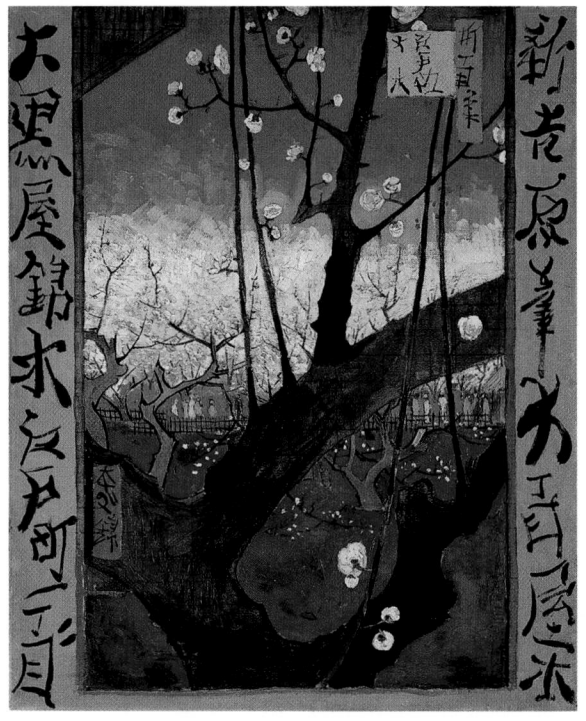

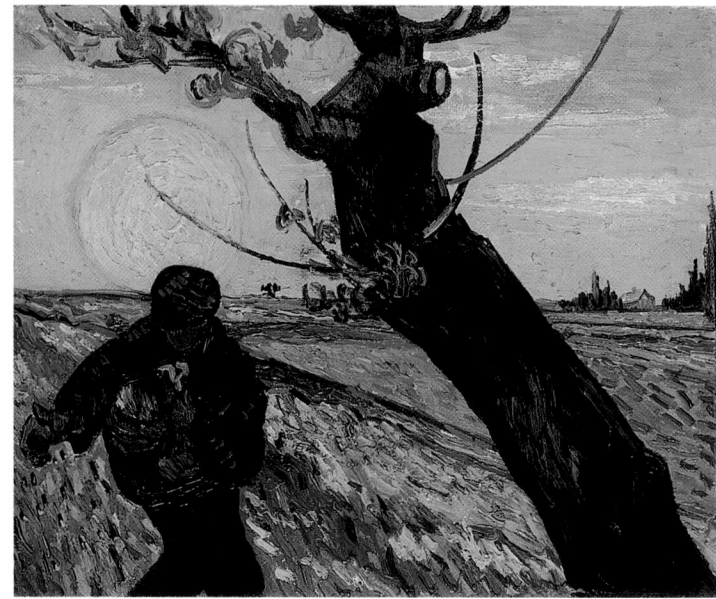

520 Vincent van Gogh.
THE SOWER. 1888.
Oil on canvas. 17⅜″ × 22⅛″.
Vincent van Gogh Foundation. Van Gogh Museum, Amsterdam.

519 Vincent van Gogh.
JAPONAISERIE: FLOWERING PLUM TREE. 1887.
Oil on canvas. 21½″ × 18″.
Vincent van Gogh Foundation. Van Gogh Museum, Amsterdam.

With Vincent van Gogh, late nineteenth-century painting moved from an outer impression of what the eye sees to an inner expression of what the heart feels and the mind knows.

From Impressionism, van Gogh learned the expressive potential of open brushwork and relatively pure color; but the style did not provide enough freedom to satisfy his desire to express his feelings. Van Gogh intensified the surfaces of his paintings with textural brushwork that recorded each gesture of his hand and gave an overall rhythmic movement to his paintings. He began to use strong color in an effort to express his emotions more clearly. In letters to his brother Theo, he wrote,

. . . instead of trying to reproduce exactly what I have before my eyes, I use color more arbitrarily so as to express myself forcibly. . . .

I am always in hope of making a discovery there to express the love of two lovers by a marriage of two complementary colors, their mingling and their opposition, the mysterious vibrations of kindred tones. To express the thought of a brow by the radiance of a light tone against somber background.[9]

As did other artists of the period, van Gogh developed a new sense of design from studying and even copying Japanese prints, as in JAPONAISERIE: FLOWERING PLUM TREE. In THE SOWER, the Japanese influence on van Gogh's sense of design is clearly seen in the bold, simplified shapes and flat color areas. The wide band of a tree trunk cuts diagonally across the composition; its strength balances the sun and its energy coming toward us with the movement of the sower.

Van Gogh was driven by a strong desire to share personal feelings and insights. In THE STARRY NIGHT, his observation of a town at night became the point of departure for a powerful symbolic

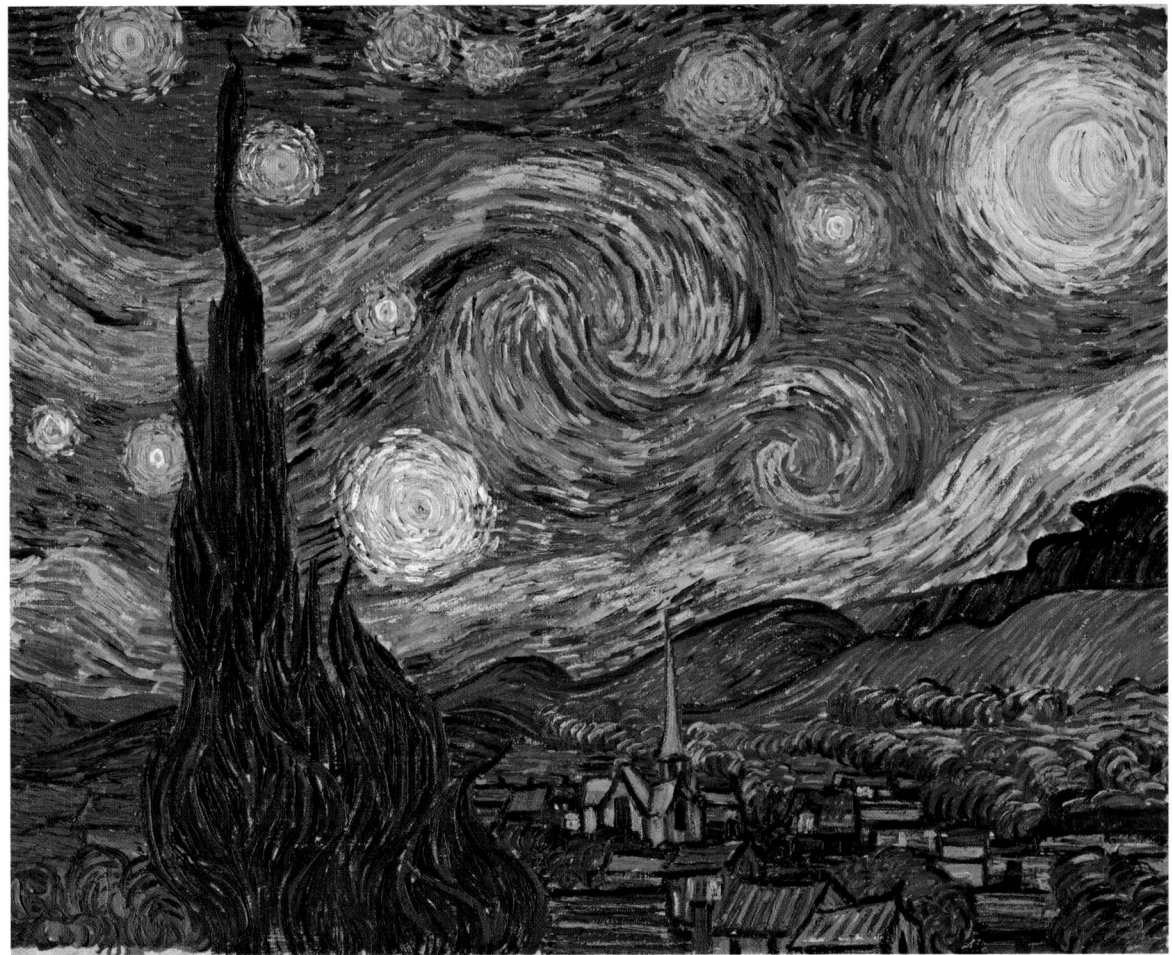

521 Vincent van Gogh.
THE STARRY NIGHT. 1889.
Oil on canvas. 29″ × 36¼″.
Acquired through the Lillie P. Bliss bequest. 472. 1941. The Museum of Modern Art, NY.
Licensed by Scala-Art Resource, NY.

image. Hills seem to undulate, echoing tremendous cosmic forces in the sky. The small town nestled into the dark forms of the ground plane suggests the scale of human life. The church's spire reaches toward the heavens, echoed by the larger, more dynamic upward thrust of the cypress trees in the left foreground. (The evergreen cypress is traditionally planted beside graveyards in Europe as a symbol of eternal life.) All these elements are united by the surging rhythm of lines that express van Gogh's passionate spirit and mystical vision. Many know of van Gogh's bouts of mental illness, but few realize that he did his paintings between seizures, in moments of great clarity.

French artist Paul Gauguin, like van Gogh, was highly critical of the materialism of industrial society. Gauguin experienced that business world firsthand during the several years that he worked as a stockbroker to support his family, painting on the weekends. He exhibited occasionally with the Impressionists, but he longed to escape what he called "the European struggle for money." This attitude led Gauguin to admire the honest life of the Brittany peasants of western France. In 1888, he

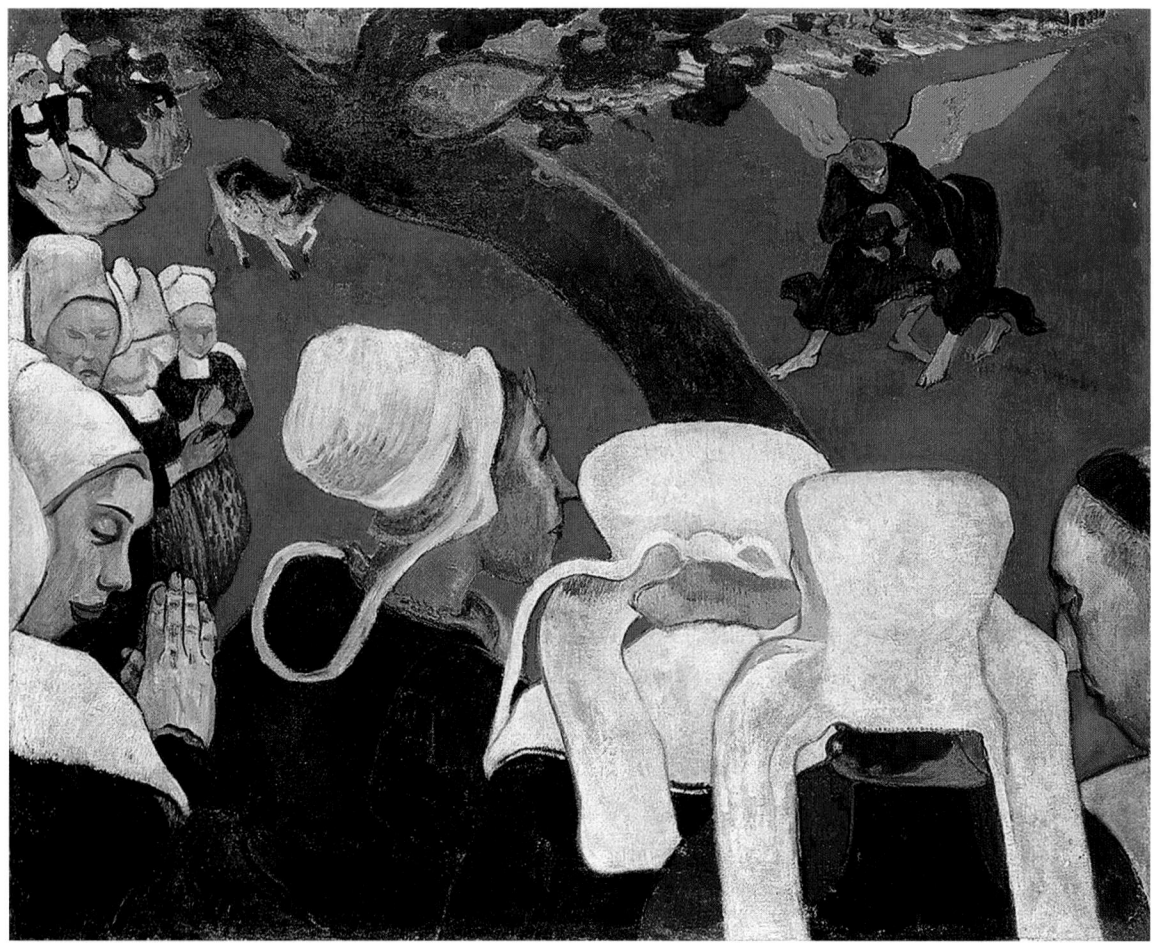

522   Paul Gauguin.
THE VISION AFTER THE SERMON (JACOB WRESTLING WITH THE ANGEL). 1888.
Oil on canvas. 28¾″ × 36½″.
National Gallery of Scotland, Edinburgh.

completed THE VISION AFTER THE SERMON, the first major work in his revolutionary new style. The large, carefully designed painting shows Jacob and the angel as they appear to a group of Brittany peasants in a vision inspired by the sermon in their village chruch.

The symbolic representation of unquestioning faith is an image that originated in Gauguin's mind rather than in his eye. With it, Gauguin took a major step toward personal expression. In order to avoid what he considered the distraction of implied deep space, he tipped up the simplified background plane and painted it an intense, "unnatural" vermilion. The entire composition is divided diagonally by the trunk of the apple tree, in the manner of Japanese prints. Shapes have been reduced to flat curvilinear areas outlined in black, with shadows minimized or eliminated.

Both van Gogh's and Gauguin's uses of color were important influences on twentieth-century painting. Their views on color were prophetic. The subject, Gauguin wrote, was only a pretext for symphonies of line and color.

In painting, one must search rather for suggestion than for description, as is done in music. . . . Think of the highly important musical role which colour will play henceforth in modern painting.[10]

Gauguin retained memories of his childhood in Peru that persuaded him that the art of ancient and

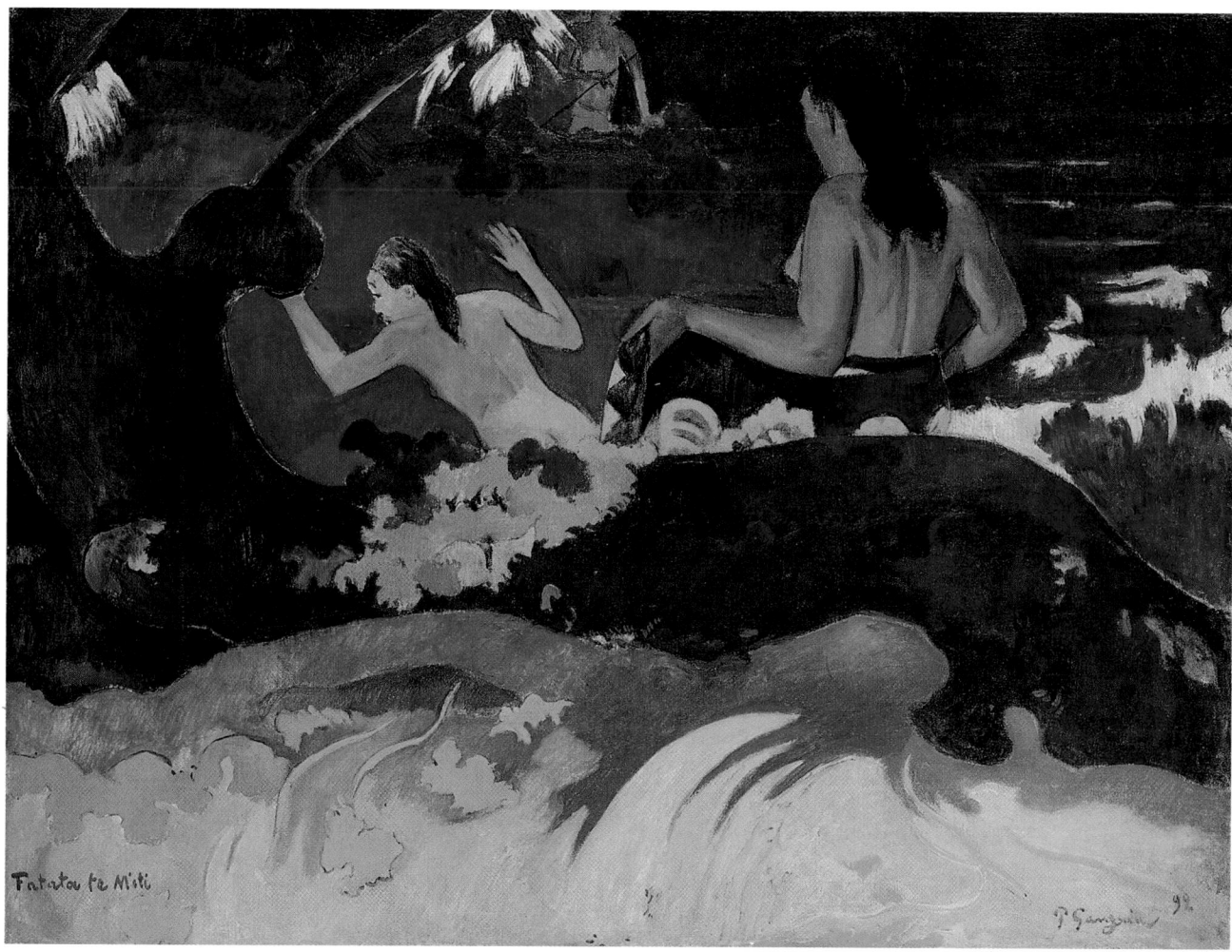

523 Paul Gauguin.
FATATA TE MITI (BY THE SEA). 1892.
Oil on canvas. 26¾″ × 36″.
Chester Dale Collection.
Photograph: © 2002 Board of Trustees, National Gallery of Art, Washington, D.C. 1963. 10.149. (1813)/PA.

non-Western cultures had a spiritual strength that was lacking in the European art of his time. He wrote:

Keep the Persians, the Cambodians, and a bit of the Egyptians always in mind. The great error is the Greek, however beautiful it may be.[11]

A great thought system is written in gold in Far Eastern art.[12]

Gauguin's desire to rejuvenate European art and civilization with insights from non-Western traditions would be shared in the early twentieth century by Matisse, Picasso, and the German

Expressionists. They adopted Gauguin's vision of the artist as a spiritual leader who could select from the past, and from various world cultures, anything capable of releasing the power of self-knowledge and inner life.

At the end of his life, Gauguin tried to break completely with European civilization by going to Tahiti. In FATATA TE MITI, he combined flat, curvilinear shapes with tropical and fanciful colors.

For Gauguin, art had become above all a means of communicating through symbols, a "synthesis," he called it, of visual form carrying memory, feelings, and ideas. These beliefs link him to *Symbolism*,

PAUL
Gauguin
Struggling Idealist
1848–1903

"I WANT TO ESTABLISH the right to dare everything," Gauguin wrote on the eve of his death.[13] Battered by bronchitis, neuralgia, syphilis, and a series of strokes, alone, impoverished, and halfway around the world from France, Gauguin had indeed dared everything—not only in his art, but in his life.

Paul Gauguin was twenty-three when a family friend introduced him to the world of art and artists. Immersing himself in the new art of his day, he collected works by Cézanne, Degas, and others, and he began to paint in his spare time. By 1879, he was exhibiting with the Impressionist artists he so admired. His job as a stockbroker had become an unbearable distraction, and when he lost it in the aftermath of a financial crash a few years later, he decided not to look for another: He would be an artist. He was then thirty-five, with a pregnant wife and four children. It quickly became clear that he could not support his family as an artist, and after two years of arguments and compromises, his wife moved back to her family, taking the children with her.

Gauguin sought a place to paint that would nourish his vision of an art in touch with the primal mysteries of life. He moved first to Brittany, drawn to the primitive lives of the Breton peasants. In 1887, he painted on the Caribbean island of Martinique, but he fell ill, ran out of money, and had to return to France. The following year he joined van Gogh in the south of France, but their idealistic plans for an artists' commune disintegrated into disastrous quarrels.

Convinced that he had to escape the "disease of civilization," Gauguin voyaged to Tahiti in 1891. He left its Westernized capital, Papeete, for a grass hut in a remote village, where he took a teenage bride, fathered a child, and steeped himself in the island's myths and legends. Despite the pressure of constant poverty, Gauguin transformed the raw material of Tahiti into a dream of earthly paradise, where a sensual people lived in harmony with their gods.

The world that Gauguin painted in FATATA TE MITI and other works was not the one that actually existed in Tahiti when he lived there. Gauguin idealized the "primitive" nature of life and left out the Western clothing, the missionaries, and the towns.

In 1893, Gauguin returned to France, confident that his Tahitian work would bring him success. It did not come. Lonely and disillusioned, he returned to Tahiti in 1895 and found it more Westernized than before. Frustrated and angry, he fought with the colonial authorities and railed against the missionaries. His health was failing rapidly, he was desperate for money, and he grew so despondent he attempted suicide. Again he set off in search of a simpler life, sailing in 1901 to the Marquesas Islands, where he died two years later.

"It is true that I know very little," Gauguin wrote to a friend. "But who can say if even this little, worked on by others, will not become something great?"[14] In Paris, in 1906, a large retrospective of Gauguin's work made the extent of his achievement clear for the first time. His achievement was considerable, and, built on by Picasso, Matisse, and many others, his "little" did indeed become something great.

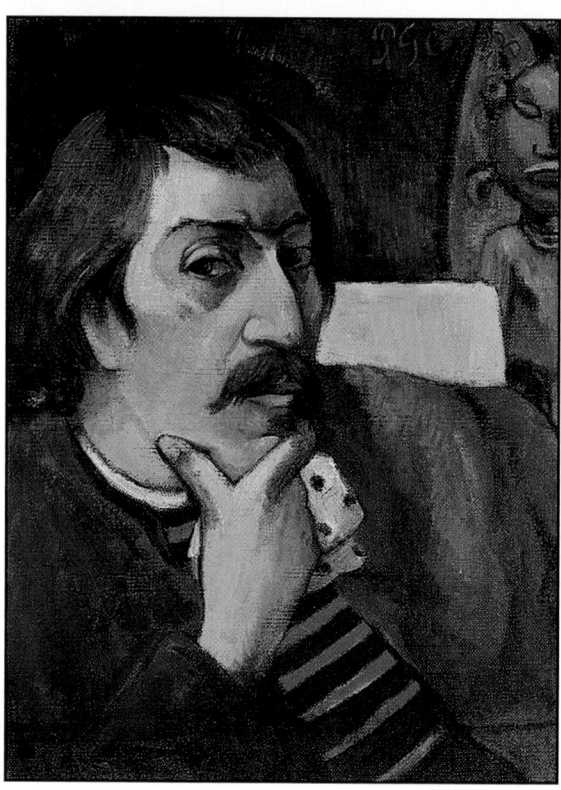

524 Paul Gauguin.
PORTRAIT OF THE ARTIST WITH THE IDOL. c. 1893.
Oil on canvas. 17¼″ × 12⅞″.
Collection of the McNay Art Museum, Bequest of Marion Koogler McNay.

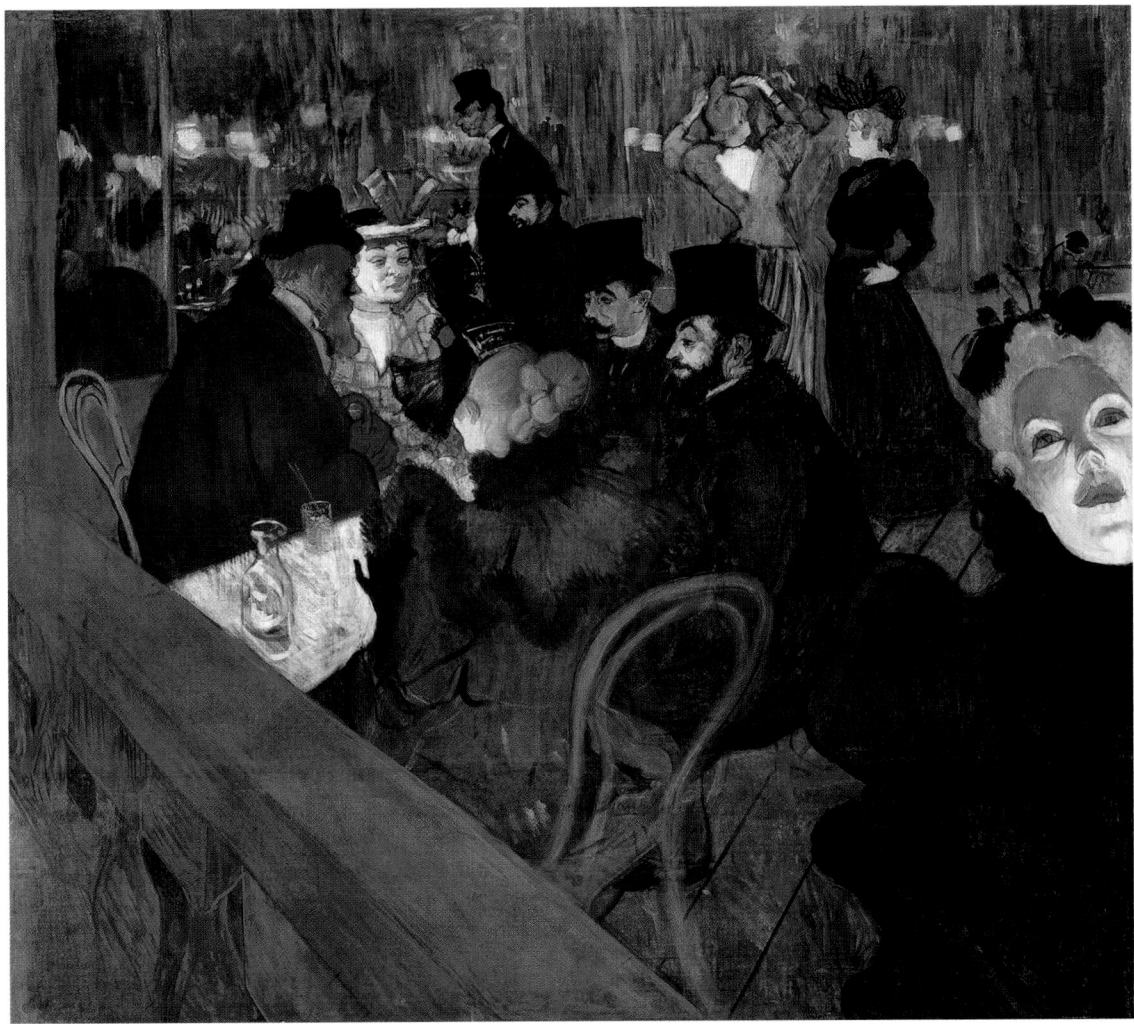

525 Henri de Toulouse-Lautrec.
AT THE MOULIN ROUGE. 1892–1895.
Oil on canvas. 48⅜″ × 55¼″.

a movement in literature and the visual arts that developed around 1885.

Reacting against both Realism and Impressionism, Symbolist poets and painters sought to lift the mind from the mundane and the practical. They employed decorative forms and symbols that were intentionally vague or open-ended in order to create imaginative suggestions. The poets held that the sounds and rhythms of words were part of their poems' deeper meaning; the painters recognized that line, color, and other visual elements were expressive in themselves. Symbolism, a trend rather than a spe-cific style, provided the ideological background for twentieth-century abstraction; it has been seen as an outgrowth of Romanticism and a forerunner of Surrealism.

Henri de Toulouse-Lautrec, another Post-Impressionist, painted the gaslit interiors of Parisian nightclubs and brothels. His quick, long strokes of color define a world of sordid gaiety. Toulouse-Lautrec was influenced by Degas (see page 369), whose work he greatly admired. In AT THE MOULIN ROUGE, Toulouse-Lautrec used unusual angles, cropped images, such as the face on the right, and

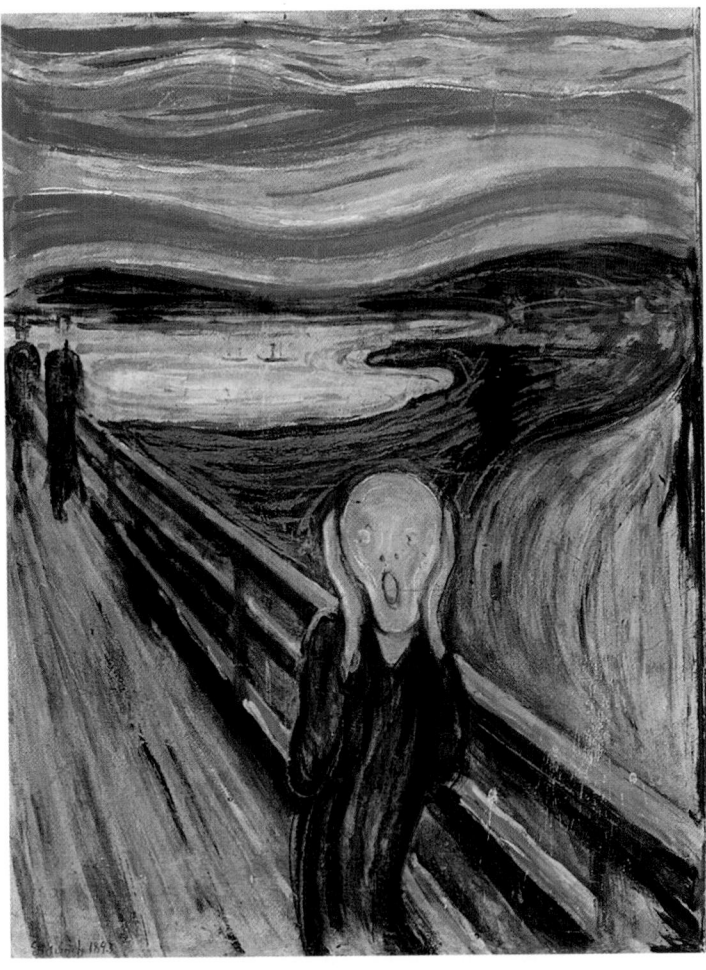

526 Edvard Munch.
THE SCREAM. 1893.
Casein on canvas. 35⅞″ × 29″
National Gallery, Oslo. © 2005. The Munch Museum–Ellingsen Group.
Artists Rights Society (ARS). NY/ADAGP, Paris. Scala. Art Resource, NY.

expressive, unnatural color to heighten feelings about the people and the world he painted. His paintings, drawings, and prints of Parisian nightlife influenced twentieth-century expressionist painters and his posters influenced graphic designers (see page 140).

Norwegian painter Edvard Munch traveled to Paris to study the works of his contemporaries, especially Gauguin, van Gogh, and Toulouse-Lautrec. What he learned from them, particularly from Gauguin's works, enabled him to carry Symbolism to a new level of expressive intensity. Munch's powerful paintings and prints explore depths of emotion—grief, loneliness, fear, love, sexual passion, jealousy, and death.

In THE SCREAM Munch takes the viewer far from the pleasures of Impressionism and extends considerably van Gogh's expressive vision. In this powerful image of anxiety, the dominant figure is caught in isolation, fear, and loneliness. Despair reverberates in continuous linear rhythms. Munch's image has been called the soul-cry of that age.

The nineteenth-century invention of photography, along with the discovery of non-Western art, strongly affected the direction of modern art. As the century progressed, artists sought a deeper reality by breaking away from the artificial idealism of officially recognized academic art.

This fresh beginning was full of self-assurance, as seen in the optimistic mood of Impressionism. Yet the process of seeing the visual world anew brought with it added levels of awareness, as the appearance of things came to be less important than the relationship between viewer and reality. Once again, it became the artist's task to probe and reveal hidden worlds, to make the invisible visible. Artists gave increasing importance to the elements of form and to the formal structure of seen and invented imagery. Nature was internalized and transformed in order to portray a greater reality as the stage was set for even bigger changes in the twentieth century.

EARLY TWENTIETH CENTURY

During the first decade of the last century, Western views of the nature of reality changed radically. In 1900, Sigmund Freud published *The Interpretation of Dreams*, a vast work that explored the structure and power of the subconscious mind. In 1903, the Wright brothers flew the first power-driven aircraft, and Marie and Pierre Curie isolated the radioactive element radium for the first time. In 1905, Albert Einstein changed our concepts of time, space, and substance with his theory of relativity. Matter could no longer be considered solid; rather, it was a form of energy.

The industrial revolution had changed life in myriad ways. Thousands of new jobs opened in city-based factories, drawing rural people into a new, crowded, and impersonal urban environment. Business-oriented capitalism moved the workplace farther from family life than it had ever been before, and most wage work became much more unpleasant. The most violent revolutions of the century—in Russia, Mexico, and China—sprang from class tensions. At the same time, the industrial system created vast amounts of wealth that engendered a middle class and gave millions a financial floor. Better vaccines and public health led to longer life expectancies and a lower birth rate. A steady stream of inventions made business more productive and made scientists into heroes. Government functions expanded into new areas such as factory inspection, education, regulation of currency, and border controls.

Simultaneously, great changes occurred in art, and some of them were inspired by scientific discoveries. In 1913, Russian artist Wassily Kandinsky described how deeply he was affected by the discovery of subatomic particles:

A scientific event cleared my way of one of the greatest impediments. This was the further division of the atom. The crumbling of the atom was to my soul like the crumbling of the whole world.[1]

The art of the twentieth century was the result of a series of revolutions in thinking and seeing. Its characteristics are those of the century itself: rapid change, diversity, individualism, and exploration—accompanied by abundant discoveries. Twentieth-century artists, as well as scientists, have helped us see the world in new ways and revealed new levels of consciousness.

The explosion of new styles of art at the beginning of this century grew from Impressionist and Post-Impressionist innovations. Yet in their search for forms to express the new age, European artists often looked to ancient and non-Western cultures for inspiration and renewal. In so doing, they overturned the authority of the Renaissance, which had dominated Western artistic thought for five hundred years.

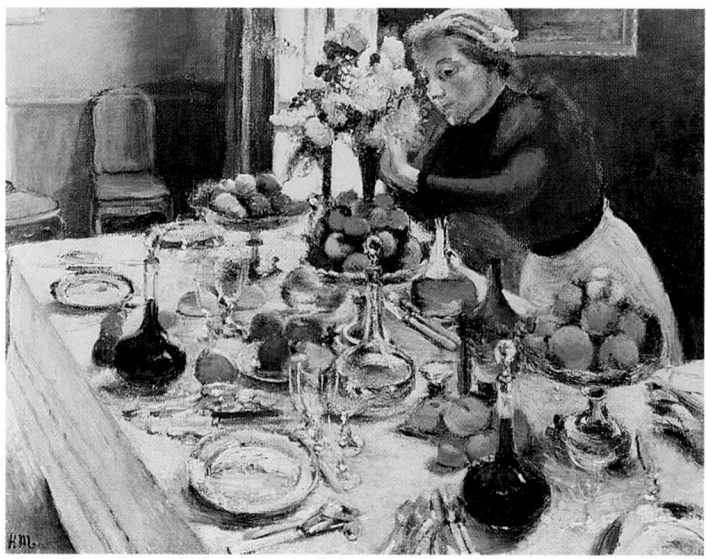

527 Henri Matisse (1869–1954).
LA DESSERTE. 1897.
Oil on canvas. 39½″ × 51½″.
Private collection/Bridgeman Art Library International Ltd., London/New York. PHD30074.
© 2005 Succession H. Matisse, Paris/Artists Rights Soceity (ARS), NY.

528 Henri Matisse (1869–1954).
HARMONY IN RED (THE RED ROOM). 1908–1909.
Oil on canvas. 70⅞″ × 86⅝″.
Hermitage Museum, St. Petersburg, Russia. Scala/Art Resource, NY.
© 2007 Succession H. Matisse, Paris/Artists Rights Society (ARS), NY.

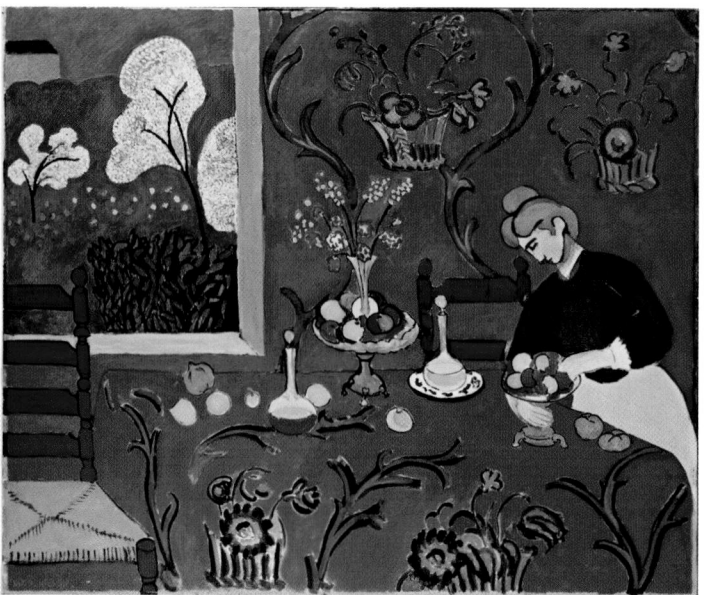

We see the new spirit in action if we compare two works by Henri Matisse, LA DESSERTE and HARMONY IN RED. These works treat the same subject in radically different ways. In LA DESSERTE, we see naturalistic color, three-dimensional perspective, and modeling of forms in light and shade. These skills were first perfected in the Renaissance. Twelve years later in HARMONY IN RED, the colors are intense and pure, spaces and forms are flattened, and the pattern of the tablecloth grows exuberantly up the wall. Matisse was a leader in the early twentieth-century movement known as Fauvism, which expanded on the innovations of Post-Impressionism.

THE FAUVES AND EXPRESSIONISM

By the turn of the century, many young painters in France had been attracted to Seurat's pointillist method (see page 372). Its formalist, rational approach seemed perfectly suited to a progressive, scientific era. For some painters just starting out, pointillism offered a systematic way to escape the weight of the past and to counter the oppressive influences of their academic teachers and the outdated Impressionists.

Soon, however, some of these artists felt imprisoned rather than liberated by pointillism. They wanted to express themselves more directly, more spontaneously. Led by Henri Matisse, a group of painters that included André Derain drew inspiration from the expressive color of Gauguin and van Gogh. They studied Cézanne's pictorial constructions in colored planes. Their own use of color grew increasingly intense and subjective.

In 1905, their first group exhibit shocked the public. A critic of that show derisively called them *les fauves* (the wild beasts). According to Matisse, the epithet was never accepted by the group; it was merely a tag the critics found useful.

Matisse was not as rebellious as his detractors claimed; rather, he was a thoughtful person who tried merely to express his enthusiasm for life. Every part of a painting by Matisse is expressive: the lines, the colors, the subject, and the composition itself. He frequently reduced his subjects to a

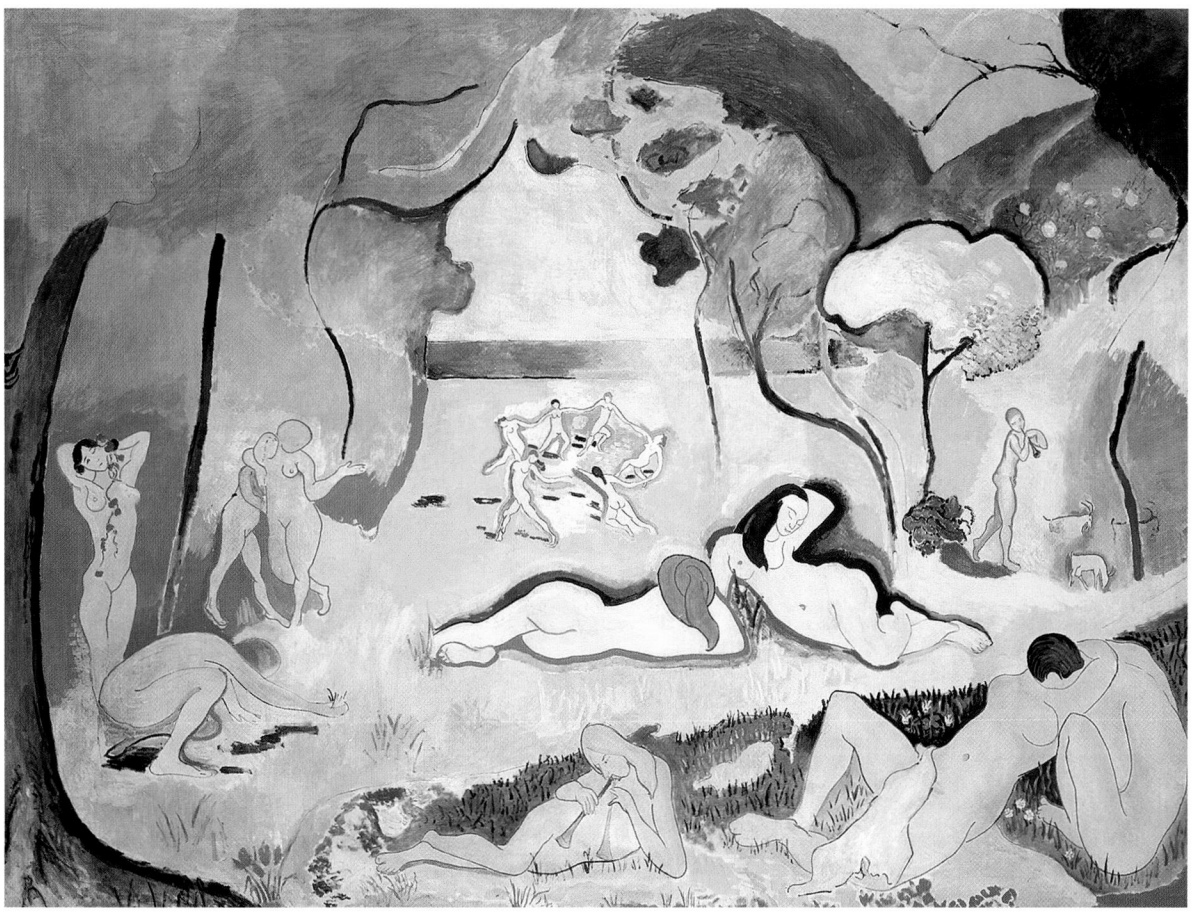

529 Henri Matisse (1869–1954).
JOY OF LIFE. 1905–1906.
Oil on canvas. 69⅛″ × 94⅞″.
Barnes Foundation, Merion, Pennsylvania. © 2005 Succession H. Matisse,
Paris/Artists Rights Society (ARS), New York. Photograph: Barnes Foundation/SuperStock.

few outlines, rather than fill in all of their details. He did this to better preserve the original impulse of feeling. More detail in a work would merely overburden the viewer and distract attention from the immediate burst of emotion. Asked if he was religious, he replied, "Only when I am painting." (See the biographical essay on page 92.)

Matisse's painting JOY OF LIFE is an early work in a long career and a masterpiece of Fauvism. Pure hues vibrate across the surface; lines, largely freed from descriptive roles, align with simplified shapes to provide a lively rhythm in the composition. The seemingly careless depiction of the figures is based on Matisse's knowledge of human anatomy and draw-

ing. The intentionally direct, childlike quality of the form serves to heighten the joyful content. Matisse said, "What I am after, above all, is expression."

In Derain's LONDON BRIDGE (on the following page), brilliant, invented color is balanced by some use of traditional composition and perspective. Derain spoke of intentionally using discordant color. It is an indication of today's acceptance of strong color that Derain's painting does not appear disharmonious.

The Fauve movement lasted little more than two years, from 1905 to 1907, yet it was one of the most influential developments in early twentieth-century painting. The Fauves took the decisive step in freeing color from its traditional role of describing

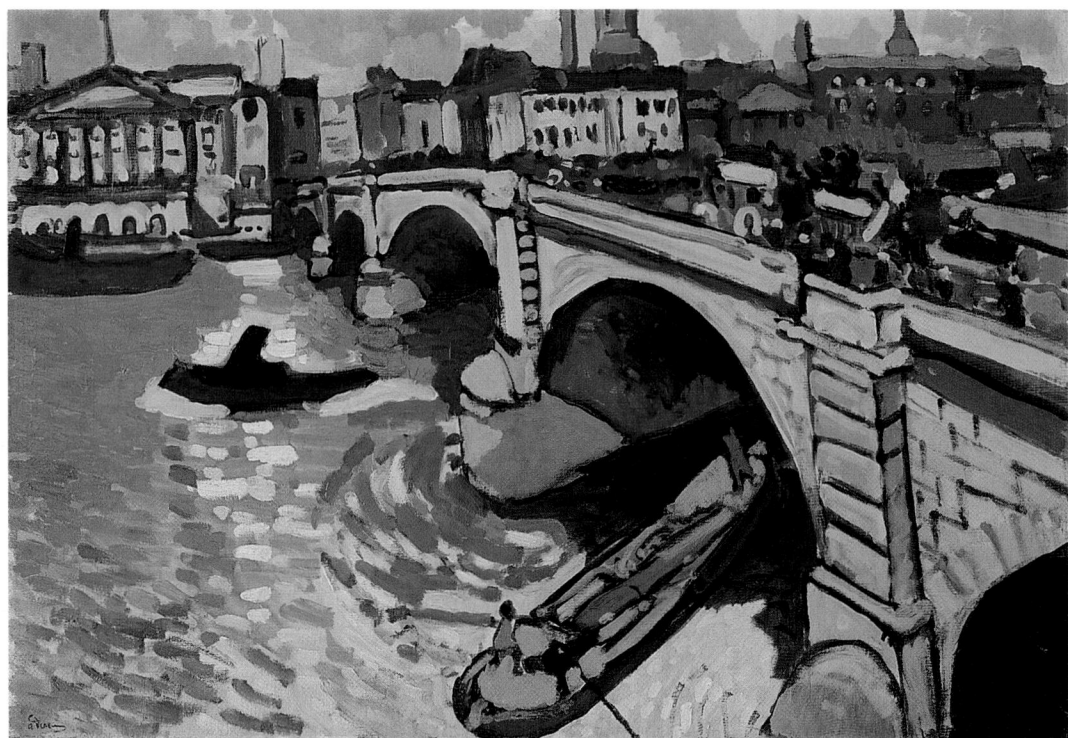

530 André Derain.
LONDON BRIDGE. 1906.
Oil on canvas. 26″ × 39″.
The Museum of Modern Art, NY. Licensed by Scala-Art Resource, NY.
Gift of Mr. and Mrs. Charles Zadok.
Photograph © 2002 The Museum of Modern Art, New York.
© 2002 Artists Rights Society (ARS), NY, ADAGP, Paris.

the natural appearance of an object. In this way, their work led to an increasing use of color as an independent expressive element.

We can categorize Fauvism as an expressive style. *Expressionism* is a general term for art that emphasizes inner feelings and emotions over objective depiction. In Europe, romantic or expressive tendencies can be traced from seventeenth-century Baroque art to the early nineteenth-century painting of Delacroix, who in turn influenced the expressive side of Post-Impressionism (particularly van Gogh).

A few German artists at the beginning of the century shared the expressionist goals of the Fauves. Their desire to express attitudes and emotions was so pronounced and sustained that we call their art *German Expressionism*. They developed imagery characterized by vivid, often angular simplifications of their subjects, dramatic color contrasts, with bold, at times crude finish. These techniques added emotional intensity to their works. Like their Fauve counterparts, the German Expressionists built on the achievements of Gauguin and van Gogh and the soul-searching paintings of Munch. They felt compelled to use the power of expressionism to address the human condition, often exploring such themes as natural life, sorrow, passion, spirituality, and mysticism. As their art developed, it absorbed formal influences from medieval German art, Fauvism, Slavic folk art, African and Oceanic art, and Cubism.

Two groups typified the German Expressionist movement of the early twentieth century: The

Bridge (*Die Brücke*) and The Blue Rider (*Der Blaue Reiter*). Ernst Ludwig Kirchner, architecture student turned painter, was the founder of the Bridge. The group included several of his fellow architectural students, Emil Nolde, and others. They appealed to artists to revolt against academic painting and establish a new, vigorous aesthetic that would form a bridge between the Germanic past and modern experience. They first exhibited as a group in 1905, the year of the first Fauve exhibition.

Kirchner's concern for expressing human emotion gave his work a quality similar to that which he admired in Munch's work. Kirchner's early paintings employed the flat color areas of Fauvism; by 1913, he had developed a style that incorporated the angularities of Cubism (discussed presently), African sculpture, and German Gothic art. In STREET, BERLIN, elongated figures are crowded together. Repeated diagonal lines create an urban atmosphere charged with energy. Dissonant colors, chopped out shapes, and rough, almost crude, brushwork heighten the emotional impact.

The Blue Rider group was led by Russian painter Wassily Kandinsky, who lived in Munich between 1908 and 1914 and who shared with his German associates a concern for developing an art that would turn people away from false values, toward spiritual rejuvenation. He believed that a painting should be "an exact replica of some inner emotion": In BLUE MOUNTAIN (on the following page), painted in 1908, he created a "choir of colors" influenced by the vivid, freely expressive color of the Fauves.[2]

Kandinsky's paintings evolved toward an absence of representational subject matter. In BLUE MOUNTAIN, subject matter had already become secondary to the powerful effect of the visual elements released from merely descriptive roles.

By 1910, Kandinsky had made the shift to totally nonrepresentational imagery in order to concentrate on the expressive potential of pure form freed from associations with recognizable sub-

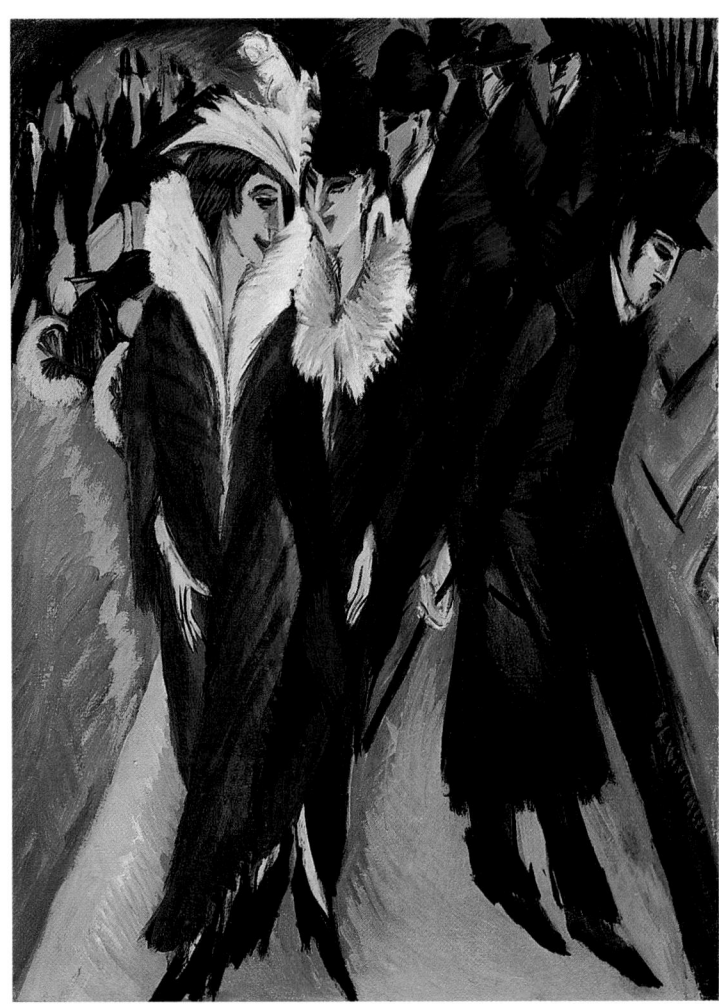

531   Ernst Ludwig Kirchner.
STREET, BERLIN. 1913.
Oil on canvas.
47½" × 35⅞".
The Museum of Modern Art, NY. Licensed by Scala-Art Resource, NY. Purchase.
Photograph © 2002 The Museum of Modern Art, New York.

jects. A person of mystical inclinations, Kandinsky hoped to create art only in response to what he called "inner necessity," or the emotional stirrings of the soul, rather than in response to what he saw in the world. He said that art should transcend physical reality and speak directly to the emotions of viewers without intervening subject matter. He sought a language of visual form comparable to the

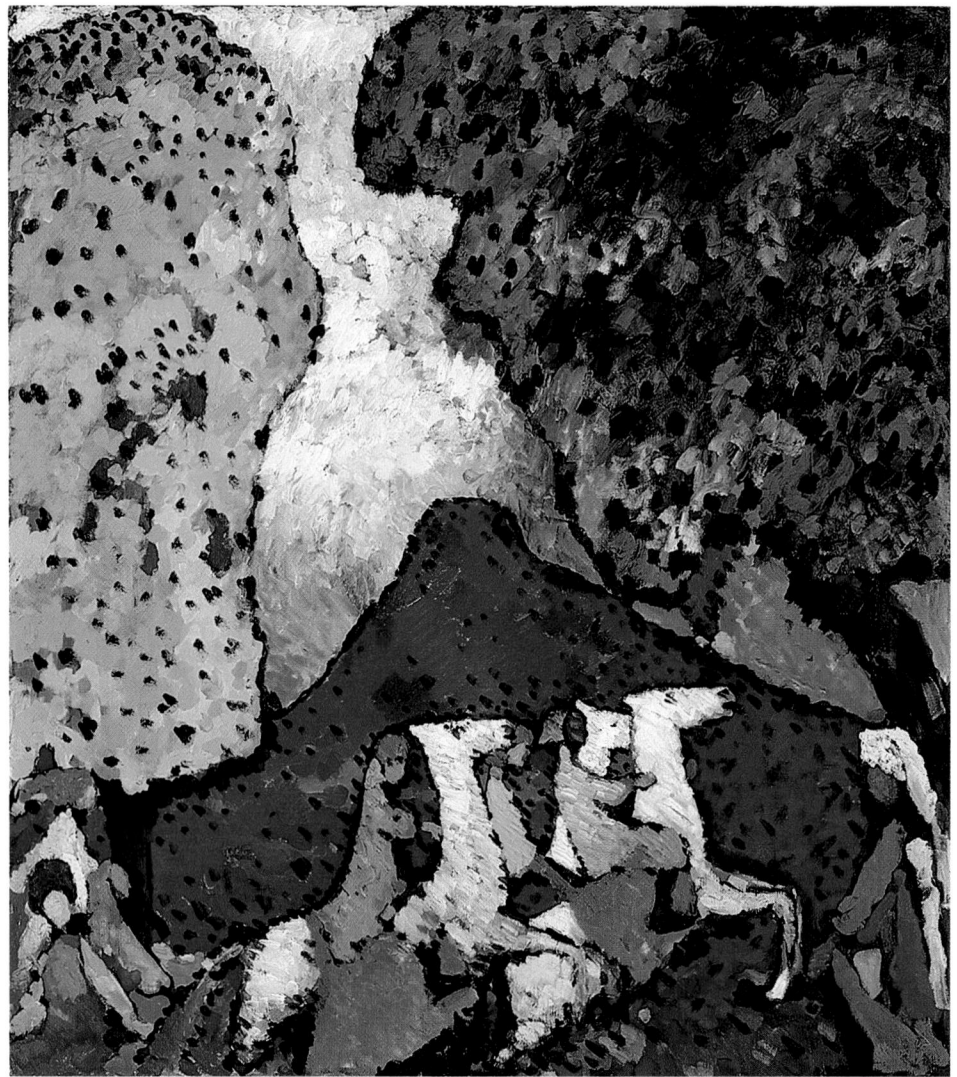

532 Wassily Kandinsky.
BLUE MOUNTAIN. 1908–1909.
Oil on canvas. 41¾″ × 38″.
The Solomon R. Guggenheim Museum, NY. Gift, Solomon
R. Guggenheim, 1941.41.505. Photograph by David Heald.
© The Solomon R. Guggenheim Foundation, NY.
© 2002 Artists Rights Society (ARS). NY/ADAGP, Paris.

independent aural language we experience in music. The rhythms, melodies, and harmonies of music please or displease us because of the way they affect us. To exploit this relationship between painting and music, Kandinsky often gave his paintings musical titles, such as COMPOSITION IV. Here we see colors and shapes that only vaguely correspond to things in the world. Rather, the artist painted out of inner necessity to make visible his personal mood at that time. Just as a composer uses harmony and melody, Kandinsky used color and form to (as he put it) "set the soul vibrating."

Kandinsky said that the content of his paintings was "what the spectator *lives* or *feels* while under the effect of the *form and color combinations* of the picture."[3] He was an outstanding innovator in the history of art, and his revolutionary nonfigurative works played a key role in the development of subsequent nonrepresentational styles. His purpose was not simply aesthetic: he saw his paintings

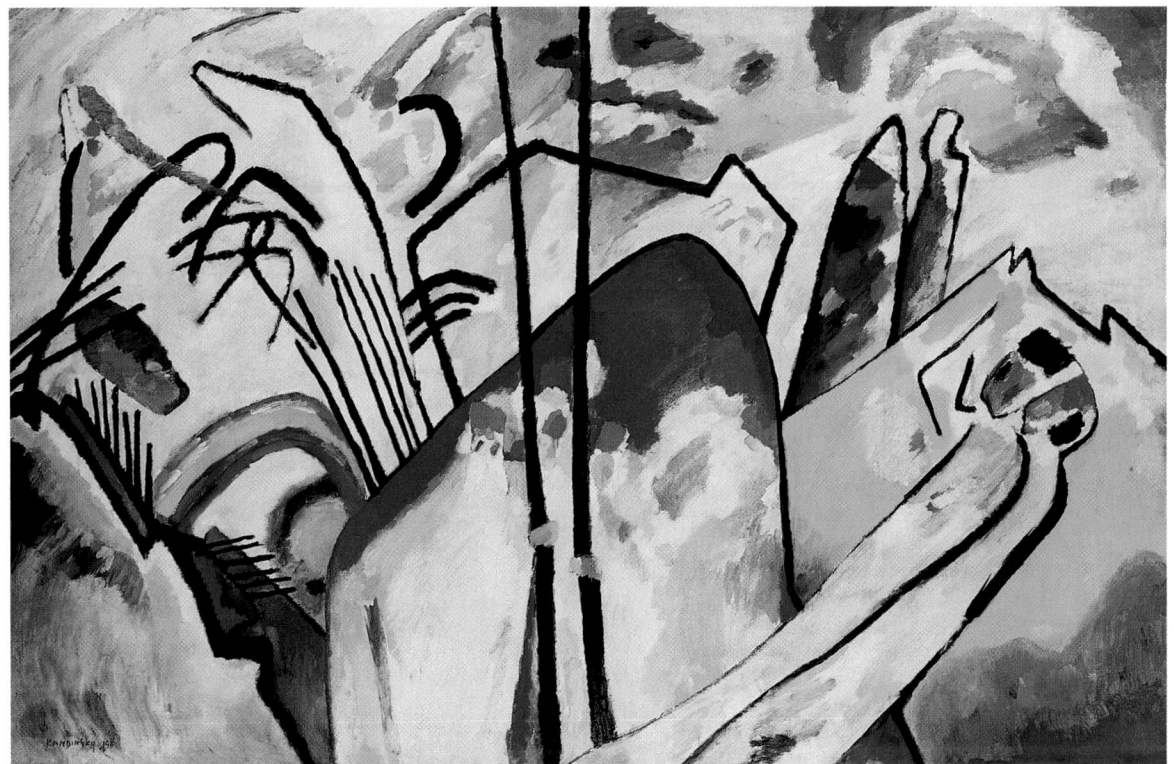

533   Wassily Kandinsky.
COMPOSITION IV. 1911.
Oil on canvas. 62¹³⁄₁₆″ × 98⅝″.
Kunstsammlung Nordrhein-Westfalen, Düsseldorf.
Photograph: Walter Klein, © 2002 Artists Rights Society (ARS),
NY/ADAGP, Paris.

as leading a way through an impending period of catastrophe to a great new era of spirituality. Kandinsky felt art could provide a spiritual nourishment for the modern world.

CUBISM

While living in Paris, Spanish artist Pablo Picasso shared ideas and influences with French artist Georges Braque. Together they pursued investigations that led to Cubism, the most influential movement of the early twentieth century. Cubism heavily influenced the spatial design (basic visual structure) of many of the notable paintings and sculptures of the century. In terms of design, Cubist color is secondary to structure. Through its indirect influence on architecture and the arts, Cubism has become part of our daily lives.

Picasso absorbed influences quickly, keeping only what he needed to achieve his objectives. His breakthrough painting, LES DEMOISELLES D'AVIGNON (on the following page), shows a radical departure from tradition. Rejecting the accepted European notion of ideal beauty, Picasso created an entirely personal vocabulary of form influenced by Cézanne's faceted reconstructions of nature and by the inventive abstraction, vitality, and power he admired in African sculpture such as the KOTA RELIQUARY FIGURE and the MASK FROM IVORY COAST (both shown on page 389). While the meanings and uses of African sculpture held little interest for him, their form revitalized his art.

Picasso's new approach astonished even his closest friends. Georges Braque, who did as much as Picasso to develop Cubism, was appalled when

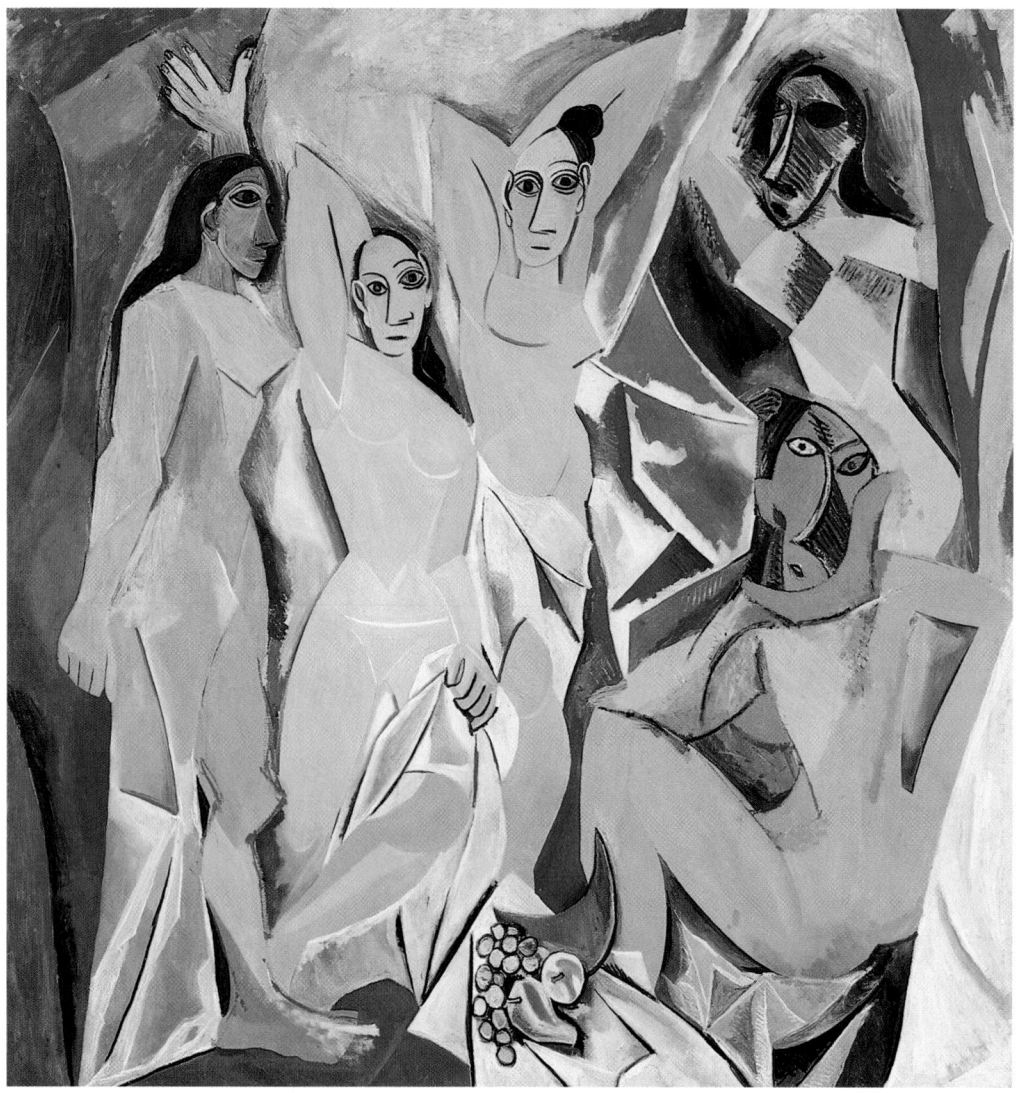

534 Pablo Picasso.
LES DEMOISELLES D'AVIGNON. 1907.
Oil on canvas. 8' × 7'8".
The Museum of Modern Art, NY. Licensed by Scala-Art Resource, NY. Acquired through the Lillie P. Bliss Bequest.
Photograph: © 2002 The Museum of Modern Art, NY. © 2002 Estate of Pablo Picasso. Artists Rights Society (ARS), NY.

he first saw LES DEMOISELLES in 1907. "You may give all the explanations you like," he said, "but your painting makes one feel as if you were trying to make us eat cotton waste and wash it down with kerosene."[4] In LES DEMOISELLES D'AVIGNON, the fractured, angular figures intermingle with the sharp triangular shapes of the ground, activating the entire picture surface. This reconstruction of image and ground, with its fractured triangulation of forms and its merging of figure and ground was the turning point. With this painting, Picasso exploded the lingering Renaissance approach to the human figure in art and the legacy of Renaissance perspective. In short, he overturned many of the traditions of Western art. LES DEMOISELLES thus set the stage and provided the impetus for the development of Cubism. Though some art historians have come to decry the work's negative depiction of women, viewers are challenged by the painting's hacked-out shapes and overall intensity.

535 KOTA RELIQUARY FIGURE. (left)
Cameroon, probably 20th century.
Brass sheeting over wood. Length 27½".
Catalog #323686, Neg. No. 36712A. Department of Anthropology,
Smithsonian Institution.

536 MASK FROM IVORY COAST. (right)
Wood. 9¾" × 6½".
Collection Musée de l'Homme, Paris. Photograph: D. Ponsard.

537 Paul Cézanne.
GARDANNE. 1885–1886.
Oil on canvas. 31½" × 25¼".
The Metropolitan Museum of Art. Gift of Dr. and Mrs. Franz H. Hirschland, 1957.
(57.181). Photograph: © 1991 The Metropolitan Museum of Art.

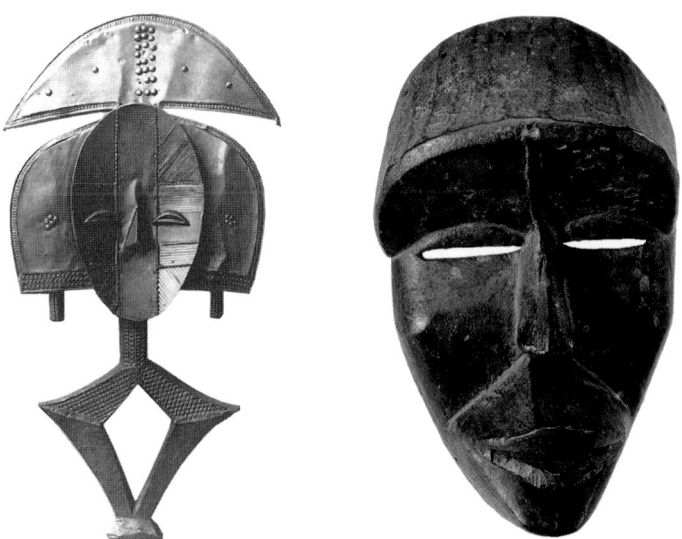

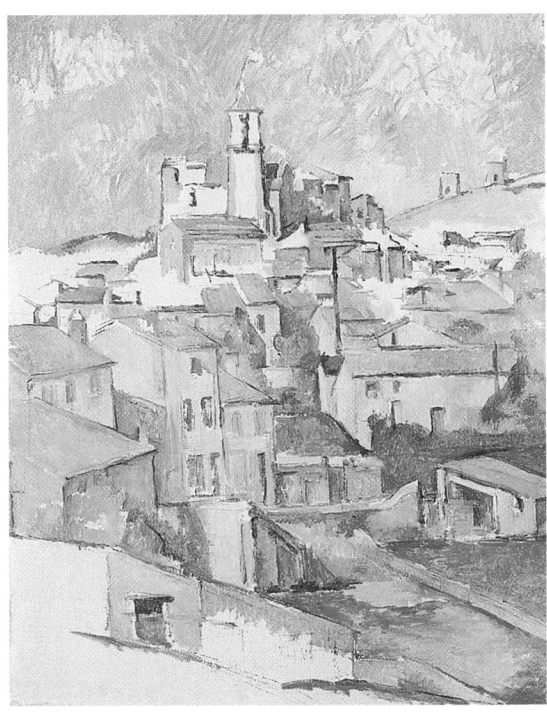

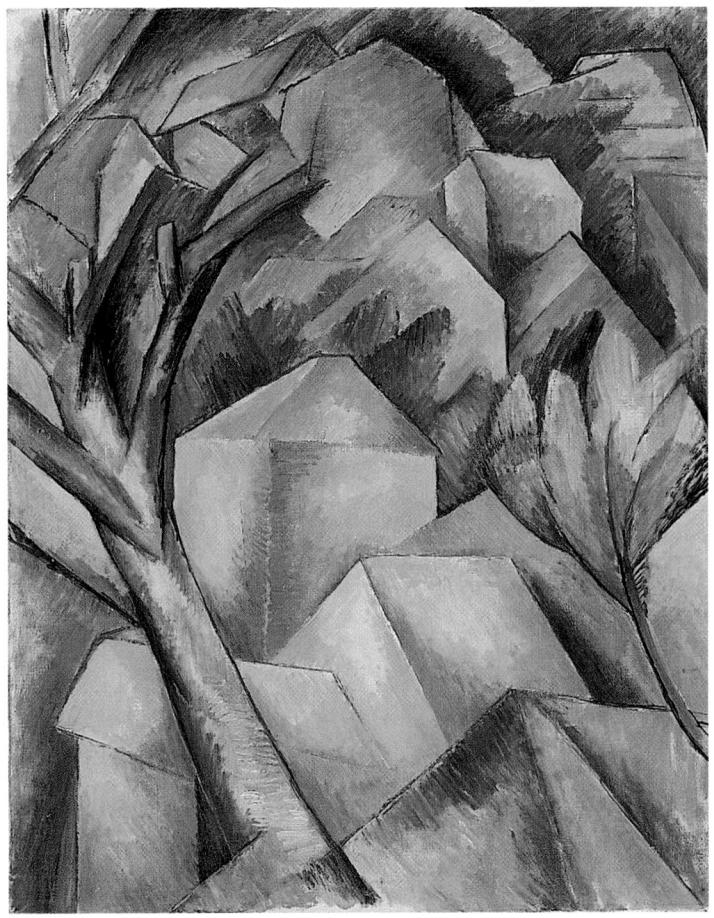

A comparison of two paintings—Cézanne's GARDANNE, completed in 1886, and Braque's HOUSES AT L'ESTAQUE, completed in 1908, shows the beginning of the progression from Cézanne's Post-Impressionist style to the Cubist approach that Braque and Picasso developed.

Picasso made the first breakthrough, but Braque did more to develop the vocabulary of Cubism. Braque admired Cézanne's continuous probing, his doubt, and his dogged determination to get at the truth of his subjects. In a series of landscapes painted in the south of France (where

538 Georges Braque.
HOUSES AT L'ESTAQUE. 1908.
Oil on canvas. 28½" × 23".
Foundation RUPF, Bern, Switzerland. Giraudon. Art Resource, NY.
© 2005 Artists Rights Society (ARS), NY/ADAGP, Paris.

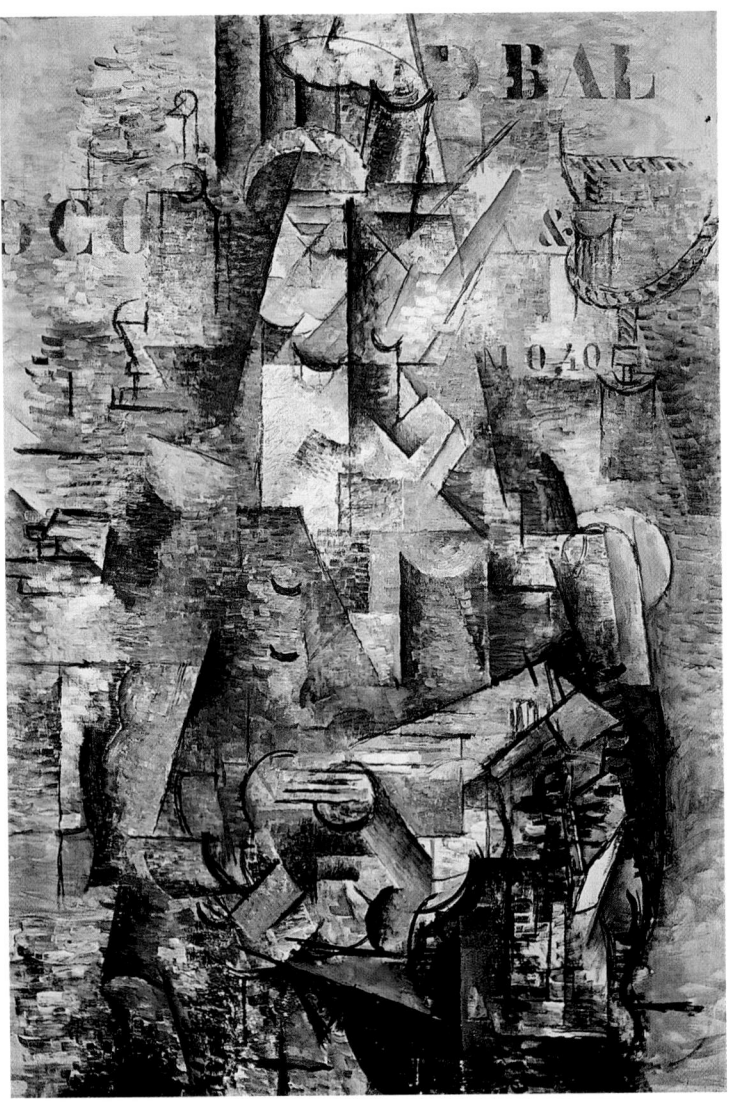

539 Georges Braque.
THE PORTUGUESE. 1911.
Oil on canvas. 46" × 32".
Kunstmuseum, Basel, Switzerland. Giraudon. Art Resource, NY.
© 2005 Artists Rights Society (ARS), New York/ADAGP, Paris.

ment's name: When Matisse saw this painting, he declared it to be a bunch of little cubes. From 1908 to 1914, Braque and Picasso were jointly responsible for bringing Cubism to maturity. They worked for a time in increasingly neutral tones, in an effort to achieve formal structure devoid of the emotional distractions of color.

By 1910, Cubism had become a fully developed style. During the *analytical* phase of Cubism (1910 to 1911), Picasso, Braque, and others analyzed their subjects from various angles, then painted abstract, geometric references to these views. Because mental concepts of familiar objects are based on experiences of seeing many sides, they aimed to show objects as the mind, rather than the eye, perceives them. Georges Braque's THE PORTUGUESE is a portrait of a man sitting at a café table strumming a guitar. The subject is broken down into facets and recombined with the background. Figure and ground thus collapse into a shallow and jagged pictorial space.

Cubism was a rational, formalist counterpart to the subjective emphasis of the Fauves and other expressionists. Above all, it was a reinvention of pictorial space. The Cubists realized that the two-dimensional space of the picture plane was quite different from the three-dimensional space we occupy. Natural objects were points of departure for abstract images, demonstrating the essential unity of forms within the spaces that surround and penetrate them. Cubism is a reconstruction of objects based on geometric abstraction. By looking first at Cézanne's GARDANNE, then at Braque's HOUSES AT L'ESTAQUE, and finally at THE PORTUGUESE, we see a progression in which forms seem to build, then spread across the surface in interwoven planes.

A new kind of construction of planes in actual space came about when Picasso assembled his sheet-metal GUITAR and thereby extended the Cubist revolution to sculpture. It began a dominant trend toward sculptural construction: Before GUITAR, most sculpture was carved or modeled. Since GUITAR, much of contemporary sculpture has been constructed.

In 1912, Picasso and Braque modified Analytical Cubism with color, textured and patterned surfaces,

Cézanne had worked), Braque took Cézanne's faceted planar constructions a step further.

Instead of the regular perspective that had been common in European painting since the Renaissance, Braque's shapes define a rush of forms that pile up rhythmically in shallow, ambiguous space. Buildings and trees seem interlocked in an active space that pushes and pulls across the picture surface.

HOUSES AT L'ESTAQUE, one of the first Cubist paintings, provided the occasion for the move-

and the use of cutout shapes. The resulting style came to be called Synthetic Cubism. Artists used pieces of newspaper, sheet music, wallpaper, and similar items, not re-presented but actually *presented* in a new way. The newspaper in VIOLIN AND FRUIT is part of a real Paris newspaper. The shapes, which in earlier naturalistic, representational paintings would have been "background," have been made equal in importance to foreground shapes. Picasso chose traditional still-life objects; but rather than paint the fruit, he cut out and pasted printed images of fruit. Such compositions, called *papier colle* in French, or pasted paper, became known as *collage* in English. Analytical Cubism involved taking apart, or breaking down, the subject into its various aspects; Synthetic Cubism was a process of building up or combining bits and pieces of material.

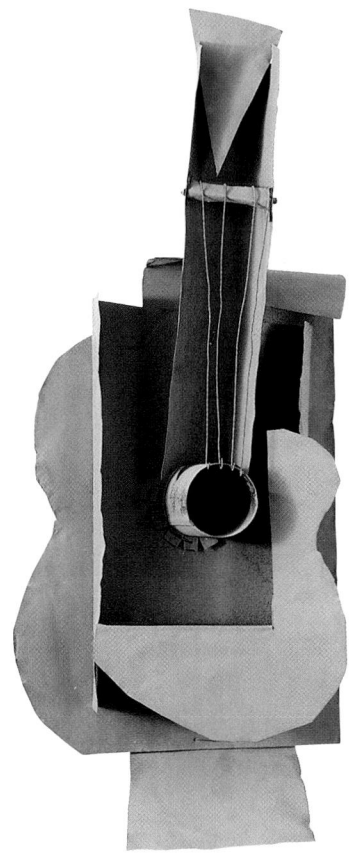

540 Pablo Picasso.
GUITAR. 1912–1913.
Construction of sheet metal and wire.
30½″ × 13¾″ × 7⅞″.
The Museum of Modern Art, NY. Gift of the artist.
Photograph © 2002 The Museum of Modern of Modern Art, NY.
Licensed by Scala-Art Resource, NY.
© 2002 Estate of Pablo Picasso. Artists Rights Society (ARS), NY.

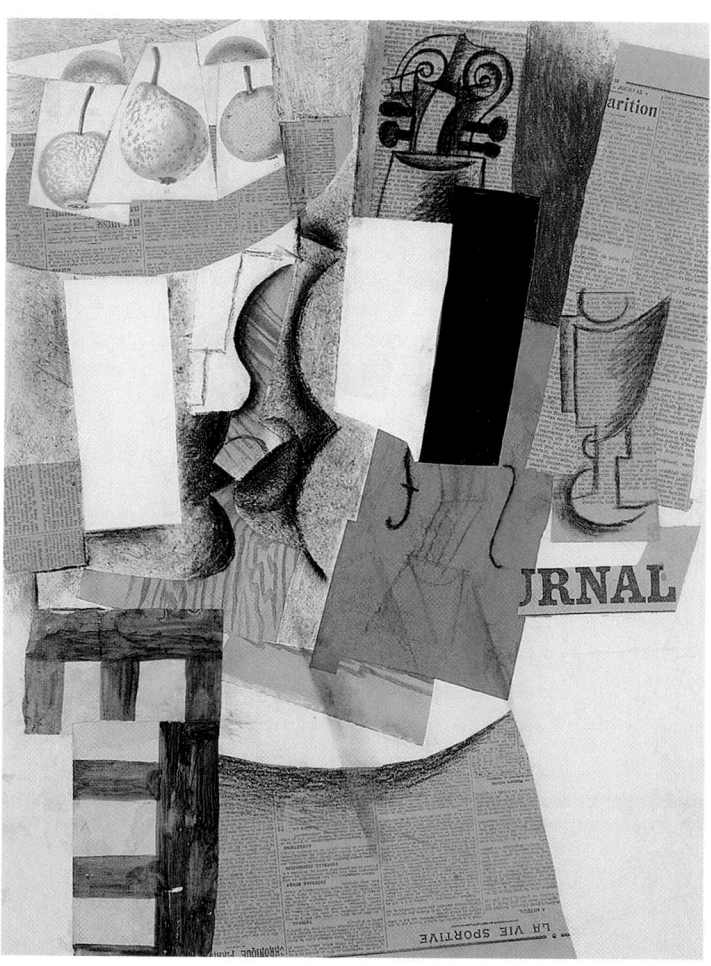

541 Pablo Picasso.
VIOLIN AND FRUIT. 1913.
Charcoal colored papers, gouache, painted paper collage. 25¼″ × 19½″.
Philadelphia Museum of Art; A.E. Gallatin Collection, 1952-61-106.
© 2002 Estate of Pablo Picasso. Artists Rights Society (ARS), NY.

Picasso

Restless Creativity

EVEN BEFORE HE COULD TALK, Pablo Picasso showed skill in drawing. Years later, he could remember the colors of things he saw in early childhood.

Born in the southern Spanish town of Málaga to artistic parents, Picasso first studied art with his father, a drawing teacher. At the age of ten he moved with his family to La Coruña on the Atlantic coast, then to Barcelona four years later, when the future Cubist was fourteen. Such was his skill at drawing, that upon arrival he passed the entrance examinations for the School of Fine Arts. He won his first gold medal at an exhibition in his hometown in 1897.

At the age of sixteen he entered the Royal Academy in Madrid, but attended only briefly because he regarded the teaching methods as oppressive. Returning to Barcelona in 1899, he began to frequent the advanced art circles where Modern art was practiced and hotly debated. His own work evolved rapidly through Symbolism and Post-Impressionism to expressive portraits of social outcasts and poor people.

From 1904 to 1945 he lived in Paris. His early work shows his ability to assimilate varied influences and his interest in exploring new modes of expression.

Picasso became fascinated with art from outside Western traditions. He became particularly interested in the African and Oceanic sculpture that Gauguin and later the Fauves had "discovered."

Accounts vary regarding when and where Picasso first saw African sculpture. He claimed that his first encounter with African sculpture and masks was in an exhibition late in 1907, after he had finished LES DEMOISELLES. Other artists and writers, including Matisse and Gertrude Stein, told of showing Picasso African sculpture in 1906. His paintings and sculpture of the period certainly show a familiarity with sculpture and masks of the Ivory Coast and the metal-covered figures of the Gabon. By 1909 Picasso had become a serious collector of African art.

In their development of Cubism, Picasso and Braque drew inspiration from the inventive abstractions of African sculpture and the paintings of Cézanne.

Picasso exhibited in the first Surrealist exhibition in Paris in 1925, but he did not sign the group's manifesto. Like the Surrealists, he became increasingly involved with the political unrest in Europe during the 1930s. After a short period of rest and retreat, Picasso produced a series of drawings and paintings that expressed his anguish over the growing violence that led to World War II (see GUERNICA, page 108).

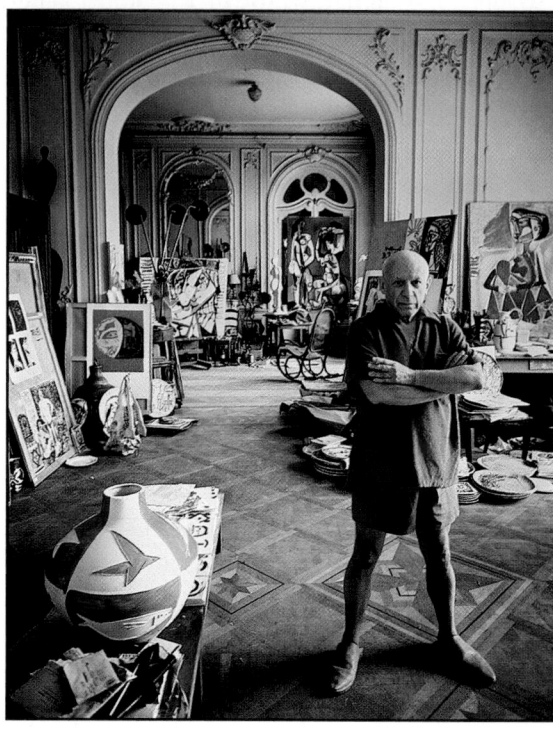

542   PICASSO IN HIS STUDIO AT CANNES. c. 1965.
© Arnold Newman/Getty Images.

Any written biography of Picasso is only a footnote to the autobiographical content of much of his art. In his many variations on the themes of the artist at work and the artist with his model, we recognize that Picasso is commenting on his own experience. Within his images there is the ebb and the flow of Picasso's turbulent love life. Five different women, who shared his life, appear again and again in his art.

His later work included ceramics and huge numbers of prints and drawings in addition to many paintings. Hardworking and prolific until the end of his life, he gave expression to the essential character of his time. In its diversity, Picasso's art relates to most of the twentieth century's art movements. With his prodigious imagination and many changes in style and media, Picasso inspired generations of younger artists.

Picasso's stature in the twentieth century is comparable to Michelangelo's during the Renaissance: both artists lived nearly a century, both became famous early in life, both lived during periods of rapid change, and both were at the forefront of the artistic developments of their times.

TOWARD ABSTRACT SCULPTURE

Early twentieth-century sculpture continued the general shift from naturalistic to abstract art begun in the late nineteenth century. The comparison in Chapter 2 of two works of sculpture, both titled THE KISS (page 34), illustrates the transition from nineteenth- to twentieth-century thinking. Rodin, the leading sculptor of the nineteenth century, created a naturalistic work. Constantin Brancusi produced an abstract interpretation.

A sequence of Brancusi's early work shows his radical break with the past. His SLEEP of 1908 has an appearance similar to Rodin's romantic naturalism. In his SLEEPING MUSE I of 1911, Brancusi simplified the subject as he moved from naturalism to abstraction. THE NEWBORN of 1915 is stripped to essentials. Brancusi said, "Simplicity is not an end in art, but one arrives at simplicity in spite of oneself, in approaching the real sense of things."[5]

Comparisons can be made between Brancusi's work and Cycladic sculpture over four thousand years old. Ancient sculpture from the Cyclades (islands of the Aegean Sea) has a distinctive, highly abstract elegance similar to Brancusi's. Just as the Cubists studied African art, Brancusi spent time in the Louvre studying the collection that included ancient sculpture, such as the CYCLADIC head.

Brancusi shared with other leading Parisian artists an interest in African and other non-Western arts, but the main influence on his sculpture was the folk art of his native Romania and his childhood in a peasant community with a strong woodcarving tradition.

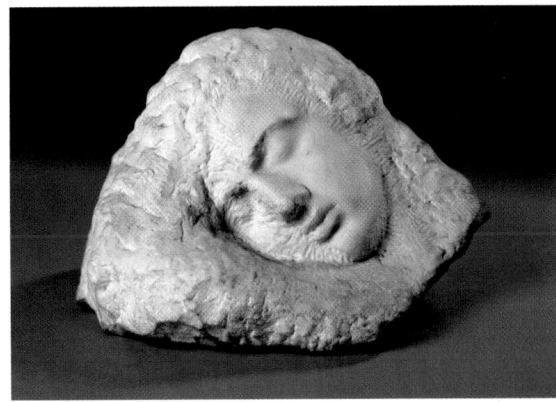

543 Constantin Brancusi.
SLEEP. 1908.
Marble. 6½″ × 12″.
Photograph courtesy Musée National d'Art Moderne, Centre National d'Art et de Culture Georges Pompidou. © VISARTA (The Romanian Visual Arts Copyright Collecting Society), Bucharest, Romania.
©2002 Artists Rights Society (ARS), New York/ADAGP, Paris.

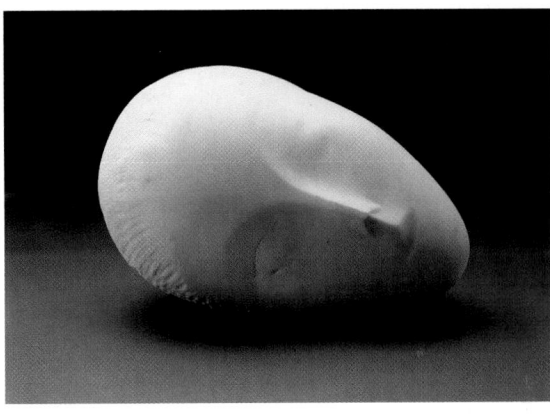

544 Constantin Brancusi.
SLEEPING MUSE I. 1909–1911.
Marble. 6¾″ × 10⅝″ × 8⅜″.
Hirschhorn Museum and Sculpture Garden, Smithsonian Institution, Gift of Joseph H. Hirschhorn (1966). © 2005 Artists Rights Society (ARS), New York/ADAGP, Paris.

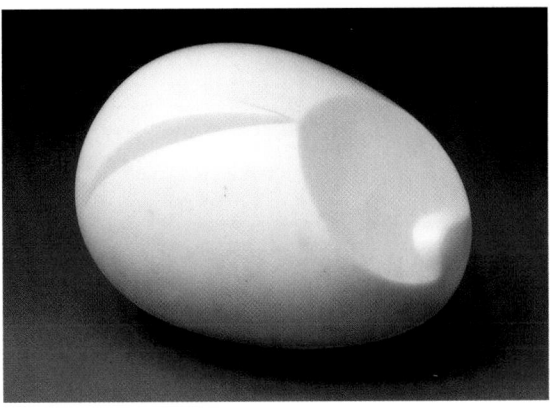

545 Constantin Brancusi.
THE NEWBORN. 1915.
Marble. 5¾″ × 8¼″ × 5⅞″.
Philadelphia Museum of Art. The Louise and Walter Arensberg Collection, 1950. [1950–134–10] © 2005 Artists Rights Society (ARS), New York/ADAGP, Paris.

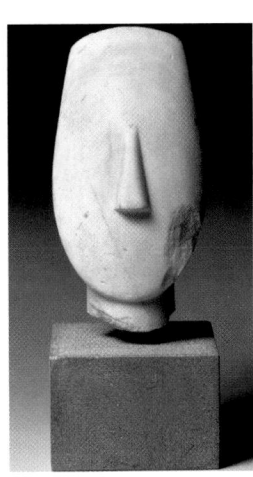

546 CYCLADIC II.
Female statuette.
2700–2300 B.C.E.
Marble. Height 10½″.
Photograph: Herve Lewandowski.
Louvre Museum, Paris, France.
© Reunion des Musées Nationaux.
Art Resource, NY.

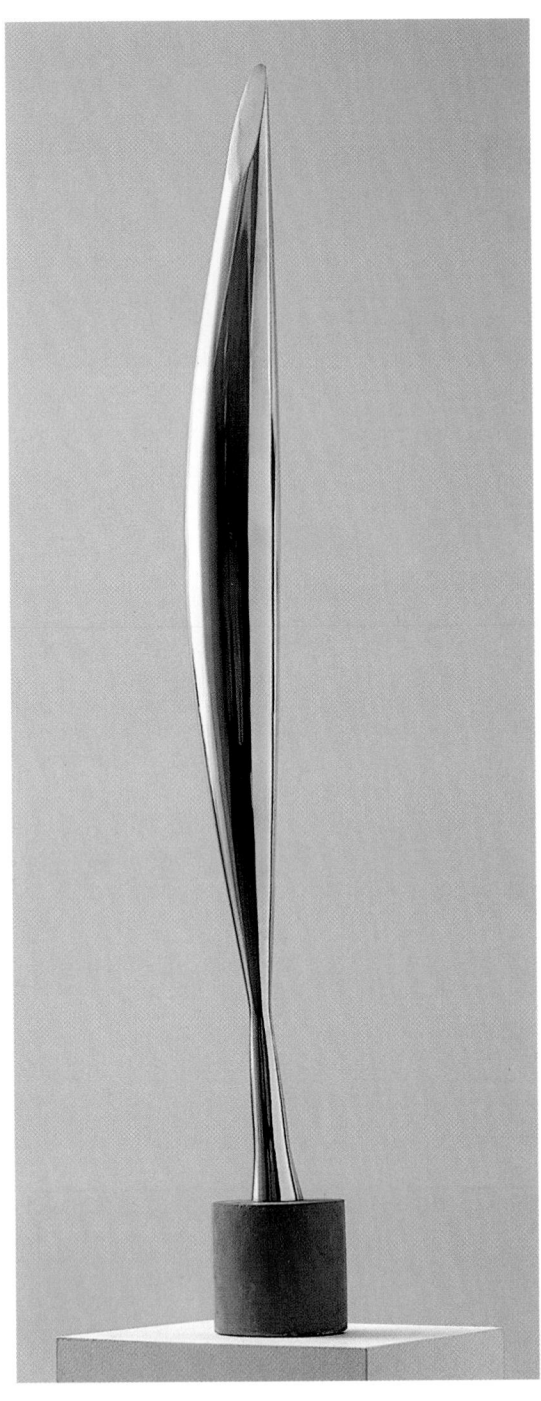

547 Constantin Brancusi.
BIRD IN SPACE. 1928.
Bronze (unique cast). 54″ × 8½″ × 6½″.
The Museum of Modern Art, NY. Licensed by Scala-Art Resource, NY.
© 2005 Artists Rights Society (ARS), NY/ADAGP, Paris.

Brancusi sought to go beyond the surface embellishments that had dominated European sculpture since the Gothic period and to make viewers conscious of form. He brought about a revival of carving. Brancusi achieved expressive strength by carefully reducing forms to their essence. As a result, his sculptures invite contemplation.

In BIRD IN SPACE, Brancusi transformed inert mass into an elegant, uplifting form. The implied soaring motion of the "bird" embodies the idea of flight. The highly reflective polish given to the bronze surface adds considerably to the form's weightless quality. Brancusi started working on this visual concept about a decade after the Wright brothers initiated the age of human flight, but long before the world was filled with streamlined aircraft, cars, pens, and telephones. Brancusi said, "All my life I have sought the essence of flight. Don't look for mysteries. I give you pure joy."[6]

THE MODERN SPIRIT IN AMERICA

As Picasso and Braque took the steps that led to Cubism, American photographer Alfred Stieglitz was also reconsidering the geometry of design on the picture plane. When Picasso saw Stieglitz's photograph THE STEERAGE, he said, "This photographer is working in the same spirit as I am."[7]

THE STEERAGE looked "chopped up" to many people. Some of the artist's friends felt that it should have been two photographs rather than one. Stieglitz, however, saw the complex scene as a pattern of interacting forces of light, shade, shape, and direction. Aboard a ship headed for Europe, he saw the composition of this photograph as "a round straw hat, the funnel leaning left, the stairway leaning right, the white drawbridge with its railings made of circular chains, white suspenders crossing on the back of a man on the steerage below, round shapes of iron machinery, a mast cutting into the sky, making a triangular shape. . . . I saw a picture of shapes and underlying that the feeling I had about life."[8] He rushed to his cabin to get his camera, hoping the relationships would not change. Nothing had shifted, and he made the photograph he considered his best.

Stieglitz made major contributions toward establishing photography as an art of comparable importance to traditional media (see page 148 for another work). He also played a key role in introducing the new European painting and sculpture to Americans. In 1907, he opened a gallery in New York and began showing the work of the most progressive European artists, including photographers. He was the first in America to show works by Cézanne, Matisse, Brancusi, Picasso, and Braque. Following the exhibition of art by these European pioneers, Stieglitz began to show work by those who would become leading American artists, including Georgia O'Keeffe (see biography on page 37).

O'Keeffe's work from the time of World War I was innovative, consisting mostly of abstractions based on nature. In 1917, while teaching in the Texas Panhandle, she took frequent walks in the lonely, windswept prairie. Finding its emptiness immensely stimulating, she made a series of pioneering abstract watercolors entitled EVENING STAR NO. VI, based on her sightings of the planet Venus in the darkening sky. Venus is the small unpainted circle that the yellow orb encloses, and this empty spot seems to radiate ever wider sweeps of rich, saturated

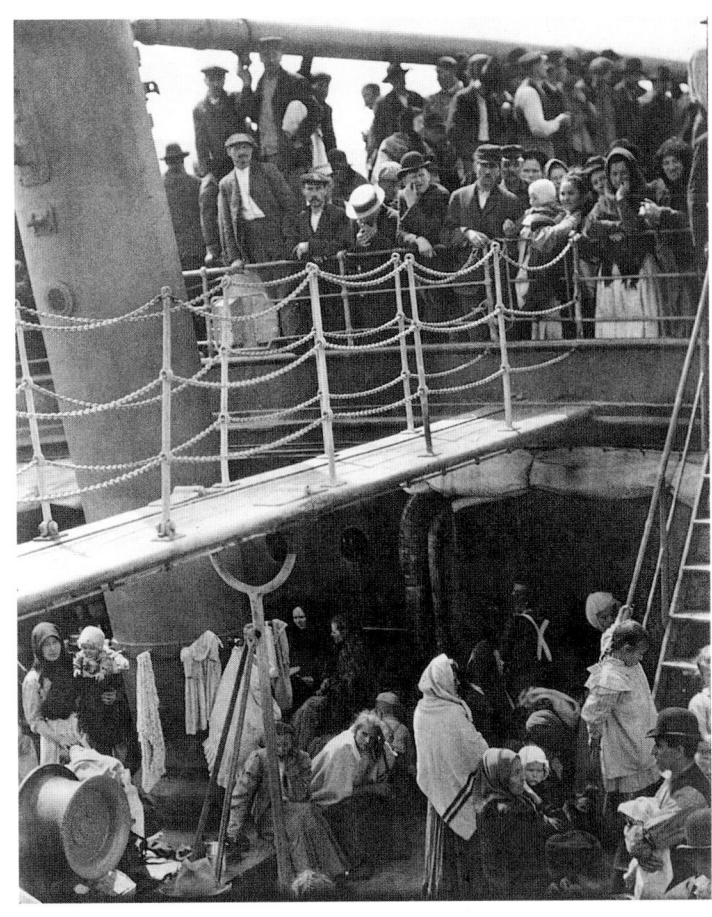

548 Alfred Stieglitz.
THE STEERAGE. 1907.
From *Camera Work*, New York, No. 34, October 1911. Photogravure. 7¾″ × 6½″.
The Museum of Modern Art, NY. Licensed by Scala-Art Resource, NY.
Gift of Alfred Stieglitz.
Copy Print © 1999 The Museum of Modern Art, New York.

549 Georgia O'Keeffe.
EVENING STAR NO. VI. 1917.
Watercolor on cream paper.
8⅞″ × 12″.
Photograph: Malcom Varon 2001. The Georgia O'Keeffe Museum, Santa Fe, New Mexico.
Gift of the Bartlett Foundation.

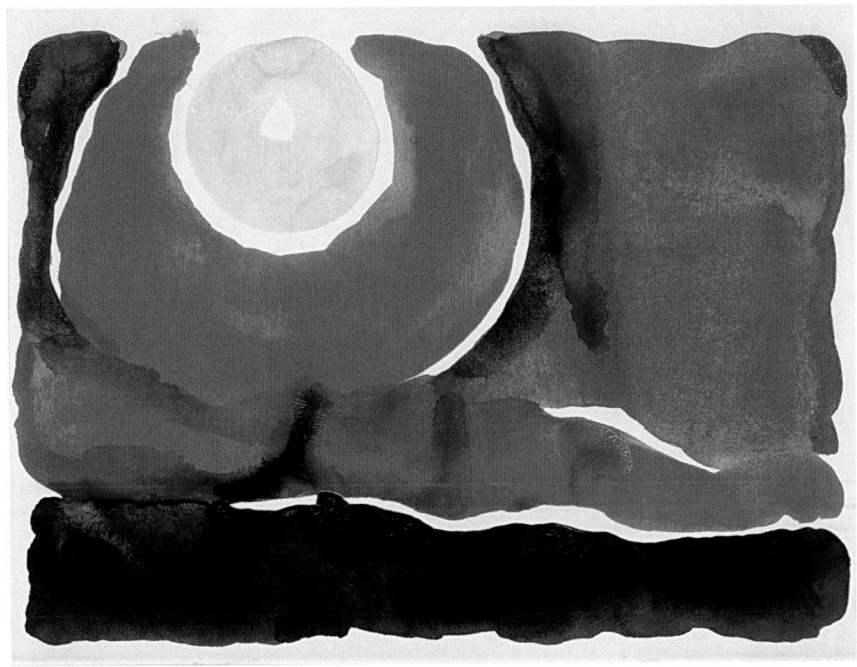

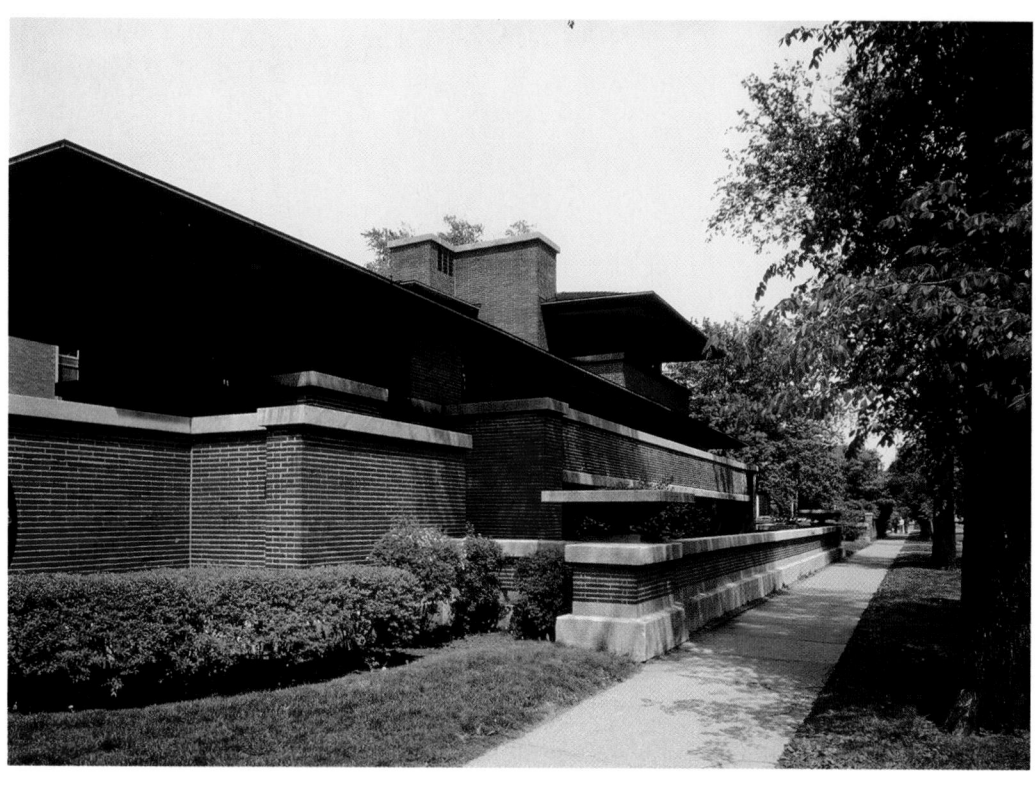

color. The "bigness" of the Texas landscape inspired her; she wrote to a friend, "It is absurd how much I love this country."

Between 1905 and 1910, architects began to challenge traditional concepts of form in space just as painters and sculptors had done. While Cubism was developing in painting, leading American architect Frank Lloyd Wright was designing "prairie houses," in which he often omitted or minimized walls between living and dining rooms and between interior and exterior spaces. Wright's concept of open plans has changed the way people design living spaces. In many contemporary homes, kitchen, dining room, and living room now join in one continuous space, and indoors often intermingles with outdoors.

In his ROBIE HOUSE of 1909, a striking cantilevered roof reaches out and unifies a fluid design of asymmetrically interconnected spaces. Through Wright's influence, the open flow of spaces became a major feature of contemporary architecture. To get a feeling of how far ahead of his time Wright was, imagine the incongruity of a new 1909 automobile that could have been parked in front of the

ROBIE HOUSE the year it was completed. (For more on Frank Lloyd Wright and his architecture, see pages 225–227.)

The American public had its first extensive look at leading developments in European art during the Armory Show, held in New York in 1913. In this show of over sixteen hundred works, American artists were able to see key works by Impressionists, Post-Impressionists, and Fauves—particularly Matisse, who was much maligned by critics. Also shown were paintings by Picasso and Braque, and sculpture by Brancusi. As a result, Cubism and other forms of abstract art spread to America.

FUTURISM AND THE CELEBRATION OF MOTION

The Italian Futurists were among the many artists who gained their initial inspiration from Cubism. To the shifting planes and multiple vantage points of Cubism, Futurists such as Giacomo Balla and Umberto Boccioni added a sense of speed and motion and a celebration of the machine.

By multiplying the image of a moving object, Futurists expanded the Cubist concepts of simultaneity of vision and metamorphosis. In 1909, the poet Filippo Tommaso Marinetti proclaimed in the *Initial Manifesto of Futurism*: "the world's splendor has been enriched by a new beauty; the beauty of speed . . . a roaring motorcar . . . is more beautiful than the Victory of Samothrace."[9]

The Futurists translated the speed of modern life into works that captured the dynamic energy of the new century. Giacomo Balla intended his work ABSTRACT SPEED—THE CAR HAS PASSED to depict the rushing air and dynamic feeling of a vehicle passing. This "roaring motorcar" is passing at about 35 miles an hour, but at that time this was the pinnacle of speed.

An abstract sculpture of a striding figure climaxed a series of Umberto Boccioni's drawings, paintings, and sculpture. Boccioni insisted that sculpture should be released from its usual confining outer surfaces in order to open up and fuse the work with the space surrounding it. In UNIQUE FORMS OF CONTINUITY IN SPACE, muscular forms seem to leap outward in flamelike bursts of energy. During this period, the human experience of motion, time, and space was transformed by the development of the automobile, the airplane, and the movies. Futurist imagery reflects this exciting period of change.

French artist Marcel Duchamp, working independently of the Futurists, brought the dimension of motion to Cubism. His NUDE DESCENDING A STAIR-CASE, NO. 2 (on the following page) was influenced by stroboscopic photography, in which sequential camera images show movement by freezing successive instants (see page 154 for an example).

Through sequential, diagonally placed, abstract references to the figure, the painting presents the movement of a body through space, seen all at once, in a single rhythmic progression. Our sense of gravity intensifies the overall feeling of motion. When the painting was displayed at the Armory Show in New York in 1913, it caused cries of dismay and was seen

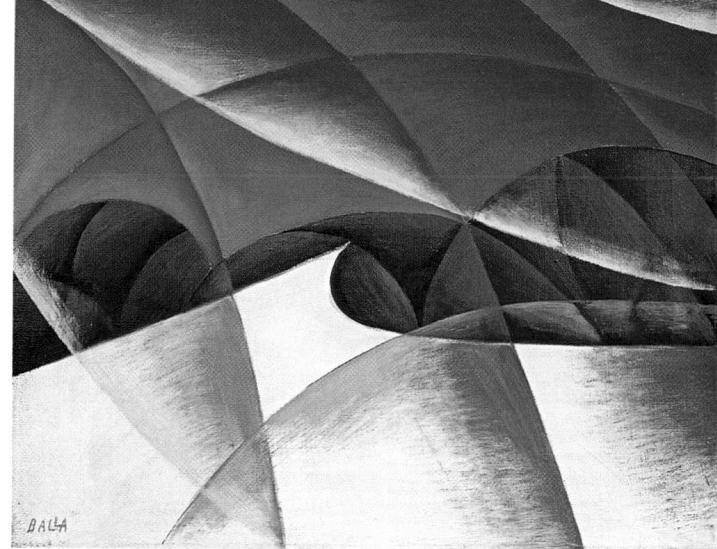

551 Giacomo Balla.
ABSTRACT SPEED—THE CAR HAS PASSED. 1913.
Oil on canvas. 19¾" × 25¼".
© Tate Gallery, London. Art Resource, NY.
© 2005 Artists Rights Society (ARS), NY/SIAE, Rome.

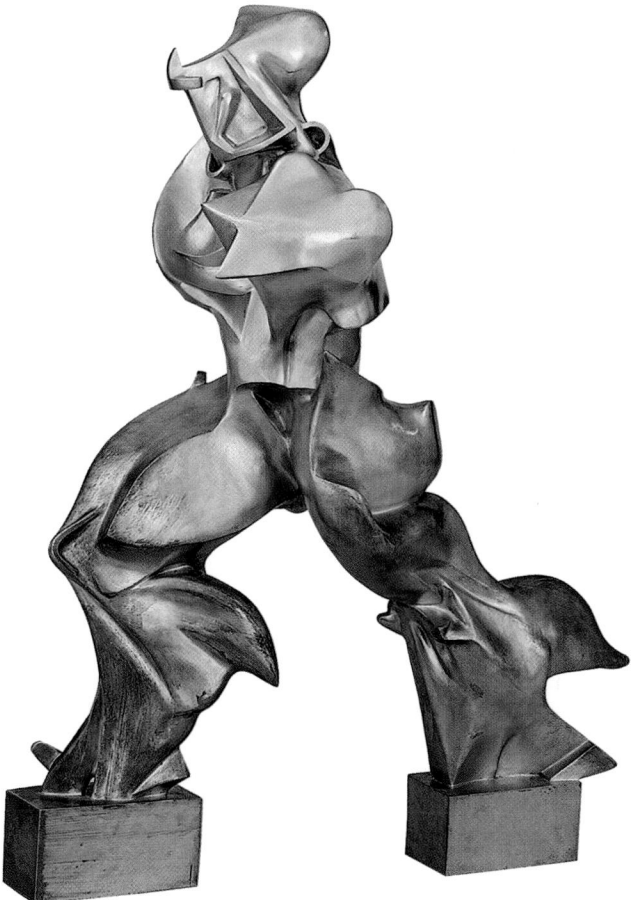

552 Umberto Boccioni.
UNIQUE FORMS OF CONTINUITY IN SPACE. 1913.
Bronze (cast in 1931). 43⅞" × 34⅞" × 15¾"
The Museum of Modern Art, NY. Licensed by Scala-Art Resource, NY.
Acquired through the Lillie P. Bliss Bequest.
Photograph © 2002 The Museum of Modern Art, New York.

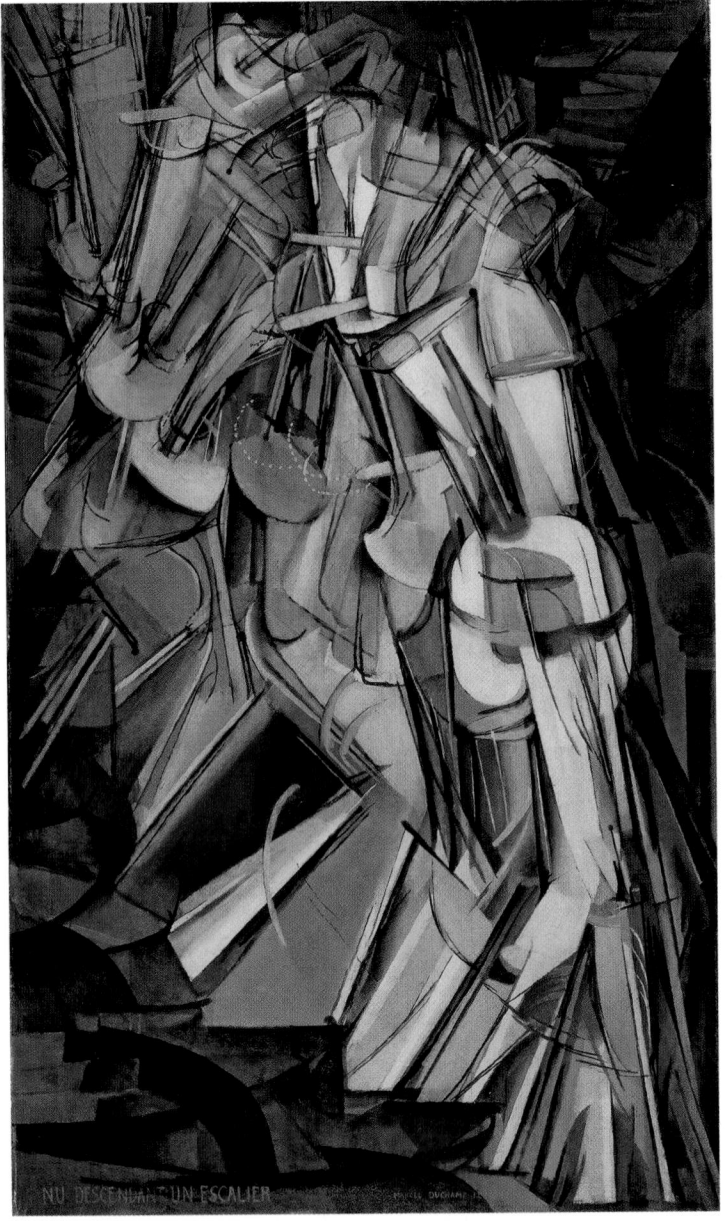

NU DESCENDANT UN ESCALIER   MARCEL DUCHAMP

553 Marcel Duchamp.
NUDE DESCENDING A STAIRCASE, NO. 2. 1912.
Oil on canvas. 58″ × 35″.
Philadelphia Museum of Art. The Louise and Walter Arensberg Collection.
1950–134–59. Photo by Graydon Wood, 1994.
© 2002 Artists Rights Society (ARS), NY. ADAGP, Paris.
Estate of Marcel Duchamp.

554 Sonia Delaunay.
BAL BULLIER. 1913.
Oil on mattress ticking. 38⅛″ × 12′8″.
Musee National d'Art Moderne. Centre National d'Art et de Culture. Collections
du Centre Georges Pompidou. Photograph: Philippe Migeat/Reunion de Musees
Nationaux/Art Resource, NY.

as the ultimate Cubist madness. The painting, once described as "an explosion in a shingle factory," has remained an inspiration to artists who use repetition and rhythm to express motion.

Sonia Delaunay expressed motion in her paintings through color contrasts. Her large work BAL BULLIER is an interpretation of couples moving about on the floor of one of Paris's leading nightclubs of the time. We see Cubist influence in the work, as it is composed of flat shapes that overlap in shallow space. But the added push and pull of contrasting color contributes both depth and motion to the composition. Stretching a canvas twelve feet across proved difficult, so the artist used mattress ticking.

Delaunay was an early crusader for the integration of Modern art into everyday things. Even as she painted, she made bookbindings, embroideries, textiles, and fashions that included ideas from the latest Modern art movements. She started her own clothing design studio in 1922, where she specialized in what she called Simultaneous Dresses. Not for many years would such ideas take hold in the mass market.

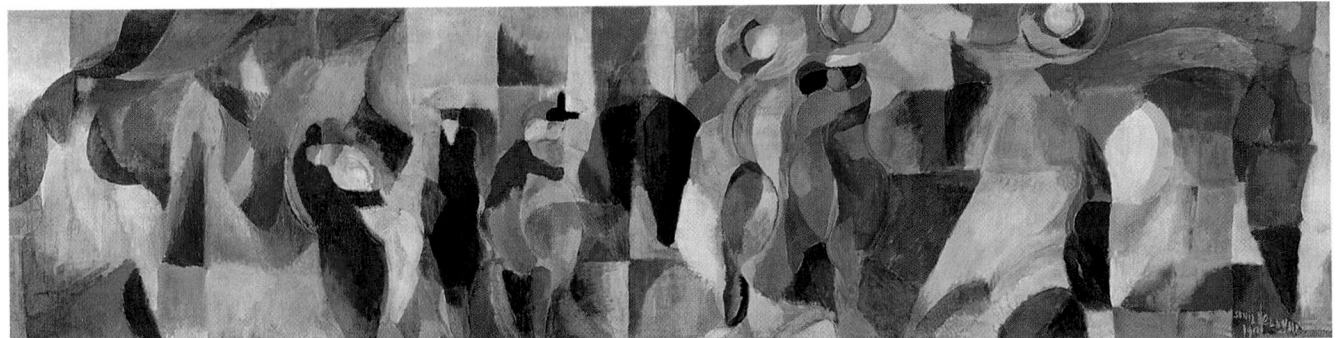

BETWEEN WORLD WARS

In 1914, enthusiasm for grand patriotic solutions to international tensions led citizens of many countries into World War I, an intense and protracted conflict that involved most European countries and eventually the United States. But the war was far more devastating than the people of the time expected: Over ten million were killed and twice that number wounded. The promise of a whole new generation was lost in the world's first experience with mechanized mass killing.

As a result of the war, the political and cultural landscape was changed forever. The war set the stage for the Russian Revolution and sowed grievances that the Nazis of Germany and the Fascists of Italy later exploited. Governments assumed new powers to mobilize people and material, to dictate economic life, to censor public expression, and, by controlling information, to manipulate the way people thought. Dissent was denounced as unpatriotic.

Writers, photographers, and artists were prevented by governments and the self-censoring press from communicating the horror of the war. Many writers and artists produced propaganda, remained silent, or fought in the war. A great many were killed.

It was not until after the war had ended that those artists and writers who survived were able to express their perceptions of the catastrophe that shaped the world. Many sensitive people either were stifled by cynicism or sought relief in idealistic schemes for reform.

During the postwar era, a wide gap opened between the older generation who accepted the propaganda and the young who had been in the trenches, between the official government line and the reality that informed people understood. In the arts, several movements emerged to protest the insanity and to mend the gulf between idealism and actuality.

DADA

Dada began in protest against the horrors of World War I as an assault on corrupt values by an international group of young writers and artists. Those who began the movement in Zurich chose the ambiguous word *Dada* as their rallying cry. One member of the group assumed that it referred to *da, da*, Slavic for "yes, yes." The two-syllable word was well suited for expressing the essence of what was an attitude, not a style. In the eyes of the Dadaists, the destructive absurdity of war was caused by traditional, narrow-minded values, which they set out to overturn. According to artist Marcel Janco:

Dada was not a school of artists, but an alarm signal against declining values, routine, and speculation, a desperate appeal on behalf of all forms of art, for a creative basis on which to build a new and universal consciousness of art.[1]

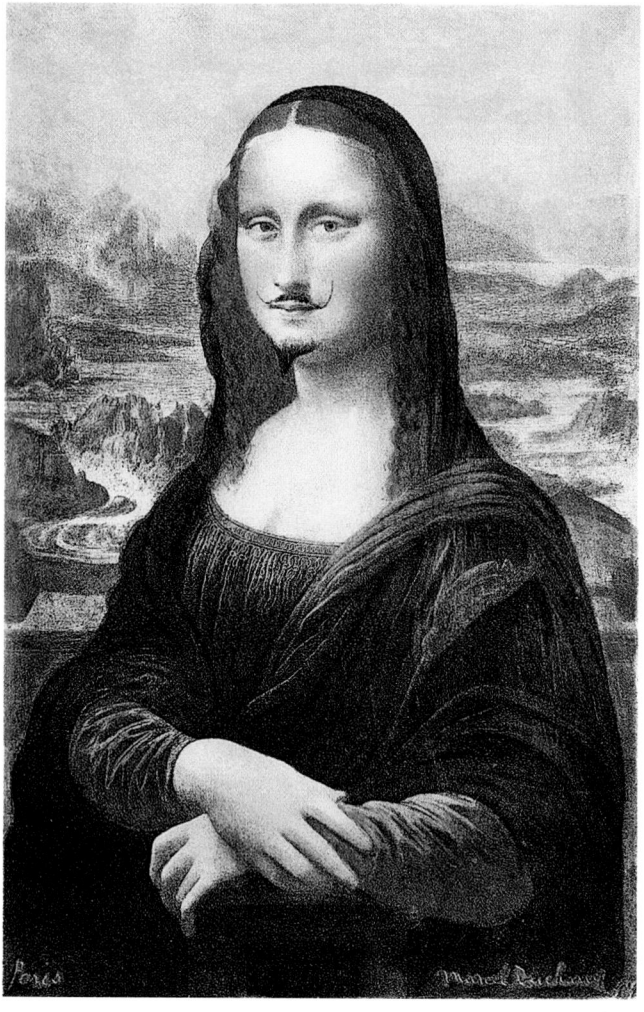

555 Marcel Duchamp.
L.H.O.O.Q. 1919.
Pencil on reproduction of Leonardo's MONA LISA. 7¾" × 4¾".
Philadelphia Museum of Art: Louise and Walter Arensburg Collection.
© 2002 Artists Rights Society (ARS) NY/ADAGP, Paris/Estate of Marcel Duchamp.

French artist and poet Jean Arp said:

While the thunder of guns rolled in the distance, we sang, painted, glued, and composed for all our worth. We are seeking an art that would heal mankind from the madness of the age.[2]

The insanity of the war proved to Dadaists that European culture had lost its way. To make a new beginning, the Dadaists rejected most moral,

social, political, and aesthetic values. They thought it was pointless to try to find order and meaning in a world in which so-called rational behavior had produced only chaos and destruction. They sought to shock art viewers into seeing the absurdity of the Western world's social and political situation.

The Dadaists protested, in part, through play and spontaneity. Their literature, art, and staged events were often based on chance rather than premeditation. Poets shouted words at random; artists joined elements in startling, irrational combinations.

For Marcel Duchamp, mechanically produced things were a reservoir of unselfconscious art objects. In his view, a reproduction of the MONA LISA was a ready-made object, in the same class as bicycle wheels, kitchen stools, and snow shovels. L.H.O.O.Q. is an "assisted readymade" by Duchamp, expressing his view that art had become simply a precious commodity. He poked fun with his "corrections," a penciled moustache and goatee and a new title. The unusual title is a vulgar pun in French, comprehensible to those who can hear the sentence in the sound of the letters pronounced in French. Translated into English, it reads, "She has a hot tail." Duchamp's outrageous irreverence toward one of the world's most revered paintings was an attempt to shake people out of their unthinking acceptance of dominant values.

Man Ray, an American, was a friend of Duchamp. His Dada works include paintings, photographs, and assembled objects. In 1921, in Paris, Man Ray saw an iron displayed in front of a shop selling housewares. He purchased the iron, a box of tacks, and a tube of glue. After gluing a row of tacks to the smooth surface of the iron, he titled his assemblage THE GIFT—thus creating an ironic contradiction.

One memorable Dada sculpture, Raoul Hausmann's THE SPIRIT OF OUR TIME, continues to express a truth about our culture. We would like to know ourselves, yet we succumb to the playthings of our technology and ignore the sound of silence. Have the artifacts of our mass production turned us into hollow-headed robots who simply receive and transmit information and are unable to think

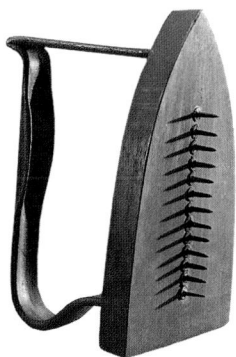

556 Man Ray.
CADEAU (THE GIFT). c. 1958.
Replica of 1921 original. Painted flatiron thirteen tacks.
6⅛″ × 3⅝″ × 4½″.
The Museum of Modern Art, NY. Licensed by Scala-Art Resource, NY. James Thrall
Soby Fund. Photograph © 2001 The Museum of Modern Art, NY.
© 2002 Man Ray Trust. Artists Rights Society (ARS), NY/ADAGP, Paris.

557 Raoul Hausmann .
THE SPIRIT OF OUR TIME. 1919.
Mixed media. Height 12¾″.
Musée National d'Art Modern, Georges Pompidou Centre, Paris.
© Artists Rights Society (ARS), NY/ADAGP, Paris.
© CNAC/MNAM/Dist. Reunion de Musées Nationaux. Art Resource, NY.

558 Hannah Höch.
THE MULTI-MILLIONAIRE. 1923.
Photomontage. 14″ × 12″.
© 2002 Artists Rights Society (ARS), NY. VG Bild-Kunst, Bonn.

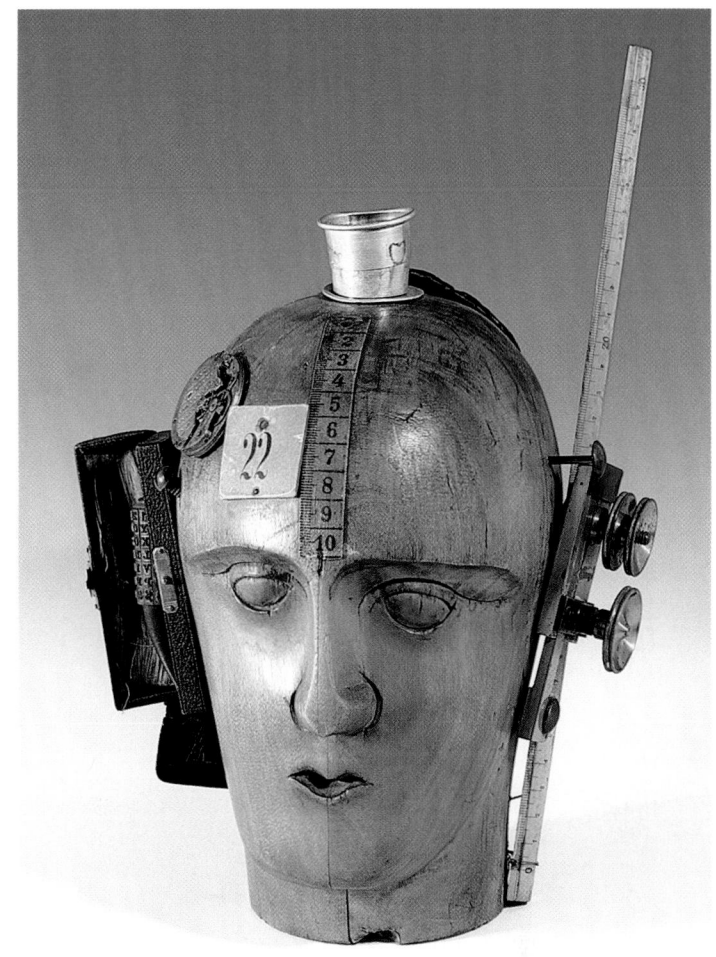

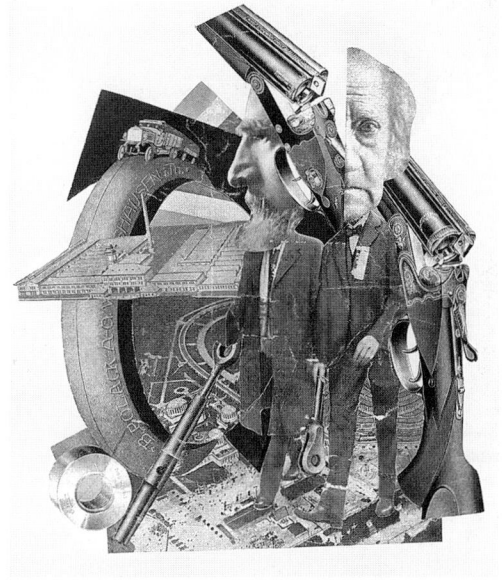

for ourselves? Hausmann seems to have anticipated the world of artificial intelligence and the ubiquitous headset radios and mp3 players.

Dadaists expanded on the Cubist idea of collage with *photomontage*, in which parts of photographs are combined in thought-provoking ways. In THE MULTI-MILLIONAIRE, by Dadaist Hannah Höch, industrial-age man stands as a fractured giant among the things he has produced.

Some Dadaists maintained that "Art is dead." By this they meant that it was useless to try to create beauty in a world that could destroy itself. They often intended to be anti-aesthetic. Ironically, they created a new aesthetic that had lasting influence on the twentieth century.

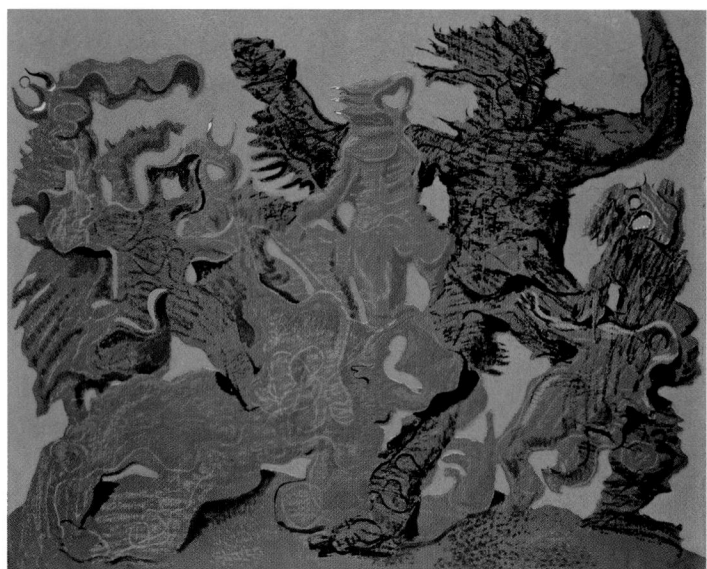

559 Max Ernst.
THE HORDE. 1927.
Oil on canvas. 45″ × 57½″.
Stedelijk Museum, Amsterdam.

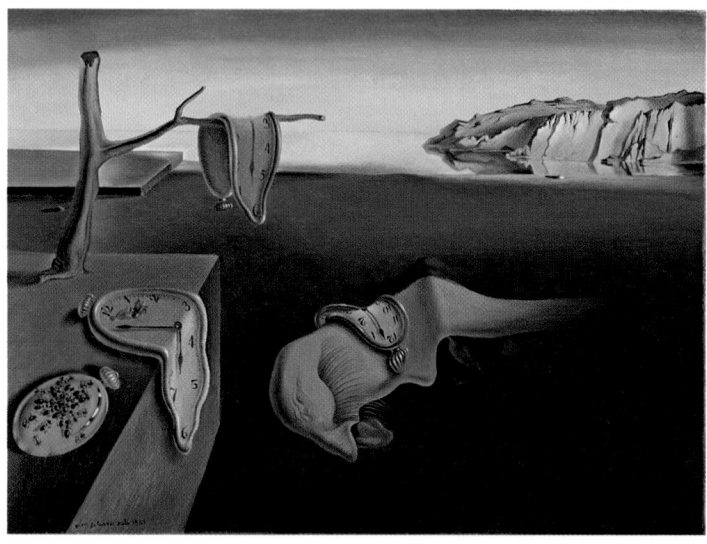

560 Salvador Dalí.
THE PERSISTENCE OF MEMORY. 1931.
Oil on canvas. 9½″ × 13″.
The Museum of Modern Art, NY. Licensed by Scala-Art Resource, NY. Anonymous gift.
Photograph © 2002 The Museum of Modern Art, New York.
© 2002 Kingdom of Spain, Gala-Salvador Dalí Foundation/Artists Rights Society (ARS), NY.

SURREALISM

In the 1920s, a group of writers and painters gathered to proclaim the omnipotence of the unconscious mind, thought to be a deeper reality than the conscious mind. Their goal was to make visible the imagery of the unconscious. They were indebted to the shocking irrationality of Dadaism, and they also drew heavily on the new psychology of Sigmund Freud.

The new movement, *Surrealism*, was officially launched in Paris in 1924 with the publication of its first manifesto, written by poet-painter André Breton. In it he defined the movement's purpose as:

the future resolution of these two states, dream and reality, which are seemingly so contradictory, into a kind of absolute reality, a surreality, if one may so speak.[3]

One of the first converts to the movement was the former Dadaist Max Ernst, who had fought in the war and was still haunted by its nightmares. To allow freer play to fantasy, he laid his canvases over textured surfaces such as asphalt pavement. In this way he could be surprised by the patterns that emerged for fertilization in his imagination. In the 1927 work THE HORDE, we see a gaggle of silhouetted monsters who tumble over one another in a violent scene. The artist's combat experience in World War I most likely influenced the chaotic nature of this work.

The Spanish artist Salvador Dalí dealt more directly with his nightmares. He simply drew them and painted them in a highly illusionistic fashion based on academic techniques. Dalí's THE PERSISTENCE OF MEMORY evokes the eerie quality of some dreams. Mechanical time wilts in a deserted landscape of infinite space. The warped, headlike image in the foreground may be the last remnant of a vanished humanity. It may also be a self-portrait, complete with protruding tongue.

Dalí's illusionary deep space and representational techniques create near-photographic dream

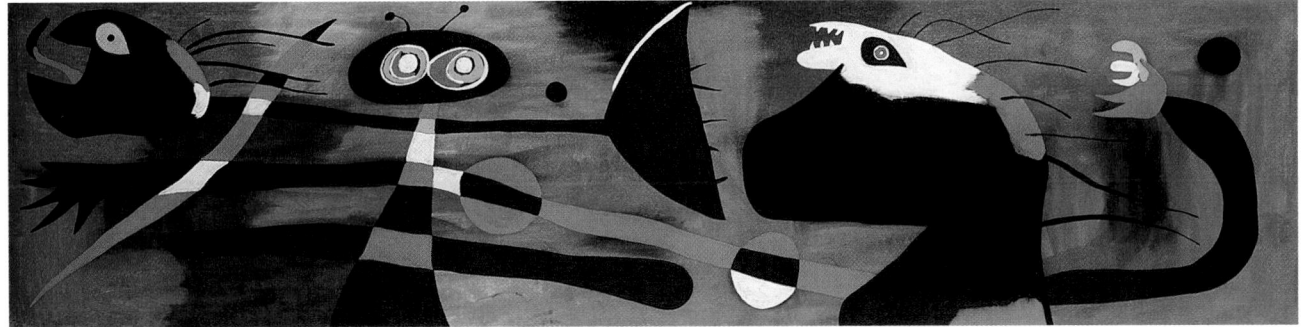

561 Joan Miró.
WOMAN HAUNTED BY THE PASSAGE OF THE DRAGONFLY, BIRD OF BAD OMEN. 1938.
Oil on canvas. 31½″ × 124″.
The Toledo Museum of Art, Toledo, Ohio. Purchased with funds from the Libbey Endowment.
Gift of Edward Drummond Libbey. 1986.25 © 2002 Artists Rights Society (ARS), NY. ADAGP, Paris.

images that make the impossible seem believable. The startling juxtaposition of unrelated objects creates a nightmarish sense of a superreality beyond the everyday world. This approach has been called Representational Surrealism. In contrast, Joan Miró's Abstract Surrealism provides suggestive elements that give the widest possible play to the viewer's imagination, and emphasize color and design rather than storytelling content.

To probe into the unconscious, Miró and others used automatic processes, sometimes called *automatism*, in which chance was a key factor. With the adoption of spontaneous and "automatic" methods, the Surrealists sought to expand consciousness by transcending limits of rational thought.

Miró's evocative paintings often depict imaginary creatures. He made them by scribbling on the canvas and then examining the results to see what the shapes suggested. The bold, organic shapes in WOMAN HAUNTED BY THE PASSAGE OF THE DRAGONFLY, BIRD OF BAD OMEN are typical of his mature work. The wild, tormented quality, however, is unusual for Miró and reflects his reaction to the times. Miró pointed out that this painting was done at the time of the Munich crisis that helped precipitate World War II. Even though there is a sense of terror here, Miró's underlying playful optimism is apparent. He loved the art of children so much that he tried to paint like one.

Belgian Surrealist René Magritte used an illogical form of realism, similar to Dalí's in surface appearance but quite different in content. Magritte's paintings engage the viewer in mind-teasing mystery and playful humor. Everything depicted in PORTRAIT (on the following page) is ordinary; the impact comes from the unsettling placement of an eye looking back at us from a plate of ham. Perhaps his best-known work is THE TREASON OF IMAGES, pictured on page 30.

EXPANDING ON CUBISM

Cubism has been one of the most influential Modern art movements. Beginning in Paris, it spread to many parts of the world. This style makes possible many ambiguities between presence and absence, representation and abstraction, figure and ground. It suggests meanings that are relative and contingent. Far from presenting the world as stable and predictable, Cubism suggests constant change and evolution. An art historian wrote, "By devaluing subject matter, or by monumentalizing simple,

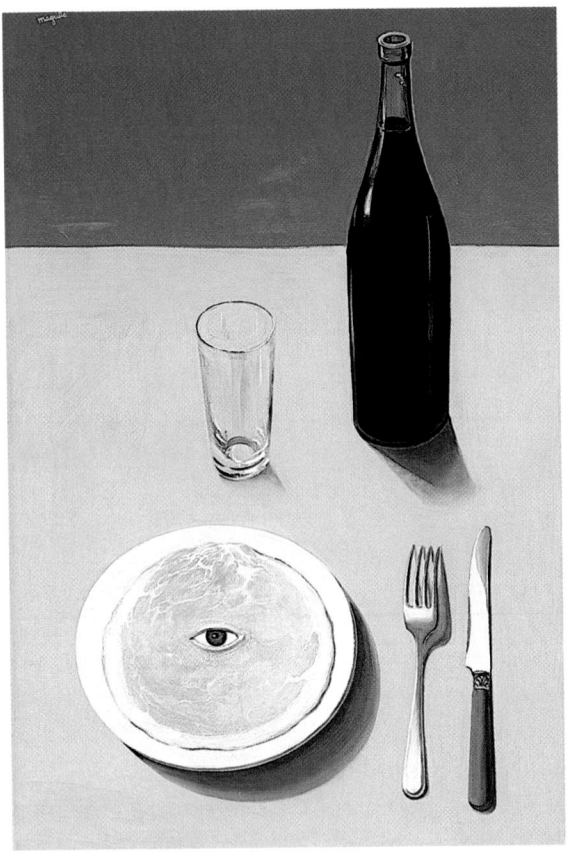

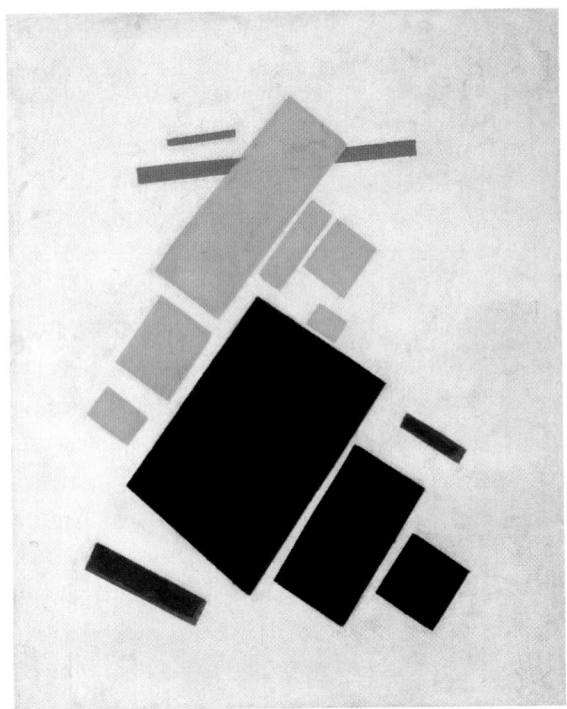

562 René Magritte.
PORTRAIT. 1935.
Oil on canvas. 28⅞″ × 19⅞″.
The Museum of Modern Art, NY. Licensed by Scala-Art Resource, NY.
Gift of Mrs. Kay Sage Tanguy.
Photograph: © 2002 The Museum of Modern Art, NY. © 2002 C. Herscovici,
Brussels. Artists Rights Society (ARS), NY.

563 Kazimir Malevich.
SUPREMATIST COMPOSITION: AIRPLANE FLYING. 1915.
(dated 1914).
Oil on canvas. 22⅞″ × 19″.
The Museum of Modern Art, NY. Licensed by Scala-Art Resource, NY. Acquisition
confirmed in 1999 by agreement with the Estate of Kazimir Malevich and made
possible with funds from the Mrs. John Hay Whitney Bequest (by exchange).
Photograph © 2002 The Museum of Modern Art.

personal themes, and by allowing mass and void to elide, the Cubists gave effect to the flux and paradox of modern life and the relativity of its values."[4] Thus, Cubism makes visible some important characteristics of modern life.

Russian artists took Cubism in the direction of complete abstraction. A leader there was Kazimir Malevich, who branded his style Suprematism. His painting SUPREMATIST COMPOSITION: AIRPLANE FLYING shows in its title that the artist was familiar with Futurism: its subject is a speeding modern airplane. Yet Malevich so simplified the Cubist pictorial language that we are left with a succession of flat irregular rectangles against a pure background.

Malevich believed that shapes and colors in a painting always communicate, no matter what the subject of the work. Ideally, he thought, art should not need subject matter. This is why he named his movement Suprematism, because he wanted to focus on the supremacy of shape and color in art over external stimuli. He shared some points of view with his fellow Russian Wassily Kandinsky, whom he knew (see page 387). But while Kandinsky (who worked in Germany) painted brash, expressive works, Malevich's constant urge to simplify makes him the more radical painter.

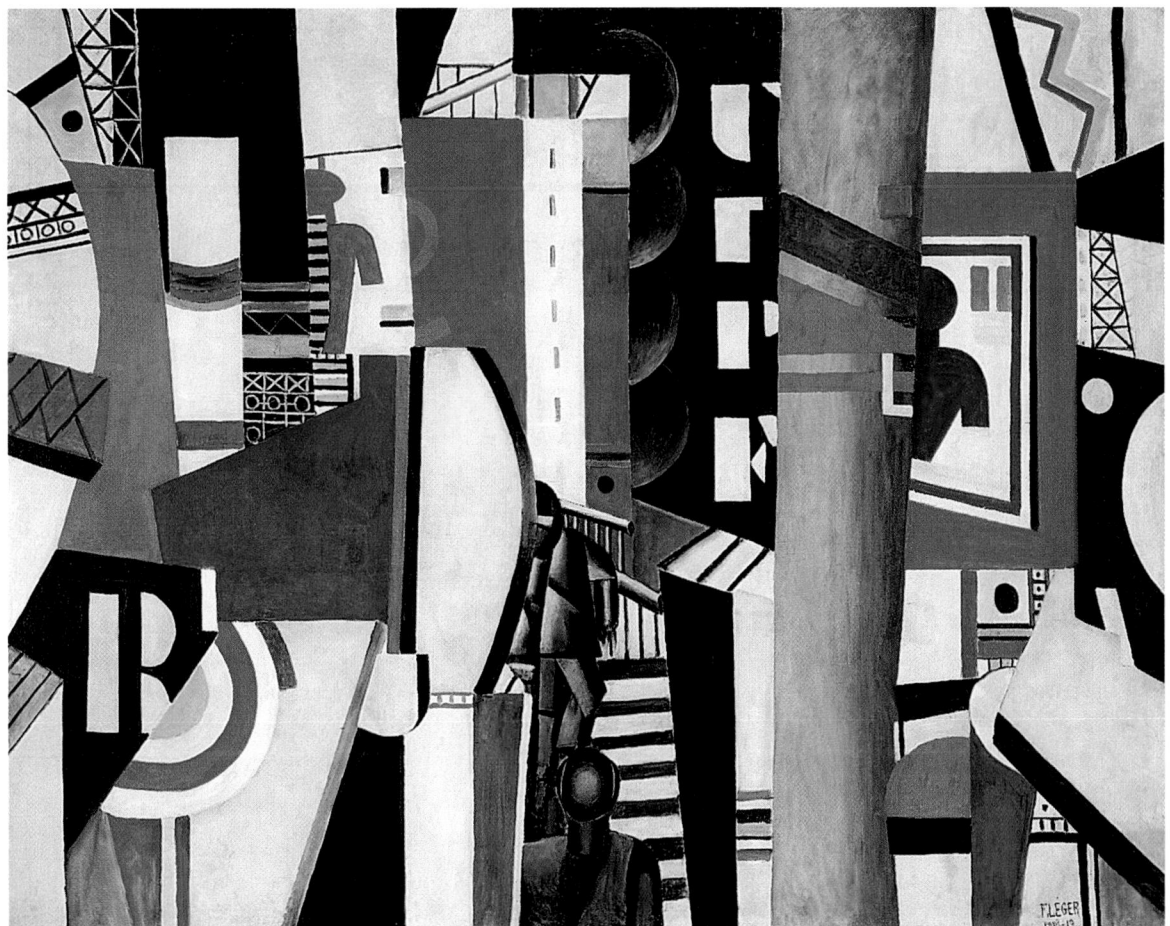

564 Fernand Léger.
THE CITY. 1919.
Oil on canvas. 91″ × 177½″.
Philadelphia Museum of Art. A. E. Gallatin Collection, 1952-61-58.
© 2002 Artists Rights Society (ARS), NY. ADAGP, Paris.

In his large painting THE CITY, Fernand Léger crushed jagged shapes together, collapsing space in a composition reminiscent of a Cubist portrait or still life. The forms in his paintings look machine-made, rounded and tubular; this is in keeping with the urban bustle that is the work's subject.

Léger soon took Cubist composition into film when he made BALLET MECANIQUE (on the following page), a 17-minute cinematic collage in which churning machines alternate with a swinging pendulum, a smiling woman, and shifting geometric shapes. Some-times these forms are distorted with a kaleidoscopic mirror, which mashes them up and flattens them in the manner of a Cubist still life. Léger intended the film to have a score by the American George Antheil, but practicalities prevented this. (Antheil composed an unforgettably riotous work for seventeen player pianos, percussion, and a siren, but because it ran twice as long as the film, the two could not be syn-chronized.) Léger's film follows no obvious logic, but it seems to argue that machines and humans are about equally rhythmic if not equally graceful.

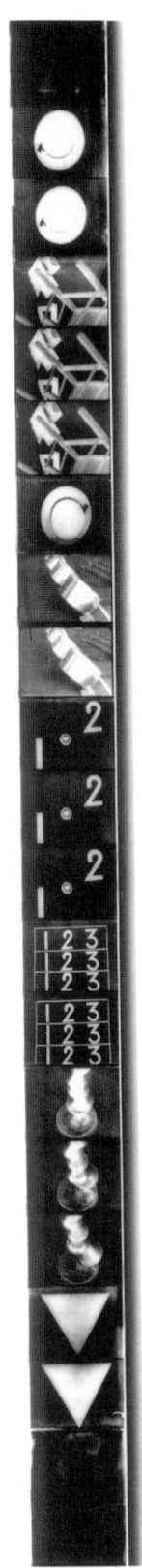

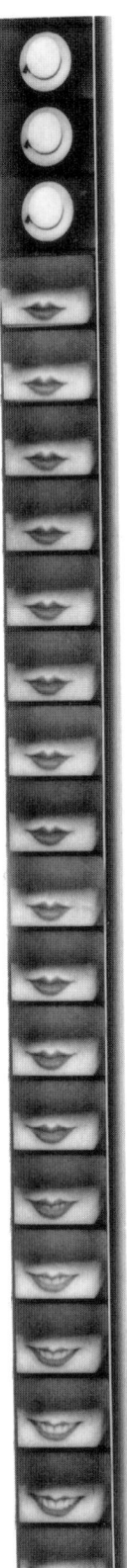

565 Fernand Léger.
BALLET MECANIQUE. 1924.
Film.

BUILDING A NEW SOCIETY

Several art movements that emerged between the wars had the goal of improving the world somehow. Surrealists, for example, hoped to liberate human consciousness. Pioneer abstractionists felt that the nonrepresentational language of form they were creating would provide an ideal basis for the utopian society they sought. Constructivism, in Russia, focused on developing a new visual language for a new industrial age. De Stijl, in Holland, advocated the use of basic forms, particularly rectangles, horizontals, and verticals. Both movements spread throughout Europe and strongly influenced many art forms.

Constructivism

Constructivism was a revolutionary sculptural movement that began in Russia, inspired in part by abstraction of Malevich and others. Seeking to create art that was relevant to modern life in form, materials, and content, Constructivists made the first nonrepresentational constructions out of such modern materials as plastic and electroplated metal.

The Constructivists were in concert with the Cubists in rejecting the traditional view of sculpture as a static volume defined by mass and created by modeling and carving. The name of the movement came from their preference for constructing planar and linear forms that suggested a dynamic quality and, whenever possible, contained moving elements. Mass had previously been the main element in sculpture; with the Constructivists, space became primary.

Vladimir Tatlin's MODEL FOR MONUMENT TO THE THIRD INTERNATIONAL embodies many Constructivist ideas. Indebted about equally to Cubist sculpture and to the Eiffel Tower, this daring structure was intended to be 1,300 feet high. Built primarily of steel and glass, with its structure on the outside, it was to house inside it three office buildings that would rotate at varying speeds: once an hour, a day, and a month. The double spiral ramps symbolized the ascent of humanity to a new stage of evolution, which Tatlin thought was the new Communist state then being established in Russia. The

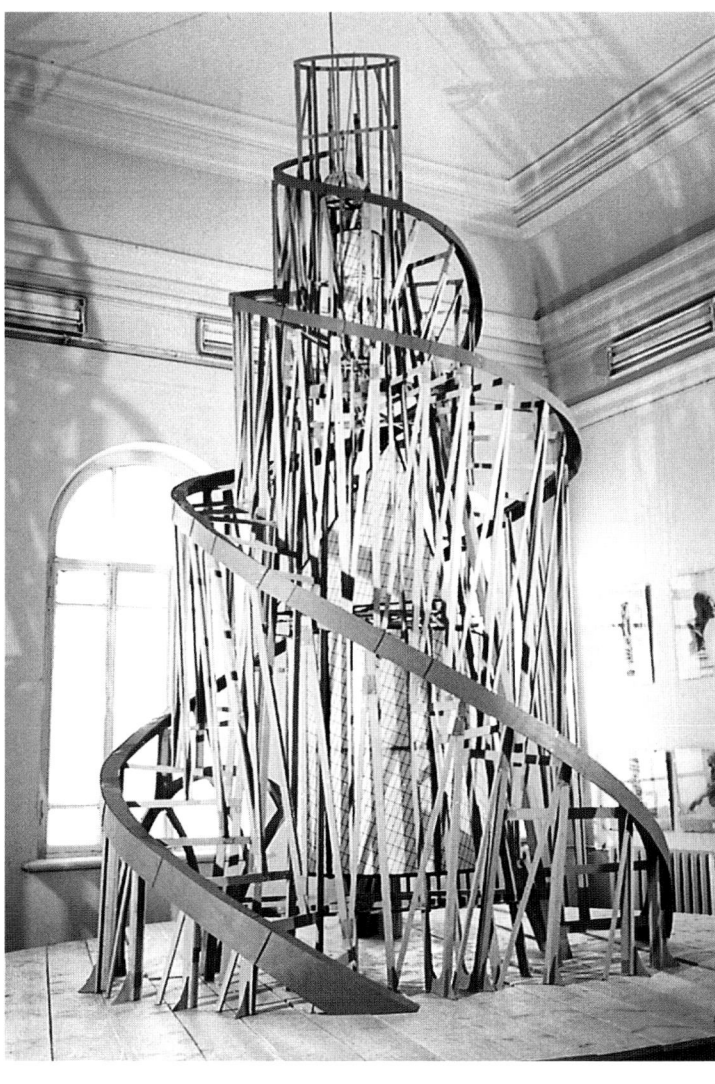

monument would reflect the dynamism and progress of that social experiment. Tatlin's model was widely exhibited in Europe, but the project was too revolutionary to be realized.

The Russian government of the middle 1920s decided to tolerate only art that the public could easily understand. This gave rise to a new movement called Socialist Realism. (A leader of this movement, Vera Mukhina, will be discussed on page 411.) Artists who resisted the new realist style had little hope of exhibiting paintings, and some were actively persecuted. Many abstract artists decided instead to use their skills to make practical objects in a new, modern style. A leader in this trend was Aleksandr Rodchenko, whose WORKERS' CLUB (on the following page) is a training ground for the Soviet mind. Rodchenko envisioned every aspect of this installation to educate workers in the new historical dynamic that would lead to the future classless society. The chairs, shelves, and desks are all made of simple, mass-produced parts, and designed to facilitate sitting upright.

De Stijl

Another of the many movements inspired by the formal qualities of Cubism was *De Stijl* (The Style). In 1917, a small group of Dutch artists, led by painter Piet Mondrian, began to employ nonrepresentational

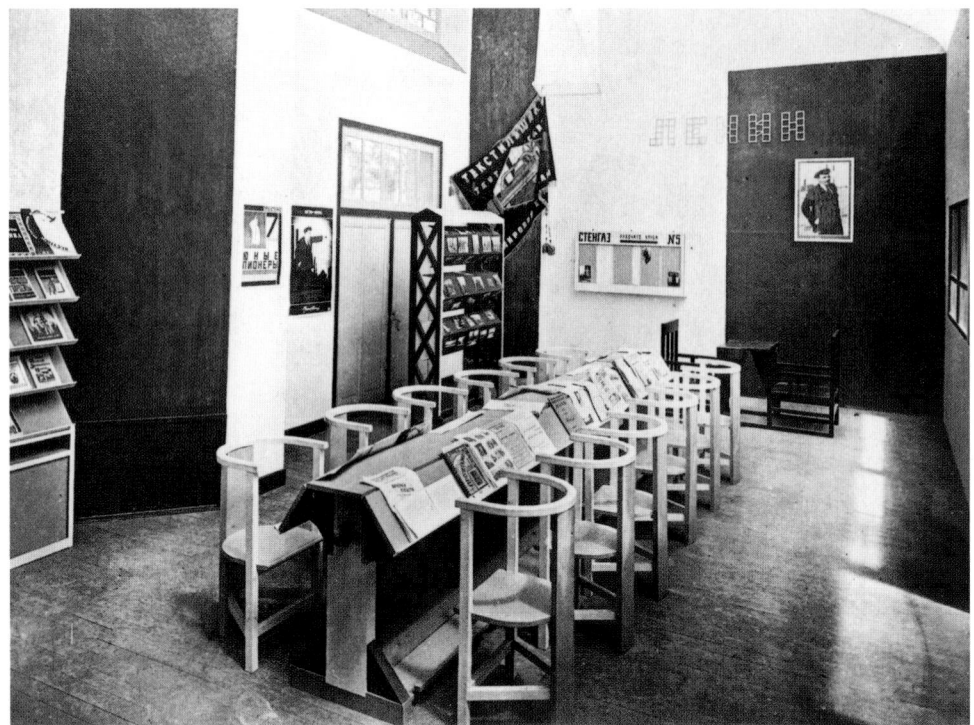

567 Aleksandr Rodchenko.
THE WORKERS' CLUB.
Exhibited at the International Exposition of Modern Decorative and Industrial
Arts, Paris. 1925.
© Estate of Aleksander Rodchenko. RAD Moscow licensed by VAGA, NY.
Rodchenko-Stepanova Archive, Moscow.

geometric elements in a group style that involved both two- and three-dimensional art forms. Their goal was the creation of a world of universal harmony. Using the newly independent vocabulary of "pure" visual form, they created an inventive body of work in painting, architecture, furniture, and graphic design.

Mondrian's evolution as an artist represents the origin and essence of De Stijl. Working to free painting completely from both the depiction of real objects and the expression of personal feelings, he developed an austere style based on the expressive potential of fundamental visual elements and their relationships. He created a new aesthetic that would provide a poetic vitality capable of setting standards of harmony for the new technological age.

From 1917 until his death in 1944, Mondrian was the leading spokesperson for an art reflecting universal order. For Mondrian, the universal elements were straight lines, the three primary colors, and rectangular shapes. He reduced painting to four elements: line, shape, color, and space. His painting TABLEAU 2 exemplifies his totally nonrepresentational later work. Mondrian hoped that the rhythms and forms of his works paralleled those of nature itself, which he viewed as rational and orderly.

International Style Architecture

The search for a new visual language engaged architects as well as painters. Ideas about form developed by the Constructivists, the De Stijl artists, and previously by American architect Frank Lloyd Wright, were carried further by architects stimulated by the structural possibilities of modern materials including steel, plate glass, and reinforced concrete.

About 1918, a new style of architecture emerged simultaneously in Germany, France, and the Netherlands and came to be called the *International Style*. Steel-frame curtain-wall construction methods made it possible to build structures characterized by undec-

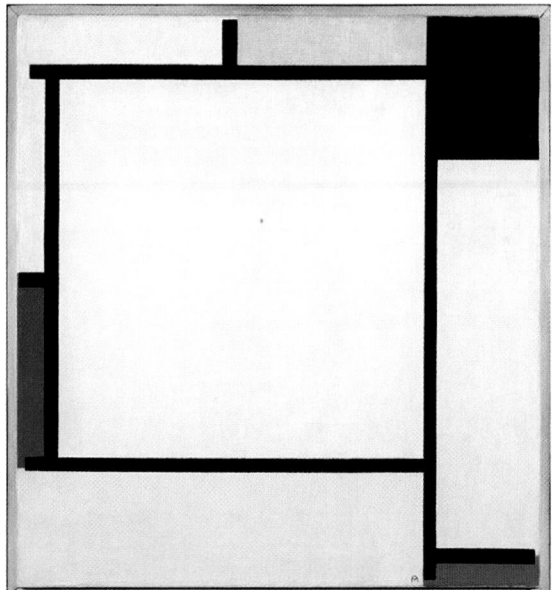

568 Piet Mondrian (1872–1944).

 TABLEAU 2 WITH YELLOW, BLACK, BLUE, RED, AND GRAY. 1922.
Oil on canvas. 21⅛″ × 21⅛″. Solomon R. Guggenheim Museum, New York.
© 2009 Mondrian/Holtzman Trust c/o HCR International, Warrenton, VA, USA.

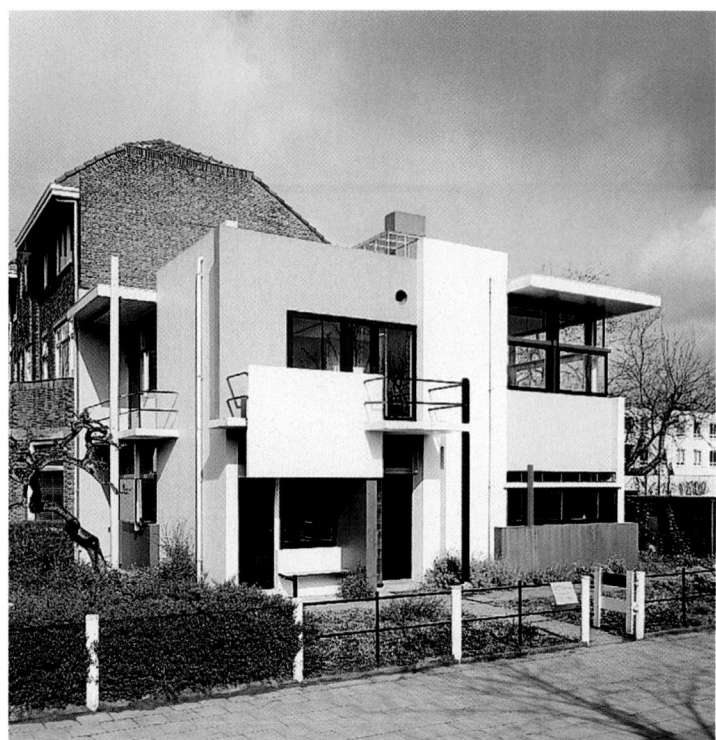

569 Gerrit Rietveld.
SCHRÖDER HOUSE. 1924.
Centraal Museum Utrecht, The Netherlands.
© 2002 Artists Rights Society (ARS), NY. Beeldrecht, Amsterdam.

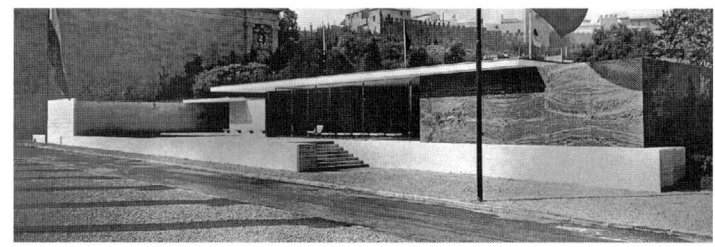

570 Ludwig Mies van der Rohe.
GERMAN PAVILION. 1929.
For International Exposition, Barcelona.
© Artists Rights Society (ARS), NY. VG Bild-Knust, Bonn.

orated rectilinear planes. Extensive use of glass in non-load-bearing exterior walls brought abundant light and flexible space to interiors. In many International Style buildings, asymmetrical designs created dynamic balances of voids and solids. Unlike Frank Lloyd Wright, who blended houses with their natural surroundings, architects working in the International Style deliberately created a visual contrast between natural and manufactured forms.

Dutch architect and furniture designer Gerritt Rietveld joined De Stijl in 1919. His SCHRÖDER HOUSE in Utrecht was an early classic of the International Style. Its design of interacting planes, spaces, and primary colors are closely related to Mondrian's paintings.

The International Style buildings designed by Walter Gropius for the Bauhaus (see page 221) clearly reflect the concepts of both De Stijl and Constructivism. Today, the spare style that Mondrian and the Bauhaus helped to initiate can be seen in the design not only of buildings, but of books, interiors, clothing, furnishings, and many other articles of daily life.

Architect and designer Ludwig Mies van der Rohe was one of the most influential figures associated with the Bauhaus and the International Style. For the Barcelona World's Fair in 1929, he designed the GERMAN PAVILION in marble, glass, and steel. Like the SCHRÖDER HOUSE, the GERMAN PAVILION is an abstract composition similar to a De Stijl painting. Mies designed the pavilion with flowing spaces so that the visitor never feels "boxed in." An attached rectangular pool on the left reflects the

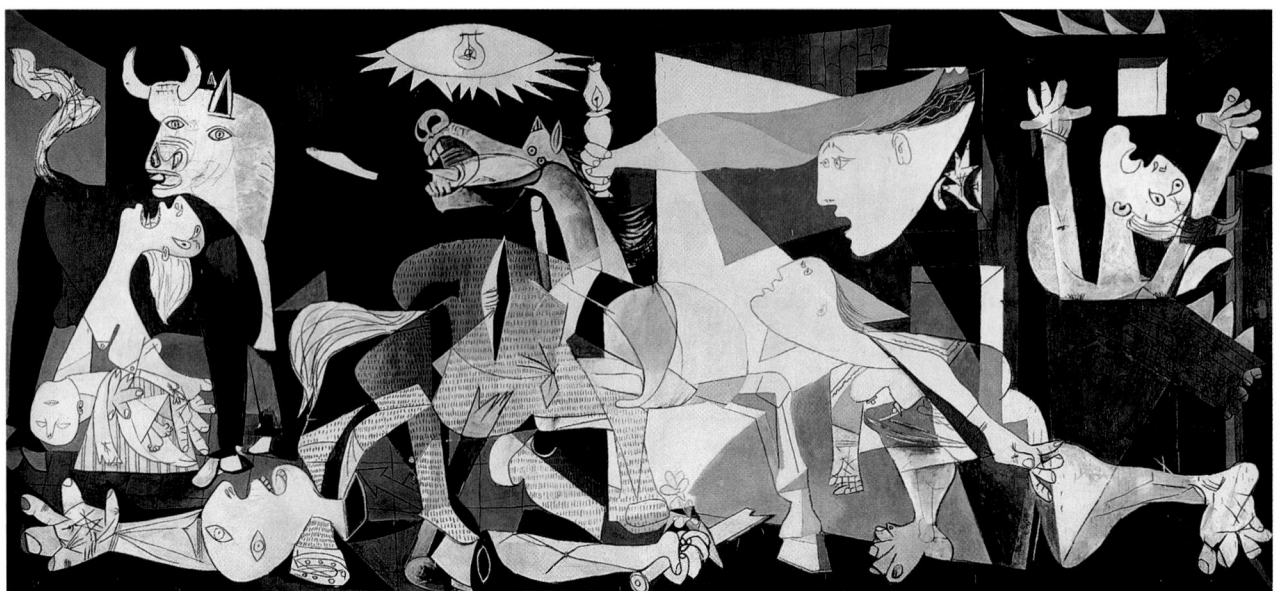

571 Pablo Picasso.
GUERNICA. 1937.
Oil on canvas. 11′5½″ × 25′5¼″.
Museo Nacional Centro de Arte Reina Sofía. Giraudon. Art Resource, NY.
© 2005 Estate of Pablo Picasso. Artists Rights Society (ARS), NY.

elegant design on the water's surface. In 1938, Mies emigrated to the United States. There, his ideas and works strongly influenced the post–World War II development steel-frame skyscraper. His SEAGRAM BUILDING is pictured on page 222.

POLITICAL PROTEST

Many artists in the interwar period focused their art on political life. Protesting against fascism and dictatorship was a dominant theme.

Throughout the 1920s and into the 1930s, Spanish-born Pablo Picasso continued to produce innovative drawings, paintings, prints, posters, and sculptures. Many of these works were filled with strange distortions and dislocations related to Surrealism. In 1937, while the Spanish Civil War was in progress, Picasso was commissioned by the doomed Spanish democratic government to paint a mural for the Paris Exposition. For several months he was unable to begin work. Suddenly, on April 26, 1937, he was shocked into action by the "experimental" mass bombing of the defenseless Basque town of Guernica. To aid his bid for power,

General Franco had allowed Hitler to use his war machinery on the town as a demonstration of military power. The bombing, which leveled the fifteen-square-block city center, was the first incidence of saturation bombing in the history of warfare. Hundreds died, and more were strafed with machine gun fire from German aircraft as they fled the city into neighboring fields.

Picasso, appalled by this brutality against the people of his native country, called upon all his powers to create the mural-size painting GUERNICA. Although Picasso's GUERNICA stems from a specific incident, it is a statement of protest against the senseless brutality of all war.

GUERNICA covers a huge canvas more than 25 feet long. It is painted in somber black, blue-blacks, whites, and grays. A large triangle embedded under the smaller shapes holds the whole scene of chaotic destruction together as a unified composition. GUERNICA combines Cubism's intellectual restructuring of form with the emotional intensity of earlier forms of Expressionism and Abstract Surrealism. Details show some of the personal symbolism

Picasso used to portray ideas and feelings beyond the protest of a single incident. In dream symbolism, a horse often represents a dreamer's creativity. Here the horse is speared and is dying in anguish. Beneath the horse's feet a soldier lies in pieces; near his broken sword a faint flower suggests hope. Above, a woman reaches out from an open window, an oil lamp in hand. Near the old-fashioned lamp and above the horse's head is an eyelike shape with an electric lightbulb at the center. Jagged rays of light radiate out from the bottom edge. The sun? An eye? Sometimes an eye representing the eye of God was painted on the ceiling of medieval churches. The juxtaposition between old and new sources of illumination could be a metaphor relating to enlightenment. God's eye, in this context, may symbolize the creative energy of God subverted by human beings for destructive rather than creative ends.

Interviewed during the war, Picasso remarked that "painting is not done to decorate apartments. It is an instrument of war for attack and defense against the enemy."[5] Unfortunately, the type of aerial bombardment that he decried in GUERNICA soon became a common strategy that all sides adopted.

Between the world wars, a socially and politically committed form of art called *social realism* became common in many countries. This style took many forms, but they all include a retreat from the radical innovations of Modern art and a desire to communicate more readily with the public about social causes and issues. In Nazi Germany and in Communist Russia this style became an officially sponsored "norm" for art, which artists could ignore only if they did not care to have a successful career. A good example of Russian social realism is Vera Mukhina's MONUMENT TO THE PROLETARIAT AND AGRICULTURE. Her huge statue, which depicts a male factory worker and a female farm worker in stainless steel 78 feet high, was first exhibited at the Paris World's fair of 1937. Later set up in Moscow, it expresses the hopes and ideals of the workers' state, which came crashing down in 1991 with the fall of the Communist regime.

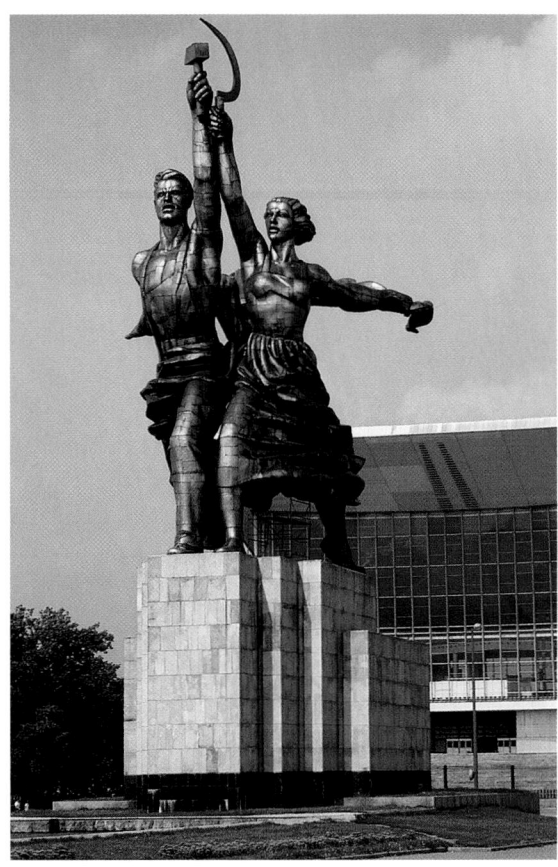

572 Vera Mukhina.
MONUMENT TO THE PROLETARIAT AND
AGRICULTURE. 1937.
Stainless steel. 78′ high.
All-Russia Exposition Grounds, Moscow.
© Estate of Vera Mukhina. Licensed by VAGA, NY.

Mexican social realism took the form of mural paintings that embodied the ideals of the revolution of 1910–1917, when a popular uprising overthrew a long-entrenched dictatorship. The Mexican government in 1921 embarked on a program to pay artists an hourly wage to decorate public buildings with murals that spoke to the people about the recent revolution and about their long history. Inspired by the murals of the Italian Renaissance and by pre-Columbian wall paintings of ancient Mexican cultures, the muralists envisioned a national art that would glorify the traditional Mexican heritage and promote the new post-revolutionary government. Diego Rivera's fresco

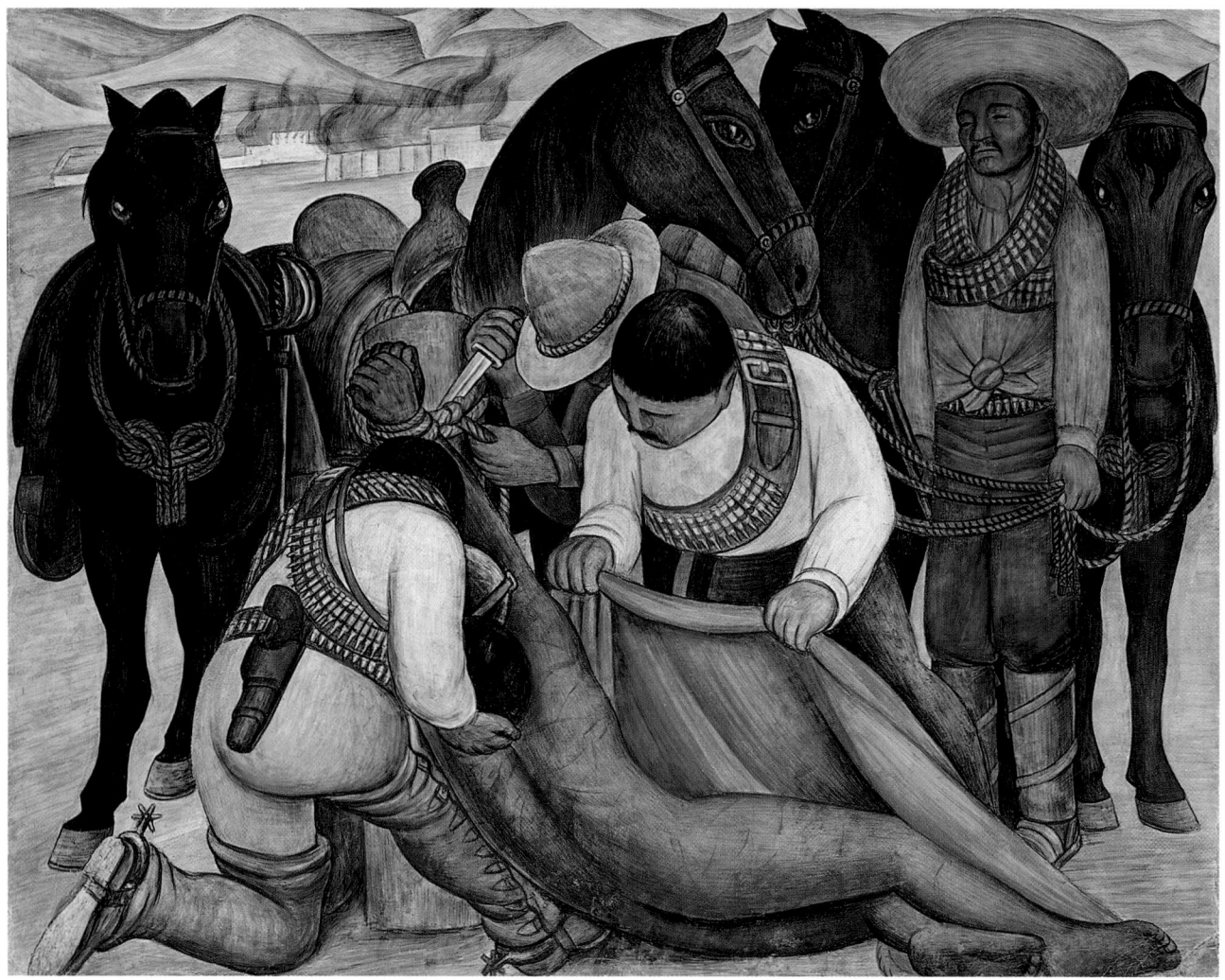

573 Diego Rivera.
THE LIBERATION OF THE PEON. 1931.
Fresco. 73″ × 94¼″.
Philadelphia Museum of Art. Given by Mr. and Mrs. Herbert Cameron. 1943–46–1. Photo by Graydon Wood, 1994.
© 2002 Banco de Mexico Diego Rivera & Frida Kahlo Museums Trust. Av. Cinco de Mayo No. 2, Col. Centro Del.
Cuauhtemoc 06059, Mexico, D.F. Reproduction authorized by the Instituto National de Bellas Artes and Literature.

THE LIBERATION OF THE PEON is a good example that deals with a common event of the revolution: the landlord's house burns in the background, while revolutionary soldiers untie the peon from a stake and cover his naked body, which is scarred by repeated lashings. This work is a variation of a large painting on a wall of the Ministry of Education in Mexico City. Both Diego Rivera and fellow muralist José Clemente Orozco visited the United States, where they influenced American mural painting (a work by Orozco is pictured on page 86).

During the Depression years of the 1930s, the United States government maintained an active program of subsidy for the arts. The Works Progress Administration (WPA) commissioned painters to paint murals in public buildings, and the Farm Security Administration (FSA) hired photographers and filmmakers to record the eroding dustbowl and its workworn inhabitants. With government support, the art of documentary filmmaking reached a peak of achievement.

This book was a major force behind the cultural flowering known as the Harlem Renaissance, which included poets, musicians, and novelists along with visual artists. Some important figures associated with the Renaissance include Langston Hughes, Paul Robeson, Zora Neale Hurston, and many others both in Harlem and elsewhere in the United States. Visual artists were an integral part of the movement; they illustrated books, designed interior spaces, and photographed the teeming life around them.

The principal vehicle for displaying the painting and sculpture of African Americans at that time was the annual traveling exhibition sponsored by the Harmon Foundation. One artist who was repeatedly honored in that show was Sargent Johnson. A resident of California, he produced painted wood sculptures such as FOREVER FREE that expressed his view of the black identity. A motherly woman shelters two smaller figures, all of whom show pronounced African-American features. The title of the work comes from the Emancipation of 1863, which ended slavery in the Confederate states. He wrote of this expression of cultural roots: "I am producing strictly a Negro Art, studying not the culturally mixed Negro of the cities, but the more primitive slave type as existed in this country during the period of slave importation."[6]

During the Depression of the 1930s, the Works Progress Administration (WPA) set up community art centers in one hundred cities. Jacob Lawrence was a product of one of these centers in Harlem, where he met most of the leaders of the Renaissance. In 1938, he made a series of forty-one paintings on Toussaint L'Ouverture, the black leader of the revolt that made Haiti the first independent nation in Latin America in 1804. GENERAL TOUSSAINT L'OUVERTURE DEFEATS THE ENGLISH AT SALINE shows his style, which he called "dynamic Cubism." Lawrence was not practicing the French Cubism of Braque and Picasso, however; he made his own investigation of African art and reinterpreted it in his own way.

Archibald Motley of Chicago took a realist view of African-American culture. His painting BARBECUE (on the following page) of 1934 is ebullient and full

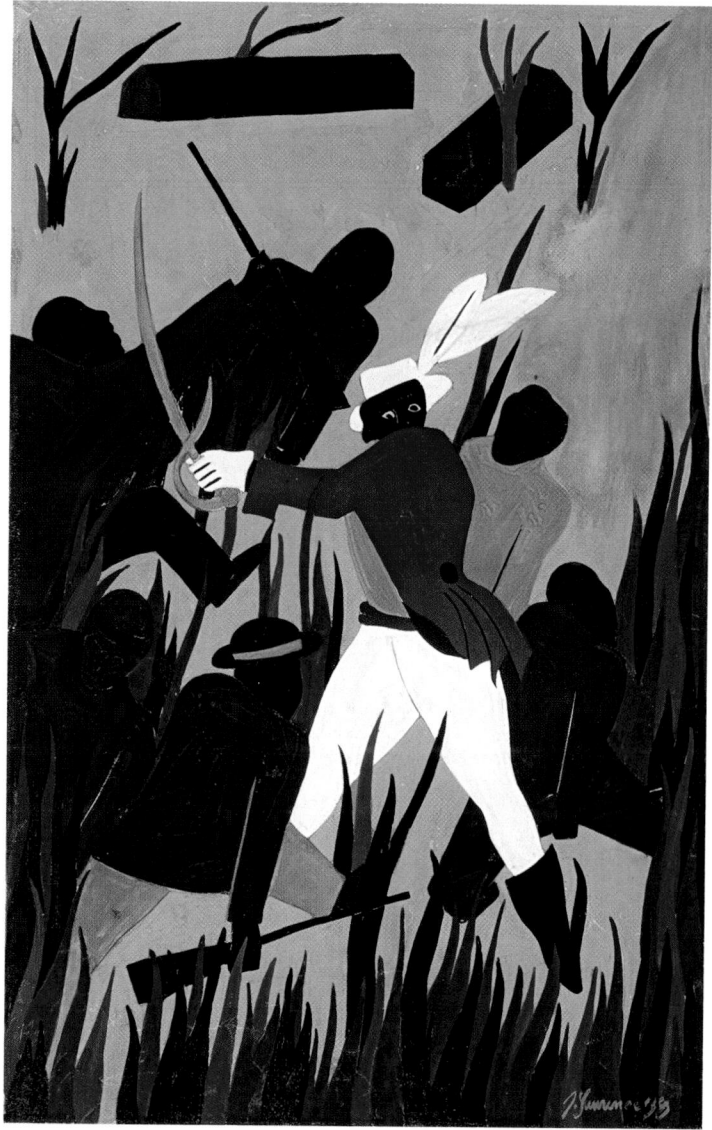

584   Jacob Lawrence.
GENERAL TOUSSAINT L'OUVERTURE DEFEATS THE ENGLISH AT SALINE. 1937–1938.
Gouache on paper. 19″ × 11″.
Aaron Douglas Collection, The Amistad Research Center, Tulane University,
© 2005 The Estate of Gwendolyn Knight Lawrence.
Artists Rights Society (ARS), NY.

of motion, and also shows an interest in how figures look under artificial light. Motley specialized in depicting all aspects of the urban black experience, including on occasion gamblers and drinkers during Prohibition. Such subject matter did not endear him to pretentious art patrons, but Motley replied, "I have tried to paint the Negro as I have seen him

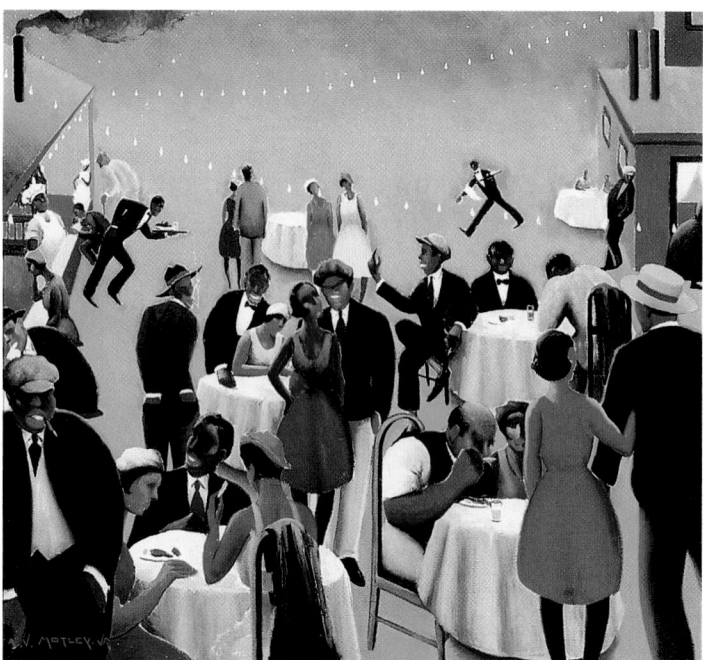

585 Archibald Motley, Jr.
BARBECUE. 1934.
Oil on canvas. 36¼" × 40⅛".
Howard University Gallery of Art, Washington, D.C.

and as I feel him, in my self without adding or detracting, just being frankly honest."[7]

GLOBAL INFLUENCES

Non-Western cultures continued to influence European modern art during the interwar period. Paul Klee exhibited with the members of the Blue Rider group prior to a trip to Tunisia in 1914. The effect of the desert light and the exposure to Muslim culture stayed with him for years to come; he wrote to a friend enthusiastically, "I am now an artist." He made several watercolors of the Great Mosque at Kairouan and later created some paintings that show influence of Islamic calligraphy, such as INSULA DULCAMARA. His curving and dipping lines are of course illegible, but they reveal his belief that writing uses the expressive power of line just as painting does.

English sculptor Henry Moore came to non-Western art through a different route. After serving in World War I, he used a veteran's grant to study art in London. While there, he spent long hours studying the collections of tribal arts in the British Museum and the Victoria and Albert Museum. His

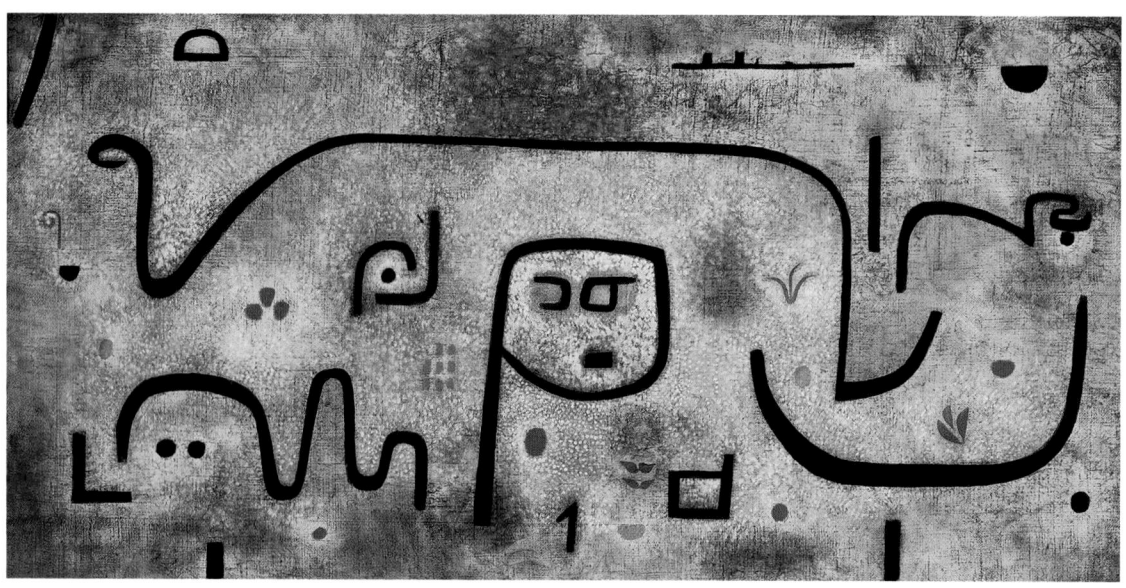

586 Paul Klee.
INSULA DULCAMARA. 1938.
Oil and black paste on newspaper, mounted on burlap. 34⅞" × 69¼".
Courtesy of the Paul Klee Foundation, Berne.
© 2004 Artists Rights Society (ARS), NY. VG Bild-Kunst, Bonn.

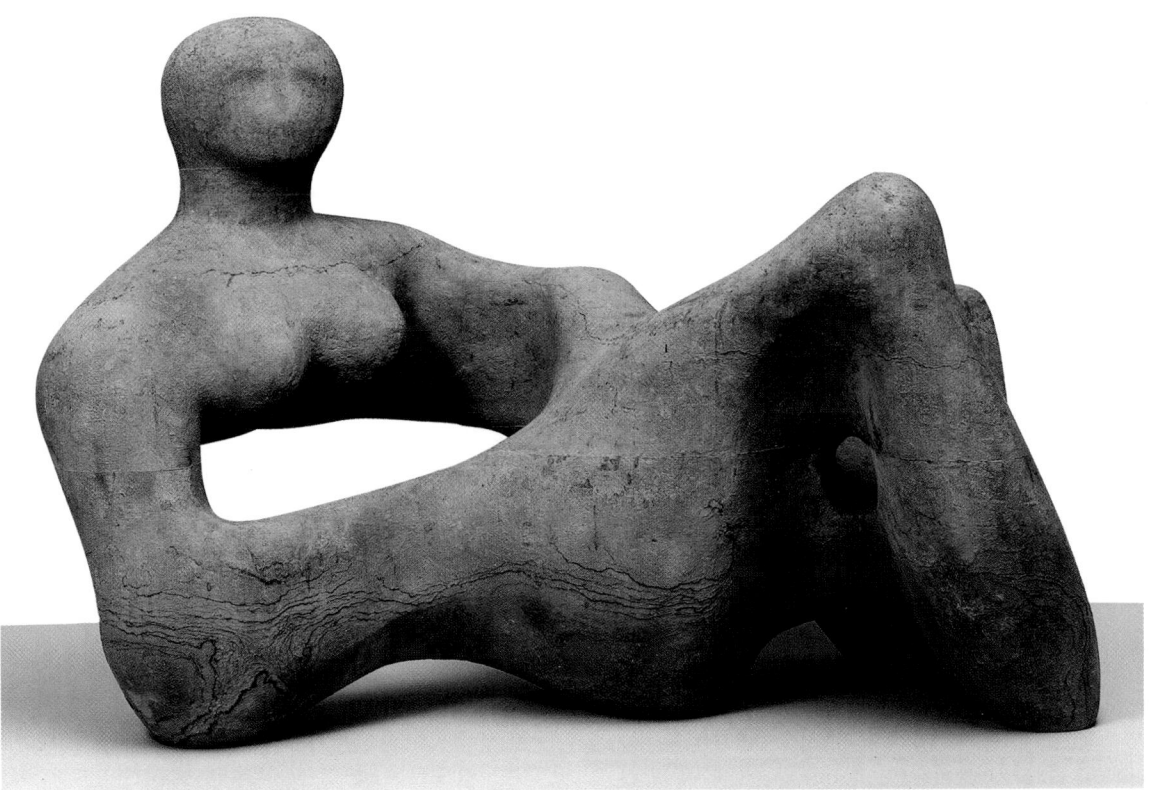

587   Henry Moore.
RECUMBENT FIGURE. 1938.
Green hornton stone. 35″ × 52¼″ × 29″.
© Henry Moore Foundation. Tate Gallery, London/Art Resource, NY.

RECUMBENT FIGURE from 1938 is an elaboration of the **CHACMOOL** of the Toltecs (see page 346). Moore smoothed the stone into an organic abstract shape that suggests the human form without exactly depicting it. He also left voids in the center of the work to lighten the density of the stony mass.

The outbreak of World War II in Europe in 1939 took humanity to the brink of destruction yet again. Besides the suffering that it created, the war also redrew the world map of artistic innovation. Many European artists migrated to the Americas and fertilized modern movements there.

POSTWAR MODERN
MOVEMENTS IN THE WEST

At the end of World War II, Europe lay in ruins—financially, emotionally, and physically. The war took the lives of over a quarter million English people, six hundred thousand French, five million Germans, and twenty million Russians. The Nazi holocaust alone consumed the lives of six million Jews, Romany (gypsies), and homosexuals. Refugees and displaced persons numbered forty million. England's wartime Prime Minister Winston Churchill in 1947 described Europe as "a rubble heap, a charnel house, a breeding ground for pestilence and hate." Many prominent European artists had fled from Nazi oppression to the United States, which emerged from the war economically strong and optimistic.

Among the artists who settled in New York were Mondrian, Léger, Duchamp, Dalí, and Hans Hofmann. They worked, taught, exhibited, and generally stirred things up, opening new possibilities for American artists. The Solomon Guggenheim collection opened to the public in 1930 as the Museum of Non-Objective Art, specializing in abstract European works (today known as the Guggenheim Museum). The Museum of Modern Art opened in New York in 1929, showing a comprehensive history of the modern movement; ten years later it reopened in the larger space in midtown Manhattan that it still occupies. Mexican muralists Diego Rivera and David Siqueiros exhibited and taught in New York during the 1930s, encouraging artists away from traditional easel painting. Modernism was no longer a distant, European phenomenon; its leading practitioners were in the United States.

War had altered the consciousness of the developed world in subtle but profound ways. The Nazi genocide machine had taken human cruelty to a new low, and the atomic bomb gave humankind terrifying new powers: People were now living in a world they had the power to destroy in minutes. These conditions formed the background for art and life in Europe and the United States for most of the postwar period.

ABSTRACT EXPRESSIONISM AND RELATED ART

The horrors of World War II, in which millions of people lost their lives in battle or in concentration camps, led artists to rethink the relationship between art and life. Again, dislocations caused by war led artists to explore visual realms other than the representational and narrative. The result was *Abstract Expressionism,* a culmination of the expressive tendencies in painting from van Gogh and Gauguin through Fauvism and German Expressionism. Immediate inspiration came from the motives and spontaneous methods of Surrealism—in particular, the abstract Surrealism of Miró.

The new émigrés influenced many American painters, leading them to move away from realist styles dominant in the 1930s and experiment with more expressive and inventive ways of creating art. The unparalleled crisis of the World War also led them to move away from public issues of history and social comment that Depression-era painting emphasized. As a result, they began to paint in styles that were both stylistically innovative and personal.

Jackson Pollock, the leading innovator of Abstract Expressionism, studied in the 1930s with both Thomas Hart Benton and the Mexican muralist David Siqueiros. The rhythmic structure of Benton's style, and the mural-scale art of the Mexicans influenced Pollock's poured paintings of the late 1940s and early 1950s. Searching for ways to express primal human nature, Pollock also studied Navajo sand painting and psychologist Carl Jung's theories of the unconscious.

The act of painting itself became a major part of the content of Pollock's paintings. Pollock created AUTUMN RHYTHM by dripping thin paint onto the canvas rather than brushing it on. By working on huge canvases placed on the floor, Pollock was able to enter the space of the painting physically and psychologically. The huge format allowed

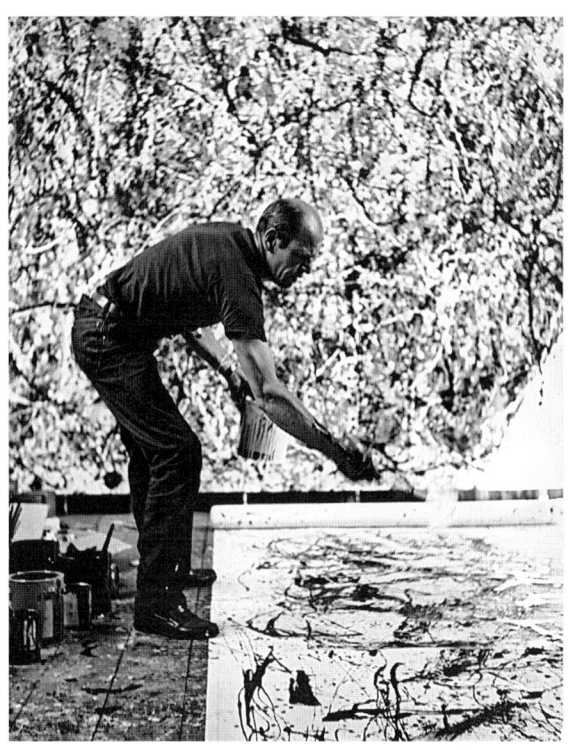

588 Hans Namuth. JACKSON POLLOCK. 1950.
Gelatin silver print.
National Portrait Gallery, Smithsonian Institution.
Gift of the Estate of Hans Namuth.

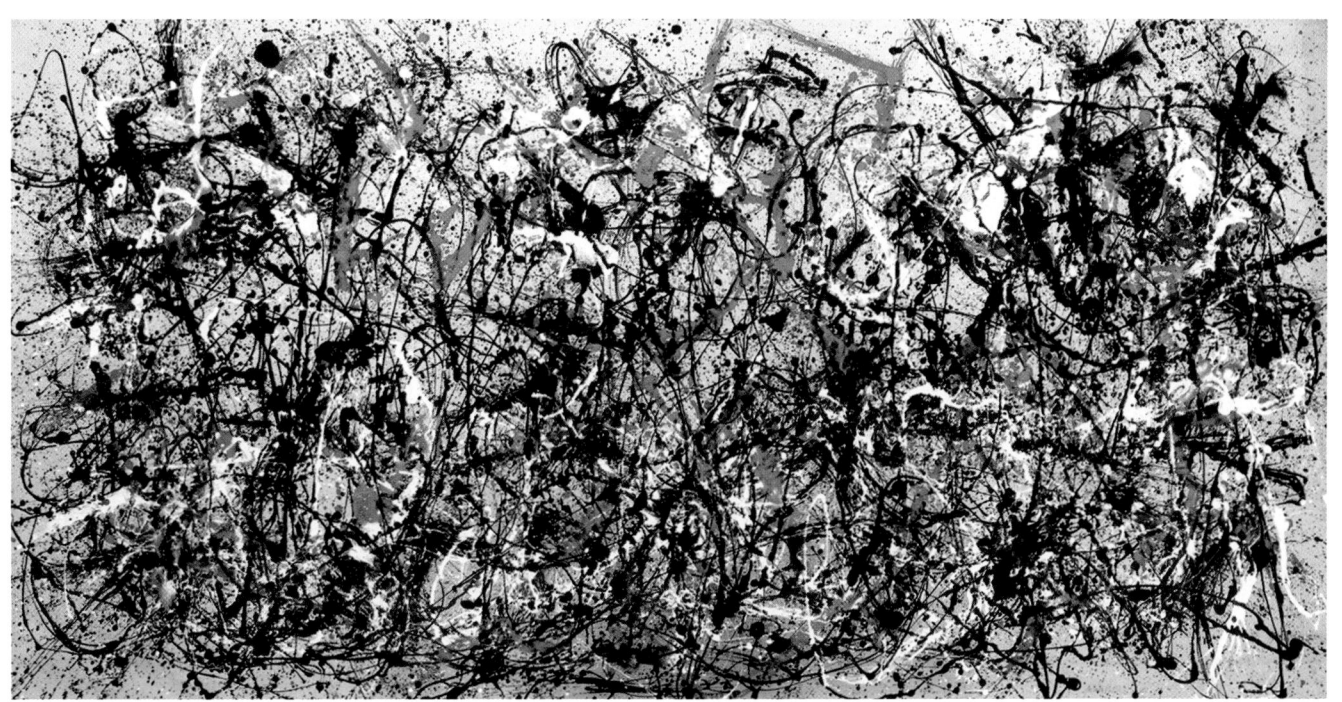

589 Jackson Pollock.
AUTUMN RHYTHM. (NUMBER 30). 1950.
Oil on canvas. 105″ × 207″.
The Metropolitan Museum of Art, George A. Hearn Fund, 1957. (57.92).
Photograph: © 1998 The Metropolitan Museum of Art. © 2004 The Pollock-Krasner Foundation. Artists Rights Society (ARS), NY.

590 Mark Rothko.
BLUE, ORANGE, RED. 1961.
Oil on canvas. 90¼″ × 81¼″.
Hirschhorn Museum and Sculpture Garden, Smithsonian Institution,
Washington,D.C. Gift of Joseph H. Hirschhorn Foundation (1966).
Photograph: Lee Stalsworth. © 2005 Kate Rothko Prizel and Christopher Rothko.
Artists Rights Society (ARS), NY. HMSG 66.4420.

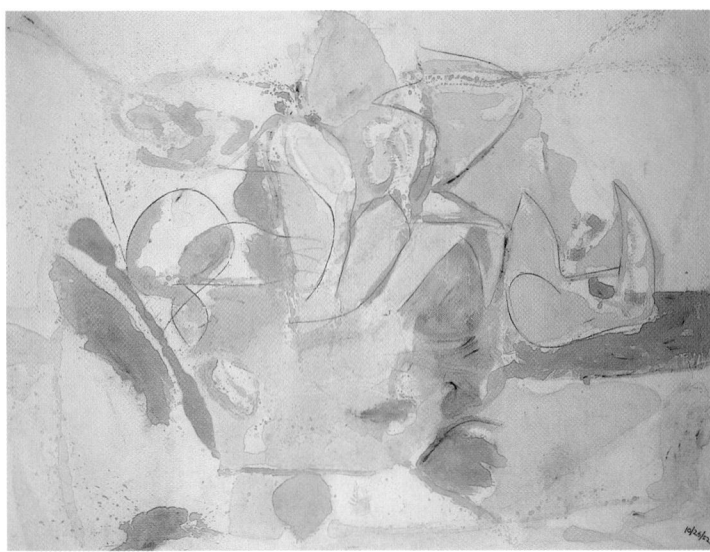

591 Helen Frankenthaler.
MOUNTAINS AND SEA. 1952.
Oil on canvas. 7′2⅝″ × 9′9¼″.
Collection of the artist, on loan to The National Gallery of Art, Washington, D.C.
© Helen Frankenthaler 1999.

ample room for his sweeping gestural lines. Pollock dripped, poured, and flung his paint, yet he exercised control and selection by the rhythmical, dancing movements of his body. A similar approach in the work of many of his colleagues led to the term *action painting*.

A different, but related, painting style that evolved at about the same time was *color field*, a term for painting that consists of large areas of color, with no obvious structure, central focus, or dynamic balance. The canvases of color field painters are dominated by unified images, images so huge that they engulf the viewer. They are not about environments; they are environments in themselves.

Mark Rothko is now best known as a pioneer of color field painting, although his early works of the 1930s were urban scenes. By the 1940s, influenced by Surrealism, he began producing paintings inspired by myths and rituals. In the late 1940s, he gave up the figure and began to work primarily through color. In works such as BLUE, ORANGE, RED Rothko was able to use color to evoke moods ranging from joy and serenity to melancholy and despair. By superimposing thin layers of paint, he achieved a variety of qualities from dense to atmospheric to luminous. Rothko's paintings have sensuous appeal and monumental presence.

Helen Frankenthaler's work also evolved during the height of Abstract Expressionism. In 1952, she pioneered staining techniques as an extension of Jackson Pollock's poured paint and Mark Rothko's fields of color. Brush strokes and paint texture were eliminated as she spread liquid colors across horizontal, unprimed canvas. As the thin pigment soaked into the raw fabric, she coaxed it into fluid, organic shapes. Pale, subtle, and spontaneous, MOUNTAINS AND SEA marked the beginning of a series of paintings that emphasize softness and openness and the expressive power of color. The twenty-four-year-old Frankenthaler painted it in one day, after a trip to Nova Scotia.

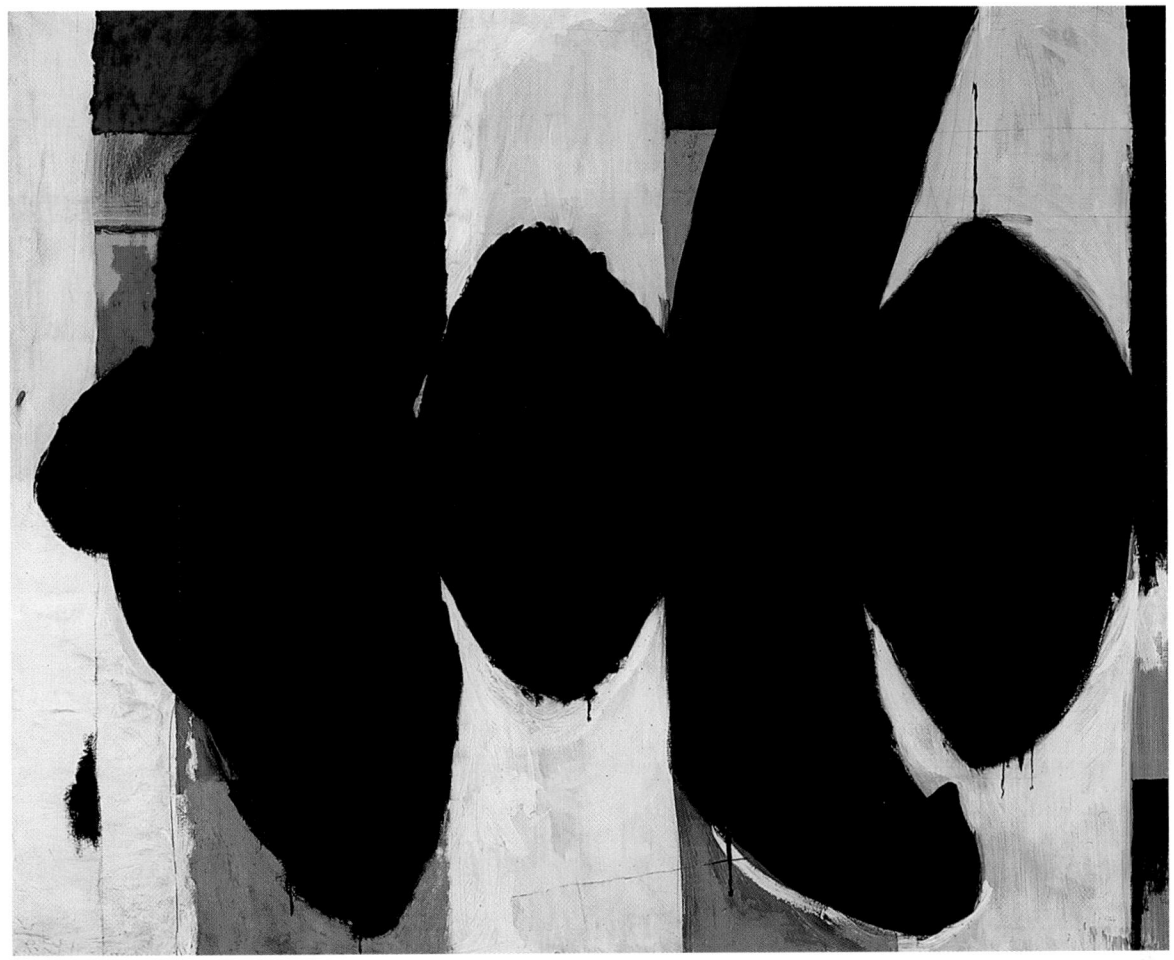

592 Robert Motherwell.
ELEGY TO THE SPANISH REPUBLIC NO. 34. 1953–1954.
Oil on canvas. 80″ × 100″.
Albright-Knox Art Gallery, Buffalo, NY. Gift of Seymour H. Knox, Jr. (1957).
© Dedalus Foundation, Inc. Licensed by VAGA, NY.

Robert Motherwell's series of paintings titled ELEGY TO THE SPANISH REPUBLIC is permeated with a tragic sense of history. Unlike many Abstract Expressionists, Motherwell began with a specific subject as his starting point. His elegies brood over the destruction of the young Spanish democracy by General Franco in the bloody Spanish Civil War of the 1930s. Heavy black shapes crush and obliterate the lighter passages behind them.

The influence of Expressionist and Surrealist attitudes on Willem de Kooning's work is evident in his spontaneous, emotionally charged brushwork and provocative use of shapes. Throughout his career, de Kooning emphasized abstract imagery, yet he felt no compulsion to ban recognizable subject matter. After several years of working without subjects, he began a series of large paintings in which ferocious female figures appear. These canvases, painted with slashing attacks of the brush, have an overwhelming presence. In WOMAN AND BICYCLE (on the following page), the toothy smile is repeated in a savage necklace that caps tremendous breasts. While it explodes with the energies of Abstract Expressionism, this work is controversial for the horrendous image of women that it presents.

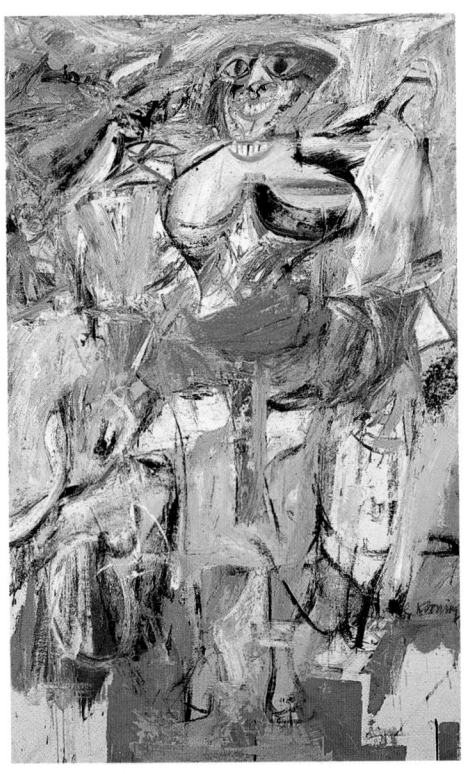

Norman Lewis was an African-American artist who participated in Abstract Expressionism from its inception. Like most of the Abstract Expressionists, during the 1930s Lewis painted in a social realist style, depicting urban poverty that he observed in his neighborhood of Harlem. During and after World War II, he was increasingly influenced by Modern art. His UNTITLED work from 1947 documents his shift toward a more spontaneous and improvisational style. Lewis's art differs from other Abstract Expressionists in that it seems more poetic and reserved. In addition, his painting at times shows traces of nature or, as we see in this work, city life.

In the ten years following the end of the war, European art differed from American art in two principal ways: First, many Europeans ventured less into abstraction, often retaining some trace of the human figure in their art. A prime example of this is the sculptor Alberto Giacometti, whose MAN POINTING is illustrated on page 48. In painting, Danish artist Asger Jorn made explosive figural

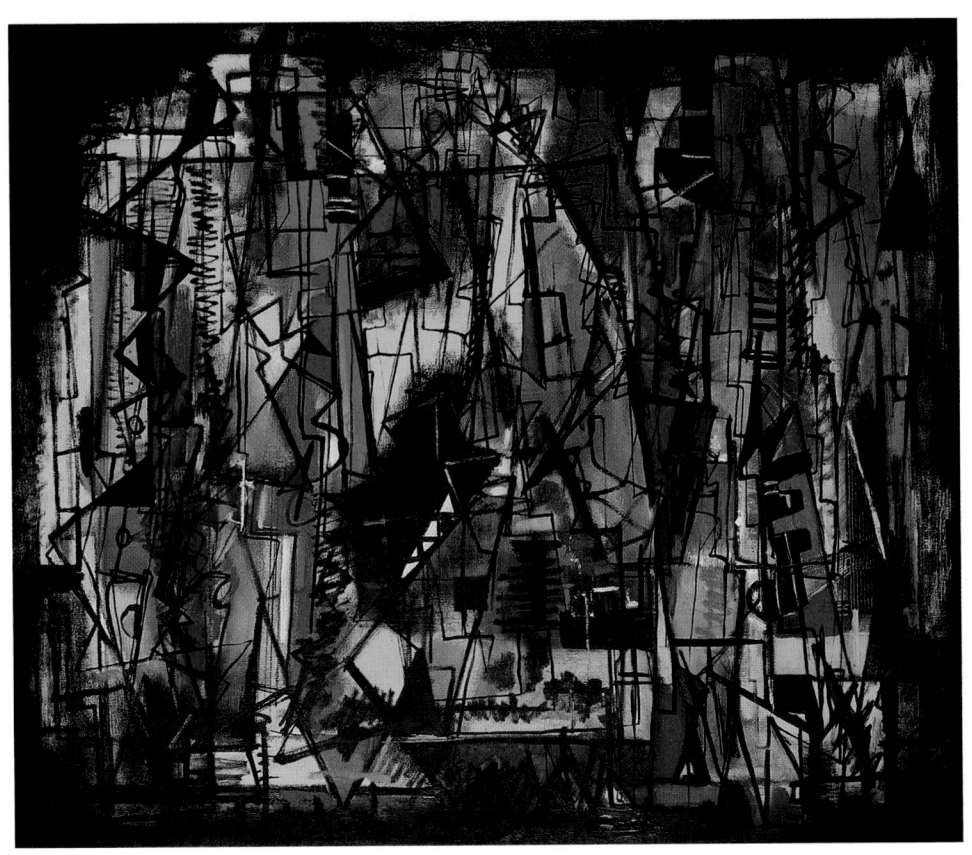

593 Willem de Kooning.
WOMAN AND BICYCLE. 1952–1953.
Oil on canvas. 76½″ × 49″.
Collection of Whitney Museum of Art, NY. Purchase, 55.35.
Photograph © 2000: Whitney Museum of American Art, NY.
© 2005 Willem de Kooning Foundation. Artists Rights Society (ARS), NY.

594 Norman Lewis.
UNTITLED. c. 1947.
Oil on canvas. 30″ × 36″.
Private Collection, NY.
Courtesy of Michael Rosenfeld Gallery, NY and Landor Fine Arts, NJ.

works that often combined heavily worked paint surfaces with ironic titles. In his painting THE GREAT VICTORY, instead of a scene of triumph we see a group of leering, monstrous heads emerging from murky depths. With their art, Giacometti and Jorn often commented on the basic aloneness of individuals, and the disappointments of an exhausted and devastated postwar European society.

Second, some Europeans were more innovative than Americans in their use of materials. Alberto Burri, for example, used burlap sacks in a series of works in the early 1950s. His COMPOSITION includes tattered pieces of fabric crudely stitched to the surface of the canvas. During the war, the artist served in the Italian army as a doctor; his use of red is meant to symbolize blood, and the burlap represents a temporary bandage. Burlap had a further symbolic significance in that it held grain that the United States sent to Italy as postwar foreign aid. These burlap works are Burri's effort to symbolically bind up Europe's wounds after the havoc of the war.

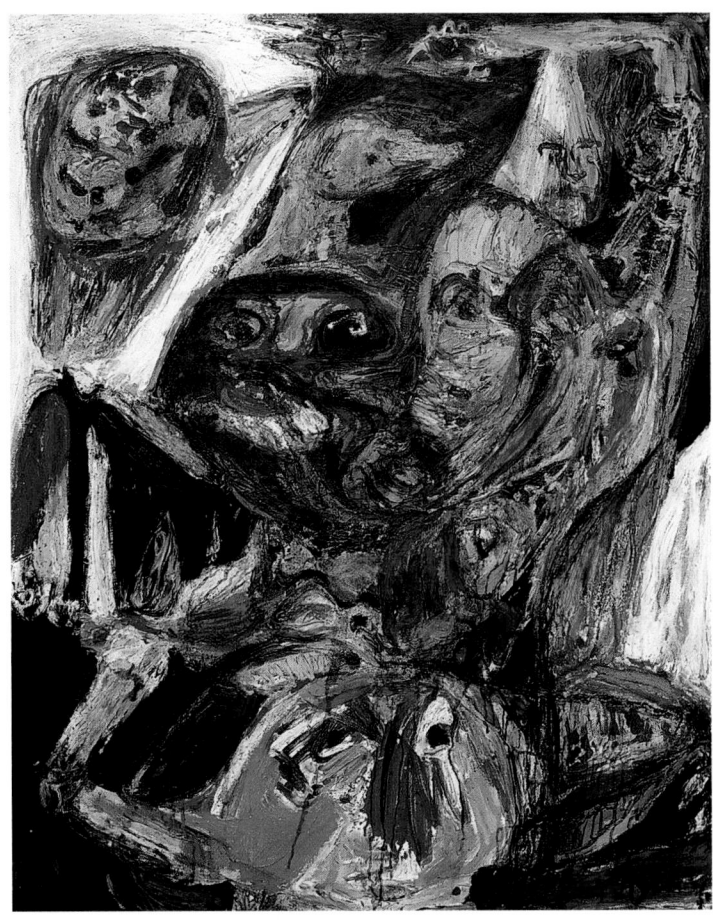

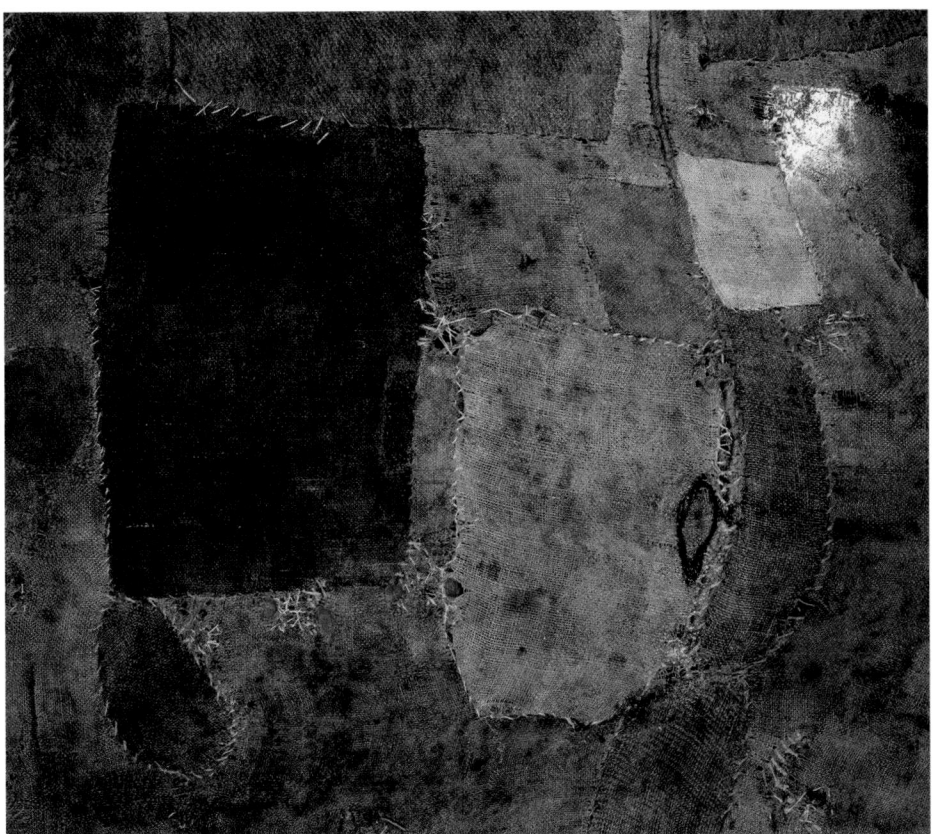

595 Asger Jorn.
THE GREAT VICTORY. 1955–1956.
Oil on canvas. 50″ × 41″.
Photograph: Lars Bay. © Silkeborg Kunstmuseum, Silkeborg, Denmark. © 2005 fam. Jorn. Artists Rights Society (ARS), NY. COPY-DAN, Copenhagen.

596 Alberto Burri.
COMPOSITION. 1953.
Oil, gold paint, and glue on burlap and canvas. 33⅞″ × 39½″.
Solomon R. Guggenheim Museum, New York. Photograph: David Heald and Myles Aronowitz. © The Solomon R. Guggenheim Foundation, NY. (FN53.1364).

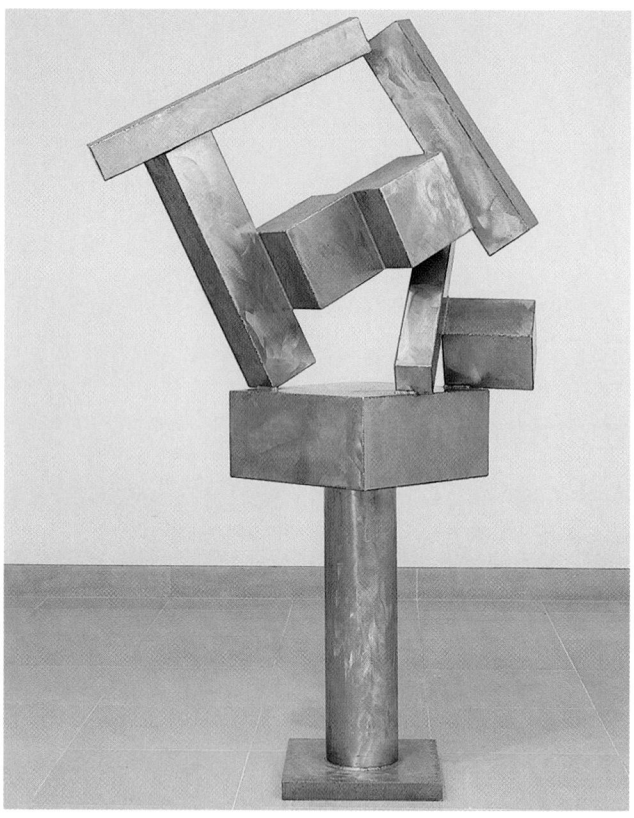

David Smith, for many critics the most important American sculptor of the postwar period, took the formal ideas of Cubism and gave them an American vigor. His assembled metal sculpture balanced formal qualities with the elemental energy of Abstract Expressionist painting. His use of factory methods and materials provided new options for the next generation of sculptors. Smith's late work included the stainless steel CUBI series, based on cubic masses and planes balanced dynamically above the viewer's eye level. The scoured surfaces of the steel reflect light in ways that seem to dissolve their solidity. Smith intended the sculpture to be viewed outdoors in strong light, set off by green landscape.

PHOTOGRAPHY AND ARCHITECTURE AT MID-CENTURY

In the late 1940s, at the dawn of the age of television, camera imagery began to proliferate into what has become today's mass-media environment. During this period some "art" photographers made their own contributions to the way we see. Both straight and manipulated approaches to image making were employed as photographers explored new frontiers of experience. There was an active exchange of visual ideas among photographers and painters, another phase in the dialog between these artists that started when photography was invented.

New York photographer Aaron Siskind pioneered an abstract style of photography based on documenting urban life. He focused on walls and buildings, isolating parts of them in order to "create an altogether new object, complete and self-contained," as he described it. His CHICAGO 4C is a tattered urban wall turned into an abstract composition.

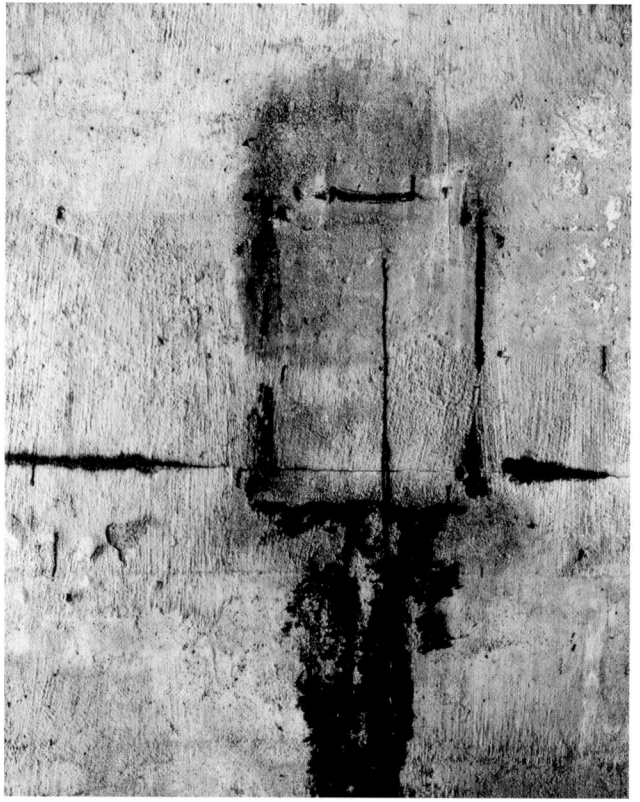

597 David Smith.
  CUBI XVII. 1963.
  Polished stainless steel. 107¾" × 64⅜" × 38⅛".
  Dallas Museum of Art. The Eugene and Margaret McDermott Fund.
  © Estate of David Smith. Licensed by VAGA, NY.

598 Aaron Siskind.
  CHICAGO 4C. 1948.
  Gelatin silver print. 14" × 11".
  Museum of Contemporary Art, Los Angeles. Gift of Marjorie and Leonard Vernon.
  Aaron Siskind Foundation. Courtesy of Robert Mann Gallery.

Most architects at mid-century were still involved with the International Style (introduced on page 408), but in a more reserved and austere way. LEVER HOUSE in New York City heralded the future of office buildings for the next twenty-five years: It is a steel-and-glass box that looks slick, convenient, and modern. Most American cities have such buildings; another is pictured on page 222. Later architects would revolt against it, but for a generation this ultra-clean look represented the image of the American corporation.

Following the words of American architect Louis Sullivan ("Form follows function"), International Style architects built practical buildings that clearly showed structural supports and banished all ornament. While many such buildings (such as LEVER HOUSE) looked elegant and distinguished, the glass-box regularity of the style began to seem limiting. For example, Brazilian architect Oscar Niemeyer seized the opportunity that his country presented when it commissioned a new capital city to open in 1960.

His PLANALTO PALACE participates in the glass-box style yet departs from it in important ways. The

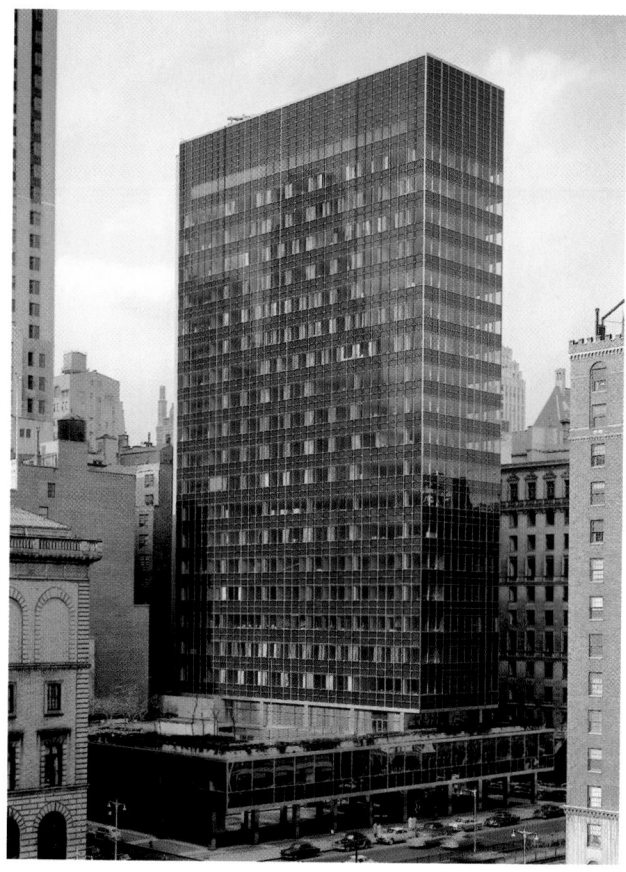

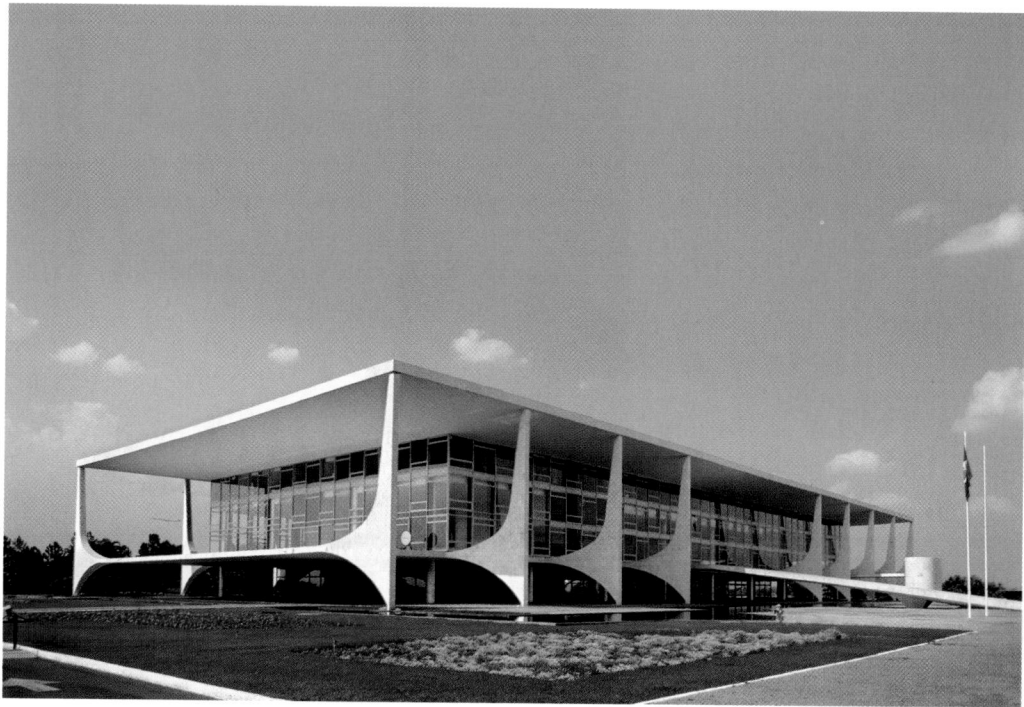

599 Skidmore, Owings, and Merrill.
LEVER HOUSE. 1952.
New York City.
Photograph: Ezra Stoller © Esto. All rights reserved.

600 Oscar Niemeyer.
PLANALTO PALACE.
Presidential Residence, Brasília, Brazil. 1960.
Photograph: Bernard Boutrit.

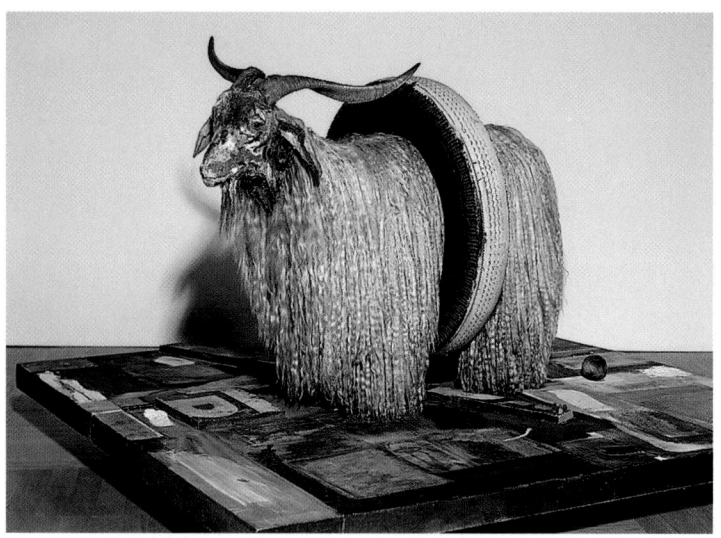

601 Robert Rauschenberg.
MONOGRAM. 1955–1959.
Freestanding combine. 42″ × 64″ × 64½″.
Moderna Museet, Stockholm.
© Robert Rauschenberg. Licensed by VAGA, NY.

entrance ramp hardly looks practical, and the sweeping, curved struts of the external skeleton take on a decorative life of their own. Such imaginative building soon became a hallmark of the Postmodern movement, as we shall see in Chapter 25.

ASSEMBLAGE

Most leading artists of the 1940s and 1950s chose not to deal with recognizable subject matter. They avoided any reference to the appearance of the environment in which they lived. In the mid-1950s, a few young artists began to acknowledge, confront, and even celebrate the visual diversity of the urban scene; they wanted to move beyond the exclusive, personal nature of Abstract Expressionism. In their effort to re-engage art with ordinary life, these artists created loose conglomerations of seemingly random objects, often called assemblages. The art of assemblage took the Dada collage of Hannah Höch (see page 401) into three dimensions.

Under the influence of avant-garde composer John Cage, who urged artists to pay attention to the lives they were living, Robert Rauschenberg began combining ordinary objects and collage materials with Abstract Expressionistic brushwork in what he called "combine-paintings." The essence of creative thinking involves combining elements of the world in order to make an unexpected, previously unthinkable new thing. Such is the startling presence of Rauschenberg's MONOGRAM. What is a stuffed, long-haired angora goat doing standing in the middle of a collage-painting with a tire around its middle? The artist is acting as a prankster, in the spirit of the Surrealist artists such as Magritte (see page 404).

This strange assemblage offers glimpses of seemingly unrelated objects and events and acts as a symbol for the wild juxtapositions of modern life. Instead of blocking out the chaotic messages of city streets, TV, and magazines, Rauschenberg incorporates the trash of urban civilization in his art, renewing our sense of mystery.

In the early 1960s, with the aid of the new technique of photographic screen printing, Rauschenberg brought together images from art history and documentary photographs. In TRACER he combined expressionist painting with modified parts of art reproductions and news photographs so that art history, the Vietnam War, and street life interact with one another. Just as we can move from sports to dinner to televised wars and sitcoms, Rauschenberg's work assembles the unrelated bits and pieces of everyday experience.

Assemblage artists on the West Coast made more direct social comments. For example, JOHN DOE by Edward Kienholz makes the average American into an outrageous caricature. Half of a store mannequin rides on a baby stroller with his chest blown out (revealing a cross). Paint drips add to the ridiculous effect. An inscription below adapts a sarcastic riddle: "How is John Doe like a piano? Because he is square, upright, and grand." Kienholz was friendly with many writers of the Beat movement, who similarly despaired over the blandness of middle-class life.

Rauschenberg often discussed art-making with Jasper Johns during their formative years in the 1950s. Whereas Rauschenberg's work is filled with visual complexity, Johns's work is deceptively simple.

His large early paintings were based on common graphic forms such as targets, maps, flags, and numbers. He was interested in the difference between signs (emblems that carry meaning) and art. In Johns's work, common signs play a dual role: they have the power of Abstract Expressionist forms in their size, bold design, and painterly surface qualities, yet they represent familiar objects and thus bring art back to everyday life. In his TARGET WITH FOUR FACES (on the following page), a sign (target) becomes a painting, while the faces (sculpture) are perceived as a sign.

As with Man Ray's THE GIFT (page 401), Johns's common subjects are now objects of contemplation. His irony relates back to Dada and forward to Pop Art. The Neo-Dada works of Johns and Rauschenberg provided a bridge between Abstract Expressionism and later Pop Art. Johns and Rauschenberg are champions of art in an environment saturated with media-promoted icons of popular culture.

The Neo-Dada spirit also broke out in Europe, where in 1958 Yves Klein greeted visitors at an empty gallery, in a show he called "The Void." Italian artist Piero Manzoni turned people into "works

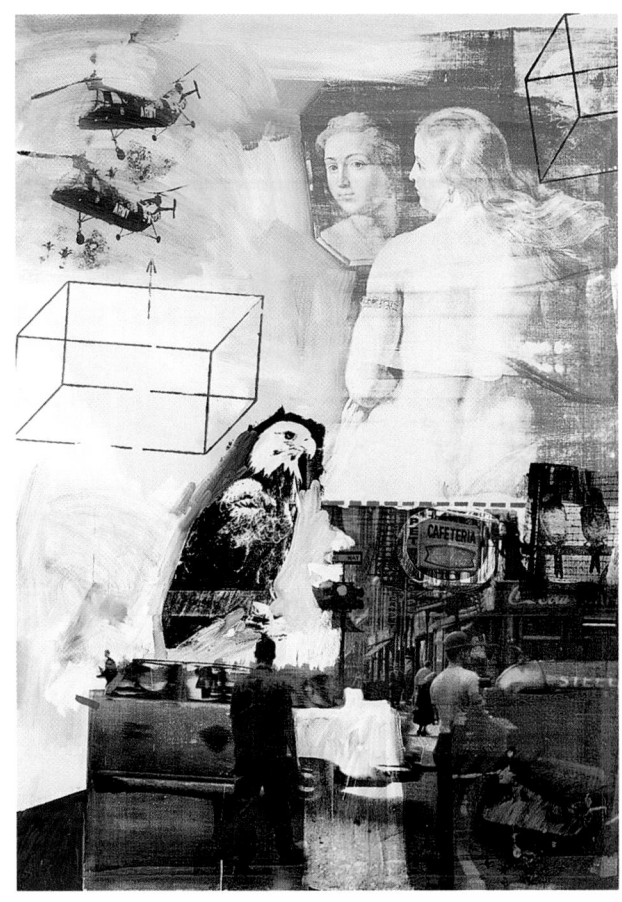

602 Robert Rauschenberg.
TRACER. 1963.
Oil and silkscreen on canvas. 84⅛″ × 60″.
Photograph: Jamison Miller © 2002 The Nelson Gallery Foundation.
The Nelson-Atkins Museum of Art, Kansas City, Missouri, (Purchase) F84–70.
© Robert Rauschenberg. Licensed by VAGA, New York, NY.

603 Edward Kienholz.
JOHN DOE. 1959.
Oil and paint on mannequin parts; perambulator, wood, metal, plaster, plastic, rubber.
39½″ × 19″ × 31½″.
The Menil Collection, Houston.

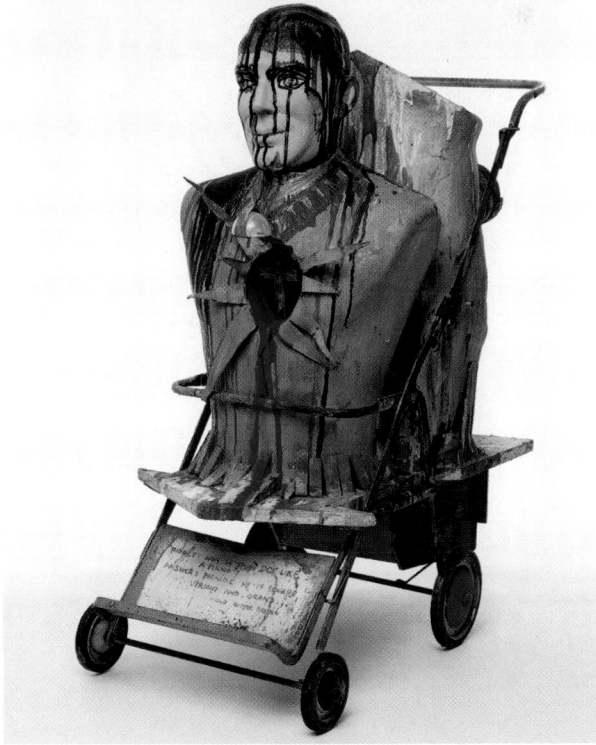

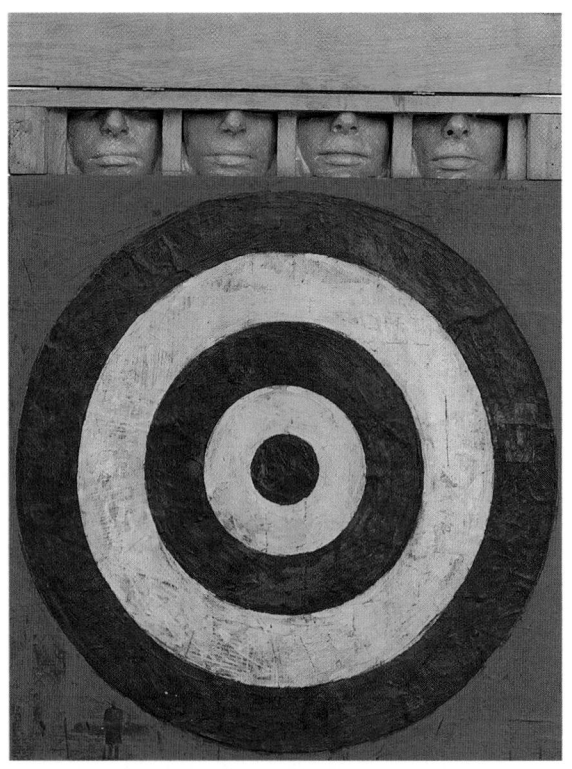

604   Jasper Johns.
TARGET WITH FOUR FACES. 1955.
Assemblage: encaustic on newspaper and collage on canvas with objects, surmounted by four tinted plaster faces in wood box with hinged front. Overall dimensions with box open, $33\frac{5}{8}'' \times 26'' \times 3''$.
The Museum of Modern Art, NY. Licensed by Scala-Art Resource, NY. Gift of Mr. and Mrs. Robert C. Scull, Photograph: © 2002 The Museum of Modern Art, NY. © Jasper Johns. Licensed by VAGA, NY.

of art" by signing their bodies and clothing. Niki de Saint Phalle made paintings and collages, and then symbolically killed them by piercing them with nails, darts, or even gunshots. ST. SEBASTIAN, OR THE PORTRAIT OF MY LOVE contains one of her husband's shirts and neckties below a dartboard. The artist drove dozens of nails into the shirt, and then threw darts at the board. These works by Saint Phalle and others continue the irreverent aspects of the spirit of Dada. Saint Phalle's target carries a far more direct meaning than that of Jasper Johns in his TARGET WITH FOUR FACES.

EVENTS AND HAPPENINGS

Artists have continued to extend the boundaries of the visual arts until they can no longer simply be defined as aesthetic objects. In addition to easel paintings, there are now room-size installation pieces; in addition to traditional sculpture, there are earthworks. And, in addition to stationary art objects, there are living, moving art events.

For Swiss sculptor Jean Tinguely, life was play, movement, and perpetual change. Tinguely made machines that do just about everything except work in the manner we expect. Although much kinetic art has celebrated science and technology, Tinguely enjoyed a mocking yet sympathetic relationship to machines and machine fallibility. "I try to distill the frenzy I see in the world, the mechanical frenzy of our joyful, industrial confusion."[1]

In 1960, Tinguely built a large piece of mechanized sculpture that he put together from materials

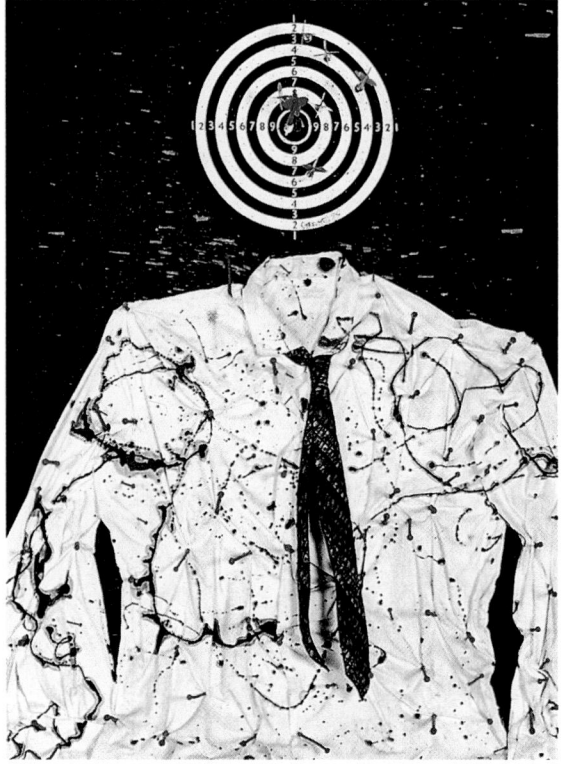

605   Niki de Saint Phalle.
ST. SEBASTIAN, OR THE PORTRAIT OF MY LOVE. 1960.
Oil, fabric, darts, and nails on wood and dartboard.
$28\frac{1}{2}'' \times 21\frac{3}{4}'' \times 2\frac{3}{4}''$.
Collection of the artist.
© 2002 Artists Rights Society (ARS), NY/ADAGP, Paris.

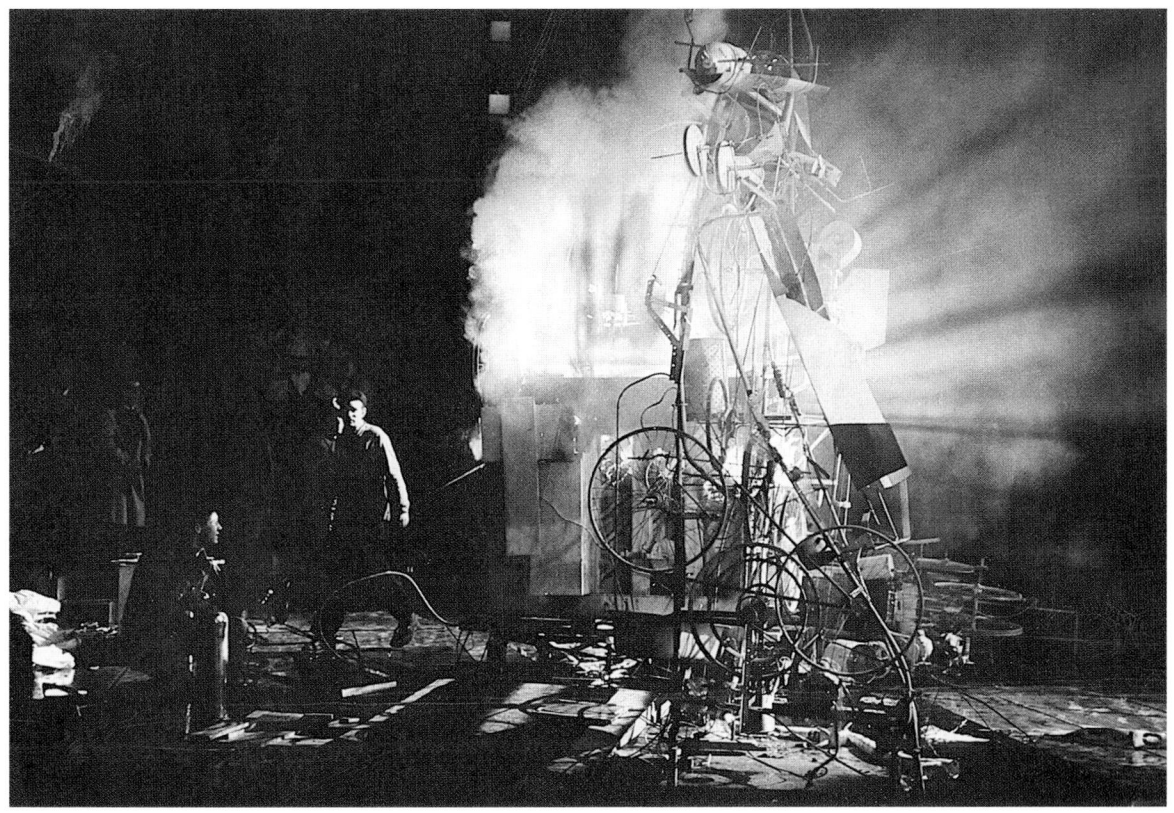

606 Jean Tinguely.
HOMAGE TO NEW YORK: A SELF-CONSTRUCTING,
SELF-DESTRUCTING WORK OF ART. 1960.
Photograph: David Gahr.
© 2002 Artists Rights Society (ARS), NY/ADAGP, Paris.

gathered from junkyards and stores in and around
New York City. The result was a giant assemblage
designed to destroy itself at the turn of a switch—
which it did in the courtyard of the Museum of
Modern Art in New York City on March 17, 1960.
The environmental sculpture was appropriately called
HOMAGE TO NEW YORK: A SELF-CONSTRUCTING, SELF-
DESTRUCTING WORK OF ART. Tinguely's HOMAGE
TO NEW YORK was an event, similar in its effect to a
Happening.

Happenings are cooperative events in which
viewers become active participants in partly
planned, partly spontaneous performances that
combine loose scenarios and considerable improvi-
sation. Strictly speaking, Happenings are drama
with "structure but no plot, words but no dialogue,
actors but no characters, and above all, nothing
logical or continuous."[2] Unlike Dada and Surrealist

events, the first Happenings were frequently
nihilistic, without a relieving sense of humor. No
help was given the viewer, who was expected to
find his or her own answers. Happenings led to
more controlled, more focused types of art events.

The term *Happening* was first used by Allan
Kaprow in the late 1950s. There were no spectators
at Kaprow's Happening, HOUSEHOLD (on the following page). At a preliminary meeting, participants were given parts. The action took place at an
isolated rural dump, amid smoldering piles of
refuse. The men built a wooden tower on a trash
pile while the women constructed a nest on
another mound. During the course of a series of
interrelated events, the men destroyed the nest and
the women retaliated by pulling down the men's
tower. In the process, participants gained a new
perspective on the theater of life in our time.

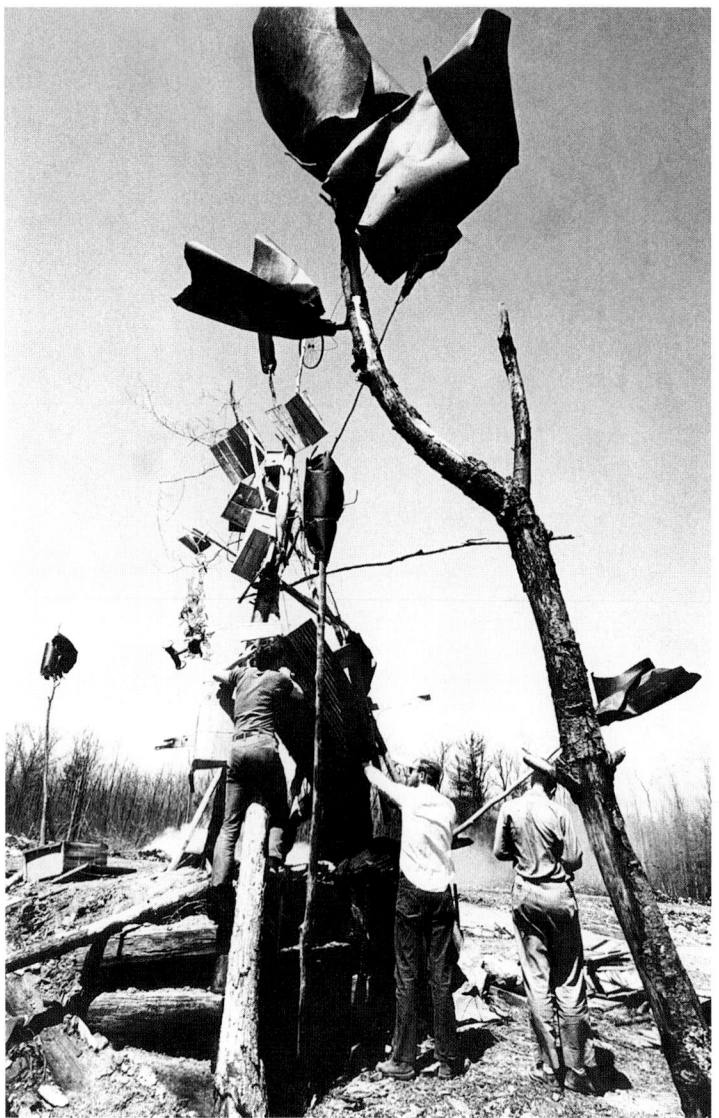

607 Allan Kaprow.
HOUSEHOLD.
Happening commissioned by Cornell University, performed May 1964.
Photograph: Solomon A. Goldberg.

POP ART

Pop artists use real objects or mass-production techniques in their art. Like the Dadaists before them, Pop artists wanted to challenge cultural assumptions about the definition of art; they also made ironic comments on contemporary life.

Commercial art, long denigrated by fine artists, became a source of inspiration. Pop painters used photographic screenprinting and airbrush techniques to achieve the surface characteristics of such anonymous mass-produced imagery as advertising, food labels, and comic books.

Pop Art flowered most brilliantly in the United States, but it first appeared in London, where a group of young artists made collages with images cut from popular magazines. In 1957, English artist Richard Hamilton published a list of characteristics of Pop Art for the London artists who were beginning to work in this vein. The list includes qualities of contemporary mass culture these artists addressed. Hamilton wrote that Pop Art should be:

Popular (designed for a mass audience)
Transient (short-term solution)
Expendable (easily forgotten)
Low-cost
Mass-produced
Young (aimed at youth)
Witty
Sexy
Gimmicky
Glamorous
Big business[3]

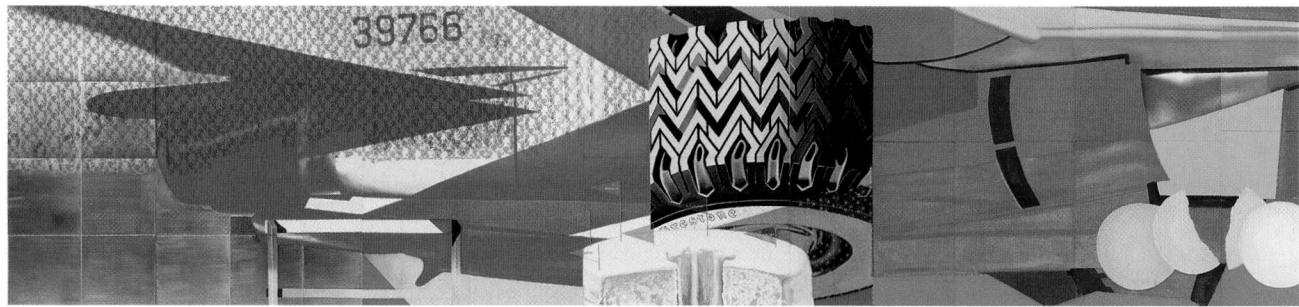

Pop Art's media sources include the comic strip, the advertising blowup, the famous-name-brand package, and the visual clichés of billboard, newspaper, movie theater, and television. Elements from all these mass media are included in Hamilton's collage JUST WHAT IS IT THAT MAKES TODAY'S HOMES SO DIFFERENT, SO APPEALING? Hamilton's work is a hilarious parody of the superficiality and materialism of modern popular culture. The word "pop" on the giant sucker gave the movement its name.

American artist James Rosenquist worked as a billboard painter after attending art school and college. Later, he incorporated his billboard experiences in a mature style that presents impersonally rendered montages of contemporary American popular culture. He drew on the techniques and imagery of sign painting, rendering huge close-up details of faces, natural forms, and industrial objects with a mechanical airbrush.

Rosenquist's huge mural F-111 filled all four walls of the Leo Castelli Gallery in New York City when it was first presented in 1965. The image of an F-111 fighter jet sweeps across his wall-to-wall environment of 1960s Americana. Rosenquist mixed symbols of affluence and destruction in his billboard-sized painting, which includes—in addition to a jet fighter plane—a hair dryer, a child of ambitious parents, a tire, lightbulbs, a beach umbrella, and a mushroom cloud from a nuclear bomb.

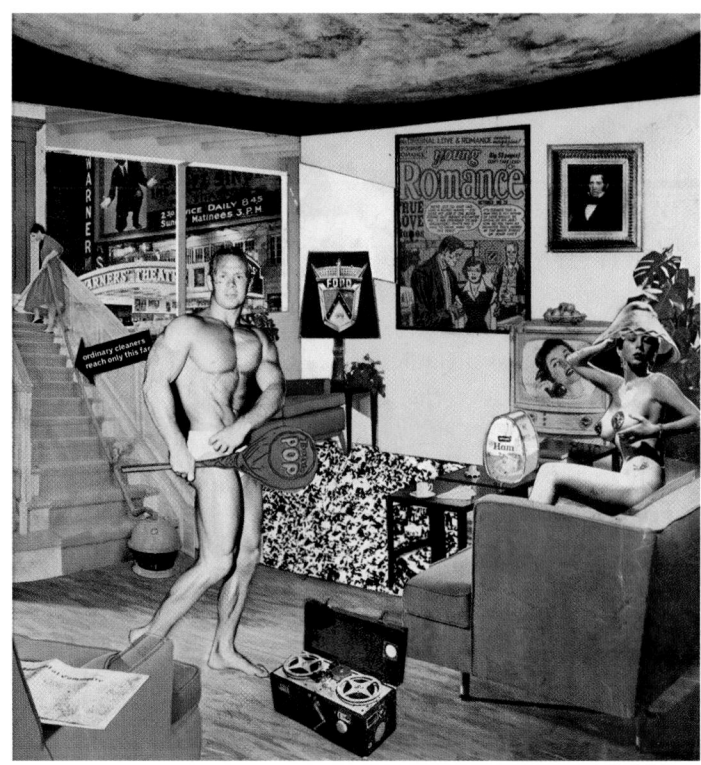

608 Richard Hamilton.
JUST WHAT IS IT THAT MAKES TODAY'S HOMES SO DIFFERENT, SO APPEALING? 1956.
Collage. 10¼″ × 9¾″.
Kunsthalle, Tübingen, Germany. © 2005 Artists Rights Society (ARS), NY. DACS, London.

609 James Rosenquist.
F-111. 1965.
Oil on canvas with aluminum, four parts. 10′ × 86′.
Private collection.
© James Rosenquist/Licensed by VAGA, NY.

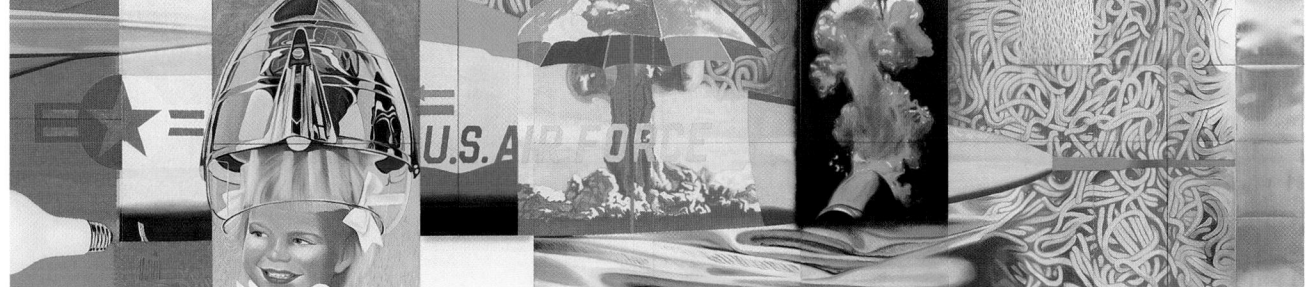

No American artist in the 1960s sparked more public indignation than Andy Warhol. He did not invent Pop Art, but he was its most visible and controversial exponent. Like Rosenquist, Warhol began his career as a commercial artist. When he moved into the fine-art sphere in the early 1960s, Warhol came as an inventive subversive.

Warhol's art shows us, in new ways, the effect of mass media and mass marketing on all of us. Among his most common subjects were consumer products such as Coca-Cola and Campbell's Soup. He blew up images of these products, silkscreened them onto canvas, and presented them as art. These works were made at a time when nationally standardized brands were just becoming the norm, as Americans began to prefer them to locally-produced goods. If multiple rows of identical cans in a store make us happy, then why not make them into art?

Another subject that he frequently treated was the mass media. He borrowed melodramatic images from news photographs and re-created them, singly or in identical rows. His works take no position on the event pictured; rather, they repackage for us their sensational aspect. He discovered that repeated exposure to events in the media desensitizes us to them, and his works re-enact the boredom. Indeed, boredom was another of his major themes, because it seems to characterize so much of modern life.

MARILYN DIPTYCH is his meditation on celebrity status. The work gives us the actress's face

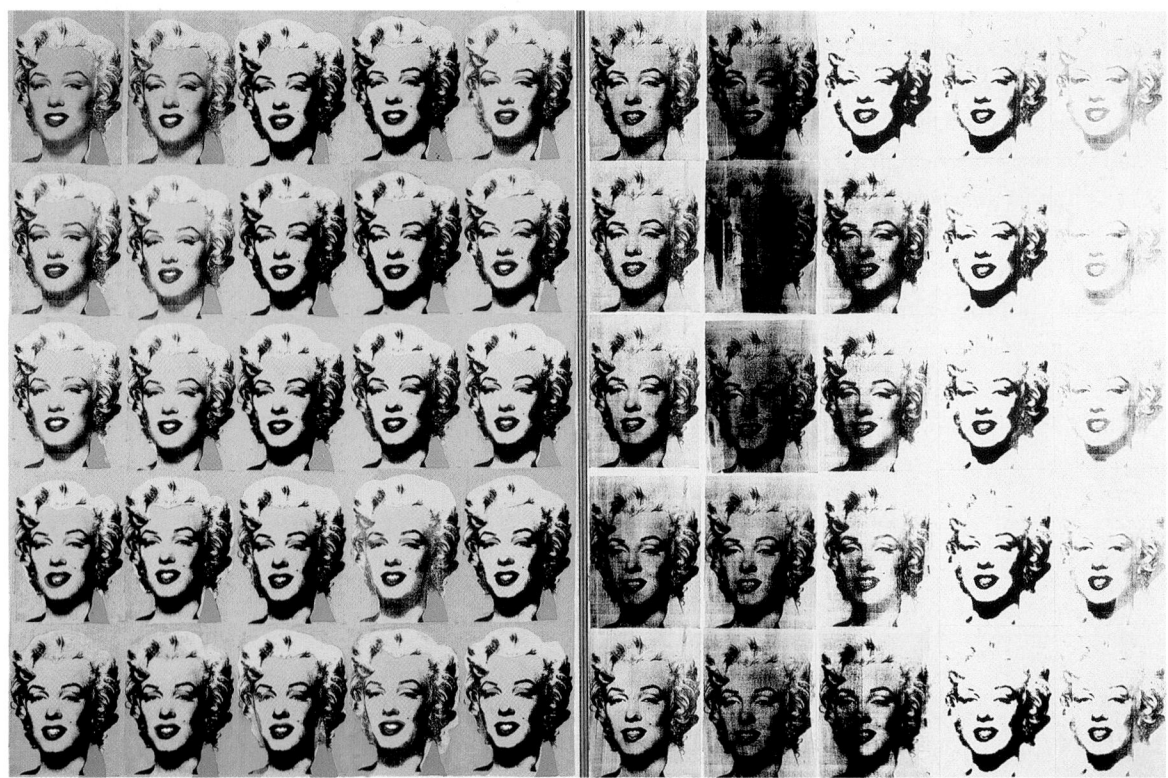

610 Andy Warhol.
MARILYN DIPTYCH. 1962.
© Tate Gallery, London. Art Resource, NY.
© 2005 Andy Warhol Foundation for the Visual Arts. Artists Rights Society (ARS), NY.
™2002 Marilyn Monroe LLC under license authorized by CMG Worldwide Inc.
Indianapolis, Indiana 46256 USA. www.MarilynMonroe.com.

611 Andy Warhol.
THIRTEEN MOST WANTED MEN.
1964.
Silkscreen ink on masonite.
25 panels each 48″ × 48″.
Photograph of installation on exterior of American Pavilion, New York World's Fair (destroyed).
Photograph © Eric Pollitzer. © 2009 The Andy Warhol Foundation for the Visual Arts. Artists Rights Society (ARS), NY.

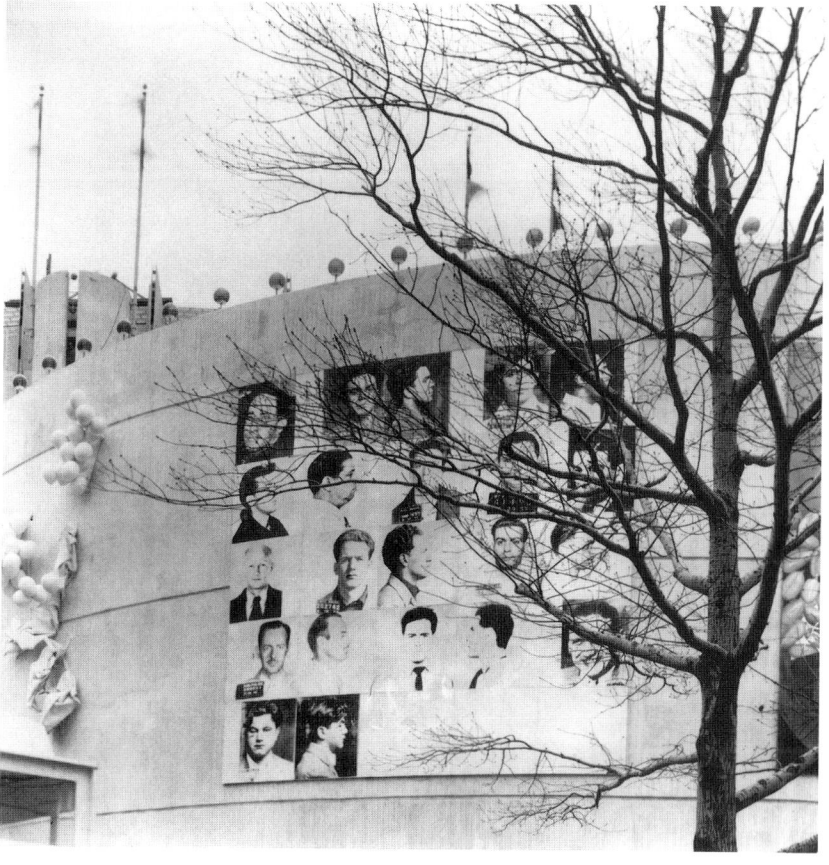

fifty times over, in smudged black-and-white and garish color. The work seems to be telling us that a celebrity is a packaged commodity. This was news in the 1960s; today most people seem to realize it. Warhol's work called attention to the pervasive and insistent character of our commercial environment. The repetition of mass imagery has become our cultural landscape and our mythology; the "canned" popular image sells us everything from processed foods to presidential candidates.

One of his most audacious projects was created—but never displayed—for the United States Pavilion at the New York World's Fair of 1964. At the invitation of the architect, Warhol installed

THIRTEEN MOST WANTED MEN, a twenty-foot-square mural of the faces of criminals gleaned from FBI "wanted" posters. A controversy immediately followed, centering on the potential glorification of crime, and whether the poster photos were art or not. Warhol's point was that crime is already a glamorous part of our culture and life, filling much of our media. We "want" these men, after all. When the Fair organizers demanded removal of the work, Warhol offered to put in its place a huge portrait of the Fair's chief organizer. When this was declined, officials removed THIRTEEN MOST WANTED MEN before the fair opened. See the essay at the end of this chapter for more information about censorship of modern art.

Warhol

The Pope of Pop

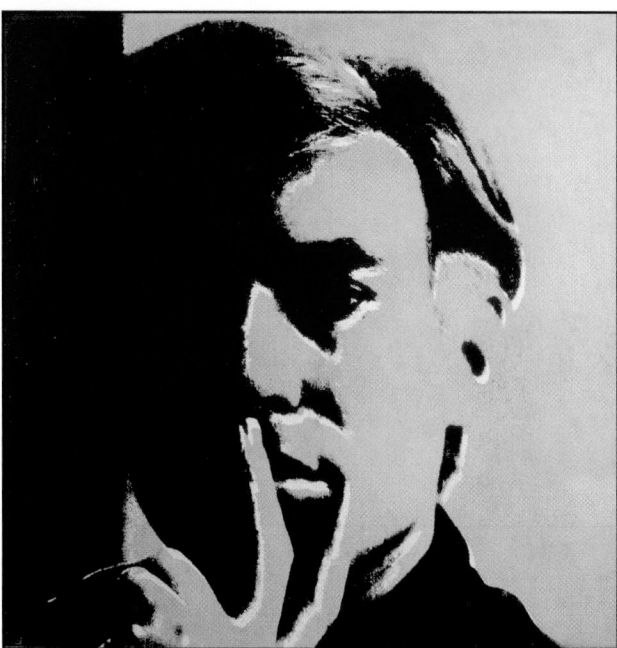

612 Andy Warhol.
SELF-PORTRAIT. 1966.
Silkscreen on silver coated paper. 23⅟₁₆″ × 23″.
The Museum of Modern Art. Licensed by Scala-Art Resource, NY. Philip Johnson Fund.
Photograph: © 2002 The Museum of Modern Art, NY.

PROBABLY NO ARTIST OF THE TWENTIETH CENTURY foreshadowed today's culture more than Andy Warhol. His treatment of themes such as celebrities, consumerism, and the mass media of the 1960s has become part of most people's standard way of thinking today.

His work functioned in the same way that his SELF-PORTRAIT does. His cool and detached face stares blankly back at us, just as his art reflects in a straightforward fashion our culture of celebrities, consumer products, and the media. Taking these phenomena wholesale into the art gallery raises our awareness of how they function.

He should be as famous for his philosophical pronouncements as for his art. Here are a few examples: "In the future everyone will be world famous for fifteen minutes." "When you see a gruesome picture over and over again, it doesn't really have any effect." "Being good in business is the most fascinating kind of art." "Department stores are kind of like museums." "I don't know where the artificial stops and the real starts." "Hollywood films are just planned-out commercials."

His early life gave little hint of his later importance: Born in Pittsburgh to a family of Ukrainian immigrants, he studied commercial art at the Carnegie Institute. On graduation in 1949 he moved to New York City, where he began to rise in the ranks of designers, making advertising layouts. His first paintings in 1960 served as backdrop for a department store display.

Following the lead of early Pop artists such as Richard Hamilton and Robert Rauschenberg, Warhol began to borrow the media's popular imagery and mass production for his own art. Most art critics in the early sixties panned his work, deeming it insincere, lacking in craftsmanship, and boring. But Warhol's defenders replied that he is only showing us our culture, where most of our public life is staged to look good in the media, craftsmanship vanished with the dawn of mass production, and boredom is common even in households with 250 TV channels. If contemporary culture is obsessed with celebrities and spectacles, Warhol foreshadowed this in works that isolate those phenomena in a memorable way.

He gave up painting in 1962 because it was, he said, too much work; instead he favored silkscreen, which yields hundreds of identical copies. His assistants made these works in a studio that he ironically called The Factory; it became a gathering place for the glamorous and the avant-garde.

Warhol was active in many realms besides the visual arts: He made several notorious movies on the theme of boredom. His first film in 1963 was *Sleep*, a six-hour film of a man sleeping. He promoted rock concerts featuring The Velvet Underground, a band that influenced many later groups. He also started the magazine *Interview*, which still functions today.

He reduced his activities somewhat after a disaffected member of The Factory crew shot him in 1968. This was Valerie Solanas, the subject of the documentary film *I Shot Andy Warhol*. (She had created a feminist group called The Society to Cut Up Men, or SCUM. Charged with attempted murder, she was judged not guilty by reason of insanity. The Scum Manifesto foreshadowed many concerns that later feminists developed.)

In the seventies, Warhol devoted himself mostly to making portraits of the rich and famous, who lined up to sit for him. The portraits were not based on the sitter's individual personality but rather on how they appeared in the media. Warhol apparently doubted that an individual's deeper soul even existed. Here is how he described himself: "If you want to know all about Andy Warhol, just look at the surface of my paintings and films and there I am. There's nothing behind it." His influence outlasted modern art, as we shall see in Chapter 25.

In DROWNING GIRL and other paintings, Roy Lichtenstein used comic book images with their bright primary colors, impersonal surfaces, and characteristic printing dots. His work is a commentary on a world obsessed with consumer goods, sex, and violence. He saw Pop Art as "involvement with what I think to be the most brazen and threatening characteristics of our culture, things we hate, but which are also powerful in their impingement on us."[4]

For several decades, Claes Oldenburg has been finding inspiration in the common, mass-produced artifacts of American society. His lumpy, gloopy TWO CHEESEBURGERS WITH EVERYTHING (known as DUAL HAMBURGERS) needs no explanation. There it is! Oldenburg enjoys taking mundane objects and remaking them into icons; see another project on page 87. Rather than turn away from the funk of neo-America, Oldenburg embraces it:

I am for Kool-Art, 7-UP art, Pepsi-art, Sunshine art, 39 cents art . . . Menthol art . . . Rx art . . . Now art . . . I am for U.S. Government Inspected Art, Grade A art, Regular Price art, Yellow Ripe art, Extra Fancy art, Ready-to-eat art.[5]

Since prehistoric times, art has helped people to describe, to understand, and to gain a sense of positive interaction with their surroundings. Cave dwellers, our ice-age ancestors, painted the animals that were a major feature of their environment; modern city dwellers draw inspiration from an urban environment, making art of the signs and symbols of popular culture.

MINIMAL AND HARD-EDGE

Pop Art was just one reaction against the self-absorbed quality of Abstract Expressionism. In the late 1950s and early 1960s, a number of artists who began as painters rejected painting because they felt it lacked the concreteness and presence of three-dimensional forms. However, their minimalist sculpture frequently has more in common with architecture and painting than it does with traditional sculpture. Instead of being emotionally

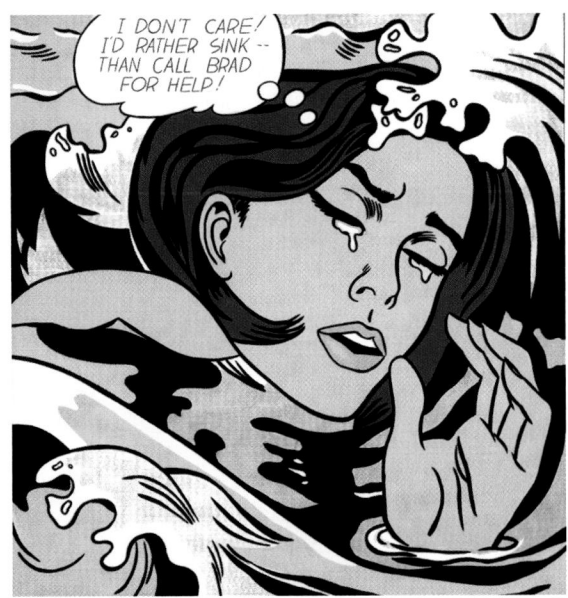

613 Roy Lichtenstein.
DROWNING GIRL. 1963.
Oil and synthetic polymer paint on canvas. 67⅝" × 66¾".
The Museum of Modern Art, NY. Licensed by Scala-Art Resource, NY.
Philip Johnson Fund and gift of Mr. and Mrs. Bagley Wright.
Photograph: © 2002 The Museum of Modern Art, NY.

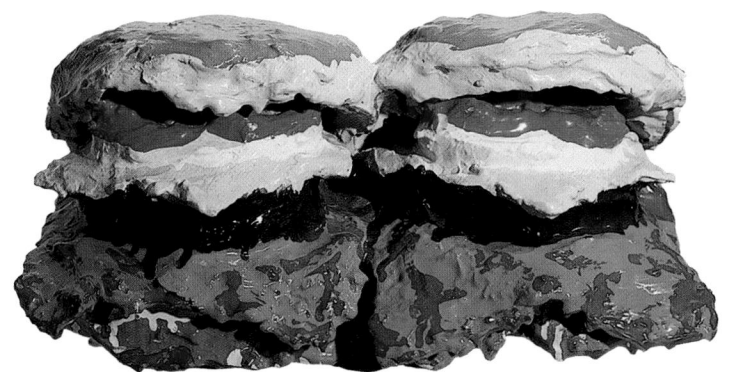

614 Claes Oldenburg.
TWO CHEESEBURGERS WITH EVERYTHING
(DUAL HAMBURGERS). 1962.
Burlap soaked in plaster, painted with enamel.
7" × 14¾" × 8⅝".
The Museum of Modern Art, NY. Licensed by Scala-Art Resource, NY.
Philip Johnson Fund. Photograph: © 2002 The Museum of Modern Art, NY.

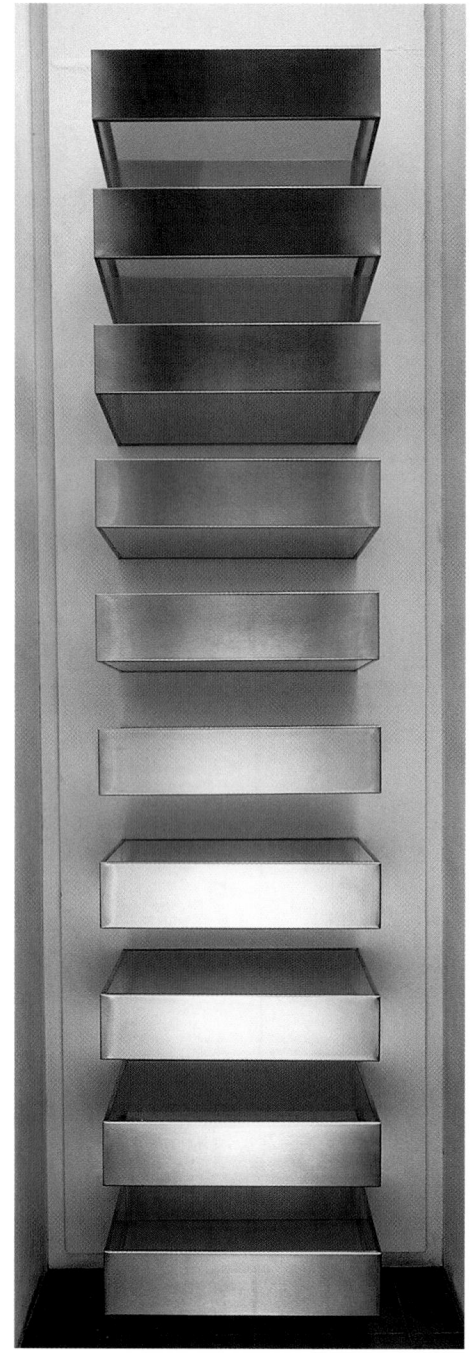

615 Donald Judd.
UNTITLED. 1967.
Stainless steel and plexiglass, ten units.
9⅛″ × 40″ × 31″.
Collection of the Modern Art Museum of Fort Worth. Museum Purchase,
The Benjamin J. Tillar Memorial Trust.
© Donald Judd Foundation. Licensed by VAGA, New York, NY.

charged, the works are nonsensual, impersonal, geometric structures.

Among those who went from painting to sculpture was Donald Judd. He worked with industrial materials such as sheet metal, aluminum, and molded plastics, which had not previously been used for art; his UNTITLED combines stainless steel and plexiglass. Judd was a leading artist and the major spokesman for the Minimalist movement. In his essay "Specific Objects," he wrote about the aims of his art:

It isn't necessary for a work to have a lot of things to look at, to compare, to analyze one by one, to contemplate. The thing as a whole, its quality as a whole, is what is interesting. . . . In the new work the shape, image, color, and surface are single, and not partial and scattered.[6]

Other painters and sculptors took different approaches. Some painters shared an interest in what they saw as the essence of painting: a flat, colored surface. Quick-drying acrylic paints, which were developed at this time, lend themselves to uniform application and to the use of tape to obtain shapes with precise edges—a style called *hard-edge*. This somewhat misleading term refers to works concerned not only with linear definition but with the relationship of color to form.

The most complete application of Minimalism occurs in sculpture, yet painters were also involved. As paintings became objects rather than reflections of objects, they began to function as environments in themselves instead of as representations of environments.

Ellsworth Kelly's bold paintings are richly hued studies of color and form. BLUE, GREEN, YELLOW, ORANGE, RED is self-explanatory in at least a superficial sense. At a deeper level, Minimalism is a quest to see if art can still be art without representation, storytelling, or personal feeling. If the work had curved lines, modeled color, or paint strokes, it would not be as pure. Rather, the subject seems to be color itself: how we respond to it, and how different colors interact with each other in our field of

616 Ellsworth Kelly.
BLUE, GREEN, YELLOW, ORANGE, RED. 1966.
Oil on canvas, 5 panels. Overall: 60″ × 240″.
Solomon R. Guggenheim Museum, NY. Photograph by Ellen Labenski.
© The Solomon R. Guggenheim Foundation, NY. (FN 67. 1833).

view. It is an optical experiment that throws away a great many of the traditional rules. Such quests for the essence of art motivated many in those years.

Frank Stella's rigorous hard-edge paintings of the 1960s emphasize the flatness of the picture plane and its boundaries. He treated his paintings like constructed objects rather than pictures. In AGBATANA III, Stella replaced the traditional rectangular format with a distinctive outer profile to further extend the concept of the surface as an object in its own right rather than as a field for illusions. External boundaries of the overall shape are arrived at internally. There is no figure-ground relationship; within the painting, everything is figure. Interwoven bands of both muted and intense colors pull together in a tight spatial weave.

Stella's intellectual conception of the painting-as-object brought him close to the realm of sculpture and aligned him with Minimalism. Minimalists admired the unified, all-at-once, nonrelational character of works by such artists as Pollock and Rothko. Minimalism depends on such a total impression. Formal properties are reduced to essentials.

CONCEPTUAL ART

During the 1960s and 1970s, artists reacted ever more quickly to each successive aesthetic movement. Pushing back the limits, the next reductive step after Minimalist art became no art at all—that

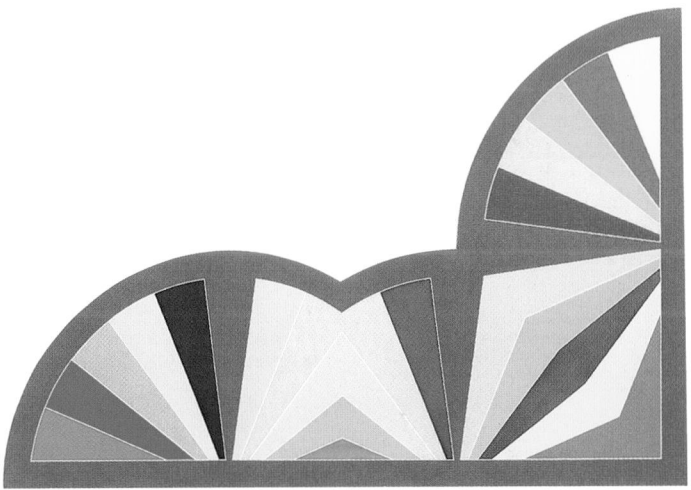

617 Frank Stella.
AGBATANA III. 1968.
Fluorescent acrylic on canvas. 120″ × 180″.
© Allen Memorial Art Museum, Oberlin College, Ohio.
Ruth C. Roush Fund for Contemporary Art and National Foundation
for the Arts and Humanities Grant, 1968.
© 2002 Frank Stella. Artists Rights Society (ARS), NY.

is, an art of ideas rather than objects. Conceptual Art, in which an idea takes the place of the art object, was an outgrowth of Minimalism and a reaction to Pop. The Conceptual movement was heavily indebted to Marcel Duchamp, the first champion of an art of ideas.

Joseph Kosuth, the most rigorous early Conceptualist, was angered at the materialism of the art market and Pop Art's embrace of commercialism. In 1965, he produced ONE AND THREE CHAIRS,

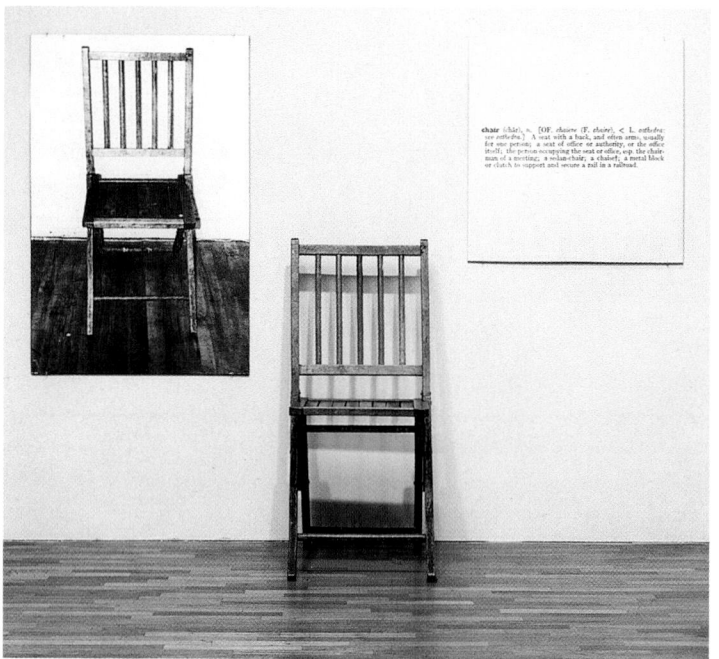

618 Joseph Kosuth.
ONE AND THREE CHAIRS. 1965.
Wooden folding chair, photographic copy of a chair, and photographic
enlargement of dictionary definition of a chair. Chair, 32⅜″ × 14⅞″ × 20⅞″.
Photo panel, 36″ × 24⅛″. Text panel, 24″ × 24⅛″.
The Museum of Modern Art, NY. Licensed by Scala-Art Resource, NY.
Larry Aldrich Foundation Fund. Photograph: © 2002 The Museum of Modern Art, NY.
© 2002 Joseph Kosuth. Artists Rights Society (ARS), NY.

which consisted of a wooden chair, a photograph of
the same chair, and a photographic enlargement of
a dictionary definition of the word "chair." The
piece shows that we apprehend each of the three
forms of a chair somewhat differently.

Conceptual art is based on the fact that a work
of art usually begins as an idea in the artist's mind. A
great work of art is a great idea first, and its creator
merely carries out the idea. If this is true, then art
can still be art without a unique, artist-made object.
If we "get the idea," then we have understood the
piece. Creativity is, after all, a mental process.

Rather than making things, Conceptual artists
present us with enough information so that we
grasp the concept they have in mind. Another early
leader in the movement was Yoko Ono, whose
pieces are generally instructions to viewers. One
example: Take 15 minutes to pronounce the word
south. The best way to illustrate this work is to try it
yourself and see what happens.

SITE WORKS AND EARTHWORKS

In the late 1960s, a number of artists working
under the influence of Minimalism and Conceptual Art went beyond the prevailing idea of sculpture as a portable precious object. They began creating works that are inseparable from the sites for
which they were designed. In *site-specific* works, the
artist's sensitivity to the location determines the
composition, scale, medium, and even the content
of each piece.

When Bulgarian artist Christo was a student,
he was alienated by the narrowness of his country's
officially prescribed social realist art. His enthusiasm was aroused, however, by government-
sponsored trips to the countryside, during which
he and other art students advised farmers on how
to improve the appearance of the landscape for foreigners traveling on the *Orient Express*.

Christo first made his living as a portrait
painter. Later, he joined a group of artists in Paris
who were presenting objects as art rather than making painted or sculpted representations of objects.
In collaboration with his wife he began wrapping
in fabric objects ranging in size from a motorcycle
to a mile of sea cliffs in Australia.

One of Christo and Jeanne-Claude's most ambitious projects was RUNNING FENCE, a temporary
environmental artwork that was as much a process
and an event as it was sculpture. The eighteen-foot-
high white nylon fence ran from the ocean at
Bodega Bay in Sonoma County, California,
through 24.5 miles of agricultural and dairy land.
RUNNING FENCE was a unique event, ultimately
involving thousands of people. The project required
political action, the agreement of landowners, and
the help of hundreds of workers. They raised the
necessary funds for this and other projects by selling
drawings and collages of their works.

The seemingly endless ribbon of white cloth
made the wind visible and caught the changing
light as it stretched across the gently rolling hills,
appearing and disappearing on the horizon. The
simplicity of RUNNING FENCE relates it to Minimalist art, but the fence itself was not presented as an
art object. Rather, it was the focal point for a work
that interwove people, process, object, and place.

Walter De Maria's THE LIGHTNING FIELD is a site sculpture designed to be viewed over a period of time. The work consists of four hundred stainless-steel poles arranged in a rectangular grid over an area measuring one mile by one kilometer (0.6 mile) in west central New Mexico. The sharpened tips of the poles form a level plane, a kind of monumental bed of nails. Each of the poles can act as a lightning conductor during the electrical storms that occur frequently over the desert. (Actual strikes are rare, however.) Early and late in the day the poles reflect the sun, creating accents of technological precision in sharp contrast to the otherwise natural landscape. Purposely isolated from the art-viewing public, THE LIGHTNING FIELD combines aspects of both Conceptual and Minimalist art. Viewers must arrange their visits through the Dia Foundation, which commissioned the piece. Once there, they are left to study the work and make their own interpretations.

Site works are environmental constructions, frequently made of sculptural materials, designed to interact with, but not permanently alter, the

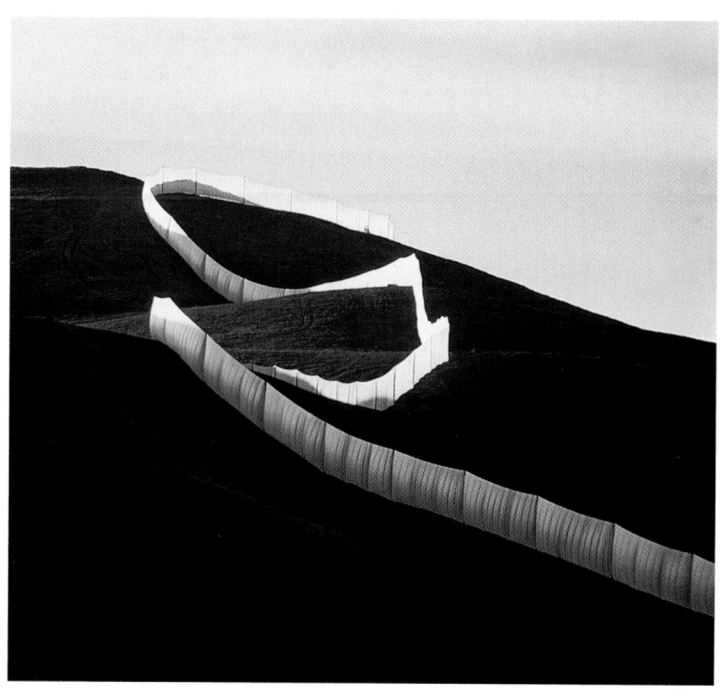

619 Christo and Jeanne-Claude.
RUNNING FENCE. 1972–1976.
Sonoma and Marin Counties, California. 18 feet × 24½ miles. Nylon fabric and steel poles.
© 1976 Christo. Photograph: Walfgang Volz.

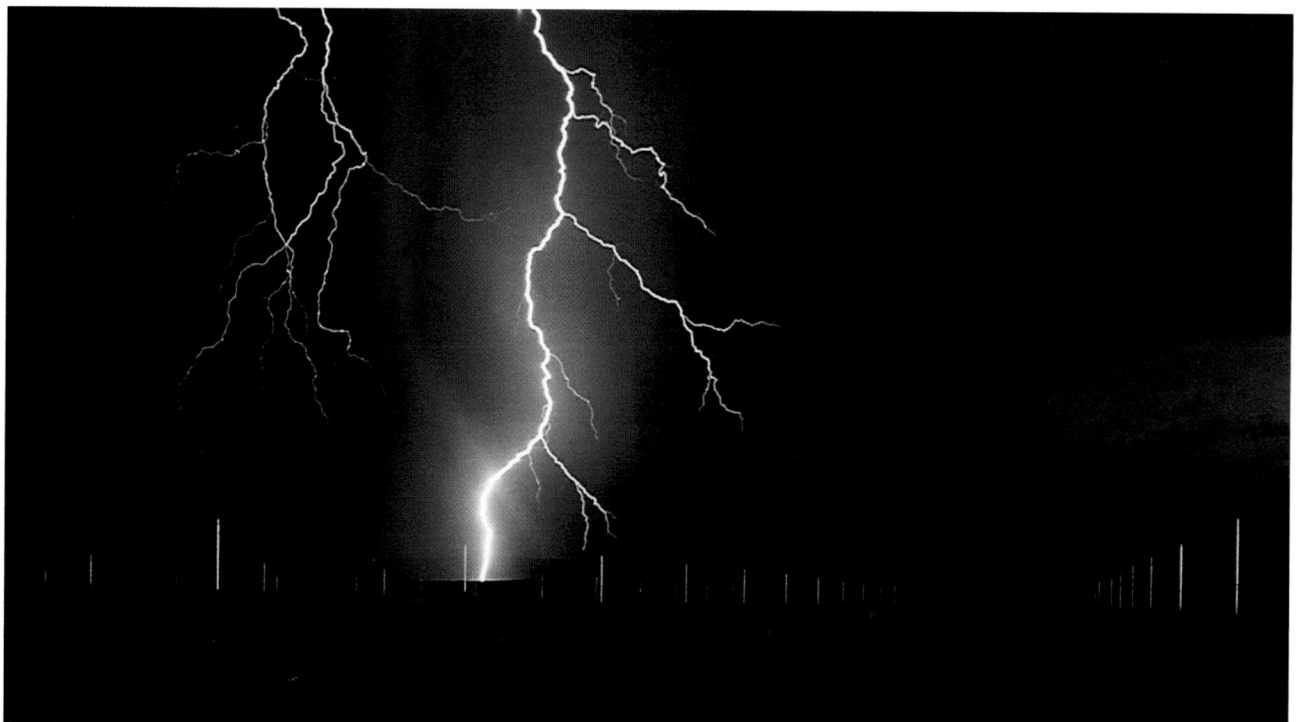

620 Walter De Maria. THE LIGHTNING FIELD. 1977.
Quemado, New Mexico. 400 stainless-steel poles, average height 20′7″; land area 1 mile × 1 kilometer.
Photograph: John Cliett. © Dia Center for the Arts, New York.

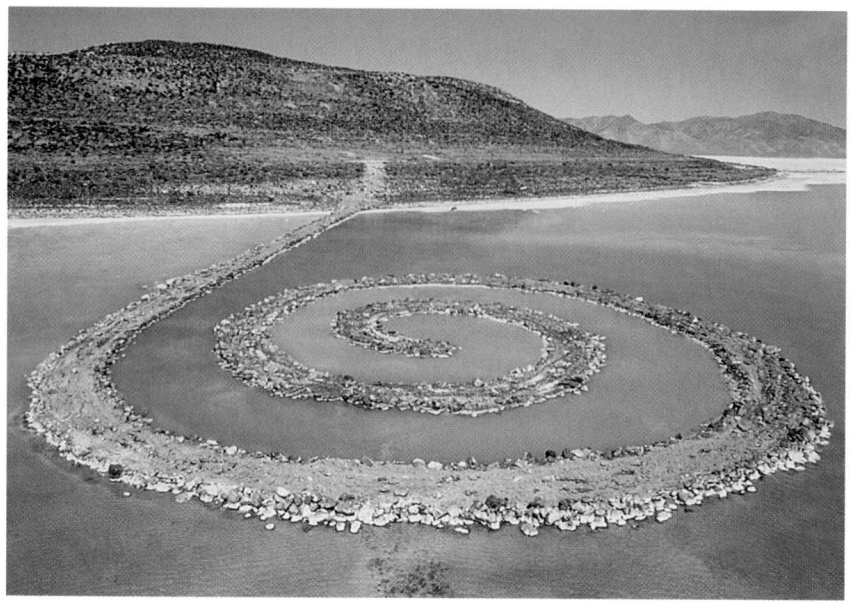

621 Robert Smithson.
SPIRAL JETTY. 1970.
Great Salt Lake, Utah. Earthwork.
Length 1500′, width 15′.
© Gianfranco Gorgoni Art. © Estate of Robert
Smithson. Licensed by VAGA, NY.

environment. *Earthworks* are sculptural forms made of materials such as earth, rocks, and sometimes plants. They are often very large, and they may be executed in remote locations. Earthworks are usually designed to merge with or complement the landscape. Many site works and earthworks show their creators' interest in ecology and in the earthworks of ancient America.

Robert Smithson was one of the founders of the earthworks movement. His SPIRAL JETTY, completed at Great Salt Lake, Utah, in 1970, has since gone in and out of view several times with changes in the water level. Its natural surroundings emphasize its form as willful human design. Although our society has no supportive, agreed-upon symbolism or iconography, we instinctively respond to universal signs like the spiral, which are found in nature and in ancient art.

The earthworks and site works movements have helped redirect relationships among architecture, sculpture, and the environment.

Although site-specific works can be commissioned, they are almost never resold unless someone buys the land they occupy. Artists who create conceptual art, earthworks, site works, and performance art share a common desire to subvert the gallery-museum-collector syndrome, to present art as an experience rather than as a commodity.

INSTALLATIONS AND ENVIRONMENTS

While some artists were creating outdoor earthworks and site works, others were moving beyond the traditional concepts of indoor painting and sculpture. Since the mid-1960s, artists from diverse backgrounds and points of view have fabricated interior installations and environments rather than portable works of art. Some installations alter the entire spaces they occupy; others are experienced as large sculpture; most of them assume the viewer to be a part of the piece.

James Turrell's installations challenge assumptions about the truth of what we see. By manipulating light and space, Turrell creates environments that cause shifts in viewers' perceptions. His work goes beyond the lean physical structures of Minimalism, and beyond Conceptualism's reliance on words and ideas, to dwell on the mysterious and at times awe-inspiring interaction of light, space, and time. Light becomes a tangible physical presence in works such as AMBA, where viewers are coaxed into paying attention to their own perceptions.

The work is about your seeing. It is responsive to the viewer. As you move within the space or as you decide to see it, one way or another, its reality can change.[7]

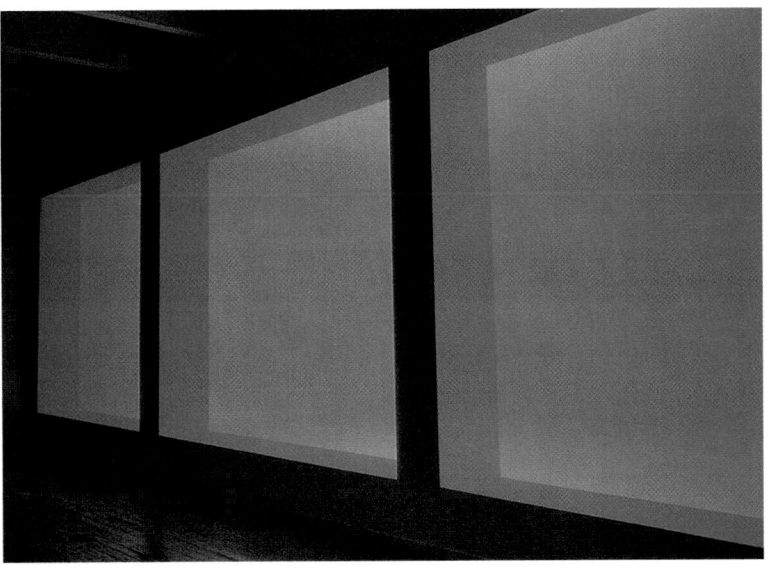

622 James Turrell.
AMBA. 1982.
Light installation.
Photograph courtesy of the artist.

What really interests me is having the viewer make discoveries the same way the artist does . . . instead of having the viewer participate vicariously, through someone else. . . . You determine the reality of what you see. The work is the product of my vision, but it's about your seeing. The poles of the realm in which I operate are the physical limitations of human vision and the learned limits of perception, or what I call "prejudiced perception." Encountering these prejudices can be an amazing experience, and if someone can come to these discoveries directly, the way the artist does, the impact is greater and so is the joy.[8]

Turrell has also created what he calls Skyspaces, windowless rooms with a portion of the ceiling removed to expose the sky. He encourages viewers to visit them near sunset, when the daylight is changing to evening.

As San Francisco's de Young Museum was moving into its new building in 2005, the directors engaged British artist Andy Goldsworthy to create an installation at the entrance. For his creation DRAWN STONE, the artist broke off huge blocks of paving stones to make benches. He then pierced the courtyard with a long, thin crack that meanders crazily

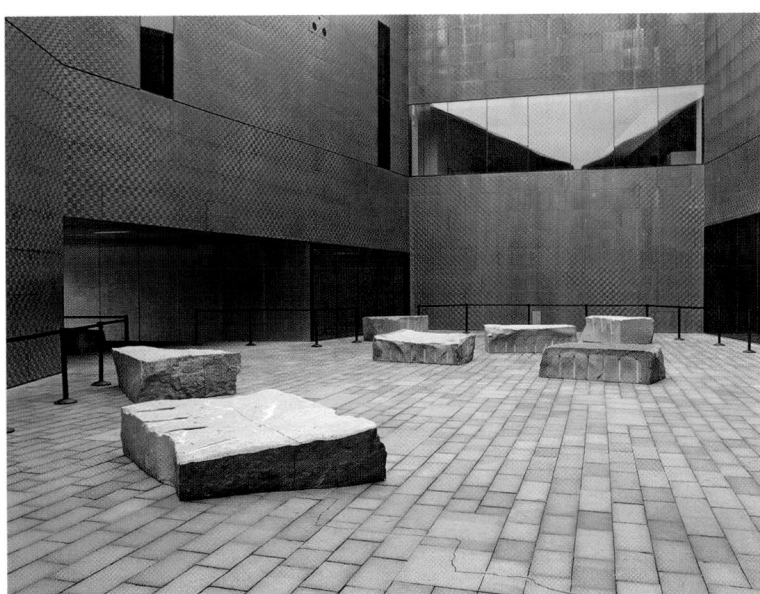

623 Andy Goldsworthy.
DRAWN STONE. 2005.
Site-specific stone installation at the
de Young Museum, San Francisco.
Fine Arts Museums of San Francisco, Museum
Purchase. Gift of Lonna and Marshall Wais,
2004–2005.

from the sidewalk to the front door, passing through some of the benches. This crack is a subtle reference to the earthquake that ruined the museum's previous building. Goldsworthy said:

Holes and cracks have always been for me a way of reaching below the surface of a material—a way of entering a stone, and a release of the energy contained within. These ideas inevitably take on greater significance and meaning in California.[9]

EARLY FEMINISM

In the late 1960s, many women artists began to speak out against the discrimination they faced in their careers. It was rare for women to be taken seriously in artists' groups; galleries were more willing to exhibit the work of men than of women; and museums collected the work of men far more often than that of women. Moreover, it seemed to the early feminists that making art about their experience as women might doom them to obscurity in a male-dominated art world. In the early 1970s in New York and California, they began to take action.

Lucy Lippard, an art critic and feminist, argues, "The overwhelming fact remains that a woman's experience in this society—social and biological—is simply not like that of a man. If art comes from the inside, as it must, then the art of men and women must be different, too."[10] The work of some women artists definitely is influenced by their gender and their interest in feminist issues.

California feminists tended to work collaboratively, and to make use of media that have been traditionally associated with "craft work" and with women: ceramics and textiles. THE DINNER PARTY was a collaboration of many women (and a few men), organized and directed by Judy Chicago over a period of five years. This cooperative venture was in itself a political statement about the supportive nature of female experience, as opposed to the frequently competitive nature of the male.

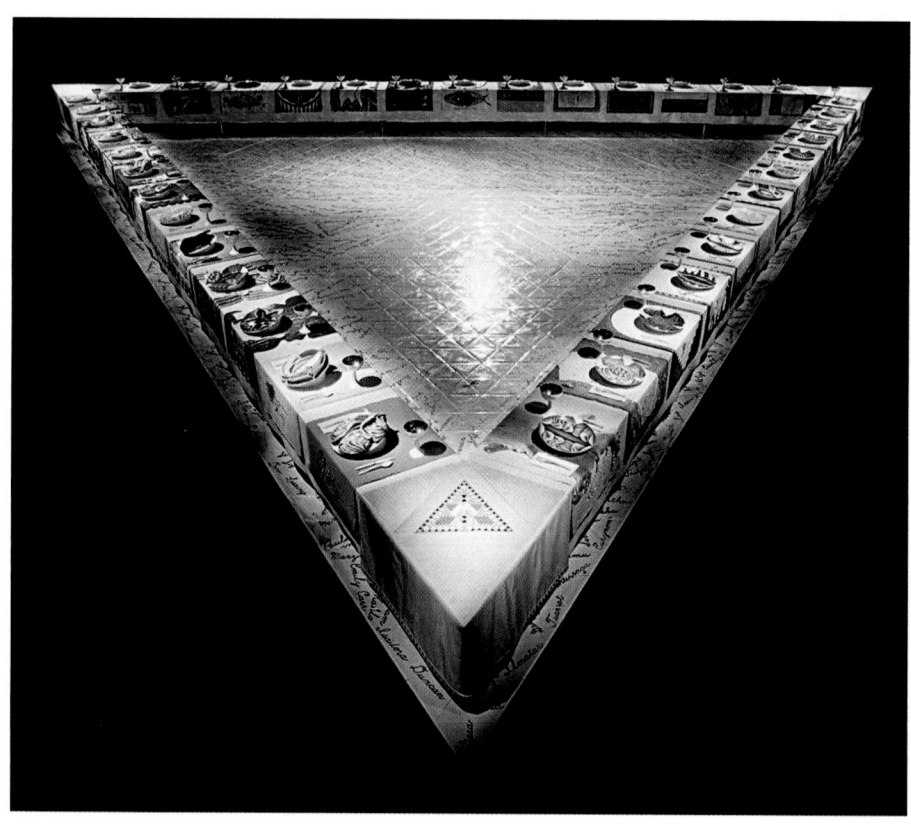

624 Judy Chicago.
THE DINNER PARTY. 1979.
Mixed Media. $48' \times 48' \times 42' \times 3'$.
Triangular table on white tile floor.
Collection of the Brooklyn Museum of Art, Gift of the Elizabeth A. Sackler Foundation.
Photograph: © Donald Woodman. © 2005 Judy Chicago. Artists Rights Society (ARS), NY.

A large triangular table contains place settings for thirty-nine women who made important contributions to world history. These run a wide gamut, from Egyptian Queen Hatshepsut to Georgia O'Keeffe. The names of 999 additional women of achievement are inscribed on ceramic tiles below the table. Each place setting includes a hand-embroidered fabric runner and a porcelain plate designed in honor of that woman. Some of the plates are painted with flat designs; others have modeled and painted relief motifs; many are explicitly sexual, embellished with flowerlike female genitalia.

East Coast feminists were more pointed in their protests. Some of them formed the group Women Artists in Revolution (WAR), which picketed museums. In response to private dealers who were reluctant to show work by women, they formed their own collaborative gallery, Artists in Residence (AIR). Nancy Spero, a leader in East Coast feminist circles, participated in both groups. Her work from the late 1960s and early 1970s used uncommon media such as paper scrolls, stencils, and printing to document subjects such as the torture and abuse of women. Her later scrolls, such as REBIRTH OF VENUS, attempt to present images of women different from those commonly seen in art. In the segment illustrated here, an ancient statue of the love goddess Venus is split open to reveal a woman sprinter who runs directly toward the viewer. The contrast between the two images is difficult to miss. Woman as love object gives way to woman as achiever. (Compare this work to Botticelli's Renaissance BIRTH OF VENUS on page 270.)

One of the most radical feminists in Europe was Orlan, who, like Judy Chicago, rejected the name she was born with. Her persistent theme has been the woman's body as the site of cultural debate and struggle. In 1974, she donned a nun's costume based on Bernini's ECSTASY OF ST. TERESA (see page 283), and performed a strip-tease that she documented in a series of photographs. Thus she passed between the two poles of identity (virgin and whore) that she saw the culture allotting to women. She also photographed parts of her body and sold them at a street market in Portugal.

Her most controversial work came in 1977 when she crashed a contemporary art exhibition in Paris with LE BAISER DE L'ARTISTE (The Artist's Kiss) (on the following page). She was not invited to this show, but rather set up her exhibit at the staircase leading to it. On a large black pedestal, viewers approached either Orlan the Saint (a photo from the earlier strip-tease act) or Orlan the Body (the artist herself sitting behind an invented vending machine). A soundtrack invited viewers to either bring a candle to the virgin, or insert a coin in the slot below the artist's chin. As the coin ran down to its receptacle, the artist dispensed kisses. This rather scandalous performance forcefully raised the issue of woman as virginal ideal or as marketable commodity; it also cost the artist her teaching position.

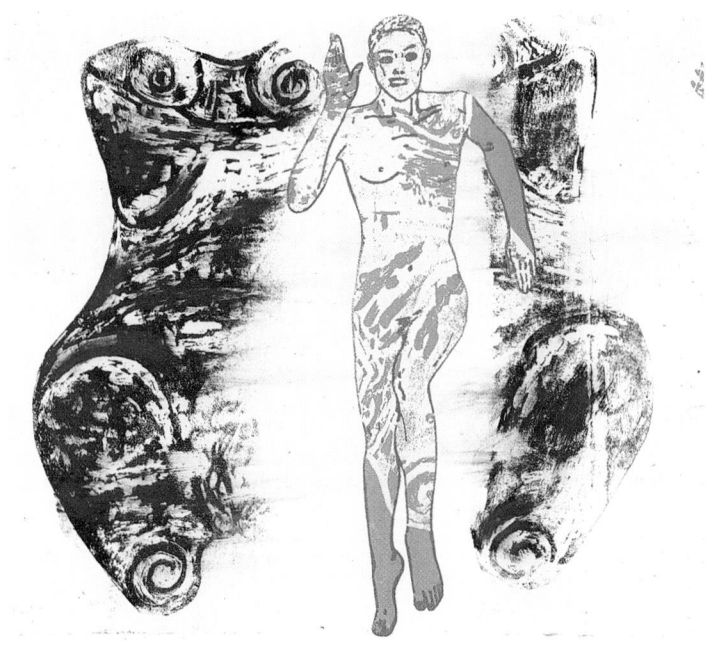

625 Nancy Spero.
REBIRTH OF VENUS. Detail. 1984.
Handprinting on paper. 12″ × 62′.
Courtesy of the artist.
Photograph: David Reynolds

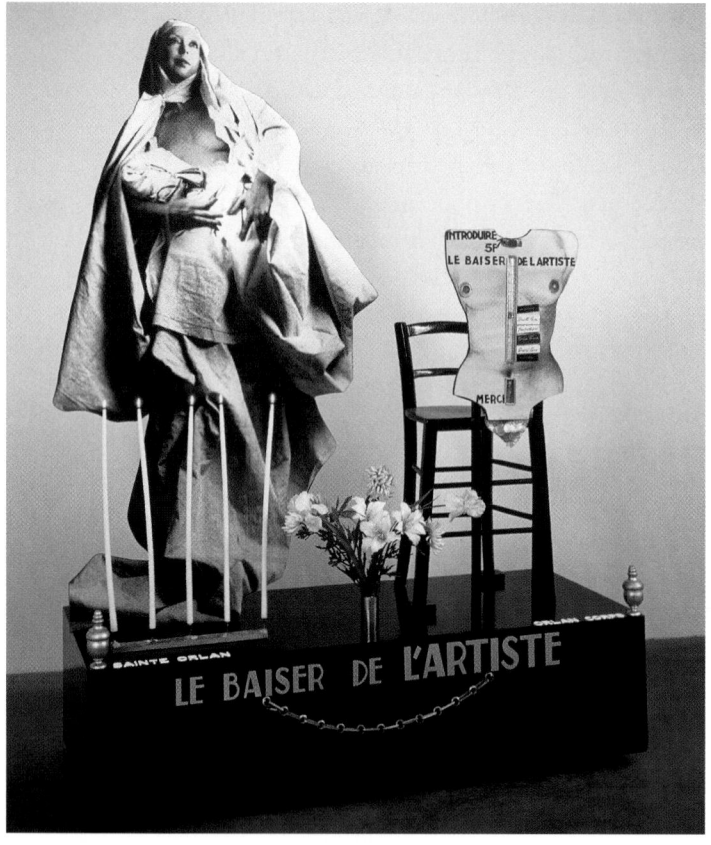

626 Orlan.
LE BAISER DE L'ARTISTE (The Artist's Kiss). 1977.
Mixed media with paint, metal chain, photographs, wood,
blinking diode, artificial candles, artificial flowers, and CD.
86½" × 67" × 23½".
In the collection of the Fonds Regional d'art Contemporian, Pays de la Loire,
France © ORLAN © 2009 Artists Rights Society (ARS), NY.

Researchers and art historians continue to uncover and publicize work by women throughout history, and each edition of this book has benefited from the effort by including more of them. Because Feminism has influenced most contemporary art movements since the 1970s, it makes little sense to separate feminist artists in discussions of the styles of the last quarter-century.

PERFORMANCE ART

In performance art, artists do not use traditional media at all. Rather, they perform actions before an audience or in nature. Thus this art form contains both visual art and drama, and has historical antecedents in Dada performances of the early twentieth century as well as in Expressionist painting. An Abstract Expressionist painting is the frozen record of an event (the act of making a painting). The next step was easy: eliminate the record and concentrate on the event itself. The record was in the remembered experience of the participants and in a few photographs. The Happenings movement is another important antecedent. Forms of art such as Conceptual art, which emphasize idea and process, are related to performance art.

One of the most influential performance artists of the 1960s and 1970s was German-born Joseph Beuys. He carried out actions that resonated with deep symbolic significance, as if he were a healer or shaman. For one 1965 piece, he swathed his head in honey and gold leaf, and carried a dead rabbit around an art gallery explaining to it the paintings on view, touching the rabbit's lifeless paw to each. Some people, he later said, were as insensitive in their daily lives as the rabbit was in the art gallery. Arriving in New York for the first time in 1974, he immediately plunged into a work called COYOTE: I LIKE AMERICA AND AMERICA LIKES ME. Met at the airport by an ambulance, he was wrapped in felt and taken to a gallery, where he lived for a week with a coyote. The animal symbolized the wild West; copies of the *Wall Street Journal* were delivered daily to represent contemporary, business-oriented culture. He meant to heal the breach between the two.

Cuban émigré Ana Mendieta used her own body in several works as a symbol of the earth and natural cycles. In the TREE OF LIFE SERIES, she coated her body with mud and grasses and stood against ancient tree trunks. She intended in these pieces to show the essential equivalence between femaleness and natural processes such as birth and growth. For her, as for many early feminists, biology accounted for most of the differences between women and men. Through the natural cycles of their bodies, she seems to be saying, women are closer to the rhythms of the earth.

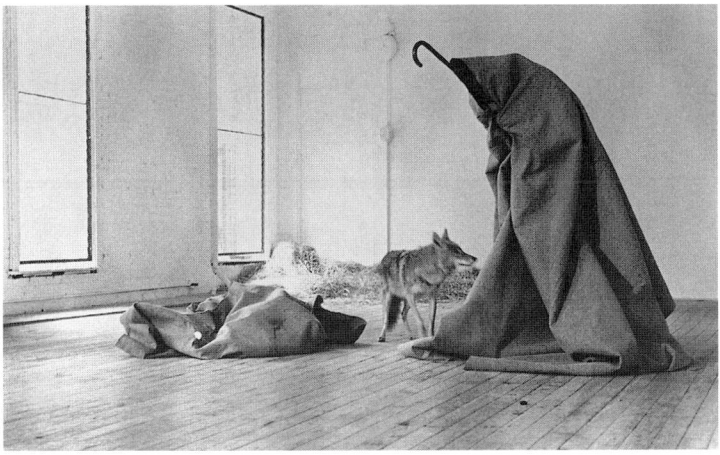

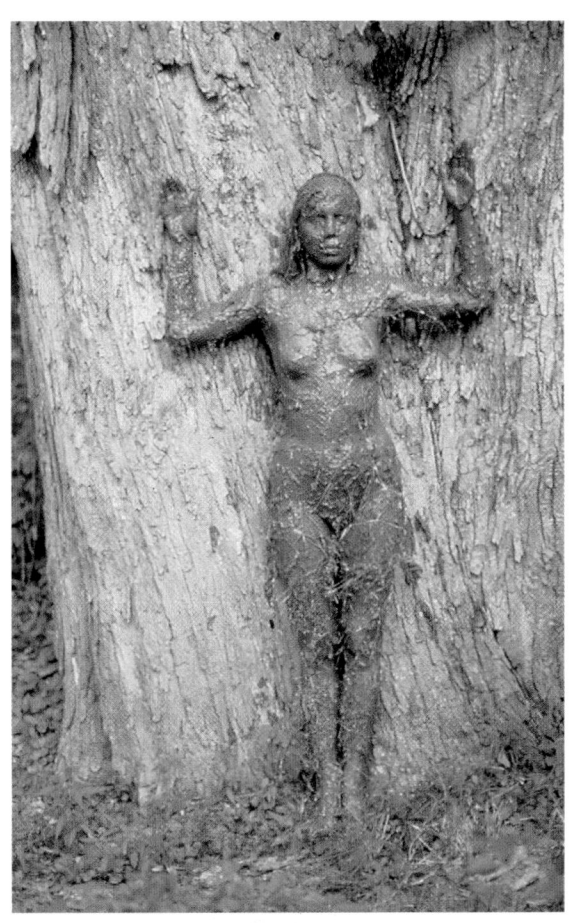

627 Joseph Beuys.
COYOTE: I LIKE AMERICA AND AMERICA LIKES ME. 1974.
Performance at Rene Block Gallery.
Courtesy of Ronald Feldman Fine Arts, NY. Photograph: © Caroline Tisdall.
© 2005 Artists Rights Society (ARS), NY/VG Bild-Kunst, Bonn.

628 Ana Mendieta.
TREE OF LIFE SERIES. 1977.
Performance at Old Man's Creek, Iowa City, Iowa.
Photograph: Collection Ignacio C. Mendieta.
Courtesy of the estate of Ana Mendieta and Galerie Lelong, NY.
© Estate of Ana Mendieta.

ARTISTS AT WORK

Mierle Ukeles

Like Conceptual Art and Minimalism, Performance can take art to its very edges. Mierle Ukeles's 1974 work A.I.R. WASH was one such occasion. For three hours, this artist kept a stretch of New York City sidewalk spotless. She scrubbed until her rags tore. She wiped the street behind passers-by. Each hour she announced four times, "I am washing this street as a work of art!" When asked what made this a work of art, she replied, "It's a work of art because I say it is; I'm the boss." But then can anyone declare their daily acts a work of art? "Yes, because you're the boss too." Then why scrub the street? "Because maintenance workers in our society don't get enough credit," she said. A video of this conversation is on the *Artforms* Web site. Was A.I.R. WASH art? If art is supposed to use visual experience to challenge our usual way of thinking, then the answer is yes.

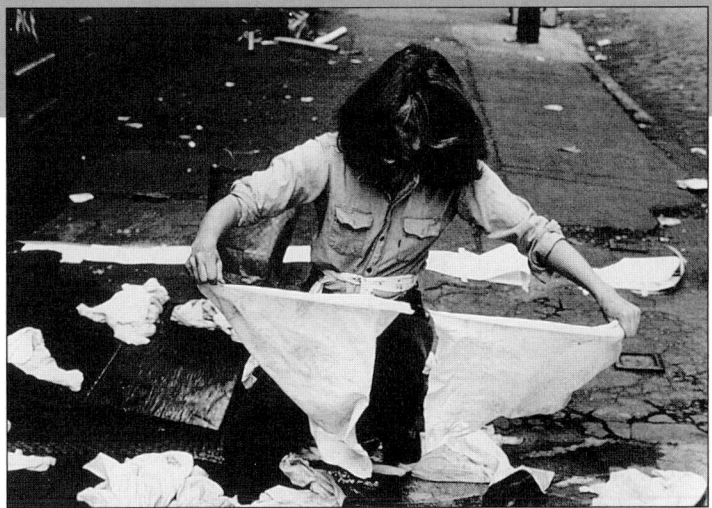

629 Mierle Laderman Ukeles.
A.I.R. WASH. 1974.
Performance.
Courtesy Ronald Feldman Fine Arts, NY.

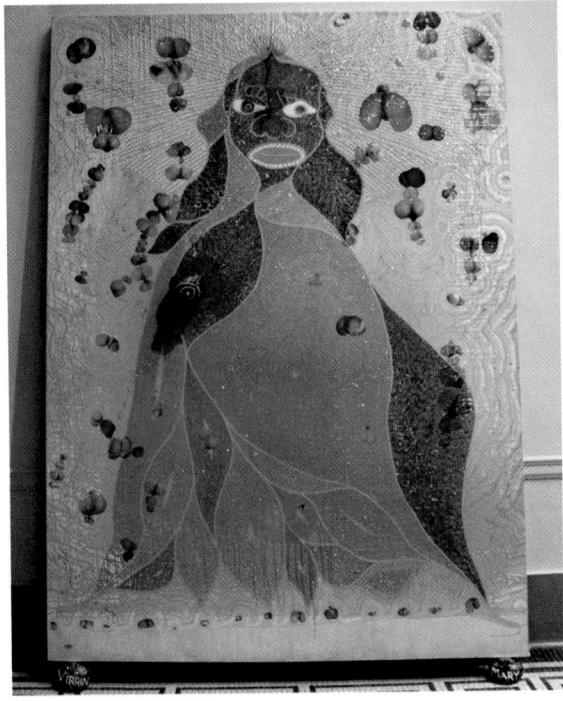

630 Chris Ofili.
THE HOLY VIRGIN MARY. 1996.
Mixed media on canvas. $8' \times 6'$.
Courtesy of Chris Ofili-Afroco and Victoria Miro Gallery.

SIMPLY DEFINED, censorship is the alteration or removal of works of art from public view. Censorship may be carried out for religious, moral, or political reasons, when civil authorities decide that the artist's freedom matters less than other important values. Consider the following recent cases:

New York Mayor Rudolph Giuliani tried to close the Brooklyn Museum in the fall of 1999 because of the painting THE HOLY VIRGIN MARY by Chris Ofili. Giuliani found the work offensive to Roman Catholicism because it portrayed Mary as a black woman with exaggerated features, and because the work had pieces of elephant dung attached to it. Because the museum operates in a city-owned building, the mayor went to court to try to evict it and cut off its maintenance funds if the directors did not remove the work from view. The court sided with the artist and the museum. Far from suppressing Ofili's work, the mayor's lawsuit brought record-breaking crowds.

In early 2004, a large tapestry called *Eye Speak* was unveiled in a display case at Los Angeles International Airport. Created by a group of 115 artists, the work was a response to the attacks of September 11, 2001. After several employees objected to one part of the work that showed a bare-breasted woman, airport authorities ordered the piece removed, calling it "inappropriate for the airport." Artists protested on First Amendment grounds, and after local newspapers reported the story, the airport authorities rescinded their decision.

Brandeis University in Boston staged an exhibition in May 2006 that was censored. The exhibition, part of a seminar called "Arts of Building Peace," consisted of drawings and paintings by Palestinian teenagers about their lives in a refugee camp. It drew protests from several Jewish students who deemed the art inflammatory. Administrators closed the show after four days because they said it had been hung "without any educational context."

The Southern California city of Alhambra staged an art show in early 2007 at City Hall that divided the community. The show of local Asian-American artists was installed as part of an observation of Chinese New Year; it included a silkscreen print by Jeffrey Ma, which depicted Communist leader Mao Zedong next to George Washington. After a city resident complained that the work glorified a dictator who he thought was as bad as Adolf Hitler, city officials removed it from the show. The artists protested the removal, and when the city officials refused to rehang the print, the artists removed all their work.

Not all these cases led to censorship, but all demonstrate that artistic creation is often contested territory in which wider struggles over values, culture, and politics resonate.

Artists in the United States seem to enjoy wide latitude to create as they please. This right was best codified in a 1973 court case, *Miller v. California*, which held that a work may be censored only if it is demonstrably obscene; that is, if the "average person, applying contemporary community standards," finds it so, and if "the work taken as a whole lacks serious literacy, artistic political or scientific value." Thus our society, which places high value on individual achievement and personal self-expression, seems to tip the balance in favor of freedom for artists. However, when an exhibition benefits from public funds or an official finds it inflammatory, attempts to censor often ensue.

MODERN ART BEYOND THE WEST

As we have seen, cultural interaction influenced the evolution of modern art in the West. Exploration, the colonial system, and other trading relationships brought the art of many cultures into Western museums and collections. Thus the art of Africa, Asia, the Pacific, Native America, and Islamic lands all influenced Modern art at various times.

This visual exchange went in both directions. Artists around the world were also exposed to the art and culture of the West, and soon they began to borrow and reinterpret what they saw, adding elements of Western art to their own traditional styles. Generally speaking, modern artists outside the West were more interested in using art to explore cultural and national identity than were modern artists in Europe. Formal experimentation for its own sake was rare outside the West. Most artists experimented with modern styles as they searched for new ways to express their roots. In this chapter we will examine some of these new creations.

JAPAN

Commodore Perry's 1854 visit to Japan provoked a crisis in Japan's aristocracy. How should the closed and secluded country deal with this new influence? An 1868 revolt overthrew Japan's military rulers and reinstated the emperor. He embarked on an intensive program of cultural exchanges with Europe and the United States that included artists and art historians. Under these programs, Japanese artists went abroad with grants and returned to teach Western painting techniques. Thus Japanese art, which had influenced the development of Impressionism in the West, was in turn influenced by that movement (see UPSTAIRS by Kunishiro on page 318).

Later artists continued these exchanges as they incorporated later developments. For example, Fujishima Takeji studied Western art at the Tokyo School of Fine Arts before visiting Europe from 1905 to 1909. While in Paris, he studied the work of Post-Impressionist artists such as Edvard Munch, whose severely simplified style influenced him. That Fujishima should be attracted to Post-Impressionist art seems natural, because that style already owed a debt to the Japanese art that had influenced its European painters such as Vincent van Gogh (see page 374). Back home during the 1930s, Fujishima traveled throughout Japan, sketching and painting the landscape; SUNRISE OVER THE EASTERN SEA (on the following page) shows the results of all his journeys. The work resembles a Post-Impressionist painting in the flatness of its forms and its bold color choices. Yet the painting includes distinctly Japanese elements: Green and orange were nationalistic colors in Japan at that time, and the rising sun has been a symbol of Japan since ancient times.

Japan's defeat in the Second World War radically altered its culture. Most of the old norms were swept away, and there was little market for contemporary

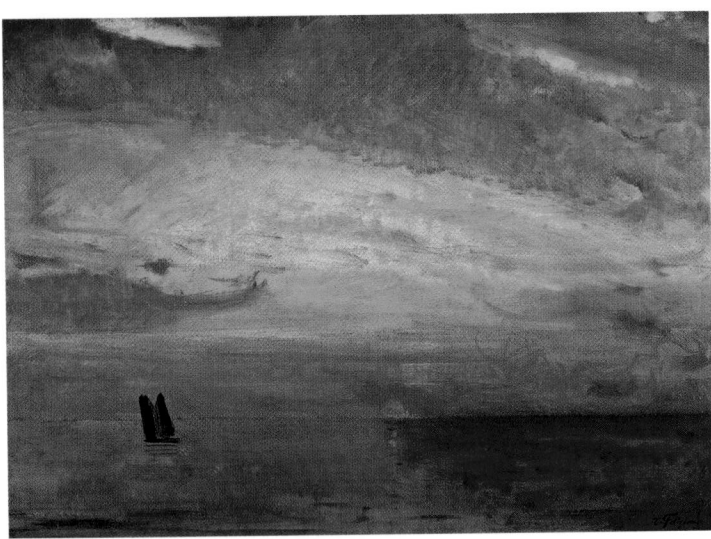

631　Fujishima Takeji.
SUNRISE OVER THE EASTERN SEA. 1932.
Oil on canvas. 25½″ × 35¾″.
Bridgestone Museum of Art, Tokyo.

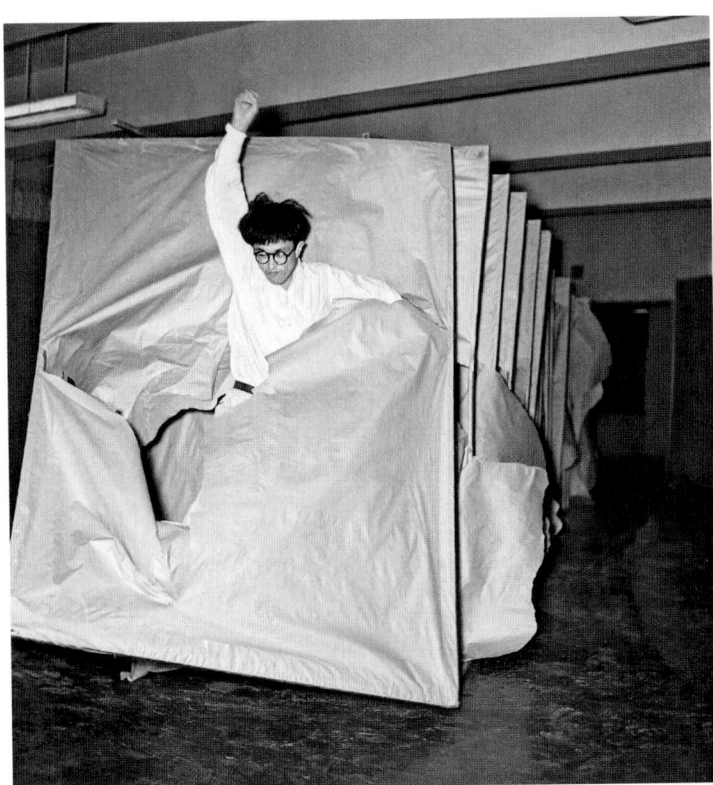

632　Saburo Murakami.
PASSING THROUGH (21 PANELS OF 42 PAPERS). 1956.
Performance.
© Murakami Makiko and the former members of the Gutai group.
Courtesy of the Ashiya City Museum of Art and History.

art. This led Japanese artists into a period of restless questioning of art's very basis. The most radical of these artists joined a group called Gutai ("embodiment"), which functioned from 1954 to 1972. One artist made paintings with his feet; another shot pigment-filled bullets at his canvases. The Gutai manifesto proclaimed the end of traditional art making, and the members "decided to pursue the possibilities of pure and creative activity with great energy."

Saburo Murakami mounted blank sheets of paper in frames and destroyed them in performances that he called PASSING THROUGH. Because paper is a treasured material in Japan, traditionally thought to manifest a sacred spirit, Murakami's performance symbolized the rebellious, questioning attitude of the postwar period. Performances like his by members of the Gutai group also anticipated several aspects of Happenings and Performance Art that emerged later in the West.

CHINA

The Chinese have been less eager than the Japanese to embrace ideas from the West. In the early twentieth century, the most creative artists were following the examples of individualist painters such as Bada Shanren (see his CICADA ON A BANANA LEAF on page 311). An artist who painted this way well into the twentieth century was Qi Baishi (see his LANDSCAPE on page 121). The leader of the first movement of Chinese artists that combined influences from Asia and the West was Gao Jianfu.

After a thorough course of study in traditional Chinese painting techniques, Gao spent three years in Japan, where he came to admire the Japanese openness to Western art. Returning home in 1908, he became politically active in the overthrow of the last emperor, who fell in 1911. Gao established a magazine urging China's modernization and taught art in Shanghai; in 1920 he relocated to Hangzhou in the South. There his studio came to be known as the Lingnan School, and it upset the traditionalists as it produced students who combined diverse influences.

Gao and his students borrowed cautiously, however, as THE FIVE-STORIED PAVILION shows. The perspective and colors are influenced by the West, but Gao took a traditional Asian subject and used traditional Chinese and Japanese brush techniques. This work exudes melancholy and nostalgia, as the tower sits forlornly in the sunset. Gao wrote on the painting:

All that remains of the perilous high tower after myriad destructive calamities are creeping grass and empty mist, distant crows and fading dusk.[1]

The work illustrates the mood of China in that period. The fall of the Empire in 1911 brought not a new era but more disorder, as advocates of a Western-style economy (Nationalists) vied with Communists for influence in the post-imperial republic.

Nationalists and Communists agreed that China's old imperial traditions needed re-examination if not outright rejection. Thus writers and artists alike took a new and deeper interest in Western ideas in the 1920s and 1930s. In literature, the authors connected with the May Fourth Movement took up new, modern subjects. Artists (fewer in number than their literary counterparts) traveled to Japan or to Europe to learn about new currents such as Impressionism, Post-Impressionism, Expressionism, and Cubism. The Chinese port cities of Shanghai and Hangzhou were centers of these new cosmopolitan influences; both cities hosted organized groups devoted to the exhibition and study of modern art.

The Japanese invasion of 1937 brought much of this ferment to a close, as resistance to foreign domination became a paramount concern. The invading troops sacked many Chinese cities, including Shanghai and Hangzhou, destroying hundreds of works of art. Chinese painters who explored modern currents were not numerous, but few of their works survived the turmoil.

The Communists urged a socially progressive, low-cost art that could be widely disseminated and that clearly depicted the current political and economic situation in the country. During the 1930s,

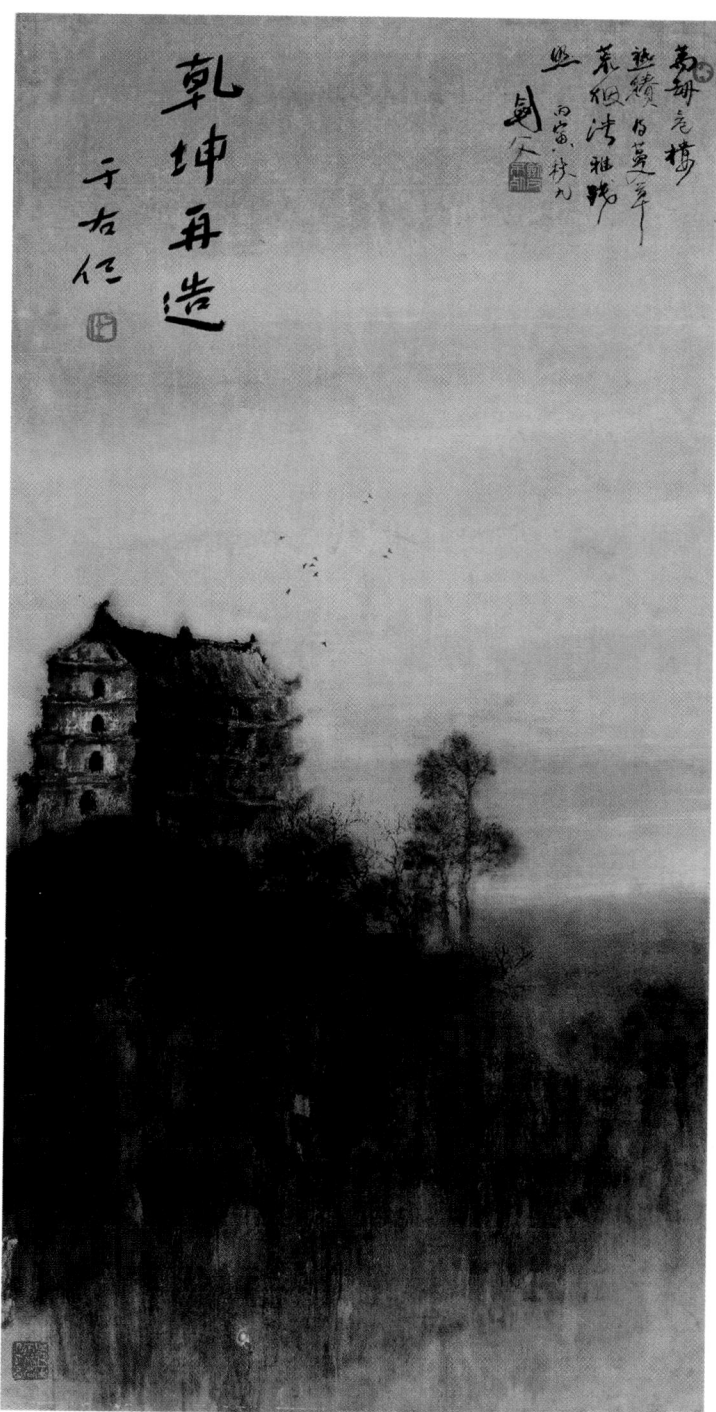

633 Gao Jianfu.
THE FIVE-STORIED PAVILION. 1926.
Ink and color on paper. 31½" × 16½".
Hong Kong Museum of Art Collection.
FA1978.100.

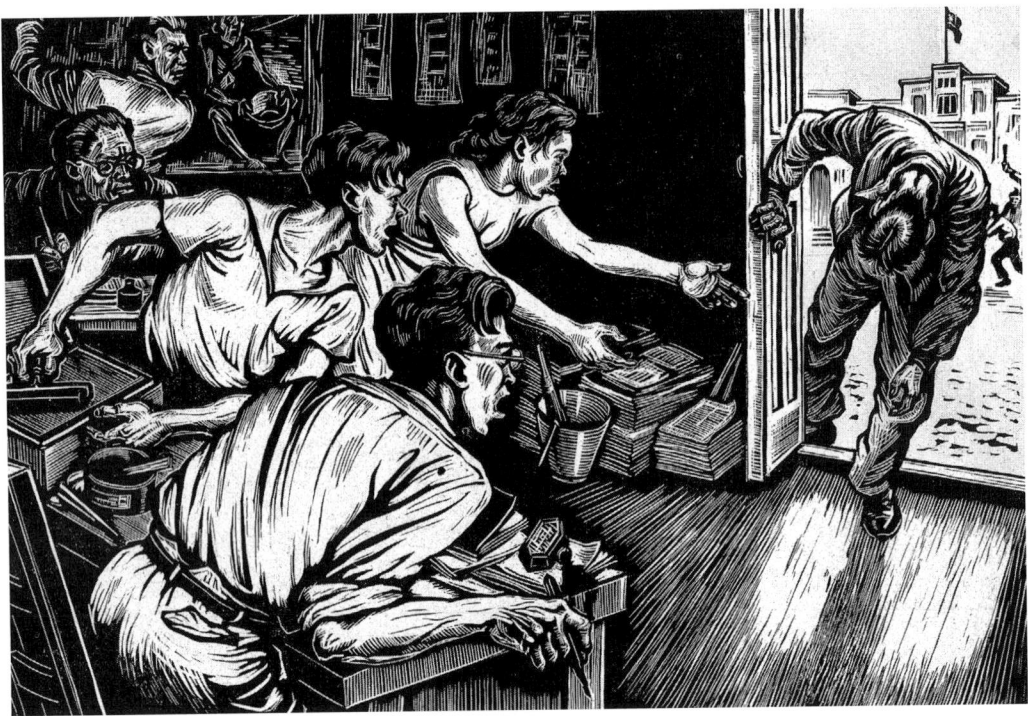

634 Li Hua.
TAKE HIM IN! 1946.
Woodcut. 21½ cm × 32½ cm.
Gift of Mr. and Mrs. Theodore Herman. Courtesy of The Picker Art Gallery,
Colgate University, (1980.120)

members of the League of Left-Wing Artists pursued these ideals by making woodcuts in a social realist style (see page 412 for a Western example of social realism). They illustrated books and made posters that encouraged resistance to the Japanese occupation.

With the Japanese surrender in 1945, the Communists and the Nationalists resumed their civil war for control of China. Former League member Li Hua depicted one such moment in his woodcut TAKE HIM IN! Here we see a wounded protester taking refuge from the disorder outside; he enters a printmaking studio where artists interrupt their work to care for their wounded comrade. This realist style became the government-sponsored norm for China after the Communist victory of 1949, as it had in Russia after Josef Stalin took power.

INDIA

When the Indian subcontinent was still a British colony, a small group of Indian artists hoped to create an art of global reach by synthesizing Asian and Western techniques into a seamless new style. An early leader in this cause was Rabindranath Tagore, a poet and painter who won the Nobel Prize for literature in 1913. Tagore established a university near Calcutta devoted to this fusion in 1921. The program had a cosmopolitan influence on Indian culture, urging artists away from over-dependence on the European Academic styles then taught at the British-sponsored art schools.

The first artist to achieve this synthesis was Amrita Sher-Gil, who was herself half Indian and half Hungarian. Her formative years were divided between Europe and India, and she studied the painting of both. Returning to India in 1934 in search of her roots, she made a visit to the Ajanta caves (see page 295 for an illustration). Seeing much common ground between Western modern art and that of ancient India, she wrote to a friend:

Modern art has led me to the comprehension and appreciation of Indian painting and sculpture. It seems paradoxical but I know for certain that had we not come away to Europe, I should perhaps never have realized that a fresco from Ajanta or a small piece of sculpture in the Musée Guimet is worth more than a whole Renaissance.[2]

Her 1940 work THE SWING exemplifies her concerns. The color scheme and flat patterns owe a great deal to both the ancient caves at Ajanta and the Post-Impressionism of Paul Gauguin (see page 377). Her subject is Indian women of different races, whom she hoped to elevate by depicting in a noble way. While she influenced many artists, her early death in 1941 at the age of twenty-nine kept her from developing her ideas.

M. F. Husain was working as a designer of children's toys when he saw an exhibition of work by Sher-Gil in 1941. He decided from that moment to be an artist, but not to follow in her footsteps. He respected the fusion of styles that she had created, but he wanted his art to be more personal and less idealizing.

Husain found allies in the Progressive Art Group, which formed just as India was becoming independent in 1947. These artists wanted to embody the complex reality of India as it became a modern state. Husain was inspired by these ideas; his major creation from those years was the large painting MAN. Here we see a dark figure seated at the center, surrounded by other figures of different colors (some of them inverted) symbolizing the various races of

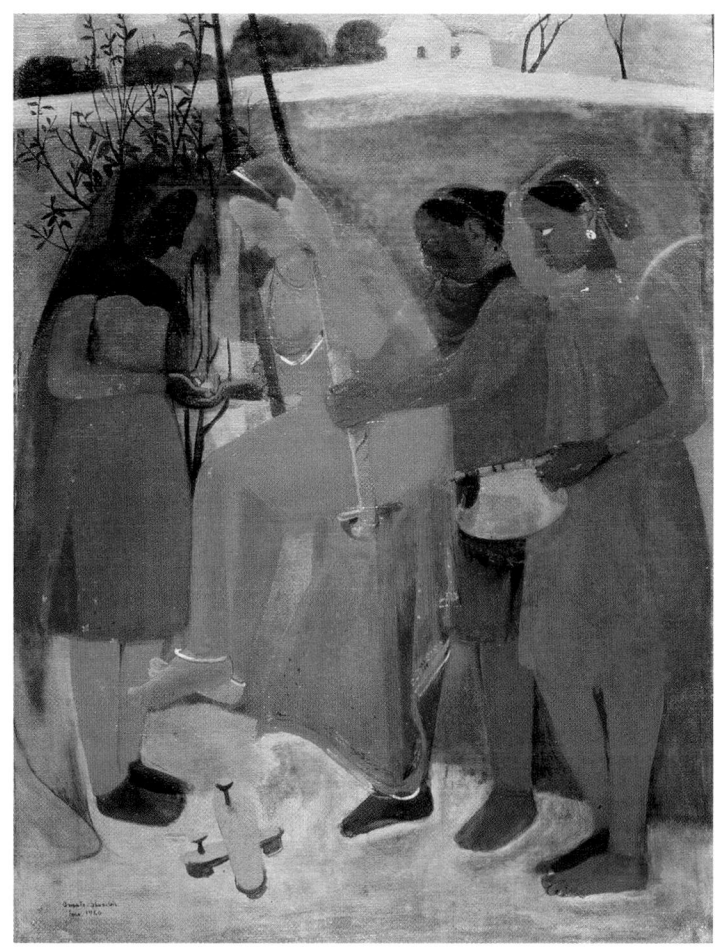

635 Amrita Sher-Gil.
THE SWING. 1940.
National Museum, New Delhi, India.
Giradon/Art Resources, NY.

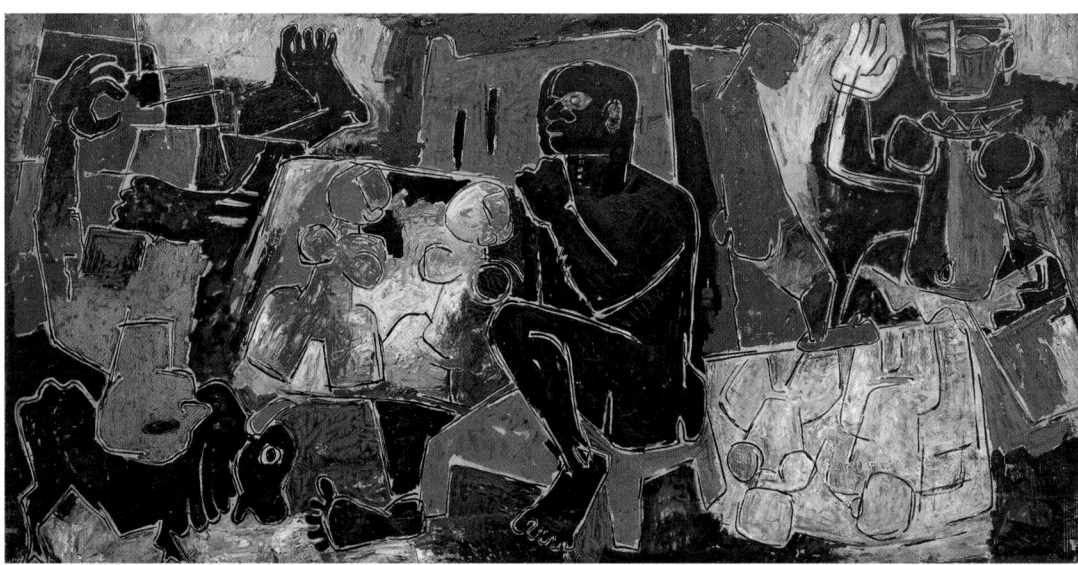

636 M. F. Husain.
MAN. 1951.
Oil on canvas.
47″ × 95″.
The Chester and Davida Herwitz Collection. Courtesy of the Peabody Essex Museum. Photograph: Jeffrey Dykes.

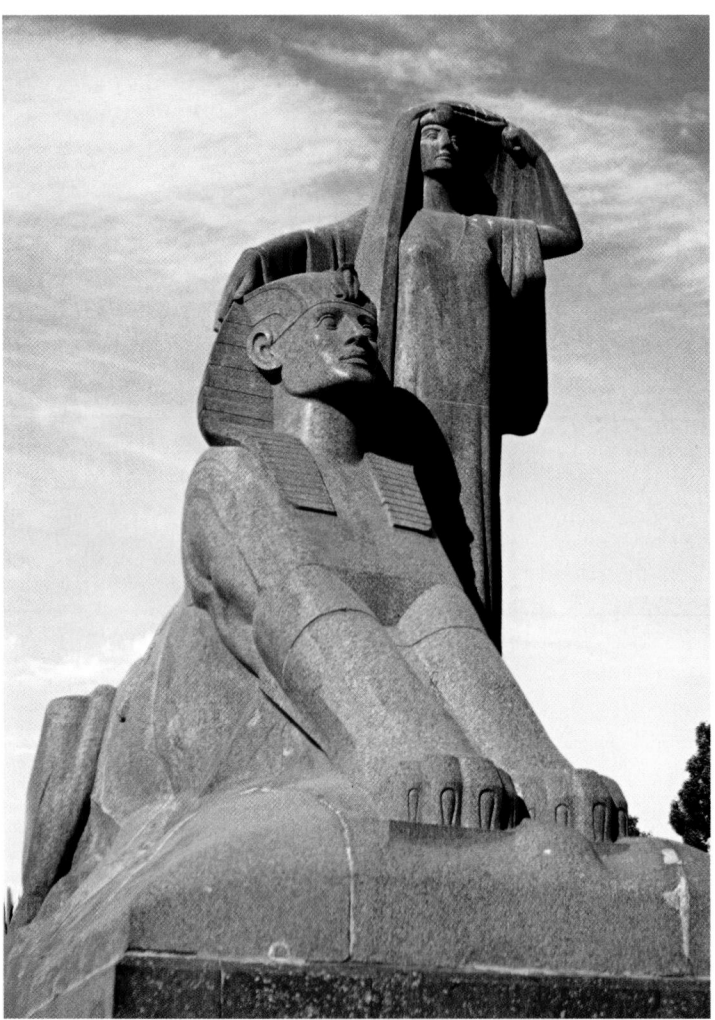

637 Mahmoud Mukhtar.
EGYPT AWAKENING. 1919–1928.
Schist. Height 20′.
Bernard O'Kane.

India. The two flat tablets on either side allude to ancient sculpture of the Indus valley, just as the color scheme and outlined silhouettes refer to 17th-century Indian book illustrations (see page 298). From European sources, the central figure seems to quote THE THINKER by Auguste Rodin (see page 371), and the jagged overlapping forms owe something to the Cubism of Picasso. The work as a whole presents a multifaceted image of an India that is fragmented, divided, and problematic. Husain said:

India was never a nation . . . This is the first time it is struggling to become a nation. It might collapse . . . The very fact that it is struggling is dangerous and exciting.[3]

ISLAMIC LANDS

The first school in the Arab world to teach Western art, The School of Fine Arts, opened in Cairo in 1908 with all foreign teachers. Among the first students was Mahmoud Mukhtar, who later became a national hero for his monumental sculpture EGYPT AWAKENING.

Mukhtar was studying in Paris when the news of the 1919 revolts against British rule reached him. He was electrified, and immediately began planning a statue to embody the new spirit of a liberated Egypt. His project attracted the attention of Egyptian political leaders, who lured the artist home with a promise to erect it in a prominent place.

Mukhtar carved the work from huge blocks of the same dense schist that ancient Egyptians had used in Pharaonic times. EGYPT AWAKENING shows influence from that ancient style and from the simplified sculpture of Brancusi (see page 393). We see a sphinx rising and stretching its catlike front legs; at its side is a woman opening her eyes as she pulls back a veil. The work thus uses a modern language to reach far back to Egypt's pre-Islamic past. It attempts to symbolize a national spirit much as the *Statue of Liberty* does for the United States.

The pace of reception of Western art in Islamic lands was very uneven, as the Islamic opposition to figural art in a religious context weighed against some kinds of artistic experimentation. Artists in many countries, however, combined the ancient tradition of calligraphy with modern painting techniques to create a distinctly Muslim type of modern art.

An early leader in this calligraphic movement was the Sudanese Ibrahim el-Salahi. He was first exposed to modern art techniques during studies in London in the 1950s as Sudan was becoming independent. On his return to his homeland he began exploring its visual traditions, which combine African, Muslim, and Christian influences. His 1963 work FUNERAL AND A CRESCENT is a remembrance of his father, a Muslim cleric. The faces in the work resemble traditional African masks, painted using the strokes of Arabic calligraphy. The earth tones recall the soil of Sudan. The deceased figure looks upward to a crescent moon, the symbol of Islam.

movement culminated in the International Style, a glass-box look that swept most Western cities in the years after World War II. However, a growing discontent with the sterile anonymity of the International Style (see the LEVER HOUSE on page 429) led many architects to rebel and to look once again at meaning, history, tradition, and context. Their departure from architectural modernism was dubbed Postmodern in the late 1970s.

Postmodernists thought that the unadorned functional purity of the International Style made all buildings look the same, offering no identity relative to purpose, no symbolism, no meaning, no mystery, no excitement. Postmodern architects celebrate the very qualities of modern life that the proponents of machine aesthetics rejected: complexity, ambiguity, contradiction, nostalgia, romance, and the popular taste.

Postmodern architects embraced an eclectic mix of historical influences, decorative tendencies, and the popular styles of architecture and applied arts for the general public to relate to. The Postmodernists divorced themselves and their work from the accepted meanings of "traditional" and "modern" and did not value one more than the other. The attitudes associated with Postmodernism are a part of all the arts, including literature. In the visual arts, the Postmodern style is perhaps best seen in architecture.

Architect Philip Johnson's career has spanned both the Modern and Postmodern movements. He has been known since mid-century as an advocate of Modernism and, with Mies van der Rohe, designed the SEAGRAM BUILDING (page 222), a landmark of the International Style. But the pure glass-enclosed box, repeated a thousand times in cities throughout the world, became too severe, too limited for Johnson and his younger colleagues. In high-rise buildings such as the AT&T BUILDING in New York City, he reversed himself. Here Johnson and John Burgee brought back warmth and delight with a decorative upper story that brings together elements from several historical styles: The huge round-arched portal recalls Roman architecture. The round windows at the side are merely decora-

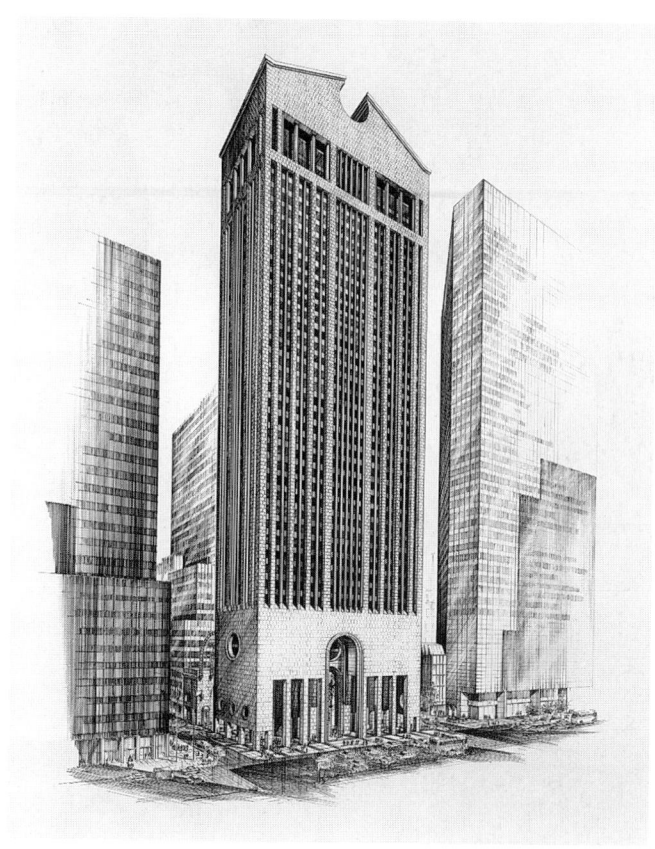

641   Johnson and Burgee.
AT&T BUILDING.
New York City. 1978–1984.
Photo by Gil Amiaga, NYC.

tive, having no structural function. The top of the building with its curved gable quotes colonial-style American furniture. Moreover, the exterior is sheathed in warm brick rather than modern concrete or steel.

The architecture of Michael Graves reflects a personal blend of traditional classicism and inventive irony. His PUBLIC SERVICES BUILDING (on the following page) is both formal and playful. The exterior refers to a pair of fluted classical columns sharing a single huge capital. These off-color vertical elements are set in a pool of reflecting mirror windows, which detaches them from any function in the building's structure. The remainder of the façade consists of anonymous rows of square openings, an ironic reference to the bureaucrats inside.

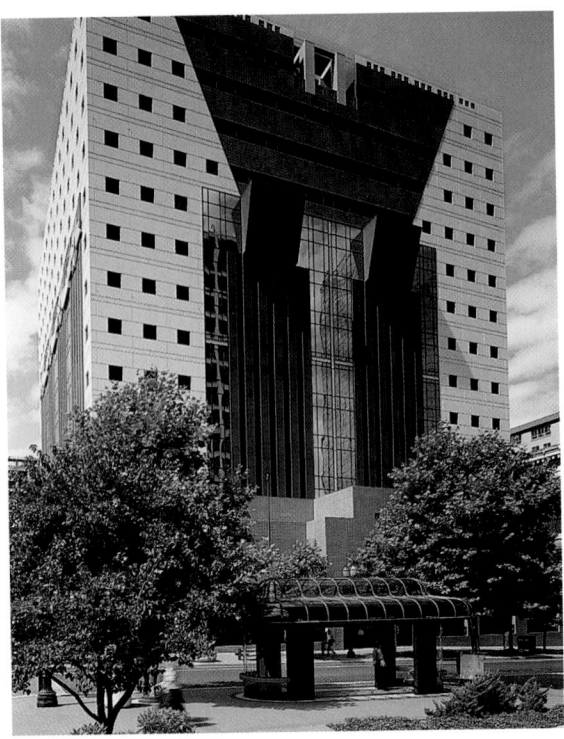

642 Michael Graves.
PUBLIC SERVICES BUILDING.
Portland, Oregon. 1980–1982.

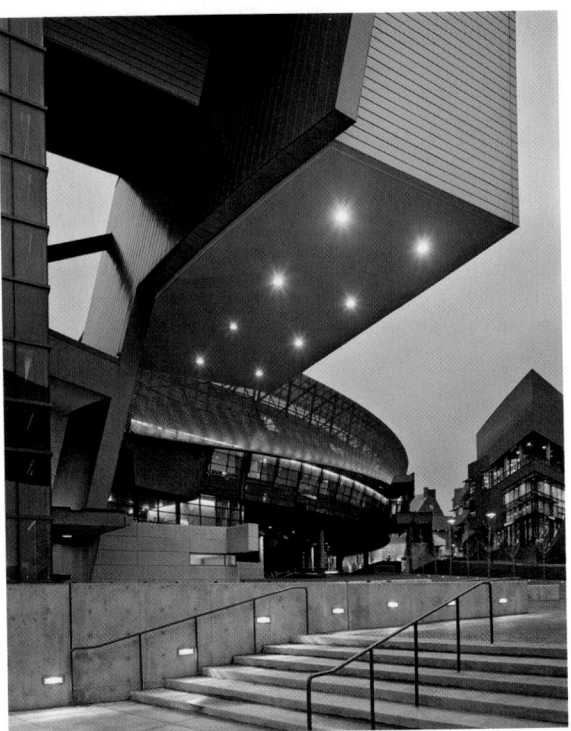

643 Thom Mayne and Morphosis.
CAMPUS RECREATION CENTER.
University of Cincinnati. 2006.
Photo: Roland Halbe.

The most creative architects today neither rebel against tradition like the modernists, nor quote tradition whimsically like postmodernists. Rather, they try to make visually stunning buildings that fulfill their functions with ease. Californian Thom Mayne is a leader in this new trend in combining aesthetics and utility. His CAMPUS RECREATION CENTER at the University of Cincinnati answers a list of tasks: A full gymnasium, classrooms, a food court, and student housing occupy an irregularly shaped building that responds to the surrounding topography and channels foot traffic over the shortest paths to and from surrounding buildings. "I wanted to make a village," he said of this building, and it fits seamlessly into the fabric of existing structures with an attractive, high-tech look. His firm is called Morphosis, an invented word that roughly means "taking shape," and the freedom with which his buildings take shape earned him architecture's highest honor, the Pritzker Prize, in 2005.

PAINTING

As Modernism came to an end, many painters in America and Europe began to revive expressive, personal styles in a movement known as Neo-Expressionism. This was partly in response to the impersonality and generally aesthetic orientation of movements such as Conceptual Art and Minimalism, and to the ironic, tongue-in-cheek quality of Pop Art and related trends.

One of the first Neo-Expressionists was Susan Rothenberg, who in the 1970s began making symbolic, heavily brushed works in which subject matter teeters on the brink of recognizability. After the cleansing blankness of Minimalism, Rothenberg could return to figurative images with original vision; what emerges is almost ethereal.

THOM
Mayne

Building on the Edge

1944–

THOM MAYNE is among today's most honored architects, but he has always been in some sense a rebel. He founded the studio Morphosis back in 1972 because, he said, most architects failed to address the dislocations in modern society. Rather than leaning toward one style or approach, Morphosis would approach a task without any preconceptions, and arrive at the final design through interaction with the client and discussion among themselves. Said one early partner, "It was not really a practice as much as it was a garage band."

Mayne graduated from the University of Southern California in 1968, near the peak years of the student protest movement. To this day, he numbers among his heroes Malcolm X and Jimi Hendrix. His first job was teaching at Cal Poly in Pomona, but his unconventional approach got him fired. Along with some colleagues, he founded an alternative school: The Southern California Institute of Architecture (SCI-Arc), which still functions.

Morphosis made its name in the 1970s, designing private homes for offbeat clients and putting innovative touches on small businesses such as restaurants and bookshops. The firm had a local reputation for outlandish creativity, but it almost never built the sort of large-scale projects that lead to public recognition.

Mayne was never fully on board with the historical quotations of Postmodernism, so the firm went into a slump in the 1980s. Discussions with clients became confrontations. Building contractors balked at his ideas. Commissions dwindled. Frustration mounted. "I was a raving maniac in those days," Mayne recalled. His question-everything approach was too radical for the times, so he devoted more time to teaching, both at SCI-Arc and at UCLA.

The turnaround came in the early 1990s, when the firm began competing for and winning high-visibility projects, such as the MTV Studios in Los Angeles and the Sun Office Tower in Seoul, South Korea. To each, Mayne brought the same creative spark that had nourished him all along, but now his personal style was less confrontational, and the clients more receptive.

The firm is still on the cutting edge for building in response to today's needs and demands. For example, the 2005 United States Courthouse in Eugene, Oregon, little resembles a classical courthouse with a gleaming, translucent skin over an asymmetrical façade. The courtrooms inside make allowance for all of today's high-tech presentation media, and each is shaped like a teardrop, with the judge at the small end, to save space. The building received a Gold certification from the U.S. Green Building Council.

A 2007 Federal office building in San Francisco includes a sky garden on the eleventh floor, where employees can literally breathe fresh air in an atrium three stories high. To respond to demands for energy conservation, the building's elevators stop only every third floor, forcing employees to walk up or down to their offices (and perhaps to socialize on the sun-drenched landings as they do).

Many of Mayne's old friends wonder at the fact that the former sixties radical is now designing for the government, but the projects speak for themselves. The bureaucracy responsible for maintaining California's multitudinous freeways and bridges (Caltrans) in 2005 got a gleaming new headquarters in Los Angeles that is sheathed in perforated aluminum screens that a computer opens and closes in response to weather conditions. The outdoor lobby boasts a light installation by Keith Sonnier (MOTORDOM) that recalls time-lapse photos of car taillights moving on a road at night. (This work is pictured on page 63.) At the same time, the Caltrans building is secured against truck bombs by a set of firmly anchored curving pipes that resemble sculpture.

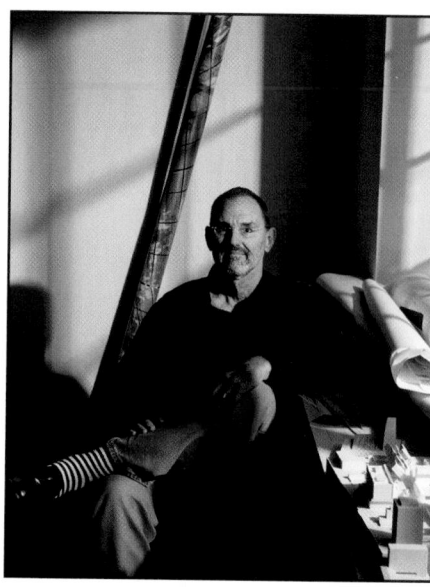

644 Thom Mayne.
Photograph: Mark Hanauer, Morphosis.

Projects continue to pour out of the Morphosis Santa Monica office: An open-air arena in Mexico, a jazz center for New Orleans, a public housing project in Madrid, a skyscraper outside Paris that will be Europe's tallest office building when complete in 2012. They all embody the Mayne/Morphosis philosophy, which he summarized in his usual intense fashion: "I'm a (expletive) dreamer, and I was always told I couldn't do it. But here it is . . . And you could do it. Don't let anybody tell you, you can't do it. That's their problem."[1]

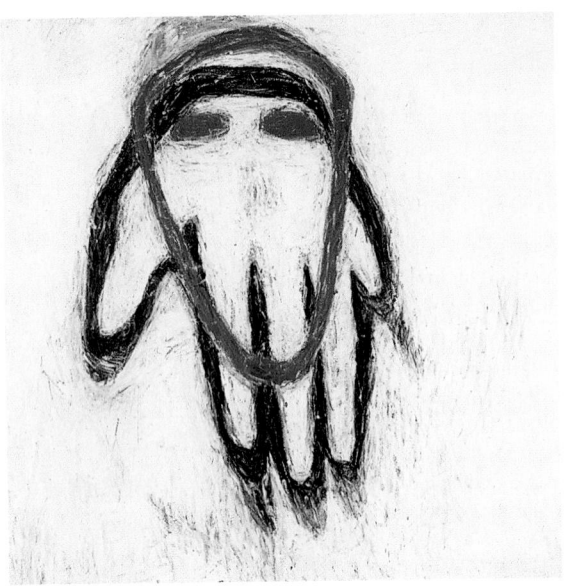

645 Susan Rothenberg.
BLUE HEAD. 1980–1981.
Acrylic on canvas. 114″ × 114″.
Virginia Museum of Fine Arts, Richmond.
Gift of The Sydney and Frances Lewis Foundation.
© Virginia Museum of Fine Arts.
© 2002 Susan Rothenberg/Artists Rights Society (ARS), NY.

She works in a narrow range of tones, using a muted palette of white, beige, silvery or dark gray, with a bit of color. Her BLUE HEAD, which outlines a horse's head in front of a human hand, is a haunting image that resists explanation. It is a primal sign operating between the material world and the mystery beyond.

The German painter Anselm Kiefer combines the aggressive paint application of Abstract Expressionism with nineteenth-century feelings for history and mythology. Kiefer gives equal attention to moral and aesthetic issues. A student of performance artist Joseph Beuys, Kiefer, in the late 1960s, did a highly controversial series of performances that he called *Occupations*, which he documented with photographs. For these performances, he donned a military uniform and stood in various famous places across Europe, giving a Nazi salute. He said that he wanted to better understand Fascism by re-enacting some of its rituals. His paint-ings, loaded with symbolism, mythology, and religion, speak to the rest of us through powerful stories in dramatic compositions.

OSIRIS AND ISIS retells the ancient Egyptian myth of the cycle of death and rebirth. Osiris symbolized the indestructible creative forces of nature; according to legend, the god was slain and cut into pieces by his evil brother. Isis, sister and wife of Osiris, found and buried the pieces, making each burial place sacred. In another version of the story, Isis collected the pieces and brought Osiris back to life. In Kiefer's huge painting, a network of wires attached to fragments of the dismembered Osiris connects to the goddess Isis in the form of a TV circuit board atop a pyramid. The heavily textured surface of paint, mud, rock, tar, ceramic, and metal intensifies the image's epic treatment of the afterlife theme.

The Neo-Expressionists tend to favor painting because a seemingly infinite variety of surface textures and colors are possible. Every creative decision can leave a trace on the finished work, registering every twitch in sensibility. Other artists use the painting media because they facilitate storytelling, allowing the artist to create a two-dimensional world with the utmost freedom. This interest in narration is a dominant tendency in contemporary painting.

Elizabeth Murray combines personal meanings with explosively innovative form in works such as MORE THAN YOU KNOW. The painting dates from the time between the birth of her two children; however, beyond the general outlines of a room with two red chairs, there is little here to suggest the experience of motherhood. Her personal information is only the launching pad for a fascinatingly jagged array of canvas fragments that do not fit together, but still seem to cohere. Murray's vibrant and exuberant paintings leave a great deal of the story for the viewer to make up from the suggestive shapes.

Kerry James Marshall grew up in housing projects in Alabama and Los Angeles, and he wants to

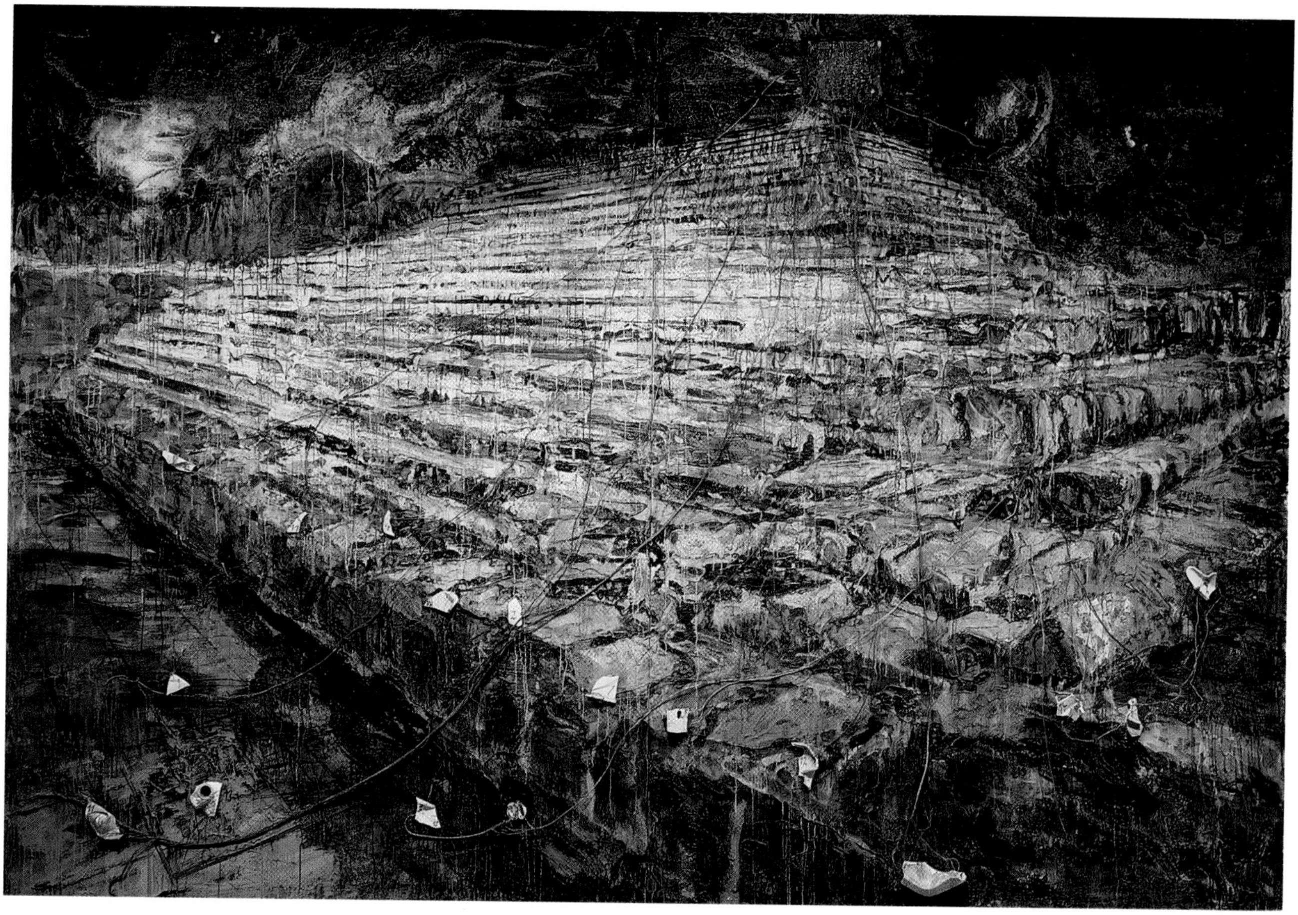

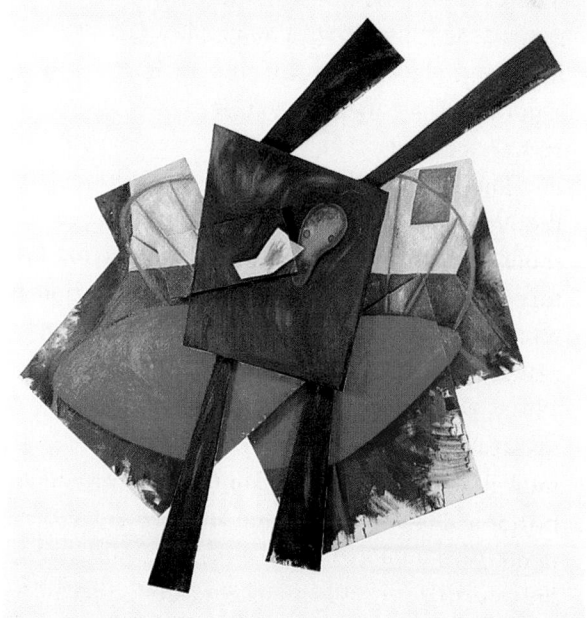

646 Anselm Kiefer.

OSIRIS AND ISIS. 1985–1987.

Oil, acrylic, emulsion, clay, porcelain, lead copper wire,
and circuit board on canvas.

150″ × 229½″ × 6½″.

San Francisco Museum of Modern Art. Purchased through a gift of Jean Stein,
by exchange, the Mrs. Paul L. Wattis Fund, and the Doris and Donald Fisher Fund.
Photograph by Ben Blackwell. © Artists Rights Society (ARS), NY.

647 Elizabeth Murray.

MORE THAN YOU KNOW. 1983.

Oil on nine canvases. 108″ × 111″ × 8″.

Collection of The Edward R. Broida Trust, Florida.
© 1983 Elizabeth Murray. Photograph courtesy of Pace
Wildenstein.

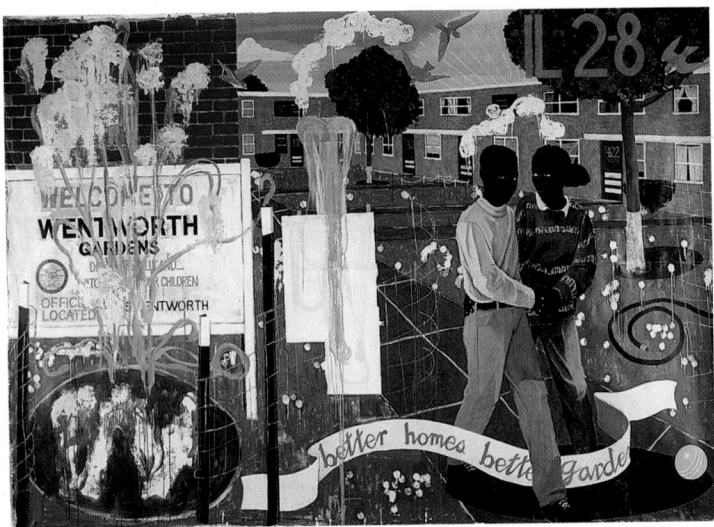

648 Kerry James Marshall.
BETTER HOMES BETTER GARDENS. 1994.
Acrylic and collage on canvas. 8′4″ × 12′.
Collection of Denver Art Museum. Photograph courtesy Jack Shainman Gallery, New York.

correct a popular vision of those places as crime-ridden. His 1994 work BETTER HOMES BETTER GARDENS is part of a series of paintings that he made on Chicago housing projects that contain the word "garden" in their names. This one is obviously set in Wentworth Gardens, and it depicts a couple walking down a flowered pathway in a low-rise setting. At the left is a fenced area enclosing a communal flower garden. Three of the artist's trademark bluebirds fly across the upper portion of the scene, and all seems peaceful. Whatever else happens in housing projects, they are places of community and neighborhood feeling, he seems to be telling us.

Yet for all its optimism, there are ironic touches in this work. The perfectly spiraled garden hose, the white blotches over the heads of the couple, and the flowered entry with the "Welcome" sign add a note of complexity to the mood, casting a flickering shadow over its sweetness. The inscription "IL 2-8" in the upper right reminds us that this is both an illustration and a painting that is in fact rigorously composed. It is based on a solid grid of horizontals, verticals, and a few diagonals. Although the work is optimistic, Marshall is not merely painting an idealistic scene.

Los Angeles painter Gajin Fujita began his art career as a graffiti tagger in a crew known as K2S (Kill to Succeed). His recent works draw on both his past as a tagger and the high culture of Asia, in a mix that is thoroughly up-to-date in its wide cross-cultural sampling. His 2005 painting STREET FIGHT begins with a layer of spray-painted graffiti, some of it by the members of his old tagging crew. A layer of gold leaf provides a sense of the sacred, alluding to ancient Buddhist and Medieval Christian art; the buildings in silhouette quote both urban landscape photography and crossword puzzles in newspapers. The sky has abstract patterns based on Japanese screens by Sotatsu and others (see page 315). The two foreground figures come from traditional Japanese woodblock prints, and the lettering style of the title resembles urban graffiti that decorate most cities worldwide. The theme of the work is both ancient and modern, as the title alludes to contemporary gang life. If this painting borrows from many sources, it is also inspiring others: the L. A. Latino hiphop group Ozomatli wrote the songs for its 2007 album *Don't Mess With the Dragon* while working in a gallery where STREET FIGHT and other works by Fujita hung.

PHOTOGRAPHY

The Postmodern movement has been a primary influence on recent photography. The principal new insight that Postmodernists brought to the medium was the perhaps unsurprising notion that a photograph is not merely a "straight" record of fact. There are ways of composing, taking, developing, and printing pictures that serve to encode information and influence viewers. Photographers influenced by Postmodernism show through their pictures that they know their medium is not an objective one. Even the most straightforward scenes can have hidden meanings. Postmodernists want to show us that the camera can influence us in ways we may not suspect, and the camera itself has a certain way of seeing.

Cindy Sherman's photographs of the late 1970s were among the first to be called Postmodern. She

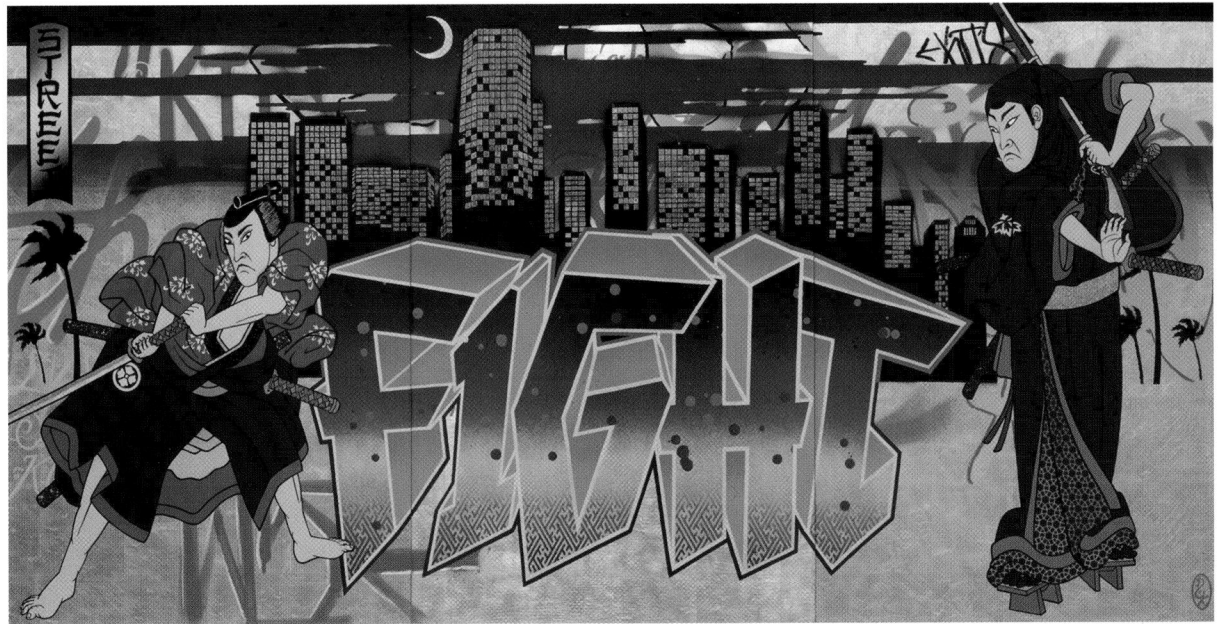

649 Gajin Fujita.
STREET FIGHT. 2005.
24-karat gold leaf, spray paint, Mean Streak, paint marker
on wood panel triptych. 24″ × 48″.
Private collection, courtesy L.A. Louver Gallery, Venice, CA.

650 Cindy Sherman.
UNTITLED FILM STILL #48. 1979.
Black and white photograph.
Courtesy Cindy Sherman and Metro Pictures.

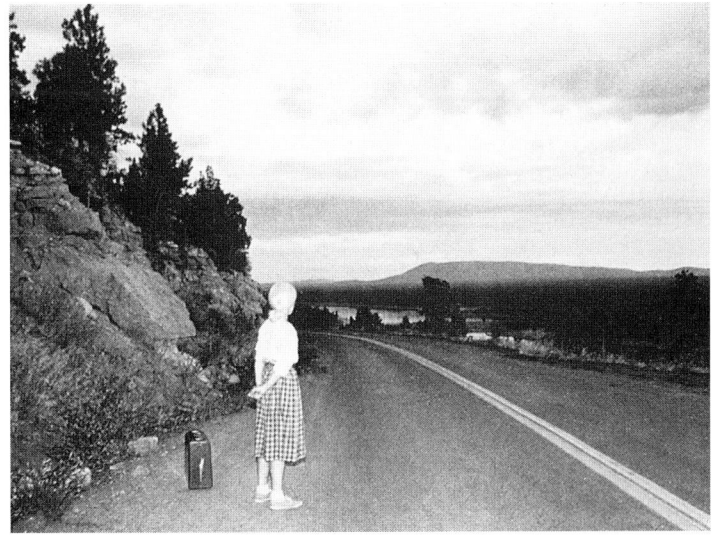

took black-and-white photos of herself, posing with props in scenes that corresponded to stereotyped female characters from popular culture. In UNTITLED FILM STILL #48, for example, she stands on a deserted road at dusk, her back to us, hastily packed suitcase at her side. As in many "teen movies" of the 1950s and 1960s, she is the misunderstood daughter running away from home. Other photos from the series depict the girl next door, daddy's little girl, the anxious young career woman, the oppressed housewife. Without referring to specific movies, Sherman's photos are imagined stills from popular film types that have helped to form stereotypical images of women. She seems to be saying that our culture typecasts women in certain roles, and these roles keep women from realizing themselves.

Sherman's work is influenced about equally by Pop Art, Performance Art, and Feminism. She differs from the early feminists, though, in presenting women as a product of the culture and not of biology. In her eyes, culture has a much larger role than nature in forming women's identities.

Andreas Gursky's photographs use the latest technological tricks to depict contemporary, sterile spaces. Using the new Cibachrome process, he

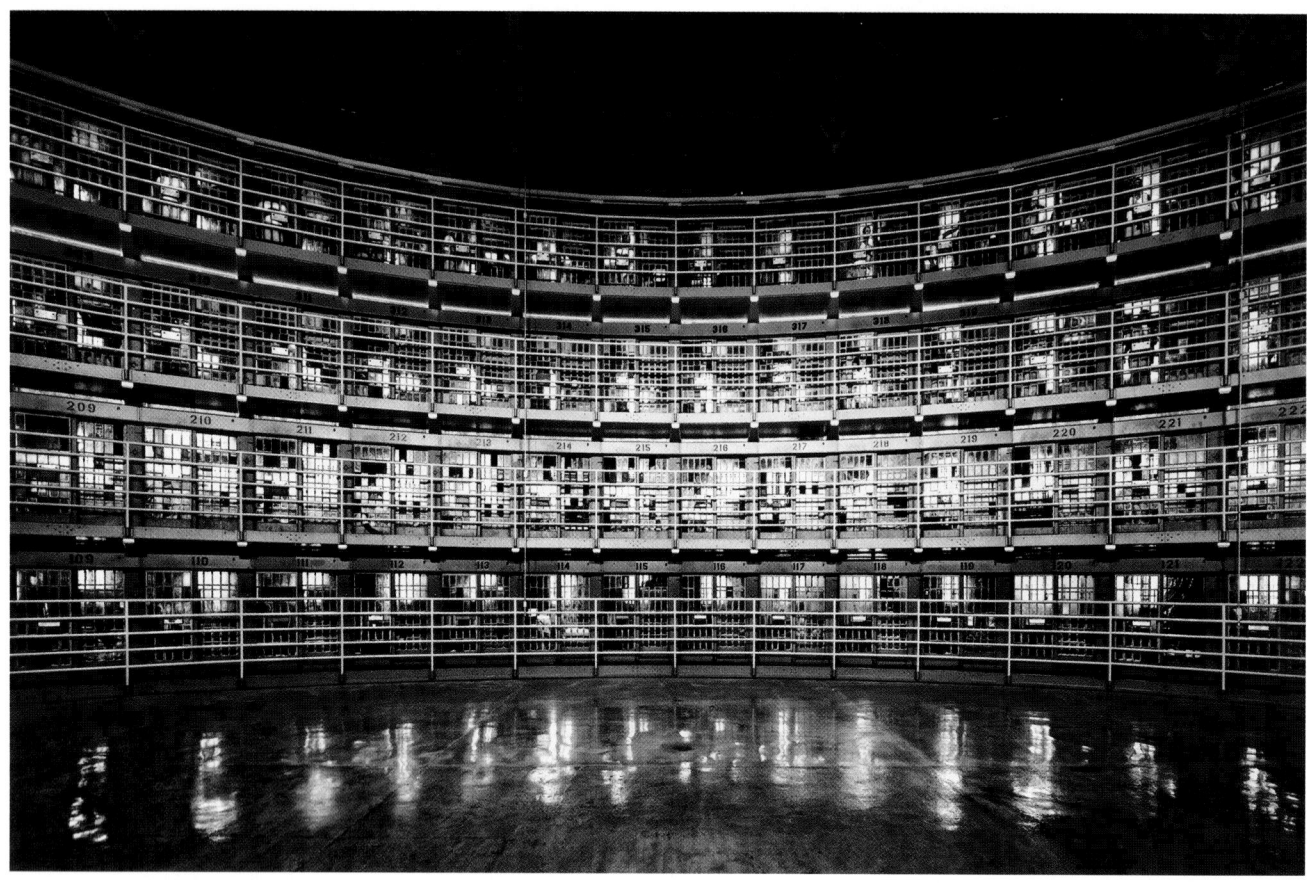

651 Andreas Gursky.
STATEVILLE, ILLINOIS. 2002.
C-Print mounted on Plexiglas in artist's frame. 81″ × 120½″.
Courtesy of Matthew Marks Gallery, New York, and Monika Spruth/Philomene Magers, Cologne/Munich.
© 2004 Andreas Gursky/Artists Rights Society (ARS), NY/VG Bild-Kuns, Bonn.

stretched STATEVILLE, ILLINOIS out to seven by ten feet, as big as a mural. The space he photographed looks lived-in, but curiously hushed. This is a prison that could be almost anywhere on earth. Gursky achieved this spotless, tightly focused look with the help of digital editing; he typically removes blemishes, adjusts lighting, adds or removes people, and improves contrast, much as a painter may manipulate the surface of a canvas. His most common subject is the public spaces that we all use today: airports, auditoriums, stores. His pictures are dazzling in a way that the "reality" is not; in this regard, his works resemble advertising photography, but the world they create is eerie.

The photos of Lebanese artist Walid Raad are even more complicated in their relationship to "reality." Raad witnessed firsthand the Lebanese civil war of the 1980s as a teenager; he often ascended to his roof and took pictures of the sky over Beirut, blackened by the smoke of aerial bombardments or artillery fire. When he developed and printed these negatives years later, he found them discolored and pockmarked, aged like the buildings of his native city. For a 2007 exhibition, he reprinted the pictures in a large format that magnified the flaws of time. BEY82 CITY VI is a blurry and smudged photo of a bomb landing behind a hospital. The degraded quality gives the image a haunted, distant appearance that contradicts the violence that it originally recorded. His photographs thus resemble faded memories, recording not only the events, but also the tide of history since they happened.

SCULPTURE

The range of options available to sculptors has rarely been wider. Partly in reaction to the simplicity of

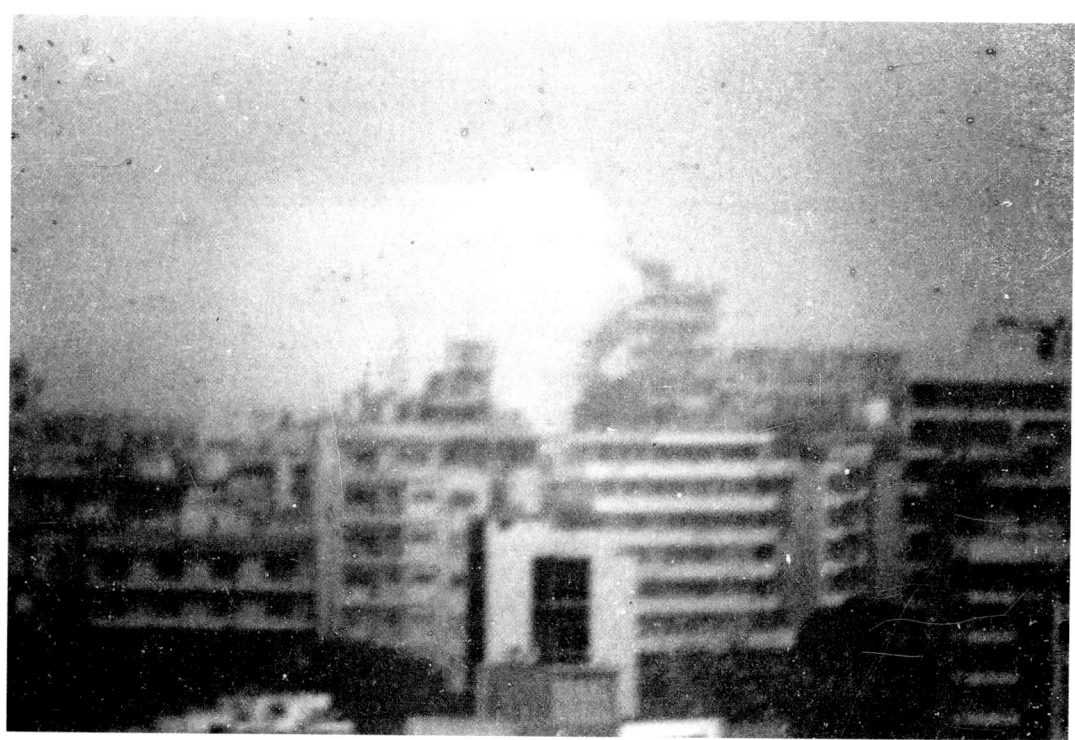

652 Walid Raad.
BEY82 CITY VI. From series "Untitled (1982–2007)."
Archival color inkjet print. 44″ × 67″.
Courtesy Paula Cooper Gallery, New York.

Minimal and Conceptual art, sculptors today draw on a range of techniques and materials. One task that seems to motivate many sculptors in recent years is exploring the symbolic value of shapes. How can a shape "mean something"? What range of memories and feelings are viewers likely to attach to a given figure? At what point does a form "take shape" so that a viewer can recognize it? Are they likely to see what the creator had in mind? These are some of the questions that sculptors have posed in recent years.

Martin Puryear, an African American, thoughtfully probes some of these issues. Combining elegant craftsmanship, organic creativity, and humor, Puryear's deceptively simple sculptures include references to shelters, canoes, trestle bridges, coffins, and basketry. Puryear's work has a distinctly American eloquence that arises from the pioneer traditions of self-reliance and craftsmanship. His OLD MOLE recalls the delicate skeleton of an animal as it combines the whimsical humor of a folktale with the austere sophistication of Minimalist sculpture.

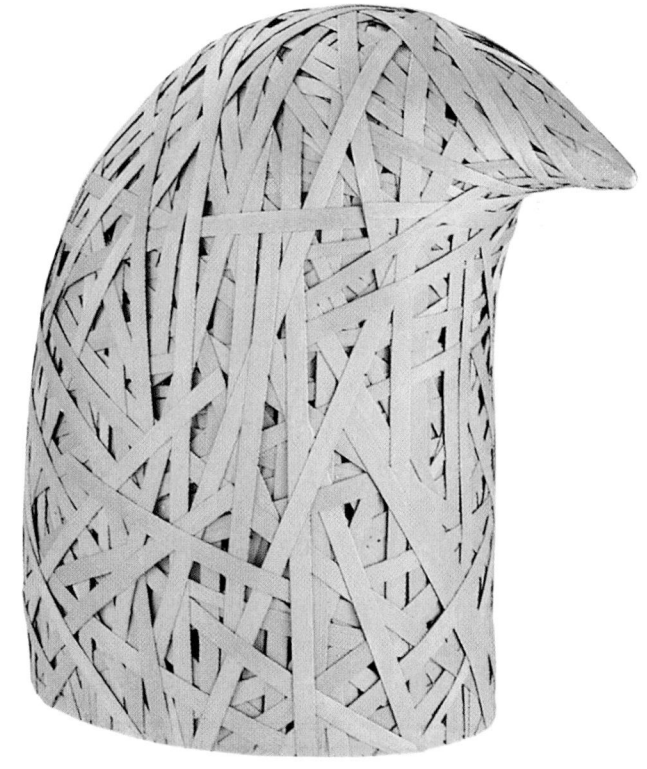

653 Martin Puryear.
OLD MOLE. 1985.
Red cedar. 61″ × 61″ × 32″.
Philadelphia Museum of Art. Purchased with gifts (by exchange) of Samuel S. White, III, and Vera White, Mr. and Mrs. C.G. Chaplin, and with funds contributed by Marion Boulton Stroud, Mr. and Mrs. Robert Kardon, Mr. and Mrs. Dennis Alter, and Mrs. H. Gates Lloyd. 1986-70-1.

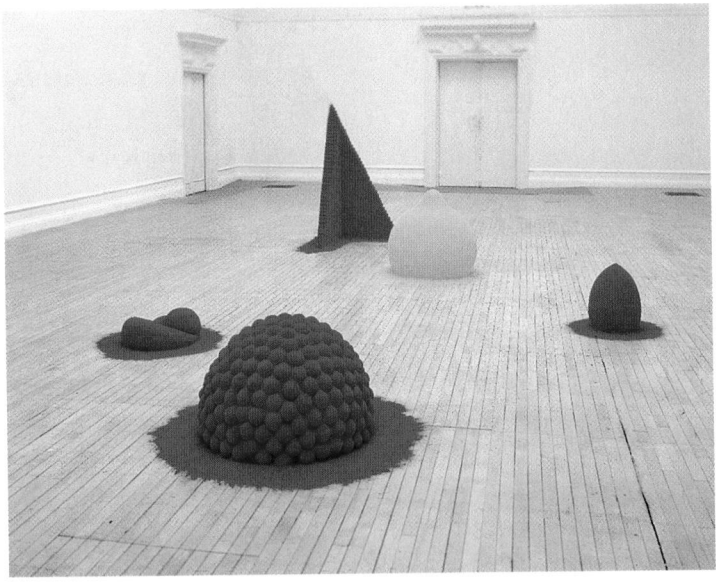

654 Anish Kapoor.
TO REFLECT AN INTIMATE PART OF THE RED. 1981.
Pigment and mixed media. Installation: 78″ × 314″ × 314″.
Photo: Andrew Penketh, London. Courtesy Barbara Gladstone.

Indian-born English sculptor Anish Kapoor takes such explorations in a more ritualistic direction in his work TO REFLECT AN INTIMATE PART OF THE RED. He deployed across a gallery floor several shapes that allude to ancient religious structures such as Maya pyramids, Indian stupas, and onion-shaped domes. Kapoor sprinkled his sculpture with powder, an action that also seems ritualistic. The translation of these shapes into an art gallery raises questions about how their spiritual meanings come about, and how much of that meaning persists in the new context.

Probably the most potent symbol in sculpture is the human body, and many artists today continue to find new meaning in the figure as a subject. These sculptors see it not as a vehicle for idealism or beauty, but rather for commenting on the ways in which culture shapes our bodies and how we think about them.

Kiki Smith is a hero to many feminists because of the way she has modeled, in resin, wax, and papier mâché, full-body depictions of wounded women. These pieces drew attention to the silent suffering of many victims of domestic violence, but in recent years she has broadened her focus. She is as likely now to concentrate attention on the inside of the body and its functions, some of which are infrequently dealt with in art. Like many artists today, she is also influenced by current events. In 1995, when the frozen body of a Stone Age man was found intact in the Alps, she fashioned ICE MAN as a commentary. The piece, showing the unclothed man in the frozen position in which he was found, is modeled life-size and cast in silicon bronze. The material gives the surface a dark color similar to that of the dead man's skin. Smith simplified the facial features, leaving the work's title the only sure clue to the source of the piece. She hung the work on the wall of the gallery, slightly above eye level, attached by its back. Thus it became for viewers an object of curiosity, a specimen, just as

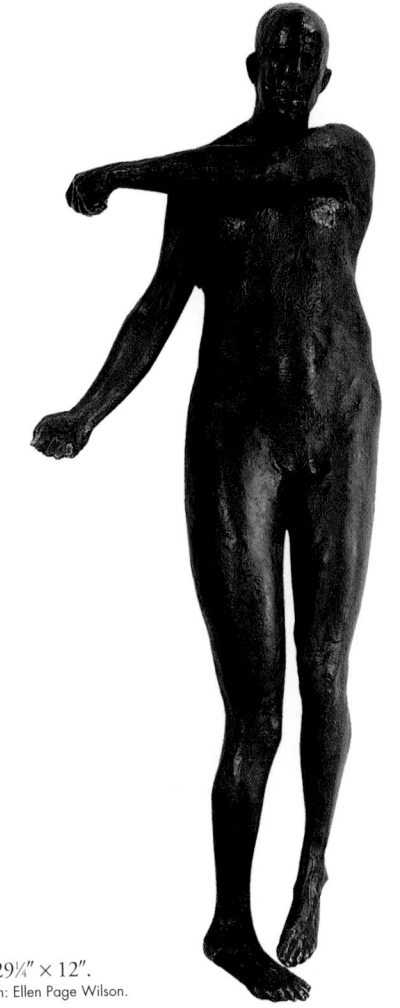

655 Kiki Smith.
ICE MAN. 1995.
Silicon bronze. 80″ × 29¼″ × 12″.
© 1995 Kiki Smith. Photograph: Ellen Page Wilson.
Courtesy of Pace Wildenstein.

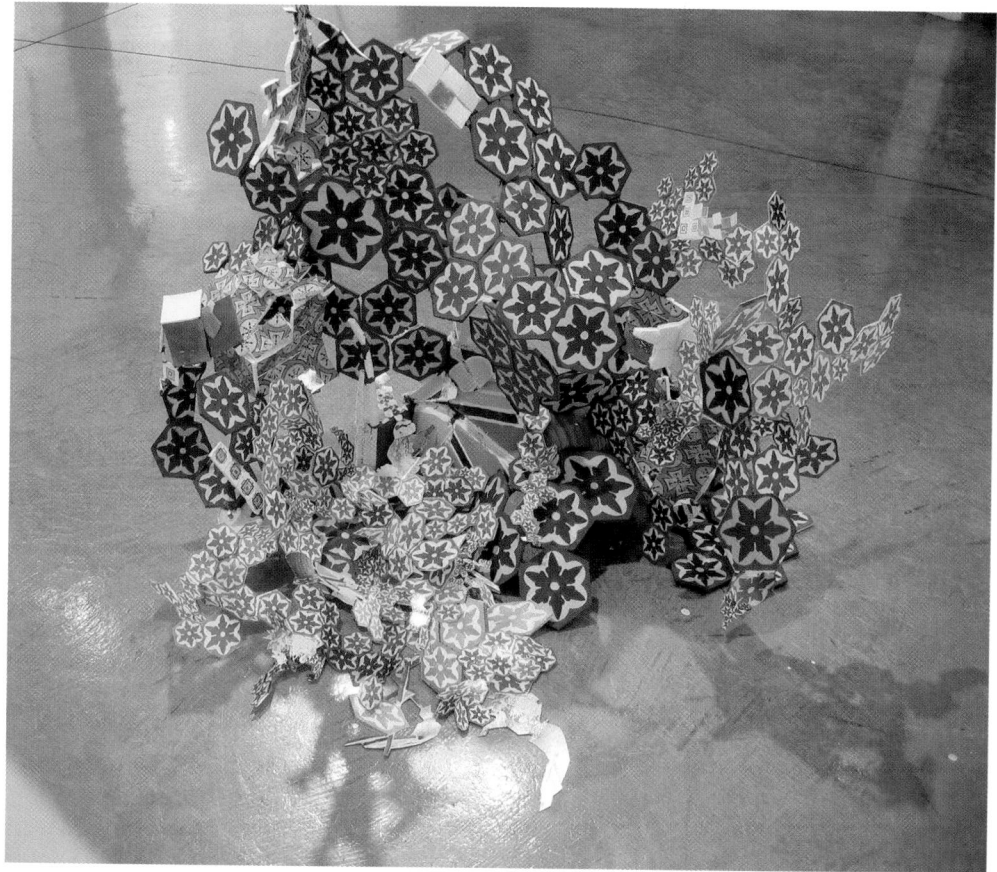

656 Renée Lotenero.
SPAGGIA. 2005.
Handmade tiles, photographs,
found objects.
24″ × 34″ × 21″.
Patricia Sweetow Gallery, San Francisco.

the frozen Stone Age man was for the anthropologists who studied it.

We might think the forms of a sculpture are fixed by the artist for all time, but the recent work of Renée Lotenero seems to show pieces in a process of becoming something. She makes her own ceramic tiles, and then arranges them into constellations that seem frozen in motion. The 2005 work SPAGGIA, for example, seems poised to explode or implode, we don't know which. The piece also includes photographs of the artist in the process of making it, adding to the complexity. Tiles usually decorate flat, static areas, but the artist here put them to work to give a lively sense of uncertainty.

PUBLIC ART

The idea of public art goes back to ancient times. Government and religious leaders have commis-sioned many of history's best-known artists to execute works for the public. However, only in recent decades have commissions for public art gone to large numbers of American artists.

During the 1960s, government leaders began to spend money in new areas. Because the arts are considered beneficial for individuals and communities, it seemed appropriate that city, state, and national governments become involved in bringing the arts to the public. A high percentage of today's public art is now commissioned by government agencies.

Among the largest sponsors of public art is the federal government's General Services Administration (GSA) Art-in-Architecture program, begun in 1962. The program requires that one-half of one percent of the cost of each new government building be spent for art to decorate it. States, cities, and countries later implemented similar programs, with

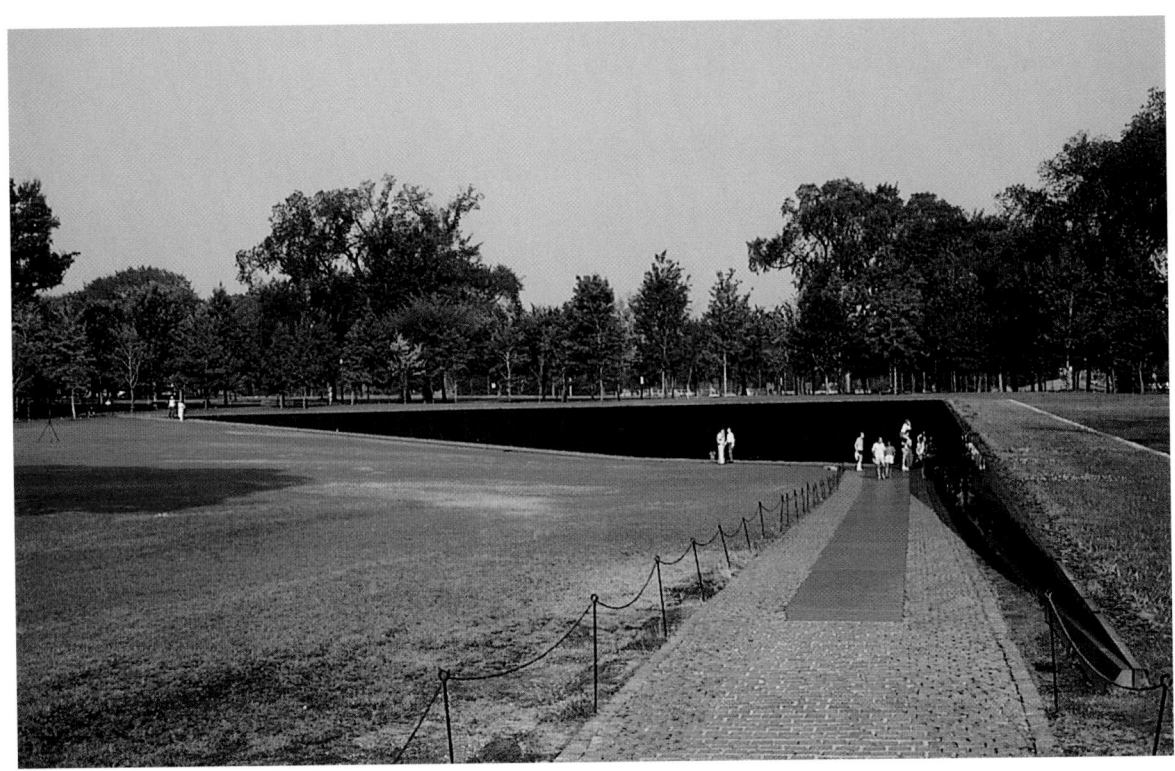

657 Maya Lin.
VIETNAM VETERANS MEMORIAL.
The Mall, Washington, D.C. 1980–1982. Black granite.
Each wall 10′1″ × 246′9″.
Photograph: Duane Preble.

varying percentages designated for the purchase or commissioning of works of art.

The VIETNAM VETERANS MEMORIAL, located on the Mall in Washington, D.C., is America's best-known public art piece. The 250-foot-long, V-shaped black granite wall bears the names of the nearly sixty thousand American servicemen and women who died or are missing in Southeast Asia. The nonprofit Vietnam Veterans Memorial Fund, Inc. (VVMF) was formed in 1979 by a group of Vietnam veterans who believed that a symbol of recognition of the human cost of the war would help speed the process of national reconciliation.

After examining 1,421 entries, the jury of internationally recognized artists and designers unanimously selected the design of twenty-one-year-old Maya Lin of Athens, Ohio, then a student at Yale University. Lin had visited the site and created a design that would work with the land rather than dominate it. "I had an impulse to cut open the earth . . . an initial violence that in time would heal. The grass would grow back, but the cut would remain, a pure, flat surface, like a geode when you cut it open and polish the edge. . . . I chose black granite to make the surface reflective and peaceful."[2]

Lin's bold, eloquently simple design creates a memorial park within a larger park. It shows the influence of Minimalism and Site Works of the 1960s and 1970s. The polished black surface reflects the surrounding trees and lawn, and the tapering segments point to the Washington Monument in one direction and the Lincoln Memorial in the other. Names are inscribed in chronological order by date of death, each name given a place in history. As visitors walk toward the center, the wall becomes higher and the names pile up inexorably. The monument's

R. M. Fischer

Battery Park City in New York is an effort to combine the expertise of specialists with input from citizens to integrate public art into a mixed commercial and residential area. This new neighborhood, which took shape in the early 1980s, was planned as a redevelopment project in a run-down area of Manhattan. Apartments, hotels, schools, and shops now occupy the 982-acre site.

R. M. Fischer's RECTOR GATE marks a strategic location between an apartment complex and a riverside park. Visitors and residents walking from one to the other pass under this fanciful structure, which is laden with symbolic motifs from science fiction movies, heroic engineering projects, and more practical TV towers or antennae.

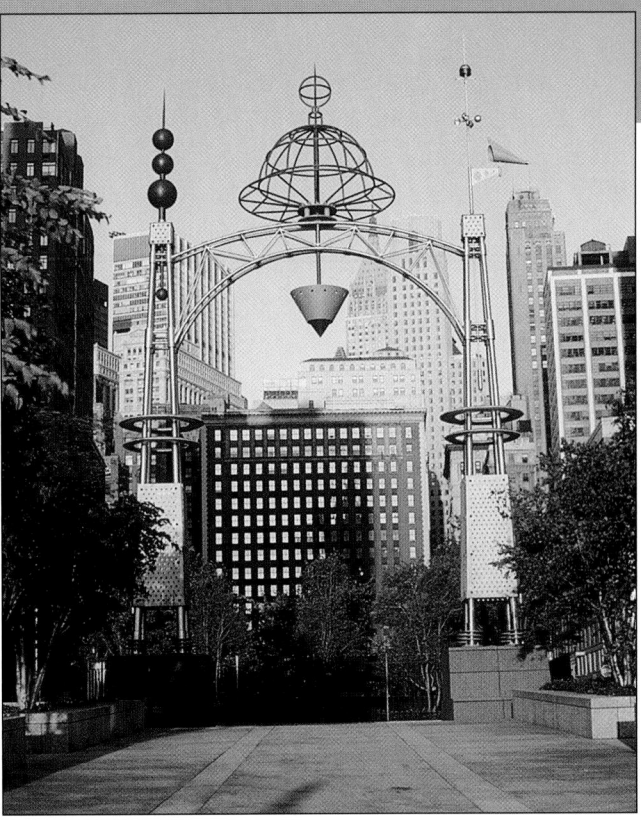

658 R. M. Fischer.
RECTOR GATE. 1988.
Stainless steel, bronze, granite, lighting.
50′ × 28′.
Courtesy of the artist.

thousands of visitors seem to testify to the monument's power to console and heal.

The fragmented nature of contemporary American culture presents a dilemma for both artists and those who sponsor public art. Should the freedom of the artist be unquestioned, with the hope that the public will follow, or at least accept, the art that results? Or should the public have a voice in setting guidelines for selection or actually select the art that becomes part of the public environment— particularly when the art is paid for by tax dollars? Just how democratic should the process be? On the one hand, we could rely entirely on experts, whose tastes are often different from those of the public; at the other extreme, with a lot of public input, we might yield to the lowest common denominator of popular taste.

When the Museum of Modern Art in New York expanded in 2004, the neighbors in high-rise buildings complained about having to look down onto new ugly roof structures. The museum responded by turning to landscape architect Ken Smith, who made the humorous MOMA ROOF GARDEN out of colored gravel, asphalt, and plastic bushes. The composition

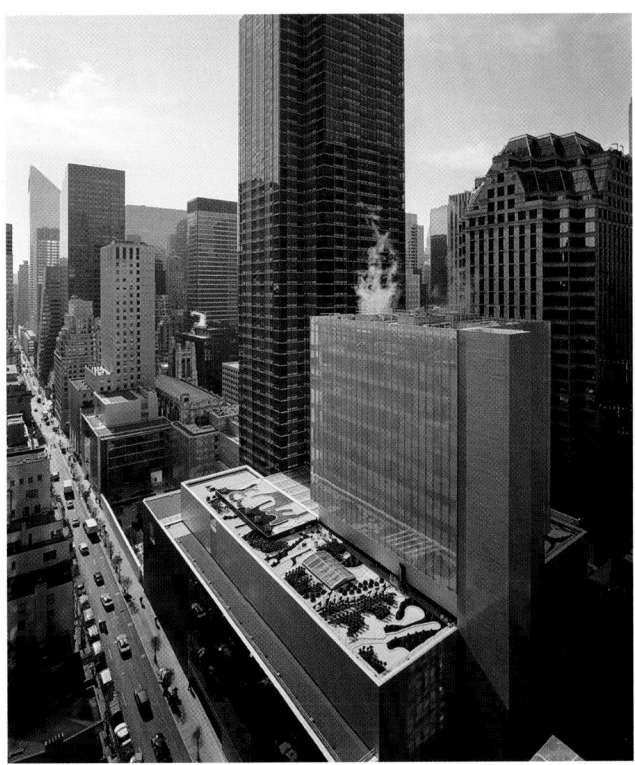

659 Ken Smith.
MOMA ROOF GARDEN. 2005.
Outdoor garden at the Museum of Modern Art, New York.
Photograph Peter Mauss, Esto. Artists Rights Society (ARS), NY.

is a camouflage pattern, the better to "hide" the building. This piece of public art is not visible from inside the museum and, more important, requires no maintenance. When the neighbors complained yet again that the garden was completely fake, Smith responded that it was about as fake as Central Park itself, which had been carefully planted on a leveled field. Thus his ROOF GARDEN pointedly poses the question of what is real and what is fake, an important dilemma in today's culture.

ISSUE-ORIENTED ART

Many artists in the past twenty years have sought to link their art to current social questions. Issue-oriented artists believe that if they limit their art to aesthetic matters, then their work will be only a distraction from pressing problems. Furthermore, they recognize that what we see influences how we think, and they do not want to miss an opportunity to influence both.

Photographer Richard Misrach presents new kinds of landscape in new ways. His photograph SUBMERGED LAMPPOST, SALTON SEA captures the silent yet ironic beauty of a small town in California that was flooded by a misguided irrigation system. In other works he has documented in chilling detail the bloated carcasses of animals killed on military proving grounds in Nevada. His brand of nature photography is the opposite of the common calendars that include soothing views of pristine landscapes. He wants us to know that such scenes are fast disappearing.

Barbara Kruger was trained as a magazine designer, and this profession shows in her piece UNTITLED (I SHOP THEREFORE I AM). She invented the slogan, which sounds as though it came from advertising. The position of the hand, too, looks like it came from an ad for aspirin or sleeping medication. Do our products define us? Are we what we shop for? Often we buy a product because

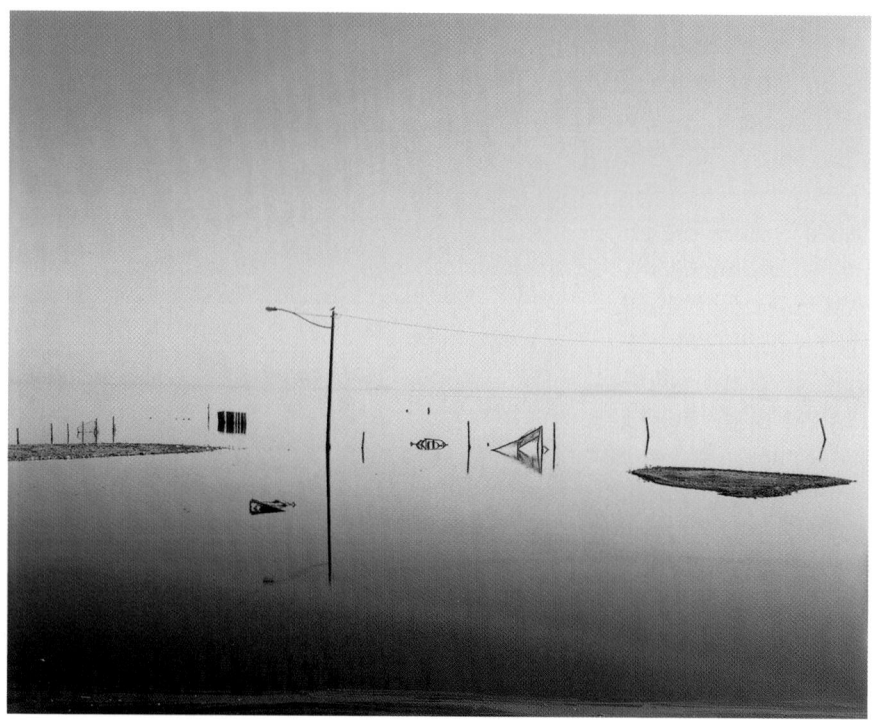

660 Richard Misrach.
SUBMERGED LAMPPOST,
SALTON SEA. 1985.
Photograph (chromogenic color print).
Courtesy of the Robert Mann Gallery.
© Richard Misrach.

of what it will say about us and not for the thing itself. These are some of the messages present in this simple yet fascinating work. Perhaps its ultimate irony is that the artist had it silkscreened onto a shopping bag.

Artists who create works about racism and class bias show how common practices of museum display contribute to such problems. In 1992, the Maryland Historical Society invited African-American artist Fred Wilson to rearrange the exhibits on one floor to create an installation called MINING THE MUSEUM. He spent a year preparing for the show, rummaging through the Society's holdings and documentary records; the results were surprising. He found no portraits, for example, of noted African-American Marylanders Benjamin Banneker (who laid out the boundaries of the District of Columbia), Frederick Douglass (noted abolitionist and journalist), or Harriet Tubman (founder of the Underground Railroad). He found instead busts of Henry Clay, Andrew Jackson, and Napoleon Bonaparte, none of whom ever lived in Maryland. He exhibited those three busts next to three empty pedestals to symbolize the missing African Americans. He set out a display of Colonial Maryland silverware and tea utensils, and included a pair of slave shackles. This lesser-known form of metalwork was perhaps equally vital to the functioning of nineteenth-century Maryland. He dusted off the Society's collection of wooden cigar-store Indians and stood them, backs to viewers, facing photographs of real Native Americans who lived in Maryland. In an accompanying exhibition brochure he wrote that a museum should be a place that can make you think. When MINING THE MUSEUM went on display, attendance records soared.

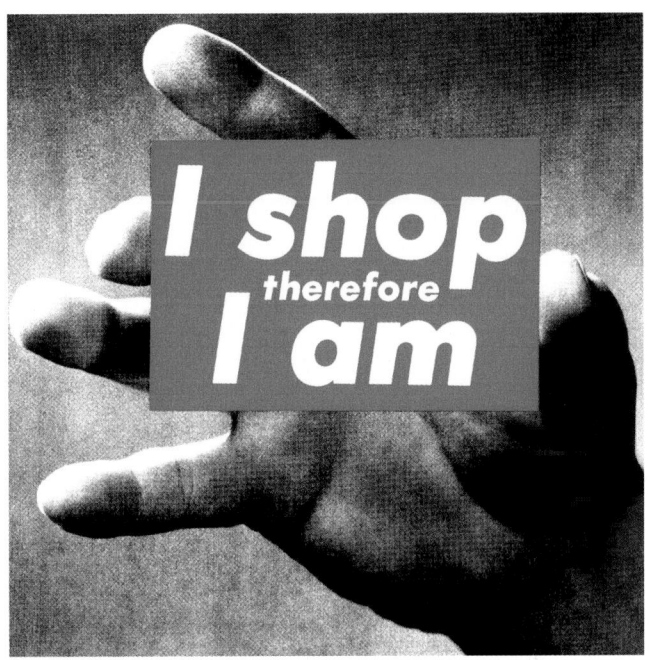

661 Barbara Kruger.
UNTITLED (I SHOP THEREFORE I AM). 1987.
Photographic silkscreen/vinyl. 111″ × 113″.
Courtesy Mary Boone Gallery, New York.

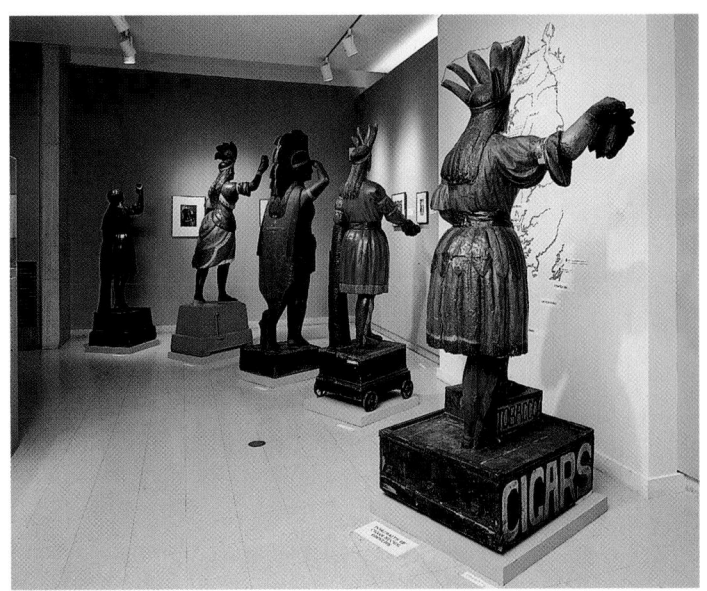

662 Fred Wilson.
MINING THE MUSEUM. 1992.
Installation. Cigar-store Indians facing photographs of Native American Marylanders.
Museum and Library of Maryland History.
Photograph: Jeff D. Goldman.

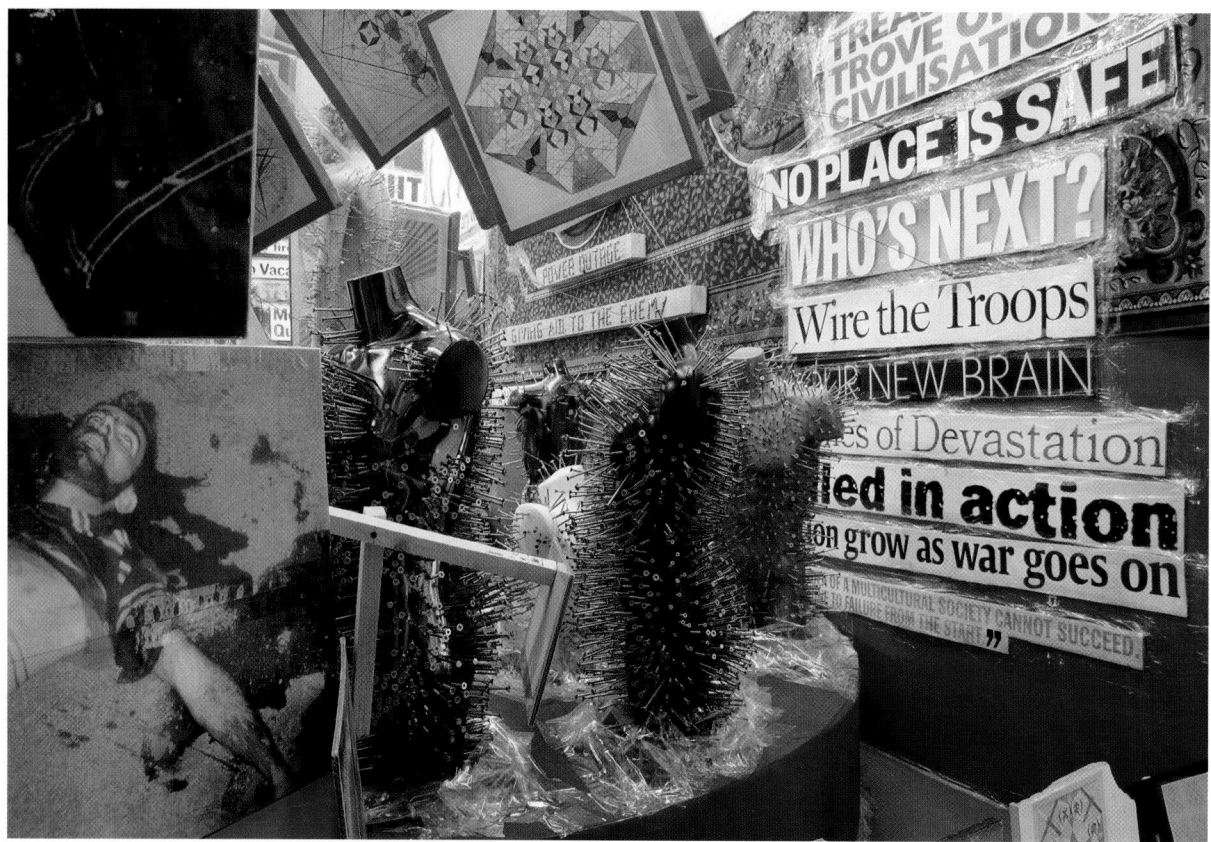

663 Thomas Hirschhorn.
SUPERFICIAL ENGAGEMENT. 2006.
Installation view.
Barbara Gladstone Gallery, New York.
Photograph: David Regen.

The Swiss-born Thomas Hirschhorn took up the issue of the Iraq war, but only indirectly, in the context of today's media-saturated society. His 2006 installation **SUPERFICIAL ENGAGEMENT** filled the entire gallery space with a dizzying array of objects that resembled a parade float on drugs, or a cross between an insane asylum and a grocery store. Photos of mangled war dead competed for space with coffins, nail-studded mannequins, blaring headlines, and reproductions of abstract artworks. The nailed bodies refer to traditional African magic sculptures (see the NKONDE on page 331), and the abstract art was mostly copied from the Austrian mystic Emma Kunz in what the artist called "friendly piracy." The headlines shout the aimless alarmism of cable news channels: "Decision Time Approaches," "Broken Borders," "An Assault on Hypocrisy," "The Real Cri-

sis." The artist used only cheap materials (cardboard, plastic, plywood, package tape) in an effort to avoid art-world pretense and make it more accessible. He said of his brash style, "Art is a tool, a tool to encounter the world, to confront the reality and the time I am living in." The shrill volume of this exhibition only paralleled the strident intensity of today's news, where a disaster might follow a fashion show. At the opening reception, the artist provided hammers and screwdrivers, and the crowd joined in attaching nails and screws, thus finishing the piece.

STREET ART

In the late 1990s, many galleries in various cities began to exhibit work by artists who had previously made illegal graffiti. Many of these "street artists" were based in the culture of skateboards and

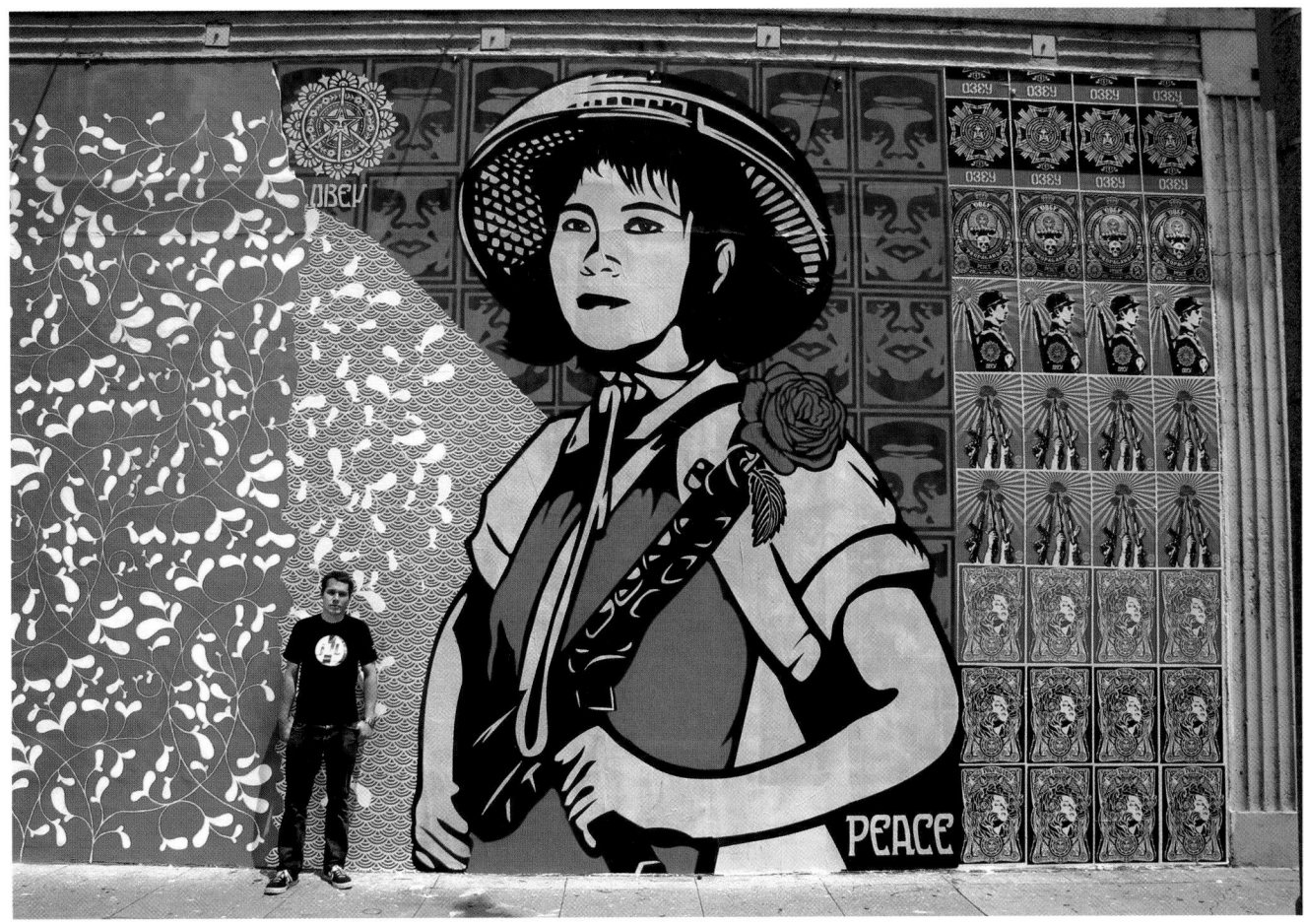

664   Shepard Fairey.
REVOLUTION GIRL. 2006.
Screenprinted temporary mural. 16′ × 19′.
Outdoor location, Los Angeles. Obey Giant Art, CA.

punk music, and they used materials bought at the hardware store rather than the art supply house. Their creations were only rarely related to gang-oriented graffiti, which usually mark out territories of influence. Nor were they autobiographical or personal. Rather, the street artists made much broader statements about themselves and the world in a language that was widely understandable. The ancestors of the movement in the 1980s were Keith Haring (see page 70) and Jean-Michel Basquiat (see page 21), both of whom worked illegally for years before exhibiting in galleries. By the turn of the twenty-first century, Street Art was a recognized movement, and most of its main practitioners work both indoors and out.

The career of Shepard Fairey is exemplary. He studied at the Rhode Island School of Design, but was never satisfied in the art world, which seemed to him closed-off and elitist. He began working outdoors, and quickly acquired notoriety for posting dozens of signs and stickers with the single word "Obey" below the ominous-looking face of wrestler Andre the Giant. His vocabulary soon expanded to include advertising symbols, propaganda posters, and currency, even as the scale of his work increased to billboard size.

His 2006 work REVOLUTION GIRL is an anti-war mural created on a legal wall for a three-month show in West Hollywood. The dominant motif is a huge female Communist soldier from

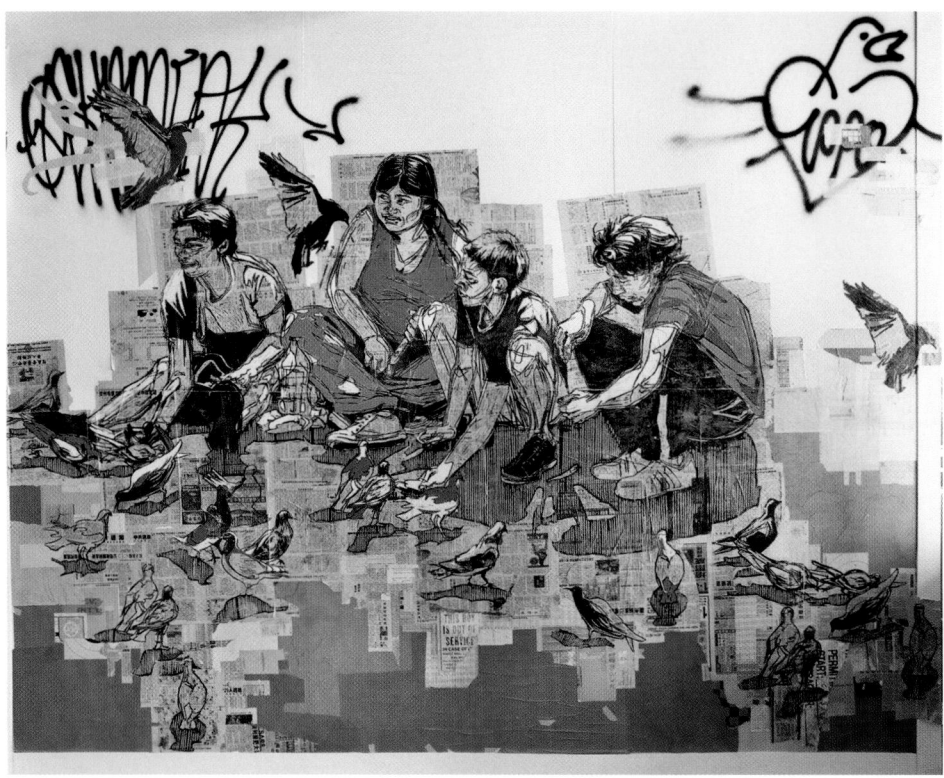

665 Swoon.
UNTITLED. 2005.
Linoleum cut, newsprint, ink and wheat paste. Variable dimensions.
Deitch Projects, New York.

the Vietnam War that the artist borrowed from Chinese propaganda, but her rifle has a flower protruding; her weapon has become an elaborate vase. Other motifs from Chinese propaganda decorate the center right, re-purposed for a peace campaign. In the lower corner, posters of a female face with flowery hair symbolize nurturing. The message of the mural is anti-war, but the artist made the statement positive rather than negative, expressing the hope that we can convert our weapons into flower holders. His friend and fellow street artist Blake Marquis provided the vivid leafy patterns at the left. We see the artist himself in the foreground.

Some of today's most skillful street art is created by Swoon, a woman who uses the pseudonym to avoid prosecution. She carves large linoleum blocks and makes life-sized relief prints from them, usually portraits of everyday people. She prints them on large sheets of cheap (usually recycled)

newsprint and pastes them on urban walls, beginning on the Lower East Side of Manhattan but now in cities on every continent. Her UNTITLED installation at Deitch Projects was a recent indoor work. Against objections that her work is mostly illegal, she replies that her creations are far easier to look at than advertising, that they lack any persuasive agenda, and that they glorify common people. Moreover, the newsprint that she uses decays over time so that her work is impermanent. Although she works mostly outdoors, she sometimes shows in galleries because, she admits, "I have to make a living," but she charges far less for her work than most other artists of wide repute.

Probably the most famous street artist is Banksy (who also uses a pseudonym). He placed his own art in the collections of several major museums in 2005 by merely entering the galleries and sticking his pieces to the wall. His street graffiti is generally witty, as we see in his GRAFFITI

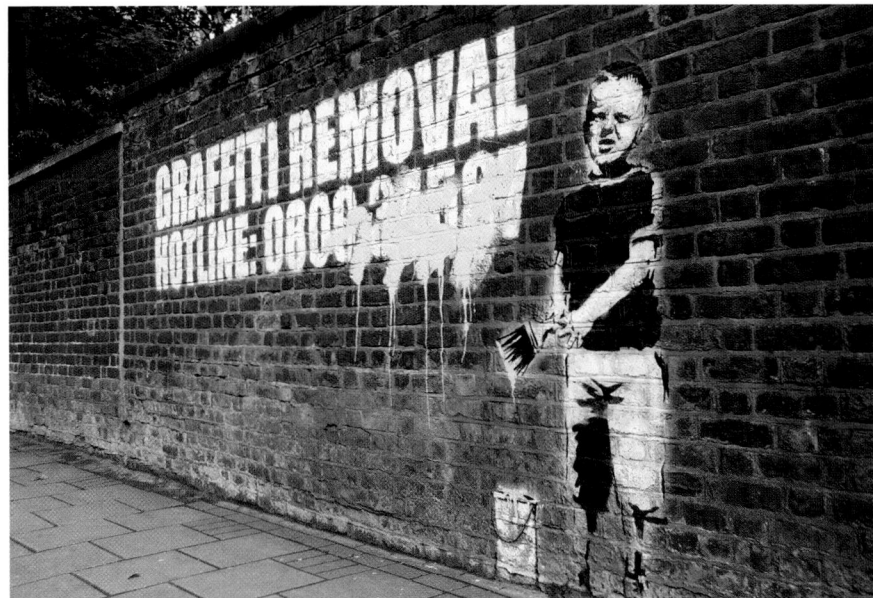

666 Banksy.
GRAFFITI REMOVAL HOTLINE,
PENTONVILLE ROAD. 2006.
Steve Cotton/artofthestate.co.uk.

REMOVAL HOTLINE, PENTONVILLE ROAD. There is no such thing as a graffiti removal hotline; the artist stenciled the words and then created the youth who seems to paint out the phone number. Banksy is currently one of the most popular artists in England, and many of his outdoor works have been preserved. When a prominent work of his was recently defaced by another graffiti artist, protests ensued and the defacer was arrested for vandalism! Thus street artists often blur the line between legal and illegal. Other artists in this book who partake of a street art style are Barry McGee (page 117) and Gajin Fujita (page 467).

THE GLOBAL PRESENT

Communication and travel technologies are making the world smaller and smaller. The Internet, air travel, mobile phones, cable television, and international migration are bringing us all into ever closer proximity. Since the fall of Communism, the world is not as divided as it was for the preceding half-century, thus contributing to a more fluid world culture. Many businesses, for example, are not confined by national boundaries anymore; they may raise money in one country, buy raw materials in another, set up manufacturing facilities in a third, and sell the final product around the world.

The trend toward globalization has had some interesting consequences: Mexican soap operas are extremely popular in the Philippines. Residents of Papua New Guinea can watch reruns of the 1980s television show *Dallas* in local bars. Latin American novels influenced Chinese filmmakers of the 1980s and 1990s. During the invasion of Iraq, Saddam Hussein followed the conflict on CNN. The world's tallest building is a bank in Taipei. By 2012, buildings in Moscow, Dubai, Seoul, and Katanji, India, will rise higher. Ethnic "minorities" already make up the majority of students in many American public school systems. By the year 2015, according to the United Nations, only one of the world's fifteen largest urban areas will be located in the United States (New York City, tied for eighth place with Tianjin, China). None of the top fifteen will be European. To function successfully and to live peacefully, it is increasingly necessary that we understand cultures beyond our own.

The globalization of culture has had a profound impact on art. Contemporary art forms such as conceptual, installation, and performance art have spread around the world. Innovative work is emerging in unexpected places, as artists in many countries use increasingly international modes of expression to interpret the contemporary world in the light of their own traditions. This union of the cosmopolitan and the local is a major source of the new creative effort that has always fertilized art. A few examples from disparate continents will have to suffice to indicate the directions that art is taking. All these works comment on issues our world faces today.

Japanese artist Mariko Mori created WAVE UFO as a refuge for hyperactive workers in the new global service sector. Her piece is a teardrop-shaped vessel that appears to have arrived from outer space to land in the lobby of a Manhattan office building. Viewers (three at a time) enter in order to experience technological enlightenment. They lie on couches connected to brain-wave detectors, where computer programs convert their brain activity into light displays. These last three minutes, followed by four more of abstract film designed by the artist to show a "cosmic-dream world." Buddhist meditation meets high technology in this work, which drew harried office workers for two months.

Jaune Quick-to-See Smith highlighted an important demographic shift in THE BROWNING OF AMERICA. Here we see a map of the continent almost covered in brown paint drips. The work

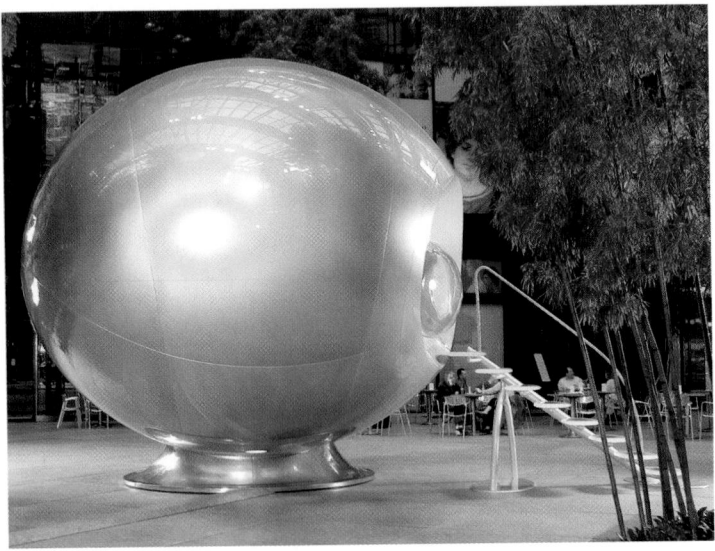

667 Mariko Mori.
WAVE UFO. 2003.
Installation in New York City.
The Public Art Fund. Photograph: Tom Powel Imaging.

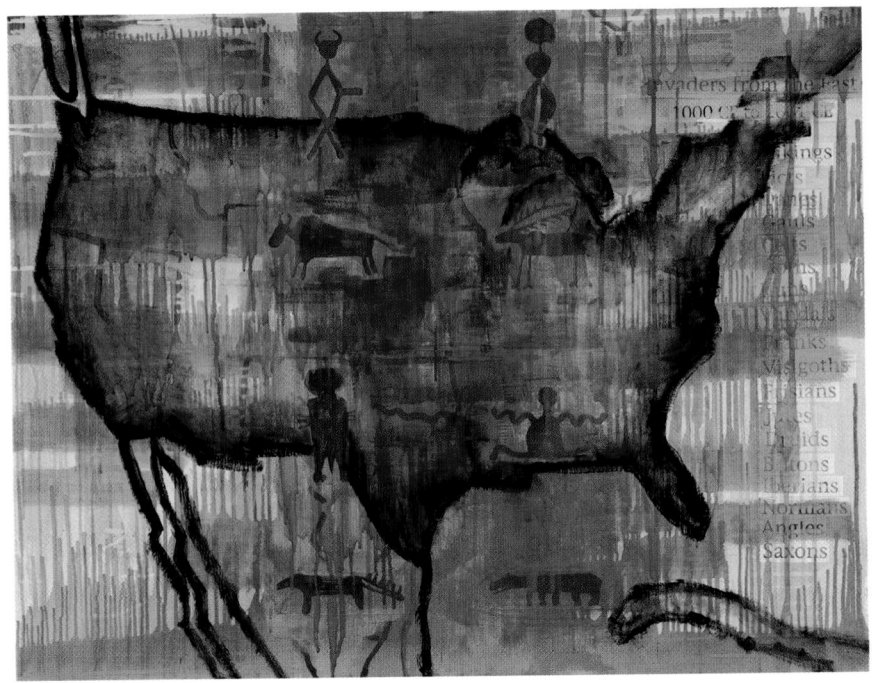

668 Jaune Quick-to-See Smith.
THE BROWNING OF
AMERICA. 2000.
Oil, collage, and mixed
media on canvas.
36" × 48".
Crocker Art Museum, Sacramento.
Partial gift of Anton Gallery,
Monterey.

seems to say that America is no longer black and white, but rather getting browner as races intermingle and immigrants arrive. Native Americans are symbolized by the shapes in the center, a strategy that gives primacy to the first Americans. (The artist counts herself among these, a member of the Flathead Indian Nation.) The first wave of immigrants, white European ethnic groups, is listed at the right, or East side from which they came. Most of the paint drips run upward, symbolizing the south-to-north movement of people that is helping to transform the ethnic basis of the United States. To make the paint run this way, she had to turn the United States upside down, a hugely symbolic act.

The issue of personal and ethnic identity provokes increasing soul-searching in this shrinking world. Does an artist from one part of the world need to stick with the traditional styles still associated with that part of the world? Is it appropriate for an American artist to paint in a traditional Chinese style or vice versa?

Shahzia Sikander answers many of these questions by taking a middle ground, drawing on her roots while giving her work a contemporary look. Born in Pakistan, she was trained first as a traditional illustrator in the ancient gouache medium (see page 324 for an example). After moving to the West in the mid-1990s, she studied at the Rhode Island School of Design. Her 2001 painting PLEASURE PILLARS is a layered arrangement of women in various guises and poses. At the center we see a headless figure in traditional garb flanked by a classical Greek nude. At the top center is a tail view of the airliner that facilitates travel between these two worlds. Other figures allude to traditional dance movements and domestic scenes. The symbolic ram's head and bird imagery complete the inventory of this work without exhausting its metaphoric meanings.

The Iranian-born Shirin Neshat similarly reflects on the complex question of a woman's identity in today's global society. She grew up before the Islamic revolution of 1979, studied in the West, and has returned to Iran several times since. She

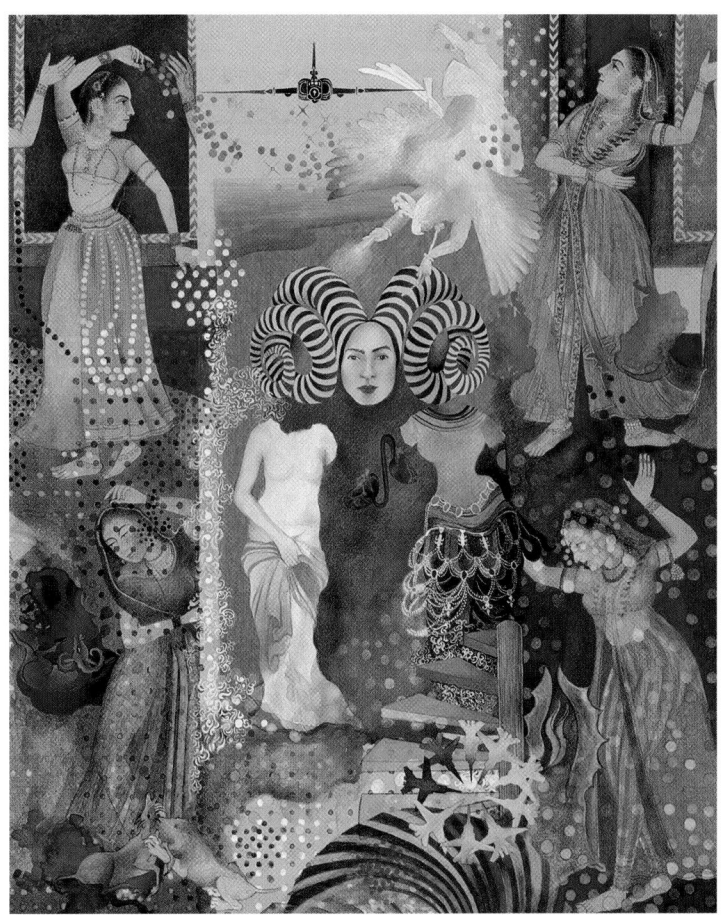

669 Shahzia Sikander.
PLEASURE PILLARS. 2001.
Watercolor, dry pigment on Wasli paper. 12″ × 10″.
Brent Sikkema Gallery, New York.

works in various media, but most recently has made films. PASSAGE (on the following page) tells a story of death and rebirth in the desert. This eleven-minute film, shot without dialogue, shows a line of men in uniform carrying a body toward a group of veiled mourning women who have dug a shallow grave. A young girl, symbolizing the next generation, sits a few yards away. She arranges stones in a circle and places sticks at the center, symbolically yet playfully re-enacting the burial. As the black-clad men approach the women and deposit the body, a ring of fire encircles all except the girl.

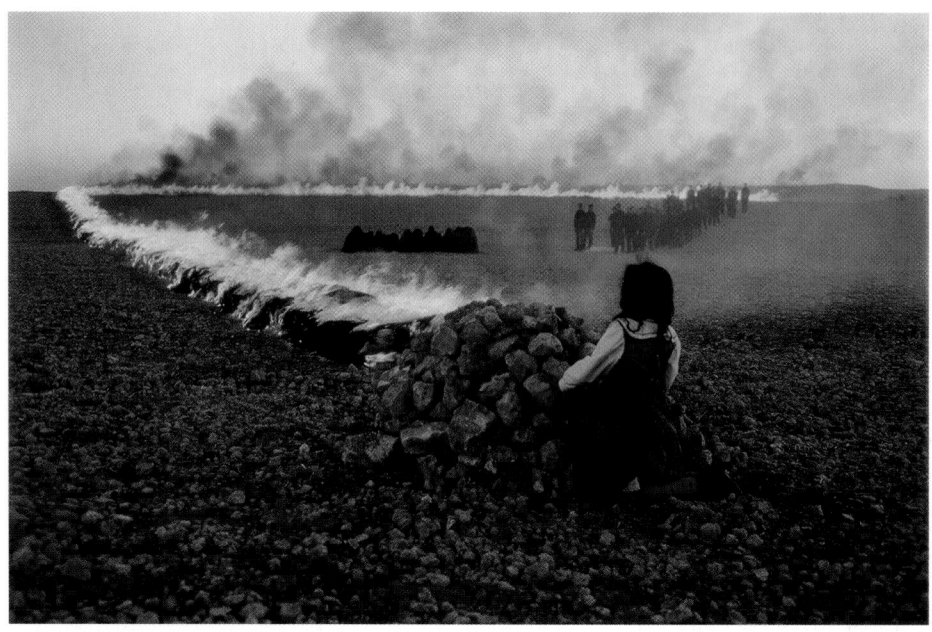

670 Shirin Neshat.
PASSAGE. 2001.
Still from film.
© 2001 Shirin Neshat.
Courtesy of the Gladstone Gallery.

Contemporary artists are unlikely to specialize in one medium or another; most prefer to work out their ideas in whatever medium best answers the urge to communicate. Indian artist Shilpa Gupta has worked with sculpture, cloth, and the Internet as she comments on how the world appears from her perspective in Mumbai, the country's largest city. Her 2004–2005 UNTITLED work is a video projection that shows seven figures wearing various styles of clothing based on camouflage patterns (which she says is an increasingly important fashion statement since the War on Terror began in 2001). Gallery viewers can use a mouse to manipulate the figures and cause them to bend, pivot, or gesture, all to the accompaniment of electronic sounds, as the command words appear on the floor. The work thus resembles a video game, but viewers soon realize that the figures do not respond perfectly to the mouse commands: Some figures imitate what others do,

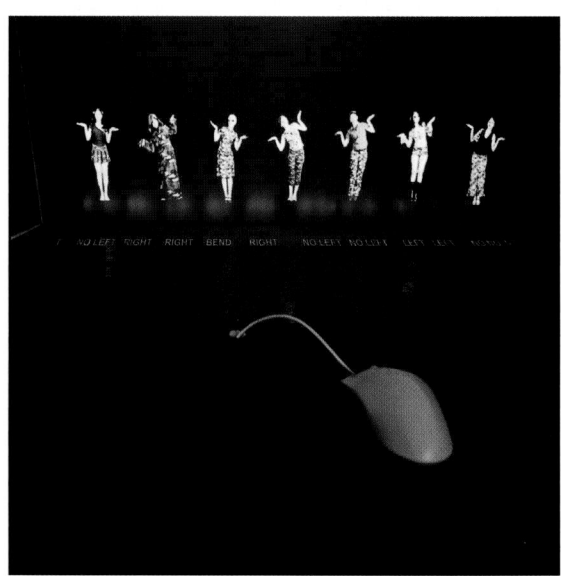

671 Shilpa Gupta.
UNTITLED. 2004–2005.
Interactive video projection;
computer and projector.
Eight minutes with sound.
Courtesy of Bose Pacia Gallery, New York.

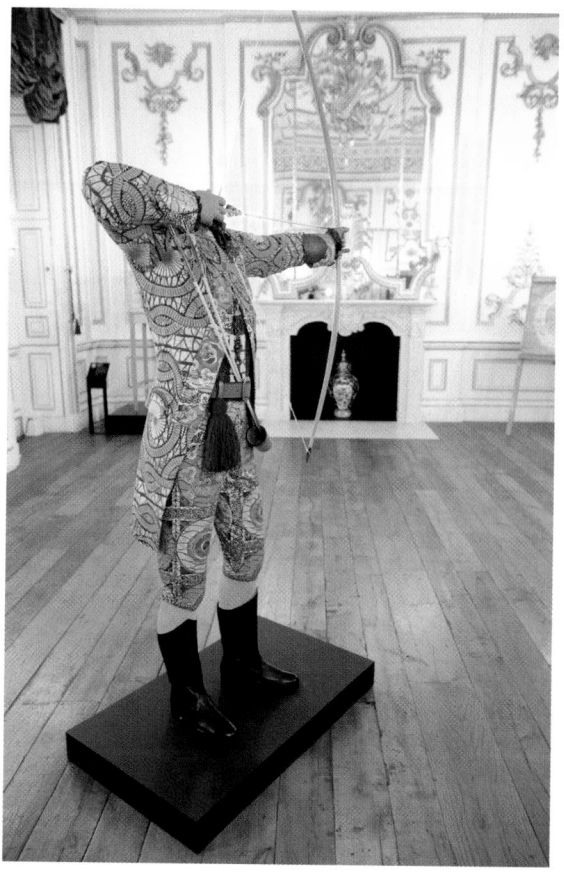

672   Yinka Shonibare, MBE.
SIR FOSTER CUNLIFFE PLAYING.
2006.
Mixed media.
Dimensions variable.
Victoria and Albert Museum, London.

and sometimes a figure makes a threatening gesture to its neighbor. Thus, the artist says, the work gives us an illusion of control similar to that which we enjoy on our daily lives. In a humorous twist, all seven figures are clones of the artist, allowing viewers to seemingly reverse the creative process by symbolically manipulating the artist.

While Gupta's work shows subtle sarcasm, Yinka Shonibare uses pointed cross-cultural satire in his work SIR FOSTER CUNLIFFE PLAYING. First, a little background: The subject of the work is a British aristocrat of the eighteenth century who pioneered the hobby of archery, founding the Royal British Bowmen in 1787 as a leisure and social club for well-off people. Soon archery matches became outdoor feasts as members donned green uniform jackets and shot arrows, often to musical accompaniment, before sitting down to an elaborate banquet. This work depicts a headless Sir Foster, on a pedestal like a Greek statue, aiming an arrow at a target. His incredibly colorful costume of African textiles is a knowing reference to his family's source of wealth: His grandfather of the same name was one of England's leading slave traders. Thus the artist, a Londoner of Nigerian descent, shows Sir Foster clothed by the Africans that his family bought and sold in the years before England's moral outrage forced the abolition of the trade in 1807. Shonibare created this work for a 2007 exhibition about the slave trade on the tricentennial of its abolition. Perhaps

the final irony is that the British government recently honored Shonibare for his witty visual critiques by making him a Member of the Order of the British Empire, the first step toward knighthood; hence the MBE after his name.

Some artists use their work to excite debate about the ever-increasing surveillance that watches us all in this new century. In response to the threat of terrorism, governments are assuming increasing powers to watch premises, intercept communication, and detain persons. Christian Moeller installed the public art commission MOJO (on the following page) in 2007 to raise awareness of the surveillance issue. Two cameras attached to buildings track the movements of people at night across

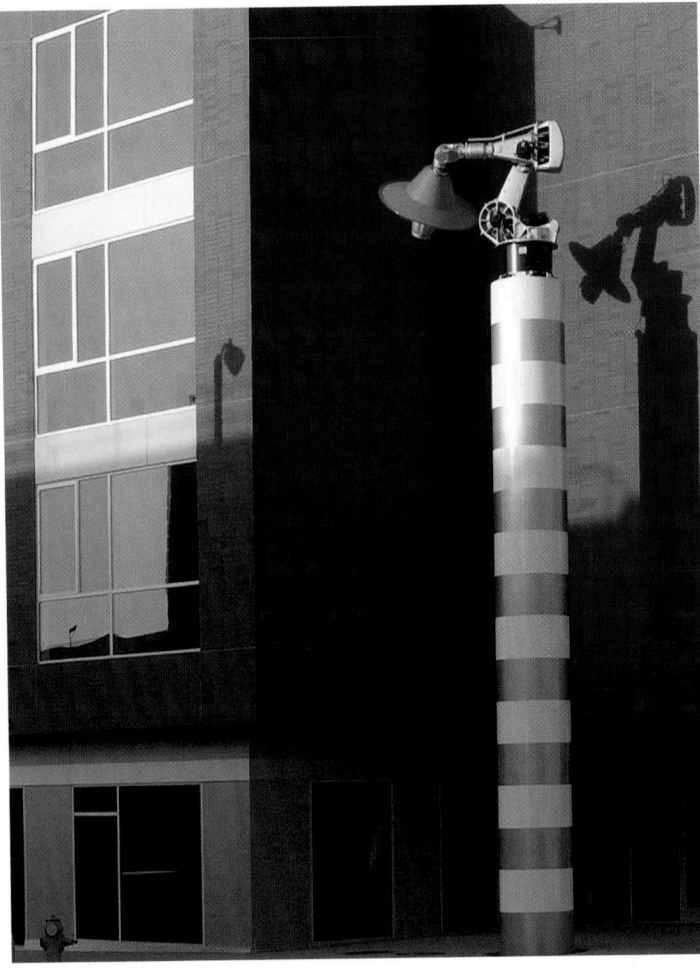

673 Christian Moeller.
MOJO. 2007.
Computer-driven sidewalk installation, San Pedro, California.
Height 40'.
Courtesy of the artist.

a corner sidewalk near the port of Los Angeles. Computer software uses this input to order a spotlight (atop the striped tower) to select and follow one passerby at a time with its intense glare. The work is part lighthouse and part toy; its title seems like a pet name, but the work has caused controversy. Some resent its spying eye, but MOJO is only doing what passes unnoticed many times a day in most people's lives. The artist, who has installed similarly high-tech pieces in London and Tokyo, does not mind the controversy. He said, "Successful public art is indicated by how much people talk about it."

We will close this book with a performance piece by an artist who inserted himself into the middle of one of the world's most dangerous hot spots. Francis Alÿs, a Belgian-born resident of Mexico, went to Jerusalem in 2004 and took a fifteen-mile walk through the city over two days, trailing a thin stream of green paint. The route he chose was the armistice line between Arabs and Jews that ended the 1948 war and established the state of Israel. This line came to be known as the Green Line, and like the old Iron Curtain, it is one of humanity's most tense borders. Across this war-torn landscape, the artist passed checkpoints, climbed hills, avoided swerving cars, and generally endured the stares and comments of Jerusalem's jittery population, stopping every five hundred yards to refill his can. The artist's "painting" re-drew the line in a way that was utterly peaceful. He gave the work a long title that hints at his intent: SOMETIMES DOING SOMETHING POETIC CAN BECOME POLITICAL AND SOMETIMES DOING SOMETHING POLITICAL CAN BECOME POETIC.

The culmination of the piece came in the next year when he edited the video of the walk down to a seventeen-minute film and showed it to activists on various sides of the Israeli/Palestinian divide. Here is a sample of what they said:

- "If you go around and ask, 'What's the Green Line?' the response is, 'It's the border.' But it was never a border. It's a ceasefire line that declared that the fire didn't cease."
- "We have the same problem, I think, on both sides: that we do not recognize that we are sick. But we are sick."
- "A lot of Israelis would find this a form of terrorism."
- "How can you make a line without a ruler? People will argue that it is maybe two centimeters from here or there. We will have to leave it for the Final Phase Negotiations. I don't think you are a good man to put frontiers or

borders. You are too disorganized, you are too artistic, too open to put these separations."

■ "I would like to see this whole area without lines, without blockades, without borders, without anything."

Alÿs wanted to find out whether an artistic act could, as he put it, "truly bring about an unforeseen way of thinking." Although the piece did not settle any of the conflicts that have persisted for generations in that part of the world, his poetic/political re-inscription did cause a lot of people to think about their divisions in a new way.

This book has attempted to present a small portion of the boundless variety of art that characterizes human expression. We have seen that art comes from basic feelings that all of us share. Through their work, artists interact with life, to find purpose and meaning in it. Art and human life vary considerably across time and space, but the art endures. Creative expression is a response to being alive.

Appreciation for the artistic dimension within each of us is as important as the recognition of the roles of art and artists in society at large. In the process of strengthening our understanding and appreciation for the art produced by recognized masters, we must not neglect the art within ourselves. To prevent such a dead end, it is necessary to give equal care and attention to the development of the artist within.

Art offers us a way to go beyond mere physical existence. The ideas, values, and approaches that constitute the basis of the visual arts can continue to enrich our lives and surroundings. We form art. Art forms us.

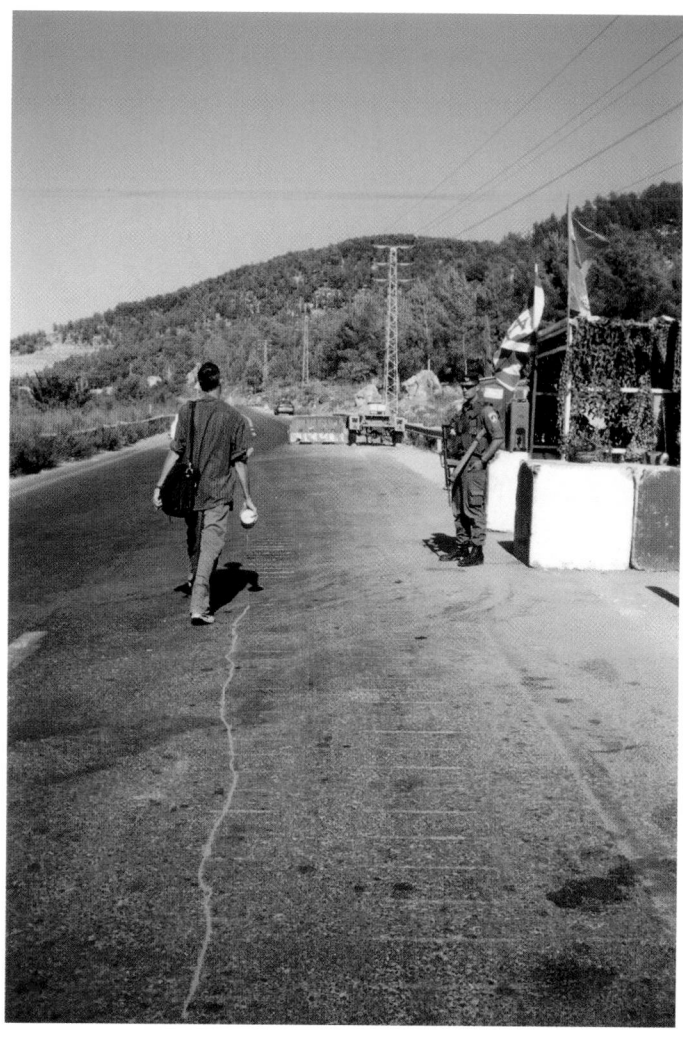

674 Francis Alÿs.
SOMETIMES DOING SOMETHING POETIC CAN BECOME POLITICAL AND SOMETIMES DOING SOMETHING POLITICAL CAN BECOME POETIC. 2005.
Performance/video projection.
David Zwirner Gallery, New York.

TIMELINE

| 30,000 | 20,000 | 10,000 | 5000 | 3000 | 2000 | 1000 | 500 | 250 | B.C.E. 0 C.E. | 200 | 400 | 600 | 800 |

Americas

Los Manos
Cave Paintings

OLMEC

Massive Stone Head

Hopewell
Hand

NAZCA

MAYA
Temple I

Man & Woman

Russia

Woman of
Willendorf

Bison

SCYTHIANS
ANIMAL STYLE

VIKINGS

Book of
Kells

NORTHERN Europe

Lascaux
Cave Paintings

Chauvet Cave Paintings

Stonehenge

Purse Cover

**CHRISTIAN ERA
BEGINS**

**POMPEII
BURIED**

ROMAN EMPIRE

Euphronios
Krater

CLASSICAL
Parthenon
Warrior

Pantheon

Division of
Empire

Head of Constantine

Fall of Western
Empire

SOUTHERN Europe

Earthenware Beaker

ARCHAIC
Kore Kouros

HELLENISTIC
Laocoön

BYZANTIUM

SUMERIAN CITIES
Bull-headed Harp
Ziggurats

**BRONZE
AGE BEGINS**

AKKADIANS
Head of Ruler

**BIRTH OF
CHRIST 4 B.C.E.**

**BIRTH OF
MOHAMMED 570**

MIDDLE East

**NEOLITHIC
REVOLUTION
BEGINS**

OLD KINGDOM
Mycerinus
Pyramids

NEW KINGDOM
Qennefer
Tomb Paintings

Mummy Portraits

Africa

Blombos Cave

NOK CULTURE
Head

IFE

India

**INDUS VALLEY
CIVILIZATION**
Harappa Torso

**BIRTH OF
BUDDHA 563**

Great
Stupa

**GUPTA
DYNASTY**

Standing Buddha

China

SHANG DYNASTY

Burial
Urn

Great Wall

Flying
Horse

BUDDHISM SPREAD TO CHINA

Xian Tomb Figures

PAPER INVENTED

**CHAN (LATER ZEN)
BUDDHISM**

Japan

Ritual
Vessel

**BUDDHISM
SPREAD
TO JAPAN**

Ise Shrine

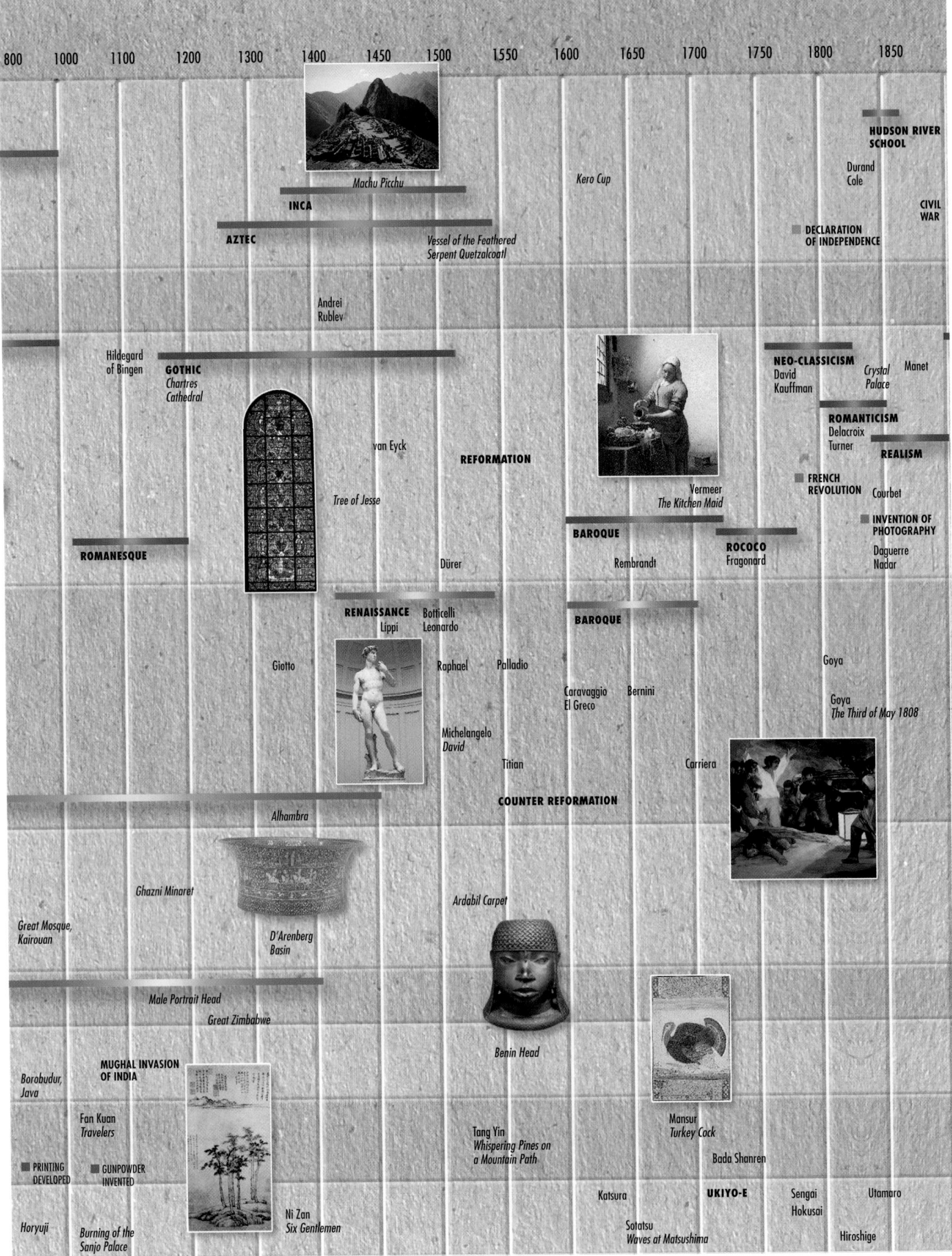

800 1000 1100 1200 1300 1400 1450 1500 1550 1600 1650 1700 1750 1800 1850

Machu Picchu

INCA

AZTEC

Vessel of the Feathered Serpent Quetzalcoatl

Kero Cup

HUDSON RIVER SCHOOL

Durand
Cole

CIVIL WAR

DECLARATION OF INDEPENDENCE

Andrei
Rublev

Hildegard
of Bingen

GOTHIC
Chartres Cathedral

van Eyck

REFORMATION

Tree of Jesse

NEO-CLASSICISM
David
Kauffman

Crystal Palace

Manet

ROMANTICISM
Delacroix
Turner

REALISM

FRENCH REVOLUTION

Courbet

Vermeer
The Kitchen Maid

Dürer

ROMANESQUE

BAROQUE

ROCOCO
Fragonard

INVENTION OF PHOTOGRAPHY

Daguerre
Nadar

RENAISSANCE Botticelli
Lippi Leonardo

BAROQUE

Giotto

Raphael Palladio

Goya

Michelangelo
David

Caravaggio Bernini
El Greco

Goya
The Third of May 1808

Titian

Carriera

COUNTER REFORMATION

Alhambra

Ghazni Minaret

Ardabil Carpet

Great Mosque,
Kairouan

D'Arenberg Basin

Male Portrait Head
Great Zimbabwe

Benin Head

Borobudur,
Java

MUGHAL INVASION OF INDIA

Fan Kuan
Travelers

Tang Yin
Whispering Pines on a Mountain Path

Mansur
Turkey Cock

Bada Shanren

PRINTING DEVELOPED

GUNPOWDER INVENTED

Katsura

UKIYO-E

Sengai
Hokusai

Utamaro

Horyuji

Burning of the
Sanjo Palace

Ni Zan
Six Gentlemen

Sotatsu
Waves at Matsushima

Hiroshige

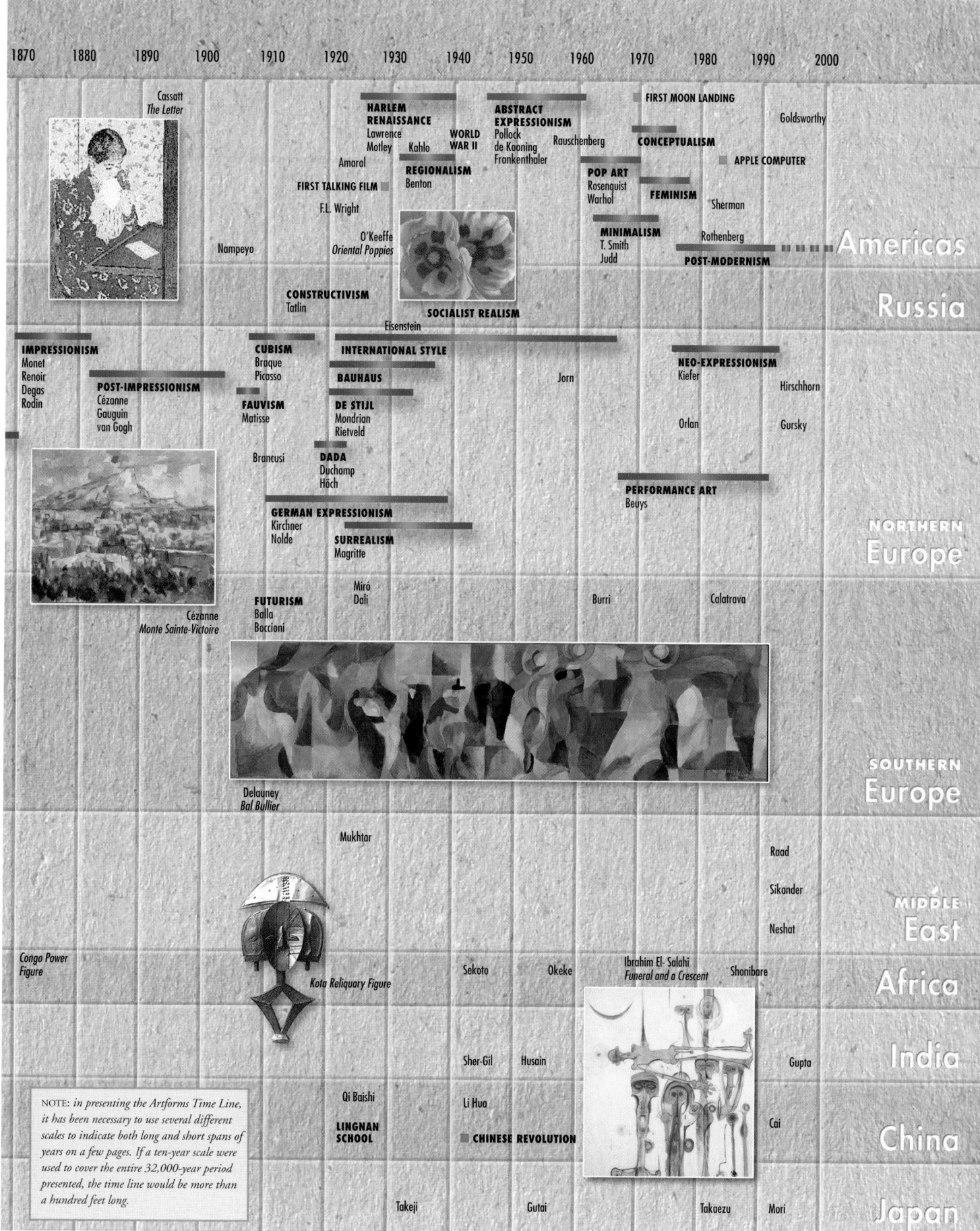

1870 1880 1890 1900 1910 1920 1930 1940 1950 1960 1970 1980 1990 2000

Cassatt
The Letter

HARLEM RENAISSANCE
Lawrence
Motley
Amaral
Kahlo

ABSTRACT EXPRESSIONISM
Pollock
de Kooning
Frankenthaler
Rauschenberg

FIRST MOON LANDING

Goldsworthy

WORLD WAR II

CONCEPTUALISM

FIRST TALKING FILM

REGIONALISM
Benton

POP ART
Rosenquist
Warhol

APPLE COMPUTER

F.L. Wright

FEMINISM

Sherman

Nampeyo

O'Keeffe
Oriental Poppies

MINIMALISM
T. Smith
Judd

Rothenberg

Americas

POST-MODERNISM

CONSTRUCTIVISM
Tatlin

SOCIALIST REALISM

Eisenstein

Russia

IMPRESSIONISM
Monet
Renoir
Degas
Rodin

CUBISM
Braque
Picasso

INTERNATIONAL STYLE

Jorn

NEO-EXPRESSIONISM
Kiefer

Hirschhorn

POST-IMPRESSIONISM
Cézanne
Gauguin
van Gogh

BAUHAUS

FAUVISM
Matisse

DE STIJL
Mondrian
Rietveld

Orlan

Gursky

Brancusi

DADA
Duchamp
Höch

PERFORMANCE ART
Beuys

GERMAN EXPRESSIONISM
Kirchner
Nolde

SURREALISM
Magritte

Cézanne
Monte Sainte-Victoire

FUTURISM
Balla
Boccioni

Miró
Dali

Burri

Calatrava

NORTHERN Europe

Delauney
Bal Bullier

SOUTHERN Europe

Mukhtar

Raad

Sikander

Neshat

MIDDLE East

Congo Power
Figure

Kota Reliquary Figure

Sekoto

Okeke

Ibrahim El- Salahi
Funeral and a Crescent

Shonibare

Africa

Sher-Gil

Husain

Gupta

India

Qi Baishi

Li Hua

Cai

China

LINGNAN SCHOOL

CHINESE REVOLUTION

NOTE: *in presenting the Artforms Time Line, it has been necessary to use several different scales to indicate both long and short spans of years on a few pages. If a ten-year scale were used to cover the entire 32,000-year period presented, the time line would be more than a hundred feet long.*

Takeji

Gutai

Takaezu

Mori

Japan

GLOSSARY

The following terms are defined according to their use in the visual arts. Words in *italics* are also defined in the glossary.

abstract art   Art that departs significantly from natural appearances. Forms are modified or changed to varying degrees in order to emphasize certain qualities or content. Recognizable references to original appearances may be very slight. The term is also used to describe art that is *nonrepresentational*.

Abstract Expressionism   An art movement, primarily in painting, that originated in the United States in the 1940s and remained strong through the 1950s. Artists working in many different styles emphasized spontaneous personal expression in large paintings that are *abstract* or *nonrepresentational*. One type of Abstract Expressionism is called *action painting*. See also *Expressionism*.

abstract Surrealism   See *Surrealism*.

academic art   Art governed by rules, especially works sanctioned by an official institution, academy, or school. Originally applied to art that conformed to standards established by the French Academy regarding composition, drawing, and color usage. The term has come to mean conservative and traditional art.

academy   An institution of artists and scholars, originally formed during the Renaissance to free artists from control by guilds and to elevate them from artisan to professional status. In an academy, art is taught as a humanist discipline along with other disciplines of the liberal arts.

achromatic   Having no color (or *hue*); without identifiable hue. Most blacks, whites, grays, and browns are achromatic.

acrylic (acrylic resin)   A clear plastic used as a *binder* in paint and as a casting material in sculpture.

action painting   A style of *nonrepresentational* painting that relies on the physical movement of the artist by using such gestural techniques as vigorous brushwork, dripping, and pouring. Dynamism is often created through the interlaced directions of the paint's impact. A subcategory of *Abstract Expressionism*.

additive color mixture   The mixture of colored light. When light colors are com-bined (as with overlapping spotlights), the mixture becomes successively lighter. Light primaries, when combined, create white light. See also *subtractive color mixture*.

additive sculpture   Sculptural form produced by adding, combining, or building up material from a core or *armature*. Modeling in clay and welding steel are additive processes.

aerial perspective   See *perspective*.

aesthetic   Pertaining to the sense of the beautiful and to heightened sensory perception in general.

aesthetics   The study and philosophy of the quality and nature of sensory responses related to, but not limited by, the concept of beauty. Within the art context: The philosophy of art focusing on questions regarding what art is, how it is evaluated, the concept of beauty, and the relationship between the idea of beauty and the concept of art.

afterimage   The visual image that remains after an initial stimulus is removed. Staring at a single intense *hue* may cause the cones, or color receptors, of the eye to become fatigued and perceive only the complement of the original hue after it has been removed.

airbrush   A small-scale paint sprayer that allows the artist to control a fine mist of paint.

analogous colors or **analogous hues** Closely related *hues*, especially those in which a common hue can be seen; hues that are neighbors on the color wheel, such as blue, blue-green, and green.

analytical Cubism   See *Cubism*.

aperture   In photography, the *camera* lens opening and its relative diameter. Measured in f-stops, such as f/8, f/11, etc. As the number increases, the size of the aperture decreases, thereby reducing the amount of light passing through the *lens* and striking the film.

apse   A semicircular end to an aisle in a *basilica* or a Christian church. In Christian churches an apse is usually placed at the eastern end of the central aisle.

aquatint   An *intaglio* printmaking process in which value areas rather than lines are etched on the printing plate. Powdered resin is sprinkled on the plate, which is then immersed in an acid bath. The acid bites around the resin particles, creating a rough surface that holds ink. Also, a *print* made using this process.

arcade   A series of *arches* supported by columns or piers. Also, a covered passageway between two series of arches or between a series of arches and a wall.

arch   A curved structure designed to span an opening, usually made of stone or other masonry. Roman arches are semicircular; Islamic and Gothic arches come to a point at the top.

armature   A rigid framework serving as a supporting inner core for clay or other soft sculpting material.

art criticism   The process of using formal analysis, description, and interpretation to evaluate or explain the quality and meanings of art.

Art Nouveau   A style that originated in the late 1880s based on the sinuous curves of plant forms. It was used primarily in architectural detailing and the applied arts.

artist's proof   A trial print, usually made as an artist works on a plate or block, to check the progress of a work.

assemblage   Sculpture using preexisting, sometimes "found" objects that may or may not contribute their original identities to the total content of the work.

asymmetrical   Without *symmetry*.

atmospheric perspective   See *perspective*.

automatism   The condition of being automatic; action without conscious control. Employed by *Surrealist* writers and artists to allow unconscious ideas and feelings to be expressed.

balance   An arrangement of parts achieving a state of equilibrium between opposing forces or influences. Major types are symmetrical and *asymmetrical*. See *symmetry*.

Baroque   The seventeenth-century period in Europe characterized in the visual arts by dramatic light and shade, turbulent *composition*, and exaggerated emotional expression.

barrel vault See *vault*.

bas relief See *relief sculpture*.

basilica A Roman town hall, with three aisles and an *apse* at one or both ends. Christians appropriated this form for their churches.

Bauhaus German art school in existence from 1919 to 1933, best known for its influence on design, leadership in art education, and its radically innovative philosophy of applying design principles to machine technology and mass production.

beam The horizontal stone or timber placed across an architectural space to take the weight of the roof or wall above; also called a *lintel*.

binder The material used in paint that causes *pigment* particles to adhere to one another and to the *support*; for example, linseed oil or acrylic polymer.

biomorphic A shape in a work of art that resembles a living organism or an *organic shape*.

bodhisattva A type of Buddhist holy person who is about to achieve enlightenment, but postpones it to remain on earth to teach others. Frequently depicted in the arts of China and Japan.

buttress A *support*, usually exterior, for a wall, *arch*, or *vault* that opposes the lateral forces of these structures. A flying buttress consists of a strut or segment of an arch carrying the thrust of a vault to a vertical pier positioned away from the main portion of the building. An important element in *Gothic* cathedrals.

Byzantine art Styles of painting, design, and architecture developed from the fifth century C.E. in the Byzantine Empire of ancient eastern Europe. Characterized in architecture by round *arches*, large *domes*, and extensive use of *mosaic*; characterized in painting by formal design, *frontal* and *stylized* figures, and rich use of color, especially gold, in generally religious subject matter.

calligraphy The art of beautiful writing. Broadly, a flowing use of line, often varying from thick to thin.

camera A mechanical or digital device for taking photographs. It generally consists of a light-proof enclosure with an *aperture*, which allows a controlled light image to pass through a shuttered *lens* and be focused on a photosensitive material.

camera obscura A dark room (or box) with a small hole in one side, through which an inverted image of the view outside is pro-

jected onto the opposite wall, screen, or mirror. The image is then traced. This forerunner of the modern *camera* was a tool for recording an optically accurate image.

cantilever A beam or slab projecting a substantial distance beyond its supporting post or wall; a projection supported only at one end.

capital In architecture, the top part, cap stone, or head of a column or pillar.

cartoon 1. A humorous or satirical drawing. 2. A drawing completed as a full-scale working drawing, usually for a *fresco* painting, *mural*, or tapestry.

carving A *subtractive* process in which a sculpture is formed by removing material from a block or mass of wood, stone, or other material, with the use of sharpened tools.

casting A substitution or replacement process that involves pouring liquid material such as molten metal, clay, wax, or plaster into a mold. When the liquid hardens, the mold is removed, and a form in the shape of the mold is left.

catacombs Underground burial places in Ancient Rome. Christians and Jews often decorated the walls and ceilings with paintings.

ceramics Clay hardened into a relatively permanent material by firing. A practitioner of the ceramic arts is a ceramist.

chiaroscuro Italian word meaning "light-dark." The gradations of light and dark *values* in *two-dimensional* imagery; especially the illusion of rounded, three-dimensional form created through gradations of light and shade rather than line. Highly developed by *Renaissance* painters.

chroma See *intensity*.

cinematography The art and technique of making motion pictures, especially the work done by motion picture camera operators.

classical 1. The art of ancient Greece and Rome. In particular, the style of Greek art that flourished during the fifth century B.C.E. 2. Any art based on a clear, rational, and regular structure, emphasizing horizontal and vertical directions, and organizing its parts with special emphasis on balance and proportion. The term classic is also used to indicate recognized excellence.

closed form A self-contained or explicitly limited form; having a resolved balance of tensions, a sense of calm completeness implying a totality within itself.

coffer In architecture, a decorative sunken panel on the underside of a ceiling.

collage From the French *coller*, to glue. A work made by gluing various materials, such as paper scraps, photographs, and cloth, on a flat surface.

colonnade A row of columns usually spanned or connected by *beams* (lintels).

color field painting A movement that grew out of *Abstract Expressionism*, in which large stained or painted areas or "fields" of color evoke aesthetic and emotional responses.

color wheel A circular arrangement of contiguous spectral *hues* used in some color systems. Also called a color circle.

complementary colors Two *hues* directly opposite one another on a *color wheel* which, when mixed together in proper proportions, produce a neutral gray. The true complement of a color can be seen in its *afterimage*.

composition The combining of parts or elements to form a whole; the structure, organization, or total form of a work of art.

Conceptual art An art form in which the originating idea and the process by which it is presented take precedence over a tangible product. Conceptual works are sometimes produced in visible form, but they often exist only as descriptions of mental concepts or ideas. This trend developed in the late 1960s, partially as a way to avoid the commercialization of art.

content Meaning or message contained and communicated by a work of art, including its emotional, intellectual, symbolic, thematic, and narrative connotations.

contrapposto Italian for "counterpose." The counterpositioning of parts of the human figure about a central vertical axis, as when the weight is placed on one foot causing the hip and shoulder lines to counterbalance each other—often in a graceful S-curve.

cool colors Colors whose relative visual temperatures make them seem cool. Cool colors generally include green, blue-green, blue, blue-violet, and violet. Warmness or coolness is relative to adjacent hues. See also *warm colors*.

crosshatching See *hatching*.

Cubism The most influential style of the twentieth century, developed in Paris by Picasso and Braque, beginning in 1907. The early mature phase of the style, called analytical Cubism, lasted from 1909 through 1911. Cubism is based on the simultaneous presentation of multiple views, disintegration, and geometric reconstruction of subjects in flattened, ambiguous pictorial space; figure and ground merge into one interwoven surface of shifting planes. Color is limited to *neutrals*. By 1912, the more decorative phase called synthetic or collage Cubism began to appear; it was characterized by fewer, more solid forms, conceptual rather than observed subject matter, and richer color and texture.

curtain wall   A non-load-bearing wall.

curvilinear   Formed or characterized by curving lines or edges.

cutting ratio   The ratio of film actually used in a movie after editing to the amount that was shot during production.

Dada   A movement in art and literature, founded in Switzerland in the early twentieth century, which ridiculed contemporary culture and conventional art. The Dadaists shared an antimilitaristic and anti-aesthetic attitude, generated in part by the horrors of World War I and in part by a rejection of accepted canons of morality and taste. The anarchic spirit of Dada can be seen in the works of Duchamp, Man Ray, Hoch, Miro, and Picasso. Many Dadaists later explored *Surrealism*.

daguerreotype   An early photographic process developed by Louis Daguerre in the 1830s, which required a treated metal plate. This plate was exposed to light, and the chemical reactions on the plate created the first satisfactory photographs.

depth of field   The area of sharpness of focus in front of and behind the subject in a photograph. Depth of field becomes greater as the *aperture* is decreased and the f-stop number is increased.

De Stijl   A Dutch purist art movement begun during World War I by Mondrian and others. It involved painters, sculptors, designers, and architects whose works and ideas were expressed in De Stijl magazine. *De Stijl*, Dutch for "the style," was aimed at creating a universal language of *form* that would be independent of individual emotion. Visual form was pared down to *primary colors* plus black and white, and rectangular shapes. The movement was influential primarily in architecture.

direct painting   Executing a painting in one sitting, applying wet over wet colors.

divisionism   See *Pointillism*.

dome   A generally hemispherical roof or *vault*. Theoretically, an *arch* rotated 360 degrees on its vertical axis.

dressed stone   Stone used for building that is cut to fit into a masonry wall.

drypoint   An *intaglio* printmaking process in which lines are scratched directly into a metal plate with a steel needle. Also, the resulting *print*.

earthenware   A type of clay used for ceramics. It fires at 1100°C–1150°C, and is porous after firing.

earthworks   Sculptural forms made from earth, rocks, or sometimes plants, often on a vast scale and in remote locations. Some are deliberately impermanent.

eclecticism   The practice of selecting or borrowing from earlier styles and combining the borrowed elements.

edition   In printmaking, the total number of *prints* made and approved by the artist, usually numbered consecutively. Also, a limited number of multiple originals of a single design in any medium.

elevation   In architecture, a scale drawing of any vertical side of a given structure.

encaustic   A painting medium in which *pigment* is suspended in a *binder* of hot wax.

engraving   An *intaglio* printmaking process in which grooves are cut into a metal or wood surface with a sharp cutting tool called a burin or graver. Also, the resulting *print*.

entasis   In *classical* architecture, the slight swelling or bulge in the center of a column, which corrects the illusion of concave tapering produced by parallel straight lines.

etching   An *intaglio* printmaking process in which a metal plate is first coated with acid-resistant wax, then scratched to expose the metal to the bite of nitric acid where lines are desired. Also, the resulting *print*.

Expressionism   The broad term that describes emotional art, most often boldly executed and making free use of distortion and symbolic or invented color. More specifically, Expressionism refers to individual and group styles originating in Europe in the late nineteenth and early twentieth centuries. See also *Abstract Expressionism*.

Fauvism   A style of painting introduced in Paris in the early twentieth century, characterized by areas of bright, contrasting color and simplified shapes. The name *les fauves* is French for "the wild beasts."

feminism   In art, a movement among artists, critics, and art historians that began in an organized fashion in the 1970s. Feminists seek to validate and promote art forms that express the unique experience of women, and to redress oppression by men.

feng shui   An ancient Chinese method of interior design that seeks to align spiritual forces within the space to be arranged.

figure   Separate shape(s) distinguishable from a background or *ground*.

flying buttress   See *buttress*.

folk art   Art of people who have had no formal, academic training, but whose works are part of an established tradition of style and craftsmanship.

font   The name given to a style of type. The text of *Artforms* is printed in the Adobe Garamond font.

foreshortening   The representation of *forms* on a *two-dimensional* surface by shortening the length in such a way that the long axis appears to project toward or recede away from the viewer.

form   In the broadest sense, the total physical characteristics of an object, event, or situation.

format   The shape or proportions of a *picture plane*.

fresco   A painting technique in which *pigments* suspended in water are applied to a damp lime-plaster surface. The pigments dry to become part of the plaster wall or surface. Sometimes called *true fresco* or *buon fresco* to distinguish it from painting over dry plaster.

frieze   A narrow band of *relief sculpture* that usually occupies the space above the columns of a classical building.

frontal   An adjective describing an object that faces the viewer directly, rather than being set at an angle or *foreshortened*.

Futurism   A group movement that originated in Italy in 1909. One of several movements to grow out of *Cubism*. Futurists added implied motion to the shifting planes and multiple observation points of the Cubists; they celebrated natural as well as mechanical motion and speed. Their glorification of danger, war, and the machine age was in keeping with the martial spirit developing in Italy at the time.

gesso   A mixture of glue and either chalk or plaster of Paris applied as a *ground* or coating to surfaces in order to give them the correct properties to receive paint. Gesso can also be built up or molded into *relief* designs, or carved.

glaze   In *ceramics*, a vitreous or glassy coating applied to seal and decorate surfaces. Glaze may be colored, transparent, or opaque. In oil painting, a thin transparent or translucent layer brushed over another layer of paint, allowing the first layer to show through but altering its color slightly.

Gothic   Primarily an architectural style that prevailed in western Europe from the twelfth through the fifteenth centuries, characterized by pointed *arches*, ribbed *vaults*, and flying *buttresses*, which made it possible to create stone buildings that reached great heights.

gouache   An opaque, water-soluble paint. *Watercolor* to which opaque white has been added.

ground   The background in *two-dimensional* works—the area around and between *figure(s)*. Also, the surface onto which paint is applied.

Happening   An event conceived by artists and performed by artists and others, usually unrehearsed and without a specific script or stage.

hard-edge   A term first used in the 1950s to distinguish styles of paintings in which shapes are precisely defined by sharp edges, in contrast to the usually blurred or soft edges in *Abstract Expressionist* paintings.

hatching   A technique used in drawing and linear forms of printmaking, in which lines are placed in parallel series to darken the value of an area. Crosshatching is drawing one set of hatchings over another in a different direction so that the lines cross.

Hellenistic   Style of the later phase of ancient Greek art (300–100 B.C.E.), characterized by emotion, drama, and interaction of sculptural forms with the surrounding space.

hierarchic proportion   Use of unnatural *proportions* or *scale* to show the relative importance of figures.

high key   Exclusive use of pale or light *values* within a given area or surface.

horizon line   In linear *perspective*, the implied or actual line or edge placed on a *two-dimensional* surface to represent the place in nature where the sky meets the horizontal land or water plane.

hue   That property of a color identifying a specific, named wavelength of light such as green, red, violet, and so on. Often used synonymously with *color*.

humanism   A cultural and intellectual movement during the *Renaissance*, following the rediscovery of the art and literature of ancient Greece and Rome. A philosophy or attitude concerned with the interests, achievements, and capabilities of human beings rather than with the abstract concepts and problems of theology or science.

icon   An image or symbolic representation (often with sacred significance).

iconography   The symbolic meanings of subjects and signs used to convey ideas important to particular cultures or religions, and the conventions governing the use of such forms.

impasto   In painting, thick paint applied to a surface in a heavy manner, having the appearance and consistency of buttery paste.

implied line   A line in a composition that is not actually drawn. It may be a sight line of a figure in a composition, or a line along which two *shapes* align with each other.

Impressionism   A style of painting that originated in France about 1870. (The first Impressionist exhibit was held in 1874.) Paintings of casual subjects were executed outdoors using divided brush strokes to capture the light and mood of a particular moment and the transitory effects of natural light and color.

installation   A type of art medium in which the artist arranges objects or artworks in a room, thinking of the entire space as the medium to be manipulated. Also called environments.

intaglio   Any printmaking technique in which lines and areas to be inked and transferred to paper are recessed below the surface of the printing plate. *Etching*, *engraving*, *drypoint*, and *aquatint* are all intaglio processes. See also *print*.

intensity   The relative purity or saturation of a *hue* (color), on a scale from bright (pure) to dull (mixed with another hue or a *neutral*).

intermediate color   A *hue* between a primary and a secondary on the *color wheel*, such as yellow-green, a mixture of yellow and green.

International Style   An architectural style that emerged in several European countries between 1910 and 1920. Related to purism and *De Stijl* in painting, it joined structure and exterior design into a noneclectic form based on rectangular geometry and growing out of the basic function and structure of the building.

Isometic perspective   See *perspective*.

iwan   A high, vaulted porch frequently used in Islamic architecture to mark an important building or entrance.

kachina   One of many deified ancestral spirits honored by Hopi and other Pueblo Indians. These spiritual beings are usually depicted in doll-like forms.

kiln   An oven in which pottery or *ceramic* ware is fired.

kinetic art   Art that incorporates actual movement as part of the design.

kore   Greek for "maiden." An archaic Greek statue of a standing clothed young woman.

kouros   Greek for "youth." An archaic Greek statue of a standing nude young male.

lens   The part of a *camera* that concentrates light and focuses the image.

linear perspective   See *perspective*.

linoleum cut   A *relief* process in printmaking, in which an artist cuts away negative spaces from a block of linoleum, leaving raised areas to take ink for printing.

lintel   See *beam*.

literati painting   In Asian art, paintings produced by cultivated amateurs who are generally wealthy and devoted to the arts, including calligraphy, painting, and poetry. Most commonly used to describe work of painters not attached to the royal courts of the Yuan, Ming, and Qing dynasties (fourteenth to eighteenth centuries) in China.

lithography   A planographic printmaking technique based on the antipathy of oil and water. The image is drawn with a grease crayon or painted with *tusche* on a stone or grained aluminum plate. The surface is then chemically treated and dampened so that it will accept ink only where the crayon or tusche has been used.

local color   The actual color as distinguished from the apparent color of objects and surfaces; true color, without shadows or reflections. Sometimes called *object color*.

logo   Short for "logotype." Sign, name, or trademark of an institution, a firm, or a publication, consisting of letter forms, borne on one printing plate or piece of type.

loom   A device for producing cloth by interweaving fibers at right angles.

lost wax   A *casting* method. First a model is made from wax and encased in clay or casting plaster. When the clay is fired to make a mold, the wax melts away, leaving a void that can be filled with molten metal or other self-hardening liquid to produce a cast.

madrasa   In Islamic tradition, a building that combines a school, prayer hall, and lodging for students.

Mannerism   A style that developed in the sixteenth century as a reaction to the classical rationality and balanced harmony of the High *Renaissance*; characterized by dramatic use of space and light, exaggerated color, elongation of figures, and distortions of *perspective*, *scale*, and *proportion*.

mass   Three-dimensional form having physical bulk. Also, the illusion of such a form on a *two-dimensional* surface.

mat   Border of cardboard or similar material placed around a picture as a neutral area between the frame and the picture.

matte   A dull finish or surface, especially in painting, photography, and *ceramics*.

medium   (pl. media or mediums) 1. A particular material along with its accompanying technique; a specific type of artistic technique or means of expression determined by the use of particular materials. 2. In paint, the fluid in which *pigment* is suspended, allowing it to spread and adhere to the surface.

mihrab   A niche in the end wall of a *mosque* that points the way to the Muslim holy city of Mecca.

minaret   A tower outside a *mosque* where chanters stand to call the faithful to prayer.

Minimalism   A *nonrepresentational* style of sculpture and painting, usually severely restricted in the use of visual elements and often consisting of simple geometric shapes or masses. The style came to prominence in the late 1960s.

mixed media   Works of art made with more than one *medium*.

mobile   A type of sculpture in which parts move, often activated by air currents. See also *kinetic art*.

modeling   1. Working pliable material such as clay or wax into *three-dimensional* forms. 2. In drawing or painting, the effect of light falling on a three-dimensional object so that the illusion of its *mass* is created and defined by *value* gradations.

monochromatic   A color scheme limited to variations of one *hue*; a hue with its *tints* and/or *shades*.

montage   1. A composition made up of pictures or parts of pictures previously drawn, painted, or photographed. 2. In motion pictures, the combining of separate bits of film to portray the character of a single event through multiple views.

mosaic   An art medium in which small pieces of colored glass, stone, or ceramic tile called *tessera* are embedded in a background material such as plaster or mortar. Also, works made using this technique.

mosque   House of public prayer in the Muslim religion. From the Arabic *masjid*, "place of prostration."

mural   A large wall painting, often executed in *fresco*.

narrative editing   A filmmaking process in which a film editor makes a version of a scene by combining many shots from various camera angles.

naturalism   An art style in which the curves and contours of a subject are accurately portrayed.

nave   The tall central space of a church or cathedral, usually flanked by side aisles.

negative shape   A background or *ground* shape seen in relation to foreground or *figure* shape(s).

Neoclassicism   New classicism. A revival of classical Greek and Roman forms in art, music, and literature, particularly during the eighteenth and nineteenth centuries in Europe and America. It was part of a reaction against the excesses of *Baroque* and *Rococo* art.

Neolithic art   A period of ancient art after the introduction of agriculture but before the invention of bronze. *Neolithic* means "new stone age" to distinguish it from *Paleolithic*, or "old stone age."

neutrals   Not associated with any single *hue*. Blacks, whites, grays, and dull gray-browns. A neutral can be made by mixing complementary hues.

nonobjective   See *nonrepresentational art*.

nonrepresentational   Art without reference to anything outside itself—without representation. Also called "nonobjective"—without recognizable objects.

object color   See *local color*.

offset lithography   Planographic printing by indirect image-transfer from photomechanical plates. The plate transfers ink to a rubber-covered cylinder, which "offsets" the ink to the paper. Also called photo-offset and offset lithography.

oil paint   Paint in which the *pigment* is held together with a *binder* of oil, usually linseed oil.

opaque   Impenetrable by light; not transparent or translucent.

open form   A form whose contour is irregular or broken, having a sense of growth, change, or unresolved tension; form in a state of becoming.

optical color mixture   Apparent rather than actual color mixture, produced by interspersing brush strokes or dots of color instead of physically mixing them. The implied mixing occurs in the eye of the viewer and produces a lively color sensation.

organic shape   An irregular, non-geometric shape. A shape that resembles any living matter. Most organic shapes are not drawn with a ruler or a compass.

original print   A print done by an artist or under his or her direct supervision. Not a reproduction.

painterly   Painting characterized by openness of form, in which shapes are defined by loose brushwork in light and dark color areas rather than by outline or contour.

Paleolithic art   A very ancient period of art coincident with the Old Stone Age, before the discovery of agriculture and animal herding.

pastels   1. Sticks of powdered pigment held together with a gum binding agent. 2. Pale colors or *tints*.

performance art   Dramatic presentation by visual artists (as distinguished from theater artists such as actors and dancers) in front of an audience, usually apart from a formal theatrical setting.

persistence of vision   An optical illusion that makes cinema possible. The eye and mind tend to hold seen images for a fraction of a second after they disappear from view. Quick projection of slightly differing images creates the illusion of movement.

perspective   A system for creating an illusion of depth or *three-dimensional* space on a *two-dimensional* surface. Usually used to refer to linear perspective, which is based on the fact that parallel lines or edges appear to converge and objects appear smaller as the distance between them and the viewer increases. Atmospheric perspective (aerial perspective) creates the illusion of distance by reducing color saturation, value contrast, and detail in order to imply the hazy effect of atmosphere between the viewer and distant objects. *Isometric perspective* is not a visual or optical interpretation, but a mechanical means to show space and volume in rectangular forms. Parallel lines remain parallel; there is no convergence. A work executed in *one-point perspective* has a single *vanishing point*. A work in *two-point perspective* has two of them.

petroglyph   An image or a symbol carved in shallow relief on a rock surface. Usually ancient.

photo screen   A variation of *silkscreen* in which the stencil is prepared photographically.

photomontage   The process of combining parts of various photographs in one photograph.

picture plane   The *two-dimensional* picture surface.

pigment   Any coloring agent, made from natural or synthetic substances, used in paints or drawing materials.

plate mark   An impression made on a piece of paper by pressing a printing plate onto it.

A plate mark is usually a sign of an *original print.*

Pointillism   A system of painting using tiny dots or "points" of color, developed by French artist Georges Seurat in the 1880s. Seurat systematized the divided brushwork and *optical color mixture* of the *Impressionists* and called his technique "Divisionism."

Pop Art   A style of painting and sculpture that developed in the late 1950s and early 1960s, in Britain and the United States; based on the visual cliches, subject matter, and impersonal style of popular mass-media imagery.

porcelain   A type of clay for *ceramics*. It is white or grayish and fires at 1350°C–1500°C. After firing, it is translucent and rings when struck.

positive shape   A *figure* or foreground shape, as opposed to a *negative* ground or background shape.

post-and-beam system (post and lintel) In architecture, a structural system that uses two or more uprights or posts to support a horizontal beam (or lintel) that spans the space between them.

Post-Impressionism   A general term applied to various personal styles of painting by French artists (or artists living in France) that developed from about 1885 to 1900 in reaction to what these artists saw as the somewhat formless and aloof quality of *Impressionist* painting. Post-Impressionist painters were concerned with the significance of form, symbols, expressiveness, and psychological intensity. They can be broadly separated into two groups—expressionists, such as Gauguin and van Gogh, and formalists, such as Cezanne and Seurat.

Post-Modern   An attitude or trend of the 1970s, 1980s, and 1990s. In architecture, the movement away from or beyond what had become boring adaptations of the *International Style*, in favor of an imaginative, eclectic approach. In the other visual arts, Post-Modern is characterized by influence from all periods and styles, including modernism, and a willingness to combine elements of all styles and periods. Although modernism makes distinctions between high art and popular taste, Post-Modernism makes no such value judgments.

primary colors   Those *hues* that cannot be produced by mixing other hues. *Pigment* primaries are red, yellow, and blue; light primaries are red, green, and blue. Theoretically, pigment primaries can be mixed together to form all the other hues in the spectrum.

prime   In painting, a primary layer of paint or sizing applied to a surface that is to be painted.

print (artist's print)   A multiple original impression made from a plate, stone, wood block, or screen by an artist or made under the artist's supervision. Prints are usually made in *editions*, with each print numbered and signed by the artist.

proportion   The size relationship of parts to a whole and to one another.

realism   1. A type of *representational art* in which the artist depicts as closely as possible what the eye sees. 2. Realism. The mid-nineteenth-century style of Courbet and others, based on the idea that ordinary people and everyday activities are worthy subjects for art.

registration   In color printmaking or machine printing, the process of aligning the impressions of blocks or plates on the same sheet of paper.

reinforced concrete (ferroconcrete) Concrete with steel mesh or bars embedded in it to increase its tensile strength.

relief printing   A printing technique in which the parts of the printing surface that carry ink are left raised, while the remaining areas are cut away. Woodcuts and linoleum prints (linocuts) are relief prints.

relief sculpture   Sculpture in which *three-dimensional* forms project from the flat background of which they are a part. The degree of projection can vary and is described by the terms high relief and low relief.

Renaissance   Period in Europe from the late fourteenth through the sixteenth centuries, which was characterized by a renewed interest in human-centered *classical* art, literature, and learning. See also *humanism*.

representational art   Art in which it is the artist's intention to present again or represent a particular subject; especially pertaining to realistic portrayal of subject matter.

reproduction   A mechanically produced copy of an original work of art; not to be confused with an original *print* or art print or artist's print.

rhythm   The regular or ordered repetition of dominant and subordinate elements or units within a design.

ribbed vault   See *vault*.

Rococo   From the French "rocaille" meaning "rock work." This late *Baroque* (c. 1715–1775) style used in interior decoration and painting was characteristically playful, pretty, romantic, and visually loose or soft; it used small *scale* and ornate decoration, *pastel* colors, and asymmetrical arrangement of curves. Rococo was popular in France and southern Germany in the eighteenth century.

Romanesque   A style of European architecture prevalent from the ninth to the twelfth centuries with round *arches* and barrel *vaults* influenced by Roman architecture and characterized by heavy stone construction.

Romanticism   1. A literary and artistic movement of late eighteenth- and nineteenth-century Europe, aimed at asserting the validity of subjective experience as a countermovement to the often cold formulas of *Neoclassicism*; characterized by intense emotional excitement, and depictions of powerful forces in nature, exotic lifestyles, danger, suffering, and nostalgia. 2. Art of any period based on spontaneity, intuition, and emotion rather than carefully organized rational approaches to form.

Salon   An official art exhibition in France, juried by members of the offical French *Academy*.

santero   Literally "saint-maker." A person in Hispanic traditions who carves or paints religious figures.

saturation   See *intensity*.

scale   The size or apparent size of an object seen in relation to other objects, people, or its environment or *format*. Also used to refer to the quality or monumentality found in some objects regardless of their size. In architectural drawings, the ratio of the measurements in the drawing to the measurements in the building.

screenprinting (serigraphy)   A printmaking technique in which stencils are applied to fabric stretched across a frame. Paint or ink is forced with a squeegee through the unblocked portions of the screen onto paper or other surface beneath.

secondary colors   Pigment secondaries are the *hues* orange, violet, and green, which may be produced in slightly dulled form by mixing two *primaries*.

serif   Any short lines that end the upper and lower strokes of a letter.

serigraphy   See *screenprinting*.

setback   The legal distance that a building must be from property lines. Early setback requirements often increased with the height of a building, resulting in step-like recessions in the rise of tall buildings.

shade   A *hue* with black added.

shape   A *two-dimensional* or implied two-dimensional area defined by line or changes in value and/or color.

shutter   In photography, the part of the *camera* that controls the length of time the light is allowed to strike the photosensitive film.

silk screen   See *screenprinting*.

simultaneous contrast   An optical effect caused by the tendency of contrasting forms and colors to emphasize their difference when they are placed together.

site-specific art   Any work made for a certain place, which cannot be separated or exhibited apart from its intended environment.

size   Any of several substances made from glue, wax, or clay, used as a filler for porous material such as paper, canvas, or other cloth, or wall surfaces. Used to protect the surface from the deteriorating effects of paint, particularly oil paint.

slip   Clay that is thinned to the consistency of cream, and used as paint on *earthenware* or *stoneware* ceramics.

stoneware   A type of clay for ceramics. Stoneware is fired at 1200°C–1300°C and is nonporous when fired.

storyboard   A series of drawings or paintings arranged in a sequence, used by directors and editors to help visualize the narrative flow of a film or video.

stupa   The earliest form of Buddhist architecture, a dome-like structure probably derived from Indian funeral mounds.

style   A characteristic handling of *media* and elements of form, which give a work its identity as the product of a particular person, group, art movement, period, or culture.

stylized   Simplified or exaggerated visual *form* that emphasizes particular or contrived design qualities.

subtractive color mixture   Mixture of colored *pigments* in the form of paints, inks, *pastels*, and so on. Called subtractive because reflected light is reduced as pigment colors are combined. See *additive color mixture*.

subtractive sculpture   Sculpture made by removing material from a larger block or form.

support   The physical material that provides the base for and sustains a *two-dimensional* work of art. Paper is the usual support for drawings and prints; canvas or panels are supports in painting.

Surrealism   A movement in literature and visual arts that developed in the mid-1920s and remained strong until the mid-1940s; grew out of *Dada* and *automatism*. Based upon revealing the unconscious mind in dream images, the irrational, and the fantastic, Surrealism took two directions: *representational* and *abstract*. Dali's and Magritte's paintings, with their uses of impossible combinations of objects depicted in realistic detail, typify representational Surrealism. Miro's paintings, with his use of abstract and fantastic shapes and vaguely defined creatures, are typical of abstract Surrealism.

symbol   A form or image implying or representing something beyond its obvious and immediate meaning.

symmetry   A design (or composition) with identical or nearly identical form on opposite sides of a dividing line or central axis; formal *balance*.

Synthetic Cubism   See *Cubism*.

tempera   A water-based paint that uses egg, egg yolk, glue, or casein as a *binder*. Many commercially made paints identified as tempera are actually *gouache*.

tessera   Bit of colored glass, ceramic tile, or stone used in a *mosaic*.

texture   The tactile quality of a surface or the representation or invention of the appearance of such a surface quality.

three-dimensional   Having height, width, and depth.

throwing   The process of forming clay objects on a potter's wheel.

tint   A *hue* with white added.

trompe l'oeil   French for "fool the eye." A *two-dimensional* representation that is so naturalistic that it looks actual or real (or *three-dimensional*).

true fresco   See *fresco*.

truss   In architecture, a structural framework of wood or metal based on a triangular system, used to span, reinforce, or support walls, ceilings, piers, or beams.

tunnel vault (barrel vault)   See *vault*.

tusche   In *lithography*, a waxy substance used to draw or paint images on a lithographic stone or plate.

two-dimensional   Having the dimensions of height and width only.

typography   The art and technique of composing printed materials from type.

unity   The appearance of similarity, consistency, or oneness. Interrelational factors that cause various elements to appear as part of a single complete form.

value   The lightness or darkness of tones or colors. White is the lightest value; black is the darkest. The value halfway between these extremes is called middle gray. Sometimes called "tone."

vanishing point   In linear *perspective*, the point on the *horizon line* at which lines or edges that are parallel appear to converge.

vantage point   The position from which the viewer looks at an object or visual field; also called "observation point" or "viewpoint."

vault   A masonry roof or ceiling constructed on the principle of the *arch*. A tunnel or barrel vault is a semicircular arch extended in depth; a continuous series of arches, one behind the other. A groin vault is formed when two barrel vaults intersect. A ribbed vault is a vault reinforced by masonry ribs.

vehicle   Liquid emulsion used as a carrier or spreading agent in paints.

vertical placement   A method for suggesting the third dimension of depth in a two-dimensional work by placing an object above another in the composition. The object above seems farther away than the one below.

video art   An art form first developed in the 1970s, in which artists use video equipment to stage and film performances or capture spontaneous events.

volume   1. Space enclosed or filled by a three-dimensional object or figure. 2. The implied space filled by a painted or drawn object or figure. Synonym: *mass*.

warm colors   Colors whose relative visual temperature makes them seem warm. Warm colors or *hues* include red-violet, red, red-orange, orange, yellow-orange, and yellow. See also *cool colors*.

warp   In weaving, the threads that run lengthwise in a fabric, crossed at right angles by the *weft*. Also, the process of arranging yarn or thread on a *loom* so as to form a warp.

wash   A thin, transparent layer of paint or ink.

watercolor   Paint that uses water-soluble gum as the *binder* and water as the *vehicle*. Characterized by transparency. Also, the resulting painting.

weft   In weaving, the horizontal threads interlaced through the *warp*. Also called woof.

woodcut   A type of *relief print* made from an image that is left raised on a block of wood.

PRONUNCIATION GUIDE

Magdalena Abakanowicz (mahg-dah-*lay*-nuh ah-bah-kah-*no*-vich)
Ácoma (*ah*-koh-mah)
Alhambra (al-*am*-bra)
Tarsila do Amaral (tar-*see*-lah doo ah-mah-*rahl*)
Angkor Wat (*ang*-kohr waht)
Sofonisba Anguissola (so-fah-*niss*-bah ahn-*gwees*-so-la)
Ardabil (ar-*dah*-bil)
Arroyo Hondo (ar-*roy*-yo *ohn*-doh)
'Aumakua (ahow-mah-*koo*-ah)
avant garde (ah-vahn *gard*)
Judy Baca (*bah*-kah)
Giacomo Balla (*jah*-koh-moh *bahl*-la)
Jean-Michel Basquait (jawn mee-*shell* bos-kee-ah)
Bauhaus (*bow*-house)
Benin (ben-een)
Gianlorenzo Bernini (jahn-low-*ren*-tsoh ber-*nee*-nee)
Umberto Boccioni (oom-*bair*-toh boh-*choh*-nee)
Bodhisattva (boh-dee-*saht*-vah)
Germaine Boffrand (zher-*main* bof-*frohn*)
Rosa Bonheur (buhn-*er*)
Borobudur (boh-roh-boo-*duhr*)
Sandro Botticelli (bought-tee-*chel*-lee)
Louise Bourgeois (boorzh-*wah*)
Constantin Brancusi (*kahn*-stuhn-teen brahn-*koo*-see)
Georges Braque (zhorzh brahk)
Pieter Bruegel (*pee*-ter *broy*-guhl)
Joseph Bueys (*yo*-sef boyce)
Michelangelo Buonarroti, see *Michelangelo*
Alberto Burri (ahl-*bair*-toe *boo*-ree)
Cai Guo Qiang (tseye gwoh *chyang*)
Callicrates (kah-*lik*-rah-teez)
Michelangelo da Caravaggio (mee-kel-*an*-jay-loe da car-ah-*vah*-jyoh)
Annibale Carraci (ahn-*nee*-bahl-lay cah-*rah*-chee)
Rosalba Carriera (roh-*sal*-bah car-*yair*-ah)
Henri Cartier-Bresson (on-*ree* car-tee-*ay* bruh-*sohn*)
Mary Cassatt (cah-*sat*)
Paul Cézanne (say-*zahn*)
Marc Chagall (shah-gahl)
Chartres (*shahr*-truh)
Chauvet (show-*vay*)

Dale Chihuly (chi-*hoo*-lee)
Chilkat (*chill*-kaht)
chola (*choh*-lah)
Christo (*kree*-stoh)
Constantine (*kahn*-stuhn-teen)
conté (kahn-tay)
contrapposto (kohn-trah-*poh*-stoh)
Gustave Courbet (*goos*-tahv koor-*bay*)
Cycladic (sik-*lad*-ik)
Louis Jacques Mandé Daguerre (loo-*ee* zhahk mon-*day* dah-*gair*)
Honoré Daumier (awn-ohr-*ay* doh-mee-ay)
Jacques-Louis David (*zhahk* loo-*ee* dah-*veed*)
Edgar Degas (ed-gahr duh-*gah*)
Willem de Kooning (*vill*-em duh *koe*-ning)
Eugène Delacroix (oo-*zhen* duh-lah-*kwah*)
André Derain (on-*dray* duh-*ran*)
de Stijl (duh steel)
Richard Diebenkorn (*dee*-ben-korn)
Donatello (dohn-ah-tell-loh)
Marcel Duchamp (mahr-*sell* doo-*shahm*)
Albrecht Dürer (*ahl*-brekht *duh*-ruhr)
Thomas Eakins (*ay*-kins)
Sergei Eisenstein (sair-gay *eye*-zen-schtine)
Olafur Eliasson (o-la-fur ee-*lie*-ah-sun)
M. C. Escher (*esh*-uhr)
Fan Kuan (fahn kwahn)
feng shui (fung shway)
Jean-Honoré Fragonard (zhon oh-no-*ray* fra-go-*nahr*)
Helen Frankenthaler (frank-en-*thahl*-er)
fresco (*fres*-coh)
Ganges (*gan*-jeez)
Gao Jianfu (gow jen-*foo*)
Paul Gauguin (go-*gan*)
Frank Gehry (*ger*-ree)
Artemisia Gentileschi (ahr-tuh-*mee*-zhyuh jen-till-*ess*-kee)
Jean Léon Gérôme (zhon *lay*-on zhay-*roam*)
Lorenzo Ghiberti (low-*rent*-soh ghee-*bair*-tee)
Alberto Giacometti (ahl-*bair*-toh jah-ko-*met*-tee)
Giotto di Bondone (*joht*-toe dee bone-*doe*-nay)
Francisco Goya (fran-*sis*-coe go-yah)

Walter Gropius (*val*-tuhr *grow*-pee-us)
Guan Yin (*gwan* yeen)
Guernica (*ger*-nih-kah)
Zaha Hadid (*zah*-hah hah-*deed*)
Hagia Sophia (hah-zhah so-*fee*-ah)
Hangzhou (hung-joe)
Suzuki Harunobu (soo-*zoo*-key hah-roo-*noh*-boo)
Hatshepsut (hah-*shep*-soot)
Heiji Monogatari (hay-jee mo-no-gah-*tah*-ree)
Hannah Höch (*hahn*-nuh *hohk*)
Hokusai (hohk-*sy*)
Pieter de Hooch (*pee*-tuhr duh *hohk*)
Victor Horta (*veek*-tohr *ore*-tah)
Horyuji (hohr-*yoo*-jee)
Ictinus (ick-*tee*-nuhs)
Inca (*eenk*-ah)
Ise (*ee*-say)
Asger Jorn (*az*-ger yorn)
kachina (kah-*chee*-nah)
Frida Kahlo (*free*-dah *kah*-loh)
Kandarya Mahadeva (gan-dahr-reeah mah-hah-*day*-vuh)
Vasily Kandinsky (vass-see-lee can-*din*-skee)
Anish Kapoor (ah-*neesh* kah-*puhr*)
Katsura (kah-*tsoo*-rah)
Khamerernebty (kahm-er-er-*neb*-tee)
Anselm Kiefer (*ahn*-sehlm *kee*-fuhr)
Ernst Ludwig Kirchner (*airnst loot*-vik *keerkh*-ner)
Torii Kiyonobu (tor-ee-ee kee-oh-*noh*-boo)
Torii Kiyotada (tor-ee-ee kee-oh-*tah*-dah)
Paul Klee (clay)
Rem Koolhaas (cole-hahss)
Krishna (*krish*-nuh)
Mistutani Kunishiro (meet-soo-*tah*-nee koo-nee-*shee*-roh)
Laocoön (lay-*ah*-koh-ahn)
Lascaux (lass-coe)
Le Corbusier (luh core-boo-zee-ay)
Fernand Léger (fair-*non* lay-*zhay*)
Li Hua (lee hwa)
Roy Lichtenstein (*lick*-ten-steen)
Maya Lin (*my*-uh *lin*)
Fra Filippo Lippi (frah fill-*leep*-poh *leep*-pee)
Marshall Lomokema (loh-moh-kem-ah)

Machu Picchu (*mah*-choo *peek*-choo)
René Magritte (ruh-*nay* muh-*greet*)
mandala (mahn-dah-lah)
Edouard Manet (ay-*dwahr* mah-*nay*)
Mansur (mahn-soor)
Maori (mow-ree)
Marisol (mah-ree-*sohl*)
Masaccio (mah-*sach*-chyo)
Henri Matisse (on-*ree* mah-*tees*)
Mato Tope (*mah*-toh *toh*-pay)
Chaz Maviyane-Davies (mah-vee-*yah*-neh)
Maya (*my*-uh)
de Medici (deh *meh*-dee-chee)
Ana Mendieta (*ah*-nah men-*dyet*-ah)
Michelangelo Buonarroti (mee-kel-*an*-jay-loe bwoh-nah-*roe*-tee)
Ludwig Mies van der Rohe (*loot*-vik *mees* vahn dair *roh*-eh)
Mihrab (*mee*-rahb)
Richard Misrach (*miz*-rahk)
Moai (moe-eye)
Piet Mondrian (*peet* mohn-dree-ahn)
Claude Monet (*klohd* muh-*nay*)
Berthe Morisot (*bairt* moh-ree-*zoh*)
mosque (mahsk)
Mu Qi (moo-chee)
Vera Mukhina (*vir*-ah moo-*kee*-nah)
Edvard Munch (*ed*-vard *moonk*)
Murujuga (mu-ru-*ju*-ga)
Eadweard Muybridge (*ed*-wurd *my*-brij)
Mycerinus (miss-uh-*ree*-nuhs)
Nadar (Felix Tournachon) (nah-*dar* fay-leeks toor-nah-*shohn*)
Nampeyo (nam-pay-oh)
Ni Zan (knee dzahn)
Emil Nolde (*ay*-meal *nohl*-duh)
Notre Dame de Chartres (*noh*-truh dahm duh *shahr*-truh)
Uche Okeke (*oo*-chay oh-*keh*-keh)
Claes Oldenburg (klahs ol-den-burg)
Olmec (*ohl*-mek)
José Clemente Orozco (ho-*say* cleh-*men*-tay oh-*rohs*-coh)
Nam June Paik (nahm joon pahk)

Andrea Palladio (ahn-*dray*-uh pahl-*lah*-dyo)
Giovanni Paolo Pannini (jyo-*vahn*-nee *pah-oh*-lo pah-*nee*-nee)
parfleche (par-*flesh*)
Pablo Picasso (pab-lo pee-*cah*-so)
pietá (pee-ay-*tah*)
Jackson Pollock (*pah*-lock)
Polyclitus (pol-ee-*cly*-tus)
Pompeii (pahm-*pay*)
Pont du Gard (pohn duh *gahr*)
Nicholas Poussin (nee-coh-*law* poo-*san*)
Qennifer (*ken*-eh-fer)
Qi Baishi (chee bye-shr)
Quetzalcoatl (kets-ahl-*kwah*-til)
Radha (*rad*-dah)
Robert Rauschenberg (*roh*-shen-buhrg)
Gerrit Reitveld (*gair*-it *ryt*-velt)
Rembrandt van Rijn (*rem*-brant van *ryne*)
Pierre August Renoir (pee-*err* oh-*goost* ren-*wahr*)
Gerhardt Richter (*gair*-hart *rick*-ter)
Diego Rivera (dee-*ay*-goh ree-*vay*-rah)
Sabatino Rodia (roh-*dee*-uh)
Francois August Rodin (frahn-*swah* oh-*goost* roh-*dan*)
Henri Rousseau (on-*ree* roo-*soh*)
Andre Rublev (*ahn*-dray *ru*-blof)
Niki de Saint Phalle (*nee*-kee duh san *fall*)
Ibrahim Salahi (ee-brah-*heem* sah-*lah*-hee)
Sanchi (*sahn*-chee)
Raphael Sanzio (ra-fay-el *sahn*-zee-oh)
Sassetta (suh-*set*-tuh)
scythian (*sith*-ee-ahn)
Sesshû (seh-shoo)
Georges Seurat (zhorzh sir-*ah*)
Bada Shanren (*bah*-dah *shan*-ren)
Yinka Shonibare (sho-ni-*bar*-ee)
Shiva Nārtarāja (*shih*-vuh nah-tah-*rah*-jah)
Katsukawa Shunsho (kaht-soo-*kah*-wah *shun*-so)
Sinan (*see*-nahn)
Tawaraya Sōtatsu (tah-wa-*rah*-ya *soh*-taht-soo)
Alfred Stieglitz (*steeg*-lits)

stupa (*stoo*-pah)
Toshiko Takaezu (tosh-ko tah-kah-*ay*-zoo)
Tang Yin (tahng yin)
Vladimir Tatlin (vlah-*dee*-meer taht-lin)
Teotihuacan (tay-oh-tee-wah-*cahn*)
Jean Tinguely (zhon tan-*glee*)
Tlingit (*kling*-git)
Félix Gonzáles Torres (*feh*-leeks gohn-*sa*-les *tohr*-res)
Henri de Toulouse-Lautrec (on-*ree* duh too-*looz* low-*trek*)
tuku-tuku (*too*-koo-*too*-koo)
James Turrell (tuh-*rell*)
Tutankhamen (too-tahn-*kahm*-uhn)
Mierle Laderman Ukeles (merl lay-duhr-man *yoo*-kuh-lees)
Unkei (ung-kay)
Ur (er)
Kitagawa Utamaro (kit-ah-*gah*-wah ut-ah-*mah*-roh)
Theo van Doesburg (*tay*-oh van dohz-*buhrg*)
Jan van Eyck (*yahn* van *ike*)
Vincent van Gogh (*vin*-sent van goe; also, van *gawk*)
Diego Velázquez (dee-*aye*-goh bay-*ahth*-kehth; also, vay-*las*-kes)
Robert Venturi (ven-*tuhr*-ee)
Jan Vermeer (*yahn* ver-*mair*)
Versailles (vair-*sy*)
Elizabeth Vigee-Lebrun (vee-*zhay* leh-*broon*)
Leonardo da Vinci (lay-oh-*nahr*-doh dah *veen*-chi)
Peter Voulkos (*vool*-kohs)
Wang Xizhi (shee-jur)
Andy Warhol (*wohr*-hohl)
Willendorf (*vill*-en-dohrf)
Xul Solar (shool so-*lar*)
ziggurat (*zig*-uh-raht)

NOTES

CHAPTER 1

1. Georgia O'Keeffe, *Georgia O'Keeffe* (New York: Viking, 1976), opposite plate 13.

2. Charles Glueck, "A Brueghel from Harlem," *New York Times* (February 22, 1970): sec. 2, 29.

3. Quoted in "Romare Bearden," *Current Biography* (1972): 30.

4. Julia Marcus, "Romare Bearden," *Smithsonian* (March 1981): 74.

5. Ibid., 72.

6. Félix González-Torres, interview with Tim Rollins, in *Félix González-Torres* (New York: Artpress, 1993), 23.

7. Clive Bell, "The Aesthetic Hypothesis," *Art in Theory 1900–1990*, edited by Charles Harrison and Paul Wood (London: Blackwell, 1992), 115.

8. *Concise Oxford English Dictionary.* Tenth Edition, Revised ed. Judy Pearsall (London: Oxford University Press, 2002), 75.

CHAPTER 2

1. Don Fabun, *The Dynamics of Change* (Englewood Cliffs, NJ: Prentice Hall, 1968), 9.

2. Lawrence Weschler, *Seeing Is Forgetting the Name of the Thing One Sees: A Life of Contemporary Artist Robert Irwin* (Berkeley: University of California Press, 1982), 64.

3. Edward Weston, *The Daybooks of Edward Weston*, edited by Nancy Newhall (Millerton, NY: Aperture, 1973), vol. 2, 181.

4. Henri Matisse, "The Nature of Creative Activity," *Education and Art*, edited by Edwin Ziegfeld (New York: UNESCO, 1953), 21.

5. Douglas Davis, "New Architecture: Building for Man," *Newsweek* (April 19, 1971): 80.

6. Betty Burroughs, ed., *Vasari's Lives of the Artists* (New York: Simon & Schuster, 1946), 191.

7. Leo Tolstoy, *What Is Art?* (London: Walter Scott, 1899), 50.

8. André Derain, *ArtNews* (April 1995): 118.

9. John Holt, *How Children Fail* (New York: Pitman, 1964), 167.

10. Bergen Evans, *Dictionary of Quotations* (New York: Delacorte Press, 1968), 340.

11. Erich Fromm, "The Creative Attitude," *Creativity and Its Cultivation*, edited by Harold H. Anderson (New York: HarperCollins, 1959), 44.

12. Oswald Sirén, *The Chinese on the Art of Painting* (New York: Schocken, 1963), 56.

13. Gyorgy Kepes, *The Language of Vision* (Chicago: Paul Theobald, 1944), 9.

14. "Notes d'un peintre sur son dessin," *Le Point* IV (1939): 14.

15. Jean Schuster, "Marcel Duchamp, vite," *le surréalisme* (Spring 1957): 143.

16. Georgia O'Keeffe, *Georgia O'Keeffe* (New York: Viking, 1976), opposite plate 23.

CHAPTER 3

1. Maurice Denis, *Theories 1870–1910* (Paris: Hermann, 1964), 13.

2. Quoted in "National Airport: A New Terminal Takes Flight," *Washington Post* (July 16, 1997). http://www.washingtonpost.com/wp-srv/local/longterm/library/airport/architect.htm (accessed May 14, 2000).

3. Faber Birren, *Color Psychology and Color Theory* (New Hyde Park, NY: University Books, 1961), 20.

CHAPTER 4

1. R. G. Swenson, "What Is Pop Art?" *Art News* (November 1963): 62.

2. Elizabeth McCausland, "Jacob Lawrence," *Magazine of Art* (November 1945): 254.

3. Jack D. Flam, *Matisse on Art* (New York: Dutton, 1978), 36; originally in "Notes d'un peintre," *La Grande Revue* (Paris, 1908).

4. Ibid.

5. Henri Matisse, "Notes of a Painter," translated by Alfred H. Barr, Jr., *Problems of Aesthetics*, edited by Eliseo Vivas and Murray Krieger (New York: Holt, 1953), 259–260; originally in "Notes d'un peintre."

6. Ibid., 260.

CHAPTER 6

1. Quoted in David Bayles, *Art and Fear* (Santa Barbara, 2001), 79.

2. Frederick Franck, *The Zen of Seeing: Seeing/Drawing as Meditation* (New York: Vintage, 1973), 6.

3. Vincent to Theo van Gogh, April 1884, Letter 184. *Vincent van Gogh: The Complete Letters*. http://www.vangoghgallery.com (accessed Oct. 21, 2004). Edited by Robert Harrison.

4. Robert Wallace. *The World of Van Gogh* (New York: Time-Life, 1969), 90.

5. Anthony Blunt, *Picasso's Guernica* (New York: Oxford University Press, 1969), 28.

6. Ichitaro Kondo and Elsie Grilli, *Katsushika Hokusai* (Rutland, VT: Tuttle, 1955), 13.

7. Marjane Satrapi, "On Writing *Persepolis*," http://www.randomhouse.com/pantheon/graphicnovels/satrapi2.html (accessed July 26, 2007).

8. June Wayne, quoted in Barbara Isenberg, "Prices of Prints." *Los Angeles Times,* May 14, 2006.

CHAPTER 7

1. Quoted in Erika Doss, *Spirit Poles and Flying Pigs: Public Art and Cultural Democracy in American Communities* (Washington, D.C.: Smithsonian Institution Press, 1995), 176.

2. Ibid., 179.

3. Ibid., 180.

CHAPTER 9

1. Minor White, Foreword to *Ansel Adams*, edited by Liliane De Cock (New York Graphic Society, 1972).

2. "Edwin Land," *Time* (June 26, 1972): 84.

3. Henri Cartier-Bresson, *The Decisive Moment* (New York: Simon & Schuster, 1952), 14.

4. Margaret Bourke-White, *Portrait of Myself* (New York: Simon & Schuster, 1963), 13.

5. Ibid., 64.

6. Ibid.

7. Ibid., 142.

8. Ibid., 308.

CHAPTER 10

1. "Do You Know Your ABCs?" *Advertising Age,* June 19, 2000.

2. All quotes this article from "Chaz Maviyane-Davies, Artist and Designer," *The Idea: Indian Documentary of Electronic Arts* No. 5, July 2002.

CHAPTER 11

1. Henry Hopkins, *Fifty West Coast Artists* (San Francisco: Chronicle Books, 1981), 25.

2. Ruth Butler, *Western Sculpture: Definitions of Man* (New York: HarperCollins, 1975), 249; from an unpublished manuscript in the possession of Roberta Gonzáles, translated and included in the appendices of a Ph.D. dissertation by Josephine Whithers, "The Sculpture of Julio González: 1926–1942" (New York: Columbia University, 1971).

3. Brassaï, *Conversations with Picasso* (Paris: Gallimard, 1964), 67.

4. Brandon Taylor, *Avant-Garde and After: Rethinking Art Now* (New York: Prentice Hall, 1995), 157.

CHAPTER 12

1. Quoted in Thalia Gouma-Peterson, *Miriam Schapiro: Shaping the Fragments of Art and Life* (New York: Abrams, 1999), 29.

2. Ruth Bunzel, *The Pueblo Potter* (New York: Columbia University Press, 1929), 56.

3. Quoted in Rose Slivka and Karen Tsujimoto, *The Art of Peter Voulkos* (Tokyo: Kodansha, 1995), 50.

4. John Coyne, "Handcrafts," *Today's Education* (November–December 1976): 75.

5. Grace Glueck, "In Glass, and Kissed by Light," *New York Times*, Aug. 29, 1997: Bl.

6. Quoted in *Expressions in Wood: Masterworks from the Wornick Collection* (Oakland: Oakland Museum of California, 1996), 64.

7. Kathleen McCann, "Diane Itter: Paying Tribute to the Artist," *Fiberarts* (September–October 1992): 46. Reprinted by permission of the publisher, Altamont Press, Inc., Asheville, NC.

8. *Abakanowicz* (New York: Abbeville, 1982), 127.

9. Faith Ringgold, *We Flew Over the Bridge: The Memoirs of Faith Ringgold* (Boston: Little, Brown, 1995), 26.

10. Ibid.

11. Ibid.

CHAPTER 13

1. Louis Sullivan, "The Tall Office Building Artistically Considered," Lippincott Monthly Magazine, March 1986: 408.

2. *Zaha Hadid: Complete Buildings and Projects* (New York: Rizzoli, 1998), 43.

3. Frank Lloyd Wright, *The Future of Architecture* (New York: Horizon Press, 1953), 227.

4. Will Durant, *The Story of Philosophy*, 2nd ed. (New York: Simon & Schuster, 1933), 141.

5. Humphry Osmond, "Some Psychiatric Aspects of Design," in *Who Designs America*, ed.

6. Laurence B. Holland (Garden City: Anchor Books, 1966), 316.

CHAPTER 14

1. "Picasso Speaks," *The Arts* (May 1923): 319.

CHAPTER 15

1. Quoted in Michael Kimmelman, "Is It All Loot? Tackling the Antiquities Problem," *New York Times*, March 29, 2006.

2. Suzan Mazur, "Interview: Italy's Antiquities Prosecutor Fiorilli," *Scoop News*, December 28, 2006.

3. Titus Burckhardt, *Chartres and the Birth of the Cathedral* (Bloomington, IN: World Wisdom Books, 1996), 47.

CHAPTER 16

1. David Piper, *The Illustrated History of Art* (New York: Crescent Books, 1991), 130.

2. Jacob Bronowski, "Leonardo da Vinci," *Renaissance Profiles*, ed. J. H. Plumb (New York: HarperCollins, 1976), 84.

3. *The World of Michelangelo* (New York: Time-Life Books, 1966), 192.

4. Saint Teresa of Jesus, *The Life of Saint Teresa of Jesus*, translated by David Lewis, edited by Benedict Zimmerman (Westminster, MD: Newman, 1947), 266.

5. Linda Nochlin, "Why Have There Been No Great Women Artists?" *Art News* (January 1971): 22–39ff.

6. Mira Bank, *Anonymous Was a Woman* (New York: St. Martins, 1979).

CHAPTER 17

1. Wen C. Fong, "The Literati Artists of the Ming Dynasty," Wen C. Fong and James C. Y. Wyatt, *Possessing the Past: Treasures from the National Palace Museum, Taipei* (New York: Metropolitan Museum of Art, 1996), 387.

CHAPTER 18

1. McGuire Gibson, "Cultural Tragedy in Iraq: A Report on the Looting of Museums, Archives, and Sites," *IFAR Journal* 6, nos. 1–2 (2003): 41–47.

2. Marie Woolf, "Desecration of the Cradle of Civilisation," *The Independent* (London), April 15, 2007.

CHAPTER 20

1. Katherine Solender, *Dreadful Fire! The Burning of the Houses of Parliament* (Cleveland: Cleveland Museum of Art, 1984), 42–56.

2. Beaumont Newhall, "Delacroix and Photography," *Magazine of Art* (November 1952): 300.

3. Margaretta Salinger, *Gustave Courbet, 1819–1877, Miniature Album XH* (New York: Metropolitan Museum of Art, 1955), 24.

4. From *Reminiscences of Rosa Bonheur*, published in 1910 and quoted in Wendy Slatkin, ed., *The Voices of Women Artists* (Englewood Cliffs, NJ: Prentice Hall, 1993), 132.

5. Ibid.

6. William Seitz, *Claude Monet* (New York: Abrams, 1982), 13.

7. Albert E. Elsen, *Rodin* (New York: Museum of Modern Art, 1963), 53; from a letter to critic Marcel Adam, published in an article in *Gil Blas* (Paris: July 7, 1904).

8. John Rewald, *Cézanne: A Biography* (New York: Abrams, 1986), 208.

9. Vincent van Gogh, *Further Letters of Vincent van Gogh to His Brother, 1886–1889* (London: Constable, 1929), 139, 166.

10. Ronald Alley, *Gauguin* (Middlesex, England: Hamlyn, 1968), 8.

11. Paul Gauguin, *Lettres de Paul Gauguin à Georges-Daniel de Monfried* (Paris: Georges Cres, 1918), 89.

12. John Russell, *The Meanings of Modern Art* (New York: HarperCollins, 1974), 35.

13. Jean Leymarie, "Paul Gauguin," *Encyclopedia of World Art* (London: McGraw-Hill, 1971), vol. 6, 42.

14. Yann Le Pichon, *Gauguin: Life, Art, Inspiration* (New York: Abrams, 1987), 240.

CHAPTER 21

1. Wassily Kandinsky, "Reminiscences," *Modern Artists on Art*, ed. Robert L. Herbert (Englewood Cliffs, NJ: Prentice Hall, 1964), 27.

2. William Fleming, *Art, Music and Ideas* (New York: Holt, 1970), 342.

3. Ibid.

4. Roland Renrose, *Picasso: His Life and Work* (New York: Schocken, 1966), 125.

5. Alfred H. Barr, Jr., ed., *Masters of Modern Art* (New York: Museum of Modern Art, 1955), 124.

6. H. H. Arnason, *History of Modern Art*, rev. ed. (New York: Abrams, 1977), 146.

7. Nathan Lyons, ed., *Photographers on Photography* (Englewood Cliffs, NJ: Prentice Hall, 1966), 133.

8. Beaumont Newhall, *The History of Photography* (New York: Museum of Modern Art, 1964), 111.

9. Joshua C. Taylor, *Futurism* (New York: Museum of Modern Art, 1961), 124.

CHAPTER 22

1. Hans Richter, *Dada 1916–1966* (Munich: Goethe Institut, 1966), 22.

2. Paride Accetti, Raffaele De Grada, and Arturo Schwarz, *Cinquant'annia Dada—Dada in Italia 1916–1966* (Milan: Galleria Schwarz, 1966), 39.

3. André Breton, *Manifestos of Surrealism*, translated by Richard Seaver and Helen R. Lane (Ann Arbor: University of Michigan Press, 1972), 14.

4. Sam Hunter and John Jacobus, *Modern Art* (New York: Harry N. Abrams, 1985), 148.

5. Herbert Read, *A Concise History of Modern Painting* (New York: Praeger, 1959), 160.

6. *San Francisco Chronicle,* October 6, 1935; quoted in Evangeline Montgomery, "Sargent Claude Johnson," *Ijele: Art Journal of the African World* (2002), 1–2.

7. Romare Bearden and Harry Henderson, *A History of African American Artists from 1792 to the Present* (New York, 1993), 152.

CHAPTER 23

1. Edward Lucie-Smith, *Sculpture Since 1945* (London: Phaidon, 1987), 77.

2. Calvin Tomkins, *The World of Marcel Duchamp* (New York: Time-Life Books, 1966), 162.

3. Richard Hamilton, *Catalogue of an Exhibition at the Tate Gallery*, March 12–April 19, 1970 (London: Tate Gallery, 1970), 31.

4. R.G. Swenson, "What Is Pop Art?" *Art News* (November 1963): 25.

5. Claes Oldenburg, "I am for an art . . ." from *Store Days*, Documents from the Store (1961) and Ray Gun Theater (1962), selected by Claes Oldenburg and Emmett Williams (New York: Something Else Press, 1967).

6. Donald Judd, "Specific Objects," *Arts Yearbook* 8 (1965): 78.

7. Julia Brown, *Occluded Front: James Turrell* (Los Angeles: Fellows of Contemporary Art, Lapis Press, 1985), 15.

8. Patricia Failing, "James Turrell's New Light on the Universe," *Art News* (April 1985): 71.

9. Andy Goldsworthy, "Artist's Statement," http://www.thinker.org/deyoung/about/subpage.asp?subpagekey = 847 (accessed July 20, 2007).

10. Lucy R. Lippard, *From the Center: Feminist Essays on Women's Art* (New York: Dutton, 1976), 48.

CHAPTER 24

1. Christina Chu, "The Lingnan School and Its Followers: Radical Innovation in Southern China"; Julia F. Andrews and Kuiyi Shen, *A Century in Crisis: Modernity and Tradition in the Art of Twentieth-Century China* (New York: Guggenheim Museum, 1998), 70.

2. Quoted in Vivian Sundaram, "Amrita Sher-Gil: Life and Work;" *Sikh Art*, http://www.sikh-heritage.co.uk/arts/amritashergil/amshergil.htm (accessed June 21, 2004).

3. Daniel Herwitz, *Husain* (Bombay, 1988), 17.

4. Uche Okeke, "Natural Synthesis," Art Society, Zaire, Nigeria, October 1960. Found in Okui Enwezor, *The Short Century: Independence and Liberation Movements in Africa, 1945–1994* (Munich: Prestel, 2001), 453.

CHAPTER 25

1. Adam Davidson, "Thom Mayne's Moment," *Metropolis*, March 2003, 68–73ff.

2. Joel L. Swerdlow, "To Heal a Nation," *National Geographic* (May 1985): 557.

SUGGESTED READINGS

PART 1
Art Is...

Canaday, John. *What Is Art? An Introduction to Painting, Sculpture & Architecture.* New York: Knopf, 1980.

Dictionary of Art, The. 34 vols. New York: Grove's Dictionaries, 1996.

Dissanayake, Ellen. *Homo Aestheticus: Where Art Comes From and Why.* New York: Free Press, 1992.

Edwards, Betty. *Drawing on the Artist Within: A Guide to Innovation, Invention and Creativity.* New York: Simon & Schuster, 1986.

Johnson, Jay. *American Folk Art of the Twentieth Century.* New York: Rizzoli, 1983.

London, Peter. *No More Secondhand Art: Awakening the Artist Within.* Boston: Shambhala, 1989.

Lowenfeld, Viktor. *Creative and Mental Growth,* 8th ed. New York: Macmillan, 1987.

Lucie-Smith, Edward, ed. *The Thames and Hudson Dictionary of Art Terms.* New York: Thames and Hudson, 1984.

May, Rollo. *The Courage to Create.* New York: W. W. Norton, 1975.

McKim, Robert. *Experiences in Visual Thinking,* 2nd ed. Monterey, California: Brooks/Cole, 1980.

Read, Herbert, and Nikos Stangos, eds. *The Thames and Hudson Dictionary of Art and Artists.* London: Thames and Hudson, 1985.

Samuels, Mike, M.D., and Nancy Samuels. *Seeing with the Mind's Eye: The History, Techniques and Uses of Visualization.* New York: Random House, 1975.

PART 2
The Language of Visual Experience

Arnheim, Rudolf. *Art and Visual Perception,* rev. ed. Berkeley: University of California Press, 1974.

Baudrillard, Jean. *The Ecstasy of Communication,* trans. Bernard and Caroline Schutze. Brooklyn, NY: Semiotext(e), 1988.

Berger, John. *The Sense of Sight.* New York: Vintage International, 1985.

Gage, John. *Color and Meaning: Art, Science, and Symbolism.* Berkeley: University of California Press, 1999.

Sayre, Henry. *Writing About Art.* Upper Saddle River, NJ: Prentice Hall, 2006.

Shahn, Ben. *The Shape of Content.* New York: Random House, 1957.

Varley, Helen, ed. *Colour.* London: Mitchell Beazley, 1980.

PART 3
The Media of Art

Bacon, Edmund N. *The Design of Cities,* rev. ed. New York: Penguin, 1976.

Camusso, Lorenzo, and Sandro Bortone, *Ceramics of the World: From 4000 B.C. to the Present.* New York: Abrams, 1991.

Carlin, John, et al. *Masters of American Comics.* New Haven: Yale University Press, 2005.

Cartier-Bresson, Henri. *The Decisive Moment.* New York: Simon & Schuster, 1952.

Cooper Union for the Advancement of Science and Art, *Techo-Seduction.* New York: Cooper Union, 1997.

Fairey, Shepard. *Obey: Supply & Demand.* Corte Madera: Ginko Press, 2006.

Franck, Frederick. *The Zen of Seeing: Drawing as Meditation.* New York: Random House, 1973.

Gardiner, Stephen. *Introduction to Architecture.* Oxford: Equinox, 1983.

Goldstein, Nathan. *The Art of Responsive Drawing,* 4th ed. Englewood Cliffs, NJ: Prentice Hall, 1992.

Hammer Museum. *Thing: New Sculpture from Los Angeles.* Los Angeles, Hammer Museum, 2005.

Hollis, Richard. *Graphic Design: A Concise History.* New York: Thames and Hudson, 2001.

Ivins, William M. *Prints and Visual Communication.* New York: Plenum, 1969.

Le Normand-Romain, Antoinette, et al. *Sculpture: The Adventure of Modern Sculpture in the Nineteenth and Twentieth Centuries.* New York: Rizzoli, 1986.

London, Barbara, with John Upton. *Photography,* 5th ed. New York: Longman, 1994.

Lucie-Smith, Edward. *The Story of Craft: The Craftsman's Role in Society.* Ithaca, NY: Cornell University Press, 1981.

Lupton, Ellen. *Mixing Messages: Graphic Design in Contemporary Culture.* New York: Cooper-Hewitt National Design Museum, 1996.

Macaulay, David. *Cathedral: The Story of Its Construction.* Boston: Houghton Mifflin, 1973.

Mast, Gerald. *A Short History of the Movies.* New York: Macmillan, 1986.

Mau, Bruce, et al. *Massive Change.* New York: Phaidon, 2004.

Mayer, A. Hyatt. *Prints and People: A Social History of Printed Pictures.* Princeton: Princeton University Press, 1980.

Mayer, Barbara. *Contemporary American Craft Art.* Salt Lake City: Gibbs M. Smith, 1988.

Mayer, Ralph. *Artists Handbook of Materials and Techniques,* 5th ed. New York: Viking, 1991.

McCloud, Bruce. *Understanding Comics: The Invisible Art.* Northampton, MA: Kitchen Sink Press, 1993.

McFadden, David Revere. *Radical Lace and Subversive Knitting.* New York: Museum of Arts and Design, 2007.

Newhall, Beaumont. *The History of Photography,* rev. ed. New York: Museum of Modern Art, 1982.

Raizman, David. *History of Modern Design.* Upper Saddle River, NJ: Prentice Hall, 2004.

Rubinstein, Charlotte Streifer. *American Women Sculptors: A History of Women Working in Three Dimensions.* Boston: G. K. Hall, 1990.

Rush, Michael. *New Media in Late 20th-Century Art.* New York, Thames and Hudson, 1999.

Salvadori, Mario. *Why Buildings Stand Up.* New York: W. W. Norton, 1980.

Saunders, Gill and Rosie Miles. *Prints Now: Directions and Definitions.* London: Victoria and Albert Museum Publications, 2006.

Scully, Vincent, Jr. *Modern Architecture: The Architecture of Democracy.* New York: Braziller, 1977.

Smith, Stan, and Friso Ten Holt, eds. *The Artist's Manual: Equipment, Materials, Techniques.* New York: Mayflower Books, 1980.

Speight, Charlotte and John Toki. *Hands in Clay: An Introduction to Ceramics,* 3rd ed. Mountain View, CA: Mayfield, 1994.

Thomas, Michel, Cristine Mainguy, and Sophie Pommier. *Textile Art.* New York: Rizzoli, 1985.

Tribe, Mark and Jana Reena. *New Media Art*. Cologne: Taschen, 2006.

Turcotte, Bryan Ray, ed. *Fucked Up and Photocopied: Instant Art of the Punk Movement*. Corte Madera, CA: Ginko Press, 1999.

Watkin, David A. *A History of Western Architecture*. London: Barrie & Jenkins, 1986.

Wines, James. *De-Architecture*. New York: Rizzoli, 1987.

Wye, Deborah. *Thinking Print: From Books to Billboards, 1980–95*. New York: Abrams and Museum of Modern Art, 1996.

PART 4
Art as Cultural Heritage

Bahn, Paul G. *Journey Through the Ice Age*. Berkeley: University of California, 1997.

Blair, Sheila, and Jonathan M. Bloom. *The Art and Architecture of Islam, 1250–1800*. New Haven: Yale University Press, 1994.

Blier, Suzanne Preston. *The Royal Arts of Africa: The Majesty of Form*. New York: Abrams, 1998.

Chadwick, Whitney. *Women, Art, and Society*, 2nd rev. ed. London: Thames and Hudson, 1996.

Coe, Ralph T. *Lost and Found Traditions: Native American Art 1965–1985*. New York: American Federation of the Arts, 1986.

Cole, Herbert M. *Icons: Ideals and Power in the Art of Africa*. Washington, D.C.: Smithsonian, 1989.

Dreamings: The Art of Aboriginal Australia. New York: Braziller and the Asia Society Galleries, 1988.

Ettinghausen, Richard. *The Art and Architecture of Islam, 650–1250*. New York: Penguin, 1987.

Feest, Christian. *Native Arts of North America*. New York: Thames and Hudson, 1992.

Fine, Elsa H. *Women and Art: A History of Women Painters and Sculptors from the Renaissance to the 20th Century*. Montclair, NJ: Allanheld & Schram, 1978.

Gombrich, E.H. *The Story of Art*, 15th ed. Englewood Cliffs, NJ: Prentice Hall, 1989.

Guerrilla Girls, *The Guerrilla Girls' Bedside Companion to the History of Western Art*. New York: Penguin, 1998.

Heller, Nancy G. *Women Artists: An Illustrated History*. New York: Abbeville, 1987.

Kennedy, Jean. *New Currents, Ancient Rivers: Contemporary African Artists in a Generation of Change*. Washington, D.C.: Smithsonian, 1992.

Lee, Sherman. *A History of Far Eastern Art*, 5th rev. ed. New York: Abrams, 1997.

Mason, Penelope. *History of Japanese Art*. New York: Abrams, 1993.

Mead, S. M. *Exploring the Visual Arts of Oceania*. Honolulu: University Press of Hawaii, 1979.

Metropolitan Museum of Art. *Mexico: Splendors of Thirty Centuries*. New York: Metropolitan Museum, 1990.

Pfeiffer, John E. *The Creative Explosion: An Inquiry into the Origins of Art and Religion*. New York: Harper & Row, 1982.

Reti, Ladislao, ed. *The Unknown Leonardo*. New York: McGraw-Hill, 1974.

Ruspoli, Mario. *The Cave of Lascaux: The Final Photographic Record*. London: Thames and Hudson, 1987.

Stanley-Baker, Joan. *Japanese Art*. New York: Thames and Hudson, 1984.

Stokstad, Marilyn. *Art History*. Upper Saddle River, NJ: Prentice Hall, 2008.

Sullivan, Michael. *The Arts of China*, 4th ed. Berkeley: University of California Press, 2000.

Summers, David. *Real Spaces: World Art History and the Rise of Western Modernism*. New York: Phaidon, 2003.

Visonà, Monica Blackmun, et al. *A History of Art in Africa*. Upper Saddle River, NJ: Prentice Hall, 2008.

PART 5
The Modern World

Ali, Wijdan. *Modern Islamic Art: Development and Continuity*. Gainesville: University Press of Florida, 1997.

Andrews, Julia F., and Kuiyi Shen. *A Century in Crisis: Modernity and Tradition in the Arts of Twentieth-Century China*. New York: Guggenheim Museum, 1996.

Arnason, H. H. *History of Modern Art: Painting, Sculpture, Architecture, Photography*, 4th ed. New York: Abrams, 1986.

Bearden, Romare, and Harry Henderson. *A History of African-American Artists from 1792 to the Present*. New York: Pantheon, 1993.

Beardsley, John. *Earthworks and Beyond*. New York: Abbeville, 1984.

Blazwick, Iwona, ed. *Century City: Art and Culture in the Modern Metropolis*. London: Tate Gallery, 2001.

Broude, Norma, and Mary D. Garrard, eds. *The Expanding Discourse: Feminism and Art History*. New York: HarperCollins, 1992.

Butler, Cornelia. *Wack! Art and the Feminist Revolution*. Los Angeles: Museum of Contemporary Art, 2007.

Canaday, John. *Mainstreams of Modern Art*, 2nd ed. New York: Henry Holt, 1981.

Cockcroft, Eva, John Weber, and James C. Cockcroft. *Toward a People's Art: A Contemporary Mural Movement*. New York: Dutton, 1977.

Dickerman, Leah, et al. *Dada*. Washington: National Gallery of Art, 2006.

Enwezor, Okwui. *The Short Century: Independence and Liberation Movements in Africa, 1945–1994*. Munich: Prestel, 2001.

Fineberg, Jonathan. *Art Since 1940: Strategies of Being*. Upper Saddle River, NJ: Prentice Hall, 2006.

Friedman, Mildred. *De Stijl: 1917–1931*. New York: Abbeville, 1992.

Goldberg, Vicki. *The Power of Photography: How Photographs Changed Our Lives*. New York: Abbeville, 1991.

Harrison, Charles, and Paul Wood (eds.). *Art in Theory 1900–2000: An Anthology of Changing Ideas*. Oxford: Blackwell, 2003.

Henri, Adrian. *Total Art: Environment, Happenings, and Performance*. New York: Praeger, 1974.

Hughes, Robert. *American Visions: The Epic Story of Art in America*. New York: Knopf, 1997.

Merewether, Charles, and Rika Iezumi Hiro. *Art, Anti-Art, Non-Art. Experimentations in the Public Sphere in Postwar Japan 1950–1970*. Los Angeles: Getty Research Institute, 2007.

Quirarte, Jacinto. *Mexican American Artists*. Austin: University of Texas Press, 1973.

Ramírez, Mari Carmen, and Héctor Olea, eds. *Inverted Utopias: Avant-Garde Art in Latin America*. New Haven: Yale University Press, 2004.

Rickey, George. *Constructivism: Origins and Evolution*. New York: Braziller, 1967.

Rosenblum, Naomi. *A History of Women Photographers*. New York: Abbeville, 1994.

———. *A World History of Photography*, 3rd ed. New York: Abbeville, 1997.

Sandler, Irving. *American Art of the 1960s*. New York: Harper & Row, 1988.

Sonfist, Alan, ed. *Art in the Land: A Critical Anthology of Environmental Art*. New York: Dutton, 1983.

Stern, Robert A. M. *American Architecture: Innovation and Tradition*. New York: Rizzoli, 1985.

Stich, Sidra. *Anxious Visions: Surrealist Art*. Berkeley: University Art Museum, 1990.

Stiles, Kristine, and Peter Selz. *Theories and Documents of Contemporary Art: A Sourcebook of Artists' Writings*. Berkeley: University of California Press, 2008.

Sullivan, Edward J., ed. *Latin American Art in the Twentieth Century*. London: Phaidon, 1996.

Tuchman, Maurice, *The Spiritual in Art: Abstract Painting 1890–1985*. New York: Abbeville, 1986.

PART 6
The Postmodern World

Asia Society Galleries. *Contemporary Art in Asia: Traditions/Tensions*. New York: Asia Society, 1996.

Cohn, Melanie Franklin (ed.). *Who Cares?* New York: Creative Time Books, 2006.

Daftari, Fereshteh. *Without Boundary: Seventeen Ways of Looking*. New York: Museum of Modern Art, 2006.

Fleming, Ronald Lee, and Renata von Tscharner. *Place Makers: Creating Public Art That Tells You Where You Are*. New York: Harcourt, Brace, Jovanovich, 1986.

Foster, Hal, ed. *The Anti-Aesthetic: Essays on Postmodern Culture*. Seattle: Bay Press, 1983.

Golden, Thelma, and Christine Y. Kim. *Frequency*. New York: Studio Museum in Harlem, 2006.

Jencks, Charles. *A New Paradigm: The Language of Post-Modernism*. New Haven: Yale University Press, 2002.

Kocur, Zoya, and Simon Leung, eds. *Theory in Contemporary Art Since 1985*. London: Blackwell, 2005.

Lippard, Lucy. *Mixed Blessings: New Art in a Multicultural America*. New York: Pantheon, 1990.

Murakami, Takashi, ed. *Little Boy: The Arts of Japan's Exploding Subculture*. New York: Japan Society, 2005.

Njami, Simon. *Africa Remix: Contemporary Art of a Continent*. London: Hayward Gallery, 2005.

Rose, Aaron, ed. *Beautiful Losers: Contemporary Art and Street Culture*. New York: Iconoclast and Distributed Art Publishers, 2004.

Sambrani, Chaitanya. *Edge of Desire: Recent Art in India*. Perth: Art Gallery of Western Australia, 2005.

Sandler, Irving. *Art of the Postmodern Era*. New York: Icon, 1996.

Thompson, Natto, et al. (eds.). *The Interventionists: Users' Manual for the Creative Disruption of Everyday Life*. North Adams: Mass Moca, 2004.

SUGGESTED WEB SITES

General Reference

The Web Museum
http://sunsite.unc.edu/wm/

Artlex: Art Dictionary
http://www.artlex.com

Researching Your Art Object
http://www.ilpi.com/artsource/weidman.html

Mark Harden's Artchive
http://www.artchive.com

The Artcyclopedia
http://www.artcyclopedia.com

Metropolitan Museum of Art Timeline of Art History
http://www.metmuseum.org/toah

Mother of All Art and Art History Links
http://art-design.umich.edu/mother/

Major Museum Web Sites

Detroit Institute of Art
http://www.dia.org

The Louvre Museum, Paris
http://www.louvre.fr

The Prado Museum, Madrid
http://museoprado.es

Hermitage Museum, St. Petersburg
http://www.hermitagemuseum.org

Art Institute of Chicago
http://www.artic.edu/aic/index.html

PART 1
Art Is ...

Rene Magritte and Contemporary Art
http://www.lacma.org/art/MagritteIndex.aspx

Museum of International Folk Art
http://www.moifa.org

Simon Rodia Builds the Watts Towers (film)
http://www.archive.org/details/TowersTh1957

PART 2
The Language of Visual Experience

Color Matters
http://www.colormatters.com/

The Web Museum: Impressionism
http://sunsite.unc.edu/wm/paint/glo/impressionism/

Claes Oldenburg: An Anthology
http://www.artnetweb.com/oldenburg

Museum of Bad Art
http://www.museumofbadart.org

Tate Etc., Contemporary Art
http://www.tate.org.uk/tateetc/

Modern Art Notes Blog
http://www.artsjournal.com/man

PART 3
The Media of Art

Modern Paint Podcasts
http://www.tate.org.uk/learning/learnonline/modernpaints/intro.htm

TypoGRAPHIC
http://www.rsub.com/typographic

George Eastman House
http://www.geh.org

Walker Art Center Gallery 9
http://www.walkerart.org/gallery9

One Thousand Words
http://spot.colorado.edu/~johnsoja/1KWords.html

Spencer Museum Graphic Arts Page
http://www.spencerart.ku.edu/prints.html

TWA Termina 360 Degree Panorama
http://fieldofview.com/flickr/?page=photos/nylocations/177590740/

The Henry Moore Foundation
http://www.henry-moore-fdn.co.uk/

Christo and Jeanne-Claude Home Page
http://www.christojeanneclaude.net/

Nineteenth-Century Sculpture
http://www.bc.edu/bc_org/avp/cas/fnart/art/19th_sculp.html

How Paint is Made
http://www.theblueprinter.com/artcolony/makepaint.htm

Stardust Studios (Motion Graphics)
http://stardust.tv

Origins of American Animation
http://lcweb2.loc.gov/ammem/oahtml/oahome.html

U. S. Green Building Council
http://www.usgbc.org

Design Museum, London
http://designmuseum.org

PART 4
Art as Cultural Heritage

The Chauvet Cave
http://www.culture.gouv.fr/culture/arcnat/chauvet/en

Australian Rock Art Research Association
http://mc2.vicnet.net.au/home/aura/web/index.html

Universes in Universe
http://www.universes-in-universe.de/english.htm

Universal Leonardo da Vinci
http://www.universalleonardo.org/

Islamic Arts and Architecture
Organization
http://islamicart.com/

Discover Islamic Art
http://www.discoverislamicart.org

Kyoto Museum of Art
http://www.kyohaku.go.jp/indexe.htm

How a Japanese Print is Made
http://www.fitzmuseum.cam.ac.uk/pharos/
sections/making_art/index_japan.html

National Palace Museum, Taiwan
http://www.npm.gov.tw

Virtual Views of Ancient Rome
http://www.romereborn.virginia.edu/

World Monuments Fund Watch List
http://www.worldmonumentswatch.org

Vatican Museums: The Sistine Chapel
http://mv.vatican.va/3_EN/pages/
MV_Visite.html

British Library Manuscript Pages
http://www.bl.uk/collections/treasures/
digitisation2.html

Illicit Cultural Property Blog
http://illicit-cultural-property.blogspot.com/

PART 5
The Modern World

The Age of Enlightenment
http://mistral.culture.fr/files/imaginary_
exhibition.html

The Online Picasso Project
http://picasso.tamu.edu/

The Andy Warhol Museum
http://www.warhol.org

Wack! Art and the Feminist Revolution
http://www.moca.org/wack/

Kandinsky: Compositions
http://www.glyphs.com/art/kandinsky/

The International Dada Archive
http://www.lib.uiowa.edu/dada

Smithsonian American Art Museum
http://nmaa-ryder.si.edu/

Vincent Van Gogh Gallery
http://www.vangoghgallery.com/

Frida Kahlo Retrospective Exhibition
www.tate.org.uk/modern/exhibitions/kahlo

Museum of Modern Art YouTube Channel
http://www.youtube.com/profile?user=
MoMAvideos

Art of the Sixties Exhibition
http://www.neue-digitale.de/projects/
summer-of-love/

PART 6
The Postmodern World

Artnet Magazine
http://www.artnet.com/magazineus/
frontpage.asp

Public Art in Indianapolis
http://www.publicartindianapolis.org/

010101: Art in Technological Times
http://010101.sfmoma.org/

**Museum of Contemporary Art,
Los Angeles**
http://www.moca-la.org

Contemporary Arts Center, Cincinnati
http://www.contemporaryartscenter.org

PBS: Art 21 Series
http://www.pbs.org/art21/series/index.html

The Wooster Collective: Street Art
http://woostercollective.com/

INDEX

Hopewell culture, 338–339
Hopi art, 199, 200
HOPI KACHINA, HUMIS KATSINA
  FIGURE, Marshall Lomakema, 341
Hopper, Edward, NIGHTHAWKS, 415,
  417
HORDE, THE, Max Ernst, 402
horizon lines, 52, 53
HORSE FAIR, THE, Rosa Bonheur, 360
HORSE IN MOTION, THE, Eadweard
  Muybridge, 153–154
HORYUJI TEMPLE, 312
HOSTAGE, Dara Birnbaum, 162, 163
HOUSE, 22
HOUSEHOLD, Allan Kaprow, 433, 434
HOUSE POST, Olembe Alaye, 330–331
HOUSES AT L'ESTAQUE, Georges
  Braque, 389–390
How Children Fail (Holt), 23
Howling Wolf
  biography, 343
  CLASSROOM AT FORT MARION, 343
  drawings, 342
Huai-su, AUTOBIOGRAPHY, 304, 305
Hudson River School, 355
hues, 64, 65
Hughes, Langston, 419
HUGO BOSS COMMERCIAL, Stardust
  Studios, 177, 178
human figures in Islamic art, 319
humanism, 266
HUMMINGBIRD, 347
HUNTERS IN THE SNOW, Pieter
  Bruegel, 279
Hurston, Zora Neale, 419
Husain, M.F., MAN, 455–456

I

I AND THE VILLAGE, Marc Chagall, 46
I CAN RIDE, I CAN RIDE MY UNICYCLE,
  23
ICE MAN, Kiki Smith, 470–471
Iconoclastic Controversy, 257–258
iconography, 36, 38–40, 258–259,
  444
Ictinus, PARTHENON, 246–247, 248
Ife, 328
Ikemoto, Howard, 102
Imperial Hotel, Tokyo, Frank Lloyd
  Wright, 227
implied light, 61–62
implied line, 46
implied motion, 59–60
implied textures, 70
IMPRESSION: SUNRISE, Claude Monet,
  366

Impressionism
  evaluating art, 93
  Japanese Modern art, 451
  Latin American Modernism,
    414–415
  painting style, 365–371
Incas, 347–348
Indian art
  Buddhist art, 291, 292–295
  DANCING KRISHNA, Chola dynasty,
    59
  early cultures, 291–292
  Hindu art, 296–298
  iconography, 38–40
  Modern, 454–456
  Mughal empire, 297, 323, 325
industrial design, 177–180
Industrial Light and Magic, 159
Indus Valley culture, 291
INFANT IN THE WOMB, THE, Leonardo
  da Vinci, 271
Inferno (Dante Alighieri), 114
Initial Manifesto of Futurism
  (Marinetti), 397
ink, 113–114
installations, 194–195, 444–446
INSULA DULCAMARA, Paul Klee, 420
intaglio
  drypoint, 136, 137
  engraving, 133–135
  etching, 135–137
  process, 133
intensity of a color, 65
INTERIOR OF A DUTCH HOUSE, Pieter
  de Hooch, 76
INTERIOR OF THE PANTHEON, ROME,
  THE, Giovanni Paolo Panini, 252
intermediate hues, 65, 66
International Style, 220–222,
  408–410, 429
INTERNET DWELLER: WOL.FIVE.YDPB,
  Nam June Paik, 193–194
Interpretation of Dreams, The (Freud),
  381
Interview, 438
in-the-round sculpture, 181
INTOLERANCE, D. W. Griffith, 155
Ionic capitals, 248
Iraq, looting of art in, 326
Irwin, Robert, 18
Islamic art
  Arab lands, 320
  calligraphy, 321, 420
  carpets, 204–205, 322
  history of, 319
  India, Mughal empire, 297, 323,
    325

looting in Iraq, 326
  map of, 322
  Modern Art, 456, 457
  Persia, 322–323, 324
  Spain, 321
ISOMETIC PERSPECTIVE, 55, 56
issue-oriented art, 474–476
Itter, Diane, PATTERN SCAPE, 205

J

JACK-IN-THE-PULPIT NO. V, Georgia
  O'Keeffe, 36
JACKSON POLLOCK, Hans Namuth,
  423
Jainism, 292
Janco, Marcel, 399
JANE AVRIL, Henri de
  Toulouse-Lautrec, 140, 141
JANE AVRIL DANSANT, Henri de
  Toulouse-Lautrec, 138–139
Japanese art
  architecture, 311–312, 316–317
  Modern, 451–452
  pagodas, 293, 294
  painting, 313–315, 317–318
  sculpture, 313
  woodblock printing, 131–132,
    315–316
JAPONAISERIE: FLOWERING PLUM TREE,
  Vincent van Gogh, 374
JAR, Ácoma Pueblo, 340
Jeanne-Claude, RUNNING FENCE, 442,
  443
Jefferson, Thomas, MONTICELLO, 352
JEPPESEN TERMINAL BUILDING, 223
Jigagian, Dawn Marie, SHY GLANCE,
  94
JOCKEYS BEFORE THE RACE, Edgar
  Degas, 80–81, 82, 83
JOHN DOE, Edward Kienholz, 430,
  431
Johns, Jasper
  simplicity of work, 430–431
  TARGET WITH FOUR FACES, 431,
    432
Johnson, James
  biography, 165
  ONE THOUSAND WORDS, 165
Johnson, Philip
  AT&T BUILDING, 461
  SEAGRAM BUILDING, 221–222, 461
Johnson, Sargent, FOREVER FREE, 418,
  419
Jonas, Joan, VOLCANO SAGA, 162
Jones, Kristin, MNEMONICS, 58
Jorn, Asger, GREAT VICTORY, THE, 427

PUBLIC SERVICES BUILDING, Michael Graves, 461, 462
Pueblo people, 340, 341
PURSE COVER, 260
Puryear, Martin, OLD MOLE, 469
PYGMALION AND GALATEA, Jean Léon Gérôme, 360, 362
PYRAMID OF THE SUN, 344
pyramids
    Egyptian, 240, 241
    Maya, 345
    Olmec, 342

Q

qalam, 321
QENNEFER, STEWARD OF THE PALACE, 48–49
qi, 303
Qi Baishi, LANDSCAPE, 121, 452
Qin dynasty, 301–303
Qing dynasty, 310, 311
quilt making, 206, 207, 209, 210

R

Raad, Walid, BEY82 CITY VI, 468, 469
rag paper, 119–120
RAILS AND JET TRAILS, Ansel Adams, 43
RAISING OF THE CROSS, THE, Peter Paul Rubens, 284
Raphael Sanzio
    MADONNA OF THE CHAIR, 84, 85, 276–277
    PAUL PREACHING AT ATHENS, 277
    SCHOOL OF ATHENS, THE, 53–55, 277
    tondo format, 88
Rauschenberg, Robert
    MONOGRAM, 430
    TRACER, 430, 431
Raw magazine, 114
Ray, Charles, SELF-PORTRAIT, 185
Ray, Man
    CADEAU (THE GIFT), 400, 401
    RAYOGRAPH, 149
RAYOGRAPH, Man Ray, 149
Realism, 358–365
REBIRTH OF VENUS, Nancy Spero, 447
RECTOR GATE, R. M. Fischer, 473
RECUMBENT FIGURE, Henry Moore, 420–421
REFLECTED BEAUTY, SEVEN BEAUTIES APPLYING MAKE-UP: OKITA, Kitagawa Utamaro, 316

registered inked blocks, 131
Reid, Jamie, GOD SAVE THE QUEEN, 176
reinforced concrete, 220–222
relief
    printmaking, 131–133
    sculpture, 181–182
Rembrandt van Rijn
    art as personal expression, 9–10
    CHRIST PREACHING, 135–136, 285
    RETURN OF THE PRODIGAL SON, 285
    SELF-PORTRAIT, 10, 124, 286
    SELF-PORTRAIT IN A CAP, OPEN MOUTHED AND STARING, 87
Renaissance
    defined, 266–267
    high, 271–277
    Italian frescoes, 128
    Italy, 267–270
    late, 280–281, 289
    northern Europe, 277–280
Renoir, Pierre-Auguste, LUNCHEON OF THE BOATING PARTY, THE, 368
repetition in design, 84–86
replacement process, casting as, 184
representational art, 29–30
Representational Surrealism, 403
restoration of artworks, 290
RETURN OF THE PRODIGAL SON, Rembrandt van Rijn, 285
Reverón, Armando, UNTITLED, 414–415
REVOLUTION GIRL, Shepard Fairey, 477–478
rhythm in design, 84–86
Richter, Gerhard, ABSTRACT PAINTING, 118, 119
Rietveld, Gerrit, SCHRÖDER HOUSE, 409
Riley, Bridget, CURRENT, 44
Ringgold, Faith
    biography, 208
    CHANGE: FAITH RINGGOLD'S OVER 100 POUND WEIGHT LOSS PERFORMANCE STORY QUILT, 208
    MRS. JONES AND FAMILY, 207
    SLAVE RAPE SERIES, THE, 208
    SONNY'S QUILT, 208
    TAR BEACH, 208, 209
Rintaro, METROPOLIS, 160
ritual, art for, 7–9
RITUAL VESSEL (LA TIGRESSE), Shang dynasty, 301
Rivera, Diego
    DETROIT INDUSTRY, 127, 128
    Frida Kahlo, 416

LIBERATION OF THE PEON, THE, 411–412
Robeson, Paul, 419
ROBE WITH MATO TOPE'S EXPLOITS, 342
ROBIE HOUSE, Frank Lloyd Wright, 396
Robusti, Marietta, 289
ROCKET TO THE MOON, Romare Bearden, 11
Rococo style, 287–288
Rodchenko, Aleksandr
    GIVE ME SUN AT NIGHT, 169–170
    WORKERS' CLUB, THE, 407, 408
Rodia, Sabatino, NUESTRO PUEBLO, 26
Rodin, Auguste
    Brancusi and, 393
    CAMBODIAN DANCER, 102
    Gates of Hell, The, 371
    KISS, THE, 34, 71, 371
    THINKER, THE (LE PENSEUR), 371
ROETTGEN PIETÀ, 89
Roman art
    arches, 215
    architecture, 251–253
    painting, 253
    politics and culture, effects of, 249, 251
    sculpture, 250, 251
    tempera, 122
    typeface, 172
Romanesque art, 261–262
ROMAN PAINTING, 253
Romanticism, 352–356
ROSA BONHEUR, W. H. Mote, 361
ROSE DE FRANCE window, 264
Rosenquist, James, F-111, 434–435
ROSENTHAL CENTER FOR CONTEMPORARY ART, Zaha Hadid, 224
Rothenberg, Susan
    BLUE HEAD, 464
    early work, 462
Rothko, Mark, BLUE, ORANGE, RED, 424
Rubens, Peter Paul
    influence of, 283–284
    RAISING OF THE CROSS, THE, 284
Rublev, Andrei, OLD TESTAMENT TRINITY, 259
RUE TRANSNONAIN, Honoré Daumier, 138
RUNNING FENCE, Christo and Jeanne-Claude, 442, 443

S

Saar, Betye, LIBERATION OF AUNT
JEMIMA, THE, 40
Saarinen, Eero, SHELL STRUCTURE
(TWA TERMINAL), 222–223
Saint Phalle, Niki de, ST. SEBASTIAN,
OR THE PORTRAIT OF MY LOVE, 432
SAKS FIFTH AVENUE LOGO, Michael
Bierut, 171
Salon, 358
SALON DE LA PRINCESSE, HÔTEL DE
SOUBISE, Germain Boffrand, 287
sans serif, 172
santeros, 27, 28
santos, 27, 28
SAN VITALE, 256, 257
Sanzio, Raphael. See Raphael Sanzio
SARAH BERNHARDT, Nadar, 358
Sassetta, MEETING OF SAINT ANTHONY
AND SAINT PAUL, THE, 57
Satrapi, Marjane, PERSEPOLIS, 115–116
saturation of a color, 65
Saxe, Adrian, FUTURE KINGS OF THE
WORLD, 198, 200
scale in design, 86–89
SCALE RELATIONSHIPS, 86–87
SCANNER DARKLY, A, Richard
Linklater, 161
Schapiro, Miriam
HEARTLAND, 16
PERSONAL APPEARANCE #3, 197
Schnitger, Lara, GRIM BOY, 193
SCHOOL OF ATHENS, THE, Raphael,
53–55, 277
SCHRÖDER HOUSE, Gerrit Rietveld,
409
SCREAM, THE, Edvard Munch, 380
screenprinting (silkscreen, serigraphy),
139, 141–142
sculpture
carving, 186–188
casting, 184–186
constructing and assembling,
188–191
freestanding and relief, 181–182
installations, 194–195
kinetic, 192
methods and materials, 182–191
mixed media, 192–194
modeling, 182–184
sculpture, styles of
Abstract, 393–394
Abstract Expressionism, 428
African-American modernism,
418, 419
Aztecs, 346

Baroque, 283
Constructivism, 406–407, 408
Cubism, 390, 391
Dada, 400–401
Egyptian, 242
Gothic, 264–265
Greek, 181, 244–246, 248–249,
250
Hindu, 182, 187, 296–297,
300–301
Impressionism, 371
Indian Buddhist, 294–295
Indus Valley culture, 291
Japanese, 313
Maya, 345
Minimalism, 439–440
Oceanic art, 335–336
Postmodern art, 468–471
Renaissance, early, 269–270
Renaissance, high, 274, 275
Roman, 250, 251
Romanesque, 262
site works and earthworks,
442–444
Toltec civilization, 346
SCYTHIAN ANIMAL, 260
SEAFORM SERIES, Dale Chihuly, 202
SEAGRAM BUILDING, Ludwig Mies van
der Rohe and Philip Johnson,
221–222, 461
SEARCHING FOR BUGS IN THE PARK,
Kojyu, 22
secco fresco, 127–128
secondary hues, 65, 66
seeing, 18, 20
Sekoto, Gerard, STREET SCENE,
457–458
SELF-PORTRAIT, Andy Warhol, 438
SELF-PORTRAIT, Charles Ray, 185
SELF-PORTRAIT, Leonardo da Vinci,
273
SELF-PORTRAIT, Rembrandt, 10
SELF-PORTRAIT, Rembrandt van Rijn,
124
SELF-PORTRAIT, Sofonisba Anguissola,
289
SELF-PORTRAIT IN A CAP, OPEN
MOUTHED AND STARING,
Rembrandt van Rijn, 87
SELF-PORTRAIT IN A STRAW HAT,
Elizabeth Vigee-Lebrun, 94
SELF-PORTRAIT WITH CROPPED HAIR,
Frida Kahlo, 416
SELF-PORTRAIT WITH GRAY HAT,
Vincent van Gogh, 106
Senmut, FUNERARY TEMPLE OF QUEEN
HATSHEPSUT, 240, 241

sequential art, comics as, 114
serifs, 172
serigraphy, 141
Sesshū, HABOKU LANDSCAPE, 314
set-back laws, 221
Seurat, Georges
DETAIL OF A SUNDAY ON LA
GRANDE JATTE, 67
L'ECHO, 111
SUNDAY ON LA GRANDE JATTE, A,
372–373
SE7EN, title sequence for, Kyle
Cooper, 177
747 WING HOUSE, David Hertz,
228–229
sfumato, 271
shades of a hue, 65
Shang dynasty, 301
shape, 46–47
SHAPE OF SPACE, A, 47
SHARECROPPER, Elizabeth Catlett, 133
SHELL STRUCTURE (TWA TERMINAL),
Eero Saarinen, 222–223
Shen Zhou, POET ON A MOUNTAIN
TOP, 56, 95
Sher-Gil, Amrita
modern art, 454–455
SWING, THE, 455
Sheridan, Sonia Landy, FLOWERS, 153
Sherman, Cindy, UNTITLED FILM
STILL #48, 466–467
Shinto, 311
Shonibare, Yinka, SIR FOSTER
CUNLIFFE PLAYING, 483
shots, film, 154
SHUTTLECOCKS, Claes Oldenburg and
Coosje van Bruggen, 87
SHY GLANCE, Dawn Marie Jigagian, 94
Siddhartha Gautama, 292–293
Sikander, Shahzia, PLEASURE PILLARS,
481
SILENCE=DEATH, 172–173
silkscreen, 141, 438
simulated textures, 70
SIR FOSTER CUNLIFFE PLAYING, Yinka
Shonibare, 483
Siskind, Aaron, CHICAGO 4C, 428
Sistine Chapel ceiling, 107–108, 128,
274, 275, 276
site-specific works, 442–444
Six Dynasties Period, 304
SIX GENTLEMEN, Ni Zan, 97–98, 307
SIX PERSIMMONS, Mu Qi, 52
SKETCHBOOK, Guillermo del Toro,
103
sketchbooks/notebooks, 103, 271,
273

WOMAN OF LESPUGUE, 233–234
WOMAN OF WILLENDORF, 233–234
women. *See also* specific artists
    feminism, early, 446–448
    Renaissance and Baroque painters,
        289
Women Artists in Revolution, 447
wood
    carving, 203–204
    structures, 213
Wood, Beatrice, CHALICE, 8
Wood, Grant
    AMERICAN GOTHIC, 417
    realistic style, 415, 417
wood carvings
    Incas, 348
    Oceanic art, 333–335, 337
woodcut (woodblock) printing,
    131–132, 315–316
wood engravings, 131
Woodman, Betty, DIVIDED VASES
    (CHRISTMAS), 198
WORKERS' CLUB, THE, Aleksandr
    Rodchenko, 407, 408
Works Progress Administration
    African-American modernism, 419
    arts programs, 412

World Monuments Fund, 290
World Wide Web, 164–168
worship, art for, 7–9
Wright, Frank Lloyd
    biography, 227
    building own dwellings, 212
    FALLINGWATER, 81, 225–226, 227
    Guggenheim Museum, 225, 227
    Imperial Hotel, Tokyo, 227
    ROBIE HOUSE, 396
Wu Chen, ALBUM LEAF FROM MANUAL
    OF INK BAMBOO, 307

X

XTNZ, Rui Filipe Antunes, 166

Y

Yong Soon Min, DWELLING, 10–11
Yoruba
    ADIRE CLOTH, 332–333
    DANCE WAND IN HONOR OF ESHU,
        9
    HOUSE POST, 330–331
    MALE PORTRAIT HEAD, 328

You Have Seen Their Faces, Erskine
    Caldwell and Margaret Bourke-
    White, 150
YOU SEE THE HUT YET YOU ASK
    "WHERE SHALL I GO FOR SHELTER,"
    Roberto Visani, 191
Yuan dynasty, 98, 309
Yu Ko, 24

Z

ZAPATISTAS, José Clemente Orozco,
    86
Zappa, Frank, 114
Zemankova, Anna, UNTITLED (M), 25
Zen Buddhism, 314
Zen of Seeing, The (Franck), 104
ZIGGURAT OF UR-NAMMU, 239
ziggurats, 238–239

SINGLE PC LICENSE AGREEMENT AND LIMITED WARRANTY

READ THIS LICENSE CAREFULLY BEFORE OPENING THIS PACKAGE. BY OPENING THIS PACKAGE, YOU ARE AGREEING TO THE TERMS AND CONDITIONS OF THIS LICENSE. IF YOU DO NOT AGREE, DO NOT OPEN THE PACKAGE. PROMPTLY RETURN THE UNOPENED PACKAGE AND ALL ACCOMPANYING ITEMS TO THE PLACE YOU OBTAINED THEM [[FOR A FULL REFUND OF ANY SUMS YOU HAVE PAID FOR THE SOFTWARE]]. ***THESE TERMS APPLY TO ALL LICENSED SOFTWARE ON THE DISK EXCEPT THAT THE TERMS FOR USE OF ANY SHAREWARE OR FREEWARE ON THE DISKETTES ARE AS SET FORTH IN THE ELECTRONIC LICENSE LOCATED ON THE DISK:***

1. GRANT OF LICENSE and OWNERSHIP: The enclosed computer programs <<and data>> ("Software") are licensed, not sold, to you by Pearson Education, Inc. publishing as Prentice Hall ("We" or the "Company") and in consideration [[of your payment of the license fee, which is part of the price you paid]] [[of your purchase or adoption of the accompanying Company textbooks and/or other materials,]] and your agreement to these terms. We reserve any rights not granted to you. You own only the disk(s) but we and/or our licensors own the Software itself. This license allows you to use and display your copy of the Software on a single computer (i.e., with a single CPU) at a single location for <u>academic</u> use only, so long as you comply with the terms of this Agreement. You may make one copy for back up, or transfer your copy to another CPU, provided that the Software is usable on only one computer.

2. RESTRICTIONS: You may <u>not</u> transfer or distribute the Software or documentation to anyone else. Except for backup, you may <u>not</u> copy the documentation or the Software. You may <u>not</u> network the Software or otherwise use it on more than one computer or computer terminal at the same time. You may <u>not</u> reverse engineer, disassemble, decompile, modify, adapt, translate, or create derivative works based on the Software or the Documentation. You may be held legally responsible for any copying or copyright infringement that is caused by your failure to abide by the terms of these restrictions.

3. TERMINATION: This license is effective until terminated. This license will terminate automatically without notice from the Company if you fail to comply with any provisions or limitations of this license. Upon termination, you shall destroy the Documentation and all copies of the Software. All provisions of this Agreement as to limitation and disclaimer of warranties, limitation of liability, remedies or damages, and our ownership rights shall survive termination.

4. LIMITED WARRANTY AND DISCLAIMER OF WARRANTY: Company warrants that for a period of 60 days from the date you purchase this SOFTWARE (or purchase or adopt the accompanying textbook), the Software, when properly installed and used in accordance with the Documentation, will operate in substantial conformity with the description of the Software set forth in the Documentation, and that for a period of 30 days the disk(s) on which the Software is delivered shall be free from defects in materials and workmanship under normal use. The Company does <u>not</u> warrant that the Software will meet your requirements or that the operation of the Software will be uninterrupted or error-free. Your only remedy and the Company's only obligation under these limited warranties is, at the Company's option, return of the disk for a refund of any amounts paid for it by you or replacement of the disk. THIS LIMITED WARRANTY IS THE ONLY WARRANTY PROVIDED BY THE COMPANY AND ITS LICENSORS, AND THE COMPANY AND ITS LICENSORS DISCLAIM ALL OTHER WARRANTIES, EXPRESS OR IMPLIED, INCLUDING WITHOUT LIMITATION, THE IMPLIED WARRANTIES OF MERCHANTABILITY AND FITNESS FOR A PARTICULAR PURPOSE. THE COMPANY DOES NOT WARRANT, GUARANTEE OR MAKE ANY REPRESENTATION REGARDING THE ACCURACY, RELIABILITY, CURRENTNESS, USE, OR RESULTS OF USE, OF THE SOFTWARE.

5. LIMITATION OF REMEDIES AND DAMAGES: IN NO EVENT, SHALL THE COMPANY OR ITS EMPLOYEES, AGENTS, LICENSORS, OR CONTRACTORS BE LIABLE FOR ANY INCIDENTAL, INDIRECT, SPECIAL, OR CONSEQUENTIAL DAMAGES ARISING OUT OF OR IN CONNECTION WITH THIS LICENSE OR THE SOFTWARE, INCLUDING FOR LOSS OF USE, LOSS OF DATA, LOSS OF INCOME OR PROFIT, OR OTHER LOSSES, SUSTAINED AS A RESULT OF INJURY TO ANY PERSON, OR LOSS OF OR DAMAGE TO PROPERTY, OR CLAIMS OF THIRD PARTIES, EVEN IF THE COMPANY OR AN AUTHORIZED REPRESENTATIVE OF THE COMPANY HAS BEEN ADVISED OF THE POSSIBILITY OF SUCH DAMAGES. IN NO EVENT SHALL THE LIABILITY OF THE COMPANY FOR DAMAGES WITH RESPECT TO THE SOFTWARE EXCEED THE AMOUNTS ACTUALLY PAID BY YOU, IF ANY, FOR THE SOFTWARE OR THE ACCOMPANYING TEXTBOOK. BECAUSE SOME JURISDICTIONS DO NOT ALLOW THE LIMITATION OF LIABILITY IN CERTAIN CIRCUMSTANCES, THE ABOVE LIMITATIONS MAY NOT ALWAYS APPLY TO YOU.

6. GENERAL: THIS AGREEMENT SHALL BE CONSTRUED IN ACCORDANCE WITH THE LAWS OF THE UNITED STATES OF AMERICA AND THE STATE OF NEW YORK, APPLICABLE TO CONTRACTS MADE IN NEW YORK, AND SHALL BENEFIT THE COMPANY, ITS AFFILIATES AND ASSIGNEES. HIS AGREEMENT IS THE COMPLETE AND EXCLUSIVE STATEMENT OF THE AGREEMENT BETWEEN YOU AND THE COMPANY AND SUPERSEDES ALL PROPOSALS OR PRIOR AGREEMENTS, ORAL, OR WRITTEN, AND ANY OTHER COMMUNICATIONS BETWEEN YOU AND THE COMPANY OR ANY REPRESENTATIVE OF THE COMPANY RELATING TO THE SUBJECT MATTER OF THIS AGREEMENT. If you are a U.S. Government user, this Software is licensed with "restricted rights" as set forth in subparagraphs (a)-(d) of the Commercial Computer-Restricted Rights clause at FAR 52.227-19 or in subparagraphs (c)(1)(ii) of the Rights in Technical Data and Computer Software clause at DFARS 252.227-7013, and similar clauses, as applicable.

Should you have any questions concerning this agreement or if you wish to contact the Company for any reason, please contact in writing: Prentice Hall, One Lake Street Upper Saddle River, NJ 07458.